W9-AFU-073

Praise for *The Principles of Banking*

Moorad Choudhry's *The Principles of Banking* opens up a portal into the world of sophisticated, dynamic, capital markets-based commercial banking. He gives us the big picture, the precise details and a framework for analyzing the enormous risks facing these firms. The book is an invaluable resource.

Jean Helwege
J. Henry Fellers Professor of Business Administration,
Department of Finance, University of South Carolina

This book is a "must read" for all senior bankers. There is no writer better than Moorad Choudhry for communicating the vital principles of liquidity, capital and asset-liability management and bank corporate governance.

Professor Carol Alexander
Chair of Financial Risk Management, ICMA Centre, University of Reading
Chair of the Board, Professional Risk Manager's International Association

The Principles of Banking is ideal reading for anyone planning or developing a career in banking. Professor Choudhry's coverage is fully integrated, clear, and authoritative. There is no better practitioner's guide to this subject.

Darrell Duffie
Dean Witter Distinguished Professor of Finance
Graduate School of Business, Stanford University

The failure of the US banking system in 2007–2008 can be effectively described by failing to apply the principles and strategies discussed by Moorad Choudhry. Indeed, banks should understand the dynamic interaction of the economy, credit losses and interest rates, and utilize the strategies within to balance the extremes, and prioritize strategies based upon return of capital and return on capital.

Joe Jennings CFA
Former Managing Director,
Sterne Agee & Leach, Inc.,
Memphis, TN

Asset and liability management (ALM) is at the heart of any bank. Among many of its functions, keeping the bank liquid and fixing the "value" of money (for the bank) are key to a bank's survival and success. Moorad Choudhry has a wealth of experience in this area. *The Principles of Banking* is an invaluable practical guide on how banks can lift their conduct to meet the challenges of the post-crash era.

Abhijit Patharkar
Senior Business Manager,
Asset and Liability Management,
Standard Chartered Bank, Singapore

Moorad continues to make a substantial contribution both to academia and the finance profession. His latest book, *The Principles of Banking*, is a comprehensive coverage of best-practice concepts and his own recommended strategies which are set out in a very lucid manner. Moorad, who is a Visiting Professor at CARISMA, makes us proud; well done Moorad!

Gautam Mitra
Professor of Computational Optimisation and Modelling &
Emeritus Professor, Brunel University
Director of CARISMA: The Centre for the Analysis of Risk and
Optimisation Modelling Applications

Yet again, a work of excellence.

Rafael Hurtado
Vice-President Risk Management, Banco de Credito, Lima

Professor Choudhry puts financial instruments and their derivatives within the context of banks' asset and liability management, constituting a masterful and unique reference work in the field. This book covers bank liquidity risk analysis and management, as well as stress testing. On these topics Professor Choudhry's book is indispensable reading and is set to become the principal reference.

Nuno Cassola e Barata
Adviser, Market Operations, European Central Bank, Frankfurt

Moorad has hit the mark. Whether you are a newcomer to the subject area or a practitioner of many years experience *The Principles of Banking* is a valuable insight into the simple yet complex world of finance. Illustrating the importance of having sound Asset & Liability Management at the heart of the bank, and the potential pitfalls where ALM principles are overlooked, with *The Principles of Banking* he has produced a book invaluable for academia and practitioners alike.

Colin Johnson
Head of ALM & Liquidity Oversight, Santander UK, London
Education Secretary, UK Asset-Liability Management Association

As a banker and bank regulator, asset and liability management has remained a high priority area for me. Professor Choudhry's inclusive and incisive book on the nitty-gritty and nuances of this extremely important subject will help both practitioners and researchers better understand and analyse new tools and models for measuring and managing risk, as well as to keep up with the innovation challenges.

Dr. K C Chakrabarty
Deputy Governor, Reserve Bank of India, Mumbai

Professor Choudhry has been recommending for years what bank regulatory authorities only started writing about after the crash. *The Principles of Banking* is the last word on the subject, the definitive rulebook on bank governance and risk management for senior directors, board members and supervisors.

Martin Barber
Global Head of ITO Delivery, Hewlett-Packard Corporation, EMEA

A really comprehensive and approachable text – an invaluable companion for any financial market practitioner.

Mark Miller
Global Economist, Lloyds TSB Corporate Markets, London

A very highly rated book in the Group CFO performance management office! The office ALM bible, our main reference point on ALM matters.

Vasilis Kosmas
Head of Structured Finance, National Bank of Greece, Athens

Asset and liability management is without doubt a priority in banking; it is essential that proper controls are in place to ensure the best returns on, and also efficient use of, capital. This book covers all essential topics in a straightforward manner and builds, from basic to complex, a very useful tool for everyone in this environment.

Tom O'Connor
Head of Treasury, KBC Bank NV, London

Professor Choudhry's book takes us along all of the subtle issues of Asset and Liability Management, Capital, Liquidity and well beyond. The text is a comprehensive sum of all techniques and concepts needed by bank practitioners, which makes it essential reading for anyone involved in the industry.

Joel Bessis
Professor of Finance, HEC Paris and author of Risk Management in Banking

This book is a real "must have" for everyone who wants to deepen his knowledge of banking governance. It is written in a straightforward way and is a great compendium for practitioners.

Aleksandar Doric
Fixed Income Trading, Baader Bank Aktiengesellschaft, Frankfurt

Professor Choudhry's *Principles of Banking* is an essential and very timely educational exercise on the global banking industry going through profound change. This book is a front-row analysis on the global financial market failures; and on the how and why that has forced the entire banking system to return to fundamental asset and balance sheet management, basic underwriting and critical, sound, best-practice risk management.

Kevin M. Cuff, MPA, IOM
Executive Director, Professional Risk Managers International Association, Boston

A comprehensive – but straightforward – tour of the realities of the banking business, from a guy who has seen it all. The main point – that banks are in the business of lending, and funding that lending, however they dress it up – may seem obvious, but it's one that has been obscured in much of traditional theory, particularly when it comes to derivatives. Similarly, while many pay lip service to liquidity being the biggest risk to the Street, few other texts have that principle as ingrained in the logic of their argument. No smoke and mirrors here, and very few mathematical jazz-hands.

Laurie Carver
Senior Staff Writer and Deputy Technical Editor, Risk *magazine, London*

As senior management at banks look to redefine their business models and strategies (either voluntarily or via regulatory change) they would be well advised to read Moorad Choudhry's *The Principles of Banking* to refresh themselves with the core fundamentals in how to effectively manage a bank's capital and liquidity exposure. This book should also be mandatory reading for all graduates entering the industry to fully appreciate the core drivers of banking.

Cris Kinrade
MD Capital and Collateral Management, Commercial Banking, Lloyds Banking Group, London

This is a must-read for anyone who wants to acquire a deep understanding of how modern banking works. This fundamental text covers the most important areas of the discipline, such as liquidity, risk and capital management, strategy and governance. With his vast practical knowledge and deep insight of the banking business, Professor Choudhry re-examines the recent banking experience and presents his view on how a modern bank should be managed in order to successfully cope with today's challenges. This handbook will provide long-term benefits to serious readers.

Dr Evgueni Ivantsov
Chairman, European Risk Management Council, London

This book impressed me in so many ways. I found it highly informative and stimulating, and recommend it to every person in the banking profession, especially for Treasury people involved in ALM, liquidity & fund management.

Sk. Matiur Rahman
EVP & Head of Treasury, Prime Bank Limited, Dhaka

Dictum Meum Pactum

—The motto of the London Stock Exchange

The Principles of Banking

MOORAD CHOUDHRY

John Wiley & Sons Singapore Pte. Ltd.

Published in 2012 by John Wiley & Sons Singapore Pte. Ltd.
1 Fusionopolis Walk, #07-01, Solaris South Tower, Singapore 138628

Other Wiley Editorial Offices

John Wiley & Sons, 111 River Street, Hoboken, NJ 07030, USA
John Wiley & Sons, The Atrium, Southern Gate, Chichester, West Sussex, P019 8SQ, United Kingdom
John Wiley & Sons (Canada) Ltd., 5353 Dundas Street West, Suite 400, Toronto, Ontario, M9B 6HB, Canada
John Wiley & Sons Australia Ltd., 42 McDougall Street, Milton, Queensland 4064, Australia
Wiley-VCH, Boschstrasse 12, D-69469 Weinheim, Germany

Library of Congress Cataloging-in-Publication Data
ISBN 978–0–470–82521–1 (Hardback)
ISBN 978–0–470–82701–7 (ePDF)
ISBN 978–0–470–82700–0 (Mobi)
ISBN 978–0–470–82702–4 (ePub)

Typeset in 10/12pt, Sabon Roman by Thomson Digital, India

10 9

For my wife,
Mrs. Lindsay Choudhry

Contents

Foreword

Rundheersing Bheenick

Professor Moorad Choudhry presented me a copy of his book, ***The Principles of Banking***, when he visited Mauritius to attend a banking conference which the Bank of Mauritius was hosting.

I was struck by his sound down-to-earth grasp of the banking scene and impressed by his academic and publishing track record. I made it a point to plough my way through his masterly tome and emerged thoroughly convinced that this book deserves a wide readership. It is, therefore, most welcome.

Banking has gone through exceptionally turbulent times over the last few years. The bankers who brought us the spectacular global financial crisis, their regulators who failed equally spectacularly, and the reformers of the banking and finance system tasked with ensuring that we minimise risks of such bust-ups in future, have all been constantly in the news. The arcana of banking are no longer the exclusive preserve of specialists. There is keen and widespread interest to understand better what goes on in the mysterious world of banking.

This book sheds light on the subject. It returns us to basics. It is indeed a delight to have in one packed volume a text that sets out all that you wanted to know about doing the honest job of banking but perhaps did not have the nerve to ask.

As we still struggle to emerge from the 2007-10 financial crisis in good shape, it is a boon to have such a clearly-written guide on the fundamental principles of good banking practice. ***The Principles of Banking*** is eminently suited to the needs of banking students, but can also enlighten experienced practitioners and bank Board members. Professor Choudhry brings to this sizeable endeavour a wealth of experience in this field as a seasoned banking practitioner and well-respected teacher.

This volume is the latest in a series he has delivered over the past decade or more covering many separate areas of banking, such as bonds, derivatives, the money market and factors underlying banking crises. With admirable skill in setting out the implications of complex numerical issues, he bridges that yawning gap between theoretical precepts of banking systems and the everyday life problems that bankers face. It is a text for everyone involved in banking from the professionals in the high street branches interacting with the public, the decision-makers in the executive suite or the board room, to the supervisors and regulators in central banks and oversight agencies in their role as arbiters of current practice and designers of safer systems for the future.

Banking has a long history of crises, from the US banking collapse of 1792, to the latest debacle, rooted in the mismanagement of cheap mortgages and the confection of evidently misleading derivatives. This latest text book is both a survival guide for wayward practitioners and a treatise for students and their academic masters, which hopefully will help to steer this sector out of its shaky immediate past.

Professor Choudhry is a master of his subject but envelopes the mathematical devices he presents so clearly with a sound sense of priorities. He closes this most valuable contribution to the literature on banking with this wise adage, which we forget at our peril:

"The first principle of banking is to have principles. Or as the motto of the London Stock Exchange puts it: *my word is my bond*."

I wish this book all the success it deserves in these troubled times for the banking profession.

Rundheersing Bheenick
Governor
Bank of Mauritius
5 May, 2014

Foreword

Ian Plenderleith

All sorts of causes can be adduced for the financial crisis of 2007–2008, from which the world is still recuperating. The globalisation of finance, as of other areas of business activity; deregulation and heightened competition; the concentration of banking groups following successive waves of mergers; the application of advanced quantitative techniques to risk control, with imperfect recognition of their limitations; innovation in the design of financial instruments and trading strategies; increased reliance on active liability management in wholesale markets; and the conjuncture of cyclical downturn in the global economy with continuing underlying imbalances between major economies – the list is long and will provide fertile soil for doctoral theses for years to come.

But one pervasive faultline is that in the process many banks somehow lost sight of the basic principles of banking. So the primer that Moorad Choudhry provides in this book is both timely and salutary. In clear, concise and uncompromising terms, he has provided a comprehensive compendium of good practice, starting with an overview of the essential elements of banking business, then drilling down into the critical areas of asset–liability management, liquidity and risk management, and then surveying the over-arching issues of strategy and governance. Not all bankers are renowned for an interest in literature, but this book is required reading.

If there is one area where this book will be most valuable in helping the present generation of bankers rebuild their business on the rubble of the financial crisis, it is in its treatment of liquidity – which Moorad Choudhry aptly describes as "the water of life" of banking. As he notes, "the crisis of 2007 and 2008 was as much a crisis of bank liquidity as it was of capital erosion". The huge expansion of wholesale markets over the past half century allowed banks to economise on the quantum and quality of liquidity they hold on the balance sheet as a cushion against unforeseen funding needs. But the result, as we have seen, has been severe exposure to liquidity strains if, as happened, wholesale market funding suddenly evaporates. The result has been much more substantial liquidity requirements set by bank supervisors, which, as Moorad Choudhry rightly remarks, are not new, but rather "a turning of the clock back to earlier times, when conservative principles in liquidity management were actually quite common place". Our forefathers could not have put it better.

It is not easy, in a book on the principles of banking, to bring the narrative to a thrilling climax. But Moorad Choudhry delivers a remarkable denouement with his chapter on corporate governance principles, which concludes with a clinical dissection of the weaknesses that undermined banks, large and small, in the recent crisis. This spine-chilling post mortem of what went wrong brings the principles of banking blazingly alive. If reading it keeps bankers awake at night, this admirable book will have served its purpose.

Ian Plenderleith
Former Executive Director
Bank of England
31 March 2011

Preface

Aficionados of science fiction will be familiar with *Dune*, a seminal work in that genre written by the late Frank Herbert. A complex, interwoven tale of imperial rivalry, medieval mysticism, clan fighting and religious hero worship, as well as an old-fashioned story of good guys versus bad guys, it is set on the desert planet Arrakis. Among a range of peculiar geophysical features, this planet suffers from an almost complete lack of water. The native inhabitants of Arrakis, the *Fremen,* appreciated this lack so much that they took great pains to preserve and recycle every drop of moisture, even to the extent of recycling water from the bodies of their dead. Water was life. Anything that was vital to the maintenance of life itself was known by the Fremen as "the water of life".[1]

And so to banking. Banks have always been a part of recorded history. Latin texts describe a form of borrowing and lending activity in Roman times, and before that the ancient Babylonians practised an elementary form of banking. In his excellent and thought-provoking book *Zero* (London: Souvenir Press, 2000), Charles Seife tells us "before Arabic numerals came around, money [lenders] had to make do with an abacus or counting board. The Germans called the counting board a *Rechenbank*, which is why we call moneylenders *banks*". So now we know. Banks are the lifeblood of society, because without them nothing would get done. By that I mean nothing productive. Nothing would be built, nothing would be traded, and very little would be consumed. This would result in all of us being much worse off than we are now. As Simon Johnson and James Kwak note in their book *13 Bankers* (New York: Pantheon, 2010), because an advancing society in the process of industrialisation requires "investments in new technology, it also [requires] credit . . . long-run prosperity requires

1 Actually, it turns out that my own initial interpretation of this elegant expression was entirely erroneous. The story in fact refers to a powerful narcotic drug that is taken by the *Bene Gesserit*, a female order of exceptionally clever thinkers, as part of a developmental ritual, which ends either in death or in enhanced prescient powers on the part of the user. Reading *Dune* for the first time as a 15-year-old, I understood it as a general expression for the importance of water to life. And first impressions last . . .

large-scale commerce and industry, both of which require banks". Banks are vital to societal development and civilisation. And right from the start, banks have always had to rely on the availability of continuous funding, or *liquidity*. This is a definition of banking. For banks, liquidity is the water of life.

Because they are such an important part of society and human development, it is evident that banks must be managed properly. This is not as obvious as one might think. During the global financial crisis of 2007–2009, a number of small and large banks around the world failed, some of them quite spectacularly. Many of these banks were shown to have been managed with monumental incompetence by people who had seemingly been at the top of their game. People boasting MBAs, feted around the world with invitations to dine at prime ministerial and presidential levels. People who had in many cases never actually bothered to obtain any professional qualifications in banking, but who would have us believe their self-generated hype that they were the Masters of the Universe. Many of them thought that they could beat the market, that as long as the music was playing they should still be in the game, even as all the indications suggested that a recession was already enveloping them. In the end it was a case of the emperor's new clothes, because it became apparent that many of these star bankers had done what any literate teenager could do: they'd made money in a bull market. Or, as Quentin Letts writes in his brilliant polemic *50 People Who Buggered Up Britain* (London: Constable, 2009), "They were bull-market innocents caught short by change". Come the crash, they were shown to be naked. These people, through a combination of hubris, arrogance, conceit, perverse empire-building obsession, greed, herd mentality, monstrous egotism, poor understanding of finance, simple ineptitude, and a lack of appreciation of the basic principles of banking, inadvertently conspired to bring about the worst banking crisis since the Great Depression, if not of all time.

This book is for them. It is not for beginners, it is for senior staff. Of course, it is also for junior staff who may or may not aspire to reach the heights of the Board, but who want to understand *before* they get there what they don't teach you at Harvard Business School: the practical but vital principles of bank liquidity, capital and asset–liability management.

This book is also about the principles of bank strategy and corporate governance. These principles are, in the main, not new (although some of them are). But they deserve to be renewed and never forgotten, especially during the next bull market run. Being about basic principles, *The Principles of Banking* omits a lot of product detail and complex mathematics on the more technical aspects of finance, much of which was covered to considerable depth in my book *Bank Asset and Liability*

Management (John Wiley & Sons, 2007). That book discussed such issues as analysing the yield curve, bank capital, securitisation, Basel II, value-at-risk (VaR) methodology, interest-rate risk hedging, derivatives pricing, determinants of the swap spread, and money markets trading. It also included detailed coverage of all the various products, both cash products such as bonds and floating-rate notes and derivatives such as credit default swaps (CDS) and caps/floors. We do not repeat that material here (and, as that book was over 1,400 pages long, that's just as well!), although we do repeat the material that remains very relevant, and more important than ever in the light of recent events: the four chapters on bank asset–liability management (ALM) and the asset–liability committee (ALCO). But otherwise in this book we focus on key issues in bank strategy and liquidity management. So if you require detailed product technical knowledge, please consult the earlier book.

Where we do get detailed and technical is in the field of liquidity risk management and management reporting. The 2007–2009 financial crisis highlighted the need for banks to "get back" to the roots of banking and concentrate on liquidity management, which is the essence of banking. In my earlier book I devoted four chapters to ALM and liquidity risk management, but clearly that wasn't enough! In this book we dedicate a lot more page space to this essential topic. Liquidity is a key focus of bank regulators in the post-crisis age, so it is important to be up to speed with this subject at a detailed level.

We also get very detailed and technical in Chapter 5. This chapter covers the yield curve, which is a very important topic. All senior management should be familiar with the yield curve, with the no-arbitrage principles of finance that drive its use, and how to analyse and interpret it. Why? Quite simply, because the curve drives everything. A bank sets the price of its assets and the cost of its liabilities from what its own internal risky yield curve implies. An understanding and appreciation of what the correct valuation of balance sheet items should be, requires an understanding of what drives the yield curve. It is worth taking the time and effort to become thoroughly *au fait* with Chapter 5. It has been kept deliberately technical, although still accessible, for the specific enjoyment of senior management and board members.

This book looks at the high-level principles of finance. The first principle of banking is common sense. Being cautious and sensible is an essential prerequisite for sound and efficient bank management. Beyond this we cover further basic principles in the following chapters, but here is a flavour of them to start with:

1. Secure your funding base – that is, your liquidity – for all contingencies, *before* you start lending beyond your deposit base.

2. Establish a sound base of customer deposits, and ensure that a majority of lending is funded from core, stable deposits.
3. Lend prudently, and with sound judgement (that is, not following the herd), and if necessary across a diverse range of customers (but not to customers or sectors outside your area of expertise: know your risk).
4. Maintain a strong capital base of equity, sufficient to absorb all losses and *unexpected* losses, and still continue as a going concern.
5. See (1).

The essential message for bankers and regulators is one of conservatism. Liquidity crises are rare events, and it is possible for a person to spend his or her entire time in a senior managerial position at a bank and never experience one. The temptation to relax some of the conservative principles recommended in this book is strong. However, because of the importance of banks to the world's economic system, it is imperative that when a liquidity crisis does occur, a bank is able to survive it without support from the taxpayer. This is harder to do if one adopts a less-than-strict view about the liquidity and ALM risks involved in banking.

Traditionally, we describe a bank as a financial institution that is in the business of taking deposits and advancing loans, and which makes money from the difference in interest rates paid and received on these two products (the "net interest income"). This picture is still true today; even for the most complex banks with operations across multiple jurisdictions and product lines, it all still boils down to managing funding costs and running a sensible funding policy. While today even small banks deal in a variety of cash and derivative instruments across time zones, reflecting the high product sophistication in the finance industry, and the sources of revenue for banks are now quite diverse, the basic principles of running both a simple and a complex bank are unchanged, and identical. So while the modern banking institution is a complex beast, basic management objectives have remained unchanged. Or at least, they should have. In the lead-up to the financial crash, some senior bank management forgot this fact. Or quite possibly they were never aware of it in the first place.

So to reiterate, this book covers essential principles of banking that will guide senior management towards a more sustainable business model for their banks, and regulators towards a more stable banking system. It is something of a handbook for competent management. Incidentally, *The Principles of Banking* does not review the causes of the financial crash of 2007–2009. Also, it does not offer macro-level prescriptions for the economy as a whole. These subjects are discussed in my book *The Future of Finance* (John Wiley & Sons, 2010).

We must remember that at the core of *all* capital markets activity lies the need to bring together the suppliers of capital with the borrowers of capital. This was the original business logic behind the very first banks, and in that respect very little has changed. There is much other activity surrounding this basic function in the markets, but this function is paramount. As Mr. Letts goes on to say, "The first duty of the high street bank, surely, is stability. To be entrusted with the savings of small-time customers is a heavy responsibility". And the key ingredient in discharging this responsibility is the management of the bank's assets and liabilities. It is this that we focus on in this book, high-level ALM and its twin siblings, capital and liquidity management. On the ALM desk in a bank, the cash assets and liabilities are king and must be managed prudently. Liquidity and disciplined ALM are the water of life in banking. That's something the Fremen would have understood.

LAYOUT OF THE BOOK

The book is divided into five parts, covering the various different but relevant aspects of banking principles. These are:

Part I – A primer on banking
Part II – Bank asset–liability management
Part III – Bank liquidity risk management
Part IV – Bank strategy and governance
Part V – Application software, spreadsheets and teaching aids.

For newcomers to the market, junior bankers and students, we include a primer on banking basics in Chapter 1. A detailed background on financial instruments, a summary of financial market arithmetic, and a comprehensive glossary of banking and finance terms are included in the author's earlier book *Bank Asset and Liability Management*.

Highlights of *The Principles of Banking* include:

- a detailed look at the ALM function as undertaken by banks and securities houses, including risk management and management reporting;
- comprehensive coverage of liquidity risk management, including liquidity metrics, reporting, contingency planning and the liquid asset buffer;
- the role and function of the bank ALM committee (ALCO); including the organisation of the Group ALCO (GALCO) function in a multinational or multi-entity banking group;
- a detailed technical analysis of internal funds pricing, and how it should be set up in a bank;

- capital and liquidity risk reporting and stress testing;
- strategy formulation, and capital and funding management;
- recommended best-practice on effective bank corporate governance.

Files on the Wiley website, www.wiley.com/go/principlesofbanking, accompany this book. They hold policy document templates, risk report samples, teaching aids, applications software and Excel spreadsheets. These are discussed in Chapter 19, and hopefully should be of some use to practitioners.

Note that we do not discuss operational risk in this book. The principles of operational risk are not unique to banks, and would be applicable in any corporate environment. That said, bank management will need to be aware of the operational risk charge element in their regulatory capital requirement, so this is discussed in Chapter 2.

As always, the aim is to remain accessible and practical throughout; we hope this has been achieved. Comments on the text are most welcome and should be sent to the author care of John Wiley & Sons Singapore Pte. Ltd.

Acknowledgements

Love and affection to my wife Linzi, the most fantastically gorgeous woman in the world, for inspiring this book, title and all, during a visit to the Bank of England Museum in February 2009.

Thank you to my Father, Mr A.K.M.S. Choudhry, for everything. If it wasn't for you Da, I wouldn't be in England, in Surrey, in the City, in banking and in academia. I owe everything to you, thank you for inspiring me to work hard towards my goals, and for inspiring those goals. Thank you to my Mum for always making sure I know right from wrong. Thank you to Anika, Millie and Leela, an exotic and unbeatable combination.

Thanks to Clax, Khurram, the *Raynes Park Footy Boys* (Abukar Ali, Abubakar, Rod Pienaar, Richard Pereira, Mohamoud Dualeh, Zhuoshi Liu, Harry Cross and Farooq Jaffrey), Shareef C, Dave Beech, Nik Slater, Phil Broadhurst, the JP Morgan Chase ITS Footy Boys (Alan Fulling, Rich Lynn, Neil Lewis, Michael Nicoll, Jonathan Rossington, Stuart Medlen, Tony Fulling, Michael Beddow and Matthew Neville), Mike Brand, Didier Joannas, Martin Barber, Melvin Chan, Professor Carol Alexander, Andrew Benson, Suleman Baig, Stuart Turner, Mark Burgess, and Suraj Gohil. *A Solid Bond In Your Heart.*

Thanks to Mr. Tim Leonard, Professor Darrell Duffie, Brian Eales, Professor Gautam Mitra, Professor Christine Oughton, Rob Lynn, Gino Landuyt, Zena Deane, Ee Sing Wong and everyone at CNBC, Naomi Kerbel, Camy Boey, Jim Harrison, Tom O'Connor, Maira Chatziperou, Balamurali Radhakrishnan, Mike Hellmuth, Professor Radu Tunaru, David Lemmon and his Kiwi colleagues, Jaffar Hussain, Stafford Bent, Jas Singh Ghag, Jim Croke, Libon Fung, Professor Roman Matousek, Remi Bola, Wei Lei Goh, Emma and Maureen at Traveltime, Lamiaa Mohammed, Tony Holloway, Dr. James Berriman, Andre Stander, David Wileman, Sean Baguley, Professor Jean Helwege, Arno Kratky, Irving Henry, Eric Burg, Mark Miller, Jim Byrne, Colin Johnson, Vikki Spooner, Nayan Sthanakiya, Eric Scotto di Rinaldi, Ghislain Lafont, David Moskovic, Chris Ko, Nicola Conway, Paul Bennett, Liam Coleman, Lisa Sheehy, Jeff Skillman, Cathryn Warner, Matt Foss, Gareth Walters, David Connolly, Phil Smith,

Cris Kinrade, Stephen Fox, Janet Adams, Anita Berthier, Sarah Small, Jenny Organ, Eleanor Lavan and everyone who has helped, guided or inspired me through the years. Respect.

For their help when I really needed it, I'd like to thank Dan Cunningham at KBC Bank, Adam Lawson at Beltane Ventures, Abhijit Patharkar at Standard Chartered Bank, Frank Spiteri at Peel Hunt, Sharad Samy at Aladdin Capital, Graeme Wolvaardt at Europe Arab Bank, Tope Fasua and Syed Ahmed at Global Analytics Consulting, Richard Mitchell at the CISI, Lisa Hughes at Coutts, Ravi Biant, Roger Drayton at UK ALMA, and Bill Rickard, Martyn Hoccom and Ani Lassus at The Royal Bank of Scotland. I won't forget it.

Thanks to the team at Wiley Asia, easily the best publishers in the world, especially Janis Soo, Joel Balbin, Cynthia Mak, Sharifah Sharomsah, Jules Yap, Nick Wallwork and the rest of the gang, and to the fantastic Edward Caruso, for every step of the way from commissioning to publication.

Thank you to you – my readers. This time, it really is my last ever book. I'd like to sign off with two of the best from Derek Taylor at King & Shaxson Limited, a gentleman who's looked after me right from the start when I joined Hoare Govett Securities back in 1992. The first one below is from my days at ABN Amro Hoare Govett, and the second from my time at KBC Financial Products:

Moorad: I like the long gilt right now, I've just bought 50 lots . . .
Derek [shouting to the rest of the floor]: Sell 1,000 gilt! I don't care what it costs, just get it done!

Moorad: I'm looking to diversify our funding sources, do you know any counterparties who might be long cash and looking to lend?
Derek: Try Mervyn King at the Bank of England, I hear he's a lender of last resort!

Goodbye! Stay handsome.

Goodbye . . .

Moorad Choudhry
Surrey, England
New Year's Day, 2012

About the Author

Moorad Choudhry is Treasurer, Corporate Banking Division at The Royal Bank of Scotland. He was previously Head of Treasury at Europe Arab Bank, Head of Treasury at KBC Financial Products, and Vice President in Structured Finance Services at JPMorgan Chase Bank. He began his career at the London Stock Exchange in 1989.

He is Visiting Professor at the Department of Mathematical Sciences, Brunel University; Honorary Professor at Kent Business School, University of Kent; and Visiting Teaching Fellow at the Department of Management, Birkbeck, University of London.

Moorad is a Fellow of the Chartered Institute for Securities and Investment, a Fellow of the Global Association of Risk Professionals, a Fellow of the Institute of Sales and Marketing Management, and member of the Board of Governors of *ifs University College* and Board of Directors of PRMIA. He is Managing Editor of the *International Journal of Monetary Economics and Finance*, and a member of the Editorial Boards of *Qualitative Research in Financial Markets, Securities and Investment Review*, the *Journal of Structured Finance*, and *American Securitization.*

How does one define leadership? Simple. Look at the people sitting around you at the Boardroom table, your senior leadership team. How many of them would follow you to your next job for a cut in pay? If the answer is none of them, then you're not a leader. A true leader commands respect and loyalty in equal measure, and that goes far beyond a wage packet.

— Sherif Choudhry, Vice President, CapGemini

PART I

A Primer on Banking

Part I is a primer on banking, and sets the scene for newcomers, be they students or practitioners. It is essential to be familiar with the nature of banking business, as well as the types of instruments used in money market trading. We also need to be familiar with banking capital and financial statements, the former preparatory to a discussion on regulatory capital and the Basel rules, the latter simply for general knowledge purposes. So the first part of this book covers these areas.

We begin with a look at the fundamentals of banking business, and the different elements of bank capital. We also look at financial ratio analysis, used when reviewing metrics such as return on capital.

The remainder of Part I looks at regulatory capital, credit risk and credit limits, the use of securitisation and the yield curve.

CHAPTER 1

A Primer on Bank Business and Balance Sheet Risk

This chapter is intended for newcomers to the market, junior bankers and finance students. Everyone else should read it as an essential refresher course. The purpose of this primer is to introduce all the essential basics of banking necessary to gain a strategic overview of what banks do and to manage what risk exposures they face. We begin with the concept of banking, and follow with a description of bank cash flows, calculation of return, the risks faced in banking, and organisation and strategy.

A summary of the bank product line is given in the Appendix at the end of the chapter.

AN INTRODUCTION TO BANKING

Banking has a long and honourable history. Banking operations encompass a wide range of activities, all of which contribute to the asset and liability profile of a bank. Table 1.1 shows selected banking activities, and the type of risk exposure they represent. The terms used in the table, such as "market risk", are explained elsewhere in this book. In Chapter 2 we discuss elementary aspects of financial analysis, using key financial ratios, that are used to examine the profitability and asset quality of a bank. We also discuss bank regulation and the concept of bank capital.

Before considering the concept of asset and liability management (ALM), all readers should be familiar with the way a bank's earnings and performance are reported in its financial statements. A bank's income statement will break down the earnings by type, as we have defined in Table 1.1. So we need to be familiar with interest income, trading income and so on. The other side of an income statement is the costs, such as operating expenses and bad loan provisions.

TABLE 1.1 Selected banking activities and services.

Service or function	Revenue generated	Risk
Lending		
– Retail	Interest income, fees	Credit, Market
– Commercial	Interest income, fees	Credit, Market
– Mortgage	Interest income, fees	Credit, Market
– Syndicated	Trading, interest income, fees	Credit, Market
Credit cards	Interest income, fees	Credit, Operational
Project finance	Interest income, fees	Credit
Trade finance	Interest income, fees	Credit, Operational
Cash management		
– Processing	Fees	Operational
– Payments	Fees	Credit, Operational
Custodian	Fees	Credit, Operational
Private banking	Commission income, interest income, fees	Operational
Asset management	Fees, performance payments	Credit, Market, Operational
Capital markets		
– Investment banking	Fees	Credit, Market
– Corporate finance	Fees	Credit, Market
– Equities	Trading income, fees	Credit, Market
– Bonds	Trading income, interest income, fees	Credit, Market
– Foreign exchange	Trading income, fees	Credit, Market
– Derivatives	Trading income, fees	Credit, Market

That the universe of banks encompasses many different forms is evident from the way they earn their money. Traditional banking institutions, perhaps typified by a regional bank in the United States (US) or a building society in the United Kingdom (UK), will generate a much greater share of their revenues through net interest income than trading income, and vice versa for a bank such as Goldman Sachs or Morgan Stanley. The latter firms will earn a greater share of their revenues through fees and trading income.

During 2007 a regional European bank reported the following earnings breakdown, as shown in Table 1.2.

However, this breakdown varies widely across regions and banks, and in fact would be reversed at an "investment bank" whose core operating activity was market-making and proprietary trading.

Let us now consider the different types of income stream and costs.

TABLE 1.2 European regional bank, earnings structure 2007.

Core operating income	% share
Net interest income	62
Fees and commissions	27
Trading income	11

Source: Bank financial statements.

Interest Income

Interest income, or net interest income (NII), is the main source of revenue for the majority of banks worldwide. As we saw from Table 1.2, it can form upwards of 60% of operating income, and for smaller banks and building societies it reaches 80% or more.

NII is generated from lending activity and interest-bearing assets, the "net" return is this interest income minus the cost of funding the loans. Funding, which is a cost to the bank, is obtained from a variety of sources. For many banks, retail deposits are a key source of funding, as well as one of the cheapest. They are generally short term, though, or available on demand, so are often supplemented with longer term funding. Other sources of funds include senior debt, in the form of bonds, securitised bonds and money market paper.

NII is sensitive to both credit risk and market risk. Market risk, which we will look at later, is essentially interest-rate risk for loans and deposits. Interest-rate risk will be driven by the maturity structure of the loan book, as well as the match (or mismatch) between the maturity of the loans against the maturity of the funding. This is known as the interest-rate gap.

Fees and Commissions

Banks generate fee income as a result of the provision of services to customers. Fee income is very popular with bank senior management because it is less volatile and not susceptible to market risk like trading income or NII. There is also no credit risk because the fees are often paid up front. There are other benefits as well, such as the opportunity to build up a diversified customer base for this additional range of services.

Fee income uses less capital and also carries no market risk, but does carry other risks such as operational risk.

Trading Income

Banks generate trading income through trading activity in financial products such as equities (shares), bonds and derivative instruments. This includes acting as a dealer or market-maker in these products, as well as taking proprietary positions for speculative purposes. Running positions in securities (as opposed to derivatives) in some cases generates interest income; some banks strip this out of the capital gain made when the security is traded to profit, while others include it as part of overall trading income.

Trading income is the most volatile income source for a bank. It also carries relatively high market risk, as well as not inconsiderable credit risk. Many banks, although by no means all, use the value-at-risk (VaR) methodology to measure the risk arising from trading activity, which gives a statistical measure of expected losses to the trading portfolio under certain selected market scenarios.

Costs

Bank operating costs comprise staff costs, as well as other costs such as regulatory costs, premises, information technology and equipment costs. Further, significant elements of cost are provisions for loan losses, which are a charge against the loan revenues of the bank. The provision is based on a subjective measure by management of how much of the loan portfolio can be expected to be repaid by the borrower.

THE CAPITAL MARKETS

"Capital markets" is the term used to describe the market for raising and investing finance. The economies of most countries are based on financial systems that contain investors and borrowers, markets and trading arrangements. A market can be one in the traditional sense such as an exchange where financial instruments are bought and sold on a trading floor, or it may refer to one where participants deal with each other over the telephone or via electronic screens. The basic principles are the same in any type of market. There are two primary users of the capital markets: lenders and borrowers. The source of lenders' funds is, to a large extent, the personal sector made up of household savings and those acting as their investment managers such as life assurance companies and pension funds. The borrowers are made up of the government, local governments and companies (called corporates). There is a basic conflict in the financial objectives of borrowers and lenders, in that those who are investing funds wish to remain *liquid*, which means they have easy access to their investments. They also wish to maximise the return on their investment. A borrower, on the other hand, will wish to generate maximum net profit on its activities, which will require continuous investment in plant, equipment, human resources and so on. Such investment will therefore need to be as long term as possible. Government borrowing, as well, is often related to long-term projects such as the construction of schools, hospitals and roads. So while investors wish to have ready access to their cash and invest short, borrowers desire funding to be as long as possible. The economist John Hicks[1] referred to this conflict as the "constitutional weakness" of financial markets, especially when there is no conduit through which to reconcile the needs of lenders and borrowers. To facilitate the efficient operation of financial markets and the price mechanism, intermediaries exist to bring together the needs of lenders and borrowers. A bank is the best example of this. Banks accept deposits from investors, which make up the *liability* side of their balance sheet, and lend funds to borrowers, which form the *assets* on their balance sheet. If a bank builds up a sufficiently large asset and liability base, it will be able to meet the needs of both investors and borrowers, as it can maintain liquidity to meet investors' requirements, as well as create long-term assets to meet the needs of borrowers. The bank is exposed to two primary risks in carrying out its operations, one that a large number of investors decide to withdraw their funds at the same time (a "run" on the bank), or that large numbers of borrowers go bankrupt and default on their loans. In acting as a financial intermediary, the bank reduces the risks it is exposed to by spreading and pooling risk across a wide asset and liability base.

Corporate borrowers wishing to finance investment can raise capital in various ways. The main methods are:

- continued reinvestment of the profits generated by a company's current operations;
- selling shares in the company, known as equity capital, equity securities or *equity*, which confirm on buyers a share in ownership of the company. The shareholders as owners have the right to vote at general meetings of the company, as well as the right to share in the company's profits by receiving dividends;
- borrowing money from a bank, via a bank loan. This can be a short-term loan such as an overdraft, or a longer term loan over two, three, five years or even longer. Bank loans can be at either a fixed or more usually, variable rate of interest;

1 Hicks, J. (1939), *Value and Capital*, Oxford University Press, Oxford.

- borrowing money by issuing debt securities, in the form of *bills*, *commercial paper* (CP) and *bonds* that subsequently trade in the debt capital market.

The first method may not generate sufficient funds, especially if a company is seeking to expand by growth or acquisition of other companies. In any case a proportion of annual after-tax profits will need to be paid out as dividends to shareholders. Selling further shares is not always popular among existing shareholders as it dilutes the extent of their ownership; there are also a host of other factors to consider, including if there is any appetite in the market for that company's shares. A bank loan is often inflexible, and the interest rate charged by the bank may be comparatively high for all but the highest quality companies. However, it is often the first source of corporate finance. Hence the importance of banks.

BANKING BUSINESS AND CAPITAL

We introduced the different aspects of banking business at the beginning of this chapter. For the largest banks these aspects are widely varying in nature. For our purposes we may group them together in the form shown in Figure 1.1. Put simply, "retail" or "commercial" banking covers the more traditional lending and trust activities, while "investment" banking covers trading activity and fee-based income such as stock exchange listing and mergers and acquisitions (M&A). The one common objective of all banking activity is return on capital. Depending on the degree of risk it represents, a particular activity will be required to achieve a specified return on the capital it uses. The issue of banking capital is vital to an appreciation of the banking business; entire new business lines (such as securitisation) have been originated in response to a need to generate more efficient use of capital.

We can see the scope of banking business from Figure 1.1. There is a vast literature on all these activities, so we do not need to cover them here. However, it is important to have good knowledge of the main products.

ALM is concerned with, among other things, the efficient management of banking capital. It therefore concerns itself with all banking operations, even if the day-to-day contact between the ALM desk (or Treasury desk) with other parts of the bank is remote. The ALM desk will be responsible for the treasury and money markets activities of the entire bank. So if we wish, we could draw a box with ALM in it around the whole of Figure 1.1. This is not to say that the ALM function does all these activities; rather,

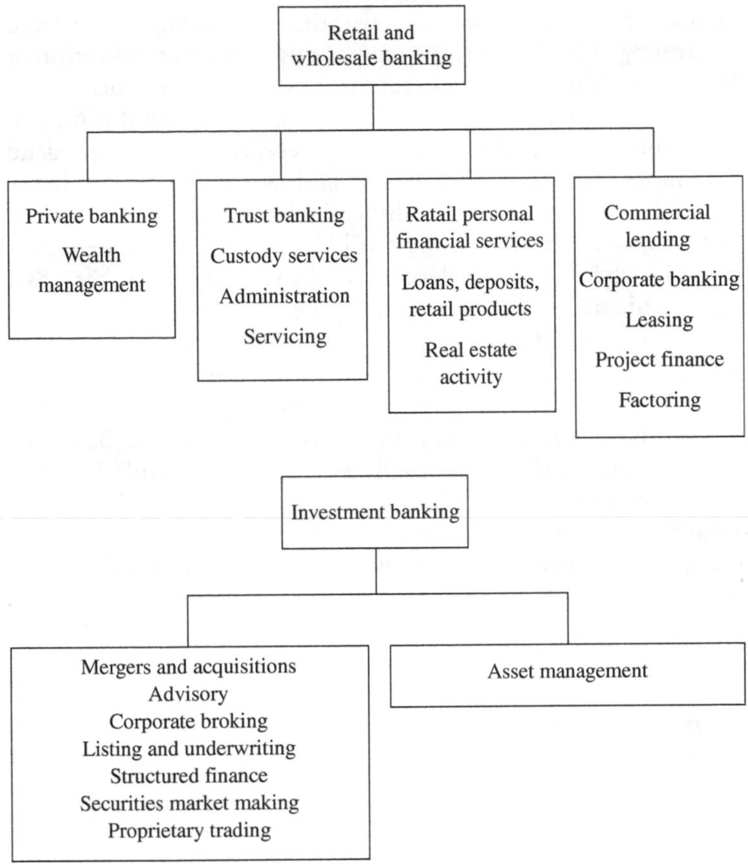

FIGURE 1.1 Scope of banking activities.

it is just to make clear that all the various activities represent assets and liabilities for the bank, and one central function should be responsible for the management of this side of these activities. In other words, the ALM function is responsible for the overall management of the balance sheet.

For capital management purposes a bank's business is organised into a "banking book" and a "trading book". We consider them next; first though, a word on bank capital.

Capital

Bank capital is the equity of the bank. It is important as it is the cushion that absorbs any unreserved losses that the bank incurs. By acting as this cushion, it enables the bank to continue operating *as a going concern* and thus avoid insolvency or bankruptcy during periods of market correction or economic downturn. When the bank suffers a loss or writes off a loss-making or otherwise economically untenable activity, the capital is used to absorb the loss. This can be done by eating into reserves, freezing dividend payments or (in more extreme scenarios) writing down equity capital. In the capital structure, the rights of capital creditors, including equity holders, are subordinated to senior creditors and deposit holders. A capital base that is not sufficient to absorb losses and still maintain the viability of the bank as a going concern is inadequate and not fit for purpose.

Banks occupy a vital and pivotal position in any economy, as suppliers of credit and financial liquidity, so bank capital is important. As such, banks are heavily regulated by central monetary authorities, and their capital is subject to regulatory rules governed by the Bank for International Settlements (BIS), based in Basel, Switzerland. For this reason its regulatory capital rules are often called the Basel rules. Under the original Basel rules ("Basel I") a banking institution was required to hold a minimum capital level of 8% against the assets on its book.[2] Total capital is comprised of:

- equity capital;
- reserves;
- retained earnings;
- preference share capital;
- hybrid capital instruments
- subordinated debt.

Capital is split into Tier 1 capital and Tier 2 capital. The first three items above comprise Tier 1 capital while the remaining items are Tier 2 capital.

The quality of the capital in a bank reflects its mix of Tier 1 and 2 capital. Tier 1 or "core capital" is the highest quality capital, as it is not obliged to be repaid, and moreover there is no impact on the bank's reputation if it is not repaid. Tier 2 is considered lower quality as it is not "loss absorbing"; it is repayable and also of shorter term than equity capital. Assessing the financial strength and quality of a particular banking institution often requires calculating key capital ratios for the bank and comparing these to market averages and other benchmarks.

---

2 There is more to this than just this simple statement, and we consider the subject in chapters 2 and 17.

TABLE 1.3 Bank analysis ratios for capital strength.

Ratio	Calculation	Notes
Core capital ratio	Tier 1 capital/ Risk-weighted assets	A key ratio monitored in particular by rating agencies as a measure of high-quality non-repayable capital, available to absorb losses incurred by the bank
Tier 1 capital ratio	Eligible Tier 1 capital/ Risk-weighted assets	Another important ratio monitored by investors and rating agencies. Represents the amount of high-quality, non-repayable capital available to the bank
Total capital ratio	Total capital/ Risk-weighted assets	Represents total capital available to the bank
Off-balance sheet risk to total capital	Off-balance sheet and contingent risk/Total capital	Measure of adequacy of capital against off-balance sheet risk including derivatives exposure and committed, undrawn credit lines

Source: Higson (1995).

Analysts use a number of ratios to assess bank capital strength. Some of the more common ones are shown in Table 1.3.

Banking and Trading Books

Banks and financial institutions make a distinction between their activities for capital management, including regulatory capital, purposes. Activities are split into the "banking book" and the "trading book". Put simply, the banking book holds the more traditional banking activities such as commercial banking; for example, loans and deposits. This would cover lending to individuals as well as corporates and other banks, and so will interact with investment banking business.[3] The trading book records wholesale market transactions, such as market making and proprietary trading in bonds and derivatives. Again, speaking simply, the primary difference between the two books is that the over-riding principle of the

3 For a start, there will be a commonality of clients. A corporate client will borrow from a bank, and may also retain the bank's underwriting or structured finance departments to arrange a share issue or securitisation for it, as well as arrange interest-rate risk hedging via the bank's derivatives desk.

banking book is one of "buy and hold"; that is, a long-term acquisition. Assets may be held on the book for up to 30 years or longer. The trading book is just that, it employs a trading philosophy so that assets may be held for very short terms, less than one day in some cases, and usually no longer than six months. The regulatory capital and accounting treatment of each book differs. The primary difference here is that the trading book employs the "mark-to-market" approach to record profit and loss (P&L), which is the daily "marking" of an asset to its fair market value. An increase or decrease in the mark on the previous day's mark is recorded as an unrealised profit or loss on the book: on disposal of the asset, the realised profit or loss is the change in the mark at disposal compared to its mark at purchase.

The Banking Book

Traditional banking activity such as deposits and loans is recorded in the banking book. Accounting treatment for the banking book follows the accrual concept, which accrues interest cash flows as they occur. There is no mark-to-market. The banking book holds assets for which both corporate and retail counterparties as well as banking counterparties are represented. So it is the type of business activity that dictates whether it is placed in the banking book, not the type of counterparty or which department of the bank is conducting it. Assets and liabilities in the banking book generate interest-rate and credit risk exposure for the bank. They also create liquidity and term mismatch ("gap") risks. Liquidity refers to the ease with which an asset can be transformed into cash, as well as to the ease with which funds can be raised in the market. So we see that "liquidity risk" actually refers to two related but separate issues.

All these risks form part of ALM. Interest-rate risk management is a critical part of Treasury policy and ALM, while credit risk management will be set and dictated by the credit policy of the bank. Gap risk creates an excess or shortage of cash, which must be managed. This is the cash management part of ALM. There is also a mismatch risk associated with fixed-rate and floating-rate interest liabilities. The central role of the financial markets is to enable cash management and interest-rate management to be undertaken efficiently. ALM of the banking book will centre on interest-rate risk management and hedging, and liquidity management. Note how there is no "market risk" for the banking book in principle, because there is no marking-to-market and all interest-rate risk should be hedged. However, the interest rate exposure of the book (floating-versus fixed-rate interest risks) creates an exposure that is subject to market movements in interest rates, and so in reality the banking book is indeed exposed to market risk that requires hedging.

The Trading Book

Wholesale market activity, including market making and proprietary trading, is recorded in the trading book. Assets on the trading book can be expected to have a high turnover, although not necessarily so, and are usually subject to a "churn" rule, which means they must be sold after a period of 180 days on the book. Assets are marked-to-market daily. The counterparties to this trading activity can include other banks and financial institutions such as hedge funds, corporates and central banks. Trading book activity generates the same risk exposure as that on the banking book, including market risk, credit risk and liquidity risk. It also creates a need for cash management. Much trading book activity involves derivative instruments, as opposed to "cash" products. Derivatives include futures, swaps and options. These can be equity, interest-rate, credit, commodity, foreign exchange (FX), weather and other derivatives. Derivatives are known as "off-balance sheet" instruments because they are recorded off the (cash) balance sheet.

Off-balance sheet transactions refer to "contingent liabilities", which are so-called because they refer to a future exposure contracted now. These are not only derivatives contracts such as interest-rate swaps or writing an option, but include guarantees such as a credit line to a third-party customer or a group subsidiary company. These represent a liability for the bank that may be required to be honoured at some future date. In most cases they do not generate cash inflow or outflow at inception, unlike a cash transaction, but represent future exposure. If a credit line is drawn on, it represents a cash outflow and that transaction is then recorded on the balance sheet. However, it is risk-managed as if a current exposure.

FINANCIAL STATEMENTS AND RATIOS

A key information tool for bank analysis is the financial statement, which is comprised of the balance sheet and the P&L account. Assets on the balance sheet should equal the assets on a bank's ALM report, while receipt of revenue (such as interest and fees income) and payout of costs during a specified period is recorded in the P&L report or income statement.

The Balance Sheet

The balance sheet is a statement of a company's assets and liabilities as determined by accounting rules. It is a snapshot of a particular point in time, and so by the time it is produced it is already out of date. However, it is an important information statement. A number of management

TABLE 1.4 Components of a bank balance sheet.

Assets	Liabilities
Cash	Short-term liabilities
Loans	Deposits
Financial instruments (long)	Financial instruments (short)
Fixed assets	Long-dated debt
Off-balance sheet (receivables)	Equity
	Off-balance sheet (liabilities)

information ratios are used when analysing the balance sheet and these are shown at Table 1.6.

For a bank there are usually four parts to a balance sheet, as it is split to show separately:

- lending and deposits, or traditional bank business;
- trading assets;
- treasury and inter-bank assets;
- off-balance sheet assets;
- long-term assets, including fixed assets, shares in subsidiary companies, together with equity and Tier 2 capital.

This is illustrated in Table 1.4. The balance sheet of a retail or commercial bank will differ from that of an investment bank in the relative importance of their various business lines.

Profit & Loss Report

The income statement for a bank is the P&L report. It records all the income, and losses, during a specified period of time. A bank income statement will show revenues that can be accounted for as either NII fees and commissions, and trading income. The precise mix of these sources will reflect the type of banking institution and the business lines it operates in. Revenue is offset by operating (non-interest) expenses, loan loss provisions, trading losses and tax expense.

A more "traditional" commercial bank will have a much higher dependence on interest revenues than an investment bank that engages in large-scale wholesale capital market business. Table 1.5 shows the components of a UK retail bank's income statement.

The composition of earnings varies widely among different institutions. Figure 1.2 shows the breakdown for a UK building society and the UK branch of a US investment bank in 2007, as reported in their financial accounts for that year.

TABLE 1.5 Components of a bank income statement, typical structure for a retail bank.

	%	Expressed as percentage of
Core operating income	100	
Net interest income	64	/core operating income
Commissions and fee income	31	/core operating income
Trading income	8	/core operating income
+ Net other operating income	8	/core operating income
– Operating expenses	61	/revenues
Personnel	38	/revenues
Other, depreciation		
– Loan loss provisions	23	/pre-provision net income
= Net operating income		
+ Other non-operating income		
= Profit before tax		
– Tax		
= Net income		
– Minority interest		
= Attributable income		

UK building society, core earnings split 2007

Net interest income	80%
Fee income	18%
Trading profit	2%

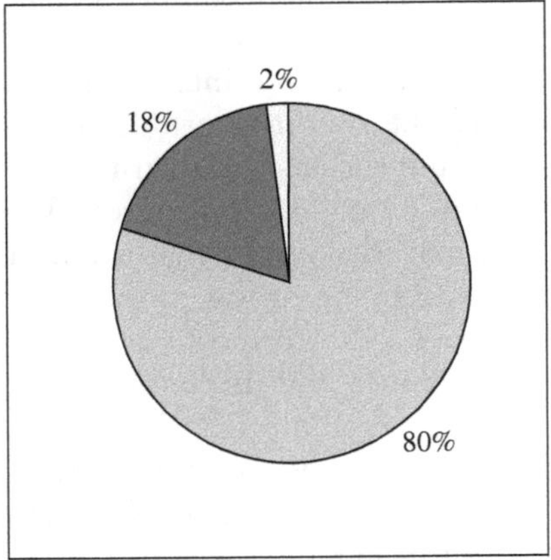

UK branch, US investment bank, core earnings split 2007

Net interest income	22%
Fee income	52%
Trading profit	26%

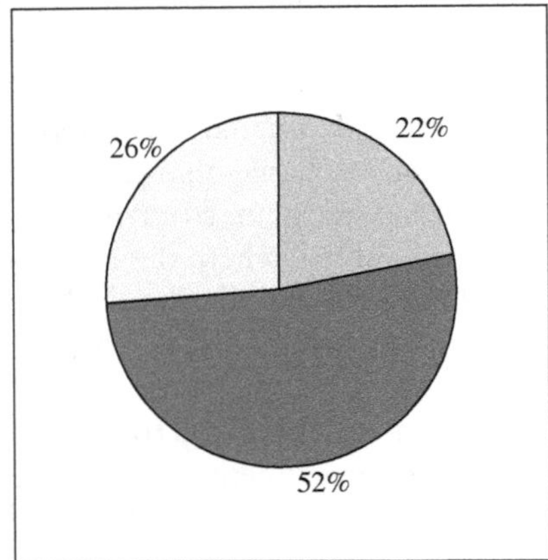

FIGURE 1.2 Composition of earnings.
Source: Bank financial statements.

Net Interest Income

The traditional source of revenue for retail banks, NII, remains as such today (see Figure 1.2). NII is driven by lending and interest-earning asset volumes, and the net yield available on these assets after taking into account the cost of funding. While the main focus is on the loan book, the ALM desk will also concentrate on the bank's investment portfolio. The latter will include coupon receipts from money market and bond market assets, and dividends received from any equity holdings.

The cost of funding is the key variable in generating overall NII. For a retail bank the cheapest source of funds is deposits, especially non-interest-bearing deposits such as cheque accounts.[4] Even in an era of high-street competition, the interest payable on short-term liabilities such as instant access deposits is far below the wholesale market interest rate. This is a funding advantage for retail banks when compared to investment banks, which generally do not have a retail deposit base. Other funding sources include capital markets (senior debt), wholesale markets (the inter-bank money market), securitised markets and covered bonds. The overall composition of funding affects significantly net interest margin, and if constrained, can reduce the activities of the bank.

The risk profile of the asset classes that generate yields for the bank should lead to a range of net interest margins being reported across the sector, such that a bank with a strong unsecured lending franchise should seek significantly higher yields than one investing in secured mortgage loans; this reflects the different risk profiles of the assets. The proportion of NIBLs will also have a significant impact on the net interest margin of the institution. While a high net interest margin is desirable, it should also be an adequate return for the risk incurred in holding the assets.

Bank NII is sensitive to both credit risk and market risk. Interest income is sensitive to changes in interest rates and the maturity profile of the balance sheet. Banks that have assets that mature earlier than their funding liabilities will gain from an environment of rising interest rates. The opposite applies where the asset book has a maturity profile that is longer dated than the liability book. Note that in a declining or low interest-rate environment, banks may suffer from negative NII irrespective of their asset–liability maturity profile, as it becomes more and more difficult to pass on interest rate cuts to depositors.

While investment banks are less sensitive to changes in rates, as their overall NII expectations are low due to their lower reliance on NII itself, their trading book will also be sensitive to changes in interest rates.

4 These are referred to as *NIBLs* (non-interest bearing liabilities).

Fee and Commission Income

Fee revenue is generated from the sale and provision of financial services to customers. The level of fees and commissions will be communicated in advance to customers. Fee income, separate from trading income and known as non-interest income, is desirable for banks because it represents a stable source of revenue that is not exposed to market risk. It is also attractive because it provides an opportunity for the bank to cross-sell new products and services to existing customers, and the provision of these services does not expose the bank to additional credit or market risk. Fee income represents diversification in a bank's revenue base.

Note that although fee-based business may not expose the bank to market risk directly, it does bring with it other risks, and these can include indirect exposure to market risk.[5] In addition, an ability to provide fee-based financial services may require significant investment in infrastructure and human resources.

Trading Income

Trading income arises from the capital gain earned from buying and selling financial instruments. These instruments include both cash and derivative (off-balance sheet) instruments, and can arise from undertaking market-making business, which in theory is undertaken to meet client demands, and from proprietary business for the bank's own trading book. Note that interest income earned while holding assets on the trading book should really be considered as NII and not trading income, but sometimes this is not stripped out from the overall trading book P&L. There is no uniformity of approach among banks in this regard.

Trading income is the most volatile form of bank revenue. Even a record of consistent profit in trading over a long period is no guarantee of future losses arising out of market corrections or simply making the wrong bet on financial markets.

Operating Expenses

Banking operating costs typically contain the human resources costs (remuneration and other personnel-related expenses), together with other operating costs such as premises and infrastructure costs, depreciation

5 For example, a strategy pursued by banks in the 1990s was to merge with or acquire insurance companies, so-called *bancassurance* groups. Although much insurance business is fee-based, the acquisition of insurance portfolios brought with it added market risk to the banking group.

TABLE 1.6 Common bank cost–income ratios.

Ratio	Calculation	Notes
Pre-tax ROE	Pre-tax income/Average shareholders' equity	Measures the pre-tax return on equity. A measure above 20% is viewed as above average and strong
ROE	Attributable net income/Average shareholders' equity	Measures return on equity. A measure above 10% is considered strong
ROA	Net income/Average assets	Measures return on assets. A measure above 1% is considered strong
Cost–income ratio	Non-interest costs/ Total net revenues	Non-interest costs minus non-cash items such as goodwill or depreciation of intengible assets. The cost to produce one unit of net interest and non-interest income. The lower the ratio, the more efficient the bank
Net interest margin	Net interest income/ Average earning assets	The difference between tax-equivalent yield on earning assets and the rate paid on funds to support those assets, divided by average earning assets
Loan loss provision	Loan-loss provision/ Pre-provision, pre-tax income	The proportion of pre-tax income that is being absorbed by loan losses. This is the credit cost of conducting the business
Non-interest income	Non-interest income/ Net revenues	Non-interest income includes service charges on deposits, trust fees, advisory fees, servicing fees, net trading profits from trading books, and commissions and fees from off-balance sheet items. Generally, the higher the ratio, the greater the bank's sensitivity to changes in interest rates

charges and goodwill.[6] Cost is generally measured as a proportion of revenue. A number of cost–income ratios are used by analysts, some of which are given in Table 1.6.

The return on equity (RoE) measure is probably the most commonly encountered, and is usually integrated into bank strategy, with a target RoE level stated explicitly in management objectives. Note that there is a difference

6 These are accounting terms common to all corporate entities, and are not solely used to describe bank operating costs.

between the accounting RoE and the market return on equity; the latter is calculated as a price return, rather like a standard P&L calculation, which is taken as the difference between market prices between two dates. The RoE target needs to reflect the relative risk of different business activity.

The return on assets (RoA) is another common measure of performance, and for a number of reasons a better measure to employ. This is calculated as follows:

$$\frac{\text{Current income (Interest income + Fees)}}{\text{Asset value}}.$$

Both financial statement P&L reports and measures such as RoE and RoA are bland calculations of absolute values. They do not make any adjustment for relative risk exposure so cannot stand too much comparison with the equivalent figures of another institution. This is because the risk exposure, not to mention the specific type of business activity, will differ from one bank to another. However, there are general approximate values that serve as benchmarks for certain sectors, such as the 15% RoE level for investment banks.

Provisions

Banks expect a percentage of loan assets, and other assets, to suffer loss or become unrecoverable completely. Provisions are set aside out of reserves to cover for these losses each year, and are a charge against the loan revenues of the bank. The size of the provision taken is a function of what write-offs may be required against the loan portfolio in the current portfolio in the current period and in the future, and the size and adequacy of loan loss reserves currently available. In some jurisdictions there are regulatory requirements that dictate the minimum size of the provision. Provisions fund the bank's loan loss reserve, and the reserve will grow in size when the bank provides more for expected credit losses than the actual amount that is written off. If the bank believes subsequently that the size of the reserve built up is in excess of what is currently required, it may write back a percentage of it.

THE MONEY MARKETS

The money markets are part of the global financial system. The various markets that make up this system are all, in one form or another, channels through which fund flows between the users and the suppliers of capital move. This flow of funds takes place in different markets, depending on the characteristics of the funds themselves and the needs of the market participants. The money market is where transactions in short-term funds take place. This is the borrowing and lending of funds that have a repayment date of within 12 months of the loan start date. However, the money market is not just made up of loans or cash products. There is a wide range of instruments used in the market, both cash and derivative, and it is these products and the uses to which they are put that are a significant focus of this book.

So, the money market is the centre in which market participants – which can be governments, banks, other corporate institutions, fund managers or individuals – meet to transform a short-term shortage (or surplus) of funds into a surplus (or shortage). As such, the money market enables market participants to manage their liquidity positions.

The suppliers of funds in financial systems worldwide are generally commercial banks, as well as savings institutions such as money market mutual funds. Other institutions such as local authorities and corporations are also long of cash at certain times. The borrowers of funds include the government, banks (again), local authorities and corporations (also, again).

In terms of trading volumes the money markets are the largest and most active market in the world. As money market securities are securities with maturities of up to 12 months, they are short-term debt obligations. Money market debt is an important part of the global financial markets, and facilitates the smooth running of the banking industry, as well as providing working capital for industrial and commercial corporate institutions. Money market instruments allow issuers to raise funds for short-term periods at relatively low interest rates. These issuers include sovereign governments, who issue Treasury bills (T-bills), corporates issuing CP, and banks issuing bills and certificates of deposit. The T-bill market in any country is that country's lowest risk instrument, and consequently carries the lowest yield of any debt instrument. Indeed, the first market that develops in any country is frequently the T-bill market.

Although the money market has traditionally been defined as the market for instruments maturing in one year or less, frequently the money market desks of banks trade instruments with maturities of up to two or three years, both cash and off-balance sheet.[7] In addition to the cash instruments that go to make up the market, the money markets also consist

7 The author has personal experience in market making on a desk that combined cash and derivative instruments of up to two years' maturity, as well as government bonds of up to three years' maturity. In his capacity on other bank Treasury desks the longest maturity of trades in cash and derivatives varied between 18 and 36 months, including products such as loans and deposits and overnight-index swaps of up to 18 months' maturity, medium-term notes (MTNs) of up to 24 months' maturity and liquidity portfolios of up to five years maturity.

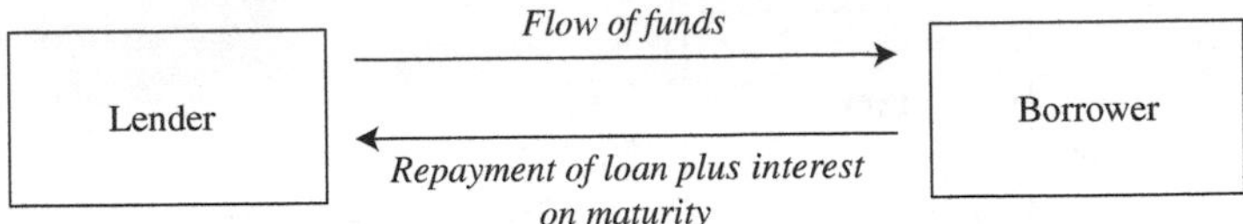

FIGURE 1.3 Direct financing.

of a wide range of over-the-counter (OTC) off-balance sheet derivative instruments. These instruments are used mainly to establish future borrowing and lending rates, and to hedge or change existing interest-rate exposure. This activity is carried out by both banks, central banks and corporates. The main derivatives are short-term interest rate futures, forward rate agreements, and short-dated interest rate swaps. Other derivatives such as total return swaps are also used.

Financial Transactions

All financial systems exist to facilitate one basic transaction: the moving of funds from cash-rich entities to cash-poor ones. This transaction involves the exchange of money for financial assets, or an interest in a financial asset. This exchange can be undertaken directly between participants, via an intermediary or indirectly.

Direct Finance

This involves two parties, one of which lends funds directly to the other for an agreed term and rate of interest. This transaction is shown in Figure 1.3. The funds can be lent in exchange for security (known as *collateral*) or on an unsecured basis. Direct financing is the simplest method for undertaking a financial transaction. Its drawbacks are that parties must know about each other and each other's requirements; they must also possess sufficient information on their counterparties such that they are satisfied in entering into the transaction. For this reason, direct financing, while very common among larger institutions or where the central government is involved, often gives way to financing via intermediaries.

Financing via an Intermediary

In terms of volume, the majority of money market transactions are carried out in semi-direct form, via intermediaries. We include banks among our list of intermediaries. These can be distinguished as follows:

- Brokers: a broker simply acts to bring lenders and borrowers together, and charges a commission for doing so. However, the involvement of

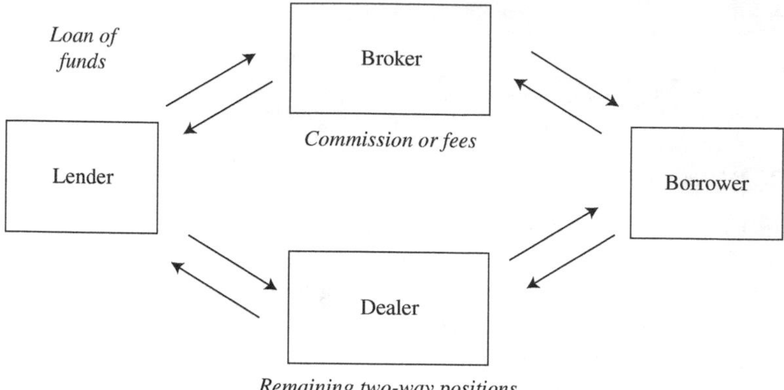

FIGURE 1.4 Intermediary financing.

a broker introduces greater transparency and information into the market.

- Market-makers: known as *dealers* in the US market, who also serve as intermediaries between borrowers and lenders, but take the cash position onto their own books and charge a two-way price in this cash to all other market participants. As such, dealers run a risk exposure position in the cash they own directly, as their profit depends on the value of the cash, which fluctuates in line with market dynamics and supply and demand.

Of course, the same institution can act in both capacities, according to who its counterparties are or what market it is trading in. This transaction is illustrated in Figure 1.4.

Indirect Financing

The existence of an active secondary market in money market securities reflects the extent of indirect financing. This covers a number of areas, such as banks issuing their own securities to fund their loans to corporates and individuals, and the trading of these securities after the initial finance has been raised. Financial intermediaries that are part of this market include commercial banks, insurance companies, credit institutions such as automobile manufacturer credit arms, finance companies, savings and loan associations (known as building societies in the UK), pension funds, mutual funds and so on. Their role in the market is to act essentially as both borrowers and lenders themselves in a way that serves the market's ultimate borrowers and lenders. Table 1.7 lists the types of firms involved in indirect financing.

TABLE 1.7 Financial institutions and intermediaries active in the money markets.

Deposit-taking institutions	Contractual institutions	Wholesale market counterparties
Commercial banks Retail banks Non-banking institutions: – Savings & Loan ("Building Societies") – Credit Unions Mutual funds ("Unit Trusts") – Money market funds Finance companies Government-lending institutions	Life insurance companies Life assurance companies Pension fund managers Mutual Funds ("Unit Trusts") Investment trust companies	Investment banks Securities houses ("Broker-Dealers") Brokers

Characteristics of the Money Market

The money market, worldwide, acts as a channel through which market participants exchange financial assets for cash, or raise cash on a secured and unsecured basis. Its key defining point is that it serves short-term needs. These are the short-term financing needs of participants who are short of cash, and the short-term investment needs of participants who are long cash. Figure 1.5 shows a stylised structure of the money market as it would exist in most countries.

Interest rates set in the money market act as benchmarks and guidelines for all other rates used. The importance of the money markets to this activity is often over-looked.

The size of the market means that it, in most countries and certainly in all developed economies, carries considerable breadth and depth. It is possible to transact very large volumes of business and for this not to impact the money market in an observable way. Money market dealing is "OTC", meaning it is not conducted on an exchange but over the telephone or computer terminal.

Interest rates in the money market – the rates at which participants borrow and lend funds – are set by the market and reflect a number of factors, from macroeconomic issues and global supply and demand, to more market-specific issues such as liquidity and transparency. There are a large number of interest rates, for different products and different counterparties. The cornerstone of the market's various rates is the T-bill rate. T-bills are issued by the government to raise short-term cash (the typical maturity is

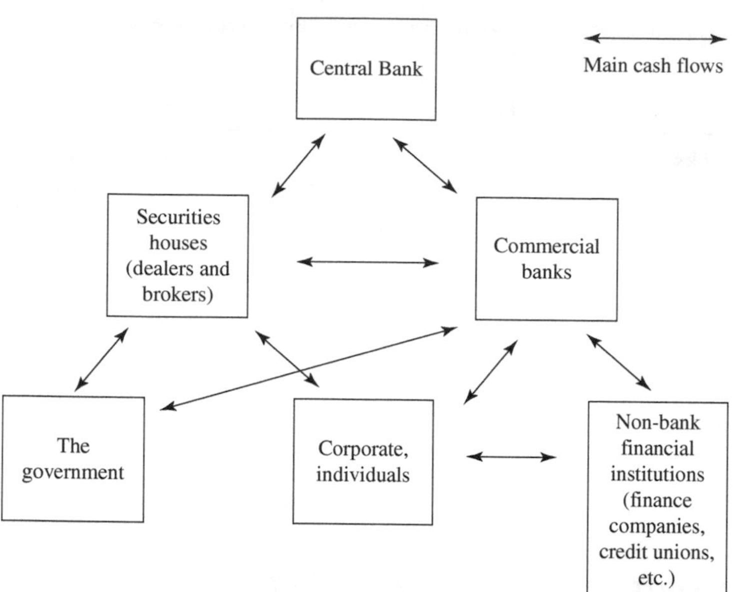

FIGURE 1.5 The structure of the money market.

90 days). Because the bills are backed by the government, they carry the lowest default risk in that market. Hence the rates payable on these bills are the lowest in that market. All other rates in the market (and the bond market) will be at a positive spread over the T-bill rate.

Readers interested in detailed coverage of the various instruments that go to make up the money markets may wish to consult the author's book *Bank Asset and Liability Management*. That book includes a primer on financial markets arithmetic. This is required background for an understanding of interest rate mechanics.

Money Market Conventions

Many money market instruments trade under similar market conventions. For example, for most currencies the basis used to calculate interest on a loan assumes a 360-day year, although sterling is an important exception to this. Again, while it is the norm for many currencies to float freely, their exchange rates to other currencies set by market supply and demand, some other important currencies are pegged to the US dollar and move with that currency. A small number of currencies are not convertible and cannot be traded.

Table 1.8 shows the characteristics of a sample of world currencies. It serves to highlight the individual detail differences that exist in the market. Terms such as "day-count" and "value date" are explained in the author's book noted above.

TABLE 1.8 Selected global currency conventions.

Country	Currency	FX rate	Day-count	Spot FX value date
Argentina	Peso	Free-floating	ACT/360	T+2
Australia	Dollar	Free-floating	ACT/365	T+2
Brazil	Real	Free-floating	ACT/360	T+3
Canada	Dollar	Free-floating	ACT/365 (domestic)	T+1
			ACT/360 (int'l)	T+2
China	Renminbi	Pegged to USD	ACT/360	N/A
Czech Republic	Koruna	Free-floating	ACT/360	T+2
Denmark	Krone	Free-floating	ACT/360	T+2
Egypt	Pound	Free-floating	ACT/360	T+2
Euro Area[1]	Euro	Free-floating	ACT/360	T+2
Hong Kong	Dollar	Pegged to USD, HKD 7.70 per USD 1	ACT/365	T+2
Hungary	Forint	Managed floating	ACT/360	T+2
Japan	Yen	Free-floating	ACT/360	T+2
Latvia	Lats	Pegged to Special Drawing Right (SDR)[2]	ACT/360	T+2
Lithuania	Litas	Pegged to euro, LTL 3.4528 to EUR 1	ACT/360	T+2
Malaysia	Ringgit	Pegged to US dollar	ACT/365	T+2
New Zealand	Dollar	Free-floating	ACT/365	T+2
Norway	Krone	Free-floating	ACT/360	T+2
Poland	Zloty	Free-floating	ACT/365	T+2
Singapore	Dollar	Managed floating	ACT/365	T+2
South Africa	Rand	Free-floating	ACT/365	T+2
South Korea	Won	Free-floating	ACT/365	T+2
Switzerland	Franc	Free-floating	ACT/360	T+2
Taiwan	Dollar	Free-floating	ACT/365	T+2
Thailand	Baht	Free-floating	ACT/365	T+2
United Kingdom	Pound	Free-floating	ACT/365	T+2
United States	Dollar	Free-floating	ACT/360	T+2

[1]Austria, Belgium, Cyprus, Estonia, Finland, France, Germany, Greece, Ireland, Italy, Luxembourg, Malta, Netherlands, Portugal, Slovakia, Slovenia and Spain.
[2] The "currency" of the International Monetary Fund.

Sources: Bloomberg L.P. and Reuters.

Practitioners with access to Bloomberg can look up individual currency details by selecting:

[Ticker] [Currency yellow key] DES <Go>.

We show this page for Australian dollar, Brazilian real and Egyptian pound in Figures 1.6, 1.7 and 1.8 respectively.

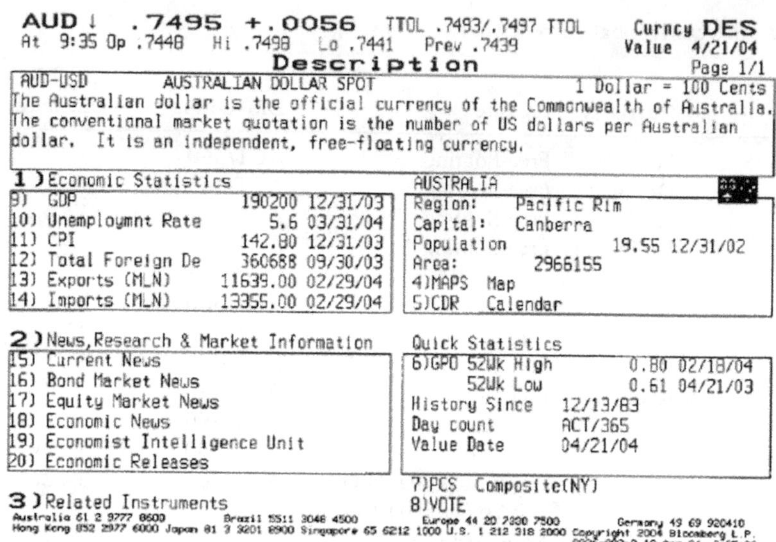

FIGURE 1.6 Bloomberg page DES for Australian dollar.

BRL 2.9130Y as of close 4/16 Curncy DES

Description Page 1/3

USD-BRL BRAZILIAN REAL SPOT 1 Real = 100 Centavos

The Brazilian real is the official currency of the Federative Republic of Brazil. The conventional market quotation is the number of reals per US dollar. It is an independent free-floating currency.

1) Economic Statistics

9) GDP% Qtr/Qtr 1.50 12/31/03
10) Unemploymnt Rate 7.08 11/30/02
11) CPI .12 03/31/04
12) Government Debt 926680.65 02/29/04
13) Total revenue 13053.0 11/30/99
14) Total Expenditur 12742.0 11/30/99

BRAZIL
Region: South America
Capital: Brasilia
Population 179.91 12/31/02
Area: 3286500
4)MAPS Map
5)CDR Calendar

2) News,Research & Market Information

15) Current News
16) Equity Market News
17) Economist Intelligence Unit
18) Economic Statistics
19) IMF Data
20) Related Instruments

Quick Statistics
6)GPO 52Wk High 3.11 08/04/03
52Wk Low 2.77 01/13/04
History Since 1/15/92
Day count ACT/360
Value Date 04/22/04
7)PCS Composite(NY)
8)VOTE

3) Related Instruments

Australia 61 2 9777 8600 Brazil 5511 3048 4500 Europe 44 20 7330 7500 Germany 49 69 920410
Hong Kong 852 2977 6000 Japan 81 3 3201 8900 Singapore 65 6212 1000 U.S. 1 212 318 2000 Copyright 2004 Bloomberg L.P.
6926-802-0 19-Apr-04 9:35:52

FIGURE 1.7 Bloomberg page DES for Brazilian real.

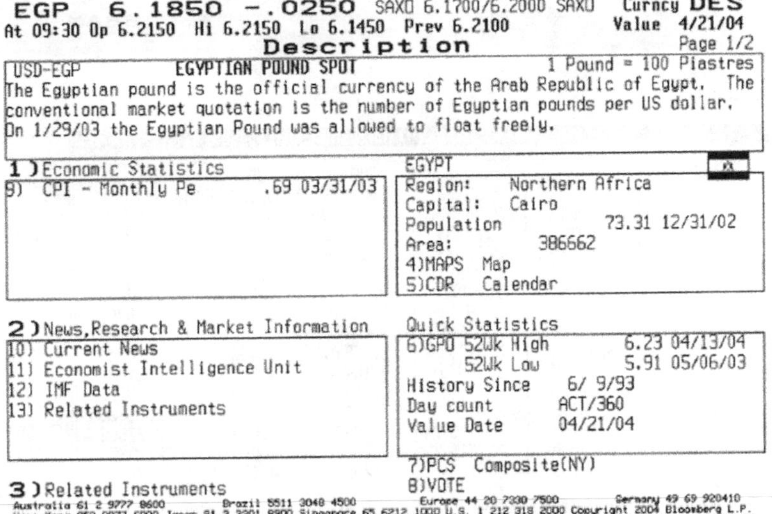

FIGURE 1.8 Bloomberg page DES for Egyptian pound.

LIBOR

The term Libor or "LIBOR" is the acronym for London Inter-bank Offered Rate and is the interest rate at which one London bank expects to pay for funds from another London bank of acceptable credit quality. The rate is fixed by the British Bankers' Association (BBA) at 11 a.m. every business day morning (in practice, the fix is usually about 20 minutes later) by taking the average of the rates supplied by member banks. The term "Libid" is the bank's "bid" rate; that is, the rate at which it pays for funds in the London market. The quote spread for a selected maturity is therefore the difference between Libor and Libid. The convention in London is to quote the two rates as Libor–Libid, thus matching the yield convention for other instruments. In some other markets the quote convention is reversed. Euribor is the interbank rate offered for euros as reported by the European Central Bank, fixed in Brussels.

Figure 1.9 shows the Libor fixing page from the BBA on Bloomberg, for the Libor rate fix on 31 August 2004.

(*continued*)

BBAM1 N1211a Govt **BBAM**

BRITISH BANKERS' ASSOCIATION

Page 1 of 4

08/31 11:03 GMT [BRITISH BANKERS ASSOCIATION LIBOR RATES] 3750

[31/08/04] RATES AT 11:00 LONDON TIME 31/08/2004 31/08 10:39 GMT

CCY	USD	GBP	CAD	EUR	JPY	EUR 365
O/N	1.62500	4.69375	2.03500	2.07625	SN0.03375	2.10509
1WK	1.57375	4.78625	2.06000	2.06863	0.03500	2.09736
2WK	1.58375	4.82156	2.12333	2.06938	0.03625	2.09812
1MO	1.67000	4.85375	2.16333	2.07575	0.03813	2.10458
2MO	1.73000	4.89500	2.23833	2.09300	0.04563	2.12207
3MO	1.80000	4.96250	2.32000	2.11313	0.05188	2.14248
4MO	1.86000	5.00250	2.38333	2.13300	0.05500	2.16263
5MO	1.92125	5.04125	2.44667	2.14925	0.05838	2.17910
6MO	1.99000	5.07625	2.51000	2.16575	0.06300	2.19583
7MO	2.04875	5.10625	2.56500	2.18450	0.06875	2.21484
8MO	2.10000	5.13625	2.61667	2.20138	0.07313	2.23195
9MO	2.15000	5.16375	2.66667	2.22000	0.07875	2.25083
10MO	2.20000	5.18750	2.71167	2.24438	0.08450	2.27555
11MO	2.25000	5.20750	2.76167	2.26800	0.08875	2.29950
12MO	2.30000	5.22750	2.81167	2.29575	0.09313	2.32764

Australia 61 2 9777 8600 Brazil 5511 3048 4500 Europe 44 20 7330 7500 Germany 49 69 920410
Hong Kong 852 2977 6000 Japan 81 3 3201 8900 Singapore 65 6212 1000 U.S. 1 212 318 2000
G926-802-3 31-Aug-04 12:03:31

FIGURE 1.9 BBA Libor fixing page, 31 August 2004.

EURIBOR

The official euro fixing is known as Euribor, which is set in Brussels at 1100 hours local time each euro business day. This should not be confused with the euro Libor fixing. The fixing operates in the same way as Libor, with a panel of Euribor banks contributing their rates each morning. The average rate of all contributions is taken as the fix.

Figure 1.10 shows the main menu page for euro fixing on Bloomberg, which is EBF. The rates fix page is shown in Figure 1.12, which is the fix for 11 June 2004. The fix is for spot value, and this is confirmed on the page, where we see that the value date is 15 June 2004, two business days later. The same menu page can be used to access both Euribor and the EONIA fix, which is the euro overnight interest rate.[8] This is shown at Figure 1.12, again for 11 June 2004. This shows the same fixings seen in Figure 1.11, as well as the previous days' fixing and the EONIA rate fixing at the bottom of the screen.

8 EONIA is the rate used with regard to an overnight-index swap (OIS), which we discuss in Chapter 8.

EBF N217 n M-Mkt **EBF**

email: pricecontrib@bloomberg.net

EONIA – EUREPO – EURIBOR

1) OFFICIAL EURIBOR FIXING
2) OFFICIAL EONIA FIXING
3) OFFICIAL EURIBOR FIXING (ACT/365)
4) EURIBOR & EONIA HISTORICAL DATA
5) EURIBOR PANEL BANK DATA
6) EURIBOR DEFINITIONS
7) EONIA DEFINITIONS
8) OFFICIAL EUREPO FIXING
9) EUREPO PANEL BANK DATA
10) EURIBOR OFFICIAL WEB PAGE
11) EUREPO OFFICIAL WEB PAGE
12) FBE OFFICIAL WEB PAGE

Australia 61 2 9777 8600 Brazil 5511 3048 4500 Europe 44 20 7330 7500 Germany 49 69 920410
Hong Kong 852 2977 6000 Japan 81 3 3201 8900 Singapore 65 6212 1000 U.S. 1 212 318 2000 Copyright 2004 Bloomberg L.P.
G926-802-2 11-Jun-04 11:49:34

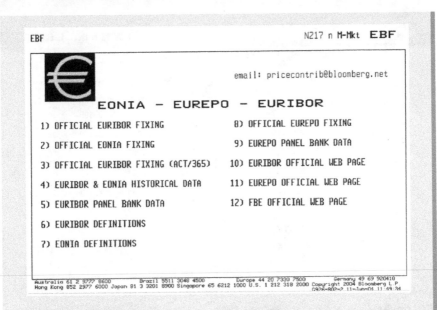

FIGURE 1.10 Euribor menu page EBF on Bloomberg.

1
Screen Printed N121 a M-Mkt **EBF**

EUROPEAN BANKING FEDERATION

Page 1 of 1

06/11 12:48 GMT [EURIBOR FBE/ACI] 248

EURIBOR RATES ACT/360 AT 11H00 BRUSSELS TIME 11/06/2004 11/06 09:12 GMT

		ACT/ 360	
	1WK	2.054	[FIXED]
	2WK	2.058	VALUE DATE 15/06/04
	3WK	2.070	[EURIBOR NOTE ON PAGE 47893]
	1MO	2.078	
	2MO	2.093	
	3MO	2.112	
	4MO	2.148	
	5MO	2.177	[WARNING] EITHER EURIBOR FBE,
	6MO	2.199	NOR EURIBOR ACI, NOR THE EURIBO
	7MO	2.240	PANEL BANKS, NOR THE EURIBOR
	8MO	2.280	STEERING COMMITTEE, NOR MONEYLI
	9MO	2.312	TELERATE LTD CAN BE HELD LIABLE
[HISTORY] THIS CAN BE	10MO	2.345	FOR ANY IRREGULARITY OR
DOWNLOADED FROM THE	11MO	2.390	INACCURACY OF THE EURIBOR RATE.
WEBSITE WWW.EURIBOR.ORG	12MO	2.426	(FOR DETAILS SEE PAGE 47896)

Australia 61 2 9777 8600 Brazil 5511 3048 4500 Europe 44 20 7330 7500 Germany 49 69 920410
Hong Kong 852 2977 6000 Japan 81 3 3201 8900 Singapore 65 6212 1000 U.S. 1 212 318 2000 Copyright 2004 Bloomberg L.P.
G926-802-2 11-Jun-04 13:48:35

FIGURE 1.11 Euribor rates fix page, 11 June 2004.

4 N2N299 M-Mkt EBF
Screen Printed
11:47 EURIBOR & EONIA FIXINGS PAGE 1 / 1

EURIBOR ACT/360	RATE	PREVIOUS RATE	TIME	EURIBOR ACT/365	RATE	PREVIOUS RATE	TIME
1) 1 WK	2.054	2.054	10:12	17) 1 WK	2.083	2.083	10:12
2) 2 WK	2.058	2.058	10:12	18) 2 WK	2.087	2.087	10:12
3) 3 WK	2.070	2.069	10:12	19) 3 WK	2.099	2.098	10:12
4) 1 MTH	2.078	2.077	10:12	20) 1 MTH	2.107	2.106	10:12
5) 2 MTH	2.093	2.093	10:12	21) 2 MTH	2.122	2.122	10:12
6) 3 MTH	2.112	2.109	10:12	22) 3 MTH	2.141	2.138	10:12
7) 4 MTH	2.148	2.132	10:12	23) 4 MTH	2.178	2.162	10:12
8) 5 MTH	2.177	2.155	10:12	24) 5 MTH	2.207	2.185	10:12
9) 6 MTH	2.199	2.178	10:12	25) 6 MTH	2.230	2.208	10:12
10) 7 MTH	2.240	2.211	10:12	26) 7 MTH	2.271	2.242	10:12
11) 8 MTH	2.280	2.247	10:12	27) 8 MTH	2.312	2.278	10:12
12) 9 MTH	2.312	2.281	10:12	28) 9 MTH	2.344	2.313	10:12
13) 10 MTH	2.345	2.313	10:12	29) 10 MTH	2.378	2.345	10:12
14) 11 MTH	2.390	2.349	10:12	30) 11 MTH	2.423	2.382	10:12
15) 12 MTH	2.426	2.386	10:12	31) 12 MTH	2.460	2.419	10:12
EONIA	TODAY'S RATE	PREVIOUS RATE	TIME	in millions of EURO			
16) EONIA	2.030	2.030	6/10	32) EONIA VOLUME	27567		6/10

Eonia updates at 7 PM CET
Use ER <GO> to monitor additional European money market rates.

Australia 61 2 9777 8600 Brazil 5511 3048 4500 Europe 44 20 7330 7500 Germany 49 69 920410
Hong Kong 852 2977 6000 Japan 81 3 3201 8900 Singapore 65 6212 1000 U.S. 1 212 318 2000 Copyright 2004 Bloomberg L.P.
G926-802-2 11-Jun-04 11:47:02

FIGURE 1.12 Euribor and EONIA rates fix page, 11 June 2004.

BANK CASH FLOWS AND OTHER BASIC CONCEPTS

The essentials of banking are a familiarity with the principles of banking cash flows and the concept of credit risk. The former creates the ALM risk and liquidity risk, and the latter creates default risk, which impacts bank capital. In later sections we introduce these two basic principles. First we get to the starting point with a look at basic cash flows and how to calculate the required interest rate on a loan.

Bank Cash Flows: The Conventional Bank Business Model

Figure 1.13 is an overview diagram of the cash flow profile of a commercial bank. Notice how these are managed through the Treasury function. This hypothetical bank deals with corporate and retail customers and other banks; it also has a loan facility at the central bank, where it deposits reserve funds.

Treasury is the cornerstone of a bank and indeed a microcosm of the conventional bank business model. In essence, banking is based on the following:

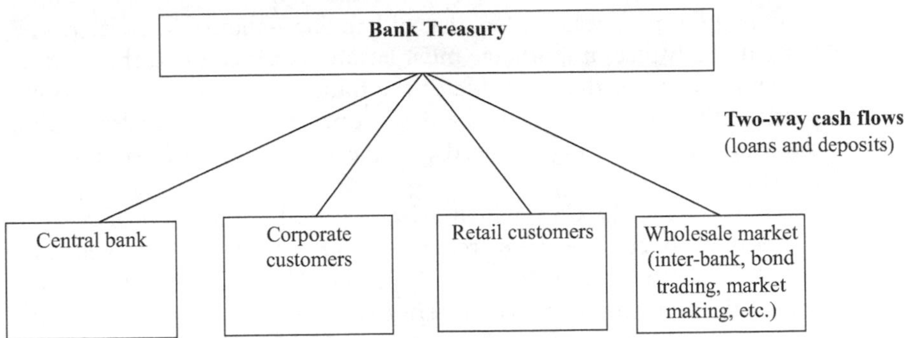

FIGURE 1.13 Two-way cash flows for a commercial bank.

- Capital and leverage: the capital of any corporation is defined as the difference between the firm's assets and its liabilities. For a bank it also includes capital set aside to cover expected loan losses, as well as certain types of long-dated debt. A bank's capital is the pool of funds that are its own funds: shareholders funds. For this reason it is also called the *capital buffer*. In banking, a small capital base is levered up into an asset pool that can be 10, 20, 30 times greater, or even higher. The equity base of a bank, that is the bank's own funds, is only a small element of the total balance sheet, perhaps 8% to 12% on average. It therefore forms only a small share of the bank's total funding, although business best-practice dictates that the capital itself is not actually used to lend to customers (not unless they are risk-free customers! More about this later). The balance of the balance sheet is made up of borrowed cash, which is then lent out to generate revenue. If we take the 10% equity capital base as an example, then a bank will be levered 10 times on this amount – the balance of 90 is borrowed and lent out. Managing the capital base, and ensuring its sufficiency, as well as controlling the level of leverage, are vital to the well-being of the bank.
- The "Gap": this is the difference in maturity between the legal contractual maturity of the assets and the legal contractual maturity of the liability. In simple terms, it is *funding short* to *lend long*. Consider a financial institution with a simple business model, such as a UK building society. Such a firm will have two main businesses, lending funds in the form of residential mortgages to retail customers (private individuals), and accepting deposits from retail customers. The legal final maturity of a residential mortgage might be 20 or 25 years, whereas deposits can be very short notice indeed, and unlikely to exceed two or three years in behavioural maturity. This is the basic business of banking; in formal terms this practice is known as "maturity transformation". The very act of

banking itself produces the key risk of banking – that of liquidity risk. A bank that advances a mortgage must ensure that it can find the funds to match the loan for the entire life of the transaction; failure to do so will result in the dissolution of the bank. So one can see how understanding the Gap,[9] and meeting its needs, is the cornerstone of banking risk management.

- The yield curve: the Gap, which arises naturally as a result of banking business, produces an extreme reliance on a positively sloping yield curve to help generate much of the bank's profits. This is because the shorter end of the yield curve, at which tenor the bank borrows money, has a lower interest rate than the longer end, at which tenor it lends money. So an understanding of yield curve risks is important. The author covers the yield curve in great detail in his earlier book, *Bank Asset and Liability Management*, and we reprise some of this material in Chapter 5.
- Liquidity: the business of maturity transformation contains an implicit, and explicit, assumption that one will always be able to rollover funding as it becomes due. Without this assumption, no bank would ever advance a 25-year loan. Therefore the business of banking assumes continuous liquidity. One can see immediately that managing the liquidity risk of the bank is vital, no less than a matter of life or death for the bank.
- Risk management: an understanding of default risk. Advancing a loan to a customer – any customer – carries with it the risk that the customer will default on the loan. An understanding of the credit risk presented by all customers is crucial to the survival of the bank, because excess defaults will erode the bank's capital and finish it as a going concern. Of equal importance to understanding customer default risk is the maintenance of loan origination standards. If these standards, which govern how creditworthy a customer must be before being eligible for a loan, are allowed to deteriorate, the bank will find itself sitting on a larger pool of poor-quality loans than is prudent.

These are the essential principles of banking. The reader is correct in thinking that they do not appear excessively complex. The art of banking is not technically difficult, it simply requires good judgement and common sense. Successful management of a financial institution does not require a PhD in mathematics or physics.[10]

Note that Figure 1.13 refers to cash flows that are both on-balance sheet and off-balance sheet. Managing the risks that arise from the latter are as important as those that arise from the former. Off-balance sheet cash

9 In continental Europe they do not use the term "Gap". They appear to prefer the term "mismatch" instead. The terms are synonymous. The author prefers "Gap".

10 Or in Econometrics . . .

flows are potentially more complex to model and measure, but this need not necessarily be the case. They do not only arise from derivative trading, but also from plain vanilla business such as letters of credit, guarantees and stand-by agreements. Such instruments create a forward-dated cash flow requirement, which must be incorporated into risk reports.

Measuring Return

Elsewhere in this book we will discuss the importance of a coherent, articulate strategy being in place at any bank, and the need for this strategy to target an explicit RoE or return on capital (RoC). To clarify exactly what we are referring to, we illustrate with a simple example.

Table 1.9 shows an hypothetical bank income statement and balance sheet. Using the values in these simplified statements, we can calculate the following:

Return on equity: 18.4/100 = 18.4%

Return on capital: 18.4/120 = 15.3%

Return on assets: 18.4/1200 = 1.53%

Earnings on assets: (120 + 65 − 12)/1200 = 14.4%

Leverage ratio: 1080/100 = 10.8

Average cost of debt: 90/1080 = 8.3%

Operating expenses: 60/1200 = 5%

Operating margin: 14.4% − 8.3% = 6.1%

Taxation rate: 4.6/23 = 20%

A glance at the above ratios shows that they are all related. All of the six variables below the RoE/RoC ratio will impact the final RoE number, so

TABLE 1.9 Hypothetical bank income statement and balance sheet.

Income statement EUR m		Balance sheet Assets	Liabilities	
Interest income	120	Loans 1200	Deposits	1080
Fees and services	65		Equity	100
			Retained profits	20
Interest expense	(90)			
Expenses	(60)			
Loss provisions	(12)			
Operating profit	23			
Taxation	(4.6)			
Profit after tax	18.4			

it is possible to generate higher return by altering only one of them (the taxation variable is outside the control of the bank of course). We see also that higher leverage produces a higher RoE, so it can become tempting for senior management to gear up ever higher, with more and more debt, in an effort to generate higher shareholder returns. This is of course a risky strategy, because in a market downturn a high level of borrowing causes debt-servicing problems. It is also why we recommend targeting return on assets (RoA) as the preferred measure.

The above would be sufficient analysis if the bank consisted of just one line of business. Most banks have more than one business line, so it is necessary to calculate returns adjusted for the amount of risk exposure each business creates, and the amount of capital it uses. The standard calculation is the risk-adjusted return on capital, or RAROC, which is given by:

RAROC = business line profit/business line equity allocation.

Using RAROC enables senior management to compare the genuine value-added of each business line. By definition the RAROC achieved by each business should exceed the bank's cost of equity. If it does not, that is an unsustainable business.

Loan Valuation

This section may seem obvious to many readers, as well as very basic, but one would be surprised how often its main tenets are not followed in corporate and commercial bank loan origination desks. So think of this as a refresher course.

The concept of shareholder value-added arises the instant one sets a target RoE at the strategy level. Holding all else equal, the bank shareholder will not continue to hold shares in the bank unless its target return is met. This target therefore drives strategy. All business undertaken by the bank must meet this target, otherwise it is not creating value. Thus the target RoE, together with the other variables introduced in the previous section, drives loan pricing. This is shown in the simple illustration at Example 1.1. Economic value-added, with respect to the capital employed, must be the guiding principle of all bank business.[11] In other words, the business must

11 Beware of arguments advanced along the lines of "in the real world, it is not as simple as that". Thus we observe "loss leader" products, we observe loss-making overseas subsidiaries being maintained because the bank's competitors are based there, we observe loss-making businesses retained for a tax write-off advantage. We observe a myriad of businesses being maintained in existence that, far from creating value, actively destroy it. Ultimately, this is all complete nonsense. Any business line that destroys value must be discontinued. It really is as simple as that.

generate a return that exceeds the target RoE. If it does not, then it is creating zero value, which means the shareholder would not rationally embark upon it.

EXAMPLE 1.1 LOAN PRICING ILLUSTRATION

Asset		Liability	
Loan	100	Deposit	90
		Equity	10

The equity base of the bank is exclusively Tier 1 (equity and retained profits)

Assumptions

Loan maturity =	1 year
The customer deposit pay rate =	5%
The target RoE =	10%
The corporate tax rate =	20%
Loan interest rate =	X%

The main principle is that the business, in this case the loan, must create value that exceeds the RoE target of equity invested.

We set the following relationship, which equates the capital employed with the after-tax discounted cash flow of the business:

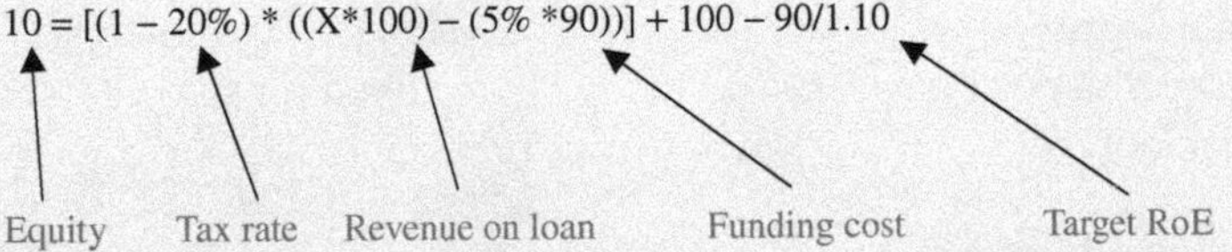

Rearranging for X we obtain an interest rate of 5.75%. The interpretation of this is as follows: by setting an interest rate of 5.75%, the present value of the revenue earned on the loan, after tax, is equal to 10, which is the capital set aside for the loan.

Therefore the loan interest rate must be set above 5.75%. At this rate or below, there is zero value creation.

Note that the break-even loan rate of 5.75% is 75 bps (basis points) above the funding rate of 5%. This is the break-even margin.

Following naturally from this illustration in Example 1.1, we see that a bank should calculate the break-even interest rate charge on business as a function of its funding rate, the break-even margin, as well as its RoE and the corporate tax rate. This is of course a very simple example that ignores all other operating costs, but these additional expenses can be incorporated in the analysis easily enough.

Note that the break-even margin is what is required to create shareholder value. For business lines that do not require any capital, for example AAA-rated government bonds, the margin can be lower. In our simple example, the loan is backed with the full capital base. In reality, the amount of capital required will depend on the "risk weighting" of the asset (loan). But the essential principle remains the same.

Let us now make the illustration more like the real world (see Example 1.2).

EXAMPLE 1.2 LOAN PRICING INCORPORATING DEFAULT RISK

Asset		Liability	
Loan	100	Deposit	90
		Equity	10

The equity base of the bank is exclusively Tier 1 (equity and retained profits)

Assumptions

Loan maturity =	2 years (annual interest)
Customer deposit pay rate =	5% (fixed for two years)
Target RoE =	10%
Corporate tax rate =	20%
Loan default probability (Year 1) =	0%
Loan default probability (Year 2) =	5%
Recovery rate =	40%
Loan interest rate =	X%

The same principle is applied again, whereby the break-even loan rate of X% must be set such that the present value of the expected cash flow of the loan, after tax, equates the value of the equity used to back the loan. Thus we have:

(*continued*)

$10 = [(X*100) - (90 *5\%)] * (1 - 0.2) / 1.10$ ← Year 1 cash flow present value (zero default probability)

Year 2 cash flow present value (incorporates default probability)

plus

$95\% * [(1 - 0.2) * X*100 + 100] + 5\% * [40 + (0.2 * 60)] / 1.10^2$

Allowing for no default (95% probability) Allowing for default (5% probability)

minus

$90 * 5\% * (1 - 0.2) + 90 / 1.10^2$ ← Year 2 funding cost

Rearranging for X we obtain an interest rate of 7.72%. This is the break-even loan rate that must be applied to the loan.

In this example, we allow for the possibility of default by the borrower in Year 2 of the two-year loan. There are now two parameters to allow for in addition to the equity backing the loan, and these are the default probability of the loan and the amount of recovery in the event of default (called the "recovery rate", in the manner of the credit derivative market). Should default occur, the bank will recover 40 cents on the dollar. We also allow for a tax recovery on the amount that is lost in the event of default, which is the tax rate of 20% multiplied by the loss amount of 60 cents on the dollar.

We see then that in setting the loan rate at a level that creates value, we need to adjust the expected cash flows for the possibility of customer default, and the amount we expect to recover should there be a default. From this point on, we have introduced an element of subjectivity in the calculation: the recovery rate is an *assumed* value (we have no firm idea what we will recover in the event of a customer going into bankruptcy) and the default probability of any customer can never be known with certainty, although one can infer it from observing the prices of loans and bonds in the market.[12] But one can see how once one enters the real world, pricing loans to create shareholder value and allow for credit risk becomes as much an art as a science.

This example also highlights the issue of setting aside part of each year's profit to cover for future loan defaults. This is known as loan provisioning; it is the method by which a proportion of bank capital is earmarked as a buffer to enable the bank to withstand losses arising from customer default in the future. In this process, part of the profit generated by the loan at the

12 See pages 815–18 of the author's book *Bank Asset and Liability Management* (John Wiley & Sons, 2007) for a detailed look from first principles on how to extract default probabilities from bond market prices.

end of Year 1, which is essentially the interest income minus the funding cost and expenses, after tax, is not recorded as profit but is instead set aside as a loan loss provision for the following year. In other words, loan provisions reduce the after-tax profit of the business.

What should the amount of loss provision be? The calculation of this amount again uses the default probability and recovery rate parameters (which may have changed from the time the loan was originated). We illustrate this in Example 1.3.

EXAMPLE 1.3 LOAN LOSS PROVISION

Net loan value:

$0.95^*[100 + (11.1)^*(1 - 0.2)] + 0.05^*[40 + (0.2^*60)]/1.10$
minus
$[90^*0.05^*(1 - 0.2)) + 90]/1.10$
$=$
9.305

Interest margin after tax:

$(1 - 0.2)^*[(11.1\%^*100) - (5\%^*90)]$
$= 5.28$

Attributable profit

$= 5.28 - 0.695$
$= 4.585$

We see that the net loan value is now 9.305. At loan origination the loan value was 10, so the loan has fallen in value by [10 – 9.305] or 0.695.

The fall in the net value of the loan at the end of the year is used to calculate the amount of interest income from it that can be attributed as profit, and what should be set aside as a loan provision. This is given as:

Attributable profit = Post-tax interest margin – fall in loan value.

This is shown in the second half of Example 1.3. The balance of the interest income not assigned to attributable profit is set aside as a credit provision.

We see then that to arrive at a sensible lending rate for any type of business that it undertakes, a bank must have a good idea of its cost base as well as a good idea of what the expected frequency of bad loans will be in the following 12 months. It also needs to have a target RoE to aim for. The interest rate on a loan is then set as a spread over the bank's funding cost, being calculated as a function of the target RoE, a credit spread to cover anticipated loan losses, and any additional spread to cover its operating expenses.

The above may be obvious, but one would be surprised just how many banks do not observe this very basic principle.

Capital Requirement

In principle, the amount of capital that a bank should hold is that amount which is sufficient to preserve it *as a going concern* in the event of losses. The italics in the previous sentence are deliberate. The capital level must be able to absorb all expected losses, and a certain level of unexpected losses, and leave enough in place to enable the bank to continue operating. This implies the following:

- the bank must have a reasonable estimate of what its expected losses, together with an add-on for unexpected losses, are likely to be; call this amount X;
- the level of capital in place must be at least X more than the minimum level required by the regulatory authority.

The first requirement is self-evident, the second less so. However, if the level of capital in place is the minimum required, and the bank suffers X expected losses, unless the second requirement has been met, the bank will be under-capitalised for regulatory purposes, which will result in a loss of confidence, a bank run and either bankruptcy or taxpayer bailout. It is important to bear this in mind when setting capital levels.

The starting point for capital allocation is the regulatory requirement. This is the simplest approach to take and quite common. The regulatory capital amount required can be compared to the "earnings-at-risk" (EaR) approach for measuring capital. This method involves observing the historical distribution of earnings, and its volatility, to determine the extent of earnings risk. The volatility level of earnings then drives the capital requirement. EaR is measured in different ways, including loan revenue, interest margin, mark-to-market volatility, accounting profit and so on. The volatility (standard deviation) of the distribution of earnings then sets the capital required.

RISK EXPOSURES IN BANKING

We need to be familiar with the risks inherent in the business of banking. The obvious ones are better known, but all risks need to be adequately managed, and the direction for this risk management must come from the top, at board level. In Chapter 18 we provide a detailed look at the ideal bank governance structure, which should allow for an effective risk management framework. Here we summarise the key risk exposures that must be measured and mitigated.

In Choudhry (2006) we define and describe the main bank risk exposures. It is worth summarising that content here.

The Main Bank Risks

Any transaction or undertaking with an element of uncertainty as to its future outcome carries an element of risk: risk can be thought of as uncertainty. To associate particular assets such as equities, bonds or corporate cash flows with types of risk, we need to define "risk" itself. It is useful to define it in terms of a risk *horizon*, the point at which an asset will be realised, or turned into cash. All market participants, including speculators, have a horizon. Essentially then the horizon is the time period within which risk is being considered.

Once we have established a notion of horizon, a working definition of risk is *the uncertainty of the future total cash value of an investment on the investor's horizon date*. This uncertainty arises from many sources. For participants in the financial markets risk is essentially a measure of the volatility of asset returns, although it has a broader definition as being any type of uncertainty as to future outcomes. The types of risk that a bank is exposed to as part of its operations in the loan and debt capital markets are described below.

Credit Risk

Also called *issuer risk*, this is the primary risk in banking. It is the risk that a customer will default on a loan. It is also the risk, short of default, that the credit quality of the obligor will deteriorate, which affects book value because there is an increased probability of default. Credit risk exists in the banking portfolio and trading portfolio. Banking book assets are not marked-to-market.

Credit risk is described by exposure, or notional value at risk; probability of default; and loss in event of default. The most common measure of credit risk is the formal credit rating. However, all banks will rate their customers according to their own internal rating methodology, which is part of their credit analysis process. An internal rating scale is essential in a bank because most bank customers (in the case of small and medium-size corporates, or SMEs, virtually all bank customers) will not have a formal public credit rating.

Sovereign risk is a type of credit risk specific to government debt. A country may default on its obligation (or declare a debt "moratorium") if debt payments relative to domestic product reach unsustainable levels.

Performance is an extension of the notion of credit risk; it relates primarily to OTC derivative instruments. It would apply, for instance, to financial agreements that do not involve an extension of credit; little or no cash is exchanged at the agreement's inception. Instead the contract calls for counterparties to exchange cash payments on a pre-set future date, according to a schedule based on the values of specific assets or indices.

Related to credit risk is "performance risk", which is the risk of underperformance by the borrower on a specific transaction. However, it is best to roll this into overall credit risk for the obligor.

A bank will have credit risk at an individual level, to each borrowing customer, as well as at the aggregate portfolio level. Portfolio risk will need to take into account the diversification impact of a group of loans, although in a bear market there is a strong case for arguing that diversity disappears and that correlation of assets is effectively unity. However, portfolio risk will differ according to the number of borrowers and their variation across industries, sectors and geographical regions.

Modelling individual and portfolio default probability is a problematic exercise at the best of times because it relies on assumptions, and unrealistic or inaccurate assumptions will produce flawed results. As such, in stress scenarios it may make more sense to assume a zero recovery and a unity correlation when determining economic capital at risk.

Market Risk

This is risk of loss arising from movements in prices in financial markets. Examples include FX risk, interest-rate risk and basis risk. In banks the key market risk is interest-rate risk, and it is sometimes measured and reported separately to other market risk.

Market risk is essentially mark-to-market risk and does not apply to non-trading assets held in a banking book or accrual books.

Interest-rate risk is the risk of loss of earnings due to movement in interest rates. A significant share of bank earnings arises as a result of interest earnings on assets. Hence this is a significant risk. Even in a banking book, with no mark-to-market revaluation, fixed rate assets will produce lower profit if the interest rate payable on liabilities funding that asset rises. Interest-rate risk includes reset risk, the risk of rates changing in between re-fixing dates on a floating-rate asset or liability.

Specific market risks will differ according to the type of asset under consideration.

Currency Risk This arises from exposure to movements in FX rates. Currency risk is often sub-divided into *transaction* risk, where currency fluctuations affect the proceeds from day-to-day transactions, and *translation* risk, which affects the value of assets and liabilities on a balance sheet.

Interest-rate Risk This arises from the impact of fluctuating interest rates and will directly affect any entity borrowing or investing funds. The most common exposure is simply to the level of interest rates, but some institutions run positions that are exposed to the changes in the shape of the yield curve.

Equity Risk This affects anyone holding a portfolio of shares, which will rise and fall with the level of individual share prices and the level of the stock market.

Reinvestment Risk This is essentially interest-rate risk: if an asset makes any payments before the investor's horizon, whether it matures or not, the cash flows will have to be reinvested until the horizon date. Since the reinvestment rate is unknown when the asset is purchased, the final cash flow is uncertain.

Prepayment Risk This is specific to mortgage assets. For example, mortgage lenders allow the homeowner to repay outstanding debt before the stated maturity. If interest rates fall prepayment will occur, which forces reinvestment at rates lower than the initial yield.

Model Risk Some of the latest financial instruments are heavily dependent on complex mathematical models for pricing and hedging. If the model is incorrectly specified, is based on questionable assumptions or does not accurately reflect the true behaviour of the market, banks trading these instruments could suffer extensive losses.

Other Market Risk There are residual market risks that fall into this category. Among these are *volatility* risk, which affects option traders, and *basis* risk, which has a wider impact. Basis risk arises whenever one kind of risk exposure is hedged with an instrument that behaves in a similar, but not identical manner. One example would be a company using 3-month interest rate futures to hedge its short-term money market notes. Although

TABLE 1.10 Summary of market risks.

	Market	Reinvestment	Credit	Sovereign	FX	Basis	Performance	Prepayment
Government bond								
– developed country	■	■	■	■				
– developing country	■	■	■	■				
Zero-coupon bond	■		■					
Corporate bond	■	■	■					
Asset-backed bond	■		■					■
Bank deposit			■					
FRA	■		■				OTC	
Futures contract	■							
Forward contract			■				OTC	
Interest-rate swap	■		■				OTC	
Repo	■		■					
Equity (listed exchange)	■	■	■					

Eurocurrency rates, to which futures prices respond, are well correlated with money market rates, they do not invariably move in lock step. If rates moved up by 50 bps but futures prices dropped by only 35 bps, the 15 bp gap would be the basis risk in this case.

Table 1.10 assigns sources of risk for a range of fixed interest, FX, interest rate derivative and equity products.

Liquidity Risk

This refers to two different but related issues: for a Treasury or money markets person, it is the risk that a bank has insufficient funding to meet commitments as they arise. That is, the risk that funds cannot be raised in the market as and when required. This is also known as *rollover risk*, for obvious reasons. Funding risk can be affected by events in the market, affecting all but the most creditworthy of banks, or by events specific to the individual bank. So, in August 2007 the UK bank Northern Rock plc found that it was unable to access inter-bank lines as these had been withdrawn from it, and was forced to go to the Bank of England for funding. Once this fact became public, a run on the bank sealed its fate. In September 2008 the collapse of the US investment bank Lehman Brothers resulted in a general drying up of liquidity in the inter-bank market, so that even large AA-rated banks were forced to pay substantially over Libor to secure term inter-bank money.

The credit rating and general perception of a bank in the market is its best protection against funding risk.

For a securities or derivatives trader, liquidity risk is the risk that the market for assets becomes too thin to enable fair and efficient trading to take place. This is the risk that assets cannot be sold or bought as and when required – in other words, the risk that an asset, once purchased, becomes illiquid and cannot be sold. Of course, many bank assets are illiquid at the start; for example, an SME loan. Therefore, it becomes important to fund such assets with a secure source of funds. It is also imperative, as we shall see later, that a sufficient share of the bank's balance sheet is held in liquid assets that may be easily realised whenever needed.

Operational Risk

This is the risk of loss associated with non-financial matters such as fraud, system failure, accidents and ethics. Operational risk can be mitigated by defining strict procedures for all aspects of a bank's business functions, from front to back office, and ensuring adherence to them. The bank's risk management function should assign a dedicated person or team to managing operational risk and each department of the bank should appoint an operational risk liaison who will work as the primary contact for the head of operational risk.

Country Risk

The primary "other" risk is country risk. A bank that undertakes operations outside its home country will be exposed to this, the risk of a crisis or other market event in a country. The most obvious example of course is war or revolution, but it can also include a sovereign downgrade or balance of payments crisis. General economic deterioration, for example high inflation rates, is another example of country risk.

The Risk Management Function

While there is some variety in the way a bank risk management function is organised, the following may be taken as being business best-practice:

- having an independent department responsible for drawing up and explicitly stating the bank's approach to risk, and defining trading limits and the areas of the market that the firm can have exposure to;

- having the head of the risk function report to an independent senior manager, who is a member of the Executive Board. This person is usually styled as the chief risk officer (CRO);
- monitoring the separation of duties between front, middle and back office, often in conjunction with an internal audit function;
- reporting to senior management, including the firm's overall exposure and adherence of the front office to the firm's overall risk strategy;
- communicating risks and risk strategy to shareholders.

The risk management function is more likely to deliver effective results when there are clear lines of responsibility and accountability. It is also imperative that the department interacts closely with other areas of the front and back office.

In addition to the above the following are often accepted as ingredients of a risk management framework in an institution engaged in investment banking and trading activity:

- proactive management involvement in risk issues;
- daily overview of the risk exposure profile and P&L reports;
- VaR as a common measure of risk exposure, alongside modified duration, but not as a sole measure of risk exposure;
- defined escalation procedures to deal with rising levels of trading loss, as well as internal "stop-loss" limits;
- independent daily monitoring of risk utilisation by a middle-office risk management function;
- independent production of daily P&L, and independent review of front-office closing prices on a daily basis;
- independent validation of market pricing, and pricing and VaR models.

These guidelines, adopted universally in the banking community, should help to develop an influential and effective risk management function for all financial institutions.

The different stakeholders in a bank or financial institution will have slightly different perspectives on risk and its management. If we were to generalise, shareholders will wish for stable earnings, as well as the highest possible return on capital. From the point of view of business managers though, the perspective may be slightly different and possibly shorter term. For them, risk management often takes the following route:

- create as diversified a set of business lines as possible, and within each business line diversify portfolios to maximum extent;
- establish procedures to enable some measure of forecasting of market prices;

- hedge the portfolio to minimise losses when market forecasts suggest that losses are to be expected.

A robust risk measurement function is central to bank strategy and management. It is used to provide an accurate idea of risk exposure for shareholders and senior management, so that banks can stay within risk exposure limits.

DRIVERS OF CREDIT RISK

Notwithstanding that liquidity risk is the primary risk management concern for a bank, it should be fairly evident that an understanding of credit risk is also fundamental. We would argue that a proper understanding of credit is not possible without a deep familiarity with the market that one is operating in. That is, to know one's risk is to know one's market. Banks have attempted to measure the extent of their credit risk, and hence the amount of capital needed to cover this risk, through the use of credit risk models. It is worthwhile considering what parameters drive these models, because that is to understand what drives credit risk. Of course, the experience of 2007–2009 demonstrated that it is not possible to model credit risk accurately for all of the time, or to cover all eventualities. This brings us back to the importance of knowing one's market. An over-reliance on mathematical models of risk exposure can prove literally fatal.

Credit risk itself is the risk of loss in event of borrower default or borrower credit standing deterioration. The management of credit risk seeks to address the issues of (i) the probability of loss and (ii) the amount of loss. Credit risk and credit ratings are discussed further in Chapter 3.

Parameters of Credit Risk Models

Since the 1990s many, if not most, banks have employed a form of credit risk model to determine the extent of their credit risk, and in some cases to calculate their capital requirement. These might be "off-the-shelf" models such as those devised by the KMV corporation, Moodys or RiskMetrics, or an in-house proprietary one. Generally these models, known as "portfolio models", use two parameters to determine the extent of credit risk: the probability of default and the "loss-given-default (LGD)", which is also sometimes referred to via the "recovery rate (RR)", since (100 – RR) is also the LGD. They also involve a third parameter: default correlation. The logic behind default correlation is as follows: one can benefit from portfolio diversification if one has a varied range of borrower names in the portfolio.

TABLE 1.11 The drivers of credit risk.

Credit risk exposure	Cash instruments: notional (face) amount Derivative instruments: current mark-to-market
Credit risk drivers	Default probability Credit rating change Recovery rate
Default correlation	Commonality of risk drivers across portfolio names
Capital at risk	Implied capital at risk from default

Equally, if there is a factor that drives changes in status, such as credit ratings, across more than one reference name in the portfolio, it as well to be aware of it because changes in this factor will produce the same impact on all the names in the portfolio. Common factors that impact in large parts of a portfolio, or an entire portfolio, may include macro-level indicators such as the base interest rate or the level of housing mortgage defaults. However, since default correlation is a statistic that cannot be observed in the market, using it to determine your credit risk exposure becomes a little problematic.

Table 1.11 is an overview of the drivers of credit risk as viewed by bank credit models.

Looking at Table 1.11, we perceive fairly quickly that there is not inconsiderable uncertainty in calculating credit risk. The only parameter we know with certainty is the notional amount of cash at risk in a loan. Default probability is usually taken from credit ratings, or in some cases it is extracted from market prices such as credit default swap (CDS) spreads or corporate bond yields. However, credit ratings become notoriously unreliable the closer we get to a market downturn or recession, as do market-implied default probabilities. Risk managers often use published data on default rates and credit rating transition matrices, but again these suffer from the same drawback as all historical data; namely, in not being necessarily a guide to future default rates. We see then that a model will always, at all times, never be more than a best endeavours estimate of what the risk exposure actually is. Therefore we conclude principally that an over-reliance on models is unwise. At precisely the moment when a bank needs to be as fully aware as possible of its risk exposures, for example as an overheating economy is about to enter recession, this will be the time when the model will be at its most inaccurate. It is important to exercise sound judgement in assessing credit risk, and this is best facilitated by knowing one's market. An unfamiliarity with the markets and customers that one is dealing with is more likely to result in a greater reliance on model output.

Credit Rating

A credit rating from one or more of the three principal ratings agencies – Standard & Poor's, Moody's and Fitch, or a bank internal credit rating – is a qualitative and quantitative measure of an obligor's default probability over the next 12 months. In essence, ratings are a function of both quantitative factors, such as financial ratios, balance sheet strength and so on, and qualitative factors such as competitive pressures and management competence. There are two main types of model: ratings models, which assign a credit rating from which is inferred a default probability; and default models, which model the default probability and map this onto a ratings scale. Details apart, both represent the same methodology. An overview of the process of undertaking credit ratings analysis is given in Chapter 4 of the author's book *Structured Credit Products* (2nd edition, John Wiley & Sons 2010).

Under the bank regulatory capital regime known as Basel II, credit ratings play a big part in determining the risk weighting of a particular asset, and hence the capital that must be set against it. The experience of 2007–2009 shows that ratings remain an inaccurate measure of credit risk under market crisis conditions. Again, the use of credit ratings does not obviate the need for sound judgement when assessing credit risk. This is particularly true when undertaking the investment decision.

Figures 1.14A to C are a stylised illustration of credit risk. The credit risk distribution of a portfolio looks somewhat like this. What the exhibit is saying is that the extent of risk is highest for the equity capital of the bank

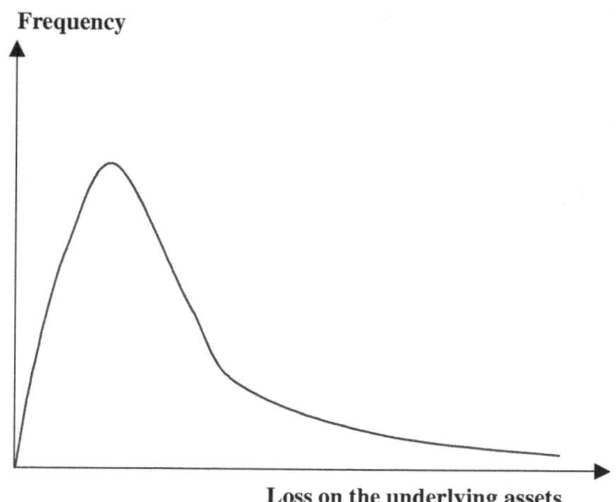

FIGURE 1.14A Credit loss distribution.

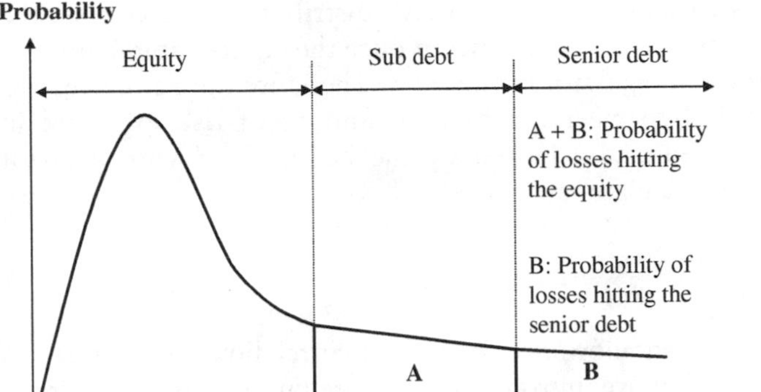

FIGURE 1.14B Expected loss distribution for the different constituents of the bank capital structure.

and lowest for the senior debt (a similar approach is taken when modelling the credit risk of a structured credit instrument such as a collateralised debt obligation). The subordinated debt holders will only suffer loss once a certain part of the portfolio has experienced loss. The credit model

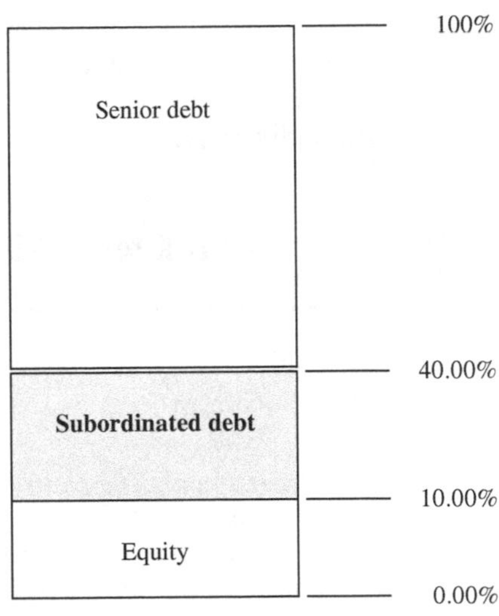

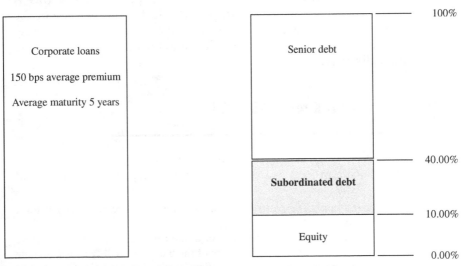

FIGURE 1.14C Capital structure of bank liabilities.

approach attempts to model this credit risk distribution. Of course, the bank is no longer viable as a going concern once the equity capital amount falls below the required regulatory minimum. Therefore the bank needs to have sufficient capital to meet the highest amount of risk exposure in the portfolio. The credit model used by the bank, allied with prudent judgement, is used to calculate this figure.

Correlation

All credit models make an allowance for default correlation. The use of this parameter, as we noted above, introduces still more uncertainty in the credit risk measurement calculation. It is accepted that corporate defaults, as well as ratings migrations, are more frequent in a recessionary market. Therefore when assessing portfolio credit risk, it is understandable to incorporate a positive correlation between the default rate of different names in the portfolio. How positive is positive? If we assign unity correlation to the assets, this means the entire portfolio defaults as soon as the first default occurs. Clearly this is unrealistic. Moreover, the joint-default correlation between two corporate names is an unobservable statistic. So at what level should the correlation parameter be set? This debate can get quite involved, and is outside the scope of this book. Again, the best approach is to apply good judgement: an element of positive correlation is sensible when assessing portfolio risk.

Modern portfolio theory states that there is a diversity benefit in correlation terms when one constructs a mixed portfolio. But this is dangerous for banking credit risk and capital calculations, because of the high positive correlation of assets during economic downturns.[13] In essence, it is not business best-practice to reduce the capital requirement based solely on portfolio diversity.

MACRO-LEVEL RISK MANAGEMENT AND STRATEGY

The high-level strategy and risk appetite of a bank is set by its Board of Directors.[14] Such a process is a very real, serious one, or at least it should

13 See the author's book *The Future of Finance* (John Wiley & Sons, 2010) for a discussion of this.

14 Just to be clear, the Board of Directors of a bank will comprise the executive directors, who are full-time senior officers of the bank and will typically include the chief executive officer (CEO) and the finance director, plus (say) one to five other senior officers (such as the head of investment banking or the head of

be, because board direction must set the overall approach of the bank. In other words, this direction must be a practical working document because the bank's entire appreciation of its risk-reward profile will come from it. An unclear or ambiguous board direction can come back to haunt the bank's shareholders, and embarrass its directors, if the bank ends up taking large losses on a particular trade or line of business.

We summarise now the correct process by which this overall risk appetite for a bank should be set.

Setting the Formal Risk-Reward Profile

The Board sets the high-level guidelines for the bank's risk appetite and its expected return. Risk appetite is in the form of upper limits on risk exposures. We do not mean that the Board sets trading limits; we mean that the Board defines broad measures such as capital ratio ranges and leverage ratios. If it does not, then it will be held accountable if the bank is seen to have taken on too much risk exposure or allowed its capital base to fall to unacceptable levels. So in this context, when we refer to "limits" we mean the broad upper limit – in other words, the risk tolerance and risk appetite.

The same applies to expected return. The Board should set the target, or benchmark, levels of return on an annual basis. Of course, traditionally higher risk means higher reward, so the return expected should reflect the risk tolerance of the bank.

We described the various bank risk exposures earlier. For a commercial bank the key risk exposure is credit risk. At this level, the Board is not setting credit risk limits for individual borrowers. Rather, it should set

---

commercial banking), and the non-executive directors (NEDs), who are not employees of the bank but retained as members of the Board (they are paid a fee for this). Often, significant shareholders of the bank may also have representation on the Board. Generally, the NEDs should be individuals with considerable banking and finance experience and/or expertise, but it is not uncommon to find some whose experience and expertise lie in other, very different fields. The chairman of the Board is often, in effect, a NED because he/she will not have a formal line function at the bank. NEDs usually chair the various board sub-committees of the bank, so one would hope that they do indeed possess extensive banking experience, as well as a proven track record of excellence within banking, and an ability to take decisions. A strong track record in other fields such as retail (supermarkets, shops and so on) is no indicator of effective judgement and decision-making ability when applied in a bank. We discuss bank corporate governance in Chapter 18.

aggregate or upper limits for countries and sectors. Below this, risk limit setting is delegated to operating business lines. Credit risk setting and monitoring is a discipline that is as old as banking itself, and its basic principles remain unchanged; essentially, credit risk management starts and ends with avoiding concentration – concentration with a single customer, industry, sector or country. The capital base of the bank also acts as a constraint on lending. Other risk limits, for market risk and FX risk for instance, are set at a lower operating level.

The point of setting a high-level risk tolerance guideline is to ensure that the bank's risk exposure does not exceed the appetite of the Board and shareholders. For this reason, limits on capital structure may be set; for instance, these could include:

- leverage limits: a limit on how much a multiple of the bank's capital base it can lever up to;
- funding gap limits: how much of a tenor mismatch between assets and liabilities a bank can run;
- wholesale funding limits: how much of the bank's balance sheet can be funded by wholesale, as opposed to retail deposit, funds.

By definition, staying within the overall risk culture, and adhering to the formal limits that are part of it, acts as a brake on business volume. That is the point. The whole concept of "risk management" is to prevent a bank over-reaching itself in a bull market or expanding economy, and to maintain its business within manageable levels. Hence procedures to constrain unlimited growth are vital.

Banking is a relationship business. The customer relationship must always remain the most important principle in banking. Viewed purely from a business angle, the logical approach might be to continuously enhance the relationship through more and more transactions. This implies a continuous increase in risk exposure as more and more business was put on the balance sheet. This would be an unsustainable strategy, because it would come unstuck at the first sign of an economic downturn. The risk management framework acts as a limit to continuous new business, thus constraining risk exposure to a manageable level. The same principle applies to market risks and capital structure risks.

Of course, it is possible to hedge risk exposures. Interest-rate risk can be neutralised, at least in theory, using derivatives. Credit risk can be removed using credit derivatives, insurance or some form of securitisation. In this way a bank can increase its business volume, but still remain within both the high-level risk culture and the specific risk limits. This is true only if the bank's senior management remains aware of the bank's true risk. In other words, to what extent in reality, and under all market conditions, is the risk really hedged? Risk hedging does not remove the need for the bank to "know your risk".

Target Return Rates

It is essential that a bank's Board sets the target return rates for business lines to meet. The level of return is itself part of the risk culture of a bank. A high target, relative to, for instance, long-run average return rates or the bank's peer group average, sends a message from management that the bank is willing to take greater risks in order to meet the higher return.

The key objective in return setting is sustainability. A bank must set targets that it believes can be sustained over the business cycle. If they are too high, then they risk being unwound at the next downturn; conversely, if they are too low then shareholders may find it unacceptable. Of course, a key part of the Board's role is to educate shareholders about the concept of a sustainable return.

There are a number of return measures that can be set. They will usually include RoE or its close relation RoC, and RoA. It is quite common to set different RoE targets for different business lines, reflecting the different risk exposures across each business line. An important ingredient in the target-setting discipline is the cost at which a business line obtains its funds. This is known as the internal funding rate (IFR), internal funds pricing or funds transfer pricing (FTP or just TP). We prefer the first term because the cost at which a Treasury desk lends funds to the other business lines of the bank is not really a "transfer" and it isn't really a "price" either; however, FTP is the most commonly used expression. FTP is important because it itself is a discipline, and also because it feeds into the return calculation. It is therefore a vital part of risk management policy. It is discussed in Chapter 15.

Another ingredient in return target setting is the risk-adjusted return. This allows for the different risk exposure of a particular business line, and is allied to how much capital it consumes. The amount of capital consumed by a business should be commensurate with the risk exposure it represents and also the return it generates. The Sharpe ratio is commonly used to compare returns levels for different businesses in order to make a fair risk-adjusted comparison.[15]

15 There are countless references in the financial literature, as well as on the Internet, to this calculation.

A sustainable return target, together with a robust FTP mechanism and a logical capital allocation methodology, are essential ingredients in the high-level risk management mechanism in a bank.

Dynamic Risk Management

The process of risk management in a bank is a dynamic and not static one. In other words, it is not enough to simply set up the infrastructure and then leave it at that. The Board and senior management need to remain aware of changes in market conditions, and act accordingly. What seemed like a worthwhile transaction a few months ago may not be now, in light of other events, and bank management must be able to react to these. Of course, prevention is better than cure. Ideally, the risk impact of all ongoing business should be captured and assessed as part of the decision-making process; that is, before the decision is made rather than after. Once a transaction is entered into, changing circumstances may dictate that the exposure is no longer worth maintaining, in which case the risk management response should be to re-hedge it or otherwise dispose of the transaction.

The risk management process is therefore dynamic with regard to the existing portfolio of business and all new business. Each new business transaction decision, both at the individual as well as portfolio level, should seek to answer clearly the following questions:

- Does it adhere to existing risk-reward guidelines and bank risk culture?
- What is the impact of the transaction(s) on risk exposure?
- Does it meet specified return-on-capital requirements?

Notice how we placed the revenue question last. This is deliberate. It is not sufficient to consider only the revenue raised and the net profit generated. To do so would result in excessive risk generation, often beyond the acceptable tolerance of the shareholders. Therefore it is imperative that the risk review process stays within an acceptable framework.

Exactly the same process applies to off-balance sheet transactions. Derivative and other OTC transactions, whether undertaken for hedging or speculative purposes, or as part of a customer product offering, must still fall under the high-level risk review process.

Bank Risk Management Structure and Organisation

A 20th century development in banks worldwide has been the introduction of a bank-wide risk management function. This was a response to the increasing sophistication and internationalisation of banking operations.[16] Risk management is now a centralised operation, whereas previously credit risk would have been managed separately to market risk, liquidity risk, operational risk and so on. These are still individual departments within a bank, but are overseen by a head of risk or chief risk officer (CRO). The CRO will typically report to the chief operating officer (COO) or a non-executive member of the Board.

By definition a firm-wide risk management function will mean a separation between the business lines and the risk supervising lines of a bank. This is an essential organisational requirement. The ALM function of the bank, usually delegated to the Treasury division, is part of this centralised risk management framework. The ALM desk is usually a separate desk within Treasury (in small banks it can be just two persons) and is responsible for the entire bank's interest-rate risk and liquidity management. For banks that have overseas branches, the head office ALM desk is ultimately responsible for the entire bank's ALM risk. Global banking groups, with overseas subsidiaries, will still place overall firm ALM risk management supervision with its Global Treasury, even if the foreign subsidiaries are required to be independent stand-alone entities with their own funding.

Placing interest-rate risk and liquidity management within one centralised function is essential for efficient ALM. Individual bank business lines cannot be allowed to run interest-rate or liquidity risk, otherwise there would be a severe danger of the bank's senior management being unable to effectively control it. Each business line, be it project finance or corporate banking or private banking, generates interest-rate risk, and this is managed at an aggregate portfolio level by the ALM desk. Transferring this risk from the individual businesses to Treasury also means that the business lines do not have to worry about interest-rate and liquidity risk: this is managed for them. The banking portfolio also generates credit risk, which is monitored by the credit risk unit. The hedging of credit risk, either by securitisation or the use of credit derivatives, insurance or guarantees, may be left to the business line (or, in the case of securitisation, to Treasury) or a dedicated unit.

---

16 Globalisation was an indirect causal factor of the 2007–2009 financial crisis. What began as a downturn in one particular sector of the US housing market ended up as global recession, and banking failure, partly arising as a result of the extensive cross-border and integrated nature of banking operations.

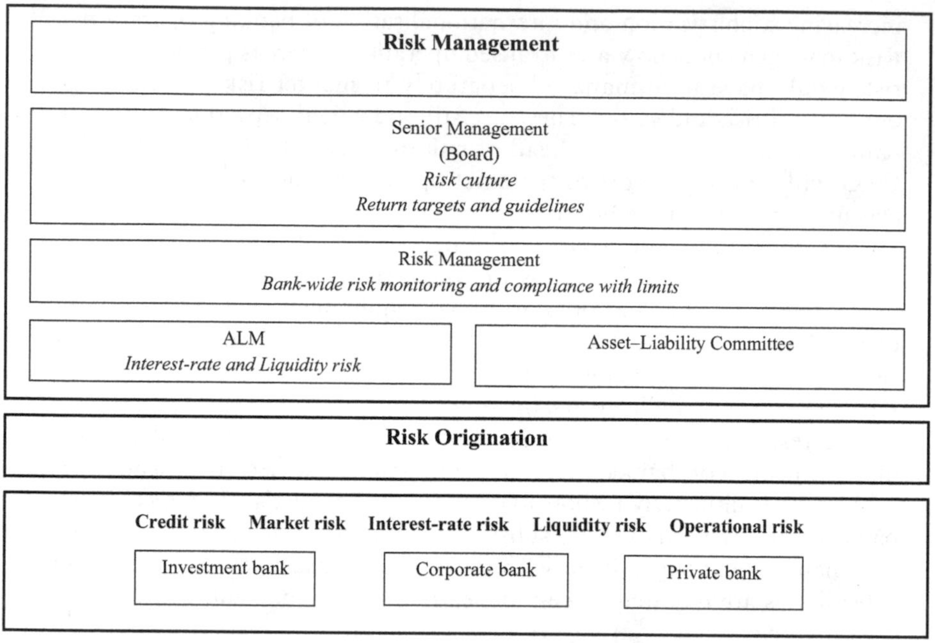

FIGURE 1.15 Centralised bank risk management, overseeing bank business lines.

Centralised Risk Management

Figure 1.15 is a stylised view of the centralised risk management function in a bank. We observe that the business lines originate the various risk exposures, and these are overseen, monitored and managed by the risk function. The senior management – which we can take to be the Board – will set the overall risk culture and this must be dynamic and up-to-date with events.

The centralised risk function will break down into individual departments monitoring specific risks. This is illustrated at Figure 1.16. Note that the Valuation Control function is sometimes situated within the Finance department. It is also sometimes known as "product control", although this term does not describe what it actually does, which is the independent checking of market prices. All three of the principal department heads will meet regularly on the ALCO. The role, objectives and responsibility of ALCOs are described in detail in Chapter 9.

Asset–Liability Management and the ALM Committee

The art of banking is the art of asset and liability management or ALM. Or rather we should say that the art of banking is maturity transformation.

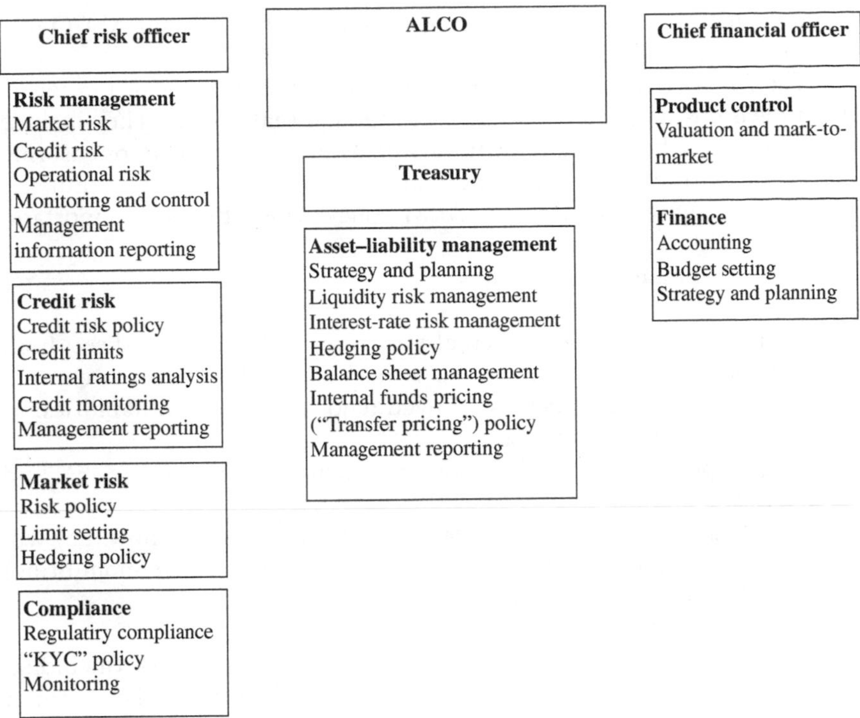

FIGURE 1.16 Centralised bank risk management, breakdown into individual risk departments.

This is the term for the mechanism by which banks "lend long" and "borrow short". This is an unavoidable fact of life for banks, and the need for ALM arises precisely because assets (loans) are always, on average, longer dated than liabilities (borrowings). It is not really practical to run a bank, except one with a very narrow and specific remit, any other way. Customer assets such as corporate loans and mortgages will always have a longer legal final maturity than liabilities such as customer deposits.

The ALM department, which is organised in different ways in different banks, is the unit responsible for managing the bank's liquidity, its interest rate and foreign exchange risk, and also its internal funds pricing. The stewardship of ALM is in the hands of the ALM Committee or ALCO. The ALCO sets policy for a number of different areas in the bank, and is the most important committee in the bank, including the bank's Board. It is possible to have an incompetent Board and still survive a market crisis;

however, it is not possible for a bank to have an incompetent ALCO and survive the same crisis.

The ALCO terms of reference are larger than mere implementation of ALM decisions, important and onerous though that task is. They include overall balance sheet management, as well as the responsibility of ensuring that policies adopted by the individual business lines fall within the boundaries required by the global ALM policy. This latter is an important, "political" task.

ALM itself addresses the following:

- defining the extent of the actual structure of the balance sheet, both assets and liabilities: one sees how this must perforce drill down into more detailed issues such as allowed tenor of assets and liabilities, as well as sources of liabilities;
- hedging policy for all risk exposures, including interest-rate, FX and liquidity risk;
- defining actual risk measures: how risks will be measured, how they will be reported, and what the limits are; monitor (or delegate monitoring) the risk exposures themselves.

We state at the outset that liquidity risk and market risk (including interest-rate risk) are inter-related and inter-dependent issues. They cannot be managed, monitored or controlled separately or independently of each other. This reflects a number of factors, the main one being that an expectation of funding difficulty in the future must be addressed today, with consequent impact on the funding cost and interest rate exposure.

Notwithstanding that larger and more sophisticated banks will have different levels of complexity compared to smaller or more narrowly focused banks, the scope of the ALM function will be identical at all banks. The one key functional difference across banks is whether the ALM, and Treasury, function, operates as a cost centre or a profit centre. We discuss this further in Chapter 9. However, setting up the ALM desk as a profit centre does not obviate the need for it to adhere to all the required levels of ALM control.

The ALCO then is the controlling arm for bank ALM. It is not an administrative function, however, as it also sets policy and guidelines. Note that banks comprised of more than one legal entity, for example across multiple legal jurisdictions, will have a Group ALCO that sets policy for the banking group as a whole. In some banks ALCO is known as the ALMAC (Asset–Liability Management Action Committee) or ALPCO (Asset–Liability Policy Committee). We discuss the ALCO function in detail in chapters 6, 7, 8, 9 and 10.

APPENDIX 1.1 SUMMARY OVERVIEW OF BANK PRODUCT LINE

DEFINITION OF BANKING

A definition of banking is available in any number of textbooks; the author recommends *Modern Banking* by Shelagh Heffernan (Wiley 2005). As a matter of interest the following are just two of many hundreds of definitions on the Internet:

> *Engaging in the business of keeping money for savings and checking accounts or for exchange or for issuing loans and credit etc.*
>
> www.wordnetweb.princeton.edu/perl/webwn

> *A bank is a financial institution that accepts deposits and channels those deposits into lending activities. Banks primarily provide financial services to customers while enriching investors. Government restrictions on financial activities by banks vary over time and location.*
>
> www.en.wikipedia.org/wiki/Banking

We will keep the definition even briefer, and refer readers to Figure A1.1.

PRODUCT LINE

As part of the primer on banking we provide a summary of the main product line offered by banks. Not all banks offer all these products, but these instruments are available in virtually every banking market. More detailed information is available in the following books by the author: *The Money Market Handbook*, *Fixed Income Markets* and *Bank Asset and Liability Management*, all published by John Wiley & Sons (Asia) Pte Ltd.

Interest-bearing and Non-interest-bearing Current Accounts

These are also known as cheque accounts or (in the US) checking accounts, and are the simplest form of short-term deposit or investment instrument.

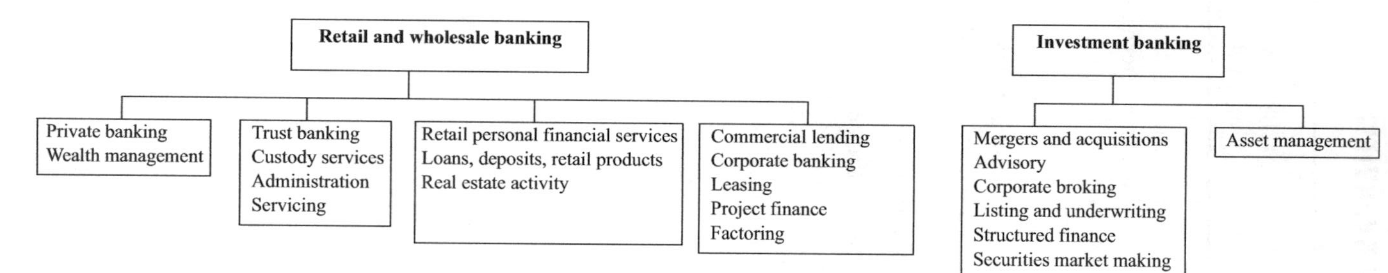

FIGURE A1.1 Banking activities.

Customer funds may be withdrawn instantly on demand, and banks generally pay interest on surplus balances, although not in all cases. Current accounts are a cheap source of funding for banks, as well as a stable one, but because their balances are instant access, the funds are less valuable from a liquidity metrics point of view.

Demand Deposits

These are also referred to as sight deposits, similar to a cheque account, but they are always interest bearing. The funds are available on demand, but cannot be used for cheques or other similar payments.

Time Deposits

Time or term deposits are interest-bearing deposit accounts of fixed maturity. They are usually offered with a range of maturities ranging from one month to five years, with the longer dated deposits attracting higher interest. This reflects the positive yield curve, which reflects the funding value to the bank of longer term liabilities. Most time deposits pay a fixed rate of interest, payable on maturity. Accounts of longer than 1-year maturity often capitalise interest on an annual basis.

Certificates of Deposit

Certificates of deposit (CDs) are receipts from banks for deposits that have been placed with them. They were first introduced in the sterling market in 1958. The deposits themselves carry a fixed rate of interest related to Libor and have a fixed term to maturity, so they cannot be withdrawn before then. However, the certificates themselves can be traded in a secondary market; that is, they are negotiable. CDs therefore are very similar to negotiable money market deposits, although the yields trade below the equivalent tenor deposit rates because of the added benefit of secondary-market liquidity. Most CDs issued are of between one and three months' maturity, although they do trade in maturities of one to five years. Interest is paid on maturity except for CDs lasting longer than one year, where interest is paid annually or occasionally, semi-annually.

Banks, investment banks and building societies issue CDs to raise funds to finance their business activities. A CD will have a stated interest rate and fixed maturity date, and can be issued in any denomination. On issue a CD is sold for face value, so the settlement proceeds of a CD on issue are always equal to its nominal value. The interest is paid, together with the face amount, on maturity. The interest rate is sometimes called the coupon, but unless the CD is held to maturity this will not equal the yield, which is of course the current rate available in the market and varies over time. The largest group of CD investors are banks, money market funds, corporates and local authority treasurers.

Commercial Paper

Commercial paper (CP) is a short-term money market funding instrument issued by banks and corporates. In most markets, including the US and UK, it is a discount instrument. Companies' short-term capital and working capital requirement is usually sourced directly from banks, in the form of bank loans. An alternative short-term funding instrument is CP, which is available to corporates that have a sufficiently strong credit rating. CP is a short-term unsecured promissory note. The issuer of the note promises to pay its holder a specified amount on a specified maturity date. CP normally has a zero coupon and trades at a *discount* to its face value. The discount represents interest to the investor in the period to maturity. CP is typically issued in bearer form, although some issues are in registered form.

CP issued in the US dollar domestic market differs in detail from Euromarket CP, which is known as EuroCommercial Paper (ECP). We highlight the main differences in Table A1.1

Asset-backed Commercial Paper

Securitisation technology led to the creation of short-term money market instruments backed by the cash flows from other assets, known as asset-backed commercial paper (ABCP). Securitisation is the practice of using the cash flows from a specified asset, such as residential mortgages, car loans or commercial bank loans, as backing for an issue of bonds. The assets

TABLE A1.1 Comparison of USCP and ECP.

	USCP	ECP
Currency	US dollar	Any Euro currency
Maturity	1–270 days	2–365 days
Common maturity	30–60 days	30–90 days
Interest	Zero coupon, issued at discount	Zero-coupon, issued at discount
Quotation	On a discount rate basis	On a yield basis
Settlement	T + 0 or T + 1	T + 2
Registration	Bearer form	Bearer form
Negotiable	Yes	Yes

themselves are transferred from the original owner (the *originator*) to a specially created legal entity known as a *special purpose vehicle* (SPV), so as to make them separate and bankruptcy-remote from the originator. In the meantime, the originator is able to benefit from capital market financing, often charged at a lower rate of interest than that earned by the originator on its assets.

Issuing ABCP enables an originator to benefit from money market financing that it might otherwise not have access to because its credit rating is not sufficiently strong. ABCP trades as conventional CP, except generally at a higher yield due to the perceived lower liquidity compared to straight CP. The administration and legal treatment is more onerous, however, because of the need to establish the CP trust structure and issuing SPV.

An ABCP conduit has the following features:

- it is a bankruptcy-remote legal entity that issues CP to finance a purchase of assets from a seller of assets;
- the interest on the CP issued by the conduit, and its principal on maturity, will be paid out of the receipts on the assets purchased by the conduit.

The assets that can be funded via a conduit programme are many and varied; to date they have included:

- trade receivables and equipment lease receivables;
- credit card receivables;
- auto loans and leases;
- corporate loans, franchise loans and mortgage loans;
- real-estate leases.

Conduits are classified into a "programme type", which refers to the makeup of the underlying asset portfolio. This can be single-seller or multi-seller, which indicates how many institutions or entities are selling assets to the conduit.

Figure A1.2 illustrates a typical ABCP structure issuing to the USCP and ECP markets.

Foreign Exchange

A *spot* FX trade is an outright purchase or sale of one currency against another currency, with delivery two working days after the trade date. Note that in some currencies, generally in the Middle East, markets are closed on Friday but open on Saturday. A settlement date that falls on a public holiday in the country of one of the two currencies is delayed for

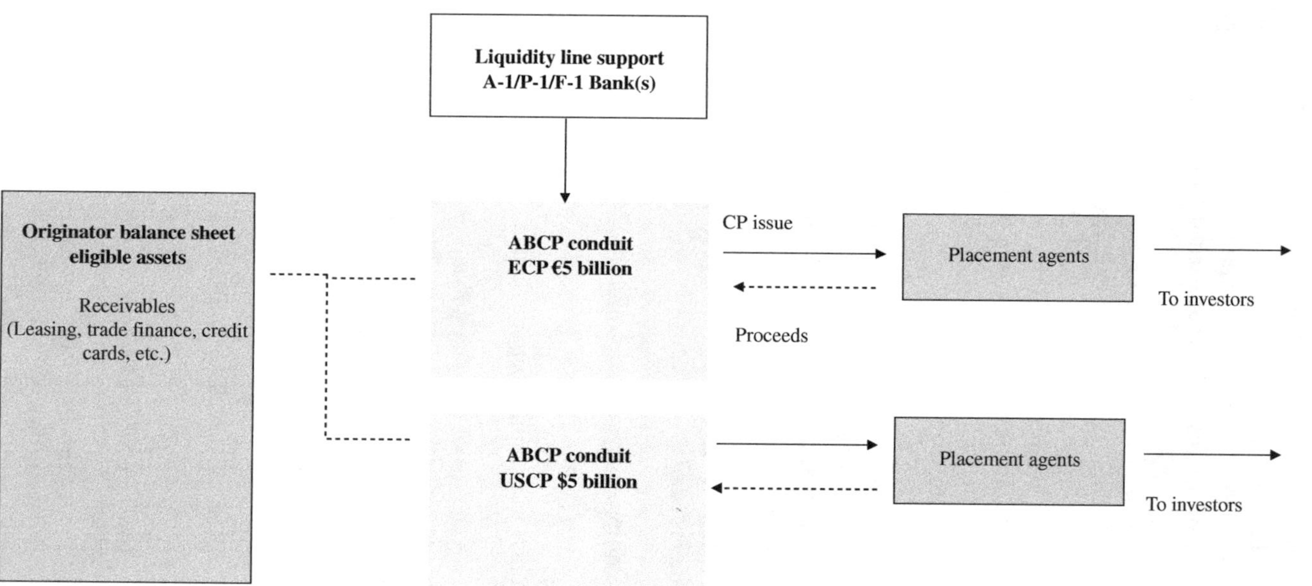

FIGURE A1.2 Single-seller ABCP conduit.

settlement by that day. An FX transaction is possible between any two currencies; however, to reduce the number of quotes that need to be made, the market generally quotes only against the US dollar or occasionally against sterling or euro, so that the exchange rate between two non-dollar currencies is calculated from the rate for each currency against the dollar. The resulting exchange rate is known as the *cross-rate*. Cross-rates themselves are also traded between banks in addition to dollar-based rates. This is usually because the relationship between two rates is closer than that of either against the dollar; for example, the Swiss franc moves more closely in line with the euro than against the dollar, so in practice one observes that the dollar/Swiss franc rate is more a function of the euro/franc rate.

The spot FX quote is a two-way bid–offer price and indicates the rate at which a bank is prepared to buy the base currency against the variable currency; this is the "bid" for the variable currency, so it is the lower rate. The other side of the quote is the rate at which the bank is prepared to sell the base currency against the variable currency. For example, a quote of 1.6245–1.6255 for GBP/USD means that the bank is prepared to buy sterling for \$1.6245, and to sell sterling for \$1.6255. The convention in the FX market is uniform across countries, unlike the money markets. Although the money market convention for bid–offer quotes is for example, $5^1/_2\%$ – $5^1/_4\%$, meaning that the "bid" for paper – the rate at which the bank will lend funds, say in the CD market – is the higher rate and always on the left, this convention is reversed in certain countries. In the FX markets the convention is always the same one just described.

The difference between the two sides in a quote is the bank's dealing spread. Rates are quoted to 1/100th of a cent, known as a *pip*. In the quote above, the spread is 10 pips; however, this amount is a function of the size of the quote number, so that the rate for USD/JPY at, say, 110.10 – 110.20, indicates a spread of 0.10 yen. Generally, only the pips in the two rates are quoted, so that for example the quote above would be simply "45–55". The "big figure" is not quoted.

EXAMPLE A1.1 EXCHANGE CROSS-RATES

Consider the following two spot rates:

EUR/USD	1.0566–1.0571
AUD/USD	0.7034–0.7039

The EUD/USD dealer buys euros and sells dollars at 1.0566 (the left side), while the AUD/USD dealer sells Australian dollars and buys

(*continued*)

US dollars at 0.7039 (the right side). To calculate the rate at which the bank buys euros and sells Australian dollars, we need to do

$$1.0566/0.7039 = 1.4997$$

which is the rate at which the bank buys euros and sells Australian dollars. In the same way, the rate at which the bank sells euros and buys Australian dollars is given by:

$$1.0571/0.7034 \text{ or } 1.5028.$$

Therefore the spot EUR/AUD rate is 1.4997 – 1.5028.

The derivation of cross-rates can be depicted in the following way. If we assume two exchange rates XXX/YYY and XXX/ZZZ, the cross-rates are:

$$\text{YYY/ZZZ} = \text{XXX/ZZZ} \div \text{XXX/YYY}$$
$$\text{ZZZ/YYY} = \text{XXX/YYY} \div \text{XXX/ZZZ}$$

Given two exchange rates, YYY/XXX and XXX/ZZZ, the cross-rates are:

$$\text{YYY/ZZZ} = \text{YYY/XXX} \times \text{XXX/ZZZ}$$
$$\text{ZZZ/YYY} = 1 \div (\text{YYY/XXX/ZZZ})$$

Figure A1.3 shows the Bloomberg major currency FX monitor, page FXC, as at 10 May 2004.

Government Bonds

The secondary market in government bonds is provided by banks, those that choose to be market-makers or primary dealers. Sovereign debt is essentially a plain vanilla market, with the vast majority of bonds being fixed coupon and fixed maturity. Governments also issue index-linked bonds that offer returns linked to the rate of inflation.

Floating Rate Notes

Floating rate notes (FRNs) are bonds that have variable rates of interest; the coupon rate is linked to a specified index and changes periodically as

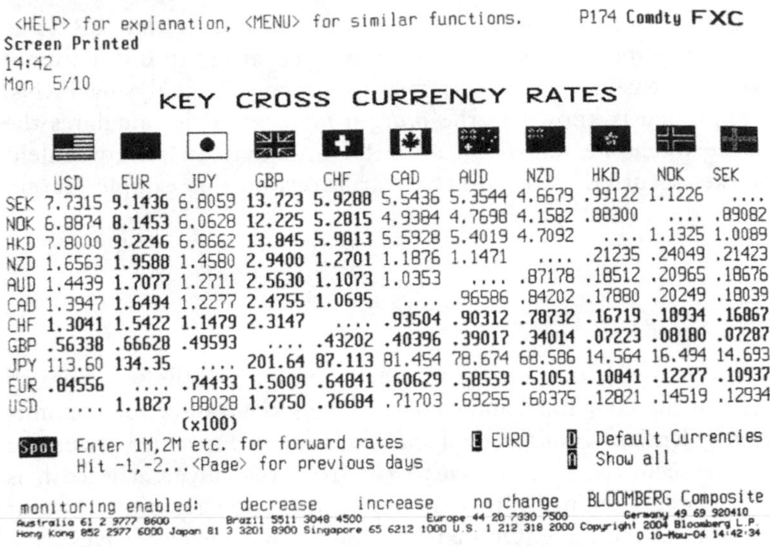

<HELP> for explanation, <MENU> for similar functions. P174 Comdty FXC

Screen Printed

14:42

Mon 5/10

KEY CROSS CURRENCY RATES

	USD	EUR	JPY	GBP	CHF	CAD	AUD	NZD	HKD	NOK	SEK
SEK	7.7315	9.1436	6.8059	13.723	5.9288	5.5436	5.3544	4.6679	.99122	1.1226	....
NOK	6.8874	8.1453	6.0628	12.225	5.2815	4.9384	4.7698	4.1582	.88300	....	.89082
HKD	7.8000	9.2246	6.8662	13.845	5.9813	5.5928	5.4019	4.7092	....	1.1325	1.0089
NZD	1.6563	1.9588	1.4580	2.9400	1.2701	1.1876	1.1471	....	.21235	.24049	.21423
AUD	1.4439	1.7077	1.2711	2.5630	1.1073	1.0353	....	.87178	.18512	.20965	.18676
CAD	1.3947	1.6494	1.2277	2.4755	1.0695	....	.96586	.84202	.17880	.20249	.18039
CHF	1.3041	1.5422	1.1479	2.3147	....	.93504	.90312	.78732	.16719	.18934	.16867
GBP	.56338	.66628	.49593	....	.43202	.40396	.39017	.34014	.07223	.08180	.07287
JPY	113.60	134.35	....	201.64	87.113	81.454	78.674	68.586	14.564	16.494	14.693
EUR	.84556	....	.74433	1.5009	.64841	.60629	.58559	.51051	.10841	.12277	.10937
USD	....	1.1827	.88028	1.7750	.76684	.71703	.69255	.60375	.12821	.14519	.12934
			(x100)								

Spot Enter 1M,2M etc. for forward rates E EURO D Default Currencies

Hit -1,-2...<Page> for previous days A Show all

monitoring enabled: decrease increase no change BLOOMBERG Composite

Australia 61 2 9777 8600 Brazil 5511 3048 4500 Europe 44 20 7330 7500 Germany 49 69 920410

Hong Kong 852 2977 6000 Japan 81 3 3201 8900 Singapore 65 6212 1000 U.S. 1 212 318 2000 Copyright 2004 Bloomberg L.P.

0 10-May-04 14:42:34

FIGURE A1.3 Bloomberg major currency monitor page, 10 May 2004.

the index changes. An FRN is usually issued with a coupon that pays a fixed spread over a reference index; for example, the coupon may be 50 bps over the 6-month Libor rate. Since the value for the reference benchmark index is not known, it is not possible to calculate the redemption yield for an FRN. Additional features have been added to FRNs, including *floors* (the coupon cannot fall below a specified minimum rate), *caps* (the coupon cannot rise above a maximum rate) and *callability*.

Generally, the reference interest rate for FRNs is the London inter-bank offered rate or Libor. An FRN will pay interest at Libor plus a quoted margin (or spread). The interest rate is fixed for a 3-month or 6-month period, and is reset in line with the Libor *fixing* at the end of the interest period. Hence, at the coupon reset date for a sterling FRN paying 6-month Libor + 0.50%, if the Libor fix is 7.6875%, then the FRN will pay a coupon of 8.1875%. Interest therefore will accrue at a daily rate of £0.0224315.

On the coupon reset date an FRN will be priced precisely at par. Between reset dates it will trade very close to par because of the way in which the coupon is reset. If market rates rise between reset dates an FRN will trade slightly below par; similarly, if rates fall the paper will trade slightly above. This makes FRNs very similar in behaviour to money market instruments traded on a yield basis, although of course

FRNs have much longer maturities. Investors can opt to view FRNs as essentially money market instruments or as alternatives to conventional bonds. For this reason one can use two approaches in analysing FRNs. The first approach is known as the *margin method*. This calculates the difference between the return on an FRN and that on an equivalent money market security. There are two variations on this: simple margin and discounted margin.

Repos

A repo agreement is a transaction in which one party sells securities to another, and at the same time, and as part of the same transaction commits to repurchase identical securities on a specified date at a specified price. The seller delivers securities and receives cash from the buyer. The cash is supplied at a predetermined rate – the *repo rate* – that remains constant during the term of the trade. On maturity the original seller receives back collateral of equivalent type and quality, and returns the cash plus repo interest. One party to the repo requires either the cash or the securities and provides *collateral* to the other party, as well as some form of compensation for the temporary use of the desired asset. Although legal title to the securities is transferred, the seller/lender retains both the economic benefits and the market risk of owning them. The purpose of the transaction of course is to provide secured lending of cash.

Repo is a short-term secured cash instrument that should always be labelled as part of the money markets. There is a wide range of uses to which repo might be put. In the equity market, repo is often conducted in a basket of stocks, which might be constituent stocks in an index such as the FTSE100 or CAC40, or user-specified baskets. Market-makers borrow and lend equities with differing terms to maturity, and generally the credit rating of the institution involved in the repo transaction is of more importance than the quality of the collateral. Central banks' use of repo also reflects its importance; it is a key instrument in the implementation of monetary policy in many countries. Essentially then, repo markets have vital links and relationships with global money markets, bond markets, futures markets, swap markets and OTC interest-rate derivatives.

For practical purposes, repo is essentially a secured loan. The term comes from *sale and repurchase agreement*; however, this is not necessarily the best way to look at it. Although in a classic repo transaction the legal title of an asset is transferred from the "seller" to the "buyer" during the term of the repo, this should not detract from the essence of the instrument: a secured loan of cash. The main value of repo lies in the fact that, for the lender of cash it provides collateral backing to help mitigate counterparty credit risk, and for the borrower of cash it enables the financing of asset positions in the security that is being repo'd out.

Letter of Credit

A letter of credit (LoC) is a standard vanilla product available from a commercial bank. It is an instrument that guarantees that a buyer's payment to a seller will be received at the right time and for the specific amount. The buyer is the customer of the bank. If the buyer is unable to make payment on the due date, the bank will cover the full amount of the purchase. The bank therefore takes on the credit risk of the buyer when it writes a LoC on its behalf. The buyer therefore pays a fee for the LoC that reflects its credit standing.

LoCs are used in domestic and international trade transactions. Cross-border trade transactions involve both parties in issues such as distance, different legal jurisdictions and lack of due diligence available on the counterparties. A LoC is a valuable tool that eases the process for the buying and selling parties. The bank also acts on behalf of the buyer (the purchaser of the LoC) because it would only make payment when it knows that the goods have been shipped. For the seller, a LoC substitutes the credit of the buyer for that of the bank, which is an easier risk exposure for the seller to take on.

There are essentially two types of LoC: commercial and standby. The commercial LoC is the primary payment mechanism for a transaction, while the standby LoC is a secondary payment mechanism.

Commercial Letter of Credit

A commercial LoC is a contract between a bank, known as the issuing bank, on behalf of one of its customers, authorising another bank, known as the advising or confirming bank, to make payment to the beneficiary. The issuing bank makes a commitment to guarantee drawings made under the credit. The beneficiary is normally the provider of goods and/or services. An advising bank, usually a foreign correspondent bank of the issuing bank, will advise the beneficiary but otherwise has no other obligation under the LoC.

A LoC is generally negotiable; this means that the issuing bank is obliged to pay the beneficiary, but also at its request any bank nominated by the beneficiary. To be negotiable, the LoC features an unconditional promise to pay on demand at a specified time.

Standby Letter of Credit

The standby LoC is a contract issued by a bank on behalf of a customer to provide assurances of its ability to perform under the terms of a contract between it and the beneficiary. In other words, the standby LoC is more of a guarantee, as both parties to the transaction do not expect that the LoC will be drawn on. It essentially provides comfort to the beneficiary, as it enhances the credit worthiness of its customer.

Structured Deposits

A structured deposit is a deposit whose payoff or return profile is structured to match a specified customer requirement. The structuring results from the use of an embedded derivative in the product, which links the deposit to changes in interest rates, FX rates or other market levels. There is a wide range of different products available that fall in the class of "structured deposit". An example is the following: a customer places funds on deposit at a specified interest rate and fixed term. Under the agreement, if the central bank base interest rate remains between 4% and 5%, then the return is enhanced by 100 bps. If the rate moves below 4% or above 5%, then the deposit forfeits all interest for the remaining term of its life. This is an example of a "collared range accrual" deposit.

Liquidity Facilities

Liquidity facility is the generic term for a standing loan agreement, against which a borrower can draw down funds at any time up to the maximum value of the line. The borrower pays a fee, even if the line is not used, called the standing fee, and then pays the agreed rate of interest on any funds that it does draw.

We distinguish between the following:

- Back-up facility: a facility that is not used in the normal course of business. It is generally drawn down if the borrower is experiencing some difficulty in obtaining funding from its usual sources.
- Revolving credit facility (RCF): a commitment from a bank to lend on a revolving basis under pre-specified terms. Under an RCF there is usually a regular drawdown and repayment of funds during the life of the facility.
- Term loan: this is distinct from liquidity lines in that it is a non-revolving facility and will be drawn down at execution. It has a fixed repayment date, although this may be on an amortised basis.

TABLE A1.2 Typical priorities of corporate bonds and loans of investment grade and sub-investment grade borrowers.

	Investment-grade borrower	Sub-investment-grade borrower
Bonds	• Senior unsecured	• Senior unsecured (*high-yield bonds*)
Loans	• Senior unsecured	• Senior secured • (*leveraged loans/syndicated loans*)

Source: Choudhry (2010).

Liquidity facilities require full regulatory capital backing, as the capital treatment is to assume that they are being fully used at all times.

Syndicated Loans[17]

To raise debt capital, companies may issue bonds or loans (as well as other debt-like instruments), both of which are associated with a certain seniority or ranking. In a liquidation or winding-up, the borrower's remaining assets are distributed according to a priority waterfall: debt obligations with the highest seniority are repaid first, and only if assets remain thereafter are obligations with lower seniorities repaid. Further, debt instruments may be secured or unsecured: if a certain number of the borrower's assets are ring-fenced[18] to serve as collateral for the lenders under a particular obligation only, this obligation is deemed to be "secured". Together, seniority and collateral determine the *priority* of an obligation. As illustrated in Table A1.2, bonds and loans issued by investment-grade companies, as well as bonds issued by sub-investment grade companies, called "high-yield bonds", are typically senior unsecured. However, loans issued by sub-investment grade companies are typically senior secured. Often, these are called "leveraged loans" or "syndicated secured loans". The market often uses both terms interchangeably.

The definition of "leveraged loan" is not universal, however. Various market participants define a leveraged loan to be a loan with a sub-investment grade rating, while other users view it as one with a certain spread over Libor

17 This section is an extract from Chapter 11 of Choudhry (2010). It was co-written with Timo Schlafer and Marliese Uhrig-Homburg.

18 Ring-fencing is a legal term that refers to the practice of segregating assets, for the benefit of one entity, such that they cannot be touched by other creditors during a bankruptcy or administration proceeding.

(say 100 bps or more) and sometimes a certain debt/earnings before interest, taxes, depreciation and amortisation (EBITDA) ratio of the borrower. S&P, for instance, calls a loan "leveraged" if it is rated sub-investment grade or if it is rated investment grade but pays interest of at least Libor + 125 bps. Bloomberg uses a hurdle rate of Libor + 250 bps. Essentially, the market refers to leveraged loans and high-yield bonds as "high-yield debt".

Leveraged loans may be arranged either between a borrower and a single lending bank, or, more commonly, between a borrower and a syndicate of lending banks. In the latter case, one (or more) of the lending banks acts as lead arranger. Before any other lending banks are involved, the lead arranger conducts detailed due diligence on the borrower. Also, lead arranger and borrower agree on the basic transaction terms such as size of the loan, interest rate, fees, loan structure, covenants and type of syndication. These terms are documented in a "loan agreement". Based on the information received in the due diligence process, the lead arranger prepares an information memorandum, also called "bank book", which is used to market the transaction to other potential lending banks or institutional investors. Together, the lead arranger and the other lenders constitute the primary market. If the transaction is an "underwritten syndication", the lead arranger guarantees the borrower that the entire amount of the loan will be placed at a predefined price. If the loan is undersubscribed at that price, the lead arranger is forced to absorb the difference. If the transaction is a "best-efforts syndication", the lead arranger tries to place the loan at the predefined terms but will, if investor demand is insufficient, adjust these terms to achieve full placement.

Leveraged loans typically consist of a revolving credit facility or "revolver" and "term loans". The term loans are usually tranched into an amortising term loan (term loan A), provided by the syndicate banks, and institutional tranches (term loans B, C and D), provided by institutional investors. In the US market, amortising term loans have become increasingly rare as institutional investors are now the primary buyers of leveraged loans. The term loan D may represent a further subdivision, called "second lien tranche", which is subordinated to term loans A, B and C, called "first lien tranches", but ranks senior to all other debt of the borrower. Historically, this structure has resulted in significantly higher recovery rates of first lien tranches compared to second lien tranches.

The term loan A is usually repaid on scheduled repayment dates during its life, whereas term loans B, C and D are mostly subject to bullet repayment; that is, a one-off repayment on the maturity date. Once repaid, term loans cannot be re-borrowed. This is the principal difference to the revolving credit facility, usually provided by syndicate lenders, which allows the borrower to borrow, repay, and re-borrow funds during the life of the

TABLE A1.3 Typical structure of leveraged loans.

<table>
<tr><th></th><th></th><th>Lien</th><th>Lender</th><th>Repayment</th></tr>
<tr><td>Revolving credit facility</td><td></td><td rowspan="4">First lien</td><td rowspan="2">Banks</td><td>Discretionary</td></tr>
<tr><td>Term loans</td><td>A</td><td>Amortising</td></tr>
<tr><td></td><td>B</td><td rowspan="3">Institutional investors</td><td rowspan="3">Bullet</td></tr>
<tr><td></td><td>C</td></tr>
<tr><td></td><td>D</td><td>Second lien</td></tr>
</table>

Source: Choudhry (2010).

loan in accordance with predetermined conditions. In addition to interest on borrowed funds, borrowers are charged a commitment fee on unused funds. Revolvers are often used to fund working capital and capital expenditure requirements that can fluctuate significantly over time. Table A1.3 summarises the above discussion.

Leveraged loans pay floating rate coupons. These are composed of Libor (or another inter-bank rate, depending on the loan's currency) plus a certain spread (that is, risk premium) and are typically payable quarterly. Floating rate coupons provide an effective hedge against interest-rate risk: if interest rates rise, so does the coupon and vice versa. Consequently, floating rate coupons are particularly popular in times of rising interest rates. Often, the spread of leveraged loans is not fully fixed but moves according to a pricing grid predefined in the loan agreement: if the borrower's credit condition improves, for instance indicated by a decline of financial leverage and/or a rating upgrade, the spread decreases and vice versa.

Leveraged loans commonly mature between 7 to 10 years after issuance. The *effective* life of leveraged loans, however, tends to be significantly shorter as the borrower is typically allowed to prepay or "call" the loan at any time at no or limited premium. Prepayment is generally seen as negative by lenders. This is because borrowers tend to prepay when their refinancing costs decrease; for instance, when they are upgraded to investment grade or acquired by an investment grade-rated company or when interest rates decrease. For lenders, this means that they bear all the downside (that is, rising interest rates or a deterioration in the borrower's credit condition) but retain limited upside. Generally, floating-rate coupons mitigate lenders' risk associated with rising interest rates.

REFERENCES

Choudhry, M. (2013), *An Introduction to Value-at-Risk*, 5th edition, Chichester: John Wiley & Sons Ltd.

Choudhry, M. (2010), *Structured Credit Products: Credit Derivatives and Synthetic Securitisation*, 2nd edition, Singapore: John Wiley & Sons (Asia) Pte. Ltd.

Choudhry, M., S. Turner, G. Landuyt and K. Butt, "Modern portfolio theory and the myth of diversification", *World Commerce Review*, Vol. 3, Issue 1, 2009.

Higson C. (1995), *Business Finance*, 2nd edition, Oxford: Butterworth.

CHAPTER 2

Bank Regulatory Capital

In Chapter 1 we noted the importance of capital to the basic business of banking. The ratio of a bank's capital to its overall balance sheet is a sign of the firm's overall health, and as the capital buffer is required to cover all losses suffered by the bank, it is the target of bank regulators' rulings. In this chapter we provide a primer on bank capital, its calculation, treatment and allocation. This includes a review of the standard Bank for International Settlements (BIS) regulatory capital rules, known as the Basel rules, to which all bank jurisdictions adhere to. We also introduce the main requirements of the Basel III rules. The second part of the chapter looks at the capital calculation and the concept of return on capital.

BANK REGULATORY CAPITAL

We review a topic of fundamental importance to bank ALM, that of regulatory capital and the Basel capital ratios. The cost of capital is the driver behind return on capital calculations, and a prime objective of banking operations is to meet return on capital targets. Hence, regulatory capital issues play an important part in bank strategy.

The need for adequate regulation of the banking industry is widely recognised, and a string of banking failures in the 1990s emphasised this. Lessons were not learned, however, as capital inadequacy was again an issue during the "credit crunch" of 2007–2008.

By the nature of their activities, bank trading and lending desks are risk-takers, and the reward culture in many banks provides strong incentives for perhaps excessive risk-taking. However, the regulators are more concerned with *systemic risk*, the risk that, as a result of the failure of one bank, the whole banking system is put in danger, due to knock-on effects. This did not arise in 1995 in the UK when Barings collapsed, because the bank was not a large enough part of the monetary system. However, the integrated nature of the global financial industry means that banks are closely entwined, and the failure of one bank generates a risk of failure for all those banks that have lent funds to the failed bank. This was the reasoning behind the "bail out" in 2008 of banks such as Lloyds TSB, UBS and KBC Bank. So systemic risk management is a major challenge for regulators. While a bank will be concerned with risk management of its own operations, regulators are concerned with the risk to the whole financial system. The interrelationships between banks mean that they have exposures to one another, while the profit motive encourages risk-taking. The systemic risk inherent in the banking system means that it is important to have sufficiently adequate financial regulation, of which the capital requirements rules are one example.

Following the bank crash in 2008, further rules were introduced in consultative form in 2010, known as Basel III. These are discussed at the end of the chapter.

REGULATORY CAPITAL REQUIREMENTS

Banks and financial institutions are subject to a range of regulations and controls; the primary one is concerned with the level of capital that a bank holds, and that this level is sufficient to provide a cushion underpinning the activities that the bank enters into. Typically, an institution is subject to regulatory requirements of its domestic regulator, but may also be subject to cross-border requirements such as the European Union's Capital Adequacy Directive.[1] A capital requirements scheme proposed by a committee of central banks acting under the auspices of the BIS in 1988 has been adopted universally by banks around the world. These are known as the BIS regulatory requirements or the Basel capital ratios, from the town in Switzerland where the BIS is based.[2] The BIS is not a regulatory body in itself, and its pronouncements carry no legislative weight; however, national authorities are keen to demonstrate that they follow the Basel rules

1 In the UK, banking regulation is the responsibility of the Financial Services Authority, which took over responsibility for this area from the Bank of England in 1998. In 2012, this body was subsumed into the Bank of England. In the US, banking supervision is conducted by the Federal Reserve; it is common for the central bank to be a country's domestic banking regulator.

2 Bank for International Settlements, Basle Committee on Banking Regulations and Supervisory Practice, *International Convergence of Capital Measurement and Capital Standards*, July 1988.

at a minimum, to maintain investor and public confidence. Under the Basel requirements all cash and off-balance sheet instruments in a bank's portfolio are assigned a risk weighting, based on their perceived credit risk, that determines the minimum level of capital that must be set against them.

A bank's *capital* is, put simply, the difference between assets and liabilities on its balance sheet, and is the property of the bank's owners. It may be used to meet any operating losses incurred by the bank, and if such losses exceeded the amount of available capital, then the bank would have difficulty in repaying liabilities, which may lead to bankruptcy. However, for regulatory purposes capital is defined differently; again in its simplest form regulatory capital is comprised of those elements in a bank's balance sheet that are eligible for inclusion in the calculation of capital ratios. The ratio required by a regulator will be that level deemed sufficient to protect the bank's depositors. Regulatory capital includes equity, preference shares and subordinated debt, as well as the general reserves. The common element of these items is that they are all *loss-absorbing*, whether this is on an ongoing basis or in the event of liquidation. This is crucial to regulators, who are concerned that depositors and senior creditors are repaid in full in the event of bankruptcy.

THE BASEL I RULES

The BIS rules set a minimum ratio of capital to assets of 8% of the value of the assets. Assets are defined in terms of their risk, and it is the weighted risk assets that are multiplied by the 8% figure. Each asset is assigned a risk-weighting, which is 0% for risk-free assets such as certain country government bonds, to 20% for inter-bank lending, and up to 100% for the highest risk assets such as certain corporate loans. So while a loan in the inter-bank market would be assigned a 20% weighting, a loan of exactly the same size to a corporate would receive the highest weighting of 100%. The risk weights are given at Table 2.1.

Formally, the BIS requirements are set in terms of the type of capital that is being set aside against assets. International regulation defines the following types of capital for a bank:

- *Tier 1*: perpetual capital, capable of absorbing loss through the non-payment of a dividend. This is shareholders' equity and also non-cumulative preference shares;
- *Upper Tier 2*: this is also perpetual capital, subordinated in repayment to other creditors; this may include, for example, undated bonds such as building society PIBS, and other irredeemable subordinated debt;

- *Lower Tier 2*: this is capital that is subordinated in repayment to other creditors, such as long-dated subordinated bonds.

The level of capital requirement is given by (2.1):

$$\frac{\text{Tier 1 capital}}{\text{Risk-adjusted exposure}} > 4\%$$
$$\frac{\text{Tier 1} + \text{Tier 2 capital}}{\text{Risk-adjusted exposure}} > 8\%. \tag{2.1}$$

The ratios in (2.1) therefore set minimum levels. A bank's *risk-adjusted exposure* is the cash risk-adjusted exposure, together with the total risk-adjusted off-balance sheet exposure. For cash products on the banking book the capital charge calculations (risk-adjusted exposure) is given by:

$$\text{Principal value} \times \text{Risk weighting} \times \text{Capital charge } [8\%]$$

calculated for each instrument.

The sum of the exposures is taken. Firms may use netting or portfolio modelling to reduce the total principal value.

The BIS makes a distinction between *banking book* transactions as carried out by retail and commercial banks (primarily deposits and lending) and *trading book* transactions as carried out by investment banks and securities houses. Capital treatment differs between banking and trading books. A repo transaction, for example, attracts a charge on the trading book. The formula for calculating the capital allocation is:

$$CA = max.\,(((C_{mv} - S_{mv}) \times 8\% \times RW),\ 0) \tag{2.2}$$

where

C_{mv} = is the value of cash proceeds
S_{mv} = is the market value of securities
RW = is the counterparty risk-weighting (as a percentage).

EXAMPLE 2.1 BASEL I CAPITAL CHARGE ILLUSTRATION

Calculate the capital adequacy directive (CAD) charge for a repo transaction with the following terms:

Clean price of collateral: 100

Accrued interest: 0

Cash proceeds on £50 m nominal: £50,000,000

Counterparty: OECD bank

Counterparty risk-weighting: 20%

$$CA = (((50{,}000{,}000 - 50{,}000{,}000) \times 8\% \times 20\%), 0)$$
$$= 0.$$

The CAD charge for a loan/deposit transaction of the same size is as follows:

Unsecured loan: £50,000,000

Counterparty: OECD bank

Counterparty risk weighting: 20%

$$CA = \max((50{,}000{,}000 \times 8\% \times 20\%), 0)$$
$$= £800{,}000.$$

The detailed risk weights for market instruments are given in Table 2.1.

TABLE 2.1 Risk weightings of typical banking book assets, Basel I.

Weighting	Asset type	Remarks
0%	■ Cash ■ Claims on own sovereign and Zone A sovereigns and central banks ■ Claims on Zone B sovereign issuers denominated in that country's domestic currency	Zone A countries are members of the OECD and countries that have concluded special lending arrangements with the IMF. Zone B consists of all other countries. Under certain regulatory regimes, holdings of other Zone A government bonds are given 10% or 20% weightings, and Zone B government bonds must be funded in that country's currency to qualify for 0% weighting, otherwise 100% weighting applies.
20%	■ Claims on multilateral development banks ■ Claims on regional governments or local authorities in own or Zone A countries	Under certain regulatory regimes, claims on Zone B banking institutions with residual maturity of less than one year also qualify for 20% weighting.

(continued)

TABLE 2.1 (*Continued*)

Weighting	Asset type	Remarks
	■ Senior claims on own country or guaranteed by Zone A banking institutions ■ Senior claims on Zone B banking institutions with an original maturity of under one year	
50%	■ Claims secured on residential property ■ Mortgage-backed securities	
100%	■ All other claims	

Under the original Basel rules, assets are defined as belonging to a bank's banking book or its trading book. The banking book essentially comprises the traditional activities of deposit taking and lending, with assets booked at cost and not revalued. Trading book assets, which include derivatives, are marked-to-market on a daily basis, with a daily unrealised profit or loss recorded. Such assets are risk-weighted on a different basis to that shown in Table 2.1, on a scale made up of market risk and credit risk. Market risk is estimated using techniques such as VaR, while credit risk is a function of the type of asset. The calculation of capital requirements for trading book assets is more complex than that for banking book assets.

The process of determining the capital requirement of a banking institution involves calculating the quantitative risk exposure of its existing operations and comparing this amount to the level of regulatory capital of the bank. The different asset classes are assigned into the risk buckets of 0%, 20%, 50% and 100%. Not surprisingly, this somewhat rigid classification led to distortions in the pricing of assets, as any movement between the risk buckets has a significant impact on the capital required and the return on capital calculation. Over time the impact of the Basel rules led to the modified rules of Basel II.

Table 2.2 summarises the elements that comprised the different types of capital that made up regulatory capital in the EU's CAD for Basel 1. Tier 1 capital supplementary capital is usually issued in the form of non-cumulative preference shares, known in the US as preferred stock. Banks generally build Tier 1 reserves as a means of boosting capital ratios, as well as to support a reduced pure equity ratio. Tier 1 capital now includes certain securities that have similar characteristics to debt, as they are structured to

TABLE 2.2 European Union regulatory capital rules, Basel I.

	Limits	Capital type	Deductions
Tier 1	■ No limit to Tier 1 ■ "Esoteric" instruments such as trust-preferred securities are restricted to 15% of total Tier 1	■ Equity share capital, including share premium account ■ Retained profits ■ Non-cumulative preference shares and other hybrid capital securities	■ Bank holdings of its own Tier 1 instruments ■ Goodwill and other intangible assets ■ Current-year unpublished losses
Tier 2	■ Total Tier 2 may not exceed 100% of Tier 1		
Upper Tier 2		■ Perpetual subordinated, loss-absorbing debt ■ Cumulative preference shares ■ General reserves ■ Revaluation reserves	■ Holdings of other banks' own fund instruments in excess of 10% of the value of own capital ■ Holding of more than 10% of another credit institution's own funds ■ Specified investments in non-consolidated subsidiaries ■ Qualified investments, defined as a holding of more than 10% of a company
Lower Tier 2	■ Cannot exceed 50% of Tier 1 ■ Amount qualifying as capital amortises on a straight-line basis in the last five years	■ Fixed maturity subordinated debt ■ Perpetual subordinated non-loss absorbing debt	
Other	■ Capital to only include fully paid-up amounts ■ Issues of capital cannot include cross-default or negative pledge clauses ■ Default of Lower Tier 2 capital is defined as non-payment of interest or a winding-up of the bank ■ No rights of set-off to be included in capital issues documentation ■ Early repayment of debt must be approved by the bank's regulator ■ Interim profits must be audited accounts, and net of expected losses, tax and dividends		

allow interest payments to be made on a pre-tax basis rather than after tax; this means they behave like preference shares or equity, and improve the financial efficiency of the bank's regulatory capital. Such securities, along with those classified as Upper Tier 2 capital, contain interest deferral clauses so that they may be classified similar to preference shares or equity.[3]

Example 2.2 illustrates a simple capital adequacy calculation for a hypothetical bank. To illustrate, consider a bank with a loan book made up of the following assets:

- £100 million gilts;
- £315 million corporate loans;
- £600 million residential mortgages.

The risk-adjusted exposure of the bank's portfolio is $(0.0 \times 100) + (1.0 \times 315) + (0.5 \times 600)$ or £615 million. Therefore the bank would require a minimum Tier 1 capital level of £24.6 million (that is, 4% × 615 million). If the capital available to support the loan book comprised both Tier 1 and Tier 2 capital, the minimum amount required would be higher, at £49.2 million.

There is of course a cost associated with maintaining capital levels, which is one of the main reasons for the growth in the use of derivative (off-balance sheet) instruments, as well as the rise in securitisation. Derivative instruments attract a lower capital charge than cash instruments, because the principal in a derivative instrument does not change hands and so is not at risk, while the process of securitisation removes assets from a bank's balance sheet, thereby reducing its capital requirements.

The capital rules for off-balance sheet instruments are slightly more involved. Certain instruments, such as FRAs and swaps with a maturity of less than one year, have no capital requirement at all. Briefly, the regulatory capital rules for derivatives are:

$$EAD = \left(\sum [max(0, MTM) + PFE\right) - Coll + Coll\,Haircut \qquad (2.3)$$

where

EAD = Exposure at default
PFE = Potential future exposure
$Coll$ = Collateral value

3 Note that under Basel III, which we discuss later in the chapter, the concept of Tier 3 capital has been abolished.

TABLE 2.3 Add-on risk adjustment for interest-rate swaps, percentage of nominal value.

Maturity	Plain vanilla	Floating/Floating swaps	Currency swaps
Up to 1 year	0.0	0.0	1.0
Over 1 year	0.5	0.0	5.0
Over 5 years	1.5	0.0	7.5

PFE is given by

$$PFE_{Gross} = Contract\ Value \times Add\ On \tag{2.4}$$

The Add-on multiple is given at Table 2.3.

If the bank has a "netting" agreement in place with a counterparty, formalised in the legal agreement between them, then the portfolio-level capital calculation is given by:

$$EAD = \left(\sum [MTM + PFE_{Net}\right) - Coll + Coll\, Haircut \tag{2.5}$$

where

$$PFE_{\text{Gross}} = (0.4 \times PFE_{Gross}) + (0.6 \times NGR \times PFE_{Gross}) \tag{2.6}$$

and NGR is the net gross ratio, given by

$$NGR = \frac{\sum MTM}{\sum Max(0, MTM)}.$$

The capital calculations for derivatives have detail differences between them, depending on the instrument that is being traded. For example, for interest-rate swaps the exposure includes an "add-on factor" to what is termed the instrument's "current exposure". This add-on factor is a percentage of the nominal value, and is shown in Table 2.3.

EXAMPLE 2.2 SIMPLE ILLUSTRATION OF CALCULATION OF CAPITAL ADEQUACY, BASEL I RULES

The assets of ABC Bank plc are £2.536 billion, which are balanced by shareholders' funds and long-term borrowings, as well as the deposit base of the bank. The Basel risk-weighting assigns the various types of assets a certain risk-weighting, and using the rules we calculate a

(*continued*)

capital at risk value of £1.298 billion. The capital required is 8% of this sum, or just over £103 million. The Basel rule states that at least 50% of this amount must be sourced from Tier 1 capital. We see from Table 2.4 that the level of Tier 1 capital is well above the sum required. The combination of Tier 1 and Tier 2 capital is also well above the minimum required.

TABLE 2.4 Example of capital adequacy calculation.

ABC Bank plc Balance Sheet			
Assets	**Weighting (%)**	**Value (£m)**	**Capital risk-weighting (£m)**
T-Bills	0	250	0
Cash	0	30	0
Inter-bank loans	20	790	158
Mortgage book	50	652	326
Commercial loan book	100	814	814
TOTAL		2536	1298
Capital charge (8%)			103.84
Liabilities			
Shareholders' funds	100		
Reserves	356	456	
Long-term debt	500		
Deposits	1580	2080	
		2536	

THE BASEL II RULES[4]

The perceived shortcomings of the 1988 Basel capital accord attracted much comment from academics and practitioners alike, almost as soon as they were adopted. The main criticisms were that the requirements made no allowance for the credit risk ratings of different corporate borrowers, and that they were too rigid in their application of the risk-weightings.

4 The actual title of the document, published by the Basel Committee on Banking Supervision of the Bank for International Settlements on 26 June 2004, is *International Convergence of Capital Measurements and Capital Standards.*

That these were valid issues was recognised when, on 3 June 1999, the BIS published proposals to update the capital requirements rules. The new guidelines were designed "to promote safety and soundness in the financial system, to provide a more comprehensive approach for addressing risks, and to enhance competitive equality". The proposals were also intended to apply to all banks worldwide, and not simply those that are active across international borders. The 1988 accord was based on very broad counterparty credit requirements, and despite an amendment introduced in 1996 to cover trading book requirements, it remained open to the criticism of inflexibility. The Basel II rules have three pillars, and were designed to be more closely related to the risk levels of particular credit exposures. These are discussed below.

Elements of the Basel II Rules

Basel II is split into three approaches or pillars, which we consider in this section.

Pillar 1 – The Minimum Capital Requirements

(1) **Credit risk** The capital requirements are stated under two approaches:

- the standardised approach;
- the internal ratings-based (IRB) approach. Within IRB there is a foundation approach and an advanced approach, the latter of which gives banks more scope to set elements of the capital charges themselves.

Standardised Approach

In the standardised approach banks risk-weight assets in accordance with a set matrix, which splits assets according to their formal credit ratings. The matrix is detailed in Table 2.5, which shows the new risk weights as percentages of the standard 8% ratio.

The revised ruling redistributed the capital required for different types of lending and also added an additional category for very low-rated assets. For sovereign lending there is a smooth scale from 0% to 150%, while the scale is more staggered for corporates. An unusual feature is that low-rated companies attract a higher charge than non-rated borrowers. For lending to other banks there are two options; in the first, the sovereign risk of the home country of the bank is used, and the bank is placed in the next lower category. In the second option, the credit rating of a bank itself is used.

TABLE 2.5 Basel II capital requirement risk weights, percentage weightings.

	Credit rating						
Asset	AAA to AA	A+ to A−	BBB+ to BBB−	BB+ to B−	B+ to B−	Below B−	Unrated
Sovereign	0%	20%	50%	100%	100%	150%	100%
Banks –							
option 1[1]	0%	20%	50%	100%	100%	150%	100%
option 2[2]							
< 3 months	20%	20%	20%	50%	50%	150%	20%
> 3 months	20%	50%	50%	100%	100%	150%	50%
Corporates	20%	50%	100%	100%	150%	150%	100%

[1] Based on the risk-weighting of the soveraign in which the bank is incorporated.
[2] Based on the assessment of the individual bank.
Source: BIS.

National regulators select which of the two approaches to use for inter-bank exposures. Under option 1, loans are categorised in accordance with the rating of their sovereign domicile, while under option 2 loans are slotted according to the bank's own rating. If using the latter approach, assets of below three months receive preferential treatment.

Loans made to unrated borrowers are placed in a separate band that carries the full risk weighting of 100%, although regulators should review the historical default experience of the relevant market and assess whether this weighting is sufficient. Short-term credit facilities with corporates that remain undrawn, which under Basel I attract a zero weighting, are weighted at 20% under Basel II. Compared to Basel I, under Basel II there is a greater allowance for credit risk reduction, principally in the form of recognition of securities as collateral. The following assets are recognised as collateral:

- cash and government securities (as currently recognised under Basel I);
- securities rated BB− and above issued by a sovereign or public-sector entity;
- securities rated BBB− and above;
- equities that are constituents of a main index, or listed on a recognised investment exchange;
- gold.

Securities placed as collateral are given a "haircut" to their market value to reflect their price volatility.

Internal Ratings-based (IRB) Approach

In the IRB approach, banks' assets are categorised in accordance with their own internal risk assessment. To undertake this approach a bank must have its internal systems recognised by its relevant supervisory body, and systems and procedures must have been in place for at least three years previously. This includes a system that enables the bank to assess the default probability of borrowers. If using an IRB approach a bank will use its own internal ratings to categorise loans in *probability-to-default* (PD) bands. The number of PD bands set up is at the discretion of the bank. The BIS has compiled a formula that enables the bank to calculate the capital allocation requirement in accordance with its PD bands. Table 2.6 sets out the capital requirements under Basel I, and both the standard and IRB approaches under Basel II.

If using the advanced approach, banks may recognise any form of collateral and set their own parameters when using the BIS formula for calculating capital, following approval from their banking supervisory body. For the first two years after such approval, the credit risk element of capital allocation cannot be lower than 90% of the allocation calculated under the foundation approach.

(2) **Operational Risk** An element of Basel II is the capital charge to cover banks' operational risk. There are three different approaches for calculating the operational risk capital charge. These are:

- the basic indicator approach, under which 20% of total capital would be allocated;
- a standardised approach, under which different risk indicators will be allocated to different lines of business within a bank; this would be the

TABLE 2.6 Capital requirements under specified PD bands.

	%			
	PD band	Basel I	Standard approach	IRB foundation approach
AAA	0.03	8.0	1.6	1.13
AA	0.03	8.0	1.6	1.13
A	0.03	8.0	4.0	1.13
BBB	0.20	8.0	8.0	3.61
BB	1.40	8.0	8.0	12.35
B	6.60	8.0	12.0	30.96
CCC	15.00	8.0	12.0	47.04

Source: BIS.

level of average assets for a retail bank and assets under management for a fund manager. The Committee would set the capital charge level for each business line, in accordance with its perceived level of risk in each national jurisdiction, and the total operational risk would be the sum of the exposures of all business lines;
- an internal estimation by a bank of the expected losses due to operational risk for each business line. Operational risk here would be risk of loss as a result of fraud, IT failures, legal risk and so on.

(3) **Total Minimum Capital** The sum of the capital calculation for credit risk exposure, operational risk and the bank's trading book will be the total minimum capital requirement. This capital requirement will be expressed as an 8% risk-asset ratio, identical to the rules under Basel I.

Pillar 2 – Supervisory Approach

In Basel II there is a requirement for a supervision approach to capital allocation. This is based on three principles. First, banks must have a procedure for calculating their capital requirements in accordance with their individual risk profile. This means they are required to look beyond the minimum capital requirement as provided for under Pillar 1, and assess specific risk areas that reflect their own business activities. This would consider, for instance, interest-rate risk exposure within the banking book, or prepayment risk as part of mortgage business. This process is reviewed constantly by banking supervisory authorities. Second, the risk-weighted capital requirement calculated under Pillar 1 is viewed as a minimum only, and banks are expected to set aside capital above this minimum level to provide an element of reserve. Supervisors are empowered to require a bank to raise its capital level above the stipulated minimum. Finally, supervisors are instructed to constantly review the capital levels of banks under their authority, and act accordingly in good time so that such levels do not fall below a level deemed sufficient to support an individual bank's business activity.

Pillar 3 – Disclosure

Basel II sets out rules on core disclosure that banks are required to meet, and which supervisors must enforce. In addition there are supplementary disclosure rules; these differ from core rules in that banks have more flexibility on reporting them if they are deemed not relevant to their specific operating activities, or of they are deemed non-material. The disclosures include:

- *capital*: the elements that make up the bank's capital, such as the types of instruments that make up the Tier 1 and Tier 2 capital;
- *capital adequacy*: this covers the amount of capital required against credit, market and operational risk, as well as capital requirements as a percentage of the total capital of the bank;
- *risk exposure*: the overall risk exposure of a bank, as measured by credit risk, market risk, operational risk and so on. Hence, this would include a profile of the ALM book, including maturity profile of the loan book, interest-rate risk, other market risk, essentially the sum of the exposures measured and monitored by a bank's risk management department.

Note that the definition of bank capital remains as it is under Basel I, and the minimum capital ratios of 4% for Tier 1 and 8% for total capital also remain in place. So Pillar 1, and Basel II as a whole, is concerned only with the denominator of the capital ratio calculation as established under Basel I, and not the numerator, which stays unchanged.[5]

IMPLEMENTATION APPROACHES

Basel II rules can be implemented under three alternative approaches: the standardised, foundation IRB and advanced IRB approaches. Briefly, these can be described as follows:

- *standardised approach*: the most straightforward to apply, with risk weights being assigned according to asset class or formal credit ratings. The assets are described as residential mortgages, corporate loans and so on;
- *foundation IRB*: under this the capital calculation is made after the bank itself sets default probabilities for each class of assets. The bank assigns PD to each asset class, or each asset in accordance with credit rating; using Basel II guidelines it then sets the LGD, exposure-at-default (EAD) and maturity (M) parameters. These inputs are then used to calculate risk-weights for each asset class using the Basel II capital calculation formula. Foundation IRB may be used as a stepping-stone before implementation of the advanced IRB methodology, or retained as a calculation method in its own right;

5 There is a slight change to the numerator in the ratio under Basel II in circumstances where deductions of capital for certain asset classes must be made, but this will not apply to all banks.

- *advanced IRB*: under this a bank will calculate risk-weights using its own parameters, which are arrived at from its own default data and internal models.

Under the IRB approach the banks may use their own data, significantly including data for PD, LGD and EAD. Their own model can be used to calculate risk-weights, which is then adjusted by a scaling factor. In practice this means a scaling factor of 1.06 will be applied. Note that a bank must adopt the same approach for both its banking book and its trading book.

The vast majority of banks in the world employ the standardised approach. Only the large integrated multinational banks apply the advanced IRB approach, which requires significant investment in internal systems. Banks that implement the advanced IRB approach must obtain supervisory approval of their systems and models from their national regulator.

IMPACT ON SPECIFIC SECTORS

To illustrate Basel II further, we consider it with regard to specific selected asset classes. We review sovereigns first, followed by bank assets, structured finance securities, liquidity facilities, corporate and retail lending, and credit derivatives.

Sovereign Assets

The treatment of sovereign debt under Basel I was very simple. Sovereigns were divided into OECD and non-OECD debt.[6] OECD sovereign debt was risk-weighted at 0%, while non-OECD sovereigns were weighted at 100%. Under Basel II there is a deeper distinction, with the risk-weighting assigned by credit rating (under the standardised approach). This is shown at Table 2.7.

Both IRB approaches use the banks' own internal measures of risk. Under the standardised approach, formal credit ratings from the "external credit assessment institutions" (ECAIs) assume a high importance. Basel II states that if a country carries a rating each from S&P, Moody's and Fitch, and one of these is lower than the other two, then the higher one can be

---

6 The Organisation for Economic Cooperation and Development (OECD) member countries are Australia, Austria, Belgium, Canada, Czech Republic, Denmark, Finland, France, Germany, Greece, Hungary, Iceland, Ireland, Italy, Japan, Korea, Luxembourg, Mexico, the Netherlands, New Zealand, Norway, Poland, Portugal, Slovakia, Spain, Sweden, Switzerland, Turkey, the UK and US.

TABLE 2.7 Basel II sovereign debt risk weightings (standardised approach).

Basel I		Basel II	
OECD	0%	AA− and above	0%
Non-OECD	100%	A	20%
		BBB	50%
		BB+ to B−	100%
		Below B−	150%
		Unrated	100%

Source: BIS.

assumed. For a bank holding the debt of a country rated A/A2/A− this rule has no impact; however, for a bank holding sovereign debt rated A1/BBB+/A, this is significant. It means that the bank can take the two higher ratings, which enable it to apply a 20% risk weighting. This is a considerable saving compared to the Basel I weighting of 100%.

An illustration of the change under Basel II is as follows: consider a bank holding two bonds, each of USD10 million nominal, issued by Korea and South Africa respectively. In 2011 these countries were rated A/A1/A+ and BBB+/A3/BBB+. Under Basel I, and taking the minimum 8% capital requirement, the capital charges for each are:

Korea government bond capital:

$$\text{USD}0.00$$

South Africa government bond capital:

$$[10{,}000{,}000 \times 100\% \times 8\%] \text{ or USD}800{,}000.00$$

Under the Basel II standardised approach the charges are:

Korea

$$[10{,}000{,}000 \times 20\% \times 8\%] \text{ or USD}160{,}000.00$$

South Africa

$$[10{,}000{,}000 \times 50\% \times 8\%] \text{ or USD}400{,}000.00$$

So in this stylised example the impact is quite significant. The makeup and composition of government bond portfolios in banks will be reviewed and heavily influenced by each sovereign credit ECAI. As capital charges rise for certain borrowers compared to others, those sovereigns that suffer an adverse impact in terms of the capital that a bank investor is required to hold against them may find their issuance yields rise. It is not necessarily emerging-market sovereigns that are so impacted. In 2011 Italy was rated at A+ by S&P (although it was rated Aa2 by Moody's and AA– by Fitch). If one of the other agencies also downgraded Italian sovereign debt, then such debt would lose its 0% risk-weighting under Basel II standardised approach rules. This point also highlights an advantage of adopting the IRB rules. Under foundation IRB, certain countries that attract a 20% weighting under a standardised approach may be weighted at 0% under a bank's own PD values for sovereign debt. However, generally higher rated non-OECD sovereigns gain under Basel II. Lower-rated OECD members generally attract a higher charge.[7]

Description of Calculation

Much of the calculation framework for Basel II is the same for corporates as well as sovereign assets. Under Basel II the standardised approach applies risk-weights in accordance with asset credit rating, as shown in Table 2.5. Under the IRB approach, banks that meet minimum specified requirements, and have obtained their regulator's approval, can use their internal estimates of risk parameters to determine their capital requirements. These parameters are:

- probability-of-default (*PD*): this is key to the IRB approach, and is the 1-year probability that an obligor will default;
- loss-given-default (*LGD*): this is a measure of the expected average loss that a bank will suffer per unit of asset or exposure, in the event of counterparty default. Whereas a borrower can only have one credit rating and hence only one PD, different sets of exposure to the same borrower may have different LGDs; for example, if one exposure is collateralised and another is not;
- exposure-at-default (*EAD*): this is a measure of the extent to which a bank is exposed to a counterparty in the event of the latter's default. For cash transactions, this amount is the nominal amount of the exposure. For derivative transactions and transactions with variable drawdown options, a credit conversion factor is applied to convert notional amounts to nominal values;
- maturity (*M*): generally speaking, longer dated loans represent higher credit risk. Up to a point, the longer the maturity of an exposure the higher the probability of decrease in its credit quality; hence, the higher

7 Bloomberg users can access up-to-date sovereign credit ratings from screens CSDR <go> and WCDM <go>.

the PD. Somewhat counter-intuitively, this effect is higher for better rated entities, because the higher the credit rating the more downward categories, short of default, there are for the entity to migrate to. Hence the risk-weight, in terms of M, is actually higher.

- *Foundation IRB*: a bank adopting this approach may use its internal credit risk-scoring model to estimate PD,[8] but must use BIS-prescribed LGD, EAD and M values. Senior unsecured claims on corporates, sovereigns and banks are assigned a 45% LGD; subordinated unsecured borrowings are assigned a 75% LGD. There is an assigned value of 2.5 for M. For EAD a credit conversion factor of 75% is applied for undrawn liquidity facilities and unused credit lines.
- *Advanced IRB*: banks that implement the advanced IRB approach will use their own values for PD, EAD and LGD, and calculate their own M value. Because national regulatory authorities will also be setting their own prescribed levels for these parameters, adopting the advanced approach will be beneficial for banks that believe their own estimates will be lower than those of the regulator. The calculation of M is dependent on the cash flows of the actual assets on the book. Generally, if the M value is below 2.5, then the risk-weight will be lower under the advanced approach compared to the foundation approach. If M lies above 2.5, then the opposite is true. The maximum value for M is 5.0.
- *Formulas*: for all assets not in default, the formulas for calculating the risk-weights and capital requirements under both foundation and advanced approaches are:

Correlation $(R) =$

$$0.12 \times \frac{[1 - exp(-50 \times PD)]}{[1 - exp(-50)]} + 0.24 \times \left[1 - \frac{[1 - exp(-50 \times PD)]}{[1 - exp(-50)]}\right]. \quad (2.7)$$

Maturity adjustment $(b) =$

$$(0.11852 - 0.05478 \times ln(PD))^2. \quad (2.8)$$

Capital requirement $(K) =$

$$\left[LGD \times N\left((1 - R)^{0.5} \times G(PD) + \left[\frac{R}{(1 - R)}\right]^{0.5} \times G(0.999)\right) - (PD \times LGD)\right]$$
$$\times \left(\frac{1}{1 - 1.5 \times b}\right) \times [1 + (M - 2.5) \times b] \quad (2.9)$$

8 There is a minimum level of 0.03% specified by BIS for corporates and banks.

where

$N()$ = is the cumulative distribution function for a standard normal variable with $N(0, 1)$

$G(z)$ = is the inverse cumulative distribution function for a standard normal variable (that is, the value of x is such that $N(x) = z$).

Risk-weighted assets $(RWA) = K \times 12.5 \times EAD$.

The formula for K says that, ignoring the correlation and maturity factors, the capital requirement represents the difference between the loss under the worst case scenario (assumed to be an event with a probability less than 0.1%) and the expected loss (given by $PD \times LGD$).

Of course, the correlation parameter is key, because the defaults of different obligors are not independent of each other. General macroeconomic factors impact all obligors, more so for higher rated entities (on the assumption that lower rated firms are more likely to experience difficulty due to firm-specific issues rather than the general state of the economy). The correlation parameter value in the formula lies between 0.12 and 0.24; the value increases from 0.12 for entities with a higher credit rating. The maturity adjustment factor b is a correction to allow for the fact that the tenor of the exposure will be shorter or longer than the benchmark value of 2.5.

The standard formula given here is not used for assets in default. For such exposures the capital requirement is given by:

$$Max\,[0,\ LGD - (PD \times LGD)]$$

where the expected loss $(PD \times LGD)$ is the bank's best estimate. This estimate is used to calculate loan loss provision and set-off charges for each asset in default.

Example Illustration

To illustrate the calculation rules, and as an indication of how capital requirements can be significantly different under Basel II when compared to Basel I, we present a stylised example using two sovereign assets. Imagine that a bank holds the following two sovereign bonds, with ratings at the time as shown:

- USD100 million, Republic of Turkey 10-year, rated BB–;
- USD100 million, Malaysia 10-year, rated A–.

Under Basel I the regulatory capital requirement for this portfolio is zero for the Turkey bond, because the country is an OECD member, and USD8 million for the Malaysia bond, which is 100% risk-weighted.

Under Basel II this requirement changes, with the exact calculation being dependent on the approach being adopted.

Standardised Approach Under the standardised approach, the ratings of each sovereign determine its risk-weighting.[9] So the capital calculation is:

- Turkey: USD4 million;
- Malaysia: USD1.6 million.

This illustrates a general comment on the impact of Basel II compared to Basel I: under the simple standardised approach, asset portfolios that gain include those of higher rated non-OECD obligations such as China, Chile, Hong Kong and South Africa, while portfolios that would suffer higher capital charges would include OECD-member countries that are lower rated, such as Mexico, Poland, Slovakia, South Korea and, as shown here, Turkey. In our example, the holding of the Turkey sovereign bond suffers a significant increase in capital charge, while the Malaysia bond benefits from a much-reduced requirement.

Foundation IRB For this example we extract statistical data from debt market prices in January 2008. This is given in Table 2.8. For the PD values these are unnecessarily severe, and rating agency PD would for both countries be nearer to zero.[10] However, the illustration works better using our unrealistic estimates, which produce the risk-weights shown in Table 2.9. The M and LGD values are those prescribed in the BIS document for the foundation approach.

With the calculated risk-weights, we produce a capital requirement of:

- Turkey: USD5.1 million;
- Malaysia: USD3.3 million.

So under foundation IRB we have a still higher capital charge for Turkey, and a lower requirement for Malaysia.

---

9 In our example there is one uniform rating for each exposure. Very broadly speaking, if a sovereign or other entity is rated differently across different agencies, the lower rating applies.

10 And this is significant: at a zero PD there would be a zero capital requirement, because there is no minimum level of PD for sovereign exposures. For corporate exposures, a minimum floor PD applies irrespective of rating.

TABLE 2.8 Comparison of Basel I and Basel II risk-weights: selected countries.

Country	Basel I (%)	Standardised Basel II (%)	Foundation IRB (%)	Advanced IRB (%)
Australia	0	20	0	0
Chile	100	20	30	47
China	100	20	44	68
Czech Republic	0	20	0	0
Hong Kong	100	20	0	0
Indonesia	100	100	143	153
Malaysia	100	50	0	0
Poland	0	50	44	68
Portugal	0	50	44	47
Slovakia	0	50	0	0
South Africa	100	50	57	86
South Korea	0	20	57	86

Sources: BIS based on S&P rating agency data.

Advanced IRB Under the advanced IRB, as sovereign Malaysia has a lower PD value its impact is, somewhat counter-intuitively, greater over a longer period compared to Turkey. This produces a greater increase in capital charge for a 10-year exposure for Malaysia compared to Turkey. The risk-weight for Malaysia rises from 41% to 66%, while that for Turkey rises from 66% to 100%.

Note that the values arrived under advanced IRB are heavily influenced by the PD, M and LGD parameters used. Significant differences in results can emerge based on what values are assigned for these inputs. For example, rating-agency PDs often differ from CDS-implied PD values. In the case of

TABLE 2.9 Calculation parameters.

	PD	Correlation factor	M	LGD[1]
Turkey	0.34	0.2	2.5	45%
Malaysia	0.15	0.2	2.5	45%
	Risk-weights			
Turkey	66%			
Malaysia	41%			

[1] Senior-level debt.

sovereign exposures, because PDs can assume zero value, the choice of which number to use is significant.

Bank Assets

Banks are significant holders of short- and medium-term bank-issued debt, and may rebalance liquidity portfolios when assets are affected by capital rules.[11]

Short-term Debt

The rules for short-term bank debt can be summarised as follows:

- debt of 1-year maturity or less is assigned 20% risk-weighting, assuming it is rated at A–1/P–1.[12] Short-term bank debt rated at A–2/P–2 is assigned a 50% weighting, while A–3/P–3 paper is weighted at 100%;
- very short-term debt of 3-month maturity or less that is unrated, but whose issuer has a long-term rating equivalent to A–3/P–3, and is weighted at 20%.

Essentially, most short-term bank paper is rated at 20%, which is unchanged from the Basel I regime. The preferential treatment of very short-term debt, which enables even low-rated (A–3/P–3) assets to be weighted at 20% is prescribed in Option 2 of the standardised approach to bank debt (see Table 2.10). It is not available under Option 1, so banks that are required to adopt the latter by their national regulator will not have this flexibility. Under Option 1 short-term assets will be rated at 20%, 50% and 100% for A–1/P–1, A–2/P–2 and A–3/P–3 ratings respectively. In the event that a sovereign or bank has three ratings, the two highest ratings will apply.

Table 2.10 summarises the Option 1 and Option 2 risk-weights.

We identify certain anomalies that may arise under these two alternative rulings. For all assets of over 3-month maturity, there is a clear difference at the BBB+ to BBB– rating band. Under Option 1 a bank in that rating range would be 100% risk-weighted, whereas under Option 2 it would carry only a 50% risk-weighting. Another anomaly is a BBB-rated bank incorporated in an A-rated country: under Option 1 it would carry a 50% weighting,

11 Banks hold a large part of their liquidity book in short-term bank debt such as CDs, CP and FRNs.

12 Note that the highest S&P short-term rating is A–1+, while the highest Moody's short-term rating is P–1.

TABLE 2.10 Basel II bank debt capital charge, Option 1 and Option 2.

Option 1: Central government risk-weight-based method						
Rating of sovereign	**AAA to AA−**	**A+ to A−**	**BBB+ to BBB−**	**BB+ to B−**	**Below B−**	**Unrated**
Risk-weight for senior bank debt	20%	50%	100%	100%	150%	100%

Option 2: Credit assessment-based method						
Rating of bank	**AAA to AA−**	**A+ to A−**	**BBB+ to BBB−**	**BB+ to B−**	**Below B−**	**Unrated**
Risk-weight for senior bank debt	20%	50%	50%	100%	150%	50%
Risk-weight for very short-term senior debt (< 3-month maturity)	20%	20%	20%	50%	150%	20%

Source: BIS.

compared to a 100% weighting under Option 2. Note also the preferential treatment for very short-term bank debt under Option 2.

From Table 2.10 we would conclude that banks of lower credit rating, but which are incorporated in a highly rated country, would benefit from the adoption of Option 1, while in the case of the converse Option 2 would be advantageous.[13] Note that the UK's regulatory agency, the Financial Services Authority, has stated that Option 2 is the more risk sensitive of the two approaches and should be the one that is used.[14]

IRB Approach The procedure for applying the IRB rules in both foundation and advanced form for bank assets is virtually identical to that used for sovereign assets. The only significant difference is that a minimum value of 0.03% for the PD parameter must be applied for bank assets when calculating the risk-weighting. If applying foundation IRB, a bank may use its own internal credit analysis results when estimating the PD parameter (subject to the 0.03% minimum), while the values for the EAD, LGD and M parameters are set in the BIS guidelines. Senior unsecured bank debt is assigned a 45% LGD value, with subordinated unsecured debt given a 75% LGD level. The value for M is 2.5. If applying advanced IRB, a bank may use its own internally calculated values for PD, EAD, LGD and M.

Under Option 2 of Basel II, risk-weighting for bank assets that are rated at A or BBB will rise to 50% from the previous level of 20%. The capital required to be held against instruments issued by weaker rated banks will therefore be substantially higher under Basel II.

Covered Bonds[15] Under Basel I covered bonds were risk-weighted at 10%, which made them particularly attractive for both issuers and bank investors.[16] In the Basel II standardised approach regime, covered bonds are assigned the same weighting as senior subordinated debt, which places them at 10% risk-weight for banks rated AA and above, and 20% for other banks. However, if a bank applies foundation or advanced IRB this

13 Note that the rating agencies do not rate a corporate entity, including a bank, at a higher rating than the rating of its country of incorporation (although an equivalent rating is possible). Hence, such banks are rare beasts.

14 Consultation Paper 189, FSA.

15 Covered bonds are described in Chapter 20 of the author's book *Bank Asset and Liability Management*.

16 Covered bonds issued by banks in Italy, Portugal, Sweden and the UK were assigned 20% risk-weighting by their respective national regulators, thus making them equal in capital charge terms to other bank debt instruments in these jurisdictions.

weighting is likely to fall to below 10%. Therefore these assets could become more attractive for banks employing the IRB approach, with the attendant implications for both yield spreads and further issuance.

A consideration for banks with large residential mortgage portfolios is the choice of whether to concentrate on issuing covered bonds or residential mortgage-backed securities (RMBS). Securitising mortgage books not only achieved capital relief for banks under Basel I, it is also an important liquidity and funding mechanism for many banks. In the UK, banks such as Northern Rock plc and Bradford & Bingley plc followed the example of credit card banks in the US, and were able to significantly grow their mortgage books after employing securitisation techniques. Unfortunately, the rapid asset growth that such instruments allowed was a factor in those two banks' demise. Under Basel II and associated with genuine risk-transfer regulatory rules, for many banks there is no longer a capital advantage in securitising residential mortgages – it will be cheaper, in capital charge terms, to keep them on their balance sheet. Therefore covered bonds are more attractive for these banks, rather than RMBS.

Repo Agreements and Securities Lending

A 0% risk-weight is applied to an exposure that is collateralised under a repo agreement if the counterparty is a "core market participant". Otherwise, the risk-weight is 10%. This assumes that (i) the loan and the collateral are denominated in the same currency, (ii) the position is marked-to-market on a daily basis and margin taken where necessary, and (iii) the transaction takes place under a standard legal agreement such as the Global Master Repurchase Agreement (GMRA).[17]

Any other collateralised exposure is also risk-weighted at 0%, provided that the collateral is in the form of cash or sovereign debt issued by a country also risk-weighted at 0% under the standardised approach, and there is a haircut of at least 20%.[18]

Derivative Positions

Banks are the largest users of off-balance sheet derivatives such as swaps. Under Basel I, banks calculated the credit exposure arising from derivatives trading using the "current exposure" method, which entailed taking the mark-to-market value of each position and basing the exposure on that.

---

17 See Chapter 12 of the author's book *Bank Asset and Liability Management* for detail on the GMRA.

18 This is a substantial haircut. The haircut for A-rated assets would seldom exceed 10% in a repo under GMRA.

Basel II continues essentially with this approach. The counterparty charge for derivatives transactions is given by:

$$\text{Counterparty charge} = [(RC + \text{Add-on}) - CA] \times r \times 0.08 \qquad (2.10)$$

where

RC = is the replacement cost
Add-on = is the potential future exposure
CA = is the collateral value
r = is the counterparty risk-weight.

Note that this applies to OTC derivative contracts only, not exchange-traded ones, for which no counterparty charge is required. Formula (2.10) shows that a bank will obtain capital relief for any of its derivative trades that are collateralised by the counterparty.

Structured Finance Assets

Basel I applied a very simple regime to structured finance securities. There was a 100% risk-weight for all asset-backed securities (ABS), with the exception of AAA-rated senior tranche RMBS bonds, which were weighted at 50%.[19] Under Basel II different risk weights are applied according to the rating of the individual tranche. The key areas of impact arise from the following:

- the capital charge requirement against assets such as residential mortgages and credit card debt reduced under Basel II;
- banks that invest in ABS (certain tranches) are required to hold less capital against these assets under Basel II.

From an ALM point of view, banks have a continuing incentive to securitise lower rated mortgage books such as commercial mortgages.

Approach under Basel II

The standardised approach for ABS follows a similar procedure as that for sovereign and bank assets. Risk-weights that are assigned to ABS tranches, depending on whether the bank is originating the instrument or investing in it, are shown in Table 2.11. These weights are prescribed by the BIS. Note that all unrated tranches require that a deduction be made from capital, unless the tranche concerned is the most senior in a securitisation, when in such cases the tranche is assigned the average risk-weight of the underlying assets.

19 Junior tranches rated below BB– are deducted from capital under Basel I.

TABLE 2.11 Basel II standardised approach for ABS tranches.

ABS tranches risk-weighting	%	
	Investor	Originator
Long-term		
AAA to AA−	20	20
A+ to A−	50	50
BBB+ to BBB−	100	100
BB+ to BB−	350	Deduction
B+ to below/unrated	Deduction	Deduction
Short-term		
A–1/P–1	20	20
A–2/P–2	50	50
A–3/P–3	100	100
Unrated	350	350

Source: BIS.

The procedure for the IRB method is slightly more complex, with three different methods depending on the rating of the ABS tranche. These are the:

- ratings-based approach (RBA);
- supervisory formula (SF);
- internal assessment approach (IAA).

These are considered further below.

Ratings-based Approach (RBA) The RBA is applied where a structured finance security is rated, or where a rating can be implied from the formal rating of a reference entity. The tranche rating governs the risk-weight applicable, as does three other parameters, which are:

- the seniority of the tranche;
- the long-term or short-term rating;
- the granularity of the underlying asset pool.

Granularity in this case refers to how many individual assets are in the underlying asset pool.[20] For Basel II purposes, a pool is said to be granular if it holds six or more assets.

20 While a large RMBS transaction may contain many hundreds, if not thousands, of individual assets in the asset pool, other securitisations such as commercial mortgage-backed securities (CMBS) may contain only a handful of assets. Esoteric asset securitisations may contain only one asset (for example, a museum entry fee receivables securitisation).

TABLE 2.12A RBA risk-weights (%).

Rating	Tranches and eligible senior notes	Base case	Non-granular pool
Aaa	7	12	20
Aa	8	15	25
A1	10	18	
A2	12	20	35
A3	20	35	
Baa1	35		50
Baa2	60		75
Baa3		100	
Ba1		250	
Ba2		425	
Ba3		650	
Below Ba3		Deduction	

Source: BIS.

The risk-weights applied under RBA to the most senior tranche of a securitisation transaction, which are governed by the tranche's rating, are shown in Table 2.12B. Note that these apply to originating as well investing banks. Table 2.12A shows the risk weight for a non-granular pool, as well as the base case.

For all tranches ranked below the senior note in a structured finance transaction, the risk-weightings are as listed in Table 2.13A for granular pools and Table 2.13B for non-granular pools.

Supervisory formula (SF) The SF is applied where no external formal rating is available for a structured finance security. The calculation of the capital charge using the SF, which is given in the BIS document, is quite involved. Note that an ALM desk will rarely, if ever, need to apply the SF because unrated ABS tranches outside the first-loss ("equity") piece are invariably rated. Therefore we do not reproduce the SF here.[21]

21 The SF calculation assumes five drivers of credit risk. These are: (i) K, the capital charge if the assets were not securitised; (ii) L, any credit enhancement; (iii) T, thickness of the exposure (which is the ratio of the nominal size of the ABS tranche to the total size of the underlying pool); (iv) N, the effective number of exposures, which is the ratio of the square of the sum of the individual exposures to the sum of squares of individual exposures; and (v) LGD, the loss-given-default.

TABLE 2.12B Structured finance securities: senior tranche risk-weightings (%).

Long-term	RW %
AAA	7
AA	8
A+	10
A	12
A−	20
BBB+	35
BBB	60
BBB−	100
BB+	250
BB	425
BB−	650
Below BB−/Unrated	Deduction from capital
Short-term	**RW %**
A–1/P–1	7
A–2/P–2	12
A–3/P–3	60
Unrated	Deduction from capital

Source: BIS.

TABLE 2.13A Structured finance securities: all tranches (except senior tranche) risk-weightings (%): granular asset pool.

Long-term	RW %
AAA	12
AA	15
A+	18
A	20
A−	35
BBB+	50
BBB	75
BBB−	100
BB+	250
BB	425
BB−	650
Below BB−/Unrated	Deduction from capital
Short-term	**RW %**
A–1/P–1	12
A–2/P–2	20
A–3/P–3	75
Unrated	Deduction from capital

Source: BIS.

TABLE 2.13B Structured finance securities: non-granular asset pool.

Long-term	RW %
AAA	20
AA	25
A+	35
A	35
A–	35
BBB+	50
BBB	75
BBB–	100
BB+	250
BB	425
BB–	650
Below BB–/Unrated	Deduction from capital
Short-term	**RW %**
A–1/P–1	20
A–2/P–2	35
A–3/P–3	75
Unrated	Deduction from capital

Source: BIS.

Internal Assessment Approach (IAA) The IAA is an approach applicable in the case of ABCP programmes, specifically where credit enhancements, including liquidity facilities, are unrated. Note that the ABCP programme itself must be rated. When calculating the risk-weighting for unrated liquidity and other credit enhancements, a bank can apply its own internal assessment of the exposures. The BIS prescribes that the internal assessment approach must be similar to the methodology employed by the rating agencies.

Liquidity Facilities

Liquidity facilities are a key credit-enhancement mechanism in the securitisation market, and are particularly important in the ABCP market. The providers of such facilities are usually banking groups. Under Basel I not all liquidity lines were subject to capital rules, but this changed under Basel II when all such facilities become subject to regulation.[22] All banks will be required to hold capital against liquidity facilities; as such, the ALM

22 Note that this impacts the providers of the liquidity lines only (that is, the banks), not the issuing vehicle that has a line in place.

Unrated facility
 100% × SF risk-weight

Rated facility
 100% × RBA risk-weight
 For < 1-year maturity:
  50% × risk-weight determined by rating
 For < 1-year maturity:
  100% × risk-weight determined by rating
 For facility only available in market corrections:
  20% × SF risk-weight

FIGURE 2.1 Liquidity facility risk weighting: IRB approach.
Source: BIS.

approach has to allow for the extent to which these are made available to customers, at least in their traditional form. The treatment of liquidity facilities differs according to whether the standardised or IRB approach is adopted. Banks that adopt the IRB should see a smaller capital charge compared to the charge calculated under the standardised method. The standardised approach states that the risk-weight of an unrated facility is given by:

$$100\% \times RW$$

where RW is the risk-weight of the lowest rating category for which the facility is granted.

The risk-weight for a rated facility of less than 1-year maturity is 20%, while if the maturity is greater than one year it is 50%. If a facility is only made available in the event of severe market correction or other market disturbance, the risk-weight is 0%. The IRB approach is summarised in Figure 2.1.

Corporate and Retail Lending

Corporate lending is, in many cases, the largest proportion of a bank's balance sheet. Under Basel II banks have found it harder to lend to unrated or low-rated corporates compared to middle-rated corporates.

Corporate Assets

The simple 100% risk-weight for corporate lending that applied under Basel I was discarded under Basel II. In its place is the ratings-based methodology for the standardised approach shown in Table 2.14. Under

TABLE 2.14 Basel II standardised approach: corporate risk-weights.

Rating	Risk-weight (%)
AAA to AA−	20
A+ to A−	50
BBB+ BB−	100
Below BB−	150
Unrated	100

Source: BIS.

the foundation IRB approach the capital charge reduces for higher rated corporates, so that AA-rated companies, previously rated 100% under Basel I, would now be at around 15%. The class of assets termed "small and medium-sized enterprises" (SMEs) gained under Basel II when compared to non-SME corporates; under the IRB approach the weighting is 20% lower for small SMEs.[23]

Retail assets risk-weighting under Basel II are at 75% in the standardised approach, compared to 100% under Basel I. Residential mortgages risk-weighting decreased from 50% to 35%; under the IRB method they are expected to fall to lower than this, around 15%. Thus banks with large pools of residential mortgages benefitted in capital charge terms compared to non-mortgage banks.

Corporate Assets: Standardised Approach Under the blanket 100% risk weighting of Basel I, banks had a greater incentive, somewhat perversely, to lend to lower rated corporates because this resulted in higher return on capital. This anomaly is better addressed under Basel II. In the standardised approach the obligor's formal credit rating determines the capital charge risk-weighting. Broadly, the only unchanged case is corporates rated from BBB+ to BB− that remain at 100%. All other corporates have changed risk-weights. Banks adopting the standardised approach then have little incentive to lend to entities in this rating category, whereas they have an incentive to lend to un-rated corporates compared to those rated below BB−. An un-rated corporate will have no incentive to apply for a credit rating unless this is likely to be better than BBB+, as the lending rate to it may be prohibitive.

23 An SME is defined for Basel II purposes as a corporate with annual sales of €50 million or less.

Corporate Assets: IRB Approach Banks implementing the foundation IRB methodology are allowed to use their internal credit-risk models to estimate the PD values for each obligor;[24] the values for the LGD, EAD and M parameters are prescribed by the BIS. Under the advanced IRB a bank may use its own estimates of all four parameters.

Illustration Using Hypothetical Example We use a simple example to illustrate Basel II. Consider a bank lending to two entities:

- a utility company rated AA;
- an industrial company rated BB−.

Under Basel I a loan of $10 million to each company would each attract a minimum capital charge of $800,000.00. Under the standardised approach of Basel II the charge for the loan to the utility company would be $160,000, while the requirement for the industrial company would be unchanged at $800,000.

Under the foundation approach, the bank would use its PD value to calculate the risk-weighting; assuming the calculation came to 15% for the utility company the capital charge would now be $120,000. Again, we assume the risk-weight for the industrial company was worked out as 95%; this leads to a capital charge of $760,000. The risk-weight values under the advanced IRB would use the bank's internal data for all the calculation parameters, but may well be higher for the industrial company, making this asset an even more expensive one when compared to the Basel I regime.

Retail Assets

Under Basel I there was a blanket 100% risk-weight for all retail assets, except for residential mortgages, which were weighted at 50%. Under Basel II more types of retail assets are specifically defined, as residential mortgages were under the earlier regime, so that there is less blanket coverage. A retail asset is defined as:

- an exposure to an individual person, or to an SME;
- an exposure that is one of a "significant number" of similar such assets;
- a total exposure to an individual exposure that does not exceed €1 million.

Standardised Approach Under the standardised approach the risk weighting for retail assets falls to 75%, which is a substantial reduction from the Basel I 100% risk-weight. For residential mortgages the risk-weight is

24 There is a BIS-imposed minimum PD of 0.03%.

35% (down from 50%) and for commercial mortgages the risk-weight is 50%, which is reduced from 100%. Non-performing loans (NPLs) are risk-weighted at (i) 150% if the value adjustment is less than 20% of the unsecured portion of the exposure; (ii) 100% if the value adjustment is above 20% of the unsecured portion of the exposure; or (iii) 50% if the value adjustment is above 50%. The value adjustment is the amount of loss transferred to the P&L account for that loan. Non-performing residential mortgages are risk-weighted at 100%.

IRB Approach Retail assets are described somewhat differently under the IRB approaches compared to sovereign or corporate assets. There is only one IRB approach; that is, we do not have separate foundation and advanced approaches. A bank adopting the IRB method for retail assets may use its own internal PD, LGD and EAD values. Unlike for large corporates and sovereigns, where there is a wealth of historical and other published data, this may prove problematic for retail assets. A bank would need sufficient statistical data for each retail borrower, which may not be available.

Credit Derivatives

Credit derivatives are classed as a "credit risk mitigation" tool. Basel I allowed for such instruments, but only explicitly named collateral and bank guarantees. Exposures backed by collateral are risk-weighted at the risk-weight of the collateral, be it cash, sovereign bonds or other suitable securities. Exposures backed by a bank guarantee are risk-weighted at 20% if the bank is an OECD bank. Credit derivatives are treated as implicit guarantees under Basel I, so an exposure backed by a CDS is risk-weighted at the level of the entity that is selling protection. This would be 20% for an OECD bank. If there is a currency mismatch between the exposure and the denomination of a swap, this is taken to be an 8% reduction in protection. Exposures protected by a basket CDS are risk-weighted according to the type of instrument it is; for example, in a first-to-default (FtD) CDS, only one asset in the basket is recognised as being under protection, and the bank can nominate which one this is and which receives the 20% weighting. The remaining assets would be weighted as if they had no credit risk mitigation treatment.

Basel II explicitly identifies a larger number of credit risk mitigation instruments, and these include credit derivatives. In addition to collateral and guarantees, they include:

- netting agreements;
- third-party guarantees;
- buying credit protection using credit derivatives.

An instrument is recognised as a credit risk mitigation tool if it is transacted under standard documentation that can be enforced in all legal jurisdictions. The procedure is slightly different, depending on what type of risk mitigation tool is used; however, certain factors are common to all three types. The most important of these is the maturity mismatch. A hedging tool of different maturity to the exposure is only considered if the maturity of the latter is one year or more. The BIS prescribes an adjustment factor that reduces the amount considered to be under protection for all hedges that do not match the exposure maturity.

We consider only credit derivatives in this section.

Standardised and IRB Approach

Under the standardised approach of Basel II, if an asset is protected with a credit derivative its risk-weight is deemed to be equal to the risk-weight of the credit protection seller. This is identical treatment to that under Basel I. For capital charge purposes then, there is an advantage to obtaining credit protection only from counterparties whose risk-weight is lower than the asset being protected; post-crash, this may not necessarily be a majority of cases with regard to corporate and certain emerging market sovereign assets. The BIS document states that the credit events protected under the credit derivative must include failure to pay, bankruptcy and restructuring. These are all included under standard International Swap and Derivative Association (ISDA) credit derivative documentation. If the contract excludes restructuring, then the level of capital charge relief is reduced.

The foundation IRB approach to treating credit derivatives is similar to the standardised approach. The PD value that is used in the calculation will be that of the entity that is providing the credit risk protection. Under the advanced IRB approach, a bank's own PD and LGD values can be adjusted to account for the CDS protection.

Selling Protection via CDS

The Basel II capital treatment of a CDS contract used to sell protection assumes it is a cash instrument. Thus, capital must be allocated to the position as if it were a cash asset in the name of the reference entity. This is the same principle as Basel I, although now of course the reference entity rating is the key factor. For example, under Basel I selling protection on an A-rated corporate entity would attract a 100% risk-weighting, whereas under standardised Basel II the risk-weight would be 50%. Under the foundation IRB this weighting would be lower still.

TABLE 2.15 Standardised approach for synthetic CDO tranches: risk-weights (%).

	Risk-weight %	
Tranche rating	**Investing banks**	**Originating banks**
AAA to AA−	20	20
A+ to A−	50	50
BBB+ to BBB−	100	100
BB+ to BB−	350	Deduction from capital
B+ and below	Deduction from capital	Deduction from capital
Unrated	Deduction from capital	Deduction from capital

Source: BIS.

Credit Derivatives and Synthetic Securitisation

The use of credit derivatives in a structured finance transaction produces a so-called synthetic securitisation, in which the credit risk transfer of a pool of assets is achieved via the credit derivatives rather than a "true sale" of the assets to a specially incorporated legal entity. For synthetic collateralised debt obligations (CDOs) (see the author's book, *Structured Credit Products*) the Basel II rules prescribe separate approaches for originators and investors.

Standardised Approach: Synthetic CDO The risk-weights to use for synthetic CDO note tranches are shown in Table 2.15.

IRB Approach When calculating the capital charge for CDO note assets, banks have less freedom to use their own internal data, even under the IRB approach. This stands it apart from other asset classes. An originating bank must nevertheless apply the IRB approach if it is using this same approach to assign risk-weights for the underlying assets of the CDO. If the tranche is rated, then the bank must apply the RBA approach; if not, then the SF calculation method will apply. If neither of these methods can be used, then the CDO asset must be deducted from capital. The RBA approach is essentially identical to that described earlier for ABS assets.

Basel II and Securitisation

In Chapter 4 we discuss securitisation and its importance as a tool and technique in ALM. Given that so much securitisation business is driven by regulatory capital issues, a bank will regard it as imperative to assess the economic effects of Basel II rules and position itself accordingly. We discuss some scenarios of likely interest to ALM strategists.

Change from Basel I to Basel II

A direct result of the original Basel accord, albeit an unplanned one, was the widespread adoption of securitisation as a balance sheet management tool among banks. This reflected the blanket coverage of the rules to a wide range of assets held on bank balance sheets, of widely varying credit quality. Basel I created a strong incentive to reduce regulatory capital charges by removing exposures, particularly higher quality ones, from balance sheets by securitising them. In order to help place the deal in the market, originators often retained the "first-loss" or equity tranche of the structure, which meant that the highest risk part of the asset pool was retained by the bank. The somewhat ironic result of such a procedure is that, while the regulatory capital requirement would have been reduced, the economic risk to the bank would not have been. This was one of the main areas of complaint on the original accord, that it did not align closely enough the regulatory capital requirement to actual economic risk exposure of a bank's asset pool. Basel II attempted to address this issue, and even in the standardised approach it managed to produce less of a "shotgun" approach to risk capital calculations compared to Basel I. The IRB approach attempts to align regulatory capital with economic risk closer still. In addition, Basel II carries a high capital charge for securitised assets where the junior tranche is retained by the bank, so the deal economics in a securitisation will no longer be as attractive as before if the first-loss piece is retained. As we noted above, though, a significant influence on whether securitisation should be undertaken depends on whether the standardised or IRB approach is adopted. For instance, the capital charge against investment in an AA-rated ABS tranche is higher for a standardised bank than an IRB bank. Table 2.16, which is reproduced with the kind permission of Fitch Ratings Ltd, shows the difference in capital charges between the two approaches in a securitisation issue. The figures are for banks that invest in ABS tranches.

One further significant impact of Basel II is the distinction it introduced between investment-grade and sub-investment-grade assets. The increased capital charge that results once one moves into a sub-investment-grade rating is pronounced. This has the effect of creating a wall of higher charges across just one notch in rating; for example, from Table 2.16 we observe that under the RBA method a BBB– note tranche attracts an 8% charge, whereas a note rated one notch lower at BB+ requires more than double this amount of capital (20%). This sudden steep increase gives banks an incentive to minimise the number and size of un-rated tranches. In practice, usually only the equity tranche is un-rated, so to reduce the regulatory capital charge to the lowest possible amount this note piece will need to be as small as possible. Balanced against this is the need for the

TABLE 2.16 Basel II risk-weights under securitisation: standardised versus IRB approach (%).

External rating	Standardised securitisation charges[1]	Basel II IRB securitised[2]	IRB vs standardised securitisation charges
AAA	1.60	0.56	(65)
AA	1.60	0.64	(60)
A	4	0.96	(76)
BBB+	8	2.80	(65)
BBB	8	4.80	(40)
BBB−	8	8	0
BB+	28	20	(29)
BB	28	34	21
BB−	28	52	86
B	Full deduction	Full deduction	NA
CCC+	Full deduction	Full deduction	NA

[1] Applies to investing standardised banks only; originating standardised banks are required to deduct non-investment-grade tranches. Rated BB+ and below out of capital.

[2] For positions rated BBB and above, the most favourable RBA charges available for granular and senior positions are used in this comparison, given the severe stress scenarios and conservative enhancement levels needed to achieve an investment-grade rating.

IRB – internal ratings based

NA – not applicable

equity piece to be of sufficient size such that it provides sufficient credit enhancement and protection for the tranches lying above it, as required by the rating agencies.

Under Basel II not only are banks penalised if they retain an un-rated securitisation note and/or the equity notes, other banks have no incentive to hold these as investments.

Transaction Structuring

We note in Chapter 4 that regulatory capital management is one of three main strategic motivations behind the origination of a securitisation deal. The final structure of a deal reflects tactical issues including:

- market conditions such as supply and demand for specific assets, and interest-rate spreads;

- rating agency requirements;
- legal, tax and administrative considerations.

Basel II introduced another element in the structuring decision; namely, the lower attraction of sub-investment-grade tranches. Therefore from a capital charge perspective, and also the viewpoint of potential bank investors in the issued notes, the liability structure of an ABS deal would be expected to minimise the size, or eliminate entirely, all tranches rated below BBB–. There will always be a junior piece to an ABS deal, the first-loss piece, but under Basel II its size is as small as possible (the minimum required to create the necessary subordination to enable the required rating on senior tranches).

OPERATIONAL RISK

The operational risk capital charge introduced in Basel II is the most significant departure in regulatory capital rules when compared to the previous regime. The primary objective of the new charge is to cover for the possibility of catastrophic loss situations *à la* Barings or Kidder Peabody.

The Nature of Operational Risk

The BIS defines operational risk as "the risk of loss resulting from inadequate or failed internal processes, people and systems or from external events".[25] Put in this way, operational risk covers a very wide range of risk exposures; some of these include the following:

- *fraud*: the risk of loss arising from fraudulent activity, both internal to the bank undertaken by employees and external to the bank and undertaken by a third party. This would cover trading fraud of the type perpetrated by Nick Leeson at Barings, and (allegedly) by Kweku Adoboli at UBS;
- *system failures*: the risk of loss arising from a breakdown of systems and processes;
- *employment practice and workplace safety*: risk of loss due to litigation for personal or other injury, including sexual harassment claims;
- *physical plant and assets*: risk of loss arising from damage to office property and buildings, say from natural disaster or other such events.

25 BIS document of 26 June 2004.

The above is only a small sample. We observe then that the operational risk category is a wide one, and in fact can be taken as a catch-all for all unforeseen risks and losses that are not market risks. Essentially, the operational risk capital charge is designed to protect against low-frequency, but large-impact, rare events.

Calculation Methodology

The BIS specifies three methods by which the operational risk charge may be calculated. These are the:

- basic indicator approach (BIA);
- standardised approach (SA);
- advanced measurement approach (AMA).

The BIS has suggested that banks adopt the more sophisticated SA or AMA methods over the BIA approach. Banks are allowed to select more than one method if they wish to apply different approaches for different parts of their business.

Basic Indicator Approach (BIA)

This is fairly simple calculation which states that the operational risk charge is the average over the bank's last three years of 15% of its positive annual gross income. It is given by:

$$BIA = \frac{(15\% \times \sum \text{Years } 1-3 \text{ Annual gross income})}{3}. \qquad (2.11)$$

The definition of gross income is given as net interest income plus net non-interest income: a fairly wide coverage. However, it would exclude the insurance income of bancassurance groups.

Standardised Approach (SA)

The SA method is slightly more sophisticated. It divides a bank's activities into eight different business lines, which are:

- corporate finance;
- trading and sales;
- retail banking
- commercial banking;
- payment and settlements;
- agency services;

- asset management;
- retail brokerage.

Gross income is taken for each business line; the capital charge is the product of the gross income and a factor termed the *beta* for that business line. Beta is prescribed by the BIS, and is meant to denote the relationship between the level of operational risk for that business line and the aggregate level of gross income for that line. The formula for the capital charge is:

$$SA = \frac{(\sum \text{Years } 1\text{–}3 \text{ max.}[\sum(\text{Annual gross income}_{1-8} \times \beta_{1-8}), 0])}{3}. \quad (2.12)$$

The business line beta factors are:

Corporate finance:	18%
Trading and sales:	18%
Retail banking:	12%
Commercial banking:	15%
Payment and settlements:	18%
Agency services:	15%
Asset management:	12%
Retail brokerage:	12%.

The beta factors are lower for more "traditional" banking factors, which suggests that the SA method would be favoured by retail and commercial banks; conversely, investment banks may prefer the BIA approach, or adopt the AMA approach.

Advanced Measurement Approach (AMA)

The AMA might be said to be the advanced IRB approach for operational risk, as it uses a bank's internal operational risk measurements and requires the approval of the national supervisor. A 5-year database of internal operational risk measurement data is required to implement AMA. This includes five years of historical observation.

Calculating the capital charge requires that the bank maps the historical loss data for each of the eight business lines from its internal measures, for each of the risk types that are defined to be "operational risk". This requires complex and sophisticated systems, which not all banks will have in place.

Insurance Policy Mitigation

Under Basel II a bank can make use of insurance policies to offset a maximum of 20% of its operational risk capital charge. The BIS prescribes the circumstances in which a bank can use insurance to achieve this. These include terms such as: (i) the insurance policy must have a minimum initial term of one year with a minimum 90-day cancellation notice period; (ii) the policy must contain no exclusions for events triggered by supervisory action; and (iii) the policy must be provided by a third-party institution. The maximum relief that can be granted is 20% of a bank's operational risk capital charge. The insurance policy cannot cover any fines levied by bank regulatory authorities.

BASEL III

In December 2010 the Basel Committee for Banking Supervision (BCBS), which comprises the regulators and central bankers of 27 countries, released details of the new banking regulatory capital rules, which were termed Basel III. The rules require banks to hold a higher amount of core Tier 1 capital than was required under the Basel I and II regimes.

The main provisions of Basel III are as follows:

- The minimum level of core Tier 1 capital is to be 4.5% of risk-weighted assets. This compares to the 2% level required under the Basel II accord.
- A "capital conservation" buffer of 2.5% will also be required, as protection against periods of economic and financial stress.
- There will be a Tier 1 "leverage ratio" of 3%.

Although this additional reserve is not compulsory, a bank that does not put it in place will be restricted from paying dividends to shareholders; therefore, for practical purposes the minimum Tier 1 capital ratio is actually 7%.

In addition, a "countercyclical" capital buffer of up to 2.5% will be allowable, with national regulators having the authority to impose this requirement when they deem it necessary, as a response to overheating markets.

The definition of core Tier 1 capital is also being simplified under Basel III; going forward, it will comprise only equity, retained reserves and undated preference shares. The timeline for implementation is January 2015, with the capital conservation buffer not required until January 2019.

As at the time of writing, Basel III had not made any modifications to the process of assigning risk weightings to assets. This remains identical to the methodology implemented under Basel II.

Initial Impact

The Basel III rules are possibly more onerous for banks than a first reading might suggest, particularly when the Tier 1 capital ratio is taken together with the proposals for a leverage ratio and liquidity buffers. However, although banks will need to hold more high-quality capital, they have been allowed a long transition phase to implement the new requirements. They will need to hold common equity to the value of 4.5% of their assets by the start of 2015, up from the current 2%. Beyond that, by January 2019 banks will need to hold the 2.5% capital conservation buffer of common equity. The rationale of the buffer is that it is just that – a buffer that can be run down during periods of market stress, without hitting the regulatory reserve and thus preserving the bank as a going concern. The total requirement comprises the common equity ratio of 7% stated above. This is a considerable increase on the previous minimum of 2%.

In addition, the BCBS introduced new rules from 2012 that demand a more onerous capital regime for trading activities and securitised assets held on the trading book. This is three times the level required against banking book assets. Large systemically important banks will, at a point in the future, face a capital surcharge on top of the standard requirements.

The more problematic area of the new rules is the countercyclical buffer. If regulators believe that banks are in the midst of a credit bubble they may levy a countercyclical buffer of up to 2.5% of assets, which will be made up of common stock or other equally loss-absorbing instruments.

The Tier 1 leverage ratio of 3% will limit banks to lending 33 times their capital, a significantly lower value than that observed at some banks during the lead-in to the financial crash of 2008. This represents a cap on bank risk irrespective of the impact from the higher capital numbers. Although this limit is not due to be introduced until 2018, banks will need to disclose the level to the market from 2015 onwards.

Overview

We summarise the provisions being implemented under Basel III.

Tier 1 Capital

Under Basel III, the Tier 1 capital ratio is pegged at 6%, with core Tier 1 at 4.5%. Implementation will start in January 2013, when core Tier 1 rises from 2% to 3.5%, with full phase-in of the Tier 1 rules to be completed by January 2015. Deferred taxes and mortgage-servicing rights will not count towards Tier 1 capital from January 2018.

This compares to the current regime, under which banks are required to have a Tier 1 capital ratio of 4%, with half of this, or 2%, dubbed "core" Tier 1 in the form of equity and retained earnings.

Capital Conservation Buffer

Basel III introduces a capital conservation buffer of 2.5% that will sit on top of Tier 1 capital. A bank whose capital ratio fails to stay above the buffer will be restricted from making payouts such as dividends, share buybacks and bonuses. The buffer will be composed of common equity, after the application of deductions such as deferred taxes. The buffer will be phased in from January 2016 and will be fully effective in January 2019.

Countercyclical Capital Buffer

This buffer is set at 0%–2.5% of common equity or other full loss-absorbing capital. The aim of the buffer is to force banks to start building up such an extra buffer when supervisors see excessive credit in the system that threatens to spark loan losses later on. Banks would then tap the buffer to offset such losses without having to raise fresh capital immediately. At the time of writing there is no confirmed timeline for the implementation of this buffer.

Definition of Capital

The predominant form of Tier 1 capital must be common equity and retained earnings. Banks may include deferred tax assets, mortgage-servicing rights and investments in financial institutions to an amount no more than 15% of the common equity component. The capital requirement of a minority interest in a bank can be counted in the group's capital only if the investment represents a genuine common equity contribution.

Leverage Ratio

The aim of the leverage ratio is to place a cap on the level of leverage in the banking sector on a global basis. In theory this will help to reduce the risk that eventual deleveraging could destabilise the sector. The leverage ratio will be calculated in a comparable manner across jurisdictions, adjusting for any remaining differences in accounting standards. A leverage ratio of 3% of Tier 1, meaning that balance sheets cannot exceed 33 times Tier 1 capital, is to be implemented on a trial basis before a mandatory leverage ratio is introduced in January 2018.

Liquidity

Banks will be required to maintain a short-term liquidity buffer, comprised mainly of sovereign debt. A 1-year horizon liquidity buffer, known as the net stable funding ratio, will be implemented on a trial basis and become mandatory in January 2018.

Risk Coverage

There will be a risk-weighting of 1%–3% on banks' mark-to-market and collateral exposures to a central counterparty. The risk-weighting on non-centrally cleared derivative contracts will be higher, but at the time of writing the exact level had not been announced.

Summary of Basel III Requirements

Capital Ratios

The new minimums and capital buffers are set out in Table 2.17:

TABLE 2.17 Basel III capital ratios.

	Core Tier 1 common equity (after deductions)	Tier 1 capital (%)	Total capital (%)
Minimum ratio	4.5	6.0	8.0
Capital conservation buffer	2.5	–	–
Minimum plus capital conservation buffer	7.0	8.5	10.5
Countercyclical capital buffer range	0 –2.5	–	–
SIFI surcharge/buffer	To be determined	–	–

Source: BIS.

Liquidity Issues

The BCBS confirmed the following:

- *Liquidity coverage ratio (LCR)*: the definition of "high-quality liquid assets" covers an extended portfolio of government and public sector entity assets, as well as high-quality corporate and covered bonds (rated AA– and above), subject to a cap and with a 15% haircut. The LCR is defined as follows:

$$\frac{\text{Stock of high-quality liquid assets}}{\text{Total net cash outflows over the next 30 calendar days}} > 100\%$$

- *Net stable funding ratio (NSFR)*: the definition of this metric is as follows:

$$\frac{\text{Available amount of stable funding}}{\text{Required amount of stable funding} > 100\%}$$

- The NSFR limit is 100%, which is the minimum. "Stable funding" is described as those types and amounts of equity and other liabilities that are expected to be reliable sources of funds of over a 1-year time horizon, under conditions of expected stress.

The full details of the Basel III provisions can be viewed at www.bis.org.

Definition of Capital

The Basel III capital rules will have the effect of improving the overall quality of bank capital. There is also a greater emphasis on capital being able to absorb losses on a going concern basis. Figure 2.2 illustrates the change.

Core Tier 1 consists of:

- ordinary shares
- retained earnings.

This capital takes the first and proportionately greatest share of losses. It is the most deeply subordinated, and is perpetual, with no expectation that the liability will be bought back or redeemed. With regard to dividends, these are:

- fully discretionary, with no fixed rate;
- paid out only after all distributable items;
- paid after all other obligations.

Basel II	Basel III
Tier 1	*Tier 1*
Core	Core
Non-innovative	Non-core
Innovative	
Tier 2	*Tier 2*
Upper Tier 2	Tier 2
Lower Tier 2	
Tier 3	
Upper Tier 3	
Lower Tier 3	

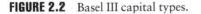

FIGURE 2.2 Basel III capital types.

Non-core Tier 1 consists of contingent convertible (CoCo) and preference share-type instruments that exhibit the following features:

- fully discretionary coupon, which is non-cumulative;
- perpetual, with no incentive to redeem (for example, a step-up coupon);
- call feature allowed, but not expectation of call.

In addition these instruments must have conversion (to equity) or write-down features to absorb losses on a going concern basis.

Tier 2 capital consists of long-dated subordinated debt, with no incentives to redeem early.

THE CAPITAL CALCULATION AND RETURN ON CAPITAL TARGETS

The 2007–2009 financial crisis and taxpayer-funded bank bailouts in the US, UK and Europe demonstrated that the capital rules in place at that time were insufficient to prevent the bankruptcy of many banks.[26] In many cases, failed banks had reported capital ratios that were well above the Basel minimum very shortly before they went under or were rescued by their government. The capital buffers in place were insufficient to preserve the bank in the face of large losses.

The key to bank capital sufficiency is that it must be at a level that *preserves the bank as a going concern*. That is, even after suffering all expected losses as well as unexpected losses, the capital buffer must be sufficient to maintain confidence in the bank. Taking this to its ultimate logical conclusion, a bank therefore has to calculate its capital requirement to cover expected losses, add in a contingency reserve for unexpected losses, and then add these two amounts to the minimum regulatory capital amount. The experience of 2008 showed that capital in place after all losses has to be above the regulatory minimum, otherwise the bank is viewed as non-viable and will suffer a loss of confidence and bank run. Put simply, to ensure its survival in a crash scenario, a bank needs to have a capital base that is at least twice the regulatory minimum.

In this section we review the main principles behind the capital calculation.

26 We include the nationalised banks, or banks such as UBS that were not formally nationalised, but received large state cash injections, among the number of failed banks. If they had not received government aid, they would certainly have gone bust.

Credit Risk and Capital Calculation

A bank will calculate the credit risk exposure of its portfolio using a statistical model of default risk and expected losses. The parameters used in the loss distribution were discussed in the previous chapter. The other issue that needs to be formulated is the time horizon that the model is calculating against. The time horizon chosen will depend on the risk approach of the bank; it may reflect either the time needed to change the risk profile of the portfolio, or the time needed to raise more capital. An asset portfolio is not something that can be adjusted easily or quickly; once originated, the bank is pretty much stuck with it. Hence, the time horizon used in the credit risk calculation needs to be one that allows the bank sufficient time to raise more capital. This is usually set at one year or two years, but in practice would need to be longer. Once the time horizon is set, the capital requirement is essentially the portfolio expected and unexpected losses, minus portfolio revenue. However, portfolio income should be assumed as still available at the horizon date only for performing assets. Most default models calculate the expected loss as the amount of decrease in value arising from default.

Time Horizon

In the previous decade there was a growing philosophy and practice that active portfolio management enabled a bank to set lower capital levels. That is, the use of securitisation and credit derivatives, as well as the secondary loan market, created an ability to manage the risk exposure of a portfolio. This in turn meant that lower capital could be allocated because the portfolio was no longer a "hold-to-maturity" one, which is essentially what a banking book is. However, the financial crisis has shown that such active risk management is far less effective than was supposed.

The time horizon to select for making the capital calculation is one that allows the bank to adjust the portfolio to alter its risk exposure, and to raise more capital if required, given the portfolio's existing risk. The first action will only be possible under benign economic conditions; in a crisis situation it will not be possible to sell or hedge assets for anything much less than a total loss. The second action will take time, and will be progressively more difficult and expensive the more negative the market conditions. For these reasons, most banks elect to set a 1-year time horizon, and dynamically manage their capital levels. It is also a user-friendly time span, because it fits in with the standard finance department annual budget process. Other banks will set a 1-year, 2-year, 3-year and 5-year horizon and calculate a value for each; these are then used in capital planning.

Given that the majority of a bank's assets mature beyond one year, the credit risk model will assign default probabilities for each sub-period of

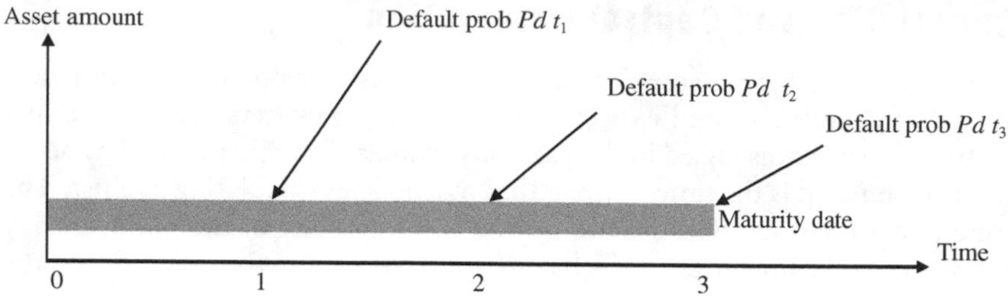

FIGURE 2.3 Assigning default probability to asset maturity sub-periods.

an asset's life until maturity. A default probability for an asset's sub-period is the marginal default probability for that period. We illustrate this at Figure 2.3.

Most bank assets will mature beyond the standard 1-year risk horizon. For those maturing within the horizon, the bank can adjust the default probability to allow for this shorter horizon. Otherwise it should apply the selected horizon time period when calculating the default probability. Thus at Figure 2.3 the asset matures in three years; however, for capital allocation we require the default probability as at one year. Note that it is not only default that needs to be allowed for, credit ratings migrations also need to be accounted as these can cause credit risk losses due to changes in asset valuation.

Portfolio Loss Distribution

To calculate expected loss, we require a loss probability distribution. This distribution then drives the loss statistics and capital VaR. The market generally assumes a lognormal distribution of credit losses, of the kind shown at Figures 2.4A and 2.4B. This is not the standard normal distribution shown for market risk analysis, but rather the standard lognormal distribution of credit losses.

Figure 2.5 shows how applying the credit loss distribution profile works on a portfolio basis. We select our time horizon and can then work out how much capital is required. In qualitative terms,

Time today:	t
Horizon date:	T
Portfolio current value:	M_t
Maximum portfolio loss at *i* confidence interval:	$L_{(i)}$
Capital required at the *i* confidence interval:	$C_{(i)}$
Portfolio expected loss:	EL
Portfolio revenue:	R
Net revenue:	$[R - EL] = S$

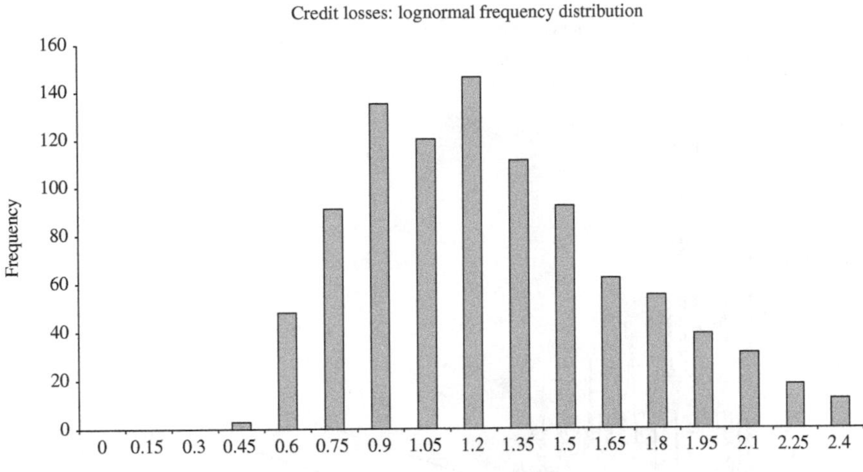

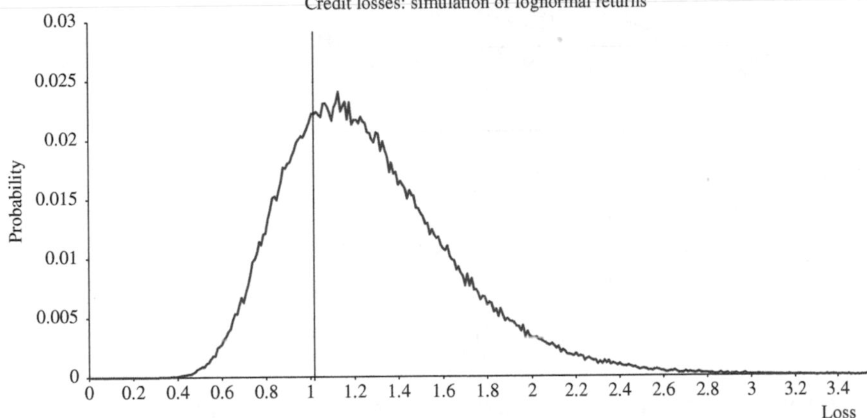

FIGURES 2.4A AND 2.4B Credit losses: probability distribution.

The capital required is a function of the portfolio loss L, adjusted for the expected loss EL. The net revenue of the portfolio enables the amount required C to be reduced. The calculation of expected loss is based on assumptions. Because of this, it is not sufficient to base C on EL only. The calculation of EL is based on the starting or current value of the portfolio, an implied default probability and recovery rate, and the expected value at the horizon date.

If one assumes no default, the expected value at the horizon date is the current portfolio book value. As the portfolio accrues revenue, this can (at year end) be added to reserves and enhance the loss-absorbing buffer. Only revenues over and above all operating expenses and expected losses can be

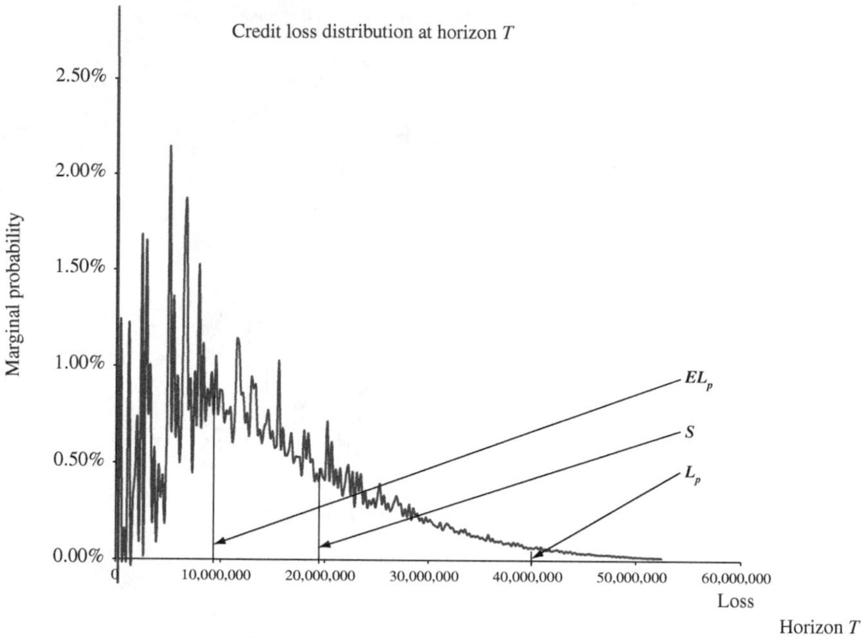

FIGURE 2.5 Credit loss distribution.

used in this way. This means that capital required is the net of excess revenues over expected loss, given by:

$$C_{(i)} = [L_{(i)} + R] - EL.$$

This approach is too simplistic once one allows for portfolio defaults. Incorporating this feature, the portfolio expected value at horizon time T is given by:

$$E[M_T] = E\left(M_{T|nodefault}\right) \times [1 - Pd(t,T)] + M_{T|default} \times Pd(t,T)$$

where M is the portfolio current value.

That is, the expected value is given by the expected value with no default multiplied by the probability of no default, together with the value given default, or, (1 – probability of no default).

The expected loss EL of a portfolio is the value of all the losses in the portfolio at horizon T. Simply it is given by:

$$EL = (E[M_T]) - M_t.$$

In other words, it is the value of the portfolio under no default minus the value of the portfolio given default.

Defining Capital in Portfolio Loss Distribution Terms

We can see from the above that given a portfolio loss distribution, and an expected loss, we can calculate required capital. Note that this is capital to absorb losses in the portfolio, it is not driven by regulatory requirements. If we are concerned about the level of capital available being sufficient, or of anticipated future difficulties in raising more capital, then we should target a low-risk asset origination strategy.

From the logic of what we introduced above, the maximum capital amount would be represented by the maximum portfolio loss L, minus either a zero loss, the expected loss EL or the net revenue S. The approach adopted will depend on the risk aversion, or conservatism, of the bank. Thus, in order of decreasing risk aversion, capital can be one of the following:

- Capital as an excess of the no-loss amount, with no reduction for expected loss or offset due to net revenue, so that the level is able to absorb both the expected loss and any unexpected losses. This is given by $C = L$.
- Capital as an excess of the expected loss, with the addition of loss provisioning. This is given by $C = L - EL$.
- Capital as an excess of the net revenue, less the expected losses at the horizon point. This is given by $C = L - S$. Under this logic, the net revenues will serve to absorb unexpected losses.

The decision as to which approach to use should remain dynamic, ready for adjustment as economic conditions warrant. In the aftermath of the financial crisis, "macroprudential" capital management requires that the capital base respond to the business cycle. We consider this further in Chapter 17.

In calculating the capital provision, the concept of present value still applies. Thus, the amount of EL and S at the horizon point T should be discounted back to today's present value. The discount rate to be used would be the appropriate tenor government bond yield, or risk-free rate. The logic behind this is that the capital itself, if it were not being used to back the bank's loan assets, would be invested at this rate. This is the main reason why business best practice is that the bank's capital should be invested in risk-free assets. Capital should never be used to invest directly in risk-bearing assets, because by exposing capital to risk, this would in itself generate a higher capital requirement. If a bank invests any of its capital base in risk-bearing assets, then by definition its capital base will not be sufficiently high enough.

The Return on Capital Target

It is important to remember that the capital base itself is not designed to be used to generate revenue, and any income accrued from its investment is not part of shareholders' value-added. This is contrary to what one may read in some textbooks, which state that the revenues from capital invested in risk-free assets can and/or should be added to returns generated by the risk-bearing assets, and this amount should then be used in the return on capital (RoC) calculations. This is not business best-practice, and is also logically untenable.

Shareholders do not need to invest in a bank in order to generate risk-free returns. Rather, they are looking to generate shareholder value-added by investing in the bank. Including the revenues from the capital investment in the RoC calculation will boost it artificially. Therefore, this is bad practice and must not be followed. Any income accruing from the investment of capital in risk-free assets should be accounted to the ALCO book, rather than any business lines, and is simply added to shareholder reserves. It should not form part of the net returns attributable to the business.

A consistent definition of RoC is important because the RoC value itself drives the rest of the business strategy. Table 2.18 illustrates the calculation of RoC based on the three definitions of capital discussed earlier. We apply the rule that revenue generated from capital invested at the risk-free rate is not included in the total revenue figures.

TABLE 2.18 RoC calculations for different calculations of capital.

Portfolio notional, M	1000		
Portfolio revenue, R	100		
Expected loss, EL	30		
Portfolio loss, L	500		
Capital calculations, C_i	$L_{(i)}$	$L_{(i)} - EL$	$L_{(i)} - (R - EL)$
	500	\	430
RoC revenue base	Revenue R	$R - EL$	$R - EL$
	100	70	70
RoC calculation	$R/[L_{(i)}]$	$[R - EL]/[L_{(i)} - EL]$	$[R - EL]/[L_{(i)} - (R - EL)]$
	20%	14.89%	16.28%

The portfolio is generating a return on assets (RoA) of 10%. The RoC is higher because the capital base required to support the portfolio is set at the maximum portfolio loss level, set here at 500. In the third approach shown, we adjust this for the revenue minus the expected loss *EL*, and this gives an RoC of just over 16%. This is therefore also the target shareholder value return for new business. Is this approach conservative enough for risk purposes? Certainly more so than the first approach, which gives an over-optimistic calculation of RoC. The key to capital calculation and RoC setting is the presentation of the bank as a going concern through the business cycle. For this reason, the most appropriate return measure is in fact RoA.

BIBLIOGRAPHY

Dermine, J. and Bissada, Y. (2002), *Asset and Liability Management*, London: FT Prentice Hall.

Duffle, D. and Singleton, K. (2003), *Credit Risk*, New Jersey: Princeton University Press.

Gup, B. (2004), *The New Basel Capital Accord*, New York, NY: Thomson Corporation.

CHAPTER 3

Banking and Credit Risk

In Chapter 1 we observed that the essence of bank risk management is effective supervision of liquidity risk and credit risk. Liquidity risk is reviewed in detail in Part III. In this chapter we provide a primer on understanding and managing credit risk. We look first at the elements of credit risk exposure; we then consider credit risk limit setting policy and principles of loan origination standards. We also look at the approach and methodology of applying credit ratings to obligors, both internally within a bank and externally at the credit rating agencies.

CREDIT RISK PRINCIPLES

While the concept of "credit risk" is as old as banking itself, it would appear that bank management are less aware of it during periods of economic growth, only to become reacquainted with its principles following an economic downturn, which increases dramatically the level of loan losses.

For example, consider the following developments:

- credit spreads tightened during 1992–1999 and again during 2002–2007, to the point where blue-chip companies were being offered syndicated loans for as little as 10–12 bps over Libor. To maintain margin, or the increased return on capital, banks increased lending to lower rated corporates, thereby increasing their credit risk both overall and as a share of overall risk;
- investors were finding fewer opportunities in interest rate and currency markets, and therefore moved towards yield enhancement through extending and trading credit across lower rated and emerging market assets;
- the rapid expansion of high-yield and emerging market sectors, again lower rated assets, increased the magnitude of credit risk for investors and the banks that held and traded such assets.

The growth in credit risk exposure would naturally be expected to lead to more sophisticated risk management techniques than those employed hitherto. It was accompanied, however, by a rise in the level of corporate defaults and consequently higher losses due to credit deterioration, which led to a rigorous test of banks' risk management systems and procedures. It also led to a demand for the type of product that resulted in the credit derivative market. The development of the credit derivatives market, and hence the subsequent introduction of structured credit products, was a response to the rising importance attached to credit risk management. For this reason, it is worthwhile beginning this chapter with a look at credit ratings, default and credit risk measurement.

In this chapter we look at the concept of credit risk, before considering the main way that it is measured in banks and financial institutions, using credit VaR. Finally, we look at credit risk limit setting and loan origination standards.

CREDIT RISK

There are two main types of credit risk that a portfolio of assets, or a position in a single asset, is exposed to. These are credit default risk and credit spread risk.

Credit Default Risk

This is the risk that an issuer of debt (obligor) is unable to meet its financial obligations. This is known as *default*. There is also the case of technical default, which is used to describe a company that has not honoured its interest payments on a loan for (typically) three months or more, but has not reached a stage of bankruptcy or administration. Where an obligor defaults, a lender generally incurs a loss equal to the amount owed by the obligor less any recovery amount that the firm recovers as a result of foreclosure, liquidation or restructuring of the defaulted obligor. This recovery amount is usually expressed as a percentage of the total amount and is known as the *recovery rate*. All portfolios with credit exposure exhibit credit default risk.

The measure of a firm's credit default risk is given by its credit rating. The three main credit rating agencies are Moody's, Standard & Poor's (S&P) and Fitch. These institutions undertake qualitative and quantitative analysis of borrowers and formally rate the borrower after their analysis. The issues considered in the analysis include:

- the financial position of the firm itself, for example, its balance sheet position and anticipated cash flows and revenues;
- other firm-specific issues such as the quality of management and succession planning;
- an assessment of the firm's ability to meet scheduled interest and principal payments, both in its domestic and in foreign currencies;
- the outlook for the industry as a whole, and competition within it, together with general assessments of the domestic economy.

The range of credit ratings awarded by the three main rating agencies is shown at Table 3.1. Ratings can also be seen on Bloomberg page RATD, shown at Figure 3.1. We discuss credit ratings again shortly.

Credit Spread Risk

Credit spread is the excess premium, over and above government or risk-free risk, required by the market for taking on a certain assumed credit exposure.

TABLE 3.1 Long-term bond credit ratings.

Fitch	Moody's	S&P	Summary description
Investment grade–High creditworthiness			
AAA	Aaa	AAA	Gilt-edged, prime, maximum safety, lowest risk
AA+	Aa1	AA+	
AA	Aa2	AA	High-grade, high-credit quality
AA−	Aa3	AA−	
A+	A1	A+	
A	A2	A	Upper medium grade
A−	A3	A−	
BBB+	Baa1	BBB+	
BBB	Baa2	BBB	Lower medium grade
BBB−	Baa3	BBB−	
Speculative–Lower creditworthiness			
BB+	Ba1	BB+	
BB	Ba2	BB	Low grade; speculative
BB−	Ba3	BB−	
B+	B1		
B	B2	B	Highly speculative
B−	B3		

(*continued*)

TABLE 3.1 (*Continued*)

Predominantly speculative, substantial risk or in default

CCC+		CCC+	
CCC	Caa	CCC	Substantial risk, in poor standing
CC	Ca	CC	May be in default, very speculative
C	C	C	Extremely speculative
		CI	Income bonds–no interest being paid
DDD			
DD			Default
D		D	

For example, Figure 3.2 shows the credit spreads in May 2009 for US dollar corporate bonds with different credit ratings (AAA, A and BBB). The benchmark is the on-the-run or active US Treasury issue for the given maturity. Note that the higher the credit rating, the smaller the credit spread; note also the higher yields on financial names. Credit spread risk is the risk of financial loss resulting from changes in the level of credit spreads used in the marking-to-market of a product. It is exhibited by a portfolio for which the

GRAB Govt RATD

LONG-TERM RATING SCALES COMPARISON Page 1/2

MOODY'S	Aaa	Aa1	Aa2	Aa3	A1	A2	A3	Baa1	Baa2	Baa3
S&P	AAA	AA+	AA	AA-	A+	A	A-	BBB+	BBB	BBB-
COMP	AAA	AA1	AA2	AA3	A1	A2	A3	BBB1	BBB2	BBB3
TBW	AAA	AA+	AA	AA-	A+	A	A-	BBB+	BBB	BBB-
FITCH	AAA	AA+	AA	AA-	A+	A	A-	BBB+	BBB	BBB-
CBRS	AAA	AA+	AA	AA-	A+	A	A-	BBB+	BBB	BBB-
DOMINION	AAA	AAH	AA	AAL	AH	A	AL	BBBH	BBB	BBBL
R&I	AAA	AA+	AA	AA-	A+	A	A-	BBB+	BBB	BBB-
JCR	AAA	AA+	AA	AA-	A+	A	A-	BBB+	BBB	BBB-
MI	AAA		AA			A			BBB	

Note: white = investment grade, yellow = non-investment grade

Australia 61 2 9777 8600 Brazil 5511 3048 4500 Europe 44 20 7330 7500 Germany 49 69 920410
Hong Kong 852 2977 6000 Japan 81 3 3201 8900 Singapore 65 6212 1000 U.S. 1 212 318 2000 Copyright 2003 Bloomberg L.P.
G926-802-1 03-Nov-03 14:07:10

FIGURE 3.1 Bloomberg screen RATD, long-term credit ratings.

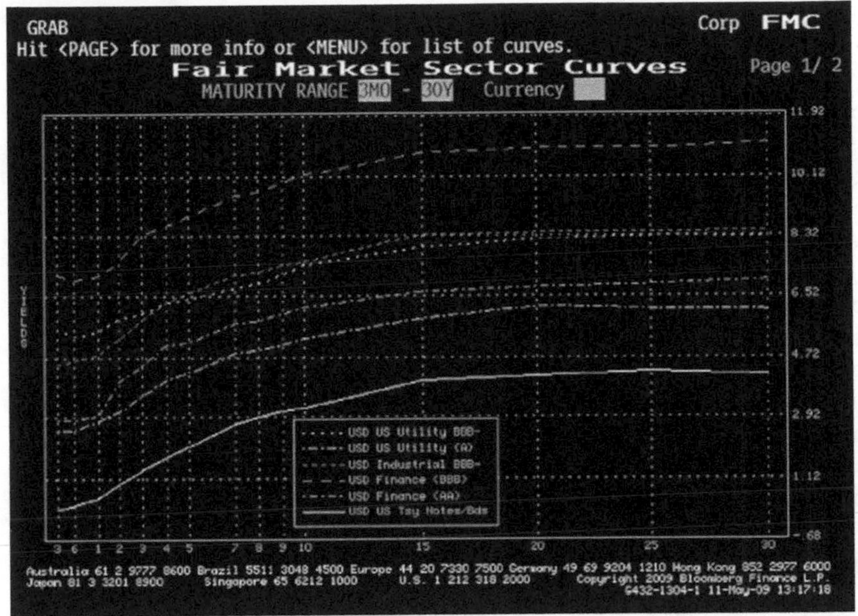

FIGURE 3.2 US dollar bond yield curves, May 2009.

credit spread is traded and marked-to-market. Changes in observed credit spreads affect the value of the portfolio and can lead to losses for investors.

CREDIT RATINGS

The risks associated with holding a fixed interest debt instrument are closely connected with the ability of the issuer to maintain the regular coupon payments as well as redeem the debt on maturity. Only the highest quality government debt and a small amount of supra-national debt are considered to be entirely free of credit risk. Therefore, at any time, the yield on a bond reflects investors' views on the ability of the issuer to meet its liabilities as set out in the bond's terms and conditions. In order to determine the ability of an issuer to meet its obligations for a particular debt issue, for the entire life of the issue, judgmental analysis of the issuer's financial strength and business prospects is required. There are a number of factors that must be considered, and larger banks, fund managers and corporates carry out their own credit analysis of individual borrowers' bond issues. The market also makes considerable use of formal credit ratings that are assigned to individual bond issues by a formal credit rating agency.

The specific factors that are considered by a ratings agency, and the methodology used in conducting the analysis, differ slightly among the individual ratings agencies. Although in many cases the ratings assigned to a particular issue by different agencies are the same, they occasionally differ and in these instances investors usually seek to determine what aspect of an issuer is given more weight in an analysis by which individual agency. Note that a credit rating is not a recommendation to buy (or equally, sell) a particular bond, nor is it a comment on market expectations. Credit analysis does take into account general market and economic conditions, but the overall point of credit analysis is to consider the financial health of the issuer and its ability to meet the obligations of the specific issue being rated. Credit ratings play a large part in the decision-making of investors, and also have a significant impact on the interest rates payable by borrowers. This became an issue of contention during the 2007–09 crash.

Purpose of Credit Ratings

Investors in securities accept the risk that the issuer may default on coupon payments or fail to repay the principal in full on the maturity date. Generally, credit risk is greater for securities with a long maturity, as there is a longer period for the issuer potentially to default. For example, if company issues 10-year bonds, investors cannot be certain that the company will still exist in 10 years' time. It may have failed and gone into liquidation some time before that. That said, there is also risk attached to short-dated debt securities; indeed, there have been instances of default by issuers of commercial paper, which is a very short-term instrument.

The prospectus or offer document for an issue provides investors with some information about the issuer so that some credit analysis can be performed on the issuer before the bonds are placed on the market. The information in the offer document enables investors to perform their own credit analysis by studying this information before deciding whether or not to invest in the bonds. Credit assessments take up time, however, and also require the specialist skills of credit analysts. Large institutional investors employ specialists to carry out credit analysis; however, often it is too costly and time-consuming to assess every issuer in every debt market. Therefore investors commonly employ two other methods when making a decision on the credit risk of debt securities:

- name recognition;
- formal credit ratings.

Name recognition is when the investor relies on the good name and reputation of the issuer and accepts that the issuer is of such good financial standing, or sufficient financial standing, that a default on interest and principal payments is unlikely. An investor may feel this way about companies such as Microsoft or British Petroleum. However, the collapse of Barings Bank in 1995 suggested to many investors that it may not be wise to rely on name recognition alone in today's marketplace. The tradition and reputation behind the Barings name allowed the bank to borrow at sub-Libor interest rates in the money markets, which put it on a par with highest quality clearing banks in terms of credit rating. The Barings case illustrated that name recognition needs to be augmented by other methods to reduce the risk of loss due to unforeseen events. Credit ratings are increasingly used to make investment decisions about corporate or lesser developed government debt.

On receipt of a formal request, the credit rating agencies carry out a rating exercise on a specific issue of debt capital. The request for a rating comes from the organisation planning the issue of bonds. Although ratings are provided for the benefit of investors, the issuer must bear the cost. However, it is in the issuer's interest to request a rating as it raises the profile and "saleability" of the bonds, and investors may refuse to buy paper that is not accompanied with a recognised rating. Although the rating exercise involves a credit analysis of the issuer, the rating is applied to a specific debt issue. This means that, in theory, the credit rating is applied not to an organisation itself, but to specific debt securities that the organisation has issued or is planning to issue. In practice, it is common for the market to refer to the creditworthiness of organisations in terms of the rating of their debt. A highly rated company such as Rabobank is therefore referred to as a 'triple-A rated' company, although it is the bank's debt issues that are rated as triple-A.

The rating for an issue is kept under review and if the credit quality of the issuer declines or improves, the rating will be changed accordingly. An agency may announce in advance that it is reviewing a particular credit rating, and may go further and state that the review is a precursor to a possible downgrade or upgrade. This announcement is referred to as putting the issue under *credit watch*. The outcome of a credit watch is, in most cases, likely to be a rating downgrade; however, the review may reaffirm the current rating or possibly upgrade it. During the credit watch phase the agency will advise investors to use the current rating with caution. When an agency announces that an issue is under credit watch, the price of the bonds will fall in the market as investors look to sell out of their holdings. This upward movement in yield will be more pronounced if an actual downgrade results. For example, in October 2008 the government of Ireland was placed under credit watch (and subsequently lost its AAA credit rating); as a result, there was an immediate and sharp sell-off in Irish government Eurobonds, before the rating agencies had announced the actual results of their credit review.

RATINGS CHANGES OVER TIME

Ratings Transition Matrix

We have noted that the rating agencies constantly review the credit quality of firms they have rated. As may be expected, the credit rating of many companies will fluctuate over time as they experience changes in their corporate well-being. As a guide to the change in credit rating that might be expected over a 1-year period, Moody's and S&P publish historical transition matrices, which provide average rating transition probabilities for each class of rating. An example is shown at Table 3.2, which is Moody's 1-year ratings transition matrix for 2006. These results are obtained from a sample of a large number of firms over many years. In Table 3.2, the first column shows the initial rating and the first row the final rating. For instance, the probability of an A-rated company being downgraded to Baa in one year is 4.63%. The probability of the A-rated company defaulting in this year is 0.00%.

There are some inconsistencies in the ratings transition table, and this is explained by Moody's as resulting from scarcity of data for some ratings categories. For instance, an Aa-rated company has a 0.02% probability of being in default at year-end, which is higher than the supposedly lower rated A-rated company. Hence such results must be treated with caution. The conclusion from Table 3.2 is that the most likely outcome at year-end is that the company rating remains the same. It may be that a 1-year time

TABLE 3.2 Moody's 1-year rating transition matrix, 2006.

	Aaa	Aa	A	Baa	Ba	B	Caa	Default
Aaa	93.40%	5.94%	0.64%	0.00%	0.02%	0.00%	0.00%	0.00%
Aa	1.61%	90.55%	7.46%	0.26%	0.09%	0.01%	0.00%	0.02%
A	0.07%	2.28%	92.44%	4.63%	0.45%	0.12%	0.01%	0.00%
Baa	0.05%	0.26%	5.51%	88.48%	4.76%	0.71%	0.08%	0.15%
Ba	0.02%	0.05%	0.42%	5.16%	86.91%	5.91%	0.24%	1.29%
B	0.00%	0.04%	0.13%	0.54%	6.35%	84.22%	1.91%	6.81%
Caa	0.00%	0.00%	0.00%	0.62%	2.05%	4.08%	69.20%	24.06%

Source: Moody's. Reproduced with permission.

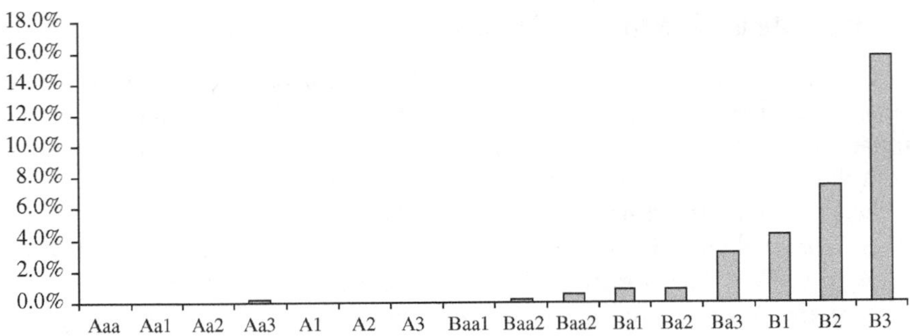

FIGURE 3.3 One-year cumulative default rates, 1985–2006.
Source: Moody's. Reproduced with permission.

horizon provides little real value; hence, the rating agencies also publish transition matrices for longer periods, such as five and 10 years.

We might expect an increased level of default as we move lower down the credit ratings scale. This is borne out in Figure 3.3, which is a reproduction of data published by Moody's. It shows 1-year average cumulative default rates by credit rating category, for the period 1985–2006. We see that the average 1-year default rate rises from zero for the highest rated Aaa, to 15.7% for the B3 rating category. However, investors generally attach little value to 1-year results. Figure 3.4 shows average cumulative default rates for 5- and 10-year time horizons, for the same period covered in Figure 3.3. This repeats the results shown in Figure 3.3, with higher default rates associated with lower credit ratings.

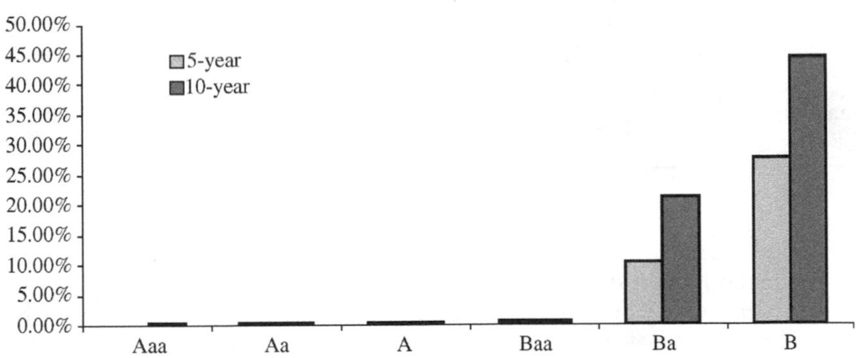

FIGURE 3.4 Five- and 10-year average cumulative default rates, 1985–2006.
Source: Moody's. Reproduced with permission.

Structured Finance Rating Transitions

In March 2009 Moody's published a *Special Comment* on ratings transitions for structured finance securities for the period 1983–2008, which covered the impact of the 2007–08 financial crisis.[1] The extent of the impact was evident from the statistics observed; for example, the 12-month rate for downgrades in the global structured finance market reached a historical high of 35.5% in 2008, from a figure of 7.4% in 2007, while the upgrade rate reduced from 2.2% to 0.7%.[2] The primary driver of these results was the poor performance of the most recent structured finance deals, which had sourced the most recent (and poor quality) US sub-prime mortgage assets.

Table 3.3 shows the global structured finance and global corporate finance 12-month rating transition matrices for the year 2008 and also for the period 1984–2008. Although structured finance assets performed worse than straight corporate bonds during 2008, it is noteworthy that over the longer term the former outperformed the latter.

Further illustration of the impact of the crisis on the structured finance market is given at Table 3.4, which is a summary of rating transition trends.

TABLE 3.3 Global structured finance and global corporate finance 12-month rating transition matrices.

	Structured finance in 2008						
	Aaa	Aa	A	Baa	Ba	B	Caa and below
Aaa	73.89%	7.23%	6.31%	5.32%	2.84%	1.74%	2.66%
Aa	1.00%	55.51%	7.29%	5.68%	4.83%	7.98%	17.71%
A	0.27%	0.92%	58.86%	7.72%	4.78%	6.39%	21.07%
Baa	0.10%	0.05%	0.82%	55.42%	5.47%	6.26%	31.88%
Ba	0.05%	0.02%	0.05%	0.67%	54.67%	3.81%	40.74%
B				0.09%	0.21%	45.65%	54.04%
Caa and below						0.13%	99.87%

(continued)

1 This report is entitled *Structured Finance Rating Transitions: 1983–2008* and is dated March 2009. It is the seventh such annual report from Moody's. It may be obtained from www.moodys.com. Structured finance securities include ABS and mortgage-backed securities (MBS), as well as CDOs, which are discussed in Chapter 4.

2 Source: Moody's Investors Service.

TABLE 3.3 *(Continued)*

Structured finance; 1984–2008 average over 12-month horizon

	Aaa	Aa	A	Baa	Ba	B	Caa and below
Aaa	97.79%	0.76%	0.53%	0.37%	0.19%	0.14%	0.21%
Aa	5.27%	87.19%	2.14%	1.12%	0.80%	1.72%	1.77%
A	1.10%	3.26%	85.61%	3.28%	1.39%	2.02%	3.34%
Baa	0.37%	0.47%	2.46%	83.17%	3.46%	2.92%	7.14%
Ba	0.15%	0.07%	0.45%	2.46%	82.33%	3.56%	10.98%
B	0.07%	0.04%	0.08%	0.34%	1.95%	83.63%	13.89%
Caa and below	0.03%			0.07%	0.08%	0.51%	99.30%

Corporate finance in 2008

	Aaa	Aa	A	Baa	Ba	B	Caa and below
Aaa	95.85%	4.15%					
Aa	4.43%	91.25%	4.12%	0.10%		0.10%	
A		10.02%	87.10%	2.69%	0.06%		0.13%
Baa		0.18%	7.30%	88.63%	3.60%	0.28%	
Ba			0.18%	8.06%	83.70%	7.33%	0.73%
B	0.10%			0.19%	6.67%	83.60%	9.44%
Caa and below						15.12%	84.88%

Corporate finance: 1984–2008 average over 12-month horizon

	Aaa	Aa	A	Baa	Ba	B	Caa and below
Aaa	92.76%	6.97%	0.26%		0.02%		
Aa	1.26%	91.45%	6.95%	0.27%	0.05%	0.02%	0.01%
A	0.07%	3.01%	90.91%	5.30%	0.55%	0.11%	0.04%
Baa	0.05%	0.21%	5.37%	88.33%	4.53%	1.00%	0.51%
Ba	0.01%	0.06%	0.43%	6.48%	81.47%	9.56%	2.00%
B	0.01%	0.05%	0.18%	0.40%	6.16%	81.72%	11.47%
Caa and below		0.03%	0.04%	0.19%	0.67%	11.44%	87.63%

Source: Moody's Investors Service. Reproduced with permission.

TABLE 3.4 Summary of rating transition trends, 1983–2008.

	Structured finance		Corporate finance	
	2008	1984–2008	2008	1984–2008
Downgrade rate	35.50%	6.25%	18.22%	13.47%
Upgrade rate	0.69%	2.24%	4.64%	9.86%
Average number of notches downgraded	8.30	6.99	1.64	1.78
Average number of notches upgraded	2.12	2.37	1.34	1.49

Source: Moody's Investors Service. Reproduced with permission.

Again, over the longer term structured finance assets have outperformed corporate assets, as shown in the table.

It is apparent that straight corporate credit ratings are actually much less stable than ratings on structured finance securities, but that when rating changes do take place, the scale of the change is, on average, lower for the corporate ratings. In other words, the statistics appear to confirm that the higher return (on average) of structured finance securities compared to corporate bonds of the same rating reflects their higher risk, which manifests itself during extreme bear market situations.

UNDERSTANDING CREDIT RISK

Credit risk management is a judgement call. The one single factor that most assists effective credit risk management is knowing one's market. An unfamiliarity with a particular market or customer set, or an over-reliance on "black box" models to assess loan origination quality, hampers the application of credit risk, because it renders it too susceptible to the business cycle. So beyond understanding the drivers of credit risk, and their dynamics, the over-riding principle remains to understand the market one is operating in. Never originate loans or invest in assets that one does not understand. This principle does not change, irrespective of the level of sophistication of the product or customer. In other words, the complexity of a product or transaction does not alter the requirement to understand the borrower and its business risks. That is what credit risk is. Even with sophisticated transactions or complex products, while the evaluation of the risk exposure may be more difficult, the need to understand the nature of the risk does not alter. Ultimately, the question of credit risk management remains the same: what is the chance that the investment will incur losses, and how much will the lender lose if the borrower is unable to repay? And is the lender able to survive this potential loss? The answer to these questions, which are dynamic, guides the approach to bank credit risk management.

In this section we define credit risk and exposure, and consider recovery rate in the event of default.

Definition of Credit Risk

Credit risk is the risk of loss due to a "credit event". This was the case before the advent of the credit derivative market placed this term into regular usage. A credit event can be a number of things, from outright default due to bankruptcy, liquidation or administration, or it can be something short of full default. It can also mean loss due to credit migration, such as a downgrade in credit rating. In the credit derivatives market, the range of credit events is defined in the legal documentation governing the market. In a full default, the extent of loss can be observed immediately to be the full notional amount of the loan; however, typically over time the lender will receive an amount of the loan back from the administrators, known as the "recovery value". In a credit loss event short of default, the amount of loss is determined by applying mark-to-market valuation.

Default itself is defined in more than one way. Generally it is one or more of the following:

- non-payment of interest 90 days after the interest-due date;
- non-payment of loan 90 days after the loan maturity date;
- a restructuring of the borrower's loans;
- filing for bankruptcy, appointment of administrators, liquidation and so on.

Late payment is often termed an NPL or a delinquent loan rather than a defaulted loan if the borrower itself is still undertaking business. However, at some point, irrespective of the state of the borrower, an NPL will be written off as a default loss. The write-down, which must be funded out of the bank's capital, is often at 100% of outstanding notional value, even though the bank will probably recover a percentage, however small, at some later date. Another definition of default is that presented by Merton in his 1974 paper. This states that default occurs when the value of a company falls below the value of its debts. The definition of default is relevant because for some models it is a driver of the calculation of default probability; it is also relevant to credit rating agencies when they compile the historical frequency of default. Rating agencies generally apply the delay in payment definition.

The Asset Exposure

The notional, or absolute level of risk exposure is the first port of call. It is also the easiest to calculate. It is given by the amount of the loan or investment with the customer or "counterparty".[3] This amount may be fixed, sometimes called a "bullet" loan, or it may reduce steadily, which is an amortising loan. If the exposure is a vanilla loan that is recorded in the bank's balance sheet, the amount will not change from the origination date to the maturity date. If it is a loan that is tradeable, such as a bond, or otherwise subject to mark-to-market valuation, then the exposure amount will vary according to its valuation, but should always be 100% of notional by the maturity date. Figure 3.5 is a stylised representation of the behaviour of asset risk exposure by type of asset, each of which has the same maturity date.[4]

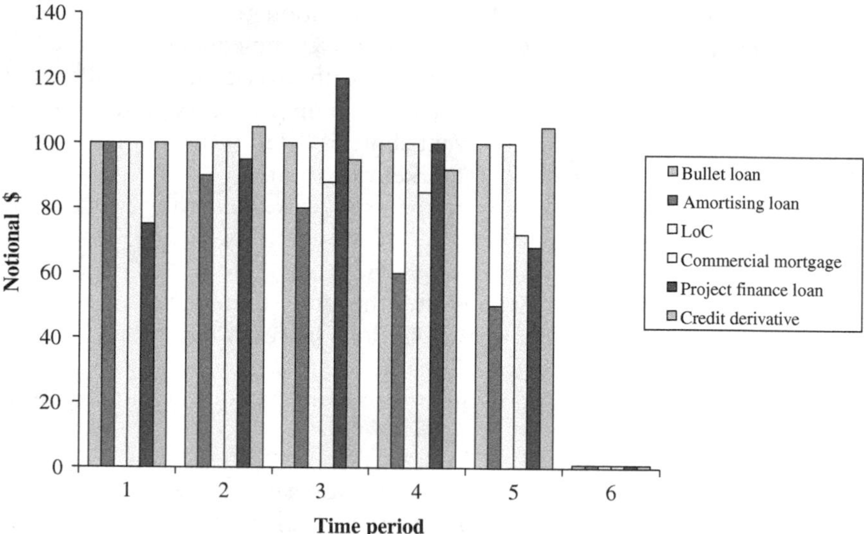

FIGURE 3.5 Notional value risk exposure profiles of different product types.

3 We have to be careful with the use of the word "investment". Here we mean it from the viewpoint of the bank. In general conversation, investment is often used to mean an equity investment, by a shareholder in the business. A bank is advancing debt funds to the customer, but this is of course also an investment in the future well-being of the company.

4 This is for illustration. It is highly uncommon to observe this different range of asset types with identical maturity dates. Mortgage and project finance loans have the longest legal final maturity dates.

Trading book assets apply mark-to-market. The value of a loan that is under mark-to-market will change because of changes to the general level of interest rates, and/or changes to the credit standing of the borrower (or the borrower's industrial sector, or to credit conditions generally in the market). As such, trading book assets capture changes in value, at least theoretically, that arise due to, for instance, changes in credit rating. This is known as credit migration risk. The banking book, which does not apply mark-to-market, cannot by definition capture migration risk of its assets. It only captures the risk of loss due to default. This might be seen to be some sort of disadvantage, because the changes in credit standing of a borrower also change its probability of default. However, use of mark-to-market in a trading book is less of an advantage than one might think, and in stressed market conditions it can be self-defeating (lower mark-to-market values can generate a vicious circle of falling prices that impacts confidence and can itself lead to default).

The asset exposure on a balance sheet is not comprised solely of live loans. It also includes potential future liabilities, such as letters of credit (LoC), third-party liquidity lines and other guarantees. The notional amount of such off-balance sheet exposures is also part of the bank's credit risk exposure.

The main risk management mechanism for asset exposure risk is by means of credit limits. This is the maximum amount that can be outstanding at any time to the individual customer, the industrial sector, the country and so on. Limits can also be set by currency.

Recovery Value

It is quite common for banks to write down the entire notional value of an NPL. In practice, virtually all defaulted assets return an element of recovery value, although the time taken to realise this value can be very long indeed. In general therefore a prudent approach is to assign a 0% recovery value for risk management purposes.

The concept of recovery value is relevant in the credit derivative markets as well, as it is a parameter that feeds into pricing.

Recovery Rates

The concept of RR is a key parameter in credit derivative valuation. This is somewhat unfortunate, because the nature of markets is such that an assumed rate must be used. In the real world, actual recovery value from a defaulted obligation may not be known for years.

The procedure for determining RR in the cash market is a long drawn-out affair. Debt investors take their place in the queue with all other creditors and receive their due after the administrators have completed their work. This process can take a matter of months or over 10 years. The rating agencies make an assumption of what the final recovery amount will be from the market price of the debt asset at the time bankruptcy or default is announced. This approach is carried over to an extent into the credit derivative market.

The definition of recovery rate in the CDS market differs slightly from that in the cash bond market, for reasons of practicality. This is because the contract must settle fairly soon after the notice of a credit event has been announced, and the real "RR" is not at that point. At the same time, the model approach under which the CDS would have been priced and valued up to now would have used a "RR" as one of its parameters. So in the CDS market, recovery is defined as the market value of the "delivered obligation". This market value is determined by a poll of CDS dealers bidding for the defaulted assets of the reference entity.

Note that recovery rates for the two markets will therefore differ from those in the cash market in practice. This arises for a number of reasons, one of which is that in the CDS market a credit event will encompass circumstances that fall short of full default in the cash market. For example, Moody's notes three categories of default for the purposes of its ratings and historical default statistics:

- delayed or failed coupon or principal payments;
- bankruptcy or receivership;
- distressed exchange that results in investors having a lower obligation value, undertaken by the obligor in order to avoid default.

Recovery rates in practice vary widely, as we note below. In essence, what the 2007–08 credit crunch has taught us is that if one is using CDS to hedge credit risk, the safest approach is to assume a 0% recovery rate. This is because in the event of default it will be some time before the investor receives the recovery value, while in the meantime the payment from the CDS that was used to hedge the asset will be (100 – RR) so the investor will actually have lost out on some of the investment until recovery is received. In the meantime, the investor's accountants would most probably have written down the entire par value of the investment. Therefore for complete hedging it is best to assume a zero recovery value when calculating the notional amount of the CDS used to hedge the investment.

Despite the RR being a key parameter in CDS pricing models, it is not apparent that it is influencing CDS premiums heavily, or that actual historical RRs are used when selecting the input level. A look at CDS spreads during the

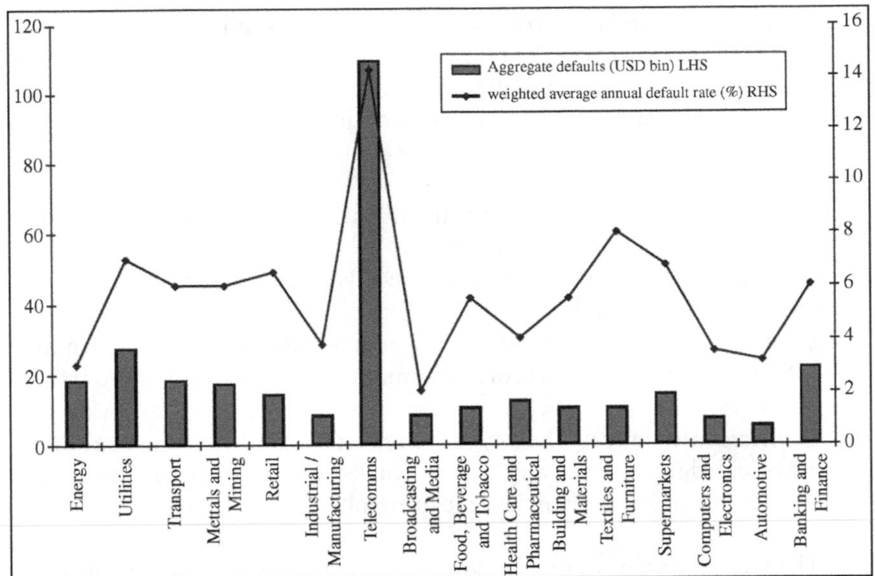

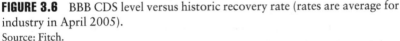

FIGURE 3.6 BBB CDS level versus historic recovery rate (rates are average for industry in April 2005).
Source: Fitch.

period 2000–2004 shows that while "RR" varies widely, the CDS premium across all industries is fairly similar (see Figure 3.6).

We observe that most industries were trading at levels fairly close: within 10 or 20 bps of each other. Industries traditionally regarded as higher risk (for example, computers and electronics), or in more difficult circumstances such as automotive, are marked up. But otherwise the closeness is significant.

These observations are noteworthy because RR assumption is a required, and important, parameter in CDS pricing. However, it is usually set at 40% for all reference names (for example, the Bloomberg page CDSW defaults to this value. Post the credit crunch and global recession, however, it is more usually set at 50% for most names). The chart is interesting because it implies there is little variation in RR assumption – if we adjusted for it we should have observed greater variation in CDS prices.

Note the approximation of market implied default probability in a flat term structure environment, which uses the RR assumption, showing the relationship between them which is as follows:

$$P(\text{default}) = \text{CDS spread}/[1 - \text{RR}].$$

Generally, the market gives little weight to the RR assumption when the probability of default is low. But during a recession or in a bear market environment when default probability is higher, this approach is risky and can lead to less accuracy in hedging. A report from Fitch[5] (that pre-dated the credit crunch) suggests the following reasons behind the small differences between industry spread, given that the variation in recovery rate is so much larger:

- at the time, the low-default environment may have made this a non-issue;
- when actual recovery values are received, the ultimate result will probably be very similar;
- given the real difficulty in estimating actual recovery values, which may be many years into the future, the market may prefer a standardised assumption;
- historical rates may not be any more realistic a guide to future rates;
- historical data on recovery values varies widely year-to-year across industries, rendering them less meaningful.

The recovery value of an investment-grade reference name can be more difficult to estimate than a high-yield name given that for the former, any default is likely to occur further in the future.

In practice, as we might expect, there is considerable variation in default rates over time. Average default and recovery rate by industry and loan seniority for the US market (see Table 3.5 and Figure 3.7) shows the variation over time historically, although if we standardised by credit rating some of this variation would reduce.

TABLE 3.5 Moody's recovery rates for varying levels of loan seniority, 2006.

Recovery rates according to loan seniority		
Seniority	**Mean (%)**	**Standard deviation (%)**
Senior secured bank loans	60.70	26.31
Senior secured	55.83	25.41
Senior unsecured	52.13	25.12
Senior subordinated	39.45	24.79
Subordinated	33.81	21.25
Junior subordinated	18.51	11.26
Preference shares	8.26	10.45

5 Fitch special report, 8 June 2005.

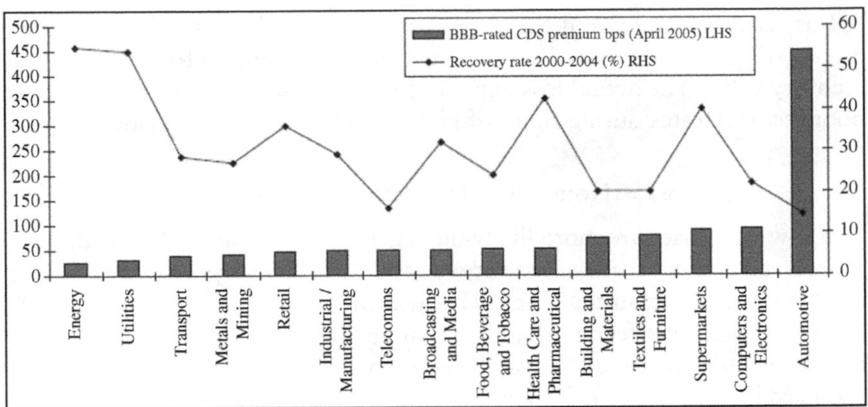

FIGURE 3.7 Default rate versus recovery rate.
Source: Fitch.

Recovery rates also exhibit great variation. In practice, recovery rates and default rates tend to be inversely related: high default rates are associated with lower average recovery rates (see Figure 3.8). Note that most market practitioners, and the Fitch report we quote from, measure

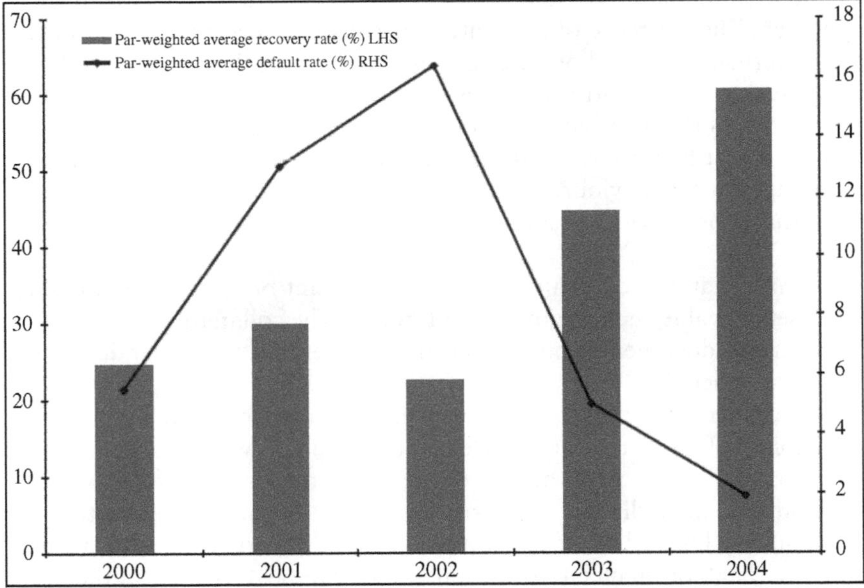

FIGURE 3.8 High yield sector default rate versus recovery rate.
Source: Fitch.

RR as recovery value, and the market price of the defaulted loan 30 days after default. As we noted above this will be different from the actual recovery value. The actual loss experienced by investors will be increased by poor recovery rates during times of high default rate. A rough calculation is given by:

$$\text{Loss} = \text{Notional} \times [\text{Default rate} \times (1 - \text{RR})].$$

Low recoveries are more likely during a period of high defaults and this reflects economic reality, as supply and demand depresses secondary market price for defaulted loans. This was observed during the 2008–2009 recession and is in effect a "double whammy" for investors. It also means it is difficult to estimate a "normal" recovery rate (one more reason for the standard level used in CDS pricing).

Collateral and Third-Party Guarantees

Much bank lending involves the use of collateral and/or guarantees from third parties to back the loan. The existence of these features complicates the credit risk management process. From a prudent, perhaps conservative viewpoint, the assessment of risk exposure should take no account of these features. It is always the credit quality of the borrower, and that only, that should drive the loan origination process and the credit risk management approach. The existence of guarantees or collateral also does not influence the performance of the borrower and hence the loan. In practice banks do factor such security features into their risk calculations, especially when to do so enables them to reduce their regulatory capital requirement. While this might not be business best-practice, the fact that Basel II allows for it encourages such behaviour.

Security or backing for a loan can be arranged in the following forms:

- Loan collateral: company assets such as plant or machinery, or other assets of value such as government bonds. The collateral is written into the loan documentation as security transferable to the lender in the event of default.
- Guarantee: this may be in the form of third-party that assumes the liability of the borrower in the event of default, in which case the lender is exposed to the credit quality of the guarantor, or in the form of credit insurance or credit protection such as a credit derivative contract.
- Liquidity line: a line of credit arranged by the borrower, from a third-party bank or financial institution, which can be drawn on in the event of financial difficulty of the borrower. This type of facility is common in structured finance transactions that involve the use of an SPV legal

entity. It exposes the cash lender to the credit quality of the third-party institution, as well as the soundness and strength of the legal documentation governing the obligations of the third party.

These arrangements do not impact the fortunes of the borrower or the performance of the loan. An arrangement that does so to an extent, but does not provide any additional security for the lender, is a loan covenant. A covenant is a provision written in the legal documents describing the loan that requires the borrower to adhere to certain specific requirements, such as the absolute level of borrowing or the leverage ratio. Some covenants also describe certain business activities that the borrower is prohibited from entering into. Whatever their form, they serve to restrict the borrower in certain ways and thus are a risk management mechanism for the lender.

In practice, collateral and guarantees often serve to reduce a lender's risk aversion, under the impression that the risk exposure is less than it might otherwise be. However, whatever their form, they do not eliminate credit risk (unless the third-party guarantor is a AAA-rated government), and so should not be viewed ultimately as risk mitigating tools. In the event of default, the lender will still suffer some form of loss. Equally, an "implicit" guarantee is often worthless, because unless the guarantor is legally obliged to back the loan, it may walk away from it in the event of default (even at risk to its reputation). A bank should always ensure that third-party backing is written into the loan documentation, otherwise it has no value.

The impact of a guarantee on credit risk calculations is assessed using the recovery rate assumption for the loan. We discussed recovery rate earlier. The LGD of a loan is given by:

$$\text{LGD} = \text{Notional value} \times (100\% - \text{RR})$$

where RR is the recovery rate as before.

As we saw earlier, recovery rates vary widely across industry and even within industries, and also by the seniority of the loan in the corporate capital structure. Historically, recovery rates have been higher for senior loans and secured loans than for subordinated loans and unsecured loans. The bank must therefore make a distinction between recovery rate assumptions according to the type of guarantee and the type of loan in question.

For risk management practice that is adequate throughout the business cycle, the impact of the credit risk reducing measures described above should be set at negligible or zero. This is because in the event of default, there is a legal process to be followed, affecting all creditors, which may take many months or years. Recovery of any kind – including collateral – may be some distance away. Even a third-party guarantee may not be enforceable, while a covenant clause is of no value if the borrower is in breach of them. As a going concern, a bank cannot rely on a legal process as part of its support to ensure that it can carry on business as usual. Also, in a stress situation such as a recession or financial market crisis, the legal process may take even longer than usual.

The bottom line for senior management is this: credit enhancements in themselves should not be viewed as alternatives to sound loan origination and credit risk management.

EXTERNAL RATING AGENCY CREDIT RATINGS

Credit analysis is concerned with issuer-specific considerations (as opposed to macro considerations). This will include a quantitative analysis and a qualitative analysis that results in the assignment of an internal credit rating. Investors sometimes substitute the credit rating given by a third-party company such as Moody's or S&P. The qualitative factors to consider include those both internal and exogenous to the company.

In this section, we introduce the process of credit analysis, as this is an essential element of banking.

Credit Analysis

When ratings agencies were first set up, the primary focus of credit analysis was on the default risk of the bond, or the probability that the investor would not receive the interest payments and the principal repayment as they fell due. Although this is still important, credit analysts now also consider overall macroeconomic conditions, as well as the chance that an issuer will have its rating changed during the life of the bond. There are differences in approach, depending on which industry or market sector the issuing company is part of.

Here we review the main issues of concern to a credit analyst when rating bond issues. Analysts usually adopt a "top-down" approach, or a "big picture" approach, and concentrate on the macro issues first before looking at the issuer-specific points in detail. The process therefore involves reviewing the issuer's industry, before looking at its financial and balance sheet strength, and finally the legal provisions concerning the bond issue. There are also detail differences in analysis depending on which industry the issuer is in.

The Issuer Industry

In the first instance the credit analysis process will review the issuer's industry. This is in order to place the subsequent company analysis in context. For example, a company that has recorded growth rates of 10% each year may appear to be a quality performer, but not if its industry has been experiencing average growth rates of 30%. Generally, the industry analysis will review the following issues:

- *Economic cycle*. The business cycle of the industry and its correlation with the overall business cycle are key indicators. That is, how closely does the industry follow the rate of growth of its country's GNP? Certain industries such as the electricity and food retail sectors are more resistant to recession than others. Other sectors are closely tied to changes in population and birth patterns, such as residential homes, while the financial services industry is influenced by the overall health of the economy, as well as by the level of interest rates. As well as the correlation with macro-factors, credit analysts review traditional financial indicators in context; for example, the issuing company's earnings per share (EPS) against the growth rate of its industry.
- *Growth prospects*. This review is of the issuer industry's general prospects. A company operating within what is considered a high-growth industry is generally deemed to have better credit quality expectations than one operating in a low-growth environment. A scenario of anticipated growth in the industry has implications for the issuing company; for example, the extent to which the company will be ablc copc with capacity demands and the financing of excess capacity. A fast-growth industry also attracts new entrants, which will lead to over-supply, intensified competition and reduced margins. A slow-growth industry has implications for diversification, so that a company deemed to have plans for diversifying when operating in stagnant markets will be marked up.
- *Competition*. A review of the intensity of competitive forces within an industry, and the extent of pricing and over- or under-capacity, is an essential ingredient of credit analysis. Competition is now regarded as a global phenomenon and well-rated companies are judged able to compete successfully on a global basis while concentrating on the highest growth regions. Competition within a particular industry is related to that industry's structure and has implications for pricing flexibility. The type of market – for example, monopoly, oligopoly and so on – also influences pricing policy and relative margins. Another issue arises if there is obvious overcapacity in an industry; this has been exemplified

in the past in the airline industry and financial services when overcapacity often leads to intense price competition and price wars. This is frequently damaging for the industry as a whole, as all companies suffer losses and financial deterioration in the attempt to maintain or grow market share.

- *Supply sources.* The availability of suppliers in an industry influences a company's financial well-being. Monopoly sources of supply are considered a restrictive element and have negative implications. A vertically integrated company that is able to supply its own raw materials is less susceptible to economic conditions that might affect suppliers or leave it hostage to price rises. A company that is not self-sufficient in its factors of production, but is nevertheless in strong enough a position to pass on its costs, is in a good position.
- *Research and development.* A broad assessment of the growth prospects of a company must also include a review of its research and development (R&D) position. In certain industries, such as telecommunications, media and information technology, a heavy investment in R&D is essential simply in order to maintain market share. In a high technology field it is common for products to obsolesce very quickly, therefore it is essential to maintain high R&D spending. In the short term, however, a company with a low level of research expenditure may actually post above-average (relative to the industry) profits because it is operating at higher margins. This is not considered a healthy strategy for the long term, though. Evaluating the R&D input of a company is not necessarily a straightforward issue of comparing ratios, however, as it is also important to assess correctly the direction of technology. That is, a successful company needs not only to invest a sufficient amount in R&D, it must also be correct in its assessment of the direction the industry is heading, technology-wise. A heavy investment in developing Betamax videos, for example, would not have assisted companies in the early 1980s.
- *Level of regulation.* The degree of regulation in an industry, its direction and its effect on the profitability of a company are relevant in a credit analysis. A highly regulated industry such as power generation, production of medicines or (in certain countries) telecommunications can have a restrictive influence on company profits. On the other hand, if the government has announced a policy of deregulating a particular industry, this is considered a positive development for companies in that sector.
- *Labour relations.* An industry with a highly unionised labour force or generally tense labour relations is viewed unfavourably compared to one with stable labour relations. Credit analysts will consider historic

patterns of, say, strikes and production days lost to industrial action. The status of labour relations is also more influential in a highly labour-intensive industry than one that is more automated for example.
- *Political climate.* The investment industry adopts an increasingly global outlook and the emergence of sizeable tradeable debt markets in, for example, "emerging" countries means that ratings agencies frequently must analyse the general political and economic climate in which an industry is operating. Failure to foresee certain political developments can have far-reaching effects for investors.

Financial Analysis

The traditional approach to credit analysis concentrated heavily on financial analysis. The more modern approach involves a review of the industry the company is operating in first, discussed above, before considering financial considerations. Generally, the financial analysis of the issuer is conducted in three phases, namely:

- the ratio analysis for the bonds;
- analysing the company's return on capital;
- non-financial factors such as management expertise and the extent of overseas operations.

Ratio Analysis

In themselves ratios do not present very much insight, although there are various norms that can be applied. Generally, ratio analysis is compared to the levels prevalent in the industry, as well as historical values, in an effort to place the analysis in context and compare the company with those in its peer group. The ratios that can be considered are:

- pre-tax interest cover, the level of cover for interest charges in current pre-tax income;
- fixed interest charge level;
- *leverage*, which is commonly defined as the ratio of long-term debt as a percentage of total capitalisation;
- level of leverage compared to industry average;
- nature of debt, whether fixed- or floating-rate, short- or long-term;
- cash flow, which is the ratio of cash flow as a percentage of total debt. Cash flow itself is usually defined as net income from continuing operations, plus depreciation and taxes, while debt is taken to be long-term debt;

TABLE 3.6 S&P ratio benchmarks, 2007.

Credit rating	Pre-tax interest cover	Leverage	Cash flow
AAA	17.99	13.2	97.5
AA	9.74	19.7	8.5
A	5.35	33.2	43.8
BBB	2.91	44.8	29.9

Source: S&P.

- net assets, as a percentage of total debt. The liquidity of the assets – meaning the ease with which they can be turned into cash – is taken into account when assessing the net asset ratio.

The ratings agencies maintain benchmarks that are used to assign ratings, and these are monitored and if necessary modified to allow for changes in the economic climate. For example, Standard & Poor's guidelines for pre-tax interest cover, leverage level and cash flow in 2007 are shown in Table 3.6. A pre-tax cover of above 9.00, for example, was consistent with a double-A rating.

Other ratios that are considered include:

- intangibles; that is, the portion of intangibles relative to the asset side of a balance sheet;
- unfunded pension liabilities; generally a fully funded pension is not seen as necessary; however, an unfunded liability that is over 10% of net assets would be viewed as a negative point;
- the age and condition of the plant;
- working capital.

These are general ratios. Analysis is specific to the type of company under consideration.

Return on Equity

There is a range of performance measures used in the market that are connected with return on equity (generally, the analysis concentrates on return on capital, or more often RAROC). In analysing measures of return, analysts seek to determine trends in historical performance and comparisons with peer group companies. Different companies also emphasise different target returns in their objectives, usually an expression of their corporate philosophy, so it is common for companies in the same industry to have different return ratios. The range of ratios used by the credit ratings agencies is shown below. Note that EBIT is "earnings before interest and tax".

The agencies make available data that may be consulted by the public; for example, default rates, recovery rates and so on.

$$\text{Return on net assets} = \frac{\text{Profit}}{\text{Net assets}} \times 100$$

$$\text{Return on sales} = \frac{\text{Profit}}{\text{Sales turnover}} \times 100$$

$$\text{Return on equity} = (\text{Return on net assets} \times \text{Gearing}) \times 100$$

$$\text{Pre-tax interest cover} = \frac{\text{Pre-tax income from continuing operations}}{\text{Gross interest}}$$

$$\text{EBIT interest cover} = \frac{\text{Pre-tax income from continuing operations} + \text{Interest expense}}{\text{Gross interest}}$$

$$\text{Long-term debt as \% of capitalisation} = \frac{\text{Long-term debt}}{\text{Long-term debt} + \text{Equity}} \times 100$$

$$\text{Funds flow as \% of debt} = \frac{\text{Funds from operations}}{\text{Total debt}} \times 100$$

$$\text{Free cash flow as \% of debt} = \frac{\text{Free cash flow}}{\text{Total debt}} \times 100.$$

Non-financial Factors

The non-financial element of a company credit analysis has assumed a more important role in recent years, especially with regard to companies in exotic or emerging markets. Credit analysts review the non-financial factors relevant to the specific company after they have completed the financial and ratio analysis. These include the strength and competence of senior management, and the degree of exposure to overseas markets. The depth of overseas exposure is not always apparent from documents such as the annual report, and analysts sometimes need to conduct further research to determine this. Companies with considerable overseas exposure, such as petroleum companies, also need to be reviewed with respect to the political situation in their operating locations. A bank such as Standard Chartered, for example, has significant exposure to more exotic currencies in Asian, Middle-Eastern and African countries, and so is more at risk from additional market movements than a bank with almost exclusively domestic operations. The global, integrated nature of the bond markets also means that the foreign exchange exposure of a company must be evaluated and assessed for risk. The quality of management is a subjective, qualitative factor that can be reviewed in a number of ways. A personal familiarity with senior directors, acquired over a period of time, may help in the assessment. A broad breadth of experience, diversity of age and strong internal competition for those aspiring to senior roles is considered positive. A company that had been founded by one individual, and in which there were no clear plans of "succession", might be marked down.

Industry-specific Analysis

Specific industries will be subject to a review that is more relevant to the particular nature of the operations of the companies within them. In this section we briefly consider two separate industries: power generation, water and certain other public service companies (or utilities); and financial companies.

Utility Companies

The industry for power generation, water supply and until recently telecommunications has a tradition of being highly regulated. Until the mid-1980s, utility companies were public sector companies, and the first privatisation of such a company was British Telecom in 1984. In certain European countries, utility companies are still nationalised companies, and their debt trades virtually as government debt. Credit analysis for utility companies therefore emphasises non-financial factors such as the depth of regulation and the direction in which regulation is heading; for example, towards an easing or tightening. Even in a privatised industry, for example, new government regulation maybe targeted only at the utility sector. For example, in March 2011, the coalition Conservative–Liberal Democrat government in the UK imposed a specific industry tax on petroleum companies involved in North Sea oil extraction.

Another consideration concerns government direction on how the companies may operate, such as restrictions on where a power generation company may purchase coal. In some countries coal must be bought from the country's own domestic coal industry only, which imposes costs on the generating company that it would escape if it were free to purchase coal from other, lower cost producers. The financial analysis of a utility company essentially follows the pattern we described earlier.

Financial Sector Companies

The financial sector encompasses a large and diverse group of companies. At its simplest, financial service companies such as banks earn profit by taking the spread between funds lent and borrowed. In analysing a financial sector company the credit analyst will consider the type of customer base served by the company; for example, how much of a bank's lending is to the wholesale sector, how much is retail and so on. The financial strength and prospects of its customer base are important elements of a bank's credit rating.

Financial analysis of banks and securities houses is concerned with the asset quality of the institution; for example, the extent of diversification of a bank's lending book. Diversification can be across customer base as well as geographically. A loan book that is heavily concentrated in one sector is considered to be a negative factor in the overall credit assessment of the bank. A credit analyst will be concerned with the level of loans compared with levels in peer companies and the risk involved with this type of lending. For example, the expected frequency of bad loans from direct unsecured retail customer loans is higher than for retail customer loans secured by a second mortgage on a property. The higher lending rate charged for the former is designed to compensate for this higher lending risk.

There is a range of financial ratios that can be used to assess a bank's asset quality. These include:

- loss reserves/net charge-off level;
- net losses/average level of receivables;
- NPLs/average level of receivables.

However, unlike the more "concrete" financial ratios given earlier, there is a higher subjective element with these ratios as banks themselves will designate which loans are non-performing and those loans against which have been assigned charges. Nevertheless, these ratios are useful indicators and may be used to identify trends across the sector as well. The loss reserves/net charge-off ratio is perhaps the most useful as it indicates the level of "cushion" that a bank has; a falling ratio suggests that the bank may not be adding sufficient reserves to cover for future charge-offs. This trend, if continued, may then result in a future increase in the reserves and therefore a decrease in earnings levels as the expense of the reserves increase.

The leverage ratio is particularly important for financial sector companies, as the industry and business itself are highly leveraged. Banks and securities companies are therefore permitted a significantly higher leverage level than other companies. For example, in a diversified banking group with a high level of asset quality, a leverage ratio of 20:1 or even higher is considered satisfactory by ratings agencies. Another important measure for financial companies is *liquidity*. Due to the nature of the industry and the capital structure of banks, liquidity or, more accurately, the lack of liquidity is the primary reason behind banking failures. A bank that is unable to raise funds sufficiently quickly to meet demand will most probably fail, and certainly so if external support is not provided. An inability to raise funds may arise due to internal factors, such as a deterioration in earnings or a very poorly performing loan book, connected perhaps with a downgrade in credit rating, or from external factors such as a major structural fault in the money markets. The latter helped speed the demise of Northern Rock in 2007.

For credit analysis purposes the traditional liquidity measures are:

- cash;
- cash equivalents;
- level of receivables under one year/level of short-term liabilities.

A higher ratio indicates a greater safety cushion. A further consideration is the extent of lines of credit from other banks in the market. Other measures of strength for financial companies are *asset coverage*, the bank's earnings record including *earnings per share* (profit attributable to shareholders/number of shares in issue) and finally, the size of the institution. There is an element of thought which states that a very large institution, measured by asset size, cannot go bankrupt. This type of thinking can lead to complacency however, and it did not prevent several large Japanese banks from getting into financial difficulty in the 1990s.[6] It was also plainly no defence against the problems suffered by certain large banks in 2008.

6 In fact, the Japanese government gave an implicit guarantee for the largest 20 "city" banks at one stage, shortly after the collapse of Yamaichi Securities in 1997.

BANK INTERNAL CREDIT RATINGS

All banks will employ some form of internal credit rating methodology for their customers. The rating criteria for bank internal systems are similar in concept to those of external agencies. That is, they include qualitative and quantitative factors. Criteria are tweaked in accordance with the type of borrower being assessed. For example, financial institutions will be assessed by bank-specific metrics such as the loan-to-deposit ratio or the level of loan loss reserves.

In recent years there has been a tendency for banks to adopt a "black box" approach, in which loan agents input the required parameters into their system, and the model output is either an approval or disapproval. A reduced level of human judgement in the loan origination process has limitations that are exposed during a recession or economic crash, mainly because black box models are not immune to being "sucked" into a bull market. For this reason, it is important that the loan approval process includes an element of operator judgement, which is of value when the operator is familiar with the market.

Internal ratings are similar to external ones in assigning a grade, on either a letter or number scale, to borrowers that rank their credit standing. For many banks, the customers in question will be SMEs, and so will not possess an external agency credit rating. For SMEs it is mainly the internal bank rating that will drive the loan approval process. A bank's credit analysis department will consider the obligor risk of default, the credit quality of any parent or supporting company, the risk of the loan product itself and the backing of any other banking institution when calculating its internal rating. The borrower risk of default assessment is similar to the qualitative and financial review used by external rating agencies.

A bank operating across more than one legal jurisdiction will also want to have an internal rating for each country. This is important because depending on the country concerned, it may be difficult or impossible to recover cash or assets in the event of default, or to enforce a legal ruling. Therefore a foreign country rating is required as well. This remains important even if the obligor is rated higher than its domicile country, because of potential legal problems just referred to. Note that the external rating agencies have a rule that no company borrower can be rated higher than the rating of its domicile country. This rule is not applied universally in bank internal credit rating processes.

The Basel II rules crystallised the use of credit ratings by making explicit reference to them in its standardised approach (see Chapter 2). However, for many banks the standardised approach is no less risk-insensitive than Basel I, because their customers are not externally rated. Such banks

TABLE 3.7 Moody's rating statistics 2007.

Rating	Yearly average default rate	Yearly volatility of default rate (1970–2007)
Aaa	0.00%	0.00%
Aa	0.05%	0.12%
A	0.08%	0.05%
Baa	0.20%	0.29%
Ba	1.80%	1.40%
B	8.30%	5.03%

Source: Moody's Inc. Reproduced with permission.

can map external ratings to their internal system and assign risk-weights accordingly, providing they have obtained regulator approval for their internal model. Generally this mapping process involves applying the external rating, and their implied default probabilities, to the internal rating and obtaining an external rating equivalent for the internal grade. This can be undertaken using an off-the-shelf credit model. Although this process is in common use, it is inherently flawed because of its reliance on the two usual parameters, default probability and RR. The rating criteria reflects the expected loss (EL) of an asset, given by:

$$\text{EL} = \mathit{DefaultProb} \times (1 - \text{RR}).$$

We see then that EL can alter significantly even if default probability stays unchanged, by changing RR. This in turn can change the external rating. Table 3.7 shows Moody's statistics for ratings and default, and the equivalent for each rating grade. It is possible to alter a ratings-equivalent default rate by changing the recovery rate, and thereby obtain a different rating. Business best practice, and prudent risk management, dictates therefore that banks assume a 0% recovery in their internal ratings systems.

CREDIT VALUE-at-RISK

Credit risk is different in nature to market risk. Typically, market return distributions are assumed to be relatively symmetrical and approximated by normal distributions. In credit portfolios, value changes are relatively small as a result of minor up/downgrades, but can be substantial upon default. This remote probability of large losses produces skewed distributions with heavy downside tails that differ from the more normally distributed returns assumed for market VaR models. This is shown in Figure 3.9.

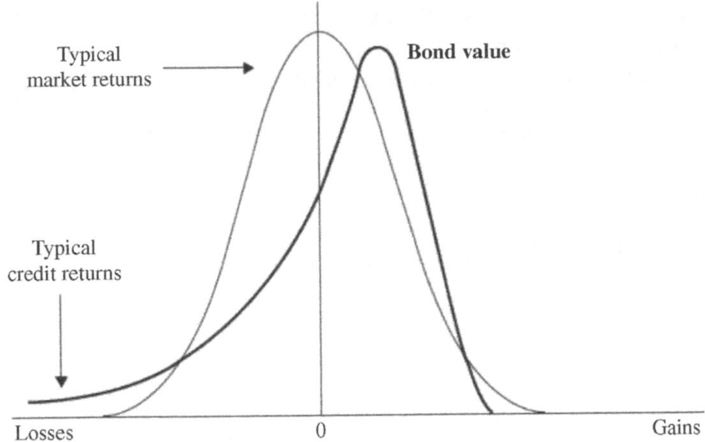

FIGURE 3.9 Comparison of distribution of market returns and credit returns.

This difference in risk profiles does not prevent us from assessing risk on a comparable basis. Analytical method market VaR models consider a time horizon and estimate VaR across a distribution of estimated market outcomes. Credit VaR models similarly look to a horizon and construct a distribution of value given different estimated credit outcomes.

When modelling credit risk the two main measures of risk are:

- distribution of loss: obtaining distributions of loss that may arise from the current portfolio. This considers the question of what the expected loss is for a given confidence level;
- identifying extreme or catastrophic outcomes: this is addressed through the use of scenario analysis and concentration limits.

To simplify modelling, no assumptions are made about the causes of default. Mathematical techniques used in the insurance industry are used to model the event of an obligor default.

Time Horizon

The choice of time horizon will not be shorter than the timeframe over which risk-mitigating actions can be taken. Essentially there are two alternatives:

- a constant time horizon such as one year;
- a hold-to-maturity time horizon.

The constant time horizon is similar to that used for market risk measures. It is more suitable for bank trading desks. The hold-to-maturity approach is used by institutions such as insurance companies and fund managers.

Data Inputs

Modelling credit risk requires certain data inputs; these include the following:

- credit exposures;
- obligor default rates;
- obligor default rate volatilities;
- recovery rates.

These data requirements present some difficulties. There is a lack of comprehensive default and correlation data and assumptions need to be made at certain times. The most accessible data are compiled by the credit ratings agencies such as Moody's and Standard & Poor's.

We now consider the variance–covariance methodology used for measuring credit VaR.

VARIANCE–COVARIANCE CREDIT VaR

The parametric credit VaR approach was first introduced by JPMorgan in 1994. We describe it here.

Methodology

There are two main frameworks in use for quantifying credit risk. One approach considers only two scenarios: default and no default. This model constructs a binomial tree of default versus no default outcomes until maturity. This approach is shown in Figure 3.10.

The other approach holds that risk is the observed volatility of corporate bond values within each credit rating category, maturity band and industry grouping. The idea is to track a benchmark corporate bond (or index) that has observable pricing. The resulting estimate of volatility of value is then used as a proxy for the volatility of the exposure (or portfolio) under analysis.

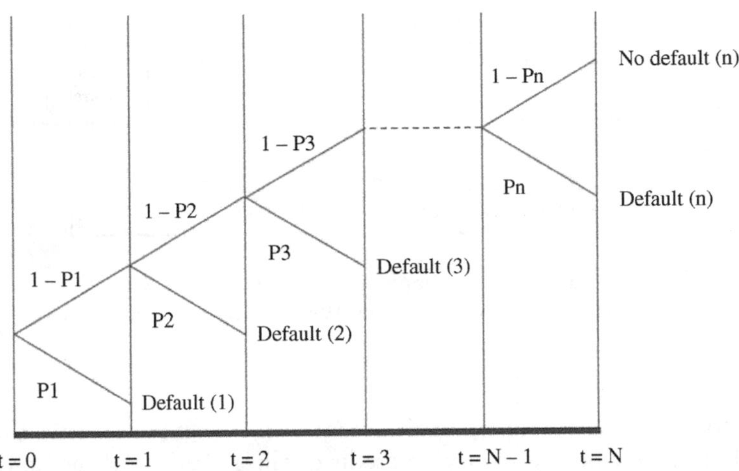

FIGURE 3.10 A binomial model of credit risk.

The variance–covariance methodology sits between these two approaches. The model estimates portfolio VaR at the risk horizon due to credit events that include upgrades and downgrades, rather than just defaults. Thus it adopts a mark-to-market framework. As shown in Figure 3.11, bonds within each credit rating category have volatility of

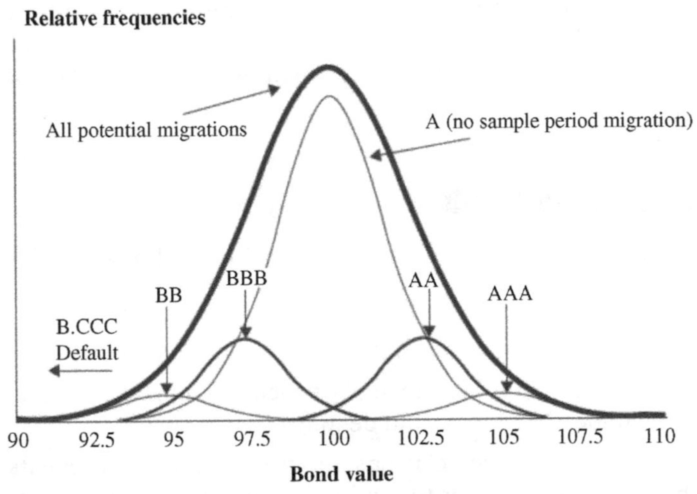

FIGURE 3.11 Distribution of credit returns by rating.

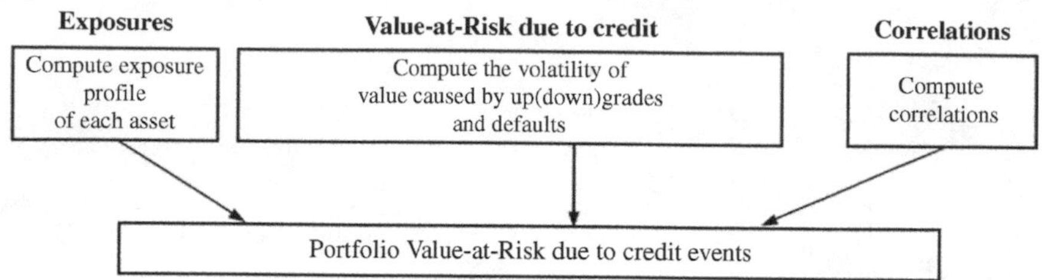

FIGURE 3.12 Analytics road map for variance-covariance credit VaR.
Source: JPMorgan; *RiskMetrics*™ technical document, 1997. Reproduced with permission.

value due to day-to-day credit spread fluctuations. The exhibit shows the loss distributions for bonds of varying credit quality. Credit VaR assumes that all credit migrations have been realised, weighting each by a migration likelihood.

Time Horizon

Credit VaR typically adopts a 1-year risk horizon. The justification given is that this is because much academic and credit agency data are stated on an annual basis. This is a convenient convention similar to the use of annualised interest rates in the money markets. The risk horizon is adequate as long as it is not shorter than the time required to perform risk-mitigating actions. Users must therefore adopt their risk management and risk adjustments procedures with this in mind.

The steps involved in VaR measurement methodology are shown in Figure 3.12.

Calculating the Credit VaR

The calculation methodology assesses individual and portfolio credit VaR in three steps:

Step 1 it establishes the exposure profile of each obligor in a portfolio.

Step 2 it computes the volatility in value of each instrument caused by possible upgrade, downgrade and default.

Step 3 taking into account correlations between each of these events, it combines the volatility of the individual instruments to give an aggregate portfolio risk.

Step 1 Exposure Profiles

This incorporates the exposure of instruments such as bonds (fixed or floating-rate), as well as other loan commitments and off-balance sheet instruments such as swaps. The exposure is stated on an equivalent basis for all products.

Step 2 Volatility of Each Exposure from Up/Downgrades and Defaults

The levels of likelihood are attributed to each possible credit event of upgrade, downgrade and default. The probability that an obligor will change over a given time horizon to another credit rating is calculated. Each change (migration) results in an estimated change in value (derived from credit spread data and in default, recovery rates). Each value outcome is weighted by its likelihood to create a distribution of value across each credit state, from which each asset's expected value and volatility (standard deviation) of value are calculated.

There are three steps to calculating the volatility of value in a credit exposure:

- the senior unsecured credit rating of the issuer determines the chance of either defaulting or migrating to any other possible credit quality state in the risk horizon;
- revaluation at the risk time horizon can be by either (i) the seniority of the exposure, which determines its recovery rate in case of default or (ii) the forward zero-coupon curve (spot curve) for each credit rating category, which determines the revaluation upon up/downgrade;
- the probabilities from the two steps above are combined to calculate volatility of value due to credit quality changes.

Step 3 Correlations

Individual value distributions for each exposure are combined to give a portfolio result. To calculate the portfolio value from the volatility of individual asset values requires estimates of correlation in credit quality changes. This is because of frequent difficulty in obtaining directly observed credit quality correlations from historical data.

Our discussion of credit risk, and the VaR methodology for measuring such risk, is useful background for an understanding of the way credit risk exposure might be managed.

CREDIT LIMIT SETTING AND RATIONALE

For many commercial banks, and certainly all smaller banks, on a day-to-day basis credit limits and credit exposure are perhaps the most important aspects of the risk management process, given that such institutions should not be running much market risk. The latter is more of an issue for larger banks, multinational banks and market-making banks. While liquidity risk management is universal to all banks, maintaining effective credit risk origination standards and limit setting policy is essential for the vast majority of banks that do not carry material market risk. Smaller banks are less likely to be rescued by the central bank or the government if they fail, because they would not be deemed "systemically important", so a prudent credit risk management culture and through-the-cycle macro-prudential procedures are of primary importance for such firms.[7]

We discuss now business best practice principles of credit limit setting, and the loan origination process.

Credit Limit Principles

The point of credit risk limits is to set an upper bound to the loss that can be suffered by a bank at any one time.

The basic principles of credit limit setting are universal for every bank, and follow the essential requirements of prudence and concentration. In other words, an element of diversification in the loan portfolio is necessary, although at all times the bank should practise the basic principle of "know your risk". In other words, diversity as an end in itself is not recommended good practice; a bank should diversify only into sectors that it has a thorough understanding of, and in which it has some competitive advantage or valuable skill base.

In standard textbooks on finance and banking, one will read that the capital base drives the limit-setting process. Essentially, what this is saying in practice is that one takes the amount of capital available, and allocates it

7 In the US alone, according to the FDIC website, there were 25 bank failures in 2008, 140 in 2009 and 157 in 2010. This compares to just 11 bank failures during the period 2003–2007. With the exception of Washington Mutual Bank, these failing banks did not make the mainstream media headlines, due to their small size and domestic business base; nevertheless, a failed bank in any jurisdiction and of any size is a gross failure of management and corporate governance. Regulatory authorities should have an objective of treating all banks as systemically important, as we suggest in Chapters 17–18.

as per credit limit buckets for each of the businesses. Actually, as we suggest in Chapter 16, the proper and intellectually robust way to do this is the other way around: the bank should determine its strategy and business model, and prepare budgets based on risk exposure that it considers it has the expertise to manage. This process then drives a level of capital, and regulatory capital, that the bank should then set up. Once this amount is known and achieved, it can then be allocated to specific business lines as lower level credit limits by geography, industry, product and so on.

The essential principles governing limit setting include the following:

- All single exposures should be sufficiently sized such that a complete default, with 0% recovery, can be contained within the existing capital base and does not endanger the bank as a going concern. In other words, after the loss the bank will still be within its regulatory capital limits.
- The loan portfolio should be diversified by industrial sector, geography and product line, but *at all times* within the knowledge base and expertise of the bank.
- A minimum internal (and if desired, external) rating criteria is established. Below this the bank will not lend. For example, this may be "investment-grade rated only" or "no lending to entities with an internal rating equivalent to BB/Ba2".
- Not lending to obligors any amount that as a result over-extends the borrower and creates a situation in which repayment is at put at risk. This requires that the "know-your-risk" dictum be applied equally to understanding one's customers' risks. This should be assessed via an analysis of the borrower's financial indicators, including leverage ratio, debt service coverage ratio and so on.
- Limit categories are set to avoid concentration, and also according to borrower rating.

As part of a transaction origination process, reviewers must consider what "ancillary business" can be generated from the same borrower. The bank must set a policy that dictates how much this ancillary business drives the origination process, whether the lending business can be a "loss leader" to an extent, or must be creating sufficient shareholder value-added in its own right.

Credit Limit Setting

The process of setting credit limits is very important to all banks, and vanilla commercial banks in particular, insofar as credit risk exposure generates the highest losses for such institutions. It should follow prudent and robust policy, and be run according to economic cycle-proof principles to avoid over-extension during a bull market, when loan origination standards are relaxed. Credit limits are set for a range of criteria, which are deliberately set as overlapping so as to ensure that all the various different category of risk exposure is captured.

Macro-level credit limits are set per individual obligor, originated within the business lines, but approved by the Executive Credit Committee, with secondary approval from the bank's ALCO. If necessary, if the size of a transaction dictates it, further approval may be needed by the Executive Management Committee (ExCo) and the Board itself (see Chapter 18). The level of capital allocation required for a particular limit application determines how far up the governance structure it needs to go. Formal limits on capital allocation are therefore set at ExCo approval level.

The limit-setting process produces overlapping limits, by design. Limits will be set in the following categories:

- *Individual obligor*: this is further split into limit by product class; a limit globally and a limit locally. Sub-limits do not necessarily aggregate to the overall obligor limit: this is to prevent excess exposure in one product class or geographical region. Sub-limits are also set per currency. At all times, the obligor exposure cannot exceed its overall limit.
- *Geographical region*: this is further split into country limits and individual regions within a country.
- *The industrial sector*: this is split by sector, and again individual sub-limits may not aggregate to the overall limit. They are placed to prevent over-exposure in specific sectors.

As no individual limit can be breached, any new capital-using transaction must fit into the capacity allowed by all three limit categories.

A limit excess is a serious breach of management governance and must be reported to ALCO (and if necessary ExCo) for corrective action. This can be one or more of the following: (i) cease further business with the specific obligor; (ii) transferring some of the exposure, either with secondary market sale, securitisation, or hedging with credit derivatives; (iii) increasing the limit; (iv) transferring some capacity from another part of the business and/or another obligor; and (v) if possible, undertaking assets disposal.

LOAN ORIGINATION PROCESS STANDARDS

The loan origination process differs across banks. The detail of an individual specific process is not of tremendous interest to us. What is important is that this origination process adheres to basic principles of prudence, and that these are controlled and managed to ensure they are "through-the-cycle". That is, a reduction in standards, or a relaxation of them during a period of economic growth, is something that should require board approval if it is not to be explicitly avoided. Enlarging the balance sheet during the bull market is a risky strategy, because it is during this time that standards are lowered and low-quality and/or under-priced assets are put on the book.

An example of this occurred at the failed UK banks, Northern Rock and Bradford & Bingley, which originated large numbers of 100% loan-to-value (LTV) and 125 LTV mortgages, as well as risky buy-to-let mortgages. The failed bank HBOS (in common with many banks at the time) operated a loan origination process for retail and corporate loans that delegated the approval decision to a "black box" computer model, which rated all applications in a tick-box process that assigned a credit score and then approved the loan on that basis. This is understandable for high-volume business models, but sacrifices a large element of "know your customer" that is essential to a robust approval process.

The essential guidelines for a through-the-cycle asset origination standards process include:

- *Know your customer*: for one-off and/or big-ticket transactions this principle is straightforward to apply. It is more difficult for large volume business, particularly when the bank has adopted a "black box" system in which the approval is granted by a model (the applicant's details are input to the system and the system generates the approval. No loan officer or credit expert reviews the application). This is common practice for retail business such as credit card and mortgage applications, especially for business conducted over the telephone or internet. The danger is that, in a commoditised and competitive market, origination standards are lowered and the bank creates a pool of lower quality assets, the obligors for which it is not familiar with and whose financial strength it cannot be certain of.[8] This was an acute problem for retail mortgage banks in the US, UK, Ireland and Spain (among other countries) during 2002–2007, all of whom experienced a housing boom and bust in this period. Business best-practice dictates that for all origination business, banks must know their customer base at all times (see below on mortgages). This means that the "black box" application

8 The practice of originating "self-certified" loans also generates risk that is difficult to quantify accurately, because ultimately the bank will have no real idea of the obligor's true income, and therefore its ability to service and repay the loan satisfactorily.

process must be supplemented with a review by an experienced loan analyst.

- *Loan security*: the collateral acceptable for a loan should at all times be of sufficient liquidity, as well as value. The bank must be able to realise the collateral if the obligor defaults. Genuine liquidity through all market conditions is restricted to sovereign liabilities only, so to cover for the loss of liquidity in other types of collateral, the bank must ensure sufficient margin over and above the loan value.
- *Sub-prime lending restrictions*: assets against which no collateral is taken, or insufficient collateral, should at all times be subject to restrictions and severe limits because these types of assets are the first to experience default when the economy experiences a downturn. Mortgages that are not covered by sufficient collateral, such as 100 LTV or 125 LTV loans where the advance is greater than the value of the security, and other sub-prime mortgages or higher risk mortgages such as "self-certified" loans, should similarly be subject to restriction.

With the exception of loans that originated at the top of an economic cycle (when market levels are at their historic highs) that is followed by the economy falling into recession, loan defaults typically do not occur at the start or end of a loan's term. The exception is right at the end of the bull market, when bank loan origination standards have been lowered and asset prices (credit spreads) are at their most undervalued, when banks write much low-quality business. Leaving that aside, the most common time of default is generally between 45–55 months after the loan start date. This means that default statistics are very much in a lag to the actual state of the economy. Given historical default rates, which banks use to assist them in setting their credit limits, there is a danger that business continues to be written, at lower credit standards, at precisely the time when the bank should be undertaking less risky business. This is why the basic principles we summarise above should be observed at all times, and made a guiding light for a bank's Executive Credit Committee.

EXAMPLE 3.1 CREDIT SCORING PROCESSES

The credit approval process for high-volume business often follows credit scoring methods such as the "FICO" score. While grounded in statistical logic, the danger of relying overmuch (or exclusively) on such techniques when conducting the credit approval process is that the bank becomes remote from its customer. This erodes the "know-your-risk" principle.

An individual's credit score is a number based on the information in the applicant's credit file, which implies a probability of the borrower repaying a new loan. The higher the score, the less risk (in theory) the borrower represents. The score not only determines whether a loan is granted, it also drives the interest rate paid on the loan. Lower score borrowers pay a higher rate. A commonly used credit score is the "FICO" score, developed by the Fair Isaac Corporation in the 1950s. FICO scores range from 350 to 850, and are based on a number of factors, including payment history, account balances, types of credit used, length of credit history and new credit applications. Note that certain factors that one might expect to influence the FICO score in fact do not, such as the applicant's income, location of residence, age, occupation or employment history. Rather, the credit score changes as an individual changes the way that she/he handles bills and credit accounts. The length of an individual's credit history, how long the loan accounts have been open and how long it has been since they have seen activity, are also influential.

Although bank "black boxes" that are used to process mortgage and credit card applications do take income and occupation into account, they also build credit scores on a similar basis to the FICO score. On its own, this is insufficient risk management procedure, particularly during a bull market.

Credit Process

Banks generally operate one of two types of approval process: (i) via a credit committee and (ii) via delegated authority from the credit committee to a business line head. The committee process is designed to ensure that there is proper scrutiny of any transaction that commits the bank's capital. The sponsor bringing the transaction to committee is the front office business line, and the committee will approve or decline based on the risk-reward profile of the transaction.

Procedure (ii) is common for high-volume business, for which the committee process, because it is time consuming, would not be practical. As we noted above, there is a risk that the "know your risk" principle can be diluted, particularly in a competitive environment where a bank is trying to build volume. Given this risk, "market share" should not be a performance indicator, or target, for a bank's business line. Rather, performance should be measured only via the amount of genuine shareholder value-added that the business generates.

Capital Allocation Process

We illustrate now a business best practice procedure for obtaining approval for a credit-risky transaction that generates a risk-weighted capital exposure for a bank. Figure 3.13 is an example of a "Capital Request Form" for a corporate loan, as might be used at a commercial bank. This would be completed and submitted by the business line, for example Corporate Banking, to the ExCo and ALCO. At large banks, the approval authority may be delegated down to the credit committee in the business line itself, with large-size transactions or new business-type transactions being reserved for the Executive Credit Committee (ECC) and ALCO. The purpose of this form is to facilitate the discussion of the transaction in the capital allocation approval process; it outlines how much capital is required, the expected RoC and the shareholder value-added (SVA) (given no default). The expected ancillary business is also quantified.

The approval process should consider not only the deal economics, which is all that the form at Figure 3.13 describes, but also that it fits within the bank's overall strategy and business model. This is dictated by the bank's policy guidelines on strategy, capital management and risk-reward culture.

The key risk element in this process is that (i) anticipated "ancillary business" arising from a transaction should be assessed against what is actually received from the client and (ii) the underlying transaction should be profitable in line with business line RoC and RoA targets *in its own right*. In other words, undertaking loss-making transactions because they are expected to generate subsequent profitable business is a tenuous strategy at best.

Collateral Enablement

Bank funding models are likely to move towards a greater share of secured funding, which dictates that as much as possible of the assets of the balance sheet be either repo-able or securitisable. As part of the capital request and loan origination process, banks should adopt a "collateral enablement" template. This is a checklist that enables the bank to determine how straightforward it is to later securitise or secure-fund the asset that is being originated. All else being equal, the bank would seek to originate assets that lend themselves better to being funded in this respect.

An example of an asset origination template for collateral enablement purposes would include:

- Legal framework: is the asset written under English law, US law or in another jurisdiction? Some legal jurisdictions are more user-friendly to

	Bank's role								
	Relationship manager				[Sole lender/Syndicate/Debt capital market/etc.]				
	Approval								
Facility	**Currency/ Notional**	**Tenor**	**Internal rating**	**Recovery rate**	**Proposed spread**	**Risk weighting**	**Capital allocated ($m)**	**Internal funding cost**	**SVA ($m)**
Term loan	USD 500 m	5 year	5	40%	200 bps	50%	25	80 bps	6
Amortising loan									
Revolving credit facility									
Liquidity line									
Committed lending facility									
								Interest income	6
Ancillary business expected	**Potential revenue ($m)**	**Partner approval**						Fees	0.5
FX	0.1								
FX hedge									
Interest rate hedge	0.5								
Underwriting									
Syndicate									
M&A									
Other									
	0.6							→	0.6
								Transaction economics	7.1
								RoC	

FIGURE 3.13 Capital allocation process, new asset origination application form.

the lender for securitisation and contract enforcement purposes than others. In addition, legal review costs may be higher.

- Transferability: how straightforward is it to transfer the loan to another legal entity, for example, another bank or as part of a true sale in securitisation? If the asset is a revolving facility, are there any difficulties in transferring? Are there any stated restrictions on transfer?
- Disclosure: what is the minimum information that must be disclosed to third parties, and to the obligor on transfer?
- Currencies of drawdown: loan facilities that grant the borrower to draw down in multiple currencies present more issues on securitisation than single currency loans.
- Vanilla or exotic: vanilla loans of fixed coupon or fixed spread and fixed maturity are more straightforward to securitise than loans that incorporate exotic features such as interest rate options, prepayment facilities and so on.

In practice a bank will seek to meet the requirements of customers that it wishes to service, and who fit its strategic objectives. This is a higher priority than collateral enablement; if it is not then it should re-define its strategy. Within this objective however, applying collateral enablement principles to the asset origination process is sensible practice.

SHAREHOLDER VALUE ADDED AND CREDIT STRATEGY

In the modern era of finance, which we can take to be the period after the collapse of the Bretton Woods fixed exchange rate mechanism, and brought on by the US and UK easing currency restrictions at the start of the 1980s, bank lending business has provided a decreasing share of total bank income. In many cases, it may well be the business line with the lowest level of return on capital employed (ROCE). Under these circumstances it is important to exercise discipline in the loan origination process to ensure that the business generates genuine SVA, and that the ROCE generated is above the bank's cost of capital. It is common for banks to treat the lending business as a "loss leader", necessary to create customer relationships that then generate higher value transaction business. If this is part of the bank's strategy, it is important that the aggregate SVA produced from any particular client be worthwhile, from an ROCE perspective. If it is not, the bank should strongly consider withdrawing from that business or the specific client. A common error made by banks is to mistake an artificial funding profit for genuine SVA; one reason this might happen is if the bank is merely undertaking a "funding arbitrage" and viewing this profit as SVA. Funding arbitrage was the business model employed by a form of structured credit product known as a structured investment vehicle (SIV). SIVs bought long-dated assets such as bonds or loans, and funded them with short-dated liabilities in the form of CP. When the CP market temporarily disappeared in the crisis of August 2007, many SIVs were found to be unsustainable. Bank lending businesses that operate as a form of SIV may be in danger of writing business that is not only at higher risk in a liquidity squeeze, it may also not be generating true SVA, but merely reporting an artificial funding profit made possible by a positive-sloping yield curve.

Business lines originating loans should aim for uniformity in the loan origination, execution and documentation process. This will facilitate a more straightforward use of the loans as collateral in a repo, securitisation or other such liquidity and/or capital relief transaction. A balance sheet that is comprised of loans of widely heterogeneous format will be harder to manage, for collateral and balance sheet purposes, at a later date. For example, if there are 100 assets on a balance sheet and they are all of the same type, such as bullet loans with no fluctuating revolving facility and all documented under one legal jurisdiction, that will make them much more straightforward to manage than a balance sheet of 100 loans that was originated in 10 different country locations, under 10 different legal jurisdictions and with monthly variations in notional size. In the latter case, for instance, each loan document would have to be reviewed by a lawyer with an expertise in the particular jurisdiction, a process that would add considerably to a securitisation transaction's cost and timescale.

BIBLIOGRAPHY

Choudhry, M. (1999), *An Introduction to Value-at-Risk*, London: Securities Institute (Services) Publishing.

Duffie, D. and Singleton, K. (2003), *Credit Risk*, Princeton: Princeton University Press.

Kimber, A. (2004), *Credit Risk: From Transaction to Portfolio Management*, Oxford: Elsevier.

Merton, R. (1974), "On the Pricing of Corporate Debt: The Risky Structure of Interest Rates", *Journal of Finance*, 29, pp. 449–70.

CHAPTER 4

A Primer on Securitisation

Securitisation has been an important technique in bank ALM from the 1990s onwards. Its use was curtailed significantly as a result of the financial crash of 2007–2009; however, as a balance sheet management tool it retains its value and importance in ALM for banks. For this reason we include a chapter on this subject in Part I of this book. We introduce the basic concepts of securitisation and look at the motivation behind its use, as well as its economic impact. We also illustrate the process with an hypothetical case study.

THE CONCEPT OF SECURITISATION

Securitisation is a well-established practice in the global debt capital markets. It refers to the sale of assets, which generate cash flows from the institution that owns the assets, to another company that has been specifically set up for the purpose of acquiring them, and the issuing of notes by this second company to fund the asset purchase. These notes are collateralised by the cash flows from the original assets. The technique was introduced initially as a means of funding for US mortgage banks. Subsequently, the technique was applied to other assets such as credit card payments and equipment leasing receivables. It has also been employed as part of bank ALM, as a means of managing balance sheet risk.

Securitisation allows institutions such as banks and corporations to convert assets that are not readily marketable – such as residential mortgages or car loans – into rated securities that are tradeable in the secondary market. The investors that buy these securities gain exposure to these types of original assets that they would not otherwise have access to. The technique was first introduced by mortgage banks in the US during the 1970s. The synthetic securitisation market was established more recently, dating from 1997. The key difference between cash and synthetic securitisation is that in the former the assets in question are actually sold to a separate legal company, known as a special purpose vehicle (SPV)[1]. This does not occur in a synthetic transaction, as we shall see.

Sundaresan (1997, p. 359) defines securitisation as:

> *. . . a framework in which some illiquid assets of a corporation or a financial institution are transformed into a package of securities backed by these assets, through careful packaging, credit enhancements, liquidity enhancements and structuring.*

The process of securitisation creates *asset-backed bonds*. These are debt instruments that have been created from a package of loan assets on which interest is payable, usually on a floating basis. Techniques employed by investment banks today enable an entity to create a bond structure from virtually any type of cash flow. Assets that have been securitised include loans such as residential mortgages, car loans and credit card loans. The interest payments on the original loans form the cash flows used to service the new bond issue. Traditionally, mortgage-backed bonds are grouped in their own right as MBS, while all other securitisation issues are known as asset-backed bonds or ABS.

MARKET PARTICIPANTS

The securitisation process involves a number of participants. In the first instance there is the originator, the firm whose assets are being securitised. The most common process involves an issuer acquiring the assets from the originator. The issuer is usually a company that has been specially set up for the purpose of the securitisation and is the SPV, and is usually domiciled offshore. The creation of an SPV ensures that the underlying asset pool is held separate from the other assets of the originator. This is done so that in the event that the originator is declared bankrupt or insolvent, the impact on the original assets is minimised.

This last is often the responsibility of a trustee. The issuer trustee is responsible for looking after the interests of bondholders. Its roles include:

- representing the interests of investors (note holders);
- monitoring the transaction and issuer to see if any violation of the deal covenants has occurred;

1 An SPV is also referred to as a special purpose entity (SPE) or a special purpose company (SPC). See Example 4.1 in this chapter for more information on SPVs.

- enforcing the rights of the note holders in the event of bankruptcy.

The security trustee is responsible for undertaking the following duties:

- holding the security interest in the underlying collateral pool;
- liaising with the manager of the underlying collateral;
- acting under the direction of the note trustee in the event of default.

By holding the assets within an SPV framework, defined in formal legal terms, the financial status and credit rating of the originator becomes almost

EXAMPLE 4.1 SPECIAL PURPOSE VEHICLES

The key to undertaking securitisation is the special purpose vehicle or SPV. They are also known as SPEs or SPCs. They are distinct legal entities that act as the "company" through which a securitisation is undertaken. They act as a form of repackaging vehicle, used to transform, convert or create risk structures that can be accessed by a wider range of investors. Essentially, they are a legal entity to which assets such as mortgages, credit card debt or synthetic assets such as credit derivatives are transferred, and from which the original credit risk/reward profile is transformed and made available to investors. An originator will use SPVs to increase liquidity and to make liquid risks that cannot otherwise be traded in any secondary market.

An SPV is a legal trust or company that is not, for legal purposes, linked in any way to the originator of the securitisation. As such it is *bankruptcy-remote* from the sponsor. If the sponsor suffers financial difficulty or is declared bankrupt, this will have no impact on the SPV, and hence no impact on the liabilities of the SPV with respect to the notes it has issued in the market. Investors have credit risk exposure only to the underlying assets of the SPV.

To secure favourable tax treatment, SPVs are frequently incorporated in offshore business centres such as Jersey or the Cayman Islands, or in jurisdictions that have set up SPV-friendly business legislation such as Ireland or The Netherlands. The choice of location for an SPV is dependant on a number of factors as well as taxation concerns, such as operating costs, legal requirements and investor considerations.[2]

(*continued*)

2 For instance, investors in some European Union countries will only consider notes issued by an SPV based in the EU, so that would exclude many offshore centres.

The key issue is taxation, however; the sponsor will want all cash flows both received and paid out by the SPV to attract low or no tax. This includes withholding tax on coupons paid on notes issued by the SPV. In other words, the SPV must be set up as a tax-neutral entity.

SPVs are used in a wide variety of applications. For example, one established application is in conjunction with an asset swap, when an SPV is used to securitise the asset swap so that it becomes available to investors who cannot otherwise access it. Essentially, the SPV will purchase the asset swap and then issue notes to the investor, who gains an exposure to the original asset swap albeit indirectly. This is illustrated in Figure 4.1.

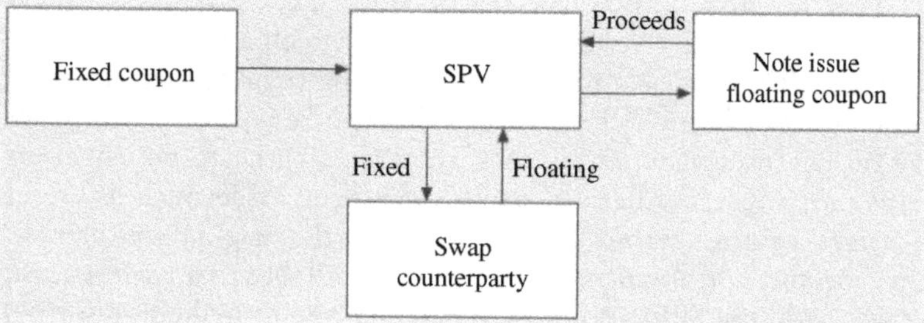

FIGURE 4.1 Asset swap package securitised and economic effect sold on by SPV.

The most common purpose for which an SPV is set up is a cash flow securitisation, in which the sponsoring company sells assets off its balance sheet to the SPV, which funds the purchase of these assets by issuing notes. The revenues received by the assets are used to pay the liability of the issued overlying notes. Of course, the process itself has transformed previously untradeable assets such as residential mortgages into tradeable ones, and in theory created more room on the balance sheet of the originator.

SPVs are also used for the following applications:

- converting the currency of underlying assets into another currency more acceptable to investors, by means of a currency swap;
- issuing credit-linked notes (CLNs). Unlike CLNs issued by originators direct, CLNs issued by SPVs do not have any credit-linkage to the sponsoring entity. The note is linked instead

to assets that have been sold to the SPV, and its performance is dependent on the performance of these assets. Another type of credit-linked SPV is when investors select the assets that (effectively) collateralise the CLN and are held by the SPV. The SPV then sells credit protection to a swap counterparty, and on occurrence of a credit event the underlying securities are sold and used to pay the SPV liabilities. Yet another type of SPV-issued CLN references a third-party bond or bonds that are not used by the SPV, but to which its returns are linked;

- transforming illiquid assets into liquid ones. Certain assets such as trade receivables, equipment lease receivables or even more exotic assets such as museum entry-fee receipts are not tradeable in any form, but can be made into tradeable notes via securitisation.

For legal purposes an SPV is categorised as either a Company or a Trust. The latter is more common in the US market, and its interests are represented by a Trustee, which is usually the Agency services department of a bank such as the Bank of New York or Deutsche Bank, or a specialist Trust company such as Wilmington Trust. In the Euromarkets, SPVs are often incorporated as companies instead of trusts.

After the Enron episode, when SPVs were used to assist fraudulent activity, accounting rules were changed to the extent that banking groups must now consolidate all legal entities into one set of accounts. Under the US accounting rule, Fin 46 R, banks that report their result under US Generally Accepted Accounting Principles (GAAP) are required to consolidate SPVs. However, it is possible to avoid the consolidation requirement if the originator can show that the first-loss piece in a transaction has been sold or otherwise transferred to a genuine third-party. This is an incentive for banks to not retain the equity tranche in a securitisation; there are also advantages to so doing under the Basel II regime (see Chapter 2).

The SPV-consolidation issue is also relevant in Europe, where it is required under International Accounting Standards (ISA) rules. Again, in some cases consolidation of an SPV into the group accounts may be avoidable if the first-loss piece in the deal is held by a third party.

irrelevant to the bondholders. In legal terms, the assets held in the SPV are bankruptcy-remote.

REASONS FOR UNDERTAKING SECURITISATION

The driving force behind securitisation has been the need for banks to realise value from the assets on their balance sheet. Typically, these assets are residential mortgages, corporate loans, and retail loans such as credit card debt. Let us consider the factors that might lead a financial institution to securitise part of its balance sheet. These might be the following:

- if revenues received from assets remain roughly unchanged, but the size of assets has decreased, there will be an increase in the return on equity ratio;
- where the level of capital required to support the balance sheet will be reduced, which again can lead to cost savings or allow the institution to allocate the capital to other, perhaps more profitable, business;
- to obtain cheaper funding: frequently the interest payable on ABSs is considerably below the level receivable on the underlying loans. This creates a cash surplus for the originating entity.

In other words, the main reasons that a bank securitises part of its balance sheet is for one or all of the following reasons, all of which form part of bank ALM to one degree or another:

- funding the assets it owns;
- balance sheet capital management;
- risk management and credit-risk transfer.

We consider each of these in turn.

Funding

Banks can use securitisation to: (i) support rapid asset growth; (ii) diversify their funding mix, and reduce the cost of funding; and (iii) reduce maturity mismatches.

The market for ABS is large, with an estimated size of USD1,000 billion invested in ABS issues worldwide annually, of which over USD200 billion is in the European market alone.[3] Access to this source of funding enables a bank to grow its loan books at a faster pace than

3 Sources include Bloomberg and investment bank research reports.

if they were reliant on traditional funding sources alone. For example, in the UK a former building society turned bank, Northern Rock plc, employed securitisation to back its growing share of the UK residential mortgage market. As we now know of course, ultimately that was a flawed, and failed, strategy that contributed to its demise. This does not mean that securitisation is not an effective funding tool, rather that it must be employed sensibly.

Securitising assets also allows a bank to diversify its funding mix. Banks generally do not wish to be reliant on a single or just a few sources of funding, as this can be high risk in times of market difficulty. Banks aim to optimise their funding between a mix of retail, inter-bank and wholesale sources. Securitisation has a role to play in this mix. It also enables a bank to reduce its funding costs. This is because the securitisation process de-links the credit rating of the originating institution from the credit rating of the issued notes. Typically, most of the notes issued by SPVs will be higher rated than the bonds issued directly by the originating bank itself. While the liquidity of the secondary market in ABS is frequently lower than that of the corporate bond market, and this adds to the yield payable by an ABS, it is frequently the case that the cost to the originating institution of issuing debt is still lower in the ABS market because of the latter's higher rating. Finally, there is the issue of maturity mismatches. The business of banking is one of maturity mismatch, since a bank often funds long-term assets such as residential mortgages, with short-term asset liabilities such as bank deposits or inter-bank funding. This mismatch can be reduced via securitisation, as the originating bank receives funding from the sale of the assets, and the economic maturity of the issued notes frequently matches that of the assets.

Balance Sheet Capital Management

Banks use securitisation to improve balance sheet capital management. This provides: (i) regulatory capital relief; (ii) economic capital relief; and (iii) diversified sources of capital.

As stipulated in BIS capital rules,[4] banks must maintain a minimum capital level for their assets, in relation to the risk of these assets. Under Basel I, for every $100 of risk-weighted assets, a bank must hold at least $8 of capital; however, the designation of each asset's risk weighting is restrictive. For example, with the exception of mortgages, customer loans are 100% risk-weighted regardless of the underlying rating of the borrower or

4 For further information on this see Chapter 2.

the quality of the security held. The anomalies that this raises were addressed in part by the Basel II rules. But the original Basel I rules were a driving force behind securitisation. As an SPV is not a bank, it is not subject to Basel rules and it therefore only needs such capital that is economically required by the nature of the assets they contain. This is not a set amount, but is significantly below the 8% level required by banks in all cases.

To the extent that securitisation provides regulatory capital relief, it can be thought of as an alternative to capital raising, compared with the traditional sources of Tier 1 (equity), preferred shares, and perpetual loan notes with step-up coupon features. By reducing the amount of capital that has to be used to support the asset pool, a bank can also improve its ROE value. This is received favourably by shareholders.

Risk Management

Once assets have been securitised, the credit risk exposure on these assets for the originating bank is reduced considerably and, if the bank does not retain a first-loss capital piece (the most junior of the issued notes), it is removed entirely. This is because assets have been sold to the SPV. Securitisation can also be used to remove non-performing assets from banks' balance sheets. This has the dual advantage of removing credit risk as well as freeing up regulatory capital. Further, there is a potential upside from securitising such assets; if any of them start performing again, or there is a recovery value obtained from defaulted assets, the originator will receive any surplus profit made by the SPV.

EXAMPLE 4.2A SUMMARY OF MOTIVATIONS FOR UNDERTAKING SECURITISATION

A summary of reasons why banks undertake securitisation is given below; many transactions fulfil a number of these objectives simultaneously:

- reducing and releasing regulatory capital;
- increasing RoE and RoA;
- increasing mortgage lending capacity, and growing asset books quicker than would be possible through the normal course of business;
- improving the bank's cost-to-income ratio;
- diversifying funding sources;
- increasing market share;

- preserving customer relationships with obligor clients whose assets are securitised;
- with regard to NPL assets:
  - transferring the risk associated with NPL assets
  - freeing up capital for employment elsewhere;
- providing positive research material for equity analysts.

In the post-crash environment of Basel III, not all of these benefits may be available unless specific structural requirements are met. However, the technique remains of value as a credit-risk transfer mechanism and as a funding diversification mechanism.

EXAMPLE 4.2B PARTIES TO THE DEAL

Rating Agencies

Rating agencies undertake due diligence on the transaction and assign the rating to the issued liabilities.

Lawyers

The originator, arranger and Trustee will assign external counsel to draft and review the legal documents that describe the deal.

Servicer/Administrator

The servicer administers the underlying assets in the portfolio. This includes monitoring of loans/bonds, collection of interest, enforcing late payments and producing statements. This role is often retained by the administrator, although third-party servicing firms also exist. The quality and reputation of the servicer is considered by the rating agencies when they assign the transaction rating.

Monoline Insurer

A specialist class of investor, known as a monoline insurer, may provide a "wrap", or guarantee of the ABS notes, in return for a fee.

(*continued*)

This acts as a credit enhancement to the transaction, particularly if a AAA rating for the senior note is dependent on the availability of a monoline insurance wrap. Monolines must understand their risk exposure.

Bank Counterparty Services

A transaction may require one, more or all of the following in its structure:

- interest-rate swap and/or FX swap, to hedge interest-rate and FX risk where there is a mismatch of rates and/or FX between the assets and liabilities of the vehicle;
- a committed liquidity line, to be drawn on to cover principal and interest payments in the event that the SPV cannot make them;
- guaranteed investment contract (GIC), to act as a reserve in which the proceeds of note issuance are invested.

These services are provided by a bank or banks, which act as a counterparty to the SPV.

Depositary

The depositary for a Eurobond issue is responsible for the safekeeping of securities. The common depositary is responsible for:

- representing Euroclear and Clearstream, and facilitating delivery-versus-payment of the primary market issue by collecting funds from the investors, taking possession of the temporary global note (which allows securities to be released to investors), and making a single payment of funds to the issuer;
- holding the temporary global note in safe custody, until it is exchanged for definitive notes or a permanent global note.

Trustee

An issuer may appoint a trustee to represent the interests of investors. In the event of default, the trustee is required to discharge its duties on behalf of bondholders. A trustee has a variety of powers and discretion, which are stated formally in the issue trust deed, and these include its duties in relation to the monitoring of covenants, and duties to bondholders.

Custodian

A custodian provides safekeeping services for securities belonging to a client. The client may be an institutional investor, such as a pension fund, that requires a portfolio of securities in many locations to be kept in secure custody on their behalf. As well as holding securities, the custodian usually manages corporate actions such as dividend payments.

EXAMPLE 4.2C ABS TERMINOLOGY

Master Trust

This is a legal structure that allows for repeat issuances of notes from the same vehicle, usually where the underlying asset pool that is being securitised is a revolving pool. This is common for credit card ABS and residential MBS transactions.

Static Pool

A pool of assets that does not change; that is, the assets in the pool at deal inception remain there to the end of the deal's life. There is no removal or addition of assets.

Soft Bullet

A bond that has an expected redemption date, but this date is not its formal legal maturity. If the bond does not redeem on this date, it is not an event of default.

Pass-through

Where the repayments of underlying assets are used to redeem overlying bonds as and when they occur. This creates uncertainty when determining weighted-average life (WAL) of the notes.

(*continued*)

Sequential Pay

A term referring to the process whereby senior bonds in the liability structure are redeemed fully, before amortisation of the junior note classes can begin.

Pro-rata

Senior and junior bonds are redeemed at the same time pro-rata. However, triggers are in place that kick in to revert to a sequential pay structure should the collateral pool performance deteriorate, such that it cannot support the liabilities in full.

THE PROCESS OF SECURITISATION

We look at the process of securitisation, the nature of the SPV structure and issues such as credit enhancements and the cash flow "waterfall".

The securitisation process involves a number of participants. In the first instance there is the *originator*, the firm whose assets are being securitised. The most common process involves an *issuer* acquiring the assets from the originator. The issuer is usually a company that has been specially set up for the purpose of the securitisation, which is the SPV (see Example 4.1).

By holding the assets within an SPV framework, defined in formal legal terms, the financial status and credit rating of the originator becomes almost irrelevant to the bondholders. The process of securitisation often involves *credit enhancements*, in which a third-party guarantee of credit quality is obtained, so that notes issued under the securitisation are often rated at investment grade and up to AAA-grade.

The process of structuring a securitisation deal ensures that the liability side of the SPV – the issued notes – carries a lower cost than the asset side of the SPV. This enables the originator to secure lower cost funding that it would not otherwise be able to obtain in the unsecured market. This is a benefit for institutions with lower credit ratings.

Figure 4.2 illustrates the process of securitisation in simple fashion.

Mechanics of Securitisation

Securitisation involves a "true sale" of the underlying assets from the balance sheet of the originator. This is why a separate legal entity, the SPV,

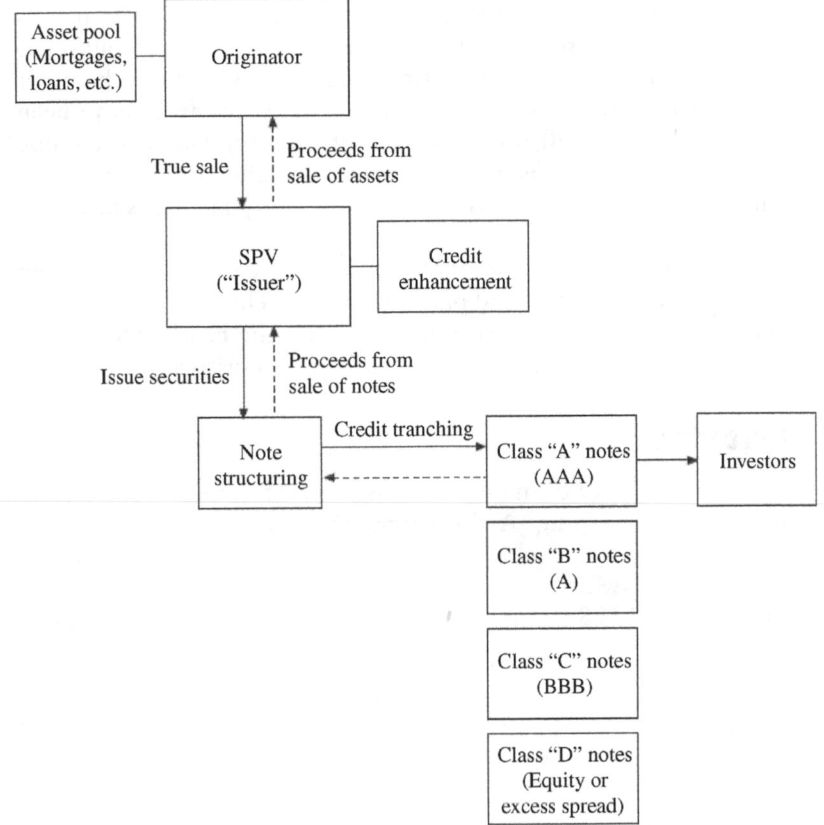

FIGURE 4.2 Securitisation structure.

is created to act as the issuer of the notes. The assets being securitised are sold on to the balance sheet of the SPV. The process involves:

- undertaking "due diligence" on the quality and future prospects of the assets;
- setting up the SPV and then effecting the transfer of assets to it;
- underwriting loans for credit quality and servicing;
- determining the notes' structure, including how many tranches are to be issued, in accordance with originator and investor requirements;
- rating notes by one or more credit-rating agencies;
- placing notes in the capital markets.

The sale of assets to the SPV needs to be undertaken so that it is recognised as a true legal transfer. The originator obtains legal counsel to advise it in such matters. The credit rating process considers the character and quality of the assets, and also whether any enhancements have been made to the assets that will raise their credit quality. This can include *over-collateralisation*, which is when the principal value of notes issued is lower than the principal value of assets, and a liquidity facility is provided by a bank.

A key consideration for the originator is the choice of the underwriting bank, which structures the deal and places the notes. The originator awards the mandate for its deal to an investment bank on the basis of fee levels, marketing ability and track record with assets being securitised.

SPV Structures

There are essentially two main securitisation structures: amortising (pass-through) and revolving. A third type, the master trust, is used by frequent issuers.

Amortising Structures

Amortising structures pay principal and interest to investors on a coupon-by-coupon basis throughout the life of the security, as illustrated in Figure 4.3. They are priced and traded based on expected maturity and WAL, which is the time-weighted period during which principal is outstanding. A WAL approach incorporates various prepayment assumptions, and any change in this prepayment speed will increase or decrease

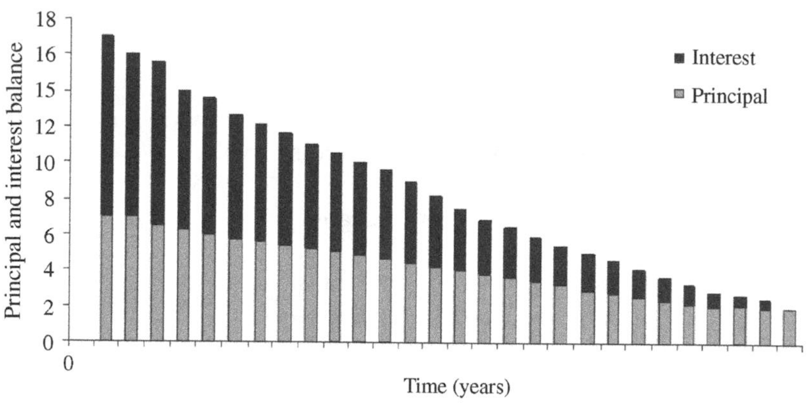

FIGURE 4.3 Amortising cash flow structure.

the rate at which principal is repaid to investors. Pass-through structures are commonly used in residential and commercial MBSs, and consumer loan ABS.

Revolving Structures

These structures revolve the principal of the assets; that is, during the revolving period, principal collections are used to purchase new receivables that fulfil the necessary criteria. The structure is used for short-dated assets with a relatively high prepayment speed, such as credit card debt and auto-loans. During the amortisation period, principal payments are paid to investors either in a series of equal instalments (*controlled amortisation*), or principal is "trapped" in a separate account until the expected maturity date and is then paid in a single lump sum to investors (soft bullet).

Master Trust

Frequent issuers under US and UK law use *master trust* structures, which allow multiple securitisations to be issued from the same SPV. Under such schemes, the originator transfers assets to the master trust SPV. Notes are then issued out of the asset pool based on investor demand. Master trusts are used by MBS and credit card ABS originators.

Cash Flow Waterfall

All securitisation structures incorporate a *cash waterfall* process, whereby all the cash that is generated by the asset pool is paid in order of payment priority. Only when senior obligations have been met can more junior obligations be paid. An independent third-party agent is usually employed to run "tests" on the vehicle to confirm that there is sufficient cash available to pay all obligations. If a test is failed, then the vehicle will start to pay off the notes, starting from the senior notes. The waterfall process is illustrated in Figure 4.4.

Impact on Balance Sheet

Figure 4.5 illustrates, by way of an hypothetical example, the effect of a securitisation transaction on the liability side of an originating bank's balance sheet. Following the process, selected assets have been removed from the balance sheet, although the originating bank will usually have retained the first-loss piece. With regard to the regulatory capital impact, this first-loss amount is deducted from the bank's total capital position. For example, assume a bank has $100 million of risk-weighted

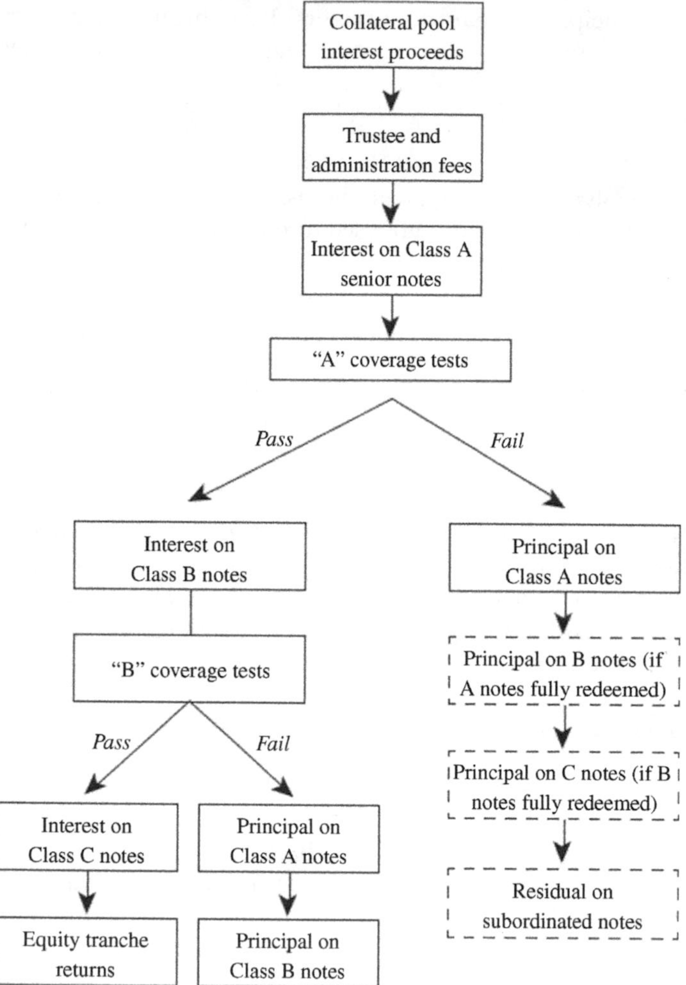

FIGURE 4.4 Cash flow waterfall (priority of payments).

assets and a target Basel ratio of 12%,[5] and it securitises all $100 million of these assets. It retains the first-loss tranche that forms 1.5% of the total issue. The remaining 98.5% will be sold onto the market. The bank will still have to set aside 1.5% of capital as a buffer against future losses, but it has been able to free itself of the remaining 10.5% of capital.

5 The minimum is 8%, but many banks prefer to set aside an amount in excess of this minimum required level.

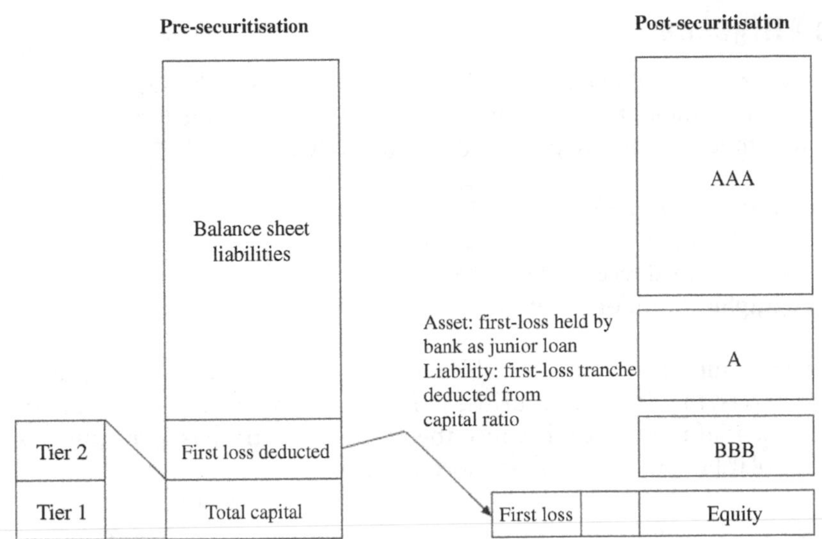

FIGURE 4.5 Regulatory capital impact of securitisation.

ILLUSTRATING THE PROCESS OF SECURITISATION: AIRWAYS NO. 1 LIMITED

To illustrate the process of securitisation, we consider an hypothetical airline ticket receivables transaction, originated by a fictitious company called ABC Airways plc and arranged by the equally fictitious XYZ Securities Limited. The following illustrates the kind of issues that are considered by the investment bank that is structuring the deal. Note that this example is a very esoteric transaction.

Originator: ABC Airways plc

Issuer: "Airways No. 1 Ltd"

Transaction: Ticket receivables airline future flow securitisation bonds, €200 m 3-tranche floating-rate notes, legal maturity 2010
Average life 4.1 years

Tranches: Class "A" note (AA), Libor plus [ ] bps[6]
Class "B" note (A), Libor plus [ ] bps
Class "E" note (BBB), Libor plus [ ] bps

Arranger: XYZ Securities plc

6 The price spread is determined during the marketing stage, when the notes are offered to investors during a "road show".

Due Diligence

XYZ Securities undertakes due diligence on the assets to be securitised. In this case, it examines the airline performance figures over the last five years, as well as modelling future projected figures, including:

- total passenger sales;
- total ticket sales;
- total credit card receivables;
- geographical split of ticket sales.

It is the future flow of receivables, in this case credit card purchases of airline tickets, that is being securitised. This is a higher risk asset class than, say, residential mortgages, because the airline industry has a tradition of greater volatility of earnings than mortgage banks.

Marketing Approach

The investment bank's syndication desk seeks to place the notes with institutional investors across Europe. The notes are first given an indicative pricing ahead of the issue, to gauge investor sentiment. The notes are "benchmarked" against recent issues with similar underlying asset classes, as well as the spread level in the unsecured market of comparable issuer names. This marketing phase can take several months.

Deal Structure

The deal structure is shown in Figure 4.6.

The process leading to the issue of notes is as follows:

- ABC Airways plc sells its present and all future flow credit card ticket receivables to an offshore SPV set up for this deal, incorporated as Airways No. 1 Ltd;
- the SPV issues notes in order to fund its purchase of the receivables;
- the SPV pledges its right to the receivables to a fiduciary agent, the Security Trustee, for the benefit of the bondholders;
- the Trustee accumulates funds as they are received by the SPV;
- the bondholders receive interest and principal payments, in the order of priority of the notes, on a quarterly basis.

In the event of default, the Trustee will act on behalf of the bondholders to safeguard their interests.

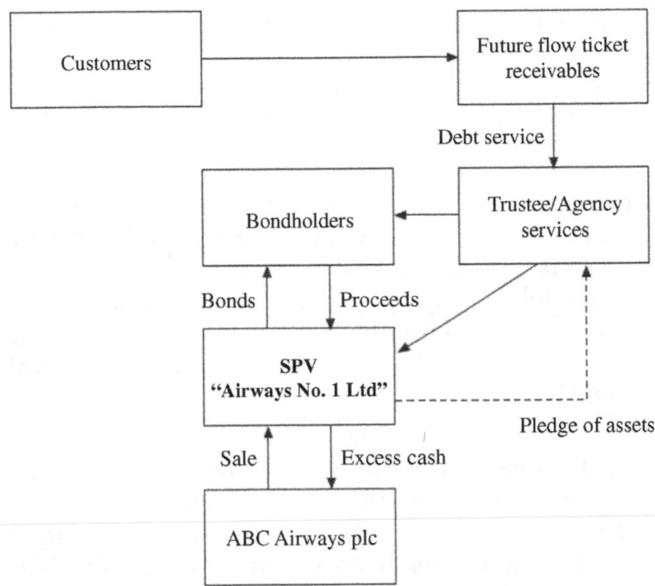

FIGURE 4.6 Airways No. 1 Limited deal structure.

Financial Guarantors

The investment bank decides whether or not an insurance company, known as a monoline insurer, should be approached to "wrap" the deal by providing a guarantee of backing for the SPV in the event of default. This insurance is provided in return for a fee.

Financial Modelling

XYZ Securities constructs a cash flow model to estimate the size of the issued notes. The model considers historical sales values, any seasonal factors in sales, credit card cash flows and so on. Certain assumptions are made when constructing the model; for example, growth projections, inflation levels and tax levels. The model considers a number of different scenarios, and also calculates the minimum asset coverage levels required to service the issued debt. A key indicator in the model is the debt service coverage ratio (DSCR). The more conservative the DSCR, the more comfort there is for investors in the notes. For a residential mortgage deal, this ratio may be approximately 2.5–3.0; however, for an airline ticket receivables deal, the DSCR is unlikely to be lower than 4.0. The model therefore calculates the amount of notes that can be issued against the assets, while maintaining the minimum DSCR.

Credit Rating

It is common for securitisation deals to be rated by one or more of the formal credit ratings agencies such as Moody's, Fitch or Standard & Poor's. A formal credit rating makes it easier for XYZ Securities to place the notes with investors. The methodology employed by the ratings agencies takes into account both qualitative and quantitative factors, and differs according to the asset class being securitised. The main issues in our hypothetical Airways No. 1 deal would be expected to include:

- corporate credit quality: these are risks associated with the originator, and are factors that affect its ability to continue operations, meet its financial obligations, and provide a stable foundation for generating future receivables. This might be analysed according to the following:
  - ABC Airways' historical financial performance, including its liquidity and debt structure;
  - its status within its domicile country; for example, whether or not it is state-owned;
  - the general economic conditions for industry and for airlines;
  - the historical record and current state of the airline; for instance, its safety record and age of its aeroplanes;
- the competition and industry trends: ABC Airways' market share, the competition on its network;
- regulatory issues, such as the need for ABC Airways to comply with forthcoming legislation that will impact its cash flows;
- legal structure of the SPV and transfer of assets;
- cash flow analysis.

Based on the findings of the ratings agency, the arranger may redesign some aspect of the deal structure so that the issued notes are rated at the required level.

Legal Documentation

All securitisation transactions, indeed all capital market transactions generally, are characterised by a set of legal documentation describing the deal. This is drafted by external counsel to the issuing party or originator.

The third parties involved in the deal, such as the Trustee and the underwriter, also engage external counsel to advise them.

The documentation involved in a bond issuance includes the following:

- Mandate letter: a legal document that confirms that the arranger to the deal has obtained a mandate from the issuer (which for securitisation transactions will be the SPV) to execute the transaction.
- Offering circular: this is also known as the Offering Memorandum or Prospectus, and contains a description of the conditions of the bond and the issuer. This is a detailed document, cast in legal language, and will describe the terms of the bond issue, the nature of the issuer, financial analysis, use of proceeds, tax considerations and other relevant details.
- Trust deed and agency agreement: describes the legal obligations of the issuer and functions of other third-party agents such as the bond paying agent.

There will be further legal documentation as required, for example, Listing Particulars if the bond being issued is listed on an exchange. For an introduction to legal documentation issues see Villar-Garcia and Patel (2004).

This is a selection of the key issues involved in the process of securitisation. Depending on investor sentiment, market conditions and legal issues, the process from inception to closure of the deal may take anything from 3 to 12 months or more. After the notes have been issued, the arranging bank no longer has anything to do with the issuc; however, the bonds themselves require a number of agency services for their remaining life until they mature or are paid off (see Procter and Leedham 2004). These agency services include the paying agent, cash manager and custodian.

CREDIT RATING CONSIDERATIONS

The originator in a securitisation will take a keen interest in the various factors that are of importance to the credit-rating agencies.[7] These factors

7 These are Standard & Poor's, Moody's and Fitch ratings. There are other agencies, but in the capital markets it is invariably that at least one, and often all three, of these agencies will be retained to provide the rating. Their dominance is illustrated by the fact that many fund managers, especially money market funds, will not invest in a security unless it has an S&P rating.

must be met if the transaction is to be rated at the required level, otherwise it will be difficult to place the liabilities. We consider some of the key issues here.

True Sale and Ownership of Assets

A prime consideration is that, in the event of default, the underlying assets are able to be liquidated and the proceeds used to repay note holders. The true sale of the assets to the SPV, which then ring-fences them, ensures this. However, it also means that the assets must be able to be sold to the SPV and transferred into its ownership. If the assets cannot be sold easily in the traditional manner, such as hedge fund assets, then a synthetic securitisation may be more appropriate. In such a deal, typically the assets are referenced synthetically and cash flows from them transferred via means of a swap such as a total return swap.

Asset Quality and Loss Rate

As part of the process of assigning a rating, the agencies will undertake due diligence on the asset pool. This includes reviewing the nature of the cash flows, the state of interest servicing payments to date, the status and ability to pay of the obligors. In their modelling process they will calculate probabilities of default for the assets. This includes looking at historical default rates and recovery rates. These two values are used to calculate a potential loss rate, which is of interest to investors.

The loss rate is calculated as follows: if the historical default rate is 1% and the RR is 30%, then the loss rate is 0.7%. This rate states that for every \$100 of assets, \$1 will default. If \$0.30 of this is recovered, then the ultimate loss is \$0.70. Hence the loss rate is 0.7%.

Agencies will also be interested in the diversity of the asset pool, and its concentration in one borrower or one type of borrower.

Asset Servicing

We noted earlier that in many, if not most, securitisation transactions the servicing function is retained by the originator. This is logical because the originator will be familiar with the obligors and the industry, and should be best placed to administer the assets. From the point of view of the credit rating agency, this is the best arrangement. If the servicing function is transferred to a third party, the rating agency will review this entity and assess its ability to undertake the servicing function. The assessment will consider the servicer's experience in the industry and other facets of its expertise. In some transactions, a back-up servicer is assigned to the deal – who is on stand-by to take over the role if necessary, for any reason.

Cash Flow Modelling

The rating process will project cash flows for the deal, and hence determine the likelihood of the vehicle to meet its payment obligations. The obligations include not only the principal and interest payments on the notes, but also fees for third parties such as the Trustee, the sub-administrator and the rating agencies. Cash flow projections are based on assumptions about default and recovery rates.

The arranging bank will also undertake modelling for the deal, as they work towards putting together its final structure. There is a distinct difference in the objective of their modelling, in that they seek to structure to meet the rating agency requirements and so be assigned the rating they need. The rating agencies on the other hand run the deal mechanics through their model, which then produces a result based on these inputs. From the point of view of the arranging bank, there is further distinction between the two main types of structure: ABS/MBS and CDO. The models differ as follows:

- In a CDO model, cash flows are less of a concern. Instead the model is used to determine the final form of the underlying portfolio. The model runs various permutations on a subset of a pool of securities (bonds and/or loans) to achieve the necessary diversity and note spread. The diversity requirement is a rating agency consideration. The key objective is to construct the most efficient portfolio in order to enable the CDO to achieve the rating agency requirements at the lowest funding costs.
- In an ABS transaction, the originator is not concerned overly much with the portfolio: the portfolio is given and there is little quantifiable diversity. For example, the entire portfolio will be residential mortgages or credit card debt. The arrangers will be concerned with the cash flows to ensure they have the mechanics right, but the focus is on structuring around the mechanical obstacles that the portfolio brings. For example, if the deal is concerned with residential mortgages in a certain jurisdiction, then that jurisdiction may state that there is set-off risk (that is, customers can offset mortgage balances that belong to the SPV against current account deposits that do not).

Of these two deal types, probably the static balance sheet CDO is the closest to the ABS type in terms of modelling aspect.

Loan-to-value Ratio

The LTV ratio is the ratio of the amount of the loan to the market value of the asset. The value of the asset is a market value, which can be estimated from secondary market trading of similar assets, or independently valued when it is sold to the SPV. An LTV ratio of 0.8 indicates that the value of the loan is 80% of the market value of the asset. The difference between the value of an asset and the loan amount is known as the "borrower's equity". If the LTV is below 1, this means that the borrower has positive equity in the asset and so is less likely to default. If the LTV is higher than 1 it means that the amount borrowed is above the market value of the asset and it may be advantageous to default. Rating agencies view LTV as an important indicator of the likelihood of default.

$$\text{Loan to value ratio} = \frac{\text{Loan amount}}{\text{Market value of the asset}}$$

Payment-to-income Ratio

The payment-to-income ratio (PTI) is the ratio of the amount of the monthly loan interest payment to the income available each month to make the loan interest payment. A higher PTI means that a higher amount of a borrower's income needs to be set aside to meet the interest servicing.

A related ratio is the DSCR, which we referred to earlier in this chapter. This is the mortgaged property's net operating income as a percentage of the debt service cost. A low ratio is indicative of potential default as the income may not be sufficient to cover interest costs.

SECURITISATION AS IN-HOUSE DEAL TO CREATE COLLATERAL

Following the July–August 2007 implosion of the asset-backed commercial paper market, investor interest in ABS product reduced considerably. The growing illiquidity in the inter-bank market, which resulted in even large AA-rated banks finding it difficult to raise funds for tenors longer than one month, became acute following the collapse of Lehman Brothers in September 2008. To assist banks in raising funds, central banks, starting with the US Federal Reserve and the European Central Bank (ECB), and then the Bank of England (BoE), began to relax the criteria under which they accepted collateral from banks that raised terms funds from them. In summary, the central banks announced that ABS, including MBS and other securitised products, would now be eligible as collateral at their daily liquidity window.

As originally conceived, the purpose of these moves was to enable banks to raise funds, from their respective central bank, using existing ABS on their balance sheet as collateral. Very quickly, however, the banks began to originate new securitisation transactions, using illiquid assets held on their balance sheet (such as residential mortgages or corporate loans) as collateral in the deal. The issued notes would be purchased by the bank itself, making the deal completely in-house. These new purchased ABS tranches would then be used as collateral at the central bank repo window. We discuss these central bank-led deals in this section.

Structuring Considerations

Essentially a central bank deal is like any other deal, except that one has a minimum requirement to be central bank eligible. There are also haircut considerations and the opportunity to structure it without consideration for investors. To be eligible for repo at the ECB, deals had to fulfil certain criteria. These included:

- Minimum requirements:
  - public rating of triple-A or higher at first issue;
  - only the senior tranche can be repo'd;
  - no exposure to synthetic securities. The ECB rules stated that the cash flow in generating assets backing the ABSs must not consist in whole or in part, actually or potentially, of CLNs or similar claims resulting from the transfer of credit risk by means of credit derivatives. Therefore, the transaction should expressly exclude any types of synthetic assets or securities;
  - public presale or new issue report issued by the credit rating agency that rates the transaction;
  - bonds listed in Europe (for example, on the Irish Stock Exchange);
  - book entry capability in Europe (for example, settlement in Euroclear, Clearstream);
- Haircut considerations:
  - collaterised loan obligations (CLOs) securities denominated in euro will incur a haircut of 12% regardless of maturity or coupon structure;

  - for the purposes of valuation, in the absence of a trading price within the past five days, or if the price is unchanged over that period, a 5% valuation markdown is applied. The ECB will apply its own valuation to the notes, rather than accept the borrower's valuation;
  - CLO securities denominated in US dollars will incur the usual haircuts, but with an additional initial margin of between 10% and 20% to account for FX risk;
- Other considerations:
  - the deal can incorporate a revolving period (external investors normally would not prefer this);
  - it can be a simple 2-tranche set-up. The junior tranche can be unrated and subordinated to topping up the cash reserve;
  - it can be structured with an off-market interest rate swap, but penalties are imposed if it is an in-house swap provider;
  - it must be rated by at least two rating agencies;
  - there can be no in-house currency swap (this must be with an external counterparty).

The originator also must decide whether the transaction is to be structured to accommodate replenishment of the portfolio or whether the portfolio should be static. ECB transactions are clearly financing transactions for the bank, and as such the originating bank will retain the flexibility to sell or refinance some or all of the portfolio at any time should more favourable financing terms become available to it. For this reason there is often no restriction on the ability to sell assets out of the portfolio provided that the price received by the issuer is not less than the price paid by it for the asset (par), subject to adjustment for accrued interest. This feature maintains maximum refinancing flexibility and has been agreed to by the rating agencies.

Whether or not replenishment is incorporated into the transaction depends on a number of factors. If it is considered likely that assets will be transferred out of the portfolio (in order to be sold or refinanced), then replenishment enables the efficiency of the CDO structure to be maintained by adding new assets rather than running the existing transaction down and having to establish a new structure to finance additional/future assets. However, if replenishment is incorporated into the transaction the rating agencies carry out diligence on the bank to satisfy themselves on the capabilities of the bank to manage the portfolio. Also, the recovery rates assigned to a static portfolio are higher than those assigned to a managed portfolio. The decision on whether to have a managed or static transaction will have an impact on the documentation for the transaction and the scope of the bank's obligations and representations.

Closing and Accounting Considerations: Case Study of ECB-led ABS Transaction ("Red Sea Master Series")

We provide here a case study of an in-house ABS transaction undertaken for ECB funding purposes. Although modelled on an actual deal, we have made the specific details hypothetical. However, this deal is not a typical in-house deal; it features an additional SPV as part of its structure, designed to allow the originator's parent group entity to use the vehicle for further issuances. Note that this structure does not feature a currency swap, because the overlying notes are issued in three separate currencies to match the currencies of the underlying assets. This was because a currency swap with an outside provider would add substantial costs to the deal, and an in-house currency swap was expressly forbidden under ECB eligibility rules.

Background

To meet the dual objectives of securing term liquidity and cheap funding, and to benefit from the liquidity facility at the ECB, XYZ BANK undertakes an ABS securitisation of XYZ BANK's balance sheet of approximately EUR2 billion of corporate loans. During 2008, such deals were undertaken by many banks throughout Europe. The transaction was conducted entirely in-house and all the notes issued were purchased by XYZ BANK. This was a funding transaction and not a revenue generation transaction.

We detail here the accounting treatment adopted by XYZ BANK on execution of the transaction and the capital adequacy issues arising therein.

Accounting Treatment

As noted in the transaction structure, there will effectively be three legal entities directly influenced by the transaction:

1. XYZ BANK.
2. The Master Series Purchase Trust Limited ("the Trust").
3. The Master Series Limited 1 ("the Issuer").

The closing process of events is summarised as follows:

- A true (legal) sale of XYZ BANK assets between XYZ BANK and the Trust against cash.
- The Trust issues pass-through certificates that will be purchased by the Issuer for cash.
- The Issuer issues re-tranched pass-through ABS securities purchased by XYZ BANK for cash.

The transaction structure is illustrated at Figure 4.7.

All the above transactions occur simultaneously and in contemplation of one another. From an accounting perspective, the following questions were addressed as part of the closing process:

Would XYZ BANK Be Required to Consolidate the Trust and the Issuer?

The IAS 27 accounting standard requires consolidation of all entities that are controlled (subsidiaries) by the reporting entity (XYZ BANK). The SIC-12 rule further explains consolidation of SPVs, when the substance of the relationship between an entity and the SPV indicates that the SPV is controlled by the entity. Given the above two standards, XYZ BANK would be required to consolidate the SPVs established due to following reasons:

- In substance, the activities of the SPVs are being conducted on behalf of XYZ BANK, according to its specific business needs so that XYZ BANK obtains benefits from their operations.
- In substance, XYZ BANK has the decision-making powers to obtain the majority of the benefits of the activities of the SPVs, albeit through an autopilot mechanism.
- In substance, XYZ BANK will have rights to obtain the majority of the benefits of the SPVs and will therefore be exposed to the risks inherent to the activities of the SPVs.
- In substance, XYZ BANK retains the majority of the residual risks related to the SPVs or its assets in order to obtain benefits from its activities.

Although share capital issued by both the Trust and the Issuer will be owned by third parties (the Charitable Trust ownership structure that is common in finance market SPV arrangements), the SIC-12 conditions would require XYZ BANK to consolidate them by virtue of having control over the SPVs.

Would the True (Legal) Sale Between XYZ BANK and the Trust Meet the De-recognition Criteria?

Although a true (legal) sale of the underlying assets will be achieved, a transfer can be recognised from an accounting perspective only when it meets the de-recognition criteria under IAS 39 rules. The decision whether a transfer qualifies for de-recognition is made by applying a combination of risks and rewards and control tests. De-recognition cannot be achieved merely by transferring the legal title to an asset to another party. The substance of the arrangement has to be assessed in order to determine

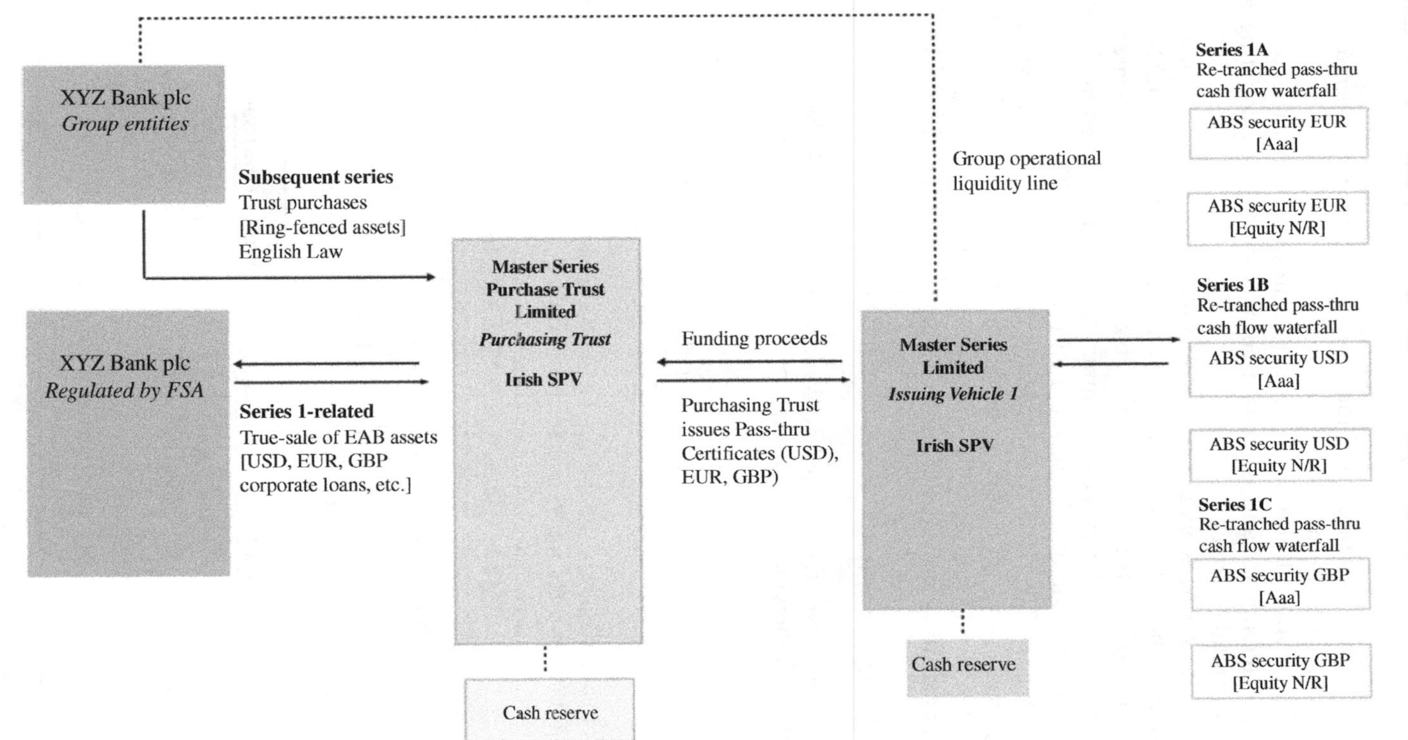

FIGURE 4.7 "Red Sea Master Series" Transaction structure, in-house ECB-led securitisation.

whether an entity has transferred the economic exposure associated with the rights inherent in the asset.

In other words, an in-house transaction has no practical accounting or risk transfer impact and is recognised as such in its accounting and regulatory capital treatment.

Hence, XYZ BANK would continue to recognise the underlying loans on its balance sheet. This is primarily due to the fact the XYZ BANK will continue to retain substantially all the risks and rewards associated with the underlying loans by virtue of owning all the Notes issued by the SPV, without any intention of onward sale to a third party. This would include all tranches issued by the SPV irrespective of the rating or subordination. Furthermore, in case of a loss occurred on any of the underlying loans, XYZ BANK would indirectly be affected through either reduction in the interest payments or principal of the Notes held.

Detailed Accounting

Based on the above, the detailed accounting entries would be as follows, and under the following assumptions:

- The SPVs are consolidated under SIC 12.
- The transaction sale does not meet the de-recognition criteria under IAS 39.

On closing day, the accounting entries to be produced on day 1 of the transaction in the three individual entities would be as follows:

On legal sale of loans from XYZ BANK to the Trust		
XYZ BANK	**The Trust**	**The Issuer**
Cash – Dr	Inter-company loan (loans and receivables) – Dr	N/A
Inter-company loan (loans and receivables) – Cr	Cash – Cr	N/A
On issue of pass-through certificates by the Trust to the Issuer		
XYZ BANK	The Trust	The Issuer
N/A	Cash – Dr	Notes issued by the Trust (loans and receivables) – Dr
N/A	Notes (financial liabilities at amortised cost) – Cr	Cash – Cr

On issue of Notes by the Issuer and acquisition by XYZ BANK		
XYZ BANK	The Trust	The Issuer
Notes issued by the Issuer (loans and receivables) [see note below*]–Dr	N/A	Cash–Dr
Cash–Cr	N/A	Notes (financial liabilities at amortised cost)–Cr

Although the Notes issued by the Issuer were listed on the Irish Stock Exchange, they could still be classified as "loans and receivables" as they were not quoted in an active market. As per AG71 in the IAS 39 rules, a financial instrument is regarded as quoted in an active market if quoted prices are readily and regularly available from market sources and those prices represent actual and regularly occurring market transactions on an arm's-length basis. Since all the Notes issued by the Issuer were to be held by XYZ BANK and would not be traded, they are deemed to be not quoted in active markets.

Therefore on day 1, the balance sheets of each of the entities would reflect the following on execution of the transaction, assuming an EUR2 billion transaction size:

XYZ BANK (Extract Only)	**The Trust**	**The Issuer**
Notes (investment in Issuer)–2 bn	Assets	Assets
	Cash–X Inter-company loan to XYZ BANK – 2 bn Total assets 2 bn + X	Cash – X Notes issued by the Trust – 2 bn Total 2 bn + X
Liabilities Inter-company borrowing from the Trust–2 bn	Liabilities Notes (Pass-thru certificates) – 2 bn	Liabilities Liabilities Notes issued AAA – XXXm BBB – XXXm Non-rated sub-debt–XXXm Total – 2 bn
	Equity–X Total liabilities and equity – 2 bn + X	Equity – X Total liabilities and equity – 2 bn + X

In XYZ BANK consolidated financial statements, all the above balances will net off except for cash balances held by the SPVs (if external) and the minority interest in equity of the SPVs. The financial statements will effectively continue to reflect the underlying loans as "loans and receivables" as they do at present. If the Notes issued by the Issuer were subsequently used as collateral for repo purposes, XYZ BANK would reflect third-party borrowing in its financial statements while disclosing the underlying collateral.

Swap

As part of the proposed transaction, an interest-rate swap (IRS) will be entered into between XYZ BANK and the Trust to manage the basis risk. Both the entities will mark-to-market the swap in their individual financial statements, while in the XYZ BANK consolidated financial statements the balances will net off with zero mark-to-market impact.

Transaction Costs

The transaction costs incurred by the Issuer on the issuance of Notes and the set-up of the structure will be deducted from the fair value of the Notes issued on initial recognition in the financial statements of the Issuer. These costs would include the one-off fees including legal, rating agencies and so on. These would then form part of the effective interest rate calculations of the Notes issued and will be amortised through the profit or loss over the economic life of the Notes issued. The annual running costs would be accounted for in the profit and loss as and when occurred.

In the XYZ BANK consolidated financial statements, these transaction costs were reflected as an asset to be amortised over the economic life of the Notes issued. An asset has been defined "as a resource controlled by the enterprise as a result of past events and from which future economic benefits are expected to flow to the enterprise".

For XYZ BANK the objective of the structure was to secure term liquidity and cheap funding, and to benefit from the liquidity facility at the ECB. Therefore the expected future economic benefits flowing to XYZ BANK justified the recognition of these costs as an asset. The asset would be subject to impairment review on at least an annual basis.

Other Considerations

Capital adequacy assumes that XYZ BANK prepares its regulatory returns on a solo consolidated basis. This allows elimination of both the major intra-group exposures and investments of XYZ BANK in its subsidiaries when calculating capital resource requirements. Therefore as described above for XYZ BANK consolidated financial statements, there would be no additional capital adequacy adjustments to arise subject to the treatment of costs incurred on the transaction. XYZ BANK would, however, be required to make a waiver application to its regulatory authority (in this case the UK's Financial Services Authority (FSA) under BIPRU 2.1 explaining the proposed transaction and its objectives). The key points FSA would consider in approval of the waiver request include:

- The control XYZ BANK will have over the subsidiaries/SPVs.
- The transferability of capital/assets from the subsidiaries to XYZ BANK.
- The total amount of capital/assets solo consolidated by XYZ BANK.

XYZ BANK would reflect the investment in Notes issued by the Issuer at 0% risk-weighting to avoid double-counting. Therefore, there would be no further capital charge on the Notes issued by the Issuer and held by XYZ BANK.

SPVs are not regulated entities and therefore would not be required to comply with the European Union Capital Requirements Directive.

THE SECURITISATION MARKET POST-2008

The impact of the 2007–2009 financial crash on the securitisation market can be illustrated as follows; for example, in 2007 US market public and Rule 144A ABS issuance amounted to USD863 billion. In 2008 and 2009 the same asset issuance was USD230 billion.[8] This is a tremendous decline; indeed, the majority of the issuance was under the term asset-backed loan facility (TALF), a support programme for the market introduced by the US government. What this statistic also tells us is that securitisation remains a viable and valuable asset class for both originators and investors, given that issuance did not disappear completely. Therefore in this section we look briefly at the market in the immediate post-crash era and also discuss salient features of interest to bank ALM practitioners.

8 Source: Thomson Financial Securities Data.

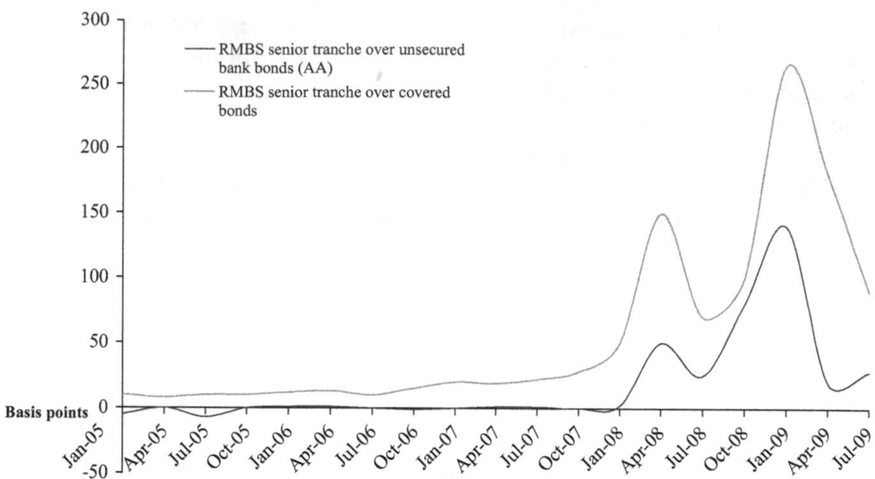

FIGURE 4.8 UK RMBS spreads over bank debt and covered bonds.
Source: Bloomberg L.P.

Market Observation

A standard feature during the recovery in an economic cycle is that risk aversion reduces once the worst of the recession is over. For example, during 2009, UK AAA-rated residential MBS spreads tightened over 300 bps and were trading at 180 bps over Libor. This is considerably below the yields seen only six months previously. Figure 4.8 shows UK RMBS spreads over alternative bank funding sources (straight bank debt-rated AA and bank covered bonds) for the period 2005–2009.

In the post-crash market in the US the most common type of issuance was for auto-loan and credit card underlying. Figure 4.9 is a breakdown of ABS issuance in 2009. Note the virtual disappearance of the "CDO" asset class. Figure 4.10 illustrates the impact on note spreads following the financial crisis.

The number of synthetic securitisation transactions fell considerably, to virtually zero, in the wake of the crash. Such deals returned only in 2010, in considerably reduced volumes.[9]

9 For a detailed discussion and analysis of synthetic securitisation, see the author's book *Structured Credit Products: Credit Derivatives and Synthetic Securitisation*, 2nd edition (John Wiley & Sons, 2010).

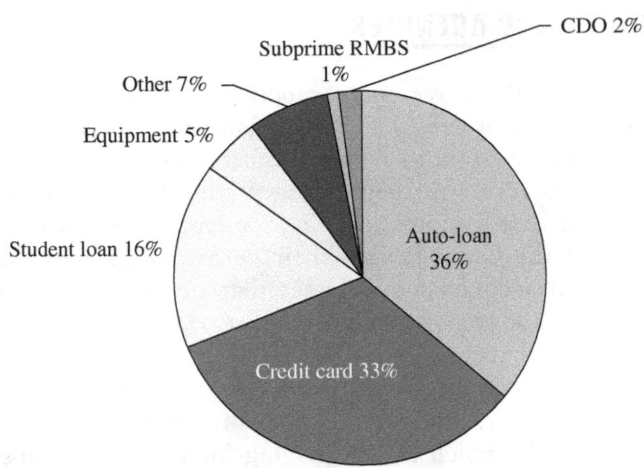

FIGURE 4.9 US ABS sector breakdown 2009.
Source: Thomson Financial Securities Data.

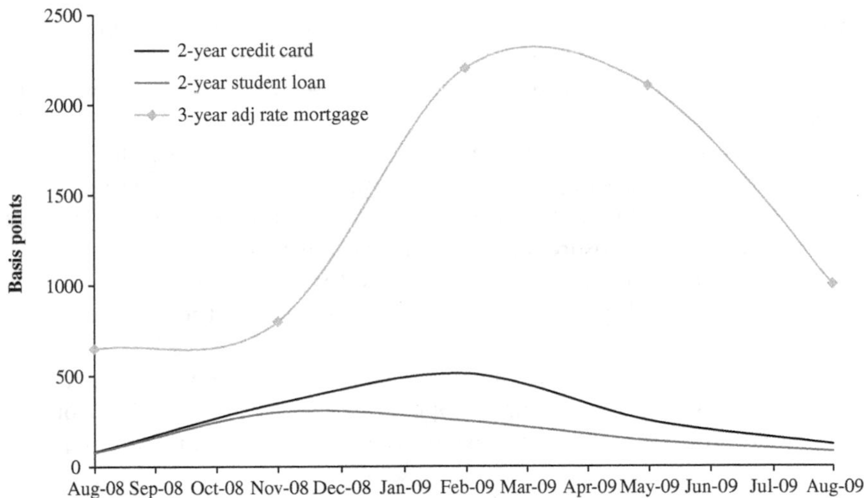

FIGURE 4.10 US floating rate spreads 2009.
Source: Bloomberg.

IMPACT ON RATING AGENCIES

The reputation of the three main credit rating agencies (CRA) was impacted in the wake of the 2007–2009 financial crisis. This issue caused many former ABS investors to refrain from re-entering the market. As a result the agencies reviewed their rating methodologies and criteria, as well as their base case assumptions. The immediate impact of the review process was that the CRAs revised their performance and loss assumptions to take into account actual losses that occurred in the recession. The CRAs also took steps to publish more transparent disclosures as part of their ratings process.

The stability of credit ratings was most heavily damaged in the mortgage market sector. Investors in sub-prime and prime RMBS, CMBS and CDO of ABS (in which the underlying included MBS) observed the greatest deterioration in ratings during 2008–2009. CRAs publish "ratings transition" tables detailing the percentage of securities that were still the same rating after one year (or longer). Moody's also publishes "downgrade rates", which are defined as the number of securities downgraded divided by the total number of outstanding securities at the beginning of the observation period.

In a report from 2009, Moody's reported that 7.38% of all the structured finance securities that it rated were downgraded in the period 1999–2008. This is a surprisingly low figure. If CDO of ABS, home equity ABS and RMBS are excluded the figure is 3.18%.[10] For 2008 only, however, the downgrade rate was 35.5%, and 12.1% when mortgage-related securities were excluded.

In response to the crisis the CRAs modified their approach. However, in essence their methodology remained in place, and changes were largely technical in nature. The definition of a rating itself did not change, but certain underlying assumptions were changed to reflect the observations from 2007–2009. In addition, all CRAs undertook to provide greater transparency and disclosures as part of the ratings process.

One significant change that was adopted was that the ratings process now considers the liquidity and funding scenario for the originating or sponsoring entity: this had not been reviewed prior to the crash. The impact of this change is material, because the CRAs now take into account the liquidity position of the originator. Sponsors that are overly reliant on the ABS market, or have few alternative sources for their funding, are required

10 See Moody's Investors Service, *Structured Finance Rating Transitions: 1983–2008*, Special Report, March 2009.

to provide a higher level of credit enhancements for the structure. In some cases, the top AAA/Aaa rating is not available to such sponsors.

We provide a summary comparison of the new approaches of each of the major CRAs.

Moody's Investors Service

According to its website, a Moody's rating is a qualitative description of a quantitative measure of relative creditworthiness of a security. It is a forward-looking, 12-month risk assessment. The analysis undertaken to arrive at a rating is both qualitative and quantitative, although for a structured finance security the qualitative review is limited in comparison. The rating itself represents a probability of the likelihood of a security making full and timely payment of its principal and interest liabilities.

Moody's rating approach is essentially unchanged from its pre-crisis model, but has been modified in certain aspects of its detail. Greater weight is now given to operational features of the structure, the relationship of the structure with the sponsor and the sponsor's access to alternative sources of liquidity. Based on this approach, some asset class ABS product is now no longer assigned a Aaa rating irrespective of the amount of credit enhancement that is built into the vehicle; this has been observed, for example, with specific types of auto-ABS securities, as well as certain credit card issuers and equipment lease deals.[11]

Included in the new Moody's approach is the provision of "V-scores" and "parameter sensitivities" in its ratings report. The V-score is a measure of the potential variability of the inputs to the ratings process, and is designed to highlight the risk of such fluctuations to investors. Parameter sensitivities are a sensitivity analysis of these rating inputs.

Standard & Poor's

An S&P rating is a qualitative measure of relative creditworthiness of a security within the rated population; however, it is also a measure specifically of the probability of default. The S&P review process also includes payment priority, recovery rate and credit stability. Since the 2007 crisis, S&P has emphasised that its ratings are comparable across security

11 Some of the so-called "credit card banks" had relied excessively on the securitisation market to raise finance and grow their balance sheet. For such firms, the lack of alternative sources of finance means that their ABS product is now unlikely to be assigned a Aaa/AAA rating unless the sponsor arranges for funding diversity.

type and asset class, and that they represent an ability to withstand specific macroeconomic scenarios. An AAA-rated bond in theory would not default in an economic scenario similar to the 1930s Depression, while a BBB-rated bond would survive an equity market fall of 50% and unemployment rate of 10% (statistics that are similar to those observed in the 2007–2009 crash).

Fitch

Similar to the other CRAs, a Fitch rating is a measure of relative creditworthiness, with an emphasis (as with S&P) on probability of default. Fitch has also adopted a similar approach to Moody's in taking into account the liquidity and funding position of an originating entity when assigning the rating.

Alone among the CRAs, Fitch publishes an outlook for each rating, which is a medium-term view of rating stability alongside the 12-month formal rating. Two additional measures introduced by Fitch are "loss severity ratings" and "recovery ratings". Loss severity ratings measure the adequacy of the size of the tranche under specified loss scenarios. The recovery rating is a measure of recovery value.

SECURITISATION OBJECTIVES IN THE BASEL III ENVIRONMENT

In the post-Enron era of consolidated accounting, and the later requirements of Basel II and specific regulatory requirements such as the UK FSA's "BIPRU 9" ruling, it is not possible to achieve regulatory capital relief unless the first-loss risk exposure to the underlying assets is placed elsewhere. In a true-sale cash securitisation, this means placing the entire liabilities capital structure, including the junior note or equity note, with an external third-party investor (see Figure 4.11). A cash ABS or CLO deal that closed without placing its junior tranche in the market, so that the note had to be bought by the originating bank itself, would be a funding transaction only, and not a regulatory capital relief transaction.

If the securitisation is a synthetic one, then regulatory capital relief will be obtained to the extent that there will be a reduced capital requirement, but there will also be a counterparty risk weighting to the investor who has bought the synthetic note or sold protection on the junior tranche.

However, Basel III requirements include regulations for securitisation originators to retain an economic interest in a portion of the credit risk of any asset (except "qualified residential mortgages") that the originator,

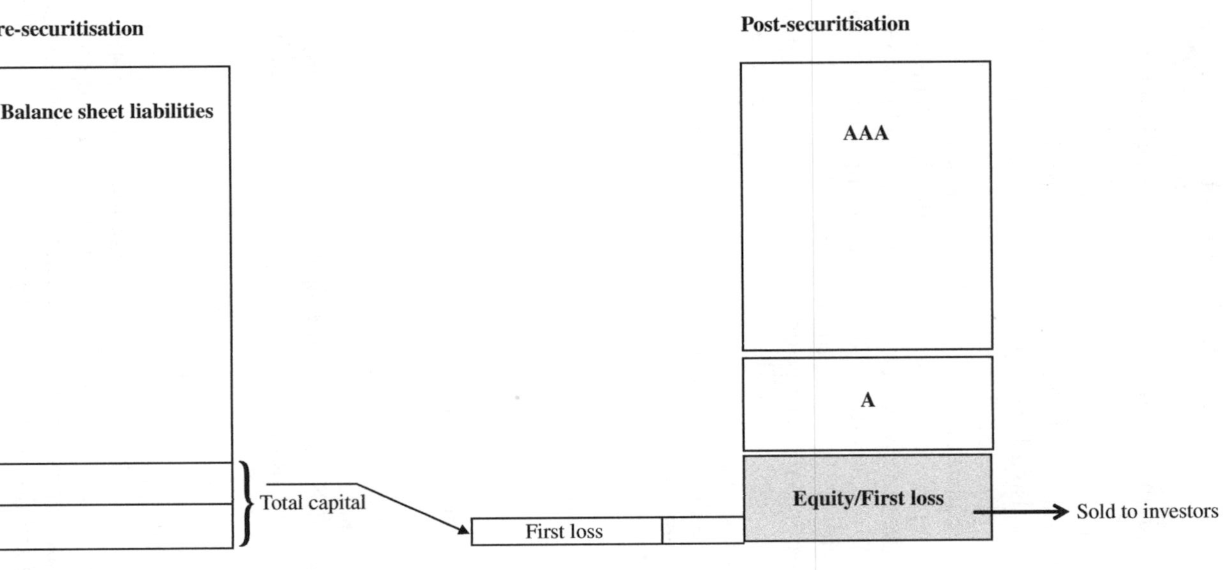

FIGURE 4.11 Securitisation realising regulatory capital relief.

through the issuance of asset-backed securities, sells or transfers to a third party. This does not have to be the first-loss piece though. The ruling also prohibits the direct or indirect hedging of retained credit risk. These requirements are to ensure that the interests of originators and investors are aligned.

The key requirement under the UK FSA ruling is for a transaction to incorporate "significant risk transfer" (SRT) if it is to result in regulatory capital relief. SRT refers to the need to demonstrate that the reduction in risk-weighted assets on the balance sheet is in line with a reduction in actual credit risk. This is also a legal criteria. The originator also has an ongoing responsibility to prove SRT over the life of the transaction. On the other side of the requirement, as stated under Basel III, is the need for the originator to retain an economic interest in the deal. This sounds slightly paradoxical to the requirements stated in the preceding sentence. Under FSA BIPRU 9.15, the investor will have to be supplied with confirmation that the originator or sponsor to the deal has retained at least a 5% economic interest in the securitisation. The retention commitment must be disclosed by the originator on the deal closure, and on an ongoing basis. The retained exposure cannot be sold or hedged. A failure to comply may result in additional risk-weights being assigned to the securitised assets.

For a transaction designed to achieve regulatory capital relief it must meet the possibly conflicting requirements of SRT and retention rules. One way to achieve this would be for the originator to retain a 5% nominal value of each securitised asset, at the true sale stage, and sell 100% of the issued liabilities.

SECURED FUNDING VALUE

We note in Chapter 17 that bank funding models will target a move away from unsecured wholesale market funding and towards a greater share of secured funding. Such funding will typically be in the form of securitised issuance and covered bonds. Relying more on secured funding will place more of the bank's assets into an encumbered state, which has implications for investors in the event of bankruptcy, as the LGD for unsecured creditors will be higher. This is an issue for further debate.

From a funding perspective, the value from secured term issuance is realised from lower funding levels. For example, Figure 4.12 shows the difference in yields between unsecured term issuance and secured (RMBS) issuance for a panel of European banks. Although funding costs are lowered over time, there are also implications for the business model and issues such as net interest margin.

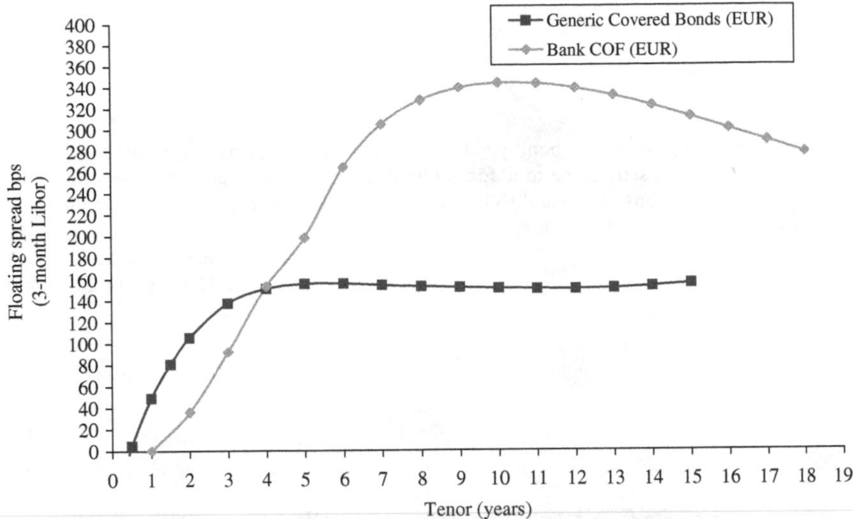

FIGURE 4.12 Generic secured and unsecured curves in EUR, December 2011.

REFERENCES

Procter, N. and Leedham, E. (2004), "Trust and Agency Services in the Debt Capital Market", in Fabozzi, F. and Choudhry, M., *The Handbook of European Fixed Income Securities*, New Jersey: John Wiley & Sons, Inc.

Sundaresan, S. (1997), *Fixed Income Markets and Their Derivatives*, Cincinnati: South-Western Publishing, Chapter 9.

Villar-Garcia, L. and Patel, T. (2004), "Legal and Documentation Issues on Bonds Issuances", in Fabozzi, F. and Choudhry, M., *The Handbook of European Fixed Income Securities*, New Jersey: John Wiley & Sons, Inc.

> The long-term government bond yield is the single most important variable in any market economy, setting the tone for equity and house prices, governing business investment decisions and establishing the discount rate for pension liabilities and insurance policies.
>
> —Anatole Kaletsky, "Economic View",
> *The Times*, 22 February 2005

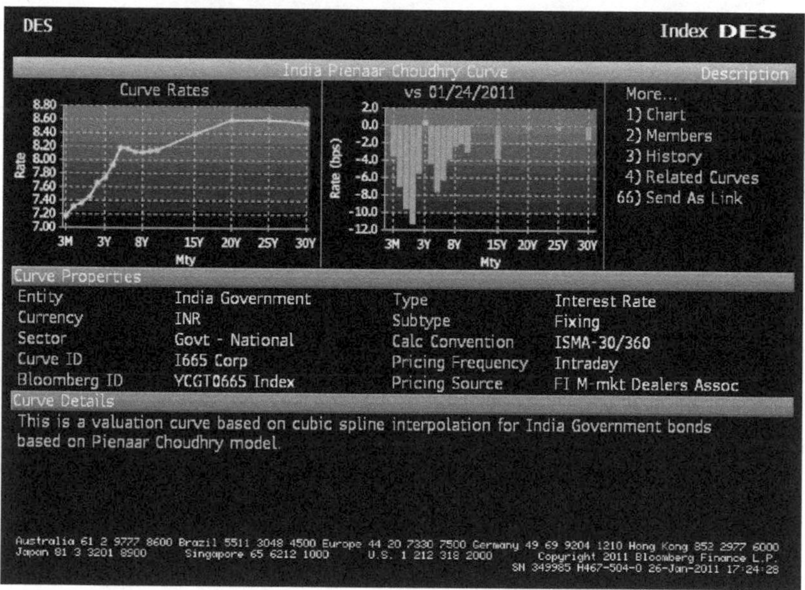

CHAPTER 5

The Yield Curve

The art of banking, indeed all of finance, revolves around the yield curve. Understanding and appreciating the curve is important to all financial market participants. It is important to debt capital market participants, and especially important to bank ALM practitioners. So if one is reading this book it is safe to assume that the yield curve is a very important subject.

This is a long chapter but well worth the close attention of all bankers, irrespective of their function or seniority. In it, we discuss the main concepts behind the yield curve, as well as its uses and information content. An ability to interpret the yield curve is vital for all market practitioners. We discuss the zero-coupon (or spot) and forward yield curves, and present the main theories that seek to explain their shape and behaviour. We will see that the spread of different curves to another, such as the swap yield curve compared to the government yield curve, is also noteworthy and so we seek to explain the determinants of these spreads in this chapter.

We begin with an introduction to the curve and interest rates in general.

IMPORTANCE OF THE YIELD CURVE

As we noted in Chapter 1, banks deal in interest rate and credit risk, as well as liquidity risk. These are the fundamental tenets of banking, as important today as they were when banking first began. The first of these, interest rates, is in effect an explicit measure of the cost of borrowing money, and is encapsulated in the yield curve. For bankers, understanding the behaviour and properties of the yield curve is an essential part of the risk management process. The following are some, but not all, of the reasons that this is so:

- changes in interest rates have a direct impact on bank revenue; the yield curve captures the current state of term interest rates, and also presents the current market expectation of the future state of the economy;

- the interest-rate gap reflects the state of bank borrowing and lending; gaps along the term structure are sensitive to changes in the shape and slope of the yield curve;
- current and future trading strategy, including the asset allocation and credit policy decision, will impact interest-rate risk exposure and therefore will take into account the shape and behaviour of the yield curve;
- the balance sheet itself, from both an asset and a liability viewpoint, is sensitive to changes in the shape, level and slope of the yield curve;
- balance sheet management and valuation requires an accurate yield curve, reflecting liquid market.

We see then that understanding and appreciating the yield curve is a vital part of banks' ALM operations, at both a strategic and tactical level. This chapter provides a detailed look at the curve from the banker's viewpoint. It is divided into three parts – Parts I and II focus on interest rates and interpreting the yield curve, and other curves; and Part III looks at fitting the curve.

Part I

THE MONEY MARKET YIELD CURVE

The main measure of return associated with holding debt market assets is the yield-to-maturity (YTM) or *gross redemption yield*. In developed markets, as well as certain emerging economies, there is usually a large number of bonds trading at one time, at different yields and with varying terms to maturity. Investors and traders frequently examine the relationship between the yields on bonds that are in the same class; plotting yields of bonds that differ only in their term to maturity produces what is known as a *yield curve*. This curve is an important indicator and knowledge source of the state of a debt capital market. It is sometimes referred to as the *term structure of interest rates*, but strictly speaking this is not correct, as this expression should be reserved for the zero-coupon yield curve only. We shall examine this in detail later.

Much of the analysis and pricing activity that takes place in the capital markets revolves around the yield curve. This curve describes the relationship between a particular redemption yield and that yield's maturity. Plotting the yields along the term structure will give us our yield curve. It is very important that only rates from the same class of issuer or with the same degree of liquidity are used when plotting the yield curve; for example, a curve may be constructed for UK gilts or for AA-rated sterling Eurobonds, but not a mixture of both, because gilts and Eurobonds are bonds from different class issuers. The primary yield curve in any domestic capital market is the government bond yield curve, so for example in the US market it is the US Treasury yield curve. In the eurozone, in theory any euro-currency government bond can be used to plot a euro yield curve. In practice, only bonds from the same government are used, as for various reasons different country bonds within euro-land trade at different yields (the *de facto* euro benchmark is the German bund).

Outside the government bond markets yield curves are plotted for money-market instruments, off-balance sheet instruments; in fact, virtually all debt market instruments. Money market instruments trade on a simple yield basis, as the cash market is comprised essentially of bullet interest payment securities. So the money market yield curve is simple to construct. The "Libor curve" for money markets is the main measure of money market return, and in theory goes out to 12 months only. In fact, money market derivatives frequently trade out to 18 months and two years, and for tenors beyond that the interest-rate swap fixed rate is also referred to as "Libor". We show in Figures 5.1 and 5.2 the Bloomberg screen for Libor

1 P3007a Govt **BBAM**
Screen Printed

BRITISH BANKERS'
ASSOCIATION Page 1 of 4

05/10 13:34 GMT [BRITISH BANKERS ASSOCIATION LIBOR RATES] 3750
[10/05/04] RATES AT 11:00 LONDON TIME 10/05/2004 10/05 11:18 GMT

CCY	USD	GBP	CAD	EUR	JPY	EUR 365
O/N	1.05250	4.27875	2.07000	2.00125	SN0.03250	2.02905
1WK	1.08000	4.32813	2.06833	2.04613	0.03375	2.07455
2WK	1.08125	4.37500	2.07000	2.05063	0.03500	2.07911
1MO	1.10000	4.40500	2.07500	2.06263	0.03750	2.09128
2MO	1.16000	4.43875	2.08500	2.08038	0.04313	2.10927
3MO	1.24000	4.47188	2.10833	2.08950	0.04750	2.11852
4MO	1.34000	4.52750	2.13167	2.10613	0.05075	2.13538
5MO	1.43750	4.59500	2.15833	2.12275	0.05525	2.15223
6MO	1.53000	4.65625	2.20000	2.14038	0.05975	2.17011
7MO	1.62000	4.70750	2.23833	2.16150	0.06250	2.19152
8MO	1.71250	4.76375	2.27500	2.19150	0.06750	2.22194
9MO	1.81000	4.82125	2.32667	2.22363	0.07188	2.25451
10MO	1.89375	4.86875	2.37000	2.25275	0.07750	2.28404
11MO	1.98125	4.91625	2.41000	2.27788	0.08438	2.30952
12MO	2.07000	4.95875	2.46333	2.31538	0.08875	2.34754

FIGURE 5.1 Bloomberg screen BBAM, daily Libor fixing page, as at 10 May 2004.

ICAU2
Screen Printed
14:34 USD OIS - ICAU

P1P300 Govt ICAU

PAGE 1 / 1

USD OIS	Ask	Bid	Time
1) 1 Month	1.0230	1.0030	14:12
2) 2 Month	1.0670	1.0470	14:12
3) 3 Month	1.1350	1.1150	14:26
4) 4 Month	1.2430	1.2230	14:31
5) 5 Month	1.3220	1.3020	14:31
6) 6 Month	1.4030	1.3830	14:31
7) 7 Month	1.4920	1.4720	14:31
8) 8 Month	1.5810	1.5600	14:34
9) 9 Month	1.6680	1.6470	14:34
10) 10 Month	1.7490	1.7290	14:34
11) 11 Month	1.8280	1.8070	14:34
12) 12 Month	1.9120	1.8920	14:34
13) 15 Month	2.1590	2.1390	14:34
14) 18 Month	2.3900	2.3690	14:34
15) 21 Month	2.6120	2.5920	14:34
16) 24 Month	2.8010	2.7810	14:34

FIGURE 5.2 Bloomberg screen ICAU2, Garban ICAP broker's price screen for US dollar OIS swaps, 10 May 2004.

fixing and a broker's screen (Garban ICAP) for US dollar overnight-index swaps (OIS) swaps. These show that the maximum accepted maturity for the money market yield curve is 24 months. Another money market yield curve, in fact the most widely used by participants, is the exchange-traded futures curve for short-dated deposits; for instance, the Eurodollar curve or the short-sterling curve. This is taken as the most reliable and liquid indicator of expected money market rates. Figure 5.3 shows the Eurodollar curve as at 10 May 2004.

Figure 5.4 shows the inter-bank fixings for HKD and SGD, and the AUD deposit rates as at 6 September 2004, as money market yield curves on Bloomberg screen MMCV.

The principles behind the money market yield curve are exactly the same as those behind the longer dated bond market yield curve. So in this chapter we will consider the YTM yield curve and how to derive spot and forward yields from a current redemption yield curve.

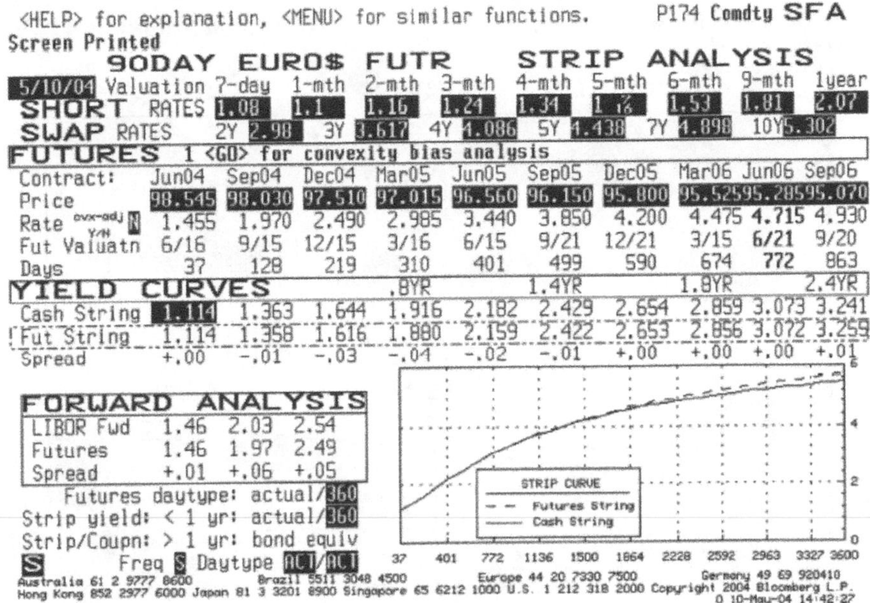

<HELP> for explanation, <MENU> for similar functions. P174 Comdty SFA
Screen Printed
90DAY EURO$ FUTR STRIP ANALYSIS
5/10/04 Valuation 7-day 1-mth 2-mth 3-mth 4-mth 5-mth 6-mth 9-mth 1year
SHORT RATES 1.08 1.1 1.16 1.24 1.34 1 7/16 1.53 1.81 2.07
SWAP RATES 2Y 2.98 3Y 3.617 4Y 4.086 5Y 4.438 7Y 4.898 10Y 5.302
FUTURES 1 <GO> for convexity bias analysis
Contract: Jun04 Sep04 Dec04 Mar05 Jun05 Sep05 Dec05 Mar06 Jun06 Sep06
Price 98.545 98.030 97.510 97.015 96.560 96.150 95.800 95.525 95.285 95.070
Rate cvx-adj Y/N N 1.455 1.970 2.490 2.985 3.440 3.850 4.200 4.475 4.715 4.930
Fut Valuatn 6/16 9/15 12/15 3/16 6/15 9/21 12/21 3/15 6/21 9/20
Days 37 128 219 310 401 499 590 674 772 863
YIELD CURVES .8YR 1.4YR 1.8YR 2.4YR
Cash String 1.114 1.363 1.644 1.916 2.182 2.429 2.654 2.859 3.073 3.241
Fut String 1.114 1.358 1.616 1.880 2.159 2.422 2.653 2.856 3.072 3.259
Spread +.00 -.01 -.03 -.04 -.02 -.01 +.00 +.00 +.00 +.01
FORWARD ANALYSIS
LIBOR Fwd 1.46 2.03 2.54
Futures 1.46 1.97 2.49
Spread +.01 +.06 +.05
Futures daytype: actual/360
Strip yield: < 1 yr: actual/360
Strip/Coupn: > 1 yr: bond equiv
S Freq S Daytype ACT/ACT
STRIP CURVE
Futures String
Cash String
6
4
2
0
37 401 772 1136 1500 1864 2228 2592 2963 3327 3600
Australia 61 2 9777 8600 Brazil 5511 3048 4500 Europe 44 20 7330 7500 Germany 49 69 920410
Hong Kong 852 2977 6000 Japan 81 3 3201 8900 Singapore 65 6212 1000 U.S. 1 212 318 2000 Copyright 2004 Bloomberg L.P.
0 10-May-04 14:42:27

FIGURE 5.3 Eurodollar yield curve, 10 May 2004.

USING THE YIELD CURVE

All participants in the capital markets have an interest in the current shape and level of the yield curve, as well as what this information implies for the future. Its main uses are summarised below.

Setting the Yield for all Debt Market Instruments

The yield curve essentially fixes the cost of money over the maturity term structure. The yields of government bonds from the shortest maturity instrument to the longest set the benchmark for yields for all other debt instruments in the market, around which all debt instruments are analysed. Issuers of debt (and their underwriting banks) therefore use the yield curve to price bonds and all other debt instruments. Generally, the zero-coupon yield curve is used to price new issue securities, rather than the redemption yield curve.

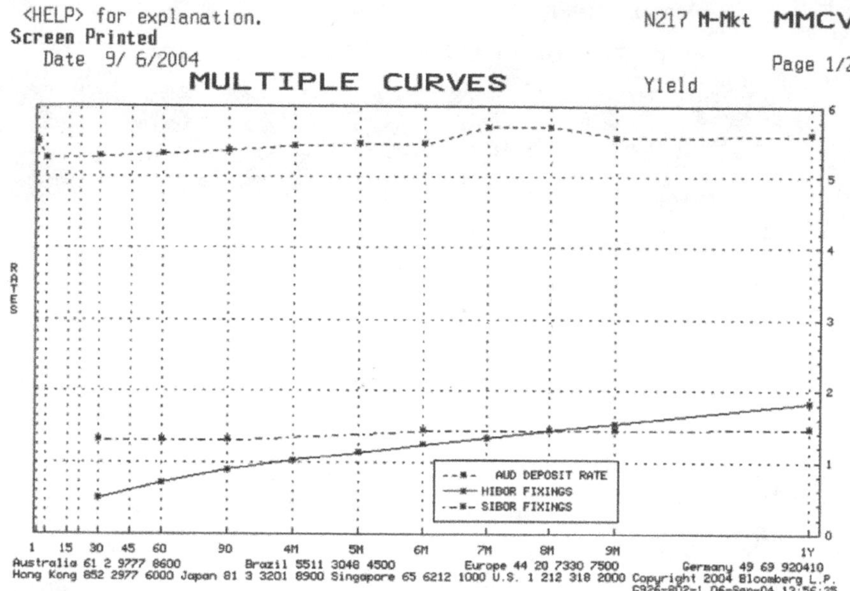

FIGURE 5.4 Bloomberg screen MMCV, inter-bank fixings for HKD and SGD, and AUD deposit rates as at 6 September 2004.

Acting as an Indicator of Future Yield Levels

As we discuss later in this chapter, the yield curve assumes certain shapes in response to market expectations of future interest rates. Bond market participants analyse the present shape of the yield curve in an effort to determine the implications regarding the future direction of market interest rates. This is perhaps one of the most important functions of the yield curve. The yield curve is scrutinised for its information content, not just by bond traders and fund managers, but also by corporate financiers as part of the project appraisal process. Central banks and government treasury departments also analyse the yield curve for its information content, with regard to expected inflation levels.

Measuring and Comparing Returns Across the Maturity Spectrum

Portfolio managers use the yield curve to assess the relative value of investments across the maturity spectrum. The yield curve indicates the returns that are available at different maturity points and is therefore very important to fixed-income fund managers, who can use it to assess which point of the curve offers the best return relative to other points.

Indicating Relative Value Between Different Bonds of Similar Maturity

The yield curve can be analysed to indicate which bonds are cheap or dear to the curve. Placing bonds relative to the zero-coupon yield curve helps to highlight which bonds should be bought or sold either outright or as part of a bond spread trade.

Pricing Interest-rate Derivatives

The price of derivatives revolves around the yield curve. At the short-end, products such as forward rate agreements (FRAs) are priced off the futures curve, but futures rates reflect the market's view on forward 3-month cash deposit rates. At the longer end, interest-rate swaps are priced off the yield curve, while hybrid instruments that incorporate an option feature such as convertibles and callable bonds also reflect current yield curve levels. The "risk-free" interest rate, which is one of the parameters used in option pricing, is the T-bill rate or short-term government repo rate, both constituents of the money market yield curve.

TYPES OF YIELD CURVE

Yield-to-maturity Yield Curve

The most commonly occurring yield curve is the YTM yield curve. The equation used to calculate the YTM is available in countless fixed income textbooks. The curve itself is constructed by plotting the YTM against the term to maturity for a group of bonds of the same class. Three different types are shown in Figure 5.5. Bonds used in constructing the curve will only rarely have an exact number of whole years to redemption; however, it is often common to see yields plotted against whole years on the *x*-axis. This is because once a bond is designated the *benchmark* for that term, its yield is taken to be the representative yield. For example, the then 10-year benchmark bond in the UK gilt market, the $4\frac{3}{4}\%$ of 2020, maintained its benchmark status throughout 2010 and into 2011, even as its term to maturity fell below 10 years. The YTM yield curve is the most commonly observed curve simply

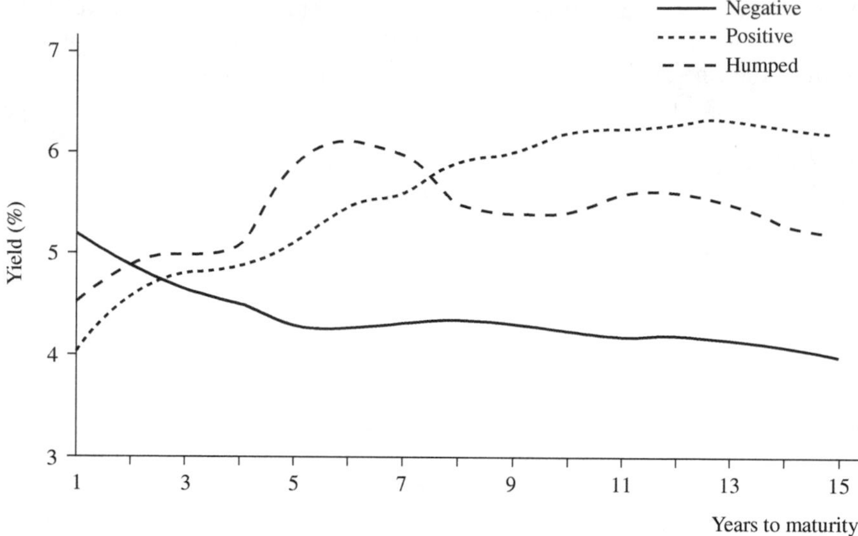

FIGURE 5.5 YTM yield curves.

because YTM is the most frequent measure of return used. The business sections of daily newspapers, where they quote bond yields at all, usually quote bond yields to maturity. As we might expect, given the source data from which it is constructed, the YTM yield curve contains some inaccuracies. The main weakness of the YTM measure is the assumption of a constant rate for coupon reinvestment during the bond's life at the redemption yield level. Since market rates will fluctuate over time, it will not be possible to achieve this (a feature known as *reinvestment risk*). Only zero-coupon bondholders avoid reinvestment risk as no coupon is paid during the life of a zero-coupon bond.

The YTM yield curve does not distinguish between different payment patterns that may result from bonds with different coupons; that is, the fact that low-coupon bonds pay a higher portion of their cash flows at a later date than high-coupon bonds of the same maturity. The curve also assumes an even cash flow pattern for all bonds. Therefore in this case cash flows are not discounted at the appropriate rate for the bonds in the group being used to construct the curve. To get around this, bond analysts may sometimes construct a *coupon yield curve*, which plots YTM against term to maturity for a group of bonds with the same coupon. This may be useful when a group of bonds contains some with very high coupons; high coupon bonds often trade "cheap to the curve"; that is, they have higher yields than corresponding bonds of the same maturity but lower coupon. This is usually because of reinvestment risk and, in some markets, for tax reasons.

```
GRAB                                                        Govt   IYC
Enter curve selection <go>
                        SINGLE YIELD CURVE
                        Curves for UNITED STATES            Page  1 / 1
 1) US Treasury Actives          I25
 2) US On/Off The Run Govt       I111
 3) US Government Strips         I39
 4) US Treas. Inflation Index    I169
 5) US Dollar Swap Rates         I52
 6) US Dollar Swap Spreads       I48
 7) US Swap Act/360              I205
 8) US Swap Spreads Act/360      I207
 9) US Agency                    I26
10) US Fannie Mae Benchmarks     I168
11) US Freddie Mac Notes         I197
12) US FHLB Issues               I199
13) Supranational Eurodollar     I27
14) World Bank Global            I80
15) BMA-FNMA Benchmark           I252
16) BMA-FHLMC Reference          I267

Australia 61 2 9777 8600    Brazil 5511 3048 4500    Europe 44 20 7330 7500    Germany 49 69 920410
Hong Kong 852 2977 6000 Japan 81 3 3201 8900 Singapore 65 6212 1000 U.S. 1 212 318 2000 Copyright 2003 Bloomberg L.P.
                                                                  G657-802-2 15-Aug-03  8:37:53
```

FIGURE 5.6 US menu page from screen IYC on Bloomberg.

The market often uses other types of yield curve for analysis when the YTM yield curve is deemed unsuitable. That there are a number of yield curves that can be plotted, each relevant to its own market, can be seen from Figure 5.6, which shows the curves that can be selected for the US dollar market, from screen IYC on Bloomberg. We see that curves can be selected for US Treasuries, US dollar swaps, strips, agency securities and so on. Figure 5.7 shows the curves for Treasuries, interest-rate swaps and strips as at August 2006.

The Coupon Yield Curve

The coupon yield curve is a plot of the YTM against term to maturity for a group of bonds with the same coupon. If we were to construct such a curve we would see that in general high-coupon bonds trade at a discount (have higher yields) relative to low-coupon bonds, because of reinvestment risk and for tax reasons (in the UK, for example, on gilts the coupon is taxed as income tax, while any capital gain is exempt from capital gains tax; even in jurisdictions where capital gain on bonds is taxable, this can often be deferred, whereas income tax cannot). It is frequently the case that yields

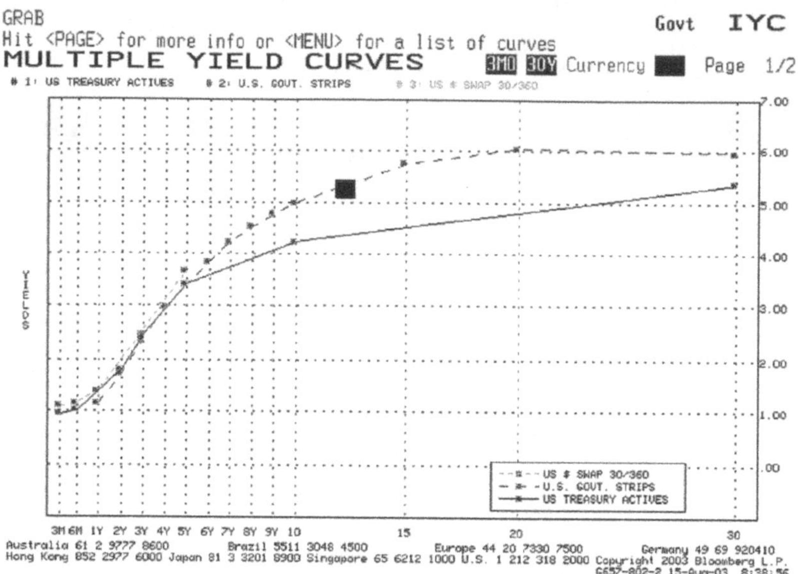

FIGURE 5.7 US yield curves, August 2006.

vary considerably with coupons for the same term to maturity, and with term to maturity for different coupons. Put another way, usually we observe different coupon curves not only at different levels but also with different shapes. Distortions arise in the YTM curve if no allowance is made for coupon differences. For this reason bond analysts frequently draw a line of "best fit" through a plot of redemption yields, because the coupon effect in a group of bonds will produce a curve with humps and troughs. Figure 5.8 shows a hypothetical set of coupon yield curves. However, since in any group of bonds it is unusual to observe bonds with the same coupon along the entire term structure this type of curve is observed rarely.

The Par Yield Curve

The *par yield curve* is not usually encountered in secondary market trading; however, it is often constructed for use by corporate financiers and others in the new issues or *primary* market. The par yield curve plots YTM against term to maturity for current bonds trading at par.[1] The par yield is therefore

1 Par price for a bond is almost invariably 100%. Certain bonds have par defined as 1,000 per 1,000 nominal of paper.

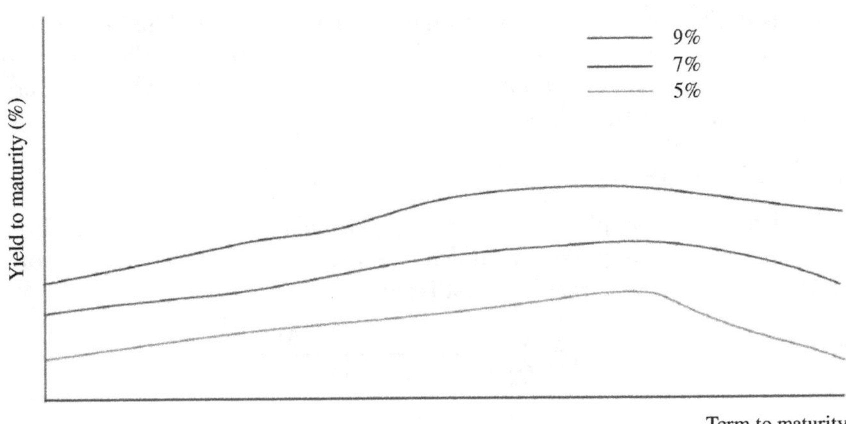

FIGURE 5.8 Coupon yield curves.

equal to the coupon rate for bonds priced at par or near to par, as the YTM for bonds priced exactly at par is equal to the coupon rate. Those involved in the primary market will use a par yield curve to determine the required coupon for a new bond that is to be issued at par. This is because investors prefer not to pay over par for a new-issue bond, so the bond requires a coupon that will result in a price at or slightly below par.

The par yield curve can be derived directly from bond yields when bonds are trading at or near par. If bonds in the market are trading substantially away from par then the resulting curve will be distorted. It is then necessary to derive it by iteration from the spot yield curve. As we would observe at almost any time, it is rare to encounter secondary market bonds trading at par for any particular maturity. The market therefore uses actual non-par vanilla bond yield curves to derive *zero-coupon yield curves* and then constructs hypothetical par yields that would be observed were there any par bonds being traded.

The Zero-coupon (or Spot) Yield Curve

The *zero-coupon* (or *spot*) yield curve plots zero-coupon yields (or spot yields) against term to maturity. A zero-coupon yield is the yield prevailing on a bond that has no coupons. In the first instance if there is a liquid zero-coupon bond market we can plot the yields from these bonds if we wish to construct this curve. However, it is not necessary to have a set of zero-coupon bonds in order to construct the curve, as we can derive it from a coupon or par yield curve; in fact, in many markets where no zero-coupon bonds are traded, a spot yield curve is derived from the conventional YTM yield curve. This is of course *a theoretical* zero-coupon (spot) yield curve, as opposed to the *market* or *observed* spot curve that can be constructed using the yields of actual zero-coupon bonds trading in the market.[2]

Basic Concepts

Spot yields must comply with equation (5.1). This equation assumes a bond with annual coupon payments and that the calculation is carried out on a coupon date so that accrued interest is zero.

$$\begin{aligned} P_d &= \sum_{n=1}^{N} \frac{C}{(1+rs_n)^n} + \frac{M}{(1+rs_N)^N} \\ &= \sum_{n=1}^{N} C \times df_n + M \times df_N \end{aligned} \tag{5.1}$$

where

rs_n = is the spot or zero-coupon yield on a bond of dirty price P_d with n years to maturity

df = is the corresponding *discount factor*.

In (5.1) rs_1 would be the current 1-year spot yield, rs_2 the current 2-year spot yield and so on. Theoretically the spot yield for a particular term to maturity is the same as the yield on a zero-coupon bond of the same maturity, which is why spot yields are also known as zero-coupon yields.

This last is an important result, as spot yields can be derived from redemption yields that have been observed in the market. As with the yield-to-redemption yield curve, the spot yield curve is commonly used in the market. It is viewed as the true term structure of interest rates because there is no reinvestment risk involved; the stated yield is equal to the actual annual return. That is, the yield on a zero-coupon bond of n years maturity is regarded as the true n-year interest rate. Because the observed government bond redemption yield curve is not considered to be the true interest rate, analysts often construct a theoretical spot yield curve. Essentially, this is done by breaking down each coupon bond that is being observed into its

2 It is common to see the terms "spot rate" and "zero-coupon rate" used synonymously. However, the spot rate is a theoretical construct and cannot be observed in the market. The definition of the spot rate, which is the rate of return on a single cash flow that has been dealt today and is received back almost instantaneously, comes very close to that of the yield on a very short-dated zero-coupon bond, which can be observed directly in the market. Zero-coupon rates can therefore be taken to be spot rates in practice, which is why the terms are frequently used interchangeably.

constituent cash flows, which become a series of individual zero-coupon bonds. For example, £100 nominal of a 5% 2-year bond (paying annual coupons) is considered equivalent to £5 nominal of a 1-year zero-coupon bond and £105 nominal of a 2-year zero-coupon bond.

Let us assume that in the market there are 30 bonds all paying annual coupons. The first bond has a maturity of one year, the second bond of two years and so on, out to 30 years. We know the price of each of these bonds, and we wish to determine what the prices imply about the market's estimate of future interest rates. We naturally expect interest rates to vary over time, but assume that all payments being made on the same date are valued using the same rate. For the 1-year bond we know its current price and the amount of the payment (comprised of one coupon payment and the redemption proceeds) we will receive at the end of the year; therefore, we can calculate the interest rate for the first year: assume the 1-year bond has a coupon of 5%. If the bond is priced at par and we invest £100 today we will receive £105 in one year's time; hence, the rate of interest is apparent and is 5%. For the 2-year bond we use this interest rate to calculate the future value of its current price in one year's time: *this is how much we would receive if we had invested the same amount in the 1-year bond.* However, the 2-year bond pays a coupon at the end of the first year; if we subtract this amount from the future value of the current price, the net amount is what we should be giving up in one year in return for the one remaining payment. From these numbers we can calculate the interest rate in year 2.

Assume that the 2-year bond pays a coupon of 6% and is priced at 99.00. If the 99.00 were invested at the rate we calculated for the 1-year bond (5%), it would accumulate £103.95 in one year, made up of the £99 investment and interest of £4.95. On the payment date in one year's time, the 1-year bond matures and the 2-year bond pays a coupon of 6%. If everyone expected that at this time the 2-year bond would be priced at more than 97.95 (which is 103.95 minus 6.00), then no investor would buy the 1-year bond, since it would be more advantageous to buy the 2-year bond and sell it after one year for a greater return. Similarly, if the price was less than 97.95 no investor would buy the 2-year bond, as it would be cheaper to buy the shorter bond and then buy the longer dated bond with the proceeds received when the 1-year bond matures. Therefore the 2-year bond must be priced at exactly 97.95 in 12 months' time. For this £97.95 to grow to £106.00 (the maturity proceeds from the 2-year bond, comprising the redemption payment and coupon interest), the interest rate in year 2 must be 8.20%. We can check this by using the standard present value formula. At these two interest rates, the two bonds are said to be in equilibrium.

This is an important result and shows that (in theory) there can be no arbitrage opportunity along the yield curve; using interest rates available today the return from buying the 2-year bond must equal the return from buying the 1-year bond and rolling over the proceeds (or *reinvesting*) for another year. This is the known as the *break-even principle*, the law of no-arbitrage.

Using the price and coupon of the 3-year bond we can calculate the interest rate in year 3 in precisely the same way. Using each of the bonds in turn, we can link together the *implied 1-year rates* for each year up to the maturity of the longest dated bond. This process is known as *bootstrapping*. The "average" of the rates over a given period is the spot yield for that term: in the example given above, the rate in year 1 is 5% and in year 2 it is 8.20%. An investment of £100 at these rates would grow to £113.61. This gives a total percentage increase of 13.61% over two years, or 6.588% per annum (the average rate is not obtained by simply dividing 13.61 by 2, but – using our present value relationship again – by calculating the square root of "1 plus the interest rate" and then subtracting 1 from this number). Thus, the 1-year yield is 5% and the 2-year yield is 8.20%.

In real-world markets it is not necessarily as straightforward as this; for instance, on some dates there may be several bonds maturing, with different coupons, and on some dates there may be no bonds maturing. It is most unlikely that there will be a regular spacing of bond redemptions exactly one year apart. For this reason it is common for analysts to use a software model to calculate the set of implied spot rates which best fits the market prices of the bonds that do exist in the market. For instance, if there are several 1-year bonds, each of their prices may imply a slightly different rate of interest. We choose the rate that gives the smallest average price error. In practice all bonds are used to find the rate in year 1, all bonds with a term longer than one year are used to calculate the rate in year 2 and so on. The zero-coupon curve can also be calculated directly from the coupon yield curve using a method similar to that described above; in this case the bonds would be priced at par and their coupons set to the par yield values.

The zero-coupon yield curve is ideal to use when deriving implied forward rates, which we consider next, and defining the term structure of interest rates. It is also the best curve to use when determining the *relative value*, whether cheap or dear, of bonds trading in the market, and when pricing new issues, irrespective of their coupons. However, it is not an absolutely accurate indicator of average market yields because most bonds are not zero-coupon bonds.

Zero-coupon Discount Factors

Having introduced the concept of the zero-coupon curve in the previous paragraph, we can illustrate more formally the mathematics involved. When deriving spot yields from redemption yields, we view conventional bonds as being made up of an *annuity*, which is the stream of fixed coupon payments, and a zero-coupon bond, which is the redemption payment on maturity. To derive the rates we can use (5.1), setting $Pd = M = 100$ and $C = rm_N$ as shown in (5.2) below. This has the coupon bonds trading at par, so that the coupon is equal to the yield. So we have:

$$\begin{aligned} 100 &= rm_N \times \sum_{n=1}^{N} df_n + 100 \times df_n \\ &= rm_n \times A_N + 100 \times df_n \end{aligned} \tag{5.2}$$

where rm_N is the par yield for a term to maturity of N years, where df_n, the discount factor, is the fair price of a zero-coupon bond with a par value of £1 and a term to maturity of N years, and where

$$A_N = \sum_{n=1}^{N} df_n = A_{N-1} + df_N \tag{5.3}$$

is the fair price of an annuity of £1 per year for N years (with A_0 by convention). Substituting (5.3) into (5.2) and rearranging them will give us the expression below for the N-year discount factor, shown in (5.4):

$$df_N = \frac{1 - rm_N \times A_{N-1}}{1 + rm_N}. \tag{5.4}$$

If we assume 1-year, 2-year and 3-year redemption yields for bonds priced at par to be 5%, 5.25% and 5.75% respectively, we will obtain the following solutions for the discount factors:

$$\begin{aligned} df_1 &= \frac{1}{1 + 0.05} = 0.95238 \\ df_2 &= \frac{1 - (0.0525)(0.95238)}{1 + 0.0525} = 0.90261 \\ df_3 &= \frac{1 - (0.0575)(0.95238 + 0.90261)}{1 + 0.0575} = 0.84476. \end{aligned}$$

We can confirm that these are the correct discount factors by substituting them back into equation (5.2); this gives us the following results for the 1-year, 2-year and 3-year par value bonds (with coupons of 5%, 5.25% and 5.75% respectively):

$$\begin{aligned} 100 &= 105 \times 0.95238 \\ 100 &= 5.25 \times 0.95238 + 105.25 \times 0.90261 \\ 100 &= 5.75 \times 0.95238 + 5.75 \times 0.90261 + 105.75 \times 0.84476. \end{aligned}$$

Now that we have found the correct discount factors it is relatively straightforward to calculate the spot yields using equation (5.1), and this is shown below:

$$df_1 = \frac{1}{(1 + rs_1)} = 0.95238, \text{which gives } rs_1 = 5.0\%$$

$$df_2 = \frac{1}{(1 + rs_2)} = 0.90261, \text{which gives } rs_2 = 5.256\%$$

$$df_3 = \frac{1}{(1 + rs_3)} = 0.84476, \text{which gives } rs_3 = 5.784\%.$$

Equation (5.1) discounts the n-year cash flow (comprising the coupon payment and/or principal repayment) by the corresponding n-year spot yield. In other words, rs_n is the *time-weighted rate of return* on an n-year bond. Thus, as we said in the previous section the spot yield curve is the correct method for pricing or valuing any cash flow, including an irregular cash flow, because it uses the appropriate discount factors. That is, it matches each cash flow to the discount rate that applies to the time period in which the cash flow is paid. Compare this to the approach for the YTM procedure, which discounts all cash flows by the same yield to maturity. This illustrates neatly why the N-period zero-coupon interest rate is the true interest rate for an N-year bond.

The expressions above are solved algebraically in the conventional manner, although those wishing to use a spreadsheet application such as Microsoft Excel® can input the constituents of each equation into individual cells and solve using the "Tools" and "Goal Seek" functions.[3]

---

3 To calulate these values the steps are summarised below:

$$Df = \frac{1}{(1 + rs_1)}$$

$$(1 + rs_1) = \frac{1}{Df}$$

$$rs = \left[\frac{1}{Df}\right] - 1$$

$$Df = \frac{1}{(1 + rs_2)^2}$$

$$rs_2 = \left[\sqrt{\frac{1}{Df}}\right] - 1$$

In the example in the text the working is:

Par yields	0.05	Df	0.952381		
	0.0525		0.9026128		
	0.0575		0.8447639	Working	0.1066621
					0.8933379
					1.0575
Spot yields	0.05				
	0.0525658 ←	Working			1.1078947
					1.0525658
					0.0525658
	0.0578438 ←	Working			1.1837627
					1.0578438
					0.0578438

With special thanks to Praveen Murthy, iflexsolutions, for assistance with the calculations.

EXAMPLE 5.1 ZERO-COUPON YIELDS

Consider the following zero-coupon market rates:

1-year (1y): 5.000%
2y: 5.271%
3y: 5.598%
4y: 6.675%
5y: 7.213%.

Calculate the zero-coupon discount factors and the prices and yields of:

a. a 6% 2-year bond;
b. a 7% 5-year bond.

Assume both are annual coupon bonds.

The zero-coupon discount factors are:

$$1y: 1/1.05 = 0.95238095$$
$$2y: 1/(1.05271)^2 = 0.90236554$$
$$3y: 1/(1.05598)^3 = 0.84924485$$
$$4y: 1/(1.06675)^4 = 0.77223484$$
$$5y: 1/(1.07213)^5 = 0.70593182.$$

The price of the 6% 2-year bond is then calculated in the normal fashion using present values of the cash flows:

$$(6 \times 0.95238095) \times (106 \times 0.90236554) = 101.365.$$

The YTM is 5.263%, obtained using the iterative method, with a spreadsheet function such as Microsoft Excel® "Goal Seek" or a Hewlett Packard (HP) calculator. The price of the 7% 5-year bond is:

$$(7 \times 0.95238095) + (7 \times 0.90236554) + (7 \times 0.84924485) + (7 \times 0.77223484) + (107 \times 0.70593182) = 99.869.$$

The yield to maturity is 7.05%.

Formula Summary

Example 5.1 illustrates that if the zero-coupon discount factor for n years is df_n and the par yield for N years is rp, then the expression in (5.5) is always true.

(*continued*)

$$(rp \times df_1) + (rp \times df_2) + \ldots + (rp \times df_N) + (1 + df_N) = 1$$
$$rp \times (df_1 + df_2 + \ldots + df_N) = 1 - df_N$$
$$rp = \frac{1 - df_N}{\sum_{n=1}^{N} df_N} \tag{5.5}$$

Using Spot Rates in Bond Analysis

The convention in the markets is to quote the yield on a non-government bond as a certain *spread* over the yield on the equivalent maturity government bond, usually using gross redemption yields. Traders and investment managers will assess the relative merits of holding the non-government bond based on the risk associated with the bond's issuer and the magnitude of its yield spread. For example, in the UK at the beginning of 2006 companies such as National Grid, Severn Trent Water, Abbey National plc and Tesco plc issued sterling-denominated bonds, all of which paid a certain spread over the equivalent gilt bond.[4] Figure 5.9A, B and C shows the yield spreads of corporate bonds of different rating sectors in the USD, EUR and GBP markets in 2005 and 2006, relative to the government yield curve. Yield source is Bloomberg L.P. in all cases.

Traditionally, investors will compare the redemption yield of the bond they are analysing with the redemption yield of the equivalent government bond. As with the redemption yield measure, there is a flaw with this approach, in that the spread quoted is not really comparing like for like, as the yields do not reflect the true term structure given by the spot rate curve. There is an additional inaccuracy if the cash flow stream of the two bonds do not match, which in practice they will do only rarely.

Therefore the correct method for assessing the yield spread of a corporate bond is to replicate its cash flows with those of a government bond, which can be done in theory by matching the cash flows of the corporate bond with a package of government zero-coupon bonds of the same nominal value. If no zero-coupon bond market exists, the cash flows can be matched synthetically by valuing a coupon bond's cash flows on a zero-coupon basis. The corporate bond's price is of course the sum of the present value of all its cash flows, which should be valued at the spot rates in place for each cash flow's maturity.

4 The spread is, of course, not fixed and fluctuates with market conditions and supply and demand.

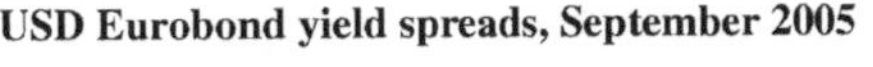

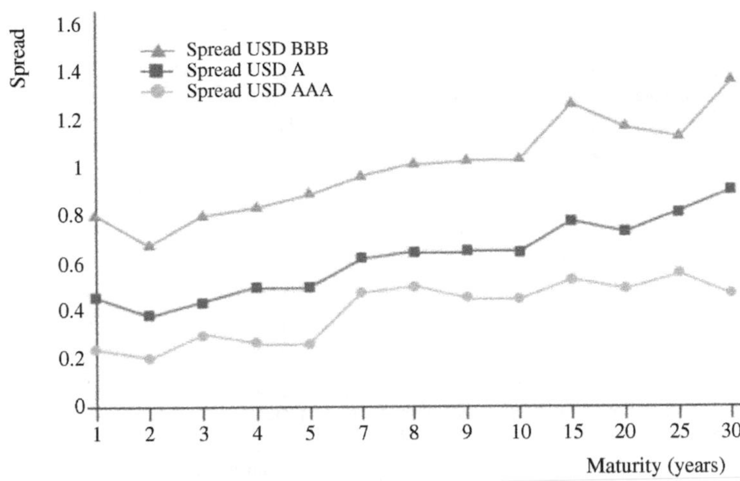

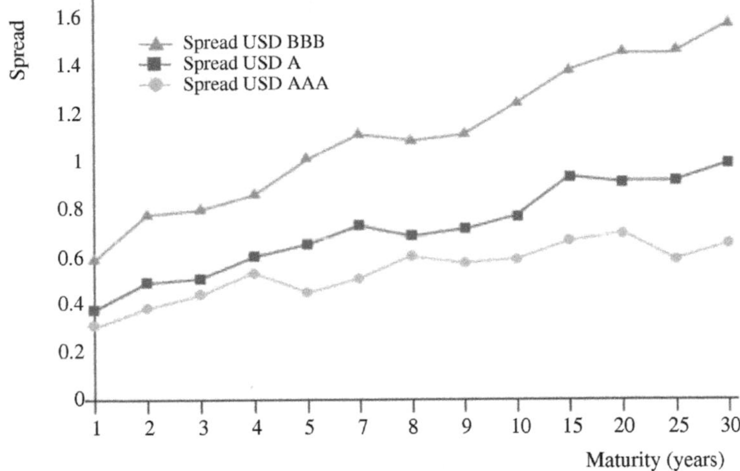

FIGURE 5.9A USD Eurobond yield spreads, 6 September 2005 and 6 September 2006.

It is the yield spread of each individual cash flow over the equivalent maturity government spot rate that is then taken to be the true yield spread.

This measure is known in US markets as the *zero-volatility spread* or *static spread*, and it is a measure of the spread that would be realised over

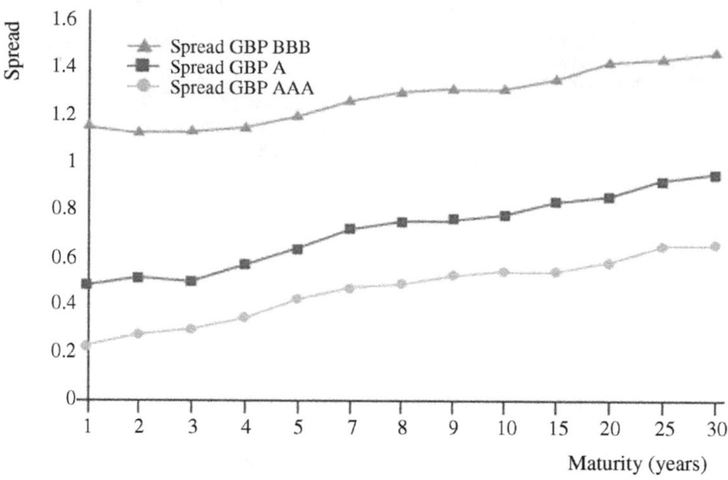

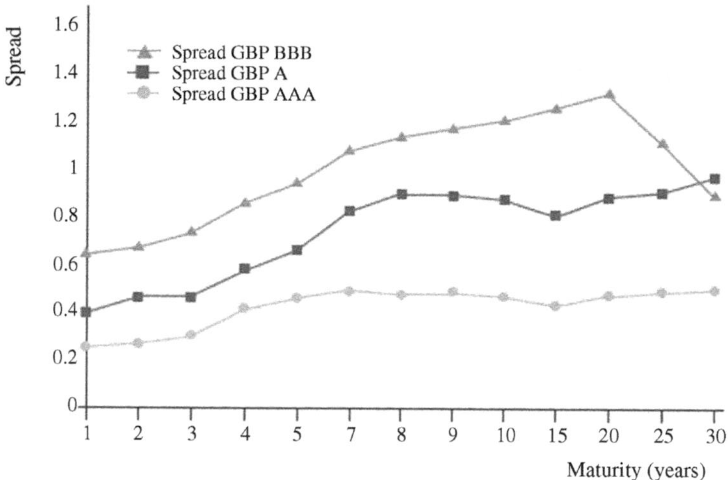

FIGURE 5.9B GBP Eurobond yield spreads, 6 September 2005 and 6 September 2006.

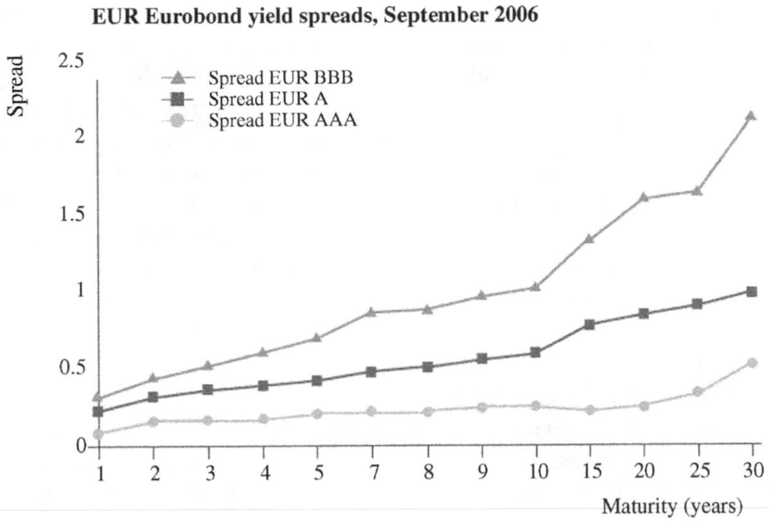

EUR Eurobond yield spreads, September 2006

Maturity (years)	1	2	3	4	5	7	8	9	10	15	20	25	30

Spread; legend: Spread EUR BBB, Spread EUR A, Spread EUR AAA; y-axis: 0, 0.5, 1, 1.5, 2, 2.5

FIGURE 5.9C EUR Eurobond yield spreads, 6 September 2006.

the government spot rate yield curve if the corporate bond were to be held to maturity. It is therefore a different measure to the traditional spread, as it is not taken over one point on the (redemption yield) curve but over the whole term to maturity. The zero-volatility spread is that spread which equates the present value of the corporate bond's cash flows to its price, where the discount rates are each relevant government spot rate. The spread is found through an iterative process, and it is a more realistic yield spread measure than the traditional one.

The Forward Yield Curve

Forward Yields

Most transactions in the market are for immediate delivery, which is known as the *cash* market, although some markets also use the expression *spot* market, which is more common in foreign exchange. Cash market transactions are settled straight away, with the purchaser of a bond being entitled to interest from the settlement date onwards.[5] There is a large market in

5 We refer to "immediate" settlement, although of course there is a delay between trade date and settlement date, which can be anything from one day to seven days, or even longer in some markets. The most common settlement period is known as "spot" and is two business days.

forward transactions, which are trades carried out today for a forward settlement date. For financial transactions that are forward transactions, the parties to the trade agree today to exchange a security for cash at a future date, but at a price agreed today. So the forward rate applicable to a bond is the spot bond yield as at the forward date. That is, it is the yield of a zero-coupon bond that is purchased for settlement at the forward date. It is derived today, using data from a present-day yield curve, so it is not correct to consider forward rates to be a prediction of the spot rates as at the forward date. Rather, the correct way to view forward rates is simply the forward-starting equivalent of spot rates; that they are saying one-and-the-same thing is immediately apparent when one considers the mathematical relationships below.

Forward rates can be derived from spot interest rates. Such rates are then known as implied forward rates, since they are implied by the current range of spot interest rates. The *forward* (or *forward–forward*) *yield curve* is a plot of forward rates against term to maturity. Forward rates satisfy expression (5.6):

$$
\begin{aligned}
P_d &= \frac{C}{(1+{}_0rf_1)} + \frac{C}{(1+{}_0rf_1)(1+{}_0rf_2)} + \dots + \frac{M}{(1+{}_0rf_1)\dots(1+{}_{N-1}rf_N)} \\
&= \sum_{n=1}^{N} \frac{C}{\prod_{n=1}^{n}(1+{}_{i-1}rf_i)} + \frac{M}{\prod_{n=1}^{N}(1+{}_{i-1}rf_i)}
\end{aligned}
\tag{5.6}
$$

where ${}_{n-1}rf_n$ is the implicit forward rate (or forward–forward rate) on a 1-year bond maturing in year N, with coupons C and redemption payment M.

As a forward or forward–forward yield is implied from spot rates, the forward rate is a forward zero-coupon rate. Comparing (5.1) and (5.6) we see that the spot yield is the geometric mean of the forward rates, as shown below:

$$(1+rs_n)^n = (1+{}_0rf_1)(1+{}_1rf_2)\dots(1+{}_{n-1}rf_n). \tag{5.7}$$

This implies the following relationship between spot and forward rates:

$$
\begin{aligned}
(1+{}_{n-1}rf_n) &= \frac{(1+rs_n)^n}{(1+rs_{n-1})^{n-1}} \\
&= \frac{df_{n-1}}{df_n}.
\end{aligned}
\tag{5.8}
$$

TABLE 5.1 Coupon, spot and forward yields.

Year	Coupon yield (%)	Zero-coupon yield (%)	Forward rate (%)
1	5.000	5.000	5.000
2	5.250	5.2566	5.5138
3	5.750	5.7844	6.8479

Using the spot yields we calculated in the earlier paragraph we can derive the implied forward rates from (5.8). For example, the 2-year and 3-year forward rates are given by:

$$(1 + {}_1rf_2) = \frac{(1 + 0.05256)^2}{(1 + 0.05)} = 5.5138\%$$

$$(1 + {}_2rf_3) = \frac{(1 + 0.05778)^3}{(1 + 0.05256)^2} = 6.8479\%.$$

Using our expression gives us ${}_0rf_1$ equal to 5%, ${}_1rf_2$ equal to 5.514% and ${}_2rf_3$ as 6.848%. This means, for example, that given current spot yields, which we calculated from the 1-year, 2-year and 3-year bond redemption yields (which were priced at par), the market would set the yield on a bond with one year to mature in three years' time at 6.848% (that is, the 3-year 1-period forward–forward rate is 6.848%).

The relationship between the par yields, spot yields and forward rates is shown in Table 5.1.

Figurc 5.10 highlights our results for all three yield curves graphically. This illustrates another important property of the relationship between the three curves, in that as the original coupon yield curve was positively sloping, so the spot and forward yield curves lie above it. The reasons behind this will be considered later in the chapter.

Let us now consider the following example. Suppose that a 2-year bond with cash flows of £5.25 at the end of year 1 and £105.25 at the end of year 2 is trading at par, hence it has a redemption yield (indeed, a par yield) of 5.25% (this is the bond in Table 5.1 above). To be regarded as equivalent to this a pure zero-coupon bond or discount bond making a lump-sum payment at the end of year 2 only (so with no cash flow at the end of year 1) would require a rate of return of 5.257%, which is the spot yield. That is, for the same investment of £100 the maturity value would have to be £110.79 (this figure is obtained by multiplying 100 by $(1 + 0.05257)^2$).

This illustrates why the zero-coupon curve is important to corporate financiers involved in new bond issues. If we know the spot yields, then we

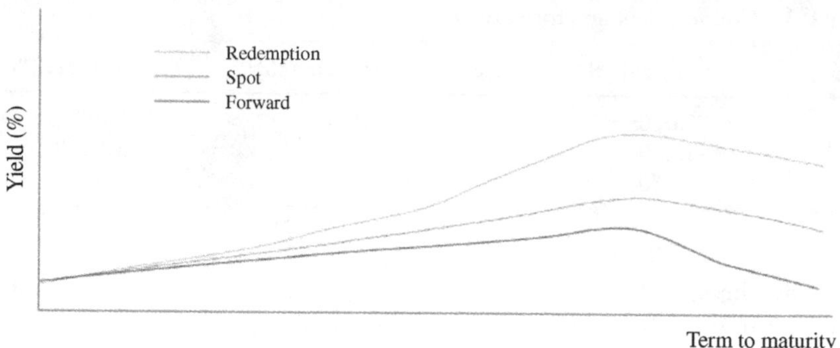

FIGURE 5.10 Redemption, spot and forward yield curves: traditional analysis.

can calculate the coupon required on a new 3-year bond that is going to be issued at par in this interest-rate environment by making the following calculation:

$$100 = \frac{C}{(1.05)} + \frac{C}{(1.05257)^2} + \frac{C + 100}{(1.05784)^3}.$$

This is solved in the conventional algebraic manner to give C equal to 5.75%.

The relationship between spot rates and forward rates was shown in (5.8). We can illustrate it as follows. If the spot yield is the average return, then the forward rate can be interpreted as the marginal return. If the marginal return between years 2 and 3 increases from 5.514% to 6.848%, then the average return increases from 5.257% up to the 3-year spot yield of 5.784% as shown below:

$$\{[(1.05257)^2(1.06848)]^{1/3} - 1\} = 0.05784$$

or 5.784%, as shown in Table 5.1.

FORMULA SUMMARY

The forward zero-coupon rate from interest period a to period b is given by (5.9):

$$_{\mathrm{a}}rf_{\mathrm{b}} = \left[\frac{(1 + rs_b)^b}{(1 + rs_a)^a}\right]^{1/(b-a)} - 1 \qquad (5.9)$$

where rs_a and rs_b are the a and b period spot rates respectively, and $_{\mathrm{a}}rf_{\mathrm{b}}$ is an annualised forward rate.

The forward rate from interest period a to period $(a + 1)$ is given by (5.10):

$$_{a}rf_{a+1} = \frac{(1 + rs_{a+1})^{a+1}}{(1 + rs_a)^a} - 1. \tag{5.10}$$

Calculating Spot Rates from Forward Rates

The previous section showed the relationship between spot and forward rates. Just as we have derived forward rates from spot rates based on this mathematical relationship, it is possible to reverse this and calculate spot rates from forward rates. If we are presented with a forward yield curve, plotted from a set of one-period forward rates, we can use this to construct a spot yield curve. Equation (5.7) states the relationship between spot and forward rates, rearranged as (5.11) to solve for the spot rate:

$$rs_n = [(1 + {_1rf_1}) \times (1 + {_2rf_1}) \times (1 + {_3rf_1}) \times \ldots \times (1 + {_nrf_1})]^{1/n} - 1 \tag{5.11}$$

where ${_1rf_1}$, ${_2rf_1}$, ${_3rf_1}$ are the 1-period versus 2-period, 2-period versus 3-period forward rates up to the $(n - 1)$ period versus n-period forward rates.

Remember to adjust (5.11) as necessary if dealing with forward rates relating to a deposit of a different interest period. If we are dealing with the current 6-month spot rate and implied 6-month forward rates, the relationship between these and the n-period spot rate is given by (5.11) in the same way as if we were dealing with the current 1-year spot rate and implied 1-year forward rates.

EXAMPLE 5.2A SPOT RATES

The 1-year cash market yield is 5.00%. Spot prices imply 1-year rates in one year's time at 5.95% and in two years' time at 7.25%. What is the current 3-year spot rate that would produce these forward rate views?

To calculate this we assume an investment strategy dealing today at forward rates, and calculate the return generated from this strategy. The return after a 3-year period is given by the future value relationship, which in this case is $1.05 \times 1.0595 \times 1.0725 = 1.1931$.

(continued)

(*continued*)

The 3-year spot rate is then obtained by:

$$\left(\frac{1.1931}{1}\right)^{1/3} - 1 = 6.062\%.$$

EXAMPLE 5.2B FORWARD RATES

Consider the following 6-month implied forward rates, when the 6-month spot rate is 4.0000%.

$_1rf_1$ 4.0000%
$_2rf_1$ 4.4516%
$_3rf_1$ 5.1532%
$_4rf_1$ 5.6586%
$_5rf_1$ 6.0947%
$_6rf_1$ 7.1129%

An investor is debating between purchasing a 3-year zero-coupon bond at a price of £72.91028 per £100 nominal, or buying a 6-month zero-coupon bond and then rolling over her investment every six months for the 3-year term. If the investor was able to reinvest her proceeds every six months at the actual forward rates in place today, what would her proceeds be at the end of the 3-year term? An investment of £72.91028 at the spot rate of 4% and then reinvested at the forward rates in our table over the next three years would yield a terminal value of:

$$\begin{aligned}&72.91028\\&\quad \times (1.04)(1.044516)(1.051532)(1.056586)(1.060947)(1.071129)\\&\quad = 100.\end{aligned}$$

This merely reflects our spot and forward rates relationship, in that if all the forward rates are indeed realised, our investor's £72.91 will produce a terminal value that matches the investment in a 3-year zero-coupon bond priced at the 3-year spot rate. This illustrates the relationship between the 3-year spot rate, the 6-month spot rate and the implied 6-month forward rates. So what is the 3-year zero-coupon bond trading at? Using (5.11) the solution to this is given by:

$$rs_6 = [(1.04)(1.044516)(1.051532)(1.056586)(1.060947)(1.071129)]^{1/6} - 1 = 5.4068\%$$

which solves our 3-year spot rate rs_6 as 5.4068%. Of course, we could have also solved for rs_6 using the conventional price/yield formula for zero-coupon bonds; however, the calculation above illustrates the relationship between spot and forward rates.

An Important Note on Spot and Forward Rates

Forward rates that exist at any one time reflect everything that is known in the market *up to that point*. Certain market participants believe that the forward rate curve is a forecast of the future spot rate curve. This is implied by the *unbiased expectations hypothesis* that we consider below. In fact, this interpretation of implied forward rates is incorrect; for an excellent analysis of this see Jarrow (1996). It is possible, for example, for the forward rate curve to be upward sloping at the same time that short-dated spot rates are expected to decline, but this is simply explained by the mathematical properties of forward rates (the best explanation for this is given in Campbell, Lo and MacKinlay (1997), see also Example 5.9 on page 284). To view the forward rate curve as a predictor of rates is a misuse of it. The derivation of forward rates reflects all currently known market information. Assuming that all developed country markets are at least in a semi-strong form,[6] to preserve market equilibrium there can only be one set of forward rates from a given spot rate curve. However, this does not mean that such rates are a prediction because the instant after they have been calculated new market knowledge may become available that alters the market's view of current interest rates. This will cause the forward rate curve to change.

Forward rates are important because they are needed if we are to make prices today for dealing at a future date. For example, a bank's corporate customer may wish to fix today the interest rate payable on a loan that begins in one year from now; what rate does the bank quote? The forward rate is used by market-makers to quote prices for dealing today, and is the best *implied expectation* of future interest rates given everything that is known in the market up to now, but it is not a prediction of future spot rates. What would happen if a bank were privy to insider information;

6 See Fama (1970).

for example, it knew that central bank base rates would be changed very shortly? A bank in possession of such information (if we ignore the ethical implications) would not quote forward rates based on the spot rate curve, but would quote rates that reflected its insider knowledge.

The Bootstrapping Approach Using Discount Factors

In this section we describe how to obtain zero-coupon and forward rates from the yields available from coupon bonds, using the *bootstrapping* technique. In a government bond market such as US Treasuries, the bonds are considered to be default-free. The rates from a government bond yield curve describe the risk-free rates of return available in the market today; however, they also *imply* (risk-free) rates of return for future time periods. These implied future rates, known as *implied forward rates*, or simply *forward rates*, can be derived from a given discount function or spot yield curve using bootstrapping. This term reflects the fact that each calculated spot rate is used to determine the next period spot rate, in successive steps. We illustrate the technique using discount factors. Once we have obtained the discount curve, it is a straightforward process to obtain the spot rate curve, as we saw earlier when we described the relationship that exists between discount factors, spot rates and forward rates.

A t-period discount factor is the present value of \$1 that is payable at the end of period t. Essentially it is the present value relationship expressed in terms of \$1. If $d(t)$ is the t-year discount factor, then the 5-year discount factor at a discount rate of 6% is given by:

$$d(5) = \frac{1}{(1+0.06)^5} = 0.747258.$$

The set of discount factors for the time period from one day to 30 years (or longer) is termed the *discount function*. Discount factors are used to price any financial instrument that is comprised of a future cash flow. For example, if the 6-month discount factor is 0.98756, the current value of the maturity payment of a 7% semi-annual coupon bond due for receipt in six months' time is given by 0.98756×103.50 or 102.212.

Discount factors may be used to calculate the future value of any current investment. From the example above, \$0.98756 would be worth \$1 in six months' time, so by the same principle a present sum of \$1 would be worth at the end of six months:

$$1/d(5) = 1/0.98756 = 1.0126.$$

As we saw earlier in the chapter, the interrelationship between discount factors and spot and forward rates means we may obtain discount factors from current bond prices. Assume a hypothetical set of semi-annual coupon

TABLE 5.2 Hypothetical set of bonds and bond prices

Coupon	Maturity date	Price
7%	7/6/2001	101.65
8%	7/12/2001	101.89
6%	7/6/2002	100.75
6.50%	7/12/2002	100.37

bonds and bond prices as given in Table 5.2, and assume further that the first bond matures in precisely six months' time. All other bonds then mature at 6-month intervals.

Taking the first bond, this matures in precisely six months' time, and its final cash flow will be 103.50, comprised of the \$3.50 final coupon payment and the \$100 redemption payment. The market-observed price of this bond is \$101.65, which allows us to calculate the 6-month discount factor as:

$$d(0.5) \times 103.50 = 101.65$$

which gives us $d(0.5)$ equal to 0.98213.

From this step we can calculate the discount factors for the following 6-month periods. The second bond in Table 5.2, the 8% 2001, has the following cash flows:

- \$4 in six months' time
- \$104 in one year's time.

The price of this bond is 101.89, the bond's present value, and this is comprised of the sum of the present values of the bond's total cash flows. So we are able to set the following:

$$101.89 = 4 \times d(0.5) + 101 \times d(1).$$

However, we already know $d(0.5)$ to be 0.98213, which leaves only one unknown in the above expression. Therefore we may solve for $d(1)$ and this is shown to be 0.94194.

If we carry on with this procedure for the remaining two bonds, using successive discount factors, we obtain the complete set of discount factors as shown in Table 5.3. The continuous function for the 2-year period is shown as the discount function in Figure 5.11.

TABLE 5.3 Discount factors calculated using the bootstrapping technique.

Coupon	Maturity date	Term (years)	Price	*dn*
7%	7/6/2001	0.5	101.65	0.98213
8%	7/12/2001	1	101.89	0.94194
6%	7/6/2002	1.5	100.75	0.92211
6.50%	7/12/2002	2	100.37	0.88252

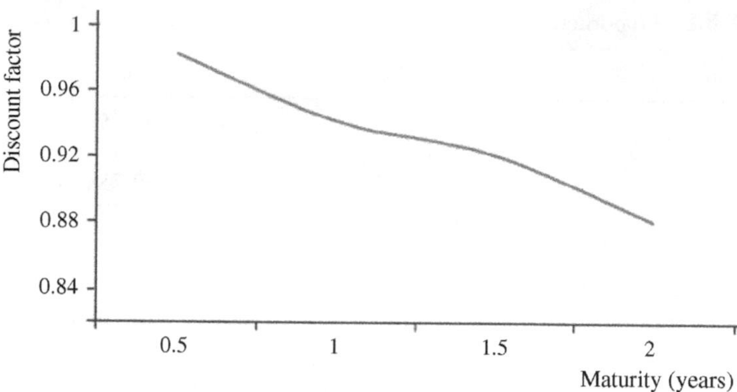

FIGURE 5.11 Discount function.

Once we have the discount function we are able to compute the zero-coupon rates and hence also the forward rates. As a result, we can fit the yield curve from the discount function.

The theoretical approach described above is neat and appealing, but in practice there are a number of issues that will complicate the attempt to extract zero-coupon rates from bond yields. The main problem is that it is highly unlikely that we will have a set of bonds that are both precisely six months (or one interest) apart in maturity and priced precisely at par. We also require our procedure to fit as smooth a curve as possible. Setting our coupon bonds at a price of par simplified the analysis in our illustration of bootstrapping, so in reality we need to apply more advanced techniques. A standard approach for extracting zero-coupon bond prices is described in Choudhry (2004b).

EXAMPLE 5.3 FORWARD RATES: BREAK-EVEN PRINCIPLE

Consider the following spot yields:

1y: 10%

2y: 12%.

Assume that a bank's client wishes to lock in today the cost of borrowing 1-year funds in one year's time. The solution for the bank (and the mechanism to enable the bank to quote a price to the client) involves raising 1-year funds at 10% and investing the proceeds for two years at 12%. The no-arbitrage principle means that the same return must be generated from both fixed rate and reinvestment strategies.

In effect, we can look at the issue in terms of two alternative investment strategies, both of which must provide the same return.

Strategy 1: Invest funds for two years at 12%.

Strategy 2: Invest funds for one year at 10%, and reinvest the proceeds for a further year at the forward rate calculated today.

The forward rate for strategy 2 is the rate that will be quoted to the client. Using the present value relationship we know that the proceeds from strategy 1 are:

$$FV = (1 + r_2)^2$$

while the proceeds from strategy 2 would be:

$$FV = (1 + r_1) \times (1 + R).$$

We know from the no-arbitrage principle that the proceeds from both strategies will be the same; therefore, this enables us to set:

$$\begin{aligned}(1 + r_2)^2 &= (1 + r_1)(1 + R)\\ R &= \frac{(1 + r_2)^2}{(1 + r_1)} - 1.\end{aligned}$$

From this we calculate the forward rate that can be quoted to the client (together with any spread that the bank might add) as follows:

$$\begin{aligned}&(1 + 0.12)^2 = (1 + 0.10) \times (1 + R)\\ &(1 + R) = (1 + 0.12)^2/(1 + 0.10)\\ &(1 + R) = 1.14036\\ &R = 14.04\%.\end{aligned}$$

This rate is the 1-year forward–forward rate, or the implied forward rate.

EXAMPLE 5.4 SIMPLE CALCULATION OF THE FORWARD RATE FROM ZERO-COUPON RATE

A customer asks you to fix a yield at which he could issue a 2-year zero-coupon USD Eurobond in three years' time. At this time the US Treasury zero-coupon rates are:

1y: 6.25%

2y: 6.75%

3y: 7.00%

4y: 7.125%

5y: 7.25%.

Ignoring the customer's borrowing spreads over these risk-free benchmark yields, as a market-maker you could cover the exposure created by borrowing funds for five years on a zero-coupon basis and placing these funds in the market for three years before lending them on to your client. Assume annual interest compounding (even if none is actually paid out during the life of the loans).

$$\text{Borrowing rate for five years: } \left[\frac{R_5}{100}\right] = 0.0725$$

$$\text{Lending rate for three years: } \left[\frac{R_3}{100}\right] = 0.0700.$$

The key arbitrage relationship is:

Total cost of funding = Total return on investments

$$(1 + R_5)^5 = (1 + R_3)^3 \times (1 + R_{3\times5})^2.$$

Therefore the break-even forward yield is:

$$(1 + R_{3\times5})^2 = \frac{(1 + 0.0725)^5}{(1 + 0.0700)^3}$$

$$(1 + R_{3\times5}) = \sqrt{\left[\frac{(1 + 0.0725)^5}{(1 + 0.0700)^3}\right]}$$

$$R_{3\times5} = \sqrt{\left[\frac{(1 + 0.0725)^5}{(1 + 0.0700)^3}\right]} - 1$$

$$= 7.63\%.$$

EXAMPLE 5.5 FORWARD RATE CALCULATION FOR MONEY MARKET TERM

Consider two positions:

- a borrowing of £100 million from 5 November for 30 days at 5.875%;
- a loan of £100 million from 5 November for 60 days at 6.125%.

This is an example of a funding gap. The bank will have to "roll over" its funding after 30 days, at which point it stands to lose money if interest rates have risen in the meantime. Therefore the two positions can be viewed as a 30-day forward 30-day interest-rate exposure (a 30- versus 60-day forward rate).

The bank can hedge this exposure by dealing today, eliminating the interest-rate gap exposure. What forward rate must be used if the trader wished to hedge this exposure? The 30-day by 60-day forward rate can be calculated using the following formula:

$$rf_i = \left[\left(\frac{1 + \left(rs_{L\%} \cdot \frac{n_L}{B}\right)}{1 + \left(rs_{S\%} \cdot \frac{n_S}{B}\right)}\right) - 1\right] \times \frac{B}{n_L - n_S}$$

where

rf_i = is the forward rate
$rs_L\%$ = is the long-period rate
$rs_S\%$ = is the short-period rate
n_L = is the long-period term in days
n_S = is the short-period term in days
B = is the day-count base, either 360 or 365.

Using this formula we obtain a 30v60 day forward rate of 6.3443%.

This interest-rate exposure can be hedged using interest-rate futures or FRAs. Either method is an effective hedging mechanism.

EXAMPLE 5.6 QUICK CALCULATION METHOD

[A]

Given the following zero-coupon yields, what does the par yield curve look like? The results as shown in Figure 5.12.

Term	Zero-coupon yield	Par yield	
1-year	4.5000	4.5	
2-year	4.7800	4.77	
3-year	5.1250	5.1	
4-year	5.3640	5.32	
5-year	5.8210	5.74	
		Discount factor	
1-year	1/(1.045)	0.956938	
2-year	1/(1.0478)^2	0.910842	
3-year	1/(1.05125)^3	0.860760	
4-year	1/(1.053640)^4	0.811393	
5-year	1/(1.058210)^5	0.753600	
1-year par yield			4.50%
2-year par yield	1−0.910842/(0.956939+0.910842)	0.047734718	4.77%
3-year par yield	1−0.86076/(0.956938 +0.910842+0.86076)	0.051030954	5.10%
4-year par yield	1−0.811393/(0.956938 +0.910842+0.86076+0.811393)	0.053279822	5.32%
5-year par yield	1−0.753600/(0.956938+0.910842 +0.86076+0.811393+0.753600)	0.057388635	5.74%

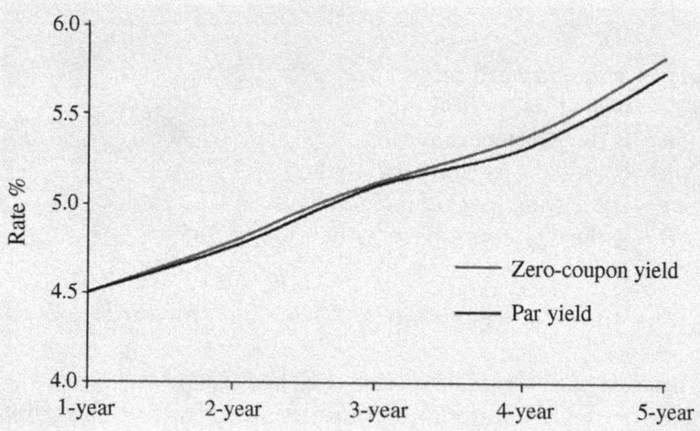

FIGURE 5.12 Par and zero-coupon curves.

[B]

Given the same zero-coupon yield curve as above, what are the 1-year versus 2-year, 2-year versus 3-year, 3-year versus 4-year and the 4-year versus 5-year forward–forward yields?

The zero-coupon discount factors are the same as before.

The solution is shown at Table 5.4.

Term	Zero-coupon yield	Discount factor
1-year	4.5000	0.956938
2-year	4.7800	0.910842
3-year	5.1250	0.860760
4-year	5.3640	0.811393
5-year	5.8210	0.753600
1-year versus 2-year fwd–fwd yield = (0.956938/0.910842) – 1	0.050608119	5.06%
2-year versus 3-year fwd–fwd yield = (0.910842/0.860760) – 1	0.058183466	5.81%
3-year versus 4-year fwd–fwd yield = (0.860760/0.811393) – 1	0.06084228	6.08%
4-year versus 5-year fwd–fwd yield = (0.811393/0.753600) – 1	0.076689225	7.67%

TABLE 5.4 Forward rates calculation.

[C]

The 1-year market interest rate is at 4.50%. Market expectations are for a rise in the 1-year rate to 5.00% in the next year and 5.50% in the year following that. Given this consensus, what should the current 2-year and 3-year zero-coupon yields be?

2-year zero-coupon yield $= (1.045 \times 1.05)^{1/2} - 1$
$= 0.47497 = 4.75\%$
3-year zero-coupon yield $= (1.045 \times 1.05 \times 1.055) \wedge 1/3 - 1$
$= 1.049992 = 5.00\%$

CASE STUDY 5.1 DERIVING A DISCOUNT FUNCTION[7]

In this example we present a traditional bootstrapping technique for deriving a discount function for yield curve fitting purposes. This technique has been called "naïve" (for instance, see James and Webber 2000, p. 129) because it suffers from a number of drawbacks; for example, it results in an unrealistic forward rate curve, which means that it is unlikely to be used in practice. This does not mean that the method does not have practical application though. We review the drawbacks at the end of the case study.

Today is 14 July 2000. The following rates are observed in the market. We assume that the day-count basis for the cash instruments and swaps is act/365. Construct the money market discount function.

Money market rates	Rate (%)	Expiry	Days
One month (1-m)	$4\frac{7}{32}$	14/8/00	31
3-m	$4\frac{1}{4}$	16/10/00	94
6-m	$4\frac{1}{2}$	15/1/01	185
Futures prices			
Sep-00	95.60	20/9/00	68
Dec-00	95.39	20/12/00	159
Mar-01	95.25	21/3/01	250
Jun-01	94.80	20/6/01	341
Swap rates			
One year (1-y)	4.95	16/7/01	367
2-y	5.125	15/7/02	731
3-y	5.28	14/7/03	1095
4-y	5.55	14/7/04	1461
5-y	6.00	14/7/05	1826

Creating the Discount Function

Using the cash money market rates we can create discount factors up to a maturity of six months, using the expression below:

7 In this illustration, the discount function is derived using interest-rate data from two off-balance sheet derivative instruments, futures and swaps, as well as money market deposit rates. For readers unfamiliar with these products, futures and swaps are covered in chapters 15 and 16 of the author's book *Fixed Income Markets* (Wiley 2004). For the market benchmark see Hull (2011).

$$Df = \frac{1}{\left(1 + \left(r \times \frac{days}{365}\right)\right)}.$$

The resulting discount factors are:

From	To	Days	r%	Df
14/7/00	14/8/00	31	$4\frac{7}{32}$	0.99642974
	16/10/00	94	$4\frac{1}{4}$	0.98917329
	15/1/01	185	$4\frac{1}{2}$	0.97770040

We can also calculate forward discount factors from the rates implied in the futures prices, which are shown below.

From	To	Days	r%	Df
20/9/00	20/12/00	91	4.40	0.98903014
20/12/00	21/3/01	91	4.61	0.98850658
21/3/01	20/6/01	91	4.75	0.98815753
20/6/01	19/9/01	91	5.20	0.98703562

In order to convert these values into zero-coupon discount factors, we need first to derive a cash "stub" rate up to the expiry of the first futures contract. The most straightforward way to do this is by linear interpolation of the 1-month and 3-month rates, as shown in Figure 5.13.

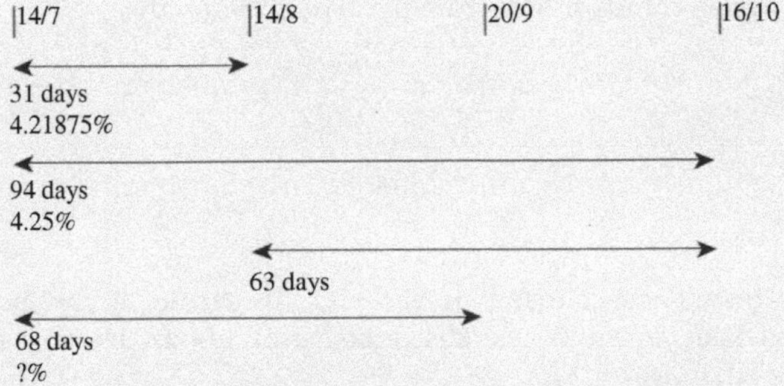

FIGURE 5.13 Linear interpolation of money market and futures rates.

(continued)

For instance, the calculation for the term (68−31) days marked is:

$$4.21875 + \left((4.25 - 4.21875) \times \frac{37}{63}\right) = 4.237\%.$$

Converting this to a discount factor:

$$\frac{1}{\left(1 + \left(0.04237103 \times \frac{68}{365}\right)\right)} = 0.99216804.$$

From the futures implied forward rates, the zero-coupon discount factors are calculated by successive multiplication of the individual discount factors. These are shown below.

From	To	Days	*Df*
14/7/00	20/9/00	68	0.992168043
	20/12/00	159	0.981284095
	21/3/01	250	0.9700058
	20/6/01	341	0.9585185
	19/9/01	432	0.94609192

For the interest-rate swap rates, to calculate discount factors for the relevant dates we need to use the bootstrapping technique.

1-y Swap

We assume a par swap, so the present value is known to be 100, and as we know the future value as well, we are able to calculate the 1-year zero-coupon rate as shown from the 1-year swap rate:

$$Df_1 = \frac{1}{1+r} = \frac{100}{104.95}$$

$$= 0.95283468.$$

2-y Swap

The coupon payment occurring at the end of period 1 can be discounted back using the 1-year discount factor above, leaving a zero-coupon structure as before.

$$Df_2 = \frac{100 - \mathrm{C} \times Df_1}{105.125}$$

This gives Df_2 equal to 0.90479641.

The same process can be employed for the 3-, 4- and 5-year par swap rates to calculate the appropriate discount factors:

$$Df_3 = \frac{100 - C \times (df_1 + df_2)}{105.28}.$$

This gives Df_3 equal to 0.8566842. The discount factors for the 4-year and 5-year maturities, calculated in the same way, are 0.80469494 and 0.74420697 respectively.

The full discount function is given in Table 5.5 and illustrated graphically in Figure 5.14.

TABLE 5.5 Discount factors

From	To	Days	Zero-coupon (%)	Discount factor	Source
14/07/2000	14/08/2000	31	4.21875	0.996429744	Money market
	20/09/2000	68	4.23710	0.992168043	Futures
	16/10/2000	94	4.25000	0.989173295	Money market
	20/12/2000	159	4.37836	0.981284095	Futures
	15/01/2001	185	4.50000	0.977700395	Money market
	21/03/2001	250	4.51457	0.970005780	Futures
	20/06/2001	341	4.63225	0.958518520	Futures
	16/07/2001	367	4.92237	0.952834683	Swap
	19/09/2001	432	4.81426	0.946091918	Futures
	15/07/2002	731	5.12230	0.904796407	Swap
	14/07/2003	1095	5.29145	0.856684155	Swap
	14/07/2004	1461	5.57863	0.804694935	Swap
	14/07/2005	1826	6.08334	0.744206971	Swap

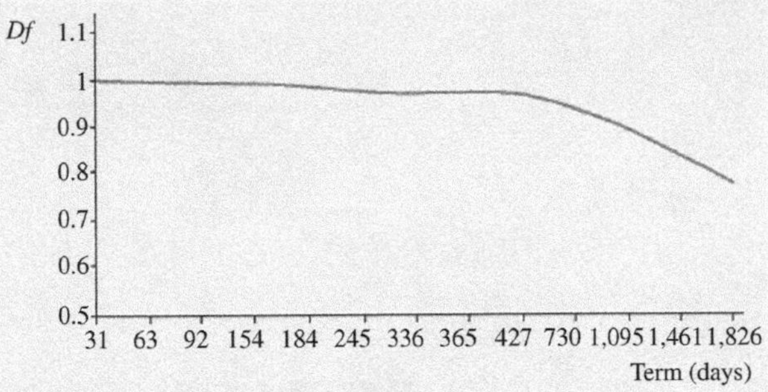

FIGURE 5.14 Discount function.

Critique of the Traditional Technique

The method used to derive the discount function in Case Study 5.1 used three different price sources to produce an integrated function and hence yield curve. However, there is no fully effective method by which the three separate curves, which are shown in Figure 5.15, can be integrated into one complete curve. The result is that a curve formed from the three separate curves will exhibit distinct kinks or steps at the points at which one data source is replaced by another data source.

The money market and swap rates incorporate a credit risk premium, reflecting the fact that inter-bank market counterparties carry an element of default risk. This means that money market rates lie above government repo rates. Futures rates do not reflect default risk, as they are exchange-traded contracts and the exchange clearing house takes on counterparty risk for each transaction. However, futures rates are treated as 1-point period rates, in effect making them equivalent to FRA rates. In theory, as the cash flow from FRAs is received as a discounted payoff at one point, whereas futures contract trades require a daily margin payment, a *convexity adjustment* is required to convert futures accurately to FRA rates. This adjustment is considered in Choudhry (2004b).

The original rationale for a convexity adjustment was articulated in Burghardt and Hoskins (1994). In the Technical Note No.1 to Hull (2011), the author states that when converting a futures rate to a forward rate, we need to make an adjustment because of the following (assume two contracts initiated at time 0 and maturing at time T):

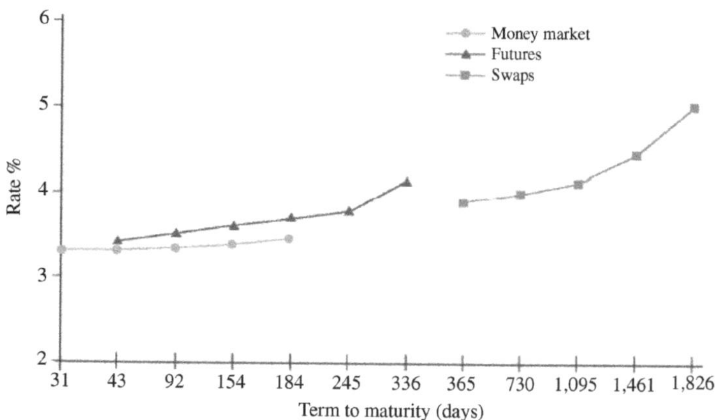

FIGURE 5.15 Comparison of money market curves.

- the difference between a futures contract that is settled daily, for example because of daily margining at the futures exchange, and a similar contract that is settled entirely at time T (for example an OTC FRA);
- the difference between a contract that is settled at T_1 and a similar contract settled at T_2.

This is essentially the longstanding Burghardt-articulated correction needed to move from an uncollateralised FRA (a contract that is fixed in advance and whose payoff is a discounted value at the crystallised rate in advance), to a purely linear futures contract which pays out a fixed PV01 times the basis points of intrinsic value, also fixed in advance and paid in advance, and on which daily variation margin is settled throughout its life.

However in the inter-bank market, under a 2-way CSA agreement that permits only cash collateral, this settlement distinction no longer applies and the payoff from a FRA and a future of identical tenor can be regarded as riskless, in the sense that the mark-to-market gain/loss from both contracts will be continually funded overnight. This brings the two instrument types close to equal, because their terminal payoffs can be discounted at very similar rates. In other words, in a daily collateralised OTC derivative environment, the original rationale for the convexity adjustment, to all practical intents and purposes, no longer applies.

That said, there is *still* a need to make an adjustment, which we also refer to as a convexity adjustment, because in fact the payoffs from the two contract types are different. A USD1 million Eurodollar contract will pay or cost:

USD25 $*$ (Fixing rate – Contracted rate).

A USD1 million FRA will pay or cost:

PV01 {(End date – Start date)/360; Fixing rate} $*$ (Fixing rate – Contracted rate).

The futures contract is linear in the fixing rate, while the PV01 of the FRA varies, making it non-linear (concave) in the fixing rate. So if one was to short the futures contract and sell the FRA against it, one would be un-hedged unless one "topped up" the hedge with a portfolio of out-the-money caplets, or otherwise dynamically adjusted the futures position over time.

For yield curve fitting purposes, we summarise as follows: an uncollateralised FRA rate compared to a futures rate requires correction because of the payoff difference and the counterparty credit risk factor. Collateralising the FRA deals with the latter issue but not the former, so a convexity adjustment still needs to be made. This adjustment, together with any *quanto* adjustment, is the drift correction necessary when moving between the two measures.

Swap rates also incorporate an element of credit risk. As liquid swap rates are only available for set maturity points, linear interpolation is used to plot points in between available rates. This results in an unstable forward rate curve calculated from the spot rate curve (see James and Webber 2000), due to the interpolation effect. Nevertheless, market-makers sometimes still price intermediate-dated swaps based on this linear interpolation method. Another drawback is that the bootstrapping method uses near-maturity rates to build up the curve to far-maturity rates. One of the features of a spot curve derived in this way is that even small changes in short-term rates cause excessive changes in long-dated spot rates, and large oscillations in the forward curve. In other words, tiny errors at the short end are magnified at the long end. Finally, money market rates beyond the "stub" period are not considered once the discount factor to the stub date is calculated, so their impact is not felt.

For these reasons the traditional technique is not used very often in the markets, although its use, especially for analysis purposes, is not uncommon.

ANALYSING AND INTERPRETING THE YIELD CURVE

From observing yield curves in different markets at any time, we notice that a yield curve can adopt one of four basic shapes. These are:

- *normal or conventional:* in which yields are at "average" levels and the curve slopes gently upwards as maturity increases;
- *upward sloping or positive or rising:* in which yields are at historically low levels, with long rates substantially greater than short rates;
- *downward sloping or inverted or negative:* in which yield levels are very high by historical standards, but long-term yields are significantly lower than short rates;
- *humped:* where yields are high with the curve rising to a peak in the medium-term maturity area, and then sloping downwards at longer maturities.

Sometimes yield curves will incorporate a mixture of the above features. A great deal of effort is expended by bond analysts and economists in analysing and interpreting yield curves. There is often considerable information content associated with any curve at any time. For example, Figure 5.16 shows the UK gilt redemption yield curve at three different times in the 10 years from June 2001 to June 2011. What does the shape of each curve tell us about the UK debt market, and the UK economy at each particular time?

In this section we will consider the various explanations that have been put forward to explain the shape of the yield curve at any one time. None of

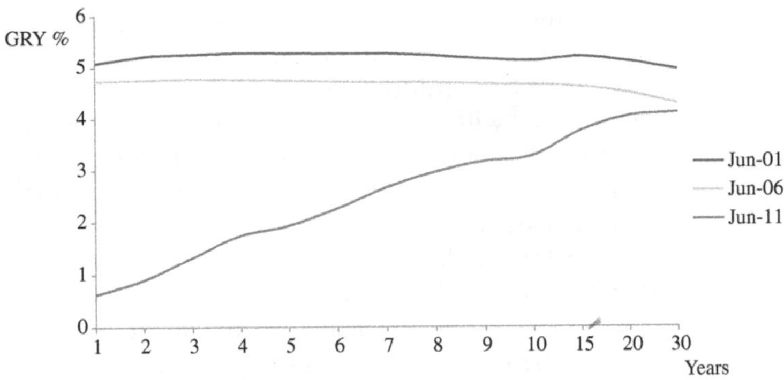

FIGURE 5.16 UK gilt redemption yield curves.

the theories can adequately explain everything about yield curves and the shapes they assume at any time, so generally observers seek to explain specific curves using a combination of the accepted theories. This subject is a large one; indeed, we could devote several books to it, so at this stage we will introduce only the main ideas; readers wishing to read about this in further detail may consult the author's book *Advanced Fixed Income Analysis* (Elsevier 2004).

The existence of a yield curve itself indicates that there is a cost associated with funds of different maturities, otherwise we would observe a flat yield curve. The fact that we very rarely observe a flat yield suggests that investors require different rates of return depending on the maturity of the instrument they are holding. In this section we review the main theories that have been put forward to explain the shape of the yield curve, which all have fairly long-dated antecedents.

By the way, an excellent account of the term structure is given in *Theory of Financial Decision Making* by Jonathan Ingersoll (1951), Chapter 18. In fact, it is worth purchasing this book just for that chapter alone. Another quality account of the term structure is by Shiller (1990). In the following section we provide an introductory review of the main research in this space.

The Expectations Hypothesis

The expectations hypothesis suggests that bondholders' expectations determine the course of future interest rates. There are two main competing versions of this hypothesis, the *local expectations hypothesis* and the *unbiased expectations hypothesis*. The *return-to-maturity expectations* hypothesis and *yield-to-maturity expectations* hypothesis are also referred to (see Ingersoll 1951). The local expectations hypothesis states that all bonds of the same class, but differing in term to maturity, will have the same expected holding period rate of return. This suggests that a 6-month bond and a 20-year bond will produce the same rate of return, on average, over the stated holding period. So if we intend to hold a bond for six months, we will receive the same return no matter what specific bond we buy. The author feels that this theory is not always relevant, despite being mathematically neat; however, it is worth spending a few moments discussing it and related points. Generally, holding period returns from longer dated bonds are on average higher than those from short-dated bonds. Intuitively we would expect this, with longer dated bonds offering higher returns to compensate for their higher price volatility (risk). The local expectations hypothesis would not agree with the conventional belief that investors, being risk averse, require higher returns as a reward for taking on higher risk; in addition, it does not provide any insight about the shape of the yield curve. Cox, Ingersoll and Ross (1981) show that the local expectations hypothesis reflected best the equilibrium between spot and forward yields. This was demonstrated using a feature known as Jensen's inequality, which is described in Appendix 5.1. Furthermore, Robert Jarrow (1996) states:

> *. . . in an economic equilibrium, the returns on . . . similar maturity zero-coupon bonds cannot be too different. If they were too different, no investor would hold the bond with the smaller return. This difference could not persist in an economic equilibrium.*
>
> *Jarrow (1996), p. 50*

This reflects economic logic, but in practice other factors can impact on holding period returns between bonds that do not have similar maturities. For instance, investors will have restrictions as to which bonds they can hold; for example, banks and building societies are required to hold short-dated bonds for liquidity purposes. In an environment of economic disequilibrium, these investors would still have to hold shorter dated bonds, even if the holding period return was lower.

So although it is economically neat to expect that the return on a long-dated bond is equivalent to rolling over a series of shorter dated bonds, it is often observed that longer term (default-free) returns exceed annualised short-term default-free returns. So an investor who continuously rolled over a series of short-dated zero-coupon bonds would most likely receive a lower return than if she had invested in a long-dated zero-coupon bond. Rubinstein (1999) gives an excellent, accessible explanation of why this should be so. The reason is that compared to the theoretical model, in reality future spot rates are not known with certainty. This means that short-dated zero-coupon bonds are more attractive to investors for two reasons; first, they are more appropriate instruments to use for hedging purposes, and second they are more liquid instruments, in that they may be more readily converted back into cash than long-dated instruments. With regard to hedging, consider an exposure to rising interest rates. If the yield curve shifts upwards at some point in the future, the price of long-dated bonds will fall by a greater amount. This is a negative result for holders of such bonds, whereas the investor in short-dated bonds will benefit from rolling over his funds at the (new) higher rates. With regard to the second issue, Rubinstein (1999) states:

> *. . . it can be shown that in an economy with risk-averse individuals, uncertainty concerning the timing of aggregate consumption, the partial irreversibility of real investments (longer-term physical investments cannot be converted into investments with earlier payouts without sacrifice), . . . real assets with shorter-term payouts will tend to have a "liquidity" advantage.*
>
> *Rubinstein (1999), pp. 84–5*

Therefore the demand for short-term instruments is frequently higher, and hence short-term returns are often lower than long-term returns over the same period.

The *pure* or *unbiased expectations hypothesis* is more commonly encountered and states that current implied forward rates are unbiased estimators of future spot interest rates.[8] It assumes that investors act in a way that eliminates any advantage of holding instruments of a particular maturity. Therefore if we have a positive-sloping yield curve, the unbiased expectations hypothesis states that the market expects spot interest rates to rise. Equally, an inverted yield curve is an indication that spot rates are expected to fall. If short-term interest rates are expected to rise, then longer yields should be higher than shorter ones to reflect this. If this were not the case, investors would only buy the shorter dated bonds and roll over the investment when they matured. Likewise, if rates are expected to fall then longer yields should be lower than short yields. The unbiased expectations hypothesis states that the long-term interest rate is a geometric average of expected future short-term rates. This was in fact the theory that was

---

8 For original discussion, see Lutz (1940) and Fisher (1986), although he formulated his ideas earlier.

used to derive the forward yield curve using (5.5) and (5.7) previously. This gives us:

$$(1 + rs_N)^N = (1 + rs_1)(1 + {}_1rf_2) \ldots (1 + {}_{N-1}rf_N) \qquad (5.12)$$

or

$$(1 + rs_N)^N = (1 + rs_{N-1})^{N-1}(1 + {}_{N-1}rf_N) \qquad (5.13)$$

where rs_N is the spot yield on a N-year bond and ${}_{n-1}rf_n$ is the implied 1-year rate n years ahead.

For example, if the current 1-year spot rate is rs_1 and the market is setting the 1-year rate in a year's time to be ${}_1rf_2 = 5.539\%$, then the market is expecting a £100 investment in two 1-year bonds to yield:

$$£100(1.05)(1.05539) = £110.82$$

after two years. To be equivalent to this an investment in a 2-year bond has to yield the same amount, implying that the current 2-year rate is rs_2 as shown below:

$$£100(1 + rs_2)^2 = £110.82$$

which gives us rs_2, equal to 5.27%, and gives us the correct future value as shown below:

$$£100(1.0527)^2 = £110.82.$$

This result must be so, to ensure no arbitrage opportunities exist in the market and in fact we showed as much earlier in the chapter when we considered forward rates. According to the unbiased expectations hypothesis, therefore the forward rate ${}_0rf_2$ is an unbiased predictor of the spot rate ${}_2rs_1$ observed one period later; on average the forward rate should equal the subsequent spot rate. This hypothesis can be used to explain any shape in the yield curve.

A rising yield curve is therefore explained by investors expecting short-term interest rates to rise; that is, ${}_1rf_2 > rs_2$. A falling yield curve is explained by investors expecting short-term rates to be lower in the future. A humped yield curve is explained by investors expecting short-term interest rates to rise and long-term rates to fall. Expectations, or views on the future direction of the market, are a function mainly of the expected rate of inflation. If the market expects inflationary pressures in the future, the yield curve will be positively shaped, while if inflation expectations are inclined towards disinflation, then the yield curve will be negative. However, several empirical studies, including one by Fama (1976), have shown that forward rates are essentially biased predictors of future spot interest rates, and often over-estimate future levels of spot rates. The unbiased hypothesis has also been criticised for suggesting that investors can forecast (or have a view on) very long-dated spot interest rates, which might be considered slightly unrealistic. As yield curves in most developed country markets exist to a maturity of up to 30 years or longer, such criticisms may have some substance. Are investors able to forecast interest rates 10, 20 or 30 years into the future? Perhaps not, nevertheless this is the theoretical information content of, say, a 30-year bond; since the yield on the bond is set by the market, it is valid to suggest that the market has a view on inflation and future interest rates for up to 30 years forward.

The expectations hypothesis is stated in more than one way; we have already encountered the local expectations hypothesis. Other versions include the *return-to-maturity* expectations hypothesis, which states that the total return from holding a zero-coupon bond to maturity will be equal to the total return that is generated by holding a short-term instrument and continuously rolling it over the same maturity period. A related version, the *yield-to-maturity* hypothesis, states that the periodic return from holding a zero-coupon bond will be equal to the return from rolling over a series of coupon bonds, but refers to the annualised return earned each year rather than the total return earned over the life of the bond. This assumption enables a zero-coupon yield curve to be derived from the redemption yields of coupon bonds. The unbiased expectations hypothesis of course states that forward rates are equal to the spot rates expected by the market in the future. The Cox, Ingersoll and Ross article suggests that only the local expectations hypothesis describes a model that is purely arbitrage-free, as under the other scenarios it would be possible to employ certain investment strategies that would produce returns in excess of what was implied by today's yields. Although it has been suggested[9] that the differences between the local and the unbiased hypotheses are not material, a model that describes such a scenario would not reflect investors' beliefs, which is why further research is ongoing in this area.

Ultimately the unbiased expectations hypothesis does not by itself explain all the shapes of the yield curve or the information content contained within it, so it is often tied in with other explanations, including the liquidity preference theory. For a description on testing the unbiased expectations hypothesis, see Appendix 5.2.

Liquidity Preference Theory

Intuitively we might feel that longer maturity investments are more risky than shorter ones. Investors lending money for a 5-year term will usually demand a

9 For example, see Campbell (1986) and Livingstone (1990).

higher rate of interest than if they were to lend the same customer money for a 5-week term. This is because borrowers may not be able to repay the loan over the longer time period as they may, for instance, have gone bankrupt in that period. For this reason longer dated yields should be higher than short-dated yields, to recompense the lender for the higher risk exposure during the term of the loan.[10] This is a logical argument.

We can consider this theory in terms of inflation expectations as well. Where inflation is expected to remain roughly stable over time, the market would anticipate a positive yield curve. However, the expectations hypothesis cannot by itself explain this phenomenon, as under stable inflationary conditions one would expect a flat yield curve. The risk inherent in longer dated investments, or the *liquidity preference theory*, seeks to explain a positive-shaped curve. Generally, borrowers prefer to borrow over as long a term as possible, while lenders will wish to lend over as short a term as possible. Therefore, as we first stated, lenders have to be compensated for lending over the longer term; this compensation is considered a premium for a loss in *liquidity* for the lender. The premium is increased the further the investor lends across the term structure, so that the longest dated investments will, all else being equal, have the highest yield. So the liquidity preference theory states that the yield curve should almost always be upward sloping, reflecting bondholders' preference for the liquidity and lower risk of shorter dated bonds. An inverted yield curve could still be explained by the liquidity preference theory when it is combined with the unbiased expectations hypothesis. A humped yield curve might be viewed as a combination of an inverted yield curve together with a positive-sloping liquidity preference curve.

The difference between a yield curve explained by unbiased expectations and an actual observed yield curve is sometimes referred to as the *liquidity premium*. It is illustrated at Figure 5.17. This refers to the fact that in some cases short-dated bonds are easier to transact in the market than long-term bonds. It is difficult to quantify the effect of the liquidity premium, which in any cases is not static and fluctuates over time. The liquidity premium is so-called because, in order to induce investors to hold longer dated securities, the yields on such securities must be higher than those available on short-dated securities, which are more liquid and may be converted into cash more easily. The liquidity premium is the compensation required for holding less liquid instruments. If longer dated securities then provide higher yields, as is suggested by the existence of the liquidity premium, they should generate on average higher total returns over an

10 For original discussion, see Hicks (2011).

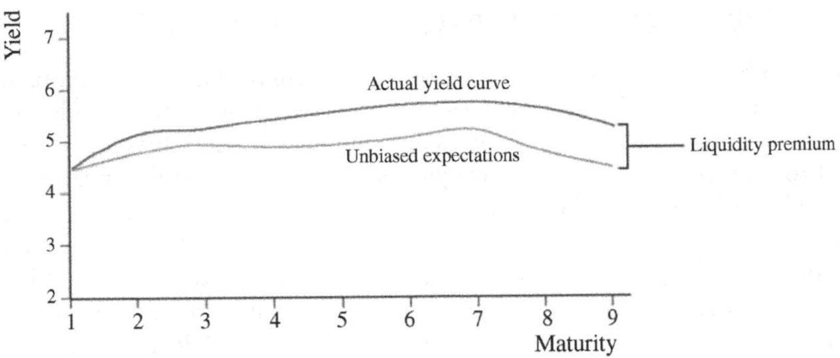

FIGURE 5.17 Yield curve explained by expectations hypothesis and liquidity preference.

investment period. This is not consistent with the local expectations hypothesis. More formally we can write:

$$0 = L_1 < L_2 < L_3 < \ldots < L_n$$
$$\text{and } (L_2 - L_1) > (L_3 - L_2) > \ldots > (L_n - L_{n-1})$$

where L is the premium for a bond with term to maturity of n years, which states that the premium increases as the term to maturity rises and that an otherwise flat yield curve will have a positively sloping shape, with the degree of slope steadily decreasing as we extend along the yield curve. This is consistent with observation of yield curves under "normal" conditions. The expectations hypothesis assumes that forward rates are equal to the expected future spot rates; that is, as shown in (5.14):

$$_{n-1}rf_n = E(_{n-1}rs_n) \tag{5.14}$$

where $E()$ is the expectations operator for the current period. This assumption implies that the forward rate is an unbiased predictor of the future spot rate, as we suggested in the previous paragraph. Liquidity preference theory, on the other hand, recognises the possibility that the forward rate may contain an element of liquidity premium that declines over time as the period approaches, given by (5.15):

$$_{n-1}rf_n > E(_{n-1}rs_n). \tag{5.15}$$

If there is uncertainty in the market about the future direction of spot rates and hence where the forward rate should lie, (5.15) is adjusted to give the reverse inequality.

Money Substitute Hypothesis

A particular explanation of short-dated bond yield curves has been attempted by Kessel (1965). In the *money substitute* theory, short-dated bonds are regarded as substitutes for holding cash. Investors hold only short-dated market instruments because these are viewed as low or negligible risk. As a result the yields of short-dated bonds are depressed due to the increased demand and lie below longer dated bonds. Borrowers, on the other hand, prefer to issue debt for longer maturities, and on as few occasions as possible to minimise costs. Therefore the yields of longer dated paper are driven upwards due to a combination of increased supply and lower liquidity. In certain respects the money substitute theory is closely related to the liquidity preference theory, and by itself does not explain inverted or humped yield curves.

Segmentation Hypothesis

The capital markets are made up of a wide variety of users, each with different requirements. Certain classes of investors will prefer dealing at the short-end of the yield curve, while others will concentrate on the longer end of the market. The *segmented markets* theory suggests that activity is concentrated in certain specific areas of the market, and that there are no interrelationships between these parts of the market; the relative amounts of funds invested in each of the maturity spectrum causes differentials in supply and demand, which results in humps in the yield curve. That is, the shape of the yield curve is determined by supply and demand for certain specific maturity investments, each of which has no reference to any other part of the curve.

For example, banks and building societies concentrate a large part of their activity at the short end of the curve, required by the routine of daily cash management (central to ALM) and for regulatory purposes (part of liquidity requirements). Fund managers such as pension funds and insurance companies are active at the long end of the market. Few institutional investors, the theory posits, have any preference for medium-dated assets. This behaviour on the part of investors will lead to high prices (low yields) at both the short and long ends of the yield curve and lower prices (higher yields) in the middle of the term structure.

Since according to the segmented markets hypothesis a separate market exists for specific maturities along the term structure, interest rates for these maturities are set by supply and demand.[11] Where there is no demand for a particular maturity, the yield will lie above other segments. Market

11 See Culbertson (1957).

participants do not hold bonds in any other area of the curve outside their area of interest,[12] so that short-dated and long-dated bond yields exist independently of each other. The segmented markets theory is usually illustrated by reference to banks and life insurance companies. Banks' and building societies' Treasury desks hold their funds in short-dated instruments, usually no longer than five years in maturity. This is because of the nature of retail banking operations, with a large volume of instant access funds being deposited in banks, and also for regulatory purposes. Holding short-term, liquid bonds enables banks to meet any sudden or unexpected demand for funds from customers. The classic theory suggests that as banks invest their funds in short-dated bonds, the yields on these bonds are driven down. When they then liquidate part of their holding, perhaps to meet higher demand for loans, the yields are driven up and prices of the bonds fall. This affects the short end of the yield curve but not the long end.

The segmented markets theory can be used to explain any particular shape of the yield curve, although it fits best perhaps with positive-sloping curves. However, it cannot be used to interpret the yield curve whatever shape it may be, and therefore it offers no information content during analysis. By definition, the theory suggests that bonds with different maturities are not perfect substitutes for each other. This is because different bonds would have different holding period returns.[13] As a result of bonds being imperfect substitutes, markets are segmented according to maturity.

The segmentations hypothesis is a reasonable explanation of certain features of a conventional positively sloping yield curve, but by itself it is not sufficient. There is no doubt that banks and building societies have a requirement to hold securities at the short end of the yield curve, as much for regulatory purposes as for yield considerations; however, other investors are probably more flexible and will place funds where value is deemed to exist. Nonetheless, the higher demand for benchmark securities does drive down yields along certain segments of the curve.

A slightly modified version of the market segmentation hypothesis is known as the *preferred habitat theory*. This suggests that different market participants have an interest in specified areas of the yield curve, but can be induced to hold bonds from other parts of the maturity spectrum if there is sufficient incentive. Hence banks may at certain times hold longer dated bonds once the price of these bonds falls to a certain level, making the return on the bonds worth the risk involved in holding them. Similar considerations may persuade long-term investors to hold short-dated debt. So higher yields

---

12 For example, retail and commercial banks hold bonds in the short dates, while life assurance companies hold long-dated bonds.

13 See footnote 10.

will be required to make bondholders shift out of their usual area of interest. This theory essentially recognises the flexibility that investors have, outside regulatory or legal requirements (such as the terms of an institutional fund's objectives), to invest in whatever part of the yield curve they identify value.

Humped Yield Curves

When plotting a yield curve of all the bonds in a certain class, it is common to observe humped yield curves. These usually occur for a variety of reasons. In line with the unbiased expectations hypothesis, humped curves will be observed when interest rates are expected to rise over the next several periods and then decline. On other occasions humped curves can result from skewed expectations of future interest rates. This is when the market believes that fairly constant future interest rates are likely, but also believes that there is a small probability for lower rates in the medium term. The other common explanation for humped curves is the preferred habitat theory.

The Combined Theory

The explanation for the shape of the yield curve at any time is more likely to be described by a combination of the pure expectations hypothesis and the liquidity preference theory, and possibly one or two other theories. Market analysts often combine the unbiased expectations hypothesis and the liquidity preference theory into an "eclectic" theory. The result is fairly consistent with any shape of yield curve, and is also a predictor of rising interest rates. In the combined theory the forward interest rate is equal to the expected future spot rate, together with a quantified liquidity premium. This is shown in (5.16):

$$_0rf_i = E(_{i-1}rs_1) + L_i \tag{5.16}$$

where L_i is the liquidity premium for a term to maturity of i. The size of the liquidity premium is expected to increase with increasing maturity.[14] An illustration is given in Example 5.7.

The combined theory is consistent with an inverted yield curve. This will apply even when the liquidity premium is increasing with maturity; for example, where the expected future spot interest rate is declining. Typically, this would be where there was a current term structure of falling yields along the term structure. The spot rates might be declining where the fall in the expected future spot rate exceeds the corresponding increase in the liquidity premium.

14 So that $L_i > L_{i-1}$.

EXAMPLE 5.7 POSITIVE YIELD CURVE WITH CONSTANT EXPECTED FUTURE INTEREST RATES

Consider the interest rate structure in Table 5.6.

TABLE 5.6 Positive yield curve with constant expected future rates

Period n	0	1	2	3	4	5
$E(rs)$		4.5%	4.5%	4.5%	4.5%	4.5%
Forward rate ${}_0rf_n$		5.0%	5.5%	6.0%	6.5%	7.5%
Spot rate rs_n	5.0%	5.3%	5.8%	6.2%	6.8%	7.0%

The current term structure is positively sloping since the spot rates increase with increasing maturity. However, the market expects future spot rates to be constant at 4.5%. The forward and spot rates are also shown; however, the forward rate is a function of the expected spot rate and the liquidity premium. This premium is equal to 0.50% for the first year, 1.0% in the second and so on.

The Flat Yield Curve

The conventional theories do not seek to explain a flat yield curve. Although it is rare to observe flat curves in any market, certainly for any length of time, at times they do emerge in response to peculiar economic circumstances. In the conventional thinking, a flat curve is not tenable because investors should in theory have no incentive to hold long-dated bonds over shorter dated bonds when there is no yield premium, so that as they sell off long-dated paper the yield at the long end should rise, producing an upward-sloping curve. In the previous circumstances of a flat curve, analysts have produced different explanations for their existence. In November 1988 the US Treasury yield curve was flat relative to the recent past; researchers contended that this was the result of the market's view that long-dated yields would fall as bond prices rallied upwards.[15] One recommendation is to buy longer maturities when the yield curve is flat, in anticipation of lower long-term interest rates, which is the direct opposite to the view that a flat curve is a signal to sell long bonds. In the case of the US market in 1988, long bond yields did in fact fall by approximately 2% in the following 12 months. This would seem

15 See Levy (1999).

to indicate that one's view of future long-term rates should be behind the decision to buy or sell long bonds, rather than the shape of the yield curve itself. A flat curve may well be more heavily influenced by supply and demand factors than anything else, with the majority opinion eventually winning out and forcing a change in the curve to a more conventional shape.

FURTHER VIEWS ON THE YIELD CURVE

In our discussion of present values, spot and forward interest rates we assumed an economist's world of the *perfect market* (also sometimes called the *frictionless* financial market). Such a perfect capital market is characterised by:

- perfect information;
- no taxes;
- bullet maturity bonds;
- no transaction costs.

Of course, in practice markets are not perfect. However, assuming perfect markets makes the discussion of spot and forward rates and the term structure easier to handle. When we analyse yield curves for their information content, we have to remember that the markets that they represent are not perfect, and that frequently we observe anomalies that are not explained by the conventional theories.

At any one time it is probably more realistic to suggest that a range of factors contributes to the yield curve being one particular shape. For instance, short-term interest rates are greatly influenced by the availability of funds in the money market. The slope of the yield curve (usually defined as the 10-year yield minus the 3-month interest rate) is also a measure of the degree of tightness of government monetary policy. A low, upward-sloping curve is often thought to be a sign that an environment of cheap money, due to a more loose monetary policy, is to be followed by a period of higher inflation and higher bond yields. Equally, a high downward-sloping curve is taken to mean that a situation of tight credit, due to more strict monetary policy, will result in falling inflation and lower bond yields. Inverted yield curves have often preceded recessions; it is well known that in the US every recession since 1955 bar one has been preceded by an inverted Treasury yield curve. The analysis is the same: if investors expect a recession they also expect inflation to fall, so the yields on long-term bonds will fall relative to short-term bonds. Hence the conventional explanation for an inverted yield curve is that the markets expect either a slow-down of the

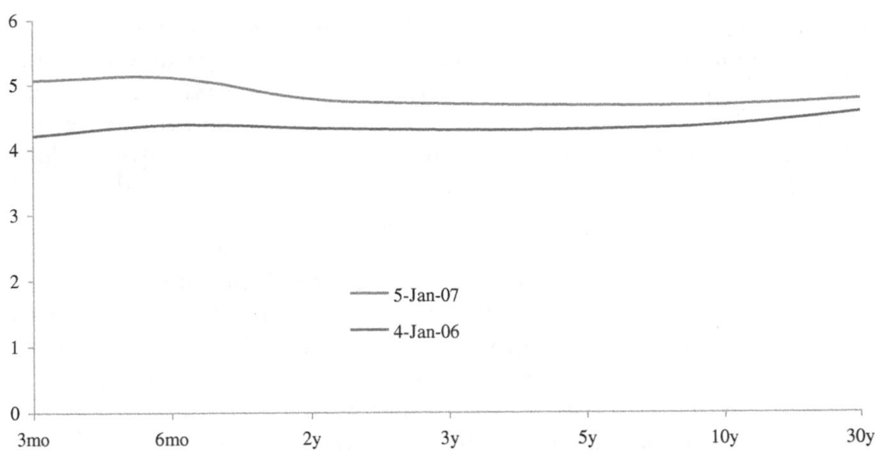

FIGURE 5.18 US Treasury yield curves, January 2006 and January 2007
Yield source: Bloomberg L.P.

economy, or an outright recession.[16] In this case one would expect the monetary authorities to ease the money supply by reducing the base interest rate in the near future; hence, an inverted curve. At the same time, a reduction of short-term interest rates will affect short-dated bonds, and these are sold off by investors, further raising their yield.

The curve maintained its predictive power for the recession of 2008–2009 in the United States. Figure 5.18 shows the US Treasury curve for January 2006 and January 2007. We see how the curve moved to inverted at the start of 2007, signalling the recession that occurred in 2008 following the sub-prime mortgages default and the bank crash.

While the conventional explanation for negative yield curves is an expectation of economic slow-down, on occasion other, structural, factors will be involved. In the UK in the period July 1997–June 1999 the gilt yield curve was inverted.[17] There was no general view that the economy was heading for recession, however. In fact, the new Labour government inherited an economy believed to be in good health. Instead the explanation behind the inverted shape of the gilt yield curve focused on two other factors:

16 A recession is formally defined as two successive quarters of falling output in the domestic economy.

17 Although the curve briefly went positively sloped out to 7–8 years in July 1999, it very quickly reverted to being inverted throughout the term structure, and remained so until certain restrictions on the need for institutional investors to hold long-dated gilts were lifted by the government in 2002.

first, the handing of responsibility for setting interest rates to the Monetary Policy Committee (MPC) of the BoE, and second, the expectation that the UK would over the medium term abandon sterling and join the euro currency. The yield curve in this time suggested that the market expected the MPC to be successful and keep inflation at a level around 2.5% over the long term (its target is actually a 1% range either side of 2.5%),[18] and also that sterling interest rates would need to come down over the medium term as part of *convergence* with interest rates in the eurozone. These are both medium-term expectations, however, and in the author's view not logical at the short-end of the yield curve. In fact, the term structure moved to a positive-sloped shape up to the 6–7-year area, before inverting out to the long-end of the curve, in June 1999. This is a more logical shape for the curve to assume, but it was short-lived and returned to being inverted after the two-year term.

There is therefore significant information content in the yield curve, and economists and bond analysts will consider the shape of the curve as part of their policymaking and investment advice. The shape of parts of the curve, whether the short-end or long-end, as well that of the entire curve, can serve as useful predictors of future market conditions. As part of an analysis it is also worthwhile considering the yield curves across several different markets and currencies. For instance, the interest-rate swap curve, and its position relative to that of the government bond yield curve, is also regularly analysed for its information content. In developed country economies the swap market is invariably as liquid as the government bond market, if not more liquid, and so it is common to see the swap curve analysed when making predictions about, say, the future level of short-term interest rates.

Government policy will influence the shape and level of the yield curve, including policy on public sector borrowing, debt management and open market operations. The market's perception of the size of public sector debt will influence bond yields; for instance, an increase in the level of debt can lead to an increase in bond yields across the maturity range. Open market operations, which refer to the daily operation by a central bank to control the level of the money supply (to which end it purchases short-term bills and also engages in repo dealing), can have a number of effects. In the short term it can tilt the yield curve both upwards and downwards; longer term, changes in the level of the base rate will affect yield levels. An anticipated rise in base rates can lead to a drop in prices for short-term bonds, whose yields will be expected to rise – this can lead to a temporary inverted curve. Finally, debt management policy will influence the yield curve. Much government debt is rolled over as it matures, but the maturity of the

18 From 2004 the BoE adopted the European Unions' harmonised consumer price index (CPI) inflation measure, and its target rate for the CPI is now 2%.

replacement debt can have a significant influence on the yield curve in the form of humps in the market segment in which the debt is placed, if the debt is priced by the market at a relatively high yield.

Part II

A FURTHER LOOK AT SPOT AND FORWARD RATES

We continue the analysis begun in this chapter using more technical terminology. First we illustrate basic concepts, followed by a discussion of yield curve analysis and the term structure of interest rates.

Basic Concepts

We are familiar with two types of fixed-income securities, *zero-coupon bonds*, also known as *discount bonds* or *strips*, and *coupon bonds*. A coupon bond may be regarded as a set of strips, with each coupon payment and the redemption payment on maturity being equivalent to a zero-coupon bond maturing on that date. This is not a purely academic concept, illustrated before the advent of the formal market in US Treasury strips, when a number of investment banks traded the cash flows of Treasury securities as separate zero-coupon securities.[19] The concepts we review in this section are set in a market of default-free bonds, whether they are zero-coupon bonds or coupon bonds. The market is assumed to be liquid so that bonds may be freely bought and sold. Prices of bonds are determined by the economy-wide supply and demand for the bonds at any time, so they are macroeconomic and not set by individual bond issuers or traders.

---

19 The term "strips" comes from Separate Trading of Registered Interest and Principal of Securities, the name given when the official market was introduced by the Treasury. Prior to this banks would purchase Treasuries, which would then be deposited in a safe custody account. Receipts were issued against each cash flow from each Treasury, and these receipts were traded as individual zero-coupon securities. The market-making banks earned profit due to the arbitrage difference in the price of the original coupon bond and the price at which the individual strips were sold. The US Treasury formalised trading in strips in 1985, after legislation had been introduced that altered the tax treatment of such instruments. The market in UK gilt strips trading began in December 1997. Strips are also traded in France, Germany and the Netherlands, among other countries.

Zero-coupon Bonds

A zero-coupon bond is the simplest form of fixed-income security. It is an issue of debt, the issuer promising to pay the face value of the debt to the bondholder on the date the bond matures. There are no coupon payments during the life of the bond, so it is a discount instrument, issued at a price that is below the face or *principal* amount. We denote as $P(t, T)$, the price of a discount bond at time t that matures at time T, with $T \geq t$. The term to maturity of the bond is denoted with n, where $n = T - t$. The price increases over time until the maturity date when it reaches the maturity or *par* value. If the par value of the bond is £1, then the YTM of the bond at time t is denoted by $r(t,T)$, where r is actually "one plus the percentage yield" that is earned by holding the bond from t to T. We have:

$$P(t, T) = \frac{1}{[r(t, T)]^n}. \tag{5.17}$$

The yield may be obtained from the bond price and is given by:

$$r(t, T) = \left[\frac{1}{P(t, T)}\right]^{1/n} \tag{5.18}$$

which is sometimes written as:

$$r(t, T) = P(tT)^{-(1/n)}. \tag{5.19}$$

Analysts and researchers frequently work in terms of logarithms of yields and prices, or continuously compounded rates. One advantage of this is that it converts the non-linear relationship in (5.18) into a linear relationship.[20]

The bond price at time t_2 where $t < t_2 < T$ is given by:

$$P(t_2, T) = P(t, T)e^{(t_2 - t)r(t, T)} \tag{5.20}$$

---

20 A linear relationship in X would be a function $Y = f(X)$, in which the X values change via a power or index of 1 only and are not multiplied or divided by another variable or variables. So, for example, terms such as X^2, $\sqrt{X}$ and other similar functions are not linear in X, nor are terms such as XZ or X/Z where Z is another variable. In econometric analysis, if the value of Y is solely dependent on the value of X, then its rate of change with respect to X, or the derivative of Y with respect to X, denoted dY/dX, is independent of X. Therefore if $Y = 5X$, then $dY/dX = 5$, which is independent of the value of X. However, if $Y = 5X2$, then $dY/dX = 10X$, which is not independent of the value of X. Hence this function is not linear in X. The classic regression function $E(Y/X_i) = \alpha + \beta X_i$ is a linear function with slope b and intercept a and the regression "curve" is represented geometrically by a straight line. For more background on regression and ordinary least squares, see Appendix 5.3.

which is consistent, given that the bond price equation in continuous time is:

$$P(t, T) = e^{-r(t,\, T)(T-t)} \tag{5.21}$$

so that the yield is given by:

$$log\, r(t, T) = -\left(\frac{1}{n}\right) log\, P(t, T), \tag{5.22}$$

which is sometimes written as:

$$P(t, T) = \sum_{t_i > t} C_i e^{-(t_i - t) r(t,T)}. \tag{5.23}$$

The expression in (5.20 and 5.21) includes the exponential function, hence the use of the term continuously compounded.

The *term structure of interest rates* is the set of zero-coupon yields at time t for all bonds ranging in maturity from $(t, t+1)$ to $(t, t+m)$ where the bonds have maturities of $\{0, 1, 2, \ldots, m\}$. A good definition of the term structure of interest rates is given by Suresh Sundaresan, who states that it:

> *. . . refers to the relationship between the yield to maturity of default-free zero coupon securities and their maturities.*
>
> Sundaresan (1997), p. 176

The *yield curve* is a plot of the set of yields for $r(t, t+1)$ to $r(t, t+m)$ against m at time t. For example, Figures 5.19–5.21 show the log

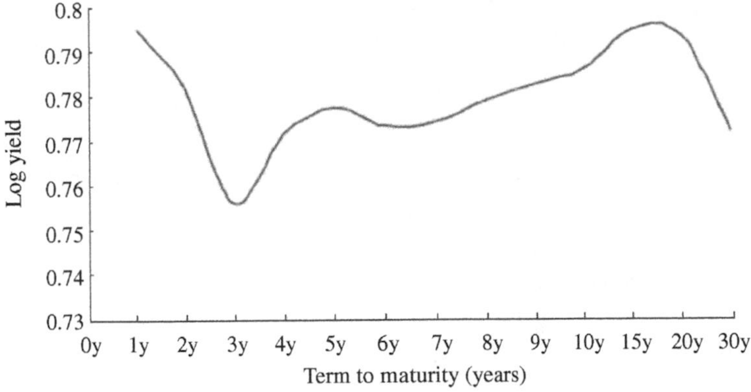

FIGURE 5.19 US Treasury zero-coupon yield curve in September 2000.
Yield source: Bloomberg L.P.

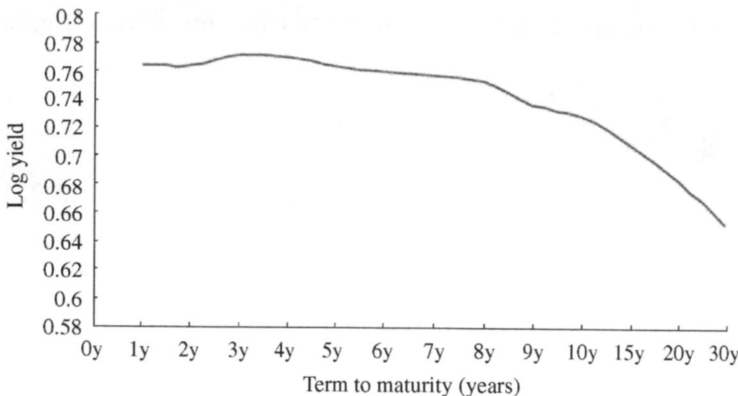

FIGURE 5.20 UK gilt zero-coupon yield curve in September 2000.
Yield source: Bloomberg L.P.

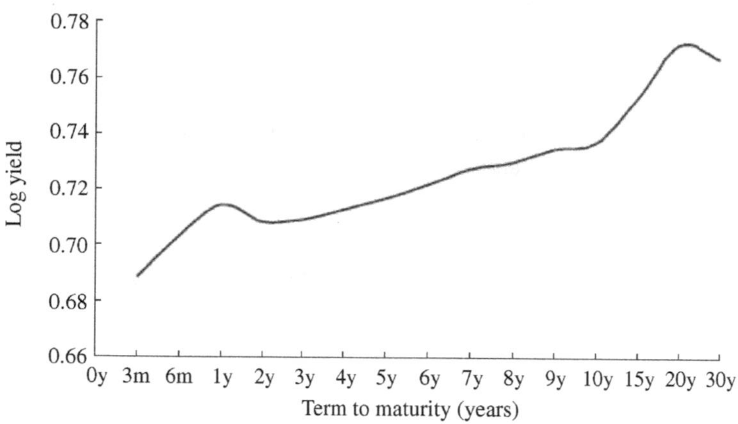

FIGURE 5.21 French OAT zero-coupon yield curve in September 2000.
Yield source: Bloomberg L.P.

zero-coupon yield curve for US Treasury strips, UK gilt strips and French OAT strips on 27 September 2000. Each of the curves exhibit peculiarities in their shape, although the most common type of curve is gently upward-sloping, as is the French curve. The UK curve is inverted.

Coupon Bonds

The majority of bonds in the market make coupon payments during their lives, and such bonds may be viewed as a package of individual zero-coupon bonds. The coupons have a nominal value that is a percentage of the nominal value of the bond itself, with steadily longer maturity dates, while the final redemption payment has the nominal value of the bond itself and is redeemed on the maturity date. We denote a bond issued at time i and maturing at time T as having a w-element vector of payment dates: ($t1$, $t2$, . . . ,$t_{w\text{-}1}$, T) and matching date payments C1, C2, . . . , $C_{w\text{-}1}$, C_w. In academic literature these coupon payments are assumed to be made in continuous time, so that the stream of coupon payments is given by a positive function of time $C(t)$, $i < t \leq T$. Investors that purchase a bond at time t, that matures at time T and pays $P(t, T)$ will receive the coupon payments as long as they continue to hold the bond.[21]

The YTM at time t of a bond that matures at T is the interest rate that relates the price of the bond to the future returns on the bond; that is, the rate that *discounts* the bond's cash flow stream C_w to its price $P(t, T)$. This is given by:

$$p(t,T) = \sum_{t_i > t} C_i e^{-(t_i - t) r(t,T)} \tag{5.24}$$

which says that the bond price is given by the present value of the cash flow stream of the bond, discounted at the rate $r(t, T)$. A zero-coupon (5.24) reduces to (5.21). In academic literature where coupon payments are assumed to be made in continuous time, the Σ summation in (5.24) is replaced by the $\int$ integral.

In some texts the plot of the YTM at time t for the term of the bonds m is described as the term structure of interest rates; but it is generally accepted that the term structure is the plot of zero-coupon rates only. Plotting yields to maturity is described as graphically depicting the yield curve, rather than the term structure. Of course, given the law of one price, there is a relationship between the YTM yield curve and the zero-coupon term structure, and given the first one can derive the second.

The expression in (5.24) obtains the continuously compounded yield to maturity $r(t, T)$. It is the use of the exponential function that enables us to describe the yield as continuously compounded.

The market frequently uses the measure known as *current yield*, which is:

$$rc = \frac{C}{P_d} \times 100 \tag{5.25}$$

21 Theoretically, this is the discounted clean price of the bond. For coupon bonds in practice, unless the bond is purchased for value on a coupon date, it will be traded with interest accrued. The interest that has accrued on a pro-rata basis from the last coupon date is added to the clean price of the bond, to give the market "dirty" price that is actually paid by the purchaser.

where P_d is the dirty price of the bond. The measure is also known as the *running yield* or *flatyield*. Current yield is not used to indicate the interest rate or discount rate and therefore should not be mistaken for the YTM.

Forward Rates

An investor can combine positions in bonds of differing maturities to guarantee a rate of return that begins at a point in the future. That is, the trade ticket is written at time t but covers the period T to $T+1$ where $t < T$ (sometimes written as beginning at T_1 and ending at T_2, with $t < T1 < T_2$). The interest rate earned during this period is known as the forward rate.[22] The mechanism by which this forward rate can be guaranteed is described in Example 5.8 below, following Jarrow (1996) and Campbell et al. (1997).

EXAMPLE 5.8 THE FORWARD RATE

An investor buys at time t one unit of a zero-coupon bond maturing at time T, priced at $P(t, T)$ and simultaneously sells $P(t, T)/P(t, T+1)$ bonds that mature at $T+1$. From Table 5.7, we can see that the net result of these transactions is a zero cash flow. At time T there is a cash inflow of 1, and then at time $T+1$ there is a cash outflow of $P(t, T)/P(t, T+1)$. These cash flows are identical to a loan of funds made during the period T to $T+1$, contracted at time t. The interest rate on this loan is given by $P(t, T)/P(t, T+1)$, which is therefore the forward rate. That is:

$$f(t,T) = \frac{P(t,T)}{P(t,T+1)}. \qquad (5.26)$$

Together with our earlier relationships on bond price and yield, from (5.26), we can define the forward rate in terms of yield, with the return earned during the period $(T, T+1)$ being:

$$f(t,T,T+1) = \frac{1}{(P(t,T+1)/P(t,T))} = \frac{(r(t,T+1))^{(T+1)}}{r(t,T)^T}. \qquad (5.27)$$

(continued)

22 See the footnote on page 639 of Shiller (1990) for a fascinating insight into the origin of the term "forward rate", which Mr Shiller ascribes to John Hicks in his book *Value and Capital*, 2nd edition, Oxford University Press (1946).

From (5.27), we can obtain a bond price equation in terms of the forward rates that hold from t to T:

$$P(t,T) = \frac{1}{\prod_{k=t}^{T-1} f(t,k)} \qquad (5.28)$$

A derivation of this expression can be found in Jarrow (1996), Chapter 3. Equation (5.28) states that the price of a zero-coupon bond is equal to the nominal value, here assumed to be 1, receivable at time T after it has been discounted at the set of forward rates that apply from t to T.

TABLE 5.7 Breaking down the forward rate principle

Transactions	Time t	T	$T+1$
Buy 1 unit of T-period bond	$-P(t, T)$	$+1$	
Sell $P(t, T)/P(t, T+1)$ of $T+1$ period bonds	$+[(P(t, T)/P(t, T+1)] \times P(t, T+1)$		$-(P(t, T)/P(t,T+1)$
Net cash flows	0	$+1$	$-(P(t,T)/P(t,T+1)$

When calculating a forward rate, it is as if we are transacting at an interest rate today that is applicable at the forward start date; in other words, we are trading a forward contract. The law of one price, or no-arbitrage, is used to calculate the rate. For a loan that begins at T and matures at $T+1$, similarly to the way we described in Example 5.8, consider the purchase of a $T+1$ period bond and the sale of p amount of the T-period bond. The cash net cash position at t must be zero, so p is given by:[23]

$$p = \frac{P(t,T+1)}{P(t,T)}$$

23 The symbol Π means "take the product of", and is defined as $\prod_{i=1}^{n} x_i = x_1 \cdot x_2 \cdot \mathrm{L} \cdot x_n$, so that $\prod_{k} = tT - 1\ f(t,k) = f(t,t) \cdot f(t+1) \cdot \mathrm{L} \cdot f(t, T-1)n$, which is the result of multiplaying the rates that obtained when the index k runs from t to $T-1$.

and to avoid arbitrage, the value of p must be the price of the $T+1$-period bond at time T. Therefore the forward yield is given by:

$$f(t, T+1) = -\frac{\log P(t, T+1) - \log P(t, T)}{(T+1) - T}. \tag{5.29}$$

If the period between T and the maturity of the later dated bond is reduced, we now have bonds that mature at T and T_2, and $T_2 = T + \Delta t$. The incremental change in time Δt becomes progressively smaller until we obtain an instantaneous forward rate, which is given by:

$$f(t, T) = -\frac{\partial}{\partial T} \log P(t, T). \tag{5.30}$$

This rate is defined as the forward rate and is the price today of forward borrowing at time T. The forward rate for borrowing today where $T = t$ is equal to the instantaneous short rate $r(t)$. At time t, the spot and forward rates for the period (t, t) will be identical, while at other maturity terms they will differ.

For all points other than at (t, t) the forward rate yield curve will lie above the spot rate curve if the spot curve is positively sloping. The opposite applies if the spot rate curve is downward sloping. Campbell et al. (1997, pp. 400–1) observe that this property is a standard one for marginal and average cost curves. That is, when the cost of a marginal unit (say, of production) is above that of an average unit, then the average cost will increase with the addition of a marginal unit. This results in the average cost rising when the marginal cost is above the average cost. Equally, the average cost per unit will decrease when the marginal cost lies below the average cost.

EXAMPLE 5.9 THE SPOT AND FORWARD YIELD CURVES

From the discussion in this section, we can see that it is possible to calculate bond prices, spot and forward rates provided that we have a set of only one of these parameters. Therefore, given the following set of zero-coupon rates observed in the market, given in Table 5.8, we calculate the corresponding forward rates and zero-coupon bond prices as shown. The initial term structure is upward sloping. The two curves are illustrated in Figure 5.22A. The mathematical explanation behind what is observed at Figure 5.22B is given at Appendix 5.4.

There are technical reasons why the theoretical forward rate has a severe kink at the later maturity.

Essentially, the relationship between the spot and forward rate curve is as stated in Campbell et al. (1997). The forward rate curve lies

TABLE 5.8 Hypothetical zero-coupon yield and forward rates

Term to maturity (0, T)	Spot rate $r(0, T)$	Forward rate $f(0, T)$	Bond price $P(0, T)$
0			1
1	1.054	1.054	0.94877
2	1.055	1.056	0.89845
3	1.0563	1.059	0.8484
4	1.0582	1.064	0.79737
5	1.0602	1.068	0.7466
6	1.0628	1.076	0.69386
7	1.06553	1.082	0.64128
8	1.06856	1.0901	0.58833
9	1.07168	1.0972	0.53631
10	1.07526	1.1001	0.48403
11	1.07929	1.1205	0.43198

*Interest rates are given as $(1 + r)$

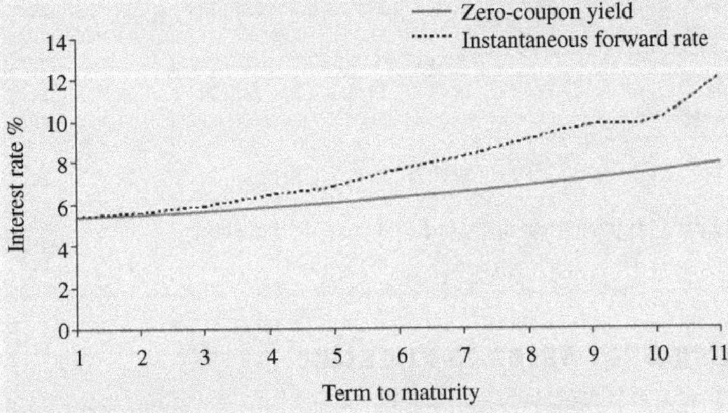

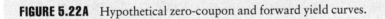

FIGURE 5.22A Hypothetical zero-coupon and forward yield curves.

above the spot rate curve if the latter is increasing, and it lies below it if the spot rate curve is decreasing. This relationship can be shown mathematically. The forward rate or *marginal rate of return* is equal to the spot rate or *average rate of return* plus the rate of increase of the spot rate, multiplied by the sum of the increases between t and T. If the spot rate is constant (a flat curve), the forward rate curve will be equal to it.

(*continued*)

(continued)

However, an increasing spot rate curve does not always result in an increasing forward curve, only one that lies above it. It is possible for the forward curve to be increasing or decreasing while the spot rate is increasing. If the spot rate reaches a maximum level and then stays constant, or falls below this high point, the forward curve will begin to decrease at a maturity point *earlier* than the spot curve high point. In the example in Figure 5.22A, the rate of increase in the spot rate in the last period is magnified when converted to the equivalent forward rate. If the last spot rate is below the previous-period rate, the forward rate curve would look like that in Figure 5.22B.

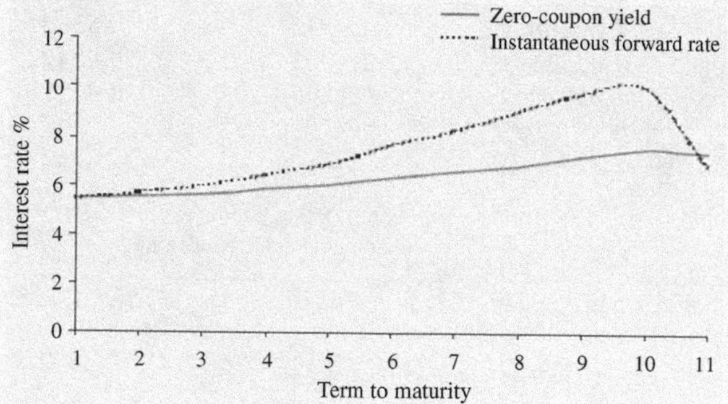

FIGURE 5.22B Hypothetical spot and forward yield curves.

Calculating Spot Rates in Practice

Researchers have applied econometric techniques to the problem of extracting a zero-coupon term structure from coupon bond prices. The most well-known approaches are described in McCulloch (1971, 1975), Schaefer (1981), Nelson and Siegel (1987), Deacon and Derry (1994), Adams and Van Deventer (1994), and Waggoner (1997), to name but a few. The most accessible article is probably the one by Deacon and Derry.[24] In addition, a good overview of all the main approaches is contained in

24 This is in the author's opinion. Those with a good grounding in econometrics will find all these references both readable and accessible. Further recommended references are given in the bibliography and selected readings at the end of this chapter.

James and Webber (2000), and chapters 15–18 of their book provide an excellent summary of the main research highlights.

We have noted that a coupon bond may be regarded as a portfolio of zero-coupon bonds. By treating a set of coupon bonds as a larger set of zero-coupon bonds, we can extract an implied zero-coupon interest-rate structure from the yields on the coupon bonds.

If the actual term structure is observable, so that we know the prices of zero-coupon bonds of £1 nominal value $P_1, P_2, \ldots, P_N$, then the price P_C of a coupon bond of nominal value £1 and coupon C is given by:

$$P_C = P_1 C + P_2 C + \cdots + P_N(1 + C). \tag{5.31}$$

Conversely, if we observe the coupon bond yield curve so that we know the prices $P_{C1}, P_{C2}, \ldots, P_{CN}$, then we may use (5.31) to extract the implied zero-coupon term structure. We begin with the one-period coupon bond, for which the price is:

$$P_{C1} = P_1(1 + C)$$

so that:

$$P_1 = \frac{P_{C1}}{(1 + C)}. \tag{5.32}$$

This process is repeated. Once we have the set of zero-coupon bond prices $P_1, P_2, \ldots, P_{N21}$ we obtain P_N using:

$$P_N = \frac{P_{CN} + P_{N-1}C - L - P_1 C}{1 + C}. \tag{5.33}$$

At this point we apply a regression technique known as *ordinary least squares* (OLS) to fit the term structure. OLS and regression techniques are summarised in Choudhry (2001).

Expression (5.31) restricts the prices of coupon bonds to be precise functions of the other coupon bond prices. In fact, this is unlikely in practice because specific bonds will be treated differently according to liquidity, tax effects and so on. For this reason we add an *error term* to (5.31) and estimate the value using cross-sectional regression against all the other bonds in the market. If we say that these bonds are numbered $i = 1, 2, \ldots, I$ then the regression is given by:

$$P_{CN} = P_1 C_i + P_2 C_i + \cdots + P_{Ni}(1 + C_i) + u_i \tag{5.34}$$

for $i = 1, 2, \ldots, I$ and where C_i is the coupon on the ith bond and N_i is the maturity of the ith bond. In (5.34), the regressor parameters are the coupon payments at each interest period date, and the coefficients are the prices of the zero-coupon bonds P_1 to P_N where $j = 1, 2, \ldots, N$. The values are obtained using OLS as long as we have a complete term structure and that $I \geq N$.

In practice, we will not have a complete term structure of coupon bonds and so we are not able to identify the coefficients in (5.34). McCulloch (1971, 1975) described a spline estimation method, which assumes that zero-coupon bond prices vary smoothly with term to maturity. In this approach we define P_N, a function of maturity $P(N)$, as a discount function given by:

$$P(N) = 1 + \sum_{i=1}^{J} a_i f_j(N). \tag{5.35}$$

The function $f_j(N)$ is a known function of maturity N, and the coefficients a_j must be estimated. We arrive at a regression equation by substituting (5.35) into (5.34) to give us (5.36), which can be estimated using OLS:

$$\prod_i \sum_{j=1}^{J} a_j X_{ij} + u_i, \quad i = 1, 2, \ldots, I \tag{5.36}$$

where:

$$\prod_i \equiv P_{C_i N_i} - 1 - C_i N_i$$
$$X_{ij} \equiv f_j(N_i) + C_i \sum\nolimits_{l=1}^{N_i} f_j(l).$$

The function $f_j(N)$ is usually specified by setting the discount function as a polynomial. In certain texts, including McCulloch, this is carried out by applying what is known as a *spline* function. Considerable academic research has gone into the use of spline functions as a yield curve fitting technique; we look at this in Part III of this book. For a specific discussion on using regression techniques for spline curve fitting methods, see Suits et al. (1978).

SPOT RATES AND FORWARD RATES IN CONTINUOUS TIME

This section analyses further the relationship between spot and forward rates and the yield curve.

The Spot and Forward Rate Relationship

In the discussion to date, we have assumed discrete time intervals and interest rates in discrete time. Here we consider the relationship between spot and forward rates in continuous time. For this we assume the mathematical convenience of a continuously compounded interest rate.

We start by saying that at the interest rate r, compounded using e^r, an initial investment of M earning $r(t, T)$ over the period $T - t$ (initial investment at time t and for maturity at T, where $T > t$) would have a value of $Me^{r(t,T)(T-t)}$ on maturity.[25] If we denote the initial value M_t and the maturity value M_T, then we can state $Me^{r(t,T)(T-t)} = M_T$ and therefore the continuously compounded yield, defined as the continuously compounded interest rate $r(t, T)$, can be shown to be:

$$r(t, T) = \frac{log(M_T/M_t)}{T - t}. \quad (5.37)$$

We can then formulate a relationship between the continuously compounded interest rate and yield. It can be shown that

$$M_T = M_t e^{\int_t^T r(s)ds} \quad (5.38)$$

where $r(s)$ is the instantaneous spot interest rate and is a function of time.

It can further be shown that the continuously compounded yield is actually the equivalent of the average value of the continuously compounded interest rate. In addition it can be shown that:

$$r(t, T) = \frac{\int_t^T r(s)ds}{T - t}. \quad (5.39)$$

In a continuous time environment we do not consider discrete time intervals over which interest rates are applicable, but rather a period of time in which a borrowing of funds would be repaid instantaneously. So we define the forward rate $f(t, s)$ as the interest rate applicable for borrowing funds where the deal is struck at time t; the actual loan is made at s (with $s > t$) and repayable almost instantaneously. In mathematics the period $s - t$ is described as infinitesimally small. The spot interest rate is defined as the continuously compounded yield or interest rate $r(t, T)$. In an

25 e is the mathematical constant 2.7182818 . . . and it can be shown that an investment of £1 at time t will have grown to e on maturity at time T (during the period $T - t$) if it is earning an interest rate of $1/(T - t)$ continuously compounded.

environment of no arbitrage, the return generated by investing at the forward rate $f(t, s)$ over the period $s - t$ must be equal to that generated by investing initially at the spot rate $r(t, T)$ and rolling over. So we may set:

$$e^{\int_t^T f(t,s)ds} = e^{r(t)dt} \tag{5.40}$$

which enables us to derive an expression for the spot rate itself, which is

$$r(t,T) = \frac{\int_t^T f(t,s)ds}{T-t}. \tag{5.41}$$

The relationship described by (5.41) states that the spot rate is given by the *arithmetic* average of the forward rates $f(t, s)$ where $t < s < T$. How does this differ from the relationship in a discrete time environment? We know that the spot rate in such a framework is the *geometric* average of the forward rates,[26] and this is the key difference in introducing the continuous time structure. Equation (5.41) can be rearranged to:

$$r(t,T)(T-t) = \int_t^T f(t,s)ds \tag{5.42}$$

and this is used to show (by differentiation) the relationship between spot and forward rates, given below:

$$f(t,s) = r(t,T) + (T-t)\frac{dr(t,T)}{dT}. \tag{5.43}$$

If we assume we are dealing today (at time 0) for maturity at time T, then the expression for the spot rate becomes:

$$r(0,T) = \frac{\int_t^T f(0,s)ds}{T} \tag{5.44}$$

so we can write:

$$r(0,T) \cdot T = \int_t^T f(0,s)ds. \tag{5.45}$$

This is illustrated in Figure 5.23 which is a diagrammatic representation showing that the spot rate $r(0, T)$ is the average of the forward rates from 0 to T, using the hypothetical value of 5% for $r(0, T)$. Figure 5.23 also shows the area represented by (5.45).

26 To be precise, if we assume annual compounding, the relationship is one plus the spot rate is equal to the geometric average of one plus the forward rates.

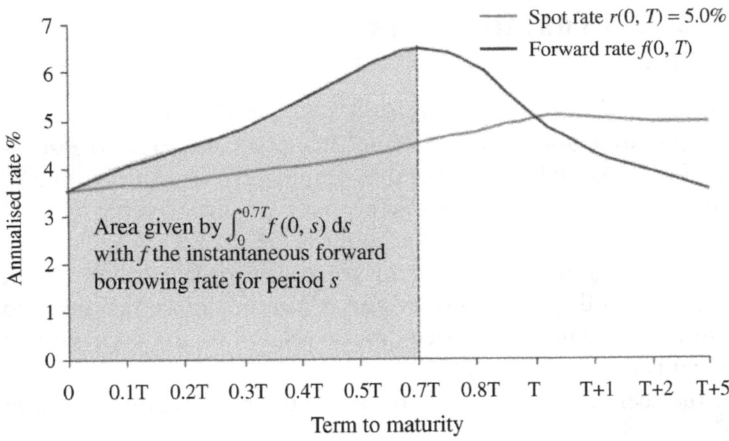

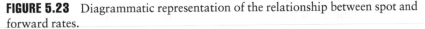

FIGURE 5.23 Diagrammatic representation of the relationship between spot and forward rates.

What (5.43) implies is that if the spot rate increases, then by definition the forward rate (or *marginal* rate, as it has been suggested that it may be called[27]) will be greater. From (5.43) we deduce that the forward rate will be equal to the spot rate plus a value that is the product of the *rate* of increase of the spot rate and the time period $(T - t)$. In fact, the conclusions simply confirm what we already discovered in the discrete time analysis described earlier in this chapter: the forward rate for any period will lie above the spot rate if the spot rate term structure is increasing, and will lie below the spot rate if it is decreasing. In a constant spot rate environment, the forward rate will be equal to the spot rate.

There is slightly more to it than that. An increasing spot rate term structure only implies that the forward rate lies above the spot rate, but not that the forward rate structure is itself also *increasing*. In fact, one can observe the forward rate term structure to be increasing or decreasing while spot rates are increasing. As the spot rate is the average of the forward rates, it can be shown that in order to accommodate this, forward rates must in fact be *decreasing* before the point at which the spot rate reaches its highest point. This confirms market observation. An illustration of this property is given in Appendix 5.4. As Campbell et al. (1997) state this is a property of average and marginal cost curves in economics.

---

27 For example, see Section 10.1 of Campbell et al. (1997), Chapter 10 of which is an excellent and accessible study of the term structure, and provides proofs of some of the results discussed here. This book is written in a very readable style and is worth purchasing for Chapter 10 alone.

Bond Prices as a Function of Spot and Forward Rates[28]

In this section we describe the relationship between the price of a zero-coupon bond and spot and forward rates. We assume a risk-free zero-coupon bond of nominal value £1, priced at time t and maturing at time T. We also assume a money market bank account of initial value $P(t, T)$ invested at time t. The money market account is denoted M. The price of the bond at time t is denoted $P(t, T)$ and if today is time 0 (so that $t > 0$), then the bond price today is unknown and a random factor (similar to a future interest rate). The bond price can be related to the spot rate or forward rate that is in force at time t.

Consider the scenario below, used to derive the risk-free zero-coupon bond price.[29]

The continuously compounded *constant* spot rate is r as before. An investor has a choice of purchasing the zero-coupon bond at price $P(t, T)$, which will return the sum of £1 at time T, or of investing this same amount of cash in the money market account, and this sum would have grown to £1 at time T. We know that the value of the money market account is given by $Me^{r(t,T)(T-t)}$). If M must have a value of £1 at time T, then the function $\mathrm{e}^{-r(t,T)(T-t)}$ must give the present value of £1 at time t and therefore the value of the zero-coupon bond is given by:

$$\mathrm{P}(t, T) = \mathrm{e}^{-r(t,T)(T-t)}. \tag{5.46}$$

If the same amount of cash that could be used to buy the bond at t, invested in the money market account, does *not* return £1 then arbitrage opportunities will result. If the price of the bond exceeded the discount function $e^{-r(t,T)(T-t)}$ then the investor could short the bond and invest the proceeds in the money market account. At time T the bond position would result in a cash outflow of £1, while the money market account would be worth £1. However, the investor would gain because in the first place $P(t, T) - e^{-r(t,T)(T-t)} > 0$. Equally, if the price of the bond was below $e^{-r(t,T)(T-t)}$, then the investor would borrow $e^{-r(t,T)(T-t)}$ in cash and buy the bond at price $P(t, T)$. On maturity the bond would return £1, the proceeds would be used to repay the loan. However, the investor would gain because $e^{-r(t,T)(T-t)} - P(t, T) > 0$. To avoid arbitrage opportunities we must therefore have:

$$P(t, T) = e^{-r(t,T)(T-t)}. \tag{5.47}$$

---

28 For more detail on this see Neftci (2000), Chapter 18, Section 3. This is an excellent, readable text.

29 This approach is also used in Campbell et al. (1997).

Given the relationship between spot and forward rates it is also possible to describe the bond price in terms of forward rates.[30] We show the result here only. First we know that

$$P(t,T)e^{\int_t^T f(t,s)ds} = 1 \tag{5.48}$$

because the maturity value of the bond is £1, and we can rearrange (5.47) to give:

$$P(t,T) = e^{-\int_t^T f(t,s)ds}. \tag{5.49}$$

Expression (5.49) states that the bond price is a function of the range of forward rates that apply for all $f(t, s)$; that is, the forward rates for all time periods s from t to T (where $t < s < T$, and where s is infinitesimally small). The forward rate $f(t, s)$ that results for each s arises as a result of a random or *stochastic* process that is assumed to start today at time 0. Therefore the bond price $P(t, T)$ also results from a random process, in this case all the random processes for all the forward rates $f(t, s)$.

The zero-coupon bond price may also be given in terms of the spot rate $r(t, T)$, as shown in (5.47). From our earlier analysis we know that:

$$\mathrm{P}(t,T)e^{r(t,T)(T-t)} = 1 \tag{5.50}$$

which is rearranged to give the zero-coupon bond price equation

$$\mathrm{P}(t,T) = e^{-r(t,T)(T-t)}. \tag{5.51}$$

as before.

Equation (5.51) describes the bond price as a function of the spot rate only, as opposed to the multiple processes that apply for all the forward rates from t to T. As the bond has a nominal value of £1 the value given by (5.51) is the discount factor for that term; the range of zero-coupon bond prices would give us the discount function.

Conclusions

What is the importance of this result for our understanding of the term structure of interest rates? First, we see (again, but here in continuous time) that spot rates, forward rates and the discount function are all closely related, and given one we can calculate the remaining two. More significantly, we may model the term structure either as a function of the

30 For instance, see Campbell et al. (1997), Section 4.2 and Ross (1999).

spot rate only, described as a stochastic process, or as a function of all of the forward rates $f(t, s)$ for each period s in the period (t, T), described by multiple random processes. The first yield curve models adopted the first approach, while a later development described the second approach.

THE DETERMINANTS OF THE SWAP SPREAD

Up to now we have been looking in detail at the risk-free yield curve. An important hedging tool in bank ALM is the interest-rate swap, and so the swap curve is also analysed by market practitioners. Therefore an important issue for interest-rate analysis is the swap spread, which is the spread of the swap curve over the government bond yield curve, and the relationship between the two yield curves. The swap spread is an indicator of value in the market, as well as an indicator of the overall health of the economy. Understanding the determinants of the swap spread is important for ALM practitioners for this reason. We also consider the impact of macro-level geo-political factors on the swap spread.

Interest-rate Swaps in Banking

Interest-rate swaps, which are described in Chapter 15 of the author's book *Fixed Income Markets*, are an important ALM and risk management tool in banking. The rate payable on a swap represents bank risk, if we assume that a swap is paying (receiving) the fixed swap rate on one leg and receiving (paying) Libor-flat on the other leg. If one of the counterparties is not a bank, then either leg is adjusted to account for the different counterparty risk; usually the floating leg will have a spread added to Libor. We can see that this produces a swap curve that lies above the government bond yield curve, if we compare Figure 5.24 with Figure 5.25. Figure 5.24 is the USD swap rates page from Tullett & Tokyo brokers, and Figure 5.25 is the US Treasury yield curve, both as at 3 July 2006. The higher rates payable on swaps represents the additional risk premium associated with bank risk compared to government risk. The spread itself is the number of basis points the swap rate lies above the equivalent maturity government bond yield, quoted on the same interest basis.

In theory, the swap spread represents only the additional credit risk of the inter-bank market above the government market. However, as the spread is variable, it is apparent that other factors influence it. An ALM desk will want to be aware of these factors, because they influence swap

2 P1P122 **Govt** **TTIS**
200<Go> to view in Launchpad
10:10 **TULLETT & TOKYO** PAGE 1 / 2

USD Swaps	Bid	Ask	Time	USD Swaps	Bid	Ask	Time
IMM SWAPS				19) 15 Year	5.7380	5.7780	1:46
1) 1st	5.6900	5.7100	10:08	20) 20 Year	5.8060	5.8460	1:46
2) 2nd	5.6580	5.6790	10:08	21) 25 Year	5.8080	5.8490	3:02
3) 3rd	5.6150	5.6350	10:10	22) 30 Year	5.7740	5.8150	1:46
4) 4th	5.5800	5.6000	10:01	SEMI-ANNUAL SWAPS			
ANNUAL SWAPS				23) 2 Year	5.6310	5.6710	7/03
5) 1 Year	5.6770	5.6970	9:36	24) 3 Year	5.6120	5.6520	7/03
6) 2 Year	5.6240	5.6650	7/03	25) 4 Year	5.6210	5.6610	7:16
7) 3 Year	5.6070	5.6480	7/03	26) 5 Year	5.6410	5.6810	0:01
8) 4 Year	5.6180	5.6590	7:16	27) 6 Year	5.6600	5.7000	0:01
9) 5 Year	5.6390	5.6790	0:01	28) 7 Year	5.6770	5.7170	0:01
10) 6 Year	5.6560	5.6970	0:01	29) 8 Year	5.6910	5.7310	0:01
11) 7 Year	5.6740	5.7150	0:01	30) 9 Year	5.7080	5.7480	0:01
12) 8 Year	5.6890	5.7300	0:01	31) 10 Year	5.7270	5.7670	7:40
13) 9 Year	5.7070	5.7470	0:01	32) 11 Year	5.7370	5.7770	0:01
14) 10 Year	5.7250	5.7650	7:40	33) 12 Year	5.4570	5.4970	1:46
15) 11 Year	5.7350	5.7760	0:01	34) 13 Year	5.7620	5.8020	0:01
16) 12 Year	5.4520	5.4920	1:46	35) 14 Year	5.7720	5.8120	0:01
17) 13 Year	5.7610	5.8020	0:01	LIVE Treasury Mid-Yields &			
18) 14 Year	5.7700	5.8110	0:01	Treasury Swap Spreads -> SMKR<GO>			

Australia 61 2 9777 8600 Brazil 5511 3048 4500 Europe 44 20 7330 7500 Germany 49 69 920410
Hong Kong 852 2977 6000 Japan 81 3 3201 8900 Singapore 65 6212 1000 U.S. 1 212 318 2000
2 04-Jul-06 10:10:46

FIGURE 5.24 Tullet & Tokyo brokers USD interest-rate swaps page on Bloomberg, as at 3 July 2006.

<HELP> for explanation. P122 **Govt** **IYC**
Cancel: Screen not saved
YIELD CURVE - US TREASURY ACTIVES Page 2/2
DATE 7/ 4/06

	DESCRIPTION	PRICE	SRC	UPDATE	YIELD	HEDGED YIELD
3MO	1) B 0 09/28/06	B 4.8900	BGN	4:00	5.0158	5.0158
6MO	2) B 0 12/28/06	B 5.0700	BGN	4:00	5.2711	5.2711
1YR	3)					
2YR	4) T 5 1/8 06/30/08	B 99.9063	BGN	4:00	5.1748	5.1748
3YR	5) T 4 7/8 05/15/09	B 99.2969	BGN	4:00	5.1400	5.1400
4YR	6)					
5YR	7) T 5 1/8 06/30/11	B100.0625	BGN	4:00	5.1104	5.1104
6YR	8)					
7YR	9)					
8YR	10)					
9YR	11)					
10YR	12) T 5 1/8 05/15/16	B 99.7813	BGN	4:00	5.1527	5.1527
15YR	13)					
20YR	14)					
30YR	15) T 4 1/2 02/15/36	B 89.4531	BGN	4:00	5.2017	5.2017
1MO	16) B 0 07/27/06	B 4.5500	BGN	4:00	4.6261	4.6261

To change price source for securities, use <FMPS>.
To change price source for swaps, use <XDF>.
Yields are based on STANDARD settlement and are Conventional

Australia 61 2 9777 8600 Brazil 5511 3048 4500 Europe 44 20 7330 7500 Germany 49 69 920410
Hong Kong 852 2977 6000 Japan 81 3 3201 8900 Singapore 65 6212 1000 U.S. 1 212 318 2000
3 04-Jul-06 10:30:31

FIGURE 5.25 US Treasury yield curve as at 3 July 2006.

rates. Swaps are an important risk hedging tool, if not the most important, for banks so it becomes necessary for practitioners to have an appreciation of what drives swap spreads.

Historical Pattern

If we plot swap spreads over the period 1997–2006, we note that they tightened in the second half of this period. Figure 5.26 shows the spread for USD and GBP for the period 1997 to the first quarter of 2006. This reflects the bull market period of 2002–2006 when credit spreads fell in all markets.

During this period the widest spread for both currencies was reached during 2000, when the 10-year sterling swap spread peaked at around 140 bps above the gilt yield. The tightest spreads were reached during 2003, when the 10-year sterling spread reached around 15 bps towards the

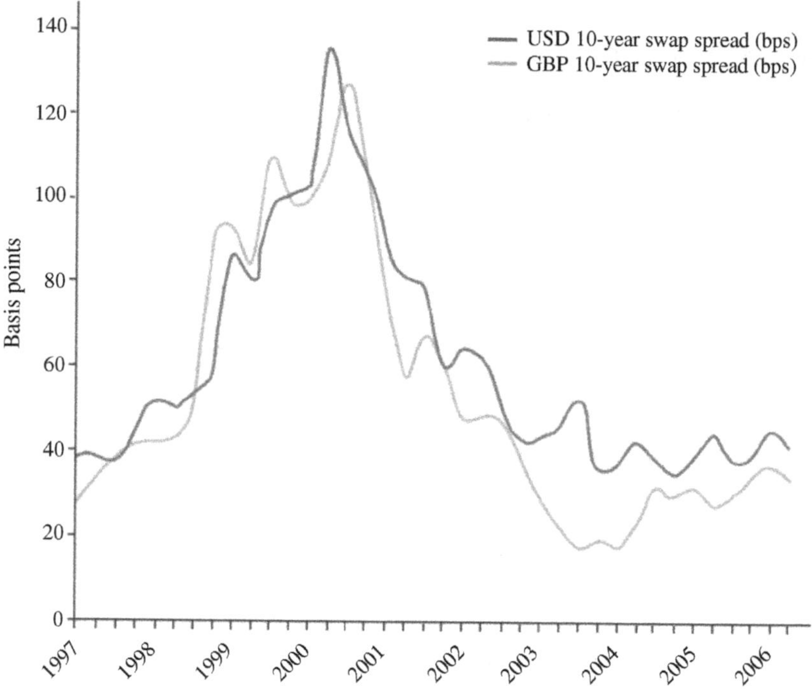

FIGURE 5.26 USD and GBP interest-rate swap spreads over government curve, 1997–2006.
Yield source: Bloomberg L.P.

end of that year. At the beginning of 2006 sterling spreads were still lower than the 10-year average of 55 bps. This implies that the perceived risk premium for the sterling capital markets had fallen.

The change in spread levels coincides with macro-level factors and occurrences. For instance, spreads moved in line with:

- the Asian currency crisis of 1997;
- the Russian government bond default and collapse of the Long Term Capital Management (LTCM) hedge fund in 1998;
- the "dot.com" crash in 2000;
- the subsequent loosening of monetary policy after the dot.com crash and the events of 9/11.

This indicates to us, if just superficially, that swap spreads react to macro-level factors that are perceived by the market to affect their business risk, credit risk and liquidity risk. Spreads also reflect supply and demand, as well as the absolute level of base interest rates.

Determinants of the Spread

We have already noted that in theory the swap spread, representing inter-bank counterparty risk, should reflect only the market's perception of bank risk over and above government risk. Bank risk is captured in the Libor rate – the rate paid by banks on unsecured deposits to other banks. So in other words, the swap spread is meant to adequately compensate against the risk of bank default. (In fact, post-crash many banks fund at a rate above Libor, so Libor itself is less accurate a gauge of bank credit risk). The Libor rate is the floating-rate paid against the fixed rate in the swap transaction, and moves with the perception of bank risk. As we implied in the previous section though, it would appear that other factors influence the swap spread. We can illustrate this better by comparing the swap spread for 10-year quarterly paying swaps with the spread between 3-month Libor and the 3-month general collateral (GC) repo rate. The GC rate is the risk-free borrowing rate, whereas the Libor rate represents bank risk again. In theory, the spread between 3-month Libor and the GC rate should therefore move closely with the swap spread for quarterly resetting swaps, as both represent bank risk. A look at Figure 5.27 shows that this is not the case. Figure 5.27 compares the two spreads in the US dollar market, but we do not need to calculate the correlation or the R_2 for the two sets of numbers. Even on cursory visual observation we can see that the correlation is not high. Therefore we conclude that other factors, in addition to perceived

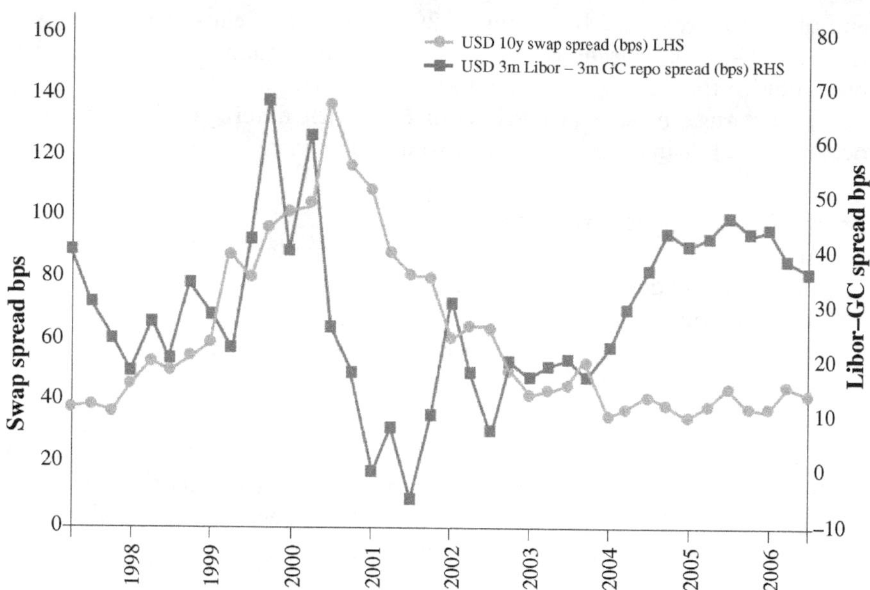

FIGURE 5.27 Comparison of USD 10-year swap spread and 3-month Libor–GC repo spread.
Yield source: Bloomberg L.P.

bank default risk, drive one or both spreads. These other factors influence swap rates and government bond yields, and hence the swap spread, and we consider them below.

Level and Slope of the Swap Curve

The magnitude of the swap spread is influenced by the absolute level of base interest rates. If the base rate is 10%, so that the government short-term rate is around 10%, with longer term rates being recorded higher, the spread tends to be greater than that seen if the base rate is 5%. The shape of the yield curve has even greater influence. When the curve is positively sloping, under the expectations hypothesis (see earlier in this chapter) investors will expect future rates to be higher; hence, floating-rates are expected to rise. This would suggest the swap spread will narrow. The opposite happens if the yield curve inverts.

Figure 5.28 shows the GBP 10-year swap spread compared to the GBP gilt yield curve spread (10-year gilt yield minus 2-year yield). We see that

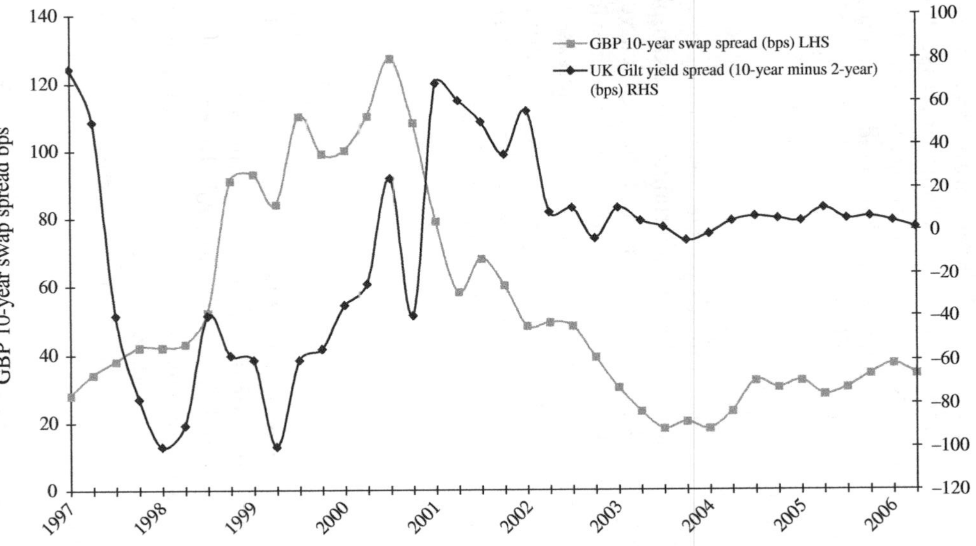

FIGURE 5.28 GBP swap spreads and gilt spreads compared 1997–2006.
Yield source: Bloomberg L.P.

the slope of the curve has influenced the swap spread; as the slope is narrowing, swap spreads are increasing and vice-versa.

Supply and Demand

The swap spread is influenced greatly by supply and demand for swaps. For example, greater trading volume in cash market instruments increases the need for hedging instruments, which will widen swap spreads. The best example of this is corporate bond issuance; as volumes increase, the need for underwriters to hedge issues increases. However, greater bond issuance also has another impact, as issuers seek to swap their fixed-rate liabilities to floating-rate. This also increases demand for swaps.

Market Volatility

As suggested by Figure 5.26, swap spreads widen during times of market volatility. This may be in times of market uncertainty (for example, the future direction of base rates or possible inversion of the yield curve) or in times of market shock such as 9/11. In some respects spread widening during periods of volatility reflects the perception of increased bank default risk. It also reflects the "flight to quality" that occurs during times of volatility or market correction: this is the increased demand for risk-free assets such as government bonds that drives their yields lower and hence swap spreads wider.

Government Borrowing

The level of government borrowing influences government bond yields, so perforce it will also impact swap spreads. If borrowing is viewed as being in danger of getting out of control, or the government runs persistently large budget deficits, government bond yields will rise. All else being equal, this will lead to narrowing swap spreads. We can see then that a number of factors influence swap spreads. An ALM or Treasury desk should be aware of these and assess them because the swap rate represents a key funding and hedging rate for a bank.

Impact of Macro-level Economic and Political Factors on Swap Spreads

The Treasury or ALM desk of a bank must always have a keen understanding of macro-level economic factors, and the overall geo-political situation, because these factors also influence swap spreads. It is worth considering the impact of these factors, in general terms, on spreads and the overall level of interest rates because the ALM desk will need to take them into account as part of its strategy. Also, geo-political events often arrive unannounced – for example, the Iraqi invasion of Kuwait in 1990, the attack on the World Trade Centre in New York ("9/11"), and the conflict between Israel and Lebanese Hezbollah guerrillas in July 2006. An ability to work effectively under the circumstances prevailing in such occurrences is crucial to efficient ALM.

Events that impact the financial markets at a macro level are often termed market "shocks" or external geo-political events. Such events invariably result in higher market volatility. The immediate impact of this is a market sell-off and a "flight to quality", which is when investors move out of higher risk assets such as equities and emerging market sovereign bonds and into risk-free assets such as US Treasuries and UK gilts. This is an almost knee-jerk reaction as investors become more risk-averse.

Swap spreads reflect the market perception about the general health of the economy and its future prospects, as well as the overall macro-level geo-political situation. Because the swap curve is an indicator of inter-bank credit quality, the swap spread can be taken to be the market perception of the health and prospects of the inter-bank market specifically and the bank sector generally.

Speaking generally, swap spreads widen during periods of increased market volatility. By implication a flight-to-quality should be reflected in a widening of the spread. This is expected because investors' new risk aversion manifests itself in lower government bond yields, arising from higher demand for government bonds. However, on occasion this analysis might be overly simplistic, because other micro-level factors will still be in play and can be expected to influence market rates. How can we consider the interaction between government yields, swap rates and possible influences on the swap spread?

The research team at Lloyds Banking Group produced a report[31] that suggests a novel way for us to analyse this, and we summarise their findings here with permission. We require an indicator of market volatility; one measure of this for the US dollar market is the VIX index. The VIX index is produced by the Chicago Board Options Exchange (CBOE) and is a proxy measure of market volatility. It uses a weighted average of implied

31 "Geo-politics Returns to the Limelight", in *Economics Perspectives*, 8 August 2006 (Lloyds Banking Group). With thanks to Mark Miller for his generous assistance.

TABLE 5.9 Correlation between the USD 10-year swap spread, the CBOE VIX index, the 10-year US Treasury yield and the CBOE VIX index.

Event	Correlation between VIX and 10-year swap spread	Correlation between VIX and 10-year US Treasury yield
Asian currency crisis (1997–1998)	0.71	−0.52
LTCM and Russian debt default (Jun.–Sept. 1998)	0.90	−0.78
9/11 to Afghan war (Sept. 2001–Mar. 2002)	−0.17	−0.67
Iraq War (Mar.–May 2003	0.54	−0.08
Ford and GM credit rating downgrade (Mar.–May 2005)	0.38	−0.53

Source: Lloyds Banking Group. Reproduced with permission.

volatilities to calculate an estimate of future volatility. An increase in the level of the index indicates increased market volatility.

We illustrate the relationship between geo-political events and the magnitude of the swap spread by looking at the correlation between the US dollar 10-year swap spread and the VIX index. Table 5.9 shows – as expected – a positive correlation between the VIX index and the swap spread during a period of both economic events, as well as macro-level geopolitical events. For instance, the period covers the 9/11 events as well as the Ford and GM credit-rating downgrades of 2005. There is a notable exception for the period September 2001 to March 2002, when there is a negative correlation. This is our first indication that the relationship is not as simplistic as we might think. Although the geo-political situation was negative, with the events of 9/11 leading to the US war in Afghanistan, suggesting that swap spreads should widen, this was also a period of successive cuts in the US base interest rate (the "Fed rate"). During this time the swap rate fell by more than 100 bps as the Fed rate was cut by 175 bps. So here we observe that the impact of specific financial market factors was greater than macro-level geo-political issues. Generally though, we observe the strong positive correlation between the swap spread the volatility index.

Figure 5.29 is a chart of the spread to the level of the VIX index.

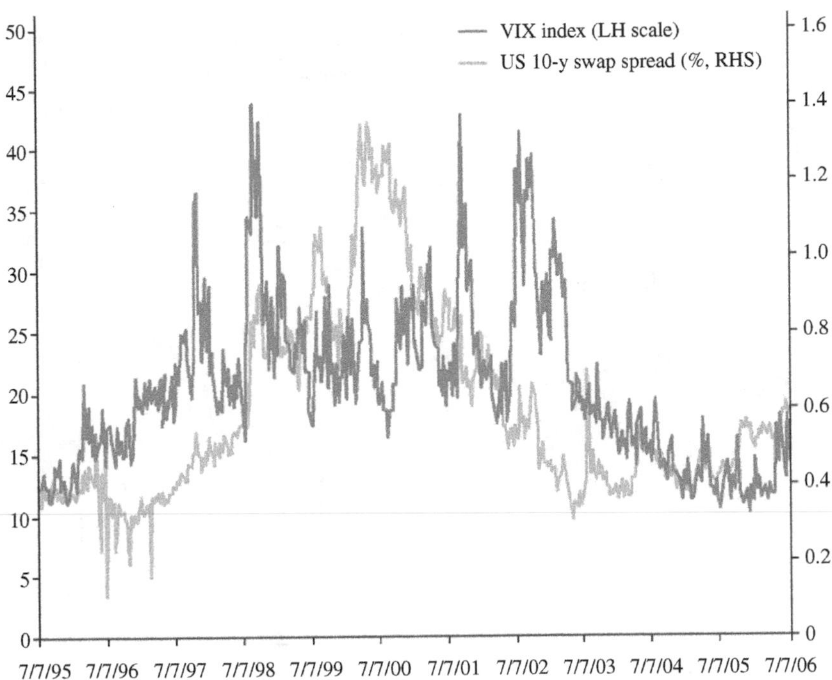

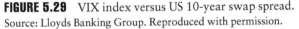

FIGURE 5.29 VIX index versus US 10-year swap spread.
Source: Lloyds Banking Group. Reproduced with permission.

By the same analysis, we can expect a negative correlation between the US Treasury yield and the VIX index level. This is generally borne out in Table 5.9. However, as with the case of the swap spread correlation, we see an occasion when other factors impact the correlation value. The low negative value for the period in 2003 leading up to, and after, the second Iraq war shows other factors influencing the Treasury yield. The flight-to-quality had taken place before the war actually began and was fully priced-in to Treasury yields.

Figure 5.30 illustrates the lower government bond yields that are observed at times of higher market volatility.

The purpose of the foregoing has been to illustrate how the swap spread interacts with macro-level geo-political factors. However, even during periods of high market tension, characterised by high levels of market volatility, the swap spread will respond also to more micro-level financial factors. ALM practitioners need to be aware of the nature of this interaction, and allow for this in their strategy and planning.

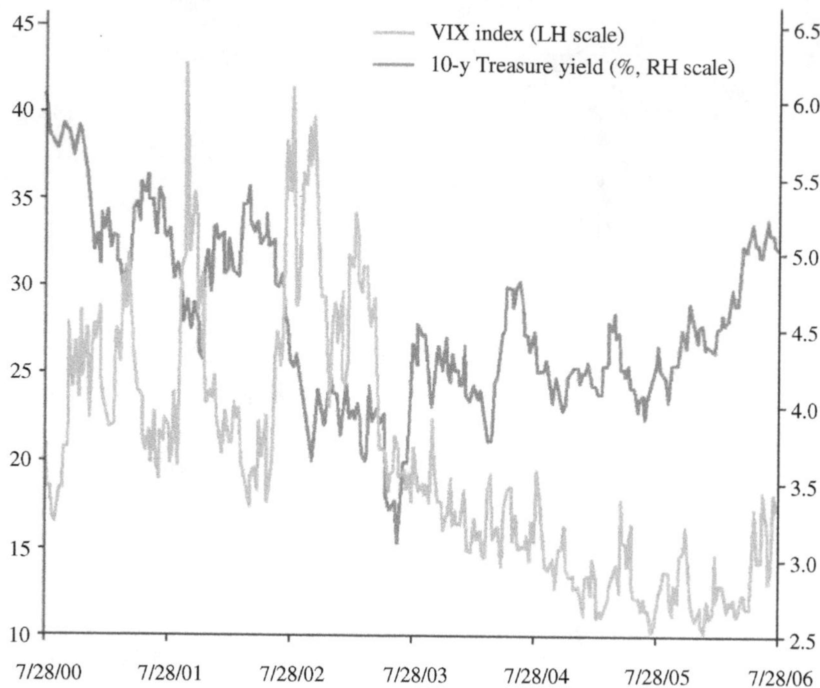

FIGURE 5.30 VIX index versus US 10-year Treasury.
Source: Lloyds Banking Group. Reproduced with permission.

Part III

FITTING THE YIELD CURVE

In this section we consider some of the techniques used to actually fit the term structure. In theory, we could use the bootstrapping approach described earlier. For a number of reasons, however, this does not produce accurate results, and so market practitioners use other methods instead. Term-structure models such as those in the academic literature define interest-rate dynamics using various assumptions about the nature of the stochastic process that drives these rates. However, the zero-coupon curve derived by models such as those described by Vasicek (1977), Brennan and Schwartz (1979); and Cox, Ingersoll and Ross (1985b) do not fit the observed market rates or spot rates implied by market yields, and generally market yield curves are found to contain more variable shapes than those derived using term-structure models. Hence, the interest-rate models described in Chapter 4 of the author's book *Fixed Income Markets* are required to be calibrated to the market and, in practice, they are calibrated to the market yield curve. This is carried out in two ways; the model is either calibrated to market instruments such as money-market products and interest-rate swaps, which are used to construct the yield curve, or the yield curve is constructed from market-instrument rates and the model is calibrated to this constructed curve. If the latter approach is preferred, there are a number of non-parametric methods that may be used. We will consider these later.

The academic literature contains a large amount of research into the empirical estimation of the term structure, the object of which is to fit a zero-coupon curve[32] that is a reasonably accurate fit to market prices *and* is a smooth function. There is an element of trade-off between these two objectives. The second objective is as important as the first, however, in order to derive a curve that makes economic sense. (It would be possible to fit the curve perfectly at the expense of smoothness, but this would be of little value).

In Part III, we present an overview of some of the methods used to fit the yield curve. An excellent account of the approaches we discuss in this chapter is given in Anderson et al. (1996). Unfortunately, this book is now out of print, but an excellent working paper that formed part of the input to this book is still available, which is Deacon and Derry (1994). A selection of other useful references is given in the bibliography.

YIELD-CURVE SMOOTHING

We know that the term structure can be described as the complete set of discount factors, the discount function, which can be extracted from the price of default-free bonds trading in the market. The bootstrapping technique described earlier may be used to extract the relevant discount factors. However, there are a number of reasons why this approach is problematic in practice. First, it is unlikely that the complete set of bonds in the market will pay cash flows at precise 6-month intervals every six months from today to 30 years or longer. An adjustment is made for cash flows received at irregular intervals, and for the lack of cash flows available at longer maturities. Another issue is the fact that the technique presented earlier allowed practitioners to calculate the discount factor for 6-month

32 The zero-coupon or spot curve, or equivalently the forward-rate curve or the discount function: all would be describing the same thing.

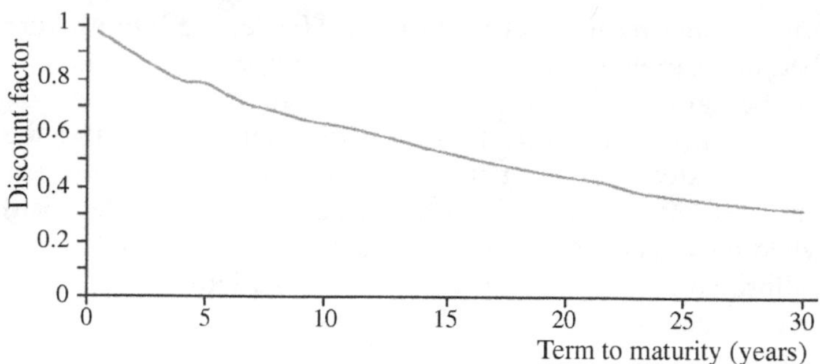

FIGURE 5.31 Discount factors from gilt prices, 12 June 2000.

maturities, whereas it may be necessary to determine the discount factor for non-standard periods, such as 4-month or 14.2-year maturities.

A third issue concerns the market price of bonds. These often reflect specific investor considerations, which include:

- the liquidity or lack thereof of certain bonds, caused by issue sizes, market-maker support, investor demand, non-standard maturity, and a host of other factors;
- the fact that bonds do not trade continuously, so that some bond prices will be "newer" than others;
- the tax treatment of bond cash flows and the effect that this has on bond prices;
- the effect of the bid–offer spread on the market prices used.

The statistical term used for bond prices subject to these considerations is error. These effects introduce noise into market prices.

To construct a fit to the yield curve that better handles the above considerations, smoothing techniques are used to derive the complete set of discount factors – the discount function – from market bond prices. Using the simple technique presented earlier we graph the discount function for the UK gilt prices as at 12 June 2000. This is shown in Figure 5.31. The yield curve plotted from gilt redemption yields is shown in Figure 5.32. Figure 5.33 shows the zero-coupon yield curve and forward rate curve that correspond to the discount function from the date.

From Figure 5.33 we see that the discount function is quite smooth, while the zero-coupon curve is also relatively smooth, although not as smooth as the discount function. The forward rate curve is distinctly unsmooth, if the reader will permit such as an expression, and there is obviously something wrong. In fact, the jagged nature of implied forward rates is one of the main concerns of the fixed-income analyst, and indicates

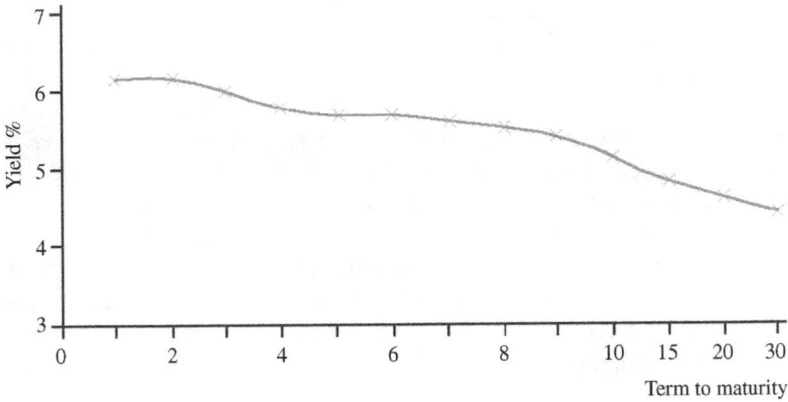

FIGURE 5.32 Gilt gross-redemption yields, 12 June 2000.

in the first instance that the discount function and zero-coupon curve are not as smooth as they appear. Using the naïve estimation method here, the main reason why the forward rates oscillate wildly is that minor errors at the discount-factor stage are magnified many times over when translated into the forward rate. That is, any errors in the discount factors (which errors may stem from any of the reasons given above) are compounded when spot rates are calculated from them, and these are compounded into larger errors when calculating forward rates. More precise techniques are required.

One approach that has been used to estimate the term structure was described by Carleton and Cooper (1976) and which assumed that default-free bond cash flows are payable on specified discrete dates, with a set of unrelated discount factors that apply to each cash flow. These discount

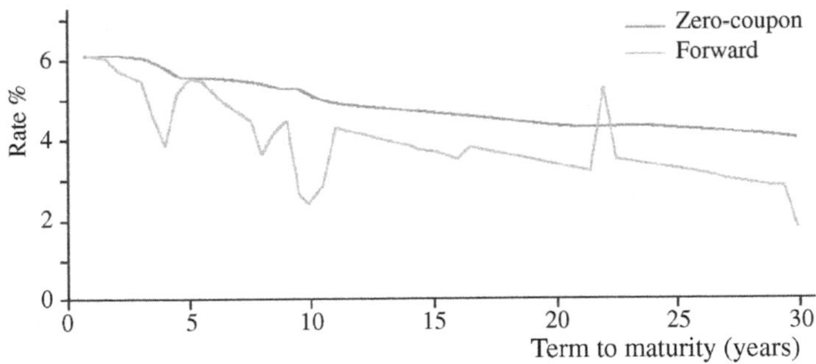

FIGURE 5.33 Zero-coupon (spot) and forward rates obtained from gilt yields, 12 June 2000.

factors were then estimated as regression coefficients, with each bond cash flow acting as the independent variables, and the bond price for that date acting as the dependent variable.[33] Using simple linear regression in this way produces a discrete discount function, not a continuous one, and forward rates that are estimated from this function are very jagged. An approach more readily accepted by the market was described by McCulloch (1971), who fitted the discount function using polynomial splines. This method produces a continuous function, and one that is linear so that the ordinary least-squares regression technique can be employed. Langetieg and Smoot (1981)[34] use an extended McCulloch method, fitting cubic splines to zero-coupon rates instead of the discount function, and using non-linear methods of estimation.

Smoothing Techniques

A common technique that may be used, but which is not accurate and so not recommended, is linear interpolation. In this approach, the set of bond prices are used to graph a redemption yield curve and where bonds are not available for the required maturity term, the yield is interpolated from actual yields. Using gilt yields for 26 June 1997, we plot this as shown at Figure 5.34. The interpolated yields are those that are not marked by a cross. Figure 5.34 looks reasonable for any practitioner's purpose. However, spot and forward yields that are obtained from this curve are apt to behave in

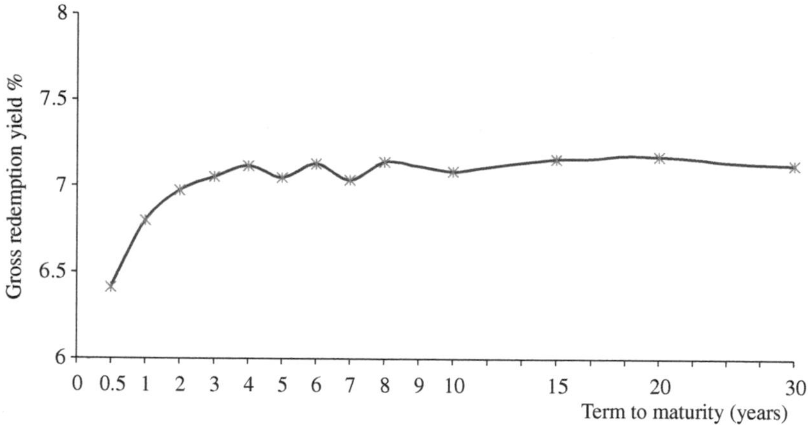

FIGURE 5.34 Linear interpolation of bond yields, 26 June 1997. Crosses represent actual data input points.

33 The basics of regression are summarised briefly in Appendix 5.3.
34 Reference in Vasicek and Fong (1982).

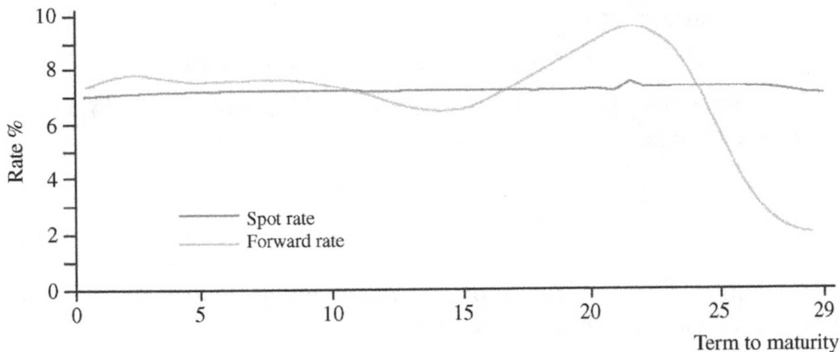

FIGURE 5.35 Spot and forward rates implied from Figure 5.34.

unrealistic fashion, as shown in Figure 5.35. The forward curve is very bumpy, and each bump will correspond to a bond used in the original set. The spot rate has a kink at 21.5 years, and so the forward curve jumps significantly at this point. This curve would not be useful for practitioners.

For this reason, market analysts do not bother with linear interpolation and instead use multiple regression or spline-based methods. One approach might be to assume a functional form for the discount function and estimate parameters of this form from the prices of bonds in the market. We consider these approaches next.

Using a Cubic Polynomial

A simple functional form for the discount function is a cubic polynomial. This approach consists of approximating the set of discount factors using a cubic function of time. If we say that $d(t)$ is the discount factor for maturity t, we approximate the set of discount factors using the following cubic function:

$$\hat{d}(t) = a_0 + a_1(t) + a_2(t)^2 + a_3(t)^3. \quad (5.52)$$

In some texts, the coefficients sometimes are written as a, b, and c rather than a_1 and so on.

The discount factor for $t = 0$, that is at time now, is 1. Therefore $a_0 = 1$, and (5.52) can then be re-written as:

$$\hat{d}(t) - 1 = a_1(t) + a_2(t)^2 + a_3(t)^3. \quad (5.53)$$

The market price of a traded coupon bond can be expressed in terms of discount factors. So at (5.54) we show the expression for the price of an N-maturity bond paying identical coupons C at regular intervals and redeemed at maturity at M.

$$P = d(t_1)C + d(t_2)C + \ldots\ldots + d(t_N)(C+M) \tag{5.54}$$

Using the cubic polynomial equation (5.53), expression (5.54) is transformed into:

$$\begin{aligned} P = C\left[1 + a_1(t_1) + a_2(t_1)^2 + a_3(t_1)^3\right] + \ldots \\ + (C+M)\left[1 + a_1(t_N) + a_2(t_N)^2 + a_3(t_N)^3\right]. \end{aligned} \tag{5.55}$$

We require the coefficients of the cubic function in order to start describing the yield curve, so we re-arrange (5.55) in order to express it in terms of these coefficients. This is shown at (5.56).

$$\begin{aligned} P = M + \textstyle\sum C + a_1[C(t_1) + \ldots + (C+M)(t_N)] \\ + a_2\left[C(t_1)^2 + \ldots + (C+M)(t_N)^2\right] \\ + a_3\left[C(t_1)^3 + \ldots + (C+M)(t_N)^3\right] \end{aligned} \tag{5.56}$$

In the same way, we can express the pricing equation for each bond in our data set in terms of the unknown parameters of the cubic function.

From (5.56) we may write

$$P - \left(M + \sum C\right) = a_1X_1 + a_2X_2 + a_3X_3 \tag{5.57}$$

where X_i is the appropriate expression in square brackets in (5.56); this is the form in which the expression is encountered commonly in text books.

EXAMPLE 5.10 SETTING THE CUBIC FUNCTION

A benchmark semi-annual coupon 4-year bond with a coupon of 8% is trading at a price of 101.25. Assume the first coupon is precisely six months from now, so that $t_1 = 0.5$ and $t_N = 4$. We wish to set up the cubic function expression.

We have $C = 4$ and $M = 100$ so therefore:

$100 + \sum C = 100 + (8 \times 4) = 132$

$P - (100 + \sum C) = 101.25 - 132 = -30.75$

$X_1 = (4\times0.5) + (4\times1) + (4\times1.5) + \ldots + (104\times4) = 472$

$X_2 = \left[4\times(0.5)^2\right] + \left[4\times(1)^2\right] + \left[4\times(1.5)^2\right] + \ldots + \left[104\times(4)^2\right] = 1{,}796$

$X_3 = \left[4\times(0.5)^3\right] + \left[4\times(1)^3\right] + \left[4\times(1.5)^3\right] + \ldots + \left[104\times(4)^3\right] = 7{,}528$

(continued)

(continued)

This means that we now have an expression for the three coefficients, which is:

$$472a_1 + 1796a_2 + 7528a_3 = -30.75.$$

The prices for all other bonds are expressed in terms of the unknown parameters. To calculate the coefficient values, we use a statistical technique such as linear regression, such as least squares to find the best fit values of the cubic equation. An introduction to this technique is given in Appendix 5.3.

In practice, the cubic polynomial approach is too limited a technique, requiring one equation per bond, and does not have the required flexibility to fit market data satisfactorily. The resulting curve is not really a curve but, rather, a set of independent discount factors that have been fit with a line of best fit. In addition, the impact of small changes in the data can be significant at the non-local level; so, for example, a change in a single data point at the early maturities can result in badly behaved longer maturities. Alternatively, a piecewise cubic polynomial approach is used, whereby $d(t)$ is assumed to be a different cubic polynomial over each maturity range. This means that the parameters a_1, a_2 and a_3 will be different over each maturity range. We will look at a special case of this use, the cubic spline, a little later.

Non-parametric Methods

Outside of the cubic polynomial approach described in the previous section there are two main approaches to fitting the term structure. These are usually grouped into *parametric* and *non-parametric* methods. Parametric curves are based on term structure models such as the Vasicek model or Longstaff and Schwartz model. Non-parametric curves are not derived from an interest-rate model and are general approaches, fitted using a set of parameters. However as they require only a few parameters, their output is reasonably stable. They include spline-based methods, which are linear, and non-linear methods such as Nelson and Siegel (1987). One advantage of the non-parametric approach is that, as James and Webber (2000, p. 433) note, the result "really is a curve, not a set of independent discount factors".

There is no one "right" or "best" method for fitting the curve. The methodology or approach selected should be the one that gives the best result for the purpose it is being used. A major reason why smooth yield curves cannot be fitted is because input data are inconsistent or have errors, so that a perfect fit to it is not possible. Therefore it is worthwhile defining first what we require the curve for, before then selecting the technique that we use to produce it. The user may require the curve for one or more of the following:

- smoothest discrete zero-coupon yields;
- smoothest continuous zero-coupon yields;
- smoothest discrete forward rates;
- smoothest continuous forward rates;
- smoothest continuous forward rates, given a forced output at the long end;
- smoothest discrete zero-coupon bond prices;
- smoothest continuous zero-coupon bond prices;
- minimised pricing error.

Van Deventer and Imai (1997) show that there is a unique solution that maximises smoothness for a given set of input parameters, and this is done by calculating the magnitude of smoothness itself; one method will produce a smoother curve than other methods. However, the user must define first whether the "best" curve is indeed the smoothest one; if it is, then one can determine mathematically which method produces the best fit. We describe later in this chapter how one can measure smoothness.

Spline-based Methods

A spline is a statistical technique and a form of linear-interpolation method. There is more than one way of applying them, and the most straightforward process is the spline function fitted using regression techniques. For the purposes of yield-curve construction, this method can cause curves to jump wildly and is over-sensitive to changes in parameters.[35] However, we feel it is the most accessible method to understand and an introduction to the basic technique, as described in Suits et al. (1978), is given in Appendix 5.5.[36] An illustration of the technique is given in Appendix 5.6.

An n-th order spline is a piecewise-polynomial approximation with n degree polynomials that are differentiable $n - 1$ times. Piecewise means that the different polynomials are connected at arbitrarily selected points known as knot points (see Appendix 5.5). A cubic spline is a 3-order spline, and is a piecewise cubic polynomial that is differentiable twice along all its points.

35 For instance, see James and Webber (2000), section 15.3.
36 The original article by Suits et al. (1978) is excellent and highly recommended.

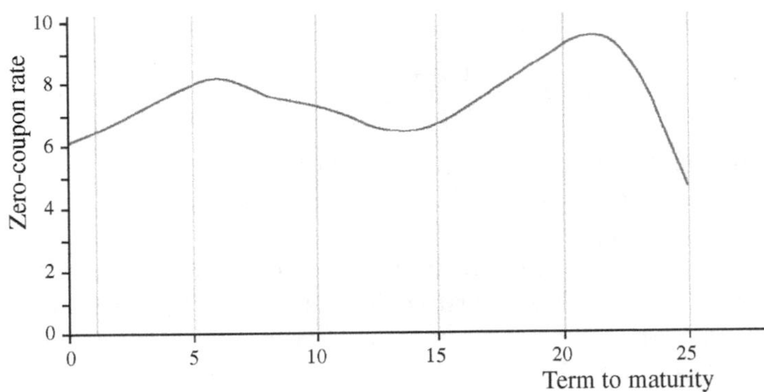

FIGURE 5.36 Cubic spline with knot points at 0, 2, 5, 10 and 25 years.

The x-axis in the regression is divided into segments at arbitrary points known as knot points. At each knot point the slopes of adjoining curves are required to match, as must the curvature. Figure 5.36 is a cubic spline. The knot points are selected at 0, 2, 5, 10 and 25 years. At each of these points, the curve is a cubic polynomial, and with this function we could accommodate a high and low in each space bounded by the knot points.

Cubic-spline interpolation assumes that there is a cubic polynomial that can estimate the yield curve at each maturity gap. One can think of a spline as a number of separate polynomials of $y = f(X)$, where X is the complete range, divided into user-specified segments, which are joined smoothly at the knot points. If we have a set of bond yields $r_0, r_1, r_2, \ldots\ldots r_n$ at maturity points $t_0,t_1,t_2, \ldots\ldots t_n$, we can estimate the cubic-spline function in the following way:

- the yield on bond i at time t is expressed as a cubic polynomial of the form $ri(t) = a_i + b_it + c_it^2 + d_it^3$ for the interval over t_i and t_{i-1};
- the coefficients of the cubic polynomial are calculated for all n intervals between the $n + 1$ data points, which results in $4n$ unknown coefficients that must be computed;
- these equations can be solved because they are made to fit the observed data. They are twice differentiable at the knot points, and these derivatives are equal at these points;
- the constraints specified are that the curve is instantaneously straight at the start of the curve (the shortest maturity) and instantaneously straight at the end of the curve, the longest maturity, that is $r''(0) = 0$.

An accessible and readable account of this technique can be found in Van Deventer and Imai (1997).

The general formula for a cubic spline is:

$$s(\tau) = \sum_{i=0}^{3} a_i \tau^i + \frac{1}{3!} \sum_{p=0}^{n-1} b_p (\tau - X_p)^3 \tag{5.58}$$

where τ is the time of receipt of cash flows and where X_p refers to the points that are joined and adjacent polynomials which are known as knot points, with $\{X_0, \ldots \ldots X_n\}$, $X_p < X_{p+1}$, $p = 0, \ldots \ldots, n - 1$. In addition, $(\tau - X_p) = \max(\tau - X_p, 0)$. The cubic spline is twice differentiable at the knot points. In practice, the spline is written down as a set of basis functions with the general spline being made up of a combination of these. One way to do this is by using what are known as B-splines. For a specified number of knot points $\{X_0, \ldots \ldots, X_n\}$ this is given by (5.59),

$$B_p(\tau) = \sum_{j=p}^{p+4} \left[\prod_{i=p, i \neq 1}^{p+4} \frac{1}{X_i - X_j} \right] (\tau - X_p)^3 \tag{5.59}$$

where $B_p(\tau)$ are cubic splines which are approximated on $\{X_0, \ldots\ldots, X_n\}$ with the following function:

$$\delta(\tau) = \delta(\tau | \lambda_{-3}, \ldots\ldots, \lambda_{n-1}) = \sum_{p=-3}^{n-1} \lambda_p B_p(\tau) \tag{5.60}$$

with $\lambda = (\lambda_{-3}, \ldots\ldots, \lambda_{n-1})$ the required coefficients. The maturity periods $\tau_1, \ldots\ldots, \tau_n$ specify the B-splines so that $B = \{B_p(\tau_j)\}_{p=-3,\ldots,n-1, j-1,\ldots,m}$ and $\hat{\delta} = (\delta(\tau_1), \ldots\ldots, \delta(\tau_m))$. This allows us to set

$$\hat{\delta} = B'\lambda \tag{5.61}$$

and therefore the regression equation

$$\lambda^* = \arg\min_{\lambda} \{\varepsilon'\varepsilon | \varepsilon = P - D\lambda\} \tag{5.62}$$

with $D = CB'$.

$\varepsilon'\varepsilon$ are the minimum errors. The regression at (5.61) is computed using ordinary least-squares regression.

An illustration of the use of *B*-splines is given in Steeley (1991) and, with a complete methodology, by Didier Joannas in Choudhry (2001) and Choudhry et al. (2010).

Appendix 5.5 provides background on splines fitted using regression methods.

Nelson and Siegel Curves

The curve-fitting technique first described by Nelson and Siegel (1987) has since been applied and modified by other authors, which is why they are sometimes described as a "family" of curves. These curves provide a satisfactory fit of the complete term structure, with some loss of accuracy at the very short and very long end. In the original curve, the authors specify four parameters. The approach is not a bootstrapping technique, but, rather, a method for estimating the zero-coupon rate function from the yields observed on T-Bills and bonds, under an assumed function for forward rates.

The Nelson and Spiegel curve states that the implied forward-rate yield curve may be modelled along the entire term structure using the following function:

$$rf(m,\beta) = \beta_0 + \beta_1 \exp\left[\frac{-m}{t_1}\right] + \beta_2\left[\frac{m}{t_{1-}}\right]\exp\left[\frac{-m}{t_1}\right] \tag{5.63}$$

where

$\beta = (\beta_0, \beta_1, \beta_2, t_1)'$ is the vector of parameters describing the yield curve, and m is the maturity at which the forward rate is calculated. There are three components; the constant term, a decay term and a term reflecting the "humped" nature of the curve. The shape of the curve will gradually lead into an asymptote at the long end, the value of which is given by β_0, with a value of $\beta_0 + \beta_1$ at the short end.

A version of the Nelson and Siegel curve is the Svensson model (1994) with an adjustment to allow for the humped characteristic of the yield curve. This is fitted by adding an extension, as shown by (5.64).

$$rf(m,\beta) = \beta_0 + \beta_1 \exp\left[\frac{-m}{t_1}\right] + \beta_2\left[\frac{m}{t_1}\right]\exp\left[\frac{-m}{t_1}\right] + \beta_3\left[\frac{m}{t_2}\right]\exp\left[\frac{-m}{t_2}\right] \tag{5.64}$$

The Svensson curve is modelled, therefore, using six parameters, with additional input of β_3 and t_2. In practice, the Svensson curve is preferred in banks because its output is less oscillating, particularly at longer tenors.

Nelson and Siegel curves are popular in the market because they are straightforward to calculate. Jordan and Mansi (2000) state that one of the advantages of these curves is that they force the long-date forward curve into a horizontal asymptote. Another is that the user is not required to specify knot points, the choice of which determines the effectiveness or otherwise of cubic spline curves. The disadvantage they note is that these curves are less flexible than spline-based curves and there is therefore a chance that they do not fit the observed data as accurately as spline models.[37] James and Webber

37 This is an excellent article, strongly recommended. A good overview to curve fitting is given in the introduction, and the main body of the article gives a good insight into the research undertaken in yield-curve analysis.

(2000, pp. 444–5) also suggest that Nelson and Siegel curves are slightly inflexible due to the limited number of parameters, and are accurate for yield curves that have only one hump, but are unsatisfactory for curves that possess both a hump and trough. In general, however, for reasons of tractability this family of curves, which includes Svensson (1994) as well as Waggoner (1997), is often selected as the interpolation method at banks wishing to fit their internal credit-risky yield curve.

IMPLEMENTING CURVES IN PRACTICE

Whichever curve is chosen will depend on the user's requirements and the purpose for which the model is required. The choice of modelling methodology is usually a trade-off between simplicity and ease of computation and accuracy. Essentially, the curve chosen must fulfil the qualities of:

- *Accuracy:* Is the curve a reasonable fit of the market curve? Is it flexible enough to accommodate a variety of yield-curve shapes?
- *Model consistency:* Is the curve-fitting method consistent with a theoretical yield-curve model such as Vasicek or Cox-Ingersoll-Ross?
- *Simplicity:* Is the curve reasonably straightforward to compute; that is, is it *tractable*?

The different methodologies all fit these requirements to greater or lesser extent. A good summary of the advantages and disadvantages of some popular modelling methods can be found in James and Webber (2000, Chapter 15).

Defining Smoothness in a Curve

As we noted earlier, term structures are constructed for a variety of purposes, and different users will have different requirements for them. The user must define what aspect of the curve output is most important to it, and then select the construction methodology that gives the "best" fit. If the requirement is to produce the smoothest curve, then the user can measure the smoothness itself mathematically.

For ease of explanation, we consider here zero-coupon bond prices in a continuously compounded environment. As we noted previously, one can represent a yield curve in any of three ways, whether as:

- discount factors, described as $Df(t_1)$, $Df(t_2)$, . . . , $Df(t_n)$;
- zero-coupon bond (or spot) interest rates, described as $r(t_1)$, $r(t_2)$, . . . , $r(t_n)$;
- forward rates, described as $f(t_0, t_1)$, $f(t_1, t_2)$, . . . ,$f(t_{n-1}, t_n)$.

We demonstrated earlier that these three are equivalent (see the Formula Summary boxes in this chapter), as shown by the following relationships:

$$Df(t_i) = e^{-r(t_i).t_i} \tag{5.65}$$

$$r(t_i).t_i = r(t_{i-1}).t_{i-1} + f(t_{i-1}, t_i)(t_i - t_{i-1}) \tag{5.66}$$

where

$$0 = t_0 < t_1 < \cdots < t_n.$$

For our purposes we define smoothness as the measure of the extent to which a function oscillates around a point. A smoothness penalty may be defined as:

$$\int (f''(t))^2 dt. \tag{5.67}$$

Spot rates are averages of forward rates so will always be smoother. An attempt to construct a curve for maximum smoothness should therefore look to maximise smoothness of the forward rates. We can measure smoothness by the proximity of a particular forward rate to those forward rates on either side of it. In other words we wish the result that minimises

$$\sum_{i=2}^{n} |f_i - f_{i-1}|. \tag{5.68}$$

In practice, we use the squared values of the differences rather than the differences themselves, given by:

$$S(f) = \sum_{i=2}^{n} (f_i - f_{i-1})^2. \tag{5.69}$$

Van Deventer and Imai (1997) note that the term structure of instantaneous forward rates $f(t), 0 \le t \le T$ that minimises (5.67) is a fourth-order polynomial spline with knot times t_i with i = 0 to n.

Practitioners should note that smooth curves are the best approach for most applications but not all. If there is insufficient market input data, then whatever methodology is selected will not make any difference, because the curve will not be smooth. Where market observable data *is* scarce, the best approach is often to specify additional inputs to force the result to the one desired; for example, lack of price data in the period from 10 to 30 years can be compensated for by using proxy inputs, or, where these are also not available, forcing the longest dated tenor to a particular value. Proxy inputs may be adjusted swap rates, CDS levels or other market indicators.

Formal Policy for Setting the Bank's Internal Funding Curve

A significant risk management decision at every bank is selecting the internal yield curve construction methodology. The internal curve is an important tool in the pricing and risk management process, driving resource allocation, business line transaction pricing, hedge construction and RAROC analysis. It is given therefore that curve construction methodology should follow business best-practice. A bank should state its procedure for constructing its internal cost of funds (COF) curve in a formal policy document.

Orthodox valuation methodology in financial markets follows the logic of risk-neutral no-arbitrage pricing.[38] The same logic should apply when setting a bank's internal pricing term structure. The risk-free curve is given by sovereign bond prices, while the banking sector risky curve was traditionally the Libor or swap curve. Banks generally fund at "cost of funds" as opposed to Libor-flat; therefore, the logic of the no-arbitrage approach dictates that a bank's risky pricing yield curve should be extracted from market prices, because the latter dictate the rate at which the bank can raise liabilities. Such an approach preserves consistency because the same no-arbitrage principles drive market prices in the first place. In other words, the logic behind setting a bank's yield curve must be identical to the logic used (say) in pricing derivatives.

The best practice at banks is to adopt an interpolation method that uses prices (yields) of the issuer's existing debt as model inputs, and extracts a discount function from these prices. The output is then used to derive a term structure that represents the issuer's current risky yield curve. To adopt such an approach requires a liquid secondary market in the issuer's bonds. Where such a liquid secondary market is not available, proxy inputs will have to be used instead (we discuss different market proxies in Chapter 15).

Recommended Procedure

Earlier in this chapter we described different interpolation methodologies, be they polynomial splines or non-parametric models. Whatever method is selected, the recommended procedure is as follows:

1. Fit the selected method to market data;
2. Extract the bank's risky yield curve. This is the baseline yield curve that determines the fixed coupon for a vanilla coupon fixed-maturity bond issued by the bank at par;

---

38 The most appropriate references in this field are Feynman-Kac (1949), Ito (1951), Markowitz (1959), Fama (1965), Black-Scholes (1973) and Merton (1973).

3. Use the continuous discount function obtained from (2) above to create a par-par asset swap curve;
4. Adopt this as the market-implied term liquidity premium (TLP) curve, which sets the spread for a vanilla FRN issued by the bank at par.

The curve at (4) is therefore the bank's TLP as dictated by market rates. By definition, under the no-arbitrage principles we refer to above, this curve is the bank's baseline pricing curve, and the source for creating all cross-currency funding curves.

The TLP curve indicates the fair-value spread a bank should pay on an FRN it issued of relevant tenor with a floating re-set based on Libor. Note that this also sets the rate it would pay on a fixed coupon bond issue that was asset-swapped, but for an uncollateralised swap.

This is because the TLP curve is an unsecured pricing curve. It would not be the correct fair-value spread to pay on an asset swap, because that would involve a secured derivative (the interest-rate swap that is part of the asset swap construction). If we assume an unsecured derivative in the asset swap, we now have the par-par asset swap curve.

We should note that the above is the market-implied curve process. The model output extrapolates where necessary if the latest tenor of a bank's issued bonds does not extend to the maturity required for the modelled curve. The user can set the model to extrapolate fair-value output to a tenor of its choice. Extrapolated rates represent the current secondary market-implied value, and hence the fair-value rate to pay for that tenor. The actual rate paid at any one time will also reflect business considerations and the impact of supply and demand. That is, a specific business case can be made at any time as to why specific tenor points at any point along the TLP curve should deviate from the market-implied prices by more than the accepted tolerance stated in the bank's procedure.

Maintenance in Line with the Market

A stated concern of regulators is the risk created by a bank's public funding curve falling out of line with market prices. To manage this risk, alongside its curve procedure policy a bank should set up a smoothing procedure, to reduce the impact of market movements producing curves that shift daily in a volatile fashion. In other words, because the bank's curve is used to price assets and liabilities daily, and some transactions are implemented over a long period, it is not practical to have the curve changing by a large margin on a daily basis due to the volatility of market price.

To address this, the bank should set up a procedure that addresses volatility and publish a smoothed curve. This can be done by not using the day's prices but by taking the 14-day or 30-day moving average of the curve and using that result each day. During extremely volatile periods, this moving average might be changed to a (say) 60-day moving average. This decision would have to be made at senior level, in practice an ALCO sub-committee that includes the Head of Treasury.

Bank assets such as syndicated loans have a long gestation period. The rate used to price these loans would be based on the bank's TLP curve, and because of the long transaction period the bank may wish to set its loans TLP at a 3-month moving average level, updated quarterly.

Finally, it should be noted that the Section 166 of the United Kingdom's Financial Services and Markets Act (2000), in its review on Funds Transfer Pricing policy, highlighted the need for a consistent pricing curve to be applied across all the business lines in a bank, and for it to be maintained in line with market prices. Setting a formal policy as described above is clearly business best-practice for a bank.

MULTI-CURRENCY YIELD CURVES

The 2007–2009 financial crisis highlighted hitherto unknown issues associated with using single-currency yield curves for pricing and valuation purposes. This reflected the multi-currency environment in which many banks now operated, where collateral is posted in different currencies to the currency of the underlying transaction, and where assets of one currency are funded by liabilities of a different currency, using forward FX swaps and cross-currency swaps for hedging. In the post-crash world, it becomes necessary to use a baseline currency yield curve, which might be in USD or EUR, and calculate the foreign currency yield curve from this, but then also allow for a basis adjustment. This is because of correlation between FX rates and yield spreads.[39] Going a step further, a bank may calculate a "multi-currency yield curve" that equalises interest rates across different currencies, using the forward FX adjustment, and then allows for "quanto" effects of correlation by making a basis adjustment. The result is then a single yield curve whose

39 Recent literature worth looking at in this space includes Ametrano and Bianchetti (2009); Hagan and West (2006); Kijima, Tanaka and Wong (2008); and Piterbarg (2010). The concept of the multi-currency yield curve is a fundamental development in term structure theory, and is worthy of greater publicity and awareness in the market.

y-axis plot is the highest rate pertaining to any individual currency, for each specific tenor.

The use of the multi-currency yield curve is most pertinent in two areas; first, the pricing of exotic cross-currency derivatives, and second, the collateral issues associated with derivatives dealing in the inter-bank market. We consider the latter issue here. The credit support annexe (CSA) side agreement to the standard ISDA derivatives agreement often allows counterparties to a derivative to post collateral in the form of cash in a different denomination to the currency of the trade. As a result, the larger banks now construct multi-currency yield curves to assist them with the funding decision when paying or receiving collateral. We consider this concept here. As this is very relevant to collateralised IRS, we place the discussion in this context.

Note that the development of multi-currency yield curves is not a new "discovery" as such; the factors that drive it were recognised prior to the crash (for example, see Tuckman and Porfirio (2003) and Hagan and West (2006)). It is just that in the pre-crash environment the cost of funding was low, and basis differentials between different currencies in multi-currency products were negligible, so that these factors were not deemed worthy of accurate measurement. In a post-crash environment, as bank funding levels rose above Libor and the basis value increased, it is good practice to be aware of these issues.

IRS Rates and Discounting Levels

Generally the market consensus has been to use Libor levels to discount swaps.[40] In a conventional positive-sloping yield curve environment, forward Libor rates will be increasing along the term structure. In this environment a vanilla IRS, paying floating and receiving fixed, will have net positive cash flows at the start of its life (when the floating rate payment, typically 3-month or 6-month Libor, is lower than the fixed rate), and net negative flows towards the end of its life (when the floating Libor fix is higher than the fixed rate). If discounting rates rise, then this will affect cash flows at the end of the swap's life by more than it affects flows at the start of the swap.

In other words, if market interest rates rise, the mark-to-market value of a receive-fixed swap will be increasing as discounting rates rise. In turn, this means that the break-even rate of the swap moves lower; hence, a

40 We refer to the BBA Libor fixings for 0–12 month and the fixed rate on inter-bank swaps for 2–30 years as "Libor rates".

market making swap bank will require a lower fixed rate if it is to price the swap correctly as discounting rates rise.

On the other hand, consider a receive-fixed IRS where the fixed payment is on an annual basis, while the floating leg pays quarterly 3-month Libor. If discounting rates rise, then this will affect the fixed leg payments by more than the floating leg payments, because fixed payments are received on a lower frequency and at a later time, so there is more time for the impact of discounting to take effect. In this case, the value of the receive-fixed swap is decreasing as discounting rates rise. Here, the break-even rate of the swap moves higher as rates rise.

The break-even rate to use when pricing an IRS is a function of the current discounting level. This is separate to the current inter-bank swap rate. The question then is what discount level to use when constructing the forward Libor curve from current swap rates. This is where the funding impact of swaps traded under a CSA agreement becomes pertinent. The party that is negative mark-to-market on a collateralised swap will, under London Clearing House and SwapClear rules, pass collateral in the local currency, which attracts the OIS interest rate.

This therefore dictates that a dealer bank should use the local currency OIS curve as inputs to construct a curve of projected Libor rates from current inter-bank swap rates. Swaps traded in euro currency would be priced off the EONIA curve, sterling swaps off the SONIA curve, and so on.[41]

Fitting Multi-currency Yield Curves

Where a swap is being priced in the local currency, it uses the projected 3-month Libor rate and OIS curve for valuation. A different issue arises when a bank posts collateral to cover a negative mark-to-market swap in a currency other than that of the swap. This means a dealer bank needs to consider using a discount curve to value a swap across different currencies. The best way to look at this is to view it from the angle of a cross-currency swap, and the spread for such products. These swaps, which exchange currencies at inception and then return the same amount, pay floating-fixed (or floating-floating) interest in two different currencies. The principle for discounting them is identical to that of vanilla IRS.

We illustrate with an example. Consider a floating-floating cross-currency swap between EUR and GBP. The latter currency has higher forward rates. If the discount rate falls in both currencies, the EUR leg value

41 The overnight-index swap in euros is the EONIA curve, and the equivalent in pounds sterling is the SONIA curve.

will decrease by more than the GBP side. This is because a higher value of the EUR cash flows than the GBP cash flows is paid at maturity on the re-exchange of principal. To allow for this, the price of the GBP leg needs to be higher, to cover against this impact.

The question here is what discount level to use when pricing the cross-currency swap. In general the market uses the OIS rate. Therefore this rate should be used when building the multi-currency curve.

The starting point is that we set discount curves in all the main currencies, which form the relevant OIS curve. We can extract the discount factors for each currency from these curves, which we call Df_{CCY} for a general discount factor and Df_{OIS} for the relevant discount factor for the OIS in that currency. If we assume that FX rates are not correlated to interest rates (an unrealistic assumption but necessary in this analysis), this implies that forward FX rates – which are a deposit product, as forward FX rates are simply spot FX rate adjusted for the deposit interest rate in each currency – are not a function of the discounting level in each currency. This further implies that the ratio of forward discount factors is constant.

This enables us to set the following relationship for any two currencies and any two rates:

$$\frac{Df^{\text{RefB}}_{\text{CCY1}}(t)}{Df^{\text{RefB}}_{\text{CCY2}}(t)} = \frac{DF^{\text{RefA}}_{\text{CCY1}}(t)}{DF^{\text{RefA}}_{\text{CCY2}}(t)}. \tag{5.70}$$

We can then use this relationship to obtain the discount factor for any currency pair. Taking the base currency of euro, we set the currency to euro and the reference level to EONIA, as follows:

$$\frac{Df^{\text{Ref}}_{\text{CCY}}(t)}{Df^{\text{Ref}}_{EUR}(t)} = \frac{Df^{EONIA}_{\text{CCY}}(t)}{DF^{EONIA}_{EUR}(t)}. \tag{5.71}$$

Setting one reference level to EONIA, we use these EONIA levels to obtain the reference level between any two currencies CCY1, CCY2, shown below:

$$\begin{aligned}\frac{Df^{REF}_{\text{CCY2}}(t)}{Df^{REF}_{\text{CCY1}}(t)} &= \left(\frac{Df^{REF}_{\text{CCY2}}(t)}{Df^{REF}_{EUR}(t)} \Big/ \frac{Df^{REF}_{\text{CCY1}}(t)}{Df^{REF}_{EUR}(t)}\right) = \left(\frac{Df^{\text{EONIA}}_{\text{CCY2}}(t)}{Df^{\text{EONIA}}_{\text{EUR}}(t)} \Big/ \frac{Df^{\text{EONIA}}_{\text{CCY1}}(t)}{Df^{\text{EONIA}}_{\text{EUR}}(t)}\right)\\ &= \frac{Df^{\text{EONIA}}_{\text{CCY2}}(t)}{Df^{\text{EONIA}}_{\text{CCY1}}(t)}.\end{aligned} \tag{5.72}$$

Using this relationship, we build the yield curve by obtaining the relevant reference rate for regular intervals on the term structure, and then obtaining the discount factors for each point along the term structure. This set of discount factors is then used to extract the yield curve.

Where the CSA in place allows a choice of two or more currencies out of EUR, GBP or USD for cash collateral, we will need to account for more than one reference level. This is done by constructing curves for each separate reference level as before, and then building a new curve by looking at each daily forward rate from the three curves, and taking the highest point for each point along the curve as the data point for the curve. This process has "equalised" the curves of the three different currencies. (Note that this process does not take into account the optionality value inherent in the fact that the bank posting collateral has a choice as to which currency it posts.) A stylised illustration of such a "hybrid" curve is shown at Figure 5.37.

The graph at Figure 5.37 shows the cross-currency basis adjusted discount curves for IRS traded under four CSA scenarios: USD cash only, EUR cash only, GBP cash only and a choice of either of the three. A hybrid curve is not like a conventional yield curve constructed using Nelson–Siegel or cubic spline, because it is not a smooth curve. As the underlying forward curve changes from one currency to another, there is a kink at the changeover

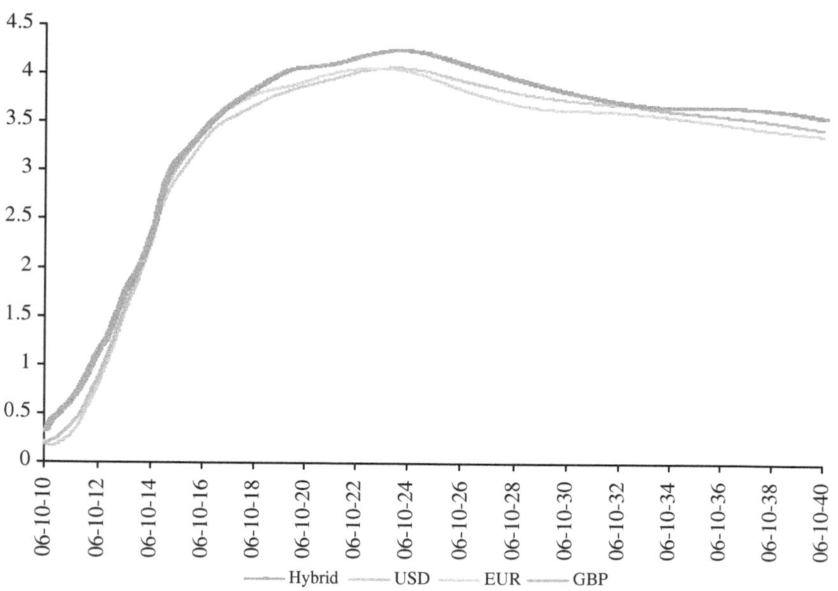

FIGURE 5.37 Hybrid yield curve, three currencies.

point. Hence as we show at Figure 5.37, at each point in time the orange hybrid curve overlaps with exactly one of the three single currency curves and only three curves can be seen at any given time. Under conventional analysis, the bank that is negative mark-to-market will post the currency of highest yield, or conversely of lowest funding cost.

The assumption of forward FX rates being uncorrelated to funding rates is perhaps the biggest issue for discussion. Certainly, one would be right to state that FX spot rates do have positive correlation with changes in interest rates. The impact is greater where one of the currencies is a core currency such as USD, EUR, GBP and possibly CHF, which are held as reserve deposits by other country central banks. However, we make the assumption with respect to forward FX rates to enable us to construct a multi-currency curve. The issue of which currency we wish to receive as collateral is a separate discussion.

In conclusion, it is accepted that the OIS curve levels should be used for the collateralised discount factors, given that the true funding cost for banks is more aligned to their specific funding rates rather than Libor rates. The purpose of the hybrid discount curve is to make sure the future cash flow is always discounted at the most conservative rate in other words, reducing the probability of underpricing a swap rate (that is, quoting a swap rate that is is lower than it should be). Practitioners should note also that that the implied forward rates of the hybrid discount curve might not always give the highest forward rates among those of the constituent discount curves. In other words, it is possible to see the forward rate of a constituent discount curve (say, the USD curve) higher than that of the hybrid curve at some tenors. To avoid this, a bank may want to construct a hybrid forward curve from the reference forward curves by the same principle and then derive the discount curve from this hybrid forward curve.

A SECURED FUNDING CURVE

A clear outcome of the 2008 bank crash has been an increase in the share of balance sheet assets that are funded with secured term liabilities. As banks reduce their levels of unsecured funding and raise their reliance on secured funding, it has become important for them to identify their secured COF, in the same way that they would always have been familiar with their unsecured funding levels and how these fed into internal transfer pricing procedures.

Earlier in the chapter we described a recommended procedure for constructing a bank's baseline unsecured risky yield curve or COF curve. The floating-rate TLP extracted from this curve described a bank's funding curve for unsecured liabilities. Here we consider an approach in principle that would enable a bank to construct a set of *secured* risky TLP curves, to be used when pricing secured liabilities.

A Liquid Funding Curve

The underlying principle of the baseline risky yield curve is that the data input points represent liquid prices. This is possible for banks that maintain a benchmark bond issuance series. When attempting to construct a secured risky curve, the practitioner is hindered by the dearth of equivalent liquid prices, as well as by the variety of asset classes and product types that are used as collateral when raising secured funding. These encompass bespoke collateral schedules, levels of recourse, legal framework and collateral pool arrangements. Appendix 5.7 is a summary of the main collateral classes, and illustrates the different types of pricing points that are available. An additional conundrum is that, due to the variety of collateral and structures employed, it is often the case that a bespoke curve may be required for specific purposes or transactions.

Any methodology that is used to construct a secured curve can therefore be generic only.

We begin with the premise that the EUR swap curve represents the funding cost for generic AA-rated bank credit in euros. The equivalent funding curve in the secured space is the EONIA curve.[42] This lies below the standard swap curve because it represents the rate paid on overnight cash collateral, and is shown at Figure 5.38.

By extension we take the OIS curve as the lower bound for the generic secured funding curve, because of the instant liquidity of the cash collateral that it represents. A bank's funding curve, of any construction, would not be expected to lie below this lower bound at any time, because its collateral quality and liquidity would never match that of overnight cash.[43] A bank's unsecured COF curve represents the upper bound. As an example, as at 22 June 2011 the position of a peer group of banks' market-implied unsecured COF curve relative to the Libor and EONIA curves shown at Figure 5.39.

---

42 The GC repo overnight (RONIA) index in the London market may also be considered here, but at the time of writing it was not a liquid term structure out to long tenors. At such time as a 0–10-year RONIA curve exists, this curve would be an alternative lower bound for any constructed secured funding curve.

43 We ignore the case of government bonds trading special, which could in practice trade in repo at below the OIS curve at specific tenor points, because banks would never be securitising pools of such assets.

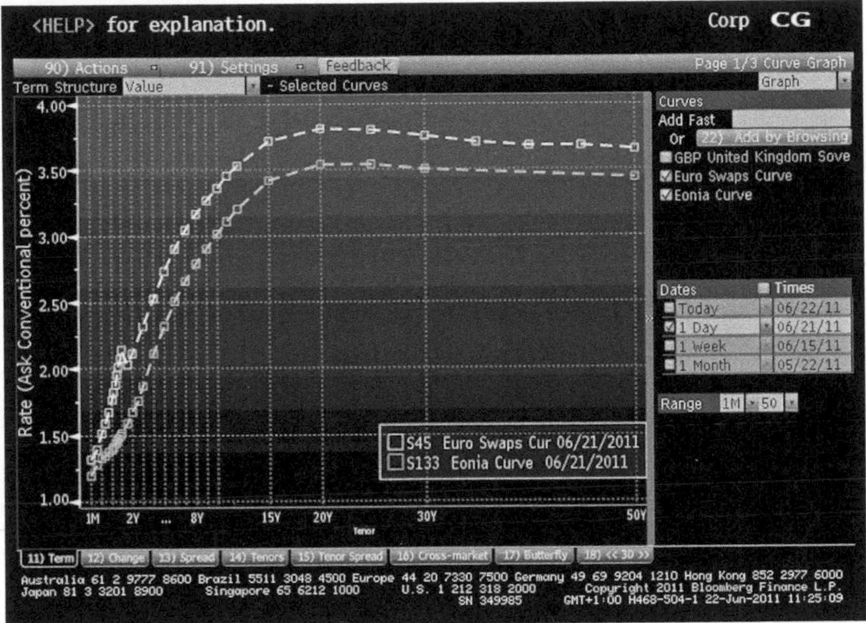

FIGURE 5.38 EUR swap and EONIA curve, 21 June 2011.

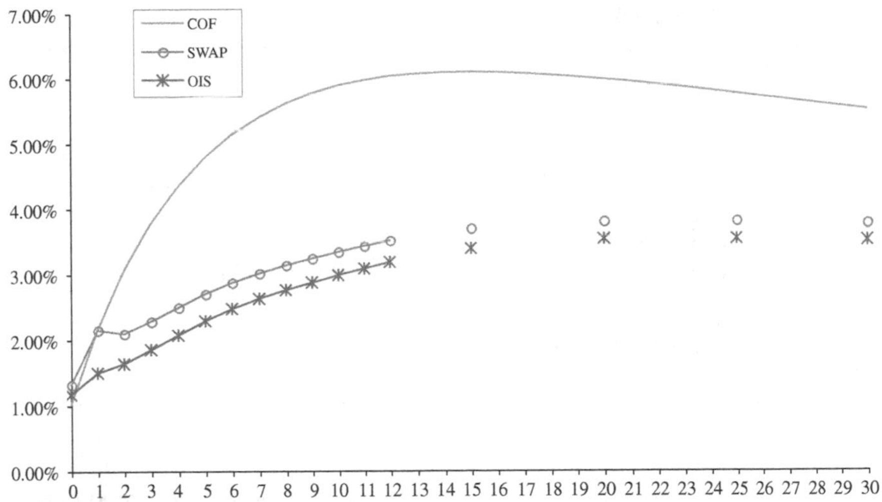

FIGURE 5.39 The EONIA, Libor and peer-group banks' COF curves as at 22 June 2011.

Pricing source: Bloomberg.

Factors in Setting the Secured Curve[44]

The issues that we need to consider when constructing the generic secured funding curve are:

- collateral asset class;
- data point transparency;
- liquidity of the collateral.

There are also issues of counterparty quality to consider, given the impact of correlation effects with the bank looking to issue secured debt; however, given the variables, this factor can be left out of the generic curve construction.

We assume a generic "residential mortgage" and "corporate loan" collateral class of prime quality. Assuming that the collateral is of sufficient quality and liquidity to be treated as liquid cash, the lower bound (once sufficient collateral is made available) would equate to the OIS funding curve.

Given the variety of collateral types that are available, it is not possible to set a construction methodology for every type. We therefore take the collateral quality as given, and adjust only for the amount of over-collateralisation (OC) that is being structured into the transaction. We also assume that the collateral is of sufficient liquidity that it can be theoretically repo'd in a stable market.

At 100% OC, the liquidity of the collateral is assumed to approach that of cash, and the secured funding curve would sit at the lower bound of the OIS curve. At 0% OC the secured funding curve is at the COF curve.

Therefore, we place the secured funding level between the OIS and COF curves as a function of the level of OC in the deal. In other words, this curve is transaction-specific.

Note that this approach would be for the senior tranche of a securitisation, and ignores the level of subordination of this tranche.

Additional Data Points

A risk-free secured funding curve is given by the government collateral repo curve. However, this is observable only to 1-year tenor, so is of limited application. It is possible to extrapolate this to 2-year tenor, but no longer. The risky secured curve is given by the corporate bond repo curve,

---

44 Parts of this section were first published in *American Securitization*, Winter/Spring 2012, Vol. 6, Issue 1, pp. 14–16.

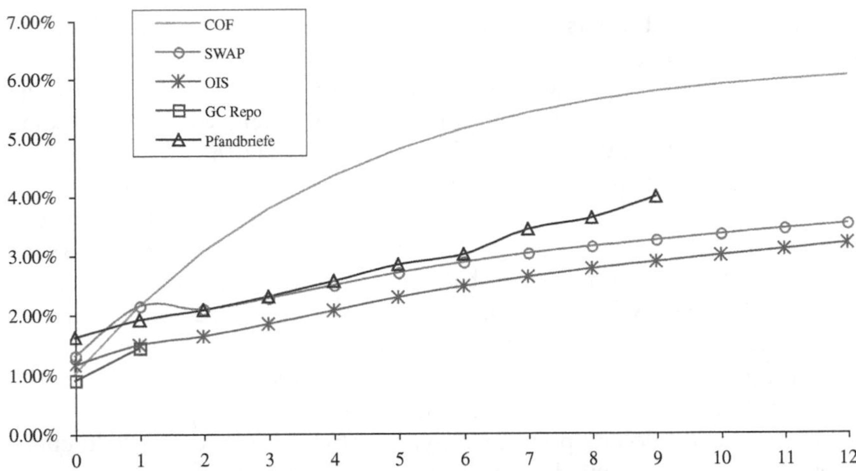

FIGURE 5.40 EUR government collateral and Pfandbrief curves as at 22 June 2011
Pricing source: Bloomberg.

but this is not transparent and is also only available at the short end. Any extrapolation of this curve could again only be out to a 2-year tenor, so is not valid for our purposes.

Instead we consider an additional lower bound given by the Jumbo Pfandbriefe curve, which is a liquid secured and transparent curve (see Figure 5.40). Its position relative to the Libor curve at longer maturities suggests that it is the lower bound for "standard" levels of OC when using high-quality collateral. Most banks' collateral does not approach this level of market-perceived quality, therefore we imply the new lower bound from the Pfandbriefe. This narrows the constraints within which the secured curve must lie.

Methodology Without Recourse to OC

At 0% OC, we suggest that a bank-issued note prices at the COF. At 100% OC, it would price at the Jumbo Pfandbriefe curve. We therefore set the pricing level as a function of the OC of the senior tranche between these bounds, assuming the highest-quality underlying asset from the bank's balance sheet.

In practice, if we wish to set a secured funding curve we will not apply the OC method because levels will be specific to each transaction, and we desire a generic pricing guide. Instead, we use the same curve methodology we selected for setting the bank's unsecured TLP curve, adapt it for use with floating-rate spread inputs, and construct the secured curve from that. We illustrate this below.

We noted earlier that two common curve interpolation methods are the cubic spline approach and the non-parametric approach. We apply the same Svensson methodology selected before for the secured curve, adapted to show a floating-rate spread output.

In the banking sector a common asset class is residential mortgages. These are securitised into residential mortgage-backed securities (RMBS) or Covered bonds. It is common for bank research desks to publish a generic yield level for the RMBS AAA tranche class, while Covered bond yields can be observed in the secondary market. We therefore have a set of liquid market inputs, based on an accessible asset class, that be used to create the generic curve.

From a methodology point of view, an issue arises because yield curve interpolation models consider specified bond yields and maturity dates. For RMBS and Covered bonds we use a floating-rate spread over Libor for each tenor point. Therefore the construction method changes slightly, in that we are fitting the Svensson (or any selected) model over floating-rate spreads. As we do not have specific bond inputs, we have no guide as to how to model the cash flows in the generic instruments. Therefore we model them all as synthetic FRNs with an annual payment, and fit the output to the 3-month Libor index.

We construct two curves, one for generic RMBS with inputs from a UK RMBS index as at October 2011, and one from the secondary market observed yields on a set of specific bank issued Covered bonds. RMBS issued by the bank whose Covered bonds we are using have been removed from the RMBS index. The generic index is comprised of 55 RMBS issues denominated in GBP, with average expected life from 0.5 to 7.5 years.

Table 5.10 shows the observed the spread levels over 3-mo Libor, as at our construction date.

TABLE 5.10 GBP generic RMBS and specific issuer Covered bond spreads (basis points)

Tenor	Generic RMBS	Tenor	Covered bond
1 year	147.2	18-mo	144.5
2 year	158	23-mo	154
3 year	157.5	35-mo	168.5
4 year	162.1	3.5 year	181
5 year	166.7	6.25 year	185
7 year	163	9 year	180

The curve fitting procedure is as follows:

1. fit the Svensson bond curve over the individual sets of data (above), and reprice at par to the synthetic annual coupon FRN;
2. plot the forward rate curve from this fitted bond curve;
3. calculate the spread at each tenor point over a given index, here 3-mo Libor.

From the input levels above we extracted the forward curve given at Figure 5.41, which was then used to produce the implied spreads shown at Figure 5.42. This is a smoothed curve that can be used to set the issuance level for secured liabilities, with adjustments on a case-by-case basis to allow for specific types of collateral, whether of lower or higher quality. Note that the covered bond curve is below the RMBS curve at the short dates then crosses over around 3-year. This is consistent with the input spreads we presented above.

For specific collateral types, the Treasury desk may wish to set issuance parameters at specified spreads below what the generic curve suggests. For example, while funds raised using mortgage assets may price at the generic RMBS curve, we expect that funds secured using higher quality assets such as agency or local authority assets will price below the generic RMBS curve. If the Treasury desk is satisfied with this general approach, there will be no requirement to construct a curve for every single asset class; rather, the generic RMBS or Covered Bond curve would suffice as the main pricing guide.

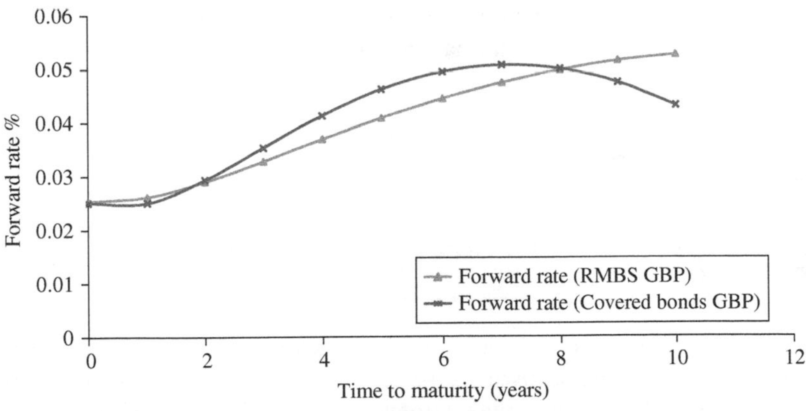

FIGURE 5.41 Forward rate curves, generic RMBS and Covered bonds

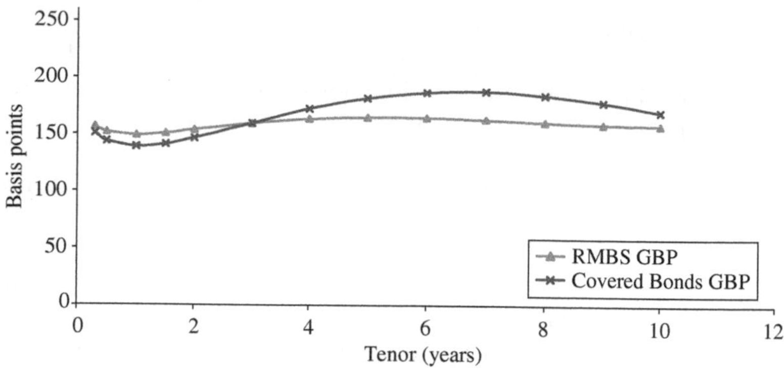

FIGURE 5.42 Implied spreads (basis points, 3-mo Libor), secured funding curve for generic RMBS and Covered Bonds

Conclusions

The efficacy of any constructed curve depends on the extent to which counterparties engage with a bank on its calculated curve. If this is not the case, it could be that any built curve is used simply as a theoretical minimum or as a set of points between an upper and lower bound, adjusted for the level of OC or for the specific type of market yield input. We are able to set an upper and lower bound with reasonable confidence, which enables us to have some confidence on a generic secured curve as a pricing guide.

Given the variety of acceptable collateral, the practical approach we recommend is to construct a generic curve only, using either an index of liquid collateral such as RMBS or a specific issuance curve where sufficient liquidity exists in the bank's name. Any incremental secured funding that lies below the generic secured curve represents added value for the bank, generated by the business line that has raised the liabilities.

Appendices

APPENDIX 5.1 JENSEN'S INEQUALITY AND THE SHAPE OF THE YIELD CURVE

In Cox, Ingersoll and Ross (1981) an analysis on the shape of the term structure used a feature known as *Jensen's inequality* to illustrate that the expectations hypothesis was consistent with forward rates being an indicator of future spot rates. Jensen's inequality states that the expected value of the reciprocal of a variable is not identical to the reciprocal of the expected value of that variable. Following this, if the expected holding period returns on a set of bonds are all equal, the expected holding period returns on the bonds cannot then be equal over any other holding period. Applying this in practice, consider two zero-coupon bonds: a 1-year bond with a yield of 11.11% and a 2-year zero-coupon bond with a yield of 11.8034%. The prices of the bonds are as follows:

1 year: 90

2 year: 80.

Assume that the price of the 2-year bond in one year's time can be either 86.89 or 90.89, with identical probability. At the end of year 1, the total return generated by the 2-year bond will be either (86.89/80) 8.6125% or (90.89/80) 13.6125%, while at this point the (now) 1-year bond will offer a return of either (100/86.89) 15.089% or (100/90.89) 10.023%. The two possible prices have been set deliberately so as to ensure that the expected return over one year for the 2-year bond is equal to the return available today on the 1-year bond, which is 11.11% as we noted at the start. The return expected on the 2-year bond is indeed the same (provided either of the two prices is available); that is, [(0.5) × (86.89/80) + (0.5) × (90.89/80)], or 11.11%. Therefore it cannot also be true that the certain return over two years for the 2-year bond is equal to the expected return for two years from rolling over the investment in the 1-year bond. At the start of the period the 2-year bond has a guaranteed return of [100/80] 25% over its lifetime. However, investing in the 1-year bond and then reinvesting at the 1-year period after the first year will produce a return that is higher than this, as shown:

$$11.11\% \times [(0.5) \times (100/86.89) + (0.5) \times (100/90.89)]$$

or 25.063%. Under this scenario, investors cannot expect equality of returns for all bonds over all investment horizons.

APPENDIX 5.2 TESTING THE UNBIASED EXPECTATIONS HYPOTHESIS

For empirical studies testing the unbiased expectations hypothesis see Kessel (1965) and Fama (1976). If we consider the expectations hypothesis to be true then the forward rate ${}_0rf_2$ should be an accurate predictor of the spot rate in period 2. Put another way, the mean of ${}_0rf_2$ should be equal to the mean of ${}_1rs_1$. In previous studies (Fama 1976) it has been shown that forward rates are in fact biased upwards in their estimates of future spot rates. That is, ${}_0rf_2$ is usually higher than the mean of ${}_1rs_1$. This bias tends to be magnified the further one moves along the term structure. We can test the unbiased expectations hypothesis by determining if the following condition holds:

$$ {}_1rs_1 = p + q({}_0rf_2). \tag{A5.2.1} $$

In an environment where we upheld the expectations hypothesis, then p should be equal to zero and q equal to one. Outside of the very short end of the yield curve, there is no evidence that this is true. Another approach, adopted by Fama (1984), involved subtracting the current spot rate rs_1 from both sides of equation (A5.2.1) and testing whether:

$$ {}_1rs_1 - {}_0rs_1 = p + q({}_0rf_2 - {}_0rs_1). \tag{A5.2.2} $$

If the hypothesis was accurate, we would again have p equal to zero and q equal to one. This is because ${}_1rs_1 - {}_0rs_1$ is the change in the spot rate predicted by the hypothesis. The left-hand side of (A5.2.2) is the actual change in the spot rate, which must equal the right-hand side of the equation if the hypothesis is true. Evidence from the earlier studies mentioned has suggested that q is a positive number less than one. This of course is not consistent with the unbiased expectations hypothesis. However, the studies indicate that the prediction of changes in future spot rates is linked to actual changes that occur. This suggests then that forward rates are indeed based on the market's view of future spot rates, but not in a completely unbiased manner.

An earlier study was conducted by Meiselman (1962), referred to as his error-learning model. According to this, if the unbiased expectations hypothesis is true, forward rates are not then completely accurate forecasts of future spot rates. The study tested whether (A5.2.3) was true.

$$ {}_1rf_n - {}_0rf_n = p + q_1rs_1 - {}_0rf_2 \tag{A5.2.3} $$

If the hypothesis is true then p should be equal to zero and q should be positive. The error-learning model suggests a positive correlation between forward rates, but this would hold in an environment where the unbiased expectations hypothesis did not apply.

The empirical evidence suggests that the predictions of future spot rates reflected in forward rates is related to subsequent actual spot rates. So forward rates *do* include an element of market interest-rate forecasts. However, this would indicate more a biased expectations theory, rather than the pure unbiased expectations hypothesis.

APPENDIX 5.3 LINEAR REGRESSION: ORDINARY LEAST SQUARES

The main purpose of regression analysis is to estimate or predict the average value of a dependent variable given the known values of an independent or explanatory variable. In one way, it measures the relationship between two sets of data. This data might be the relationship between family income and expenditure; here the income would be the independent variable and expenditure the dependent variable. More relevant for our purposes, it could be the relationship between the change in price of a corporate bond, priced off the benchmark yield curve, and changes in the price of a short-dated benchmark bond and the price of a long-term bond. In this case, the price of the corporate bond is the dependent variable, while the prices of the short- and long-term government bonds are independent variables. If there is a linear relationship between the dependent and independent variables, we may use a regression function to determine the relationship between them. In this appendix, we provide a basic overview and introduction to regression and ordinary least squares. Regression analysis is a key part of financial econometrics, and advanced econometric analysis is extensively used in fixed-income work. For a background in basic econometrics, we recommend the book of the same name by Damodar Gujarati (1995), which is excellent. Gujarati's book is very accessible and readable, and provides a good grounding in the topic. Another excellent introduction to econometrics is Brooks (2002).

If our data set consists of the entire population, rather than a statistical sample of the population, we estimate the relationship between two data sets using the population-regression function. Given an independent variable X and dependent variable Y, it can be shown that the conditional mean $E(Y|X_i)$ is a function of X_i. This would be written

$$E(Y|X_i) = f(X_i) \tag{A5.3.1}$$

where $f(X_i)$ is a function of the independent variable X_i. Equation (A5.3.1) is termed the 2-variable population-regression function and states that the

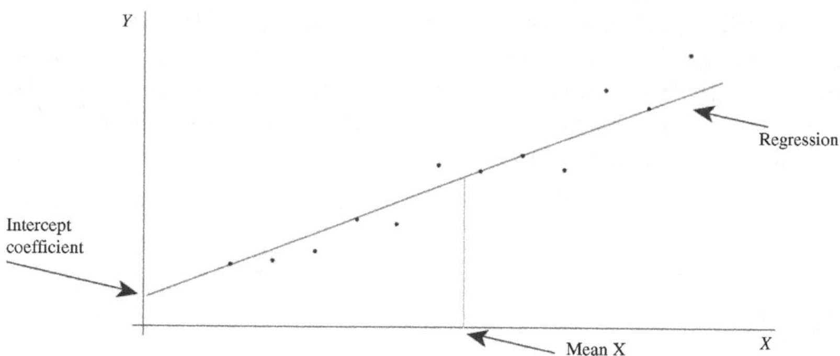

FIGURE A5.3.1 Regression line passing through values of X and Y.

average value of Y given X_i is a linear function of X_i. It can further be shown that

$$E(Y|X_i) = \alpha + \beta X_i \tag{A5.3.2}$$

where α and β are the regression coefficients; they are unknown but fixed parameters. The α term is the intercept coefficient and β is the slope coefficient. These are shown in Figure A5.3.1. The objective of regression analysis is to estimate the values of the regression coefficients using observations of the values of X and Y.

Equation (A5.3.2) is a two-variable regression; it is sometimes written as:

$$Y = \beta_1 + \beta_2 X_i. \tag{A5.3.3}$$

Where there are more than two variables, we use a multi-variable regression.

It can further be shown that given a value for X_i, the independent variable value will be clustered around the average value for Y at that X_i; in other words, around the conditional expectation. The deviation of an individual Y_i around its expected value is defined as:

$$u_i = Y_i - E(Y|X_i). \tag{A5.3.4}$$

This is rearranged to give

$$Y_i = E(Y|X_i) + u_i \tag{A5.3.5}$$

where the term u_i is an unknown random variable and is known as the stochastic disturbance, stochastic error term or simply error term. It is written as ε in some textbooks.

The value of the dependent variable is the sum of two elements: the systematic or deterministic element, which is given by the regression function above, and a random or non-systematic element, which is the error term. Essentially, the error term captures all those elements that have been missed out or left out of the regression model.

In practice it is most unlikely that we will have data sets available for the entire population, so we use statistical sample data instead. When regression is carried out on sample data we use the sample regression function (SRF), which is (A5.3.6) below.

$$Y_i = \hat{\alpha} + \hat{\beta}X_i + \hat{u}_i \qquad (A5.3.6)$$

where

$\hat{\alpha}$ = is the *estimator* of α
$\hat{\beta}$ = is the *estimator* of β

The SRF is determined using a statistical technique known as ordinary least squares or OLS. This approach is covered in any number of statistics and econometrics textbooks. We suggest Chapter 3 in Gujarati (1995). A brief description is given here.

Let us expand our regression model. Assume we have N observations and m independent variables. Say that Y_i be the ith observation on the dependent variable and X_{it} be the ith observation on the tth independent variable. The regression function of the relationship between the dependent and independent variables is given by

$$Y_i = \beta_1 X_{1i} + \beta_2 X_{2i} + \ldots\ldots + \beta_m X_{mi} + \varepsilon_i \qquad (A5.3.7)$$

and where we must estimate the $\beta_1, \beta_2, \ldots \ldots \beta_m$ regression coefficients. This is done using OLS. From (A5.3.7) ε_i is the error in the model, the random element that is left out in predicting the ith value of the dependent variable. From our earlier description we know that

$$\varepsilon_i = Y_i \beta_1 X_{1i} - \beta_2 X_{2i} - \ldots \ldots - \beta_m X_{mi} \qquad (A5.3.8)$$

We require the sum of squared errors, which is given by $\varepsilon_1^2 + \varepsilon_2^2 + \ldots\ldots + \varepsilon_i^2$, and OLS determines the coefficients that minimise this sum of squared errors.

Earlier in the chapter (Example 5.10) we illustrated a bond pricing equation, which was $472_{a1} + 1796_{a2} + 7528_{a3} = -30.75$.

What this expression tells us is that -30.75 is the value of the dependent variable. There are three independent variables with values of 472, 1796 and 7528. As there are three unknowns, we require only four such bond price equations and we can solve for a_1, a_2 and a_3. This may appear slightly daunting if it is to be carried out by hand, and software applications are used to speed the process. Using such a package, we can calculate the values that minimise the sum of squared errors on the model.

If we say that the values are $\hat{a}_1$, $\hat{a}_2$ and $\hat{a}_3$, then the OLS estimate of the discount function, given the market bond prices used to derive the coefficient equations, is given by:

$$\hat{d}(t) = 1 + \hat{a}_1 t + \hat{a}_2 t^2 + \hat{a}_3 t^3. \qquad (A5.3.9)$$

APPENDIX 5.4 ILLUSTRATION OF FORWARD RATE STRUCTURE WHEN THE SPOT RATE STRUCTURE IS INCREASING

We assume the spot rate $r(0, T)$ is a function of time and is increasing to a high point at T. It is given by:

$$r(0,T) = \frac{\int_0^T f(0,s)ds}{T}. \qquad (A5.4.1)$$

At its high point the function is neither increasing nor decreasing, so we may write:

$$\frac{dr(0,\bar{T})}{dT} = 0 \qquad (A5.4.2)$$

and therefore the second derivative with respect to T will be:

$$\frac{d^2r(0,\bar{T})}{dT^2} < 0. \qquad (A5.4.3)$$

From (5.43) and (A5.4.2) we may state:

$$f(0,\bar{T}) = r(0,\bar{T}) \qquad (A5.4.4)$$

and from (A5.4.3) and (A5.4.4) the second derivative of the spot rate is:

$$\frac{d^2r(0,\bar{T})}{dT^2} = \left[\frac{df(0,\bar{T})}{dT} - \frac{dr(0,\bar{T})}{dT}\right]\frac{1}{T} < 0 \qquad (A5.4.5)$$

From (A5.4.2) we know the spot rate function is zero at T so the derivative of the forward rate with respect to T would therefore be:

$$\frac{df(0,\bar{T})}{dT} < 0 \qquad (A5.4.6)$$

So in this case the forward rate is decreasing at the point T when the spot rate is at its maximum value. This is illustrated hypothetically in Figure 5.21(a) and it is common to observe the forward rate curve decreasing as the spot rate is increasing.

APPENDIX 5.5 REGRESSION SPLINES

This appendix summarises Suits et al. (1978), an excellent account of how a spline function may be fitted using regression methods. The article is very accessible and strongly recommended.

A standard econometric approach is that of piecewise linear regression. This method is not suitable for fitting a relationship that is not purely linear, however (such as a term structure), as illustrated by Figure A5.5.1.

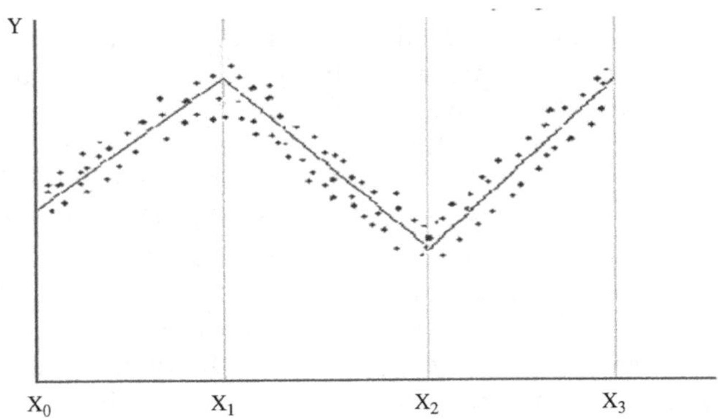

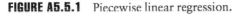

FIGURE A5.5.1 Piecewise linear regression.

To get around this problem, one approach would be to join a series of linear regressions, at arbitrary points specified by the user. This is described by:

$$Y = [a_1 + b_1(X - X_0)]D_1 + [a_2 + b_2(X - X_1)]D_2 + [a_3 + b_3(X - X_2)]D_3 + u. \tag{A5.5.1}$$

In (A5.5.1) D_1 is what is known as a dummy variable, with a value of 1 for all observations whenever $X_{i-1} \leq X \leq X_i$ and a value of 0 at other times. As it stands, (A5.5.1) is discontinuous at X_1 and X_2, but this can be removed by imposing the following constraints:

$$\begin{aligned} a_2 &= a_1 + b_1(X_1 - X_0) \\ a_3 &= a_2 + b_2(X_2 - X_1) \end{aligned} \tag{A5.5.2}$$

If (A5.5.2) is substituted into (A5.5.1), the following is obtained:

$$\begin{aligned} Y &= a_1 + b_1[(X - X_0)D_1 + (X_1 - X_0)D_2 + (X_2 - X_1)D_3] \\ &+ b_2[(X - X_1)D_2 + (X_2 - X_1)D_3] + b_3[(X - X_2)D_3] + u. \end{aligned} \tag{A5.5.3}$$

The expression at (A5.5.3) has converted a piecewise linear regression into a multiple regression. *Y* is the dependent variable and is regressed on three composite variables, the values for which are obtained from:

- the *X* data sets;
- the values for X_i at the points at which the curve is required to "bend";
- the widths of the selected intervals;
- the three dummy variables.

As Suits et al. (1978) state, it would be possible to calculate the coefficients by hand (!), but there are a number of standard software packages that the user can employ to solve the regression.

The disadvantages of piecewise linear regression if used for a number of applications, including yield-curve fitting, are twofold: first, the derivatives of the function are not continuous, and this discontinuity can seriously distort the curve at the derivative points, which would make the curve meaningless at these points. Second, and more crucial for yield-curve applications, it may not be obvious where the linear segments should be placed as the scatter diagram of observations may indicate several possibilities. This situation may make it desirable to specify X_i at user-specified (arbitrary) points, and this makes linear regression unsuitable.

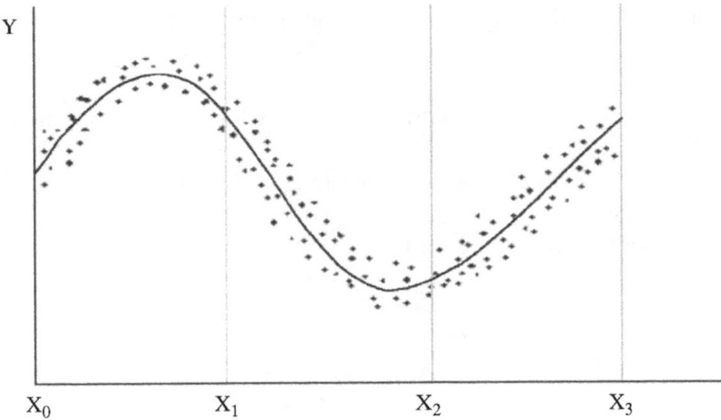

FIGURE A5.5.2 Cubic polynomial with three knot points.

To get around these problems we use a spline function. For this the linear function described by (A5.5.1) is replaced with a set of piecewise polynomial functions. It would be possible to use polynomials of any degree, but the most common approach is to use cubic polynomials. The x-axis is divided into three intervals, at the points X_0, X_1, X_2 and X_3. These points are known as knot points and are illustrated in Figure A5.5.2.

In Figure A5.5.2, the segments chosen are at equal intervals. This is not essential to the procedure, however, and for applications, including yield-curve modelling, is not undertaken. Instead, the knots are placed at points where the user thinks the relationship changes most. For example, for the term structure the knots may be placed at 0, 2-, 5- and 10-year maturities. If more than four knots are required – for instance, to go beyond to 20-and 30-year maturities – then the analyst will require a greater number of composite variables, as discussed later. The downside associated with a greater number of intervals is that, as more composite variables are required to fit the curve, additional degrees of freedom are lost.

The regression relationship now becomes:

$$\begin{aligned} Y = {} & [a_1 + b_1(X - X_0) + c_1(X - X_0)^2 + d_1(X - X_0)^3]D_1 \\ & + [a_2 + b_2(X - X_1) + c_2(X - X_1)^2 + d_2(X - X_1)^3]D_2 \\ & + [a_3 + b_3(X - X_2) + c_3(X - X_2)^2 + d_3(X - X_2)^3]D_3 + u \end{aligned} \quad (A5.5.4)$$

where D_i is a dummy variable specified by the interval i.

This time, both the function described by (A5.5.4) and its derivatives are discontinuous at the knot points, but this feature can be removed by applying constraints to the coefficients. The constraints ensure the following:

- for a_i the values of the very short end and the very long end are equal at the start and end knot points;
- for b_i the first derivatives, the slope of the left- and right-hand sides of each knot point, are equal;
- for c_i the second derivatives are equal.

The constraints are given by (A5.5.5).

$$\begin{aligned} a_2 &= a_1 + b_1(X - X_0) + c_1(X - X_0)^2 + d_1(X - X_0)^3 \\ a_3 &= a_2 + b_2(X - X_1) + c_2(X_2 - X_1)^2 + d_2(X_2 - X_1)^3 \\ b_2 &= b_1 + 2c_1(X_1 - X_0) + 3d_1(X_1 - X_0)^2 \\ b_3 &= b_2 + 2c_2(X_2 - X_1) + 3d_2(X_2 - X_1)^2 \\ c_2 &= c_1 + 3d_1(X_1 - X_0) \\ c_3 &= c_2 + 3d_2(X_2 - X_1) \end{aligned} \quad (A5.5.5)$$

Using the expression above, a spline function becomes a multiple regression of the dependent variable Y on five composite variables and Suits et al. show this to be:

$$\begin{aligned} Y = a_1 + b_1(X - X_0) + c_1(X - X_0)^2 + d_1(X - X_0)^3 \\ + (d_2 - d_1)(X - X_1)^3 D_1^* + (d_3 - d_2)(X - X_2)^3 D_2^* \end{aligned} \quad (A5.5.6)$$

where D_1^* and D_2^* are dummy variables; $D_i^* = 1$ if $X \geq X_i$, while at other times the dummy variable is equal to 0. To compute the coefficients of the regression we can use the least-squares procedure, available on standard software packages.

Finally, if we wish to select more than three intervals, that is, more than four knot points, which is common in yield-curve applications, we can use (A5.5.7) below. This is a multiple regression, a fitted spline function with $n + 1$ intervals, with knot points at X_0, X_1, X_2, ... ,X_{n+1} and corresponding dummy variables $D_1^*, D_2^*, \ldots\ldots D_n^*$.

$$\begin{aligned} Y = a_1 + b_1(X - X_0) + c_1(X - X_0)^2 + d_1(X - X_0)^3 \\ + \sum_{i=1}^{n}(d_{i+1} - d_i)(X - X_i)^3 D_1^* \end{aligned} \quad (A5.5.7)$$

With each extra interval, an extra composite variable is required and this results in the loss of one more degree of freedom.

APPENDIX 5.6 CUBIC SPLINE INTERPOLATION

Consider four observed vertices requiring three cubic equations, $rm_{(i,t)}$, each one connecting two adjacent vertices, n_i and n_{i+1}, as follows:

$$\begin{aligned} rm_{(0,t)} &= a_0 n^3 + b_0 n^2 + c_0 n + d_0, \text{ connecting vertex } n_0 \text{ with } n_1 \\ rm_{(1,t)} &= a_1 n^3 + b_1 n^2 + c_1 n + d_1, \text{ connecting vertex } n_1 \text{ with } n_2 \\ rm_{(2,t)} &= a_2 n^3 + b_2 n^2 + c_2 n + d_2, \text{ connecting vertex } n_2 \text{ with } n_3 \end{aligned}$$

where a, b, c and d are unknowns. The three equations require 12 conditions in all. The cubic spline method imposes the following set of conditions on the curves: each cubic equation must pass through its own pair of vertices. Thus, for the first equation:

$$\begin{aligned} a_0 n_0^3 + b_0 n_0^2 + c_0 n_0 + d_0 &= 4.00 \\ a_0 n_1^3 + b_0 n_1^2 + c_0 n_1 + d_0 &= 5.00. \end{aligned}$$

For the second and third equations:

$$\begin{aligned} a_1 n_1^3 + b_1 n_1^2 + c_1 n_1 + d_1 &= 5.00 \\ a_1 n_2^3 + b_1 n_2^2 + c_1 n_2 + d_1 &= 6.50 \\ a_2 n_2^3 + b_2 n_2^2 + c_2 n_2 + d_2 &= 6.50 \\ a_2 n_3^3 + b_2 n_3^2 + c_2 n_3 + d_2 &= 6.75. \end{aligned}$$

The resulting yield curve should be smooth at the point where one cubic equation joins with the next one. This is achieved by requiring the slope and the convexity of adjacent equations to be equal at the point where they meet, ensuring a smooth rollover from one equation to the next. Mathematically, the first and second derivatives of all adjacent equations must be equal at the point where the equations meet.

Thus, at vertex n_1:

$$\begin{aligned} 3a_0 n_1^2 + 2b_0 n_1 + 1 &= 3a_1 n_1^2 + 2b_1 n_1 + 1 \text{ (the first derivative)} \\ 6a_0 n_1 + 2 &= 6a_1 n_1 + 2 \text{ (the second derivative)}. \end{aligned}$$

And at vertex n_2:

$$\begin{aligned} 3a_1 n_2^2 + 2b_1 n_2 + 1 &= 3a_2 n_2^2 + 2b_2 n_2 + 1 \text{ (the first derivative)} \\ 6a_1 n_2 + 2 &= 6a_2 n_2 + 2 \text{ (the second derivative)}. \end{aligned}$$

Finally, we may impose the condition that the splines tail off flat at the end vertices, or more formally we state mathematically that the second derivatives should be zero at the end points:

$$\begin{aligned} 6a_0 n_0 + 2 &= 0 \text{ (first spline starts flat)} \\ 6a_2 n_3 + 2 &= 0 \text{ (second spline ends flat)}. \end{aligned}$$

$$
\begin{bmatrix}
n_0^3 & n_0^2 & n_0 & 1 & 0 & 0 & 0 & 0 & 0 & 0 & 0 & 0 \\
n_1^3 & n_1^2 & n_1 & 1 & 0 & 0 & 0 & 0 & 0 & 0 & 0 & 0 \\
0 & 0 & 0 & 0 & n_1^3 & n_1^2 & n_1 & 1 & 0 & 0 & 0 & 0 \\
0 & 0 & 0 & 0 & n_2^3 & n_2^2 & n_2 & 1 & 0 & 0 & 0 & 0 \\
0 & 0 & 0 & 0 & 0 & 0 & 0 & 0 & n_2^3 & n_2^2 & n_2 & 1 \\
0 & 0 & 0 & 0 & 0 & 0 & 0 & 0 & n_3^3 & n_3^2 & n_3 & 1 \\
3n_1^2 & 2n_1 & 1 & 0 & -3n_1^2 & -2n_1 & -1 & 0 & 0 & 0 & 0 & 0 \\
6n_1 & 2 & 0 & 0 & -6n_1 & -2 & 0 & 0 & 0 & 0 & 0 & 0 \\
0 & 0 & 0 & 0 & 3n_2^2 & 2n_2 & 1 & 0 & -3n_2^2 & -2n_1 & -1 & 0 \\
0 & 0 & 0 & 0 & 6n_2 & 2 & 0 & 0 & -6n_2 & -2 & 0 & 0 \\
6n_0 & 2 & 0 & 0 & 0 & 0 & 0 & 0 & 0 & 0 & 0 & 0 \\
0 & 0 & 0 & 0 & 0 & 0 & 0 & 0 & 6n_3 & 2 & 0 & 0
\end{bmatrix}
\times
\begin{bmatrix} a_0 \\ b_0 \\ c_0 \\ d_0 \\ a_1 \\ b_1 \\ c_1 \\ d_1 \\ a_2 \\ b_2 \\ c_2 \\ d_2 \end{bmatrix}
=
\begin{bmatrix} 4 \\ 5 \\ 6.5 \\ 6.75 \\ 0 \\ 0 \\ 0 \\ 0 \\ 0 \\ 0 \\ 0 \\ 0 \end{bmatrix}
$$

FIGURE A.5.6.1 Cubic spline interpolation matrix.

These constraints together give us a system of 12 equations from which we can solve for the 12 unknown coefficients. The solution is usually reached using matrices, where the equations are expressed in matrix form. This is shown at Figure A5.6.1.

In matrix notation we have:

$$[n] \times [\text{Coefficients}] = [rm],$$

therefore the solution is:

$$[\text{Coefficients}] = [n]^{-1} \times [rm].$$

Inverting the matrix n and then pre-multiplying rm with the resulting inverse, we obtain the array of required coefficients:

$$\text{Coefficients} = [0.022,\ 0.000,\ 0.413,\ 4.000,\ -0.047,\ 0.411,$$
$$-0.410,\ 4.548,\ 0.008,\ -0.249,\ 2.230,\ 1.029.$$

So the three cubic equations are specified as:

$rm_{(0,t)} = 0.022 \times n^3 + 0.413 \times n + 4.000$ for vertices $n_0 - n_1$

$rm_{(1,t)} = -0.047 \times n^3 + 0.411 \times n^2 - 0.410 \times n + 4.548$ for vertices $n_1 - n_2$

$rm_{(2,t)} = 0.008 \times n^3 - 0.249 \times n^2 + 2.230 \times n + 1.029$ for vertices $n_2 - n_3$.

APPENDIX 5.7: SUMMARY OF COLLATERAL CLASSES

Type of funding instrument	Underlying security	Term of instrument	Liquidity	Commentary
RMBS	Residential mortgages	WAL 5 years	Illiquid – pricing updated on new issue	Bootstrap existing issuance and secondary market prices. The different between primary and secondary market issuance is a consideration
CMBS	Commercial mortgage loans	WAL 8 years	Illiquid – pricing updated on new issue	(same as above)
Covered bond funding	Residential mortgages	Maturity 5 to 10 years	Liquidity – depends on currency and maturity	Bootstrap existing issuance and market prices
Repo	Government bond collateral	Less than 12 month	Liquid	Depends on type of government bond collateral
GC repo	Government bond collateral	Less than 12 month	Liquid	UK govt bond collateral – most secure
Swap rates	ISDA collateralisation terms	Depends on currency, maturity and agreed eligible collateral	Liquidity – up to 30 years (depends on ccy)	Normally collateralised
SONIA swap	ISDA collateralisation terms	Depends on currency, maturity and agreed eligible collateral	Liquidity up to 3 to 4 years (depends on ccy)	Overnight interest rates. OIS Libor is a good measure of liquidity in the swaps market. Volatility between SONIA and GC Repo also reflects differences in very short-dated unsecured lending versus secured lending

(*continued*)

APPENDIX 5.7: CONTINUED

Type of funding instrument	Underlying security	Term of instrument	Liquidity	Commentary
Unsecured funding	Bank issued senior unsecured debt	Various funding maturities	Liquid	Primary levels and secondary pricing
Collateral swaps	Illiquid – housing loans, ABS, etc	Insurance counterparties – across maturities	Medium to long-dated points. However, intense collateralisation and structural considerations due to insurance regulations and risk requirements.	Over-collateralised

REFERENCES AND BIBLIOGRAPHY

Adams, K. and Van Deventer, D. (1994), "Fitting Yield Curves and Forward Rate Curves with Maximum Smoothness", *Journal of Fixed Income*, 4, pp. 52–62.

Ametrano, F. and Bianchetti. M. (2009), "Bootstrapping the Illiquidity: Multiple Yield Curves Construction for Market Coherent Forward Rates Estimation", in *Modelling Interest Rates: Advances in Derivatives Pricing*, edited by Mercurio, F., London: RISK Books.

Anderson, N., Breedon, F., Deacon, M., Derry, A. and Murphy, M. (1996), *Estimating and Interpreting the Yield Curve*, Wiley.

Anderson, N. and Sleath, J. (November 1999), *Bank of England Quarterly Bulletin.*

Avellaneda, M. and Laurence, P. (2000), *Quantitative Modelling of Derivative Securities*, London: Chapman & Hall/CRC, chapters 10–12.

Baxter, M. and Rennie, A. (1996), *Financial Calculus*, Cambridge: Cambridge University Press, Chapter 5.

Black, F. and Scholes, M. (May–June 1973), "The Pricing of Options and Corporate Liability", *Journal of Political Economy*, 81, pp. 637–59.

Brennan, M. and Schwartz, E. (1979), "A Continuous Time Approach to the Pricing of Bonds", *Journal of Banking and Finance*, 3, p. 134*ff*.

Brennan, M. and Schwartz, E. (1980), "Conditional Predictions of Bond Prices and Returns", *Journal of Finance*, 35, p. 405*ff*.

Brooke, M., N. Cooper and C. Scholtes, "Inferring market interest rate expectations from money market rates", *Bank of England Quarterly Bulletin,* November 2000.

Brooks. C. (2002), *Introductory Econometrics for Finance*, Cambridge: Cambridge University Press.

Burghardt, G., and Hoskins, W. (1994), *The Convexity Bais in Eurodollar Futures*, Carr Futures.

Campbell, J. (March 1986), "A Defence of Traditional Hypotheses about the Term Structure of Interest Rates", *Journal of Finance*, pp. 183–93.

Campbell, J., Lo, A. and MacKinlay, A. (1997), *The Econometrics of Financial Markets*, Princeton, NJ: Princeton UP, chapters 10–11.

Carleton, W. and Cooper, I. (September 1976), "Estimation and Uses of the Term Structure of Interest Rates", *Journal of Finance*, pp. 1067–83.

Choudhry, M. (2001), *Bond Market Securities*, London: FT Prentice Hall.

Choudhry, M. (2003), *Analysing and Interpreting the Yield Curve*, Singapore: John Wiley & Sons Pte Ltd.

Choudhry, M. (2004a), *Advanced Fixed Income Analysis*, Oxford: Elsevier.

Choudhry, M. (2004b), *Fixed Income Markets*, Singapore: John Wiley & Sons.

Choudhry, M., Joannas, D., Landuyt, G., Pereira, R., Pienaar, R. (2010), *Capital Market Instruments: Valuation and Analysis*, 3rd edition, Basingstoke: Palgrave MacMillan.

Cox, J., Ingersoll, J.E. and Ross, S.A. (September 1981), "A Re-examination of Traditional Hypothesis about the Term Structure of Interest Rates", *Journal of Finance*, 36, pp. 769–99.

Cox, J., Ingersoll, J. and Ross, S. (1985a), "An Inter-Temporal General Equilibrium Model of Asset Prices", *Econometrica*, 53, pp. 81–90.

Cox, J., Ingersoll, J., and Ross S. (1985b), "A Theory of the Term Structure of Interest Rates", *Econometrica*, 53, pp. 385–407.

Culbertson, J.M. (November 7, 1957), "The Term Structure of Interest Rates," *Quarterly Journal of Economics*, 71, pp. 485–517.

Deacon, M. and Derry, A. (July 1994), "Estimating the Term Structure of Interest Rates", *Bank of England Working Paper Series*, No. 24.

Fama, Eugene F. (September/October 1965), "Random Walks In Stock Market Prices", *Financial Analysts Journal*, 21(5) pp. 55–59.

Fama, E.F. (1970), "Efficient Capital Markets: A Review of Theory and Empirical Work ", *Journal of Finance*, Vol. 25, pp. 388–417.

Fama, E.F. (October 1976), "Forward Rates as Predictors of Future Spot Interest Rates", *Journal of Financial Economics*, Vol. 3, No. 4, pp. 361–77.

Fama, E.F. (December, 1984), "The Information in the Term Structure," *Journal of Financial Economics*, 13, pp. 509–28.

Fisher, I. (August 1986), "Appreciation of Interest", *Publications of the American Economic Association*, pp. 23–39.

Gujarati, D. (1995), *Basic Econometrics*, 3rd edition, New York: McGraw-Hill.

Hagan, P. and West, G. (June 2006), "Interpolation Methods for Curve Construction", *Applied Mathematical Finance*, 13(2), pp. 89–129.

Hicks, J. (1946), *Value and Capital*, 2nd edition, Oxford: Oxford University Press.

Hull, J., (2011), *Options Futures and other Derivatives*, 8th edition, London: Pearson Education.

Ingersoll, J. (1987), *Theory of Financial Decision Making*, Savage, MA: Rowman & Littlefield, Chapter 18.

Ito, Kiyoshi (1951), "On stochastic differential equations", *Memoirs, American Mathematical Society*, 4, pp. 1–51.

James, J. and Webber, N. (2000), *Interest Rate Modelling*, Chichester: John Wiley & Sons.

Jarrow, R. (1981), "Liquidity Premiums and the Expectations Hypothesis", *Journal of Banking and Finance,* 5(4), pp. 539–46.

Jarrow, R. (1996), *Modelling Fixed Income Securities and Interest Rate Options*, New York: McGraw-Hill.

Jordan, J. and Mansi, S. (September 2000), "How Well do Constant-Maturity Treasuries Approximate the On-The-Run Term Structure?", *Journal of Fixed Income*, 10: 2, pp. 35–45.

Kac, Mark (1949), "On Distributions of Certain Wiener Functionals", *Transactions of the American Mathematical Society* 65 (1): pp. 1–13.

Kessel, R.A. (1965), "The Cyclical Behaviour of the Term Structure of Interest Rates", *Essays in Applied Price Theory*, Chicago: University of Chicago.

Kijima, M., Tanaka, K. and Wong, T. (2008), "A Multi-quality Model of Interest Rates", *Quantitative Finance*, 9(2), pp. 133–45.

Langetieg, T.C. and Smoot, S.J. (December 1981), *An Appraisal of Alternative Spline Methodologies for Estimating the Term Structure of Interest Rates*, Working Paper, University of Southern California.

Levy, H. (1999), *Introduction to Investments*, 2nd edition, Cincinnati: South-Western College Publishing.

Livingstone, M. (1990), *Money and Capital Markets*, New Jersey: Prentice Hall, pp. 254–6.

Lutz, F. (November (1940), "The Structure of Interest Rates", *Quarterly Journal of Economics*, pp. 36–63.

Mastronikola, K. (1991), "Yield Curves for Gilt-edged Stocks: A New Model", *Bank of England Discussion Paper (Technical Series)*, No. 49.

Markowitz, H. M. (1959), *Portfolio Selection: Efficient Diversification of Investments*, New York: John Wiley & Sons. Reprinted by Yale University Press, 1970; 2nd ed. Basil Blackwell, 1991.

McCulloch, J. (1971), "Measuring the Term Structure of Interest Rates", *Journal of Business*, 44, pp. 19–31.

McCulloch, J. (1975), "The Tax-Adjusted Yield Curve", *Journal of Finance*, 30, pp. 811–30.

McCulloch, J.H. (1975), "An Estimate of the Liquidity Premium," *Journal of Political Economy*, 83, Jan.–Feb. pp. 95–119.

Meiselman, D. (1962), *The Term Structure & Interest Rates*, New Jersy: Prentice Hall.

Merton, Robert C. (1973), "Theory of Rational Option Pricing", *Bell Journal of Economics and Management Science* (The RAND Corporation) 4(1): pp. 141–183.

Merton, R. Spring (1973), "Theory of Rational Option Pricing", *Bell Journal of Economics and Management Science*, 4, pp. 141–83.

Neftci, S. (2000), *An Introduction to the Mathematics of Financial Derivatives*, 2nd edition, San Francisco: Academic Press, Chapter 18.

Nelson, C. and Siegel, A. (1987), "Parsimonious Modelling of Yield Curves, *Journal of Business*, 60(4), pp. 473–89.

Piterbarg, V. (February 2010), "Funding beyond Discounting: Collateral Agreements and Derivatives Pricing", *RISK*, pp. 97–102.

Questa, G. (1999), *Fixed Income Analysis for the Global Financial Market*, Chichester: Wiley.

Ross, Sheldon, M. (1999), *An Introduction to Mathematical Finance*, Cambridge: Cambridge University Press.

Rubinstein, M. (1999), *Rubinstein on Derivatives*, London: RISK, pp. 84–5.

Ryan, R. (ed.) (1997), *Yield Curve Dynamics*, Chicago: Glenlake Publishing Company.

Schaefer, S. (1981), "Measuring a Tax-Specific Term Structure of Interest Rates in the Market for British Government Securities", *Economic Journal*, 91, pp. 415–38.

Shiller, R. (1990), "The Term Structure of Interest Rates", in Friedman, B. and Hahn, F. (eds), *Handbook of Monetary Economics*, Amsterdam: North-Holland, Chapter 13.

Steeley, J.M. (1991), "Estimating the Gilt-Edged Term Structure: Basis Splines and Confidence Intervals", *Journal of Business Finance and Accounting*, 18, pp. 513–30.

Suits, D., Mason, A. and Chan, L. (1978), "Spline Functions Fitted by Standard Regression Methods", *Review of Economics and Statistics*, 60, pp. 132–39.

Sundaresan, S. (1997), *Fixed Income Markets and Their Derivatives*, Cincinnati: South-Western.

Svensson, L. (1994), "Estimating and Interpreting Forward Rates: Sweden 1992-4," *National Bureau of Economic Research Working Paper* #4871.

The Economist, "Out of Debt", (12 February 2000), pp. 44–9.

Tuckman, B. and Porfirio, B. (2003), *Interest Rate Parity, Money Market Basis Swaps, and Cross-currency Basis Swaps*, Lehman Brothers Fixed Income Markets Research.

Van Deventer, D. and Imai, K. (1997), *Financial Risk Analytics*, New York: Irwin.

Van Horne, J. (1995), *Financial Management and Policy*, 10th edition, New Jersey: Prentice Hall.

Vasicek, O. (1977), "An Equilibrium Characterisation of the Term Structure", *Journal of Financial Economics*, 5, pp. 177–88.

Vasicek, O. and Fong, H.G. (May 1982), "Term Structure Modelling Using Exponential Splines", *Journal of Finance*, 37(2), pp. 339–48.

Waggoner, D. (1997), "Spline Methods for Extracting Interest Rate Curves from Coupon Bond Prices", *Working Paper, Federal Reserve Bank of Atlanta*, pp. 97–10.

Windas, T. (1993), *An Introduction to Option-adjusted Spread Analysis*, Princeton: Bloomberg Publishing.

Trust is the glue in all relationships. Trust is a two-way thing. The superior must trust his subordinates to make good decisions which support his overall mission. The subordinate must trust his boss to give realistic and necessary missions, with appropriate resources, and to not bite his head off if occasionally he makes a mistake. People who don't make mistakes don't make anything. Trust is at the very centre of success.

This lies at the very heart of successful leadership. If people cannot feel, even though things are bad and may get worse, that if they follow this particular person then there is a real prospect of ultimate success – then that person has failed as a leader.

— Ian Gardiner, *In the Service of the Sultan: A First Hand Account of the Dhofar Insurgency*, Pen & Sword Books 2006

Only a fool makes the same mistake twice . . .

— Saeed Choudhry

PART II

Bank Asset and Liability Management

Part I was a primer on banking, the elements of which all feed into the essence of banking, which is asset-liability management (ALM). We are in a position now to introduce ALM itself. In Part II of the book we review the main strands of the discipline, including a look at the role of the ALM Committee (ALCO) and ALCO reporting. This covers the terms of reference of the ALCO, a look at the main drivers of the ALCO agenda, and the management information (MI) content essential to effective ALCO governance. It also includes a detailed look at the organisation of the Group ALCO (GALCO) function in a multinational or multi-entity bank.

We also consider basic trading and hedging principles, and the role of risk reporting and stress testing.

CHAPTER 6

Asset–Liability Management I

Asset–liability management (ALM) is a generic term that is used to refer to a number of things by different market participants. We believe that it should be used to denote specifically the high-level management of a bank's assets and liabilities; as such it is a strategy-level discipline and not a tactical one. It is usually implemented within a bank's Treasury division, with overall policy set by the asset–liability committee (ALCO). The principal function of the ALM desk is to manage interest-rate risk and liquidity risk. It will also set overall policy for credit risk and credit risk management, although tactical-level credit policy is set at a lower level within credit committees. Although the basic tenets of ALM would appear to apply more to commercial banking rather than investment banking, in reality it is an essential discipline for all types of financial institution. The market-making desk in an investment bank still deals in assets and liabilities, and these must be managed for interest-rate risk and liquidity risk. In a properly integrated banking function the ALM desk must have a remit overseeing all aspects of a bank's operations.

In this chapter we introduce the key principles of liquidity management and ALM hedging.

BASIC CONCEPTS

In financial markets two main strands of risk management are interest-rate risk and liquidity risk. ALM practice is concerned with managing these risks. Interest-rate risk exists in two strands. The first strand is the more obvious one, the risk of changes in asset–liability value due to changes in interest rates. Such a change impacts the cash flows of assets and liabilities, or rather their present value, because financial instruments are valued with reference to market interest rates. The second strand is that associated with optionality, which arises with products such as early redeemable loans.

The other main type of risk that ALM seeks to manage is liquidity risk, which refers both to the funding liquidity of markets and the ease with which assets can be translated to cash. ALM is conducted primarily at an overview, balance sheet level. The risk that is managed is an aggregate, group-level risk. This makes sense because one could not manage a viable banking business by leaving interest-rate and liquidity risk management at individual operating levels. We illustrate this in Figure 6.1, which highlights

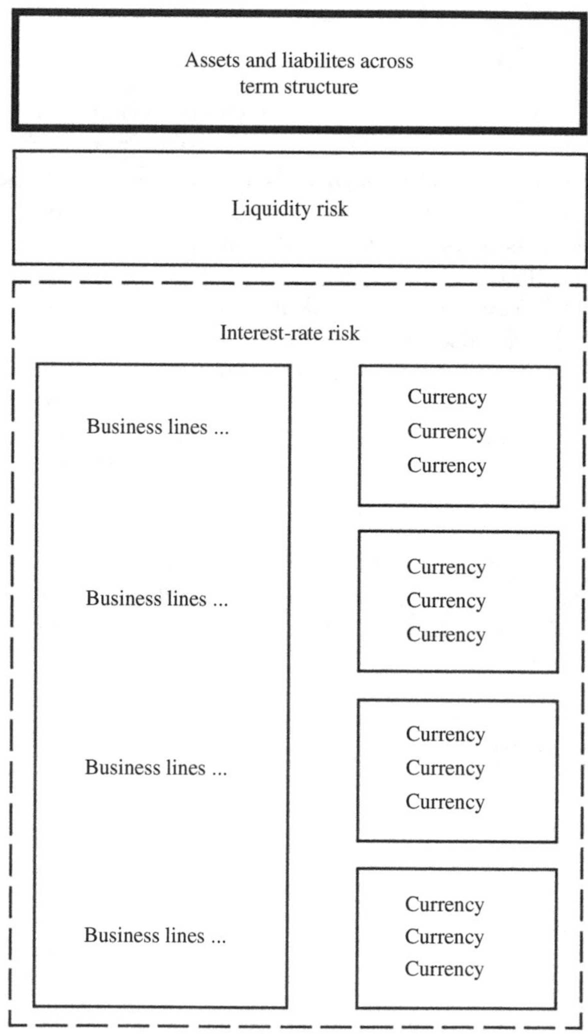

FIGURE 6.1 Cornerstone of ALM philosophy.

the cornerstones of ALM. Essentially, interest-rate risk exposure is managed at the group level by the Treasury desk. The drivers are the different currency interest rates, with each exposure being made up of the net present value (NPV) of cash flow as it changes with movements in interest rates. The discount rate used to calculate the NPV is the prevailing market rate for each time bucket in the term structure.

The interest-rate exposure arises because rates fluctuate from day to day, and continuously over time. The primary risk is that of interest-rate reset, for floating-rate assets and liabilities. The secondary risk is liquidity risk: unless assets and liabilities are matched by amount and term, assets must be funded on a continuous rolling basis. Equally, the receipt of funds must be placed on a continuous basis. Whether an asset carries a fixed or floating-rate reset will determine its exposure to interest-rate fluctuations. Where an asset is marked at a fixed rate, a rise in rates will reduce its NPV and so reduce its value to the bank. This is intuitively easy to grasp, even without recourse to financial arithmetic, because we can see that the asset is now paying a below-market rate of interest. Or we can think of it as a loss due to opportunity cost foregone, since the assets are earning below what they could earn if they were employed elsewhere in the market. The opposite applies if there is a fall in rates: this causes the NPV of the asset to rise. For assets marked at a floating-rate of interest, the risk exposure to fluctuating rates is lower, because the rate receivable on the asset will reset at periodic intervals, which will allow for changes in market rates.

We speak of risk exposure as being for the group as a whole. This exposure must therefore aggregate the net risk of all the bank's operating business. Even for the simplest banking operation, we can see that this will produce a net mismatch between assets and liabilities, because different business lines will have differing objectives for their individual books. This mismatch will manifest itself in two ways:

- the mismatch between the different terms of assets and liabilities across the term structure;
- the mismatch between the different interest rates that each asset or liability contract has been struck at.

This mismatch is known as the ALM *gap*. The first type is referred to as the *liquidity gap*, while the second is known as the *interest-rate gap*. We value assets and liabilities at their NPV; hence, we can measure the overall sensitivity of the balance sheet NPV to changes in interest rates. As such, ALM is an art that encompasses aggregate balance sheet risk management at the group level.

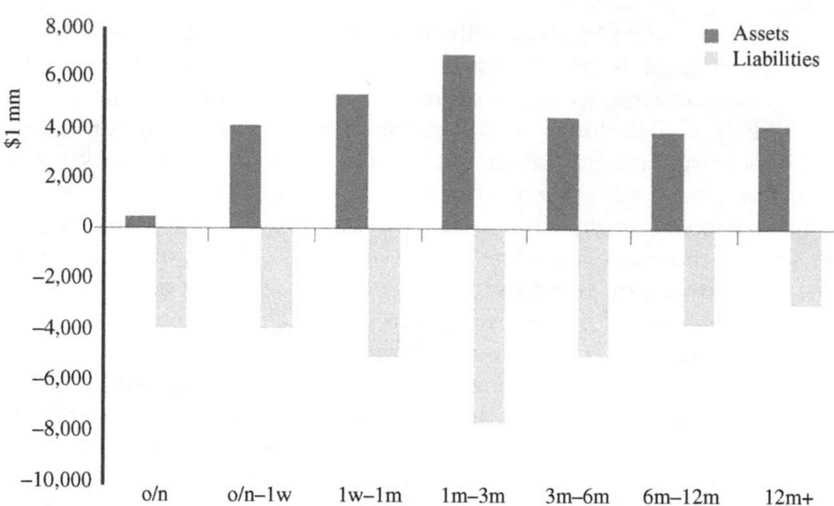

FIGURE 6.2 Securities and derivatives trading house ALM profile.

Figure 6.2 shows the aggregate group-level ALM profile for a securities and derivatives trading house based in London. There is a term mismatch as few assets are deemed to have "overnight" maturity, whereas a significant portion of funding (liabilities) is in the overnight term. One thing we do not know from looking at Figure 6.2 is how this particular institution is defining the maturity of its assets.[1] To place these in the relevant maturity buckets, we can adopt one of two approaches, which are:

- the actual contractual maturity of the assets;
- the "liquidity duration", which is the estimated time it would take the firm to dispose of its assets in an enforced or "fire sale" situation, such as a withdrawal from the business.

The method to adopt will depend on the nature of the business line and the type of assets in question, and there is an element of judgement required. The firm should select an approach and then adhere consistently to it, although both approaches may be adopted within the same firm, for different asset types and business lines. The second approach has the disadvantage of being subjective – estimating the time taken to dispose of an asset book is an inexact science. Nevertheless for long-dated and/or illiquid assets it is at least a workable method that enables practitioners to work within a specified ALM framework with regard to structuring the liability profile.

1 This report is discussed in full in the case study later in the chapter.

LIQUIDITY GAP

There is an obvious risk exposure arising because of liquidity mismatch of assets and liabilities. The maturity terms will not match, which creates the liquidity gap. The amount of assets and liabilities maturing at any one time will also not match (although overall of course, by definition assets must equal liabilities). Liquidity risk is the risk that a bank will not be able to refinance assets as liabilities become due, for any reason.[2] To manage this, the bank will hold a large portion of assets in very liquid form.[3] A surplus of assets over liabilities at any specific tenor point creates a funding requirement. If there is a surplus of liabilities, the bank will need to find efficient uses for those funds. In either case, the bank has a liquidity gap. This liquidity can be projected over time, so that one knows what the situation is each morning, based on net expiring assets and liabilities. The projection will change daily of course, due to new business undertaken each day.

We could eliminate liquidity gap risk by matching assets and liabilities across each time bucket. Actually, at individual loan level this is a popular strategy: if we can invest in an asset paying 5.50% for three months and fund this with a 3-month loan costing 5.00%, we have locked in a 50 bp gain that is interest-rate risk free. However, while such an approach can be undertaken at the individual asset level, it would not be possible at an aggregate level, or at least not possible without imposing severe restrictions on the business. For certain types of business, such as residential mortgages, it would simply not be possible. Hence, liquidity risk is an essential part of banking, and a key consideration in ALM. A bank with a surplus of long-term assets over short-term liabilities will have an ongoing requirement to fund the assets continuously, and there is the ever-present risk that funds may not be available as and when they are required. The concept of a future funding requirement is itself a driver of interest-rate risk, because the bank will not know what the future interest rates at which it will deal will be.[4] So a key part of ALM involves managing and hedging this forward liquidity risk.

---

2 The reasons can be macro-level ones, affecting most or all market participants, or more firm- or sector-specific. The former might be a general market correction that causes the supply of funds to dry up, and would be a near-catastrophe situation. The latter is best illustrated with the example of Barings plc in 1995: when it went bust overnight due to large, hitherto covered-up losses on the Simex exchange, the supply of credit to similar institutions was reduced or charged at much higher rates, albeit only temporarily, as a result.

3 Such assets would be very short-term, risk-free assets such as T-bills.

4 It can of course lock in future funding rates with forward-starting loans, which is one way to manage liquidity risk.

Definition and Illustration

To reiterate then, the liquidity gap is the difference in maturity between assets and liabilities at each point along the term structure. Because for many banks ALM concerns itself with a medium-term management of risk, this will not be beyond a 5-year horizon, and in many cases it will be considerably less than this. Notice from Figure 6.2 that the example we use to illustrate shows the longest dated time bucket in the ALM profile extending out to only "12-month plus", so that all liabilities longer than one year were grouped in one time bucket. This recognises that a significant share of liabilities are funded in the money markets, although a proportion of funding will be a much longer term, up to 30 years or so. For each point along the term structure at which a gap exists, there is (liquidity) gap risk exposure. This is the risk that funds cannot be raised as required, or that the rate payable on these funds is prohibitive.[5] To manage this risk, a bank must perforce:

- disperse the funding profile (the liability profile) over more than just a short period of time. For example, it would be excessively risky to concentrate funding in just the overnight to 1-week time bucket, so a bank will spread the profile across a number of time buckets. Figure 6.3 shows the liability profile for a European multi-currency asset-backed CP programme in 2005, with liabilities extending from one month to one year;

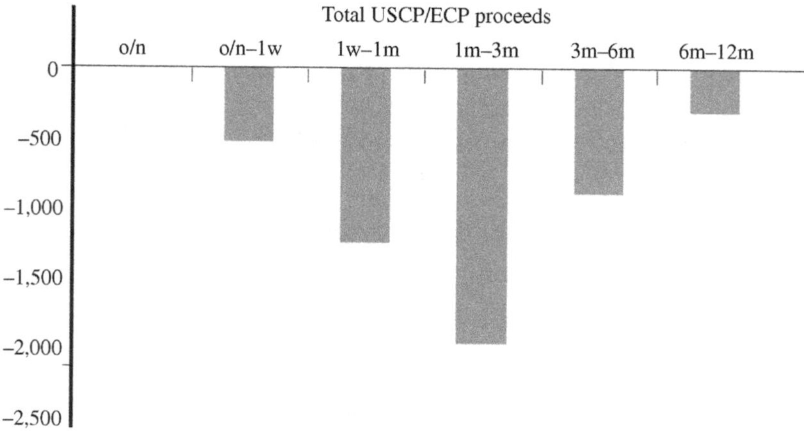

FIGURE 6.3 CP programme liability profile, European bank conduit 2005.

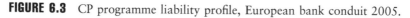

5 Of course the opposite applies: the gap risk also refers to an excess of liabilities over assets.

- manage expectations so that large-size funding requirements are diarised well in advance, as well as not planned for times of low liquidity such as the Christmas and New Year period;
- hold a significant proportion of assets in the form of very liquid instruments such as very short term risk-free cash loans (such as deposits at the central bank), T-bills and high-quality short-term bank CDs.

Observing the last guideline allows a bank to maintain a reserve of liquidity in the event of a funding crisis, because such assets can be turned into cash at very short notice.

The size of the liquidity gap at any one time is never more than a snapshot in time, because it is constantly changing as new commitments are entered into on both the asset and liability side. For this reason some writers speak of a "static" gap and a "dynamic" gap, but in practice one recognises that there is only ever a dynamic gap, because the position changes daily. Hence we will refer only to one liquidity gap.

A further definition is the "marginal" gap, which is the difference between the change in assets and change in liabilities during a specified time period. This is also known as the "incremental" gap. If the change in assets is greater than the change in liabilities, this is a positive marginal gap, while if the opposite applies this is a negative marginal gap.[6]

We illustrate these values in Table 6.1. This is a simplified asset–liability profile from a regional European bank, showing gap and marginal gap at each time period. Note that the liabilities have been structured to produce an "ALM Smile", which is recognised to follow prudent business practice. Generally, no more than 20% of the total funding should be in the overnight to 1-week time bucket, and similarly for the 9–12 month bucket. The marginal gap is measured as the difference between the change in assets and the change in liabilities from one period to the next.

TABLE 6.1 Simplified ALM profile for regional European bank.

	One week	One month	3–month	6–month	9–12 month	> 12 months	Total
Assets	10	90	460	710	520	100	1890
Liabilities	100	380	690	410	220	90	1890
Gap	−90	−290	−230	300	300	10	
Marginal gap		200	−60	−530	0	290	

6 Note that this terminology is not a universal convention.

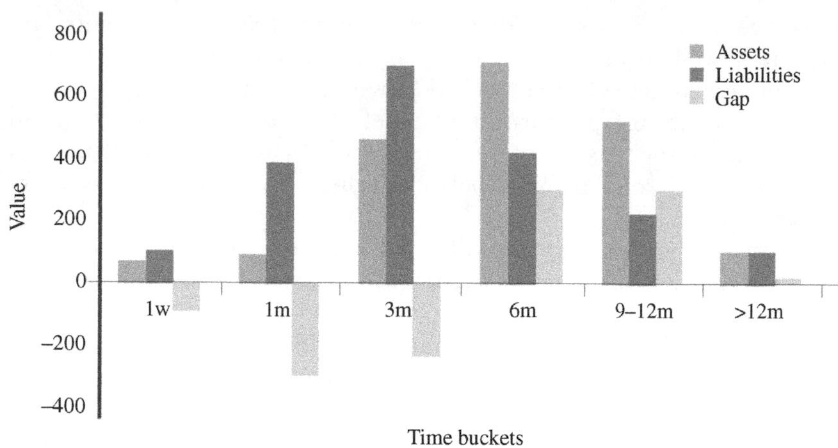

FIGURE 6.4 ALM time profile.

Figure 6.4 shows the graphical profile of the numbers in Table 6.1; and Figure 6.2 shown earlier illustrates the "ALM Smile".

Liquidity Risk

Liquidity risk exposure arises from normal banking operations. That is, it exists irrespective of the type of funding gap, be it excess assets over liabilities for any particular time bucket or an excess of liabilities over assets. In other words, there is a funding risk in any case, either funds must be obtained or surplus assets laid off. The liquidity risk in itself generates interest-rate risk, due to the uncertainty of future interest rates. This can be managed through hedging, and we discuss interest-rate hedging in Chapter 8.

If assets are floating-rate, there is less concern over interest-rate risk because of the nature of the interest-rate reset. This also applies to floating rate liabilities, but only insofar that these match floating-rate assets. Floating-rate liabilities issued to fund fixed-rate assets create forward risk exposure to rising interest rates. Note that even if both assets and liabilities are floating-rate, they can still generate interest-rate risk. For example, if assets pay 6-month Libor and matching term liabilities pay 3-month Libor, there is an interest-rate spread risk between the two terms. This is known as "basis risk". Such an arrangement has eliminated liquidity risk, but not interest-rate spread risk.

Liquidity risk can be managed by matching assets and liabilities, or by setting a series of rolling term loans to fund a long-dated asset. Generally, however, banks will have a particular view of future market conditions, and manage the ALM book in line with this view. This would leave in place a certain level of liquidity risk.

Matched Book

The simplest way to manage liquidity and interest-rate risk is the matched book approach, also known as cash matching. This is actually very rare to observe in practice, even among conservative institutions such as the smaller UK building societies. In matched book, assets and liabilities, and their time profiles, are matched as closely as possible. This includes allowing for the amortisation of assets.[7] As well as matching maturities and time profiles, the interest-rate basis for both assets and liabilities will be matched. That is, fixed loans to fund fixed-rate assets, and the same for floating-rate assets and liabilities. Floating-rate instruments will further need to match the period of each interest-rate reset, to eliminate spread risk.

Under a matched book, also known as *cash flow matching*, in theory there is no liquidity gap. Locking in terms and interest rate bases will also lock in profit. For instance, a 6-month fixed-rate loan is funded with a 6-month fixed-rate deposit. This would eliminate both liquidity and interest-rate risk. In a customer-focused business it will not be possible to precisely match assets and liabilities, but from a macro-level it should be possible to match the profiles fairly closely, by netting total exposure on both sides and matching this. Of course, it may not be possible or desirable to run a matched book, because it would be very restrictive to the business, and also this would mean the ALM book was not taking any view at all on the path of future interest rates. Hence, a part of the banking book will be left unmatched.

Managing the Gap with Undated Assets and Liabilities

We have described a scenario of liquidity management where the maturity date of both assets and liabilities is known with certainty. A large part of retail and commercial banking operations revolves around assets that do not have an explicit maturity date however. These include current account overdrafts and credit card balances. They also include drawn and undrawn lines of credit. The volume of these is a function of general economic

7 Many bank assets, such as residential mortgages and credit-card loans, are repaid before their legal maturity date. Thus the size of the asset book is constantly amortising.

conditions, and can be difficult to predict. Banks will need to be familiar with their clients' behaviour and their requirements over time to be able to assess when and for how long these assets will be utilised. In other words, a bank will apply behaviouralisation analysis to its balance sheet.

Undated assets are balanced on the other side by non-dated liabilities, such as non-interest-bearing liabilities (NIBLs), which include cheque accounts and instant-access deposit accounts. The latter frequently attract very low rates of interest, and are usually included in the NIBL total. Undated liabilities are treated in different ways by banks; the most common treatment places these funds in the shortest time bucket, the overnight to 1-week bucket. However, this means the firm's gap and liquidity profile can be highly volatile and unpredictable, which places greater strain on ALM management. For this reason some bank's take the opposite approach and place these funds in the longest dated bucket, the greater-than-12-month bucket. This is logically tenable because the statistical behaviour of such liabilities is often long-dated in practice. A third approach is to split the total undated liabilities into a "core" balance and an "unstable" balance, and place the first in the long-dated bucket and the second in the shortest dated bucket. The amount recognised as the core balance will need to be analysed over time, to make sure that it is accurate.

MANAGING LIQUIDITY

Managing liquidity gaps and the liquidity process is a continuous, dynamic one because the ALM profile of a bank changes on a daily basis. Liquidity management is the term used to describe this continuous process of raising and laying off funds, depending on whether one is long or short cash that day.

The basic premise is a simple one: the bank must be "squared off" by the end of each day, which means that the net cash position is zero. Thus, liquidity management is both very short-term, as well as projected over the long term, because every position put on today creates a funding requirement in the future on its maturity date. The ALM desk must be aware of their future funding or excess cash positions and act accordingly, whether this means raising funds now or hedging forward interest-rate risk.

The Basic Case: The Funding Gap

A funding requirement is dealt with on the day it occurs. The decision on how it will be treated will factor the term that is put on, as well as allowing for any new assets put on that day. As funding is arranged, the gap at that day will be zero. The next day there will be a new funding requirement or surplus, depending on the net position of the book.

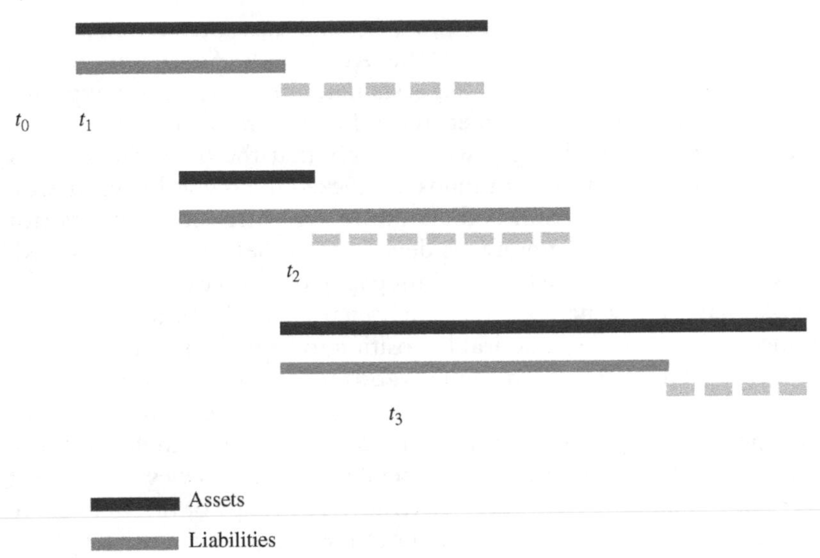

FIGURE 6.5 Funding position on a daily basis.

This is illustrated in Figure 6.5. Starting from a flat position on the first day (t_0) we observe a gap (the dotted line) on t_1, which is closed by putting on funding to match the asset maturity. The amount of funding to raise, and the term to run it to, will take into account the future gap as well as that day's banking activities. So at t_2 we observe a funding excess, which is then laid off. We see at t_3 that the assets invested in run beyond the maturity of the liabilities at t_2, so we have a funding requirement again at t_3. The decision on the term and amount will be based on the market view of the ALM desk. A matched book approach may well be taken where the desk does not have a strong view, or if its view is at odds with market consensus.

There are also external factors to take into account. For instance, the availability of funds in the market may be limited, due to both macro-level issues and to the bank's own (in)ability to raise funds. The former might be during times of market correction or recession (a "credit crunch"), while the latter includes the bank's credit lines with market counterparties. Also some funds will have been raised in the capital markets and this cash will cover part of the funding requirement. In addition, the ALM desk must consider the cost of the funds it is borrowing; if, for example, it thought that interest rates in the short term, and for short-term periods, were going to fall, it might cover the gap with only short-term funds so it can then refinance at the expected lower rates. The opposite might be done if the desk thought rates would rise in the near future.

Running a liquidity gap over time, beyond customer requirements, would reflect a particular view of the ALM desk. So maintaining a consistently underfunded position suggests that interest rates are expected to decline, at which point longer term funds can be taken at cost. Maintaining an over-funded gap would imply that the bank thinks rates will be rising, and so longer term funds are locked in now at lower interest rates. Even if the net position is dictated by customer requirements (for example, customers placing more on deposit than they take out in loans), the bank can usually manage the resultant gap in the wholesale market.

Excess liabilities generally is a rare scenario in a bank and it is not, under most circumstances, a desirable position to be in. This is because the bank will have target return on capital ratios to achieve, and this requires that funds be put to work, so to speak, by acquiring assets. In the case of equity capital it is imperative that these funds are properly employed.[8] The exact structure of the asset book will depend on the bank's view on interest rates, credit risk and the yield curve generally. The shape of the yield curve and expectations on this will also influence the structure and tenor of the asset book. The common practice is to spread assets across the term structure, with varying maturities. There will also be investments made with a forward start date, to lock in rates in the forward curve now. Equally, some investments will be made for very short periods so that if interest rates rise, when the funds are reinvested they will benefit from the higher rates.

The Basic Case: Illustration

The basic case is illustrated in Table 6.2, in two scenarios. In the first scenario, the longest dated gap is −130, so the bank puts on funding for +130 to match this tenor of three periods. The gap at period t_2 is −410, so this is matched with a 2-period tenor funding position of +280. This leaves a gap of −180 at period t_1, which is then funded with a 1-period loan. The net position is zero at each period ("squared off"), and the book has been funded with three bullet fixed-term loans. The position is not a matched book as such, although there is now no liquidity risk exposure.

In the second case, the gap is increasing from period 1 to period 2. The first period is funded with a 3-period and a 2-period borrowing of +50 and +200 respectively. The gap at t_2 needs to be funded with a position that is not needed *now*. The bank can cover this with a forward-start loan of +390

8 The firm's capital will be invested in risk-free assets such as government T-bills. It will not be lent out in normal banking operations because the ALM desk will not want to put capital in a credit-risky investment.

TABLE 6.2 Funding the liquidity gap: two examples.

(i)

Time	t_1	t_2	t_3
Assets	970	840	1,250
Liabilities	380	430	1,120
Gap	−590	−410	−130
Borrow 1: tenor 3 periods	130	130	130
Borrow 2: tenor 2 periods	280	280	
Borrow 3: tenor 1 periods	180		
Total funding	+590	+410	+130
Squared off	0	0	0

(ii)

Time	t_1	t_2	t_3
Assets	970	840	1,250
Liabilities	720	200	1,200
Gap	−250	−640	−50
Borrow 1: tenor 3 periods	50	50	50
Borrow 2: tenor 2 periods	200	200	
Borrow 3: tenor 1 periods	0	390	
Total funding	+250	+640	+50
Squared off	0	0	0

at t_1, or can wait and act at t_2. If it does the latter it may still wish to hedge the interest-rate exposure.[9]

THE LIQUIDITY RATIO

The *liquidity ratio* is the ratio of assets to liabilities. It is a short-term ratio, usually calculated for the money market term only; that is, up to one year. Under most circumstances, and certainly under a positive yield curve environment, it would be expected to be above 1.00; however, this is less common at the very short end because the average tenor of assets is often greater than the average tenor of liabilities. So in the 1-month to 3-month period, and perhaps out to six months, the ratio may well be less than one.

9 We look at the mechanics of this, using different derivative instruments, in Chapter 8.

This reflects the fact that short-term borrowing is used to fund longer term assets.

A ratio of below one is inefficient from an ROE point of view. It represents an opportunity cost of return foregone. To manage it, banks may invest more funds in the very short term, but this also presents its own problems because the return on these assets may not be sufficient. This is especially true in a positive yield curve environment. This is one scenario where a matched book approach will be prudent, because the bank should be able to lock in a bid–offer spread in the very short end of the yield curve. A more risky approach would be to lend in the short term and fund these in the long term, but this would create problems because the term premium in the yield curve will make borrowing in the long term expensive relative to the return on short-dated assets (unless we have an inverted yield curve). There is also the liquidity risk associated with the more frequent rolling over of assets compared to liabilities. We see then, that maintaining the liquidity ratio carries something of a cost for banks.

CASE STUDY 6.1 SECURITIES AND DERIVATIVES TRADING HOUSE: ALM POLICY AND PROFILE

We conclude this introduction to the concept of ALM with a look at the ALM policy and profile of a European securities and derivatives trading house, which we call XYZ Securities Limited. The business is a financial institution based in London, with a number of business lines in FX, equity, and credit derivatives trading and market-making. We outline the various firm-wide policies on ALM, cash management, liquidity and investment that have been formalised at XYZ Securities, in the firm's Treasury policy statement. We show first the initial policy set up when the Treasury desk was established, and the "enhanced" policy that was adopted subsequently. This policy remains business best practice in the post-crash environment, and is a model for all securities houses.

Policy Statement: Funding and ALM

This note outlines the approach to managing the asset–liability profile that is generated by the funding requirements of XYZ Securities Limited ("XYZ"). The principal source of funding is the parent bank. Funds are also raised from a variety of external sources, including prime brokerage, bank lines, total return swaps (TRSs) and repo lines, a repo conduit and an ABCP programme. The overall management of the ALM profile is centralised within the firm's Treasury desk.

The key objective of the Treasury desk is to undertake prudent management of XYZ's funding requirement, with regard to liquidity management, interest-rate management (gap profile) and funding diversification. This process includes management information (MI) and reporting. The primary deliverable of the Treasury desk is the ALM report. This is presented in Table 6.3.

ALM Profile

The ALM profile of all XYZ business lines is shown in Table 6.3. The report comprises the following segments:

- the ALM report;
- asset liquidity profile;
- liabilities.

We consider each part next.

ALM Report

This report summarises the total funding requirement of each of XYZ's business lines. The business lines are: FX, interest-rate and credit derivatives market-making; equity derivatives proprietary trading, asset management and equity brokerage. The funding is profiled against the asset profile to produce the firm-wide ALM profile. Liability represents the funding taken by each business line. They are set out in accordance with the maturity term structure of each constituent loan of the total funding requirement. The maturity buckets used in the report are:

- overnight
- overnight – one week
- one week – one month
- one month – three months
- three months – six months
- six months – 12 months
- over 12 months.

The asset pool is distributed along the same maturity buckets in accordance with certain assumptions. These assumptions are concerned with the expected turnover of assets in each business, and the time estimated to liquidate the business under enforced conditions.[10]

(*continued*)

10 The percentage breakdown that reflects senior management assumptions of the maturity profile of assets is an input into the ALM report.

TABLE 6.3 XYZ Securities Limited ALM report and profile.

	o/n	o/n–1	1w–1m	1m–3m	3m–6m	6m–12m	12m+	Total
Assets	481	4,104	5,325	6,954	4,478	3,845	4,128	29,315
Liabilities	–3,947	–844	–5,107	–7,579	–5,053	–3,799	–2,986	(29,315)
Gap	3,466	3,260	218	625	575	46	1,142	9,332
Percent of total funding	13%	3%	17%	26%	17%	13%	10%	100%
Gap as % of total gap	37%	35%	2%	7%	6%	0%	12%	100%
Gap as % of total funding	12%	11%	1%	2%	2%	0%	4%	
Gap limit	20%	20%	20%	20%	20%	20%	20%	
Limit breach	–	–	–	–	–	–	–	
Cumulative assets	481	4,585	9,910	16,864	21,342	25,187	29,315	
Cumulative liabilities	–3,947	–4,791	–9,898	–1,747	–22,530	–26,329	–29,315	
Net gap	–3,466	–206	12	–613	–1,188	–1,142	0	

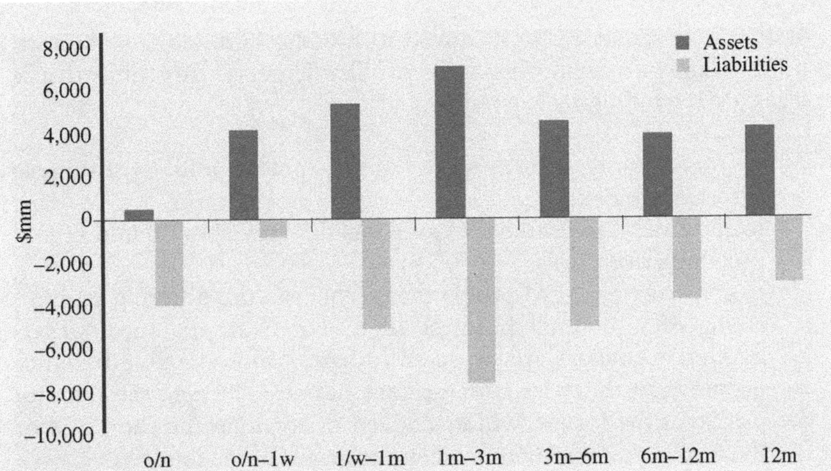

FIGURE 6.6 XYZ Securities Limited gap profile.

Underneath the ALM profile is the gap profile (see Figure 6.6). "Gap" is defined as the difference between assets and liabilities per maturity bucket; it shows how the liability profile differs from the asset profile. It is also a snapshot that reflects where the forward funding requirement lies at the time of the snapshot.

Asset Liquidity Profile

This report is a detailed breakdown of the funding requirement of each business line. Assets and liabilities are split according to desk within each business line, set out by maturity profile.

Liabilities

This is the detailed liability profile breakdown of all the business lines. Funding is split into term structure of liabilities. A separate table is given for each business line. There is also a detailed breakdown of use of funds from each source of funds.

Aims and Objectives

Historically, the funding of XYZ business was concentrated overwhelmingly on a very short-term basis. This reflected primarily the short-term trading nature of XYZ's assets, which meant that the asset profile was effectively changing on a high frequency. Over time, XYZ's business evolved into dealing in more longer term asset classes

(continued)

and as a consequence XYZ moved to funding in the longer term, to more adequately match its asset profile. The Treasury objective is based on the following reasoning:

- to match asset profile with liability profile and to minimise forward gap risk;
- to term out the funding away from the very short-dated tenors used hitherto;
- to construct an ALM profile that recognises the differing requirements of individual business lines. For example, the market-making businesses are expected to have a more flexible liquidity profile than the asset management business. Hence, the liability profile of the former will be concentrated along the short end of the funding term structure when compared to the latter;
- to even out the liability profile such that no one maturity bucket contains more than 20% of the total funding requirement. This is treated as a formal funding risk limit, to be monitored by the risk management function.

A 20% gap limit will apply to the overall XYZ funding requirement.

Application of Cost of Funds

The effect of terming out funding is to produce a cost of funds that is not explicitly observable without calculation. That is, the cost of funds must be determined as a pooled or weighted-average cost of funds (WACF). XYZ uses a simplified version of this calculation that is essentially the interest charged on each loan as a proportion of the total borrowing, or, put another way, the daily interest payable on all loans divided by the total notional amount. This is a common market practice and is used, for example, at a number of European banks. Treasury applies the WACF interest rate to each business line.

As XYZ increases in size and complexity, it becomes necessary to implement a more sophisticated ALM approach. This is described below.

ALM Report

The ALM report summarises the total funding requirement of each of XYZ's business lines. It is unchanged from the version described earlier.

Aims and Objectives

The aims and objectives remain the same as described earlier.

Modifications and Updates

The new ALM policy includes the following improvements:

- the ALM profile of XYZ has been structured in line with market good practice, with more accurate matching of liabilities to assets; it now resembles a banking ALM profile more accurately;
- the overnight funding profile of XYZ, which represented significant liquidity risk, has now been transformed such that overnight funding now represents 13% of overall funding, compared with over 40% at the start of the new policy;
- the 20% gap limit has been formalised and implemented, and now is a formal limit that is observed by Treasury and monitored by Risk Management;
- there is regular weekly reporting of ALM and funding for XYZ (see Table 6.3 and Figure 6.6);
- greater diversity in funding sources has been achieved, with bank lines in place for XYZ access to unsecured, un-guaranteed funding, secured funding using repo and TRSs, a repo conduit and an asset-backed CP programme.

The Treasury desk in charged with implementing market best practice with regard to ALM and funding policy.

Funding Cost Allocation: Revised Treasury Approach

The major change in policy is now a move from a WACF funding cost allocation to each of the business lines to a Treasury "pool" funding method. In this approach, all funding, both overnight and term loans, is placed in a central Treasury pool. These funds are lent out, on an overnight basis, to the various business lines in accordance with their funding requirement. This removes interest-rate risk hedging considerations from the business lines and places them with Treasury. All business lines receive the same funding rate, the overnight Libor + spread rate, so no business line has a funding cost advantage over another.

Treasury moves from being a cost-centre to a profit-centre, with any savings it makes in structuring the funding, below that of Libor-flat at which it lends funds, being retained within it.

(*continued*)

Interest-rate Hedge

Under the new funding regime, all interest-rate risk exposure generated when putting on term loans is hedged within the Treasury book. The policy is as follows:

- Treasury has an interest-rate exposure limit of USD30,000 total interest-rate risk, measured as present value of a basis point (PVBP, or "DV01"), for all time buckets greater than 30 days.
- This exposure is generated by the use of term loans. Exposure is offset by lending funds in matching terms, running the liquidity book of CP, CDs, sovereign bonds and FRNs.
- Remaining DV01 is hedged using Eurodollar, Bund and short-sterling futures contracts.
- The interest-rate exposure is monitored daily and subject to dynamic hedging as term loans are replaced.

Cash Management

Cash management at XYZ is undertaken by the Treasury desk. Its aim is to undertake prudent management of XYZ's funding requirement, with regard to liquidity management, interest-rate management (gap profile and gap risk) and funding diversification. It is also responsible for producing management information and ALM reporting. The Treasury desk carries out its responsibilities working in conjunction with the middle office and back office. The back office reports each day's funding requirement, and the funding itself is carried out by Treasury in accordance with its view. The middle office reports the funding allocated to each line of business as part of regular P&L reporting.

The objective of ALM policy is to apply market-standard guidelines to the XYZ business and to follow prudent market practice. It is also to make the whole funding process more transparent with regard to management reporting and to centralise funding into one desk within the group.

ALM and Funding Report

The firm-wide ALM report is shown in Table 6.3 and Figure 6.6. From Table 6.3 we observe the following:

- the "gap" is defined as the absolute value of the assets and liabilities added together, which, because liabilities are reported as negative numbers, is essentially assets minus liabilities;

- the funding within each time bucket is reported as a percent of total funding. This is a key control measure, as prudent ALM policy suggests that the liability profile should be humped in shape ("the ALM Smile"), so that each bucket should not hold more than approximately 15–20% of the total funding;
- the next control value is the "gap as percent of total gap". This is noted to prevent an excessive forward gap developing in one time bucket;
- the key control measure is the gap as percent of total funding, which at XYZ is set at a 20% limit. We see that on this date there was no breach of this limit in any of the time buckets;
- the report also lists cumulative assets and liabilities, as well as the "net gap", which is the sum of the two cumulative values for each time bucket.

We observe that the ALM profile at XYZ follows roughly the "ALM Smile" shape that is recommended as the ideal profile over the term structure, and good business practice.

The firm-wide funding report is shown in Figure 6.7. This is reported in graphical form to observe adherence to funding limits and indicate breaches. Unlike the ALM report, which is produced by Treasury (a front-office function), the funding report is produced by the bank's Middle Office (MO), which is a control function. Figure 6.8 shows the breakdown by business line.

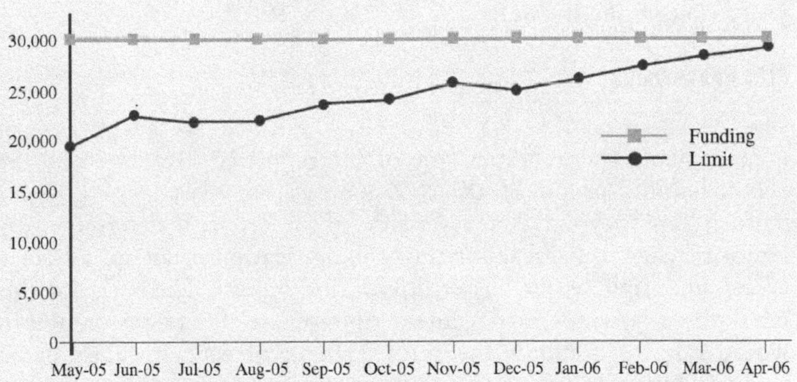

FIGURE 6.7 XYZ Securities Limited funding usage and limit report.

(*continued*)

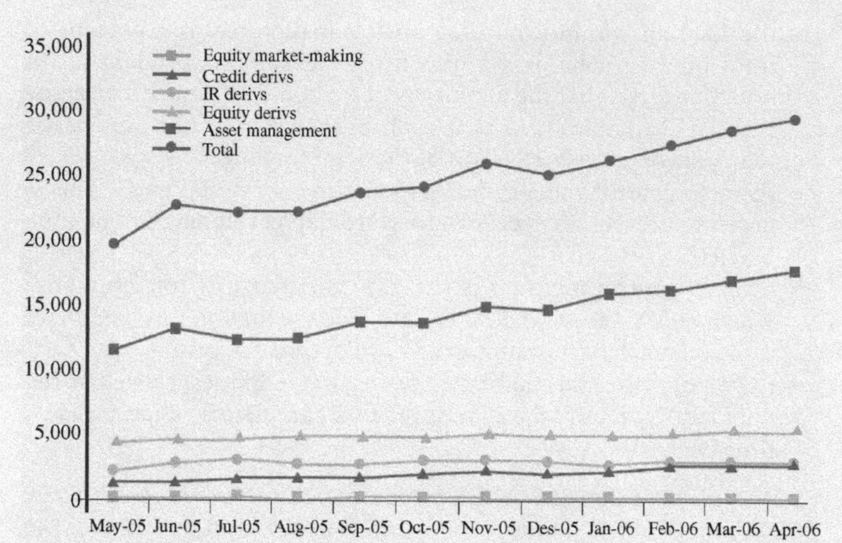

FIGURE 6.8 XYZ Securities Limited funding usage by business line.

ALM Reporting

XYZ Treasury follows the ALM policy previously described to and approved by senior management. One strand of the ALM discipline is the regular reporting of the firm's ALM profile, by means of the ALM report. This is produced by Treasury using data recorded by itself as well as data from the MO.

ALM Procedures

The ALM report for XYZ Securities Limited is sent to senior management. The liabilities side of the report is determined by the actual liability profile of all XYZ loans, from overnight to 1-year maturity and beyond. The asset side of the report is determined by senior management breakdown of the liquidation profile of all XYZ assets, and input as the "asset-liquidation input". The basis for this breakdown is senior management opinion on the length of time it would take to liquidate the trading book of each business in an enforced "fire sale" situation.[11]

11 The liquidity duration of the asset pool is unrelated to the contractual duration of the assets themselves.

The process of assigning liquidation maturity buckets is based on the subjective view of senior management. For each business line, senior management asks the question, "What reasonable time period would it take to liquidate positions if it was decided to close down the business?" The answer to this question is a function of the secondary market trading liquidity of the assets in question.[12] Hence, for frequently traded assets such as Eurobonds, we assume that one week would be sufficient time to trade out of all assets. For business lines with illiquid assets, such as some part of the asset management book, a longer time period (specifically in this case, in excess of one year) is noted. Management allocate this estimated time period in the same time buckets as we have established for the liabilities.

By definition assets equal liabilities.

The procedure for compiling the report is as follows:

- Treasury compiles its own funding report, independent of MO, from its own record of overnight and term funding for XYZ. The procedure for creating this document is documented internally;
- the Treasury report is used to populate the "Liabilities" segment on the ALM report. This segment lists the current funding profile (liabilities) of XYZ by business line;
- senior management will instruct any change to the asset liquidation breakdown, otherwise these values are retained;
- the "asset liquidity profile" segment is linked directly to the asset liquidation segment (for the asset side) and liabilities input segment (for the liability side).

The ALM graph is automatically updated when balance sheet assets and liabilities are generated.

The Treasury Liquidity Book

Following conventional banking business best practice, XYZ Treasury maintains a liquidity book of T-bills, CDs, sovereign bonds and bank FRNs. The firm's capital as well as a proportion of long-term cash is held in the liquidity book.

12 In practice, other factors (such as whether the market was aware that this was an enforced sale or not) would also influence this timing but are difficult to factor into any estimation.

In the next case study we set out the firm's policy for maintaining the FRN liquidity book.

CASE STUDY 6.2 XYZ SECURITIES LIQUIDITY BOOK: FRN PORTFOLIO

Banks maintain a pool of low-risk FRNs issued by other banks and building societies as part of their reserve and liquidity requirements. This well-established practice is favoured because of low regulatory capital requirements against these assets, and because it enables institutions that are funded at Libor to hold Libor-plus floating-rate assets with funding locked in.

The XYZ Treasury desk funds at Libor-plus spread via its commercial paper vehicle. Within the parent group funding limit of USD30 billion, Treasury maintains a low-risk portfolio of bank and building society assets to employ spare capacity by holding a low-risk, locked-in funding portfolio of bank and building society FRNs. As these are liquid assets, they can in theory be used to generate liquidity in a funding stress environment.

Objective of this Business Activity

The primary objective of the FRN book is to maintain a portfolio of short- to medium-dated bank and building society FRNs, all rated A or better, and held to maturity. These will be FRNs paying a spread over 3-month Libor, and denominated in USD, EUR or GBP.

Bonds are funded in their own currency by means of 3-month CP issued from the CP conduit, funded at Libor-plus spread. There is no gap funding risk.

Motivation Behind the Business

A portfolio of bank and building society FRNs enables XYZ Securities Ltd to:

- earn a low-risk but material return over locked-in funding;
- utilise spare capacity in funding availability.

Bonds will be purchased at par or below par so there is no capital loss if held to maturity.

Building society paper carries particular value relative to their credit rating. There has never been a default in the history of the building society movement (traditionally building societies merge or are taken over if in any financial difficulty) and this implies that their financial risk is stronger than the rating they receive.[13] In effect, the book holds conventional bank risk (A-/A3) for BBB-rated return.

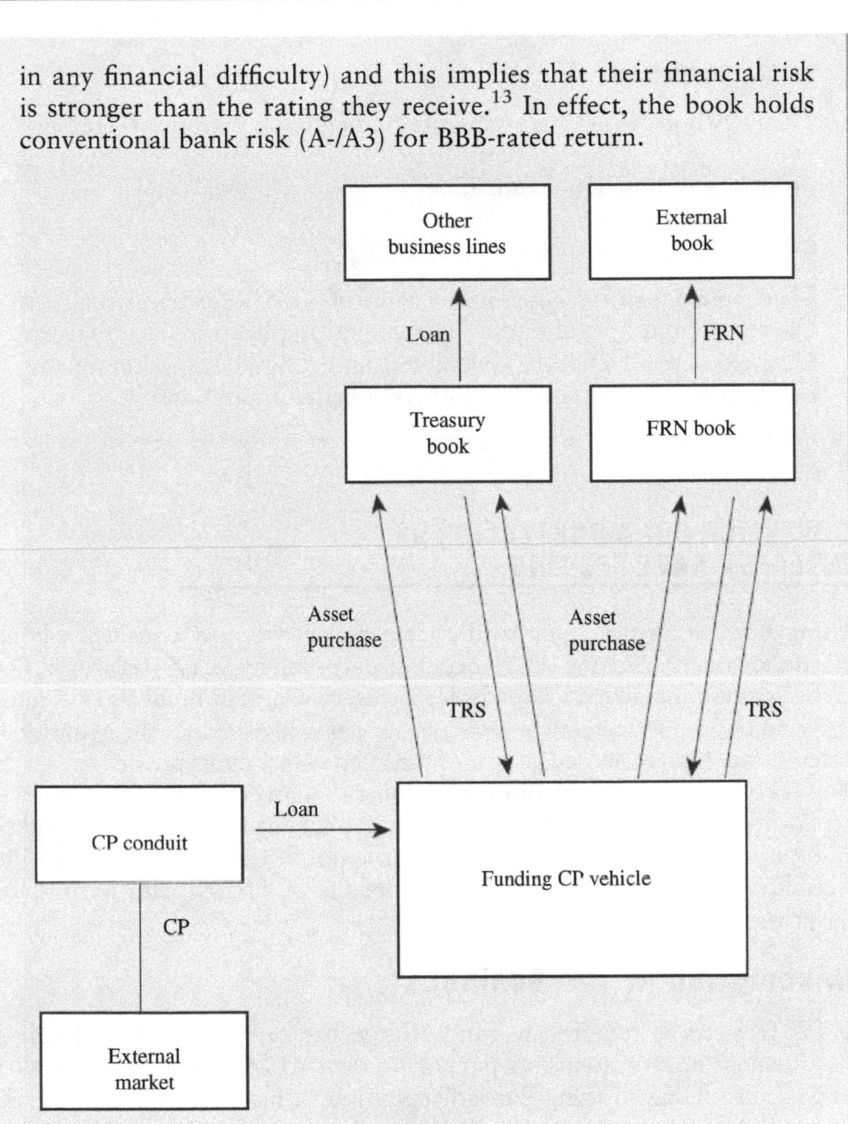

FIGURE 6.9 FRN book: schematic of booking cash flows.

(*continued*)

13 This statement holds true in the post-crash environment. The UK building societies that experienced difficulties during 2008–2009 were either taken over by other building societies or, in the case of Dunfermline Building Society, by the UK government. Bondholders did not suffer default losses.

Booking Procedure

The FRN book is held in a separate trading book within the Treasury book, in order to ring-fence the match-funded positions. The booking procedure is shown in Figure 6.9.

Capital and Taxation Issues

There are no taxation issues in the name of XYZ Securities, which is a UK-incorporated legal entity. The capital implications are that the securities are all 20% risk-weighted under Basel I, but retain this risk-weight only if they are rated AA- or better under Basel II.

SOVEREIGN BOND PORTFOLIO FOR INTEREST-RATE HEDGING

Using XYZ Securities again to illustrate policy, we now consider a bond portfolio maintained for ALM hedging purposes by XYZ Treasury. The Treasury desk maintains a book of US Treasury, German Bund and UK gilts. This is also used to facilitate a repo business, as well as reduce the quantity of interest-rate futures needed as part of the interest-rate exposure hedge.

We emphasise that the objective behind this sovereign bond portfolio is to facilitate interest-rate risk hedging: it cannot form part of the liquidity book of the firm because it is funded in repo. For it to also serve as the liquidity reserve of the bank, it would need to be funded with term funds (over 90-day tenor).

Description of the Business

XYZ Treasury is required to fund a large size of the firm-wide funding requirement in term loans, as part of prudent ALM. The resulting DV01 exposure is managed using Eurodollar futures. It has also established a US government bond portfolio as a lower cost means of managing the DV01 risk. The objective is to manage the DV01 exposure of the Treasury book by buying very short-dated Treasury notes and strips, which sets up an income stream that is diversified from other sources and that represents zero credit risk. This is achieved by:

- establishing a portfolio of very short-dated US Treasuries and Treasury strips on the balance sheet (maximum maturity recommended 1–1.5 years, majority in three to six months);

- placing the composition of the book as:
  - 200m, 3-m
  - 300m, 6-m
  - 50m, 1-year;
- having the average maturity of portfolio at around the 6-month tenor;
- funding these in Treasury repo, under the standard GMRA legal agreement;[14]
- holding Treasury securities and Treasury strips to maturity to generate a steady income stream. With ultra-short-dated strips, this also benefits from the pull-to-par effect on mark-to-market.

All funding is locked into maturity, thus there is no gap risk.

Objectives of the Business

The sovereign bond book is business that:

- allows XYZ to undertake cheaper hedging of its interest-rate risk (DV01), complementing the standard arrangement using Eurodollar, Euribor and short sterling futures;
- establishes a risk-free portfolio that generates interest income for XYZ;
- enables XYZ to use a AAA risk-free portfolio for use in setting up TRSs and repo lines with market counterparties.

The benefits to XYZ of holding such a portfolio include:

- earning the spread between yield and funding cost; a bonus that is not available when using Eurodollar futures for DV01 hedging, which do not earn any income. XYZ also saves on the commission and margin costs associated with maintaining Eurodollar futures positions;
- using the business to set up dealing relationships with bank counterparties that could then be used as sources of additional funding if required, adding to the diversity of funding (required as part of the Treasury remit);
- assisting Treasury in undertaking ALM objectives through lower cost hedging of DV01 risk, compared to futures, which impose a cost on the book.

Capital and Taxation Issues

Treasury securities are 0% risk-weighted under Basel rules, except where they create DV01 risk when the charge is 0.7%. However, if held for

14 See the author's book *The Global Repo Markets*, also published by John Wiley & Sons (Asia).

interest-rate risk hedging purposes (as is the case here), they may actually reduce overall capital requirements.

Risks

There is no gap funding risk and no credit risk.

As the positions are held on a Trading book, and not the Banking book, they are marked-to-market. The desk expects volatility in short-dated government bonds to be lower than for the term loans they are hedging, but volatility is a risk exposure and there may be periods when the desk will experience mark-to-market losses.

CASE STUDY 6.3 XYZ SECURITIES UK GILT PORTFOLIO

Banks hold their domestic sovereign debt for liquidity and reserve requirements. In the UK commercial banks and building societies are natural holders of gilts, for the following reasons:

- for liquidity purposes, as gilts are the most liquid instruments in the UK market;
- as an instrument in which to invest the firm's capital reserves;
- for income-generation purposes, given the favourable funding costs of gilt repo and the zero credit and liquidity risk (note that gilts funded via repo should not form part of a liquidity reserve, for reasons we discuss in Part III of this book);
- to intermediate between gilt, stock loan and inter-bank markets in CDs;
- to benefit from being long in gilts that go "special" and can be funded cheaper than GC repo;
- to establish an asset pool that receives favourable capital treatment (0% risk-weighted under Basel I and Basel II).

The benefits to XYZ Securities Ltd of holding such a portfolio include some of the above, as well as the following:

- earning the spread between yield and funding cost;
- using the business to set up dealing relationships with bank counterparties that could then be used as sources of additional funding if required, adding to the diversity of funding (required as part of the Treasury remit);
- assisting Treasury to undertake ALM objectives.

Business Line

This is a UK government bond portfolio at XYZ Treasury. The objective is to maintain an income stream that is diversified from current sources and that is also relatively low risk, but stable. This is achieved by:

- establishing a portfolio of very short-dated gilts and gilt strips on the balance sheet (the maximum maturity recommended is one year, the majority in three to six months). The expected makeup of the book might be:
  - 125m, 3-m
  - 200m, 6-m
  - 25m, 1-year
- average maturity of the portfolio in the first year would be around the 6-month mark;
- funding these in gilt repo, under the GMRA agreement and also funding using TRS under ISDA if required;
- the repo funding margin for gilts in the wholesale market, which is often 0%. With zero or a very low margin or "haircut", all positions will be virtually fully funded;
- holding gilts and gilt strips to maturity to generate a steady income stream. With ultra-short-dated strips, we also benefit from the pull-to-par effect.

Market Rates

Table 6.4 shows income yields and funding rates as at 2 June 2004. This shows where value was obtained from holding a book of gilts at that time. For example, all the following positions yielded funding profit:

- holding gilts and funded in GC; depending on the specific stock and the term of funding arranged, a gain ranging from 15 to 50–60 bps;
- holding strips to maturity; for example, a gain of approximately 35 bps for Dec 04 Principal strip at 1-week or 2-week funding. Locked-in funding gain (buy 6-m strip and fund in 6-m) of 9 bps for the Dec 04 strip – this is risk-free income;
- holding strips at 3-, 6- and 9-month maturities as longer dated bills and holding to maturity. Funding will be locked in if available or rolled:

(*continued*)

- for example, as at 2 June 2004, XYZ Securities Ltd purchased the Sep 04 coupon strip at 4.34% and funded in the 1-week term at 4.15% (and ran the resultant funding gap risk – but this gilt had a strong pull-to-par effect. If funding is no longer profitable in the short dates, XYZ would have sold the gilt for a probable realised mark-to-market profit);
- coupon strips are bid for in repo by the main market-makers, thereby reducing liquidity risk in these products;
- taking advantage of special rates for stocks that XYZ was long in. On 2 June 2004, a position in the 9.5% 2005 gilt was funded cheaper due to special status, from 35 bps (down from 50 bps the week before). The 6.75% 2004 gilt was being funded at 100 bps cheaper than GC. So the gain on holding that stock would be significant, as the funding cost in repo would be very low. It would be an objective of the Treasury desk to be aware of stocks expected to go special and act accordingly.

Risks

The principal risk is funding roll-over (gap risk). Where possible, XYZ Treasury would lock in funding with an expected holding period of positions, but will also look to take advantage of markets rates as appropriate and roll over funding. Gap risk will be managed in the normal way as part of overall Treasury operations. Gaps will be put on to reflect the interest-rate and yield curve view of the desk.

There is no credit risk.

The interest-rate risk and gap risk is managed as a standard banking ALM or cash book. The objective is to set up an income stream position at low risk, but if necessary DV01 risk would be managed where deemed necessary using 90-day sterling futures, an OIS or short-dated swaps. XYZ can also sell out of positions where it expects significant market movement (for example, a central bank base rate hike). The main objective, however, is to establish an income stream, in line with a view on short-term interest rates. Hedging would only be carried out when necessary for short-term periods (say, ahead of a data release or anticipated high volatility).

The interest-rate risk for longer dated stocks is shown in Table 6.4, measured as DV01 (dollar-value of loss for 1 bp in yields). Longer dated stocks expose XYZ Securities Ltd to greater interest-rate risk position when marking-to-market.

TABLE 6.4 Market rates as at 2 June 2004.

Market rates

GC rates 2 Jun					
1w	4.15	4.10	4m	4.40	4.30
2w	4.25	4.15	5m	4.43	4.33
3w	4.25	4.15	6m	4.50	4.40
1m	4.15	4.15	9m	4.67	4.57
2m	4.28	4.18	1y	4.78	4.68
3m	4.32	4.22			

Source: Bloomberg

Gilt yields 2 Jun	GRY %	DV01	Special rates
5% Jun 04	5.05		
6T Nov 04	4.33	0.00416	100 basis points
9H Apr 05	4.668	0.00817	30 basis points cheaper than GC
8H Dec 05	4.818	0.014	25 basis points cheaper, down from 1.5%
7T Sep 06	4.945	0.02141	
7H Dec 06	4.966	0.02364	10 basis points

Source: KSBB screens

Gilt strip yields 2 Jun	GRY %	DV01
P Jun 04	3.78	
C Sep 04	4.342	0.00195
C Dec 04	4.509	0.00432
C Mar 05	4.633	0.00664
C Jun 05	4.744	0.00888
C Sep 05	4.829	0.01107
P Dec 05	4.85	0.01321

Source: Bloomberg

REFERENCES

Choudhry, M. (2004), *The Global Repo Markets*, Singapore: John Wiley & Sons.

Choudhry, M. (2007), *Bank Asset and Liability Management*, Singapore: John Wiley & Sons.

Gup, B. E. and Brooks, R. (1993), *Interest Rate Risk Management*, New York: Irwin.

CHAPTER 7

Asset–Liability Management II

In our second chapter on the subject we look further at the art of ALM as essentially one of risk management and capital management. Although the day-to-day activities are run at the desk level, overall direction is given at the highest level of a banking institution. The risk exposures in a banking environment are multi-dimensional, as we have seen they encompass interest-rate risk, liquidity risk, credit risk and operational risk. Interest-rate risk is one type of market risk. Risks associated with moves in interest rates and levels of liquidity[1] are those that result in adverse fluctuations in earnings levels due to changes in market rates and bank funding costs. By definition, banks' earnings levels are highly sensitive to moves in interest rates and the cost of funds in the wholesale market. ALM covers the set of techniques used to manage interest rate and liquidity risks; it also deals with the structure of the bank's balance sheet, which is heavily influenced by funding and regulatory constraints and profitability targets.

In this chapter we review the concept of balance sheet management, the role of the ALM desk, liquidity risk and maturity gap risk. We also review a basic gap report. The increasing use of securitisation and the responsibility of the ALM desk in enhancing the return on assets on the balance sheet are also considered.

INTRODUCTION

One of the major areas of decision-making in a bank involves the maturity of assets and liabilities. Typically, longer term interest rates are higher than shorter term rates; that is, it is common for the yield

1 In this chapter the term *liquidity* is used to refer to funding liquidity.

curve in the short-term (say 0–3-year range) to be positively sloping. To take advantage of this banks usually raise a large proportion of their funds from the short-dated end of the yield curve and lend out these funds for longer maturities at higher rates. The spread between the borrowing and lending rates is in principle the bank's profit. The obvious risk from such a strategy is that the level of short-term rates rises during the term of the loan, so that when the loan is refinanced the bank makes a lower profit or a net loss. Managing this risk exposure is the key function of an ALM desk. As well as managing the interest-rate risk itself, banks also match assets with liabilities – thus locking in a profit – and diversify their loan book, to reduce default risk exposure to one sector of the economy.

Another risk factor is liquidity. From a banking and Treasury point of view the term *liquidity* means funding liquidity, or the "nearness" of money. The most liquid asset is cash money. Banks bear several interrelated liquidity risks, including the risk of being unable to pay depositors on demand, an inability to raise funds in the market at reasonable rates and an insufficient level of funds available with which to make loans. Banks keep only a small portion of their assets in the form of cash, because this earns no return for them. In fact, once they have met the minimum cash level requirement, which is something set by regulation, they will hold assets in the form of other instruments. Therefore the ability to meet deposit withdrawals depends on a bank's ability to raise funds in the market. The market and the public's perception of a bank's financial position heavily influences liquidity.

This is the key issue. In banking, confidence is everything, and the perception of confidence in a bank is vital. If this view is negative, the bank may be unable to raise funds and consequently be unable to meet withdrawals or loan demand. Or, as with Northern Rock in the UK, there may be a run on the bank. Thus liquidity management is running a bank in a way that maintains confidence in its financial position. The assets of the banks that are held in near-cash instruments, such as T-bills and sovereign bonds, must be managed with liquidity considerations in mind.

BASIC CONCEPTS

In the era of stable interest rates that preceded the breakdown of the Bretton Woods agreement, ALM was a more straightforward process, constrained by regulatory restrictions and the saving and borrowing pattern of bank customers.[2] The introduction of the negotiable CD by Citibank in the 1960s enabled banks to diversify both their investment and funding sources. With this there developed the concept of the *interest margin*, which is the spread between the interest earned on assets and that paid on liabilities. This led to the concept of the *interest gap* and the management of the gap, which is the cornerstone of modern-day ALM. The increasing volatility of interest rates, and the rise in absolute levels of rates themselves, made gap management a vital part of running the Banking book. This development meant that banks could no longer rely permanently on the traditional approach of borrowing short (funding short) to lend long, as a rise in the level of short-term rates would result in funding losses. The introduction of derivative instruments such as FRAs and swaps in the early 1980s removed the previous uncertainty and allowed banks to continue the traditional approach while hedging against medium-term uncertainty.

Foundations of ALM

The general term *asset and liability management* entered common usage from the mid-1970s onwards. In the changing interest-rate environment, it became imperative for banks to manage both assets and liabilities simultaneously, in order to minimise interest rate and liquidity risk and maximise interest income. ALM is a key component of any financial institution's overall operating strategy. ALM is defined in terms of four key concepts, which are described below. The first is *liquidity*, which in an ALM context does not refer to the ease with which an asset can be bought or sold in the secondary market, but the ease with which assets can be converted into cash.[3] A bank is required by the regulatory authorities to hold a specified minimum share of its assets in the form of very liquid instruments. Liquidity is very important to any institution that accepts deposits because of the need to meet customer demand for instant-access funds.

2 For instance, in the US banking sector the terms on deposit accounts were fixed by regulation, and there were restrictions on the geographic base of customers and the interest rates that could be offered. Interest-rate volatility was also low. In this environment, ALM consisted primarily of asset management, in which the bank would use depositors' funds to arrange the asset portfolio that was most appropriate for the liability portfolio. This involved little more than setting aside some of the assets in non-interest reserves at the central bank authority and investing the balance in short-term securities, while any surplus outside of this would be lent out at very short-term maturities.

3 The marketability definition of liquidity is also important in ALM. Less liquid financial instruments must offer a yield premium compared to liquid instruments.

In terms of a banking book the most liquid assets are overnight funds, while the least liquid are long-dated non-tradeable assets such as syndicated loans. Short-term assets such as T-bills and CDs are also considered to be liquid.

The second key concept is the money market term structure of interest rates. The shape of the yield curve at any one time, and expectations as to its shape in the short and medium term, impact to a significant extent on the ALM strategy employed by a bank. Market risk in the form of *interest-rate sensitivity* is significant, in the form of present-value sensitivity of specific instruments to changes in the level of interest rates, as well as the sensitivity of floating-rate assets and liabilities to changes in rates. Another key factor is the *maturity profile* of the book. The maturities of assets and liabilities can be matched or unmatched; although the latter is more common the former is not uncommon, depending on the specific strategies that are being employed. Matched assets and liabilities lock in return in the form of the spread between the funding rate and the return on assets. The maturity profile, the absence of a locked-in spread and the yield curve combine to determine the total interest-rate risk of the banking book. The fourth key concept is *default risk*: the risk exposure that borrowers will default on interest or principal payments that are due to the banking institution.

These issues are placed in context in the hypothetical situation described in Example 7.1.

EXAMPLE 7.1 FUNDING CONSIDERATIONS

Assume that a bank may access the markets for 3-month and 6-month funds, whether for funding or investment purposes. The rates for these terms are shown in Table 7.1. Assume no bid–offer spreads. The ALM manager also expects the 3-month Libor rate in three months to be 5.10%. The bank can usually fund its book at Libor, while it is able to lend at Libor plus 1%.

The bank could adopt any of the following strategies, or a combination of them:

- Borrow 3-month funds at 5.50% and lend this out in the 3-month period at 6.50%. This locks in a return of 1% for a 3-month period.

TABLE 7.1 Hypothetical money market rates.

Term	Libor	Bank rate
90-day	5.50%	6.50%
180-day	5.75%	6.75%
Expected 90-day rate in 90 days' time	5.10%	6.10%
3v6 FRA[1]	6.60%	

[1]FRA – forward rate agreement

- Borrow 6-month funds at 5.75% and lend in the 6-month period at 6.75%; again this earns a locked-in spread of 1%.
- Borrow 3-month funds at 5.50% and lend this in the 6-month term at 6.75%. This approach would require the bank to re-fund the loan in three months' time, which it expects to be able to do at 5.10%. This approach locks in a return of 1.25% in the first 3-month period, and an expected return of 1.65% in the second 3-month period. The risk of this tactic is that the 3-month rate in three months does not fall as expected by the ALM manager, reducing profits and possibly leading to loss.
- Borrow in the six months at 5.75% and lend these for a 3-month period at 6.50%. After this period, lend the funds in the 3-month or 6-month period. This strategy does not tally with the ALM manager's view, however, who expects a fall in rates and so should not wish to be long of funds in three months' time.
- Borrow 3-month funds at 5.50% and again lend this in the 6-month period at 6.75%. To hedge the gap risk, the ALM manager simultaneously buys a 3v6 FRA to lock in the 3-month rate in three months' time. The first period spread of 1.25% is guaranteed, but the FRA guarantees only a spread of 15 bps in the second period. This is the cost of the hedge (and also suggests that the market does not agree with the ALM manager's assessment of where rates will be three months from now!), the price the bank must pay for reducing uncertainty – the lower spread return. Alternatively, the bank could lend in the 6-month period, funding initially in the 3-month period, and buy an interest-rate cap with a ceiling rate of 6.60% and pegged to Libor, the rate at which the bank can actually fund its book.

Although simplistic, these scenarios serve to illustrate what is possible, and indeed there are many other strategies that could be

(*continued*)

adopted. The approaches described in the last option show how derivative instruments can be used actively to manage the banking book, and the cost that is associated with employing them.

Liquidity and Gap Management

We noted in Chapter 6 that the simplest approach to ALM is to match assets with liabilities. For a number of reasons, which include the need to meet client demand and to maximise return on capital, this is not practical and banks must adopt more active ALM strategies. One of the most important of these is the role of the gap, and gap management. This term describes the practice of varying the asset and liability gap in response to expectations about the future course of interest rates and the shape of the yield curve. Simply put, this means increasing the gap when interest rates are expected to rise, and decreasing it when rates are expected to decline. The gap here is the difference between floating-rate assets and liabilities, but gap management must also be pursued when one of these elements is at a fixed rate.

Such an approach is of course an art and not a science. Gap management assumes that the ALM manager is proved to be correct in his or her prediction of the future direction of rates and the yield curve. Views that turn out to be incorrect can lead to an unexpected widening or narrowing of the gap spread, and losses. The ALM manager must choose the level of trade-off between risk and return.

Gap management also assumes that the profile of the banking book can be altered with relative ease. This is not always the case, and even today this may still present problems, although the evolution of a liquid market in off-balance sheet interest-rate derivatives has eased this problem somewhat. It is difficult to change the structure of the book over a short period of time, as many loans cannot be liquidated instantly and fixed-rate assets and liabilities cannot always be changed to floating-rate ones. Client relationships must also be observed and maintained – this is a key banking issue. For this reason it is much more common for ALM managers to use off-balance sheet products when dynamically managing the book. For example, FRAs can be used to hedge gap exposure, while interest-rate swaps are used to alter an interest basis from fixed to floating, or vice-versa. The last strategy in Example 7.1 presented the use that could be made of derivatives. The widespread use of derivatives has enhanced the opportunities available to ALM managers, as well as the flexibility with which the banking book can be managed, but it has also contributed to the increase in competition and the reduction in margins and bid–offer spreads.

INTEREST-RATE RISK AND SOURCE

The Banking Book

Traditionally, ALM has been concerned with the banking book. The conventional techniques of ALM were developed for application to a bank's "banking book"; that is, the lending and deposit-taking transactions.[4] The core banking activity will generate either an excess of funds, when the receipt of deposits outweighs the volume of lending the bank has undertaken, or a shortage of funds, when the reverse occurs. This mismatch is balanced via financial transactions in the wholesale market. The banking book generates both interest-rate and liquidity risks, which are then monitored and managed by the ALM desk. Interest-rate risk is the risk that the bank suffers losses due to adverse movements in market interest rates.

Note that the asset side of the banking book, which is the loan portfolio, also generates credit risk.

The ALM desk will be concerned with risk management that focuses on the quantitative management of the liquidity and interest-rate risks inherent in a banking book. The major areas of concern in this regard are:

- *measurement and monitoring of liquidity and interest-rate risk:* this includes setting up targets for earnings and volume of transactions, and setting up and monitoring interest-rate risk limits;
- *funding and control of any constraints on the balance sheet:* this includes liquidity constraints, debt policy and the capital adequacy ratio and solvency;
- *hedging of liquidity and interest-rate risk.*

Of course, these considerations also apply in a trading book environment.

Interest-rate Risk

Put simply, interest-rate risk is defined as the potential impact, adverse or otherwise, on the net asset value of a financial institution's balance sheet and earnings resulting from a change in interest rates. Risk exposure exists whenever there is a maturity date mis-match between assets and liabilities,

4 The technical definition of what goes on the banking book is essentially of assets that are intended to be held to maturity, and which do not re-price (that is, there is no mark-to-market). The assets on the banking book are often referred to as "Loans and Receivables".

or between principal and interest cash flows. Interest-rate risk is not necessarily a negative thing; for instance, changes in interest rates that increase the net asset value of a banking institution would be regarded as positive. For this reason, active ALM seeks at some banks to position a banking book to gain from changes in rates. We split interest-rate risk into two elements: *investment risk* and *income risk*. The first risk type is the term for potential risk exposure arising from changes in the market value of fixed interest-rate cash instruments and off-balance sheet instruments, and is also known as *price risk*. Investment risk is perhaps best exemplified by the change in value of a plain vanilla bond following a change in interest rates, associated with the inverse relationship between changes in rates and the value of fixed income securities. Income risk is the risk of loss of income when there is a non-synchronous change in deposit and funding rates, and it this risk that is known as gap risk.

ALM covering the formulation of interest-rate risk policy is usually the responsibility of the asset–liability committee or ALCO, which is made up of senior management personnel. ALCO sets bank policy for balance sheet management and the likely impact on revenue of various scenarios that it considers may occur. The size of ALCO will depend on the complexity of the balance sheet and products traded, and the amount of management information available on individual products and desks.

The process employed by ALCO for ALM will vary according to the particular internal arrangement of the institution. A common procedure involves a monthly presentation to ALCO of the impact of different interest-rate scenarios on the balance sheet. This presentation may include:

- an analysis of the difference between the actual NII for the previous month and the amount that was forecast at the previous ALCO meeting. This is usually presented as a gap report, broken by maturity buckets and individual products;
- the result of discussion with business unit heads on the basis of the assumptions used in calculating forecasts and impact of interest-rate changes; scenario analysis usually assumes an unchanging book position between now and one month later, which is essentially unrealistic;
- a number of interest-rate scenarios, based on assumptions of (i) what is expected to happen to the shape and level of the yield curve, and (ii) what may happen to the yield curve; for example, extreme scenarios. Essentially, this exercise produces a value for the forecasted NII due to changes in interest rates;
- an update of the latest actual revenue numbers.

Specific new or one-off topics may be introduced at ALCO as circumstances dictate; for example, the presentation of the approval process for the introduction of a new product or business line. The role and responsibility of the bank's ALCO is covered in detail in Chapter 9.

Sources of Interest-rate Risk

Assets on the balance sheet are affected by absolute changes in interest rates, as well as increases in the volatility of interest rates. For instance, fixed-rate assets will fall in value in the event of a rise in rates, while funding costs will rise. This decreases the margins available. We noted that the way to remove this risk was to lock in assets with matching liabilities; however, this is not only not always possible, but also sometimes undesirable, as it prevents the ALM manager from taking a view on the yield curve. In a falling interest-rate environment, deposit-taking institutions may experience a decline in available funds, requiring new funding sources that may be accessed at less favourable terms. Liabilities are also impacted by a changing interest-rate environment.

There are five primary sources of interest-rate risk inherent in an ALM book, which are described below.

Gap risk is the risk that revenue and earnings decline as a result of changes in interest rates, due to the difference in the maturity profile of assets, liabilities and off-balance sheet instruments. Another term for gap risk is *mismatch risk*. An institution with gap risk is exposed to changes in the level of the yield curve, a so-called *parallel shift*, or a change in the shape of the yield curve or *pivotal shift*. Gap risk is measured in terms of short- or long-term risk, which is a function of the impact of rate changes on earnings for a short or long period. Therefore the maturity profile of the book, and the time to maturity of instruments held on the book, will influence whether the bank is exposed to short-term or long-term gap risk.

Yield curve risk is the risk that non-parallel or pivotal shifts in the yield curve cause a reduction in NII. The ALM manager will change the structure of the book to take into account their views on the yield curve. For example, a book with a combination of short-term and long-term asset or liability maturity structures[5] is at risk from a yield curve inversion, sometimes known as a *twist* in the curve.

Basis risk arises from the fact that assets are often priced off one interest rate, while funding is priced off another interest rate. Taken one step

5 This describes a *barbell* structure, although this is really a bond market term.

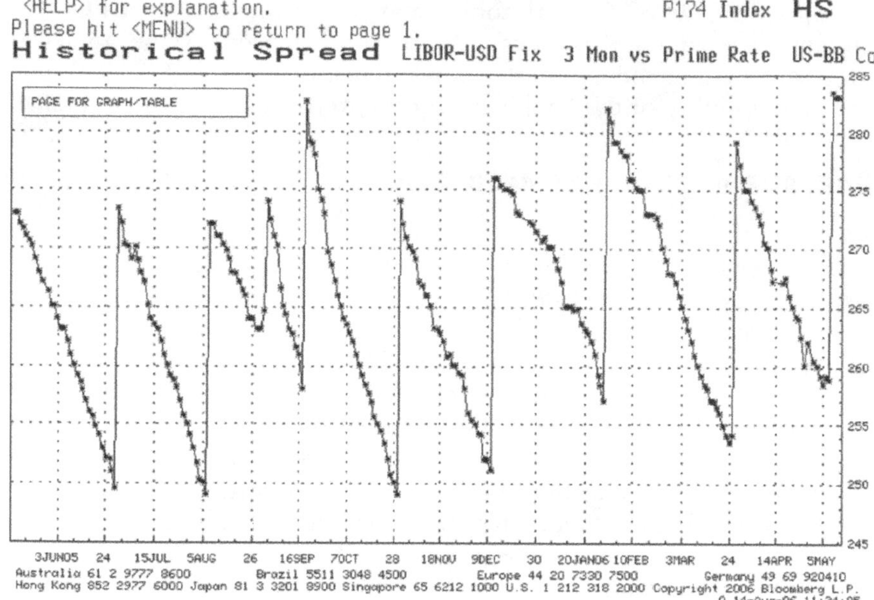

FIGURE 7.1 Change in spread between the 3-month prime rate and 3-month Libor 2005–06.

further, hedge instruments are often linked to a different interest rate to that of the product they are hedging. In the US market the best example of basis risk is the difference between the prime rate and Libor. Term loans in the US are often set at prime, or a relationship to prime, while bank funding is usually based on the Eurodollar market and linked to Libor. However, the prime rate is what is known as an "administered" rate and does not change on a daily basis, unlike Libor. While changes in the two rates are positively correlated, they do not change by the same amount, which means that the spread between them changes regularly. This results in the spread earned on a loan product changing over time. Figure 7.1 illustrates the change in spread during 2005–2006.

Another risk for deposit-taking institutions such as clearing banks is **run-off risk**, associated with the NIBLs of such banks. The level of interest rates at any one time represents an opportunity cost to depositors who have funds in such facilities. However, in a rising interest-rate environment, this opportunity cost rises and depositors will withdraw these funds, available at immediate notice, resulting in an outflow of funds for the bank. The funds may be taken out of the banking system completely; for example, for investment in the stock market. This risk is significant and therefore sufficient funds must be maintained at short notice, which is an opportunity cost for the bank itself.

Many banking products entitle the customer to terminate contractual arrangements ahead of the stated maturity term; this is referred to as **option risk.** This is another significant risk as products such as CDs, cheque account balances and demand deposits can be withdrawn or liquidated at no notice, which is a risk to the level of NII should the option inherent in the products be exercised.

Gap and Net Interest Income

We noted earlier that gap is a measure of the difference in interest-rate sensitivity of assets and liabilities that revalue at a particular date, expressed as a cash value. Put simply it is:

$$Gap = A_{ir} - L_{ir} \tag{7.1}$$

where A_{ir} and L_{ir} are the interest-rate sensitive assets and interest-rate-sensitive liabilities. Where $A_{ir} > L_{ir}$ the banking book is described as being *positively gapped*, and when $A_{ir} < L_{ir}$ the book is said to be *negatively gapped*. The change in NII is given by:

$$\Delta NII = Gap \times \Delta r \tag{7.2}$$

where r is the relevant interest rate used for valuation. The NII of a bank that is positively gapped will increase as interest rates rise, and will decrease as rates decline. This describes a banking book that is asset sensitive; the opposite, when a book is negatively gapped, is known as liability sensitive. The NII of a negatively gapped book will increase when interest rates decline. The value of a book with zero gap is immune to changes in the level of interest rates. The shape of the banking book at any one time is a function of customer demand, and the treasury manager's operating strategy and view of future interest rates.

Gap analysis is used to measure the difference between interest-rate-sensitive assets and liabilities over specified time periods. Another term for this analysis is *periodic gap*, and the common expression for each time period is maturity bucket. For a commercial bank the typical maturity buckets might be:

- 0–3 months;
- 3–6 months;
- 6–12 months;
- 1–2 years;
- 2–5 years;
- > 5 years.

Another common approach is to group assets and liabilities by the buckets or grid points of the RiskMetrics VaR methodology. Any combination of time periods may be used, however. For instance, certain US commercial banks place assets, liabilities and off-balance sheet items in terms of *known maturities*, *judgemental maturities* and *market-driven maturities*. These are defined as:

- *known maturities*: fixed-rate loans and CDs;
- *judgemental maturities*: passbook savings accounts, demand deposits, credit cards, and NPLs;
- *market-driven maturities*: option-based instruments such as mortgages, and other interest-rate sensitive assets.

The other key measure is *cumulative gap*, defined as the sum of the individual gaps up to 1-year maturity. Banks traditionally use the cumulative gap to estimate the impact of a change in interest rates on NII.

Assumptions of Gap Analysis

A number of assumptions are made when using gap analysis, assumptions that may not reflect reality in practice. These include:

- the key assumption that interest rate changes manifest themselves as a parallel shift in the yield curve; in practice, changes do not occur as a parallel shift, giving rise to basis risk between short-term and long-term assets;
- the expectation that contractual repayment schedules are met; if there is a fall in interest rates, prepayments of loans by borrowers who wish to refinance their loans at lower rates will have an impact on NII. Certain assets and liabilities have option features that are exercised as interest

rates change, such as LOCs and variable rate deposits; early repayment will impact a bank's cash flow;

- that re-pricing of assets and liabilities takes place in the mid-point of the time bucket;
- the expectation that all loan payments will occur on schedule; in practice, certain borrowers will repay the loan earlier.

Recognised weaknesses of the gap approach include:

- no incorporation of future growth, or changes in the asset–liability mix;
- no consideration of the time value of money;
- arbitrary setting of time periods.

Limitations notwithstanding, gap analysis is used extensively. Gup and Brooks (1993, p. 59) is a relatively old textbook (but still a very valuable one), and the authors' stated reasons for the continued popularity of gap analysis remain current:

- it was the first approach introduced to handle interest-rate risk, and provides reasonable accuracy;
- the data required to perform the analysis are already compiled for the purposes of regulatory reporting;
- the gaps can be calculated using simple spreadsheet software;
- it is easier (and cheaper) to implement than more sophisticated techniques;
- it is straightforward to demonstrate and explain to senior management and shareholders.

Although there are more sophisticated methods available, gap analysis remains in widespread use.

THE ALM DESK

The ALM desk or unit is a specialised business unit that fulfils a range of functions. Its precise remit is a function of the type of the activities of the financial institution that it is a part of.

If an ALM unit has a profit target of zero, it will act, in effect, as a cost centre with a responsibility to minimise operating costs. This would be consistent with a strategy that emphasises commercial banking as the core business of the firm, and where ALM policy is concerned purely with hedging interest-rate and liquidity risk.

The next level is where the ALM unit is responsible for minimising the cost of funding. That would allow the unit to maintain an element of exposure to interest-rate risk, depending on the view that was held as to the future level of interest rates. As we noted above, core banking activity generates either an excess or shortage of funds. To hedge away all of the excess or shortage, while removing interest-rate exposure, has an opportunity cost associated with it since it eliminates any potential gain that might arise from movements in market rates. Of course, without a complete hedge, there is an exposure to interest-rate risk. The ALM desk is responsible for monitoring and managing this risk, and of course is credited with any cost savings in the cost of funds that arise from the exposure. The saving may be measured as the difference between the funding costs of a full hedging policy and the actual policy that the ALM desk adopts. Under this policy, interest-rate risk limits are set, which the ALM desk ensures the bank's operations do not breach.

The final stage of development is to turn the ALM unit into a profit centre, with responsibility for optimising the funding policy within specified limits. The limits may be set as gap limits, VaR limits or by another measure, such as level of earnings volatility. Under this scenario the ALM desk is responsible for managing all financial risk.

The final development of the ALM function has resulted in it taking on a more active role. The previous paragraphs described the three stages of development that ALM has undergone, although all three versions are part of the "traditional" approach. Practitioners now think of ALM as extending beyond the risk management field, and responsible for adding value to the net worth of the bank, through proactive positioning of the book and hence, the balance sheet. That is, in addition to the traditional function of managing liquidity risk and interest-rate risk, ALM should be concerned with managing the regulatory capital of the bank and with actively positioning the balance sheet to maximise profit. The latest developments mean that the there are now financial institutions that run a much more sophisticated ALM operation than that associated with a traditional banking book.

We consider next the traditional elements of an ALM function.

Traditional ALM

Generally, a bank's ALM function has in the past been concerned with managing the risk associated with the banking book. Since then, additional functions have been added to the ALM role. There are a large number of financial institutions that adopt the traditional approach; indeed, the nature of their operations would not lend themselves to anything more. We can summarise the role of the traditional ALM desk as follows:

- **Interest-rate risk management.** This is the interest-rate risk arising from the operation of the banking book. It includes net interest income sensitivity analysis, typified by maturity gap and duration gap analysis, and the sensitivity of the book to parallel changes in the yield curve. The ALM desk will monitor the exposure and position the book in accordance with the limits as well as its market view. Smaller banks, or subsidiaries of banks that are based overseas, often run no interest-rate risk; that is, there is no short gap in their book. Otherwise the ALM desk is responsible for hedging the interest-rate risk or positioning the book in accordance with its view.
- **Liquidity and funding management.** There are regulatory requirements that dictate the proportion of banking assets that must be held as short-term instruments. The liquidity book in a bank is responsible for running the portfolio of short-term instruments. The exact makeup of the book is, however, the responsibility of the ALM desk, and will be a function of the bank's funding costs, its view of market interest rates, as well as its opinion on the relative value of one asset over another. For example, it may decide to move some assets into short-dated government bonds, above what it normally holds, at the expense of high-quality CDs, or vice-versa.
- **Reporting on hedging of risks.** The ALM desk fulfils a senior MI function by reporting on a regular basis on the extent of the bank's risk exposure. This may be in the form of a weekly hardcopy report, or via some other medium.
- **Setting up risk limits.** The ALM unit will set limits, implement them and enforce them, although it is common for an independent "middle office" risk function to monitor compliance with limits.
- **Capital requirement reporting.** This function involves the compilation of reports on capital usage and position limits as a percentage of capital allowed, and the reporting to regulatory authorities.

All financial institutions must carry out the activities described above.

EXAMPLE 7.2 GAP ANALYSIS SUMMARY

Maturity gap analysis measures the cash difference or gap between the absolute values of the assets and liabilities that are sensitive to movements in interest rates. Therefore the analysis measures the relative interest-rate sensitivities of the assets and liabilities, and thus determines the risk profile of the bank with respect to changes in rates. The gap ratio is given as (7.3):

$$\textit{Gap ratio} = \frac{\textit{Interest-rate sensitive assets}}{\textit{Interest-rate sensitive liabilities}} \tag{7.3}$$

and measures whether there are more interest-rate sensitive assets than liabilities. A gap ratio higher than one, for example, indicates that a rise in interest rates will increase the NPV of the book, thus raising the return on assets at a rate higher than the rise in the cost of funding. This also results in a higher income spread. A gap ratio lower than one indicates a rising funding cost. *Duration gap* analysis measures the impact on the net worth of the bank due to changes in interest rates by focusing on changes in market value of either assets or liabilities. This is because duration measures the percentage change in the market value of a single security for a 1% change in the underlying yield of the security (strictly speaking, this is *modified duration* but the term for the original "duration" measure is now almost universally used to refer to modified duration). The duration gap is defined as (7.4):

$$\textit{Duration gap} = \textit{Duration of assets} - w(\textit{Duration of liabilities}) \tag{7.4}$$

where w is the percentage of assets funded by liabilities. Hence, the duration gap measures the effects of the change in the net worth of the bank. A higher duration gap indicates a higher interest rate exposure. As duration only measures the effects of a linear change in the interest rate – that is, a parallel shift yield curve change – banks with portfolios that include a significant amount of instruments with elements of optionality, such as callable bonds, ABSs and convertibles, also use the *convexity* measure of risk exposure to adjust for the inaccuracies that arise in duration over large yield changes.

LIQUIDITY AND INTEREST-RATE RISK

The Liquidity Gap

Liquidity risk arises because a bank's portfolio will consist of assets and liabilities with different sizes and maturities. When assets are greater than resources from operations, a funding gap will exist that is usually sourced in the wholesale market. When the opposite occurs, the excess resources must be invested in the market. The differences between the assets and liabilities is the liquidity gap. For example, if a bank has long-term commitments that have arisen from its dealings and its resources are exceeded by these commitments, and have a shorter maturity, there is both an immediate and a future deficit. The liquidity risk for the bank is that, at any time, there are not enough resources, or funds available in the market, to balance the assets.

Liquidity management has several objectives; possibly the most important is to ensure that deficits can be funded under all foreseen circumstances, and without incurring prohibitive costs. In addition, there are regulatory requirements that force a bank to operate certain limits, and state that short-term assets be in excess of short-run liabilities, in order to provide a safety net of highly liquid assets. Liquidity management is also concerned with funding deficits and investing surpluses, with managing and growing the balance sheet, and with ensuring that the bank operates within regulatory and in-house limits. In this section we review the main issues concerned with liquidity and interest-rate risk.

The liquidity gap is the difference, at all future dates, between assets and liabilities of the banking portfolio. Gaps generate liquidity risk. When liabilities exceed assets, there is an excess of funds. An excess does not of course generate liquidity risk, but it does generate interest-rate risk, because the present value of the book is sensitive to changes in market rates. When assets exceed liabilities, there is a funding deficit and the bank has long-term commitments that are not currently funded by existing operations. The liquidity risk is that the bank requires funds at a future date to match the assets. The bank is able to remove any liquidity risk by locking in maturities, but of course there is a cost involved as it will be dealing at longer maturities.[6]

Gap Risk and Limits

Liquidity gaps are measured by taking the difference between outstanding balances of assets and liabilities over time. At any point a positive gap

6 This assumes a conventional upward-sloping yield curve.

between assets and liabilities is equivalent to a deficit, and this is measured as a cash amount. The *marginal gap* is the difference between the changes of assets and liabilities over a given period. A positive marginal gap means that the variation of value of assets exceeds the variation of value of liabilities. As new assets and liabilities are added over time, as part of the ordinary course of business, the gap profile changes.

The gap profile is tabulated or charted (or both) during and at the end of each day as a primary measure of risk. For illustration, a tabulated gap report is shown in Table 7.2 and is an actual example from a UK banking institution. It shows the assets and liabilities grouped into maturity buckets and the net position for each bucket. It is a snapshot today of the exposure, and hence funding requirement of the bank for future maturity periods.

Table 7.2 is very much a summary report, because the maturity gaps are very wide. For risk management purposes the buckets would be much narrower; for instance, the period between zero and 12 months might be split into 12 different maturity buckets. An example of a more detailed gap report is shown in Table 7.3, which is from another UK banking institution. Note that the overall net position is zero, because this is a balance sheet and therefore, not surprisingly, it balances. However, along the maturity buckets or grid points there are net positions which are the gaps that need to be managed.

Limits on a banking book can be set in terms of gap limits. For example, a bank may set a 6-month gap limit of £10 million. The net position of assets and maturities expiring in six months' time could then not exceed £10 million. An example of a gap limit report is shown at Figure 7.2, with the actual net gap positions shown against the gap limits for each maturity. Again this is an actual limit report from a UK banking institution.

The maturity gap can be charted to provide an illustration of net IR exposure, and an example is shown at Figure 7.3, from another UK banking institution. In some firms' reports both the assets and the liabilities are shown for each maturity point, but in our example only the net position is shown. This net position is the gap exposure for that maturity point. A second example, used by the overseas subsidiary of a Middle Eastern commercial bank, which has no funding lines in the inter-bank market and so does not run short positions, is shown in Figure 7.4, while the gap report for a UK high-street bank is shown in Figure 7.5. Note the large short gap under the maturity labelled "non-int"; this stands for *non-interest-bearing liabilities* and represents the balance of current accounts (cheque or "checking" accounts), which are funds that attract no interest and are in theory very short-dated (because they are demand deposits, so may be called at instant notice).

TABLE 7.2 Example gap profile, UK bank.

	Time periods											
	Total		0–6 months		6–12 months		1–3 years		3–7 years		7+ years	
Assets	40,533	6.17%	28,636	6.08%	3,801	6.12%	4,563	6.75%	2,879	6.58%	654	4.47%
Liabilities	40,533	4.31%	30,733	4.04%	3,234	4.61%	3,005	6.29%	2,048	6.54%	1,513	2.21%
Net cumulative positions	0		(2,097)		567		1,558		831		(859)	
Margin on total assets:			2.58%									
Average margin on total assets:			2.53%									

TABLE 7.3 Detailed interest-rate gap profile, UK bank.

ASSETS	Total (£m)	Up to 1 month	1–3 months	3–6 months	6 months to 1 year
Cash & inter-bank loans	2,156.82	1,484.73	219.36	448.99	3.84
CDs purchased	1,271.49	58.77	132.99	210.26	776.50
FRNs purchased	936.03	245.62	586.60	12.68	26.13
Bank bills	314.35	104.09	178.36	31.90	0.00
Other loans	13.00	0.00	1.00	0.00	0.00
Debt securities/gilts	859.45	0.00	25.98	7.58	60.05
Fixed-rate mortgages	4,180.89	97.72	177.37	143.13	964.98
Variables & capped rate mortgages	14,850.49	14,850.49	0.00	0.00	0.00
Commercial loans	271.77	96.62	96.22	56.52	0.86
Unsecured lending and leasing	3,720.13	272.13	1,105.20	360.03	507.69
Other assets	665.53	357.72	0.00	18.77	5.00
	29,239.95	17,567.91	2,523.06	1,289.77	2,345.05
Swaps	9,993.28	3,707.34	1,462.32	1,735.59	1,060.61
FRAs	425.00	0.00	50.00	0.00	220.00
Futures	875.00	0.00	300.00	0.00	175.00
TOTAL	40,533.24	21,275.24	4,335.38	3,025.36	3,800.66
LIABILITES (£m)					
Bank deposits	3,993.45	2,553.85	850.45	233.03	329.06
CDs Issued	1,431.42	375.96	506.76	154.70	309.50
CP & Euro	508.46	271.82	128.42	108.21	0.00
Subordinated debt	275.00	0.00	0.00	0.00	0.00
Eurobonds + other	2,582.24	768.75	1,231.29	121.94	53.86
Customer deposits	17,267.55	15,493.65	953.60	311.70	340.50
Other liabilities (incl capital/reserves)	3,181.83	1,336.83	0.00	0.00	741.72
	29,239.96	20,800.86	3,670.52	929.58	1,774.64
Swaps	9,993.28	1,754.70	1,657.59	1,399.75	1,254.24
FRAs	425.00	0.00	150.00	70.00	55.00
Futures	875.00	0.00	0.00	300.00	150.00
TOTAL	40,533.24	22,555.56	5,478.11	2,699.33	3,233.89
Net Positions	0.00	−1,351.09	−1,234.54	265.58	583.48

1–2 years	2–3 years	3–4 years	4–5 years	5–6 years	6–7 years	7–8 years	8–9 years	9–10 years	10+ years
0.00	0.00	0.00	0.00	0.00	0.00	0.00	0.00	0.00	0.00
92.96	0.00	0.00	0.00	0.00	0.00	0.00	0.00	0.00	0.00
45.48	0.00	0.00	19.52	0.00	0.00	0.00	0.00	0.00	0.00
0.00	0.00	0.00	0.00	0.00	0.00	0.00	0.00	0.00	0.00
7.00	0.00	1.00	0.00	0.00	2.00	2.00	0.00	0.00	0.00
439.06	199.48	26.81	100.50	0.00	0.00	0.00	0.00	0.00	0.00
1,452.91	181.86	661.36	450.42	22.78	4.30	3.65	3.10	2.63	14.67
0.00	0.00	0.00	0.00	0.00	0.00	0.00	0.00	0.00	0.00
2.16	1.12	3.64	8.85	1.06	0.16	0.17	0.16	4.23	0.00
694.86	400.84	195.19	79.98	25.45	14.06	10.03	10.44	10.82	33.42
0.00	0.00	0.00	0.00	0.00	0.00	0.00	0.00	0.00	284.03
2,734.43	783.31	888.00	659.26	49.28	20.53	15.85	13.71	17.68	332.12
344.00	146.50	537.60	649.00	70.00	5.32	200.00	75.00	0.00	0.00
5.00	150.00	0.00	0.00	0.00	0.00	0.00	0.00	0.00	0.00
400.00	0.00	0.00	0.00	0.00	0.00	0.00	0.00	0.00	0.00
3,483.43	1,079.81	1,425.60	1,308.26	119.28	25.84	215.85	88.71	17.68	332.12
21.07	1.00	0.00	5.00	0.00	0.00	0.00	0.00	0.00	0.00
60.00	20.00	3.50	1.00	0.00	0.00	0.00	0.00	0.00	0.00
0.00	0.00	0.00	0.00	0.00	0.00	0.00	0.00	0.00	0.00
0.00	0.00	0.00	0.00	0.00	0.00	200.00	75.00	0.00	0.00
9.77	13.16	150.43	150.53	0.00	7.51	0.00	0.00	0.00	75.00
129.10	6.60	24.90	0.00	7.50	0.00	0.00	0.00	0.00	0.00
0.00	0.00	0.00	0.00	0.00	0.00	0.00	0.00	0.00	1,103.28
219.93	40.76	178.83	156.53	7.50	7.51	200.00	75.00	0.00	1,178.28
1,887.97	281.44	905.06	770.52	15.76	6.48	7.27	8.13	13.06	31.30
150.00	0.00	0.00	0.00	0.00	0.00	0.00	0.00	0.00	0.00
425.00	0.00	0.00	0.00	0.00	0.00	0.00	0.00	0.00	0.00
2,682.90	322.20	1,083.90	927.05	23.26	13.99	207.27	83.13	13.06	1,209.58
929.10	803.46	341.70	404.88	104.28	11.85	8.58	5.57	4.62	−877.45

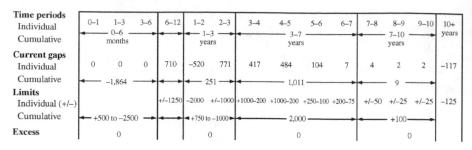

Time periods														
Individual	0–1	1–3	3–6	6–12	1–2	2–3	3–4	4–5	5–6	6–7	7–8	8–9	9–10	10+ years
Cumulative	0–6 months				1–3 years		3–7 years				7–10 years			
Current gaps														
Individual	0	0	0	710	–520	771	417	484	104	7	4	2	2	–117
Cumulative	–1,864				251		1,011				9			
Limits														
Individual (+/–)				+/–1250	–2000	+/–1000	+1000–200	+1000–200	+250–100	+200–75	+/–50	+/–25	+/–25	–125
Cumulative	+500 to –2500				+750 to –1000		2,000				+100			
Excess	0				0		0				0			

FIGURE 7.2 Gap limit report.

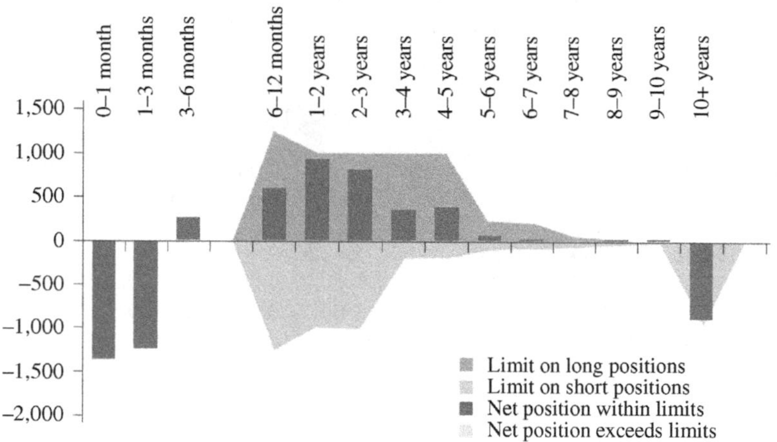

FIGURE 7.3 Gap maturity profile in graphical form.

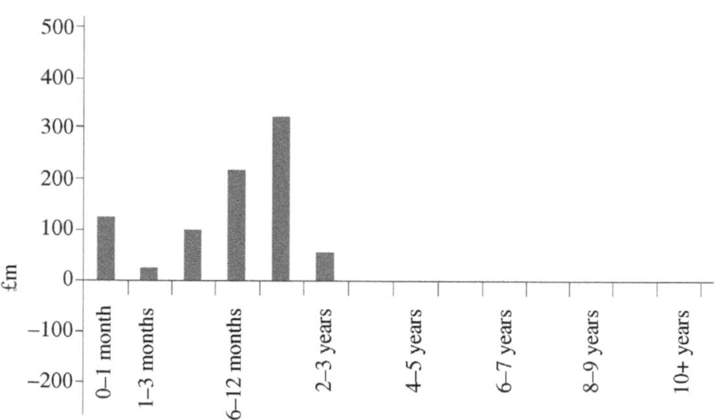

FIGURE 7.4 Gap maturity profile, bank subsidiary with no short funding allowed.

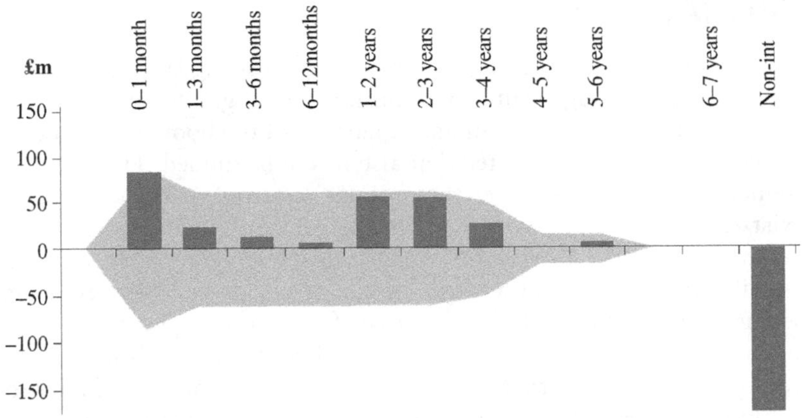

FIGURE 7.5 Gap maturity profile, UK high-street bank.

Gaps represent cumulative funding required at all dates. The cumulative funding is not necessarily identical to the new funding required at each period, because the debt issued in previous periods is not necessarily amortised at subsequent periods. The new funding between, for example, months 3 and 4 is not the accumulated deficit between months 2 and 4 because the debt contracted at month 3 is not necessarily amortised at month 4. Marginal gaps may be identified as the new funding required or the new excess funds of the period that should be invested in the market. Note that all the reports are snapshots at a fixed point in time and the picture is of course a continuously moving one. In practice the liquidity position of a bank cannot be characterised by one gap at any given date, and the entire gap profile must be used to gauge the extent of the book's profile.

The liquidity book may decide to match its assets with its liabilities. This is known as cash matching and occurs when the time profiles of both assets and liabilities are identical. By following such a course the bank can lock in the spread between its funding rate and the rate at which it lends cash, and run a guaranteed profit. Under cash matching, the liquidity gaps will be zero. Matching the profile of both legs of the book is done at the overall level; that is, cash matching does not mean that deposits should always match loans. This would be difficult as both result from customer demand, although an individual purchase of, say, a CD can be matched with an identical loan. Nevertheless, the bank can elect to match assets and liabilities once the net position is known, and keep the book matched at all times. However, it is highly unusual for a bank to adopt a cash matching strategy.

Liquidity Management

The continuous process of raising new funds or investing surplus funds is known as liquidity management. If we consider that a gap today is funded, thus balancing assets and liabilities and squaring-off the book, the next day a new deficit or surplus is generated that also has to be funded. The liquidity management decision must cover the amount required to bridge the gap that exists the following day, as well as position the book across future dates in line with the bank's view on interest rates. Usually in order to define the maturity structure of debt a target profile of resources is defined. This may be done in several ways. If the objective of ALM is to replicate the asset profile with resources, the new funding should contribute to bringing the resources profile closer to that of the assets; that is, more of a matched book looking forward. This is the lowest risk option. Another target profile may be imposed on the bank by liquidity constraints. This may arise if, for example, the bank has a limit on borrowing lines in the market so that it could not raise above a certain amount each week or month. For instance, if the maximum that could be raised in one week by a bank is £10 million, the maximum period liquidity gap is constrained by that limit. The ALM desk will manage the book in line with the target profile that has been adopted, which requires it to try to reach the required profile over a given time horizon.

Figure 7.6 is a liquidity analysis for a UK bank, showing the maturity of funding going forward and where liquidity requirements arise.

Managing the banking book's liquidity is a dynamic process, as loans and deposits are known at any given point, but new business will be taking

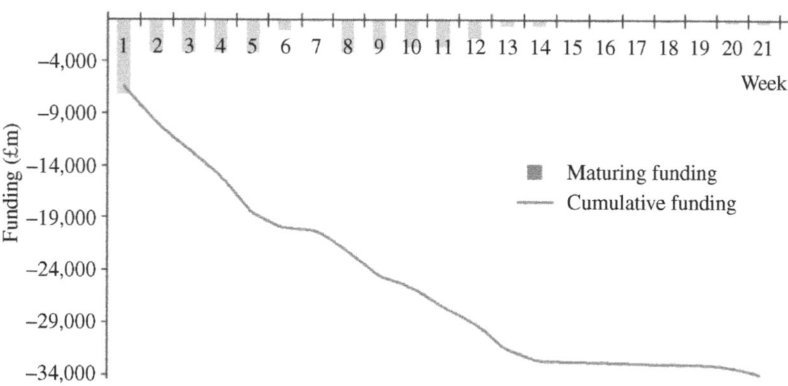

FIGURE 7.6 Liquidity analysis – example of UK bank profile of maturity of funding.

place continuously and the profile of the book looking forward must be continuously re-balanced to keep it within the target profile. There are several factors that influence this dynamic process, the most important of which are reviewed below.

Demand Deposits

Deposits placed on demand at the bank, have no stated maturity and are available on demand at the bank. Technically they are referred to as "non-interest-bearing liabilities" because the bank pays no or very low rates of interest on them, so they are effectively free funds. The balance of these funds can increase or decrease throughout the day without any warning, although in practice the balance is quite stable. There are a number of ways that a bank can choose to deal with these balances. These are:

- to group all outstanding balances into one maturity bucket at a future date that is the preferred time horizon of the bank, or a date beyond this. This would then exclude them from the gap profile. Although this is considered unrealistic because it excludes the current account balances from the gap profile, it is nevertheless a fairly common approach;
- to rely on an assumed rate of amortisation for the balances, say 5% or 10% each year;
- to divide deposits into stable and unstable balances, of which the core deposits are set as a permanent balance. The amount of the core balance is set by the bank based on a study of the total balance volatility pattern over time; for example, the last five years. The excess over the core balance is then viewed as very short-term debt. This method is reasonably close to reality, as it is based on historical observations;
- to make projections based on observable variables that are correlated with the outstanding balances of deposits. For instance, such variables could be based on the level of economic growth plus an error factor based on the short-term fluctuations in the growth pattern.

Pre-set Contingencies

A bank will have committed lines of credit, the utilisation of which depends on customer demand. Contingencies generate outflows of funds that are by definition uncertain, as they are contingent upon some event; for example, the willingness of the borrower to use a committed line of credit. The usual way for a bank to deal with these unforeseen fluctuations is to use statistical data based on past observation to project a future level of activity.

Prepayment Options of Existing Assets

Where the maturity schedule is stated in the terms of a loan, it may still be subject to uncertainty because of prepayment options. This is similar to the prepayment risk associated with a mortgage-backed bond. An element of prepayment risk renders the actual maturity profile of a loan book to be uncertain; banks often calculate an "effective maturity schedule" based on prepayment statistics instead of the theoretical schedule. There are also a range of prepayment models that may be used, the simplest of which use constant prepayment ratios to assess the average life of the portfolio. The more sophisticated models incorporate further parameters, such as one that bases the prepayment rate on the interest rate differential between the loan rate and the current market rate, or the time elapsed since the loan was taken out.

Interest Cash Flows

Assets and liabilities generate interest cash inflows and outflows, as well as the amortisation of principal. The interest payments must be included in the gap profile as well.

Interest-rate Gap

The interest-rate gap is the standard measure of the exposure of the banking book to interest-rate risk. The interest-rate gap for a given period is defined as the difference between fixed-rate assets and fixed-rate liabilities. It can also be calculated as the difference between interest-rate sensitive assets and interest-rate liabilities. Both differences are identical in value when total assets are equal to total liabilities, but will differ when the balance sheet is not balanced. This only occurs intra-day, when, for example, a short position has not been funded yet. The general market practice is to calculate interest-rate gap as the difference between assets and liabilities. The gap is defined in terms of the maturity period that has been specified for it.

The convention for calculating gaps is important for interpretation. The "fixed-rate" gap is the opposite of the "variable-rate" gap when assets and liabilities are equal. They differ when assets and liabilities do not match and there are many reference rates. When there is a deficit, the "fixed-rate gap" is consistent with the assumption that the gap will be funded through liabilities for which the rate is unknown. This funding is then a variable-rate liability and is the bank's risk, unless the rate has been locked in beforehand. The same assumption applies when the bank runs a cash surplus position, and the interest rate for any period in the future is unknown. The gap position at a given time bucket is sensitive to the interest rate that appliesto that period.

The gap is calculated for each discrete time bucket, so there is a net exposure for, say, 0–1 month, 1–3 months and so on. Loans and deposits do not, except at the time of being originated, have precise maturities like that, so they are "mapped" to a time bucket in terms of their relative weighting. For example, a £100 million deposit that matures in 20 days' time will have most of its balance mapped to the 3-week time bucket, but a smaller amount will also be allocated to the 2-week bucket. Interest-rate risk is measured as the change in present value of the deposit, at each grid point, given a 1 bp change in the interest rate. So a £10 million 1-month CD that was bought at 6.50% will have its present value move upwards if on the next day the 1-month rate moves down by a basis point.

The net change in present value for a 1 bp move is the key measure of interest-rate risk for a banking book, and this is what is usually referred to as a "gap report", although strictly speaking it is not. The correct term for such a report is a "PVBP" or "DV01" report, which are acronyms for "present value of a basis point" and "dollar value of a 01 [1 basis point]" respectively. The calculation of interest-rate sensitivity assumes a parallel shift in the yield curve; that is, that every maturity point along the term structure moves by the same amount (here 1 bp) and in the same direction. An example of a PVBP report is given in Table 7.4, split by different currency books, but with all values converted to sterling.

The basic concept in the gap report is the NPV of the banking book, which is introduced in Appendix 7.1. The PVBP report measures the difference between the market values of assets and liabilities in the banking book. To calculate NPV we require a discount rate, and it represents a

TABLE 7.4 Banking book PVBP grid report.

	1 day	1 week	1 month	2 months	3 months	6 months	12 months	2 years
GBP	8,395	6,431	9,927	8,856	(20,897)	(115,303)	(11,500)	(237,658)
USD	1,796	(903)	10,502	12,941	16,784	17,308	(13,998)	(18,768)
Euro	1,026	1,450	5,105	2,877	(24,433)	(24,864)	(17,980)	(9,675)
Total	11,217	6,978	25,534	24,674	(28,546)	(122,859)	(43,478)	(266,101)

	3 years	4 years	5 years	7 years	10 years	15 years	20 years	30 years
GBP	(349,876)	(349,654)	5,398	(5,015)	(25,334)	(1,765)	(31,243)	(50,980)
USD	(66,543)	(9,876)	(1,966)	237	2,320	(5,676)	(1,121)	0
Euro	(11,208)	(3,076)	1,365	1,122	3,354	(545)	(440)	(52)
Total	(427,627)	(362,606)	4,797	(3,656)	(19,660)	(7,986)	(32,804)	(51,032)

GBP total: (1,160,218); USD total: (56,963); Euro total: (75,974); Grand total: (1,293,155) All figures in £.

mark-to-market of the book. The rates used are always the zero-coupon rates derived from the government bond yield curve, although an adjustment is sometimes made to this to allow for individual instruments.

Gaps may be calculated as differences between outstanding balances at one given date, or as differences of variations of those balances over a time period. A gap number calculated from variations is known as a *margin gap*. The cumulative margin gaps over a period of time, plus the initial difference in assets and liabilities at the beginning of the period are identical to the gaps between assets and liabilities at the end of the period.

The interest-rate gap differs from the liquidity gap in a number of ways; note that:

- whereas for liquidity gap all assets and liabilities must be accounted for, only those that have a fixed rate are used for the interest-rate gap;
- the interest-rate gap cannot be calculated unless a period has been defined because of the fixed-rate/variable-rate distinction. The interest-rate gap is dependent on a maturity period and an original date.

The primary purpose in compiling the gap report is to determine the sensitivity of the interest margin to changes in interest rates. As we noted earlier the measurement of the gap is always "behind the curve" as it is a historical snapshot; the actual gap is a dynamic value as the banking book continually undertakes day-to-day business.

Portfolio Modified Duration Gap

Modified duration measures the change in the market price of a financial instrument that results from a given change in market interest rates. The duration gap of a net portfolio value is a measure of the interest-rate sensitivity of a portfolio of financial instruments and is the difference between the weighted-average duration of assets and liabilities, adjusted for the net duration of any off-balance sheet instruments. Hence it measures the percentage change in the net portfolio value that is expected to occur if interest rates change by 1%.

The net portfolio value, given by the NPV of the book, is the market value of assets A minus the market value of the liabilities L, plus or minus the market value OBS of off-balance sheet instruments, shown by (7.5):

$$NPV = A - L \pm OBS. \tag{7.5}$$

To calculate the duration gap of the NPV, we obtain the modified duration of each instrument in the portfolio and weight this by the ratio of its market value to the net value of the portfolio. This is done for assets, liabilities and off-balance sheet instruments. The modified duration of the portfolio is given by (7.6):

$$MD_{NPV} = MD_A - MD_L \pm MD_{OBS}. \tag{7.6}$$

The modified duration of the NPV may be used to estimate the expected change in the market value of the portfolio for a given change in interest rates, shown by (7.7):

$$\Delta NPV = NPV - MD_{NPV} \times \Delta r. \tag{7.7}$$

It is often problematic to obtain an accurate value for the market value of every instrument in a banking book. In practice book values are used to calculate the duration gap when market values are not available. This may result in inaccurate results when actual market values differ from book values by a material amount.

The other points to note about duration gap analysis are:

- the analysis uses modified duration to calculate the change in NPV and therefore provides an accurate estimate of price sensitivity of instruments for only small changes in interest rates. For a change in rates of more than, say, 50 bps the sensitivity measure given by modified duration will be significantly in error;
- the duration gap analysis, like the maturity gap model, assumes that interest rates change in a parallel shift, which is clearly unrealistic.

As with the maturity gap analysis, the duration gap is favoured in ALM application because it is easily understood and summarises a banking book's interest-rate exposure in one convenient number.

CRITIQUE OF THE TRADITIONAL APPROACH

Traditionally, the main approach of ALM is concentrated on the interest sensitivity and NPV sensitivity of a bank's loan/deposit book. The usual interest sensitivity report is the maturity gap report, which we reviewed earlier. The maturity gap report is not perfect, however, and can be said to have the following drawbacks:

- the repricing intervals chosen for gap analysis are ultimately arbitrary, and there may be significant mismatches within a repricing interval. For instance, a common repricing interval chosen is the 1-year gap and the 1–3-year gap; there are (albeit extreme) circumstances when mismatches would go undetected by the model. Consider a banking book that is composed solely of liabilities that reprice in one month's

time, and an equal cash value of assets that reprice in 11 months' time. The 1-year gap of the book (assuming no other positions) would be zero, implying no risk to net interest income. In fact, under our scenario the net interest income is significantly at risk from a rise in interest rates;
- maturity gap models assume that interest rates change by a uniform magnitude and direction. For any given change in the general level of interest rates, however, it is more realistic for different maturity interest rates to change by different amounts, what is known as a non-parallel shift;
- maturity gap models assume that principal cash flows do not change when interest rates change. Therefore it is not possible effectively to incorporate the impact of options embedded in certain financial instruments. Instruments such as mortgage-backed bonds and convertibles do not fall accurately into a gap analysis, as only their first-order risk exposure is captured.

Notwithstanding these drawbacks, the gap model is widely used as it is easily understood in the commercial banking industry, and its application does not require a knowledge of sophisticated financial modelling techniques.

THE COST OF FUNDING

Banks can choose to set up their Treasury function as either a cost centre or a profit centre. Most of the discussion up to now has assumed a profit centre arrangement, with the Treasury desk also responsible for market-making of money market instruments and being expected to position the bank's ALM requirement and trade money markets to profit. Many banks set up the Treasury function simply to arrange the firm's funding requirement, so that it is not given an explicit profit target.

In such an arrangement, the question arises as what the Treasury desk should charge the firm's lines of business for their funds. Consider a broker–dealer firm that operated the following lines of business:

- a corporate bond market-making desk;
- an equity derivatives trading desk;
- an investment portfolio that holds Eurobonds and structured finance securities for the medium term;
- a business that offers structured derivatives products, on a leveraged basis, to clients that wish to invest in hedge fund of funds or other alternative assets.

Each of these lines of business will have a different funding requirement; for example, the market-making desk would expect to have a frequent turnover of its portfolio and so its liquidity profile would be fairly short-dated. It could be funded using short-term borrowing, no more than one week to one month, with much funding on an overnight to 1-week basis. The client-focused business would have a longer dated asset profile, and so should be funded using a mixture of short-, medium- and long-dated funds. Assuming a positive-sloping yield curve, the term structure effect means that the client-focused business would have a higher cost of funds. However, the Treasury desk would not fund each desk separately (it could, but that would be inefficient and wasteful of resources). Hence, what charge should be made to the desks for their funds?

One theoretically correct but little-used option is for banks to use a weighted-average cost (WAC or WACF) of funding, sometimes called a "blended" or "pooled" rate, as the funding rate, which is passed on to the business lines.

The subject of internal funds pricing or "funds transfer pricing" (FTP) is discussed in detail in Chapter 15.

The Cost of Borrowing

There are two approaches with regard to the transfer price for loans. The first approach refers to existing assets and liabilities, and charges a cost for each loan as a proportion of the total. The second approach is to define an optimum funding solution and use this as the cost of funds. This can be the blended rate.

Using the existing resources has the appeal of simplicity. However, it raises the problems we encountered at the start of this section: each type of resource has a different cost. We could define a maturity term for all assets and match each term loan to assets of identical maturity. But this is not effective in practice. For instance, if an asset can be identified that has a precise maturity profile, then one can fund it to matching dates, either with one loan or a set of loans that all roll off in order until the final maturity date. But to do this for every asset would be impractical. Hence a WACF may be preferred.

The Blended Cost of Funds

For fixed-rate loans, the cost of funds is explicit, but when more than one loan is taken out, the funding cost will depend on the combination of amounts borrowed and their respective maturity dates. For instance, consider a funding arrangement for USD100 that is comprised of:

- 40 borrowed for two years;
- 60 borrowed for one year.

The relevant interest rates are the zero-coupon interest rates for 1- and 2-year loans. The transfer price to use for the overall funding of 100 in the first 12 months is the average cost of the funds of these two loans. It is in fact given by the discount rate that would equate the present value of the future values of each loan equal to the original amount borrowed. The future value is of course the maturity amount, which is the original principal plus interest. To be strictly accurate, we assume that the loans are zero-coupon loans and the interest rates charged are zero-coupon interest rates.

The future cash flows on the above arrangement are:

- $60\ (1 + r_1)$ in year 1;
- $40\ (1 + r_2)^2$ in year 1 and year 2.

So the WACF is given by the rate rw such that:

$$100 = 60(1 + r_1)/(1 + rw) + 40(1 + r_2)^2/(1 + rw)^2.$$

This discount rate will obviously lie somewhere between r_1 and r_2. A "back of the envelope" solution to this would be to calculate a linear approximation of the formula above, namely:

$$100 = 60(1 + r_1 - rw) + 40(1 + 2r_2 - 2rw)$$
$$rw = (60 \times r_1 + 40 \times 2 \times r_2)/(60 + 2 \times 40).$$

The rate rw is the weighted average of the two rates r_1 and r_2, which we took to be the 1- and 2-year zero-coupon rates respectively. The weighting used refers to the size of the loan in proportion to the total and its maturity. As a rough rule of thumb, a 1-year rate rolled over in a 2-year period would be weighed at twice the 2-year one. If we imagine that r_1 is 4% and r_2 is 5%, then rw in this case will be nearer to r_2, because it is the longest dated loan, but pulling in the other direction is the fact that the 1-year loan in our example was for a larger amount.

In practice, even large commercial banks calculate their WACF as the daily interest payment on each loan outstanding, added together, and then divided by the total nominal amount of all loans.We illustrate the concept of the WACF in Table 7.5. This shows a USD500 million funding requirement that has been arranged as three loans, namely:

- overnight USD200 million at 1.05%;
- 1-week loan of USD200 million at 1.07%;
- 3-month loan of USD100 million at 1.15%.

The spreadsheet shows the calculation of the WACF on a more scientific basis than the "back of the envelope" approach, as it takes into account the term structure effect of the loans (as we go further out along the term structure, we pay a higher rate of interest). However, the result is very close to the simple approach. The WACF for these three loans is shown to be 1.146%.

EXAMPLE 7.3 CASH POSITION MANAGEMENT

Starting the day with a flat position, a money market inter-bank desk transacts the following deals:

1. £100 million borrowing from 16 September to 7 October (3 weeks) at 6.375%;
2. £60 million borrowing from 16 September to 16 October (1 month) at 6.25%;
3. £110 million loan from 16 September to 18 October (32 days) at 6.45%.

The desk reviews its cash position and the implications for refunding and the interest-rate risk, bearing in mind the following:

- There is an internal overnight rollover limit of £40 million (net).
- The bank's economist feels more pessimistic about a rise in interest rates than most others in the market, and has recently given an internal seminar on the dangers of inflation in the UK as a result of recent increases in the level of average earnings.
- Today there are some important figures being released including inflation (CPI) data. If today's CPI figures exceed market expectations, the dealer expects a tightening of monetary policy by *at least* 0.50% almost immediately.
- A broker's estimate of daily market liquidity for the next few weeks is one of low shortage, with little central bank intervention required, and hence low volatilities and rates in the overnight rate.
- Brokers' screens indicate the following term repo rates:

O/N	6.350%–6.300%
1 week	6.390%–6.340%
2 week	6.400%–6.350%
1 month	6.410%–6.375%
2 month	6.500%–6.450%
3 month	6.670%–6.620%

(*continued*)

- The indication for a 1v2 FRA is:
  1v2 FRA 6.680%–6.630%
- The quote for an 11-day forward borrowing in three weeks' time (the "21v32 rate") is 6.50% bid. The book's exposure looks like this:

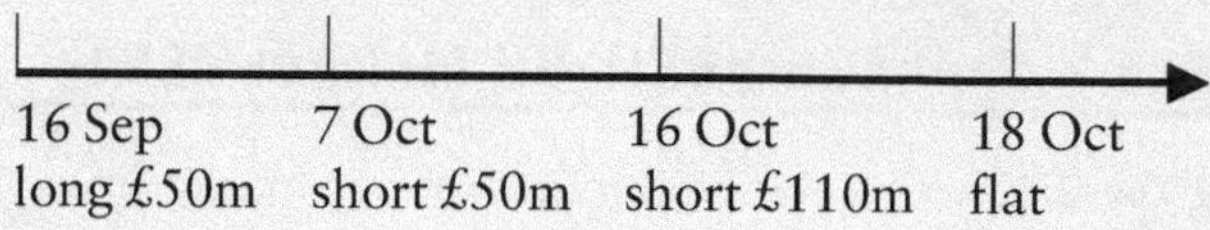

What courses of action are open to the desk, bearing in mind that the book needs to be squared off such that the position is flat each night?

POSSIBLE SOLUTIONS

Investing early surplus

From a cash management point of view, the desk has a £50 million surplus from 16/9 up to 7/10. This needs to be invested. It may be able to negotiate a 6.31% loan with the market for an overnight term, or a 6.35% term deposit for one week to 6.38% for one month.

The overnight roll is the most flexible but offers a worse rate, and if the desk expects the overnight rate to remain both low and stable (due to forecasts of low market shortages), it may not opt for this course of action.

However, it may make sense from an interest-rate risk point of view. If the desk agrees with the bank's economist, it should be able to benefit from rolling at higher rates soon – possibly in the next three weeks. Therefore it may not want to lock in a term rate now, and the overnight roll would match this view. However, it exposes them to lower rates, if their view is wrong, which will limit the extent of the positive funding spread. The market itself appears neutral about rate changes in the next month, but appears to factor in a rise thereafter.

The forward "gap"

Looking forward, the book is currently on course to exceed the £40 million overnight position limit on 7/10, when the refunding requirement is £50 million. The situation gets worse on 16/10 (for two days) when the refunding requirement is £110 million. The desk needs to fix a term deal before those dates to carry it over until 18/10 when the funding position reverts to zero. A borrowing from 7/10 to 18/10 of £50 million will reduce the rollover requirement to within limit.

However, given that interest rates are expected to rise, should the Treasury desk wait until the 7th to deal in the cash? Not if it has a firm view. It may end up paying as much as 6.91% or higher for the funding (after the 0.50% rate rise). So it would be better to transact now a forward starting repo to cover the period, thus locking in the benefits obtainable from today's yield curve. The market rate for a 21×32-day repo is quoted at 6.50%. This reflects the market's consensus that rates may rise in about a month's time. However, the desk's own expectation is of a larger rise, hence its own logic suggests trading in the forward loan. This strategy will pay dividends if their view is right, as it limits the extent of funding loss.

An alternative means of protecting the interest-rate risk alone is to buy a 1v2 month FRA for 6.68%. This does not exactly match the gap, but should act as an effective hedge. If there is a rate rise, the book gains from the FRA profit. Note that the cash position still needs to be squared off. Should the desk deal before or after the inflation announcement? That is, of course, its decision, but most dealers like, if at all possible, to sit tight ahead of releases of key economic data.

GENERIC ALM POLICY FOR DIFFERENT BANKS

The management of interest-rate risk is a fundamental ingredient of commercial banking. Bank shareholders require comfort that interest-rate risk is measured and managed in a satisfactory manner. A common approach to risk management involves the following:

- the preparation and adoption of a high-level interest-rate risk policy at managing board level; this sets general guidelines on the type and extent of risk exposure that can be taken on by the bank;
- setting limits on the risk exposure levels of the banking book; this can be by product type, desk, geographic area and so on, and will be along the maturity spectrum;
- actively measuring the level of interest-rate risk exposure at regular, specified intervals;
- reporting to senior management on general aspects of risk management, risk exposure levels, limit breaches and so on;
- monitoring of risk management policies and procedures by an independent "middle office" risk function.

The risk management approach adopted by banks will vary according to their specific markets and appetite for risk. Certain institutions will have their

TABLE 7.5 Weighted-average borrowing cost calculation, with three hypothetical loans

WACF calculation			
			0.002777778
			Amount of interest (accrued)
			1
			o/n
Term (days)		Interest rate % pa (Libor fix)	Amount of interest
1 o/n	200,000,000	1.05%	5,833.33
7 1wk	200,000,000	1.07%	5,944.44
90 3mth	100,000,000	1.15%	3,194.44
	500,000,000		1.078%
			14,972.22
		Period	1
			0.0030%
		Overall cost of funds – WAC measure	1.146%
		Total interest	1,432,055.56
			0.002777778
			Amount of interest (accrued)
SAME CALCULATION – as above – but using the effective cost of funds			
			1
			o/n
Term (days)		WAC rate	Amount of interest
1 o/n	200,000,000	1.1456%	6,364.69
7 1wk	200,000,000	1.1456%	6,364.69
90 3mth	100,000,000	1.1456%	3,182.35
	500,000,000		1.146%
			15,911.73
		Period	1
			0.0032%
		Overall cost of funds	1.146%
			1,432,055.56

0.01944444	0.25			
7	90			
1wk	3mth			
–	–	1	0	0
41,611.11	–	1	1	0
22,361.11	287,500.00	1	1	1
1.097%	1.150%	500,000,000.00	300,000,000.00	100,000,000.00
63,972.22	287,500.00	366,444.44		
6	83			
0.0183%	0.2651%	0.2864%		

0.01944444	0.25			
7	90			
1wk	3mth			
–	–	1	0	0
44,552.84	–	1	1	0
22,276.42	286,411.11	1	1	1
1.146%	1.146%	500,000,000.00	300,000,000.00	100,000,000.00
66,829.26	286,411.11	369,152.10		
6	83			
0.0191%	0.2641%	0.2864%		

activities set out or proscribed for them under regulatory rules. For instance, building societies in the UK are prohibited from trading in certain instruments under the regulator's guidelines.

In this section we present the ALM policies of three hypothetical banks, called Bank S, Bank M and Bank L. These are respectively, a small banking entity with assets of £5 billion, a medium-sized bank with assets of £25 billion and a large bank with assets of £100 billion. The following serves to demonstrate the differing approaches that can be taken according to the environment that a financial institution operates in.

ALM Policy for Bank S (Assets = £10 billion)

The aim of the ALM policy for Bank S is to provide guidelines on risk appetite, revenue targets and rates of return, as well as risk management policy. Areas that may be covered include capital ratios, liquidity, asset mix, rate-setting policy for loans and deposits, and investment guidelines for the banking portfolio. The key objectives should include:

- to maintain capital ratios at the planned minimum, and to ensure safety of the deposit base;
- to generate a satisfactory revenue stream, both for income purposes and to further protect the deposit base.

The responsibility for overseeing the operations of the bank to ensure that these objectives are achieved is lodged with the ALM Committee. This body monitors the volume and mix of the bank's assets and funding (liabilities), and ensures that this asset mix follows internal guidelines with regard to banking liquidity, capital adequacy, asset base growth targets, risk exposure and return on capital. The norm is for the committee to meet on a monthly basis; at a minimum the membership of the committee will include the finance director, head of Treasury and risk manager. For a bank the size of Bank S the ALM committee membership will possibly be extended to the chief executive, the head of the loans business and the chief operating officer.

As a matter of course the committee will wish to discuss and review the following on a regular basis:

- overall macroeconomic conditions;
- financial results and key management ratios, such as share price analysis and rates of return on capital and equity;
- the bank's view on the likely direction of short-term interest rates;
- the current lending strategy, and suggestions for changes to this, as well as the current funding strategy;

- any anticipated changes to the volume and mix of the loan book, and that of the main sources of funding; in addition, the appropriateness or otherwise of alternative sources of funding;
- suggestions for any alteration to the bank's ALM policy;
- the maturity gap profile and anticipated changes to it.

The committee will also wish to consider the interest rates offered currently on loans and deposits, and whether these are still appropriate. Interest-rate sensitivity is monitored and confirmed as lying within specified parameters; these parameters are regularly reviewed and adjusted if deemed necessary according to changes in the business cycle and economic conditions. Measured using the following ratio:

$$A_{ir}/L_{ir},$$

typical risk levels would be expected to lie between 90–110% for the maturity period 0–90 days, and between 80–100% for the maturity period over 90 days and less than 365 days.

Put simply, the objective of Bank S ALCO would be to remain within specified risk parameters at all times, and to maintain as consistent a level of earnings as possible (and one that is immune to changes in the business cycle).

ALM Policy for Bank M (Assets = £50 billion)

Bank M is our hypothetical "medium-sized" banking institution. Its ALM policy would be overseen by ALCO. Typically, the following members of senior management would be expected to be members of the ALCO:

- chief executive
- finance director
- head of retail banking
- head of corporate banking
- head of treasury
- head of risk management
- head of internal audit

together with others such as product specialists who are called to attend as and when required. Typically, the finance director will chair the meeting.

The primary responsibilities of the Bank M ALCO are detailed below.

Objectives

The ALCO is tasked with reviewing the bank's overall funding strategy. Minutes are taken at each meeting, and decisions taken are recorded on the minutes and circulated to attendees and designated key staff. ALCO members are responsible for undertaking regular reviews of the following:

- minutes of the previous meeting;
- the ratio of the interest-rate-sensitive assets to liabilities, gap reports, risk reports and the funding position;
- the bank's view on the expected level of interest rates, and how the book should be positioned with respect to this view; and related to this, the ALCO view on anticipated funding costs in the short and medium term;
- stress testing in the form of "what if?" scenarios, to check the effect on the banking book of specified changes in market conditions; and the change in parameters that may be required if there is a change in market conditions or risk tolerance;
- the current interest rates for loans and deposits, to ensure that these are in accordance with the overall lending and funding strategy;
- the maturity distribution of the liquidity book (expected to be comprised of T-bills, CDs and very short-dated government bonds);
- the current liquidity position and the expected position in the short and medium term.

As the ALCO meets on a regular monthly basis, it may not be the case that every aspect of their responsibility is discussed at every meeting; the agenda is set by the chair of the meeting in consultation with committee members. The policies adopted by ALCO should be dynamic and flexible, and capable of adaptation to changes in operating conditions. Any changes will be made on agreement of committee members. Generally, any exceptions to agreed policy can only be with the agreement of ALCO itself.

Interest-rate Risk Policy

The objective will be to keep earnings volatility resulting from an upward or downward move in interest rates to a minimum. To this end, at each ALCO meeting members will review risk and position reports and discuss these in the light of the risk policy. Generally, the 6-month and 12-month A_{ir}/L_{ir} cumulative ratio will lie in the range of 90–110%. A significant move outside this range will most likely be subject to corrective action. The committee will also consider the results of various scenario analyses on the book, and if these tests indicate a potential earnings impact of greater than, say, 10%, instructions may be given to alter the shape and maturity profile of the book.

Liquidity Policy

A primary responsibility of the ALCO is to ensure that an adequate level of liquidity is maintained at all times. We define liquidity as:

> . . . *the ability to meet anticipated and unanticipated operating cash needs, loan demand, and deposit withdrawals, without incurring a sustainednegative impact on profitability.*
>
> Gup and Brooks (1993), p. 238

Generally, a Bank M-type operation would expect to have a target level for loans to deposits of around 85–95%, and a loans to core deposits ratio of 90–95%. The loan/deposit ratio is reported to ALCO and reviewed on a monthly basis, and a reported figure significantly outside these ranges (say, by 5% or more) will be reviewed and asked to be adjusted to bring it back into line with ALCO policy.

ALM Policy for Bank L (Assets = £200 billion)

The management policy for ALM at a larger entity will build on that described for a medium-sized financial institution. If Bank L is a group company, the policy will cover the consolidated balance sheet as well as individual subsidiary balance sheets; the committee will provide direction on the management of assets and liabilities, and the off-balance sheet instruments used to manage interest-rate and credit risk. A well-functioning management process will be proactive and concentrate on direction in response to anticipated changes in operating conditions, rather than reactive responses to changes that have already taken place. The primary objectives will be to maximise shareholder value, with target returns on capital of 14–18%.

The responsibility for implementing and overseeing the ALM management policy will reside with the ALCO. The ALCO will establish the operating guidelines for ALM, and review these guidelines on a periodic basis. The committee will meet on a more frequent basis than would be the case for Bank M, usually on a fortnightly basis. As well as this, it will set policies governing liquidity and funding objectives, investment activities and interest-rate risk. It will also oversee the activities of the investment banking division. The head of the ALM desk will prepare the interest-rate risk sensitivity report and present it to the ALCO.

Interest-rate Risk Management

The ALCO will establish an interest-rate risk policy that sets direction on acceptable levels of interest-rate risk. This risk policy is designed to guide management in the evaluation of the impact of interest-rate risk on the bank's earnings. The extent of risk exposure is a function of the maturity profile of the balance sheet, as well as the frequency of re-pricing, the level of loan prepayments and funding costs. Managing interest-rate risk is, in effect, the adjustment of risk exposure upwards or downwards, which will be in response to ALCO's views on the future direction of interest rates. As part of the risk management process the committee will monitor the current risk exposure and duration gap, using rate sensitivity analysis and simulation modelling to assess whether the current level of risk is satisfactory.

Measuring Interest-rate Risk

Notwithstanding the widespread adoption of VaR as the key market risk measurement tool, funding books such as repo books continue to use the gap report as a key measure of interest-rate risk exposure. This enables ALCO to view the risk sensitivity along the maturity structure. Cumulative gap positions, and the ratio of assets revaluation to liabilities revaluation, are calculated and compared to earnings levels on the current asset/liability position. Generally, the 90-day, 6-month and 1-year gap positions are the most significant points along the term structure at which interest-rate risk exposure is calculated. The ratio of gap to earnings assets will be set at the ±15% to ±20% level.

As it is a traditional duration-based approach, gap reporting is a static measure that measures risk sensitivity at one specific point in time. It for this reason that banks combine a VaR measure as well.

Simulation Modelling

Simulation modelling is a procedure that measures the potential impact on the banking book, and hence earnings levels, of a user-specified change in interest rates and/or a change in the shape of the book itself. This process enables senior management to gauge the risk associated with particular strategies. Put simply the process is to:

- construct a "base" balance sheet and income statement as the starting point (this is derived from the current shape of the banking book, and any changes expected from current growth trends that have been projected forward);
- assess the impact on the balance sheet of changes under selected scenarios; these might be no change in rates; a 100 bp and 250 bp

upward parallel shift in the yield curve; a 100 bp and 250 bp downward parallel shift; a 25 bp steepening and flattening of the yield curve, between the 3-month and the 3-year maturity points; a combination of a parallel shift with a pivotal shift at a selected point; an increase or decrease in 3-month T-bill yield volatility levels; and a 20 bp change in swap spreads;
- compare the difference in earnings resulting from any of the scenarios to the anticipated earnings stream under the current environment.

Generally, the committee will have set guidelines about the significance of simulation results; for example, there may be a rule that a 100 bp change in interest rates should not impact NII by more than 10%. If results indicate such an impact, ALCO will determine if the current risk strategy is satisfactory or whether adjustments are necessary.

SECURITISATION

It is common for ALM units in banks to take responsibility for a more proactive balance sheet management role, and employ securitisation as a management tool. Securitisation is a process undertaken by banks both to realise additional value from assets held on the balance sheet, as well as to remove them from the balance sheet entirely, thus freeing up lending lines. Essentially, it involves selling assets on the balance sheet to third-party investors. In principle the process is straightforward, as assets that are sold generate cash flows in the future, which provide the return to investors who have purchased the securitised assets. To minimise the risk exposure for investors, the uncertainty associated with certain asset cash flows is controlled or re-engineered, and there is a range of ways that this may be done.

For balance sheet management one of the principal benefits of securitisation is to save or reduce capital charges through the sale of assets. The other added benefit of course is that if structured in the required way, the credit risk of the underlying assets is removed from the balance sheet.

The Securitisation Process

In this section we consider the implications of securitisation from the point of view of asset and liability management.

The basic principle of securitisation is to sell assets to investors, usually through an SPV or some other intermediate structure, and to provide the investors with a fixed or floating ratereturn on the assets they have purchased; the cash flows from the original assets are used to provide this return. The most common type of assets that are securitised include mortgages, car loans, and credit card loans. However, in theory virtually any asset that generates a cash flow that can be predicted or modelled may be securitised. The vehicle used is constructed so that securities issued against the asset base have a risk return profile that is attractive to the investors that are expected to by the ABS bonds.

The ALM uses and benefits of securitisation are described in Chapter 4.

EXAMPLE 7.4 SECURITISATION TRANSACTION: ILLUSTRATION OF ECONOMICS

We illustrate the impact of securitising the balance sheet with a hypothetical example from ABC Bank plc. The bank has a mortgage book of £100 million, and under Basel I the regulatory weight for this asset is 50%. The capital requirement is therefore £4 million (that is, 8% × 0.5% × £100 million). The capital is comprised of equity, estimated to cost 25% and subordinated debt, which has a cost of 10.2%. The cost of straight debt is 10%. The ALM desk reviews a securitisation of 10% of the asset book, or £10 million. The loan book has a fixed duration of 20 years, but its effective duration is estimated at seven years, due to refinancing and early repayment. The net return from the loan book is 10.2%.

The ALM desk decides on a securitised structure that is made up of two classes of security: subordinated notes and senior notes. The subordinated notes will be granted a single-A rating due to their higher risk, while the senior notes are rated triple-A. Given such ratings the required rate of return for the subordinated notes is 10.61%, and that of the senior notes is 9.80%. The senior notes have a lower cost than the current balance sheet debt, which has a cost of 10%. To obtain a single-A rating, the subordinated notes need to represent at least 10% of the securitised amount. The costs associated with the transaction are the initial cost of issue and the yearly servicing cost, estimated at 0.20% of the securitised amount. The summary information is given at Table 7.6.

TABLE 7.6 ABC Bank plc mortgage loan book and securitisation proposal.

ABC Bank plc	
Current funding	
Cost of equity	25%
Cost of subordinated debt	10.20%
Cost of debt	10%
Mortgage book	
Net yield	10.20%
Duration	7 years
Balance outstanding million	100
Proposed structure	
Securitised amount	10 million
Senior securities:	
Cost	9.80%
Weighting	90%
Maturity	10 years
Subordinated notes:	
Cost	10.61%
Weighting	10%
Maturity	10 years
Servicing costs	0.20%

A bank's cost of funding is the average cost of all the funds it employed. The funding structure in our example is capital 4%, divided into 2% equity at 25%, 2% subordinated debt at 10.20%, and 96% debt at 10%. The weighted funding cost F therefore is:

$$\begin{aligned} F_{balance\ sheet} &= 96\% \times 10\% + ((8\% \times 50\%) \times (25\% \times 50\%) \\ &\quad + (10.20\% \times 50\%)) \\ &= 10.30\%. \end{aligned}$$

This average rate is consistent with the 25% before-tax return on equity given at the start. If the assets do not generate this return, the received return will change accordingly, since it is the end result of the bank's profitability. As currently the assets generate only 10.20%, they are performing below shareholder expectations. The return actually obtained by shareholders is such that the average cost

(*continued*)

of funds is identical to the 10.20% return on assets. We may calculate this return to be:

$$\begin{aligned}\text{Asset return} &= 10.20\% \\ &= (96\% \times 10\%) + 8\% \times 50\% \\ &\quad \times (ROE \times 50\% + 10.20\% \times 50\%).\end{aligned}$$

Solving this relationship we obtain an ROE of 19.80%, which is lower than shareholder expectations. In theory the bank would find it impossible to raise new equity in the market because its performance would not compensate shareholders for the risk they are incurring by holding the bank's shares. Therefore any asset that is originated by the bank would have to be securitised, which would also be expected to raise the shareholder return. The ALM desk proceeds with the securitisation, issuing £9 million of the senior securities and £1 million of the subordinated notes. The bonds are placed by an investment bank with institutional investors. The outstanding balance of the loan book decreases from £100 million to £90 million. The weighted assets are therefore £45 million. Therefore the capital requirement for the loan book is now £3.6 million, a reduction from the original capital requirement of £400,000, which can be used for expansion in another area, a possible route for which is given in Table 7.7.

The benefit of the securitisation is the reduction in the cost of funding. The funding cost as a result of securitisation is the weighted cost of the senior notes and the subordinated notes, together with the annual servicing cost. The cost of the senior securities is 9.80%, while the subordinated notes have a cost of 10.61% (for simplicity here we ignore any differences in

TABLE 7.7 Impact of securitisation on the balance sheet.

Outstanding balances	Value (£m)	Capital required (£m)
Initial loan book	100	4
Securitised amount	10	0.4
Senior securities	9	Sold
Subordinated notes	1	Sold
New loan book	90	3.6
Total asset	90	
Total weighted assets	45	3.6

the duration and amortisation profiles of the two bonds). This is calculated as:

$$(90\% \times 9.80\%) + (10\% \times 10.61\%) + 0.20\% = 10.08\%.$$

This overall cost is lower than the target funding cost obtained direct from the balance sheet, which was 10.30%. This is the quantified benefit of the securitisation process. Note that the funding cost obtained through securitisation is lower than the yield on the loan book. Therefore the original loan can be sold to the SPV structure, issuing the securities for a gain.

MIDDLE-OFFICE TREASURY PROCEDURES AND ALM PRACTICE[7]

In this section we address the issues specifically faced by a bank MO in their support of the ALM function. While the Treasury front office has primary responsibility for managing transactions facing the external market, MO plays an important role in *controlling* the ALM function, and the corresponding internal allocations of those transactions across the various internal business units. This section describes what is meant by the term "funding cost" and the various methods of their internal allocation, as well as the logistical issues faced by many banking corporations in effecting this allocation.

Funding

Despite increasingly complex financial markets where focus is often placed on the development of new structures designed to unlock financial value, practitioners must remember the age-old banking maxim that "Cash is King". Regardless of the simplicity or complexity of a transaction, invariably there is either a payment or receipt of cash at some stage throughout its life. In fact, that is ultimately all that banking corporations are – payers and receivers of cash today made in consideration for commitments to paying or receiving cash in the future. The term "funding

7 This section was co-authored with Andrew Oliver, KBC Financial Products, London.

cost" in banking refers to the financial cost in the form of interest that is incurred when cash is borrowed to finance other trading assets. Traditionally, investment banks are net borrowers of cash, but the same principles apply to net lenders of cash.

Accordingly, regardless of its size and nature, there are some fundamental questions that an organisation which manages its cash well must address, including:

- Where is cash being borrowed from?
- What is the financial cost (interest) of borrowing this cash?
- Where is the cash being used within the organisation?
- How is the financial cost of borrowing this cash being internally allocated to the areas of the organisation that are using it?

These costs can be real costs or they can be opportunity costs, and the larger the organisation, the more complex the issues around attributing those costs to individual business areas.

Internal Funding Cost Allocation

Banking corporations are often structured with a dedicated Treasury department that is responsible for managing the cash flow of the business, and for arranging the cash borrowings required to finance trading assets. In that respect, the external funding trades are often booked in Treasury's book, which initially bears the funding cost of those borrowings. Those funding costs are then allocated internally to the areas of the business that have generated the funding requirement by internally lending the cash to whoever needs it. Treasury is therefore acting as a conduit between the external sources of funding and the internal businesses requiring it.

There are two different approaches to determining the amount of cash Treasury is required to lend internally to each business:

1. Funding "Cash";
2. Funding "Balance Sheet".

These are linked by the principles of double-entry accounting (see Figure 7.7), and differ in their treatment of funding P&L generated by each business.

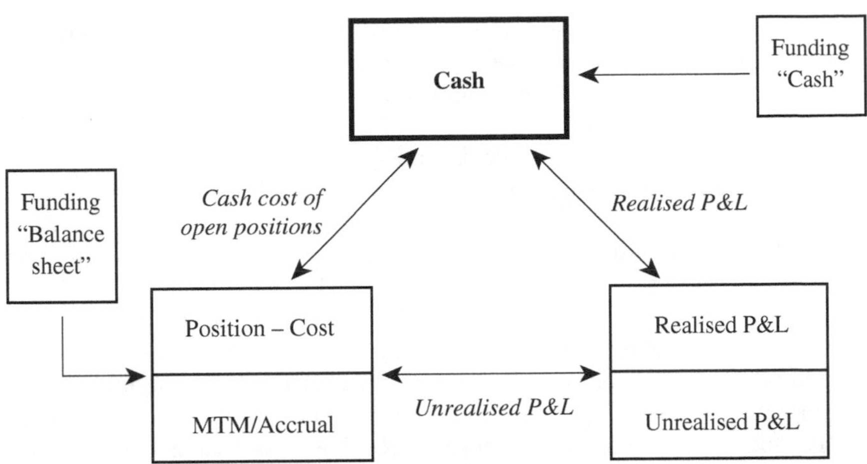

FIGURE 7.7 Double-entry accounting and funding cash allocation.

Funding "Cash"

This approach is both the simplest in theory and the simplest to apply, in that each individual business is deemed to own a portion of the overall entity's cash balance.

This portion represents that business's overall contribution since inception to the entity's cash balance. It not only includes the amount required to fund that business's current open positions, but incorporates previously generated realised P&L as well. The amount that each business is therefore required to borrow from Treasury is simply the amount that would flatten that business's own cash balance.

Funding "Balance Sheet"

This approach treats Treasury as the owner of all cash, which then lends to businesses to fund the *value* of their current trading portfolio. Figure 7.7 illustrates the difference between the cash balance of the first approach and the balance sheet value of this second approach as being the *realised* and *unrealised P&L*.

It can be less common in some organisations for there to be a clear and effective policy surrounding the funding benefit/detriment of profits earned/losses incurred.

However, particularly in trading environments, it is good practice to dictate that the funding cost/benefit of profits and losses are the property of

Treasury (or some other central element of the organisation structure), as opposed to being the property of the business that has generated them. The rationale for this policy, which applies equally to:

- current year and prior year P&L, and
- realised and unrealised P&L

is based on establishing a "level playing field" between businesses for the purpose of performance evaluation.

In trading environments where P&L is generated throughout the trading day, the assessment of the performance of that trading activity should be insulated from the ongoing funding effect of trading undertaken on previous days. Where historical profits have been *realised*, under "Cash funding", these act to increase the business's cash balance, and therefore decrease its ongoing funding requirement and associated interest cost. This funding benefit attaches itself to the businesses in perpetuity, and may have the effect of distorting the performance assessment of future trading.

Under "Balance sheet funding", however, the ongoing funding benefit of these realised profits remains with Treasury, since it continues to fund the business according to its current open trading portfolio value, but the aggregate external funding requirement of the whole entity on which Treasury pays the interest has been reduced.

Additionally, there is an opportunity cost/benefit to the entity of *unrealised P&L*, since by merely realising that P&L, there would be an immediate impact on the entity's cash borrowing cost. By funding each business based on its current open trading portfolio value, then the business is effectively paying Treasury for this opportunity cost.

By applying "Balance sheet funding", the Treasury P&L should therefore reflect the funding benefit of the entity's P&L as if it were all realised, with the businesses reflecting the opportunity cost of unrealised P&L. Businesses are therefore incentivised not to carry unrealised P&L unnecessarily. As a result, the recognition by a business of a non-cash asset/liability on the entity's balance sheet should incentivise the business concerned to use that asset/liability in a manner that generates a benefit to the entity over and above that which could be generated by Treasury just lending/borrowing the cash equivalent of that asset/liability in the overnight money market.

In practice, for logistical reasons, some organisations set up their cash management operations to adopt the cash funding basis where the amount of internal funding booked to each business flattens their cash balance, which is supplemented by an additional balance sheet charge that transfers funding P&L back to Treasury to capture the funding benefit of historic profits/losses. This method has the added benefit of capturing errors by cash management operations in assigning cash funding to each business.

Funds Transfer Pricing

A critical issue in banking is the determination of the rate at which internal businesses borrow their funding requirement from Treasury. This is often impacted by the mandate of the Treasury department, in terms of whether it is set-up as:

(1) a cost centre whose purpose is to act as a service provider to the organisation that provides a central coordination point for funding; or
(2) a profit centre whose purpose is not only to arrange funding, but is also to make P&L from trading the interest-rate risk often produced as a by-product of funding activities at the shorter end of the yield curve.

The transfer pricing rate is usually representative of the rate that Treasury pays on the external borrowings; that is, its internal COF. In some organisations a spread is applied to this rate to compensate Treasury for the operational costs involved in acting as the centralised funding provider.

However, further complications arise when the term structure of funding is taken into consideration, since different rates are payable on borrowings of different maturity, as determined by the ALM profile.

Funds transfer pricing is discussed in detail in Chapter 15.

Allocation Methodology

The Treasury book can be split between term funding portfolios and an overnight funding "pool". The term funding book would then internally lend the cash raised from term borrowings to the overnight pool at the overnight rate, with the resultant term premium P&L being captured within the term funding portfolio, along with any other gap P&L generated by Treasury electing not to swap down the term funding to OIS.

The reallocation method of the term premium P&L is to use:

(1) the asset liquidation profile from the ALM process as the basis for the amounts to be charged (the rationale being that it is this profile which the term funding is being benchmarked against to ensure satisfactory management of liquidity gaps)

in combination with:

(2) a published term premium matrix maintained by Treasury that reflects the current premium of term cash rates by maturity bucket over and above the equivalent OIS rate.

The ALM asset value per bucket is to be multiplied by the term premium for that bucket, for whatever period of time the allocation is being made (possibly in conjunction with ALM reporting), with buckets per business summed together to provide a business total.

This total allocation will not match the actual term premium P&L (since actual term funding will not perfectly match the asset liquidation profile, and the term premium matrix is only indicative), so the actual term premium P&L can then be allocated in the same proportion per business as the theoretical results calculated above.

Depending on the currency mix of the term funding, this methodology may need to be applied at a currency level.

For example, consider Table 7.8. Note how "Business F" has 25% of the total asset value, but incurs 50% of the total term premium. This reflects the disproportionate impact that Business F has on the term funding requirement under prudent ALM management.

Capital Structure

The funding cost of an entity is also impacted by its capital structure. The relative contributions of debt and share capital, including various different forms and hybrids of each, all have a bearing on the amount of interest-bearing funding required, and the rates of interest payable on that funding.

To demonstrate how the impact of the capital structure on an entity's funding cost is treated, we will address share capital and subordinated debt as examples.

Share Capital

The share capital of a legal entity represents a source of funding like any other, except it has one main defining characteristic: it bears no real interest cost. Again, there are different approaches as to where the share capital is booked and where the benefit of this free source of funding is assigned.

Since the share capital is a specific type of external funding source, it is often booked in the Treasury books of the entity in which the capital resides, with the cash forming part of the general cash funding pool of the entity that is then managed by Treasury.

The net interest benefit of the utilisation of this "free" cash is subject to the same transfer pricing issues as those discussed in the Transfer Pricing section above. It can either be:

- factored into the WACF calculation, such that the net interest benefit is distributed across the businesses. The rationale behind this approach is that the benefit is a product of conducting business from a legal entity, and therefore each business operating from that legal entity is entitled to benefit from it;
- it can be retained within Treasury, such that it forms part of the overall Treasury P&L. The rationale behind this approach is that each business should be assessed on its incremental contribution to the profitability of the entity, and should not reflect entity-level share capital that has already been injected.

Either way, the treatment should be consistent with the treatment of retained earnings discussed in the Internal Funding Cost Allocation section above. Since retained earnings and share capital are both similar sources of funding in that neither have a real interest cost, it makes sense that under cash funding, where the business benefits from retained earnings, that share capital is factored into the WACF. Alternatively, under balance sheet funding, where the benefit of retained earnings is retained within Treasury, it makes sense for Treasury to retain the benefit of share capital.

Subordinated Debt

As a mechanism of capital structure management, subordinated debt can sometimes be issued by an entity. This type of debt has characteristics of both share capital and term funding.

It has characteristics of share capital: in ranks below senior debt-holders in the pecking order of net asset distribution in the event of the entity being liquidated. In order to compensate the subordinated debt-holder for this perceived increase in credit risk relative to senior debt-holders, the entity must pay an interest premium on the subordinated debt.

Additionally, subordinated debt has characteristics of term funding in that it is generally of a longer maturity term. Therefore, the rate paid on the subordinated issue will have three elements:

- the base short-term Libor rate for short-term *senior* debt;
- the *term premium*: this will initially be captured within the Treasury P&L, and possibly reallocated as per the Transfer Pricing section above.

TABLE 7.8 Asset liquidation profile and term premium allocation

Asset liquidation profile ($m)

Business	o/n	o/n–1m	1m–6m	6m–12m	12m–2yr
Business A	42	268	150	78	43
Business B	14	113	199		
business C	32	88	266	512	478
Business D	16	503	168		
Business E	9	20	20		
Business F	7	19	23	150	220
Business G	44	448	213		
Totals	**164**	**1,459**	**1,038**	**740**	**741**

Term premium matrix (bps)

Premium	o/n	o/n–1m	1m–6m	6m–12m
Term premium (bp) 0	0	3	5	7

Annual term premium P&L allocation ($)

Business	o/n	o/n–1m	1m–6m	6m–12m	12m–2yr	2yr–5yr
Business A		80,318	75,000	54,600	43,000	
Business B		34,045	99,500			
Business C		26,398	133,000	358,400	478,000	
Business D		150,750	83,750			
Business E		5,959	9,932			
Business F		5,700	11,500	105,000	220,000	240,000
Business G		134,400	106,500			
Totals		**437,569**	**519,182**	**518,000**	**741,000**	**24,000**

2yr–5yr	5yr–10yr	10yr–15yr	15yr+	TOTAL	%
				581	12
				326	7
				1,376	28
				686	14
				49	1
200	185	300	170	1,274	25
				705	14
200	**185**	**300**	**170**	**4,997**	

12m–2yr	2yr–5yr	5yr–10yr	10yr–15yr	15yr+
10	12	15	20	25

5yr–10yr	10yr–15 yr	15yr+	Theoretical allocation	Actual allocation	%
			252,918	235,538	7
			133,545	124,368	4
			995,798	927,371	26
			234,500	218,386	6
			15,891	14,799	0
277,500	600,000	425,000	1,884,700	1,755,191	50
			240,900	224,346	6
277,500	600,000	425,000	3,758,251	3,500,000	
Actual term premium p&l:			3,500,000		

- the *subordinated premium*: this will also initially be captured within the Treasury P&L, and should be treated consistently with the return on initial share capital per the Share Capital section above.

Bid–Offer Spread

When funding larger organisations with potentially multiple legal entities, there is generally a requirement to consider the bid–offer spread. We consider the approaches in this section.

Entity Netting

Where the banking corporation is a *price-taker* in the money markets, and the funding position of multiple entities are "swept" together to generate one central funding requirement, then there is often a netting benefit across the entities within the Group in determining which side of the bid–offer spread it will pay/receive.

If the Group is a *net borrower* of cash, then all entities pay/receive the higher "*offer*" rate on their funding position.

- Individual entities that are net *borrowers* pay the *same side* of the spread as what they would pay if funded separately in an external market.
- Individual entities that are net *lenders* receive the *more beneficial side* of the spread than what they would receive if funded separately in an external market.

If the Group is a *net lender* of cash, then all entities pay/receive the lower "*bid*" rate on their funding position.

- Individual entities that are net *borrowers* pay the *more beneficial side* of the spread than what they would pay if funded separately in an external market.
- Individual entities that are net *lenders* receive the *same side* of the spread as what they would receive if funded separately in an external market.

Individual entities may therefore receive a "subsidy" from other entities in the Group by having an opposite cash position to the combined Group.

Business Netting

The same relationship as the above applies to businesses operating within an entity; that is, there is a *funding rate benefit* available to businesses whose cash position is *opposite* to that of the combined entity.

Under these circumstances, there are two policy options available:

- Apply the same side of the bid–offer spread to all internal funding tickets, thereby feeding any funding rate netting benefit down to the entities and businesses that are creating the netting benefit. Factors to consider include the implications on the tax status of an entity obtaining a benefit from other group entities, as well as the "benefit at risk" to each entity/business of the existing funding relationships with existing funding sources.
- Treat each entity and each business within an entity as a discrete price-taking funding unit that borrows at "offer" and lends at "bid". The funding rate netting benefit would then accumulate centrally in the Treasury book, both at an entity level and at a group level, and may then be available for some form of reallocation, although the possible allocation bases for this are numerous.

Example Ticket Booking Structure

Figure 7.8 is an example ticket booking structure that incorporates the above concepts. It shows the individual books within Treasury, each capturing a particular facet of the entity's funding, providing required transparency of the funding P&L.

As an alternative to actually booking this multitude of internal transactions, which do provide transparency but also require a degree of operational effort to capture and control (especially in larger and more complex organisations), there are systems in the market whose objective is to achieve the same funding P&L allocation as the above without actually capturing the internal funding as ticketed transactions per se.

When implemented correctly, these can achieve the same granularity of management information without the same degree of operational effort, although these function by applying a cost of carry to open trading positions and therefore are in extricably linked to the balance sheet funding method discussed above.

APPENDIX 7.1 NPV AND VALUE-AT-RISK (VaR)

The NPV of a banking book is an appropriate target of interest-rate policy because it captures all future cash flows and is equal to the discounted value of future margins when the discount rate is the cost of all debt. The sensitivity of the NPV is derived from the duration of the assets and liabilities. Therefore we may write the change in NPV as below:

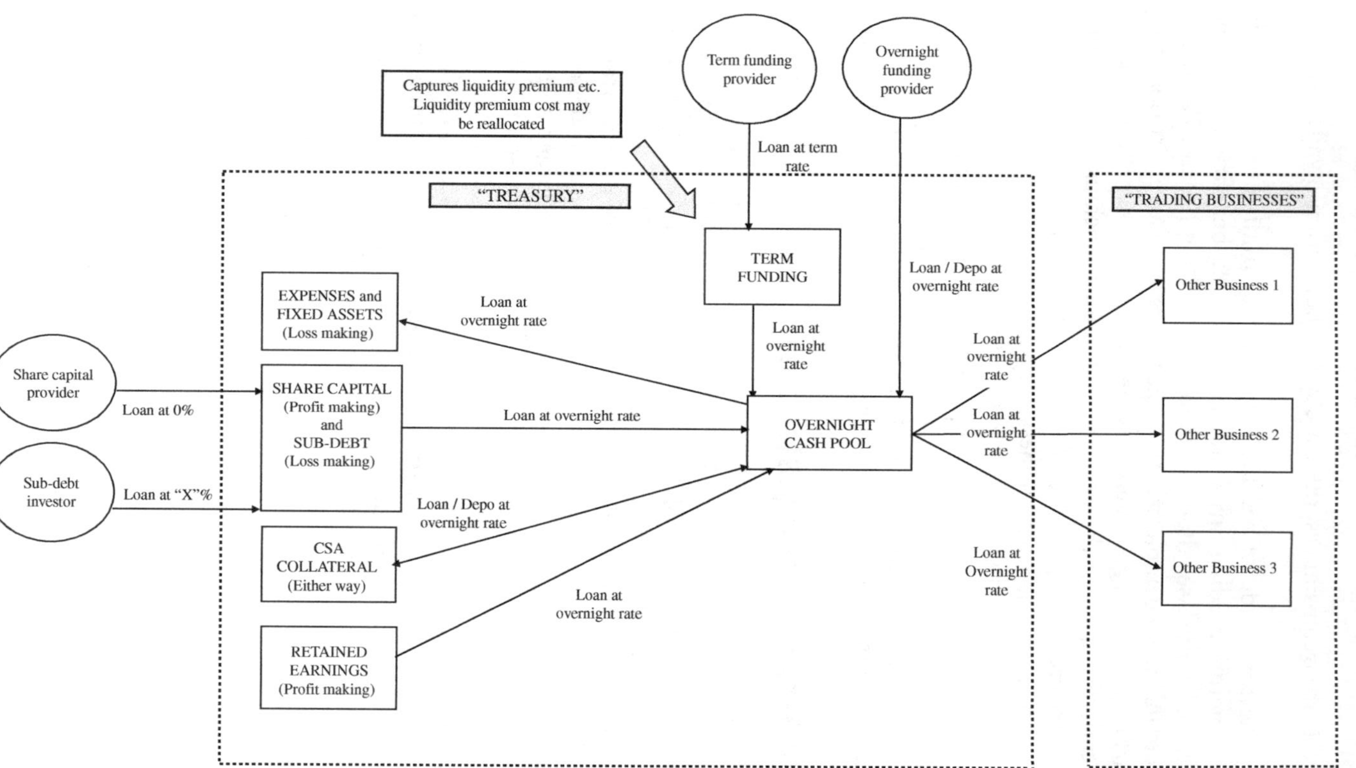

FIGURE 7.8 Ticket booking structure.

$$\frac{\Delta NPV}{\Delta r} = \left(\frac{1}{(1+r)}\right)(-D_A MV_A + D_L MV_L) \qquad (A7.1.1)$$

where D_A is the duration of assets and MV_A is the market value of assets. (A7.1.1) is applicable when only one interest rate is used for reference. The sensitivity with respect to the interest rate r is known. It is then possible to derive the VaR from these simple relationships above. With one interest rate we are interested in the maximum variation of the NPV that results from a change in the reference interest rate. The volatility of the NPV can be derived from its sensitivity and from the interest-rate volatility. If we set S_r as the sensitivity of the NPV with respect to the interest rate r, the volatility of the NPV is given by:

$$\sigma(NPV) = S_r \times \sigma(r). \qquad (A7.1.2)$$

Once the volatility is known, the maximum change at a given confidence level is obtained as a multiple of the volatility. The multiple is based on assumptions with respect to the shape of the distribution of interest rates. Under a curve of the normal distribution, a multiple of 1.96 provides the maximum expected change at a 2.5% two-tailed confidence level, so that we are able to say that the VaR of the book is as given by:

$$\text{VaR} = 1.96 \times S_r \times \sigma(r). \qquad (A7.1.3)$$

Where there is more than one interest rate, the variation of the NPV can be approximated as a linear combination of the variations due to a change of each interest rate. This is written as:

$$NPV = S_r \times \Delta r + S_s \times \Delta s + S_t \times \Delta t + L \qquad (A7.1.4)$$

where r, s and t are the different interest rates. Since all interest rate changes are uncertain, the volatility of the NPV is the volatility of a sum of random variables. Deriving the volatility of this sum requires assumptions on correlations between interest rates.

This problem is identical to the general problem of measuring the market risk of a portfolio when bearing in mind that its change in market value arises as a result of changes generated by the random variations of market parameters. The main concern is to calculate the volatility of the mark-to-market value of the portfolio, expressed as the sum of the random changes of the mark-to-market values of the various individual transactions. These random changes can be interdependent, in the same way that the underlying market parameters are. The volatility of the value of the portfolio depends upon the sensitivities of individual transactions, upon the volatilities of the individual market parameters and also upon their interdependency, if any exist. The methodology that calculates this volatility is known as *delta-VaR*. This is based on the delta sensitivity of the portfolio to changes inmarket interest rates.

REFERENCES AND BIBLIOGRAPHY

Asset & Liability Management (1998), London: RISK Books, 1998.

Bitner, J. (1992), *Successful Bank Asset-Liability Management*, New Jersey: John Wiley & Sons.

Butler, C. (1998), *Mastering Value-at-Risk*, London: FT Prentice Hall.

Cornyn, A. and Mays, E. (eds), (1997) *Interest Rate Risk Models: Theory and Practice*, Chicago, IL: Glenlake Publishing/Fitzroy Dearborn Publishers, chapters 6 and 15.

Gup, B. and Brooks, R. (1993), *Interest Rate Risk Management*, New York: Irwin.

Howe, D. (1992), *A Guide to Managing Interest-Rate Risk*, New York: New York Institute of Finance.

Johnson, H. (1994), *Bank Asset/Liability Management*, New York: Probus Publishing.

Kamakura Corporation (1998), *Asset & Liability Management: A Synthesis of New Methodologies*, London: Risk Publications.

Koch, T. (1988), *Bank Management*, New York: Dryden Press.

Marshall, J. and Bansal, V.K. (1992), *Financial Engineering*, New York: New York Institute of Finance, Chapter 20.

Schaffer, S. (May–June 1991), "Interest Rate Risk", *Business Review*, Federal Reserve Bank of Philadelphia, pp. 17–27.

Stevenson, B. and Fadil, M. Spring (1995), "Modern Portfolio Theory: Can it Work for Commercial Loans?", *Commercial Lending Review*, 10(2), pp. 4–12, London.

Toevs, A. and Haney, W. (1986), "Measuring and Managing Interest Rate Risk: A Guide to Asset/Liability Models Used in Banks and Thrifts", in Platt, R. (ed.), *Controlling Interest Rate Risk, New Techniques and Applications for Money Management*, New Jersey: John Wiley & Sons.

Wilson, J.S.G. (ed.) (1988), *Managing Banks' Assets and Liabilities*, London: Euromoney Publications.

CHAPTER 8

Asset–Liability Management III: Trading and Hedging Principles

In this chapter we introduce trading and hedging as employed by an ALM desk. Our purpose here is to acquaint the practitioner with the essential principles. The ALM and money markets desk supports the banking, fixed-interest and equities desks, hedging new issues, and working with the swaps and options desks. In some banks and securities houses it will be placed within the Treasury or money markets areas, whereas other firms will organise it as an entirely separate function. Wherever it is organised, the need for clear and constant communication between the ALM desk and other operating areas of the bank is paramount.

We look at specific uses of money market products (deposits and repo) in the context of conventional yield curve economics, and the principles of hedging using derivatives.

TRADING APPROACH

The Yield Curve and Interest Rate Expectations

When the yield curve is positively sloped, the conventional banking approach is to fund the book at the short end of the curve and lend at the long end. This is almost a definition of banking and is known as *maturity transformation.* In essence therefore if the yield curve resembled that shown in Figure 8.1 a bank would borrow, for example, 1-week funds while simultaneously lending out at, say, the 3-month maturity. This is known as funding short. The bank then continuously rolls over its funding at 1-week intervals for the 3-month period. This is known as *creating a tail*; here the "tail" is the gap between one week and three months – the interest-rate

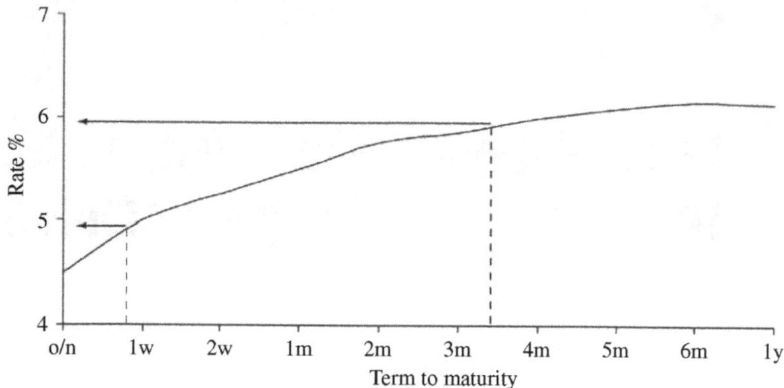

FIGURE 8.1 Positive yield curve funding.

"gap" that the bank is exposed to. During the course of the trade, as the bank has locked in a loan for three months, the bank is exposed to interest-rate risk should the slope or shape of the yield curve change. In this case if short-dated interest rates rise, the bank may see its profit margin shrink or turn into a funding loss.

As we noted in Chapter 5, there are a number of hypotheses advanced to explain the shape of the yield curve at any particular time. The Treasury desk will consider the shape of the curve and what it implies for future market conditions when implementing ALM policy.

In the case of an inverted yield curve, a bank will (all else being equal) lend at the short end of the curve and borrow at the longer end. This is known as *funding long* and is shown in Figure 8.2.

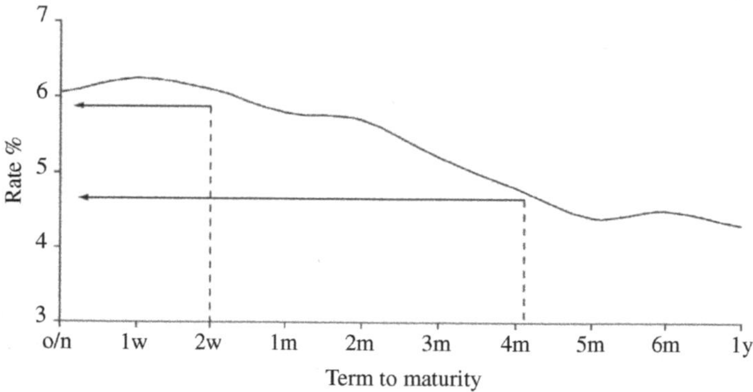

FIGURE 8.2 Negative yield curve funding.

The example in Figure 8.2 shows a short cash position of 2-week maturity against a long cash position of 4-month maturity. The interest rate gap of 10 weeks is the book's interest rate exposure. The inverted shape of the yield curve may indicate market expectations of a fall in short-term interest rates. Further along the yield curve the market may expect a benign inflationary environment, which is why the premium on longer term returns is lower than normal.

Credit Intermediation by the Repo Desk

The government bond repo market will trade at a lower rate than other money market instruments, reflecting its status as a secured instrument and the highest quality collateral. This allows the spreads between markets of different credits to be exploited. The following are examples of credit intermediation trades:

- a repo dealer lends general collateral currently trading at a spread below Libor, and uses the cash to buy bank CDs trading at a spread above Libor;
- a repo dealer borrows specific collateral in the stock-lending market, paying a fee, and sells the stock in the repo market at the GC rate; the cash is then lent in the inter-bank market at a higher rate; for instance, through the purchase of a clearing bank CD. The CD is used as collateral in the stock loan transaction. A bank must have dealing relationships with both the stock loan and repo markets to effect this trade. An example of the trade that could be put on using this type of intermediation is shown in Figure 8.3 for the UK gilt market; the details are given below, and in this instance show that the bank would gain 17 bps over the course of the 3-month trade;
- a repo dealer trades repo in the GC market, and using this cash reverse repo's in emerging market collateral at a spread, say, 400 bps higher.

These are only three examples of the way that repo can be used to exploit the interest-rate differentials that exist between markets of varying credit qualities, and between the secured and unsecured markets.

Figure 8.3 shows the potential gains that can be made by a repo dealing bank that has access to both the stock loan and general collateral repo market. It illustrates the rates available in the gilt market on 31 October 2000 for 3-month maturities, which were:

- 3-month GC repo 5.83 – 5.75%
- 3-month clearing bank CD 6 1/32 – 6.00%.

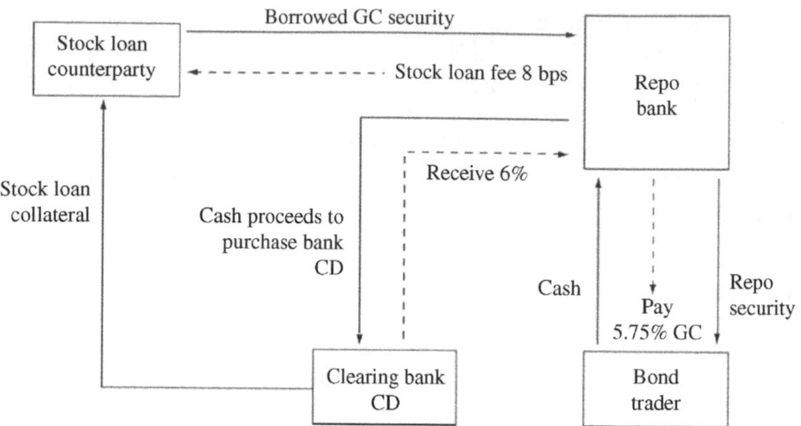

FIGURE 8.3 Intermediation between stock loan and repo markets; an example using UK gilts.

The stock loan fee for this term was quoted at 5–10 bps, with the actual fee paid being 8 bps. Therefore the repo trader borrows GC stock for three months, and offers this in repo at 5.75%; the cash proceeds are then used to purchase a clearing bank CD at 6.00%. This CD is used as collateral in the stock loan. The profit is market risk-free as the terms are locked, although there is an element of credit risk in holding the CD. On these terms in £100 million stock the profit for the 3-month period is approximately £170,000.

The main consideration for the dealing bank is the capital requirements of the trade. Gilt repo is zero-weighted for capital purposes, while the bank CD would probably be at 20% risk-weighted, so the capital cost is not onerous. The bank will need to ensure that it has sufficient credit lines for the repo and CD counterparties.

Yield Curve Trading: The Role of the Repo Funding Desk

We describe here a first-principles type of relative value trading common on fixed-interest desks, and the role played by the repo desk in funding the trade. If traders believe that the shape of the yield curve is going to change, thus altering the yield spread between two bonds of differing maturities, they can position the book to benefit from such a move. A yield spread arbitrage trade is not market directional; that is, it is not necessarily dependent on the direction that the market moves in, but rather the move in the shape of the yield curve. As long as the trade is duration weighted there is no first-order interest-rate risk involved, although there is second-order risk in that if the shape of the yield curve changes in the opposite direction to that expected, the traders will suffer a loss.

Consider the yield spread between two hypothetical bonds, one of 2-year and the other of 5-year maturity; the trader believes that this spread will widen in the near future. The trade therefore looks like this:

- buy £*x* million of the 2-year bond and fund in repo;
- sell £*y* million of the 5-year bond and cover in reverse repo.

The nominal amount of the 5-year bond will be a ratio of the respective basis point values multiplied by the amount of the 2-year bond.

The trader will arrange the repo transaction simultaneously (or instruct the repo desk to do so). The funding for both bonds forms an important part of the rationale for the trade. As repo rates can be fixed for the anticipated term of the trade, the trader will know the net funding cost – irrespective of any change in market levels or yield spreads – and this cost is the breakeven cost for the trade. A disciplined trader will have a time horizon for the trade, and the trade will be reviewed if the desired spread increase has not occurred by the expected time. In the case of the repo, however, the repo trader may wish to fix this at a shorter interval than the initial time horizon, and roll over as necessary. This will depend on the trader's (or repo desk's) view of repo rates.

Figure 8.4 illustrates the yield curve considerations involved.

The solid curve in Figure 8.4 represents the yield curve at the time the trade is put on, while the dotted curve shows the curve that is *anticipated* by the trader at the end of their time horizon for the trade. If this proves correct, at this point profit is taken and the trade is unwound. The increase

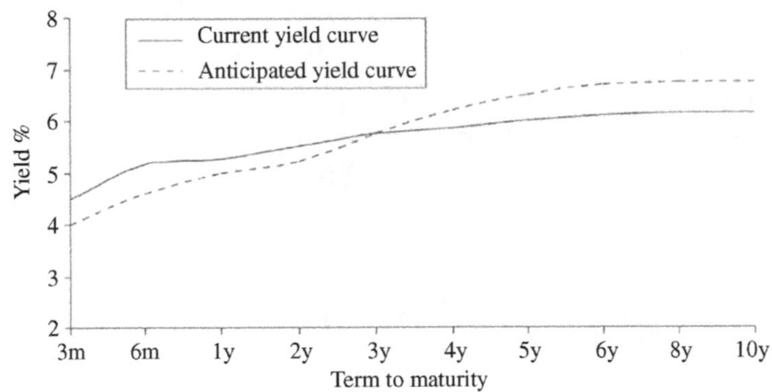

FIGURE 8.4 Yield curve relative value analysis.

in the 2-year versus 5-year spread is the profit made from the trade, minus the net funding.

This yield curve spread trade is an example of relative value trading. There are many variations on this, including trades spanning different currencies and markets.

EXAMPLE 8.1 BOND SPREAD TRADE AND FUNDING CONSIDERATIONS: EXAMPLE FROM THE GILT MARKET

The UK gilt yield curve for 1 November 2000 is shown in Figure 8.5. This is the Bloomberg screen "IYC". The trader believes that the spread between the 2-year benchmark bond, the UK Treasury 7% 2002 and the 5-year bond, the UK Treasury 8.5% 2005, will widen, and put on a spread position, sometimes referred to as a *swap* or *switch*[1] that is long the 2-year and short the 5-year. The respective bond yields also suit this

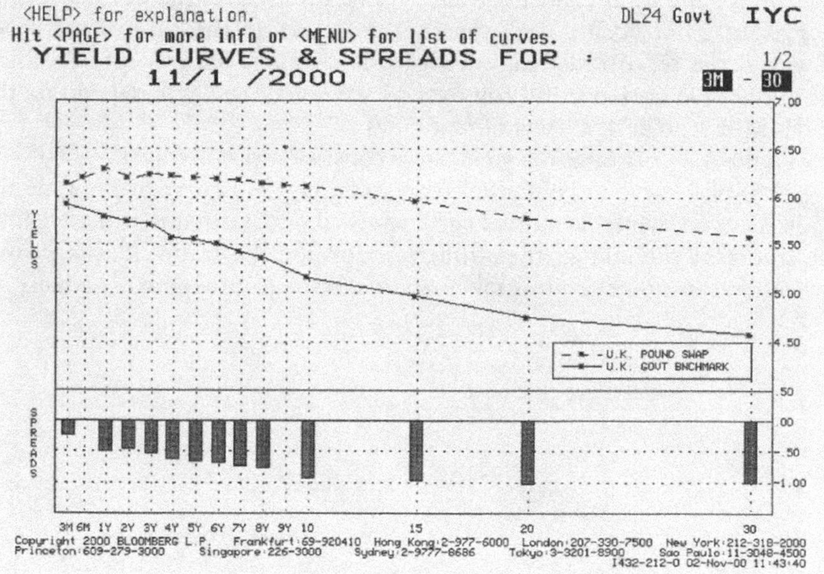

FIGURE 8.5 Bloomberg screen IYC showing yield curve.

1 Not to be confused with a swap, the derivative instrument.

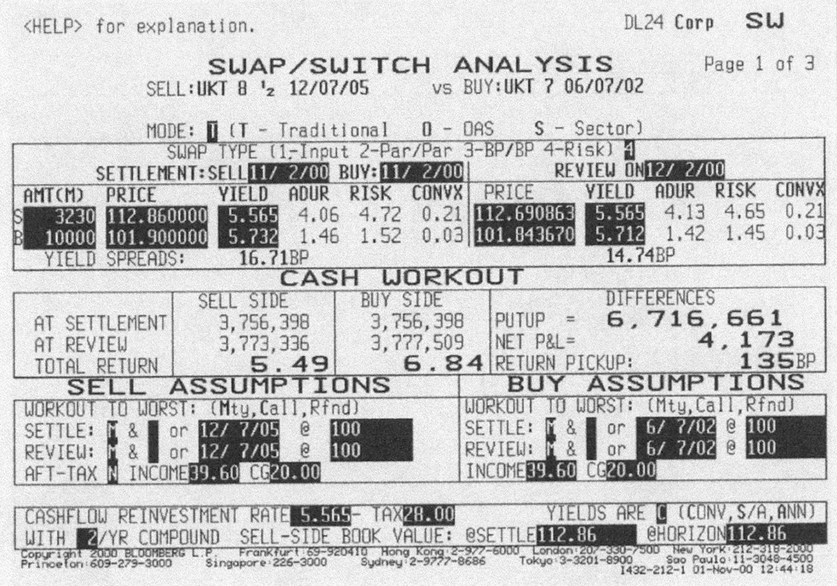

FIGURE 8.6 Bloomberg screen SW showing bond spread trade calculation.

trade because the inverted yield curve produces a higher return for the 2-year stock. If we assume the trader goes long of £10 million of the 7% 2002 bond, Bloomberg screen "SW" can be used to calculate the equivalent nominal amount of 5-year bond to short. From Figure 8.6 we see that this is £3.23 million nominal. This ratio is calculated using the respective basis point values (BPVs) for each stock, which Bloomberg terms the *risk* values. This calculation basis is user-selected, as shown by the number "4" being entered in the box marked "Swap Type" in Figure 8.6. The two-year bond has a redemption yield of 5.732%, against the yield on the 5-year of 5.565%; a yield pick-up of 16.7 bps. The trader has 1-month and 3-month horizon periods; that is, the trade will be reviewed at these points in time. The funding element is crucial. The trader obtains the following specific repo rates from the repo desk:

1-month	8.5% 2005	5.82–5.77%
	7% 2002	5.78–5.70%
3-month	8.5% 2005	5.83–5.75%
	7% 2002	5.77–5.72%.

(*continued*)

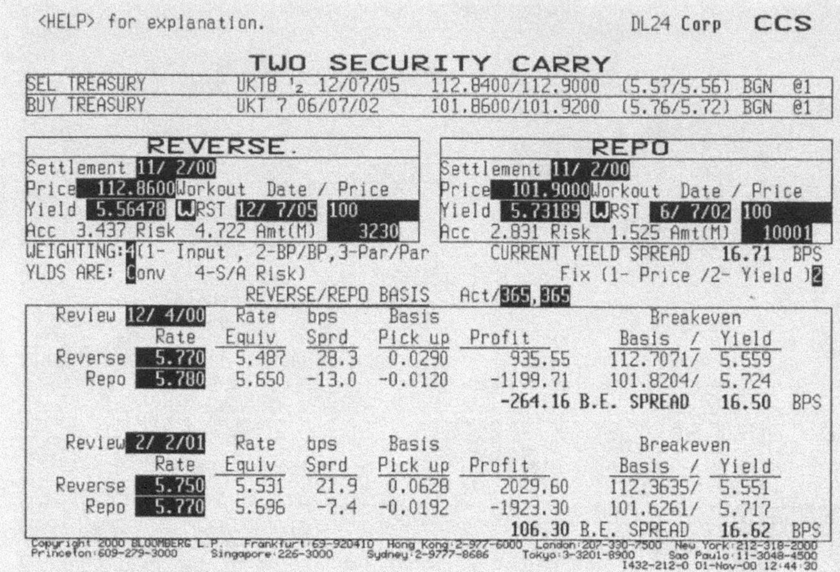

<HELP> for explanation. DL24 Corp CCS
TWO SECURITY CARRY
SEL TREASURY UKT8 ½ 12/07/05 112.8400/112.9000 (5.57/5.56) BGN @1
BUY TREASURY UKT 7 06/07/02 101.8600/101.9200 (5.76/5.72) BGN @1
REVERSE.
Settlement 11/ 2/00
Price 112.8600 Workout Date / Price
Yield 5.56478 WRST 12/ 7/05 100
Acc 3.437 Risk 4.722 Amt(M) 3230
REPO
Settlement 11/ 2/00
Price 101.9000 Workout Date / Price
Yield 5.73189 WRST 6/ 7/02 100
Acc 2.831 Risk 1.525 Amt(M) 10001
WEIGHTING: 4 (1- Input , 2-BP/BP, 3-Par/Par
YLDS ARE: C onv 4-S/A Risk)
CURRENT YIELD SPREAD 16.71 BPS
Fix (1- Price /2- Yield) 2
REVERSE/REPO BASIS Act/365, 365
Review 12/ 4/00 Rate bps Basis Breakeven
Rate Equiv Sprd Pick up Profit Basis / Yield
Reverse 5.770 5.487 28.3 0.0290 935.55 112.7071/ 5.559
Repo 5.780 5.650 -13.0 -0.0120 -1199.71 101.8204/ 5.724
-264.16 B.E. SPREAD 16.50 BPS
Review 2/ 2/01 Rate bps Basis Breakeven
Rate Equiv Sprd Pick up Profit Basis / Yield
Reverse 5.750 5.531 21.9 0.0628 2029.60 112.3635/ 5.551
Repo 5.770 5.696 -7.4 -0.0192 -1923.30 101.6261/ 5.717
106.30 B.E. SPREAD 16.62 BPS
Copyright 2000 BLOOMBERG L.P. Frankfurt:69-920410 Hong Kong:2-977-6000 London:207-330-7500 New York:212-318-2000
Princeton:609-279-3000 Singapore:226-3000 Sydney:2-9777-8686 Tokyo:3-3201-8900 Sao Paulo:11-3048-4500
1432-212-0 01-Nov-00 12:44:30

FIGURE 8.7 Bloomberg screen CCS showing bond spread trade repo funding.

The trader uses Bloomberg screen "CCS" to check the funding, inserting the rates given above. This shows the net funding cost and break-even amount for the trade; any widening of spread must be by at least the break-even amount to account for the funding cost. The calculations are shown in Figure 8.7. If the yield spread has widened by the trader's target after one month or three months, the trade is unwound and profit taken. If the spread has not widened by that amount after one month, the trade is reviewed and may be continued, but if it has narrowed by the stop-loss amount at any time it is unwound immediately.

REPO MARKET SPECIALS TRADING

The existence of an open repo market allows the demand for borrowing and lending stocks to be cleared by the price mechanism, in this case the repo rate. This facility also measures supply and demand for stocks more efficiently than traditional stock lending. It is to be expected that when specific stocks are in demand, for a number of reasons, the premium on obtaining them rises. This is reflected in the repo rate associated with the specific stock in demand, which falls below the same-maturity GC repo rate. The repo rate falls because the entity repoing out stock (that is, borrowing cash) is in possession of the desired asset: the specific bond. So the interest rate payable by this counterparty falls, as compensation for lending out the desired bond.

Factors contributing to individual securities becoming special include:

- government bond auctions; the bond to be issued is shorted by market-makers in anticipation of a new supply of stock and due to client demand;
- outright short selling, whether deliberate position-taking on the trader's view, or market-makers selling stock on client demand;
- hedging, including bond underwriters who will short the benchmark government bond that the corporate bond is priced against;
- derivatives trading such as basis ("cash-and-carry") trading creating demand for a specific stock.

Natural holders of government bonds can benefit from issues going special, which is when the demand for specific stocks is such that the rate for borrowing them is reduced. The lower repo rate reflects the premium for borrowing the stock. Note that the party borrowing the special stock is lending cash; it is the rate payable on the cash that they have lent which is depressed.

The holder of a stock that has gone special can obtain cheap funding for the issue itself, by lending it out. Alternatively, the holder can lend the stock and obtain cash in exchange in a repo, for which the rate payable is lower than the inter-bank rate. These funds can then be lent out as either secured funding (in a repo), or as unsecured funding, enabling the special stockholder to lock in a funding profit. For example, consider a situation where a repo dealer holds an issue that is trading at 5.5% in 1-week repo. The equivalent GC rate is 7%, making the specific issue very special. By lending the stock out, the dealer can lock in the profit by lending 1-week cash at 7%, or at a higher rate in the inter-bank market. This is illustrated in Figure 8.8.

There is a positive correlation between the extent to which a stock trades expensive to the yield curve and the degree to which it trades special in repo. Theory would predict this, since traders will maintain short positions for bonds with high funding (repo) costs only if the anticipated fall in the price of the bond is large enough to cover this funding premium. When stock is perceived as being expensive, for example after an auction announcement, this creates a demand for short positions and hence greater demand for the paper in repo. At other times the stock may go tight in the repo market, following which it will tend to be bid higher in the *cash* market as traders

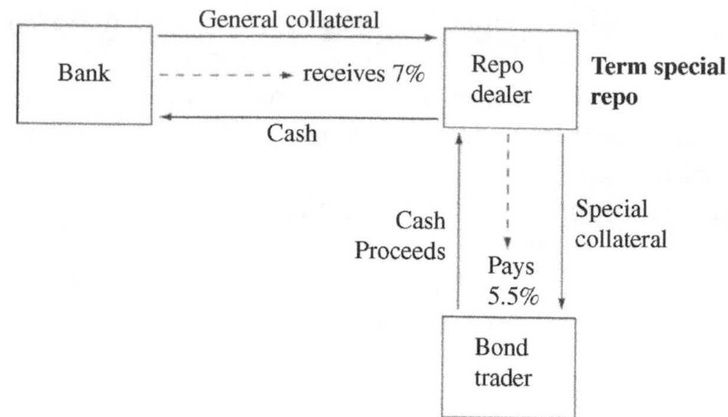

FIGURE 8.8 Funding gain from the repo of a special stock.

close out existing shorts (which becomes expensive to finance). At the same time traders and investors may attempt to buy the stock outright since it will now be cheap to finance in repo. The link between dearness in the cash market and special status in the repo market flows both ways.

INTEREST-RATE HEDGING TOOLS

Borrowing and lending cash of mismatched tenors, which is the essence of banking, creates interest-rate risk exposure. For dealers who are not looking to trade or speculate around term mismatch, there is more than one way to hedge the risk exposure. The best hedge for any trade is an exact offsetting trade. This is not always possible, nor indeed always desirable as it may reduce profit, or may use up valuable capital and credit lines. However, the advantage of a similar offsetting trade is that it reduces *basis risk* exposure.

The interest-rate risk exposure that the ALM desk seeks to hedge is part of managing the banking book. In this section we introduce the main hedging tools.

Interest-rate Futures

A forward term interest-rate gap exposure can be hedged using interest rate futures. In the sterling market the instrument will typically be the 90-day short sterling future traded on the London International Financial Futures and Options Exchange (LIFFE). The equivalents in USD and EUR are the Eurodollar and the Euribor contracts. A strip of futures can be used to hedge the term gap. The trader buys futures contracts to the value of the exposure and for the term of the gap. Any change in cash rates is then hedged by offsetting moves in futures prices.

Short-term interest rate futures fix the rate of interest on a notional fixed term deposit of money for a specified period in the future. The sum is notional because no actual sum of money is deposited when buying or selling futures; the instrument is off-balance sheet. Buying such a contract is equivalent to making a notional deposit, while selling a contract is equivalent to borrowing a notional sum.

The following examples illustrate hedging with short-term interest-rate contracts.

EXAMPLE 8.2 HEDGING A FORWARD 3-MONTH LENDING REQUIREMENT

On 1 June a Treasury desk is expecting a cash inflow of £10 million in three months' time (1 September), which it will then invest for three months. The desk expects that interest rates will fall the next few weeks and wishes to protect itself against such a fall. This can be done using short sterling futures. Market rates on 1 June are:

3-mo Libor	$6\frac{1}{2}\%$
Sep futures price	93.22

The desk buys 20 September short sterling futures contracts at 93.22, this number being equivalent to a notional sum of £10 million. This locks in a forward *lending* rate of 6.78%, if we assume there is no bid–offer quote spread.

$$\begin{aligned}\text{Expected lending rate} &= \text{rate implied by futures price}\\ &= 100 - 93.22\\ &= 6.78\%\end{aligned}$$

On 1 September market rates are as follows:

3-mo Libor	$6\frac{1}{4}\%$
Sep futures price	93.705

The desk unwinds the hedge at this price.

$$\begin{aligned}\text{Futures P\&L} &= +97 \text{ ticks } (93.705 - 93.22), \text{or } 0.485\%\\ \text{Effective lending rate} &= \text{3-mo Libor} + \text{futures profit}\\ &= 6.25\% + 0.485\%\\ &= 6.735\%\end{aligned}$$

The desk is close to achieving its target lending rate of 6.78% and the hedge has helped to protect against the drop in Libor rates from $6\frac{1}{2}\%$ to $6\frac{1}{4}\%$, due to the profit from the futures transaction.

EXAMPLE 8.3 HEDGING A FORWARD 6-MONTH BORROWING REQUIREMENT

A treasury dealer has a 6-month borrowing requirement for GBP30 million in three month's time, on 16 September. She expects interest rates to rise by at least ½% before that date and would like to lock in a future borrowing rate. The scenario is detailed below.

Date:	16 June
3-mo Libor	6.0625%
6-mo Libor	6.25
Sep futures contract	93.66
Dec futures contract	93.39

In order to hedge a 6-month GBP30 million exposure the dealer needs to use a total of 60 futures contracts, as each has a nominal value of GBP500,000, and corresponds to a 3-month notional deposit period. The dealer decides to sell 30 September futures contracts and 30 December futures contracts, which is referred to as a *strip* hedge. The expected forward borrowing rate that can be achieved by this strategy, where the expected borrowing rate is rf, is calculated as follows:

$$\left[1 + rf \times \frac{\text{days in period}}{360}\right] = \left[1 + \text{Sep implied rate} \times \frac{\text{Sep days period}}{360}\right] \times \left[1 + \text{Dec implied rate} \times \frac{\text{Dec days period}}{360}\right].$$

Therefore we have:

$$\left[1 + rf \times \frac{180}{360}\right] = \left[1 + 0.0634 \times \frac{90}{360}\right] \times \left[1 + 0.0661 \times \frac{90}{360}\right]$$

$$rf = 6.53\%.$$

The rate rf is sometimes referred to as the "strip rate".

The hedge is unwound upon expiry of the September futures contract. Assume the following rates now prevail:

3-mo Libor	6.4375%
6-mo Libor	6.8125
Sep futures contract	93.56
Dec futures contract	92.93

The futures profit and loss is:

September contract:	+10 ticks
December contract:	+46 ticks

This represents a 56 tick or 0.56% profit in 3-month interest-rate terms, or 0.28% in 6-month interest-rate terms. The effective borrowing rate is the 6-month Libor rate minus the futures profit, or:

$$6.8125\% - 0.28\% \text{ or } 6.5325\%.$$

In this case the hedge has proved effective because the dealer has realised a borrowing rate of 6.5325%, which is close to the target strip rate of 6.53%.

The dealer is still exposed to basis risk when the December contracts are bought back from the market at the expiry date of the September contract. If, for example, the future was bought back at 92.73, the effective borrowing rate would be only 6.4325%, and the dealer would benefit. Of course, the other possibility is that the futures contract could be trading 20 ticks more expensive, which would give a borrowing rate of 6.6325%, which is 10 bps above the target rate. If this happened, the dealer may elect to borrow in the cash market for three months, and maintain the December futures position until the December contract expiry date, and roll over the borrowing at that time. The profit (or loss) on the December futures position will compensate for any change in 3-month rates at that time.

Forward Rate Agreements

FRAs are similar in concept to interest-rate futures and are also off-balance sheet instruments. Under an FRA a buyer agrees notionally to borrow and a seller to lend a specified notional amount at a fixed rate for a specified period; the contract to commence on an agreed date in the future. On this date (the "fixing date") the actual rate is taken and, according to its position versus the original trade rate, the borrower or lender will receive an interest payment on the notional sum equal to the difference between the trade rate and the actual rate. The sum paid over is present-valued as it is transferred at the start of the notional loan period, whereas in a cash market trade interest would be handed over at the end of the loan period. As FRAs are off-balance sheet contracts no actual borrowing or lending of cash takes place, hence the use of the term "notional". In hedging an interest-rate gap

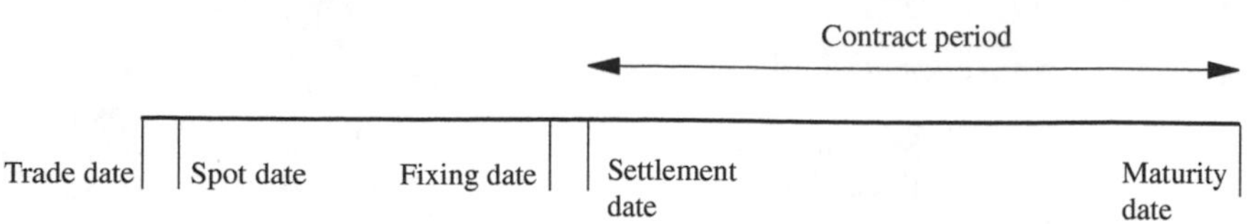

FIGURE 8.9 Key dates in FRA transaction.

in the cash period, the trader will buy an FRA contract that equates to the term gap for a nominal amount equal to their exposure in the cash market. Should rates move against them in the cash market, the gain on the FRA should (in theory) compensate for the loss in the cash trade.

Figure 8.9 shows the relevant time periods in a FRA transaction.

EXAMPLE 8.4 HEDGING WITH FRAs

A bank anticipates having to borrow GBP10 million in three month's time for a 12-month period, to fund a corporate loan. It can borrow funds today at Libor + 50 bps. Libor rates today are at 5%, but the Treasury desk expects rates to rise during the next several weeks. This presents a risk of having to fund the client transaction at higher rates unless a hedge is transacted to protect the borrowing requirement. Treasury decides to buy a 3×15 ("threes-fifteens") FRA to cover the 12-month period beginning three months from now. A dealer bank quotes $5\frac{1}{2}\%$ for the FRA, which the company buys for a notional GBP10 million. Three months from now rates have indeed gone up to 6%, thus the bank's funding rate is now $6\frac{1}{2}\%$ (the Libor rate plus spread); however, it will receive a settlement amount that will be the difference between the rate at which the FRA was bought and today's 12-month Libor rate (6%) as a percentage of GBP10 million, which will compensate for the increased borrowing costs. The FRA has enabled the bank to lock in funding rates today for a forward-starting transaction.

Interest-rate Swaps

An interest-rate swap is an off-balance sheet agreement between two parties to make periodic interest payments to each other. Payments occur on a predetermined set of dates in the future, based on a notional principal amount; one party is the *fixed-rate payer*, the rate agreed at the start of the swap, and the other party is the *floating-rate payer*, the floating-rate being determined during the life of the swap by reference to a specific market rate or index. There is no exchange of principal, only of the interest payments on this principal amount. Note that our description is for a plain vanilla swap contract; it is common to have variations on this theme – for instance, *floating–floating* swaps where both payments are floating-rate, as well as *cross-currency* swaps where there is an exchange of an equal amount of different currencies at the start- and end-dates for the swap.

An interest-rate swap can be used to hedge the fixed-rate risk arising from the purchase of a bond during a repo arbitrage or spread trade. The terms of the swap should match the payment dates and maturity date of the bond. The idea is to match the cash flows from the bond with equal and opposite payments in the swap contract, which will hedge the bond position. For example, if a trader has purchased a bond, they will be receiving fixed-rate coupon payments on the nominal value of the bond. To hedge this position the trader buys a swap contract for the same nominal value in which they will be paying the same fixed-rate payment; the net cash flow is a receipt of floating interest-rate payments. A bond issuer, on the other hand, may issue bonds of a particular type because of the investor demand for such paper, but prefer to have the interest exposure on debt in some other form. So, for example, a UK company issues fixed-rate bonds denominated in, say, Australian dollars, swaps the proceeds into sterling and pays floating-rate interest on the sterling amount. As part of the swap it will be receiving fixed-rate Australian dollars; which neutralises the exposure arising from the bond issue. At the termination of the swap (which must coincide with the maturity of the bond) the original currency amounts are exchanged back, enabling the issuer to redeem the holders of the bond in Australian dollars. (Note that this type of transaction generates cross-currency basis risk and quanto risk exposures, which must be hedged dynamically. This subject is discussed in Choudhry *et al* (forthcoming).)

INTEREST-RATE SWAP HEDGING APPLICATIONS

We review some of the principal uses of swaps as an interest-rate hedging tool.

Basic Applications

Swaps are part of the OTC market and so they can be tailored to suit the particular requirements of the user, thus they are structured so that they

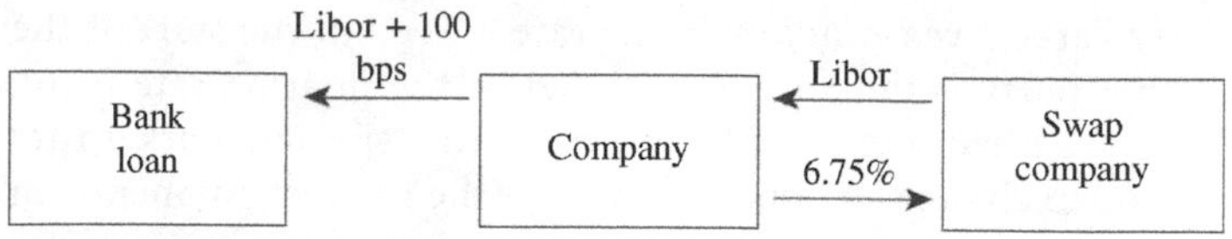

FIGURE 8.10 Changing liability from floating- to fixed-rate.

match particular payment dates, payment frequencies and Libor margins, reflecting the underlying exposure of the customer.

Swap applications can be viewed as being one of two main types: asset-linked swaps and liability-linked swaps. Asset-linked swaps are created when the swap is linked to an asset such as a bond in order to change the characteristics of the income stream for investors. Liability-linked swaps are traded when borrowers of funds wish to change the interest basis of their liabilities.

A straightforward application of an interest-rate swap is when a borrower wishes to convert a floating-rate liability into a fixed-rate one, usually in order to remove the exposure to upward moves in interest rates. For instance, a company may wish to fix its financing costs. Let us assume a company currently borrowing money at a floating-rate, say 6-month Libor + 100 bps, fears that interest rates may rise in the remaining three years of its loan. It enters into a 3-year semi-annual interest-rate swap with a bank, as the fixed-rate payer, paying say 6.75% against receiving 6-month Libor. This fixes the company's borrowing costs for three years at 7.75% (7.99% effective annual rate). This is shown in Figure 8.10.

EXAMPLE 8.5 LIABILITY-LINKED SWAP, FIXED-TO FLOATING- TO FIXED-RATE EXPOSURE

A corporate borrows for five years at a rate of $6\frac{1}{4}$% and shortly after enters into a swap paying floating-rate, so that its net borrowing cost is Libor + 40 bps. After one year, swap rates have fallen such that the company is quoted 4-year swap rates as 4.90%–4.84%. The company decides to switch back into fixed-rate liability in order to take advantage of the lower interest rate environment. It enters into a second swap paying fixed at 4.90% and receiving Libor. The net borrowing cost is now 5.30%. The arrangement is illustrated in Figure 8.11. The company has saved 95 bps on its original borrowing cost, which is the difference between the two swap rates.

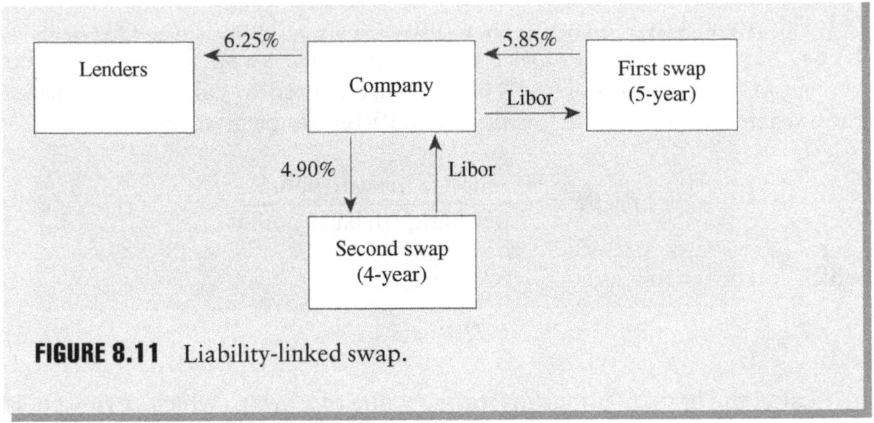

FIGURE 8.11 Liability-linked swap.

Asset-linked swap structures might be required when, for example, investors require a fixed-interest security when floating-rate assets are available. Borrowers often issue FRNs, the holders of which may prefer to switch the income stream into fixed coupons. As an example, consider a local authority pension fund holding 2-year floating-rate gilts. This is an asset of the highest quality, paying Libid minus 12.5 bps. The pension fund wishes to swap the cash flows to create a fixed-interest asset. It obtains a quote for a tailor-made swap where the floating leg pays Libid, the quote being 5.55–50%. By entering into this swap, the pension fund has in place a structure that pays a fixed coupon of 5.375%. This is shown in Figure 8.12.

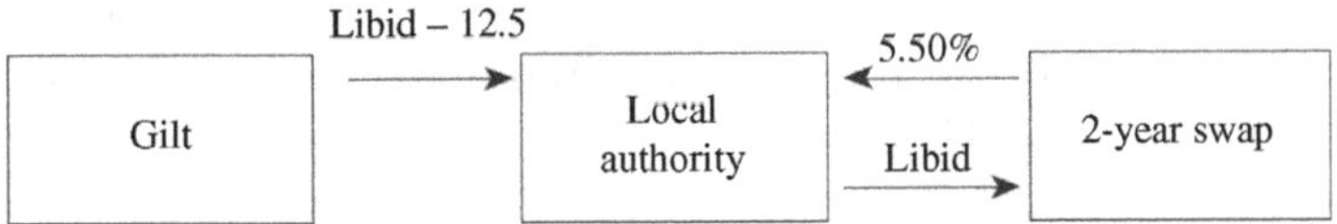

FIGURE 8.12 Transforming floating-rate asset to fixed-rate.

Hedging Interest-rate Risk Using Interest-rate Swaps

A trading desk has the option of using other bonds, bond futures or bond options, as well as swaps, when hedging the interest-rate risk exposure of a bond position. However, swaps are particularly efficient instruments to use because they display positive convexity characteristics; that is, the increase in value of a swap for a fall in interest rates exceeds the loss in value with a similar magnitude rise in rates. This is exactly the price/yield profile of vanilla bonds.

The primary risk measure we require when hedging using a swap is its PVBP.[2] This measures the price sensitivity of the swap for a basis-point change in interest rates. The PVBP measure is used to calculate the hedge ratio when hedging a bond position. The PVBP can be given by:

$$PVBP = \frac{\text{Change in swap value}}{\text{Rate change in basis points}} \tag{8.1}$$

which can be written as:

$$PVBP = \frac{dS}{dr}. \tag{8.2}$$

Using the basic relationship for the value of a swap, which is viewed as the difference between the values of a fixed-coupon bond and equivalent-maturity floating-rate bond we can also write:

$$PVBP = \frac{d\text{Fixed bond}}{dr} - \frac{d\text{Floating bond}}{dr}, \tag{8.3}$$

which essentially states that the BPV of the swap is the difference in the BPVs of the fixed-coupon and floating-rate bonds. The value is usually calculated for a notional £1 million of swap. The calculation is based on the duration and modified-duration calculations used for bonds and assumes that there is a parallel shift in the yield curve. Table 8.1 illustrates how equations (8.3) and (8.4) below can be used to obtain the PVBP of a swap. Hypothetical 5-year bonds are used in the example. The PVBP for a bond can be calculated using Bloomberg or the MDURATION function on Microsoft Excel. Using either of the two equations above we see that the PVBP of the swap is £425.00. This is shown below.

Calculating the PVBP using (8.2), we have:

$$PVBP_{swap} = \frac{dS}{dr} = \frac{4264 - (-4236)}{20} = 425$$

while we obtain the same result using the bond values:

$$\begin{aligned} PVBP_{swap} &= PVBP_{fixed} - PVBP_{floating} \\ &= \frac{1{,}004{,}940 - 995{,}171}{20} - \frac{1{,}000{,}640 - 999{,}371}{20} \\ &= 488.45 - 63.45 \\ &= 425.00. \end{aligned}$$

---

2 This is also known as DVBP, or dollar value of a basis point, or DV01.

TABLE 8.1 PVBP for interest-rate swap.

Interest-rate swap			
	Term to maturity:	5 years	
	Fixed leg:	6.50%	
	Basis:	Semi-annual, act/365	
	Floating leg:	6-month Libor	
	Basis:	Semi-annual, act/365	
	Nominal amount:	£1,000,000	
		Present value £	
	Rate change −10 bps	0 bps	Rate change +10 bps
Fixed-coupon bond	1,004,940	1,000,000	995,171
Floating-rate bond	1,000,640	1,000,000	999,371
Swap	4,264	0	4,236

The swap BPV is lower than that of the 5-year fixed-coupon bond; that is, £425 compared to £488.45. This is because of the impact of the floating-rate bond risk measure, which reduces the risk exposure of the swap as a whole by £63.45. As a rough rule of thumb, the PVBP of a swap is approximately equal to that of a fixed-rate bond that has a maturity similar to the period from the next coupon reset date of the swap through to the maturity date of the swap. This means that a 10-year semi-annual paying swap would have a PVBP close to that of a 9.5-year fixed-rate bond, and a 5.5-year swap would have a PVBP similar to that of a 5-year bond.

When using swaps as hedge tools, we bear in mind that over time the PVBP of swaps behaves differently from that of bonds. Immediately preceding an interest reset date, the PVBP of a swap will be near identical to that of the same-maturity fixed-rate bond, because the PVBP of a floating-rate bond at this time has essentially nil value. Immediately after the reset date, the swap PVBP will be near identical to that of a bond that matures at the next reset date. This means that at the point (and this point only) right after the reset the swap PVBP will decrease by the amount of the floating-rate PVBP. In between reset dates, the swap PVBP is quite stable, as the effects of the fixed and floating-rate PVBP changes cancel each other out. Contrast this with the fixed-rate PVBP, which decreases in value over time in stable fashion.[3] This feature is illustrated in Figure 8.13. A slight anomaly is that the PVBP of a swap actually increases by a small amount between

3 This assumes no sudden large-scale yield movements.

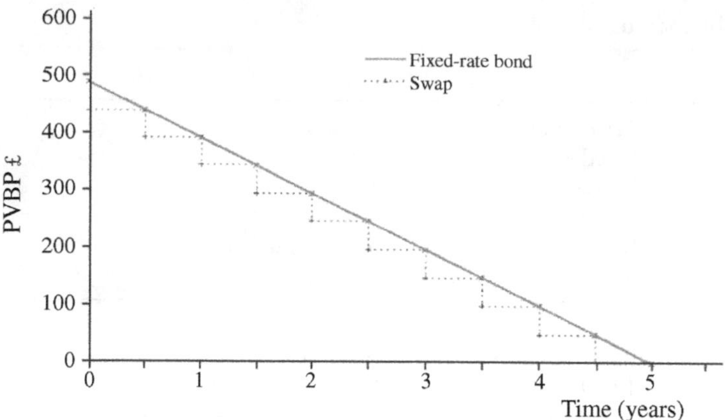

FIGURE 8.13 The PVBP of a five-year swap and fixed-rate bond.

reset dates; this is because the PVBP of a floating-rate bond decreases at a slightly faster rate than that of the fixed-rate bond during this time.

Hedging bond instruments with interest-rate swaps is conceptually similar to hedging with another bond or with bond futures contracts. If one is holding a long position in a vanilla bond, the hedge requires a long position in the swap: remember that a long position in a swap is to be paying fixed (and receiving floating). This hedges the receipt of fixed from the bond position. The change in the value of the swap will match the change in value of the bond, only in the opposite direction.[4] The maturity of the swap should match that of the bond as closely as possible. As swaps are OTC contracts, it should be possible to match interest dates as well as maturity dates. If one is short the bond, the hedge is to be short the swap, so the receipt of fixed matches the pay-fixed liability of the short bond position.

The correct nominal amount of the swap to put on is established using the PVBP hedge ratio. This is given as:

$$\text{Hedge ratio} = \frac{PVBP_{bond}}{PVBP_{swap}}. \tag{8.4}$$

This technique is still used in the market but suffers from the assumption of parallel yield-curve shifts and will lead to significant

4 The change will not be an exact mirror. It is very difficult to establish a precise hedge for a number of reasons, which include differences in day-count bases, maturity mismatches and basis differential.

hedging error over time. This is addressed through the application of *dynamic hedging*, which refers to constant adjustments to the hedge during the life of the transaction. These adjustments are sometimes referred to as *convexity adjustments*.

Overnight Index Interest-rate Swaps

Overnight index swaps (OIS) are interest-rate swaps that are traded in the money markets. Conventional swaps pay fixed against a quarterly or semi-annual floating payment. OIS swaps pay fixed against the overnight interest rate. In the sterling market they are known as sterling overnight interest-rate average swaps, or SONIA, while euro-currency OIS are known as EONIA.

SONIA Swaps

SONIA is the average interest rate of inter-bank (unsecured) overnight sterling deposit trades undertaken before 1530 hours each day between members of the London Wholesale Money Brokers' Association. Recorded interest rates are weighted by volume. A SONIA swap is a swap contract that exchanges a fixed interest rate (the swap rate) against the geometric average of the overnight interest rates that have been recorded during the life of the contract. Exchange of interest takes place on maturity of the swap. SONIA swaps are used to speculate on or to hedge against interest rates at the very short end of the sterling yield curve; in other words, they can be used to hedge an exposure to overnight interest rates.[5]

Conventional swap rates are calculated off the government bond yield curve and represent the credit premium over government yields of inter-bank default risk. Essentially they represent an average of the forward rates derived from the government spot (zero-coupon) yield curve. The fixed rate quoted on a SONIA swap represents the average level of the overnight interest rates expected by market participants over the life of the swap. In practice, the rate is calculated as a function of the BoE's repo rate. This is the 2-week rate at which the BoE conducts reverse repo trades with banking counterparties as part of its open market operations. In other words, this is the BoE's base rate. In theory one would expect the SONIA rate to follow

5 Traditionally, overnight rates fluctuate in a very wide range during the day, depending on the day's funds shortage, and although volatility has reduced since the introduction of gilt repo, it is still unpredictable on occasions.

the repo rate fairly closely, since the credit risk on an overnight deposit is low. However, in practice the spread between the SONIA rate and the BoE repo rate is very volatile, and for this reason the swaps are used to hedge overnight exposures.

EXAMPLE 8.6 USING AN OIS SWAP TO HEDGE A FUNDING REQUIREMENT

A derivatives desk at an investment bank offers a leveraged investment product to a client in the form of a participating interest share in a hedge fund. The client's investment is leveraged by funds lent to it by the investment bank, for which the interest rate charged is overnight Libor plus a spread.

The investment product has an expected life of two years. Up to now the bank's Treasury desk has been funding this requirement by borrowing overnight each day. It now wishes to match the funding requirement raised by this product by matching asset term structure to the liability term structure. Let us assume that this product creates a USD1 billion funding requirement for the bank.

The current market deposit rates are shown in Figure 8.14. The Treasury desk therefore funds this requirement in the following way:

Assets:	$1 billion, > 1-year term
	Receiving overnight Libor + 130 bps
Liabilities:	$350 million, 6-month loan
	Pay 1.22%
	$350 million, 12-month loan
	Pay 1.50%
	$300 million, 15-month loan
	Pay 1.70%.

This matches the asset structure more closely to the term structure of the assets; however, it creates an interest-rate basis mismatch in that the bank is now receiving an overnight Libor-based income, but paying a term-based liability. To remove this basis mismatch, the Treasury desk transacts an OIS swap to match the amount and term of each of the loan deals, paying overnight floating-rate interest and receiving fixed-rate interest. The rates for OIS swaps of varying terms

GRAB M-Mkt TTDE

11:37 TULLETT & TOKYO PAGE 1 / 1

	USD Cash Deposits	Non-Japanese Bid	Ask	Time		USD Cash Deposits	Japanese Bid	Ask	Time
1)	Spot	1.0000	1.0200	9:33	18)	T/N	1.0000	1.0300	11/07
2)	T/N	1.0100	1.0300	11/07	19)	1 Week	1.0400	1.0600	9:33
3)	1 Week	1.0300	1.0500	9:33	20)	2 Week	1.0500	1.0700	9:33
4)	2 Week	1.0300	1.0500	9:33	21)	3 Week	1.0600	1.0800	9:33
5)	3 Week	1.0300	1.0500	9:33	22)	1 Month	1.0800	1.1000	9:33
6)	1 Month	1.0400	1.0500	9:33	23)	2 Month	1.1800	1.2100	9:33
7)	2 Month	1.1200	1.1400	9:33	24)	3 Month	1.1900	1.2200	9:33
8)	3 Month	1.1300	1.1500	9:33	25)	4 Month	1.2000	1.2300	9:33
9)	4 Month	1.1400	1.1700	9:33	26)	5 Month	1.2100	1.2400	9:33
10)	5 Month	1.1600	1.1900	9:33	27)	6 Month	1.2300	1.2600	9:33
11)	6 Month	1.2000	1.2200	9:33	28)	7 Month	1.2700	1.3000	9:33
12)	7 Month	1.2300	1.2500	9:33	29)	8 Month	1.3100	1.3400	9:33
13)	8 Month	1.2700	1.2900	9:33	30)	9 Month	1.3800	1.4100	9:33
14)	9 Month	1.3300	1.3600	9:33	31)	10 Month	1.4600	1.4900	9:33
15)	10 Month	1.3800	1.4100	9:33	32)	11 Month	1.5300	1.5600	9:33
16)	11 Month	1.4500	1.4800	9:33	33)	12 Month	1.5500	1.5800	9:33
17)	12 Month	1.5000	1.5300	9:33					

FIGURE 8.14 Tullet US dollar deposit rates, 10 November 2003.

are shown in Figure 8.15, which show two-way prices for OIS swaps up to two years in maturity. So for the 6-month OIS the hedger is receiving fixed-interest at a rate of 1.085% and for the 12-month OIS it is receiving 1.40%. The difference between what it is receiving in the swap and what it is paying in the term loans is the cost of removing the basis mismatch, but more fundamentally reflects a key feature of OIS swaps versus deposit rates: deposit rates are Libor-related, whereas US dollar OIS rates are driven by the Fed Funds rate. On average, the Fed Funds rate lies approximately 8–10 bps below the dollar deposit rate, and sometimes as much as 15 bps below cash levels. Note that at the time of this trade, the Fed Funds rate was 1% and the market was not expecting a rise in this rate until at least the second half of 2004. This sentiment would have influenced the shape of the USD OIS curve.

The action taken above hedges out the basis mismatch and also enables the Treasury desk to match its asset profile with its liability profile. The net cost to the Treasury desk represents its hedging costs.

Figure 8.16 illustrates the transaction.

(continued)

(*continued*)

GRAB Corp ICAU

11:34 USD OIS – ICAU PAGE 1 / 1

	USD OIS	Ask	Bid	Time
1)	1 Month	1.0190	0.9990	9:30
2)	2 Month	1.0240	1.0040	9:30
3)	3 Month	1.0310	1.0110	9:30
4)	4 Month	1.0440	1.0240	10:59
5)	5 Month	1.0710	1.0510	10:59
6)	6 Month	1.1050	1.0850	11:04
7)	7 Month	1.1420	1.1220	10:59
8)	8 Month	1.1920	1.1720	11:00
9)	9 Month	1.2420	1.2220	11:05
10)	10 Month	1.2930	1.2730	11:00
11)	11 Month	1.3580	1.3380	11:00
12)	12 Month	1.4210	1.4000	11:06
13)	15 Month	1.6250	1.6040	11:00
14)	18 Month	1.8090	1.7890	11:00
15)	21 Month	2.0080	1.9880	11:00
16)	24 Month	2.2030	2.1820	11:00

Australia 61 2 9777 8600 Brazil 5511 3048 4500 Europe 44 20 7330 7500 Germany 49 69 920410
Hong Kong 852 2977 6000 Japan 81 3 3201 8900 Singapore 65 6212 1000 U.S. 1 212 318 2000
G657-802-0 10-Nov-03 11:34:17

FIGURE 8.15 Garban ICAP US dollar OIS rates, 10 November 2003.

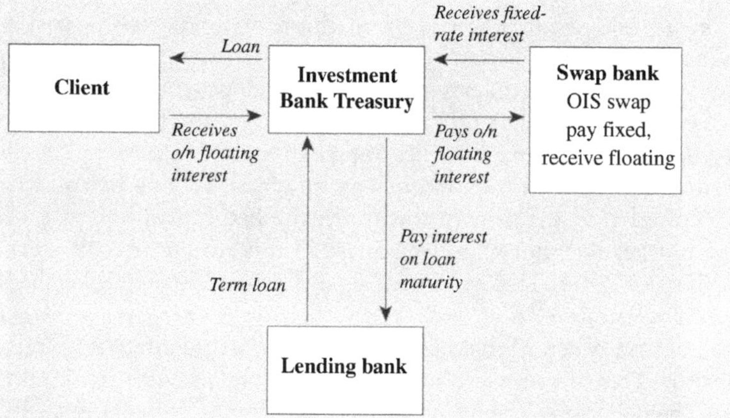

FIGURE 8.16 Illustration of interest basis mismatch hedging using OIS instrument.

EXAMPLE 8.7 CASH FLOWS ON OIS

Table 8.2 shows the daily rate fixes on a 6-month OIS that was traded for effective date 17 October 2003, at a fixed rate of 1.03%. The swap notional is USD200 million.

From Table 8.2 we see that the average rate for Fed Funds during this period was 0.99952%. Hence on settlement the fixed-rate payer would have passed over a net settlement amount of USD 30,480.

TABLE 8.2 OIS swap settlement, traded 17 October 2003.

Overnight-index swap	
Effective date	17-Oct-03
Maturity	19-Apr-04
Notional	USD200 million
Fixed-leg pay	1.030%
Floating-leg receive	Fed Funds overnight act/360
Fixed-leg pay	USD1,030,000
Floating-leg receive	USD999,520
Settlement amount	USD30,480
Average rate	0.99952%

INTEREST-RATE RISK EXPOSURE AND OPTION HEDGING

Managing interest-rate risk exposure is a significant responsibility of the bank ALM practitioner. We have seen how FRAs, futures and swaps can be used to hedge such exposure, and the flexibility and liquidity offered by these instruments means that in most cases they are all that is needed when hedging interest-rate risk. However, in certain cases a bank ALM desk may want to use option products. We illustrate such use here.

A bank that made extensive use of floating-rate liabilities in its funding is exposed to the risk of lower NII in the event that interest rates rise. It would be described as a "liability-sensitive" bank, because as interest rates rose its funding cost would increase, while its asset returns may not.[6] This would cause the net interest margin (NIM) to reduce. This risk exposure can

6 Even if all the assets are not fixed-rate, as indeed many would not be, they may still re-price on a less frequent basis than the liabilities and this also creates interest-rate risk in a rising rate environment.

be hedged by using an interest-rate cap, essentially a put option on interest rates, to reduce the extent of the risk exposure.

EXAMPLE 8.8 USING OPTIONS TO HEDGE INTEREST-RATE RISK EXPOSURE

Consider an hypothetical small-sized retail bank with a USD200 million balance sheet. Its simplified gap report is shown at Table 8.3. This shows that the majority of the bank's assets are fixed rate, while a majority of its funding (liabilities) are floating-rate. This liability sensitivity is indicated by the "instant" gap of −80.00, as shown in the table.[7] In other words, the bank exhibits an earnings stream that is at risk from a rise in interest rates. We illustrate this in Table 8.4, which shows the impact of a 100 bp parallel shift in market interest rates (we assume that all the floating-rate assets and

TABLE 8.3 Bank simplified gap report.

Asset–liability gap		
Assets	(million)	Fixed rate or current floating-rate
Loans: fixed rate	140	8%
Bonds: fixed rate	40	7%
Bonds: floating-rate	20	5%
Total assets	200	
Risk-sensitive assets (RSA)	20	
Liabilities		
Deposits: floating-rate	100	3%
Deposits: fixed rate	60	3%
NIBLs	20	0%
Capital	20	0%
	200	
Risk-sensitive liabilities (RSL)	100	
Gap	−80.0	
RSA/RSL	20%	

7 This gap report is simplified because we do not take into account the tenor of the assets and liabilities. Rather, we view this as a snapshot gap report of interest-rate sensitivity to a change in rates today.

TABLE 8.4 Net interest income scenarios.

	No rate change		−1% parallel shift		+1% parallel shift	
Interest income						
Loans: fixed rate	11.2	[140 * 0.08]	11.2	[140 * 0.08]	11.2	[140 * 0.08]
Bonds: fixed rate	2.8	[40 * 0.07]	2.8	[40 * 0.07]	2.8	[40 * 0.07]
Bonds: floating-rate	1.0	[20 * 0.05]	0.8	[20 * 0.04]	1.2	[20 * 0.06]
Total	15.0		14.8		15.2	
Interest cost						
Deposits: floating-rate	3.0	[100* 0.03]	2.0	[100 * 0.02]	4.0	[100 * 0.04]
Deposits: fixed rate	1.8	[60 * 0.03]	1.8	[60 * 0.03]	1.8	[60 * 0.03]
Total	4.8		3.8		5.8	
Net interest income (NII)	**10.2**		**11**		**9.4**	
Net interest margin (NIM)	5.10%		5.50%		4.70%	
Earnings at risk					7.84%	

(*continued*)

liabilities would re-price immediately following the change in market rates). We observe that if there is a 1% upward parallel shift in rates, NII is reduced by USD800,000.00. Thus the bank is carrying currently approximately 7.8% of EAR exposure. Put another way, the risk represents a 40-bp reduction in the NIM. We define NIM as the dollar difference between interest income and interest expenses, expressed as a percentage of average earning assets. In our example, all USD200 million of assets are earning a return – there are no non-earning assets on the balance sheet.

It may be that this is acceptable to ALCO, although typically ALCO will set a ±5% or ±10% limit on EAR. For our hypothetical bank under the current scenario the latter would not present a problem; however, the former would. The ALM desk would want to reduce the EAR to within the formal limit, and this can be undertaken in a number of ways. If derivatives are not available, the ALM desk could reduce the amount of floating-rate funding and increase fixed-rate funding; equally it could increase the amount of floating-rate assets.[8] The problem with using cash assets to reduce EAR exposure is that they cannot be effected right away.

By using derivatives the risk exposure can be adjusted immediately. An FRA can be used to cover the funding risk; or, the ALM desk can use an interest-rate cap. If it believes rates are going up, it can buy a cap. In this case, the bank can buy a cap of notional USD80 million (the amount of the funding gap at risk), which would remove the EAR completely. A lower notional would leave some exposure, and a higher notional would change the interest-rate sensitivity of the bank to one that benefited from a rise in rates. The tenor of the option would be set to match the risk horizon of the bank; if for example the ALM desk believes rates will change in the next six to 12 months, it would buy a 1-year cap. Generally, the strike price of the option would be set at the prevailing interest rate (at-the-market), so if the current 3-month Libor rate is 3% then the cap strike would be set at 3%. This removes any downside risk. For a lower option premium, the ALM desk may want to set a higher strike rate, say 4%, which is "out-of-the-money" and leaves some residual EAR. This would be done to reduce the cost of the hedge, and also if the bank feels that it can live with a small increase in rates.

8 The ALM desk might consider this if it firmly believed that the next move in interest rates was upward.

By buying a 3% strike USD80 million 1-year cap, the bank is hedged if rates rise above the strike rate. If on option maturity rates are indeed higher, the seller of the cap (usually a bank that is a market-maker in options) will pay to the buyer the difference between the current rate and the strike rate, multiplied by the notional. If rates have not risen or if they have fallen, the option expires worthless (the buyer would have paid the option premium on purchase and this remains income for the market-maker). Table 8.5 shows the effect on EAR if the bank buys the cap to hedge its interest-rate risk. The cap is an off-balance sheet instrument, but its cash flows on execution and expiry impact the bank's balance sheet position, in this case altering its risk profile. The risk exposure has been reduced such that if rates do increase, there is no negative impact for the bank.[9] The NII and NIM are unchanged even when rates have moved upward, and the EAR has been eliminated completely, so on paper this hedge looks very effective. The option premium is key to the analysis; of course, in our example it is sufficiently low to be not material, but this may not necessarily be the case in practice.

The illustration in Table 8.5 shows one advantage of using options to hedge rather than other derivatives: the ability to gain from an upside move and yet not pay – option premium excepted – on a downside move. In a falling interest-rate environment the NIM increases, but the option hedge is unused. If the hedge was constructed with an interest-rate swap or FRA, the bank would have to pay out on either of these instruments if rates moved lower. This is not the case with the option, and when the hedge is in place the only cost is the one-off premium. In other words, a swap removes earnings volatility in both a rising and a falling interest-rate environment, so while the risk protection is complete there is no chance of upside gain. With an option the bank has a chance to benefit from an upward move in rates. The cost of the hedge is the premium, which is of course paid irrespective of whether the option expires in-the-money or not. In our example, this hedge cost amounted to 5 bps in NIM terms.

Note that a bank that was "asset sensitive" would do the opposite to what is described here, it would purchase a floor option that would pay out if the Libor rate on expiry was below the strike rate.

(*continued*)

9 We have set a premium price of 0.1 to make the illustration clear. The payout on the option is shown in Table 8.5.

TABLE 8.5 Net interest income and option hedge.

	No rate change		−1% parallel shift		+1% parallel shift	
Interest income						
Loans: fixed rate	11.2	[140 ∗ 0.08]	11.2	[140 ∗ 0.08]	11.2	[140 ∗ 0.08]
Bonds: fixed rate	2.8	[40 ∗ 0.07]	2.8	[40 ∗ 0.07]	2.8	[40 ∗ 0.07]
Bonds: floating-rate	1	[20 ∗ 0.05]	0.8	[20 ∗ 0.04]	1.2	[20 ∗ 0.06]
Payments from Cap	0		0		0.8	[80mm ∗ (5% - 4%)]
Total	15		14.8		16	
Interest cost						
Deposits: floating-rate	3	[100∗ 0.03]	2	[100 ∗ 0.02]	4	[100 ∗ 0.04]
Deposits: fixed rate	1.8	[60 ∗ 0.03]	1.8	[60 ∗ 0.03]	1.8	[60 ∗ 0.03]
Cap premium	0.1		0.1		0.1	
Total	4.9		3.9		5.9	
Net interest income (NII)	**10.1**		**10.9**		**10.1**	
Net interest margin (NIM)	5.05%		5.45%		5.05%	
Earnings at risk					0.00%	

HEDGING USING BOND FUTURES CONTRACTS

A widely used risk-management instrument on ALM desks is the government-bond futures contract. This is an exchange-traded standardised contract that fixes the price today at which a specified quantity and quality of a bond will be delivered at a date during the expiry month of the futures contract. Unlike short-term interest-rate futures, which require only cash settlement, bond futures require the actual physical delivery of a bond when they are settled. They are used to hedge longer dated interest-rate risk exposures, such as a portfolio of government bonds.

There is no counterparty risk associated with trading exchange-traded futures, because of the role of the clearing house, such as the London Clearing House (LCH). This is the body through which contracts are settled. A clearing house acts as the buyer for all contracts sold on the exchange, and the seller for all contracts that are bought. So in the London market, the LCH acts as the counterparty to all transactions, so that settlement is effectively guaranteed. The clearing house requires all exchange participants to deposit margin with it, a cash sum that is the cost of conducting business (plus broker's commissions). The size of the margin depends on the size of a party's net open position in contracts (an open position is a position in a contract that is held overnight and not closed out). There are two types of margin: maintenance margin and variation margin. Maintenance margin is the minimum level required to be held at the clearing house; the level is set by the exchange. Variation margin is the additional amount that must be deposited to cover any trading losses as the size of the net open positions increases.

A bond futures contract specifies a notional coupon to prevent delivery and liquidity problems that would arise if there was a shortage of bonds with exactly the coupon required, or if one market participant purchased a large proportion of all the bonds in issue with the required coupon. For exchange-traded futures, a short future can deliver any bond that fits the maturity criteria specified in the contract terms. Of course, a long future would like to be delivered a high-coupon bond with significant accrued interest, while the short future would want to deliver a low-coupon bond with low interest accrued. In fact, this issue does not arise because of the way the invoice amount (the amount paid by the long future to purchase the bond) is calculated. The invoice amount on the expiry date is given in (8.5) below:

$$Inv_{amt} = P_{fut} \times CF + AI \tag{8.5}$$

where

Inv_{amt} is the invoice amount
P_{fut} is the price of the futures contract

CF is the conversion factor
AI is the bond accrued interest.

Any bond that meets the maturity specifications of the futures contract is said to be in the delivery basket, the group of bonds that are eligible to be delivered into the futures contract. Every bond in the delivery basket will have its own *conversion factor*, which is used to equalise coupon and accrued interest differences of all the delivery bonds. The exchange will announce the conversion factor for each bond before trading in a contract begins; the conversion factor for a bond will change over time, but remains fixed for one individual contract. That is, if a bond has a conversion factor of 1.091252, this will remain fixed for the life of the contract. If a contract specifies a bond with a notional coupon of 7%, then the conversion factor will be less than 1.0 for bonds with a coupon lower than 7% and higher than 1.0 for bonds with a coupon higher than 7%. A formal definition of conversion factor is given below.

Although conversion factors equalise the yield on bonds, bonds in the delivery basket will trade at different yields and, for this reason, they are not "equal" at the time of delivery. Certain bonds will be cheaper than others, and one bond will be the cheapest-to-deliver bond (CTD). The cheapest-to-deliver bond is the one that gives the greatest return from a strategy of buying a bond and simultaneously selling the futures contract, and then closing out positions on the expiry of the contract. This so-called cash-and-carry trading is actively pursued by proprietary trading desks in banks. If a contract is purchased and then held to maturity the buyer will receive, via the exchange's clearing house, the cheapest-to-deliver gilt. Traders sometimes try to exploit arbitrage price differentials between the future and the cheapest-to-deliver gilt, known as basis trading. This is discussed in the author's book *The Global Repo Markets* (John Wiley & Sons 2004).

CONVERSION FACTOR

The conversion factor (or price factor) gives the price of an individual cash bond such that its YTM on the delivery day of the futures contract is equal to the notional coupon of the contract. The product of the conversion factor and the futures price is the forward price available in the futures market for that cash bond (plus the cost of funding, referred to as the gross basis).

Hedging With Futures

In theory, when hedging a cash bond position with a bond futures contract, if cash and futures prices move together, then any loss from one position will be offset by a gain from the other. When prices move exactly in lock-step with each other, the hedge is considered perfect. In practice, the price of even the CTD bond (which one can view as being the bond being traded – implicitly – when one is trading the bond future) and the bond future will not move exactly in line with each other over a period of time. The difference between the cash price and the futures price is known as the *basis*. The risk that the basis will change in an unpredictable way is known as basis risk.

Futures are a liquid and straightforward way of hedging a bond position. The hedging requirement can arise for different reasons. A market-maker will wish to hedge positions arising out of client business, when she is unsure when the resulting bond positions will be unwound. A fund manager may, for example, know that he needs to realise a cash sum at a specific time in the future to meet fund liabilities, and sell bonds at that time. The market-maker will want to hedge against a drop in the value of positions during the time the bonds are held. The fund manager will want to hedge against a rise in interest rates between now and the bond sale date, to protect the value of the portfolio.

When putting on the hedge position, the key is to trade the correct number of futures contracts. This is determined by using the hedge ratio of the bond and the future, which is a function of the volatilities of the two instruments. The number of contracts to trade is calculated using the hedge ratio, which is given by:

$$Hedge\ ratio = \frac{Volatility\ of\ bond\ to\ be\ hedged}{Volatility\ of\ hedging\ instrument}.$$

Therefore one needs to use the volatility values of each instrument. We can see from the calculation that if the bond is more volatile than the hedging instrument, then a greater amount of the hedging instrument will be required. Let us now look in greater detail at the hedge ratio.

There are different methods available to calculate hedge ratios. The most common ones are the conversion factor method, which can be used for deliverable bonds (also known as the price factor method) and the modified-duration method (also known as the BPV method).

Where a hedge is put on against a bond that is in the futures delivery basket it is common for the conversion factor to be used to calculate the hedge ratio. A conversion factor hedge ratio is more useful as it is transparent and remains constant, irrespective of any changes in the price of the cash bond or the futures contract. The number of futures contracts required to hedge a deliverable bond using the conversion factor hedge ratio is determined using the following equation:

$$Number\ of\ contracts = \frac{M_{bond} \times CF}{M_{fut}} \tag{8.6}$$

where M is the nominal value of the bond or futures contract.

The conversion factor method may be used only for bonds in the delivery basket. It is important to ensure that this method is only used for one bond. It is an erroneous procedure to use the ratio of conversion factors of two different bonds when calculating a hedge ratio.

Unlike the conversion factor method, the modified-duration hedge ratio may be used for all bonds, both deliverable and non-deliverable. In calculating this hedge ratio the modified duration is multiplied by the dirty price of the cash bond to obtain the BPV. The BPV represents the actual impact of a change in the yield on the price of a specific bond. The BPV allows the trader to calculate the hedge ratio to reflect the different price sensitivity of the chosen bond (compared to the CTD bond) to interest-rate movements. The hedge ratio calculated using BPVs must be constantly updated, because it will change if the price of the bond and/or the futures contract changes. This may necessitate periodic adjustments to the number of lots used in the hedge. The number of futures contracts required to hedge a bond using the BPV method is calculated with the following:

$$Number\ of\ contracts = \frac{M_{bond}}{M_{fut}} \times \frac{BPV_{bond}}{BPV_{fut}} \tag{8.7}$$

where the BPV of a futures contract is defined with respect to the BPV of its CTD bond, as given by (8.8):

$$BPV_{fut} = \frac{BPV_{CTDbond}}{CF_{CTDbond}}. \tag{8.8}$$

The simplest hedge procedure to undertake is one for a position consisting of only one bond, the CTD bond. The relationship between the futures price and the price of the CTD given by (8.9) indicates that the price of the future will move for moves in the price of the CTD bond; therefore, we may set:

$$\Delta P_{fut} \cong \frac{\Delta P_{bond}}{CF} \tag{8.9}$$

where CF is the CTD conversion factor.

The price of the futures contract, over time, does not move tick-for-tick (although it may on an intra-day basis), but rather by the amount of the change divided by the conversion factor. It is apparent, therefore, that to hedge a position in the CTD bond we must hold the number of futures contracts equivalent to the value of bonds held multiplied by the conversion factor. Obviously, if a conversion factor is less than one, the number of futures contracts will be less than the equivalent nominal value of the cash position; the opposite is true for bonds that have a conversion factor greater than one.

THE PRIMARY HEDGE MEASURE: BOND MODIFIED DURATION AND PV 01

The main risk sensitivity measure used in calculating hedges is modified duration. The market uses variations of modified duration including the following:

- PV01: the present value of 1 bp, also referred to as PVBP or DV01 ("dollar value of an 01"). This is the change in the bond's value for a 1 bp change in market yields.
- Dollar duration: this is the change in bond value for a 1 bp change in the bond's yield.

In fact both measures are essentially the same thing, and, strictly speaking, only the first one is totally correct if one is following modified duration principles. In any case, once we know an instrument's risk sensitivity, we can construct the hedge, because the futures contract DV01 is fixed and known. Here we use Excel spreadsheets to calculate PV01 for a plain vanilla bond.

Table 8.6 shows a hypothetical 4-year 5% annual coupon bond, valued given an assumed zero-coupon curve. Table 8.7 is the same spreadsheet, but with the Excel formulas shown in the cells. The PV01 value shows the change in the value of the bond for a 1 bp parallel shift in the curve; the second calculation shows dollar durations which is the change in the bond price for a 1 bp change in the bond's yield. The difference between the two calculations is minor. Table 8.8 shows a 3-year bond, with additional calculations of convexity and the change in bond value for a 1-point change in the yield curve. Table 8.9 shows the spreadsheet formulas.

TABLE 8.6 Calculation of interest-rate risk sensitivities for a 4-year bond, given a zero-coupon curve.

A1	B	C	D	E	F	G	H	I
2								
3	Time	Cash flow	PV	Time*PV				
4	1	4	3.8095	3.8095				
5	2	4	3.6281	7.2562				
6	3	104	89.8391	269.5173				
7	Price		97.2768					
8	Macaulay duration			2.8844				
9	Modified duration			2.7470				
10	Dollar duration			0.0267				
11	Yield	5.00%						
12								
13	Example 4-year bond: assuming zero-coupon curve given, calculation of bond price, yield and interest-rate risk sensitivities							
14		Years to maturity	Interest rate	Cash flow	PV	PV × Maturity		
15		1	4.5%	5	4.78	4.78		
16		2	4.75%	5	4.56	9.11		
17		3	4.85%	5	4.34	13.01		
18		4	5%	105	86.38	345.54		
19			Macaulay duration	3.72	**100.0630**	372.45		
20								
21								
22								
23		Years to maturity	Cash flow	Interest rate	PV	Yield −1bp	PV	PV01
24		1	5	4.5%	4.7847	4.49%	4.7851	0.00046
25		2	5	4.75%	4.5568	4.74%	4.5577	0.00087
26		3	5	4.85%	4.3378	4.84%	4.3390	0.00124
27		4	105	5.0%	86.3838	4.99%	86.4167	0.03292
28					100.0630		100.0985	0.03549
29								
30		Years to maturity	Cash flow	Yield	PV	Yield −1bp	PV	Dollar duration
31		1	5	4.97%	4.7633	4.96%	4.7638	0.00045
32		2	5	4.97%	4.5379	4.96%	4.5388	0.00086
33		3	5	4.97%	4.3231	4.96%	4.3243	0.00124
34		4	105	4.97%	86.4885	4.96%	86.5214	0.03297
35					100.1128		100.1483	0.03552
36								
37			Solver objective:	0.002479757				
38								

TABLE 8.7 Table 8.6 showing Excel formulas.

A1	B	C	D	E	F	G	H	I
2								
3	Time	Cash flow	PV	Time*PV				
4	1	4	=C4/(1+$C$11)	=B4*D4				
5	2	4	=C5/(1+$C$11)^2	=B5*D5				
6	3	104	=C6/(1+$C$11)^3	=B6*D6				
7	Price		=SUM(D4:D6)					
8	Macaulay duration			=SUM(E4:E6)/D7				
9	Modified duration			=E8/(1+C11)				
10	Dollar duration			=D7*E9*0.0001				
11	Yield	5.00%						
12								
13	Example 4-year bond: assuming zero-coupon curve given, calculation of bond price, yield and interest-rate risk sensitivities							
14		Years to maturity	Interest rate	Cash flow	PV	PV × Maturity		
15		1	4.5%	5	=E16/(1+D16)	=F16*C16		
16		2	4.75%	5	=E17/(1+D17)^C17	9.11		
17		3	4.85%	5	=E18/(1+D18)^C18	13.01		
18		4	5%	105	=E19/(1+D19)^C19	345.54		
19			Macaulay duration	=G20/F20	**=SUM(F16:19)**	=SUM(G16:G19)		
20								
21								
22								
23		Years to maturity	Cash flow	Interest rate	PV	Yield –1bp	PV	**PV01**
24		1	5	=D16	=D25/(1+E25)	=E25–0.0001	=D25/(1+G25)	=H25–F25
25		2	5	=D17	=D26/(1+E26)^C26	=E26–0.0001	=D26/(1+G26)^C26	=H26–F26
26		3	5	=D18	=D27/(1+E27)^C27	=E27–0.0001	=D27/(1+G27)^C27	=H27–F27
27		4	105	=D19	=D28/(1+E28)^C28	=E28–0.0001	=D28/(1+G28)^C28	=H28–F28
28					**=SUM(F25:F28)**		=SUM(H25:H28)	=SUM(125:128)
29								
30		Years to maturity	Cash flow	Yield	PV	Yield –1bp	PV	**Dollar duration**
31		1	5	4.97%	=D32/(1+E32)	=E32–0.0001	=D32/(1+G32)	=H32–F32
32		2	5	4.97%	=D33/(1+E33)^C33	=E33–0.0001	=D33/(1+G33)^C33	=H32–F32
33		3	5	4.97%	=D34/(1+E34)^C34	=E34–0.0001	=D34/(1+G34)^C34	=H32–F32
34		4	105	4.97%	=D35/(1+E35)^C35	=E35–0.0001	=D35/(1+G35)^C35	=H32–F32
35					**=SUM(F32:F35)**		=SUM(H325:H35)	=SUM(132:135)
36								
37			Solver objective:	=(F36–F29)^2				
38								

TABLE 8.8 Bond convexity calculation.

A1	B	C	D	E	F	G	H	I	J
2	**Market interest rates**		Coupon =	**5%**	Face value =	**100**			
3	**4%**								
4	**4.25%**		Maturity	Interest rate	Cash flow	PV			
5	**4.50%**		1	4.00%	5	4.81		MaCaulay duration	**2.86**
6	**4.25%**		2	4.25%	5	4.60		Modified duration	**2.74**
7			3	4.50%	105	92.01		Convexity	**10.31**
8			Bond 1		**Price**	**101.419**		Duration–convexity approximation	
9								Yield change	**1%**
10			Maturity	**Yield**	Cash flow	PV	PV*maturity	Percentage price change	**-2.686%**
11			1	4.48%	5	4.79	4.79	Actual percentage price change	**-2.687%**
12			2	4.48%	5	4.58	9.16		
13			3	4.48%	105	92.05	276.16		
14			Bond 1	**4.48%**	0.00	101.42			
15									
16			Maturity	Yield	Cash flow	PV			
17			1	5.48%	5	4.74			
18			2	5.48%	5	4.49			
19			3	5.48%	105	89.46			
20			Bond 1	5.48%	7.43	**98.69**			
21									
22									
23									
24									

TABLE 8.9 Convexity calculation spreadsheet formulas.

A	B	C	D	E	F	G	H	I	J
1									
2	**Market Interest Rates**		Coupon =	5%	Face Value =	100			
3	4%								
4	4.25%		Maturity	Interest Rate	Cash Flow	PV			
5	4.50%		1	=B3	=$E$2*$G$2	=F5/(1+E5)		Macaulay Duration	=SUM(H11:H13)/G8
6	4.25%		2	=B4	=$E$2*$G$2	=F6/(1+E6)^D6		Modified Duration	=J5/(1+E14)
7			3	=B5	=$E$2*$G$2+G2	=F7/(1+E7)^D7		Convexity	=(2*F5/(1+E14)^3+6*F6/(1+E14)^4+12*F7/(1+E14)^5)/G8
8			Bond 1		Price	=SUM(G5:G7)		Duration-Convexity Approximation	
9								Yield Change	1%
10			Maturity	Yield	Cash Flow	PV	PV*Maturity	Percentage Price Change	=-J6*J9+0.5*J7*J9^2
11			1	=E14	=F5	=F11/(1+E11)	=G11*D11	Actual Percentage Price Change	=(G20-G8)/G8
12			2	=E14	=F6	=F12/(1+E12)^D12	=G12*D12		
13			3	=E14	=F7	=F13/(1+E13)^D13	=G13*D13		
14			Bond 1	4.48%	=(G8-G14)^2	=SUM(G11:G13)			
15									
16			Maturity	Yield	Cash Flow	PV			
17			1	=E20	=F5	=F17/(1+E17)			
18			2	=E20	=F6	=F18/(1+E18)^D18			
19			3	=E20	=F7	=F19/(1+E19)^D19			
20			Bond 1	=E14+1%	=(G14-G20)^2	=SUM(G17:G19)			
21									
22									

EXAMPLE 8.9 INTEREST RATE RISK POLICY

A bank should state interest rate risk (IRR) appetite within a formal policy document, which it updates as and when necessary. The policy should also state how the bank wishes to measure IRR.

A typical IRR policy framework would comprise the following:

- set targets and limits to IRR exposures;
- measure the actual exposure and any deviation from the target;
- execute actions to bring any exposure to the target level where necessary.

The policy document will address the banking book and trading book separately. It is standard practice for the banking book policy to state that no interest rate risk be run within the banking business, with all assets either match funded or hedged via internal swaps with the Treasury or market making desk. The policy should also state how NII and NIM sensitivity is reported and forecast, and the type of MI that is required at ALCO and BSMCO. Sensitivity tests are typically parallel and pivotal shifts of the yield curve.

Limits and target setting, and the proscribed nature of mitigating actions, form part of the IRR governance policy.

The measurement of actual IRR exposure is captured via both DV01 and VaR methods, at the following levels:

- group level;
- country/subsidiary legal entity level;
- ALCO book;
- money markets (or banking book);
- trading book;
- customer book.

Money Markets and Banking books

DV01 and VaR for IRR are measured through the trading system. The responsibility for calculation and preparation of MI resides within Market Risk Management.

Customer book

This book includes the commercial loans and deposit portfolios, which are funded via the money markets desk. IRR policy is to ensure that no IRR risk resides within the customer book itself, via a matched funding and interest-rate basis approach.

ALCO book

The ALCO book exists at the group and country/subsidiary levels. It exists to ensure proper management of the following:

- equity capital;
- liquidity buffer ("Liquid Asset Buffer");
- term placements with local branch money market desks;
- IRR hedges at group level;
- FTP sweep book.

Equity capital is treated as described in a separate policy. It is assigned an average duration of 10 years.

The IRR policy document is reviewed and updated annually by Treasury, and approved at ALCO.

HEDGING CREDIT RISK WITH CREDIT DERIVATIVES

Credit derivatives are financial contracts designed to enable traders and investors to access specific credit-risky investments in synthetic (that is, non-cash) form. They can also be used to hedge credit risk exposure by providing insurance against losses suffered due to the occurrence of a "credit event". Credit derivatives allow investors to manage the credit risk exposure of their portfolios or asset holdings, essentially by providing insurance against deterioration in credit quality of the borrowing entity. The simplest credit derivative works essentially like an insurance policy, with regular premiums paid by the protection buyer to the protection seller, and a payout in the event of a specified credit event. The flexibility of credit derivatives provides users a number of advantages, and as they are OTC products they can be designed to meet specific user requirements.

What constitutes a credit event is defined specifically in the legal documents that describe the credit derivative contract. A number of events may be defined as credit events that fall short of full bankruptcy, administration or liquidation of a company. For instance, credit derivatives contracts may be required to pay out under both technical as well as actual default.

A *technical default* is a delay in the timely payment of an obligation, or a non-payment altogether. If an obligor misses a payment, by even one day, it is said to be in technical default. This delay may be for operational reasons (and so not really a great worry) or it may reflect a short-term cash flow crisis. But if the obligor states it intends to pay the obligation as soon as it can, and specifies a time span that is within, say, one to three months, then while it is in technical default it is not in actual default. If an obligor is in *actual default*, it is in default and declared as being in default. This does not mean a mere delay of payment. If an obligor does not pay, and does not declare an intention to pay an obligation, it may then be classified by the ratings agencies as being in "default"; such assets are rated "D" by S&P.

For ALM practitioners, credit derivatives have the principle application of reducing credit exposure. A bank can reduce credit exposure either for an individual loan or for a sectoral concentration by buying a CDS. This may be desirable for assets that cannot be sold for client relationship reasons. For fixed-income managers a particular asset or collection of assets may be viewed as an attractive holding in the long term, but at risk from a short-term downward price movement. In this instance a sale would not fit in with long-term objectives; however, short-term credit protection can be obtained via a CDS. For instance, a bank can buy credit protection on a BB-rated entity from a AA-rated bank. It then has eliminated its credit risk to the BB entity, and substituted it for AA-rated counterparty risk. Notice that as the bank retains a counterparty risk to the CDS issuer, its credit risk exposure is never completely removed.

The intense competition among commercial banks, combined with rapid disintermediation, has meant that banks have been forced to evaluate their lending policy with a view to improving profitability and return on capital. The use of credit derivatives assists banks with restructuring their businesses, because they allow banks to repackage and parcel out credit risk, while retaining assets on the balance sheet (when required) and thus maintaining client relationships. As the instruments isolate credit risk from the underlying loan or bond, and transfer them to another entity, it becomes possible to separate the ownership and management of credit risk from the other features of ownership of the assets in question. This means that illiquid assets such as bank loans and illiquid bonds can have their credit risk exposures transferred; the bank owning the assets can protect against credit loss even if it cannot transfer the assets themselves.

Thus credit derivatives can be an important instrument for ALM managers, as a tool to assist balance sheet management.

Bank ALM Applications of Credit Derivatives

Banks use credit derivatives to transfer credit risk of their loan and other asset portfolios, and to take on credit exposure based on their views on the credit market. In connection with this some of them act as credit derivatives market-makers, running mismatched books in long- and short-position CDSs and TRSs. This is exactly how they operate in the interest-rate market, using interest-rate swaps.

Credit Risk Management

Credit derivatives developed as banks sought to protect themselves from loss due to default on portfolios of mainly illiquid assets, such as corporate loans and emerging-market syndicated loans. While securitisation was a well-used technique to move credit risk off the balance sheet, often this caused relationship problems with obligors, who would feel that their close relationship with their banker was being compromised if the loans were sold off the bank's balance sheet. Banks would therefore buy protection on the loan book using CDSs, enabling them to hedge their credit exposure while maintaining banking relationships. The loan would be maintained on the balance sheet, but would be fully protected by the CDSs.

To illustrate, consider Figure 8.17, which is a Bloomberg description page for a loan in the name of Haarman & Reimer, a chemicals company rated A3 by Moody's. We see that this loan pays 225 bps over Libor. Figure 8.18 shows the BBVA CDS prices page for A3-rated chemicals entities: Akzo Nobel is

GRAB Corp DES
Enter 99<GO> for options. <HELP> for Disclaimer
TRANCHE LOAN DESCRIPTION Page 1 of 1
Tranche# LN085232 Tranche A IVSXF Maturity 10/01/09 Country DE
Cusip# Type TERM Mkt Type EURO
Facility# LN085249 Amend N.A. Issue Status SIGNED

Issue Information
Borrower HAARMANN & REIMER
Industry Chemicals - Diversified
Calc Type (99) *NO CALCULATIONS*
Fac/Trnch Amts EUR 880MM /400MM
Purpose LBO
Signing Date 11/28/02
Effective Date 08/22/02
Outstanding 400MM

Sub Limit Borrowings
Not Applicable

Bank Group
Ld Arranger COBA,JPM
Agent
Participants 55<GO>

Assignment Info
Min Pc
Increment
Fee
Retain

Tranche Ratings
S&P NR
Moody's NR
FI NR

Senior Debt Ratings
S & P A+
MOODY A3

Info @ Close
EURIBOR +225.000BP

Current Sprd & Fees
Interest Typ FLOATER
Current Base EURIBOR
Spread 225.0BP

SR RTGS REFLECT: BAYER AG. TOTAL FAC INCLUDES AN ADDL €240MM MEZZANINE LOAN

Australia 61 2 9777 8600 Brazil 5511 3048 4500 Europe 44 20 7330 7500 Germany 49 69 920410
Hong Kong 852 2977 6000 Japan 81 3 3201 8900 Singapore 65 6212 1000 U.S. 1 212 318 2000 Copyright 2004 Bloomberg L.P.
G657-802-1 09-Mar-04 14:09:34

FIGURE 8.17 Haarman & Reimer loan description.

GRAB Curncy **BBCS**

14:11 **CHEMICALS/PHARMACEUTICALS** PAGE 1 / 1

CHEMICALS/ PHARMACEUTICALS		3 Y - CDS Quotes BID	/	ASK	CHG		5 Y - CDS Quotes BID	/	ASK	CHG	TIME
AKZO NOBEL	1)	20	/	28	7:29	15)	43	/	53		7:29
AVENTIS	2)	13	/	23	7:29	16)	24	/	34		7:29
BASF	3)	10	/	17	7:29	17)	10	/	20		7:29
BAYER	4)	30	/	42	7:29	18)	43	/	53		7:29
DEGUSSA	5)	10	/	23	7:29	19)	24	/	31		7:29
DSM	6)	10	/	23	7:29	20)	27	/	37		7:29
GSK	7)	2	/	12	7:29	21)	8	/	18		7:29
HENKEL KGAA	8)	23	/	33	7:29	22)	35	/	45	+2	12:28
ICI	9)	55	/	75	7:29	23)	80	/	90		7:29
LINDE	10)	25	/	35	7:29	24)	40	/	50		7:29
NOVARTIS	11)	2	/	12	7:29	25)	6	/	16		7:29
SOLVAY	12)		/			26)	25	/	32		7:29
SVENSKA AB	13)		/			27)	25	/	32		7:29
SYNGENTA AG	14)		/			28)	24	/	34		7:29

Tel: +34 91 537 6087
INDICATIVE PRICES FOR CREDIT DEFAULT SWAPS ON STANDARD
ISDA 2003 DOCUMENTATION WITH 3 CREDIT EVENTS
MATURITIES ARE ON QUARTERLY BASIS

BBVA

Australia 61 2 9777 8600 Brazil 5511 3048 4500 Europe 44 20 7330 7500 Germany 49 69 920410
Hong Kong 852 2977 6000 Japan 81 3 3201 8900 Singapore 65 6212 1000 U.S. 1 212 318 2000 Copyright 2004 Bloomberg L.P.
G657-802-3 09-Mar-04 14:11:38

FIGURE 8.18 Chemicals sector CDS prices for Banco Bilbao Vizcaya, 9 March 2004.

trading at 28 bps (to buy protection) as at 9 March 2004. A bank holding this loan can protect against default by purchasing this credit protection, and the relationship manager does not need to divulge this to the obligor.

Reducing Credit Exposure

Consider a bank that holds a large portfolio of bonds issued by a particular sector (say, utilities) and believes that spreads in this sector will widen in the short term. Previously, in order to reduce the credit exposure the bank would have to sell bonds; however, this may crystallise a mark-to-market loss and may conflict with any long-term liquidity strategy. An alternative approach would be to enter into a CDS, purchasing protection for the short term; if spreads do widen these swaps will increase in value and may be sold at a profit in the secondary market. Alternatively, the bank may enter into TRSs on the desired credits. It pays the counterparty the total return on the reference assets, in return for Libor. This transfers the credit exposure of the bonds to the counterparty for the term of the swap, in return for the credit exposure of the counterparty.

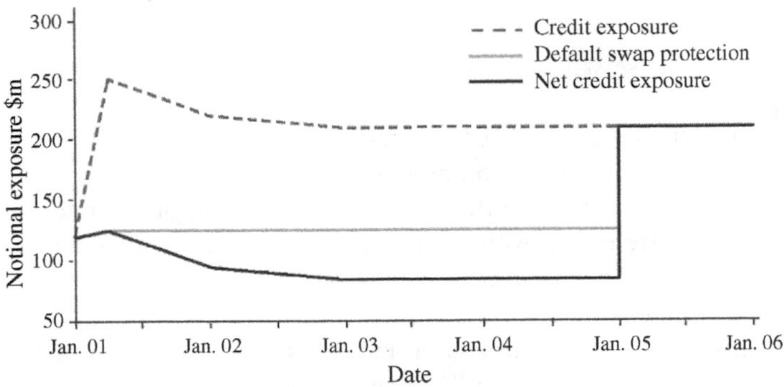

FIGURE 8.19 Reducing credit exposure.

A similar case is the case of a bank wishing to mitigate credit risk from a growing loan book. Figure 8.19 shows an example of an unhedged credit exposure to a hypothetical credit-risky portfolio. It illustrates the bank's expectation of credit risk building up to $250 million as assets are acquired, and then reducing to a more stable level as the credits become more established.[10] A 3-year CDS entered into shortly after provides protection on half of the notional exposure, shown as the broken line. The net exposure to credit events has been reduced by a significant margin.

EXAMPLE 8.10 CALCULATING THE NOTIONAL AMOUNT OF THE CREDIT RISK HEDGE[11]

It is intuitively easy to view a credit hedge as a straight par-for-par trade of notionals. That is, we would buy (or sell) USD10 million nominal of a bond against buying (or selling) USD10 million of notional in the CDS. This is still quite common practice due to its simplicity.

However, unless the cash bond in question is priced at par, this approach is not correct and the analysis will not be accurate.

(continued)

10 For instance, the fund may be invested in new companies. As the names become more familiar to the market the credits become more "established" because the perception of how much credit risk they represent falls.

11 With special thanks to Niall Considine and Suraj Gohil for their assistance with the technical details in this section.

(*continued*)
The biggest errors arise when the bond is trading significantly away from par.

To avoid the risk of being over- or under-hedged we must assess how much CDS protection to put on against a set amount of the bond. There is no one way to approach this, the key is the assumption made about the recovery rate in the event of default. In practice traders will adopt one of the following methods:

- par/par: this is a common approach. In such a trade, identical par amounts of the bond and the CDS are traded. The advantage of this method is that the position is straightforward to maintain. The disadvantage is that the trader is not accurately credit-risk hedged if the bond is priced away from par. The CDS pays out par (minus the deliverable asset or cash value on default) on default, but if the bond is priced above par greater cash value is at risk. Therefore this approach is recommended for bonds priced near to par or for trades with a long-term horizon. It is not recommended for use with bonds at higher risk of default (for instance, sub-investment-grade bonds) as default events will expose this approach to be under-hedged;
- delta-neutral: this is a similar approach used to duration-weighted bond spread trades such as butterfly/barbell trades (see Choudhry 2010). It is appropriate when the maturity of the bond does not match precisely the maturity of the CDS;
- DV01: this approach sets the CDS notional relative to the actual price of the bond. For example, if the bond is trading at 120 then we would buy 120% notional of the CDS. This is a logical approach and recommended if the bond is trading away from par.

An assumption of the recovery rate will influence the choice of hedging approach and the notional amount of CDS protection to buy.

A key risk factor is the recovery rate assumed for the bond. The rate of recovery cannot be hedged and the actual recovery after event of default will impact the final profit/loss position. The impact is greatest for bonds that are priced significantly away from par. To illustrate this, consider a bond priced at $110.00. To hedge a long position of $10 million of this bond, assume we buy protection in $11 million nominal of the CDS. We do not use a par/par approach because otherwise we would be under-hedged. Now consider, in the event of default, the following recovery rates:

- 0% recovery: we receive \$11 million on the CDS, and lose \$11 million ($1.10 \times 10{,}000{,}000$) on the bond, so net we are flat;
- 50% recovery: we receive \$5.5 million on the CDS, and lose \$6 million on the bond (the bond loss is \$5 million nominal and so we receive back \$5 million, having paid out \$11 million), so net we are down \$500,000.

So in other words, under a 50% recovery rate scenario we are under-hedged still and would need more notional of CDS to cover the loss on the bond. If the recovery rate is 30%, we still lose on the position, while at 50% or more we will lose progressively more. Note that the reverse analysis applies when the bond is priced below par. Overall then we conclude that the assumption of the recovery rate must influence the notional size of the CDS position.

Generally, the market assumes the following recovery rates:

- investment-grade 40%;
- insurance companies and corporates 30%;
- sub-investment grade 20%.

Some banks assume a 50% recovery rate in their pricing models. While a more robust approach might be to use historical data of actual defaults and ultimate recovery rates, at the current time some markets, notably those in Europe and Asia, suffer from a paucity of data and so for the time being market participants use assumed recovery rates.

To construct the correct hedge, we use the following formula for a bond priced over par:

$$Hedge = N + \left[\left(\frac{P - 100}{1 - R}\right) \times N\right] \tag{8.10}$$

where
N is the bond notional
P is the bond price
R is the (assumed) recovery rate.

In the earlier example of a bond priced at 110.00, a CDS notional of USD11,428,571 would provide an adequate hedge if the recovery rate was at 30%.

For a bond priced below par, we subtract the adjustment from the bond notional.

REFERENCES

Choudhry, M. (2010), *Structured Credit Products,* 2nd Edition, Singapore: John Wiley & Sons Singapore.

Choudhry, M., Moskovic, D., Wong, M. (2014), *Fixed Income Markets,* 2nd Edition, Singapore: John Wiley & Sons Limited.

CHAPTER 9

Asset–Liability Management IV: The ALCO

The fourth strand of our look at traditional ALM considers the reporting process, often overseen by the bank's ALM committee (ALCO). The ALCO will have a specific remit to oversee all aspects of ALM, from the front-office money market function to back-office operations and middle office reporting and risk management. In this chapter we introduce the basic elements of ALCO procedures, before taking a more detailed look at ALCO objectives and terms of reference in Chapter 10.

ALCO POLICY

The ALCO is responsible for setting and implementing ALM policy. Its composition varies in different banks but usually includes heads of business lines, as well as director-level staff such as the finance director. The ALCO also sets hedging policy.[1]

The ALM process is undertaken by the Treasury desk. In commercial banks it will be responsible for management reporting to the ALCO. The ALCO will consider the report in detail at regular meetings, usually weekly. Main points of interest in the ALCO report include variations in interest income, the areas that experienced fluctuations in income and the latest short-term income projections. The ALM report will link these three strands across the group entity and also to each individual business line. That is, it will consider macro-level factors driving variations in interest income as well as specific desk-level factors. The former includes changes in the

1 The ALCO is known by other acronyms in some banks; for example, Balance Sheet Risk and Management Committee (BRMC), Asset–Liability Policy Committee (ALPC) or Asset, Liability and Capital Management Committee (ALCMCO). The most common is ALCO.

TABLE 9.1 ALCO main mission.

Mission	Components
ALCO management and reporting	Formulating ALM strategy Management reporting ALCO agenda and minutes Assessing liquidity, gap and interest-rate risk reports Scenario planning and analysis Interest income projection
Asset management	Managing bank liquidity book (CDs, Bills) Managing the government bond and FRN book Investing bank capital
ALM strategy	Yield curve analysis Money market trading
Funding and liquidity management	Liquidity policy Managing funding and liquidity risk Ensuring funding diversification Managing lending of funds
Risk management	Formulating hedging policy Interest-rate risk exposure management Implementing hedging policy using cash and derivative instruments
Internal treasury function	Formulating transfer pricing system and level Funding group entities Calculating the cost of capital

customer behaviour and so on. Of necessity the ALM report is a detailed document, but kept as succinct as possible.

Table 9.1 is a summary overview of the responsibilities of the ALCO, and is essentially a banking ALM strategic overview.

The ALCO will meet on a regular basis, usually once a month. During stressed or crisis periods it will meet more frequently. The composition of the ALCO varies by institution, but is typically comprised of the CEO, the heads the business lines, of Treasury, and Risk Management, as well as the finance director. Representatives from the credit committee and loan syndication may also be present. A typical agenda would consider all the elements listed in Table 9.1. Thus the meeting will discuss and generate action points on the following:

- Management reporting: this will entail analysing the various management reports and either signing off on them or agreeing to items for actioning. The issues to consider include lending margin, interest income, variance from last projection, customer business and future business. Current business policy with regard to lending and portfolio management will be reviewed and either continued or adjusted.

- Business planning: existing asset (and liability) books will be reviewed, and future business direction drawn up. This will consider the performance of existing business, most importantly with regard to return on capital. The existing asset portfolio will be analysed from a risk-reward perspective, and a decision taken to continue or modify all lines of business. Any proposed new business will be discussed and if accepted in principle will be moved on to the next stage.[2] At this stage any new business will be assessed for projected returns, revenue and risk exposure.
- Hedging policy: overall hedging policy will consider the acceptance of risk exposure, existing risk limits and the use of hedging instruments. The latter also includes use of derivative instruments. Many bank ALM desks find that their hedging requirements can be met using plain vanilla products such as interest-rate swaps and exchange-traded short-money futures contracts. The use of options, and even vanilla instruments such as FRAs,[3] is much less common than one might think. Hedging policy takes into account the cash book revenue level, current market volatility levels and the overall cost of hedging. On occasion, certain exposures may be left unhedged because the cost associated with hedging them is deemed prohibitive (this includes the actual cost of putting on the hedge as well as the opportunity cost associated with expected reduced income from the cash book). Of course, hedging policy is formulated in coordination with overall funding and liquidity policy. Its final form must consider the bank's views of the following:
  - expectations on the future level and direction of interest rates;
  - balancing the need to manage and control risk exposure with the need to maximise revenue and income;
  - the level of risk aversion, and how much risk exposure the bank is willing to accept.

2 All new business should follow a formal approval process, typically involving all the relevant front, middle- and back-office departments of the bank, and culminating in a "new products committee" meeting at which the proposed new line of business will be either approved, sent back to the sponsoring department for modification or rejected.

3 See Chapter 8.

The ALCO is dependant on management reporting from Treasury, Risk, Finance and other departments. The reports are usually produced by the MO. The main report is the overall ALM report, showing the composition of the bank's ALM book. Other reports will look at specific business lines, and will consider the return on capital generated by these businesses. These reports will need to break down aggregate levels of revenue and risk by business line. Reports will also drill down by product type, across business lines. Other reports will consider the gap, the gap risk, the VaR or DV01 (interest-rate risk) report and credit risk exposures. Overall, the reporting system must be able to isolate revenues, return and risk by country sector, business line and product type. There is also an element of scenario planning; that is, expected performance under various specified macro- and micro-level market conditions.

Figure 9.1 illustrates the general reporting concept.

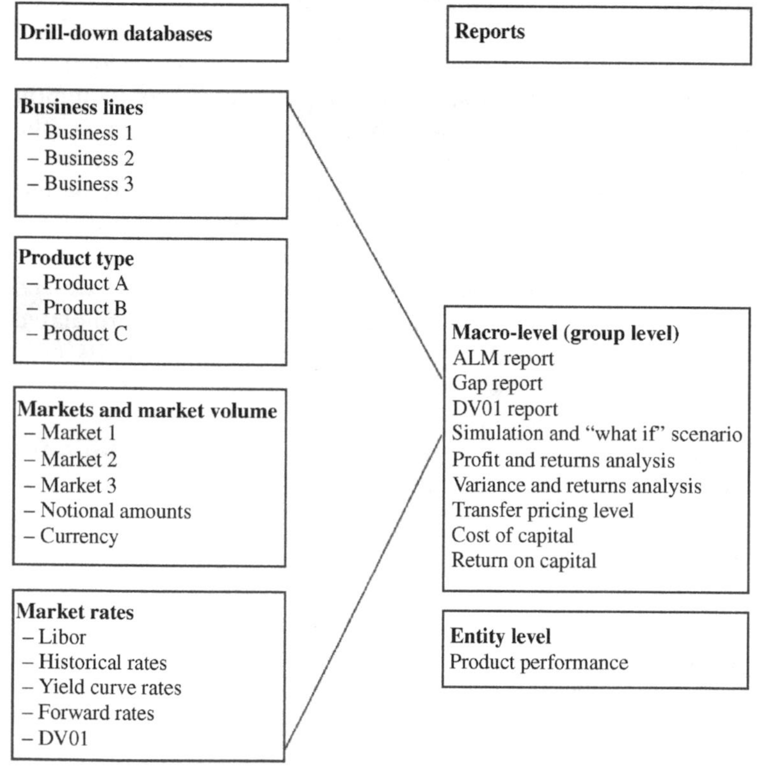

FIGURE 9.1 ALCO reporting input and output.

ALCO REPORTING

We now provide a flavour of the reporting that is provided to, and analysed by, the ALCO. This is a generalisation, reports will of course vary by the type of the institution and the nature of its business.

In Chapter 6 we showed an example of a macro-level ALM report. The ALCO will also consider macro-level gap and liquidity reports compiled for product and market. The interest-rate gap, being simply the difference between assets and liabilities, is easily set into these parameters. For management reporting purposes the report will attempt to show a dynamic profile, but its chief limitation is that it is always a snapshot of a fixed point in time, and therefore strictly speaking will always be out-of-date.

Figure 9.2 shows a typical dynamic gap, positioned in a desired ALM "Smile", with the projected interest-rate gaps based on the current snapshot profile. This report shows the future funding requirement, which the ALCO can give direction on what reflects their view on future interest-rate levels. It also shows where the sensitivity to falling interest rates, in terms of revenue, lies because it shows the volume of assets. Again, the ALCO can give instructions on hedging if they expect interest income to be affected

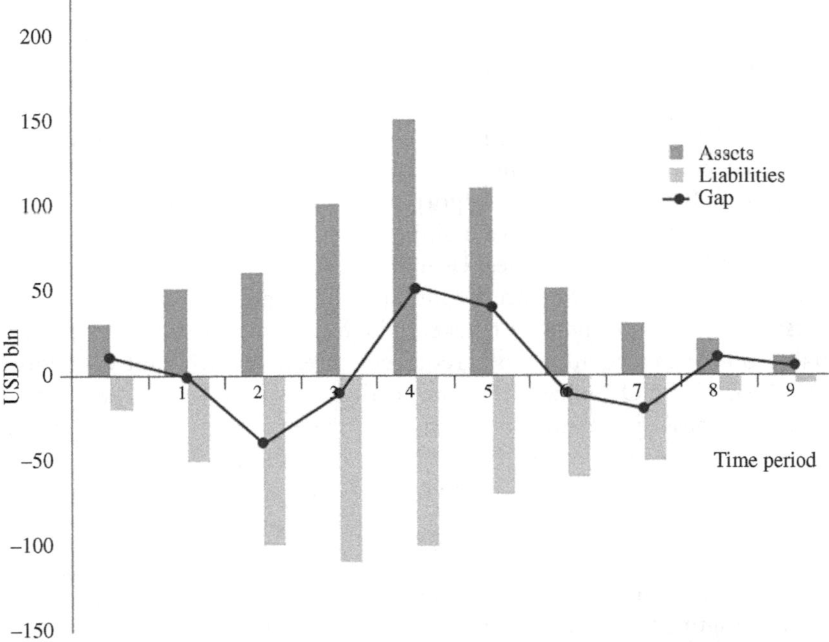

FIGURE 9.2 ALM and expected liquidity and interest-rate gap, snapshot profile.

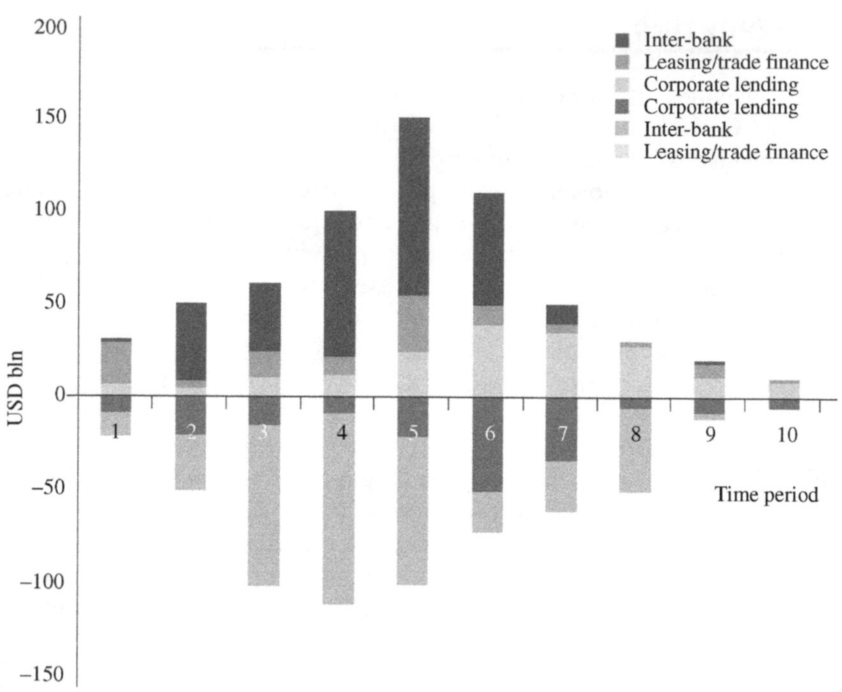

FIGURE 9.3 ALM breakdown by product (or market) segment.

adversely. The x-axis is the time buckets from overnight out to two years or beyond. Banks use different time buckets to suit their own requirements.[4]

Figure 9.3 shows the same report with a breakdown by product (or market – the report would have a similar layout). We use a hypothetical sample of different business lines. Using this format the ALCO can observe which assets and liabilities are producing the gaps, which is important because it shows if products (or markets) are fitting into overall bank policy. Equally, policy can be adjusted if required in response to what the report shows. So the ALCO can see what proportion of total assets is represented by each business line, and which line has the greatest forward funding requirement. The same report is shown again in Figure 9.4, but this time with the breakdown by type of interest rate, fixed or variable.

4 For example, a bank may have the "overnight" time bucket on its own, or incorporate it into an "overnight to one-week" period. Similarly, banks may have each period from one month to 12 in their own separate buckets, or may place some periods into combined time periods. There is more than one way.

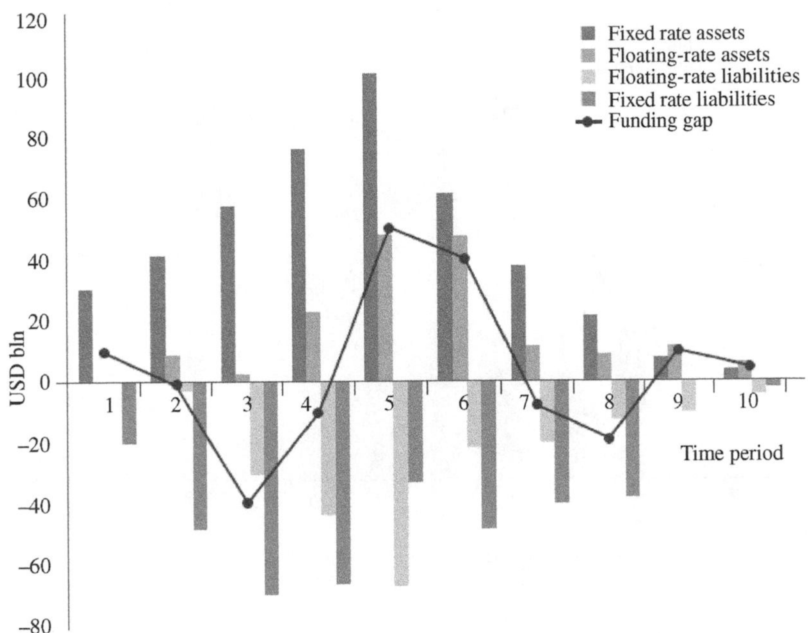

FIGURE 9.4 ALM breakdown by type of interest rate.

Another variation of this report that will be examined by the ALCO is a breakdown by income and margin, again separated into business lines or markets as required. In a pure commercial banking operation the revenue-type mix will comprise the following (among others):

- the bid–offer spread between borrowing and lending in the inter-bank market;
- corporate lending margin; that is, the loan rate over and above the bank's cost of funds;
- trading income;
- fixed fees charged for services rendered.

The ALCO will receive an income breakdown report, split by business line. The x-axis in such a report would show the margin level for each time period; that is, it shows the margin of the lending rate over the cost of funds by each time bucket. Figure 9.5 is another type of income report, which shows the volumes and income spread by business line. The spread is shown in basis points and is an average for that time bucket (across all loans and deposits for that bucket). The volumes will be those reported in the main ALM report (Figure 9.2), but this time with the margin contribution

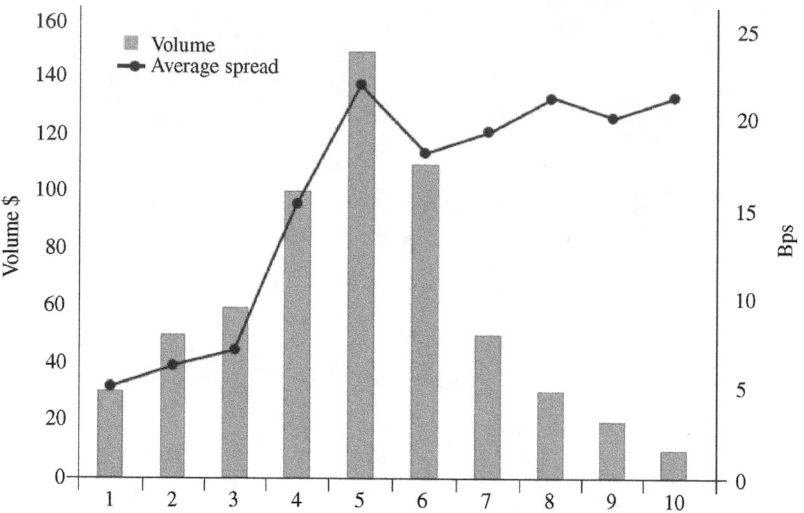

FIGURE 9.5 Asset profile volume and average income spread.

per time period. As we might expect, the spread levels per product across time are roughly similar. They will differ more markedly by product time. The latter report is shown in Figure 9.6, which is more useful because it shows the performance of each business line. In general, the ALCO will prefer low volumes and high margin as a combination, because lower

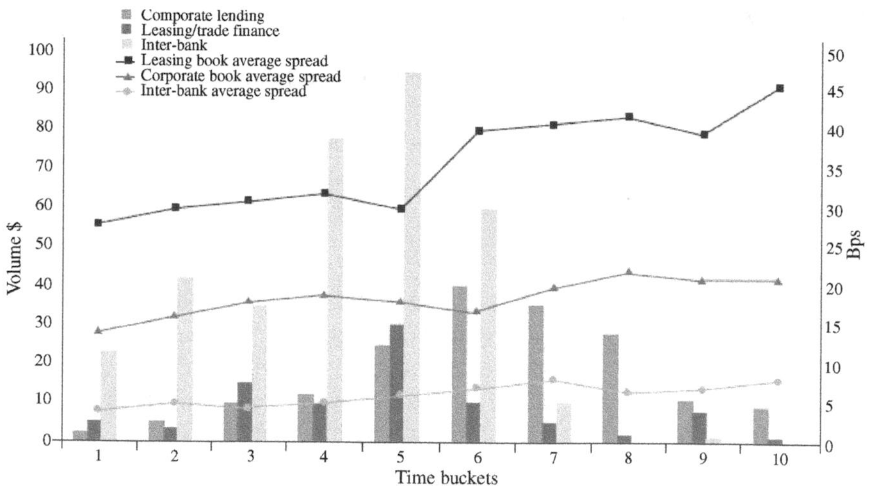

FIGURE 9.6 Business lines and average income spread.

volumes consume less capital. However, some significant high-volume business (such as inter-bank money market operations) operates at relatively low margin.

The income and return reports viewed by ALCO requires that it checks if bank policy with regard to lending and money market trading is being adhered to. Essentially, these reports are providing information on the risk-return profile of the bank. The ideal combination is the lowest possible risk for the highest possible return, although of course low-risk business carries the lowest return. The level of trade-off that the bank is comfortable with is what the ALCO will set in its direction and strategy. With regard to volumes and bank business, it might be thought that the optimum mix is high volume mixed with a high-income margin. However, high-volume business consumes the most capital, so there will be another trade-off with regard to use of capital.

The next chapter provides a formal template for setting up a bank ALCO function and procedure.

BIBLIOGRAPHY

Choudhry, M. (2007), *Bank Asset and Liability Management*, Singapore: John Wiley & Sons (Asia) Ltd, chapter 8.

CHAPTER 10

The ALCO: Terms of Reference and Treasury Operating Model

In the previous chapter we introduced the Asset–Liability Committee or ALCO, the most important operating committee in a bank. In this chapter we consider further the governance aspects of the ALCO, and a basic reporting pack that is part of ALCO MI reporting. We review a business best practice approach to ALCO governance in a group banking structure, for a bank that operates across multiple legal entities and country jurisdictions. We also describe the organisation of a business best-practice Treasury function.

A presentation summary of the ALCO role and policy is available at the Wiley website (see Chapter 19 for details). This also holds examples of ALCO reporting packs.

THE ALCO GOVERNANCE MODEL

It is important that the ALCO function be set up and run with a governance structure and authority that befits its importance. For this reason, its terms of reference (ToR) must be articulated clearly to all bank management. Regular attendance by members of the ALCO must also be stressed. A common point of discussion is the frequency with which the ALCO should meet. At the minimum it should meet once every four weeks, ideally at the same time and on the same day each month. This establishes a pattern and ensures that the meeting is embedded in the firm's risk and management culture. If for any reason a discussion is required ahead of the next scheduled meeting, for example during periods of market stress or because of a firm-specific issue of urgency, then certainly an extraordinary meeting should be able to be called at short notice.

We review here the ALCO ToR and some sample agendas.

ALCO Terms of Reference

Among the supplementary materials to this book appearing on the Wiley website (see Chapter 19 for details), we enclose a recommended sample template for an ALCO ToR. This is certainly appropriate for a small or medium-sized bank. We consider the ALCO ToR for a larger or multinational institution later in the chapter.

The most significant element of ALCO organisation is its membership, which reflects its status as a high-level management committee and key policymaking body. Table 10.1 is an extract from the ToR template. This is the criteria recommended for ALCO membership in a medium-sized bank. What one observes from Table 10.1 is the seniority as well as the slant of the ALCO, which is ultimately a risk management mechanism. Note the following:

- the committee is chaired by the Finance Director, or in case of absence, the Head of Treasury, and not by the CEO or any of the business line heads (where the Treasury desk is a profit centre and not a cost centre, the Head of Treasury is less likely to act as Chair, but if no alternative is possible, this person must be mindful to not allow any conflict of interest whenever required to act as chair in the CFO's absence);
- the head of each business line must be represented, as must the head of risk management (more often now termed the Chief Risk Officer);

TABLE 10.1 ALCO membership.

ALCO Membership
Members
CEO or Deputy CEO
Chief Financial Officer (Chair)
Head of Treasury (Deputy Chair)
Head of Corporate Banking
Head of Retail Banking
Head of Private Banking
Head of Research *or* Chief Economist
Chief Risk Officer
Guests
Head of ALM/Money Markets
Head of Market & Liquidity Risk
Head of Valuation Control/Product Control
Head of Financial Institutions Group
Secretariat
Treasury Business Manager or Liquidity team member

- selected members of staff of relevant departments can also be invited to attend as guests; for example, the head of money markets or ALM (who reports to the head of Treasury). Where this occurs, the ToR must make clear that such persons have voting powers in the absence of their department head. For effective management and decision-making, it is recommended that deputies be given such authority, so that the bank can function correctly in the absence of key senior individuals.

The author believes that the Head of Credit, or a senior person from the Credit Committee, should also attend ALCO, and certainly some banks do follow such an arrangement. However, credit decisions, including risk-related issues such as expected losses, forecasts and loss provisions, are often handled at the Executive Credit Committee level, and because the Credit department does not have a day-to-day involvement, from either an operational or policy level, with asset–liability issues it reduces the need to have it represented at the ALCO level. Ultimately, it is a decision for the CEO and ALCO chairman.

The membership of ALCO should be reasonably stable, but also flexible enough to allow for additional persons and expertise as and when necessary; for example, technical experts by invitation.

The ToR is a formal statement of the primary aims and objective of the ALCO. It should be a succinct document. We observe that its remit covers every aspect of asset, liability, liquidity and capital management of the bank's operations. We show at Figure 10.1 an extract from the ToR, which is the committee's operating agenda. The list is not exhaustive. The agenda makes clear that any aspect of the bank's operations that impact ALM issues – which is essentially anything that a bank might undertake – must be addressed, for risk management purposes, at the ALCO level.

Agenda Setting

The ALCO agenda is varied and wide ranging, and by definition dynamic in line with market and firm-specific events. On the Wiley website we include a sample of hypothetical agendas from past ALCO meetings at different banks. Figure 10.2 is an example of one of these agendas, from a bank ALCO meeting. Specific items must be the responsibility of named individuals, who will present in accordance with the agenda. The agenda and supporting documents should be circulated at least one week before the meeting date, to enable members to have sufficient time to review the contents. Where this is not possible, for example for late items or for extraordinary meetings, the emphasis should be on making the meeting documents available to the circulation list as soon as possible.

- Review gap limits, actual gaps, and their sensitivities, together with any recommendations to amend the limits;
- Review the liquidity ratio and other liquidity metrics, and adherence to regulatory and internal liquidity limits, and assess forecasted values for risk control purposes and adequacy;
- Review and discuss deposit and funding trends, including deposit concentrations, programs/products, deposit promotion campaigns, and forecasts;
- Review exceptions/excesses to internal and regulatory policies and limits as reported by the Head of Financial Planning and Control;
- Review current allocation of capital and profit contribution by business line, and present regulatory capital adequacy forecasts and requests for Board review;
- Review the market environment and potential impact on the branch's interest-rate risk and trading activities;
- Review and approve authorised instruments and permissible hedging and position-taking strategies for gap management, trading and customer sales;
- Review and discuss recommendations to change policies, objectives or limits;
- Review internal funds transfer pricing arrangements and consider whether changes are required;
- Set standards and methodology for measuring and monitoring the quantitative limits on all trading activities;
- In liaison with CRO's office, set and review stress testing scenarios;
- Review new trading activities recommended under the policy for New Products & Services; and
- Act as the centre for excellence for all ALM-related policy and governance issues.

FIGURE 10.1 ALCO operating agenda: extract from the formal ToR.

Items for inclusion at the next meeting should be discussed, informally or formally, with the Chairperson before then being sent to the committee secretary for circulation on the agenda.

ALCO REPORTING

The ALCO ToR lists the main management reports that are received and reviewed by the committee on an ongoing basis. These can be supplemented by ad hoc reports, as and when required, on request. The principle indicators are summarised in the ALCO "monthly pack", which is reviewed at each monthly meeting. It is important that this report, while kept as succinct as possible, is reviewed in depth. It is the key bank risk report. It presents aggregate level market risk, liquidity risk and capital information.

ALCO Agenda
Date: Wednesday 25 November
Time: 15:00
Location: Board Room

1) **Apologies**
2) **Minutes of last meeting**
3) **Matters arising**
4) **Review of ALCO monthly pack**
5) **ALCO Capital Investment Options for following year:** update on recommendations to replace current practice (Head of Treasury)
6) **Finance department interest-rate sensitivity: Scenario Analysis** present agreed daily analysis already in production, highlighting key aspects, and parallel limits (CFO)
7) **IPV Results for Q3** Following ALCO approval of the IPV policy, report results formally to ALCO on a calendar quarter basis, the first being Q3. (Head of Product Control)
8) **Private Bank client deposit results and targets** (Head of PB)
9) **Internal Funds "Transfer Pricing" Model – update on implementation** (Head of Financial Accounting)
10) **European Central Bank Amendment to Collateral Rules** (Head of Treasury)
11) **Update and review of the bank's Liquidity Policy Statement** (Head of Market and Liquidity Risk)
12) **Any other business**
13) **Date of next meeting**

Circulation:

CFO (Chairman)	CEO	Head of Treasury
Head of Corporate Banking	Head of Market Risk	Head of Money Markets
Head of Product Control	Head of FI	CRO
Secretariat		

Attachments:
Minutes (Item 2)
ALCO Reports Pack (Item 4)

FIGURE 10.2 Sample ALCO agenda.

The preparation of this report is the responsibility of what is generically termed the Middle Office in banks. Ultimately, it is prepared within the risk management department, although different banks will organise the arrangement differently. In general, the report is prepared by the product control department, although within larger banks it may be prepared by a specialist team in Finance or Risk Management.

The liquidity risk reports within the monthly pack are discussed in detail in Chapter 14. We show some of them here. For example, Figure 10.3 is a simple aggregate cash inflow/outflow chart, which is produced as an end-of-day snapshot on a daily basis. Note that an asset is a cash "inflow", because on maturity of the asset the cash is received at the bank. In the same way, liabilities, which are borrowings by the bank, are designated as cash "outflows". The net difference between the two is the bank's cash position for that time in the future. Note that a positive net number is therefore a funding requirement. Table 10.2 is a chart of this data.

Table 10.3 is a sample of funding reports that are to go into the monthly pack. The first is a report of the "maturity transformation" value for the bank, which is also known as the "liquidity risk factor". This metric and its uses is discussed in Chapter 13. The other two reports show sources of funds and "Top 5" individual funding counterparties, both of which are self-explanatory.

On the Wiley website we include an Excel spreadsheet file that can serve as the template to a monthly ALCO pack. The "traffic light" in the top right-hand corner of each page is a senior management reporting device, used to highlight only those parts of the report that need special attention. If the lights are "green", this indicates everything is in order, no limits have been breached and there is no need to dwell overmuch on that page. An "amber" light is an advance warning of an issue that needs to be kept under watch as a potential problem, while a "red" indication is an urgent issue that needs immediate attention. If the ALCO process has been operating effectively, there should only rarely, if ever, be a red light at the time of the meeting. The report has pages for each element of risk, such as liquidity, FX exposure, capital allocation and also large exposures. This last item is an aspect of credit risk that is included in the ALCO report.

Note that the pack is usually presented in "pdf" format when sent electronically, and reviewed at the meeting itself in hardcopy. A sample of such a report, the ALCO "Monthly Pack" as referred to in the ALCO Agenda, is included on the Wiley website. This can serve as a template for a standard ALCO report at most commercial banks.

A summary of this report, in PowerPoint format if desired, should also be prepared for review and discussion at board level. This is because time constraints at such a senior level make detailed review and understanding of long documents problematic. A succinct 2-slide summary of the ALCO monthly pack, that conveys the salient points on ALM, Liquidity and Capital risk, is therefore produced for review at this level. An example of such a 2-slide report is included as part of the supplementary material on the Wiley website.

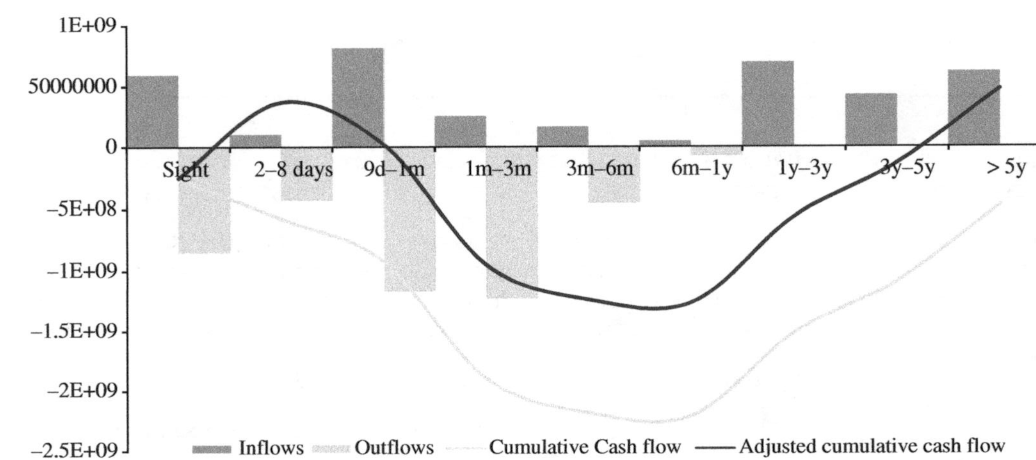

FIGURE 10.3 Aggregate cash inflow/outflow chart.

TABLE 10.2 Chart representing cash flow data shown at Figure 10.3.

	Sight	2–8 days	9d–1m	1m–3m	3m–6m	6m–1y	1y–3y	3y–5y	> 5y
Inflows	594,668,623	102,626,843	815,377,165	252,308,002	166,982,642	47,193,748	698,609,754	427,433,620	618,960,572
Outflows	(847,464,847)	(427,686,159)	(1,162,142,299)	(1,222,681,048)	(451,095,784)	(71,193,404)	(3,173,300)	0	(7,012,538)
Net mismatch	(252,796,224)	(325,059,316)	(346,765,134)	(970,373,046)	(284,113,142)	(23,999,656)	695,436,455	427,433,620	611,948,035
Cumulative cash flow	(252,796,224)	(577,855,541)	(924,620,674)	(1,894,993,720)	(2,179,106,862)	(2,203,106,518)	(1,507,670,063)	(1,080,236,443)	(468,288,409)
Adjustments		945,219,350	945,219,350	945,219,350	945,219,350	945,219,350	945,219,350	945,219,350	945,219,350
Adjusted cumulative cash flow	(252,796,224)	367,363,809	20,598,676	(949,774,370)	(1,233,887,512)	(1,257,887,168)	(562,450,713)	(135,017,093)	476,930,941

TABLE 10.3 Further examples of ALCO report liquidity metrics.

Maturity transformation report

Report date	Average liabilities tenor (days)	Average assets tenor (days)	Maturity transformation	Limit
9/30/2009	19	262	14	24

Sources of funding report

Funding source	Balance (€000,000s)	% Funding	Within limit (Y/N)
Customer – Corporate	508	12	Y
Customer – Local authority and agency	139	3	Y
Customer – Private	1,198	29	N
Institutional – Financial institutions	792	19	Y
Inter-bank	303	7	Y
Inter-group (Net balance)	249	6	Y
Other	15	0	Y
Total liabilities	3,204		

Top 5 sources of funds

Bank's top 5 counterparties	Balance (€000,000s)	% Funding	% Limit	Breach
COMMERCIAL BANK OF ABC	575	14.0	10	Y
CENTRAL BANK OF ABC	227	5.5	10	N
BANK OF XYZ	220	5.4	10	N
ABC LOCAL AUTHORITY	130	3.2	10	N
ABC BANK	105	2.6	10	N
Total		30.7		

THE GROUP ALCO

Larger banks that operate across national boundaries and/or legal entities and subsidiaries will need to organise their governance on the basis of a central Group function and outlying regional and/or legal entity functions. This applies most crucially to the ALCO function. We present here recommended best practice for a Group ALCO (GALCO) organisation structure in a multinational and/or multi-entity bank.

Group Treasury Operating Model

A large or multinational bank should put in place a formal "operating model" that states formally what the objectives, roles, responsibility and ToR of the Group Treasury and branch and subsidiary Treasuries are. This forms the basis of the Group ALCO ToR. We describe here our recommended Group Treasury operating model framework.

Treasury Roles and Responsibilities

Group Treasury is responsible for overseeing that balance sheet capital and resources are utilised at their optimum level and on a sustainable basis across the bank. This is achieved via the following parallel tracks:

- Strategic and tactical governance
  - Ensure transparent governance and communication of policies and limits across the bank
- Balance sheet management
  - Compile board-approved Treasury policy statements for governance of the balance sheet, with regard to capital, liquidity, funding, transfer pricing and interest-rate and FX risk management). Implement and ensure compliance with these policies
  - Monitor the various balance sheet limits (including capital and asset limits) across the Group, legal entities and subsidiaries
- Liaising and working with business lines
  - Ensure seamless liaison with the business lines across the Group, to facilitate application of Treasury policy guidelines at the business line level
  - Ensure that capital, liquidity, funding, transfer pricing and interest-rate and FX risk management policies are adhered to at the business line level and part of the origination process.

The above can be drilled down into a more detailed document that includes the various policy statements, limits and approval levels. This would also include department organisation and names of individuals responsible for implementing policy. The communication process would be organised as shown at Figure 10.4.

Group Treasury Role and Responsibility

At a vanilla commercial bank operating in one jurisdiction, Treasury will typically be a profit centre, while also being responsible for overall ALM, funding, liquidity risk management, and policy setting and

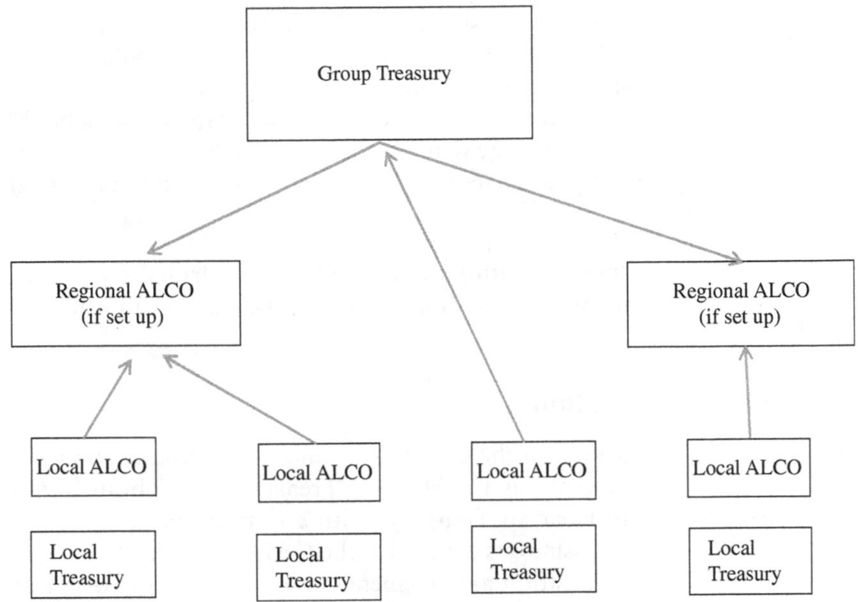

FIGURE 10.4 Group Treasury and local ALCO communication structure.

implementation. In a Group Treasury structure for a multinational and/ or multi-entity bank group, it is more likely to be organised for the latter activity only, although the home country money market desk (a profit-making activity) may also be included within it.

Generally, Group Treasury will define Treasury policy for the entire bank and implement this across the group. It will also manage and be responsible overall for the relationship with the national and all external regulators, and the credit rating agencies. Overseas entities will also manage the local regulatory relationship on a day-to-day basis.

As a standard template, GALCO on an overview basis and Group Treasury on a delegated basis are responsible for all Treasury-related issues in the bank. These include the following:

- managing the capital base of the bank;
- monitoring at aggregate level the Group's balance sheet risk;
- compiling for board approval the Group's liquidity risk appetite and funding policy. This includes responsibility for all capital raising, including equity, hybrid capital instruments, and senior and subordinated debt;

- managing the Group's funding structure, in line with approved guidelines, with respect to regulatory requirements and internal funding policy;
- managing the liquidity reporting to the national regulators;
- managing the Group's non-traded interest-rate risk for the Banking book;
- setting policy for the management of the Group's FX exposure risk, which is implemented as delegated authority to the individual local Treasury desks.

Again, this high-level operating model ToR can be drilled down into detailed policy statements and outlines of roles and responsibilities for each desk.

Local ALCO Organisation

Where the overseas business of the Group is organised as a branch, no local ALCO structure is necessary as the Head of Treasury at the branch will report direct to Group Head of Treasury (with a dotted line to the local CEO), and thus branch business is covered at the GALCO level.

A local ALCO organisation arrangement is necessary at any overseas business operation that is a subsidiary, partnership or separate legal entity to the parent. The ToR of the local ALCO will be virtually identical to that for a general ALCO of a domestic banking operation, described earlier, with the exception that the local Treasury is not responsible for any bank policy setting. The role of the local ALCO is to ensure that GALCO policy and all Treasury-related matters are adhered to in the local jurisdiction. The local ALCO ToR would include the following:

- managing the local regulatory relationship;
- ensuring that GALCO and Group Treasury policy is adhered to;
- overseeing balance sheet management for the local entity;
- in line with Group Treasury policy and principles, devising and implementing a liquidity and funding plan for the local entity;
- approving capital and funding, via the approval process at ALCO level, for local business origination, in line with overall bank strategy;
- managing the liquidity book or Liquid Asset Buffer (delegated to local Treasury).

The operating model should describe a clear delineation of roles and responsibilities, as well as a structure of transparent communication between GALCO, Group Treasury, local ALCO and the local Treasury, and thence to the business lines. For example, Table 10.4 shows how the approval levels for capital allocation may be set from GALCO downwards.

TABLE 10.4 Hypothetical capital approval limit structure.

GALCO	Any amount
Group Finance Director	Up to $100 m
Group Head of Treasury	Up to $50 m
Local ALCO	Up to $10 m
Local Head of Treasury	Up to $1 m

Local Treasury

Both branches and subsidiaries overseas will have a local Treasury desk, managed by the local Head of Treasury. This person, in conjunction with the local ALCO, is responsible for compliance with local regulations and Group Treasury policy. This includes the following:

- ensure that the local entity adheres to the requirements of the national regulator;
- compile a local market liquidity contingency funding plan;
- chair the local ALCO and compliance with the set ALCO ToR;
- manage the day-to-day relations with the local regulator.

In addition, the local Treasury is responsible for managing the branch/subsidiary liquidity requirement and risk exposure, in line with internal limits and targets to comply with local requirements. That is, liquidity is managed at local entity level (in line with Group Treasury policy) and all liquidity modelling and stress testing (see Chapter 14) is undertaken locally. Assumptions used in stress testing would follow Group standards, modified where necessary to reflect local market conditions.

Organisation Structure

There is of course more than one way to organise the GALCO governance structure at a multinational or multi-entity bank. We illustrate our recommendation at Figure 10.5. A Regional ALCO is not common and not necessarily recommended; however, for banks with a number of overseas operations in the same defined region (such as the Gulf Cooperation Council, or in Asia-Pacific), it may be logical to organise the local entities into a Regional ALCO structure. This should only be done where value is added through a regional set-up. Otherwise, incorporating both local and regional ALCOs may create unnecessary bureaucracy and duplication.

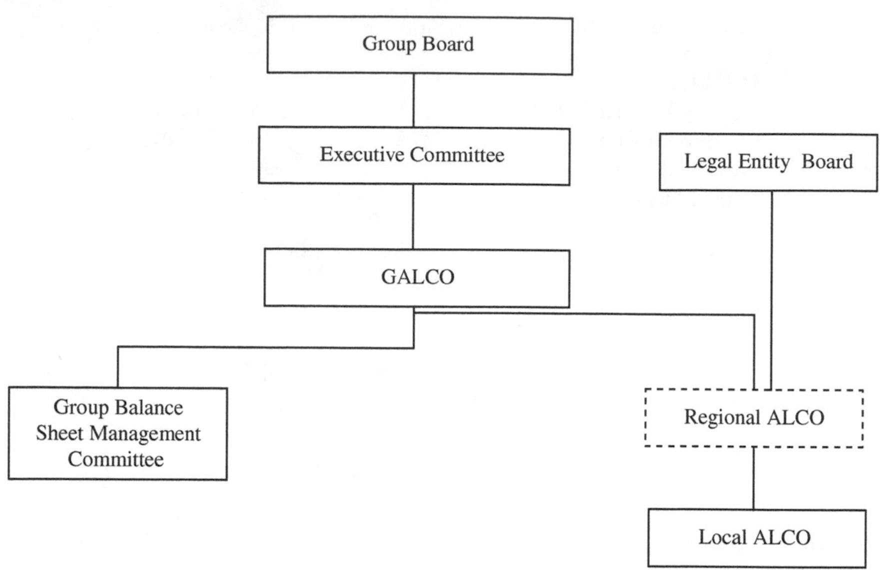

FIGURE 10.5 GALCO and Group Treasury organisation.

For larger banks and multi-entity banking groups, it is frequently the case that the ALCO does not have sufficient time to review adequately all policies and relevant aspects of the balance sheet. Where this is the case, business best-practice suggests that a separate Balance Sheet Management Committee (BSMCO) be set up to review more technical items, and feed up to ALCO where necessary. The membership of BSMCO would include:

- Head of Balance Sheet Management;
- Deputy Head of Treasury;
- Regional or Subsidiary Treasury delegates;
- Interest-rate Risk Management delegates;
- Chief Economist.

The role of BSMCO is essentially to review interest rate and liquidity risk aspects of the balance sheet from a macro-level perspective, and to recommend action in advance of expected stress events. It will also bring relevant items to the attention of ALCO, and there will be some commonality of membership between the two committees. The Chair would usually be the Deputy Head of Treasury.

Figure 10.6 shows the Treasury organisation at the subsidiary and/or overseas level for a bank that operates as a Group entity. Figure 10.6A is where the Treasury function is not also a profit centre (so that all dealing

Cost centre Treasury reporting to CEO or Finance Director

Head of Treasury

Liquidity management and liquidity buffer portfolio

Liabilities management

Balance sheet management

ALM policy and internal funds pricing

Treasury MI

Business analyis

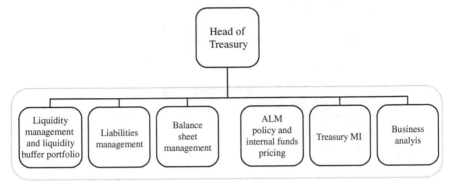

FIGURE 10.6A Treasury organisation, cost centre.

Profit-centre Treasury reporting to CEO or MD Front Office

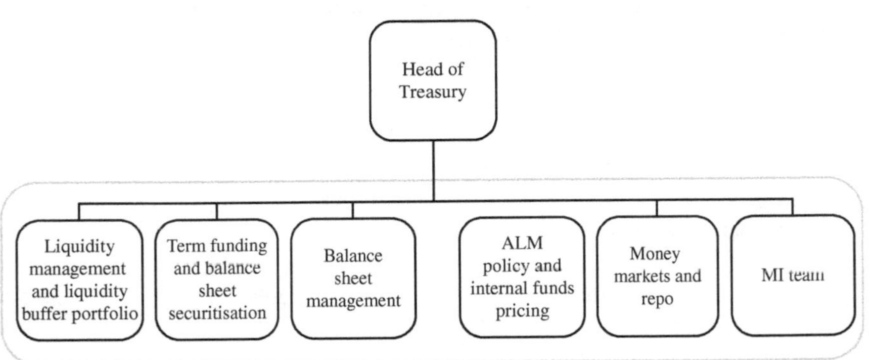

FIGURE 10.6B Treasury organisation, profit centre.

and money market trading is conducted as part of the front office environment, and Treasury is a middle office cost centre), and Figure 10.6B is the more common arrangement with the Treasury as a front-office profit centre, incorporating the money markets dealing function.

GALCO Agenda Setting

The agenda items for GALCO are conceptually identical to what we discussed earlier for the ALCO agenda. However, much of the operating level business will be discussed at the local ALCO level and, where they are set up, regional ALCO level. This means that much GALCO business concerns Group policy issues, or high-level strategic decision-making issues. A sample GALCO agenda is shown at Figure 10.7.

EXAMPLE 10.1 ALCO BEST-PRACTICE GUIDELINES: THE UK REGULATOR

The ALCO is the most important senior management and risk committee in a bank. It must always be run as a value-added committee, which means it needs to have the correct composition, review up-to-date management information that reflects accurately the balance sheet position and risk exposures of the bank and be the centre of robust discussion and debate. Policies and recommendations approved by ALCO will have a considerable influence on the bank's condition and future state, so it is important that all banks seek to manage their ALCO on best-practice lines.

The UK FSA opined on this in a publication in January 2011.[1] It presented good practice guidelines that all ALCOs should seek to adhere to, in the following areas:

- the role of ALCO;
- the composition and authority of ALCO;
- the forward-looking nature of the ALCO discussion and the decisions it makes;
- the degree of senior management challenge during meetings, and evidence of this in the approved ALCO minutes;
- regular attendance from all members.

We list the FSA's recommended guidelines here.

Role of the Committee

- Proactively controls the business in line with the bank's strategy and objectives, and focuses on the entire balance sheet;
- Ensures that risks remain within the stated risk appetite;
- Considers the impact on earnings volatility of changing economic and market conditions;

1 Financial Services Authority, *Finalised Guidance: Asset and Liability Management*, January 2011

- Ensures that an appropriate internal funds pricing mechanism is in place that correctly charges for the cost of liquidity, incentivises the desired behaviour and is in line with the bank's strategic objectives and risk appetite;
- Acts as the arbitrator in the debate and challenge process between business lines.

Committee Membership

- Attended by the CEO or Deputy CEO, and chaired by the CFO;
- Includes all business group heads, the CRO, the Head of Research/Economics and the Head of Internal Audit.

Nature of Discussion

- Is forward-looking in nature, focusing on the impact of future plans and strategy at the business line level;
- Takes proactive decisions to manage ALM risks, act to solve issues raised or otherwise escalating to the Executive Committee/Board rather than simply noting or observing the risks;
- Ensures issues are fully articulated and debated;
- Considers recommendations from a tactical sub-committee that excludes the CEO and other ExCo members. Where appropriate, delegates decision-making authority to an ALCO sub-committee;
- Ensures an active dialogue and debate among committee members, and shows evidence of a strong degree of challenge;
- Provides minutes summarising the extent of discussion and debate, and do not only record action points.

Management Information (the ALCO "Pack")

- Is content-focused on future plans and strategy;
- Presents market and economic outlook, together with impact assessment on ALM issues pertinent to the bank;
- Shows liquidity and funding metrics by currency; also provides a forecast of metrics based on current market expectations;
- Provides results of stress tests under specified stress conditions;
- Provides analysis of interest-rate risk using modified duration and VaR methodologies, NII/NIM sensitivity and basis risk, as part of an assessment of earnings volatility;

(*continued*)

(*continued*)

- Reports its current funding composition, and assesses potential refinancing risk stress points, based on its funding maturities, its market funding position and the position of the market generally;
- Presents liquidity stress testing scenarios of varying severity;
- Presents the Contingency Funding Plan (CFP) for the bank, and regularly updates it;
- Provides the required level of granularity and invites challenge from members.

The author endorses these recommendations, particularly the ones on regular attendance and management challenge.

An example of an ALCO pack is provided on the Wiley website link that accompanies this book.

ADDITIONAL MI CONTENT OF THE REGIONAL ALCO PACK

A bank operating in a multinational environment, in which the overseas entities are subsidiaries or associated legal entities rather than branches, should organise its governance via regional or legal entity ALCOs. There is then a Group ALCO (GALCO) that reviews matters at Group level. Care should be taken that the governance structure is not diluted or duplicated; either a regional or legal entity ALCO arrangement is sufficient, but there is little need for both. Business best-practice is to incorporate the legal entities that are in one defined customer region (such as MENA, GCC, Asia-Pacific and so on) into their own regional ALCO. Of course, if a particular legal entity in an overseas region is a sufficiently large business concern, then it may also have its own ALCO. There is no one definitive model, but the emphasis should be on ensuring appropriate management control, and the ability for GALCO to be abreast of all necessary MI for the overseas entities.

We illustrate the format of the inputs to a Regional ALCO here.

Above the standard constituents of the ALCO pack that we described in Chapter 9, we would expect to see the additional metrics discussed here. This is for a hypothetical multinational bank with its head office in Europe, but with a substantial presence in the Asia-Pacific region. Its reporting currency is in euros, so the aggregate regional statistics are all converted into euros.

Table 10.5 is a summary of the liquid asset buffers held in each legal entity or region. These are assets that would be available in a liquidity stress event.

For attention of GALCO
CEO
Deputy CEO
Head of Corporate Banking
Head of Portfolio Management
Head of Investment Banking
Head of Money Markets
Finance Director
Group Risk Officer
Group Head of Treasury
Deputy Group Head of Treasury

Subject
Group ALCO Agenda

Minutes/Actions:

1. **Minutes of previous GALCO**
2. **MI Pack**
3. **Macroeconomics update**

Approval items:

4. **Year-end forecast and budget update**
5. **Year-end asset and capital limits**
6. **Capital stress testing**
7. **Revised approval process, capital allocation**
8. **New business: MENA capital injection request**
9. **Private bank business organisation review**
10. **Internal funds pricing for liquidity lines**

Updated items:

11. **Risk-weighted assets limit transfer**
12. **Intra-group limits: regulatory update**
13. **Revised Funds Transfer Pricing policy**
14. **Term funding strategy**

FIGURE 10.7 Sample GALCO agenda.

TABLE 10.5 Regional liquidity buffer summary; example.

Country	Category	Currency	Market value (EUR)	WAM (years)	Liability source	Currency of liability
Australia	T-bills	AUD	615,001,300	0.21	Invested capital and reserve	AUD
	Government bonds	AUD	500,315,218	1.88	Core customer liability	AUD
Bangladesh	T-bills	BDT	28,450,000	0.22	Capital and reserves	BDT
	Central bank deposit	BDT	25,615,045	0.01	Capital and reserves	BDT
Hong Kong	T-bills	HKD	251,026,155	0.55	Core customer liability	HKD
Indonesia	T-bills	IDR	15,256,321	0.35	Capital, customer liability	IDR, USD
Malaysia	T-bills	MYR	88,255,632	0.105	Capital, customer liability	MYR, USD
	Government bonds	MYR	54,325,156	2.4	Capital, customer liability	MYR, USD
New Zealand	T-bills	NZD	156,315,255	0.33	Capital, reserves, customer deposits	NZD
	Placement with money market	NZD	105,879,954	0.61	Customer deposits	NZD
Taiwan	Government bonds	TWD	48,321,525	2.53	Capital and reserves	TWD
	Investment grade corporate bonds	TWD	56,155,421	2.87	Customer deposits, wholesale deposits	TWD

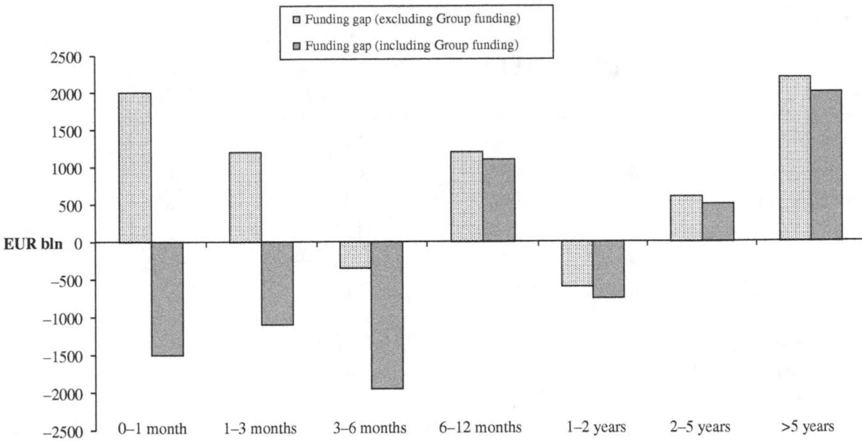

FIGURE 10.8A Regional liquidity position, regional gap.

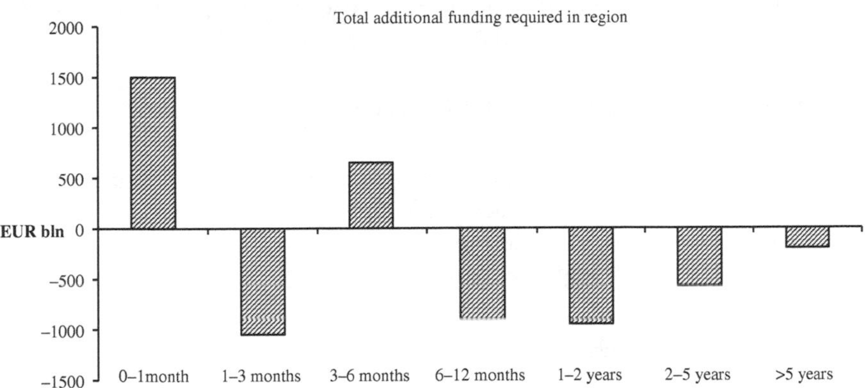

FIGURE 10.8B Regional liquidity position, total forward funding requirement.

Figure 10.8A is a regional structural liquidity and funding metrics summary. This combines all the regional entities, both branch and subsidiary. Figure 10.8A shows the funding gap as the difference between the total assets and liabilities for the region, by maturity bucket (in other words, a standard ALM gap chart, but combining a number of operating entities). Figure 10.8B is the chart of total additional funding required for the region, and shows how much funding needs to be raised by maturity bucket. The first chart also shows the extent of the reliance on parent funding. This may be a focus for attention if the home and/or local regulator imposes limits on how much parent funding is allowed, or if it decides that the local entity

TABLE 10.6 Monthly regional liquidity metrics report; example.

Country	2010 LTD ratio	2011 LTD target	2011 funding requirement[1]	Concentration risk[2] 2010	2011 limit
Australia	109%	100%	310	15%	10%
Bangladesh	68%	85%	−248	19%	15%
Hong Kong	88%	100%	−40	12%	10%
Indonesia	74%	85%	−155	18%	10%
Malaysia	115%	100%	215	8%	10%
New Zealand	102%	100%	116	11%	15%
Taiwan	98%	90%	−87	16%	10%

[1]To achieve funding self-sufficiency. EURmm
[2]Top 5 depositors

must be funding "self-sufficient". This MI is very important for banks looking to reduce overseas operations' reliance on parent funding.

Table 10.6 is the monthly liquidity metrics monitoring report for the region. The exposure to regional currencies is shown at Table 10.7.

TREASURY ORGANISATION STRUCTURE

We have described a recommended governance arrangement for a Group Treasury and local Treasury function. We also described the Balance Sheet & Capital Management function, which is the team responsible for managing and overseeing the bank's regulatory capital and economic

TABLE 10.7 Regional currency exposure report.

Currency	0–1 month	1–3 months	3–6 months	6–12 months	1–2 years	2–5 years	>5 years
AUD	56,698	(8,506)	4,499	11,361	(2,566)	(1,085)	216
BDT	(12,145)	(5,583)	2,049	18	651	(102)	34
CNY	(633)	(617)	5,811	(5,119)	387	602	(3,511)
HKD	(9,246)	(7,085)	2751	6729	(4,387)	(5,641)	2,495
IDR	(562)	(4,822)	(752)	(13)	0	(6,150)	378
JPY	36,484	(12,011)	(21,985)	(73,075)	3,379	(67,118)	56,025
MYR	(30)	697	(752)	(28)	0	(6,150)	(4,288)
SGD	(8,395)	(4,184)	(464)	(1,025)	0	(14,248)	3,754
NZD	(4,845)	(3,756)	1,025	1,799	658	(1,077)	(189)
TWD	9,874	355	(8,987)	(6,524)	(15,233)	3,265	(456)
USD	(54,437)	(25,791)	(12,980)	17,852	25,319	(50,037)	(17,849)

capital. To undertake this it will make use of both securitisation techniques and derivatives such as credit derivatives.

Different banks organise the Treasury function differently. For those banks that set up Treasury as a cost centre, the money markets trading desk (which deals in short-dated cash and derivatives for funding, trading and hedging purposes) will sit outside Treasury. Where the Treasury department is organised as a profit centre, the money markets desk will be part of Treasury. It is not uncommon, however, for the former structure to include money markets as well, which then has a "dotted-line" reporting responsibility to the head of the trading floor.

The suggested alternative organisation structures were shown at Figure 10.6.

The Liquidity Management team will devise, originate and structure more complex term funding issuance, such as a structured MTN issuance programme, secured repo and TRS trades and collateralised structured notes. Where a securitisation is undertaken for cash raising reasons, it will need to be a true-sale cash securitisation. A synthetic securitisation has no value as a funding transaction because the liabilities are either unfunded or, where they are funded (in the form of a CLN), provide cash that must be either placed in a bank account or used to buy AAA-rated collateral securities. If the former is followed, the cash in the bank account can only ever be deemed to be 30-day or 15-day cash, and so is not term funding; if the latter, the cash received from selling the CLN is no longer available to the bank.[2]

TREASURY OPERATING MODEL

As the previous section showed, there is more than one way to organise the bank Treasury function. The principle decision to take is whether it should be a profit centre, incorporating the money market trading desk, or a cost centre "middle office" that sets policy and governance but is not a market-facing function. Both approaches have their merits, but in a well-run and

2 The reason the cash can only be treated as short-dated money is due to credit rating agency rules on rating downgrade triggers. To obtain a AAA-rating on the issued synthetic note, the cash received from the note buyer must be placed with a bank that has an S&P/Moody's short-term rating of A-1/P-1. If the rating is A-1+ and the deposit-taking bank is downgraded to A-1, the synthetic note proceeds must be placed at another bank of required rating within 15 days. If the rating is A-1 and the bank is downgraded to A-2, the cash must be removed within 15 days. Hence, synthetic securitisation deals are not, for regulatory authority purposes, liquidity relief deals.

well-governed institution it is more likely that effective control and discipline can be enforced if the Treasury set-up is as a market-facing profit centre.

When organising the bank's Treasury operating model, it is recommended that a review of the functions be undertaken first, before then deciding which department they best fit in. Table 10.8 shows the relevant bank activities by discipline, illustrated as a matrix function.

There is no "right" way to organise the Treasury operating model with respect to the functions shown in Table 10.8. What is important however is that the structure that is selected is appropriate to the strategy and culture of the specific bank. All the alternative approaches shown here would be suitable. There is a large variety of models that can be selected, but in general the ones described here are a business best-practice approach; the author would not recommend structures outside what is described in Figures 10.9 to 10.12.

A common organisation structure is for Treasury to encompass both market facing and policy functions. This is shown at Figure 10.9, and describes a Treasury function that reports to the CEO, but with a "dotted line" reporting responsibility to the CFO. The areas of responsibility given to Treasury are shaded.

In a large bank the reporting line to the CEO may be replaced with one to the head of markets or the head of an operating division. We observe from Figure 10.9 that in this arrangement the Treasury desk has a P&L responsibility, but is also the control function for capital and liquidity policy. The financial reporting for Treasury therefore must separate activities conducted with the external market from internal activities, to ensure that the P&L shown is only for external business. So, for example, internal transactions undertaken as part of the internal funding policy, otherwise known as funds transfer pricing (FTP; see Chapter 15) would be reported separately, usually as part of the ALCO book and not as Treasury P&L.

The opposite to this structure is a "middle office" Treasury that is responsible for policy setting and implementation, but has no market facing function. The governance function would not encompass financial reporting, but may include regulatory reporting. In this arrangement the reporting line is typically to the CFO, although we recommend that it be to the CEO or Deputy CEO. This is shown at Figure 10.10.

The first two methodologies represent the most common arrangements. A mixture of the two, which must be implemented with care because it risks generating control and policy implementation problems, is for Treasury to manage the term liabilities functions, but not the money markets and collateral management functions. In this arrangement it has a market facing function, but not the day-to-day cash management side of this function. This is shown at Figure 10.11. This model also includes the Investor

TABLE 10.8 Bank operating functions relevant to Treasury.

<table>
<tr><th></th><th>Capital and balance sheet</th><th>Liquidity</th><th>NII/NIM</th></tr>
<tr><td>Strategic management</td><td>Capital management
Risk limits (risk-weighted assets, or RWA)
Cost of capital
Budget forecasting
Setting capital policy
Setting return metrics
Defining capital structure and ratios
Capital allocation</td><td>Liquidity risk management
Liquidity limits
Liquidity stress tests
Liquidity policy
Contingency funding plan
LAB policy
Liquidity cost calculation
Funding strategy
Internal funds pricing policy (FTP)</td><td>Banking book interest-rate risk
Interest-rate risk management
Interest-rate risk modelling
Forecasting NII/NIM</td></tr>
<tr><td rowspan="2">Market facing functions</td><td>Term Liabilities Issuance
Senior unsecured debt
Subordinated debt
Equity instruments
Securitisation
Secured
– ABS/MBS
– Covered bonds</td><td>Money Markets Desk
Cash management
Money markets
– depos
– CD/CP
Repo

Collateral management

Counterparty risk management</td><td>Swaps and Derivatives desks
Banking book
Trading book
Market risk hedging</td></tr>
<tr><td colspan="3">Investor Relations
Rating Agencies
Investors</td></tr>
<tr><td>Governance</td><td colspan="3">Finance and Risk Management
Financial control and reporting
Regulatory reporting
Risk and product control</td></tr>
</table>

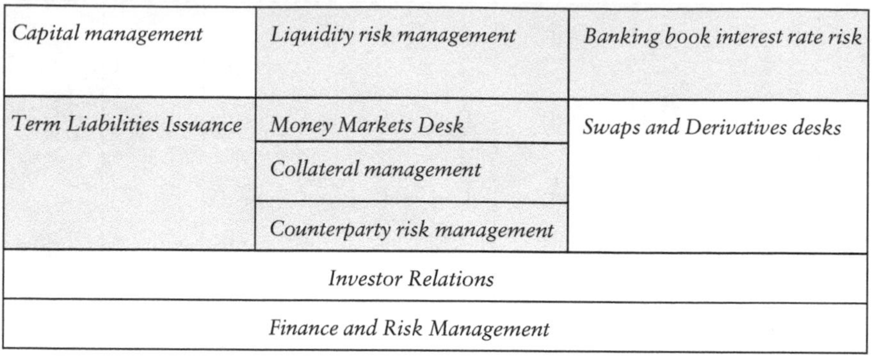

Capital management	Liquidity risk management	Banking book interest rate risk
Term Liabilities Issuance	Money Markets Desk	Swaps and Derivatives desks
	Collateral management	
	Counterparty risk management	
	Investor Relations	
	Finance and Risk Management	

FIGURE 10.9 Front office treasury operating model.

Capital management	Liquidity risk management	Banking book interest rate risk
Term Liabilities Issuance	Money Markets Desk	Swaps and Derivatives desks
	Collateral management Counterparty risk management	
	Investor Relations	
	Finance and Risk Management Regulatory reporting	

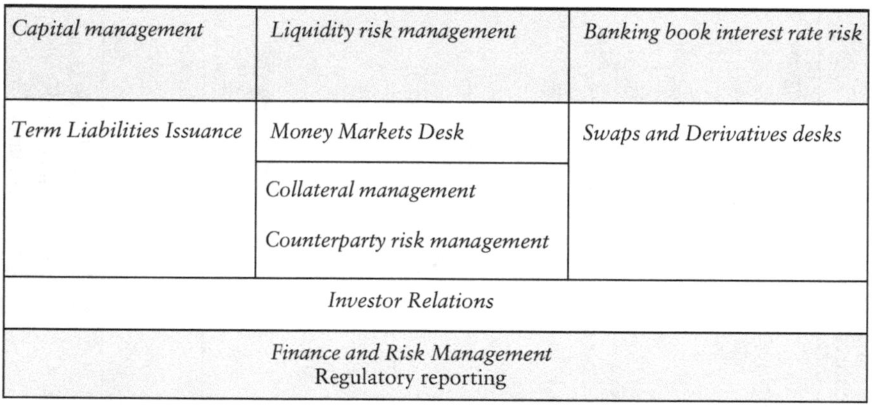

FIGURE 10.10 Middle office treasury operating model.

Capital management	Liquidity risk management	Banking book interest rate risk
Term Liabilities Issuance	Money Markets Desk	Swaps and Derivatives desks
	Collateral management Counterparty risk management	
	Investor Relations	
	Finance and Risk Management Regulatory reporting	

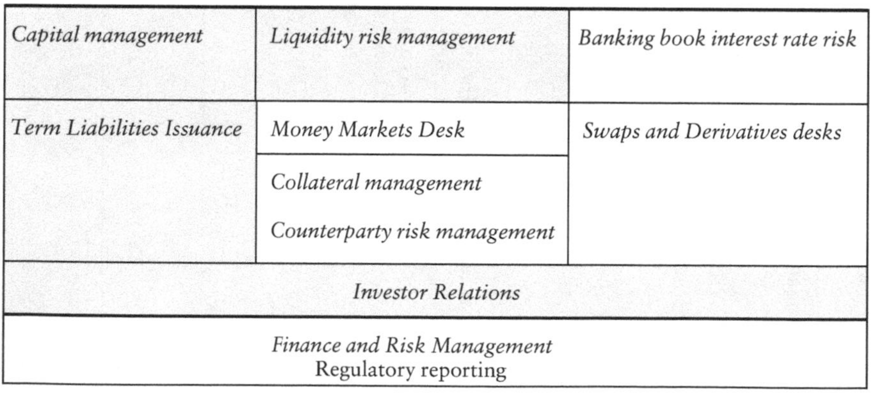

FIGURE 10.11 Treasury operating model with market facing function.

<table>
<tr><td>Capital management</td><td>Liquidity risk management</td><td>Banking book interest rate risk</td></tr>
<tr><td rowspan="2">Term Liabilities Issuance</td><td>Money Markets Desk</td><td rowspan="2">Swaps and Derivatives desks</td></tr>
<tr><td>Collateral management
Counterparty risk management</td></tr>
<tr><td colspan="3">Investor Relations</td></tr>
<tr><td colspan="3">Finance and Risk Management
Regulatory reporting</td></tr>
</table>

FIGURE 10.12 Treasury operating model with market facing and governance functions.

Relations department, and may or may not include the regulatory reporting (not shown as shaded, as this responsibility may reside within Finance). The Treasury head would report to the CFO or CEO. However, for most banks, the effective operating model would be either Figure 10.9 or Figure 10.10.

A final option is shown at Figure 10.12. This is a larger Treasury that is again front office facing and so would report to the CEO. It holds the policy and governance responsibility as well as the money market function, but the term liabilities and securitisation roles are placed elsewhere, perhaps within an investment bank division or a debt capital markets department.

As we noted at the start, there is more than one way to arrange the Treasury operating model. It is important that the method selected be fit for purpose. The critical areas of capital and liquidity management policy and operation, both day-to-day and long term, are best placed within a strong central Treasury function, which is why the author prefers the option shown at Figure 10.9.

REFERENCE

Barbican Consulting. (2011), *Asset Liability Management CEO Letter*, http://www.barbicanconsulting.co.uk/alm_ceo_letter, February 2.

CHAPTER 11

Risk Reporting, Risk Policy and Stress Testing

Successful bank management on a sustained basis requires effective risk reporting. Even the smallest banks will present difficulties in operation if the quality of high-level MI supplied to senior management is compromised. This chapter looks at the principle requirements for effective MI, and illustrates recommended best-practice with the use of hypothetical sample reports. It considers the required contents of a portfolio report, the presentation of the risk-return profile, and how the report results might be separated and shown. The introductory discussion is undertaken with reference to an hypothetical sample portfolio of 20 assets. Later in the chapter we provide samples of actual portfolio reports as part of the discussion.

The second part of this chapter discusses risk management and stress testing. As part of its strategy, a bank should formulate a high-level risk management policy to serve as the basis for the risk culture that exists within it. A bank should not leave it to operating departments to determine the extent of its risk tolerance. Rather, this should be articulated by the bank at the start. This can be done in its risk management policy. We provide a template that may serve as the basis for the formulation of risk management policy in a bank.

Stress testing and scenario analysis is now an established part of the risk management process in banks. We describe how the process should be set in a bank, again with an illustration using a template stress-testing policy suitable for a medium-sized commercial bank.

HIGH LEVEL MAPPING OF RISK

It is important to achieve a high-level understanding of exactly which parts of the bank have responsibility for each identified risk, at both operational and oversight level. Responsibilities must be identified and stated formally; for example, in the form of the "risk map" shown at Table 11.1. This is a template of identified risks (different banks will have larger or smaller risk types, according to the extent of their business operations), with operating and supervisory responsibilities stated. The ultimate supervisory oversight is carried out at senior level; for example, by the Executive Credit Committee or ALCO. This is the committee with the principal oversight responsibility; of course, other committees may have oversight of aspects of the risks, and there will be some overlap among both MI reporting as well committee membership.

After the various risks have been identified, it is the responsibility of the bank's head of risk, usually termed the Chief Risk Officer (CRO), to carry out a regular evaluation of each of the current risk exposures, in liaison with the operating departments. One way to assess the risk is to assign a current exposure level, whether "High", "Medium" or "Low", as shown at the template at Table 11.2. This is an hypothetical assessment of the extent of risk; the categorisation of the amount of potential loss will obviously differ at each bank. However, it is important for senior management to quantify the level of material and reputational loss by degree of sensitivity, if only so that operating managers know at what point to escalate potential problems.

The risk mapping report can be in the format shown at Table 11.3. This output must be maintained regularly if it is to have any value. A summary is presented by the CRO to the Executive Management Committee on a regular (say, quarterly) basis for review and comment.

PORTFOLIO CREDIT RISK: EXAMPLE ILLUSTRATION

We introduce the concept of the portfolio credit risk report using a simple, hypothetical loan portfolio.

The Portfolio Report

A bank balance sheet holds different types of asset, each of which present detail differences in their credit risk management. Notwithstanding these differences, at the aggregate level we are concerned with a summary report

TABLE 11.1 Bank risk mapping.

Risk exposures		Risk oversight		
Material risk groups	**Risks**	**1st line of defence (risk ownership)**	**2nd line of defence**	**Oversight**
Credit	Counterparty Deterioration and Default	Corporate and Retail Banking/ Credit	Credit Risk Control	Executive Credit Committee
	Country	Corporate and Retail Banking/ Credit	Credit Risk Control	Executive Credit Committee
	Concentration	Corporate and Retail Banking/ Credit	Credit Risk Control	Executive Credit Committee
	Collateral Management	Corporate and Retail Banking/ Credit	Credit Risk Control	Executive Credit Committee
	Counterparty Settlement	Corporate and Retail Banking/ Credit	Credit Risk Control	Executive Credit Committee
	Credit Documentation	Corporate and Retail Banking/ Credit	Legal	Executive Credit Committee
Liquidity	Liquidity	Treasury supported by Finance	Market & Liquidity Risk Control	ALCO
	Solvency	Treasury supported by Finance	Market & Liquidity Risk Control	ALCO
	Liquidity Concentration	Treasury supported by Finance	Market & Liquidity Risk Control	ALCO
	Regulatory Liquidity	Treasury supported by Finance	Market & Liquidity Risk Control	ALCO

(continued)

TABLE 11.1 *(continued)*

Risk exposures		Risk oversight		
Material risk groups	**Risks**	**1st line of defence (risk ownership)**	**2nd line of defence**	**Oversight**
Operational	Process	Each Department Head	Operational Risk Control	Risk & Compliance Committee
	Business Continuity	Each Department Head	Operational Risk Control	Risk & Compliance Committee
	Information Security	Each Department Head	Operational Risk Control	Risk & Compliance Committee
	Technology	Each Department supported by IT	Operational Risk Control	Risk & Compliance Committee
	Insurance	Finance department	Operational Risk Control	Risk & Compliance Committee
	Financial Reporting Risk	Each Department supported by Finance	Operational Risk Control	Risk & Compliance Committee
Legal		Each Department supported by Legal	Operational Risk Control	Risk & Compliance Committee
Capital Planning & Management	Capital	Finance supported by Treasury	Market & Liquidity Risk Control	ALCO
Regulatory	Regulatory Governance	CEO supported by Company Secretariat	Compliance	Risk & Compliance Committee
	Regulatory Compliance	Each Department	Compliance	Risk & Compliance Committee
	Financial Crime	Each Department Head	Compliance	Risk & Compliance Committee
	Statutory	Each Department	Legal	Risk & Compliance Committee

Strategy (Business, Operational, HR, IT etc.)	Setting strategy	CEO & Business Line Heads	CRO	Executive Management Committee
	Operationalising Strategy	Each Department Head	CRO	Executive Management Committee
	Strategic Decision-making	CEO	CRO	Executive Management Committee
Market	Interest Rate	Treasury supported by Product Control	Market & Liquidity Risk Control	ALCO
	FX	Treasury supported by Product Control	Market & Liquidity Risk Control	ALCO
	Hedging Strategy	Treasury supported by Product Control	Market & Liquidity Risk Control	ALCO
	Pricing	Treasury supported by Product Control	Market Risk and Credit Risk Control	ALCO
Pension Fund		Finance supported by HR (Liaison with Trustees)	CRO	CEO
Group Risk		CEO & Each Department Head	CRO	Board Risk & Compliance Committee

TABLE 11.2 Risk exposure categories.

Key	Financial risk (Annual expected loss)	Reputation risk	Regulatory risk
High	> €10 million	Reputation badly damaged, brand erosion, significant impact on parent or Group.	Intensive inspection by regulators triggered by serious and repeated market malfunctions with high visibility. Resulting in: – Deregulation – Withdrawl of individual licenses/ authorisations.
Medium/High	> €3 million – < €10 million	Negative market information and/or sentiment has a material effect on the bank's deposit base. No impact on Group.	Regulators made aware of serious incidents. Repeated, material breaches, indicative of systemic failure or significant failure in governance arrangements. Resulting in: – Public warnings – Significant fines. –Referral to Regulator.
Medium	> €0.5 million < €3 million	Some negative market information/sentiment potentially mitigated by Management action. No impact on Group.	Repeated inspections or private warnings. One-off, material breaches of the rules, requiring notification to the Regulator. Weakness in governance arrangements.
Low/Medium	> €0.1 million < €0.5 million	Minor negative market information/ sentiment mitigated by Management action.	Minor impact on Regulator. Including technical breaches of the rules, not requiring notification to the Regulator.
Low	< €0.1 million	Little negative market information/sentiment, no senior management action required.	No significant regulatory impact.

TABLE 11.3 Template for risk assessment report.

	Risk assessment						
		Effect risks (Inherent severity components)					Severity
Risk type	Inherent severity	Financial impact risk	Reputational impact risk	Regulatory impact risk	Frequency/ Probability	Controls/ Mitigation	Residual
Counterparty deterioration and default	H	H	H	H			
Liquidity concentration	M/H	M/H	L	L			
Etc.	M	M	M	L			
Etc.	L/M	L/M	L/M	L/M			
Etc.	H	H	M	M			

that states the extent of current risk exposure, and what the actual amount of credit-related losses are expected to be.

We set up an hypothetical sample portfolio used to formulate the discussion, given at Table 11.4. We observe that there are 20 assets, of varying default probability, industrial sectors and recovery rates. The portfolio report output is generated using a Monte Carlo simulation, which produces a loss distribution.[1] The risk report is shown at Table 11.5. We show the portfolio highlights at Table 11.6.

The aggregate portfolio size is £255 million, across 20 assets or "obligors". The portfolio expected loss is 0.63% of the aggregate notional value of the portfolio. The analysis is undertaken for a 12-month period, so we take each asset income spread as the expected revenue for the year. We assume a cost of capital of 10%. Running a portfolio loss distribution based on a Monte Carlo simulation, we obtain the loss distribution shown in Figure 11.1. At a 95% confidence interval the loss in the portfolio is £16.05 million, which is 6.29% of the portfolio notional and 9.83% of the portfolio loss-given-default (LGD).[2] Figure 11.2 is the cumulative loss distribution chart, which shows the portfolio loss at a 95% confidence interval.

Capital and Return on Assets

The portfolio loss distribution drives the capital calculation. We see that the default probabilities drive the EL for the portfolio, which are £1.62 million. From the cumulative loss distribution we see that the portfolio loss at the 95% interval is £16.05 million. The capital allocation for the portfolio, which is not the regulatory capital allocation but assessed for return analysis purposes, can be this amount or it can be adjusted for the portfolio EL or the portfolio expected spread revenue. This number is then used to calculate the RAROC. Assuming the cost of capital at 10%, we are able to calculate SVA, which is the portfolio expected spread revenue minus the capital costs.

At the aggregate level the portfolio loss distribution drives the capital allocation to the portfolio. Each business line will also allocate capital to

1 Note that for instructional purposes a simple Monte Carlo model is provided on the Excel spreadsheet supplementary material, available on the Wiley website. This was co-written with Abukar Ali.

2 In reality this is quite a high default rate and would indicate a poorly performing portfolio. However, the sample portfolio has only a small number of assets, and is hence quite concentrated, and the names are generally lower rated.

TABLE 11.4 Hypothetical sample portfolio.

No.	Obligor name	Notional exposure (£mln)	Sector	Internal rating	Default probability %	Recovery rate %	LGD %	Notional loss (£mln)	Credit spread bps	Portfolio weighting %
1	San Pedro Finance	10	1	3	0.75	40	60	6	160	3.92
2	Bank BV	25	1	2	0.10	40	60	15	80	9.80
3	Atlas Corp	5	2	3	1.00	40	60	3	180	1.96
4	Ringside Co	17	2	3	1.00	40	60	10.2	175	6.67
5	Atlantic Conveyer	29	3	2	0.10	40	60	17.4	78	11.37
6	Eastland Transport	5	3	3	0.75	40	60	3	155	1.96
7	Rockport Mining	15	2	4	2.00	20	80	12	230	5.88
8	Endsleigh Finance	8	1	3	1.00	40	60	4.8	190	3.14
9	Zenith Framing Co	10	2	4	2.50	20	80	8	280	3.92
10	Quality Hotels	20	5	2	0.50	40	60	12	83	7.84
11	CostCo	5	3	3	1.00	40	60	3	199	1.96
12	Tiger Manufacturing	10	2	3	1.00	40	60	6	100	3.92
13	Worldwide Markets	15	2	3	1.50	40	60	9	210	5.88
14	Anglian Television	10	4	2	0.50	40	60	6	69	3.92
15	Surrey Hills Partnership	5	3	3	0.75	40	60	3	150	1.96
16	Countrywide Building Society	30	1	2	0.25	40	60	18	50	11.76
17	The Mack Partnership	15	3	4	1.50	20	80	12	290	5.88
18	Watty Music Co	5	4	5	3.00	20	80	4	360	1.96

(*continued*)

TABLE 11.4 *(continued)*

No.	Obligor name	Notional exposure (£mln)	Sector	Internal rating	Default probability %	Recovery rate %	LGD %	Notional loss (£mln)	Credit spread bps	Portfolio weighting %
19	Slater & Burntwood Media	6	4	4	2.50	20	80	4.8	270	2.35
20	AFA Ltd	10	4	3	1.50	40	60	6	160	3.92
		255						163.2		100

Notes
Portfolio weighted average rating: 2.77
Portfolio weighted average default probability: 0.913%
Sector: 1 – Finance; 2 – Mining, Construction, Manufacturing; 3 – Transport and Utility; 4 – Media; 5 – Hotels
Rating: 1 – AAA 2– to AA– 3– to BBB– 4– to BB– 5– B+ or below

TABLE 11.5 Hypothetical sample portfolio, 1-year risk report.

No.	Obligor name	Notional exposure (£mln)	Credit spread bps	£ Spread ('000)	Default probability %	Notional loss (£ mln.)	£ Expected loss (EL)	£ (Spread – EL)
1	San Pedro Finance	10	160	160	0.75	6	45,000	115,000
2	Bank BV	25	80	200	0.10	15	15,000	185,000
3	Atlas Corp	5	180	90	1.00	3	30,000	60,000
4	Ringside Co	17	175	297.5	1.00	10.2	102,000	195,500
5	Atlantic Conveyer	29	78	226.2	0.10	17.4	17,400	208,800
6	Eastland Transport	5	155	77.5	0.75	3	22,500	55,000
7	Rockport Mining	15	230	345	2.00	12	240,000	105,000
8	Endsleigh Finance	8	190	152	1.00	4.8	48,000	104,000
9	Zenith Framing Co	10	280	280	2.50	8	200,000	80,000
10	Quality Hotels	20	83	166	0.50	12	60,000	106,000
11	CostCo	5	199	99.5	1.00	3	30,000	69,500
12	Tiger Manufacturing	10	100	100	1.00	6	60,000	40,000
13	Worldwide Markets	15	210	315	1.50	9	135,000	180,000
14	Anglian Television	10	69	69	0.50	6	30,000	39,000
15	Surrey Hills Partnership	5	150	75	0.75	3	22,500	52,500
16	Countrywide Building Society	30	50	150	0.25	18	45,000	105,000
17	The Mack Partnership	15	290	435	1.50	12	180,000	255,000
18	Watty Music Co	5	360	180	3.00	4	120,000	60,000
19	Slater & Burntwood Media	6	270	162	2.50	4.8	120,000	42,000
20	AFA Ltd	10	160	160	1.50	6	90,000	70,000
	Total (actuals)	255,000,000		3,739,700		163,200,000	1,612,400	2,127,300

TABLE 11.6 Hypothetical sample portfolio highlights.

Portfolio summary		
Portfolio aggregate value *N*	£255 million	
Aggregate LGD amount	£163.2 million	
Average LGD	64%	
Portfolio expected loss (EL) value	£1.612 million	
EL	0.63%	
Aggregate UL	£14,557,003	
Loss percentile at 95%	£16.05 million	
L(95%)/*N*	6.29%	
L(95%)/LGD	9.83%	
Capital requirement:		
C(95): L(95%) – EL	£14.438 million	
C(95)/*N*	5.66%	
Spread cash flow	3,739,700	
Expected spread (ES): Spread – EL	2,127,300	
Return on Assets (RoA): Spread/*N*	1.47%	
Expected RoA: ES/*N*	0.83%	
Capital in excess of ES: C(ES) = L(95%) – [Spread – EL])	£13.923 million	
C(ES)/*N*	5.46%	
Risk-adjusted RoC: (Spread – EL)/C(95)	14.73%	
Cost of capital (CoC) is 10%		
Funding costs at L(95%) level	£1,605,000	
Funding costs at C(95) level	£1,443,800	
Funding costs at C(ES) level	£1,392,300	
Shareholder value-added (SVA): ES – CoC		SVA/unit of portfolio exposure
–L(95%)	£522,300	0.0020
–C(95)	£683,500	0.0027
–C(ES)	£735,000	0.0029

each individual asset. The simplest capital allocation methodology is known as the "standalone loss volatility" (LV), which is given by:

$$LV = LGD \times \sqrt{DP(1 - DP)}$$

where *DP* is the default probability.

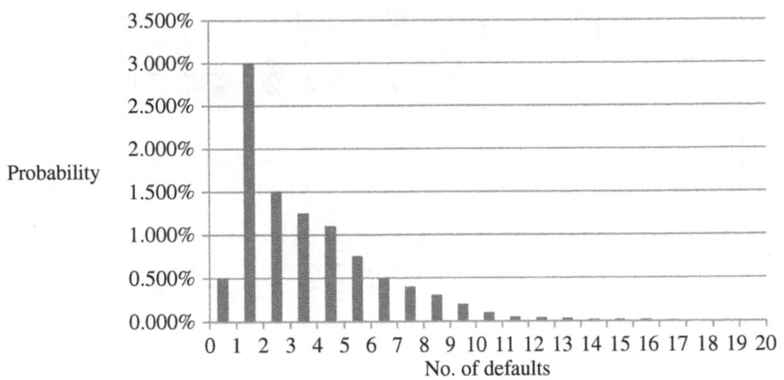

FIGURE 11.1 Sample portfolio loss distribution.

The loss volatility for each asset is calculated based on its individual default probability, and is therefore not influenced by any correlation or diversity effect. This then drives the asset capital allocation, which is calculated by applying the specific asset loss volatility to that of the complete portfolio. Calculating portfolio capital requirement by a simple aggregation of individual asset loss volatilities is a conservative approach for a bank to take.

Loss volatilities for the sample portfolio are shown at Table 11.7. We see that the capital required using individual default probabilities, which

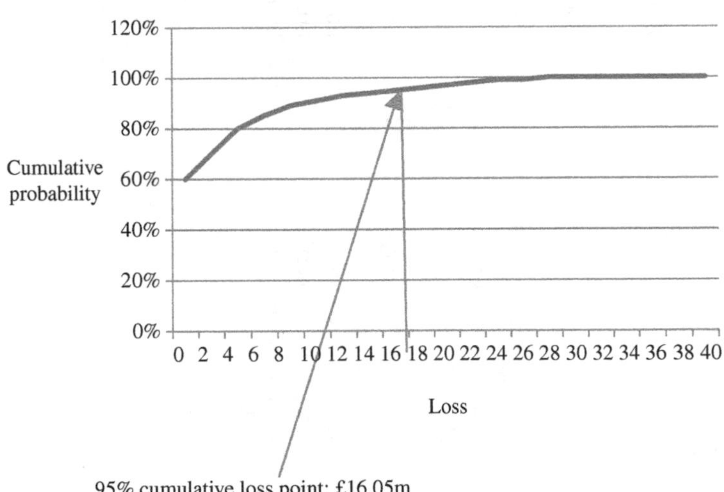

FIGURE 11.2 Cumulative loss distribution.

TABLE 11.7 Sample portfolio individual loss volatilities.

No.	Obligor name	Default probability	LGD %	Notional loss (£ mln) LGD	Loss volatility	£ Unexpected loss (UL)
1	San Pedro Finance	0.0075	60	6	0.518	517,663
2	Bank BV	0.0010	60	15	0.474	474,104
3	Atlas Corp	0.0100	60	3	0.298	298,496
4	Ringside Co	0.0100	60	10.2	1.015	1,014,887
5	Atlantic Conveyer	0.0010	60	17.4	0.550	549,961
6	Eastland Transport	0.0075	60	3	0.259	258,832
7	Rockport Mining	0.0200	80	12	1.680	1,680,000
8	Endsleigh Finance	0.0100	60	4.8	0.478	477,594
9	Zenith Framing Co	0.0250	80	8	1.249	1,249,000
10	Quality Hotels	0.0050	60	12	0.846	846,404
11	CostCo	0.0100	60	3	0.298	298,496
12	Tiger Manufacturing	0.0100	60	6	0.597	596,992
13	Worldwide Markets	0.0150	60	9	1.094	1,093,972
14	Anglian Television	0.0050	60	6	0.423	423,202
15	Surrey Hills Partnership	0.0075	60	3	0.259	258,832
16	Countrywide Building Society	0.0025	60	18	0.899	898,874
17	The Mack Partnership	0.0150	80	12	1.459	1,458,629
18	Watty Music Co	0.0300	80	4	0.682	682,349
19	Slater & Burntwood Media	0.0250	80	4.8	0.749	749,400
20	AFA Ltd	0.0150	60	6	0.729	729,315
				163.2		14,557,003

is also reported in Table 11.6 as "Aggregate UL", is within the 95% confidence interval loss distribution amount, so the portfolio capital allocation is already conservative.

PORTFOLIO RISK REPORTING: EXAMPLE ILLUSTRATION

Banks should apply both a "top-down" as well as "bottom-up" approach to credit risk management. In other words, it is necessary to be aware of and review the aggregate portfolio risk at all times, but it is also important to be aware of individual level risk, so that potentially non-performing assets can be identified in good time. The detailed risk review is undertaken at a lower level of management, who escalate to the higher level where necessary. Note that an asset may be disposed of, securitised or otherwise hedged against not only because it is non-performing or in danger of defaulting soon; such action might be taken because it no longer meets the bank's RoC or SVA requirements.

In order to meet the "bottom-up" MI requirements, the risk reports supplied to senior management need to show the risk exposure from the viewpoint of any of the parameters of credit risk, be this credit rating, default probability, LGD or so on.

Risk Parameters Reporting

We illustrate the main principles using the same sample portfolio described in the previous section. There we observed the aggregate portfolio risk exposure, EL and LGD notional amount. At the business line operating level, this will be broken down per asset, as shown in Figure 11.3. This plots

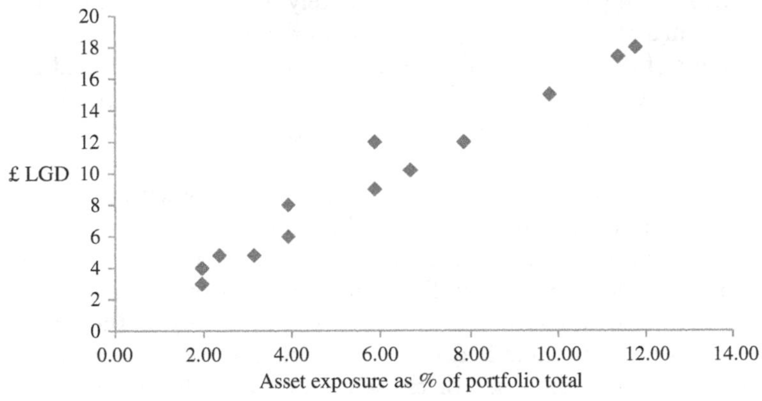

FIGURE 11.3 Portfolio risk report: asset exposure and £ LGD.

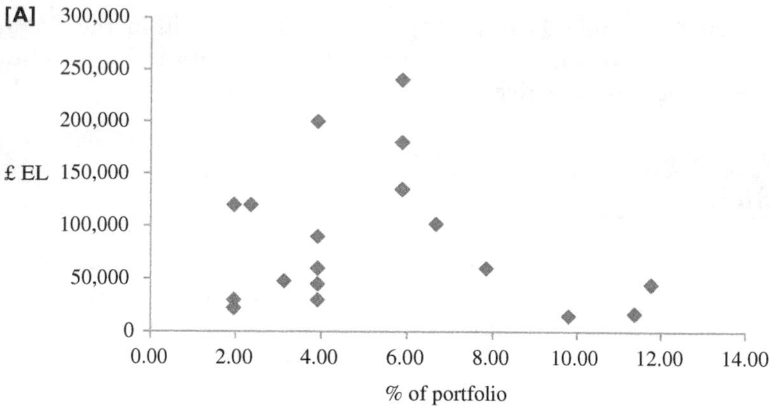

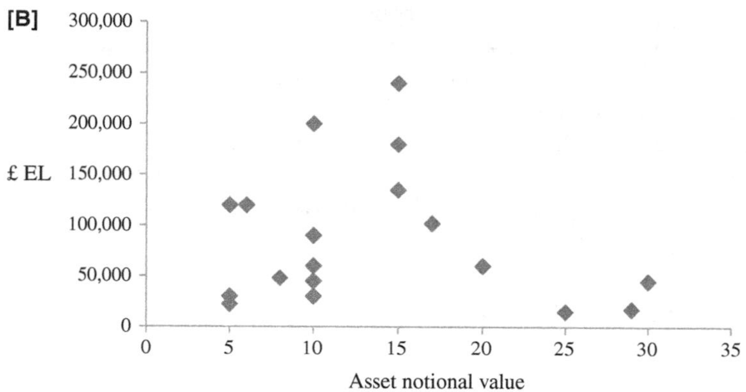

FIGURE 11.4A and B Portfolio risk report: asset exposure and £ EL.

each individual exposure's LGD against its share of the portfolio in total. In this hypothetical example, this report immediately highlights the high risk of assets that form a relatively large proportion of the portfolio.

Two variants of this report, again per individual asset, show EL and LV as a relative share of the portfolio, or we can illustrate these per actual size of each asset. Both versions are shown here, at Figure 11.4A and 11.4B for the EV parameter, and Figure 11.5A and 11.5B for the LV parameter. The reports are essentially identical; however, risk managers may wish to see the parameters relative to the portfolio or as absolute amounts.

These reports are used in limit setting, both at the portfolio level and at the individual obligor level. Setting an EL limit for each borrower, as well as by industrial sector, country, currency and so on, will force the credit manager to assess the real value-added and the risk-adjusted return. Is the return being generated by the asset, or the sub-set of a portfolio, worth the risk being generated? Viewing risk in terms of EL and LV, in addition to

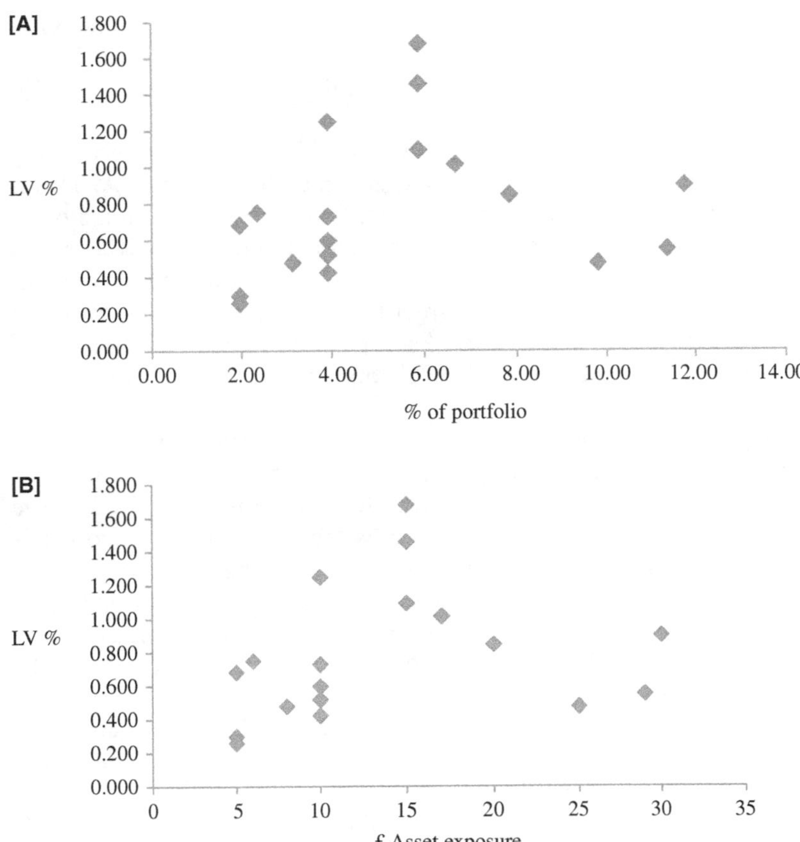

FIGURE 11.5A and B Portfolio risk report: asset exposure and £ LV.

default probabilities, is an additional discipline for the bank. If the credit quality of an asset or portfolio deteriorates, the business line managers must assess whether it is worth retaining from an SVA and RoC point of view. Adhering to EL and LV limits is therefore part of the bank's risk management process. Because LV is also used to calculate individual asset capital allocation, setting limits for LV also acts as a discipline on the use of scarce and expensive capital.

Portfolio Appraisal

In Table 11.6 we noted the RoA and RAROC values for the hypothetical sample portfolio. Both measures are used in appraising the value of the balance sheet assets; however, RoA has no "break-even" level to compare itself against, whereas the RoC or RAROC of both individual assets and the entire portfolio should always lie above the bank's CoC. The CoC is therefore the hurdle rate for all bank business, as we noted in Chapter 1.

The SVA measure takes into account both EL and CoC; all else being equal, a bank should originate assets that generate the highest SVA. This is a common refrain in textbooks on corporate finance. However, it is not an academic irrelevance, it deserves to be applied on a practical basis. For it to be applicable, business line management needs to be aware of the true cost of capital as well as the shareholder target RoC. It also needs to be aware of the full extent of all operating costs. Asset generation can then follow the SVA principle. That banks do not do this on a regular basis is a failing of senior management.

In the sample portfolio shown at Table 11.6, the absolute SVA is shown (three alternative measures are given). The average SVA is this number divided by the number of assets, so for the first value of £522,300 the average SVA is £26,115. However, the most appropriate metric to use is SVA per unit of aggregate portfolio exposure. Taking the first value of £522,300 again, the SVA/unit of exposure is (522,300/255,000,000) or 0.20%. With an established portfolio, any new asset should ideally also exceed this measure as a benchmark. An asset that produced a lower specific SVA than the portfolio average SVA is possibly under-priced. For an asset that doesn't meet the average SVA benchmark, it may be that the customer is a "loss leader" and will supply other business elsewhere, but in general it should be an exception to break this rule.

An SVA performance report at the detailed level is appropriate MI for business line management. The example for our sample portfolio is shown at Figure 11.6. This shows individual asset SVA, calculated against the portfolio SVA average value, and also shown against the average SVA/unit value. An asset exhibiting negative SVA would be a prime candidate for divestment or disposal.

Portfolio performance appraisal should also be undertaken by business lines, to enable senior management to assess which parts of the bank are the most efficient users of capital. For illustrative purposes we take the sample portfolio shown at Table 11.7 and assign them to two hypothetical business lines, which we call Corporate Banking (CB) and Treasury (Treas). This is shown at Table 11.8.

We show another format for a hypothetical bank with three business lines, namely Corporate Banking, Private Banking and Treasury, which operate across the three different geographical regions of UK, Middle East (MENA) and Asia. The revenue chart here is broken down by these regions, as shown at Figure 11.7.

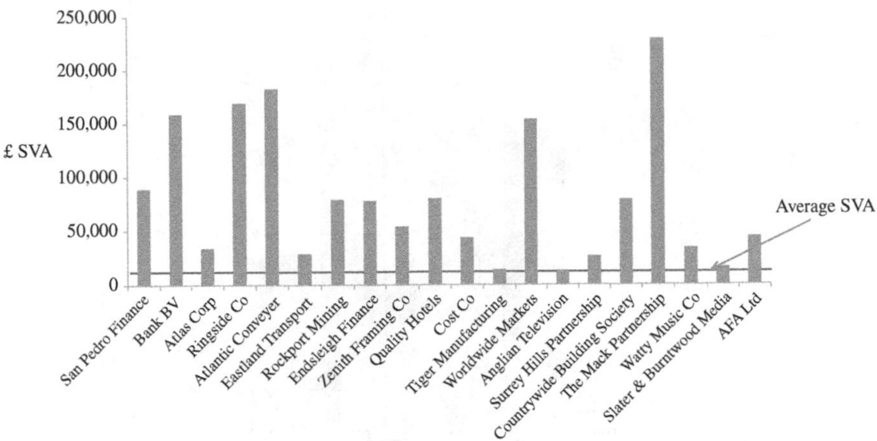

FIGURE 11.6 Sample portfolio: asset SVA and benchmark return.

TABLE 11.8 Sample portfolio assets by business line.

Obligor name	Industrial sector	Business line	£ Expected loss (EL)	SVA
San Pedro Finance	1	Treas	45,000	88,885
Bank BV	1	Treas	15,000	158,885
Atlas Corp	2	CB	30,000	33,885
Ringside Co	2	CB	102,000	169,385
Atlantic Conveyer	3	CB	17,400	182,685
Eastland Transport	3	CB	22,500	28,885
Rockport Mining	2	CB	240,000	78,885
Endsleigh Finance	1	Treas	48,000	77,885
Zenith Framing Co	2	CB	200,000	53,885
Quality Hotels	5	CB	60,000	79,885
CostCo	3	CB	30,000	43,385
Tiger Manufacturing	2	CB	60,000	13,885
Worldwide Markets	2	Treas	135,000	153,885
Anglian Television	4	CB	30,000	12,885
Surrey Hills Partnership	3	CB	22,500	26,385
Countrywide Building Society	1	Treas	45,000	78,885
The Mack Partnership	3	Treas	180,000	228,885
Watty Music Co	4	CB	120,000	33,885
Slater & Burntwood Media	4	CB	120,000	15,885
AFA Ltd	4	CB	90,000	43,885

Sector: 1 – Finance; 2 – Mining, Construction, Manufacturing; 3 – Transport and Utility; 4 – Media; 5 – Hotels.

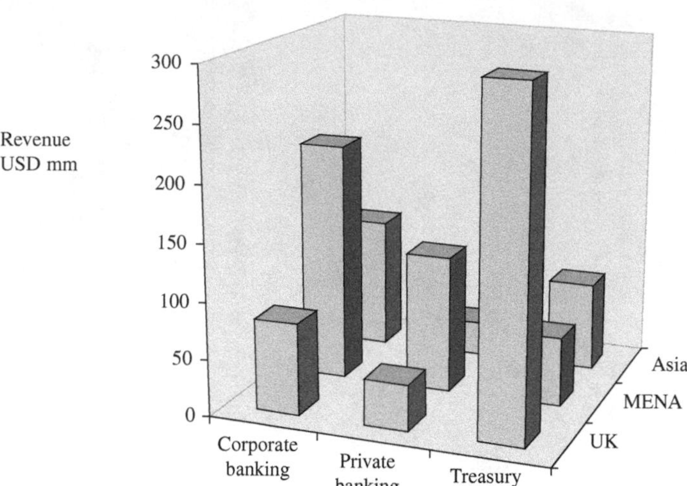

FIGURE 11.7 Sample portfolio revenue report by business line and geographical sector.

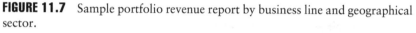

RISK POLICY

A bank must publish and circulate its high-level risk policy, to clarify its approach to risk appetite and risk management, to all staff. We discuss here a format for the banking book policy statement and the market risk policy statement.

Banking Book Policy Statement

We include a template for a standard banking book policy statement as part of the supplementary material on the Wiley website (see Chapter 19 for details). The template was drafted by the author, and is a straightforward document, suitable for a medium-sized commercial bank. It captures the essential policy guidelines of a banking book; additional sections may be added as appropriate for a bank that engages in more wide-ranging activities. However, in essence the principles behind the operation of a banking book will be identical for most, if not all, banks.

Extracting from the Policy included in this book, we note the following:

> *. . . The Bank considers trading to occur where dealers have the ability to take positions generating market risk under dealing authorities – all other transactions are considered to be non-trading. The purpose of the Banking Book Policy statement is to define how*

> *transactions are to be treated and recorded in the books of the bank and define the control and risk management framework within which the Treasury department will manage these books . . .*
>
> *The primary focus of Treasury is to manage the risks inherent in the Bank's core business, which primarily entails ensuring the bank maintains liquidity in accordance with the Liquidity Policy and manages market risk in accordance with the Market Risk Policy.*
>
> *The Banking Book relates to assets and liabilities resulting from non-trading activities. The Banking Book contains several portfolios. The assets and liabilities of each portfolio are accounted for as defined by International Financial Reporting Standards (IFRS).*
>
> *Treasury implements and develops the Bank's business activities as they relate to treasury activities. It creates and manages liquidity, market, interest rate and FX risks utilising both market opportunities and customer demands within limits defined by the ALCO. The Bank also provides treasury services and products for its customers, including transaction, payments, clearing and cash management services.*
>
> *Risks within the Banking Book can be broadly categorised as Market Risk, Liquidity Risk, Credit Risk, Operational Risk and Regulatory Risk.*
>
> *These risks are controlled through a set of limits that includes: BPV, Interest Rate Gap Limits, Trader/Desk Limits, Product Limits and Credit Risk Limit.*
>
> *Market risks are identified and reported to ALCO. The Head of Treasury can make recommendations to ALCO.*
>
> *Credit risk is managed and controlled by the Credit committee.*

The Banking Book policy statement should be maintained as a practical working document, referred to as and when necessary. It is important to assign ownership of the policy to a specific department (and individuals within this department), to ensure that it is updated regularly. In some banks this responsibility is lodged with Treasury, a procedure not without logic; however, most banks assign responsibility to a more "independent" department such as MO risk management or Product Control.

Market Risk Policy Statement

A template for a standard bank market risk policy statement is included on the Wiley website. This can be adapted to serve most banking institutions.

The point of this policy is to serve as a governance framework for market risk decisions and as a tool in training staff responsible for managing or controlling market risk. Senior management should emphasise that all procedures and policies, including the development of new products and services, must be consistent with what is stated in the policy. Therefore it should be maintained as a working document, one that sets the framework for the bank's risk culture.

Naturally, adherence to the policy should be made a directive of the Bank's Board, and thus would form an integral part of each employee's performance review where market risk (which includes interest rate risk, foreign exchange risk, and price risk) management and control is an element of that employee's position description.

Figure 11.8 is an extract from the policy, and lists the specific goals of the policy with regard to interest-rate risk management. Similar such

Market Risk Statement: Interest-rate Risk Policy

- Detail the size and stability of net interest margins and interest-sensitive fee income.
- Evaluate the component and aggregate levels of interest rate risk, including re-pricing, basis, yield curve, and option risk, relative to earnings and capital.
- Analyse the size, complexity and components of each type of interest rate risk position.
- Manage, monitor and control interest-rate risk over both the short and long term.
- Assess the character of risk, such as the volume and price sensitivity of various products.
- Determine the complexity of risk positions such as optionality of mortgage products and changing value of servicing portfolios.
- Ensure a process independent of the ALCO function that measures and analyses risk in all significant activities, including interest rate movements under a variety of scenarios.
- Examine vulnerability of earnings and capital positions under interest rate changes, such as parallel rate shifts and changes in the shape and slope of the yield curve. The rate scenarios should be compared within the context of the current rate environment.
- Assess the relative volume and future prospects of continued support from low-cost or stable funding sources, especially deposits that are non-maturing.
- Determine that satisfactory risk position changes are occurring to reflect changing market conditions.
- Ensure that appropriate levels of procedures, controls and self-monitoring techniques are implemented and properly administered.

FIGURE 11.8 Market risk policy statement: goals of interest-rate risk management.

statements for other types of market risk, such as foreign exchange risk, are also included in the policy. Figure 11.9 is an example of a product approval form, and market risk limits, that would be put in place for each branch and subsidiary of the bank.

Branch/Subsidiary:	Bank "C"
Treasurer:	AN Other

Permitted Products		
Product	**Trading/Investment**	**Fully Covered Sales**
FX Spot	☒	☐
FX Forward Outright	☒	☐
FX Swap	☒	☐
Non Deliverable Forward	☐	☒
FX Option	☐	☒
Inter-bank Deposit and Placement, Internal Deposit and Loan	☒	☐
Certificate of Deposit (CD)	☒	☐
Commercial Paper (CP)	☒	☐
Floating Rate Note (FRN)	☒	☐
Fixed Rate Bond	☒	☐
Repo and Reverse Repo, Buy-Sell-Back and Sell-Buy-Back	☒	☐
Security Borrowing and Lending	☒	☐
Interest Rate Future	☒	☐
Forward Rate Agreement (FRA)	☒	☐
Interest Rate Swap (IRS)	☒	☐
Cross-Currency Swap	☒	☐
Interest Rate Options	☐	☒
Equity	☐	☒
Structured FX Forward	☐	☒
Structured Interest Rate Product	☐	☒
Structured Equity Product	☐	☒

FIGURE 11.9 Approved market risk limits, template form (this also appears on the Wiley website).

Basis Point Value (BPV) Limits	
Total Absolute BPV Limit (USD equivalent):	130,000
Currency Sub Limits (maximum exposure per currency as a percentage of total BPV limit):	
USD	100%
GBP	30%
CHF	30%
JPY	10%
EUR	100%
Other Currencies (freely convertible)	10%

Time	Bucket #	Band #
1 Month	70%	100%
2 Month	70%	
3 Month	70%	
4 Month	70%	
5 Month	70%	
6 Month	70%	
7 Month	70%	
8 Month	70%	
9 Month	70%	
10 Month	70%	
11 Month	70%	
12 Month	70%	
15 Month	15%	15%
18 Month	15%	
21 Month	15%	
2 Year	15%	
3 Year	10%	10%
4 Year	10%	
5 Year	10%	
6 Year	10%	
7 Year	10%	
8 Year	10%	
9 Year	10%	
10 Year	10%	
15 Year	10%	
20 Year	10%	
> 20 Year	10%	

= Time bucket limits are the maximum BPV exposures per currency per time bucket. Time band limits are the maximum BPV exposures for that time band across all currencies.

FIGURE 11.9 *(continued)*

Interest Rate Stop Loss Limits (Thousand USD)		
Product	**Measure**	**USD Limit (Thousand)**
Combined Futures, FRA, IRS	Book Loss Per Day	0
	Book Loss Per Month	0
	Book Loss Per Year	0
Money Markets Warning Level	Book Warning Level Per Month	100
	Book Warning Level Per Year	300

Interest Rate Option Trading Limits (Thousand USD)	
Category	**Outstanding USD Premium Limit (Thousand)**
N/A	0

FX Trading Limits (Thousand USD)		
Category	**Daylight USD Limit (Thousand)**	**Overnight USD Limit (Thousand)**
Spot	20,000	2,000
Forward	20,000	32,000
Total	20,000	32,000

FX Option Trading Limits (Thousand USD)	
Category	**Outstanding USD Premium Limit (Thousand)**
N/A	0

FX Stop Loss Limits (Thousand USD)		
Product	**Measure**	**USD Limit (Thousand)**
FX	Book Loss Per Day	20
	Book Loss Per Month	50
	Book Loss Per Year	200

Liquidity Limits as a Percentage Ratio (Adjusted for Stickiness)	
1 Week	**1 Month**
0%	–5%

Funding through Deposits from Group HO Branches and Subsidiaries (Thousand USD)	
Funding Limit	1,000,000

FIGURE 11.9 *(continued)*

PRODUCT LINE RISK REPORTING

At the operating level a bank business line will report on specific exposures relevant to it. For instance, risk reporting will be per product or asset class. At this lower level, MI can be more detailed, and will of necessity be produced more frequently, typically on a daily (or intra-day) basis. The purpose of business line risk reporting is to enable department heads to be completely up-to-date on their risk exposure at all times, such that they are able to summarise the extent of the risk, for senior management, on request and at any time. Business line MI that does not assist line management in fulfilling this duty is not fit-for-purpose.

We illustrate with examples for FX and bond portfolio exposures, and examples of higher level summary MI reports.

FX Open Position Reporting

Table 11.9 shows an example of an open position FX limit report, produced as MI for the Head of Foreign Exchange at a commercial bank. It is a very simple report, and its contents are self-explanatory. Table 11.10 is the summary daily report for the Head of Treasury.

This template is available as part of the supplementary material accompanying this book, on the Wiley website.

Bond Portfolio Risk Reporting

The basic risk report can be in the form of a summary aggregate portfolio report presented monthly to the Head of Treasury (or Head of Fixed Income as appropriate). An example is shown at Table 11.11, and the template is also provided on the Wiley website. This report is straightforward to produce and may be updated quickly on an *ad hoc* basis if required, because the data fields are simply standing data.

This basic report can then be used to produce highlights of specific exposures as required. For example, the overall exposure by different country centre is shown at Figure 11.10, while the portfolio exposure by credit rating is shown at Figure 11.11.

Summary Management Risk Reports

Senior management risk reports are by necessity succinct. While it is important that the exact risk position of the bank is known at all times at board level, the nature of the job at that and executive director level is such that detailed reports are simply not reviewed to any sufficient extent. Therefore

TABLE 11.9 FX open position limit report.

LONDON
18-Jan-11

ALL FIGURES ARE EXPRESSED IN THOUSANDS ('000)
POSITIONS SHOULD BE INPUT IN THEIR ORIGINAL CURRENCY
LONG POSITIONS ARE EXPRESSED AS A POSITIVE NUMBER
SHORT POSITIONS ARE EXPRESSED AS A NEGATIVE NUMBER

WEEKLY FX OPEN POSITION REPORT

CURRENCY		O/N	TOM	SPOT	SUB TOTAL OF O/N, TOM AND SPOT	FORWARD	NET OPEN POSITION (SUB TOTAL + FORWARD POSITION)	USD EX RATE	NET OPEN POSITION USD EQUIVALENT	LONG	SHORT
		Settlement Day	1 Day Before Settlement	2 Days Before Settlement		> 2 Days Before Settlement					
USD	BASE CCY			–126,274	**–126,274**		–126,274	73.3722	–1,721	0	–1,721
USD				927	**927**		927	1.0000	927	927	0
EUR			150		**150**	120	270	0.7583	356	356	0
GBP		46		–35	**11**		11	0.6820	16	16	0
AUD					**0**		0	1.1980	0	0	0
CAD				566	**566**		566	1.2394	457	457	0
CHF					**0**		0	1.2072	0	0	0
CYP					**0**		0	1.0000	0	0	0
DKK					**0**		0	1.0000	0	0	0
HKD					**0**		0	7.8140	0	0	0
JPY				–209	**–209**		–209	99.7311	–2	0	–2
NOK					**0**		0	1.0000	0	0	0

(continued)

TABLE 11.9 *(continued)*

LONDON
18-Jan-11

ALL FIGURES ARE EXPRESSED IN THOUSANDS ('000)
POSITIONS SHOULD BE INPUT IN THEIR ORIGINAL CURRENCY
LONG POSITIONS ARE EXPRESSED AS A POSITIVE NUMBER
SHORT POSITIONS ARE EXPRESSED AS A NEGATIVE NUMBER

WEEKLY FX OPEN POSITION REPORT

CURRENCY	O/N	TOM	SPOT	SUB TOTAL OF O/N, TOM AND SPOT	FORWARD	NET OPEN POSITION (SUB TOTAL + FORWARD POSITION)	USD EX RATE	NET OPEN POSITION USD EQUIVALENT	LONG	SHORT
	Settlement Day	1 Day Before Settlement	2 Days Before Settlement		> 2 Days Before Settlement					
NZD				0		0	1.3437	0	0	0
SEK				0		0	1.0000	0	0	0
SGD				0		0	1.5111	0	0	0
ZAR				0		0	1.0000	0	0	0
AED				0		0	3.6718	0	0	0
BHD				0		0	0.3770	0	0	0
DZD				0		0	70.3128	0	0	0
EGP				0		0	5.6885	0	0	0
ILS				0		0	4.2300	0	0	0
INR				0		0	44.3000	0	0	0
JOD				0		0	0.7089	0	0	0
KRW				0		0	927.5000	0	0	0

KWD			**0**	0	0.2900	0	0	0
KZT			**0**	0	1.0000	0	0	0
LBP			**0**	0	1.0000	0	0	0
LYD			**0**	0	1.0000	0	0	0
MAD	5,623		**5,623**	5,623	8.2366	683	683	0
MYR		456	**456**	456	1.0000	456	456	0
OMR			**0**	0	0.3849	0	0	0
QAR			**0**	0	3.6395	0	0	0
SAR			**0**	0	3.7499	0	0	0
SDG			**0**	0	2.2950	0	0	0
SYP			**0**	0	1.0000	0	0	0
THB			**0**	0	1.0000	0	0	0
TND			**0**	0	1.4054	0	0	0
TRL			**0**	0	1.0000	0	0	0
YER			**0**	0	196.7500	0	0	0
XAG			**0**	0	1.0000	0	0	0
XAU			**0**	0	1.0000	0	0	0
XPT			**0**	0	1.0000	0	0	0
						0	**2,895**	**−1,723**
						Basel II	**2,895**	**2**

TABLE 11.10 Summary dashboard FX report (higher level MI)

LONDON
18-Jan-11

ALL FIGURES ARE EXPRESSED IN THOUSANDS ('000)
POSITIONS SHOULD BE INPUT IN THEIR ORIGINAL CURRENCY
LONG POSITIONS ARE EXPRESSED AS A POSITIVE NUMBER
SHORT POSITIONS ARE EXPRESSED AS A NEGATIVE NUMBER

FX Overnight Limit Control Panel – USD '000

AUTHORIZED SPOT/TOTAL LIMIT	3,500	OPEN POSITION	4,618
AUTHORIZED FORWARD LIMIT	1,167	EXCL. BASE CCY	2,897
FORWARD LIMIT CONSUMPTION	158	BASEL II OPEN POS.	2,895
		CAPITAL REQUIRED	232
FORWARD LIMIT BREACH	NO	LIMIT ALLOCATIONS	
SPOT LIMIT CONSUMPTION	2,738	SPOT	78.2%
SPOT LIMIT BREACH	NO	FORWARD	13.6%
		UNUSED	8.2%
REMAINING SPOT LIMIT	287		
REMAINING FORWARD LIMIT	96		

the shape of the MI presented at this level must be designed with care. The main guidelines for reporting are:

- ease of reading and assimilation;
- brevity;
- an attractive visual display.

The above may appear to be frivolous, but one of the lessons learned from the 2007–2009 financial crash is that senior management are in receipt of a large amount of electronic and hardcopy reporting, and human nature dictates that the shortest MI is read first and most diligently. This may appear to denigrate the professionalism and application of senior management, but rather the contrary: it recognises that the most important risk reports for a bank need to be the easiest to read.

Two examples of high-level MI for credit risk and market risk are included on the Wiley website, as PowerPoint files. The credit risk report is only four slides long, and the one for market risk a mere two slides. The front page of each report is shown as Figures 11.12 and 11.13, respectively.

BUSINESS LINE REPORTING

At the business line level the key to effective MI reporting is to provide a succinct summary of key ratios and indicators. We illustrate this with an example for a bank Treasury desk, which produces a monthly performance report for the bank's managing committee. The template is included as an Excel spreadsheet, supplied as part of the supplementary material on the Wiley website; we show some extracts from this report here. In this hypothetical institution, the Treasury department is comprised of the following desks:

- money markets and FX;
- liquidity book (bank bonds portfolio);
- Treasury sales;
- Treasury sales securities trading;
- financial engineering.

This is a conventional set-up for a small or medium-sized commercial bank.

Table 11.12 is the main front page and it is a conventional PnL report. The only concession to creative design is the traffic light-style

TABLE 11.11 Aggregate bond portfolio report.

GROUP SECURITIES MONTHLY AGGREGATION REPORT
Friday, 9 January 2009

Treasury Centre	Issuer Name	CUSIP/ISIN	Principal	Currency	Trade Date	Maturity Date	Payment Frequenc
Australia	Commonwealth Bank	AU0000CBAHJ1	5,074,050	AUD	10/08/2009	14/09/2009	Semi-Annu
Australia	Elders Rural Bank	AU3ECD551869	2,000,000	AUD	03/07/2009	22/12/2009	At Maturity
Australia	ABN AMRO Bank NV Australian Branch	AU3FN0008611	5,000,000	AUD	06/07/2009	06/10/2009	Quarterly
Australia	HBOS	AU3FN0004859	500,000	AUD	16/07/2009	11/02/2010	Monthly
Australia	HBOS	AU0000HBOHE2	2,000,000	AUD	28/07/2009	18/03/2010	Quarterly
London	BANQUE CENT DE TUNISIE	XS0190092204	2,000,000	EUR	15/11/2006	07/04/2011	Annual
London	ROYAL BANK OF CANADA	XS0278908222	6,700,000	GBP	06/08/2009	14/12/2011	Quarterly
London	ABBEY NATL TREASURY SERV	XS0308098317	10,000,000	GBP	22/06/2007	29/06/2010	Quarterly
London	ULSTER BANK IRELAND LTD	XS0301146634	4,000,000	EUR	11/05/2007	18/05/2010	Quarterly
London	UNICREDIT SPA	XS0308784692	10,000,000	EUR	26/06/2007	05/07/2010	Quarterly
London	BANCO ESPIRITO SANTO SA	PTBERNOM0015	10,000,000	EUR	29/10/2008	31/05/2010	Quarterly
London	DEXIA CREDIT LOCAL	XS0417874814	75,000,000	EUR	13/03/2009	23/03/2011	Annual
London	EUROPEAN COMMUNITY	EU000A1AKD47	7,500,000	EUR	17/07/2009	27/01/2015	Annual
London	KINGDOM OF SWEDEN	XS0426626312	5,000,000	EUR	29/04/2009	07/05/2014	Annual
London	NORDEA BANK AB	XS0443210090	18,000,000	EUR	29/07/2009	06/08/2012	Annual
London	SWEDBANK AB	XS0419081491	15,000,000	EUR	18/03/2009	24/03/2011	Annual
Singapore	Hongkong Land	SG7E21926922	10,000,000	SGD	09/03/2007	03/10/2010	Semi-Annua
Singapore	Hutchinson Whamp Int	XS012488068	5,000,000	USD	30/10/2006	16/02/2011	Semi-Annua
Singapore	Joynote Ltd	SG7J74932335	15,000,000	SGD	23/05/2007	26/10/2011	Semi-Annua
Singapore	Korea East West Power	XS019094987	5,000,000	USD	24/05/2006	21/04/2011	Semi-Annua
Singapore	Korea Gas Corp	XS018144484	5,000,000	USD	30/03/2006	26/11/2010	Semi-Annua
UAE	National Bank Of Dubai	XS0237182513	10,000,000	USD	06/12/2005	06/12/2010	Quarterly
UAE	National Bank Of Abu Dhabi	XS0238236243	25,000,000	USD	14/12/2005	14/12/2010	Quarterly
UAE	Abu Dhabi Commercial Bank	XS0222850686	10,000,000	USD	28/06/2005	28/06/2010	Quarterly
USA	AMERICAN EXPRESS	0258M0BX6	6,000,000	USD	2006/03/07	2010/12/02	Monthly
USA	CITIGROUP INC	172967CV1	5,000,000	USD	2007/07/17	2012/03/16	Quarterly
USA	GENERAL ELECTRIC	36962GZ49	5,000,000	USD	2008/03/03	2012/11/01	Quarterly
USA	JP MORGAN CHASE	073902PQ5	10,000,000	USD	2007/01/26	2009/09/11	Quarterly

Fixed/ Floating	Rate (Fixed or Spread)	Purchase Price	Market Price	Rating	Central Bank Eligible	Nominal Value USD	Market Value USD	Issue size
Fixed	0.0368	101.481	101.191	A-1+	Yes	4,149,995	4,138,153	
Fixed	0.0423			A-2	No	1,611,900	1,611,900	
Floating	0.0357			A-1+	Yes	4,029,750	4,029,750	675,000,000
Fixed	0.036833	100.000		A-1	Yes	402,975	402,975	1,000,000,000
Floating	0.0379	100.000		A-1+	Yes	1,611,900	1,611,900	400,000,000
Fixed	0	100.000	101.750	BBB	No	2,806,500	2,855,614	450,000,000
Floating	6	99.160	99.250	AAA	Yes	10,939,881	10,949,811	
Floating	2	99.409	99.700	AA–	Yes	16,369,183	16,417,100	350,000,000
Floating	3	99.265	98.260	A	Yes	5,571,744	5,515,333	1,500,000,000
Floating	5	99.424	99.760	AA–	Yes	13,951,672	13,998,821	1,000,000,000
Floating	7	97.110	99.560	AA–	Yes	13,626,960	13,970,756	500,000,000
Fixed	0	99.950	101.695	AA+	Yes	105,191,122	107,027,625	3,500,000,000
Fixed	0	100.000	101.280	AAA	Yes	10,524,374	10,659,086	
Fixed	0	100.000	102.209	AAA	Yes	7,016,250	7,171,239	4,000,000,000
Fixed	0	99.732	100.850	AA–	Yes	25,190,806	25,473,196	
Fixed	0	100.020	101.276	AAA	Yes	21,052,958	21,317,331	1,400,000,000
Fixed	Fixed	100.000	100.400	A–	No	6,907,986	6,935,618	325,000,000
Fixed	Fixed	100.000	106.503	A–	No	5,000,000	5,325,150	-
Fixed	Fixed	100.000	101.378	A–	No	10,361,978	10,504,767	200,000,000
Fixed	Fixed	100.000	102.734	A+	No	5,000,000	5,136,700	-
Fixed	Fixed	100.000	102.160	A	No	5,000,000	5,108,000	-
Floating	Floating	99.821	96.673	AA–	Yes	9,982,100	9,667,270	750,000,000
Floating	Floating	99.910	99.108	AA–	Yes	24,977,500	24,777,050	850,000,000
Floating	Floating	99.816	98.223	A	Yes	9,981,600	9,822,330	1,000,000,000
Floating	0.18	100.244	98.060	BBB+	No	6,014,652	5,883,600	500,000,000
Floating	0.125	100.061	92.800	A	No	5,003,050	4,640,000	1,750,000,000
Floating	0.13	96.760	92.520	AA+	No	4,838,000	4,626,000	2,575,000,000
Floating	0.19	100.077	99.177	A+	No	10,007,700	9,917,700	1,000,000,000

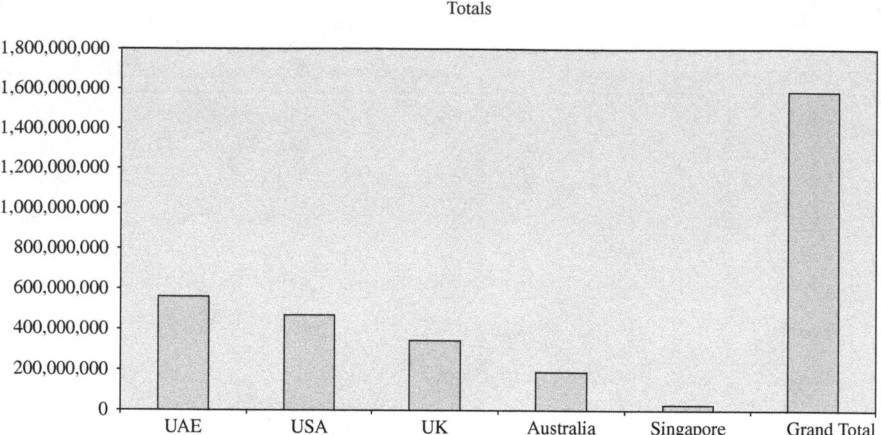

FIGURE 11.10 Bond portfolio report: country issuer mapping.

performance trend arrows placed alongside each desk. A separate trend report is also included in the monthly pack, shown here as Table 11.13. The full template has detailed breakdowns for each desk, which feed into the summary reports shown at Tables 11.12 and 11.13.

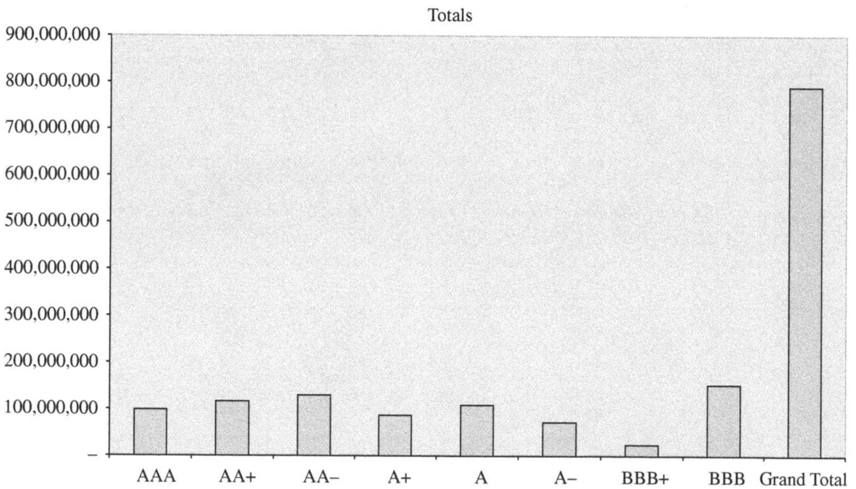

FIGURE 11.11 Bond portfolio report: exposure by credit rating.

CREDIT RISK – EXECUTIVE SUMMARY 30 NOVEMBER 2010

Executive Summary

Stats | Outlook

Problem accounts represent 22% of Corporate Exposure – slightly above last month, though some of the problem accounts have moved down a notch on the bank's internal rating scale – see tables below on this page.

The average rating on the book is 4.88 (mapping to BB- on the S&P scale) which is on the higher end of the bank's 4-5 scale but within the overall risk appetite measure for the bank approved by the Board. New limits approved are rated no less than ABC 5 (with one exception) which is within Risk Appetite but generally still at the lower end of the rating scale – higher rated credits will need to be taken on if the average is going to start improving, though the average rating for the 10 largest corporate exposures is 3.70

More detail is given this month on the larger exposures, following the policy decision by the Board to limit these to 12.5% of capital (EUR75m), both for Treasury, Corporate and Retail Banking. There are a number of limits and exposures exceeding this threshold.

The country limits have been approved at Group level and considered by Executive Credit Committee . A number of reductions have been made and these will be shown in next month's report. The industry limits are with Credit Committee to review following draft recommendations from Fisk Management.

The Quarterly Stress tests are shown for the period ending September 2010 as these are run quarterly. They indicate that the amount potentially at risk for accounts on the internal rating scale 1-6 is EUR22mm whereas, based on actual default rates compiled by Moody's , actual defaults are expected to be approximately EUR14mm. It is unlikely that these will have varied compared to last month.

Following the news about defaults in the GCC region, the corporate exposure to the UAE amounted to EUR238mm (6.9% of Total Corporate Exposure) and the banking exposure another EUR67mm (9.6% of Total Fls/Treasury Exposure) at the end of October 2010.

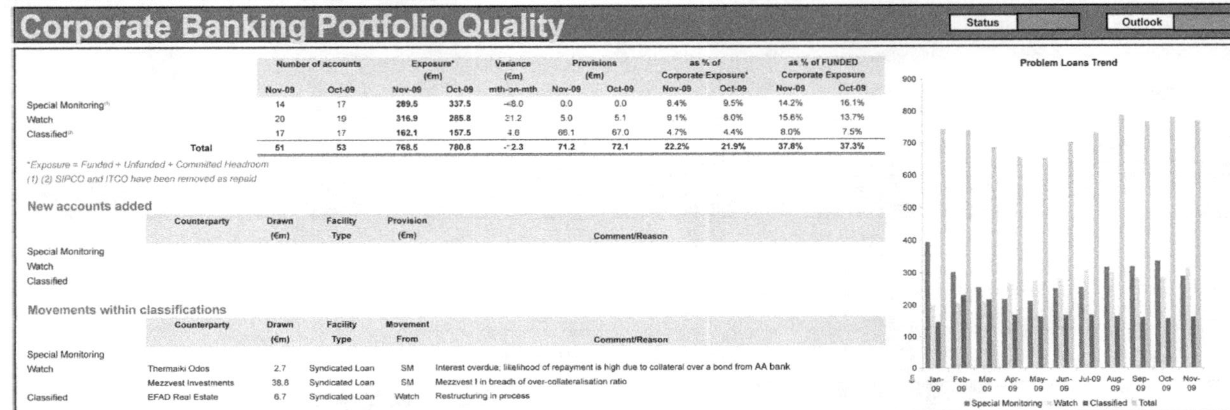

Corporate Banking Portfolio Quality

Status | Outlook

	Number of accounts		Exposure* (€m)		Variance (€m)	Provisions (€m)		as % of Corporate Exposure*		as % of FUNDED Corporate Exposure	
	Nov-09	Oct-09	Nov-09	Oct-09	mth-on-mth	Nov-09	Oct-09	Nov-09	Oct-09	Nov-09	Oct-09
Special Monitoring(1)	14	17	289.5	337.5	-48.0	0.0	0.0	8.4%	9.5%	14.2%	16.1%
Watch	20	19	316.9	285.8	31.2	5.0	5.1	9.1%	8.0%	15.6%	13.7%
Classified(2)	17	17	162.1	157.5	4.6	66.1	67.0	4.7%	4.4%	8.0%	7.5%
Total	51	53	768.5	780.8	-12.3	71.2	72.1	22.2%	21.9%	37.8%	37.3%

*Exposure = Funded + Unfunded + Commited Headroom

(1) (2) SIPCO and ITCO have been removed as repaid

New accounts added

	Counterparty	Drawn (€m)	Facility Type	Provision (€m)	Comment/Reason
Special Monitoring					
Watch					
Classified					

Movements within classifications

	Counterparty	Drawn (€m)	Facility Type	Movement From	Comment/Reason
Special Monitoring					
Watch	Thermaiki Odos	2.7	Syndicated Loan	SM	Interest overdue; likelihood of repayment is high due to collateral over a bond from AA bank
	Mezzvest Investments	38.8	Syndicated Loan	SM	Mezzvest I in breach of over-collateralisation ratio
Classified	EFAD Real Estate	6.7	Syndicated Loan	Watch	Restructuring in process

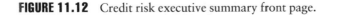

FIGURE 11.12 Credit risk executive summary front page.

MARKET RISK – EXECUTIVE SUMMARY 31 OCTOBER 2010

Report Summary

Status | Outlook

Market Risk

EUR	Oct-09	Sep-09	Limit
PV01 (max month)	-29,944	-35,324	
Stress Test (max month)	-6,093,777	-5,990,840	
BPV	56,304	56,460	101,667
Capital Markets Portfolio Value	900,803,536	878,031,355	
iTraxx Europe Crossover Index	518	570	
VaR (max month)	-834,854	-567,167	
FX Overnight Position	21,037,320	7,670,389	24,400,163

- *Interest rate risk and FX exposure remain within limits.*
- *Bond portfolio increased due to a new purchase of a €37.5mn holding in the Treasury AFS portfolio.*
- *FX open position increased due to renewal of GBP hedge of the GBP cost base*
- *The PV01 figure decreased in October due to the resetting of the IRS on the ALCO portfolio along with the rolling over of 3-month Sub debt capital (USD) on the money market book.*

Interest Rate Risk and Stress Tests

Status | Outlook

BPV and PV01 figures are well within limits due to Treasury confining their operations and limiting asset maturities. PV01 figure decreased due to the resetting of the IRS on the ALCO portfolio and the rolling over of 3-month Sub debt capital (USD) on the money market book.

Stress tests

- These stress tests show the effect on the total present value of operating assets and liabilities of the bank as reflected by funding trades in the Treasury Strategic Business Unit. The analysis shows the maximum stressed loss in the day, month and the year.
- The stress tests calculate the effect on present value of scenarios where FX rates and interest rates are flexed according to

	PV01 Analysis				Stress Tests	
(EUR)	PV01 (max mth)	PV01 (av mth)	PV01 (max yr)	PV01 (av yr)	Max stress value (mth)	Max stress value (yr)
Money Markets	-10,588	-1,215	-10,676	**3,579**	-2,090,742	-16,498,337
Capital Markets - Trading	-81	-44	-595	-110	-17,642	-112,264
Capital Markets - HTM	-5,583	-3,135	-7,036	-5,372	-1,152,729	-4,903,584
Financial Engineering	-83	-48	-8,863	-92	-220,488	-1,716,692
Foreign Exchange	-4	-1	-20	2	-752,520	-5,768,884
Treasury Sales	-4,827	-2,064	-6,509	-1,033	-1,494,989	-4,812,455
Treasury TOTAL	-21,165	-6,508	-33,698	-3,026		
ALCO	-8,779	-4,988	-45,213	-26,751	-4,311,761	-8,969,865
Overall	-29,944	-11,496	-78,911	-29,777	-6,093,777	-26,796,043

The maximum value overall resulted on 1st October from the following scenario: "Standard 200bp increase in interest rates in steps of 50bp".

Please note that the individual stress amounts will not add up to the total due to offsets.

PV01 & BPV

- PV01 = the change in the total present value generated by a 1 basis point upward parallel shift across all points on all yield curves
- BPV = the value of 1 basis point of all assets and liabilities in a time bucket over their average remaining lives and then aggregation of the absolute values of these across all time buckets.

	30 October 2009				30 September 2009			
	EUR		USD		EUR		USD	
	Value	Limit	Value	Limit	Value	Limit	Value	Limit
PV01	**13,910**				**29,763**			
BPV	**56,304**	**101,667**	83,071	150,000	**56,460**	**102,582**	82,559	150,000
FX Effect	-506	-914						

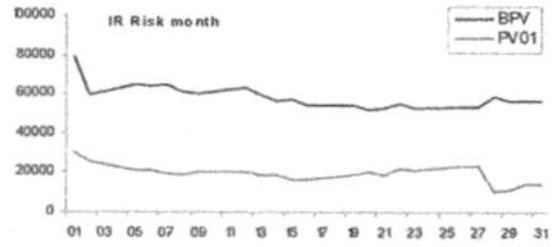

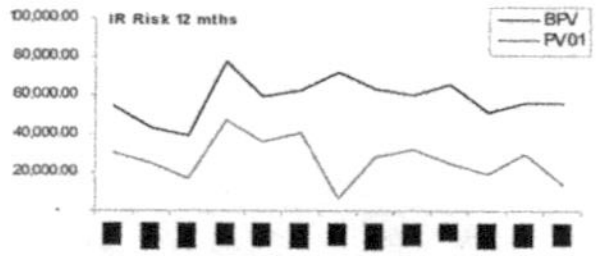

The restrictions on asset maturities remain. Treasury can invest €250mm up to 3mths, and €150mm up to 6mths. The above limits only apply to EUR. Asset maturities in all other currencies are limited to one week.
The PV01 figure decreased in October due to the resetting of the IRS on the ALCO portfolio and due to the rolling over of 3 month Sub debt capital (USD) on the money market book.

FIGURE 11.13 Market risk executive summary front page.

TABLE 11.12 Treasury monthly performance report summary.

	Actual August 2009	Budget variance August 2009	% MTD budget	Actual YTD August 2009	Budget variance YTD August 2009	% YTD budget	Full year forecast August 2009	Trend (movement month-on-month)
Money Markets	44	297	*17*	1,291	−738	*64*	933	↗
Liquidity Book	583	36	*107*	6,039	1,664	*138*	8,755	↗
Foreign Exchange	77	27	*155*	563	163	*141*	855	↗
Treasury Sales Securities	474	430	*101*	2,416	1,996	*575*	3,692	↘
Treasury Sales	7	2	*140*	−15	0	*100*	0	↘
Financial Engineering	77	9		159	77		188	
Total Revenue	1,262	205	*125*	10,453	3,161	*140*	14,423	
Direct Costs	−301	−4	*101*	−2,148	235	*90*	−3,345	↗
Treasury Business Unit Contribution	961	116	*119*	8,305	3,396	*164*	11,078	↗
Indirect Costs	−432	13	*97*	−3,827	−263	*107*	−5,668	↘
Net Contribution	529	129	*182*	4,477	3,133	*299*	5,410	
Exceptionals	−519	−519		−617	−617		0	↗
Total Profit after Exceptionals	10	−390	*(147)*	3,859	2,516	*258*	5,409	↗
Capital Usage (Basel II in EUR mn)	70	−3	*96*					

TABLE 11.13 Treasury performance trend report.

All figures in €'000

	Actual results by month										
	Dec 2008	Jan 2009	Feb 2009	Mar 2009	Apr 2009	May 2009	Jun 2009	Jul 2009	Aug 2009		Full year
	Year	Month	Month	Month	Month	Month	Month	Month	Month	YTD	forecast
Money Markets	5,061	711	400	446	231	91	(112)	(433)	44	1,291	933
Liquidity Book	5,417	1,215	884	837	715	683	547	575	583	6,039	8,755
Foreign Exchange	705	113	50	45	56	105	63	54	77	563	855
Financial Engineering	2,077						7	9	77	159	188
Treasury Sales Securities				174	369	675	175	549	474	2,416	3,692
Treasury Sales	33	0	0	0	63	(96)	11	0	7	(15)	
Total Revenue	**13,294**	**2,038**	**1,334**	**1,503**	**1,434**	**1,458**	**691**	**755**	**1,262**	**10,453**	**14,423**
Staff Costs	(2,383)	(165)	(172)	(175)	(175)	(158)	(179)	(174)	(184)	(1,378)	(2,014)
Occupancy Costs	(263)	(17)	(14)	(14)	(14)	(16)	(15)	(16)	(15)	(122)	(205)
Controllable Costs	(1,123)	(95)	(78)	(64)	(64)	(21)	(146)	28	(61)	(509)	(866)
Depreciation	(67)	(5)	(5)	(5)	(5)	(5)	(6)	(66)	(42)	(140)	(260)
Direct Costs	(3,837)	(283)	(270)	(259)	(259)	(200)	(345)	(229)	(301)	(2,148)	(3,345)
Business Unit Contribution	9,457	1,756	1,064	1,175	1,175	1,303	347	526	961	8,305	11,078
Indirect Expenses	(6,434)	(436)	(441)	(513)	(513)	(497)	(489)	(542)	(432)	(3,827)	(5,668)
Net Contribution	3,023	1,320	623	662	662	806	(142)	(16)	529	4,477	5,410
Other	0	0	0	0	0	0	0	0	0	0	0
Profit before Exceptionals	3,023	1,320	623	662	662	806	(142)	(16)	529	4,477	5,410
Exceptionals	0	0	0	0	0	0	(4)	(6)	(519)	(617)	0
Profit after Exceptionals	3,023	1,320	623	662	662	806	(146)	(22)	10	3,860	5,409
Capital usage (EURm)	70.4	74.4	73.5	81.6	81.6	72.7	74.3	93.8	70.3	70.3	70.3

STRESS TESTING POLICY

Stress testing is now a significant aspect of the bank risk management process, with considerable time and effort taken by risk management departments subjecting the balance sheet to "scenario analysis". The UK FSA has made stress testing a required part of its post-crash liquidity regime, although banks that had implemented the value-at-risk methodology in the 1990s would already have employed it in their risk management procedures.[3]

The logic behind the use of stress testing in banks is sound, but senior management must be careful not to rely overmuch on it. The one thing that is known with certainty is that the next financial crisis or market correction will be different in shape and form to any of the previous ones, so by definition it is not possible to plan for it completely and accurately in advance. Precisely because of this, in order to be prepared to cope with unexpected and exceptional events it is necessary to conduct stress testing to determine the potential impact on the bank. Paradoxically, stress testing or "what if" analysis is undertaken to mitigate the impact of unpredictable events, yet in itself will never be sufficient to prevent damage to a bank if the results are not assessed intelligently.

In essence, scenario analysis involves measuring the impact on the balance sheet of a sudden change in market parameters. Often the scenario being tested involves an extreme change in market conditions; while the probability of the various parameters taking extreme values may be remote, the testing serves to educate senior management of the consequence of a severe market correction or general economic slowdown. For the purposes of bank stress testing, the impact on the balance sheet is measured by seeing the change in asset values, liability values and default performance. The unit of measurement is usually some sort of "sensitivity" indicator, such as the amount of change in value, for a given change in the market parameter. For example, the sensitivity of a banking book to a change in interest rates may be given as the change in net interest margin for a (say) 200 bp upward parallel shift in interest rates. This type of test helps bank management to position its book in anticipation of rate changes; for instance, a book may be more "liability sensitive" than "asset sensitive", such that a rise in interest rates results in a significant loss of income. Management may then decide to alter the makeup of the book, or perhaps shift to more floating-rate assets, if they expect market rates to rise.

3 See the 1999 edition of the author's book *Introduction to Value-at-Risk* (Securities Institute Publishing), for a description of the type of risk stress testing employed during the implementation of VaR.

Stress testing therefore is an important part of bank ALM. The underlying parameters that drive valuations, such as interest rates, foreign exchange rates, equity prices and so on, are examined for the impact a change in them has on the balance sheet. For the ALM desk the key ratio that is tested for its sensitivity to market changes is the funding gap.

For it to be a value-added process, stress testing must feed through to the general risk management process. Otherwise, it becomes as worthless as a "procedures manual" compiled several years previously at great expense and effort, and immediately consigned to a filing cabinet on completion, never to be accessed or referred to. The results of stress testing need to be considered continuously by senior management, and changes made to strategy and, if possible, the balance sheet if the results suggest an unacceptable vulnerability to changes in certain market parameters. Changes to the shape and size of a balance sheet are difficult to enforce and take time to do so, which is why frequent reviews of stress test results are necessary. Once a decision has been taken to, for instance, withdraw from a business sector or reduce exposure to it, the stress testing needs to continue to see if the sensitivity of the balance sheet has been reduced. If not, further action may need to be taken.

Uncertainty about the nature of future market conditions is what drives scenario planning and "what if?" analysis. Given this uncertainty, a bank will wish to ensure that its risk exposures are manageable under unforeseen extreme conditions. The risk management department will oversee this process through the two main approaches of limit-setting and reducing sensitivities. The first approach refers to the practice of setting limits for individual borrowers, sectors and countries, as well as for market risk exposure. The second approach involves the use of derivatives (and other techniques such as securitisation) to reduce or remove the exposure.

The introduction of the VaR methodology for measuring risk exposure also resulted in the formalisation of the stress testing process, as well as something known as "back testing". Risk management departments usually run two VaR calculations, the daily 1-day or 1-week VaR exposure, and the extreme VaR number for capital adequacy estimation. The second number needs to incorporate an element of extreme scenario analysis to ensure that it is sufficiently high to protect the bank in a severe crash situation. For instance, the 1-day VaR may use a low confidence interval such as 90% or 95%, while the capital adequacy VaR calculation may run on a 99% confidence interval. Back testing is the process by which the VaR number calculated previously is checked against the actual losses suffered in the period subsequent to the calculation. Stress testing of the VaR number involves running a change in the various market parameters (such as interest rates, default rates and so on), singly and then together, and then seeing what the new VaR number is. If this is higher than the capital base of the bank, then the bank is potentially at risk in a correction situation. The stress testing needs to incorporate extreme scenarios otherwise it may not be sufficient a test.

Stress and Scenario Analysis Policy Document

A bank should formalise its stress testing and scenario analysis policy. A template suitable for application at a medium-sized commercial bank is supplied on the Wiley website. The policy sets out the framework within which stress testing and scenario analysis is conducted. It formalises the function and the responsibilities, as well as the reporting line for escalation of results.

An extract from the policy is shown at Figure 11.14. This describes the objectives of the stress testing process.

Stress Testing Objectives

The objectives of conducting for stress testing and scenario analysis (STSA) in the bank are to use the results of these tests:

- to analyse (and provide input into the setting of) the bank's risk appetite;
- to provide input into the business planning cycle;
- to allow management to plan for mitigating actions to be undertaken in stressed conditions;
- to assist in the capital planning process and to aid in capital contingency planning;
- to assist in understanding how the bank's liquidity profile could change under severe conditions and to allow liquidity contingency planning;
- to help in fulfilling regulatory requirements and expectations regarding the role of stress testing in the organisation; and
- to form part of a regular ongoing process of risk analysis and monitoring.

The following definitions of stress testing terms are used:

Stresses: these are the specific, quantified changes to risk factors required to generate the scenario. For example, the specific increase in percentage terms required to mimic the interest rate changes seen in the above scenario – 20% increase to all yield curve points longer than two weeks in EUR, GBP and USD.

Scenarios: A number of risk parameters (stresses) being varied at the same time. Scenario analyses often examine the impact of catastrophic events on the firm's financial position; for example, simultaneous movements in a number of risk categories affecting all of a firm's business operations such as business volumes, investment values and interest rate movements. These are overall descriptions of the test and are set out in plain language. For example, a scenario could be described as "the 1987 'Black Monday' scenario where equity prices fell and interest rates rose".

FIGURE 11.14 Bank stress testing objectives.

The purpose of stress and scenario testing in a bank is to:

- assist the bank in determining its risk appetite policy and provide information and results that allow the risks undertaken to be measured against this risk appetite throughout the economic cycle;
- inform the bank's business planning activities;
- demonstrate that the bank is able to survive a spectrum of severe recession scenarios (from 1 in 25 years to 1 in 100 years), while maintaining the minimum required capital adequacy ratio;
- provide additional understanding of the bank's vulnerabilities to senior management and ALCO;
- allow the bank to plan for capital adequacy both in the short term and over the economic cycle, including the development of contingency plans to be invoked in times of crisis;
- ensure that the bank can meet its liabilities as they fall due, even in severely disturbed market conditions, which should include contingency planning for stressed liquidity conditions;
- allow the bank's management to plan for mitigating actions to be undertaken in stressed conditions.

The factors that should be tested are those of material quantifiable risk and include, but are not limited to, the following:

- interest rates (market risk);
- foreign exchange rates (market risk);
- security prices (market risk and liquidity risk);
- PD (credit risk);
- LGD (credit risk);
- concentration risk (credit risk);
- funding risk (liquidity risk);
- operational loss frequency and severity (operational risk).

The results of the stress tests on the above factors will also impact the following risks:

- *Capital planning and management risk*: the risk arising from inadequacies in assessing the overall risks to which the bank may be exposed on a stressed basis, leading potentially to a failure to plan, maintain and raise capital as appropriate – particularly related to solvency and pro-cyclicality. This includes the risk of insufficient and/or inadequate regulatory capital to support the bank's risk-taking activities and its ability to fund assets at an acceptable rate.

- *Strategic risk*: the risks that affect the bank's environment/industry segment and not the bank alone. These consist of factors such as macroeconomic changes, country/industry fundamentals and competitive conditions. Such factors could impact on credit risk, market risk, interest rate risk, liquidity risk, operational risk, strategic risk and reputation risk, among others, which in turn could adversely affect earnings and capital.

The actual methodology is straightforward: assets and liabilities in the balance sheet are revalued under the market rates prevailing in the assumed stressed conditions. This is summarised in Figure 11.15.

Market Risk

Market risk is stressed across the three categories of interest rate risk, foreign exchange risk and credit spread risk.

Interest Rates

The movements in interest rates are input into a bank's trading system and then the present values of the various portfolios are calculated using the stressed rates in the calculations. The difference between these values and the unstressed values represents the profit or loss resulting from the stress.

Business best practice dictates that all interest rate risk is concentrated centrally in Treasury via funding trades; that is, all positions in other business lines should be match funded by Treasury or otherwise hedged via internal swaps. Thus all interest rate risk is represented via Treasury in the bank's trading system.

FX Rates

The movements in FX rates are input into the Treasury trading system and then the present values of the various portfolios are calculated using stressed rates in the calculations. The difference between these values in base currency and the unstressed base currency values represents the profit or loss resulting from the stress.

All FX rate risk is concentrated in Treasury via internal trades; that is, all positions in other business lines would be transferred to Treasury by internal FX trades. Thus all FX risk is represented via Treasury in the bank trading system.

Credit Spreads

The movements in credit spreads are input into the trading system and then the present values of the various bond portfolios are calculated by applying the stressed spreads only to the discount curve in the calculations. The difference

FIGURE 11.15 Sample stress testing methods of calculation.

(*continued*)

between these values and the unstressed values represents the profit or loss resulting from the stress.

Business best practice dictates that all bond portfolios are held by Treasury and/or Fixed Income business units. No other business lines should manage bond portfolios.

Credit Risk

We assume a standard bank internal credit rating system. Rating grades (usually numbered from 1 through to 6) are derived through the Moody's Risk Analyzer internal rating system. This considers quantitative and qualitative factors from financial accounts and the analyst's expert opinion and produces a number between zero and ten to two decimal points. This score is then validated against Moody's methodology, using historical company data items evaluating cause and likelihood of default against any given factor. The score is then mapped to a grade and default probability band.

Internal Ratings/Default Probabilities

Stressing internal ratings and default probabilities involves increasing the likelihood of any given client and portfolio defaulting by increasing its rating grade. The bank's grades cover wide default probability bands and each one effectively maps to three agency grades (so, for example, grade 5 maps to Moody's Ba1, Ba2 and Ba3 or S&P BB+, BB and BB–). Furthermore, grades relate to each other exponentially in terms of default probability (so a shift from the bank's 2 to 3 would have a far less severe impact on a client's default probability than a shift from 5 to 6; the same is true of agency ratings). In order to improve sensitivity and closer reflect agency grades, stress impact has been achieved by shifting a third of a grade at a time delivering a third of the default probability impact.

The stress shock used in the scenario is arrived at by shifting the various portfolios by two-thirds of a grade, observing the increase in default probability as a result and deriving a gross expected loss at default figure (that is, excluding any collateral held).

Recovery rates

Four recovery rate levels have been included in the analysis, dependent on assumed collateral and recovery levels, of 0%, 20%, 40% and 60%, demonstrating a range of scenarios.

The recovery rate considered most likely to materialise in relation to the stress period is 40%, reflecting subjective estimate of a probable recovery rate, based on Basel II guidelines for banks adopting the standardised approach. This could be confirmed when the current portfolio has fully matured and all default losses and recoveries have been analysed.

FIGURE 11.15 *(continued)*

The results of the stress shocks are calculated for the components of the balance sheet in terms of:

- P&L: This is reduced to a change in present value as a measure of the change in future cash flow streams, and has been restricted to interest streams for portions of the balance sheet that produce net interest income (NII) and change in market price for those portions of the balance sheet that represent trading portfolios.
- Capital: This would include P&L described above and changes in market price for those portions of the balance sheet that represent "available for sale" portfolios.
- Liquidity: This would include changes to cash flow values and maturities driven by the effects of stress on P&L, and capital as well as by the change in value of "held-to-maturity" portfolios.

The format of the results of the stress tests is shown in the following section.

The results of tests should be maintained by the CRO's office in the form of a stress test log. An example of the format of such a log is given at Table 11.14. The format for stress test results in banks is usually in the form of a table showing the change in present value (PV) of assets on the balance sheet in each different scenario. An example of such an output report is shown at Table 11.15.

A template for a detailed market risk stress testing policy manual is included as part of the supplementary material to this book, available on the Wiley website.

SAMPLE STRESS TEST RESULTS

For illustrative purposes we show a sample of stress test reports that would be produced by a bank MO for its Treasury department. Table 11.16 is the summary report, showing the impact on the Treasury P&L. At Figure 11.16 we show the impact of parallel shift yield curve changes on the money market book. We see from this that the book is sensitive to a rise in interest rates, be they as parallel shift, absolute shift or relative shift, and so this should inform the risk hedging actions of the bank going forward.

SCENARIO ANALYSIS: ECONOMIC DOWNTURN STRESS TEST REPORT

As part of its stress testing a bank will undertake periodic stress testing that considers the impact of a major economic downturn. An example of such a

TABLE 11.14 Stress and scenario testing log.

Bank plc
Stress testing log

Date: 31 Aug-2010

Description	Details	Unit performing	Unit reviewing	Frequency	Last run
Interest rate and FX stress tests	Thirty-four individual stress tests covering historical, bank-specific and industry standard increase and decrease shocks	Finance (Valuation Control)	Market Risk Control	Daily	31-Aug-2010
Capital adequacy ratio stress tests	Nine individual stress tests covering hypothetical shocks impacting risk-weighted assets and capital, including a "break-even" one-off loss	Finance (Valuation Control)	Market Risk Control	Monthly	31-Aug-2010
Liquidity ratio stress tests	Twelve individual stress tests covering hypothetical shocks impacting regulatory liquidity ratios, including shocks to undrawn commitments, short-dated liabilities and value of marketable securities	Finance (Valuation Control)	Market Risk Control	Monthly	31-Aug-2010

Credit risk stress tests	Counterparty specific: as part of the evaluation of a new proposal or at time of review of an individual credit. Tests will be run on cash flows, financial covenants and other break-even analyses (note *ad hoc* not monthly)	Credit Risk Control (except counterparty risk, which is assessed by the Relationship Manager when a Credit Review is conducted)	Credit Committee	Monthly	31-Aug-2010
	Total portfolio: subjecting drawn and committed undrawn exposure based on different recovery rates (0% to 60%). Then further stressing these by two notch internal rating downgrades				
	Industry specific: for major exposure concentrations using same method as for portfolios				
	Country specific for major country exposures using same method as portfolio				

TABLE 11.15 Example of stress test output: change in book PV for each scenario.

	Treasury: Stress testing scenario results – interest rates								
	Bond	Swap	Loan/Depo	MM-CD	FX	CAP	CASH	COM	Total
BankC3TA03 +100bpEUR,GBP,USD	−3,155,237	2,141,863	919,014	−728,432	−92,480	0	0	0	−915,271
BankC3TA01 +200bpEUR,GBP,USD	−6,238,082	4,213,834	1,835,619	−1,452,673	−184,427	0	0	0	−1,825,729
BankC3TX03 −100bpEUR,GBP,USD	2,716,632	−2,193,676	−454,210	470,908	20,176	0	0	0	559,830
BankC3TX01 −200bpEUR,GBP,USD	4,292,654	−3,760,224	−400,417	467,580	22,344	0	0	0	621,937
BankC3TA02 +200bpEURGBPUSDstep50	−6,243,907	4,215,754	1,601,400	−1,412,182	−149,086	0	0	0	−1,988,021
BankC3TA04 +100bpEURGBPUSDstep25	−3,093,344	2,138,458	715,150	−687,795	−71,806	0	0	0	−999,338
BankC3TX02 −200bpEURGBPUSDstep50	4,292,654	−3,760,224	−400,417	467,580	22,344	0	0	0	621,937
BankC3TX04 −100bpEURGBPUSDstep25	2,716,632	−2,193,676	−454,210	470,908	20,176	0	0	0	559,830
BankC1TA08 +20% 3m EURGBPUSD	−92,612	−4,465	74,171	−34,509	1,096	0	0	0	−56,318
BankC1TX08 −20% 3m EURGBPUSD	92,646	4,467	−74,195	34,521	−1,099	0	0	0	56,340
BankC1TA11 >1m −20% EURGBPUSD	927,397	−845,755	−38,537	84,664	4,504	0	0	0	132,272
BankC1TA12 >1m +20% EURGBPUSD	−914,453	832,470	38,812	−84,591	−4,494	0	0	0	−132,256
BankC1TA01 +20% shrt EURGBPUSD	−22,329	1,580	39,325	−8,686	55	0	0	0	9,945
BankC1TX01 −20% shrt EURGBPUSD	22,331	−1,580	−39,329	8,687	−55	0	0	0	−9,946
BankC2TA01 +20%3mUSD+40%>3mUSD	−10,058	25,180	16,139	0	−13,053	0	0	0	18,209
BankC2TA02 +20%3mEUR+40%>3mEUR	−1,744,101	1,633,386	132,236	−151,983	−11,151	0	0	0	−141,613
BankC2TA03 +20%3mGBP+40%>3mGBP	−14,219	1,063	−65,983	0	14,241	0	0	0	−64,898
BankC2TX01 −20%3mUSD-40%>3mUSD	10,101	−23,682	−15,197	0	13,063	0	0	0	−15,714
BankC2TX02 −20%3mEUR-40%>3mEUR	1,795,701	−1,684,267	−132,236	152,243	11,192	0	0	0	142,633
BankC2TX03 −20%3mGBP-40%>3mGBP	14,229	−1,074	66,199	0	−14,248	0	0	0	65,107
BankC1TA09 Curve Flatten	494,075	−712,296	271,493	−171,996	−8,744	0	0	0	−127,467

BankC1TA10 FlighttoUSD+20%EURGBP	−86,429	−3,722	46,717	−34,509	12,659	0	0	0	−65,284
Bank_ManualDelta	−32,081	21,775	8,266	−7,305	−145	0	0	0	−9,490

Treasury: Stress Testing Scenario Results – FX

	Bond	Swap	Loan/Depo	MM–CD	FX	CAP	CASH	COM	Total
SC_EUR_appreciates_10%	−18,823,132	−188,812	11,705,091	0	6,750,773	0	0	0	−556,079
SC_EUR_appreciates_20%	−37,646,263	−377,624	23,410,183	0	13,501,546	0	0	0	−1,112,159
SC_EUR_depreciates_10%	18,823,132	188,812	−11,705,091	0	−6,750,773	0	0	0	556,079
SC_EUR_depreciates_20%	37,646,263	377,624	−23,410,183	0	−13,501,546	0	0	0	1,112,159

Stress Test Results Report – Values Resulting from Tests

Note: Amounts are in euros and reflect changes in the PV for the whole portfolio resulting from each scenario

TABLE 11.16 Example of Treasury stress test results, impact on PnL.

Maximum potential loss ['000 EUR]				
	IR scenarios	FX scenarios	IR & FX combined scenarios	Maximum stress value
Money markets	−461	−270	−292	−461
Money markets	**−461**	**−270**	**−292**	**−461**
Liquidity portfolio TRADING & FUNDING	−34	0	−3	−34
Liquidity portfolio HTM	−1081	−577	−635	−1081
Liquidity portfolio FUNDING	−79	−16	−17	−79
Liquidity portfolio	**−1193**	**−590**	**−655**	**−1193**
Financial engineering	−18	−186	−186	−186
Financial engineering	**−18**	**−186**	**−186**	**−186**
FX spot and forward	0	−225	−61	−225
FX	**0**	**−225**	**−61**	**−225**
Treasury sales securities FUNDING	−544	−187	−221	−544
Treasury sales securities TRADING & FUNDING	−115	0	−10	−115
Treasury sales	0	−4	−3	−4
Treasury sales	**−659**	**−190**	**−234**	**−659**
Treasury	**−1409**	**−1195**	**−1294**	**−1409**

stress test report is included in the Wiley website, and is a template that can be adapted for use at a commercial bank.

The purpose of such a stress test is to assess the bank's likelihood of surviving as a going concern in the event of a severe economic downturn. The object of the test is to determine the impact of the downturn on three aspects of the bank's performance:

- the profit & loss position;
- the regulatory capital position;
- the liquidity position.

If the results of the report suggest it, action can be taken to alter the profile and sensitivity of the balance sheet to mitigate the impact of any

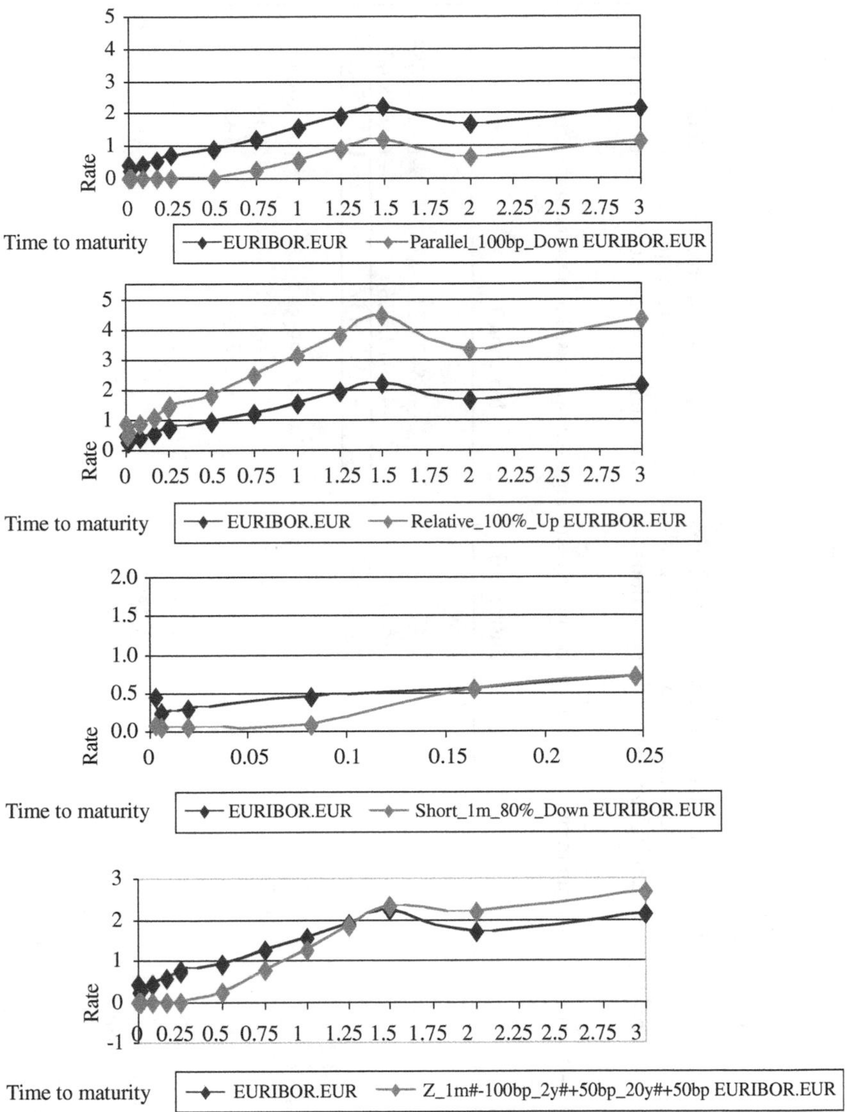

FIGURE 11.16 Example of stress test results, yield curve sensitivities.

crash. This may take the form of raising additional capital and/or contingency funding arrangements, or hedges to lower asset exposure.

In the template report provided on the Wiley website, two iterations of the stress scenario are tested and the results reported. The executive summary of this report is shown at Figure 11.17. We see from that in the

Economic Downturn: Executive Summary

This document sets out the parameters, methods and results used in ascertaining a bank's ability to withstand a severe economic downturn in terms of effect on capital, P&L and liquidity.

The risks that have been stressed include interest-rate risk, FX risk, credit risk and liquidity risk. Operational risk has not been stressed – we assume the bank has a standardised approach and a small loss history with infrequent occurrences of relatively small size. Other risks – for example, legal, pension, reputational and so on – have not been stressed as these have been insignificant historically.

This macroeconomic scenario has been run in two iterations with slightly varying assumptions. The results of the stress scenarios are as follows:

	Unstressed	**Iteration 1**	**Iteration 2**
Effect on P&L			
Market risk		−2,547,621	−61,838,086
Credit risk		−45,013,826	−60,018,435
Total		**−47,561,447**	**−121,856,521**
Effect on capital			
Risk-weighted assets	3,281,699,355	3,236,599,547	3,193,699,910
Capital	589,900,000	537,976,090	468,043,479
Capital adequacy ratio	**17.98%**	**16.62%**	**14.66%**
Effect on liquidity			
Liquidity ratio: sight	21.83%	19.41%	18.58%
Regulatory liq. ratio: sight to 8 days (limit 0%)	13.38%	11.05%	10.36%
Regulatory liq. ratio: sight to 1 month (limit −5%)	4.93%	2.69%	2.14%

FIGURE 11.17 Economic downturn stress test report: Executive summary.

The results suggest that:

- Losses appear most sensitive to changes in bond spreads, while losses due to interest-rate and FX rate changes are more modest.
- The bank is able to meet the minimum regulatory capital adequacy ratio of 15% without any management action in the unadjusted stress scenario (iteration 1), but NOT in the adjusted stress scenario (iteration 2).
- The bank would not need to seek additional funding in order to meet regulatory liquidity ratios. (In both iterations the impact of stress on liquidity did not result in breach of regulatory ratios, but in all cases the ratio deteriorated significantly.)

Thus it would appear that the bank is well placed to survive a severe economic downturn, but that some preparatory capital planning is necessary to ensure that the regulatory capital adequacy ratio can withstand large mark-to-market losses. In addition, the internal liquidity limits should reflect the sharp deterioration in liquidity possible in a downturn. This should be noted when compiling the Contingency Funding Plan.

FIGURE 11.17 *(continued)*

second iteration of the stress test, the impact on the bank is such that its regulatory capital adequacy ratio falls below (for this bank) the required level of 15%. It is the Board's decision as to whether further capital should be raised to mitigate this risk impact. The experience of the crash of 2007–2009 has shown that for a bank to maintain the confidence of the market and remain as a going concern, it is important that capital levels remain above minimum regulatory requirements, even after the worst effects of capital losses have been felt. The conclusion from this stress test, then, is that the bank should increase its capital reserves, either via a straight equity capital raising or by issuing contingent capital debt (see Chapter 18).

STRESSED VAR

Earlier in the book we introduced the VaR risk measurement technique. The standard calculation given in the Basel rules, for a 10-day time horizon market risk charge at time t and a 99% confidence interval, is:

$$MRC_t = max\left(\frac{k}{60}\sum_{i=1}^{60} VaR_{t-i}.VaR_{t-1}\right) + SRC \qquad (11.1)$$

where SRC is the specific risk charge. SRC accounts for the idiosyncratic risk of specific issuer risk, such as changes in credit spread or rating downgrade. The multiplier k is set by the regulator and is driven by the validity of the bank's internal risk model; it has a minimum value of 3.

Equation (11.1) states that the MRC is the larger of the most recent VaR or the average VaR for the last 60 days. In general, banks scale their 10-day VaR from their 1-day VaR by multiplying the latter by $\sqrt{10}$. This assumes lognormal distribution of price returns, an i.i.d. time series and a constant portfolio over the time horizon. That these are unrealistic assumptions is widely recognised, which is why the VaR measure should not be used as the sole indicator of a bank's overall risk exposure (and why banks conduct back testing to assess the accuracy of their VaR numbers).

Under Basel II banks are required to calculate a stressed VaR (SVaR), which adjusts (11.1) above for a 1-year observation period of stress. SVaR is a static risk measure that does not incorporate market movements and is essentially the VaR value arising from a stress test of the balance sheet.

A standardised calculation is

$$MRC_t = max\left(\frac{k}{60}\sum_{i=1}^{60} VaR_{t-i}, VaR_{t-1}\right) + max\left(\frac{m}{60}\sum_{i=1}^{60} SVaR_{t-i}, SVaR_{t-1}\right) + STC_t. \tag{11.2}$$

As before the multipliers k and m are set by the regulator subject to $k \geq 3$, $m \geq 3$. k is subject to back testing of the standard VaR given by (11.1).

For an accessible critique of the VaR and SVaR approach see *Bubble Value At Risk* by Max Wong (2011). As Wong notes, stress tests based on a pre-specified set of stress events and/or a long observation period suffer from an over-influence of past economic cycles and will therefore not be an accurate indicator of the impact of the next stress event, which by definition will be different in nature. He recommends the "Bubble VaR" approach to enable banks to risk manage their balance sheet in a more pro-cyclical manner.

BIBLIOGRAPHY

Moody's Analytics (2011), 2011 Stress Testing Banking Survey, https://www.efma.com/ressources/studies/2011/1-IQFY4_E_study.pdf.

I have a pet definition of discipline: it's what makes a person do the right and proper thing under many different circumstances. That doesn't mean by sheer instinct or innate ability, it means through knowledge gained by life experience, training and learned judgement . . . To do the right thing from moment to moment, a person needs to analyze and judge a situation correctly, make the right decision for the proper course of action, and then take that action.

— Robin Olds, with Christina Olds and Ed Rasimus, *Fighter Pilot: The Memoirs of Legendary Ace Robin Olds*,
New York, NY: St. Martin's Press, 2010

PART III

Bank Liquidity Risk Management

As we emphasised in the Preface, the art of banking is essentially the art of liquidity management. It is the key principle of banking. Part III of the book is dedicated exclusively to liquidity management, liquidity reporting, liquidity risk management and liquidity stress testing.

In Chapter 12 we consider the basic liquidity principles, which form the cornerstone of a sustainable bank business model. We emphasise *sustainable* here – as the experience of the financial crisis of 2007–2009 illustrated, it is easy for senior management to forget the importance of liquidity management during an extended period of plentiful and cheap liquidity. It is also easy for business line heads to think that any crisis is a rare one-off and unlikely to appear again (at least in their careers), especially when it comes to assumptions on liquidity. However, the importance of banks to the wellbeing of the economy means that it is important for them to follow a strategy, and liquidity principles, that remain successful in the long term, and continuously over the business cycle. There is no long-term viable alternative to the principles described in the next four chapters.

Chapter 13 looks at the main liquidity metrics essential for effective governance, while Chapter 14 covers liquidity risk reporting and stress testing.

Internal funds pricing in a bank, also known as funds transfer pricing (FTP) or simply transfer pricing, is an important part of the liquidity management regime in a bank. It warrants its own chapter, and is covered in Chapter 15.

CHAPTER 12

Principles of Bank Liquidity Management

The banking system in both the US and Western Europe was on the brink of collapse in September and October 2008, in the wake of the Lehman bankruptcy. Government intervention using taxpayer funds, which in many countries extended to a blanket guarantee of banks' complete liabilities, prevented this collapse from taking place. In the aftermath of the crisis, national regulators and the BIS circulated consultative papers and recommendations that addressed new requirements on bank capital, liquidity and risk management. The UK FSA was perhaps most demanding; its *Policy Statement 09/16*, which was issued in October 2009, outlined measures on capital treatment, liquidity requirements and stress testing that implied a fundamental change in the bank business model going forward.[1] Many of the elements of this change in regulatory requirements were not new, however, but rather a turning of the clock back to earlier times, when conservative principles in liquidity management were actually quite common practice. The crisis of 2007 and 2008 was as much a crisis of bank liquidity as it was of capital erosion, and the events of that period restated the importance of efficient liquidity management in banking.

In this and the next three chapters we discuss the "water of life" of banking: liquidity management. The recommended practices described in this chapter should not be followed because they are required by the national regulator or by the BIS, but because they are essential for any bank that wishes to continue in business on a sustained basis over the business cycle. In other words, sensible banking demands this practice; that regulators have to enforce it by fiat demonstrates the extent to which poor bank

1 The UK government announced shortly after it was elected in May 2010 that the banking supervision role was to be handed back to the BoE, and that the role of the FSA would be subsumed within the bank.

management exists in countries around the world. The central tenet of the principles of banking is that of liquidity risk management; therefore, by definition it should be part of the strategy of every bank to be able to survive a liquidity crisis. Liquidity management is the most important risk management function in banking, at the individual bank level and at the aggregate industry level. Failure to survive a liquidity crisis is a failure of management.

This chapter introduces and defines the concept of liquidity risk. It then covers the principles of sound liquidity management, before looking in detail at the elements of a bank liquidity policy statement, including (i) the liquid asset buffer, (ii) central bank funding facilities and (iii) the contingency funding plan.

This is a long chapter, but worth persevering with as it is perhaps the most important chapter in the book.

BANK LIQUIDITY

A search of "bank liquidity" on Google undertaken when writing this chapter returned "about 8,160,000 results" in 0.24 seconds. The first line of the first website on the list offered the following:

> *Liquidity for a bank means the ability to meet its financial obligations as they come due. Bank lending finances investments in relatively illiquid assets, but it funds its loans with mostly short-term liabilities. Thus one of the main challenges to a bank is ensuring its own liquidity under all reasonable conditions.*[2]

This definition is accurate and sufficient for our purposes, although we preferred Wikipedia's definition, which stated,

> *In banking, liquidity is the ability to meet obligations when they become due.*

In other words, maintenance of liquidity *at all times* is the paramount order of the day in banking. As we saw in Chapter 1, the business of banking itself creates maturity mismatches between assets and liabilities, and hence liquidity risk. In fact, to undertake banking is to assume a

2 The website was www.wfhummel.cnchost.com and the link was http://wfhummel.cnchost.com/bankliquidity.html, found during a Google search undertaken one night in September 2010.

continuous ability to roll over funding, otherwise banks would never originate long-dated illiquid assets such as residential mortgages or project finance loans. As it is never safe to assume anything, banks need to set in place an infrastructure and management capability to ensure that liquidity is always available, to cover for all times when market conditions deteriorate. Because banks are so important to the economy's health, central banks operate as "lenders of last resort" to come to the aid of a bank that finds itself in liquidity difficulties. However, a bank that has to resort to the central bank for funding has failed, and this is a failure of its management.

In this section we provide some historical background to the nature of liquidity risk management, and a more in-depth definition of what it involves.

Elements of Liquidity Risk Management

The importance of liquidity risk management is such that it must be addressed at the highest level of a bank's management, which is the Board of Directors. The Board will delegate this responsibility to a management operating committee, usually the ALCO, but it is the Board that owns liquidity policy. If it does not own it, then it is not following business best-practice. Given this, it is important that the Board understands every aspect of liquidity risk management. We suggest that this covers the following strands, all of which are covered in Part III of this book:

- definition of liquidity risk;
- the role of liquidity risk management;
- board responsibilities;
- liquidity strategy, policy and processes;
- regulatory requirements and reporting obligations;
- funding strategy and policy;
- liquidity risk tolerance;
- institution-specific and market-wide stress scenarios, and stress testing;
- forecasting funding cash flows over different time horizons;
- the liquidity buffer;
- intra-group and cross-border group lending;
- liquidity contingency funding plan and stress testing;
- the link between liquidity and capital adequacy;
- the benefits of robust business intelligence.

In other words, liquidity management is devised and dictated from the highest level, and influences every aspect of the bank's business strategy and operating model. The UK FSA identified the following failures in bank liquidity management during the lead-up to the 2007–2009 financial crisis:

- an inconsistent approach to qualitative and quantitative reporting, across different firms, to senior management and to the regulator;
- an excessive reliance on short-term wholesale funding and the securitisation market, to the detriment of more stable funding sources such as retail deposits;
- funding long-dated illiquid assets with short-term wholesale liabilities;
- for the branches and subsidiaries of overseas banks, an excessive reliance on parental support for funds;
- the lack of a sufficiently diverse funding base; excessive reliance on only one or two sources of liabilities, with no alternatives available in a stress situation;
- the running down, or complete abolition, of a pool of genuinely liquid assets that would have remained liquid, and providing a pool of funding, during the inter-bank liquidity crisis.

To these we would add the following:

- organisational models and processes inadequate to cope with crisis events;
- poor and ineffective tools for controlling liquidity risk, not fully implemented into banks' internal processes.

The primary lesson to be learned from the financial crisis was that banks needed to return to their roots and manage liquidity risk on a more conservative basis, along the lines that they would have done in the past. An assumption by management that inter-bank liquidity will always be available is the first step towards generating funding difficulties for itself during a period of market or economic downturn.

Liquidity crises are endemic in banking and finance. That is why it is essential to maintain liquidity principles throughout the economic cycle, a discipline that may break down during a bull market or a period of cheap and plentiful cash availability. An excellent paper by John Boyd and Mark Gertler, published in 1994, highlights the lessons learned from the US banking crisis of 1980–1982. The authors' findings and recommendations remain current, and this paper should be required reading for all bank senior management today.[3]

3 Boyd, J.H. and Gertler, M., "The Role of Large Banks in the Recent U.S. Banking Crisis", *Federal Reserve Bank of Minneapolis Quarterly Review*, Winter 1994, Volume 18, No. 1.

Among the conclusions from Boyd and Gertler were that the larger, more systemically important banks were ultimately responsible for the performance of the overall industry, and contributed disproportionately to aggregate loan losses. This they ascribed to two factors: (i) deregulation and financial innovation leading to increased overall competition in the banking industry; and (ii) the regulatory environment, which had the indirect effect of subsidising risk taking by larger banks. The second factor arises from the existence of "too-big-to-fail" banks, a term that the authors employ. Both factors were in place during 2002–2007. It is worth quoting directly from the paper, because all of the observations could be made about the later crisis; we comment on the authors' remarks with reference to the events of 2007–2008:

> *. . . rationale behind too-big-to-fail was that . . . the failure of a large bank could be contagious. It could greatly disturb the rest of the financial system and cause severe consequences for the entire US economy. But this well-intentioned policy had an unfortunate side effect: it unduly subsidized risk-taking by large banks.* (Boyd and Gertler 1994; p. 2)

The actions of US Federal Reserve chairman Alan Greenspan in assisting the market in the 10 years leading to 2007, and which became known as the "Greenspan Put", contributed to a subconscious belief that the larger banks could not be allowed to fail, and so indirectly led to ever-larger risk taking during a period of cheap liquidity.

> *Most striking are the rise in the share [of bank assets] allocated to loans and the fall in shares allocated to [liquid] securities and to cash and reserves. The drop in the latter reflects mainly a sequence of reductions in reserve requirements . . . The increased access to short-term money [markets] permitted banks to reduce precautionary holdings of securities.* (Boyd and Gertler 1994; p. 3).

Precisely this same pattern of behaviour was repeated in the period leading up to the 2007–2009 crisis.

> *Judged by a variety of criteria, the composition of bank liabilities appears to have become riskier . . . the increased use of managed liabilities relative to deposits . . . In contrast to deposits, which are relatively immobile in the short run, managed liabilities are highly interest elastic. The increased use of managed liabilities – and of money market instruments in particular – has had a number of important effects. One obvious effect is downward pressure on*

> *banks' net interest margins . . . Another effect is a rise in the interest rate sensitivity of bank liabilities . . . With the efficiency gains of the money market came the cost of increased exposure to liquidity risk.* (Boyd and Gertler 1994; p. 3).

Again, this remains an accurate description of what happened at the last crisis. As well as higher liquidity risk, lower NII often leads to banks looking at higher risk business to maintain return on capital ratios:

> *The relative use of core deposits (checkable and savings and time deposits) shrinks with size, while the relative use of money market instruments increases. About 85 percent of small bank liabilities are core deposits. Conversely, money market instruments constitute roughly 42 percent of large bank liabilities and 54 percent of money center bank liabilities. Further, the money centre banks obtain more than half of their purchased funds from abroad.*
>
> *An implication of the differences in liability structure is that larger banks have smaller net interest margins . . . In addition to holding riskier asset portfolios and employing greater use of money market instruments, larger banks have lower capital/assets ratios.* (Boyd and Gertler 1994; p. 5).

During 2002–2007 the increased use of non-core funds was not restricted to the large banks, but it is notable that the use of such liabilities rose during the bull market. Failed banks such as Northern Rock embarked on an aggressive expansion strategy that relied heavily on the use of non-core deposits.

> *The too-big-to-fail policy contributed by subsidizing risk-taking and thereby increasing the vulnerability of the banking system to these disturbances . . . With large banks as with the savings and loans, the key issue is whether the portfolio structure these financial firms adopted was distorted by regulatory bias . . . It is hard to believe that the portfolio structure of very large banks (for example, heavy investment in LDC [less-developed countries] and commercial real-estate lending, in conjunction with thin capital/assets ratios) could be explained simply by scale economies.* (Boyd and Gertler 1994; p. 8).

If we substitute US sub-prime mortgages for LDC loans above, those same words published in 1994 would apply to any analysis of 2007–2008. For example, for the UK failed bank HBOS, poor quality commercial real-estate lending was the principal factor in its demise, and which required the nationalisation of Lloyds TSB Bank (which had taken over HBOS a few months previously).

Boyd and Gertler welcomed the 1988 Basel Accord, which instituted minimum regulatory capital rules for banks worldwide, just as policymakers in 2010 welcomed the Basel III rules. They suggested that the Basel rules confronted what they saw as the main risk factor: the implicit subsidy to risk taking by large banks. They state:

> *. . . an important way the subsidy has played out has been that large banks have held less capital than they might have otherwise.* (Boyd and Gertler 1994; p. 9).

They conclude:

> *. . . the main stress on the system has not been the raw number of failures; rather it has been the poor performance of large banks.* (Boyd and Gertler 1994; p. 9).

These last two quotes would not be out of place in an analysis of the 2008 banking crisis. The liquidity crisis was, in many respects, history repeating itself. It is clear that liquidity management and risk taking remain areas of bank risk management that must be addressed throughout the business cycle. So far, they have not been. We have cited this paper in detail here for two reasons. First, to highlight that liquidity crises are not new, that similar crises have occurred in the past, often because of the same causal factors, and will occur again; and second, to note that banks that do not learn the lessons of history will be at high risk of repeating the same mistakes as the failed banks of previous crises.

Principles of Banking: Liquidity Adequacy

The lesson learned from all bank liquidity crises, of which the most recent one in 2007–2008 was the most noteworthy, is that the majority of banks do not adhere to sound principles of liquidity management during a bull market, when funds are readily available. Many firms cease maintaining an adequate liquidity buffer, and thus encounter difficulties when faced with a firm-specific and/or market-wide liquidity shock. The subsidiaries of foreign-based banks often have trouble obtaining funds from parent groups. In line with the thinking of the UK FSA, we believe that a bank's liquidity policy should be based on: (i) an adequate reserve of liquidity at all times; and (ii) in principle, the ability to be self-sufficient in funding. These can be taken to be part of the principles of banking. The key point to emphasise is that it is the responsibility of the bank itself, and thereby its Board and senior management, to undertake effective liquidity risk management, and not that of the regulator. A bank's management should incorporate sound liquidity principles into its own objectives and performance measurement, rather than wait to obtain direction from the regulator. Liquidity management is to the benefit of the bank's shareholders and stakeholders.

In principle, every bank should aim to achieve self-sufficiency in funding. For some banks, particularly the overseas branches and subsidiaries of banks headquartered elsewhere, this may not be possible; for others, the particular business model being employed may not permit it. However, funding self-sufficiency should always be the overriding goal of a bank, because that is the only way that a bank can be certain of surviving a liquidity crisis. Where self-sufficiency is not possible, the liquidity policy in place must incorporate a funding strategy that emphasises diversity on funding sources and an adequate liquidity contingency plan.

The UK FSA's *Policy Statement 09/16* states that:

> *UK banks are expected to be able to stand alone, and therefore should normally monitor and manage their own liquidity separately from the liquidity of other institutions in the group.* (page 21)

Applying this principle will help to maintain confidence in the banking system. Adopting a robust liquidity management policy will reduce the probability of a bank's failure in the event of market disruption or a specific firm bankruptcy. The rest of this chapter looks at the principles of sound liquidity management.

SUSTAINABLE BANKING: TEN PRINCIPLES OF BANK LIQUIDITY RISK MANAGEMENT

At a conference hosted by the UK FSA on 9 October 2009, there was considerable attention given to the model of liquidity management practised at HSBC plc. Given that HSBC did not suffer a liquidity crisis in 2007–2008, observers took a close interest in the HSBC model, which is inherently conservative in nature, and on what lessons could be learned from it for banking in general.

In truth, a closer look at HSBC's approach to liquidity management and asset generation shows that it is neither unique nor proprietary to the bank. For instance, it is virtually identical to the model followed at Standard Chartered Bank, BNP Paribas and Santander, among others. The

"HSBC model" would have been the norm, rather than the exception, among banks at the turn of the 21st century. In a period of excess cheap liquidity and rising markets, the basic tenets of the approach were applied by fewer and fewer banks, to the extent that by the time of the 2007–2008 financial crash they were no longer seen as a necessary ingredient of prudent bank risk management.

Nevertheless, these principles represent basic essential management standards of banking, and are not a specific response to the events of 2007–2008. They should be considered as the benchmark for general principles of banking liquidity management. Depending on their specific business model and appetite for liquidity risk, individual banks may relax some of the rules we describe here and run a higher risk funding and asset origination strategy, and this is the judgement call of senior management. There is scope for considerable variation, and a number of endogenous and exogenous factors will drive the final approach selected. However, we expect that more banks will re-adopt the more onerous aspects of these basic principles as they return to a more conservative business model, either though choice or because the requirements of the national banking regulator insist upon a more robust approach to liquidity risk management.

This section considers the most important principles of what should be taken to be the cornerstone of banking and liquidity management.

(1) Fund illiquid assets with core customer deposits Students of banking history will know that this was a founding principle of the original modern banks. In hindsight, this looks an eminently sensible guideline, but during the bull market build-up of 2001–2007 it was not applied universally. A good example of this was at Northern Rock plc, which built an asset book that far exceeded its retail deposit base in size; this pattern was observed with many banks in the US and Western Europe. It is not difficult to ascertain the logic behind this principle: core customer deposits are generally more stable than wholesale funds and also at lower risk of withdrawal in the event of a downturn in economic conditions (an apparent paradox is that they may actually increase as customers seek to deleverage and also hold off committing to cash-rich expenditure). Therefore, funding illiquid assets with core customer deposits means a bank is less likely to experience a funding problem during an economic downturn or a period of liquidity stress. It is prudent banking practice.

(2) Where core customer deposits are not available, use long-term wholesale funding sources This follows on naturally from the first principle. Where there is insufficient core deposits available, and banks resort to the wholesale funding market, they should ensure that only long-dated wholesale funds are used to fund illiquid assets. Generally, "long-dated" means over one year in maturity, although of course the appropriate tenor to source is a function of the maturity of the asset. This approach reduces rollover liquidity risk in the event that a funding stress period occurs.

(3) No over-reliance on wholesale funding. Run a sensible term structure wherever wholesale funding is used: more of it should be in long-term tenors (> 1 year) than in the short term This follows on from the primary dictum of not building up the asset base using wholesale funds unless absolutely necessary. Where recourse is made to wholesale funds, as much of this should be in the long term as possible, so as to minimise exposure to frequent short-term rollover risk of wholesale funds. A "sensible" term structure is harder to define; in an earlier book the author suggested that no more than 20%–30% of the balance sheet should be funded in the short term (less than 3-month) tenor. In a tongue-in-cheek borrowing of options traders' expression for volatility, the "ALM smile" was the term we used then (see Figure 12.1) to refer to a liability structure that matched as closely as possible to the asset structure, with only a minority of funding maintained in the shorter term.[4]

In a conventional positive-sloping yield curve environment, terming out one's funding will, all else being equal, result in lower profits for a bank. However, simply running a funding gap of very short-term liabilities against

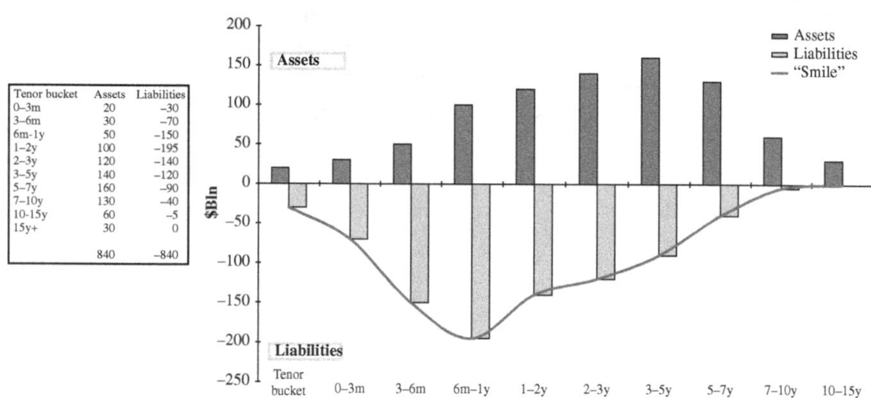

Tenor bucket	Assets	Liabilities
0–3m	20	–30
3–6m	30	–70
6m-1y	50	–150
1–2y	100	–195
2–3y	120	–140
3–5y	140	–120
5–7y	160	–90
7–10y	130	–40
10-15y	60	–5
15y+	30	0
	840	–840

FIGURE 12.1 The asset–liability management "smile".

4 The book we refer to is the author's *Bank Asset and Liability Management* (John Wiley & Sons 2007). "ALM smile" is the author's own term for it, we haven't come across it in any other literature. But a smile profile in funding is evidence of a sensible funding strategy.

long-dated assets is an effortless, non-value-added way for a bank to make money; this explains why an ALM smile was not very much in evidence among many banks during the period 2002–2008, and why much funding was concentrated at the short-end, with catastrophic results during the market panic that set in after the Lehman bankruptcy.

(4) Maintain "liquidity buffers" of instantly liquid assets, to cater for both firm-specific and market-wide stresses For UK banks this principle is no longer an option, as the regulator stipulated in its *Policy Statement 09/16* published in October 2009 that it is a formal requirement. However, before 2007 it was very common, if not universal, for banks to hold some of their assets in the form of liquid risk-free government bonds. The issue arose when the definition of what constituted "liquid" began to be relaxed.

Traditionally a bank's capital was always invested in such securities or in shorter-dated government bills, but beyond this it was accepted good practice for banks to have a proportion of their balance sheet assets in the form of sovereign securities. As these generate the lowest return, many banks' liquidity portfolios began to be extended to agency bonds, local authority bonds, bank CDs and FRNs, and corporate bonds. For the UK FSA to make it a requirement under law demonstrates the extent to which the original practice fell into disuse.

It is evident that banks reduced their holdings of government bonds so they could deploy more of their funds in higher paying risky assets. But the logic of holding a liquidity buffer is irrefutable: in periods of stress or illiquidity, government bonds are the only assets that remain liquid.[5] As such, if need be they can be sold to release liquidity. Even hitherto highly liquid assets such as high-rated bank CDs and short-dated MTNs became illiquid virtually overnight in the immediate aftermath of the Lehman collapse in 2008. This demonstrates that the liquidity buffer should be comprised of sovereign risk-free securities only.

We note, however, that both the Basel Committee and many country regulators extend their definition of liquid securities to other classes of assets. This is unfortunate. Our belief remains that if not all, then a significant portion of the liquidity buffer must be restricted to G7 sovereign bonds and/or the sovereign securities of one's home country only.

5 The author's personal experience during October 2008 confirmed that even high-quality bank CDs and FRNs could not be considered truly liquid, because the Treasury desk he managed at the time could not repo or sell its holdings of these assets. An anecdote from a friend at another bank suggested a similar experience: this person's Treasury desk could not sell or repo a AA-rated bank CD that had *three days* left to maturity! The secondary market in highly rated CDs dried up completely during this period.

(5) Establish a liquidity contingency plan A well-managed liquidity operation recognises that bank funding should be sourced from multiple origins, and that "concentration risk" should be avoided both in any specific sector and to any one lender. However, even without excess concentration, at any time particular sectors or lenders may become unavailable, for either exogenous or endogenous reasons.

Given this risk, banks needs to have contingencies to fall back on whenever particular sources of funding dry up. This may include applying for and setting up facilities at the central bank, or establishing relationships with particular sectors that, for reasons of cost or convenience, the bank does not customarily access. The contingency plan needs to be tested regularly and kept updated.

(6) Know what central bank facilities the bank can assess and test access to them This follows logically from the requirement to have a contingency funding plan in place. Once a bank has established borrowing facilities at its central bank, it needs to be aware exactly how they function and what the requirements to access them are, so that if necessary it can benefit from them without delay.

(7) Be aware of all the bank's exposures (here we are referring to the liability side, not the credit side). For example, sponsoring an ABCP conduit creates a reputational, rather than contractual, obligation to provide funding. Therefore be aware of reputational obligations, especially if it means the bank has to lend its name to another entity This is fairly straightforward to understand, but in a bull market when credit spreads are tight it is frequently forgotten. Banks may desire the fee-based income, at favourable capital levels, that comes with sponsoring a third-party entity or providing a line of liquidity, but in a stress situation one has to assume that the line will be drawn on. Is the bank prepared to take on this additional liquidity risk exposure to an entity that it might not normally, in a bear market, wish to lend funds to?

(8) Liquidity risk is not a single metric. It is an array of metrics, and a bank must calculate them all in order to obtain the most accurate picture of its liquidity. This is especially true for multinational banks and/or banks with multiple business lines Many banks, particularly the smaller banks with little or no cross-border and/or multi-entity business, often rely on just a handful of liquidity indicators, such as the loan-to-deposit ratio and the liquidity gap ratio. Given that bank ALM is more art than science, it is vital that banks use a range of liquidity measures, so as to enable as full a picture of their liquidity position to be obtained as possible. This is essential for accurate risk estimation and forecasting. We address the different metrics required in Chapter 13.

(9) The internal funding pricing ("transfer pricing") framework must be set correctly and adequately An artificial internal lending rate to the bank's business lines often results in inappropriate business decision-making, as well as the reporting of artificial profits, and this was a factor behind the growth in risky assets on bank balance sheets during the period leading to the US sub-prime crisis. A robust and disciplined internal funding policy, also known as a "transfer pricing policy" or "term liquidity premium" (TLP) policy, is an essential part of a sound liquidity strategy. We address this issue in Chapter 15.

(10) The liquidity risk management framework is "owned" by the Group Management Board. Policy is centralised The bank should formalise its liquidity and funding policy, and ensure that it applies throughout the group. This is not an issue for a bank that operates in one country, but once subsidiaries and overseas entities are set up, it is imperative that they all follow the same policy, procedures, and risk tolerances. Individual exceptions must be authorised by the Group Board in advance. That liquidity policy is owned by the Board recognises the importance attached to it, as the Board is ultimately responsible for the continued successful funding of the bank throughout all market conditions.

The above are essential basic tenets of sustainable banking practice. The business of banking is, if nothing else, the business of managing the gap between assets and liabilities ("maturity transformation"). In the history of banking, banks have never matched their asset maturity with their funding liability maturity. But it is the management of this gap risk that should be the primary concern of all banks. The above basic principles represent business best-practice, evolved over centuries of modern banking, in mitigating gap risk.

There are a number of additional principles that banks may also consider, depending on their individual risk appetite. Certain banks' management will feel that they are unnecessarily restrictive, or inhibitors of a desired target RoE level. Ideally, however, these principles would be followed by all banks; this would make the financial services industry much safer and better able to withstand economic downturns. These additional principles are as follows:

All legal entities and geographies are required to be "stand-alone" with regard to liquidity and funding; and liquidity contingency plans are required for all legal entities and geographies For banking groups that operate across country borders and via subsidiary legal entities, a reliance on the parent for funding creates a liquidity risk that is harder for the head office to manage. This is recognised by many regulators, who impose limits on lending across country borders or across different legal entities in the same group. Additionally, the local branch or subsidiary will be most familiar with the local market conditions; if it is self-sufficient in funding it is less likely that the head office will be surprised by a liquidity crisis and a demand for extra funds.

Similarly, each entity in the group across country borders should implement its own modified version of the bank's contingency funding plan, adapted to suit local conditions and requirements.

These principles follow from another core principle that is at the heart of traditional banking: that a bank creates its deposit base and raises funds (ideally retail customer deposits) before it starts lending. This requires, by definition, that overseas entities are self-sufficient in funding and not reliant on the head office for liabilities.

Maintain a high proportion of stable customer funding Banks should maintain a significant share of their customer funds in the form of "sticky" deposits. The UK regulator makes a distinction between "Type A" depositors, typically financial institutions, governments and local authorities, and "Type B" depositors such as retail customers, small businesses and clients of over 3 years standing. Type A deposits are deemed to have a higher than average likelihood of withdrawal in a stressed environment, and so are deemed less sticky.

Be aware of the liquidity of your collateral under stressed as well as normal conditions Collateral acceptable in a healthy economic environment may be less so in stressed circumstances. A bank should be aware of how collateral quality changes with changes in conditions. An equally important aspect of liquidity management is funding of collateral. Derivatives transactions in the inter-bank market are collateralised on a daily basis, usually with cash but sometimes risk-free sovereign assets. A bank that funds its collateral obligations in the overnight money market must monitor the funding risk exposure that this represents, if short-term money markets become illiquid or otherwise disconnected.

LIQUIDITY RISK MANAGEMENT: THE UNITED KINGDOM REGULATOR'S VIEW

In the aftermath of the financial crisis the UK Financial Services Authority published *Consultative Paper 08/22* and *Consultative Paper 08/24* in

2008, the recommended requirements of which were formalised in its *Policy Statement 09/16*. These publications have set a standard for bank liquidity management that is expected to be mirrored, in part if not whole, in other jurisdictions around the world. In many respects the requirements in the FSA Policy Statement are more onerous than those required in the document on liquidity risk published later (in December 2010) by the Basel Committee. As such they hint at a return to another facet of the basic bank business model, concentrated on the liabilities side of the balance sheet. In essence, the FSA recognised that the crisis of 2007 and 2008 was as much a liquidity crisis as a capital erosion crisis, and acted to mitigate this risk going forward. However, very little of the new FSA requirements is completely new to banking itself; rather, they are merely a reiteration of what was standard practice in commercial banking in previous decades.

Liquidity Management: The FSA Model

The basic tenets of the FSA proposals are grounded in market logic. Their content is expected to become business best-practice in due course, but irrespective of the regulatory jurisdiction that a bank functions in, the tenets of the FSA regime represent a sound approach to sustainable liquidity management, and the author recommends that bank boards and senior management incorporate them into their operating model. The FSA incorporates its approach into an "individual liquidity adequacy assessment" (ILAA) process, undertaken at each bank. Applying this on a general basis, the logic is that a bank conducts a liquidity adequacy assessment of its business, and takes action accordingly should the results suggest an element of unacceptable liquidity risk exposure.

In the first instance a bank must define its liquidity risk appetite in explicit terms. This should confirm the extent to which it can withstand liquidity stresses without having to access any central bank lender-of-last-resort (LoLR) facilities. These stresses should cover, but not be limited to:

- a firm-specific stress;
- a sector-specific stress;
- a market-wide stress;

and combinations of the above. The liquidity assessment should be carried out by the bank on at least an annual basis, if not more frequently. It should also be updated whenever there is any change made to the bank's strategy, operating model or product/geographic base, or whenever any new demand is placed on its liquidity resources. The liquidity assessment should be sent to the bank's regulator, as a liquidity report, irrespective of whether the regulatory demands it specifically. This is good business practice. It should also, as a matter of course, be sent to the Board.

Liquidity Assessment Report: the UK FSA Format

A bank that is required to conduct a regular liquidity assessment for its regulator, such as the ILAA required by the UK FSA, will receive direction on the format of the report from the regulator. We provide here a description of the ILAA report template that is required by the FSA, but which would be expected to be similar in content to the liquidity assessment required in other jurisdictions. In the UK the ILAA forms part of a bank's ongoing liquidity risk management process.

Liquidity Report Format

Summary A description of the liquidity assessment review process and the results. This would include a summary of the governance structure in place at the bank, the suite of liquidity reporting provided to senior management, and a description of the stress testing undertaken on liquidity exposure. Specifically, the ILAA asks for:

- the objective of the report;
- a summary of the bank's financials, including balance sheet strength and forecast profit and loss statements;
- the composition and amount of liquidity that the bank holds under "business as usual" (BAU) circumstances, and how this changes under a set of specified stress scenarios;
- description of the bank's liquidity risk management governance, process and methodologies;
- a summary of the bank's liquidity risk appetite and limits;
- description of expected liquidity risks, and the mitigating action the bank would take against them.

We now look at these sections in greater detail.

Financial and Liquidity Position This section presents the bank's current financial position and its business model, and any forecast or expected changes in either. The description of the business model will include the market that the bank operates in, its current and projected business lines and competitive position. The current liquidity position of the bank is contained in the liquidity risk profile (LRP) report. The LRP forms part of the ILAA submission.

The bank will also present here a summary of the liquid assets that form part of its sources of liquidity. The full list of each asset (government bond, etc.) would be detailed in an Appendix to the report.

Liquidity Adequacy This section provides a summary of the bank's liquidity stress testing results. The implication of the results for the bank's liquidity position, and the mitigating actions that the bank will take to address this, is also presented here. The FSA prescribes the main types of stress scenarios to be tested, and the bank will drill down into greater detail for specific stresses relevant to its market.

The liquidity risk position will cover the following:

- a formal statement articulating the firm's liquidity risk appetite, and why this appetite is appropriate to the firm and its business model;
- the list of liquidity risk metrics used and the limits set against each metric, as well as how these limits may differ under stressed conditions compared to BAU conditions;
- the bank's analysis of how its liquidity position changes under three prescribed liquidity stress tests that the FSA set out in its *CP08/22* document. Stress testing is recommended business best-practice for all banks, and while jurisdictions will differ in the detail of testing, taking the FSA papers as an example banks must implement the following stress tests:
  1. A name-specific shock
     - unforeseen name-specific shock
     - the market perceives the firm to be potentially insolvent in the short term
     - long-term impact: severity of multi-notch a downgrade in credit rating
  2. Market-wide dislocation
     - unforeseen short-term market-wide dislocation that gradually evolves into a long-term market-wide liquidity stress
     - widespread concerns on the solvency of the financial sector
     - uncertainty of value of financial assets
     - certain asset classes remain illiquid for a long period
  3. Combination of (1) and (2).

The FSA stress test main risk drivers are described later in this chapter.

Each stress test result will be reported in the ILAA, together with an assessment of whether the bank's liquidity remains within its risk appetite. If the result is negative with respect to acceptable risk appetite, it then needs to be accompanied by a description of the mitigating action that the bank will take to return the bank to acceptable liquidity parameters.

Funding Diversification Under FSA (as well as many other jurisdictions') requirements, a bank must follow a flexible funding strategy. This means a funding approach that reduces liquidity risk because it relies on a diversified group of funding sources. The ILAA submission includes therefore a description of how the various liquidity stresses impact the diversification of funding sources; that is, which sources are more volatile and vulnerable to being lost or withdrawn. A bank should describe the extent to which its funding sources are diversified according to:

- the type of funding product;
- the currency;
- the counterparties;
- its liability term structure;
- the availability of the markets it operates in as a source of funds in a stress scenario. This assessment should take into account the extent to which sources may disappear as a result of a deterioration in the firm's own position, such as a downgrade in credit rating, as well as a closure of the market itself.

Use of the ILAA in the Firm Liquidity risk appetite is part of the culture of a bank, and will necessarily differ across each one. Reflecting this fact, the ILAA submission also includes a section describing the extent to which liquidity risk management is embedded within the bank. In other words, the act of compiling the ILAA is not meant to be merely bureaucratic form-filling, but rather a process that reflects, and feeds into, the liquidity risk management process at the firm.

Impact of the UK FSA Approach to Liquidity

In its consultative papers of 2008 and policy statement of 2009, the UK FSA summarised its belief on the approach to liquidity risk regulation as follows:

- increased number of gap ("mismatch") limits and increased supervisory oversight;
- increased international cooperation between regulators;
- increased bank liquidity reporting obligations and their frequency;
- revoking or reducing certain behavioural adjustments that were previously allowed; for example, intra-group committed liquidity facilities no longer count as automatic funding self-sufficiency;

- other behavioural adjustments reviewed on a case-by-case basis; for example, the treatment of the "stickiness" of deposits;
- a requirement to hold buffers of truly liquid assets (discussed elsewhere in this chapter);
- a requirement to increase the average tenor of funding, and to diversify the sources of funds.

The main implication of these requirements is increased cost and, all else being equal, a lower RoE. Other implications for this new business model include:

- greater level of senior management and board governance and responsibility;
- an improved liquidity risk management capability (including better use of stress testing and improved contingency funding plans);
- a decreased reliance on short-term wholesale funding;
- greater incentive for a bank to attract retail time deposits, and longer term wholesale deposits;
- higher amount and quality of liquid asset stocks (including a higher proportion held in government bonds): this is the Liquid Asset Buffer;
- in theory, a reduced expansion of bank lending during favourable economic times. This impact may be as a result of more conservative liquidity requirements, but is more naturally expected to follow as a result of the need to follow "countercyclical capital" and "macroprudential regulation" rules, which are included in the Basel III provision. This is discussed in Chapter 17.

The main implication for banks is an increased likelihood of their surviving a liquidity stress event. Another aspect of the new bank model, required by regulators, is more in-depth and realistic stress testing. This subject is reviewed in more detail in Chapter 14.

The responsibility for formulating the stress tests, ensuring that they are carried out robustly and at required frequency, and reporting the results to the Board, lies with the Chief Risk Officer. Under business best-practice culture, this person will report direct to a non-executive director on the Board.

Liquidity Risk Drivers: A Regulator's Approach

The FSA prescribes the liquidity stress tests that firms must report in the ILAA submission, although the precise stress scenarios will differ across banks. The stress tests themselves are described below.

Wholesale Funding Risk

A bank will have its own definition of what constitutes its "wholesale" funding liabilities, which are generally defined as funds raised from non-customer business. Some banks include banks with whom they are deemed to have a client relationship, so-called "correspondent banks", as customers and thus include their deposits in the loan-to-deposit ratio. This is a matter for the regulatory authority to approve. In any case, for liquidity risk management purposes each bank will need to determine the behavioural characteristics of its wholesale liabilities, and then ascertain how this behaviour would be expected to change under the three main stress scenarios (see above) outlined by the FSA. Bank risk managers should note the following:

- money market funds raised via CD and CP, and capital markets funds raised via MTN issuance, are the most volatile and most likely to disappear in the event of firm- or market-wide stress. These funding sources may even dry up completely;
- wholesale deposits from lenders that are required to adhere to strict credit rating guidelines will be most sensitive to changes in the bank's credit rating; if a bank is downgraded below the required minimum, then the funds will be withdrawn overnight. Thus a bank's cash funding position is at risk of so-called "downgrade triggers", when a downgrading in credit rating below a specified minimum results in an outflow of deposits. Cash-rich institutions that generally observe ratings-led deposit guidelines include local authorities, government agencies, central banks, money market funds and insurance companies;
- depositors with whom no customer relationship exists are particularly prone to being "rate sensitive", and will also be volatile if the bank's deposit rates fall below the competition;
- deposits from large corporates that possess sophisticated Treasury functions are likely to be more volatile than those from smaller corporates and/or more passive Treasury functions;
- secured funding, such as repo, is among the most resilient in stressed conditions, and for some banks may well be the only source of funds available in a crisis. However, the ability of a bank to continue using repo to fund its balance sheet is highly dependent on the quality of collateral it can supply, and to a lesser extent whether the repo is bilateral or tri-party. Sub-investment grade and structured finance collateral may become difficult to repo in a stressed environment.

Intra-group Funding Risk

In its *PS09/16* document the UK FSA stressed the requirement of funding self-sufficiency. All UK-regulated firms were henceforth required, in principle at least, to demonstrate that they were self-sufficient in funds and not reliant on a parent entity to supply liquidity. In other words, the FSA wished to ensure that the UK banking system did not import a funding crisis that arose in another jurisdiction. Irrespective of whether this is a regulatory requirement or not, the principle of self-sufficiency is an essential ingredient of sustainable banking, and worth following in its own right.

For subsidiary entities, their liquidity strength must reflect the extent of their reliance on funds from the Group head office, and the form of any restrictions that may apply, under any condition, which would prevent them from obtaining Group funds.

Intra-day Liquidity Risk

To assess intra-day liquidity risk a bank will report its net collateral requirement, for cash and derivative exposures, and hence its expected transaction volumes across payment systems. For stress testing purposes the bank would estimate how this amount would change under the various stress scenarios, and the possibility that payments due to it from counterparties may be withheld.

Another part of this risk driver is the bank's credit policy and the process by which it extends intra-day credit to customers that are not members of a payment system. The liquidity risk that arises from such customers not honouring funds payable also needs to be estimated.

Cross-currency Liquidity Risk

This is the same risk driver as mainstream liquidity risk, except that the firm would quantify its funding exposure for each currency that it deals in, split into tenor buckets. In the stress test the bank would estimate how much of the funds' inflow and outflow would be affected in each stress scenario, and how shortfalls in each currency would be covered. This is significant risk for a bank because, unlike funding shortfalls in the home currency, it may not have access to the central bank of the country in whose currency it is suffering a shortage. In the ILAA submission a bank would:

- quantify this risk under stressed scenarios;
- list the financial instruments that it would use to raise funds in the foreign currency;
- name the main counterparties that provide funding in these currencies.

The FX funding exposure should be reported separatedly in liquidity MI.

Retail Funding Risk

Perhaps the most important source of funds for most banks, retail funding would form a significant part of a bank's liquidity reporting. As with wholesale liabilities, a bank will provide its own definition of retail funds, and determine their behavioural characteristics, under BAU and stressed conditions. In general, retail funds are more resilient than wholesale funds.

The FSA requires that the ILAA submission categorises retail liabilities by (i) value, (ii) maturity, (iii) estimated speed of outflow, (iv) product type and (v) the interest rate applied, as well as any other factor that the bank deems relevant. The following generalisations are worth observing:

- depositors with whom the bank does not maintain some sort of long-standing "relationship" are likely to be more volatile than those with whom such a relationship does exist;
- internet banking, and internet depositors, are likely to be the least resilient of any form of retail funds;
- in any country jurisdiction, where the level of a deposit is within that regime's deposit protection scheme it is more likely to remain with the bank than a deposit that is above the protection level;
- instant access and cheque account deposits are likely to be as resilient as term deposits and notice accounts during a stressed period.

Retail funding behavioural characteristics should be observable using statistics on the level and speed of withdrawal of funds.

Off-balance Sheet Liquidity Risk

While categorised as "off-balance sheet", funding liabilities arising out of derivative transactions can create significant liquidity risk for a bank during a market crisis. In assessing its off-balance sheet liquidity risk, a bank should identify all the derivative, contingent and undrawn commitment transactions that create a current or potential funding need for it, and then estimate how this funding requirement would change under the various stress scenarios. These include:

- proprietary derivative trade positions;
- contingent liabilities;

- commitments given to customers that are not drawn down, including liquidity lines and back-up lines of credit;
- letters of guarantee;
- liquidity facilities supporting conduits, asset-backed conduits and securitisation programmes.

Derivative positions are particular risk areas, as the mark-to-market on these positions may suffer markedly in a stressed environment, generating higher collateral requirements for the bank. Undrawn commitments and liquidity lines are more likely to be utilised by customers during a market crisis; hence, the bank's liquidity position will deteriorate accordingly. The purpose of stress tests is to provide an estimate of this deterioration.

Franchise Viability Liquidity Risk

In a crisis situation it might be expected that a bank, suffering from its own liquidity stresses, will withdraw liquidity lines and other forms of loan support for customers. At a more stressed level, it may withhold obligations that are already due. Such actions will have a severe impact on the bank's reputation and standing with customers and within the wider market. The purpose of this stress test is to determine the extent to which a bank can undertake such action without significantly damaging customer relationships. Ultimately, this is a qualitative judgement call.

Marketable Asset Risk

This issue feeds into the requirement for a bank to hold a liquid assets buffer of truly liquid assets. The risk exposure under consideration, and which needs to be stress tested, is the extent to which other assets that are liquid under BAU conditions become illiquid in a stressed environment. Lower rated corporate bonds and structured finance securities are good examples of this. In an extreme environment, as experienced during the last quarter of 2008, even more liquid assets, such as investment-grade-rated bank CDs and FRNs, may become illiquid. Hence, the liquidity risk position of a bank should include the extent to which its liquid assets remain liquid during the various stress scenarios. The bank should quantify:

- the likelihood that a bank can realise its tradeable assets;
- the likelihood of using its tradeable assets as collateral in repo;

- the losses arising in a forced sale scenario of now illiquid assets;
- the impact of all of the above on the bank's business and market position.

Non-marketable Asset Risk

This risk driver combines liquidity risk with credit risk. A bank should estimate the impact of a stressed liquidity environment on its non-tradeable assets, including the expected rise in non-payment of interest and loan default. Customers would also be expected to exercise any repayment options that are built into the loan terms, so the bank should quantify the increase in such an exercise that would occur.

THE BANK LIQUIDITY POLICY STATEMENT

The approach to liquidity risk management at a bank will vary depending on how conservative its liquidity policy is. A bank will be more or less risk averse than other banks, including those in its immediate peer group, in its tolerance to market and credit risk as well as liquidity risk. As such it will apply the basic principles of liquidity discussed in the previous section with more or less enthusiasm, depending on its particular business model and liquidity risk appetite. Irrespective of an individual bank's specific approach to liquidity risk, it is important that this is documented formally in a liquidity policy. This is a policy statement of the bank's "*high-level principles and concepts that provide the framework for liquidity risk measurement, management and control within the bank*".

The liquidity policy statement is designed to be a regularly updated, go-to-working document, as well as part of the bank's governance structure. We provide two templates for a standard policy statement on the Wiley website (see Chapter 19 for details), the first for a small- to medium-sized commercial bank and the second for a larger banking group that operates across multiple jurisdictions. Either would serve as a first-cut and reasonably robust framework for liquidity and funding governance, and so may be adopted by any bank for its own purposes, and modified accordingly as required. In other words, the liquidity policy templates in this book are designed to be standard frameworks that are adaptable for use at most banks. The value-added element of any policy, of course, is the section that details specific tolerances to risk and specific responses to particular market situations. This part of the policy statement is unique to each bank. We provide an example of this part of the policy statement later in this chapter.

Liquidity Policy Statement

We quote directly from page 1 of our own template framework statement (the one designed for a medium-sized commercial bank). This defines liquidity as:

> *. . . the ability to ensure that the bank will always be able to maintain or generate sufficient cash resources to meet its payment obligations in full as they fall due, on acceptable terms, under all market conditions.*

This definition should be adopted at all banks. Formally, the objectives of the liquidity policy are to:

- set out the bank's policy for measuring, monitoring and managing liquidity risk;
- set out how the bank governs its tolerance or appetite for liquidity risk;
- set out arrangements for the approval and review of liquidity policies and procedures;
- document the bank's policy for pricing liquidity risk; this includes setting a logical and appropriate internal funding policy (known variously as internal funds pricing, transfer pricing or term liquidity premium);
- document the bank's policy for managing intra-day liquidity risk;
- document the bank's policy for managing the liquidity risk related to collateral cash flows;
- if applicable, document the relationship of the bank to the group of which it is a part and the impact of this relationship on liquidity risk management;
- set out the bank's policy regarding the diversity required in sources of funds and the policy regarding the bank's access to various markets where such funds are applied;
- document the stress testing to be applied to the liquidity position of the bank;
- document the bank's contingency funding plan and policies regarding the timing, responsibility and extent of its use.

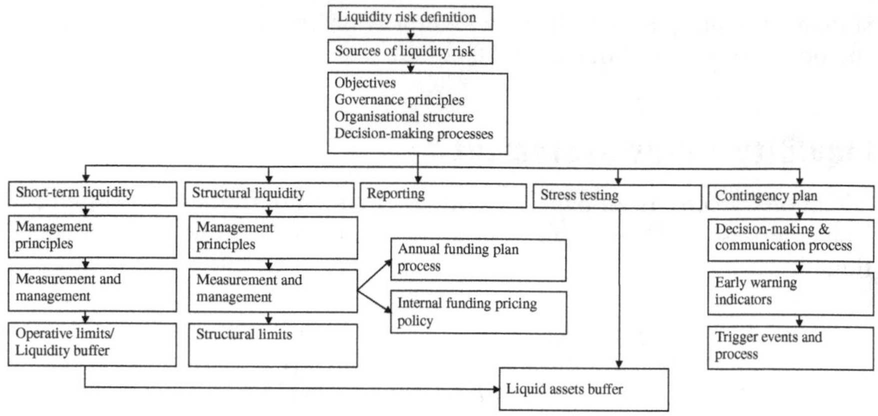

FIGURE 12.2 Liquidity policy structure.

The author's stylised depiction of this is shown at Figure 12.2.

The policy statement should be owned at board level, but disseminated and understood at dealing level. It is important that the statement provides an accurate and accessible picture of the bank's view of liquidity risk, as well as its appetite for liquidity risk. Risk appetite is described in both quantitative and qualitative terms. The former is prescribed by means of liquidity metrics and hardwired limits. As we note in our policy template:

> *In defining the bank's appetite for liquidity risk, the bank considers regulatory requirements, internal constraints, external factors and its key stakeholders' liquidity management objectives.*
>
> *The key stakeholders have been identified as:*
>
> - *shareholders*
> - *regulators*
> - *management.*

Stakeholders may also include customers, employees, the central bank and other persons or entities.

The organisation chart governing the risk management process, which is extracted from the liquidity policy, is shown at Figure 12.3.

Readers are encouraged to review the framework policy statement included as part of this book's supplementary material, available on the

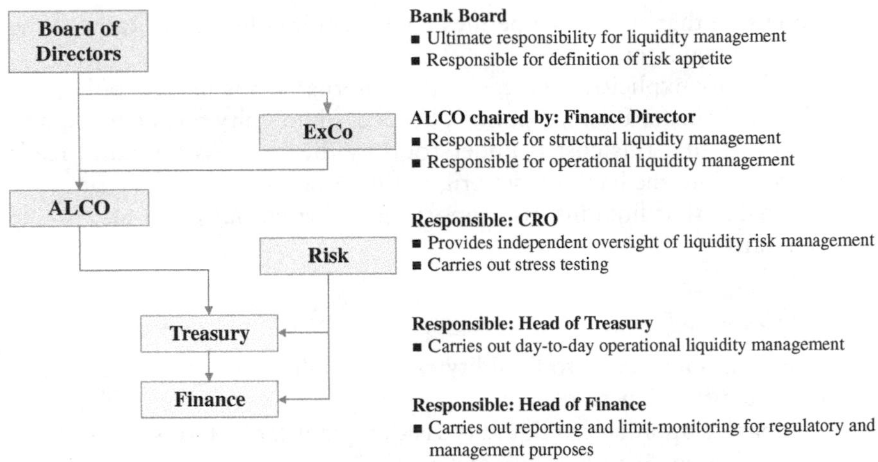

Board of Directors
ExCo
ALCO
Risk
Treasury
Finance
Bank Board
■ Ultimate responsibility for liquidity management
■ Responsible for definition of risk appetite
ALCO chaired by: Finance Director
■ Responsible for structural liquidity management
■ Responsible for operational liquidity management
Responsible: CRO
■ Provides independent oversight of liquidity risk management
■ Carries out stress testing
Responsible: Head of Treasury
■ Carries out day-to-day operational liquidity management
Responsible: Head of Finance
■ Carries out reporting and limit-monitoring for regulatory and management purposes

FIGURE 12.3 Liquidity policy statement: risk management governance structure.

Wiley website, which is supplied as a template in MS Word format. We also include a summary of the statement in PowerPoint format.

Liquidity Policy Standards

Policy statements are often augmented by policy standards, which may be used to keep the statement up-to-date; for example, with new or modified liquidity metric limits.[6] The rationale behind the liquidity policy statement is to describe in explicit terms how the bank's liquidity and funding policy should be applied. In other words, it is a lower level working document, whose primary objective is to set the framework to ensure that the bank's funding arrangements enable all the bank's assets to be funded through to asset maturity. The policy standard may be composed as follows:

Objective

- To ensure that liquidity stress for the bank is maintained within a manageable range to ensure continuous liquidity;
- To ensure that funding arrangements are maintained to enable assets to be funded through to maturity;

6 The metrics may be changed exogenously; for example, by regulatory authority fiat. Liquidity metrics are considered in Chapter 13.

- To ensure that the bank operates to all required liquidity limits of the national regulator;[7]
- To identify explicitly, via the bank's internal funds pricing policy (or "Funds Transfer Pricing" policy), the cost of liquidity for the bank, and to ensure that this cost is understood by the business lines and feeds correctly into the bank's asset origination process;
- To ensure that liquidity risk reporting is carried out to an acceptable standard.

Risk appetite

- The bank's approach to liquidity risk in qualitative terms is set out in the liquidity policy statement;
- The bank's approach to liquidity risk in quantitative terms is set out in the section on target liquidity metrics;
- All assets originated at the bank must be able to be transformed into liquid cash within [ ] days, or if not otherwise be (i) able to be funded from a contingency source; (ii) securitised into an existing programme at short notice; or (iii) eligible as collateral at the central bank;[8]
- Business-as-usual funding sources are limited to retail customer deposits, corporate customer deposits, long-dated capital market funds, and . . .

Target liquidity metrics

- Loan-to-deposit ratio of 100%;
- Liquidity gap for
  - 1-week: [ ] million
  - 1-month: [ ] million
  - 3-month: [ ] million;
- Long-dated funding (defined as over 1-year funds) minimum of 25%;
- Undrawn commitments limit of [ ] million.

7 Note that this objective is implicitly accorded a lower priority, when viewed by its position in the list, than the first objective of ensuring continuous liquidity. This is not to deny its importance – maintenance of all regulatory requirements is vital to ensure that the bank keeps its operating licence – but because simply meeting regulator limits is in itself not sufficient, the bank should apply its own sense and judgement to ensure that it can always source liquidity.

8 The target number of days is for individual bank appetite. A common figure is 90 days.

Liquidity buffer

- The bank must hold a buffer of truly liquid assets that are "unencumbered" and funded with long-dated liabilities;
- The cost of the buffer will be passed to the business lines. The exact share of each cost is a function of the amount of funding required and the extent of the balance sheet liquidity stress that the business line creates.

The liquidity buffer or "liquid asset buffer" is discussed later in this chapter.

Liquidity Policy Statement: Banking Group

The definition of liquidity and the basic ingredients of liquidity risk management are identical for all well-run banks. Additional items in a liquidity policy statement adopted at a banking group will cover the requirements necessary for operation in a multi-jurisdictional environment. We provide a template for a group liquidity policy statement on the Wiley website; the filename is "LiquidityPolicyStatement_BankGroup_Template.docx".

The governance structure for a group entity presents problems in control and monitoring. There is more than one way to organise it, but business bestpractice favours a centralised Group Treasury, tasked with formulating policy and implementing it throughout the group. Group Treasury also undertakes the money market dealing and term funding issuance at the home country location. Overseas subsidiaries and branches will have local Treasury functions to undertake the local currency dealing and liquidity management. For larger banking groups, it is useful to designate the main business centres as "Liquidity Hubs", which oversee and coordinate policy for their regional area. For example, for a UK bank the London office would be the liquidity hub for GBP and EUR, whereas its New York and Tokyo offices would be the hubs for USD and JPY. For a MENA-based bank, its overseas offices may well be the liquidity hubs for the major currencies USD, EUR and GBP.

The ALCO governance structure follows the regional arrangement of the group's Treasury desks, as we see in Figure 12.4.

The policy statement will describe the liquidity and funding policy for the group, which would be followed at all its operating locations. Regional variations are addressed at local ALCO level. The roles and responsibility of the Group ALCO ("GALCO") will include:

- liquidity risk policy
- group limits
- group liquidity buffer
- group funding plan
- pricing of liquidity risk

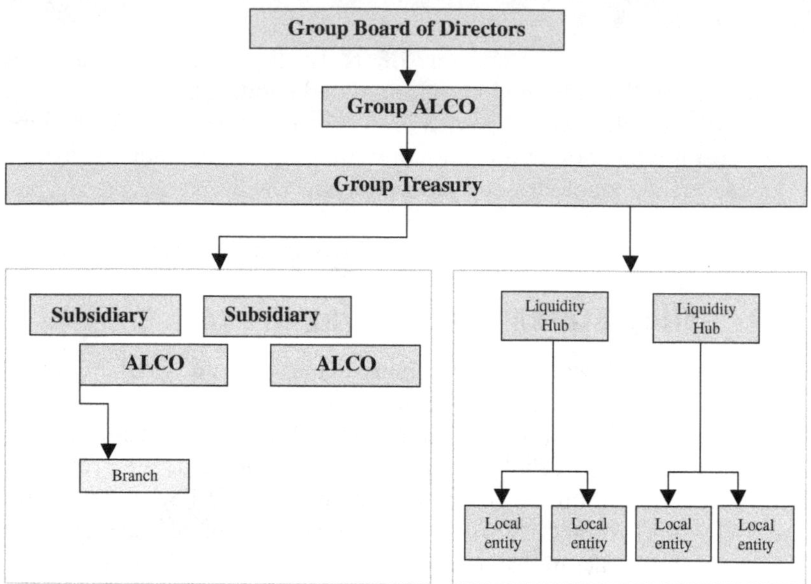

FIGURE 12.4 Bank Group ALCO governance structure.

- policy on internal funds pricing ("Funds Transfer Pricing")
- collateral management
- stress testing
- group contingency funding plan
- group liquidity risk reporting.

The subsidiary legal entity ALCOs will have responsibility for the same areas with respect to their local legal entity and balance sheet, in line with Group policy."Liquidity hub" ALCOs will coordinate policy and governance for their defined liquidity region. The policy statement will describe the escalation procedure for liquidity problems from local money market desks upwards to the GALCO level.

Table 12.1 sets out the responsibilities of the GALCO, subsidiary (local entity) ALCOs and liquidity hub ALCOs.

POLICY ON INTRA-GROUP LENDING

Intra-group lending (IGL) is a significant driver of liquidity risk exposure in a banking group and it is important to address it, at group level, in the liquidity policy statement. IGL policy must adhere to the regulatory

TABLE 12.1 Group organisation ALCO roles.

Roles and responsibilities	
Group Asset & Liability Management Committee (GALCO)	Approving liquidity management framework and liquidity policy for the Group Overseeing the implementation of balance sheet and liquidity management across the Group Monitoring and managing liquidity risk against limits set by the regulator and CRO Setting and reviewing liquidity management targets for each Subsidiary and Liquidity Hub in accordance with Group limits
Subsidiary ALCOs	Ensure compliance with Group Treasury standards and local regulatory requirements Oversee local Asset and Liability Management risks, and monitor the liquidity and funding positions in line with Group risk appetite Act as subject matter experts on local regulations and market developments Highlight any cross-border constraints and local liquidity needs
Liquidity Hub ALCOs	Undertake a coordination role between regional legal entity ALCOs Ensure that Group Treasury policy standards are understood, implemented and embedded globally and locally Provide regional summaries to GALCO

requirements of all the jurisdictions that the bank operates in, and in addition to this a bank must ensure that it puts in place adequate risk management processes to monitor IGL activity. Lending that cuts across legal entities within a group usually impacts a bank's IGL limit, although sometimes transactions across jurisdictions or country borders may also impact the IGL limit.

The regulatory environment will differ according to the jurisdiction one operates in. Among the UK FSA's four statutory objectives is consumer protection, which involves securing the appropriate degree of protection for consumers. This influences its approach to monitoring and controlling IGL exposure for UK banks. The FSA is focused on protecting UK depositors' funds and limiting the maximum risk that a bank can enter into. This drives various regulatory requirements, with the main one in relation to IGLs being to limit concentration risk.

Background

By definition, an IGL is a limit that is recorded to cover any credit equivalent exposure that arises between two connected counterparties and across legal entities within a banking group. A "connected counterparty" is usually an entity in which the group owns or controls a significant share of the equity voting rights, or in which it has significant influence. IGLs cover a number of different exposures, including (but not limited to):

- funding;
- overdrafts;
- operational facilities;
- guarantees;
- letters of credit;
- derivatives.

IGLs do not cover capital items.

Different regulators will control IGLs by various different means. The most common approach is for IGLs to be managed within the large exposure framework. In the UK this imposes a limit of 25% of the lending bank's capital base on the aggregate amount of IGLs. So for a bank capitalised at EUR 500 million, its aggregate group IGL limit would be EUR 125 million. A bank can opt to create an "Integrated Group" framework, in which all the entities in the IG can operate with no limit on exposures and a risk-weighting of 0% applied. In essence, all the members of an IG will operate as part of the same consolidated legal entity. For UK banks, for inclusion within an integrated group the entities must meet the following criteria:

- group employees have sufficient board representation to exercise majority control;
- the entity is included within the scope of consolidation on a full basis within the group;
- the nature of its business is eligible for inclusion within the integrated group (that is, it is an institution, financial holding company, financial institution, asset management company or ancillary services company as defined by the UK FSA);
- it is subject to risk evaluation, measurement and control procedures as determined by the group; and
- there is no current or foreseen material practical or legal impediment to the prompt transfer of surplus capital resources or repayment of liabilities when due from the counterparty to the firm.

Connected counterparties that fail the above criteria are classified as being in the non-integrated group (NIG) and exposures to them, in aggregate, must remain within 25% of the relevant large-exposure capital base.

The tolerance to IGL activity differs among regulators, so within a group it may depend on which entity within the group is exposed; in other words, which entity in the group is generating the exposure. For example, assume two legal entities within a banking group:

- Bank A, domiciled in Country A, regulated by Central Bank of A;
- Bank B, domiciled in Country B, regulated by Central Bank of B.

Assume further that the Country A regulator imposes a limit on IGL capacity that is stricter than that imposed by the Country B regulator. In this case, for business within this group, the impact on the bank overall, for IGL limit purposes, differs whether Bank A is lending to Bank B or Bank B is lending to Bank A.

Policy and Governance

Given regulators' strict approach to the size and extent of IGLs, it is important for a bank to formulate a policy on IGLs, to include limit size and monitoring procedures, into its liquidity policy statement.

Business best-practice requires that an intra-group exposure management policy be articulated and published as part of the statement. This should state that all business line requests for new IGLs must be authorised by:

- an executive member of the borrowing group company;
- Group Treasury and/or Group ALCO (if deemed necessary by the Group Head of Treasury).

It is the responsibility of the originating business line to seek pre-approval for obtaining these authorities ahead of any transaction being written, and for maintaining effective control mechanisms to ensure approved limits are not exceeded.

The above policy must be written into the banking group's liquidity policy statement.

THE LIQUID ASSET BUFFER

If one reviewed a bank balance sheet during the 1950s, and indeed in many cases in the 1990s, it would have been common practice to observe that on the asset side there would be a portfolio of government bonds and bills. That this practice fell into disuse reflects the flawed thinking of the first decade of the 21st century, that market liquidity could be taken for granted and bank "liquidity" portfolios could be held in the form of higher yielding bank bonds (MTNs and FRNs) and corporate bonds rather than government bonds. This would have been attractive from the return on funding point of view, as sovereign debt carries a lower yield than bank debt.

However, one of the clearest lessons of the 2008 financial crisis, in the wake of the Lehman bankruptcy, was that many types of asset considered hitherto to be liquid, such as investment-grade-rated bank FRNs and bank CDs, were not in fact truly liquid; during the last quarter of 2008 many banks found they could not sell or repo such assets. The lesson learned was that a bank's "liquidity portfolio" needed to be truly liquid, and capable of being used to generate liquidity under all market conditions. It should be composed of assets that other banks and cash lenders would accept as collateral in a financial crisis, which suggests only sovereign names. An added benefit of holding only government bonds, both at individual bank and aggregate industry level, is that it forces firms to develop their liquidity risk management ability and run a tighter ship, so to speak, with respect to their liquidity policy. This is because regulators will insist on a higher liquid asset buffer (LAB; also known as a "liquid buffer" or a "liquidity buffer"), as a proportion of total assets, for those firms with structural liquidity problems or following a poor liquidity policy. In other words, the more liquidity risk a bank runs, the larger its LAB should be. As the LAB delivers zero or negligible positive return, firms will want it to be as small as possible; this argues for a sound liquidity regime in the first place.

One idea that we must debunk right now is that a conservative approach to setting and sizing a liquidity buffer is only paramount for the large money-centre or "systemically important" banks. This is dangerous nonsense. Ultimately, every bank has the possibility of being systemically important to the system; would Northern Rock plc have been defined as systemically important prior to 2007? Even if the failure of a small bank does not lead to stress for the wider market, if it has to be bailed out by the taxpayer – like Dunfermline Building Society was in 2008 – then that is undesirable, and so every bank must take the objectives of the LAB very seriously.[9]

The UK FSA defined, on page 45 of its *Policy Statement 09/16*, a liquidity portfolio or LAB to be one composed essentially of high-quality government bonds. It also stated:

> *Our final policy will require all [UK-regulated] firms to maintain a stock of high-quality government bonds, central bank reserves and bonds issued by multi-lateral development banks.*

9 See Chapter 18 for further discussion on the failure of these two firms.

Under FSA *PS 09/16* then, an LAB is mandatory for all UK-regulated banks at all times. The logic of maintaining an LAB is irresistible though, and we would recommend that it be standard practice for all banks, irrespective of the particular business model they follow and irrespective of their operating jurisdiction, because of the obvious risk mitigation impact of maintaining such a portfolio. Because sovereign bonds pay less than other securities, the implication of this change is clear: all else being equal, a bank's RoE will be lower.

A bank should take the basic operating model for its LAB as follows:

- all regulated bank entities are required to hold buffers of liquid assets;
- a LAB comprised of high-quality sovereign and supranational assets will retain both value and liquidity in a stressed environment (the evidence from 2008 is compelling: during October and November that year, the only assets that remained liquid, and acceptable for repo, were G7 sovereign securities. Bank CDs, FRNs, corporate bonds and AAA-rated structured finance securities all became illiquid and/or were no longer acceptable as inter-bank collateral);
- the Central Bank eligibility of the LAB asset is irrelevant, on the basis that in a crisis such eligibility may be extended to illiquid assets, for political reasons. In the UK the FSA has specified which types of asset are eligible for the LAB;
- in theory the LAB cannot be funded in repo, but must be funded by long-term (at least greater than 90-day tenor, and ideally greater than 1-year) funds including retail and wholesale funds. This is to ensure that the bonds can act as a true buffer of liquidity, able to be sold or repo'd if funding availability becomes stressed for the bank;
- the LAB book should be managed as a dedicated portfolio within Treasury, or as an ALCO book. That is, it should be ring-fenced from the rest of the bank's asset portfolio.

The proportion of a bank's balance sheet that should be devoted to the LAB is a function of a number of factors, including the composition of its funding and the structural limitations in its ability to raise liabilities. The bank's regulator will also consider the quality of the firm's risk management, as well as the implications of its stress testing and scenario analysis. A bank Treasury and ALCO should be mindful of two metrics when assessing stress testing results: the funds outflow that arises during (i) a two-week firm-specific and/or market-wide liquidity crisis situation; and (ii) a 3-month market-wide stress scenario. The LAB should be of sufficient size and quality to ensure that the bank survives at least beyond these two time periods.[10] We can see therefore that the size and relative balance sheet share of the LAB will differ by firm.

A requirement of the FSA, and again of sound logic such that it deserves to be adopted in every jurisdiction, is that the LAB be demonstrably liquid. In other words, a bank should use the LAB to generate liquidity, by either selling or repo-ing some of it from time to time. This has three benefits: it demonstrates that the LAB is liquid, it removes the risk that the market will perceive the firm is in any liquidity stress whenever it is selling assets out of the LAB because this will be a routine activity, and it ensures familiarity with the operational processes involved.

EXAMPLE 12.1 GUIDELINES FROM THE COMMITTEE OF EUROPEAN BANKING SUPERVISORS

The Committee of European Banking Supervisors (CEBS; now the European Banking Authority (EBA)) published its *Guidelines on Liquidity Buffers and Survival Periods* on 9 December 2009. We reproduce with permission its key guidelines here, which should be adopted as general principles by all banks.

Certain detailed practice may differ from what CEBS has recommended; for example, the author believes that the suggestion on Guideline 3, that the survival period be "at least one month" is insufficiently rigorous, and that this should be at least three months. We also feel that bank ALCOs should apply a stricter regime than what is implied in Guideline 4. However, as basic principles they should be observed at all banks. The key guidelines are as follows:

Guideline 1 – A liquidity buffer represents available liquidity, covering the additional need for liquidity that may arise over a defined short period of time under stress conditions.

Guideline 2 – Institutions should apply three types of stress scenarios: idiosyncratic, market specific, and a combination of the two. The core of the idiosyncratic stress should assume no rollover of unsecured wholesale funding and some outflows of retail deposits. The market-wide stress should assume a decline in the liquidity value of some assets and deterioration in funding-market conditions.

Guideline 3 – A survival period of at least one month should be applied to determine the overall size of the liquidity buffer under the chosen stress scenarios. Within this period, a shorter time horizon of

10 Referred to as the "survival period" for the bank.

at least one week should also be considered to reflect the need for a higher degree of confidence over the very short term.

Guideline 4 – The liquidity buffer should be composed of cash and core assets that are both central bank eligible and highly liquid in private markets. For the longer end of the buffer, a broader set of liquid assets might be appropriate, subject to the bank demonstrating the ability to generate liquidity from them under stress within the specified period of time.

Guideline 5 – Credit institutions need to manage their stocks of liquid assets to ensure, to the maximum extent possible, that they will be available in times of stress. They should avoid holding large concentrations of particular assets, and there should be no legal, regulatory, or operational impediments to using these assets.

Guideline 6 – The location and size of liquidity buffers within a banking group should adequately reflect [sic] the structure and activities of the group in order to minimise the effects of possible legal, regulatory or operational impediments to using the assets in the buffer.

EXAMPLE 12.2 DEFINING ''LIQUID''

Generally, an asset is considered to be liquid if it can be converted into cash easily and immediately, with no loss of value as a result of its sale. Of course, the level of liquidity changes with market conditions. It is a matter of observable historical record that the only assets that maintain liquidity under any and all market conditions are high-quality sovereign bonds. But given that the liquidity of other types of assets changes according to market conditions, banks should estimate the level of liquidity pertaining at any time, an assessment that will help them determine the level of liquidity of their non-government assets.

The following proxy measures are used to estimate the level of liquidity in a market at any one time:

- bid–offer spread: a wider spread indicates lower liquidity;
- the observed theoretical price error: the difference between the market yield on a bond and its theoretical yield implied by the zero-coupon yield curve or the (CDS) term structure;
- the ratio of repo margin on structured finance securities (ABSs) over the yield spread of the ABS securities themselves.

(*continued*)

Other proxy measures are available. The following features indicate ease of maintaining liquidity in a stressed environment:

- number of market-makers: a small number of market-makers increases the risk of market manipulation as well as the chance that there will be no buyers in a falling market;
- size and depth of the particular asset class: a deep market is more likely to stay liquid in a stressed environment than a market that features small issue sizes, low trading volumes and turnover, and small transaction sizes;
- low market concentration: a diverse population of buyers and sellers is likely to assist in the maintenance of liquidity for any particular asset class.

Numerous studies have been undertaken on measuring market liquidity, and bankers should familiarise themselves with the academic literature.[11]

EXAMPLE 12.3 LIQUIDITY VALUE OF LIABILITIES

Banks fund their balance sheet using a variety of liability types. The liquidity value of each type is different, and in some cases the behavioural aspect of a certain type of liability renders it a more stable and long-term form of funding than would be implied by its contractual maturity. For this reason, regulators review liquidity management principles on both a contractual and behavioural basis. When supplying liquidity metrics to the regulator, banks will include historical analysis of certain types of liabilities such as retail current accounts (checking accounts) that will seek to demonstrate "stickiness". Retail current accounts are the best example of this: they are contractually payable on demand, so therefore of 1-day maturity as liquidity, but observation of their behaviour reveals that typically customers maintain large stable balances in such accounts over a long time period. Therefore it is in order to treat a proportion of the amount of such liabilities as term funding (the exact amount and tenor is a

11 Worthwhile references in this field include Amihud and Mendelson (1986), Fleming (2001), Fleming and Remonola (1999), and Fleming and Sarkar (1999). The author humbly adds his four published papers on the subject, see Choudhry (2009a), (2009b), (2010) and (2011).

function of the what the historical statistical behaviour of the accounts demonstrate).

On this basis it is apparent that some forms of liabilities have greater term liquidity value for a bank than others. At one end of the scale are retail current accounts; at the other are short-term unsecured wholesale liabilities, sourced in the inter-bank market, which have much more volatile characteristics in stressed market conditions and therefore are less valuable for liquidity management purposes.

Table 12.2 illustrates the author's hierarchy of value of different types of liability. It suggests that a bank should seek to maximise funding based on higher liquidity value liabilities, and minimise its reliance on wholesale inter-bank funding. This is a business best-practice principle of liquidity risk management.

TABLE 12.2 Liabilities value as liquidity.

Retail current accounts
Retail deposit accounts
Corporate cash flow accounts / call accounts
Retail savings accounts
Retail fixed term deposits
Private bank deposits
Corporate savings accounts
Corporate fixed term deposits
Private-placement MTNs
Wholesale market fixed term deposits
Money market term funding (CD/CP)
Money market deposits / inter-bank deposits

Composition and Size of LAB

It is self-evident that the liquid buffer should be comprised of cash and very liquid assets. If the latter, these must be able to be sold or repo'd easily in stressed situations, and be of the kind that will not be impacted by large downward valuations akin to a "fire sale". They must also be credit risk-free, and not correlated in performance terms with the banking sector. However, opinions differ as to what constitutes truly "liquid" securities. The experience of the last quarter of 2008 suggests that in an extreme stress situation only high-quality sovereign securities remain liquid; however, most regulators will allow other types of securities into a LAB. The guideline from CEBS has suggested a pool of assets "that are both central bank eligible and highly liquid in private markets". We suggest that it is not conservative enough to include the central bank eligibility criteria, unless these are criteria that are in place during a benign market environment; in the aftermath of the post-Lehman crisis, central banks relaxed their eligibility rules to include pools of quite illiquid assets. CEBS has recognised this, as it also states that "reference to central bank eligibility . . . excludes emergency facilities that may be offered by central banks in stressed times".[12]

The UK FSA rules stipulate that the LAB must be of sufficient quality to ensure liquidity during a 14-day and 90-day period of stressed markets (and funding cash outflow). However, the Basel Committee on Banking Supervision (BCBS) stipulates a less stringent 30-day stress period. As a driver of LAB composition, it can be argued though that the 90-day requirement can be met with assets other than sovereign bonds, such as agency securities and covered bonds. This is debateable. We recommend that the LAB must be composed of cash and high-quality sovereign assets and nothing else, because one can never know how severe, and long-lasting, a future liquidity crisis will be. Others will have a different opinion. If anything other than sovereign bonds are held in the LAB, consideration must be given to diversifying the portfolio, an issue that does not arise with government bonds. This is because a concentrated portfolio of (say) corporate bonds may give rise to further illiquidity stresses for the bank if an attempt is made to liquidate it quickly. One thing that it would be true to say is that a market-wide liquidity or funding crisis can be expected to last longer than 30 days.

A banking group entity that operates across multiple jurisdictions will need to establish multiple LABs, in observation of the principle of funding self-sufficiency for all overseas subsidiaries. Thus, overseas arms of a banking group, which will conduct business in the local currency, will need to maintain a LAB of bonds denominated in that currency. This is especially important because during a crisis individual country authorities may impose restrictions on the movement of foreign currency and liquidity across borders, so it is crucial that the local subsidiary of a bank maintains liquidity reserves to cover all its risk in the local jurisdiction.

Because many eligible bonds held in a LAB would pay lower than Libor, in other words a sub-Libor rate when held as an asset swap, banks may be inclined to hold longer dated bonds, funded with shorter dated liabilities, and thus generate a positive funding carry so as not to lose money on the portfolio. This assumes of course a positive-sloping yield curve environment. By definition the LAB is designed to be an instantly liquid book, so would not be accounted for in a hold-to-maturity (HTM) portfolio. (Although there is a case to be made to the regulator that assets held

12 CEBS 2009.

in an HTM book, and funded with long term liabilities (> 1-year), and which are occasionally repo'd out for short periods, should be considered for the LAB, provided they are of sufficient credit quality.) Being held in a trading book, the LAB will be marked-to-market, and longer dated bonds will generate significant interest-rate risk. This will need to be hedged. But in many cases the LAB will be run at a net funding loss, particularly where the term liabilities used to fund it are greater than 1-year in maturity. This can be taken to be a cost of liquidity, and this cost would be borne by the bank's business lines.

In general, irrespective of the regulatory jurisdiction of a bank, the LAB portfolio cannot be funded in repo. This would render the buffer pointless, because its assets would not be "unencumbered" and not generate funds when they were sold. The liquidity buffer must be funded using unsecured funds, retail deposits or other funds, and these must be term funds. The minimum term funding required will depend on the requirement of the bank's individual regulator; however, in principle the buffer should be funded with liabilities of at least a 90-day maturity. In the UK the FSA requires certain large banks to fund the LAB with liabilities of at least 12-months maturity; in other words, with truly long-dated funds.

Securities in the LAB

We have already suggested that a bank's LAB should be composed of cash and high-quality sovereign securities only. For a conventional commercial bank that operates within its home country only, this suggests that the LAB would hold its own government bonds only. As a bank expands into business lines in other currencies, this suggests an expansion into other country sovereign bonds. The UK FSA suggests that the LAB for most banks in Western jurisdictions would be expected to be comprised of the following (quoted from the FSA's *PS09/16*):

> *Highly liquid, high-quality government debt instruments such as gilts, plus bonds rated at least Aa3 issued by the countries of the European Economic Area (EEA), Canada, Japan, Switzerland and the United States; and*
>
> *Reserves held with the Bank of England's reserve scheme and with the central banks of the U.S., the EEA, Switzerland, Canada and Japan.*
>
> *Bonds issued by designated multilateral development banks including:*
>
> *African Development Bank*
> *Asian Development Bank*

Council of Europe Development Bank
European Bank for Reconstruction and Development
European Investment Bank
Inter-American Development Bank
International Bank for Reconstruction and Development
International Finance Corporation
Islamic Development Bank
Nordic Investment Bank

To this list we would add the sovereign bonds of other highly rated government borrowers, such as Singapore, Hong Kong and Taiwan.

That the eligible list may be wide does not necessarily suggest that a bank can hold any of the names on the list. The LAB should only consist of assets that the firm has a "natural axe" in; that is, the bank operates in these names and currencies in the normal course of business. So a domestic bank with most or all of its operations in the home country would not be expected to place foreign-currency sovereign assets in its LAB, whereas a bank with multinational business lines may well do so.

In subsequent pronouncements the UK FSA has split the required composition of the LAB into two tiers of allowable securities. These are as follows:

Level 1: sovereign securities, as described previously;

Level 2: agency securities (such as Fannie Mae and Freddie Mac); corporate bonds rated AA–/Aa3; covered bonds.

Level 2 securities can comprise a maximum 40% of the total size of the LAB, and will attract a 15% haircut. It remains to be seen if this relaxation of the rules will help to preserve a liquid market during a crisis.

The remaining question that arises is whether a reverse repo position should be considered as eligible for inclusion in the LAB. In other words, the bank does not own the asset outright but has repo'd it in. This is generally acceptable to regulators provided that:

- the asset is otherwise unencumbered;
- legal title is transferred for the time of the repo (which is the case if it is traded under the GMRA);
- the asset is of acceptable credit quality.

We should note however that certain bank internal Treasury policies do not allow reverse repos to count in the LAB, so one should question whether doing so is business best-practice.

Calculating LAB Portfolio Size

The size of the liquidity buffer is a key point. The exact proportion of a bank's balance sheet that has to be held as a LAB is a function of the type of institution it is and the structure of its funding. For a vanilla commercial bank in the UK, the basic FSA calculation methodology suggests that a bank will have to hold the aggregate total of its 3-month funding base as a liquid buffer. In other words, the more long-term funds a bank has, the smaller its buffer can be. One example calculation stipulated by the FSA on how much of a buffer a bank needs to hold is a function of how much shorter dated (0–90 day) wholesale funding a bank has. The higher this amount, the bigger the size of the LAB. In essence then, the LAB will be a function of the bank's 90-day stressed funding cash outflow value. To reduce the size of the LAB therefore, a bank needs to put in place a greater amount of long-term and/or retail liabilities. This is the key point.

Setting the Framework

Before calculating the adequate size for a LAB, it is necessary to define the survival period. Most banks will have this dictated to them by the regulator; we recommend two weeks and three months. Once that is set, banks will need to ensure that their systems are able to produce cash-flow projections of expected cash inflows and outflows, broken down by time bucket, financial instrument and business lines. We provide a simple illustration using an Excel spreadsheet later in this section. At the same time, the cash flow projections need to be accompanied by a description of the alternative funding sources, or "counterbalancing capacity", that are available to meet needs suggested by the cash flow projection. This will include the LAB. It is important that for each maturity time bucket where the cash flow projection suggests a funding shortage, the bank has in place a contingency to cover this shortfall.

Elsewhere in this chapter we discuss the need for a liquidity contingency funding plan. The LAB is not part of this plan, or, if it is, it is the first resort in the event of liquidity stress. The liquid buffer is the first port of call for the bank's counterbalancing capacity, and its use to raise liquidity should not be viewed as a sign of serious stress for the bank. The buffer exists to enable it to continue BAU operations during a time of firm-specific or market-wide stress. Thus, we define it as the excess liquidity available to a bank in the event of any kind of liquidity stress. That is why its size is a function of a bank's funding gap, under BAU as well as stressed conditions, for a set minimum period of time (say, three months).

LAB Size Principles

Liquidity risk is both firm-specific and market-wide. Of course a bank that runs a conservative liquidity regime has a greater chance of surviving both idiosyncratic and market stresses, so ultimately every bank must set its liquidity risk management to its own specific needs and business model. The bank should ensure that all sources of liquidity risk are covered within its risk management regime, including off-balance sheet commitments such as derivative trade collateral requirements, and undrawn commitments such as liquidity funding lines.

Stress tests results are a prime driver of the size of the LAB.[13] As we discuss elsewhere, this is of three types: firm-specific, market-wide and a combination of both. The largest cash flow gap in the scenarios tested dictates what the size of the LAB is. This would be the most conservative approach.

Included in the stress testing is the cash flow projection of the short and long survival periods, which we recommend are set at two weeks and three months. The size of the LAB is of course dictated by the long survival period; however, the two values can assist in the decision as to which assets to place in the LAB. The two-week survival period requirement number must be met by either cash and/or the most liquid securities – those that can be turned into cash within 1 day. The balance of the LAB requirement can, in theory at least, be placed in securities that can be liquidated within a slightly longer time period.

The analysis of cash inflow and outflow should be taken to a granular level, so that when determining cash flows and counterbalancing capacity a bank identifies contractual and behavioural flows, and applies a conservative assumption of liabilities behaviour when estimating its liquidity position. When assessing retail liabilities, however, it is reasonable to use the historical pattern of their behaviour; retail funds are generally much more "sticky" than wholesale or corporate liabilities, and most regulators allow banks to treat a percentage of such funds as being longer dated than their actual contractual maturity.[14]

---

13 Stress testing was discussed in Chapter 11.

14 The best example of this concerns retail customer call, deposit and cheque accounts, which have an instant access feature and so are contractually treated as 1-day funds, but which are in practice longer dated funds because retail customers tend to keep the balance in these accounts fairly stable over time. For example, if a bank has observed that the amount of funds kept in retail call accounts has stayed at (say) around EUR 500 million over the last five years, with a withdrawal volatility of no more than 20% from year to year, there is a case for treating 50% of these funds as 5-year funds, and the balance as 1-day liabilities. Different regulators will have differing treatments allowable for such funds.

When assessing cash flows, the bank calculates the sum of expected outflows and subtracts this from the sum of expected inflows, for each maturity bucket. Where this is a negative number – a funding gap – this amount needs to be covered by counterbalancing capacity. In the first instance this can be funds available from other time periods, if longer dated, or the LAB. A cumulative estimation of this number, up to the desired stress period, is the first-cut minimum size of the LAB. All else being equal, we see then that to minimise the size of the LAB one has to minimise the funding gap at the short-end; that is, maximise the longer dated funding.

A bank should run two cash flow projections, the first under stable BAU conditions and the second under stressed scenarios, which is used for liquidity risk management purposes. What is important is that the counterbalancing capacity be of sufficient size to enable the bank to continue *as a going concern* throughout the stress period; in other words, the LAB does not exist to enable the bank to survive during a period of stress, but to continue undertaking business. This is a subtle, but important feature of the point of maintaining a LAB. It is also another reason why using the LAB to generate liquidity should not be viewed automatically as a negative sign or crisis measure: the LAB exists to maintain liquidity access for a bank, so using it thus is not a sign of a bank in trouble. Its size, however, must facilitate a bank having access to excess liquidity over and above a BAU scenario over short-, medium- and long-term time periods.

Sample LAB Size Calculation

We illustrate the calculation of the required size of the liquidity buffer for a hypothetical commercial bank operating in the UK jurisdiction.

Table 12.3 is the basic overview liquidity gap (or "mismatch") report for the bank, showing all cash inflows and outflows broken down by maturity bucket. The remaining tables in this section all draw their data from the numbers in this report.

Table 12.4 is the wholesale funding report, showing the funding gap for each day in the next three months. This is the period for which the UK FSA requires banks to calculate a stressed cash outflow exercise in. Time buckets in this report are all for one day only, because the point here is to show the net mismatch per day. This is shown in the row "Net Mismatch per Bucket"; note that a positive number in this row indicates a funding requirement. Also note that the "adjustments" row is zero, because the bank has decided to ignore the current liquid assets buffer of FRNS and corporate bonds for liquidity purposes.

Further down the table we see the value for Cumulative Mismatch. It is the values in this row that drives the first element of the LAB calculation.

TABLE 12.3 Bank liquidity gap report.

	Sight	2–8 Days	9 Days – 1 Month	1–3 Months
Inflows				
Corporate – Overdraft	(31,915,364)	0	0	0
Corporate – Time Loan	(7,192,493)	(56,771,245)	(94,580,406)	(82,042,489)
Government – Overdraft	(5,411)	0	0	0
Government – Time Loan	0	(9,021,603)	0	(763,887)
Inter-bank – Overdraft	(88,714,071)	0	0	0
Inter-bank – Time Loan	(376,808,549)	(125,249,339)	(62,096,675)	(79,813,542)
Inter-bank – Repo	0	0	0	0
Inter-bank – Bonds, FRNs and CDs	0	(7,000,000)	(20,000,000)	0
Inter Group – Overdraft	(12,247,148)	0	0	0
Inter Group – Time Loan	(30,933,810)	(220,620,674)	(236,196,270)	(182,348,632)
Retail – Overdraft	(6,439,936)	0	0	0
Retail – Time Loan	(1,712,304)	(7,359,975)	(2,139)	(4,440,013)
Cash and Equivalents	(2,044,099)	0	0	0
Provision on Loan	0	0	0	0
Fixed Assets	0	0	0	0
Fiscal Assets	0	0	0	0
TOTAL INFLOWS	(558,013,186)	(426,022,835)	(412,875,489)	(349,408,564)
Outflows	**Sight**	**2–8 Days**	**9 Days – 1 Month**	**1–3 Months**
Corporate – Current Account	172,900,240	0	0	43,225,060
Corporate – Time Deposit	5,537,500	54,545,768	123,381,822	264,019,052
Goverment – Current Account	3,422,184	0	0	0
Government – Time Deposit	0	24,855,818	163,544,250	262,431,001
Inter-bank – Current Account	181,352,881	0	0	0
Inter-bank – Time Deposit	29,833,694	233,241,549	138,109,601	118,609,083
Inter-bank – Repo	0	0	0	0
Inter-Group – Current Account	41,616,377	0	0	0
Inter-Group – Time Deposit	193,536,183	231,246,688	319,337,144	318,936,671
Retail – Current Account	73,816,897	0	0	18,454,224
Retail – Time Deposit	7,042,496	149,575,530	93,059,664	380,487,353
Capital	0	0	0	0
Cash and Equivalents	432,703	0	0	0
Fiscal Liabilities	0	0	0	0
TOTAL OUTFLOWS	709,491,154	693,465,353	837,432,481	1,406,162,444
Behavioural Adjustments/Stress	401,516,652		(262,971,318)	324,650,603
Net Mismatch per Bucket	151,477,969	267,442,518	424,556,992	1,056,753,880
Adjustments	**Sight**	**Sight – 8 Days**	**Sight – 1 Month**	**Sight – 3 Months**
Bonds and FRNs, Non-Gov, LT 6 mo	(127,353,464)	(127,353,464)	(127,353,464)	(127,353,464)
Bonds and FRNs, Non-Gov, LT 5 yr	(687,544,654)	(687,544,654)	(687,544,654)	(687,544,654)
Bonds and FRNs, Non-Gov, GT 5 yr	(34,903,114)	(34,903,114)	(34,903,114)	(34,903,114)
Marketable Securities (CDs)	(213,750,000)	(213,750,000)	(213,750,000)	(213,750,000)
Repos	0	0	0	0
Undrawn Commitments	43,622,745	43,622,745	43,622,745	43,622,745
TOTAL ADJUSTMENTS	(1,019,928,488)	(1,019,928,488)	(1,019,928,488)	(1,019,928,488)
Cumulative Mismatch	**Sight**	**Sight - 8 Days**	**Sight - 1 Month**	**Sight – 3 Months**
	(868,450,519)	(601,008,001)	(176,451,009)	880,302,871
Liquidity Ratio	21.29%	14.74%	4.33%	–21.59%
Behavioural Adjustments/Stress Variance	–9.85%	0.00%	6.45%	–7.96%
Internal Limit	0.00%	3.00%	–3.00%	0.00%
Regulatory Limit	0.00%	0.00%	–5.00%	0.00%

3–6 Months	6 Months – 1 Year	1–3 Years	3–5 Years	5 Years and over	Total
0	0	0	0	0	(31,915,364)
(37,516,809)	(51,161,273)	(629,899,791)	(413,977,499)	(528,524,834)	(1,901,666,840)
0	0	0	0	0	(5,411)
(1,563,492)	0	(9,309,372)	(36,507,391)	(40,029,974)	(97,195,719)
0	0	0	0	0	(88,714,071)
(26,606,882)	(301,614)	(3,352,965)	0	0	(674,229,566)
0	0	0	0	0	0
0	0	0	0	0	(27,000,000)
0	0	0	0	0	(12,247,148)
(27,241,062)	(6,008,483)	(183,803)	(85,485)	0	(703,618,218)
0	0	0	0	0	(6,439,936)
(1,365)	(2,149,451)	(22,193,332)	(472,370)	(1,213,271)	(39,544,221)
0	0	0	0	0	(2,044,099)
0	0	0	0	67,109,678	67,109,678
0	0	0	0	(62,807,479)	(62,807,479)
0	0	0	0	(8,538,945)	(8,538,945)
(92,929,610)	(59,620,821)	(664,939,263)	(451,042,745)	(574,004,825)	(3,588,857,339)
3–6 Months	**6 Months – 1 Year**	**1–3 Years**	**3–5 Years**	**5 Years and over**	**Total**
0	0	0	0	0	216,125,300
27,328,802	682,297	0	0	0	475,495,242
0	0	0	0	0	3,422,184
12,719,064	15,689,450	1,121,667	0	0	480,361,250
0	0	0	0	0	181,352,881
88,486,924	0	0	0	0	608,280,851
0	0	0	0	0	0
0	0	0	0	0	41,616,377
78,671,707	12,208,430	0	0	0	1,153,936,824
0	0	0	0	0	92,271,122
136,161,861	49,080,569	2,005,951	0	0	817,413,424
0	0	0	0	0	0
0	0	0	0	0	432,703
0	0	0	0	7,526,197	7,526,197
343,368,359	77,660,747	3,127,618	0	7,526,197	4,078,234,353
93,937,391	(126,863)	(97,875,693)		(8,950,113)	450,180,659
250,438,748	18,039,926	(661,811,646)	(451,042,745)	(566,478,628)	489,377,014
Sight – 6 Months	**Sight – 1 Year**	**Sight – 3 Years**	**Sight – 5 Years**	**Sight – 5 Years**	**Total**
(127,353,464)	(127,353,464)	(127,353,464)	(127,353,464)	(127,353,464)	(1,146,181,178)
(687,544,654)	(687,544,654)	(687,544,654)	(687,544,654)	(687,544,654)	(6,187,901,883)
(34,903,114)	(34,903,114)	(34,903,114)	(34,903,114)	(34,903,114)	(314,128,030)
(213,750,000)	(213,750,000)	(213,750,000)	(213,750,000)	(213,750,000)	(1,923,750,000)
0	0	0	0	0	0
43,622,745	43,622,745	43,622,745	43,622,745	43,622,745	392,604,702
(1,019,928,488)	(1,019,928,488)	(1,019,928,488)	(1,019,928,488)	(1,019,928,488)	(9,179,356,389)
Sight – 6 Months	**Sight – 1 Year**	**Sight – 3 Years**	**Sight – 5 Years**	**Sight – 5 Years**	
1,130,741,620	1,148,781,546	486,969,900	35,927,155	(530,551,474)	
−27.73%	−28.17%	−11.94%	−0.88%	13.01%	
−2.30%	0.00%	2.40%	0.00%	0.22%	
0.00%	0.00%	0.00%	0.00%	0.00%	
0.00%	0.00%	0.00%	0.00%	0.00%	

We do not show the whole report here, because 90 columns would not fit on the page; instead the truncated version that is Table 12.4 shows days 1–3 and then days 86–91. The maximum value in the Cumulative Mismatch row is then fed through into the LAB calculation; we see that in this example it is EUR 1,240,231,393, and this is shown in Figure 12.5.

Table 12.5 is the retail funding element of the LAB calculation. For this element, the regulator recognises the "stickiness" of retail deposits, so the LAB element is simply 10% of the total liabilities base, which in the example is EUR 90,968,455. This is the second number in Figure 12.5.

Figure 12.5 is the LAB size calculation. The third element is the size of all customer ("retail") undrawn commitments, such as liquidity lines or revolving credit facilities that are as yet unused. This is taken from the summary liquidity report shown at Table 12.3, and is EUR 43,622,745. The total required LAB in this case is therefore EUR 1.375 billion, shown in Figure 12.5.

We see that in this example the basic LAB calculation is a function of the short-dated cash flow mismatch of a bank, and not of the total size of the balance sheet assets. In practice, in the UK jurisdiction and under Basel III, the size of the LAB is driven by the stress-tested cash outflow value in the next 90 (FSA) or 30 (Basel III) days.

Note that the full Excel spreadsheet that was used to provide these figures, and including the cell formulae, is supplied as supplementary material to this book on the Wiley website, under the filename "LiquidAssetBuffer_CalculationOfSize_WorkedExample.xls".

Allocating the LAB Cost

Maintaining an LAB is in some ways conceptually similar to levying a tax on the bank's business, because it takes up space on the balance sheet that would otherwise be used to hold higher paying assets. The need to hold a LAB is driven by the business itself of course, therefore the cost of running the LAB – the cost of doing business, in effect – must be borne by all the business lines of the bank. Although it is the Treasury department of a bank that usually manages the LAB, its costs (or opportunity costs) should be recharged out, on a pro-rata basis, to all the business lines.[15]

In Chapter 15 we discuss the principles of internal funds pricing in a bank. The recharge costs for the LAB operate on a similar basis. The LAB is held as a contingency to generate liquidity should the bank suffer a funding crisis, either specific to itself or within a market-wide stress event. The cost

15 Sometimes the LAB can be held in an ALCO book, as opposed to a book in Treasury, and its charge held centrally, rather than passed on via the cost allocation process we describe here. This is appropriate for many banks.

TABLE 12.4 Wholesale funding report, daily cash flow gap 0–90 days.

	Day 1	Day 2	Day 3	Day 86	Day 87	Day 88	Day 89	Day 90	Day 91	LIABILITIES OVER 90 DAYS (days 91 onwards)	
	[Time Bucket 1]	[Time Bucket 2]	[Time Bucket 3]	[Time Bucket 86]	[Time Bucket 87]	[Time Bucket 88]	[Time Bucket 89]	[Time Bucket 90]	[Time Bucket 91]	[Time Bucket 92]	Total
Inflows – ASSETS											
Corporate – Overdraft	(31,915,364)	0	0	0	0	0	0	0	0	0	(31,915,364)
Corporate – Time Loan	(117,307,751)	(5,607,569)	(2,811,342)	(977,722)	0	0	0	0	(802,091)	(1,470,054,722)	(1,820,756,612)
Government – Overdraft	(5,411)	0	0	0	0	0	0	0	0	0	(5,411)
Government – Time Loan	0	(9,017,853)	0	0	0	0	0	0	0	(87,410,229)	(97,195,719)
Inter-bank – Overdraft	(88,714,071)	0	0	0	0	0	0	0	0	0	(88,714,071)
Inter-bank – Time Loan	(376,808,549)	(6,215,053)	(35,000,000)	0	(216,358)	(25,000,000)	0	0	(3,068,403)	(111,171,688)	(755,139,793)
Inter-bank – Repo	0	0	0	0	0	0	0	0	0	0	0
Inter-bank – Bonds, FRNs and CDs	0	0	0	0	0	0	0	0	0	0	0
Inter-Group – Overdraft	(12,247,148)	0	0	0	0	0	0	0	0	0	(12,247,148)
Inter-Group – Time Loan	(30,942,348)	(72,287,365)	(74,438,479)	(6,686,503)	(4,363,134)	0	0	0	(1,328,981)	(33,518,833)	(703,626,757)
TOTAL INFLOWS	(657,940,643)	(93,127,840)	(112,249,821)	(7,664,225)	(4,579,492)	(25,000,000)	0	0	(5,199,475)	(1,702,155,472)	(3,509,600,876)
		(751,068,483)	(863,318,304)	(1,772,666,436)	(1,777,245,928)	(1,802,245,928)	(1,802,245,928)	(1,802,245,928)	(1,807,445,403)	(3,509,600,876)	
Outflows LIABILITIES	[Time Bucket 1]	[Time Bucket 2]	[Time Bucket 3]	[Time Bucket 86]	[Time Bucket 87]	[Time Bucket 88]	[Time Bucket 89]	[Time Bucket 90]	[Time Bucket 91]	[Time Bucket 92]	Total
Corporate – Current Account	216,125,300	0	0	0	0	0	0	0	0	0	216,125,300
Corporate – Time Deposit	13,226,281	14,131,656	217,233	423,981	104,829	2,738,543	0	0	672,920	20,322,318	475,495,242
Goverment – Current Account	3,422,184	0	0	0	0	0	0	0	0	0	3,422,184
Government – Time Deposit	0	12,060,312	3,736,471	29,420,514	0	0	0	0	0	29,530,181	480,361,250
Inter-bank – Current Account	181,352,881	0	0	0	0	0	0	0	0	0	181,352,881
Inter-bank – Time Deposit	116,082,304	11,003,097	53,113,558	1,093,673	0	0	0	0	0	2,238,314	608,280,851
Inter-bank – Repo	0	0	0	0	0	0	0	0	0	0	0
Inter-Group – Current Account	41,616,377	0	0	0	0	0	0	0	0	0	41,616,377
Inter-Group – Time Deposit	193,536,183	66,370,927	42,713,587	1,761,542	0	546,837	0	0	659,000	90,880,138	1,153,936,824
TOTAL OUTFLOWS	765,361,510	103,565,992	99,780,849	32,699,310	104,829	3,285,379	0	0	1,331,920	142,970,950	3,160,590,908
		868,927,502	968,708,351	3,012,897,829	3,013,002,657	3,016,288,037	3,016,288,037	3,016,288,037	3,017,619,957	3,160,590,908	

(continued)

TABLE 12.4 *(Continued)*

	Day 1	Day 2	Day 3	Day 86	Day 87	Day 88	Day 89	Day 90	Day 91	LIABILITIES OVER 90 DAYS (days 91 onwards)	
	[Time Bucket 1]	[Time Bucket 2]	[Time Bucket 3]	[Time Bucket 86]	[Time Bucket 87]	[Time Bucket 88]	[Time Bucket 89]	[Time Bucket 90]	[Time Bucket 91]	[Time Bucket 92]	Total
Behavioural Adjustments/Stress											OK
Net Mismatch per Bucket [+VE MEANS A FUNDING REQUIREMENT]	107,420,868	10,438,152	(12,468,972)	25,035,585	(4,474,663)	(21,714,621)	0	0	(3,867,555)	(1,559,184,522)	(349,009,968)
Adjustments											Total
Bonds and FRNs, Non-Gov, LT 6 mo	0	0	0	0	0	0	0	0	0	0	0
Bonds and FRNs, Non-Gov, LT 5 yr	0	0	0	0	0	0	0	0	0	0	0
Bonds and FRNs, Non-Gov, GT 5 yr	0	0	0	0	0	0	0	0	0	0	0
Marketable Securities (CDs)	0	0	0	0	0	0	0	0	0	0	0
Repos	0	0	0	0	0	0	0	0	0	0	0
Unutilised Commitments	0	0	0	0	0	0	0	0	0	0	0
TOTAL ADJUSTMENTS	0	0	0	0	0	0	0	0	0	0	0
Cumulative Mismatch [PER DAY]	107,420,868	117,859,020	105,390,048	1,240,231,393	1,235,756,729	1,214,042,109	1,214,042,109	1,214,042,109	1,210,174,554	(349,009,968) 1,240,231,393	The peak number during days 0–91 (Used as calculation number)

TABLE 12.5 Retail funding report, daily cash flow gap 0–90 days.

Inflows	**[Time Bucket 1]**	**[Time Bucket 2]**	**[Time Bucket 3]**	**[Time Bucket 90]**	**[Time Bucket 91]**	**[Time Bucket 92]**	**Total**	
Retail – Overdraft	(6,439,936)	0	0	0	0	0	(6,439,936)	
Retail – Time Loan	(1,839,168)	(7,351,044)	0	0	0	(25,902,925)	(39,544,221)	
TOTAL INFLOWS	(8,279,103)	(7,351,044)	0	0	0	(25,902,925)	(45,984,156)	
Outflows	**[Time Bucket 1]**	**[Time Bucket 2]**	**[Time Bucket 3]**	**[Time Bucket 90]**	**[Time Bucket 91]**	**[Time Bucket 92]**	**Total**	
Retail – Current Account	92,271,122	0	0	0	0	0	92,271,122	
Retail – Time Deposit	7,042,496	23,928,920	17,504,749	0	13,045,058	187,248,381	817,413,424	
TOTAL OUTFLOWS	**99,313,617**	**23,928,920**	**17,504,749**	**0**	**13,045,058**	**187,248,381**	**909,684,546**	**90,968,455** This value is 10% of the entire retail funding book (It is not a cash flow gap value)
Net Mismatch per Bucket	**91,034,514**	**16,577,876**	**17,504,749**	**0**	**13,045,058**	**161,345,456**	**863,700,389**	
Adjustments							Total	
Bonds and FRNs, Non-Gov, LT 6 mo	0	0	0	0	0	0	0	
Bonds and FRNs, Non-Gov, LT 5 yr	0	0	0	0	0	0	0	
Bonds and FRNs, Non-Gov, GT 5 yr	0	0	0	0	0	0	0	
Marketable Securities (CDs)	0	0	0	0	0	0	0	
Repos	0	0	0	0	0	0	0	
Unutilised Commitments	0	0	0	0	0	0	0	
TOTAL ADJUSTMENTS	0	0	0	0	0	0	0	
Cumulative Mismatch	91,034,514	107,612,389	125,117,139	689,309,876	702,354,934	863,700,389		

Inputs to LAB size calculation

Wholesale component	1,240,231,393	←	This is the wholesale funding maximum cumulative 90-day gap (see Table 12.4)
Retail component	90,968,455	←	This is 10% of Type B deposits and 20% of Type A deposits (type is function of depositor sensitivity to credit rating)
Credit pipeline	43,622,745	←	This is the aggregate customer lending that the bank has comitted to and is undrawn

Simplified bank liquidity buffer calculation

	(million EUR)
Wholesale component	1,240
Retail component	91
Credit pipeline	44
Total liquid assets required	**1,375**

FIGURE 12.5 LAB size calculation.

of maintaining it therefore logically sits with all of the bank's business lines that generate liquidity risk; a business line that only raised liabilities, for example, would not be charged for running it. The cost of the LAB can be calculated as a sum of the funding cost of the portfolio and the opportunity cost of holding lower yielding risk-free assets. That is, the interest charges on the funds used to run the LAB together with the difference between the risk-free yield and a typical risky yield level. The lower return is the opportunity cost that the bank pays for maintaining an LAB as insurance against a funding crisis. This total cost should be allocated, on a pro-rata basis, to the business lines. The businesses that generate the greatest need for liquidity protection (such as those with large asset–liability gaps and funded with short-term wholesale funds) will pay the greatest share of the LAB running costs.

EXAMPLE 12.4 TRANSFERRING THE COST OF RUNNING THE LAB

The opportunity cost approach to calculating the running cost of maintaining the LAB requires an element of subjectivity. Another approach is to take the asset swap return, which is a floating spread over Libor, and net this with any swap hedge costs as well the funding cost. This net cost is then allocated pro-rata to the business lines.

The concept is illustrated at Figure 12.6. We assume that all assets in the LAB have been asset swapped into floating-rate return, and that the LAB has a weighted average floating spread over 3-month Libor of 100 bps. The average funding cost is 200 bps, and the net cost of the swap hedge is 50 bps. This gives a buffer cost of:

LAB average yield	100 bps
Funding cost	−200 bps
Swap hedge	−50 bps
LAB cost	**−150 bps**

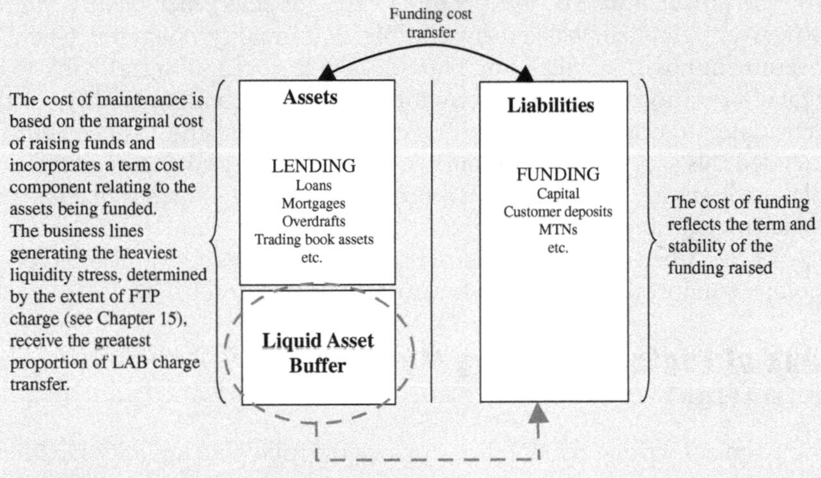

FIGURE 12.6 LAB cost allocation.

That is, the estimated cost of holding the LAB is 150 bps, so that every $1 billion of buffer produces a cost of $15 million. This is allocated to each business line in proportion to its assets, for all businesses that attract an internal funds transfer pricing at 1-year tenor or longer (see Chapter 15). The level of FTP charge is used to weight the amount of LAB charge.

CENTRAL BANK FACILITIES

A principle of bank liquidity is that a bank should be intimately familiar with the operation of its central bank funding facilities, particularly the emergency facilities, that are available to it in the event of liquidity stress. During the crisis of 2008, certain banks, which had not experienced the need to access central bank funding in their recent past, encountered difficulty in arranging central bank support because their dealing room was not aware exactly how to access it. For this reason, systems use and operational procedures on how to access central bank facilities should be practised by the dealing room, and this requirement stated in the contingency funding plan. That way, there will be no unnecessary operational delays should the bank experience funding difficulty and need to access the emergency facilities.

The specific type and level of support offered by a central bank will differ by jurisdiction. The most common type of emergency facility offered is an overnight loan backed by eligible high-quality collateral (such as government bonds or bills). For example, the European Central Bank in its regular operations offers an overnight and 1-week funding facility. In the immediate aftermath of the liquidity crisis of September–October 2008, it extended this support with 3-month, 6-month and 1-year funding facilities. All these loans are conducted as a repo, in which the ECB repos in collateral in exchange for the loan of cash.

We describe the BoE's liquidity facilities, to give an idea of the type of liquidity support that can be made available at a central bank.

Bank of England Sterling Monetary Framework

At the time of writing the BoE had in place the following liquidity facilities:

- operational standing facilities;
- reserve account facilities;
- open market operations;
- discount window facility.

For an institution to be eligible to participate in the BoE's operations under the sterling monetary framework, it must meet a number of criteria. The criteria include that the bank is:

- an eligible institution and is required to make payments of cash ratio deposits to the Bank, or is part of the clearing mechanisms CHAPS or CREST, for sterling settlement;

- operationally capable to participate in and settle transactions with the Bank efficiently;
- an institution that contributes to the Bank's market intelligence work in support of its functions as a monetary authority;
- not subject to any objection from the regulatory authority to take part in the BoE's operations;
- when part of a Group and not the primary entity within the Group, in receipt of a guarantee of the firm's liabilities from the parent entity.

Prior to the financial crisis of 2008, a participating bank had to demonstrate a continuous level of GBP 500 million in deposit liabilities. This requirement was removed in 2009, thereby widening the number of UK-domiciled banks that were able to take advantage of the bank's liquidity facilities. To apply to take part in the monetary framework, a bank must submit a template application form to the BoE, which is then followed with a meeting and the setting up of settlement links.

Collateral Eligibility

The discount window facility (DWF) is established to provide ongoing liquidity to UK-domiciled banks and building societies. It is a standing facility, under which gilt-edged securities (or sterling cash, at the Bank's discretion) is lent against eligible collateral. The collateral is required to be pre-positioned with the Bank. Each drawdown from the facility has a maturity of 30 days or 364 days.

The collateral lodged at the Bank is designated as one of four categories:

Level A: debt securities that are routinely eligible as collateral in the Bank's short-term repo open market operations; that is, high-quality sovereign and supranational securities.

Level B: third-party debt securities that are trading in liquid markets.

Level C: other third-party debt securities including those not trading in liquid markets.

Level D: own-name securitisations and covered bonds.

The haircut applied to collateral is a function of its level. To the basic haircut is added further haircuts for non-sterling securities, own-name covered bonds, structured finance securities and corporate bonds.

LIQUIDITY MANAGEMENT AND COLLATERAL

Inter-bank dealing in derivatives is collateralised under the CSA annexe of the standard ISDA Master agreement. The exact form of the CSA signed with each counterparty will differ, because there is a considerable amount of optionality available, but the identical element in every case is the requirement for the counterparty that is negative mark-to-market (MTM) in its derivative positions to pass collateral to the value of the MTM to the counterparty. An ISDA survey from 2010 suggested that cash formed 83% of all collateral posted (the balance will be made up of eligible securities such as highly rated sovereign bonds). In a stressed economic environment, there will be a tendency to increased preference for cash and high-quality government bonds as collateral, and a decline in eligibility of other assets such as corporate bonds and equities.

The above observations make clear that derivatives collateral management is simply another aspect of funding and liquidity management at a bank. It should not be viewed as a separate discipline, and should therefore be organised within the Treasury function.

Collateral Management

Collateral management policy should ensure that an increased demand for collateral does not take a bank by surprise, or become unmanageable. The best way to ensure this is to treat collateral management in the same way as funding management, and apply the same disciplines to it (such as terming out funding, applying the correct internal price to the business lines, and providing accurate and timely MI). It also requires an up-to-date awareness of the collateral position of the bank, because in a stressed environment there is a high risk of scarcity of high-quality, collateral that can be pledged.

The key considerations for collateral management policy are:

- ensure that policy and control is exercised centrally for the bank, and not separately for different business lines;
- maximise the ability to net margin calls with counterparties;
- apply general risk management considerations such as:
  - quantify the aggregate risk exposure across business lines;
  - monitor collateral concentration risk;
  - from the bank's viewpoint, ensure that collateral calls to counterparties are accurate and made on time;
  - ensure that all available eligible collateral is used efficiently, including acceptable collateral held in one business line that may be able to be

used to meet another business line's collateral requirement (this requires centralised management and high-quality MI).

The primary requirement is to ensure the most efficient use of collateral across the firm. This requires the correct pricing policy to be in place. This is best captured in the bank's Derivative Funding Policy, which we discuss in Chapter 15.

Collateral Organisation

The requirement to post collateral is a cost for a bank undertaking derivatives business. Therefore the cost must be borne by the business lines. The "ownership" of collateral is a political red-herring for bank management. While individual business lines may acquire the assets that can be used as collateral, the ultimate decision on where and how they can be deployed to meet collateral requirements should be taken by the centralised collateral management desk. This desk should come under Treasury organisation because the majority of collateral calls are met using cash; in other words, collateral management is a cash funding requirement.

Figure 12.7 shows how eligible securities may be organised across business lines, such as

- individual business areas;
- Treasury desk (includes Repo desk).

Collateral policy must ensure that no internal arbitrage takes place. For example, in a stressed liquidity scenario the bank's LAB would be sold

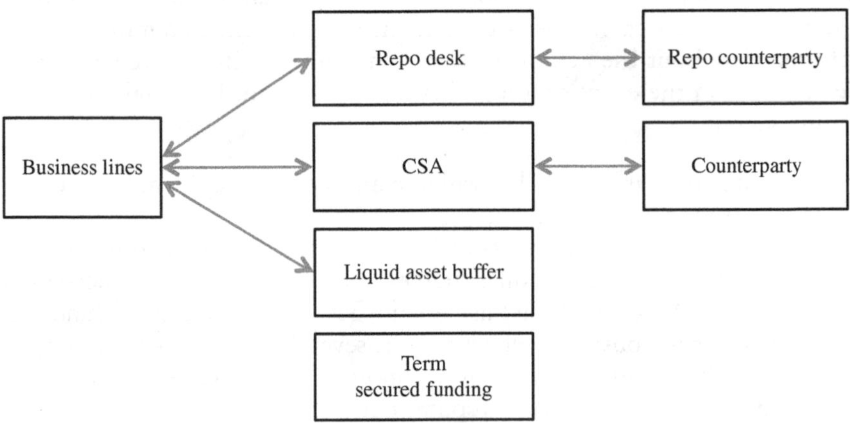

FIGURE 12.7 Collateral sources and usage.

or repo'd for cash: this places a (high) implied value on high-quality collateral.

The use of loan assets as collateral is worth exploring as it maximises efficiency in collateral management; however, even where such assets are acceptable to counterparties it can be difficult to deploy them. Securitisation may provide a solution, if the loans can be repackaged into structured note form. This was a common transaction in European banks during 2009–2011, which undertook "in-house" securitisation of loan assets and used the resulting securities as collateral at the ECB.

THE CONTINGENCY FUNDING PLAN

In some jurisdictions, a liquidity CFP is a requirement of the regulator. Irrespective of whether this is the case or not, business best-practice dictates that a bank should have a CFP in place as part of its liquidity risk management process. In fact, it could be argued that a CFP is the most important element of this process, precisely because extreme liquidity stress events are relatively rare. To be able to survive uncommon events such as liquidity crises, it is important that a bank knows how to proceed in the event of one, particularly because the majority of its staff would be unaccustomed to dealing with them. This know-how should be contained in the CFP.

Setting the CFP

A generic CFP template is provided on the Wiley website supplementary material accompanying this book. This can be adapted for use in most banks. As a practical working document, the CFP must contain detailed information about the actions to be taken, and the alternative sources to be accessed, in the event of a liquidity stress scenario. Essentially the CFP should set out:

- the range of viable, readily available and flexible deployable potential contingency funding measures;
- an estimation of the amounts of funds that can be obtained from these potential contingency funding sources, the expected lead time needed to access such funds, and the business impact of obtaining these funds. In many cases the business impact may be severely negative – for example, withholding lending lines, or in more extreme cases withholding payments, will have extreme reputational impact;
- clear and effective governance structure, policies and procedures that need to be followed if the CFP is invoked;

- appropriate communication plans;
- the steps to be followed to meet critical payments on an intra-day basis in stress situations;
- a framework under which the senior management and Board will receive timely and relevant MI.

The basic background concept of a CFP is shown in the box at Example 12.5. Table 12.7 is a more detailed "action list" that would form part of the CFP, showing the actual business lines, the primary contact for escalation and the mitigating action that could be taken to ease liquidity stress.

EXAMPLE 12.5 CFP: MANAGEMENT ACTION TO MITIGATE LIQUIDITY OUTFLOWS IN STRESSED SCENARIOS

Background

The UK FSA, as part of the ILAA process, currently requires banks to hold a liquidity buffer to offset the effects of a "combined" liquidity stress scenario. It also requires a plan of management action that would be taken by the business in response to a specific scenario called a combined stress scenario. The combined scenario lasts over three months and entails an idiosyncratic (perceived or actual 2-notch credit-rating downgrade) stress in the first two weeks, followed by a market stress after three months. Banks are required to submit a Board-approved CFP. The businesses are responsible for escalating changes in their perceived liquidity situation as per the bank's liquidity policy statement, at which point they invoke the CFP.

Management Action: Sample CFP

The CFP must describe:

- The array of potential management action to offset the combined stress scenario liquidity outflows from the bank.
- Actions that could be taken into the first two weeks (idiosyncratic stress) versus actions that could be taken after two weeks (during market-wide stress).

(*continued*)

- Quantified current impacts from these management actions with the understanding that these values are dynamic and scenario dependent

Rationale

Documenting a series of management actions within a CFP-governed stress scenario will enable the bank to:

- offset management action against cash outflows in the FSA stress scenario;
- set a lower LAB size requirement, which will free up funding capacity;
- generate customer confidence and positively influence credit-rating agency review.

Table 12.6 is a summary of possible action from the business lines. This includes quantifiable liquidity impacts, as well as other actions that could be taken in a liquidity stress scenario. It forms part of the CFP. Table 12.7 is a list of possible action from management that can be undertaken in periods of stress.

TABLE 12.6 CFP possible actions.

Product	Action	Impact	Liquidity inflow £m
Corporate Loans	Withdraw committed lines to distressed counterparties	Reputational impact	200
Corporate Loans	Withdraw non-committed lines	Reputational impact	250
Debt securities	Cease market-making activity in selected markets	Reputational impact	
Debt securities	Sell securities	PnL losses	500
Repo	Additional repo lines		100

TABLE 12.7 CFP management actions in stress.

	Action			Impact			
	Business line	Asset action	Probability of execution	Estimated liquidity impact £ mln	Contact	Treasury responsibility	Risk responsibility
Product							
ABS	Structured Finance	Repo all eligible ABS/CMBS/RMBS	Medium	200	ANO		
Debt Securities	Money Markets/Repo	Increase collateral standards (high quality)/ haircut increases	High	150	ANO		
Debt Securities	Repo funding desk	Lengthen repo	Low	100	ANO		
Debt Securities	Repo funding desk	Diversify by using additional repo counterparties	Low	50	ANO		
Debt Securities	High yield	Sell high-yield assets	Low	150	ANO		
Derivatives	MM Trading	Cash settle in the money positions at a discount	Low	25	ANO		
Equities	Equities Trading	Equities unwind long positions	Low	90	ANO		
Loans	Banking	Collateral enablement	High	100	ANO		
Loans	Banking	Pledging	High	50	ANO		
Loans	Banking	Selling	Low	300	ANO		
Loans	Banking	Withdraw unutilised lines/reduction in asset renewals	High	100	ANO		
Loans	Banking	Stop/delay pipeline	High		ANO		
Loans	Banking	Enforce legal terms/lines withdrawn on distressed counterparties	Low	250	ANO		
Transaction services	Treasury Services	Delay operational payments	Low	200	ANO		
Transaction services	Treasury Services	Optimise payment systems collateral	Medium	150	ANO		
Etc.							
Etc.							

Alternative Funding Sources

The list of alternative funding sources available to a bank is a finite and limited one. This limitation is exacerbated because in the midst of a liquidity crisis many of these sources are apt to disappear. This explains partly the importance of adhering to basic liquidity principles such as self-sufficiency in funding, satisfactory term funding, diversity in funding sources, a manageable asset–liability gap, and an adequate LAB. Of course the next crisis will be different in detail, if not in form, to previous ones, hence the need for an adequate contingency plan of alternative funding sources.

In some ways the advancement of financial markets over the 30-year period from the 1980s has created greater risk in liquidity management, as new types of financial institutions and products have entered the industry. For example, savings products such as mutual funds ("unit trusts") and money market funds have provided an alternative for investors that has reduced the amount available for banks' core deposits. At the same time, economic growth and the liberalisation of markets has resulted in high demand for loans, leading to loan-to-deposit ratios rising above 100% at many banks. This, combined with a relaxation of conservative liquidity principles, has caused banks themselves to look beyond core deposits and access alternative funding sources, including capital markets and repo, loan sales and securitisation.

Market observation suggests that it is the newer sources of funds that are the most unstable during a liquidity crisis. Given this fact, it is important for banks to have alternative funding sources available, and include them in the CFP. There is considerable variety in this alternative list, depending on the type of bank being considered and what market/jurisdiction it is operating in. The sources of alternative funding might include:

- Internet-based deposits, including via Internet brokers;
- CD and CP/ECP issuance programmes;
- credit unions;
- increasing the number of branches, with wider liability-raising ability;
- a "liquidity option facility" with a fund manager, insurance company, building society or other routine holder of AAA-rated sovereign bonds; this is similar to a back-up liquidity line which the bank can draw on, exchanging its assets for the high-quality assets held by the counterparty, which can then be repo'd for funds;
- sovereign wealth funds;
- foreign central bank reserves.

A common concern for regulators is of banks' inadequate deposit growth, declining core funding and over-reliance on wholesale market funding. Many of them, including the UK FSA, have also highlighted the volatile and unpredictable nature of non-core funding sources. The CFP is an attempt to address these concerns and is an essential part of a bank's liquidity risk management process.

REFERENCES AND BIBLIOGRAPHY

Amihud, Y. and Mendelsohn, H. (1980), "Dealership Market: Market Making with Inventory", *Journal of Financial Economics*, 8, pp. 31–53.

Amihud, Y. and Mendelson, H. (1986), "Asset Pricing and the Bid–Ask Spread", *Journal of Financial Economics*, 17, pp. 223–49.

Amihud, Y. and Mendelson, H. (1991a), "Liquidity, Asset Prices and Financial Policy", *Financial Analysts Journal*, 47, pp. 56–66.

Amihud, Y. and Mendelson, H. (1991b), "Liquidity, Maturity and the Yields on US Treasury Securities", *Journal of Finance*, 46, pp. 1411–25.

Amihud, Y., Mendelson, H. and Lauterbach, B. (1997), "Market Microstructure and Securities Values: Evidence from the Tel Aviv Stock Exchange", *Journal of Financial Economics*, 45, pp. 219–35.

Boyd, J.H. and Gertler, M., "The Role of Large Banks in the Recent U.S. Banking Crisis", *Federal Reserve Bank of Minneapolis Quarterly Review*, Winter 1994, Volume 18, No. 1.

Choudhry, M. (2009a), "United Kingdom Gilt Securities and Market Liquidity: Surveying the Impact of Structural Reforms", *Qualitative Research in Financial Markets*, Vol. 1, No. 2.

Choudhry, M. (2009b), "The Value of Introducing Structural Reform to Improve Bond Market Liquidity: Experience from the U.K. Gilt Market", *European Journal of Finance and Banking Research*, Vol. 2, No. 2.

Choudhry, M. (May–June 2010), "Measuring Bond Market Liquidity: Devising A Composite Aggregate Liquidity Score" *Applied Financial Economics*, Vol. 20, No. 10–12.

Choudhry, M. (Spring 2011), "Measuring Changes in Liquidity using the Bid–Offer Price Proxy: Determinants of Liquidity in the United Kingdom Gilt Market", *International Journal of Finance and Policy Analysis*.

Fleming, M. (July 1997), "The Round-the-Clock Market for U.S. Treasury Securities", Federal Reserve Bank of New York, *Economic Policy Review*, 3, pp. 9–32.

Fleming, M. (September 2000), "Financial Market Implications of the Federal Debt Paydown", Working Paper, Federal Reserve Bank of New York.

Fleming, M. (June 2001), "Measuring Treasury Market Liquidity", Federal Reserve Bank of New York.

Fleming, M. (March 2002), "Are Larger Treasury Issues More Liquid? Evidence from Bill Reopenings", Working Paper, Federal Reserve Bank of New York.

Fleming, M. and Remolona, E. (1999), "Price Formation and Liquidity in the US Treasury Market: The Response to Public Information", *Journal of Finance*, 52, pp. 1901–15.

Fleming, M. and Sarkar, A (1999). "Liquidity in the US Treasury Spot and Futures Markets", *Market Liquidity: Research Findings and Selected Policy Implications*, Bank for International Settlements.

CHAPTER 13

Liquidity Risk Metrics

One of the principles of bank liquidity management we introduced in the last chapter stated that liquidity risk cannot be represented by a single metric, but rather by an array of metrics. This reflects the fact that the business of liquidity risk, like the wider field of asset–liability management, is as much art as science. It is essential that banks use a range of liquidity measures for risk estimation and forecasting, and deploy the widest variety of tools available in order to produce full and accurate MI.

In some instances banks will not have a choice with regard to the liquidity metrics they report. In the wake of the 2008 crisis, national regulators and the BCBS proposed a consistent set of monitoring metrics for all firms. This was so as to assist supervisors across jurisdictions in looking at the liquidity risk in global banks, and to create a common language for MI, reducing the risk of misinterpretation of information by bank boards and regulators. (This also has the added advantage of reducing systems costs in reporting liquidity risk being run by such entities.) Thus banks can only add to the range of metrics they use, because a benchmark minimum is required under Basel III.

The point of calculating and reporting liquidity risk metrics is to enable senior management to have the most accurate, and up-to-date, estimation of the liquidity exposure of the bank at any time. This assists with planning, but more importantly it enables management to structure the bank's balance sheet and funding mix in the way that best meets its risk tolerance. It also provides management with the ability to respond more knowledgeably to market stresses. Finally, regulators oblige banks to report specified liquidity metrics on a regular basis, so the banks have no option but to implement systems that enable the liquidity numbers to be calculated.

In this chapter we detail the range of liquidity metrics that should be employed by all banks, looking beyond simply what is required under regulators' rules, and at a full set of metrics that will provide the best possible liquidity reporting for bank senior management.

SIX KEY LIQUIDITY METRICS

Liquidity reports help in providing early warning of any likely funding stress points. On their own, the reports enable the Treasury desk to estimate when or if in the future they may encounter some difficulty in rolling over their funding. When combined with the results of liquidity stress tests (see Chapter 14), they provide a reasonable idea of whether the current funding structure of the bank is acceptable. All metrics should be transparent, and ideally disclosed as public information (although often a bank will report them to the regulator, who can release peer group statistics).

We begin with six key baseline liquidity metrics, which all banks irrespective of their size or line of business should calculate and monitor as a matter of course. These are the:

- loan-to-deposit ratio;
- 1-week and 1-month liquidity ratios;
- cumulative liquidity model;
- liquidity risk factor;
- concentration and funding source report;

and one that is relevant to Group entities:

- the inter-entity lending report.

These reports measure different elements of liquidity risk. For consolidated or group entities, reports must be at country level, legal entity level and group level. Taken together, the reports provide detail on:

- the exposure of the bank to funding rollover or "gap" risk;
- the daily funding requirement, and a forecast or estimate of what this is likely to be at a forward date;
- the extent of "self-sufficiency" of a branch or subsidiary.

We examine them each individually.

Loan-to-Deposit Ratio (LTD)

This is the standard and commonly used metric, typically reported monthly. It is most pertinent to commercial banking entities. It measures the relationship between lending and customer deposits, and is a measure of the self-sustainability of the bank (or the branch or subsidiary). A level above 100% is an early warning sign of excessive asset growth, and of a potentially risky reliance on wholesale funds (which, if they are short-dated, are riskier still). Of course, a level below 70% implies excessive liquidity and implies a potentially inadequate return on funds. Generally, a limit of between 95% and 105% represents business best-practice, but this will vary widely depending on the particular business model and risk-tolerance of the individual bank. All else being equal, a value in excess of 100% is not recommended as a viable, sustainable business model.

The LTD is a good measure of the contribution of customer funding to the bank's overall funding, and as such it is worth monitoring against a specified limit. A number significantly above 100% is an indicator of funding stress for the bank in the event of market instability. However, it is not predictive and does not account for the tenor, concentration and volatility of funds. As such it is insufficient as a liquidity risk measure on its own and must be used in conjunction with other measures.

A related measure is the LTD gap, also known as the Customer Funding Gap, which is the extent to which the bank's total customer lending exceeds total customer deposits. It is used to monitor and control the bank's reliance on wholesale funding markets. A negative number indicates a funding gap; that is, customer deposits are insufficient to fund customer loans and other sources of funding are required. A maximum aggregate actual gap limit should be set to define the level of appetite for the funding gap. A bank can set a quantitative limit for this gap; this is shown at Figure 13.1. The definitions and assumptions are shown at Table 13.1.

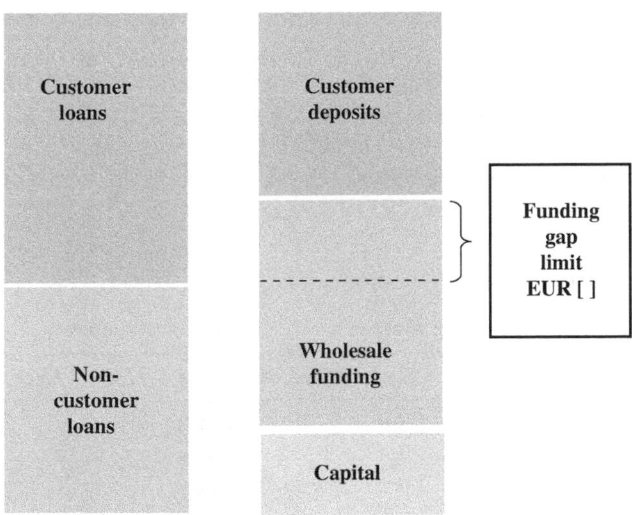

FIGURE 13.1 LTD funding gap limit.

TABLE 13.1 LTD gap assumptions and definitions.

Metric components	Definition	Measurement
Customer lending	All loans and advances to retail and corporate customers (excludes reverse repurchase arrangements)	Customer funding gap =
Customer deposits	All customer deposits including branch retail deposits and corporate deposits; excludes repurchase agreements	Total customer lending minus Total customer deposits

1-week and 1-month Liquidity Ratios

These are the standard liquidity ratios that are commonly measured against a regulatory limit requirement. An example of a report for a group-type entity comprised of four subsidiaries is shown at Table 13.2.

Liquidity ratios are an essential measure of "gap" risk. They show net cash flows, including the cash effect of liquidating "liquid" securities, as a percentage of liabilities, for a specific maturity "bucket". These are an effective measure of structural liquidity, and help to provide an early warning of likely stress points. A worsening liquidity ratio that is moving closer to an internal or regulatory limit is crucial MI that should drive a change in funding strategy, if not rapid structural changes to the composition of the balance sheet.

A more detailed liquidity ratio report is shown at Table 13.3. This shows the breakdown of cash inflows and outflows per time bucket, and also the liquidity ratio. The ratio itself is calculated by dividing the selected time bucket liability by the cumulative liability. So in this example the 8-day ratio of 17.3% is given by the fraction [781,065/4,511,294].

TABLE 13.2 Sample liquidity ratio report extract, banking group.

	1-week Gap	1-week Liquidity			1-month Liquidity		
Country	USD mm	This week	Limit	Excess	This week	Limit	Excess
F	–1586	–22.83%	–30.00%		–39.11%	–50%	
D	188	15.26%	0.00%		1.62%	–5%	
H	786	22.57%	0.00%		19.12%	–5%	
G	550	53.27%	25.00%		69.83%	25.00%	
Regional total	–62	–0.48%			–10.64%		

The "liquidity gap" is assets minus liabilities in the relevant tenor bucket. The Total Available Funds is the liquidity gap plus marketable securities and CDs, and minus committed facilities that are as yet undrawn. As we note above, the liquidity ratio is the total available funds divided by the total liabilities. Note that it is the liquidity gap element that drives the 30-day ratio much lower than the 8-day ratio.

The full model of the spreadsheet shown at Table 13.3 is provided on the Wiley website (see Chapter 19 for details).

Cumulative Liquidity Model

This is an extension of the liquidity ratio report and is a forward-looking model of inflows, outflows and available liquidity, accumulated for a 12-month period. It recognises, and helps to predict, liquidity stress points on a cash basis. A report such as this, like the liquidity ratios, will be prepared daily at legal entity level and group level.

Figure 13.2 is an example of a cumulative outflow output graph rising from the cumulative liquidity model. This gives a snapshot view of forward funding stress points.

Liquidity Risk Factor

The liquidity risk factor (LRF) measure is a static snapshot that shows the aggregate size of the liquidity gap: it compares the average tenor of assets to the average tenor of liabilities. It is also known as the "maturity transformation" value. The ratio may be calculated using years or days as the unit of time, as desired. Table 13.4 is an example of the risk factor for a bank where the unit of measurement is given in days. In this example, (262/19) is 13.79, rounded to 14 in the report.

The higher the LRF, the larger the liquidity gap and hence the greater the liquidity risk that is being run by the bank. On its own, a one-off LRF number is of little value; it is important to observe the trend over time and the change to long-run averages, so as to get early warning of the build-up of a potentially unsustainable funding structure. The limit value, which is subjective and set by ALCO, will differ according to the risk profile and funding structure of the individual bank. Clearly, a bank that wishes to run a more conservative funding profile, or that is concerned about potential future liquidity stresses, will set a lower limit.

The author recommends that the national regulator releases peer-group average and outlier values for the LRF, for banks to compare their statistics to.

TABLE 13.3 Liquidity report and liquidity ratio calculation.

XYZ Bank Liquidity Report 28-Nov-10 (EUR)				
	Sight	**2–8 Days**	**9 Days– 1 Month**	**1–3 Months**
Corporate Current/Call	24,289	0	0	0
Corporate Time Loan	28,433	14,203	151,471	106,637
Government Current/Call	342	0	0	0
Government Time Loan	250	3	805	63
Inter-bank Current/Call	41,752	0	0	0
Inter-bank Time Loan	339,276	201,745	6,251	31,906
Repos	0	0	0	47,500
Inter-Group Current/Call	4,445	0	0	0
Inter-Group Time Loan	210,177	348,414	277,964	76,268
Marketable Secs & CDs - <1Mth to Maturity	5,009	0	55,358	0
Retail Current/Call	8,215	0	0	0
Retail Time Loan	238	41	221	2,643
Additional Corporate Time Lending	0	8	1,313	43
Receivables	0	0	0	0
Total Assets	**662,426**	**564,414**	**493,383**	**265,060**
Corporate Current/Call	51,033	0	0	12,758
Corporate Time Deposit	32,303	122,955	114,627	299,551
Government Current/Call	1,946	0	0	0
Government Time Deposit	2,056	8,112	24,391	23,503
Inter-bank Current/Call	82,087	0	0	0
Inter-bank Time Deposit	83,898	83,684	349,461	86,979
Repos	0	0	0	50,000
Inter-Group Current/Call	47,095	0	0	0
Inter-Group Time Deposit	302,879	418,383	629,809	225,314
Retail Current/Call	65,273	0	0	16,318
Retail Time Deposit	203	54,128	167,090	683,288
Additional Govt/Local Authority Time Deposits	8,656	9,319	50,508	82,531
Share Capital	0	0	0	0
Payables	0	0	0	0
Total Liabilities	**677,429**	**696,581**	**1,335,886**	**1,480,242**

Ratio Calculation				
Marketable Securities				
Repos Adj				
CDs				
Unutilised Commitments				
Liquidity Gap				
Total Available Funds				
Total Liabilities				
Liquidity Ratio				
Internal Limit				
FSA Limit				
Stress testing		10% Fall in Marketable Securities		
Stress testing		10% Fall in Stickiness		
Stress testing		Combined Effect of above		

NOTES
THE Sight-8 Day AND THE Sight-30 Day RATIOS ARE SUBJECT TO FSA LIMIT. THE RATIO MUST NOT FALL BEL
THESE LIMITS. THESE REPRESENT 1-WEEK AND 1-MONTH LIQUIDITY LIMITS.
MARKETABLE SECURITIES AND CDs ARE PLACED IN A 8-DAY BUCKET WHEN MAKING THE TOTAL AVAILAB
FUNDS CALCULATION.

XYZ Bank Liquidity Report 28-Nov-10 (EUR)

3–6 Months	6 Mths to 1 Yr	1–3 Years	3–5 Years	+5 Years	Total
0	0	0	0	0	24,289
98,959	47,608	357,872	573,993	642,563	2,021,738
0	0	0	0	0	342
3,383	2,942	12,656	7,016	76,853	103,971
0	0	0	0	0	41,752
18,704	28,428	11,971	0	0	638,281
0	0	0	0	0	47,500
0	0	0	0	0	4,445
13,981	30,047	156	101	0	957,108
0	0	0	0	0	60,367
0	0	0	0	0	8,215
2,427	310	6,294	38,755	10,204	61,133
624	0	21,608	7,857	75,724	107,177
0	0	0	0	0	0
138,078	**109,335**	**410,557**	**627,722**	**805,344**	**4,076,318**
0	0	0	0	0	63,791
28,387	928	0	0	0	598,751
0	0	0	0	0	1,946
22,687	1,200	0	0	0	81,949
0	0	0	0	0	82,087
23,967	1,205	0	0	0	629,194
0	0	0	0	0	50,000
0	0	0	0	0	47,095
88,464	78,769	375	0	0	1,743,993
0	0	0	0	0	81,591
27,925	13,273	9,224	0	0	955,131
15,252	8,500	1,000	0	0	175,766
0	0	0	0	0	0
0	0	0	0	0	0
206,682	**103,875**	**10,599**	**0**	**0**	**4,511,294**

Sight	Sight – 8 Days	Sight – 1 M
0	630,536	630,536
0	0	0
0	353,219	353,219
(55,520)	(55,520)	(55,520)
(15,003)	(147,170)	(989,673)
(70,523)	781,065	(61,438)
4,511,294	4,511,294	4,511,294
−1.56%	**17.31%**	**−1.36%**
45	45	45
	3.00%	−3.00%
	0.00%	−5.00%
	15.13%	−3.54%
	17.32%	−2.79%
	15.14%	−4.97%

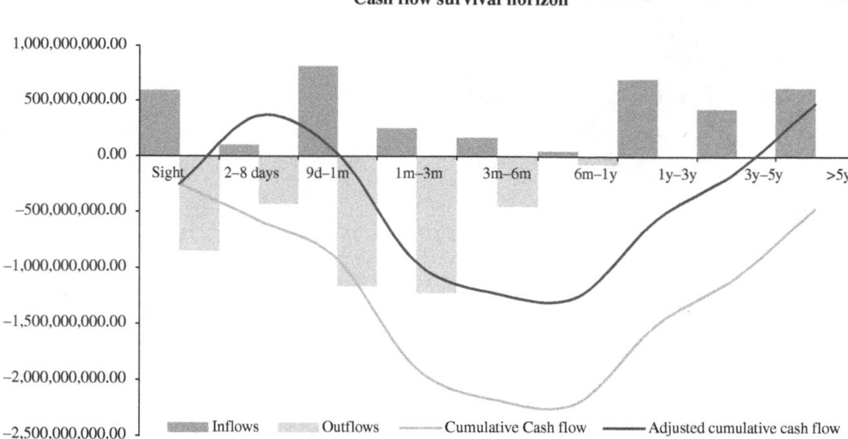

FIGURE 13.2 Cumulative liquidity model.

Concentration Report and Funding Source Report

This report shows the extent of reliance on single sources of funds. An excess concentration to any one lender, sector or country is an early warning sign of potential stress points in the event of a crash. Banks should not become over-reliant on any one source of funds; outside the retail deposit sector they should be wary of excessive reliance on one class of depositor.

An example of a concentration report is shown at Table 13.5. In Table 13.5A, "Customer 1" clearly should be the focus of a potential stress point, and a bank would need to put in a contingency in the event that this source of funds dried up. In Table 13.5B a bank is reporting its largest five depositors by name, again with the purpose of identifying potential future funding risk should one of these customers withdraw some or all of its deposits. In this example, the bank has set a limit of 10% of its aggregate funding base being sourced from one

TABLE 13.4 Liquidity risk factor.

Report date	Average liabilities tenor (days)	Average assets tenor (days)	Maturity transformation effect	Limit	Breach
9/30/2010	19	262	14	24	N

TABLE 13.5A Large depositors as percentage of total funding report.

Customer	Deposit amount	Percentage of bank funding	Percentage of group external funding
Customer 1	836,395	17.1%	2.6%
Customer 2	595,784	7.9%	1.8%
Customer 3	425,709	5.8%	1.3%
Customer 4	241,012	0.6%	0.7%
Customer 6	214,500	1.2%	0.7%
Customer 21	190,711	4.5%	0.6%
Customer 17	123,654	2.9%	0.4%
Customer 18	97,877	2.3%	0.3%
Customer 14	89,344	2.1%	0.3%
Customer 15	88,842	2.1%	0.3%
Customer 31	83,272	2.0%	0.3%
Customer 19	74,815	0.5%	0.2%
Customer 10	64,639	1.5%	0.2%
Customer 29	59,575	1.4%	0.2%
Customer 16	58,613	1.4%	0.2%
Total	6,562,116	53.3%	20.1%

TABLE 13.5B Largest depositors report.

Bank top 5 deposit counterparties	Balance (€000,000s)	% Funding	Limit	Breach
Commercial Bank of Surrey	575	14.0%	10%	Y
Central Bank of Mordor	227	5.5%	10%	N
Syldavian Sovereign Wealth Fund	220	5.4%	10%	N
Bordurian Defence Office	130	3.2%	10%	N
Arab Khemed Bank	105	2.6%	10%	N
Total		30.7%		

customer (this number is unusually high. Most banks would set a single-customer deposit limit lower than this, at between 2% and 5%); its biggest customer, the "Commercial Bank of Surrey" is well over this limit at 14%. The bank therefore needs to take action to reduce this level or otherwise increase its deposit base at the aggregate level so that this ratio comes down.

A related report is the sector funding source report, an example of which is shown at Table 13.6. This is a summary of the share of funding obtained from all the various different sectors, and is used to flag potential concentration risk by sector.

TABLE 13.6 Sector funding source report.

Source	Balance (€000,000s)	% Funding	Limit	Within limit (Y/N)
Customer – Corporate	508	15.9%	>15%	N
Customer – Local Authority	139	4.4%	>10%	Y
Customer – Private	1,198	37.4%	>30%	N
Institutional – Financial Institutions	792	24.7%	<25% or 1bn	Y
Inter-bank	303	9.5%	<25% or 1bn	Y
Inter-Group (Net balance)	249	7.8%	<25% or 1bn	Y
Other	15	0.5%	<25% or 1bn	Y
Total Liabilities	**3,204**	**100%**		

Inter-entity Lending Report

This report is relevant for Group and consolidated banking entities. Intra-group lending is common in banking entities, and in some jurisdictions subject to cross-border and cross-legal entity regulatory limits. Hence, this report is a valuable tool used to determine both how reliant a specific banking subsidiary is on Group funds, and also to what extent it is approaching regulatory limits. An example of a report for a group entity is shown at Table 13.7.

TABLE 13.7 Sample inter-group lending report.

Group Treasury			
As at (date)	**Total borrowing**	**Total lending**	**Net inter-group lending**
London	1,713,280	883,133	–830,157
Paris	3,345,986	978,195	–2,367,617
Frankfurt	17,026	195,096	178,089
Dublin	453,490	83,420	–370,070
Hong Kong	0	162,000	162,000
New York	690,949	1,516,251	825,302

The six reports above represent the primary baseline liquidity metrics. They are the benchmark essential metrics in the measurement of liquidity risk, and the minimum management information that banks and group

Treasuries will wish to prepare, both as business best-practice and as part of adherence to regulatory standards.

STRATEGIC LEVEL LIQUIDITY METRICS

High-level liquidity metrics are part of the strategic management of structural liquidity, to ensure that there is a balanced and stable liquidity profile over the medium and long term, while interacting efficiently with short-term liquidity management. Maintaining an appropriate ratio between liabilities and assets in the medium and long term will prevent pressure on present and future funding sources in the short term, during stress situations and in the normal course of business.

The main objectives of structural liquidity management are to ensure:

- that structural stability is consistent with the level of maturity transformation set by the bank's senior management. For this purpose, it is important that dependence on short-term and less stable funding (inter-bank) never exceeds acceptable levels;
- optimisation of funding costs together with the diversification of funding sources, reference markets, currencies and products (bonds, structured MTNs, securitisation, equity-linked notes and so on);
- that financing the bank's growth is via a coherent strategic funding plan, by defining an optimal structure for the bank's funding profile.

As part of this, two metrics emphasised by the UK FSA and the Basel Committee in the wake of the 2008 crisis were the LCR and the NSFR. Versions of these ratios have been monitored previously by some banks, particularly those with a more conservative approach to liquidity management. These are now viewed as minimum regulatory requirements to be maintained by all banks, enshrined in the Basel III regime.[1]

Liquidity Coverage Ratio

The LCR metric promotes short-term resilience to liquidity shocks; setting a limit for it ensures that sufficient high-quality liquid assets are maintained to offset cash outflows in a stressed environment. The LCR identifies the amount of unencumbered, high-quality liquid assets required to offset the

1 The LCR minimum standard takes effect from January 2015 and the NSFR minimum standard from January 2018.

net cash outflows arising in a short-term liquidity stress scenario. A regulatory limit for the LCR ensures that banks meet this requirement continuously.[2]

It is calculated as:

$$\frac{\text{Stock of high-quality liquid assets}}{\text{Stressed net cash outflows over a 30-day time period}} > 100\%$$

The rules in relation to eligible assets and stressed cash outflow assumptions are detailed and specific, but governed by the following principles:

- Stock of high-quality liquid assets: possessing low credit risk and market risk, ease and certainty of valuation. These are divided into Level 1 and Level 2 assets. There is a 40% cap on assets that are allowed to be in Level 2; the remaining assets in the LCR stock must be Level 1 assets. This is described further in Table 13.8.
- Stressed net cash outflows over a 30-day time period: both idiosyncratic and market-wide liquidity shocks incorporated into the firm's stress scenarios (these are often prescribed the regulator).

Note that the 30-day time period is as required under Basel III. The UK FSA has stipulated a 90-day test period when calculating the LCR. This is an important debate because the outflow value denominator of the LCR drives the liquidity buffer size requirement. On the reasonably safe assumption that a market-wide liquidity stress event would most probably last over 30 days, the author recommends that banks should aim to adopt the FSA standard.

The calculation of the stressed net cash outflow over a 30-day time period is also subject to certain provisions:

- retail deposits and unsecured funding provided by small business customers: run-off assumptions are prescribed for "stable" (5%) and "less stable" (10%) deposits maturing or callable within 30 days;
- unsecured wholesale funding provided by non-financial corporates, sovereigns, central banks and agencies: run-off assumptions are prescribed for "operational relationships" (25%) and others (75%) where deposits mature or are callable within 30 days;

2 "Unencumbered" means that the asset can be sold or offered as collateral against a loan or repo. In other words, it is either owned outright or funded with long-term liabilities, and not pledged already as collateral elsewhere.

TABLE 13.8 LCR liquid assets (Basel III).

Level 1 liquid assets	Level 2 liquid assets
Cash	**Government or agency assets qualifying for the 20% risk-weighting** under Basel II standardised approach for credit risk
Central bank reserves to the extent that they can be drawn on in times of stress	**Corporate and covered bonds subject to a haircut** (AA– or higher 15%; lower than A– is 100%); and (i) not issued by a financial institution, (ii) traded in deep and active markets (bid–offer spread not exceeded 40 bps in the last 10 years), and (iii) proven record as a reliable source of liquidity (repo and sale) during periods of market stress (i.e., market decline in price or increase in repo haircut 10% over a 30-day period during the last 10 years)
Marketable securities representing claims on sovereigns, central banks and similar institutions (e.g., IMF), where such securities would be assigned 0% risk weight under the Basel II standardised approach, deep repo markets exist and the securities are not issued by banks or other financial institutions (i.e., government-guaranteed bank debt is not eligible)	
Government or central bank debt issued in the domestic currency of the country in which liquidity risk is being taken	

- unsecured wholesale funding provided by others (including financial entities): there is an assumed 100% run-off of deposits that mature or are callable within 30 days;
- secured funding: an assumed 0% run-off of all secured funding arrangements that are backed by sovereign or central bank debt meeting the same criteria for high-quality Level 1 assets. There is an assumed 100% run-off for all other liabilities maturing within the 30-day period;
- embedded credit-rating downgrade triggers: assume 100% of any collateral to be posted in the event of a 3-notch credit rating downgrade;
- derivative and associated collateral valuation changes: collateral that is required following changes in derivative mark-to-market values

to be determined by national supervisors; a 20% add-on is required where derivative collateral is not comprised of cash or high-quality sovereign debt;

- ABCP conduits and similar vehicles: an assumed 100% run-off where debt matures or is callable within 30 days;
- required liquidity cover for bank liquidity and back-stop credit lines: the assumptions on liquidity cover for such facilities depend on the customer and facility type. For non-financial corporates and sovereigns, the cash outflow assumption is 100% for liquidity facilities and 10% for credit facilities; for financial institutions it is 100% for both types. In other words, the provision of a liquidity back-up line by a bank to a customer must assume 100% drawdown of that line in a stress scenario.[3]

The LCR is an essential liquidity metric that should be monitored against in-house limits irrespective of any local regulatory requirements.

The Net Stable Funding Ratio

A significant aspect of Basel III is a new liquidity measurement metric known as the net stable funding ratio (NSFR).The NSFR promotes funding resilience over the longer term; setting a limit for it ensures that sufficient long-term funding is in place to support the bank's balance sheet. In other words, maintaining an adequate NSFR should help considerably in ensuring a stable funding structure.

The stated objective of the NSFR is to encourage more medium and term funding, and the metric itself highlights the level of long-term funding compared to short-term liabilities. At this stage, no "limit" for the NSFR has been set, and such a limit is unlikely; however, regulators are expected to compare each bank's figure against their peer group average and range. Certainly the NSFR is not a metric that one could set a "one-size-fits-all" limit on. As such, it is expected that supervisors will view it as part of a set of other metrics before determining regulatory compliance. However, bank senior management needs to be aware of it, and structure their liabilities to be within an acceptable bound for regulatory compliance.

3 The UK FSA sets this assumption level at 20%. We can assume this will be changed to fall in line with Basel III requirements, but it may change the other way around. The facility type in the Basel requirements is also worth noting: "liquidity facilities" are defined as back-up lines in place to refinance maturing debt of customers in situations where they are unable to attract funding in financial markets; all other committed facilities are defined as "credit facilities".

The metric measures the amount of stable funding as a proportion of the total requirement for such stable funding. It is typically used to monitor and control the level of dependency on volatile, short-term wholesale markets, as a key structural balance sheet ratio. A low ratio indicates a concentration of funding in shorter maturities (under 1-year tenor) that can give rise to roll-over and mismatch risks. Setting a minimum percentage level for term funding would reduce dependency on short-term funding, while increasing the cost of business as more liabilities are moved into longer term funding.

The ratio aims to "promote more medium and long-term funding of the assets and activities of banking organisations". The BCBS defines NSFR as the following:

$$\frac{\text{Available stable funding}}{\text{Required stable funding}} > \text{c.}100\%.$$

In the December 2010 announcement the definition was confirmed, given as:

$$\frac{\text{Available amount of stable funding}}{\text{Required amount of stable funding}} > 100\%.$$

The limit is 100%, which is the minimum acceptable figure.

Table 13.9 describes the calculation in greater detail.

Assumptions used in the calculation are prescribed by the BCBS: liabilities are given conservative run-off/rollover assumptions, and callable liabilities are not considered stable funding.

Incidentally, the author prefers two alternatives for calculating the NSFR, originally put forward by the British Bankers' Association (BBA) as part of its response to the initial BCBS proposals.[4] It suggested either of the following definitions for the calculation of the NSFR:

- Capital plus term funding with residual maturity over one year plus non-wholesale funding divided by assets not marketable within one year.

$$\frac{\text{Capital} + \text{Term funding } (> 1 \text{ year}) + \text{Retail funding}}{\text{Assets} > 1 \text{ year}}$$

4 These definitions were proposed to the BBA by Group Treasury at The Royal Bank of Scotland.

TABLE 13.9 NSFR stable funding calculation.

Available stable funding The sum of:	Required stable funding The sum of:
▪ 100% of total Tier 1 and Tier 2 capital and preferred stock ▪ 100% of liabilities with a contractual maturity greater than one year ▪ 85% of "stable" retail and small business deposits with maturity less than one year ▪ 70% of "less stable" retail and small business with maturity less than one year ▪ 50% of large corporate deposits with maturity less than one year	▪ 0% cash, securities with a maturity less than one year, inter-bank loans with a maturity less than one year, securities held with an offsetting reverse repo ▪ 5% unpledged high-quality liquid securities (similar definition to central bank eligible collateral) ▪ 20% corporate & covered bonds with a proven record of liquidity (i.e., no major increases in repo haircut in the last 10 years) ▪ 50% other corporate bonds, gold, equities, loans to corporates with a maturity less than one year ▪ 85% retail loans with a maturity less than one year ▪ 100% all loans with maturity greater than one year, all other assets ▪ 10% of all undrawn committed credit lines and overdraft facilities ▪ 100% of percentage of guarantees, uncommitted credit lines, letters of credit, money market mutual fund repo obligations and so on

- Given that the problem during the 2008 crisis was one of over-reliance on short-term (< 1 year) wholesale funding, an alternative calculation of the metric could be of the form:

$$\frac{\text{Unsecured wholesale funding} < 1 \text{ year}}{\text{Total deposits} + \text{Debt securities in issue} + \text{Capital}}.$$

The second calculation would provide a useful measure of exposure to short-term funding risk, a key monitoring element of liquidity risk management. Irrespective of the form of calculation adopted, in essence the purpose of the NFSR is to control the level of maturity transformation that an institution undertakes. Although it may be considered draconian by some bankers, its implementation will reduce liquidity risk exposure in the banking system at the aggregate level.

Long-term Liquidity Limits

Many liquidity metrics are designed not only as snapshot views of a bank's liquidity position; they should also be monitored over time. A trending limit is implemented to provide an element of warning should the bank's funding structure be slowly deteriorating over an extended period. This is illustrated hypothetically at Figure 13.3. Structural thresholds are defined in terms of gap ratios for maturities greater than one year; that is, the structural liquidity profile should be stable and balanced over time, assuming all financing constraints (for example, that long-term assets cannot be funded with very short-term liabilities) are consistent with the maturity transformation limits desired by the bank. By setting long-term limits, a bank will be aware when these approach a critical warning level.

For example, the long-term trend may be set as follows:

- ratio between liabilities/assets over 1 year > 98%
- ratio between liabilities/assets over 3 year > 85%
- ratio between liabilities/assets over 5 year > 70%.

A bank that reports liquidity risk using the suite of metrics listed in the two preceding sections will be able to give a transparent picture of its liquidity position, which is essential to help ensure orderly regulatory supervision. There are additional metrics available, to help provide a more detailed picture, which are considered next.

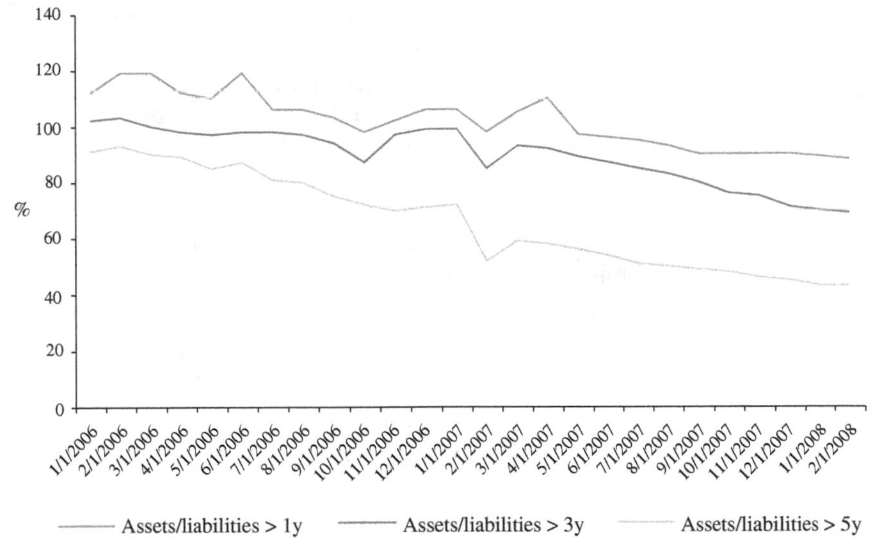

FIGURE 13.3 Trend of gap ratio.

TACTICAL LEVEL LIQUIDITY METRICS

We now describe additional liquidity metrics that we recommend banks to adopt.[5]

Contractual Maturity Mismatch

This is given by assets at their latest possible maturity against liabilities at their earliest possible maturity. It is a measure of the theoretical maximum funding risk, in gap terms, that the bank is running. The objective is to identify the gaps between the contractual inflows and outflows of liquidity for specified time bands. The metric measures contractual cash flow from all on- and off-balance sheet items. Other factors are:

- asset flows should be reported according to their latest possible maturity;
- liability cash flows should be reported according to their earliest possible date of outflow;
- contractual cash flows related to any open-maturity, callable, puttable or extendable issuance should be analysed, based on the earliest possible repayment date;
- instruments that have no specific maturity should be reported separately, with details on the instruments, with no assumptions applied.

This is a straightforward metric to calculate. However, for accurate MI analysis, the contract maturity date of an asset is often longer than its actual maturity date in practice, while the contract maturity of liabilities is for retail products often shorter than its actual maturity in practice. For example, Figure 13.4A shows the maturity profile for retail mortgages. For this reason the liquidity ratio and other metrics use adjusted tenors to consider the amortisation and "stickiness" of assets and liabilities.

Vento and La Ganga (2009) formalise two metrics that are essentially contractual maturity mismatch numbers. The first is the long-term funding ratio (LTFR), which is based on the cash flow profile arising from all on- and off- balance sheet items. It reports the share of assets with a maturity of n years or more that is funded through liabilities of the same maturity, given by:

$$LTFR = \frac{\Sigma_i \, out\ flows_i(> n\ years)}{\Sigma_i \, in\ flows_i(> n\ years)}$$

5 Thanks to Millie Teasdale at Tonbridge Grammar School for preparing the charts used in this section.

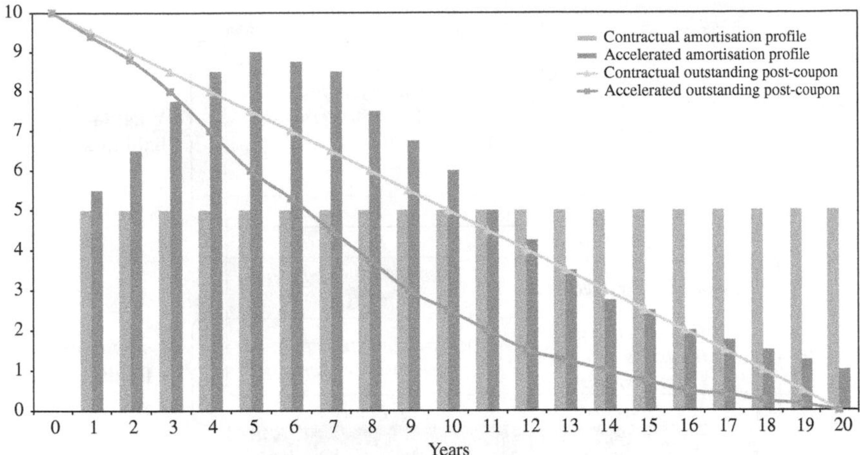

FIGURE 13.4A Contractual and accelerated amortisation profile, retail mortgages.

It is essentially the long-term contractual funding position and therefore a measure of the bank's structural funding position.

Their second metric is the cash capital position (CCP). This is calculated on the premise that to ensure a long term stable funding outlook, ideally total marketable assets (TLA) should be funded only by total volatile liabilities (TVL), and that otherwise illiquid assets should be funded only by stable liabilities. This mirrors one of the principles of liquidity we noted in Chapter 12.

The CCP approach is illustrated at Figure 13.4B. It is the difference between TLA and the sum of TVL and commitments to lend (CTL), that is,

$$CCP = TLA - TVL - CLT$$

and measures a bank's ability to fund its assets on a collateralised basis. If the result is negative, it shows that illiquid assets are greater than long-term funding and therefore a potentially unstable liquidity arrangement.

The drawback of CCP and LTFR of course is that the exact maturity of both assets and liabilities, when comparing contractual to behavioural values, may be difficult to estimate. Also, it is a judgement call as to how exactly to define "liquid", unless one takes the conservative view that only risk-free sovereign assets are genuinely liquid in a stressed situation.

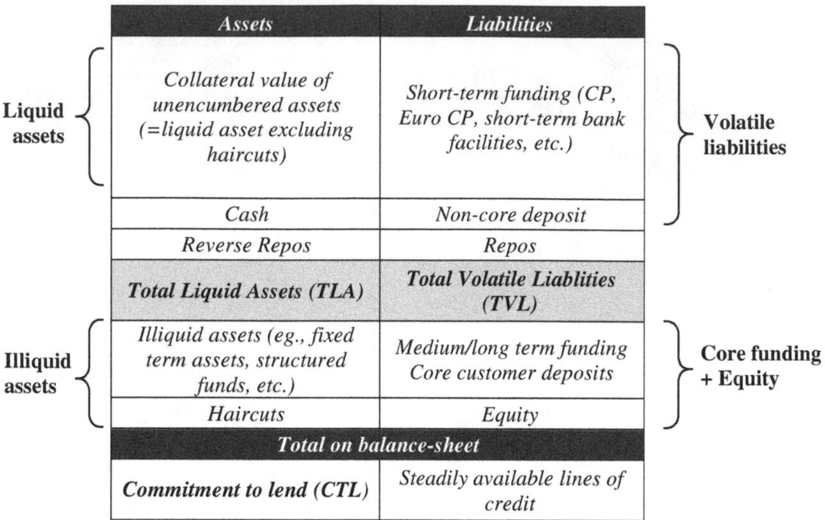

Assets
Liabilities
Liquid assets
Collateral value of unencumbered assets (=liquid asset excluding haircuts)
Short-term funding (CP, Euro CP, short-term bank facilities, etc.)
Volatile liabilities
Cash
Non-core deposit
Reverse Repos
Repos
Total Liquid Assets (TLA)
Total Volatile Liablities (TVL)
Illiquid assets
Illiquid assets (eg., fixed term assets, structured funds, etc.)
Medium/long term funding Core customer deposits
Core funding + Equity
Haircuts
Equity
Total on balance-sheet
Commitment to lend (CTL)
Steadily available lines of credit

FIGURE 13.4B The cash capital position
(Source: Vento and La Ganga (2009)).

Available Unencumbered Assets

The aggregate marketable assets are acceptable as collateral in secondary markets, and/or eligible for central banks' standing facilities, by currency. The objective of this metric is to provide supervisors with quantitative and qualitative data of the banks' available unencumbered assets, which may potentially be used as collateral to raise additional secured funding in secondary markets, and as such may potentially be additional sources of liquidity.

The parameters required for this metric include:

- the amount, type and location of available unencumbered assets that could serve as collateral for secured borrowing in secondary markets;
- the amount, type, and location of available unencumbered assets that are eligible for secured financing with relevant central banks;
- each of the above categorised by currency;
- estimated haircuts that the secondary market and/or relevant central bank would require for each asset;
- expected monetised value of the collateral (rather than the notional amount); where the assets are actually held and what business lines in the bank have access to those assets.

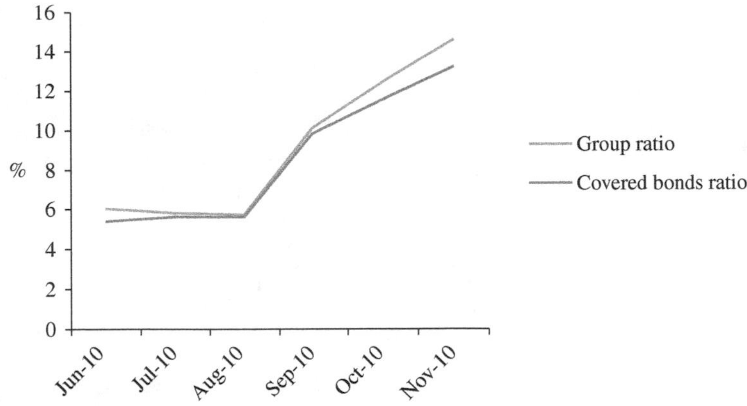

Group ratio:
All encumbered assets / Total funded balance sheet

Covered bonds ratio:
Covered bonds issed / Total assets

FIGURE 13.5 Encumbered asset ratio trend.

Again, this is a straightforward metric that provides excellent transparency for the Board and regulators. The trend of the ratio of encumbered to unencumbered assets is reported as part of the MI metrics in the ALCO pack, with an example shown at Figure 13.5.

Funding Concentration by Time Bands

This includes the following types of metric:

- Significant counterparties/Bank balance sheet total;
- Significant product or instrument/Bank balance sheet total;
- List of asset and liability balances by significant currency.

These are similar to the concentration and funding source metrics described in our key liquidity metrics section earlier. The second of these is a worthwhile metric to report, because it can highlight potentially risky reliance on one particular type of funding product.

Market Lock-out Horizon

This metric measures the number of consecutive weekdays the bank can continue to be cash flow positive if there is no access to unsecured funding

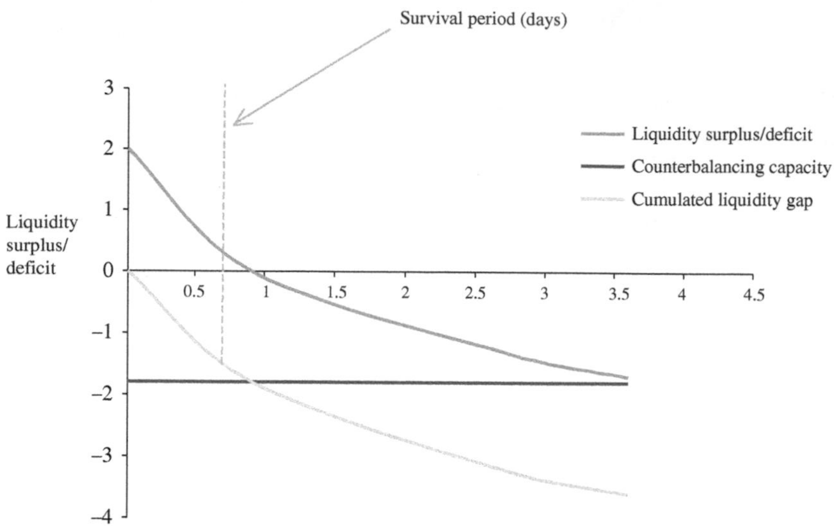

FIGURE 13.6 Market lock-out period or "survival period".

and no funding rollover is possible. A bank may apply a variety of stress scenarios against its cash flows to ensure that it is able to maintain funding in stress scenarios for a minimum period of time. One such stress scenario is a market lockout scenario where the bank has (i) no access to unsecured wholesale markets, and (ii) finds that maturing unsecured wholesale funding cannot be rolled over. In this situation, the bank will need to rely on a portfolio of unencumbered liquid assets to withstand the market lockout.The bank should then define a limit, as a minimum number of days that it can stay funding positive.

Another expression for this metric is the "survival period". It is defined in the same way as the lockout horizon: the time during which the bank is able to meet its liquidity needs without accessing the unsecured funding market. In other words, this indicator represents the "break-even point" between the gap created by the cumulative cash positions and the "counterbalancing capacity" available via the bank's stock of eligible collateral. This is illustrated at Figure 13.6.

Setting a minimum number of days for this period creates another liquidity limit for the bank.

Cash Outflow Liquidity Reserves: Survival Period

This reports the same metric as the preceding one, but we describe it separately because it is presented in a different format. Table 13.10 shows

TABLE 13.10 Cash flow survival horizon and outflow limit metric.

	1/11/2010	Compliant	1/10/2010	Compliant
Survival horizon	23 days versus target of 14 days	Y	9 days versus target of 14 days	N
2-week outflow metric	−\$56 billion versus −\$100 billion limit	Y	–\$91 billion versus –\$100 billion limit	Y
3-month outflow metric	+\$41 billion surplus versus target surplus number	Y	+\$16 bln versus target surplus number	Y

Metric reported twice-monthly to regulator

the values for the current month and the previous month, and note that in this case the bank has set a limit for the absolute dollar size of the outflow, as well as one for the survival period (which is set by the regulator in any case). The report is sent to the regulator every two weeks. In this example, we observe that the bank was within its own absolute limits throughout, but was outside the regulator 2-week limit in the previous month. The report acted as a catalyst for the mitigating action taken.

The trend over time is shown at Figure 13.7.

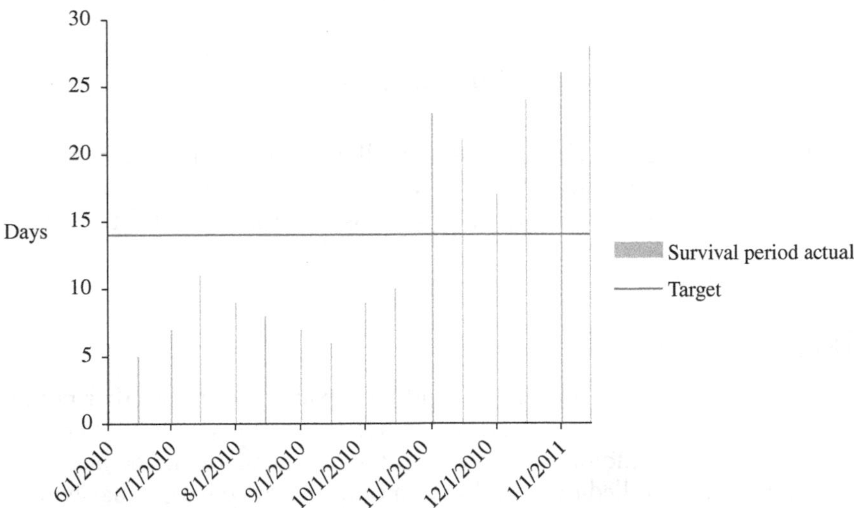

FIGURE 13.7 Trend of cash outflow survival period.

Undrawn Commitments Report

Undrawn commitments are funds which the bank has committed to make available to customers, but which have not yet been called upon. These include:

- credit card facilities;
- undrawn formal standby lending facilities and credit lines;
- liquidity facilities to customer CP programmes;
- unused overdraft facilities;
- revolving underwriting facilities;
- documentary letters of credit;
- forward asset purchases and forward deposits.

This report measures the aggregate actual level of total undrawn commitments. It is used to control the maximum amount of contractual liquidity outflow possible at a particular point in time if all the bank's customers drew upon the committed facilities that were available to them. To manage this risk a bank should set limits on the maximum cash amount of potential funded draw-downs. The higher this limit number, the larger will be the liquidity exposure for the bank.

The two common risk metrics used to monitor undrawn exposure changes are:

- undrawn commitment / aggregate lending ratio;
- undrawn commitment movements. This number may have an "early warning" limit of (say) 10% or 20% set against it, so that ALCO can monitor increases in the size of commitments.

In an LCR or LAB-related stress test, all undrawn commitments will be assumed to be drawn down and hence viewed as cash outflows. Therefore it is important to monitor this metric closely, as it is a significant driver of the liquidity buffer size.

Surplus Funding Capacity

This is a measure of the amount of funding capacity that exists after taking into account the headroom required to survive a stress event (whether a firm-specific event and/or market-wide), the extent that existing liabilities and assets will be rolled over, and the amount of new business that will be put on, over a given period of time.

Aggregate Limit Metrics

Liquidity management procedure will include the setting of actual limits for specific funding types. The level of each limit will be a function of the bank's appetite for funding risk and the structure of its funding base. Limits may be set as per the following:

Wholesale funding < 1 year (unsecured wholesale funding)	Max.[ ] bln
Liquidity reserves (cash and central bank eligible securities)	Min.[ ] bln
Amount of short-term wholesale funding (Total amount of unsecured short-term wholesale funding less than one year)	Max.[ ] bln

The composition of short-term and long-term wholesale funding is observed over time, to observe the trend and also to use in forecasting, planning and contingency planning. Figures 13.8A and 13.8B are examples of these reports. A bank will also set absolute and relative share limits against each source of funding, which these reports are used to monitor against. Table 13.11 is an example of a further breakdown of the short-term wholesale funding numbers.

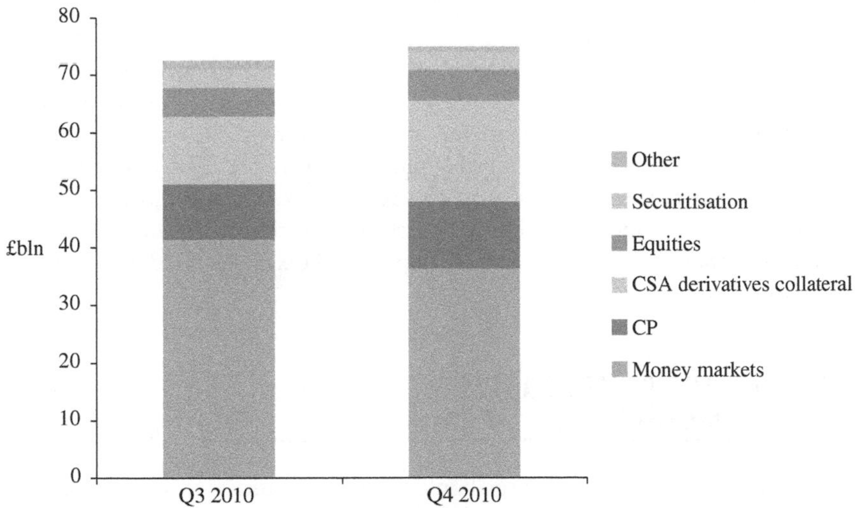

FIGURE 13.8A Wholesale liabilities: short term.

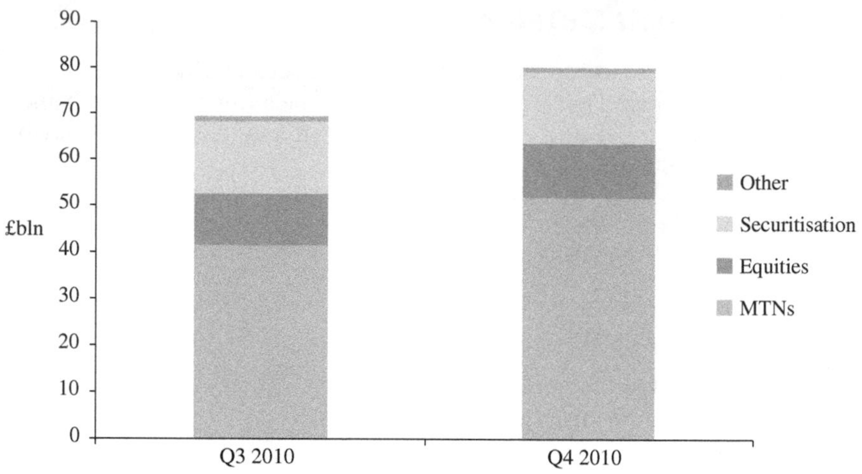

FIGURE 13.8B Wholesale liabilities: long term.

TABLE 13.11 Short-term wholesale funding report.

	Actual Q1 2010	Q2 2010	Q3 2010	Q4 2010	*Forecast* Q1 2011
Bank deposits	31.8	21.7	20.6	23.1	24.5
Debt securities	48.7	51.6	51.9	51.8	50.4

For banks that engage in significant cross-border or foreign currency operations, it is important when analysing liquidity metrics not to assume that currencies will remain transferrable in a stress situation, even for currencies which in normal times are highly convertible. The experience of the 1997 Asian currency crisis serves to remind us that individual country jurisdictions may impose restrictions on the convertibility of their currency, or on the outflow of foreign currency deposits. This cross-border risk needs to be monitored against limits.

EXTERNAL AND COMPARATIVE LIQUIDITY METRICS

Banks operate within a wider inter-bank community and economy, which are ultimately inter-connected in the global economy. A proper understanding of one's own liquidity position and risk exposure requires regular review and assessment of external indicators, including absolute levels in the market and the position of peer group banks within it. The following metrics and statistics should be collated and reported by the Treasury department, and circulated to ALCO and other senior management committees.

Market-related Monitoring Tools

This is not an internal bank liquidity metric, but rather a statement by the BCBS that a bank should use external market indicators as part of its intelligence in managing liquidity risk. In other words, a bank should wherever possible use high-frequency market data as proxy early warning indicators in monitoring potential liquidity difficulties for itself or within the market overall.

This might include the following:

- market-wide information, such as equity prices, debt market yields and spreads (money markets, medium/long-term bonds, derivatives, government bond markets, CDS indices and so on), and foreign exchange rates;
- bank-specific information, such as equity prices, CDS spreads, money-market trading prices, ease of liquidity rollover, and bank-specific rates for various tenors of funding;
- back-testing of market data. For example, back-testing analysis would (unsurprisingly) show a significant increase in spread level observed for the Euribor 3-month versus the EONIA 3-month swap following the market events of August 2007. This is shown at Figure 13.9. It is

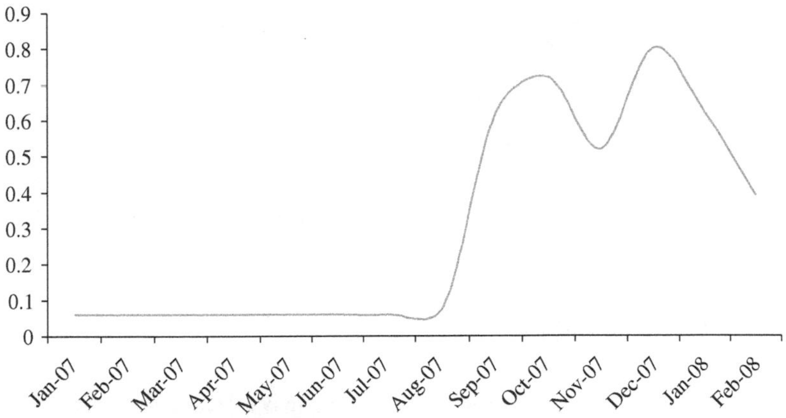

FIGURE 13.9 3-month Euribor versus 3-month EONIA spread.
Source: Bloomberg L.P.

sometimes difficult to spot a trend until one is well into it, so this type of analysis should not influence the general liquidity principles that the bank has set for itself; however, there is certainly value in observing market rates and back-testing as part of trend analysis.

Regulators will also be monitoring the same market-wide data.

Peer-group Comparison

Figure 13.10 shows a comparison of a bank's funding costs against the levels of a selected group of its peers.[6] It shows the secondary market asset-swap level for each bank, for each tenor, as a spread over 6-month Euribor. (These types of funding rates are generally straightforward to obtain, from sources such as Bloomberg and Reuters.) Under stable market conditions, a bank will not wish to be too far away from the median and average rates for these levels, for its own funding considerations as well as external market perception. Additionally, the chart reveals which banks can fund to longer tenors; in our example, "Bank 1" has no level quoted for beyond the 4-year maturity, suggesting that investors have less faith in its longer term health.

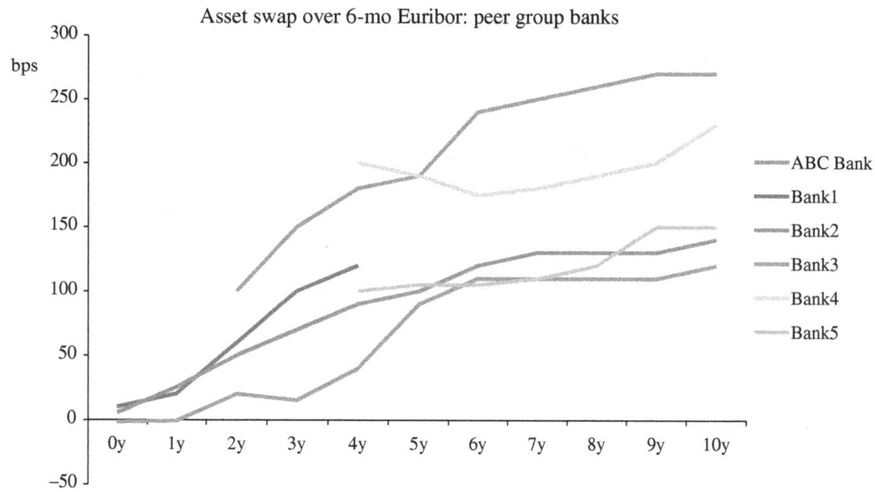

FIGURE 13.10 Comparison of funding levels, peer group of banks.

6 The peer group comparison is user-defined. A bank may select banks of the same size, same target customer base, same geographical location, same credit rating, the "leading group" of benchmark setters, or a mix of all these.

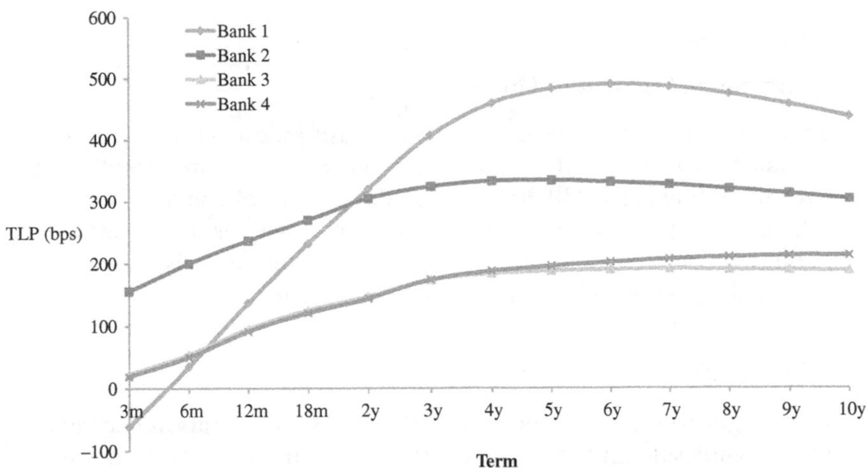

FIGURE 13.11 Peer group comparison COF curves, constructed using identical curve interpolation methodology.

Figure 13.10 represents data that can be observed in the market; for example, on Bloomberg. To ensure a complete like-for-like comparison, a bank should apply the same methodology it employs for constructing its own internal risky yield curve (described in Chapter 5) to produce an equivalent COF curve for its peer group banks, using the prices of peer bank-issued secondary market bonds. This will enable it to observe where its COF lies relative to its peer group, and is a more transparent and direct comparison.

Figure 13.11 shows an example of such a comparison COF curve for a peer group of four Tier 1 banks. The *y*-axis shows the floating-rate spread, or TLP over Libor for each bank's debt, as implied by current secondary market prices. The firm labelled "Bank 1" would conclude from this analysis that it is perceived as a higher risk in the market among investors; senior management would be expected to reign in asset origination and take measures to strengthen the bank's liquidity position.

EXAMPLE 13.1 STRATEGIC AND TACTICAL LIQUIDITY METRICS AT A MULTI-ENTITY UK BANK

A UK banking entity with extensive overseas operations includes the following suite of liquidity metrics in its Treasury MI reporting:

(*continued*)

Tactical Ratios

1. Maximum Cumulative Outflow

This metric measures the amount of net cash inflow/outflow from all on-balance sheet and off-balance sheet items under normal conditions over the following 14/30/90 calendar days. Normal conditions mean BAU customer behaviour for withdrawal and repayment of assets and liabilities. The term period that it is calculated for depends on specific bank-risk appetite and/or regulatory requirement.

2. Wholesale Borrowing Limit

A limit governing the amount that the Treasury operation can raise in the wholesale and inter-bank market, including intra-group and custodial funds. The limit must cover the requirement for all expected short-term liquidity.

3. Swapped Funds Limit

A foreign exchange liquidity limit of non-domestic funds that have been swapped into local currency.

Strategic Ratios

1. Advances/Deposits ratio: corporate and retail loans as a percentage of corporate and retail deposits. This is the LTD ratio.
2. Commitments guideline limit: a limit placed on the value of customer undrawn committed facilities.
3. Medium-term funding ratio: this is the ratio of liabilities with a maturity greater than one year to assets with a maturity greater than one year. It is similar in concept, if not in calculation, to the NSFR.
4. Liquid assets ratio: a ratio of cash and readily marketable securities to total assets.
5. Net inter-bank lending: a limit placed on the level of net inter-bank lending. This can be set as always positive; in other words, the bank can only ever be a lender to the wholesale market, not a borrower.

EXAMPLE 13.2 SPECIFYING THE LIQUIDITY RISK APPETITE

Table 13.12 is an extract from the liquidity policy statement of a medium-sized UK commercial banking institution. It articulates the liquidity risk appetite that the bank follows. This is an important part of liquidity and ALM risk management: a coherent statement of the bank's risk tolerances, defined as part of an overall ALM strategy framework. From the example illustrated, we observe that apart from the maturity transformation limit, this bank is currently within its board-approved risk tolerances. It also has an objective of reducing the ALM gap to increase its liquidity ratios, but these are to meet internal targets; it is within its regulatory limits for this metric.

TABLE 13.12 Liquidity risk appetite.

Assumptions		Actual position
1. Funding liabilities	*Total liabilities – Capital (Shareholders equity + Subordinated debt + Reserves) – Other liabilities*	£3,950 mm
2. Customer deposits	*Private customer deposits + Corporate customer deposits + Financial institutions deposits*	£1,905 mm
3. Private customer deposits	Deposits from private customers that behave in line with FSA description of *retail deposits*	£1,235 mm
4. Funding source	Counterparties with similar characteristics, especially a shared trigger that would see this funding evaporate	
5. Liquid currencies	USD, EUR, GBP, JPY, CAD, SEK, NOK, DKK, CHF, AUD, NZD	

Limits	Actual position	Target position
Liquidity ratio ("maturity mismatch")		
Regulatory		
--- Sight – 8 days > 0.00%	13.95%	N/A
--- Sight – 1 month > –5.00%	1.66%	N/A

(*continued*)

Targets	Actual position	Target position
Internal		
--- Sight – 8 days > 3.00%	13.95%	15.00%
--- Sight – 1 month > 0.00%	1.66%	2.00%
Maturity transformation		
Average asset tenor < 24 times average liability tenor	Average funding tenor = 39 days	Funding increases to 50 days
	Average lending = 1,192 days	Transformation = 24 times
	Maturity transformation = 30 times	
Funding source concentration		
No individual counterparty > 10% of funding	Largest counterparty = 95%	OK. 10% = £395 mm
No source > 25% or £1,000 mm (except private retail)	Largest source = Local authority deposits (£670 m) = 17%	OK. Max = £1,000 mm
Customer deposits > 40% of funding	£1,905 m/£3950 = 48%	
FX mismatch		
No mismatch > 50% of currency volume		
No mismatch > £50 mm per currency		
Cash buffer		
Cash buffer minimum 2% of liabilities at all times	£100 mm	OK. 2% = £80 mm

CONCLUSION

There is no right answer to the question, "How many liquidity metrics should a bank monitor against limits?". It depends on the nature of the bank's business model and the structure of its liabilities base. What is important is that the correct type and number of metrics should be employed that enable the bank to produce timely, accurate and reliable MI, and which provide senior management with the ability to understand the bank's liquidity position at all times.

Finally, it is as well to remember that banks do not exist in isolation from one another, their customers or their markets. It is possible to follow an efficient and responsible liquidity policy, supplemented by accurate and reliable MI, and still experience funding stress, perhaps because of market-wide disruption, a country-wide or regional recession or some other unpredictable factor. This chapter may imply that liquidity management is essentially a quantitative discipline. Actually it is as much a qualitative as a quantitative one. Finance is a relationship or "people" business. An understanding of the wider market, and the bank's interactions within it, is a vital part of bank ALM. A key part of ALM and liquidity risk policy is to maintain relationships with other banks, customers, stakeholders and regulators during the normal course of business. It is also important to have an understanding of peer group and investor behaviour. In stressed markets it is difficult, if not impossible, to build relationships. They need to be built and maintained during stable times beforehand.

REFERENCES AND BIBLIOGRAPHY

Vento, G., and La Ganga, P. (2009), "Bank Liquidity Risk Management and Supervision: Which Lessons from Recent Market Turmoil?", *Journal of Money, Investment and Banking*, Issue 10, pp. 79–126

CHAPTER 14

Liquidity Risk Reporting and Stress Testing

The previous chapter highlighted the nature of liquidity risk exposure measurement. We press on further with a look at benchmark liquidity risk reporting, and stress testing reporting output. We look at a range of quantitative and qualitative liquidity reports, as part of our approach to a general understanding of liquidity risk management at the aggregate overview level.

We begin with an illustration using examples of baseline liquidity reports. This is followed with a description of additional liquidity reports, together with a summary of the reporting frequency required by UK regulated banks. This regulatory reporting requirement is similar in most other jurisdictions. The second part of the chapter looks at the presentation of liquidity stress testing results.

A number of the reports shown here are available as template spreadsheets on the Wiley website supplementary material (see Chapter 19 for details).

LIQUIDITY RISK REPORTING

A bank will produce a number of liquidity reports in the normal course of business, on a daily, weekly, monthly and quarterly basis. It is important that the format of liquidity MI is both transparent and accessible. We illustrate a sample of reports that provide a benchmark framework for reporting.

Deposit Tracker Report

The deposit tracker is a simple report of the current size of deposits, together with a forecast of what the level of deposits are expected to be going forward. This report is tracked weekly and monthly because it provides an idea of the LTD ratio in the immediate short term. As we saw in the previous chapter, the LTD is a key management liquidity ratio.

Table 14.1A shows the first part of a typical deposit tracker report for a medium-sized commercial bank, as at month-end May 2009. We see that the report provides the following:

- the month-end actuals for deposits by customer type;
- the change from each month-end
- the aggregate customer assets and hence, the LTD ratio;
- a forecast of the position for the month-end for each month to the end of the year.

We see that this bank is required to meet a Board-approved LTD ratio limit of 85%, which it is just exceeding as at the date of this report, but the forecast for year-end is within this.

Table 14.1B is the second part of the deposit tracker, it shows how much liabilities will need to increase, or assets reduce, all else being equal, for the bank to meet a particular LTD ratio. Figure 14.1 is a graphical presentation of the deposit tracker report.

Figure 14.2A from the report shows the customer deposits by account type and tenor, while Figure 14.2B shows the deposits' maturity profile. This illustration assists the Treasury department to gauge the trend of the deposit balances over time. For example, from Figure 14.2A it is clear that a large percentage of the retail bank deposits are current accounts and rolling deposits, with very little fixed-term deposits. For regulatory purposes, these funds will be treated as short-term liabilities and will not assist the bank's regulatory liquidity metrics (which emphasises long-term funds), even though the local regulator may allow the bank to treat overnight balances as longer term if they can be shown to be acting as such in "behavioural" terms. In this case, it is worthwhile for the bank to undertake a marketing exercise to determine if customers may be interested in moving their deposits into fixed-term or notice accounts. Any increase in the size of the latter will improve the firm's liquidity metrics.

The forecast element of this report is based essentially on objective judgement. The historical trend up to the current date will assist in making the forecast; otherwise, it is a case of making as best an estimate as possible, with inputs from the relationship managers who look after the various customer accounts.

Daily Liquidity Report

The daily liquidity report is a straightforward spreadsheet detailing the bank's liquid and marketable assets, together with liabilities, up to 1-year

TABLE 14.1A Deposit tracker report, month-end actuals and year-end forecast.

Deposit Tracker	Month End Actuals						Forecasts						
	31/12/ 2008	31/01/ 2009	28/02/ 2009	31/03/ 2009	30/04/ 2009	28/05/ 2009	30/06/2009	31/07/ 2009	30/08/ 2009	30/09/ 2009	31/10/ 2009	30/11/ 2009	31/12/ 2009
Eligible Correspondent Banks	482,236	431,166	485,302	507,193	536,907	493,930	515,753	520,753	520,753	520,753	525,753	530,753	535,753
Corporate Client Deposits	449,871	375,849	248,677	263,267	243,710	280,248	273,893	273,893	273,893	273,893	273,893	273,893	273,893
Private Bank Client Deposits	14,168	23,334	18,990	102,174	102,582	99,119	99,123	99,123	99,123	124,123	124,123	124,123	124,123
Local Authority Deposits	196,624	195,814	192,100	226,622	267,001	325,016	333,287	343,287	348,287	373,287	393,287	413,287	433,287
Retail Bank Deposits	1,234,799	1,318,219	1,323,738	1,264,323	1,293,918	1,258,133	1,264,025	1,264,025	1,264,025	1,264,025	1,264,025	1,264,025	1,264,025
Eligible Private Bank Correspondent Banks	24,864	37,456	38,358	37,196	37,388	35,512	35,529	35,529	35,529	35,529	35,529	35,529	35,529
Treasury Sales	5,775	5,198	4,477	3,846	822	770	763	763	763	763	763	763	763
Total Customer Deposits:	2,408,337	2,387,036	2,311,642	2,404,621	2,482,328	2,492,728	2,522,373	2,537,373	2,542,373	2,592,373	2,617,373	2,642,373	2,667,373
M/M +/–		–21301	–75394	92,979	77,707	10,400	29,645	15,000	5,000	50,000	25,000	25,000	25,000
W/W +/–													
Mend +/–													
Drawdown – Month ahead							76,374	8,526	4,479	5,298	2,911	3,136	5,570
Repayment – From loans schedules							37,888	11,920	4,429	2,326	25,800	7,965	20,863
Forecast Monthly loan +/–							38,486	–3,394	50	2,972	–22,889	–4,829	–15,293
Total Customer Loans:	2,305,766	2,266,004	2,223,145	2,166,076	2,194,016	2,145,648	2,184,134	2,180,740	2,180,790	2,183,762	2,160,873	2,156,044	2,140,751
Loan-to-deposit %	95.74	94.93	96.17	90.08	88.39	86.08	86.59	85.94	85.78	84.24	82.56	81.59	80.26

TABLE 14.1B Deposit tracker, LTD ratio required cash flow changes.

							Forecasts						
Required:	LTD ratio	31/01/ 2009	28/02/ 2009	31/03/ 2009	30/04/ 2009	28/05/ 2009	30/06/ 2009	31/07/ 2009	30/08/ 2009	30/09/ 2009	31/10/ 2009	30/11/ 2009	31/12/ 2009
Liabilities increase	85	278,851	303,823	143,704	98,867	31,564	47,196	28,203	23,262	−23,241	−75,169	−105,851	−148,842
	84	310,588	334,959	174,041	129,596	61,615	77,786	58,746	53,805	7,344	−44,905	−75,654	−118,860
	83	343,089	366,846	205,109	161,065	92,390	109,113	90,025	85,085	38,666	−13,911	−44,730	−88,155
	82	376,384	399,510	236,935	193,301	123,916	141,205	122,066	117,127	70,752	17,838	−13,051	−56,701
	81	410,500	432,981	269,547	226,334	156,220	174,088	154,899	149,960	103,630	50,372	19,409	−24,470
	80	445,469	467,289	302,974	260,192	189,332	207,794	188,552	183,614	137,330	83,718	52,682	8,566
Assets reduce	85	−237,023	−258,249	−122,148	−84,037	−26,829	−40,117	−23,973	−19,773	19,755	63,894	89,973	126,516
	84	−260,894	−281,366	−146,194	−108,860	−51,756	−65,340	−49,347	−45,196	−6,169	37,720	63,550	99,842
	83	−284,764	−304,482	−170,241	−133,684	−76,684	−90,564	−74,720	−70,620	−32,093	11,547	37,126	73,168
	82	−308,634	−327,599	−194,287	−158,507	−101,611	−115,788	−100,094	−96,044	−58,016	−14,627	10,702	46,495
	81	−332,505	−350,715	−218,333	−183,330	−126,538	−141,012	−125,468	−121,468	−83,940	−40,801	−15,722	19,821
	80	−356,375	−373,831	−242,379	−208,154	−151,466	−166,235	−150,842	−146,891	−109,864	−66,975	−42,145	−6,853

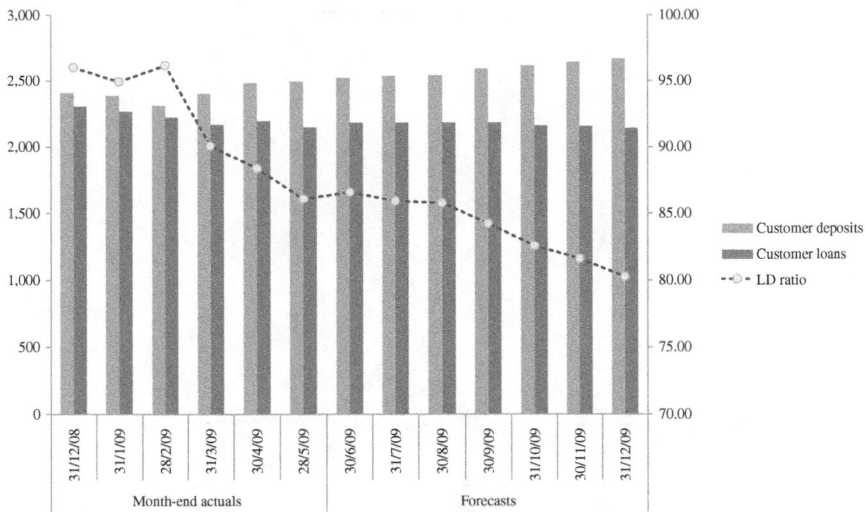

FIGURE 14.1 Deposit tracker, graphical illustration.

maturity and beyond. It provides an end-of-day of the bank's liquidity position for the Treasury and Finance departments. Each branch and subsidiary will complete one, although a bank that has only a branch structure (and no subsidiaries) may aggregate the report.

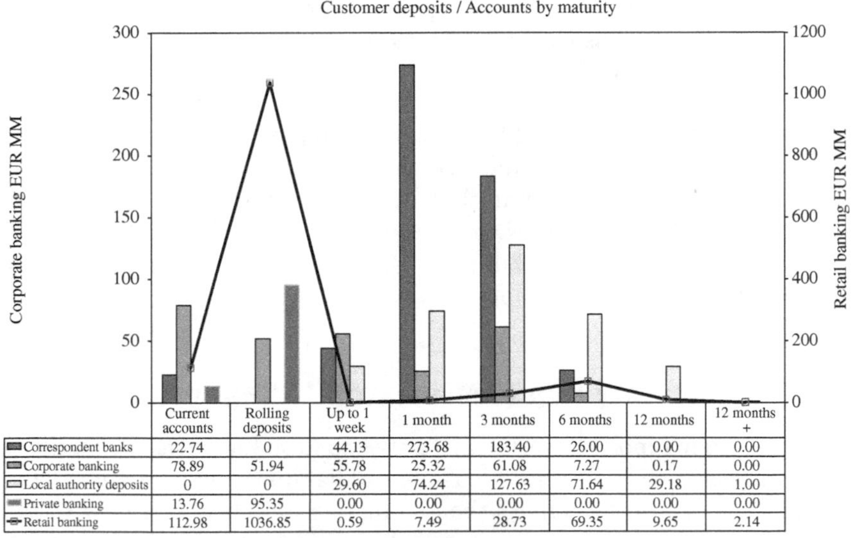

	Current accounts	Rolling deposits	Up to 1 week	1 month	3 months	6 months	12 months	12 months +
Correspondent banks	22.74	0	44.13	273.68	183.40	26.00	0.00	0.00
Corporate banking	78.89	51.94	55.78	25.32	61.08	7.27	0.17	0.00
Local authority deposits	0	0	29.60	74.24	127.63	71.64	29.18	1.00
Private banking	13.76	95.35	0.00	0.00	0.00	0.00	0.00	0.00
Retail banking	112.98	1036.85	0.59	7.49	28.73	69.35	9.65	2.14

FIGURE 14.2A Deposit tracker, deposit type and tenor.

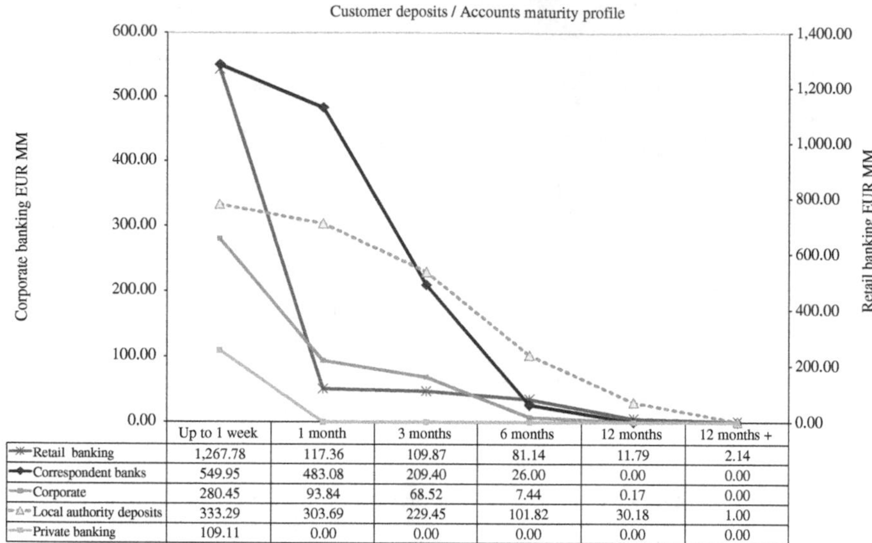

	Up to 1 week	1 month	3 months	6 months	12 months	12 months +
Retail banking	1,267.78	117.36	109.87	81.14	11.79	2.14
Correspondent banks	549.95	483.08	209.40	26.00	0.00	0.00
Corporate	280.45	93.84	68.52	7.44	0.17	0.00
Local authority deposits	333.29	303.69	229.45	101.82	30.18	1.00
Private banking	109.11	0.00	0.00	0.00	0.00	0.00

FIGURE 14.2B Deposits maturity profile.

We provide an example of a daily liquidity report for a commercial bank at Figure 14.3. This uses inputs from the bank's balance sheet accounting system to provide a summary of liquid assets, liabilities by tenor, and a cumulative liquidity report. Figure 14.3 is the summary of liquid securities; in this case these consist of government bonds, central bank eligible and non-eligible bank CDs. The value of securities deemed instantly liquid will be input to the liquidity ratio calculation report (see Chapter 13). Table 14.2A is the summary of assets and liabilities, and Table 14.2B is the cumulative liquidity report and liquidity risk factor calculation. The "counterbalancing capacity" in Table 14.2B is the sum of available securities to cover for sudden cash outflows.

This spreadsheet is available on the Wiley website supplementary material accompanying this book.

Funding Maturity Gap ("Mismatch") Report

The funding gap report shows the maturity gap (also known as the maturity mismatch) per time bucket, for all assets and liabilities, with an adjustment for liquid securities. It includes the cumulative liquidity cash flow of the previous report just described, and indeed the two reports can be combined. An extract is shown at Table 14.3. Figure 14.4 shows the maturity

SECURITIES AND CDs			
		00s	
		Input data	
Classification			
Marketable		Securities	CDs
Bank CDs: non-ECB eligible, liquid at maturity date (breakdown below)			231,645
Bank CDs: ECB eligible, liquid same day			0
ECB eligible securities, liquid in 1 week tender		649,967	
Non-ECB eligible securities, can be sold over 4 weeks		277,589	
Government securities		9,640	
TOTAL MARKETABLE SECURITIES AND CDs		**937,196**	**231,645**
Non-marketable			
Non-ECB eligible CD summary			
Average remaining tenor	Amount		
1 day			
2 days			
1 week			
2 weeks	6,645		
1 month	25,000		
2 months	50,000		
3 months	35,000		
6 months	115,000		
12 months			

FIGURE 14.3 List of liquid securities: input to daily liquidity report.

mismatch in graphical form. The key indicates the cash flow for each type of product.

The same report is used to generate the cash flow survival horizon report. This is shown at Figure 14.5. We observe that the bank in this example has a survival horizon of only seven days under normal circumstances; when the cash flow value of liquid securities and other adjustments is included, we see that the survival period is extended to 27 days. This is still below the Basel III requirement, and so on the strength of this report the bank will need to take action to address the liquidity shortage.

The full report spreadsheets, with breakdown by product type and incorporating cell formulae, are available on the Wiley website.

TABLE 14.2A Asset and liability cash flows.

	Input data										
ASSETS 000s	**1 day**	**2 days**	**1 week**	**2 weeks**	**1 month**	**2 months**	**3 months**	**6 months**	**<1 year**	**> 1 year**	**Total**
Non-marketable Securities & CDs											0
Retail call a/c	6,754	0	0	0	0	0	0	0	0	0	6,754
Retail time deposit	432	3,533	0	4	4	4,529	9	1,619	420	23,749	34,299
Inter-Group call	4,725	0	0	0	0	0	0	0	0	0	4,725
Inter-Group time	19,199	89,848	281,434	90,150	135,378	73,895	60,768	21,379	5,912	244	778,207
Other bank call	56,568	0	0	0	0	0	0	0	0	0	56,568
Other bank time	5,465	148,347	188,620	7,833	89,500	30,020	0	25,319	128	83,985	579,217
Corporate call	30,658	0	0	0	0	0	0	0	0	0	30,658
Corporate time	13,936	112,975	35,335	53,432	10,923	159,894	133,718	63,182	116,551	1,365,637	2,065,583
Government bonds	161,011	0	19,361	35	335	303	9	868	678	84,857	267,457
TOTAL ASSETS	**298,748**	**354,703**	**524,750**	**151,454**	**236,140**	**268,641**	**194,504**	**112,367**	**123,689**	**1,558,472**	**3,823,468**
Average remaining duration of assets		44.59	Months								

	Input Data										
LIABILITIES 000s	**1 day**	**2 days**	**1 week**	**2 weeks**	**1 month**	**2 months**	**3 months**	**6 months**	**<1 year**	**> 1 year**	**TOTAL**
Without any stickiness assumptions											
Retail call	97,482	0	0	0	0	0	0	0	0	0	97,482
Retail time	19,780	18,250	120,492	65,241	123,345	113,741	157,361	126,162	50,841	1,993	797,206
Inter-Group call	50,996	0	0	0	0	0	0	0	0	0	50,996
Inter-Group time	72,276	136,744	351,130	233,319	60,987	161,120	43,881	101,896	24,294	0	1,185,647
Other bank call	235,097	0	0	0	0	0	0	0	0	0	235,097
Other bank time	16,088	116,319	135,796	21,210	121,181	85,287	192,512	64,901	0	0	753,294
Corporate call	60,085	0	0	0	0	0	0	0	0	0	60,085
Corporate time	17,937	94,226	173,805	152,144	94,976	111,413	47,748	18,394	11,475	0	722,118
Government	3,689	6,005	58,163	109,046	37,671	204,339	54,477	31,341	5,902	1,122	511,755
TOTAL LIABILITIES	573,430	371,544	839,386	580,960	438,160	675,900	495,979	342,694	92,512	3,115	4,413,680
Undrawn commitments		273,242									
Average remaining duration of liabilities		7.72	Months								

TABLE 14.2B Cumulative liquidity report.

Country: London
Currency: EUR
Date: 25-Nov-10

	Cumulative liquidity report								
	1 day	2 day	1 week	2 week	1 month	2 months	3 months	6 months	1 year
Cumulative net cash balance	(111,734)	(104,480)	(301,843)	(642,230)	(738,261)	(1,040,588)	(1,884,251)	(2,122,457)	(2,099,158)
Other forecast inflows									
Other forecast outflows									
Cumulative cash gap	(111,734)	(104,480)	(301,843)	(642,230)	(738,261)	(1,040,588)	(1,884,251)	(2,122,457)	(2,099,158)
Counterbalancing capacity	8,676	8,676	797,674	804,186	828,686	877,686	979,996	1,092,696	1,092,696
Liquidity gap	(103,058)	(95,804)	495,831	161,957	90,426	(162,902)	(904,256)	(1,029,761)	(1,006,462)
Limit									
Variance	(103,058)	(95,804)	495,831	161,957	90,426	(162,902)	(904,256)	(1,029,761)	(1,006,462)

Liquidity metrics

		Limit	
1-week Ratio	11.13%	0.00%	OK
1-month Ratio	2.03%	–5%	OK
Liquidity Risk Factor	3.85		

Liquidity risk factor

	Months	
Average remaining term of assets	44.5900	*Excluding marketable securities*
Adjusted for marketable securities	34.8776	
Average remaining term of liabilities	7.7200	*With no call stickiness*
Excluding call deposits	8.0046	
Average tenor of call deposits	37.55	
Combined average remaining term of liabilities	9.0593	
LRF	3.8499	

TABLE 14.3 Extract from maturity gap report.

Data as of 2 June 2010. All figures in EUR thousands unless otherwise noted.

Liquidity Management – Maturity Mismatch

No behavioural or stress adjustments applied

Inflows	Sight	Two – Eight Days	Nine Days – One Month	One – Three Months	Three – Six Months	Six Months – One Year	One – Three Years	Three – Five Years	Five Years and on	Total
TOTAL INFLOWS	(908,203,354)	(188,005,661)	(705,398,674)	(376,131,077)	(86,328,844)	(97,212,696)	(481,473,198)	(444,603,252)	(734,632,172)	(4,021,988,928)
Outflows	Sight	Two – Eight Days	Nine Days – One Month	One – Three Months	Three – Six Months	Six Months – One Year	One – Three Years	Three – Five Years	Five Years and on	Total
TOTAL OUTFLOWS	893,940,981	397,283,377	1,379,620,964	1,251,323,695	328,027,956	105,751,557	3,219,569	0	0	4,359,168,099
Behavioural Adjustments/Stress										OK
Net Mismatch per Bucket	(14,262,374)	209,277,716	674,222,290	875,192,618	241,699,112	8,538,861	(478,253,629)	(444,603,252)	(734,632,172)	337,179,171
Adjustments	Sight	Sight – 8 Days	Sight – 1 Month	Sight – Three Months	Sight – Six Months	Sight – One Year	Sight – Three Years	Sight – Five Years	Sight – Five Years	Total
TOTAL ADJUSTMENTS	(1,256,876,281)	(1,256,876,281)	(1,256,876,281)	(1,256,876,281)	(1,256,876,281)	(1,256,876,281)	(1,256,876,281)	(1,256,876,281)	(1,256,876,281)	(11,311,886,530)
Cumulative Mismatch	Sight	Sight – 8 Days	Sight – 1 Month	Sight – Three Months	Sight – Six Months	Sight – One Year	Sight – Three Years	Sight – Five Years	Sight – Five Years	
	(1,271,138,655)	(1,061,860,938)	(387,638,649)	487,553,969	729,253,082	737,791,943	259,538,314	(185,064,938)	(919,697,110)	
Liquidity Ratio	29.16%	24.36%	8.89%	−11.18%	−16.73%	−16.93%	−5.95%	4.25%	21.10%	
Behavioural Adjustments/Stress Variance	0.00%	0.00%	0.00%	0.00%	0.00%	0.00%	0.00%	0.00%	0.00%	
Internal Limit	0.00%	3.00%	−3.00%	0.00%	0.00%	0.00%	0.00%	0.00%	0.00%	
FSA Limit		0.00%	−5.00%							

NOTE
"Outflows" are LIABILITIES
"Inflows" are ASSETS

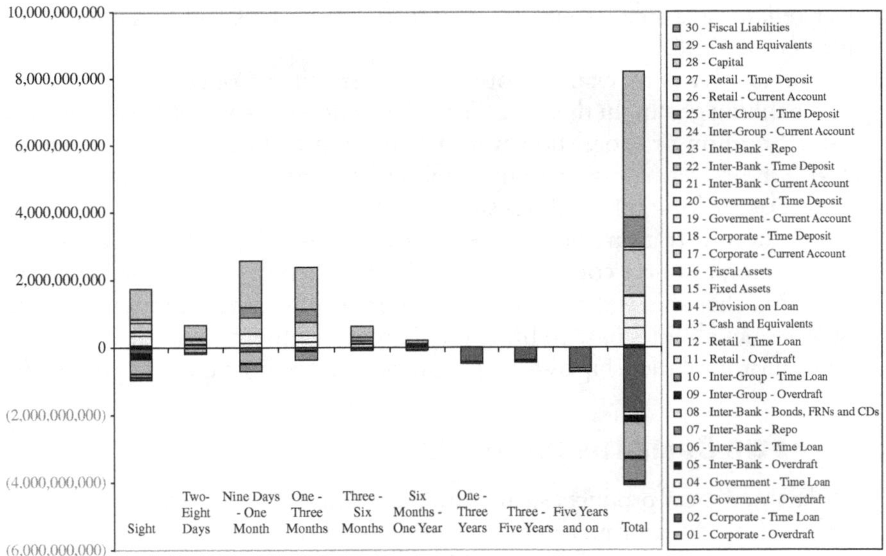

FIGURE 14.4 Graphical representation, maturity gap report.

Funding Concentration Report

Funding source concentration reports are key MI for senior Treasury and relationship managers. A central principle of liquidity management is funding diversity, and its emphasis that a bank should not become

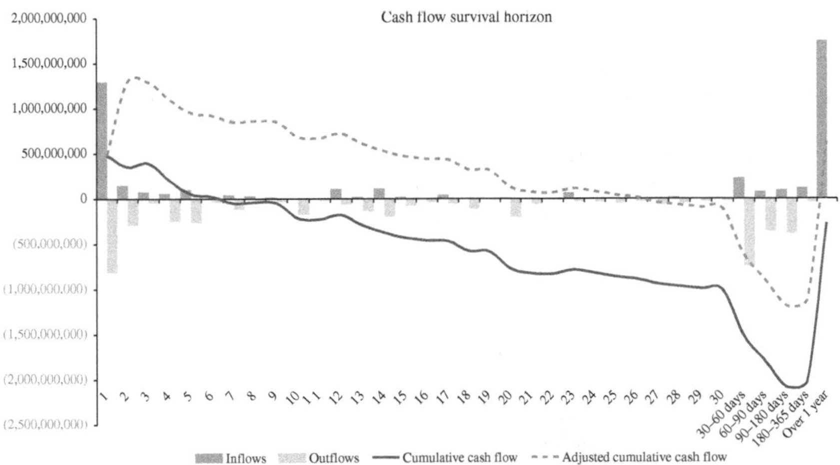

FIGURE 14.5 Cash flow survival horizon.

over-reliant on a single source, or sector, of funds. This includes reliance on intra-group funds.

Table 14.4 is an example of a Large Depositor Concentration Report for a banking group. In this case "large" is defined as someone that deposits USD50 million or more; however, a bank may define it in percentage of total liability terms rather than absolute amounts. Generally speaking, a deposit of 5% of total liabilities should be treated as large by ALCO.

In the illustration shown, the largest depositor ("CBS") exceeds the internal single-source concentration limit of 10% by a considerable margin. Assuming that this is a close customer relationship, the bank will need to increase its liabilities base to bring the share down to limit, or otherwise risk damaging the relationship by asking the depositor to remove some of the funds.

Undrawn Commitment Report

Off-balance sheet products such as liquidity lines, revolving credit facilities, letters of credit and guarantees are potential stress points for a bank's funding requirement. In a stress situation a bank can expect un-utilised liquidity and funding lines to be drawn down, as customers experience funding difficulties of their own. The existence of undrawn commitments can exacerbate funding shortages at exactly the wrong time, which is why liquidity metrics include such undrawn commitments. It is also a reason to report them separately.

Figure 14.6A is an example of an undrawn commitments report, showing trend over time, while Figure 14.6B shows the trend for both drawn and undrawn committed facilities. These are aggregate-level reports, the bank will also produce detailed breakdowns per customer.

Liability Profile

This is a simple breakdown of the share of each type of liability at the bank. An example is shown at Figure 14.7. In this case, the total liabilities of the bank are made up of the following categories:

- Customers: individuals;
- Customers: large enterprises;
- Repo (highly liquid securities);
- Repo (high-quality securities);
- Asset-backed securities;
- Unsecured: other wholesale;
- Repo (other assets);
- Conditional liabilities;

TABLE 14.4 Funding concentration report.

LARGE DEPOSITOR CONCENTRATION REPORT SUMMARY – 31 AUG 10

GROUP TREASURY Large Depositors by Country as a Percentage of Total Funding*

Country	Total Large Deposits '000s	% of External Country Funding	% of External Group Funding
A	1,652,551	44.3%	5.0%
B	1,193,328	27.0%	3.6%
C	1,061,180	33.6%	3.2%
D	818,658	10.4%	2.5%
E	119,664	4.7%	0.4%
F	50,195	3.7%	0.2%
G	40,000	4.0%	0.1%
Total	**4,935,577**		**15.0%**

* Large depositors lend Bank plc more than $50m

Large Depositors as a Percentage of Country and Total Funding

Customer	Deposit Amount 000s	Percentage of Countries External Funding								Percentage of Group External Funding **
		Bank plc	A	B	C	D	E	F	G	
CBS	844,101	16.5%		1.4%	0.8%					2.5%
CBL	588,777	7.4%			3.3%					1.8%
Customer 2	448,000		14.2%							1.4%
ACO	341,150			9.1%						1.0%

(*continued*)

TABLE 14.4 Funding concentration report (*continued*).

Bank Med	307,609	0.1%		7.1%	0.5%					0.9%
Sovereign Monetary Agency 1	300,000			8.0%						0.9%
CBJ	227,730	1.9%		2.8%			12.8%			0.7%
CBA	190,706			3.2%	0.9%					0.6%
Sovereign Monetary Agency 2	171,195	1.1%			0.9%			3.7%		0.5%
Banque Maghreb	145,000		4.6%							0.4%
Customer 1	142,516		4.5%							0.4%
Customer 3	133,080				1.7%					0.4%
AMF	122,850			3.3%						0.4%
Customer 4	102,600				1.3%					0.3%
R Bank	100,000			2.7%						0.3%
PetroCompany	94,421		3.0%							0.3%
ABC	92,819			2.3%	0.1%					0.3%
ALF	88,311		2.8%							0.3%
Retail depositor	80,000		2.5%							0.2%
Customer 5	68,116				0.9%					0.2%
Principal Bank	62,933		2.0%							0.2%
Sicon Construction	60,139								2.4%	0.2%
The Public Warehousing Co	59,526								2.3%	0.2%
GIB	54,000			1.4%						0.2%
SCB	50,000			0.3%		4.0%				0.2%
SIB	50,000			1.3%						0.2%
CBUAE	50,000			1.3%						0.2%
Total	**4,975,577**	**27.0%**	**33.6%**	**44.3%**	**10.4%**	**4.0%**	**12.8%**	**3.7%**	**4.7%**	**15.0%**

CBS is Bank plc's biggest depositor (16.5% of funding). This exceeds the Group's 10% max. depositor funding limit.

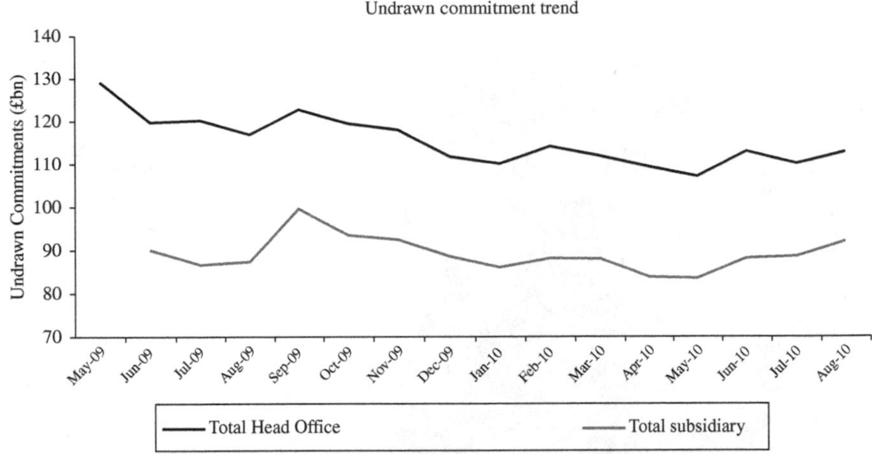

FIGURE 14.6A Undrawn commitment report, subsidiary.

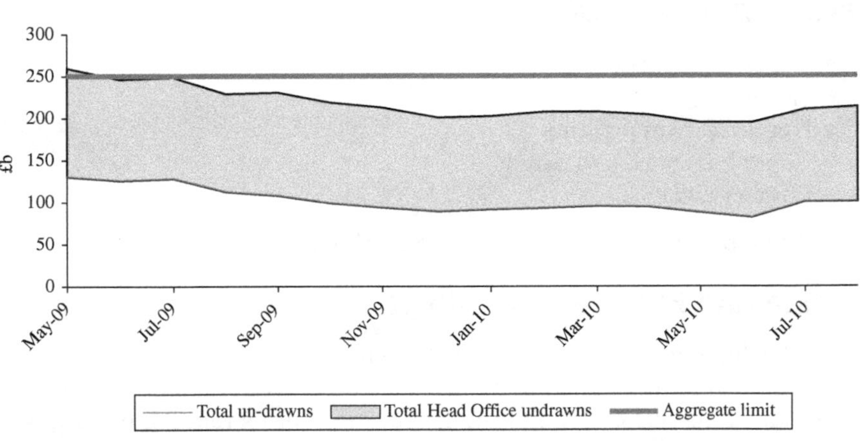

FIGURE 14.6B Undrawn commitment report, head office.

and the share of each is shown in the chart. Other types of funding sources by product type may include one or more of the following:

- Covered Bonds;
- Client free cash;
- Structured deposit products;
- Unsecured: credit institution;
- Unsecured: governments and central banks;
- Unsecured: non-bank financial;

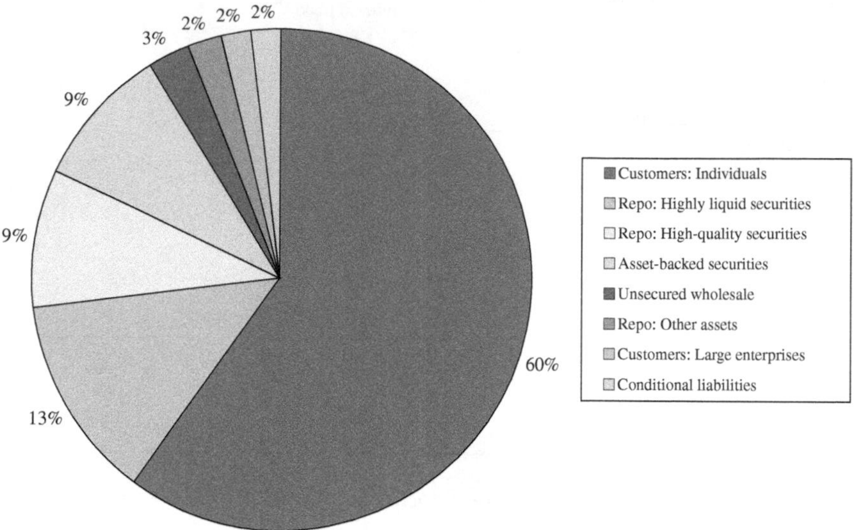

FIGURE 14.7 Liability profile.

- Customers: SME;
- Group;
- Net derivatives margin;
- Capital: undated and dated;
- Primary issuance.

The report format can be set to the user's desired choice.

Wholesale Pricing and Volume

A bank's liquidity position is not illustrated solely by its cash flow liquidity metrics. An indication of liquidity strength can also be gleaned from looking at a bank's funding costs, and the composition of its funding by product. The first, especially, is valuable market intelligence and the bank regulator will also be compiling this information. The regulatory authority can obtain an early warning of a particular bank experiencing funding stress if it observes that its funding yield curve is rising materially above that of its peer group. For individual bank senior management, it is difficult to obtain this information about other banks; however, it should be possible to get an idea of the peer group average from the regulator. A comparison to one's own funding level is a worthwhile exercise and should be undertaken on at least a quarterly basis.

Figure 14.8 is an example of a firm-specific yield curve for a UK bank. Figure 14.9 shows the breakdown of the same bank's wholesale funding by volume and product type.

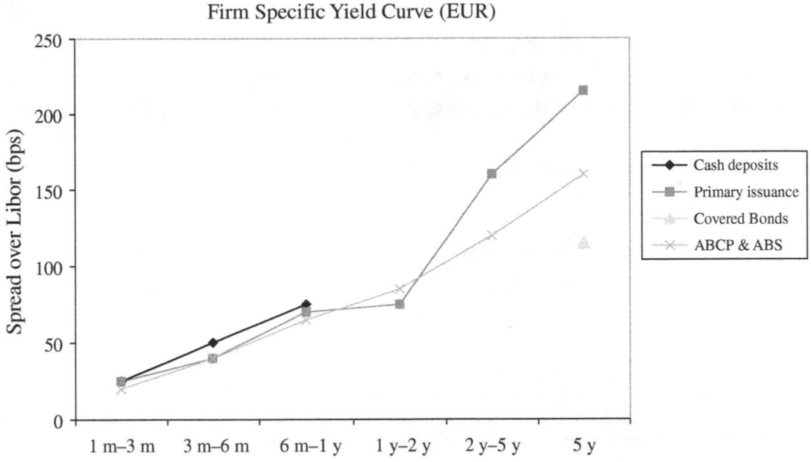

FIGURE 14.8 Firm-specific funding yield curve.

Summary and Qualitative Reports

Liquidity report MI for senior management should be presented as a 1-page summary of the key liquidity metrics. This can be distributed on a monthly basis or as directed by ALCO, although the distribution frequency may be

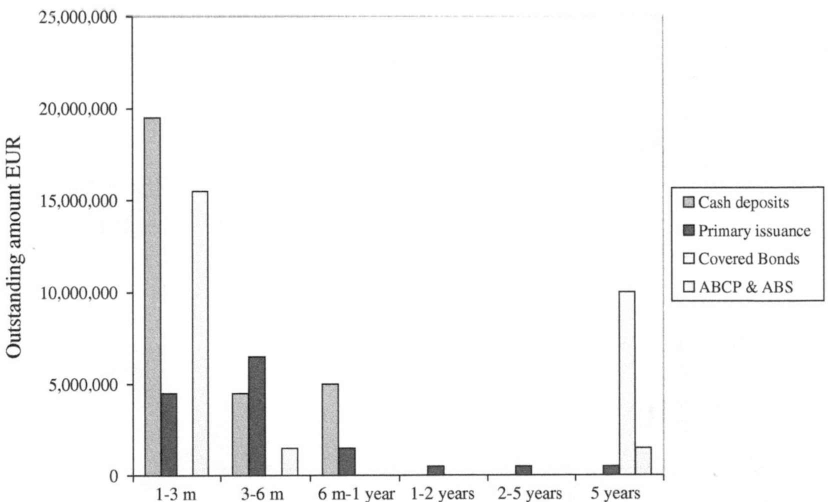

FIGURE 14.9 Wholesale funding breakdown by product and tenor bucket.

increased during a stress period. Keeping the report to one side of A4 will increase the chance that the report will actually be read and noted at senior management level, which is why these reports are an important part of liquidity MI. An example of a monthly summary report is presented at Figure 14.10.

MONTHLY LIQUIDITY SNAPSHOT

CUMULATIVE LIQUIDITY REPORT ($ '000)

Cumulative Liquidity Report									
	1 Day	**2 Day**	**1 Week**	**2 Week**	**1 Month**	**2 Months**	**3 Months**	**6 Months**	**1 Year**
Cumulative Net Cash Balance	80	80	-1,260	-1,260	-1,180	-1,408	-1,150	-850	-850
Other Forecast Inflows									
Other Forecast Outflows									
Cumulative Cash Gap	80	80	-1,260	-1,260	-1,180	-1,408	-1,150	-850	-850
Counterbalancing Capacity	180	180	635	640	748	748	1,238	1,238	1,238
Liquidity Gap	260	260	-625	-620	-432	-660	88	388	388
Limit									
Variance	**260**	**260**	**-625**	**-620**	**-432**	**-660**	**88**	**388**	**388**

* Cash gap turns negative between 2-day and 1-week
* Liquidity gap turns negative between 2-day and 1-week

LIQUIDITY RATIOS – THREE MONTH VIEW

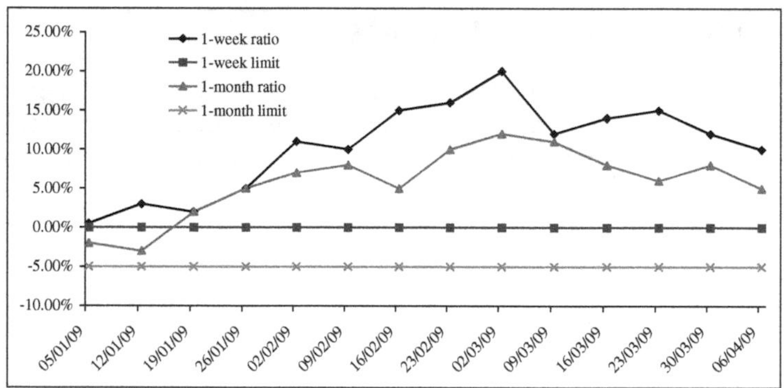

* Ratios are above the limit

	Current month	Previous month	Change
LIQUIDITY RISK FACTOR	22.2	25.1	▼
LOAN-TO-DEPOSIT RATIO	96%	93%	▲
NET INTER-GROUP LENDING	(1,228)	(1,552)	▼

FIGURE 14.10 Monthly liquidity snapshot for senior management.

GROUP TREASURY QUALITATIVE REPORTING

Monthly Liquidity Highlights

Template for Branches and Subsidiaries to Summarise Main Liquidity Changes for the Last Month

To be Provided a Fixed Specified Date Each Week

Points to consider:

1. Explain significant changes in your 1-week and 1-month liquidity ratios
2. Explain any changes to your cash and liquidity gap in your Cumulative Liquidity model
3. Explain significant changes to the Liquidity Risk Factor
4. Explain growth or shrinkage of asset books
5. Detail any changes to inter-group borrowing/lending position; detail the counterparties for any large-size deals
6. Any increase/decrease in corporate deposits, detail large dated transactions with an estimated confidence level of roll-over
7. Any increase/decrease in retail deposits
8. Average daily opening cash position

This list is not exhaustive and any other relevant points are welcome.

FIGURE 14.11 Group Treasury qualitative reporting, regular liquidity highlights.

The content is self-explanatory. An example for a bank with a group structure is shown at Figure 14.11.

For banking groups that operate across country jurisdictions and multiple subsidiaries, a qualitative report should be completed for Head Office Group Treasury, on a monthly basis. This will assist the group to better understand the liquidity position in each country.

Frequency of Reporting

In general, the main liquidity reports are required by the regulator, who stipulates their frequency. ALCO should view this obligation as a minimum requirement, and supplement it with additional MI as desired.

In the UK, quantitative liquidity reporting is an integral part of the regulatory regime. The full requirement applies to individual liquidity adequacy standards (ILAS) firms. Some smaller institutions and foreign branches are not ILAS firms, and where reporting requirements are waived or modified, the regulatory authority will agree the format and frequency of liquidity reporting on a case-by-case basis. Table 14.5 is a summary of the reporting requirements for UK standard ILAS firms.

TABLE 14.5 UK liquidity reporting requirements: standard ILAS firms.

Report	Description	Frequency	Submission deadlines
FSA047: Daily Flows	Daily cash flows out to 3 months; analyses survival period	BAU: Weekly firm-specific and/or market-wide liquidity stress: Daily	BAU: end-of-day Monday Stress: End of day following business day
FSA048: Enhanced mismatch report	ILAS risk drivers and contractual cash flows across full maturity spectrum	As above	As above
FSA050: Liquidity Buffer qualifying securities	Granular analysis of firm's marketable asset holdings	Monthly	15 business days after month-end
FSA051: Funding concentration	Firm's borrowings of unsecured wholesale funds (excludes primary issuance), by counterparty class	Monthly	15 business days after month-end
FSA052: Wholesale liabilities	Daily transaction prices and transacted volumes for wholesale unsecured liabilities	Weekly	End-of-day Tuesday
FSA053: Retail, SME and large enterprises corporate funding	Firm's retail and corporate funding profile and the stickiness of retail deposits	Quarterly	15 business days after month-end
FSA054: Currency analysis	Analysis of foreign exchange (FX) exposures on firm's balance sheet	Quarterly	15 business days after month-end
Off-balance sheet report	Aggregate undrawn committed facilities	Monthly	15 business days after month-end

Source: FSA

STRESS TEST REPORTS

The purpose of liquidity stress testing is to ascertain the extent of funding difficulties for the bank in the event of idiosyncratic or market-wide stress. In Chapter 12 we described the different types of scenario events that the UK FSA prescribes for UK-regulated banks to undertake. Stress test output results should help senior management to understand the liquidity position of the bank, enabling them to take mitigating action if deemed necessary.

The primary stress test output is the cash flow survival report. This was shown earlier in the chapter; at Figure 14.12 we illustrate an example of a report under BAU conditions and one after the mitigating actions have been taken (such as liquidating securities, and accessing contingency funding sources).

The second chart shows the stressed cumulative cash flow forecast taking into account the immediate sale or repo of marketable securities. In this example, the standard FSA-specified stresses have been applied: wholesale funding, retail liquidity, intra-day liquidity (3- and 5-day stresses), cross-currency liquidity, intra-group liquidity, off-balance sheet liquidity, marketable assets, non-marketable assets, and funding concentration. Observed behavioural forecasting (OBF), which refers to the treatment of liabilities for "stickiness", has been applied in the following way: non-interest bearing liabilities (100% every 3 days), current accounts (−5.66% every 36 days), retail time deposits (−0.41% every 344 days), capital (100% every 3 days), cash & equivalents (100% every 3 days), fiscal liabilities (100% every 3 days), repo liabilities (in this example there are no repos), other time deposits (−0.03% every 47 days) and foreign exchange (100% every 30 days). No OBF has been applied to corporate deposits, government time deposits, intra-group time deposits and inter-bank time deposits.

In this example, the survival period has been extended from 49 days to 93 days after taking into account the impact of the stress.

For senior management, a 1-slide summary of this test result is illustrated at Figure 14.13.

A line-by-line stress test result report should be produced on a quarterly basis, or as required by the regulator. We provide an example at Table 14.6. This shows the results of individual shocks on the liquidity ratio, and the probability of each result occurring. The following categories are included:

- reduction in liquid assets;
- decrease in liabilities;
- FX mismatch;
- combined shocks.

This report would be produced as part of routine stress testing, undertaken either by Treasury or Risk Management.

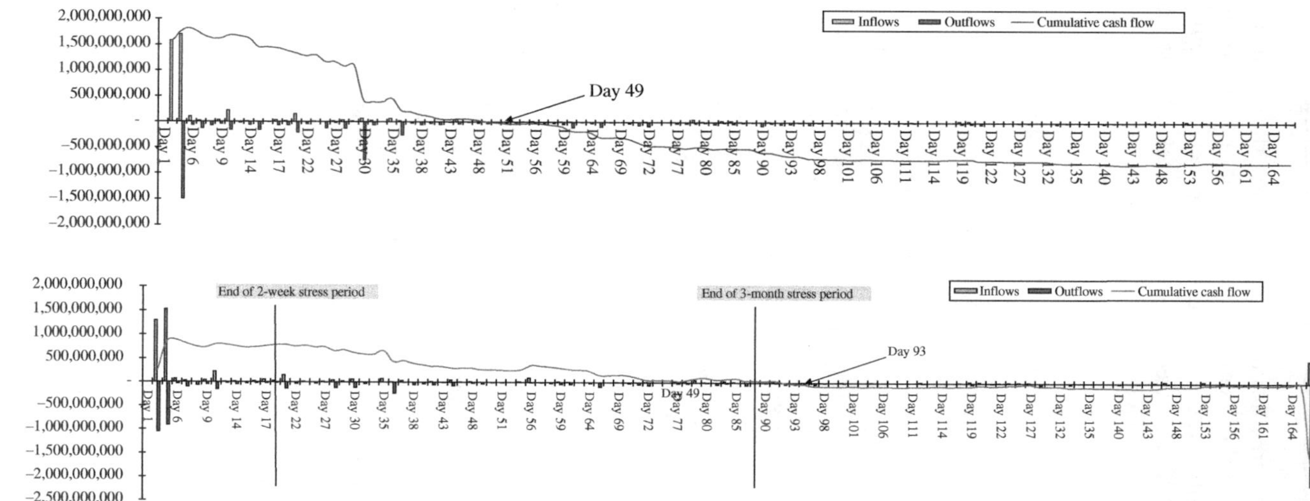

FIGURES 14.12A AND B Stress test results: cash flow survival horizon.

LIQUIDITY RISK (STRESS TESTING) WEEKLY SUMMARY 23 February 2010

Collation Grid

Assets	26/02/10 - 26/02/10	01/03/10 - 01/03/10	02/03/10 - 02/03/10	03/03/10 - 03/03/10	04/03/10 - 04/03/10	05/03/10 - 05/03/10	08/03/10 - 08/03/10	09/03/10 - 08/04/10	09/04/10 - 07/05/10	10/05/10 - 09/06/10	10/06/10 - 09/07/10	12/07/10 - 11/08/10	12/08/10 - 10/09/10
DEPOSIT	0	-241,607,851	-40,054,610	0	0	0	0	0	0	0	0	0	0
FOREIGN EXCHANGE	-44,968,540	-137,991,183	-57,139,991	-53,863,305	-58,564,187	-9,179,822	-9,053,677	-8,699,928	-9,564,882	-8,699,928	-8,699,928	-8,699,928	-8,699,928
LOAN	-3,399,632,793	-3,393,689,825	-2,673,744,068	-2,670,030,076	-2,652,419,071	-2,486,484,257	-2,449,789,080	-1,910,019,970	-1,793,858,633	-1,679,325,195	-1,642,531,170	-1,564,709,832	-1,544,267,305
SECURITIES	-1,284,200,226	-1,284,200,226	-1,284,200,226	-1,284,200,226	-1,284,200,226	-1,284,200,226	-1,284,200,226	-1,176,860,413	-1,066,883,169	-1,010,883,169	-956,385,475	-932,385,475	-818,120,475
UNDER INVESTIGATION	0	0	0	0	0	0	0	0	0	0	0	0	0
Total Assets	-4,728,801,560	-5,057,489,085	-4,055,138,895	-4,008,093,608	-3,995,183,484	-3,779,864,305	-3,743,042,983	-3,095,580,310	-2,870,306,684	-2,698,908,291	-2,607,616,573	-2,505,795,234	-2,371,087,708

Liabilities	26/02/10 - 26/02/10	01/03/10 - 01/03/10	02/03/10 - 02/03/10	03/03/10 - 03/03/10	04/03/10 - 04/03/10	05/03/10 - 05/03/10	08/03/10 - 08/03/10	09/03/10 - 08/04/10	09/04/10 - 07/05/10	10/05/10 - 09/06/10	10/06/10 - 09/07/10	12/07/10 - 11/08/10	12/08/10 - 10/09/10
DEPOSIT	4,110,991,383	4,352,599,234	3,950,075,302	3,866,815,947	3,828,122,384	3,723,005,860	3,705,910,202	1,502,417,595	890,054,066	418,752,249	336,623,349	231,403,892	187,872,880
FOREIGN EXCHANGE	45,942,962	135,799,261	57,335,715	54,356,487	60,278,274	9,513,048	9,386,774	9,125,168	10,059,444	9,125,168	9,125,168	9,125,168	9,125,168
LOAN	0	313,297	-700,000	-700,000	-700,000	-700,000	-700,000	-700,000	-500,000	-500,000	-500,000	-500,000	-500,000
UNDER INVESTIGATION	0	0	0	0	0	0	0	0	0	0	17	17	17
Total Liabilities	4,156,934,345	4,488,711,792	4,008,711,017	3,920,472,434	3,887,700,657	3,731,818,908	3,714,596,976	1,510,842,763	899,613,510	427,377,418	345,248,534	240,029,078	196,498,065
Cashflow	0	3,089,921	520,349,416	-39,193,296	-19,861,653	59,437,430	19,599,390	-1,556,291,540	-385,955,627	-300,837,700	9,162,835	-3,398,118	91,176,514
Cumulative Cashflow	0	3,089,921	523,439,337	484,246,041	464,384,388	523,821,818	543,421,208	-1,012,870,332	-1,398,825,959	-1,699,663,659	-1,690,500,824	-1,693,898,942	-1,602,722,428

Cumulative Cashflow Forecast and Stress Tests

The Cumulative Cash flow survival horizon is 42 days. Once Observed Behavioural Forecasting (OBF) is applied along with the stresses set out by the FSA, the Forecasted Cumulative Cash flow survival horizon is beyond that of the 6 months being analysed. Once relevant haircuts are applied to the Marketable Assets as part of the FSA stress testing, their value reduces by €150mm to €1.13bn

Cumulative Cashflow Forecast - Unstressed

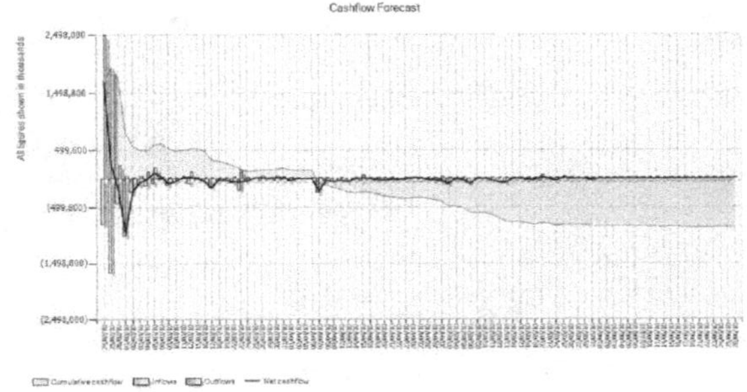

Cashflow Forecast

All figures shown in thousands

2,498,000
1,498,800
499,600
(499,600)
(1,498,800)
(2,498,000)

Cumulative cashflow · Inflows · Outflows · Net cashflow

- Graphs show daily cash flow movements over a 6 month period from 23rd Feb 2010
- The Cashflow is arrived at after factoring in sale/repo of marketable securities (bonds, FRNs, CDs). ""Overnight" data is unadjusted.
- The Cumulative cashflow is based on contractual cash flows and no adjustment has been made for asset/liability behaviour or ""stickiness".
- Data feeding graph uses same baseline data as seen in BLAST. Additional deals have been added to this data for FX swap positions.

The "cumulative cashflow" survival horizon is 42 days.

Marketable Securities	€ 1,279,200,226
Haircut Value	€ 150,116,423
Marketable Securities stressed	€ 1,129,083,803

Cumulative Cashflow Forecast – Stresses & OBF applied

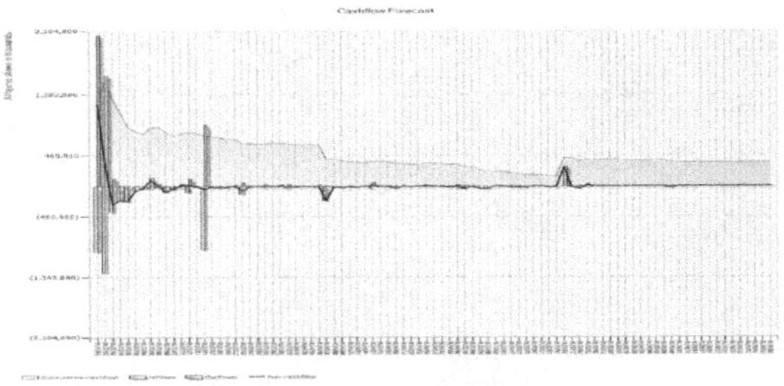

- Shows the Post-FSA stressed Cumulative Cash flow Forecast taking into account the immediate sale/repo of Marketable securities
- The following FSA stresses have been applied: Wholesale Funding, Retail Liquidity, Intraday liquidity - 3 & 5 day stresses, Cross Currency Liquidity, Intra-Group Liquidity, Off Balance Sheet Liquidity, Marketable Assets, Non-Marketable Assets, Funding Concentration.
- OBF (stickiness) applied: Non Liabilities (100% every 3 days), Current Accounts (-5.66% every 36 days), Retail Time deposits (-0.41% every 344 days), Capital (100% every 3 days), Cash & Equivalents (100% every 3 days), Fiscal Liabilities (100% every 3 days), Repo Liabilities (currently no repos), Other time deposits (-0.03% every 47 days), FX (100% every 30 days)
- OBF not applied: Corp Deposits, Govt time deposits, Intragroup time deposits, Interbank time deposits, Other Liabilities
- Forecasted Cumulative Cash flow survival horizon is beyond that of the 6 months being analysed for this report once OBF and the FSA stresses have been applied.

FIGURE 14.13 Senior management summary report, 1-slide PowerPoint.

TABLE 14.6 Liquidity management: individual stress test results report.

Stress tests – individual shocks			Sight – 8 day	Sight – 1 month	Probability	Impact
Reduction in liquid assets						
Change in repo criteria	Light	Rating category 1 notch downgrade	8.46%	1.35%	50%	30
	Moderate	Rating category 2 notch downgrade	2.34%	0.12%	20%	70
	Severe	Rating category 3 notch downgrade	−15.2%	−18.2%	1%	90
Mark-to-market reduction in value of assets	Light		8.46%	1.35%	60%	20
	Moderate		2.34%	0.12%	40%	30
	Severe		−15.2%	−18.2%	5%	70
Increased haircut on assets	Light		8.46%	1.35%	70%	25
	Moderate		2.34%	0.12%	30%	45
	Severe		−15.2%	−18.2%	8%	80
Unavailability of repo facilities	Severe	Treat all marketable securities as illiquid (i.e., allocate to final legal maturity time buckets)	−15.2%	−18.2%	5%	100
Decrease in liabilities						
Withdrawal of customer deposits	Light	Reduce customer deposits by 5%, replace with o/night funding	8.46%	1.35%	70%	20

(continued)

TABLE 14.6 *(continued)*

Stress tests – individual shocks			Sight – 8 day	Sight – 1 month	Probability	Impact
	Moderate	Reduce customer deposits by 10%, replace with o/night funding	2.34%	0.12%	15%	30
	Severe	Reduce customer deposits by 15%, replace with o/night funding	−15.2%	−18.2%	5%	40
Withdrawal of corporate deposits	Light	Reduce Local Authority deposits by 25%, other Corporate Banking deposits by 10%, replace with overnight funding	8.46%	1.35%	5%	20
	Moderate	Reduce Local Authority deposits by 50%, other Corporate Banking deposits by 35%, replace with overnight funding	2.34%	0.12%	2%	70
	Severe	Reduce Local Authority deposits by 100%, other Corporate Banking deposits by 70%, replace with overnight funding	−15.2%	−18.2%	1%	100
Withdrawal of intragroup deposits	Light	Reduce net group liability to EUR500 mm, replace with overnight funding	8.46%	1.35%	100%	5
	Moderate	Reduce net group liability to EUR250 mm, replace with overnight funding	2.34%	0.12%	70%	20

(continued)

TABLE 14.6 *(continued)*

Stress tests – individual shocks			Sight – 8 day	Sight – 1 month	Probability	Impact
	Severe	Reduce net group liability to nil, replace with overnight funding	–15.2%	–18.2%	30%	50
Withdrawal of inter-bank deposits	Light	Reduce deposits from "relationship banks" (correspondent banks) by 5%, other inter-bank deposits by 25%, replace with o/night funding	8.46%	1.35%	80%	20
	Moderate	Reduce deposits from "relationship banks" (correspondent banks) by 25%, other inter-bank deposits by 50%, replace with o/night funding	2.34%	0.12%	30%	60
	Severe	Reduce deposits from "relationship banks" (correspondent banks) by 50%, other inter-bank deposits by 100%, replace with o/night funding	–15.2%	–18.2%	10%	90
FX markets						
FX rate changes	Light	Stress GBP and USD FX rates by 5%	8.46%	1.35%	90%	20

(continued)

TABLE 14.6 *(continued)*

Stress tests – individual shocks			Sight – 8 day	Sight – 1 month	Probability	Impact
	Moderate	Stress GBP and USD FX rates by 15%	2.34%	0.12%	40%	40
	Severe	Stress GBP and USD FX rates by 25%	–15.2%	–18.2%	20%	90
Withdrawal of FX swap markets	Light	Withdrawal of less liquid swap markets	8.46%	1.35%	30%	15
	Moderate	Withdrawal of swap markets (excl. USD, EUR, GBP)	2.34%	0.12%	7%	40
	Severe	Withdrawal of all swap markets	–15.2%	–18.2%	2%	50

Stress tests – combined shocks			Sight – 8 day	Sight – 1 month	Probability	Impact
Slow-burn liquidity crunch		Detailed description of balance sheet shocks	–25.5%	–26.7%	2%	85
Severe reputational damage		Detailed description of balance sheet shocks	–42.4%	–51.2%	0.50%	100

EXAMPLE 14.1 TREATMENT OF CASH FLOWS

A common question in liquidity reporting concerns the treatment of specific types of cash flow. For example, consider the following:

1. Treatment of non-maturity items in liquidity/interest rate sensitivity analysis; for instance, demand deposits.
2. Treatment of off-balance sheet items in liquidity gap analysis:
   i. derivatives (options: equity, floors, caps and collars);
   ii. undrawn commitments.

In fact the treatment often differs for regulatory return purposes and what is in place in many banks' actual liquidity reporting models. Callable and demand deposits are treated as 1-day money for regulatory purposes, although certain regulatory authorities will allow a "behavioural" adjustment of retail deposits where it can be shown that these remain fairly stable over time. For example, 50% of such deposits may be allowed to be treated as longer term funds. Generally, however, such funds do not improve a bank's liquidity metrics, because they are viewed as 1-day funds by regulators.

For off-balance sheet items, the UK FSA treatment is as follows:

- Derivatives values/notionals are not included in the liquidity ratio calculation; however, coupons receivable or payable will be included on their pay dates.
- Commitments: 10% (specified by FSA) committed but undrawn lending is included as an outflow of cash (at sight) and included in the ratio calculations.

Bank liquidity models commonly apply the following treatment:

- Derivatives are included to the extent that collateral is payable or receivable under an ISDA/CSA agreement; coupons receivable or payable will also be included on their pay dates.
- Commitments: all committed but undrawn lending is included as an outflow of cash (at sight) and included in liquidity calculations.

In general, a conservative approach to treatment of expected cash outflows, whether as derivative collateral or undrawn commitments, is recommended business bestpractice.

CHAPTER 15

Internal Funds Pricing Policy

When describing the funding arrangements in place at a bank, the basic organisation structure involves a central Treasury function that manages all borrowing and lending requirements for the bank at an aggregate level, dealing with the external market, and acts as the internal counterparty for the funding requirements of all the bank's business lines. This is illustrated at Figure 15.1. Centralising the funding arrangement removes interest-rate risk and basis risk at the business line level, and also eliminates the funding mismatch risk at the customer face. These risks are instead centralised and managed by the Treasury desk. The terms under which the Treasury desk lends to the internal business lines has always been recognised to be an important part of the liquidity and funding management policy of the bank. This is for a number of reasons, the most important being that it is a key driver of the capital allocation decision. For efficient and disciplined business decision-making therefore, a bank's internal funding policy, known variously as funds transfer pricing, term liquidity premium or simply transfer pricing, must be both rigorous and realistic.

This is not a new concept; for instance, in the author's earlier book *Bank Asset and Liability Management* there is a discussion on the alternative approaches that may be followed when setting internal funds pricing.[1] However, poor policy setting in the build-up to the banking crisis of 2008 reaffirmed the importance of this issue, and triggered a debate on it among regulators. In the aftermath of this failure in bank governance, the CEBS stated that "the topic of an effective allocation mechanism for liquidity costs, benefits and risks has come to the fore recently. Recent regulatory initiatives have contributed to this heightened profile."[2] Recommendation

1 Discussed in Chapter 28 of the earlier book. The chapter here is a more detailed treatment of the subject.

2 CEBS, *Consultation paper on CEBS's Guidelines on Liquidity Cost Benefit Allocation (CP 36)*, 10 March 2010.

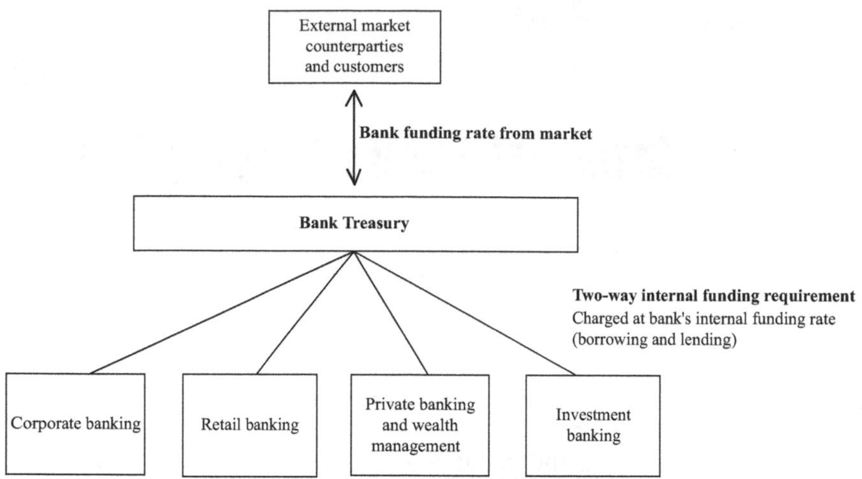

FIGURE 15.1 Bank funding structure.

2 in CEBS's technical advice to the EU commission on liquidity risk management (CEBS 2008, p. 147) states further:

> *Institutions should have in place an adequate internal mechanism – supported where appropriate by a transfer pricing mechanism – which provides appropriate incentives regarding the contribution to liquidity risk of the different business activities. This mechanism should incorporate all costs of liquidity (from short to long term, including contingent risk).*

In other words, national regulators now recognise that this issue is of fundamental importance in the bank risk management process, and therefore that they must supervise it. Certain minimum standards must be adhered to, which cannot necessarily be left to individual banks' judgement.

In this chapter we discuss the concept of internal funds pricing policy, and describe in detail a business best-practice approach for adoption as policy standard at all banks. We emphasise that this is one issue for which there is not necessarily a "right" answer; there is more than one way to organise funds transfer pricing methodology at a bank, and the more complex a bank's businesses are, the most contentious the subject becomes. In other words, there is no "one size fits all" policy. We discuss one efficacious approach, and also suggest recommended policy for different product types.

THE CONCEPT OF INTERNAL FUNDS PRICING[3]

Internal bank funds pricing, variously termed funds transfer pricing (FTP), firm liquidity pricing (FLP) or term liquidity premium (TLP), is a key ingredient in bank liquidity risk management. Here we discuss how an inappropriate or artificial internal funds pricing policy can drive poor business decision-making, before then looking at how to create and implement a more robust and disciplined internal funding framework.

The initial response of the regulators to the 2008 crisis was to look at liquidity standards and how to strengthen them. For example, as we noted in an earlier chapter, the UK FSA introduced a new liquidity regime for banks that included a requirement for:

- increased self-sufficiency in funding;
- a more diversified funding base;
- longer average tenor of liabilities
- a "liquidity buffer" of high-quality government securities.

Interestingly, the initial FSA proposals[4] did not address how bank funds are managed internally, which was surprising given that how banks structure their internal funds pricing can influence significantly the activities of individual business lines. Subsequently, both the FSA and other regulators, as well as the Basel Committee, placed banks' internal funding framework under scrutiny. This was welcome because internal funding is a driver of bank business models, which were shown to be flawed and based on inaccurate assumptions during the build-up to the bank crash.

An Effective Internal Funding Framework

Post-crash, the initial FSA coverage on bank internal liquidity pricing was peripheral.[5] This was unexpected, because essentially the price at which an individual bank business line raises funding from its own Treasury desk is a

3 Parts of this section first appeared in the article "Maintenance From Within", published in *World Finance*, Nov–Dec 2009. The author thanks Adam Lawson for his assistance and input to this article.

4 The notable FSA papers from this period were *CP 08/22 Strengthening Liquidity Standards* (December 2008); *CP 08/24 Stress and Scenario Testing* (December 2008); and *CP09/13 Strengthening Liquidity Standards 2: Liquidity Reporting* (January 2009).

5 See page 23, FSA *CP 08/22, Strengthening Liquidity Standards*, December 2008.

major parameter in business decision-making, driving sales, asset allocation and product pricing. It is also a key hurdle rate behind the product approval process and in an individual business line's performance measurement. Just as capital allocation decisions affecting front office business units need to account for the cost of that capital (in terms of return on regulatory and economic capital), so funding decisions exercised by corporate treasurers carry significant implications for sales and trading teams at the trade level. Hence, the internal funding framework is worthy of regulatory authorities' attention.

In an ideal world, the price at which cash is internally transferred within a bank should reflect the true economic cost of that cash (at each maturity band), and its impact on overall bank liquidity. This would ensure that each business aligns the commercial propensity to maximise profit with the correct maturity profile of associated funding. From a liquidity point of view, any mismatch between the asset tenor and funding tenor, after taking into account the "repo-ability" of each asset class in question, should be highlighted and acted upon as a matter of priority, with the objective to reduce recourse to short-term, passive funding as much as possible. Equally, it is important that the internal funding framework is transparent to all trading groups.

A measure of discipline in business decision-making is enforced via the imposition of minimum RoC targets. Independent of the internal cost of funds, a business line would ordinarily seek to ensure that any transaction it entered into achieved its targeted RoC. However, relying solely on this measure is not always sufficient discipline. For this to work, each business line should be set RoC levels that are commensurate with its (risk-adjusted) risk-reward profile. However, banks do not always set different target RoCs for each business line, which means that the required discipline breaks down.

The internal funding rate is as important to the discipline driving business decision-making. A uniform cost of funds, even allowing for different RoCs, will mean that the different liquidity stresses on the balance sheet, created by different types of asset, are not addressed adequately at the aggregate funding level. For example, consider the following asset types:

- a 3-month inter-bank loan;
- a 3-year floating rate corporate loan, fixing quarterly;
- a 3-year floating-rate corporate loan, fixing weekly;
- a 3-year fixed-rate loan;
- a 10-year floating-rate corporate loan fixing monthly;
- a 15-year floating-rate project finance loan fixing quarterly.

Each of these places different liquidity pressures on the Treasury funding desk (listed in increasing amount of funding rollover risk). Even allowing for different credit risk exposures and capital risk weights, the impact on the liability funding desk is different for each asset. We see therefore the importance of applying a structurally sound transfer pricing policy, dependent on the type of business line being funded.

Cost of Funds

As a key driver of the economic decision-making process, the cost at which funds are lent from central Treasury to the bank's businesses needs to be set at a rate that reflects the true liquidity risk position of each business line. If this cost is unrealistic, there is a risk that transactions are entered into that produce an unrealistic profit. This profit will reflect the artificial funding gain, rather than the true economic value-added of the business.

There is empirical evidence of the damage that can be caused by artificially low transfer pricing. In a paper published in 2008, Adrian Blundell-Wignall and Paul Atkinson[6] discussed the losses at the Swiss bank UBS AG in its structured credit business, which originated and invested in CDO assets. Quoting a UBS shareholder report,

> *. . . internal bid prices were always higher than the relevant London inter-bank bid rate (LIBID) and internal offer prices were always lower than the relevant London inter-bank offered rate (LIBOR).* (p.97)

In other words, UBS structured credit business was able to fund itself at prices better than in the market (which is implicitly inter-bank risk), despite the fact that it was investing in assets of considerably lower liquidity than inter-bank assets. There was no adjustment for tenor mismatch, to better align term funding to liquidity. The authors quote that a more realistic funding model for the bank was viewed as a "constraint on the growth strategy".

This lack of funding discipline undoubtedly played an important role in the decision-making process, because it allowed the structured credit desk to report inflated profits based on low funding costs. As a stand-alone business, a CDO investor would not expect to raise funds at sub-Libor, but rather at significantly over Libor. By receiving this artificial low pricing, the desk could report super profits and very high return-on-capital, which encouraged ever more risky investment decisions. In fact, the profit was

---

6 Blundell-Wignall, A. and Atkinson, P., "The Sub-Prime Crisis: Causal Distortions and Regulatory Reform", Working Paper, OECD, July 2008.

artificial, because much of it reflected a "funding arbitrage" involved in borrowing low-cost funds internally, which reflected the liquidity and credit profile of the parent bank, and investing it in illiquid structured finance securities of considerably greater maturity than the internal borrowing.

Another example from the bank crash involved certain other banks that entered into the "fund derivatives" business. This was lending to investors in hedge funds via a leveraged structured product. These instruments were illiquid, with maturities of two years or longer. Once originated, they could not be unwound, thus creating significant liquidity stress for the lender. However, banks funded these business lines from central Treasury at Libor-flat or Libor plus a small spread, rolling the funding in the short term. The liquidity problems that resulted became apparent during the 2007–2008 financial crisis, when inter-bank liquidity dried up.

Many banks operated on a similar model, with a fixed internal funding rate of Libor plus (say) 15 bps for all business lines, and for any tenor. But such an approach does not take into account the differing liquidity profiles of the business lines. The corporate lending desk will create different liquidity risk exposures for the bank compared to the CDO desk or the project finance desk. For the most efficient capital allocation, banks should adjust the basic internal transfer price for the resulting liquidity risk exposure of the business. Otherwise they run the risk of excessive risk taking that is heavily influenced by an artificial funding gain.

Business Best-practice

It is important that all banks put in place an internal funding structure that correctly charges for the liquidity risk placed on the balance sheet by each business line. An artificially low funding rate can create as much potentially un-manageable risk exposure as a risk-seeking loan origination culture. A regulatory requirement to impose a realistic internal funding arrangement will mitigate this risk, which is why regulators now monitor internal funding policies at banks.

At the minimum, a bank should implement the following approach: a fixed add-on spread over Libor for term loans or assets over a certain maturity, say one year, where the coupon re-fix is frequent (such as monthly or quarterly), to compensate for the liquidity mismatch. The spread would be on a sliding scale for longer term assets. Banks will need to fine-tune this policy to suit their own specific business models, and we will discuss this in the next section.

Internal funding discipline is as pertinent to bank risk management as capital buffers and effective liquidity management discipline. As banks adjust to the liquidity regime required under Basel III, it remains as important for them to consider the internal determinants of an efficient, cost-effective funding regime. In this way they can move towards embedding the true funding cost into business-line decision-making.

BENCHMARK FUNDS TRANSFER PRICING POLICY

A bank's internal funding policy should encompass both high-level guidelines on the framework for liquidity cost allocation among the various business lines, as well as a detailed description of the funding mechanism in place for each product type. The latter should include actual rates payable for each tenor; these rates should be updated on a regular basis. The funding cost that is passed on, from the Treasury funding desk to the businesses, should include the direct costs, as well as the indirect costs, associated with the liquidity contingency funding plan and liquidity buffer.

There is more than one way to structure an FTP policy, and a bank should formulate it in the way that best suits its own business model, and the level of its aversion to running liquidity risk. For instance, CEBS states in its *CP36* document that the FTP concept consists of two components: first, the costs of raising funds from an ALM perspective and interest rate costs curve, which are the direct costs; and second, the indirect liquidity costs.[7] These liquidity costs should distinguish between (i) the mismatch liquidity cost, for which the liquidity tenor and not the interest rate tenor is relevant; (ii) the cost of contingent liquidity risk, which includes the cost of holding a liquidity buffer to cover for funding stress and rollover risk; and (iii) any other categories of liquidity risk that a bank has, such as country risk arising from the imposition of capital controls.

However, the author is not convinced that this is necessarily recommended best-practice for banks. Element (i) above implies the following: for example, consider a 5-year corporate loan that is funded by 3-month CP, which is continuously rolled over. The CEBS document states that the appropriate liquidity cost is the 5-year funding cost and not the initial 3-month cost of issuing CP. This instruction ignores that banks are in the business of undertaking maturity transformation, and would rarely, if ever, undertake matched funding, for any type of asset.[8] Also, regards (ii) above, in many cases the cost of the liquidity buffer is passed on as a direct cost to

7 CEBS paper, footnote 2.

8 Taken to its ultimate conclusion, assuming all assets are funded by matching term liabilities and implementing a 100% matched funding policy for the FTP at a bank implies that it would only ever be able to lend to customers that had a poorer credit rating than itself, and/or could only fund more expensively than it could itself.

each of the business lines. While it is important to ensure that the correct cost of liquidity is allowed for in the internal funding model, it needs to be set in line with commercial and practical reality. We present our recommended FTP policy and practice next.

Setting the Bank Policy Standard

A formal internal funding policy is necessary so as to make explicit to the business lines the need for the bank to cover adequately the cost of its liquidity. The objective of the policy is to:

- ensure consistent liquidity pricing behaviour among each of the business lines;
- remove interest-rate risk from the business lines;
- include the bank's cost of liquidity in product pricing.

The policy also seeks to ensure that business lines recognise the impact of their asset and liability pricing on the balance sheet of the bank, and allow for these costs accordingly. The policy document should be formalised and approved at ALCO. It should be reviewed on a semi-annual basis, with the review responsibility delegated to Treasury.

The policy should include the treatment for each product asset class that the bank deals in.

Benchmark FTP Guidelines

We have noted previously that best-practice liquidity management principles dictate that a central unit, generally Treasury, charges the appropriate cost of liquidity to the bank's business lines. This cost is a function of the bank's overall COF.

The principle policy options driving the guidelines will be:

- Gross approach versus net approach: in a gross approach, all assets and liabilities are charged or credited with the relevant tenor FTP rate from Treasury. In the net approach, only the net position between assets and liabilities is charged or credited with the relevant tenor FTP rate. In addition, individual business lines can employ funds that they raise themselves in their own business.
- Marginal or actual funding cost: is the FTP charge of the marginal cost of funds or the actual cost of funds.

In general a gross approach at marginal cost is deemed the most effective for risk management purposes. However as we stated at the start, there is no "one size fits all" FTP for every bank.

In Figure 15.1 the FTP centre is the Treasury desk, which is also the market-facing function for funding. The business lines pay and receive the relevant FTP rate by interacting with Treasury. In a group structure, the FTP may be based on more than one pricing curve. In principle there is one baseline funding curve, given by the banks unsecured COF curve (see Chapter 5). Group Treasury would pass the relevant FTP charge to each operating business. However, the different business will each have a different COF themselves. For example, consider the following:

- Retail bank: raises term funds at below the group marginal COF, and lends at a significant margin to the COF. For example, term deposits against the mortgage lending rate;
- Investment bank: raises term funds at the COF, and lends at a margin below the COF. For example, unsecured wholesale bonds against syndicated loan assets;
- Private bank: raises funds that are in behavioural terms of long term and at significantly below the COF, and lends at a margin above COF.

Clearly there is more than one "COF" here; we are using the term to refer to the curve constructed from the bank's wholesale bond yields. Would a single FTP grid apply to all three businesses? The answer depends on what incentives the senior management wishes to set the business, and what sectors it wishes to concentrate on. Should the private bank business receive the term COF rates for funds it raises? In general one would say yes, but there is a case for setting specific COF rates more appropriate to the business line. In a group organisation structure, Group Treasury may leave it to the individual business internal Treasury desks to apply their own FTP.

The other principle to consider is how dynamic the process is. The author recommends a regular review of the policy itself as well the FTP pricing grid, at least annually but ideally on a quarterly basis. This is to ensure that the policy remains up-to-date and appropriate for changing market conditions. Figure 15.2 is an academic illustration of why this is necessary.

In Figure 15.2A the bank is running the "ALM Smile" funding profile that we recommended in Chapters 6 and 7, and so the FTP curve is set with the bank's COF curve. In Figure 15.2B the funding gap is significant in the long end, therefore we would set the FTP curve at a steeper slope to the "fair" or theoretical COF curve for the bank. This is to ensure that the right incentive is given to the business lines to raise long-term liabilities, as well as to signal that short-term funds have no real value to the bank. Equally, term

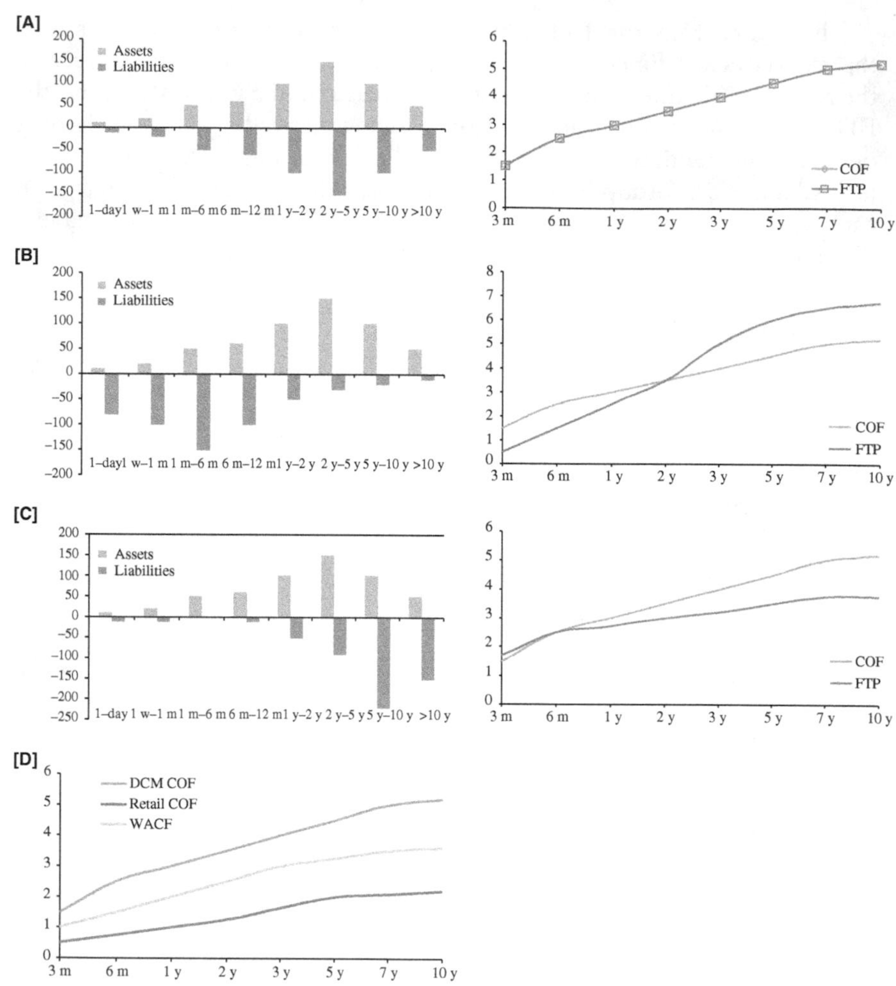

FIGURE 15.2A–D Dynamic FTP setting.

funding gaps would be penalised at the right rate. In Figure 15.2C the position is reversed, and so the FTP curve is flatter to the fair market COF curve, again to incentivise the correct behaviour.

Finally, Figure 15.2D shows how a "blended" FTP rate, which we referred to as the WACF rate in Chapter 7, might apply in practice: the question arises as to how much of each business one should do, when the asset price straddles (in this hypothetical example) the debt capital markets (DCM) COF and the Retail Bank COF rates.

Components of the Policy

The internal funding policy will cover the complete range of product types that the bank deals in. It will also define various related issues such as the reference rate for pricing (such as Libor or Euribor), bid–offer spread if any, and so on.

Funds Flow

The policy should state the reference rate used for all spot transactions. This would be Libor or the relevant index for that market. The rate to be taken is generally the fix for the date that the transaction is entered into. The general rule is that assets attract the term internal funds rate, and all liabilities receive the term internal funds rate. Exceptions can be made on a case-by-case basis, with appropriate sign-off. The approval authority may be Treasury or ALCO. Behavioural adjustments may be applied to deposits that are shown to be "sticky" and hence of longer actual maturity than their contractual maturity implies, such as for cheque accounts and call accounts.

The above is a template description. It can be expanded where necessary, and to suit specific bank business models and product suites.

Liquidity Buffer Cost Allocation

The cost of preserving liquidity, generated by the maintenance of an LAB that includes central bank balances, is recharged to the business lines and reported in the monthly management accounts. The businesses will take these costs into account when setting product pricing. Business lines (such as private banking or retail banking) that contribute to the bank's liquidity position, thereby resulting in a reduced LAB size requirement and lower costs of liquidity, will receive a credit for this business. This can be recharged (or re-credited) monthly.

Generally, this allocation of charges and credits is carried out at month-end. It is administered by the Finance department, and charges/credit are allocated on a pro-rata basis, based on average liquidity requirements and costs for the month.

Regulatory Costs

This section can be rolled up and included in the preceding one. The cost of maintaining non-interest-bearing deposits at the central bank, and the cost of supervision fees levied by the national regulator, should be recharged to the business lines on a monthly basis, pro-rata on their average liabilities or other impact on the cash balances required.

The funding cost of the central bank balance should be stated in the policy (as this is what is passed on). Generally, it will be the reference index rate, such as 1-month or 3-month Libor or Euribor.

Bid–Offer Spread

There is no strong case for setting a bid–offer spread on the bank's FTP rates. Where a spread is applied, so that internal deposits attract the bid rate and internal loans are charged at the offer rate, the extent of this should be outlined in the policy. For example, it may look like this:

Currency	Term	Bid–offer spread (bps)
GBP	0–1 year	6 bps
EUR	0–1 year	6 bps
USD	0–1 year	8 bps
CHF	0–1 year	8 bps
JPY	0–1 year	8 bps

In principle, an internal pricing function should operate to a zero P&L target, or at least seek to minimise the year-end P&L. This suggests that there should be no bid–offer spread. However, the internal funding desk will be both accepting deposits as well as advancing loans to the same business lines; in many cases it will be doing both.[9] To preserve pricing discipline, as it is dealing both ways, the internal funding desk should quote a bid rate and an offered rate. However, the spread itself should be as small as possible, perhaps 1–2 bps.

Funds Transfer Pricing Curve[10]

The actual internal funds curve, known also as the COF, FTP or TLP curve, should be included in the policy and reviewed on a regular basis. This states the rate paid or received by the business lines for assets

9 In some cases, it may be with the same desk. For instance, the MTN desk will raise term liabilities for the bank, which it will place on deposit as term funds with the internal funding desk. However, the same desk may then buy back the same MTN a short time later, from an investor that is selling back the note. When it does this, it will need to break the term deposit it made earlier. This would be done at fair value (mark-to-market), and this calls for a bid–offer spread.

10 We refer to this as the FTP "curve" but in fact it is more accurately referred to as a "grid". Bank internal ALM funding desks quote FTP rates for set maturities, so they are not really "curves", hence our preference for pricing "grid".

TABLE 15.1 FTP pricing curve, or grid.

	Matched funding FTP curve (bps)		
Term	GBP	EUR	USD
0–6 months	0	0	5
6–12 months	5	5	10
1–2 years	15	10	20
3 years	35	20	40
4 years	40	30	50
5 years	50	40	75
6 years	60	45	85
7 years	70	50	95
8 years	80	55	105
9 years	90	60	110
10 years	100	70	125
>10 years	135	90	150

and liabilities across the term structure. An example is shown at Table 15.1. Assets or liabilities with expected or contractual maturities that are not exact full years, and so fall in between the tenor grids, are priced on a straight-line interpolation basis between the shorter and longer date prices.

The example at Table 15.1 assumes matched funding, which rarely applies, and is positively sloping for each incremental increase in tenor. It is known as "full marginal cost" pricing. This is logically tenable, but may not be practical for commercial or economic reasons. We discuss later in the chapter a more practical structure of the FTP curve. The final choice for the FTP policy is a matter of individual bank judgement, approved by the ALCO.

As noted already, where behavioural analysis indicates that the term to maturity of an item differs from its contractual term to maturity, the expected maturity is used to set the appropriate FTP rate. So, for example, for a fixed term 3-year deposit that is assumed to be 80% sticky, the 3-year FTP rate would be applied to 80% of the funds, and a shorter term FTP rate to 20% of the balance. Equally, if a call account balance is shown to be 50% sticky for one year, the 1-year FTP would be earned on 50% of the funds.

For trading book assets, which are generally assumed to be liquid and expected to be sold within six months of being bought, the FTP charge would be set according to the expected holding duration and not the legal maturity of the traded asset. Typically this will be at the 6-month FTP rate;

however, this depends on the type of asset and the level of liquidity. In general, a bank will set different tiers of liquidity, with Tier 1 being the most liquid (such as G7 government bonds) and attracting a 1-week or 1-month FTP, down to Tier 3 for the least liquid and attracting the 6-month internal funds rate.

Securitisable Assests

Assets originated by a bank that are relatively straightforward to securitise, such as prime residential mortgages, have liquidity value precisely because they can be securitised subsequently. In general, each type of asset should be reviewed on a case-by-case basis; however, one approach might be to state that 50% of the relevant tenor FTP rate be applied, rather than the full rate.

Specific Product Policy

We consider now inputs to the FTP policy for specific types of product.

Eurobonds and Sovereign Securities

The FTP mechanism applied for a Trading book asset is less concerned with its duration or legal maturity. This is because assets held on the Trading book are deemed to be sufficiently liquid to trade in a secondary market, and because they are expected to be held for short-term (less than 1-year) periods. Accordingly, the internal funding mechanism for these assets should reflect their true liquidity quality.

The policy should classify securities according to their perceived liquidity. The appropriate TP to apply will be the one for what is deemed the average duration of the holding of the assets, say 3-month or 6-month. This is for judgement by ALCO; it may deem a shorter or longer tenor TP rate is preferable. The assets might be categorised as follows:

Tier 1	G7 currency bonds
Tier 2	Bonds denominated in AUD, CHF, DKK, HKD, NOK, NZD, SEK, SGD
Tier 3	Bonds rated below A–/A3

Most banks will not have FTP grids for currencies other than their domestic currency and USD and EUR. The base currency grid can be converted to a required currency rate by applying the FX basis swap rate to it. This is not an exact science, but this approach should be sufficient for most purposes.

A bank should assign one baseline funding curve, in its reporting currency, and convert that curve to pricing curves in other currencies as required. For hedging purposes, it may be necessary to apply a "quanto" adjustment to the converted curve, to allow for FX and correlation factors.

Undrawn Commitments Fee

The FTP policy for committed facilities is a crucial part of the overall discipline with regard to internal funds pricing. Back-up and other liquidity lines supplied to the bank's customers are likely to be drawn on at precisely the time when the bank will most want to be preserving liquidity and lending less: during a funding crisis. It is imperative therefore that these facilities be allocated the appropriate charge when they are originated, given the liquidity risk exposure they represent.

Until recently, commitment lines and back-up facilities usually attracted a flat standing charge, say 10 bps or 20 bps. If the line was drawn, this fee was paid on top of the actual borrowing charge. The internal charge to the business line would have been at or just below the standing charge to the customer. Based on business best-practice today, we recommend instead a flat minimum internal fee, for example 20 bps, which is then added to if required, depending on the type of facility and how its usage is expected to fluctuate over time. The latter requires the bank to perform behavioural analysis of the different types of product offerings. The standing fee, and any add-on, is also used for new business appraisal and in the calculation of RoC.

Figure 15.3 illustrates the utilisation behaviour of committed facilities, with a back-up facility and revolving credit facility shown at Figures 15.3A and 15.3B respectively, compared to a vanilla term loan shown at Figure 15.3C.

From this understanding, we conclude that a committed standing back-up facility, whether it is sold to a corporate customer or to an SPV such as a CP conduit, represents the highest risk to a bank's liquidity stress position. The FTP for this facility must therefore be set higher. This is the basic position; exceptions can be made, depending on the type of client, and to what extent the client is dependent on the facility in the event of market stress.

Table 15.2 is an example pricing grid for inclusion in the FTP policy. It should be reviewed on a semi-annual basis, to reflect changes in market conditions (the revised grid would apply to new business. For existing business, the legal documents will state how often the bank can revise prices for the facility).

Conduit Internal Funding Policy

Banks manage conduits, raising CP and ABCP, to raise funding for themselves and for third-party clients. The key element of an FTP policy for

[A] Back-up facility

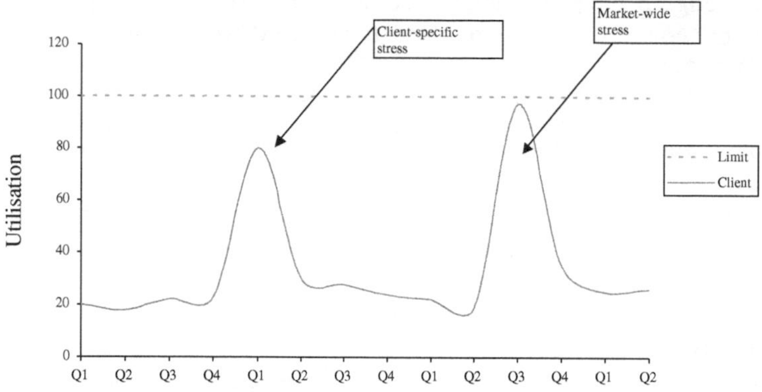

[B] Revolving credit facility

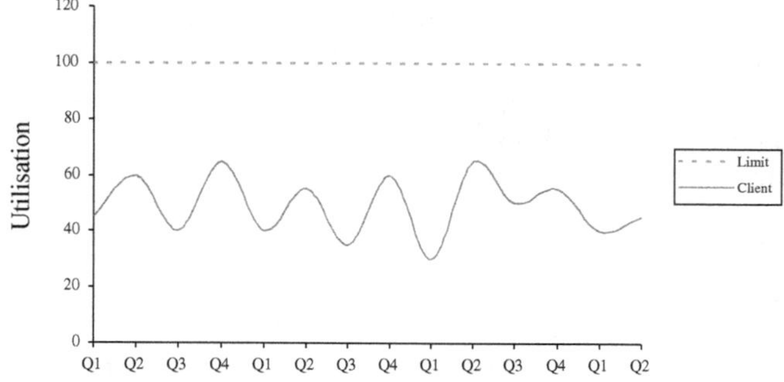

[C] Term loan

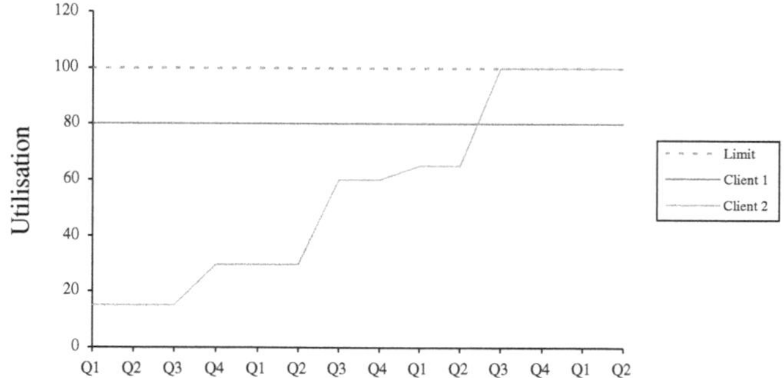

FIGURE 15.3A–C Committed facility usage behaviour profiles.

TABLE 15.2 Example, committed facilities FTP pricing structure (basis points).

		Facility tenor		
	Rating	1-year	2–4-year	> 5-year
Revolving credit facility	A1/P1	20	20	30
	A2/P2	25	25	35
Committed back-up line	A1/P1	35	40	50
	A2/P2	40	50	75
Conduit liquidity line	A1/P1	35	40	n/a
	A2/P2	40	50	n/a

conduits is to recognise that in either case, the conduit cannot be regarded as completely self-funded and therefore independent of the sponsoring bank. During a market-wide liquidity stress situation, one must assume that the entire conduit liabilities will not be able to be rolled in the CP market, and must be replaced by bank funding. For ABCP conduits, underlying assets are rarely match-funded with identical tenor liabilities. In theory, conduit outstanding balances represent a large potential liquidity stress position for a bank, with the required funding term being equal to the maturity of the longest dated asset in the conduit. (Straight bank CP, as opposed to ABCP, does not have "underlying" assets and so its funding can be replaced with the bank funding of any term).

The standard policy should be to apply the FTP rate for the tenor of the longest dated asset (for an ABCP conduit) or the tenor of the attached liquidity facility (for a CP vehicle).

FUNDING MANAGEMENT: DERIVATIVES COLLATERAL AND LIQUIDITY

This section would also be appropriate in Chapter 12 on Liquidity Risk, but we include it here because it is more naturally part of the internal funding considerations of overall liquidity strategy. Derivatives funding is a significant part of overall liquidity risk management at most banks, and must be viewed, along with all other aspects of funding, in a strategic context. We look first at funding issues associated at derivatives collateral, and then at collateral-based discounting of interest-rate swaps.

Funding Impact of Collateralising Derivatives

Transactions in derivative contracts are governed by the ISDA agreement. The CSA is an optional part of an ISDA agreement that describes the terms under which collateral between two counterparties is handled. A CSA is invariably in place between bank counterparties, but much less common for corporate and sovereign/central bank counterparties. Where a CSA is in place, a party to a derivative transaction will pass collateral to its counterparty if the derivative is offside to it (that is, it is negative mark-to-market). This collateral is usually in the form of cash, and equal to the mark-to-market value of the derivative, although sometimes it is in the form of securities.

When a CSA is not in place and the issue of collateral does not arise, the discounting curve to apply to a derivative trade should be the bank's cost of funding curve (see Chapter 5). This is usually the FTP curve, which is a spread over Libor. Where a CSA is in place, the issue is more opaque. CSA terms are standard only up to a point, and many aspects of it are negotiated; thus, they vary substantially from counterparty to counterparty. Some of the main clauses of a CSA relate to:

- the form of collateral;
- eligible currencies and securities;
- mark-to-market thresholds;
- frequency at which collateral is called;
- interest paid on collateral.

All these parameters can have a significant impact on the discount rate used to value the derivative. A standard CSA between derivative market-making banks demands a zero threshold (the mark-to-market value at which point margin is called) and daily calls. It allows for the collateral to be posted in USD, GBP or EUR, on which balances the OIS, SONIA and EONIA rate respectively is paid.

At any point in time, the discount rate on a trade is the interest rate applied to the collateral posted/received at that time. Where there is only one currency eligible and the tenor of the derivative is not very long-dated, this is a reasonably straightforward exercise. Where the CSA allows alternatives, or where the contracts are long-dated, this gives rise to complications. When a CSA allows more than one eligible currency or security, it creates a collateral option whose value is not transparent. Where only cash in the currency of the trade itself can be posted, which is a requirement of the LCH central clearing counterparty, a 30-year GBP interest-rate swap will require a 30-year SONIA curve for valuation, which until recently was not a liquid market.

The choice of which yield curve to use when pricing a derivative has become an important issue since the bank crisis of 2008. Generally, the discount curve applied to a derivatives trade reflects the funding level on that trade. Prior to the crash, when liquidity was cheap and plentiful, differences between the yield curves were negligible and so the difference in valuation discrepancy as a result of using different discount curves was minor.

A change has been required as a result of the crash, which altered the relationship between the overnight interest market and Libor. Up until the credit crunch, the convention had been to discount on Libor, and this was practised at all banks. In general, the difference between the overnight and 3-month borrowing rate was stable and the Libor term premium was on average 10–20 bps at most.[11] However, following the crash the basis became more volatile and widened considerably, and has remained so since then. For example, in October 2008 the FRA/OIS basis reached 364 bps in USD. At the same time, banks' unsecured funding spreads widened out further. This difference is expected to remain for some time. For example, Figure 15.4A shows the interest-rate swap rates for EUR on 29 December 2010. This is the vanilla swap with fixed rate against semi-annual 6-month Libor, while Figure 15.4B is the fixed-rate against overnight floating interest, which is the OIS swap (or EONIA swap as this is for euros). The difference is material even at the short-dated tenors; for the long-dated swaps the difference is considerable.

The previous convention of discounting at Libor is no longer appropriate because it does not reflect banks' true funding costs. However, for derivatives traded under a CSA agreement, the specific details of each CSA influence those funding levels. It is apparent nevertheless that collateralised derivatives trading should be conducted using the collateralised funding curve, which is the OIS curve rather than the Libor curve. Note, for example, that the derivatives clearing house LCH Clearnet has also adopted OIS discounting, in line with the change in market convention.

Banks should also be aware of the funding sensitivity of derivatives such as swaps, separate from the interest-rate mark-to-market sensitivity. Funding sensitivity arises when there is a timing mismatch between cash inflow and outflow on a swap. On a vanilla IRS, when forward–forward and spot discount curves are the same, the interest-rate risk (DV01) on the

11 See Chapter 10 in the author's book *Bank Asset and Liability Management*, "Understanding the term premium".

01 Corp ICAE
200<Go> to view in Launchpad
14:58 Intercapital-EUR Swaps PAGE 1 / 1

	EUR Swap Rates vs. EURIBOR	Ask	Bid	Time		EUR Swap Rates vs. EURIBOR	Ask	Bid	Time
1)	1 Year	1.369	1.319	14:07	21)	21 Year	3.795	3.745	14:56
2)	2 Year	1.661	1.611	14:34	22)	22 Year	3.782	3.732	14:56
3)	3 Year	1.994	1.944	14:35	23)	23 Year	3.764	3.714	14:56
4)	4 Year	2.304	2.254	14:57	24)	24 Year	3.745	3.695	14:56
5)	5 Year	2.575	2.525	14:57	25)	25 Year	3.723	3.673	14:56
6)	6 Year	2.801	2.751	14:57	26)	26 Year	3.700	3.650	14:56
7)	7 Year	2.992	2.942	14:57	27)	27 Year	3.677	3.627	14:56
8)	8 Year	3.149	3.099	14:56	28)	28 Year	3.653	3.603	14:56
9)	9 Year	3.277	3.227	14:57	29)	29 Year	3.630	3.580	14:56
10)	10 Year	3.388	3.338	14:56	30)	30 Year	3.608	3.558	14:56
11)	11 Year	3.484	3.434	14:56	31)	35 Year	3.515	3.465	14:56
12)	12 Year	3.569	3.519	14:56	32)	40 Year	3.455	3.405	14:56
13)	13 Year	3.638	3.588	14:56	33)	50 Year	3.410	3.360	14:56
14)	14 Year	3.695	3.645	14:56	34)	60 Year	3.359	3.309	14:56
15)	15 Year	3.737	3.687	14:56		Day Count: ANN 30/360 vs. 6M EURIBOR			
16)	16 Year	3.768	3.718	14:56					
17)	17 Year	3.790	3.740	14:56					
18)	18 Year	3.801	3.751	14:56					
19)	19 Year	3.806	3.756	14:56					
20)	20 Year	3.803	3.753	14:56					

Australia 61 2 9777 8600 Brazil 5511 3048 4500 Europe 44 20 7330 7500 Germany 49 69 9204 1210 Hong Kong 852 2977 6000
Japan 81 3 3201 8900 Singapore 65 6212 1000 U.S. 1 212 318 2000 Copyright 2010 Bloomberg Finance L.P.
SN 349985 29-Dec-2010 14:58:18

FIGURE 15.4A EUR vanilla interest-rate swap rates, 29 December 2010.

06 Curncy ICAE
200<Go> to view in Launchpad
14:57 EONIA Rates 1-30 Year PAGE 1 / 1

	DESCRIPTION	ASK	BID	TIME		DESCRIPTION	ASK	BID	TIME
1)	1 Year	0.811	0.761	14:07	16)	30 Year	3.305	3.235	14:56
2)	2 Year	1.128	1.058	14:57					
3)	3 Year	1.471	1.401	14:33					
4)	4 Year	1.791	1.721	14:57					
5)	5 Year	2.074	2.004	14:57					
6)	6 Year	2.315	2.245	14:56					
7)	7 Year	2.523	2.453	14:57					
8)	8 Year	2.695	2.625	14:56					
9)	9 Year	2.838	2.768	14:57					
10)	10 Year	2.963	2.893	14:56					
11)	11 Year	3.073	3.003	14:56					
12)	12 Year	3.172	3.102	14:56					
13)	15 Year	3.370	3.300	14:56					
14)	20 Year	3.468	3.398	14:56					
15)	25 Year	3.407	3.337	14:56					

ICAP

Australia 61 2 9777 8600 Brazil 5511 3048 4500 Europe 44 20 7330 7500 Germany 49 69 9204 1210 Hong Kong 852 2977 6000
Japan 81 3 3201 8900 Singapore 65 6212 1000 U.S. 1 212 318 2000 Copyright 2010 Bloomberg Finance L.P.
SN 349985 29-Dec-2010 14:57:43

FIGURE 15.4B EUR overnight-index (EONIA) swap rates, 29 December 2010.

trade is usually considered on a combined basis. However, to discount on the correct funding curve, which is usually different from the forward–forward curve, a separate funding sensitivity measurement (or funding "delta") should be calculated. For instance, zero mark-to-market on a swap does not necessarily mean a zero funding delta. Depending on payment frequency and yield curve shape, an at-the-money swap can have funding sensitivity as well. For example, in the normal positive-sloping yield curve environment, a fixed-rate payer will see net cash outflow at the start of the transaction and gradually shift to net cash inflow as rates move up.

It is imperative therefore that banks use the correct yield curve when discounting derivatives, and that the funding requirement for derivatives collateral be managed in the same way as all other funding requirements at the bank. With the former, this means using the OIS curve for secured derivatives traded under CSA, and the bank's COF curve for unsecured derivatives. For the latter, one should assume that the collateral funding will remain at current levels, whatever they are, until there is a significant change in the shape and slope of the yield curve. Therefore the funding requirement should be termed out, as per the "ALM smile" we spoke of in Part II. It is poor liquidity risk management practice if the requirement is funded wholly in the short-term.

Adjusting Yield Curves

Issues arise when a CSA agreement allows more than one currency to be posted as collateral, or allows collateral to be posted in a currency that is different from the currency of the trade.

As we noted above, the collateralised discount curves to apply depends on the CSA terms with each particular counterparty that a trade is executed. The standard CSA used by the LCH specifies the following terms:

- bilateral, daily collateral call;
- zero mark-to-market threshold;
- cash collateral only;
- collateral posting currency in accord with trade currency;
- corresponding overnight rate paid on cash collateral held;
- overnight curve in the trade currency used to discount (EONIA for EUR, OIS for USD, SONIA for GBP and so on).

The most common inter-bank CSA is similar to that of LCH, with the exception that it allows for the choice of posting EUR, USD and GBP cash. This introduces a currency collateral element into swap pricing. When a trade is settled in one currency but is funded in another, a cross-currency basis adjustment will need to be made to the standard funding curve. Under this type of CSA, a rational collateral manager would post the currency that carried the lowest funding cost; conversely, it may choose to post the currency that yields the highest return. Current practice is for a bank to construct a "hybrid" curve by comparing the forward OIS, EONIA and SONIA curves and taking the maximum value at each point in time. That is, adjust the curves for cross-currency basis and then interpose them all onto one 2-dimensional chart. An overlying plot is then made of each point along the x-axis where the yield is lowest or highest. This was discussed in Chapter 5.

DERIVATIVES FUNDING POLICY

The divergence in funding rates and bank COF from Libor since the financial crisis of 2007–09 makes it important that derivatives are valued and risk managed in a way that recognises these differences in rates. This is particularly the case for uncollateralised derivatives. The derivatives funding policy adopted at the bank should incorporate an appropriate model for discounting uncollateralised derivative cash flows.

Background

The CSA annexe to the standard ISDA derivatives agreement requires counterparties to post collateral to the value of the negative mark-to-market of their derivatives positions. Transacting a mixture of uncollateralised and collateralised derivatives creates a funding requirement of cash and/or eligible securities which, because it is akin to any other medium-term bank funding requirement, needs to be managed within an aggregate funding framework. In other words, the management of derivative collateral funding should be part of the firm's overall liquidity management policy.

A bank will fund its balance sheet at its specific COF, which splits into four categories:

- secured short-term funding costs: the rate at which the bank borrows against collateral. This is generally the OIS curve, and thus the lowest funding rate available (OIS lies below Libor). It is not relevant in an uncollateralised derivative context, because such instruments cannot be used as collateral (even if they are positive MTM);
- secured long-term funding costs: the rate at which the bank can borrow by issuing term secured liabilities such as covered bonds and mortgage-backed securities;

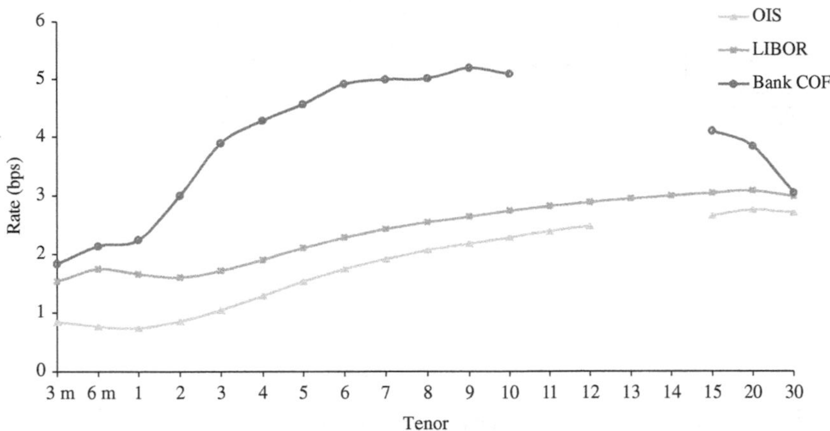

FIGURE 15.5 Graph of OIS, Libor/Swap and bank COF rates (TLP curve, spread over 3m Euribor)

- short-term unsecured funding costs: the bank's COF for short-dated (0-12 month) tenors. At its lowest this will be around Libor, although many banks' ST unsecured borrowing rate is at a spread above Libor;
- long-term unsecured funding costs: the bank's COF for long-dated (2-10 year) tenors, also referred to as the term liquidity premium (TLP).

The relative position of the OIS, Libor and TLP curves is shown in Figure 15.5.

When addressing collateral funding management, the first discipline to consider is that of the appropriate funding term structure. Generally this means terming out a proportion of collateral posting funding requirements. This creates a higher cost of business but leaves the bank at lower risk of a liquidity crisis during a funding stress event. We will address this issue again later in the chapter.

Uncollateralised derivatives

Banks deals in uncollateralised derivatives with customer counterparties. These positions are hedged in the interbank market using collateralised derivatives.

Sample illustrations In the simplest illustration, the bank will deal in an uncollateralised derivative with the customer, and a replicating hedge collateralised derivative with the hedge counterparty. Depending on where the MTM moves, the bank will either (i) receive collateral from the

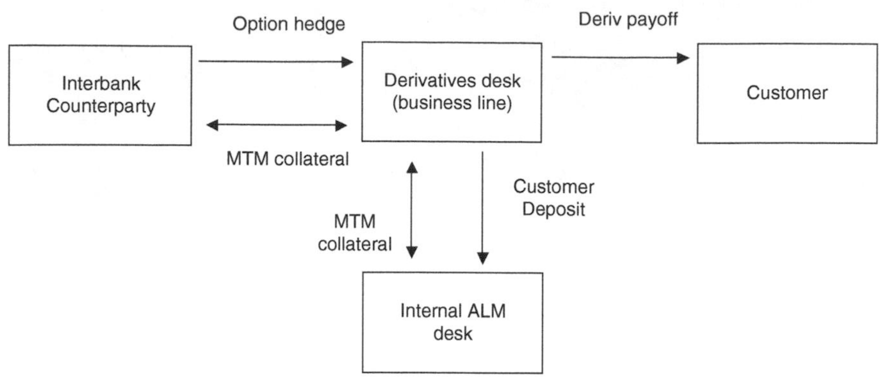

FIGURE 15.6 Uncollateralised derivative and hedge

counterparty or (ii) pass collateral to the counterparty. In the first case this cash should be placed within Treasury and managed as other interbank deposits; in the second it will be borrowed by Treasury as a funding requirement.

This is illustrated at Figure 15.6, assuming a derivative with a bullet cash flow on maturity, such as a structured zero-coupon note or an option-type product. In this arrangement, the cash deposit on Day 1 is matched to the maturity of the option. The interest on the term deposit placed under (i) above will be based on the term funding rate, and it is possible to demonstrate that this rate should also be used to discount the uncollateralised derivative. From existing literature (see Hull and White (2011)) we can state:

$$\text{Uncollateralised derivative price} = \text{Issuer bank zero-coupon bond price} \times \text{Derivative payoff}$$

It is evident then that the uncollateralised derivative will, at any time where a bank's COF lies above OIS, be discounted at a higher rate than the collateralised derivative.

Structured notes A structured note is an MTN incorporating an element of linked ("structured") payoff, for example a note linked to FX rates, equity index levels or a range of interest rates. For the issuing bank it is identical to any other form of uncollateralised liability, however its valuation will need to incorporate the LT COF because this will be directly linked to the note's payoff. Typically a structured note is valued as a combination of:

- Vanilla term deposit, valued at bank's LT COF;
- Derivative (interest-rate swap, or similar) that is hedged in the market with a collateralised swap.

In the previous illustration we suggested that the derivative is also discounted at LT COF.

Following orthodox finance theory, the valuation of the derivative would reflect the risk-neutral replicating hedge. A bank may choose to transact the derivative at a different value, for its own reasons; however the correct discounting rate used should still reflect the risk-neutral replicating hedge, and would therefore be the appropriate tenor TLP.

In both illustrations, the bank faces a borrowing requirement arising from the need to post collateral. In theory the bank should structure the borrowing so that its cash flows match that of the derivative. However this is only acceptable if the bank can fund at OIS. We assume it funds at COF, and therefore should treat this as any other form of unsecured wholesale funding. In terms of tenors, the liability profile should approach the "ALM Smile" concept discussed in Chapters 6 and 7, with a significant proportion of borrowing arranged as LT funding.

Derivative Liabilities and Assets: Credit Value Adjustment

Derivative liabilities correspond to what is termed an overall expected negative exposure (ENE), the most basic example of which is a deposit. A derivative asset corresponds to an overall expected positive exposure (EPE) and at its simplest would be a loan.

Following existing literature (for example, see Picault (2005) and Gregory (2009)), under a set of simplifying assumptions we have:

$$\begin{aligned} \text{CVA} &= \text{EPE} \times \text{PD} \times \text{LGD} \\ &= \text{EPE} \times \text{Counterparty Credit Spread} \end{aligned}$$

More formally we write

$$\text{CVA} = (1 - R) \int_{t=0}^{T} q(t)v(t)dt$$

where R is the recovery rate, q is the probability density function of counterparty default and v is the value of the derivative payoff. In discrete time we write

$$\text{CVA} = (1 - R) \sum_{i=1}^{n} q_i v_i$$

where q_i is the probability of default between times t_{i-1} and t_i, and

$$\text{DVA} = \text{ENE} \times \text{Credit Spread}$$

and

$$\text{Funding Cost} = (\text{EPE} + \text{ENE}) \times \text{Derivative Funding Spread}.$$

In other words, the discounting to be applied for valuation is at the appropriate tenor bank funding cost.

Derivative liabilities The interest payable should reflect that paid on the bank's bond. This is logical because the counterparty is providing term funding to the bank. It can be demonstrated by considering the hedge arrangement on an uncollateralised derivative, which is undertaken via a collateralised derivative. This is discounted at the term COF, by definition the rate used when issuing term liabilities. By valuing at term COF we also incorporate the DVA element and so no separate adjustment for DVA would be needed.

Therefore derivative liabilities funding and discount rate should be at LT COF; that is, the TLP.

Derivative assets Viewing a derivative asset as conceptually identical to a bond issued by the counterparty, we can treat the position as generating an EPE and therefore passing positive MTM to the bank. To discount the asset we would consider (i) the price of counterparty probability of default (implied by market prices) which is equivalent to the CVA and (ii) the funding cost.

The hedge arrangement is a collateralised derivative transacted in the interbank market. This creates a collateral posting requirement, funded by borrowing in the wholesale market. This will be charged at the bank's COF, and the bank can choose to fund in ST, LT or a mixture of the two.

The funding cost to apply can reflect what assumption one makes about the ease of unwinding the derivatives portfolio:

- Assume no easy unwind: if we cannot unwind the portfolio without punitive costs, we must assume we will have to fund the transaction for the full term. The funding cost of this commitment is given by the bank's LT COF. If we fund (value) at ST COF we run the risk that sudden spikes in the ST COF will create funding losses, or that a liquidity squeeze in general will impact our ability to rollover funding for the position. To avoid this risk, we would fund with LT borrowing, and discount unsecured derivatives off the LT COF (TLP) curve.
- Assume easy unwind: if we can unwind the position with no extraneous cost, we can apply the ST COF, say the 1-year TLP. The assumption of easy unwind means that we are not committed to rolling over funding; in the event of liquidity stress we would simply unwind the portfolio and eliminate the funding commitment. This is a strong assumption to make, particularly at a time of stress, and would be a high-risk policy.

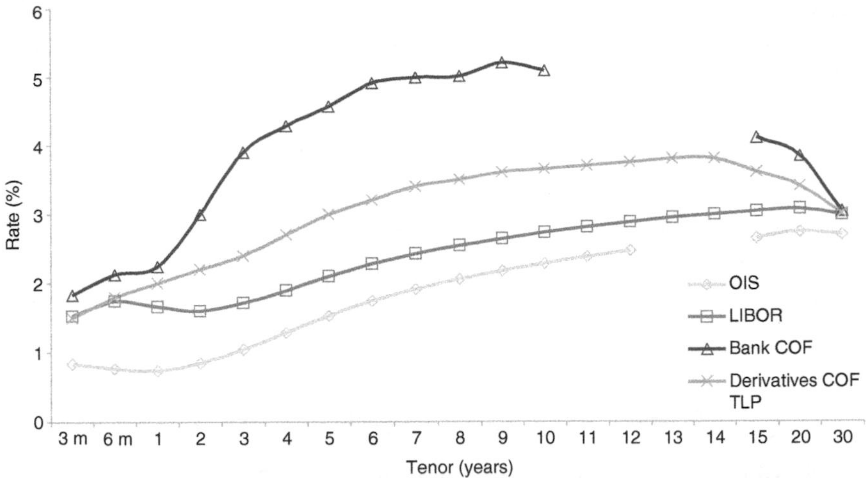

FIGURE 15.7 Derivatives funding curve as secured funding COF

Therefore in theory we recommend that the derivative asset be discounted at TLP and the funding for collateral postings be substantially term funded. That said, in some cases the funding generated from a derivative book (assuming no counterparty default) is contractually for a long maturity, and so the case may be made that this should be charged for/receive the secured funding rate as opposed to the unsecured COF rate. That being the case, the Derivatives TLP then sits below the bank's COF curve, and closer to the secured funding curve (see Chapter 9). Otherwise, it is equal to COF. The alternatives are shown at Figure 15.7.

In general when applying derivatives funding policy we assume no netting arrangements are in place, but in practice these are quite common and will have an impact on the bank's collateral funding position in the event of default.

Derivative portfolio maturity

The tenor period to apply when valuing at TLP discounting can be the contractual maturity of the derivative in question, but not necessarily so. An alternative approach is to split the portfolio into tenor buckets commensurate with the tenors at which we wish to fund the cashflows, with each bucket funded at the appropriate tenor COF.

Placing the derivative portfolio cash flows into appropriate term tenor buckets is a logical position on which to base how we choose to fund these cash flows. In practice, the derivative valuation model itself can be used to produce this tenor bucket breakdown, in the form of a

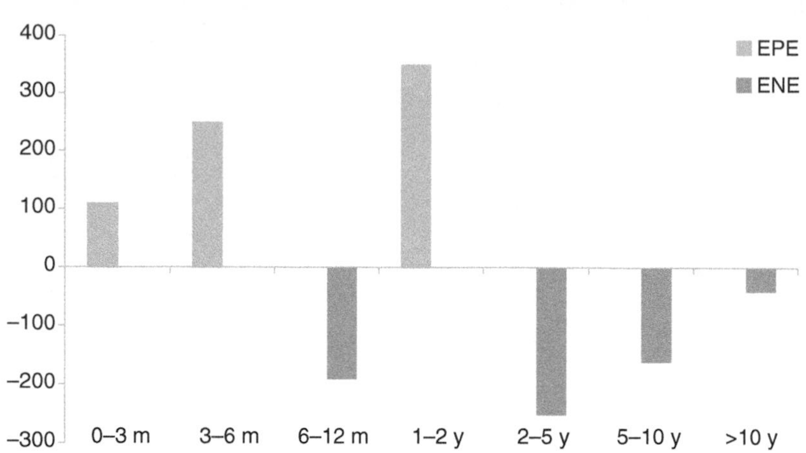

FIGURE 15.8 Uncollateralised derivatives net position FTP pricing

"funding risk per basis point" (FR01) delta ladder. Using this model output removes the need for a subjective analysis of the maturity profile of the portfolio. In other words, the maturity profile of the portfolio is given by the model output. The appropriate tenor TLP is charged on the amount in each bucket.

This is shown at Figure 15.8.

The division into derivative assets and liabilities is only relevant under certain conditions; for example, if netting arrangements are in place. However, the valuation principles are applicable in any case. If we assume we cannot unwind trades with ease, which is a reasonable assumption in a stressed environment, we would logically apply LT COF discounting in the valuation. If we assume we can unwind, we would apply ST COF.

The issue then remains what term to apply when valuing at LT COF. This can be at an average portfolio maturity, or as modelled by the derivative trading system.

Management Information

The liquidity metrics MI presented at ALCO should incorporate the collateral position for the bank. An example of such a report is given at Table 15.3.

Conclusions

Notwithstanding the strategic objective of a balanced portfolio policy, the net impact of uncollateralised derivatives transactions is to generate an

TABLE 15.3 Net collateral position report.

Currency	Total	Cash	Govt bonds	Corp. bonds	ABS/ MBS/CDO	LoC	Other
AUD	−109,151,315	23,395,812	−144,856,985	12,309,858			
CHF	381,958,058	−57,775	256,356,858	125,658,975			
EUR	60,576,080	−578,775	42,585,897	18,568,958			
GBP	1,474,737,802	850,155,878	556,898,758	−56,895,785		124,578,951	
USD	494,541,132	333,586,989	135,256,987	25,585,898		111,258	
Total	2,302,661,757	1,206,502,129	846,241,515	125,227,904		124,690,209	

ongoing unsecured funding requirement. We should expect this funding requirement to be in place as long as a bank is a going concern, in other words as ordinary business. Therefore it should be funded in LT tenors, with only a minority proportion funded in ST tenors.

As business best-practice in liquidity management policy is to maximise the proportion of funding in LT tenors, and which would cost the bank's LT COF (TLP), we conclude that uncollateralised derivative transactions should be discounted at the relevant tenor TLP rate. The derivative portfolio tenor can be broken down into appropriate tenor buckets as given by the derivatives valuation model.

EXAMPLE 15.1 COLLATERAL-BASED DISCOUNTING OF INTEREST RATE SWAPS

Collateral Types and Discount Curves

ISDA agreements generally cover three categories: single currency, multi-currency and uncollateralised derivatives. Single-currency collateral agreements include trades cleared through SwapClear, and are generally discounted using the specific currency OIS curve. For example, trades that allow posting of EUR collateral only will be discounted using the EONIA curve; with USD collateral it would be a FedFunds OIS curve. Multi-currency collateral swaps are more complex, particularly because of the optionality (allowed in some CSA agreements) in which currency collateral is allowed to be posted. The convention today is to apply a funding curve that is a hybrid

(*continued*)

of the respective single currency curves when discounting these types of swap. Uncollateralised swaps are generally discounted using the bank's COF curve for that currency.

OIS Discounting: Background and Worked Example

Since the end of the 1990s it has been common in the inter-bank market for the mark-to-market on derivatives such as interest-rate swaps to be collateralised. Until the 2008 banking crisis, inter-bank funding was always liquid (and assumed to always be liquid), so that the difference between the OIS rate and Libor was negligible. In the short dates it averaged around 2–3 bps, while at the long end of the curve it would range around 12–15 bps. Because of the lack of difference there was never any significant trading in OIS beyond the 1-year time horizon. Due to this immaterial variation, banks dealing in swaps paid little attention to the difference between OIS and Libor when discounting the cash flows on a swap. Also, there was no real market in OIS trades of longer than 1-year maturity.

This convention changed after the 2008 crash, because the funding conditions for banks altered. Inter-bank liquidity could not be taken for granted any more, and the OIS-Libor basis widened considerably (and remained wide). The impact of this in practice is that the market now places a large premium on term funding compared to overnight funding. For example, the difference between OIS and 3-month Libor averaged around 35–40 bps for EUR and USD in 2011 (it traded as high as 175 bps during the end of 2008 and beginning of 2009), and the difference between 3-month Libor and 6-month Libor averaged around 25–30 bps, again in both currencies. In fact, the basis differential is approximately the same for most currencies.

The practical impact of this is significant, and forces banks to focus on why collateralisation is important in a swap transaction. We illustrate with a simple example. We assume two banks that both fund at Libor (no bid–offer spread): Bank A and Bank B. Bank A lends Bank B £100 today, with Bank B agreeing to pay this loan back one year later. We assume further that the 1-year Libor rate is 5.00%. For the loan to be valued at par, Bank B will be paying back £105 in one year's time. Put another way, the £105 payment in one year's time is discounted back to today, using a 5% rate so that the PV of this payment is £105/(1.05) or £100.

The logic of this valuation is tenable for an uncollateralised transaction, but breaks down when a CSA agreement is signed between the two banks. The CSA means that collateral is posted on a daily basis to the net mark-to-market value by the bank that is negative mark-to-market. The bank receiving collateral, assuming it is in the form of cash, will pay interest at the overnight rate on this collateral. This is the OIS rate.

Returning to the loan transaction above, we now consider the impact of the collateral agreement. Bank A has lent Bank B £100 today and Bank B has agreed to pay Bank A £105 one year from now. Therefore the mark-to-market of the contract to pay Bank A £105 in a year's time will be £100 in Bank A's favour. So although Bank B receives £100 from Bank A today, under the collateral agreement it posts this back to Bank A as collateral immediately. Through the life of the trade Bank A pays Bank B the OIS rate on the £100 that has been placed with it (as collateral). We assume now that the 1-year OIS rate is 50 bps lower than the 1-year Libor rate of 5%, so it is 4.5%. At the end of the life of the trade, Bank B will have earned £4.50, but will have to pay Bank A £5.00. Bank B has lost the 50 bps of the OIS-Libor spread.

We conclude then that as part of its operational procedure, a bank should ensure that:

- trades that are covered by an OIS-based collateral agreement should be discounted at the OIS rate;
- it is aware of the type of collateral that is allowed in a CSA agreement, which can have a significant impact on the value of a portfolio.

As part of its liquidity funding policy therefore, a bank should modify its derivatives funding policy to incorporate the above. In addition, the daily funding needs of the derivatives portfolio must come under the same liquidity management regime of all the other liability requirements.

EXAMPLE 15.2 CEBS FTP GUIDELINES

The CEBS guidelines published in 2010 are as good an approach to adopt as any, at least in principle. We summarise and critique them here.

Guideline 1: The liquidity cost benefit allocation mechanism is an important part of the whole liquidity management framework. As such, the mechanism should be consistent with the framework of governance, risk tolerance and decision-making.

In other words, internal funds pricing is integral to bank liquidity risk management, and thereby its ALM mechanism. It is as at least as important as maintaining a satisfactory funding gap and a diverse source of funds. The methodology for setting the internal funding rate is one part of the process; the other part is the allocation of funding costs to the business lines. This can be achieved through the FTP process, and the rate at which FTP is transacted needs to be commensurate with the correct allocation of costs. Each bank should have a clearly articulated definition of its risk tolerance with regard to internal funds pricing.

Guideline 2: The liquidity cost benefit allocation mechanism should have a proper governance structure supporting it.

This makes clear that the internal funds process needs to be "owned" by senior management, delegated to the ALCO, with an explicit approval and annual review process. The internal funding methodology, and its constituent internal funding cost curve, should be applied to liquidity pricing for internal loans, as well as for the appraisal of new products or transactions.

Within this guideline CEBS goes on to state:

> *. . . the area or responsible function ultimately charged with implementing and monitoring the internal prices should be service-oriented and not have a profit target for this specific role. Equally . . . personnel working within the area should not be set profit targets for this activity.*[12]

This guideline is easy to follow for a bank that organises its Treasury desk as a middle-office function, or as a non-revenue-generating or non-P&L function. Where the bank Treasury is also a P&L centre with a profit target, the setting of FTP should be under Finance department management. Profit generated from internal funding trades should be allocated to an ALCO book.

12 CEBS 2010, p. 6.

Guideline 3: The output from the allocation mechanism should be actively and properly used and appropriate to the business profiles of the institution.

What this states is that the liquidity pricing process should be framed with practical application in mind, and set for ease of use by the business lines in their decision-making. It should be applied at the "coal face" by the business transaction managers. Equally, its rationale and objectives should be understood by everyone.

The guideline also states that "the liquidity pricing methodology should compensate the providers of liquidity and charge the users". This means that the same TLP pricing grid should be applied to both users of funds and those businesses that raise liabilities for the bank. A business line that raises long-term funds should receive the same TLP rate as that paid by a business line that lends funds of the same tenor (ignoring bid–offer spreads).

Guideline 4: The scope of application of internal prices should be significantly comprehensive to cover all significant parts of assets, liabilities and off-balance sheet items regarding liquidity.

This guideline covers a number of areas. The first one refers to applying behavioural treatment of retail deposits. It is accepted by both banks and regulators that for both fixed-term and call deposits (such as cheque accounts), retail deposits are less sensitive to market conditions than wholesale deposits. That is, retail funds are sticky, compared to wholesale funds. In practice this means that fixed-term deposits can be treated as genuine fixed term, and their overnight balances can be treated as longer term than 1-day funds. For example, if a bank can show that the stability of retail call deposits has been over 50% during the previous five years, including a period of crisis, then the bank can argue that half the value of these funds should be treated as long-term funds. The corollary of this is that those business lines raising retail liabilities should be appropriately rewarded via the FTP process.

Another aspect of this principle is that committed credit lines set up for customers should be charged at an internal rate that covers the cost of supplying these funds should the customer draw on the line. The appropriate level should reflect the fact that these lines are very likely to be drawn at the worst possible time for a bank, during a liquidity crisis. A similar internal charge should also be levied on businesses that grant uncommitted credit lines.

(*continued*)

FTP rates should be reviewed on a regular basis, and should reflect current market conditions as well as the funding position of the bank itself. CEBS states that they should "reflect both direct and indirect funding costs, including the cost of the liquidity buffer".[13] However, the author's view is that the cost of the LAB can be recharged back, on a pro-rata basis, to each business line on an arrears basis, as a separate distinct fee; it does not need to be incorporated into the FTP curve.

Guideline 5: The internal prices should be determined by robust methodologies, taking into account the various factors involved in liquidity risk.

Yield curve construction is a much-researched subject. A bank should articulate a formal procedure that describes the methodology it uses to generate its internal yield curve. As we noted earlier, the internal FTP is a significant aspect of the liquidity risk management process, because it feeds into the business appraisal decision. The net interest margin of the asset book is a function of the internal yield curve.

The basic principle is that the bank sets its internal curve with respect to the market, most commonly the Libor (or for the euro, Euribor) yield curve. For longer than 1-year tenors, this refers to the swap curve. For reference purposes, a bank should also note the levels of the CDS curve written on its own name. Where the bank is setting internal rates for tenors in which it does not have debt securities in the secondary market, it may construct the curve using a term structure model, with parameter inputs from a number of proxy rates. We discuss these proxies later in this chapter.

A key issue post-crash is the rate applied to cash collateral transferred and received under the derivative contract CSA of the standard ISDA derivative legal agreement. Collateral attracts the OIS rate, and the OIS curve is different to the Libor curve. This needs to be taken into consideration in liquidity and funding policy.[14]

Each bank will need to derive its funding curve from the market model, adjusted to reflect its own specific circumstances. The adjustment should reflect the liquidity premium for the bank in particular. This is not an exact science. The basic premise is that a bank will pay a spread above the Libor or swap rate, unless it is a higher rated bank;

13 CEBS 2010, p. 8.

14 OIS swaps are discussed in the author's book *Bank Asset and Liability Management* published by John Wiley & Sons (2007). The OIS curve, also known as the "collateralised curve", is discussed further in Chapter 5.

the spread between a bank's actual funding rate and the Libor rate incorporates both a liquidity premium and the name-specific credit risk. The challenge is extracting the liquidity element from the credit risk element when assessing the spread above Libor that a bank pays for term funding.

In essence, the basic principle here is that the product or business line approval process should be closely integrated with the internal pricing process.

Funds raised by a bank are the building block of the product that it sells (loans), which suggests by definition that the cost of funding must be included in the cost of lending. This statement has a fairly obvious logic, but it bears noting because it is vital that it is applied correctly in practice. As the CEBS document states, "selling only fairly priced products can be considered to be a major criterion for the long-term functioning of an institution".

PRICING LIQUIDITY

Market liquidity is another much-researched topic in financial economics. The trading liquidity of the secondary market in bonds and equities is usually measured with a proxy metric such as the price bid–offer spread; a narrower spread indicates a more liquid market. There are a number of other proxies that may be used, such as trading volume, market turnover, average daily trading frequency, average quote size, average trade size and theoretical yield spread, among others. No one proxy measure provides a complete picture of trading liquidity, however, so analysts often consider a range of them when attempting to determine how liquid a secondary market is.

Measuring funding liquidity is an even more opaque process. It is further complicated because there are two elements to it, the market liquidity overall and the liquidity premium specific to one bank. It is reasonably straightforward to calculate the cost of term liquidity for the larger multinational banks, because there are transparent and accurate market prices available for their secondary market debt, not to mention a ready reference of liquid CDS prices for comparison. The exercise is slightly more involved for smaller banks, which will have fewer points of external reference. Just as with trading liquidity, a bank should consider a number of proxies when setting its funding liquidity measure.

It is worth remembering what the point of an FTP mechanism is when setting the internal funds curve. Business lines originate assets that create liquidity stress for the banks, because the business of banking involves maturity transformation. The cost of sourcing that liquidity in the market needs to be covered by the business line (via the FTP charge), first so that the business can undertake its project appraisal as efficiently as possible, and second so as not to create artificial profits that do not reflect the cost of the bank's funds. Bearing this in mind is important, especially for smaller banks, because an element of judgement is called for when setting the internal funds curve.

We consider first the shape of the FTP curve, and then look at what proxies are available when setting it.

The Concept of the Term Liquidity Premium

Let us assume that a bank can always borrow at Libor-flat, and that this is the case across the entire term structure. If the bank carried out its lending on a match-funded basis, then in principle there is no need for an FTP (or, rather, the FTP can be zero). For example, say it puts on a position of the following:

Asset:	5-year corporate loan, floating rate interest received quarterly
Spread:	250 bps
Liability:	5-year FRN, paying quarterly
Spread:	0 bps

The business line will set the interest spread over Libor on the loan, and this pricing reflects the credit risk of the customer. It also drives the RoC, which is set at the required hurdle level. In this case, the Treasury desk can charge the Corporate Banking department an internal loan rate of Libor-flat. The asset generates a liquidity stress for the balance sheet for the bank, but because it is match funded on the same basis, this effectively negates the risk, and no liquidity premium need be charged.[15] The bank can raise the funding at Libor-flat, and crucially we have assumed that it will *always* be able to. When calculating the RoC, which is a function of the bank's cost of capital and the amount of capital it sets aside against the

15 Not everyone will agree with this analysis. That's life. But starting with this premise actually then makes it easier to make the logical case for adding a liquidity premium over the bank's funding rate for all other cases.

asset (itself a function of the asset risk-weighting), the Corporate Banking department will use a net profit of 250 bps.

This example is a very simple one, but it serves to make the point we wish. Consider now the following position:

Asset:	5-year corporate loan, floating rate interest received quarterly
Spread:	250 bps
Liability:	3-month inter-bank deposit, rolling quarterly
Spread:	0 bps

In this case the liquidity stress generated by the asset has not been alleviated, because the bank will need continuously to roll over the funding for the next five years. We still assume that the bank can fund at Libor-flat, but we do not know if it will always be able to roll over the funding it needs. This is liquidity risk, created by the asset–liability gap; and is of course a definition of banking, but it needs to be accounted for. In this case Treasury needs to set a liquidity premium on the internal loan, otherwise Corporate Banking will continue to use the 250 bps net profit when calculating its RoC, and this RoC will not be accurate: it will be over-stated by a funding gain. In other words, it is not true SVA, as it incorporates an element of funding spread gain that is not real. In this example, SVA is over-stated.

Therefore the Treasury desk sets an FTP of 50 bps, this being the 5-year TLP. We assume now that the bank does not fund at Libor-flat, but on average at Libor + 10 in the 0–12-month tenor range. The bank can incorporate this into the FTP grid, or it can assume that the FTP is always a spread over Libor and adjust it as necessary, say on a quarterly or semi-annual basis, to incorporate the funding cost to the bank.

This is the basic plain vanilla case for setting up an FTP mechanism. The debate now moves on to the extent of the FTP curve, and its slope. If in the above example we had used a 1-year corporate loan, the resulting liquidity stress would have been much lower for the bank and hence the FTP could be lower. In other words, the longer the tenor mismatch, the greater the FTP one should charge.

We are now in a position to set an initial FTP curve. Table 15.4 shows a continuously positively sloping FTP curve, which follows a positively sloping market yield curve. The rates are the bank's cost of liquidity, relative to its external funding cost. The derivation of these rates is discussed in the next section. This curve is the bank Treasury's official COF curve for its internal customers.

In a stable and liquid banking market, the asset–liability gap is never an issue. If one is *always* able to roll over funding, it docs not matter if the gap

TABLE 15.4 Hypothetical bank internal funds price curve ("FTP" or "TLP" curve).

Term	FTP (bps)
0–6 months	0
7–12 months	5
1–2 years	15
3 years	35
4 years	40
5 years	50
6 years	60
7 years	70
8 years	80
9 years	90
10 years	100
>10 years	135

is 12 months, 60 months or 120 months – if funding is always available, then the gap is immaterial.[16] Strangely enough, if one is not able to roll over funding, then the actual gap length is immaterial as well – any gap is fatal. In other words, in a liquidity crisis situation it does not really matter if the gap is 12 months or 120 months, if the bank cannot obtain funds then it will have to seek assistance at the central bank lender of last resort (or go bust). This is why the UK FSA focuses so emphatically on the 2-week and 90-day funding gap at UK banks, because these are the assumed critical periods in a funding crisis. Basel III takes a less conservative view and focuses on the 30-day funding gap, assuming (somewhat unrealistically) that a liquidity crisis will not last longer than 30 days.

The point of this discussion is to assert that once the liquidity stress gets beyond a material term – let us say five years for the sake of argument – then the incremental stress added for each additional gap is minor. Therefore the FTP curve does not necessarily need to follow the market yield curve completely, it can be reasonably flat after five years, and certainly flat after the 10-year point. We therefore adjust our hypothetical curve from Table 15.4, shown at Table 15.5.

16 This assumption drove the emergence of structured finance vehicles such as "funding arbitrage" asset-backed CP conduits and, the ultimate expression of gap funding across a positive-sloping yield curve, the structured investment vehicle, or SIV. The SIV suffered extinction during 2007–2008, while the ABCP vehicle was *hors de combat* for a period.

TABLE 15.5 Hypothetical FTP curve with adjustment after 5-year tenor.

Term	FTP (bps)
0–6 months	0
7–12 months	5
1–2 years	15
3 years	35
4 years	40
5 years	50
6 years	51
7 years	52
8 years	53
9 years	54
10 years	55
>10 years	60

Proxies for the Funding Liquidity Premium

The internal funds price is the cost of liquidity for the bank; that is, the additional borrowing costs the bank must pay for by raising longer term funds, chargeable solely for liquidity reasons. The perceived credit risk of the bank from the investor viewpoint has to be stripped out of its all-in borrowing costs. This is not a straightforward exercise.

The base case is for a bank that can access the wholesale markets at Libor-flat across the entire term structure. There is a case here for saying that the FTP for such a bank can be Libor-flat; however, this is the current state *now*, with the future state of the markets being unknown. That is why a zero FTP spread can be justified only on a match-funded basis. Given this logic, a bank needs to determine its cost of liquidity. There may be more than one answer, so an element of judgement is called for.

The starting point is the rate at which the bank can raise funds in the market. For a large bank, its primary issuance level will, in a stable market, lie above the secondary market level. If we ignore this difference for the time being, taking the cost of its funds in the market as the primary input to its internal funding curve is a logical first step. The two things to consider then are (i) this funding rate includes the credit risk of the bank, which needs to be stripped out, and (ii) not every bank has a public funding curve. It is necessary then to consider proxies to establish the cost of liquidity.

A number of proxy measures can be considered. The CEBS document states the following:

1. the risk-free curve + the CDS spread;
2. the risk-free rate + maturity liquidity premium + institution liquidity premium + buffer premium;
3. direct funding cost + term premium + buffer premium;
4. short-term financing cost + term funding cost (including contingent liabilities).

None of the above is an adequate proxy for pure liquidity cost, although all are worth bearing in mind. That said, for a number of reasons evident since the 2008 crash, the author does not recommend setting the TLP grid with reference to CDS levels and we have already noted that a bank may wish to account separately for the cost of the liquidity buffer premium. The proxy measure number (3) above is reasonably straightforward to ascertain, although again the "term premium" will include an element of credit spread.

Instead, the author's recommendation is to consider the following proxies for liquidity:

- the difference between the funded and the unfunded rate for the bank; that is, the swap rate versus the bond rate that the bank pays. In other words, what it pays floating in an interest-rate swap against what it pays floating in an asset swap on a bond it issues (of the same tenor);
- the difference between the risk-free rate and the swap rate. This is not exact (in theory it is the price of general bank risk plus liquidity), but is worth considering in the analysis;
- a more robust case can be made for the following, which would appear to be an implicit measure of the term liquidity premium. This is the difference between:
  - paying fixed on a term interest-rate swap; and
  - paying fixed on the same-tenor money market swap or OIS swap;
- an increase in the cost of funds for the bank for each incremental upward change in tenor. So if we consider the following bank's cost of borrowing along the term structure, as a spread over Libor:
  - 1-year: 20 bps
  - 2-year: 30 bps
  - 3-year: 35 bps
  - 4-year: 40 bps
  - 5-year: 50 bps

  then we can take the increase at each tenor point as the liquidity premium, because the credit risk element in each case is theoretically

almost identical. The difference in each case will still include some allowance for greater credit risk exposure, but this measure does begin to give an idea of the liquidity premium;
- the difference between the bank's CDS spread and the asset-swap spread (ASW) for the bank. This is the CDS basis, and in theory represents the cost of cash borrowing and liquidity premium for the bank against its pure credit risk. In theory a CDS is the price of credit only, so the basis should represent its liquidity premium. However, due to other factors driving CDS prices, this measure should not be used in isolation.

We recommend basing the FTP charge on the above, perhaps an average of all of the measures. In any case there is no transparent explicit cost of liquidity, so a bank will have to exercise some judgement when setting the rate.

Example 15.3 is a recommended input to a bank's ALCO guidance on the subject. Note that the second bullet point in Example 15.3 was not included in our list above; however, it is a useful input to the analysis.

EXAMPLE 15.3 SAMPLE POLICY GUIDANCE: THE LIQUIDITY PREMIUM

The FTP will be reviewed every six months to ensure that it is realistic to the market. There is no universal method to calculate the liquidity premium that should be added to the Libor funding cost. Rather, there are a number of proxy measures that can be used, and the bank should take a range or an average of the various proxy measures.

Approaches for TLP proxies include:

- the difference between ASW and CDS of the bank (where this is negative) for each tenor maturity;
- the difference between the funding spread over a bank of the same credit rating, or peer-group bank;
- the difference between the fixed rate on a term swap and the fixed rate on an OIS swap of the same tenor.

Additionally, a bank can consider these:

- the secondary market yields less the primary market yields of the bank's bonds;

(*continued*)

- where there is no market indicator or no liquid secondary market, the spread differential between its 2-year and its longer tenor recent issuances;
- the previous 5-year issuance (as long as within 3 months) compared against what the new issue 5-year would be today; the difference is partly a function of liquidity premium;
- a subjective add-on based on what the ALCO believes the bank will pay to raise longer dated funds, separate to the credit risk perception of the bank.

These inputs should all feed into the FTP calculation.

TEMPLATE FUNDS TRANSFER PRICING DOCUMENT

Implementing an internal funds pricing policy that explicitly charges the business lines for the cost of liquidity is not always a painless task, not least due to inertia and resistance from the business lines themselves. This is particularly acute when the businesses have historically always paid a Libor-flat or Libor + fixed spread charge. The bank's FTP policy, whether it is an update or it is being set up for the first time, should always be owned by the Board, delegated to ALCO, and implemented by the Finance department.

A simple template for a bank's funds transfer pricing policy is included at the Wiley website supplementary material accompanying this book (see Chapter 19 for details). This document would be part of a bank's liquidity policy statement; it can be used as a benchmark starting point for a bank's FTP policy. In the example given on the Wiley website, the FTP matrix is as follows:

Period to maturity	<6 mths	6 mths–12 mths	1 yr–5 yrs	>5 yrs
Liabilities	Libor	Libor + 10 bps	Libor + 30 bps	Libor + 50 bps

The actual price of the FTP needs to be calculated using one or more of the methodologies noted above. In this example, the bank is using a relatively flat term structure for its FTP curve. Note also from the template that there is no bid–offer spread in this policy. A new 2-year asset originated by a business line will attract the same TP charge that a new 2-year liability will earn.

This simple template can be added with additional sections outlining the policy for each specific product type. If a bank deals in derivatives or is a bond market-maker, or offers additional product types, the FTP treatment for each (along the lines of what we described earlier in this chapter) should be included in the FTP policy.

Another template policy is given at the Wiley website for a bank's cost allocation policy for reserves and non-interest-bearing liabilities. This document is a sub-set of the FTP policy.

REFERENCES AND BIBLIOGRAPHY

Choudhry, M. (2013), "Derivatives Funding Policy and the FVA," *Intelligent Risk*, PRMIA, February 2013, pp.16–19.

Choudhry, M. (2013), "Business best-practice bank internal funds pricing policy," *Intelligent Risk*, PRMIA, June 2013, pp. 6–11.

Gregory, J. (2009), *Counterparty Credit Risk: The New Challenge for Financial Markets*, Chichester: John Wiley & Sons.

Hull, J., and A. White (2011), *CVA and Wrong Way Risk*, Working Paper, Joseph L. Rotman School of Management, University of Toronto, August 1, 2011.

Picault, E. (2005), "Calculating and Hedging Exposure, CVA and Economic Capital for Counterparty Credit Risk," in Pykhtin, M., (editor), *Counterparty Credit Risk Modelling*, London: RISK Books.

A player like me, I freely admit, I rely on team-mates. I am better in a better team. It sounds stupid, but I could name six players who are better in a poorer team. They would almost get shown up [in a good team]. They are more physical, they don't like the ball to feet, they haven't got the sense of where the ball is going to come.

— Michael Owen, interview with Matt Dickinson in
The Times, 30 September 2009

PART IV

Bank Strategy and Governance

The final part of this book, excluding Chapter 19 which describes the Wiley website supplementary material referred to in the earlier chapters, is not necessarily more important than any of the other parts, but does describe a subject matter of the greatest influence in a bank's well-being. That is because it is open to the widest interpretation, and requires the most careful judgement in its application.

In Part IV we discuss bank strategy, capital management and corporate governance. Strategy is a nebulous, possibly nefarious concept. But it is important. In chapters 16 and 17 we provide what we consider to be business best practice guidance on how it should be formulated. In Chapter 17 we discuss bank capital and funding management, which we illustrate with a capital policy template. There is also a technical discussion on derivatives collateral funding, which needs to be included in the overall liquidity risk funding policy, and funding strategy.

Chapter 18 looks at corporate governance. This area came under the greatest scrutiny from regulators in the wake of the bank crash, but is another field where it is difficult to enforce standards solely by regulatory fiat. Incompetent senior managers and those exercising poor judgement will always be with us, in every walk of life. Regulators can only do so much to enforce minimum acceptable standards of competence and ability to exercise sound judgement. However, if the overall culture, and consensus, for strategy and management in banking changes to one of an inherent conservatism, this will result in a more sustainable business model. In this final chapter we provide recommendations on how to implement business best-practice corporate governance. We also provide a template management committee and Treasury organisation structure that should assist good governance.

CHAPTER 16

Bank Strategy I: Formulating Strategy and Direction

The global financial crisis of 2007–2009 had the effect of making all participants in the banking industry, from regulators, central banks and governments to bank boards, directors and trade associations, undertake a fundamental review of the principles of banking. Issues such as capital and liquidity management, and systemic risk, became the subject of renewed focus. In practical terms, legislators realised that they needed to address the issue of the "too-big-to-fail" bank; this issue remains unresolved, and ultimately the realisation will dawn that the global economy simply cannot withstand certain financial institutions failing. But instead of this being taken to mean that banks can operate perpetually in an environment in which their profits are privatised and losses are socialised, it should be apparent that these institutions will have to be run on principles that ensure that they survive throughout the business cycle. This will call for more enlightened strategy and management, as well as an inherent conservatism. If bankers wish to run a proprietary trading outfit, or wish to maximise market share and return on capital, or outperform their peers, then they should go and work at a hedge fund. Those who manage a retail deposit-taking institution will need to remain aware of the responsibilities they bear.

From the point of view of bank practitioners, the most important task is to address the issues of capital, liquidity and risk management, and work them into a coherent strategy that is designed to produce sustainable returns over the business cycle. In this chapter we introduce these topics as part of a wider discussion on formulating bank strategy, and consider how this strategy should be worked around the changed requirements of the post-crisis age.

THE SUSTAINABLE BANK BUSINESS MODEL

The basic bank business model has remained unchanged since banks were first introduced in modern society. Of course, as it as much an art as a science, the model parameters themselves can be set to suit the specific strategy of the individual bank, depending on whether the bank operates at a higher or lower risk-reward profile. But the basic model is identical across all banks. In essence, banking involves taking risks, and then applying effective management of that risk. This risk can be categorised as follows:

- managing the bank's capital;
- managing the liquidity mismatch: a fundamental ingredient of banking is "maturity transformation", the recognition that loans (assets) generally have a longer tenor than deposits (liabilities).

If we wished to summarise the basic ingredients of the historical bank model, we might describe it in the following terms:

- leverage: a small capital base is levered into an asset pool that can be 10, 20, 30 times greater, or even higher;
- the "gap": essentially funding short to lend long. This is a function of the conventional positively sloping yield curve, and dictated by the recognition of the asset–liability mismatch noted above;
- liquidity: an assumption that a bank will always be able to roll over funding as it falls due;
- risk management: an understanding of credit or default risk.

These fundamentals remain unchanged. The critical issue for bank management, however, is that some of the assumptions behind the application of these fundamentals *have* changed, as demonstrated by the events of 2007–2009. The changed landscape in the wake of the crisis has resulted in some hitherto "safe" or profitable business lines being viewed as risky. Although more favourable conditions for banking will return in due course, for the foreseeable future the challenge for banks will be to set their strategy only after first arriving at a true and full understanding of economic conditions as they exist today. The first subject for discussion is to consider what a realistic, sustainable return on capital target level should be, and that it is commensurate to the level of risk aversion desired by the bank's Board. The Board should also consider the bank's capital availability, and what sustained amount of business this would realistically support. These two issues need to be addressed before the remainder of the bank's strategy can be considered.

Bank Strategy

The most important function that a bank Board can undertake is to set the bank's strategy. This is not as obvious as it sounds. It would be surprising to a layperson to observe just how often banks, both large and small, sophisticated or plain vanilla, have no real articulated strategy, but it is a fact. It is vital that banks put in place a coherent, articulated strategy that sets the tone for the entire business, from the top down.

In the first instance the Board must take into account the current regulatory environment. This includes, of course, the requirements of the Basel III rules, as well as the requirements of the national regulator. A bank cannot formulate strategy without a clear and genuine understanding of the environment in which it operates. Once this is achieved, before proceeding with a formal strategy, the bank needs to determine what markets it wishes to operate in, what products it sells and what class of customer it wishes to serve. All its individual business lines should be set up to operate within the main strategy, having identified the markets and customers. In other words, all the business lines exist as ingredients of the strategy. If a business line is not a fit with the strategy, it should be divested; equally, if a bank wishes to enter into a new business, then the strategy should be reviewed and realigned if it does not naturally suggest the new business. Again, this sounds obvious, but there are many cases of banks entering piecemeal into different businesses, or maintaining business lines that have been inherited through previous growth or acquisition, that do not fit the bank's culture.

In other words, a bank cannot afford to operate by simply meandering along, noting its peer group market share and RoE, and making up strategy as it goes along. This approach, which it would seem is what many banks do indeed follow, however inadvertently, results in a senior management and Board that is not fully aware of what the bank's liabilities and risk exposures are.

The first task then is to understand one's operating environment. It is then to incorporate a specific target market and product suite as the basis of its strategy. Concurrent with this, the bank must set its RoE target, which drives much of its culture and ethos. It is important to get this part of the process right, and at the start. Prior to the crash, it was common for banks to seek to increase revenue by adding to their risk exposure. Assets were added to the balance sheet or higher risk assets were taken on. In the bull market environment of 2001–2007, and allied to low funding costs as a result of low base interest rates, this resulted in ever higher RoE figures, to the point where it was common for even "Tier 2" banks to target levels of 22%–25% RoE in their business appraisal. This process was of course not tenable in the long run.

The second task, following immediately from the first, is to set a realistic RoE target, or better still, RoA target, that is sustainable over the entire business cycle. This cannot be done without educating board directors as well as shareholders, who must appreciate the new, lower RoE targets. Managing expectations will contribute to a more dispassionate review of strategy. As important, risk-adjusted RoE should also be set at a realistic level and not be allowed to increase. Hence, the Board and shareholders must accept that lower RoE levels will become the standard. This should also be allied to lower leverage levels and higher capital ratios.

Also, concurrently with the above process, a bank must ask itself where its strength lies, and formulate its strategy around that. In other words, it is important to focus on core competencies. Again, the experience of the crash has served to demonstrate that many banks found themselves with risk exposures they did not understand. This may have been simply the holding of assets (such as structured finance securities) whose credit exposures, valuation and secondary market liquidity they did not appreciate, or embarking on investment strategies such as negative basis trading without being aware of all the risk measurement parameters of such strategies.[1] To properly implement a coherent, articulate strategy, a bank needs to be aware of exactly what it does and does not have an expertise for undertaking, and not operate in products or markets in which it has no genuine knowledge base.

Allied to an understanding of core competence is a review of core and non-core assets. Bank strategy is not a static process or document, but rather a dynamic process. Regular reviews of the balance sheet need to be undertaken to identify any non-core assets, which can then be assessed to determine whether they remain compatible with the strategy. If they are not, then a realistic disposal process should be drawn up. In the long run, this is connected with an understanding of where the bank's real strengths lie. Long-term core assets may well differ from core assets, but this needs

1 Without naming the banks, the author is aware of institutions that purchased ABS and CDO securities under a belief that the senior tranche, rated AAA, would not be downgraded even if there were a default in the underlying asset pool, presumably because the junior note(s) would absorb the losses. Of course, this loss of subordination does erode the initial rating of the senior note, with a consequent markdown in market value. Another institution, according to anecdotal evidence received by the author in an email from one of its employees, entered into negative basis trades without any consideration for the funding cost of the trade package. This resulted in losses irrespective of the performance of the basis. In this case, it is clear that the trading desks in question entered into a relatively sophisticated trading strategy without being sufficiently aware of its technical and risk implications.

to be articulated explicitly. The decision on whether an asset is core or non-core, or core or long-term core, is a function of the bank's overall strategy of what its expertise is and what markets and customers it wishes to service. This will be embedded in the strategy and the bank's business model. This drives the choice of products and business lines that the bank feels it can add value in.

Leverage Ratios

Elsewhere we discuss bank capital structure. There is no doubt that the new model for banking assumes higher capital ratios and buffers for all banks in the longer term. The higher level of capital will be substantial in some cases, because under the Basel III rules trading businesses will be required to hold up to three times as much capital as vanilla banking business. Basel III also imposes a limit on the leverage ratio, and indeed some national regulators already are doing so; this follows the example of the regulators in Canada and Australia, two jurisdictions that had imposed leverage ratio limits and which, not coincidentally, did not suffer a bank crash in 2008.

A leverage ratio is the total value of a bank's assets relative to its equity capital. The financial crash highlighted the extent of risk taking by certain banks when measured using leverage ratios. As a measure of the ratio of assets to owner's equity, they are an explicit indication of risk exposure. Lehman Brothers leverage ratio increased from approximately 24:1 in 2003 to over 31:1 by 2007. Such aggressive asset growth generated tremendous profits during the boom years, but exposed the bank to such an extent that even a 3% or 4% decline in the value of its assets would eliminate completely its equity. This duly happened.

This is why Basel III has introduced a limit on leverage ratios as an added safety measure, alongside minimum capital requirements. In the aftermath of the crash it is accepted that bank leverage ratios have to adjust downwards, and the prevailing sentiment today dictates that boards should be wary of a business model that ramps up the ratio to an excessive level. Figure 16.1 shows levels during 2007–2009; prudent management suggests average levels will be much lower than these figures over the next 10–15 years. This is not only business best-practice, but will also contribute to greater systemic stability.

Bank management will have to adjust to a concept of an explicit leverage ratio limit, the rationale for which is clear. The experience of the last and previous crises has shown that during a period of upside growth, banks' risk models tend to underestimate their exposure. This has two consequences: first, the bank takes on ever greater risk, as it targets greater revenue and profit during a bull market, and second the amount of capital

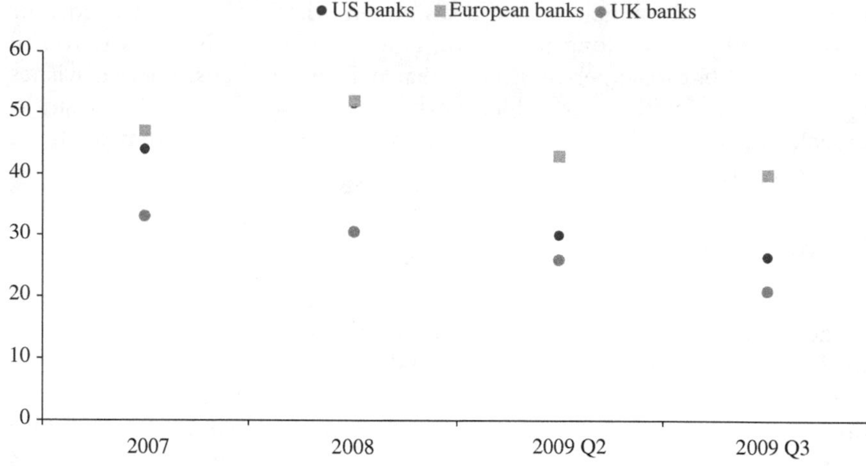

FIGURE 16.1 Bank median leverage ratios, 2007–2009.
Source: Bank of England (2009).

set aside is below what is adequate at the time the crash occurs. Figure 16.2, which shows a sample of "bulge-bracket" banks, suggests that banks focused on trading assets as they expanded their balance sheets.

In such an environment, capital ratio requirements are an insufficient safeguard against instability, and it becomes necessary to monitor leverage ratios. Hence, in the post-crash environment banks need to adjust their business strategy to allow for this constraint.

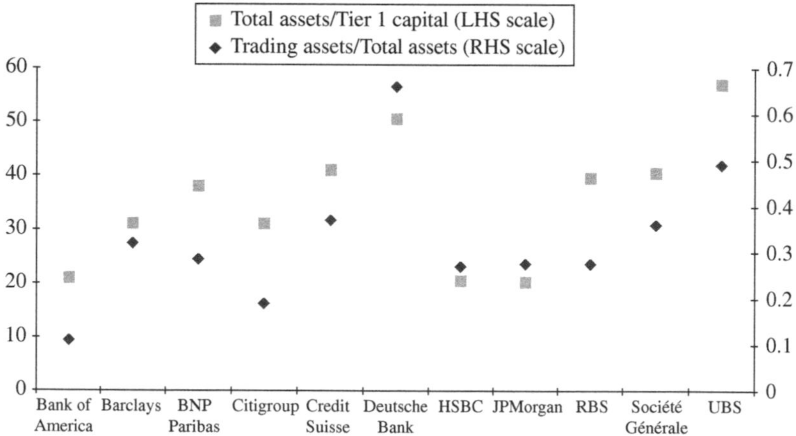

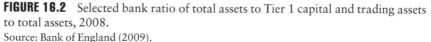

FIGURE 16.2 Selected bank ratio of total assets to Tier 1 capital and trading assets to total assets, 2008.
Source: Bank of England (2009).

Canada	Tier 1 and Tier 2 capital must be at least 5% of on-balance sheet assets plus qualifiying off-balance sheet assets.
Switzerland	Tier 1 capital must be at least 3% of on-balance sheet assets less Swiss domestic lending for bank holding companies, and at least 4% for individual institutions. This rule applies only to Credit Suisse and UBS.
US	Tier 1 capital must be at least 3% of on-balance sheet assets for "strong" bank holding companies and at least 4% for all other bank holding companies.

FIGURE 16.3 Summary of selected regulatory leverage ratio limits.
Source: Bank of England (2009).

As we noted above in the case of Lehmans, excessively high leverage results in a higher sensitivity of the balance sheet to trading and/or default losses. Limiting the amount of leverage acts as an additional risk control measure, backing up the safety net provided by a regulatory capital buffer. But when one thinks about it, this is a sensible measure on its own. It should not have to be imposed by regulatory fiat. In advance of the introduction of the standardised ratio as part of Basel III, banks should have addressed this issue anyway as part of their prudential capital and risk management.

A number of jurisdictions already employ a leverage ratio limit, although there is no uniform definition (see Figure 16.3). Under Basel III the rules will incorporate a limit, with a common definition of capital and an agreed measure of all assets, both on- and off-balance sheet.

Capital Structure

The efficient management of capital is a vital function of bank senior management. In the aftermath of any recession, capital is of course a scarce commodity. However, this fact itself leads to one of the lessons learned from the crisis: the need for "countercyclical" capital management. In other words, boards should treat capital as scare at all times, and build up capital bases even as a bull market is helping to generate higher profits. The level of capital needs to be sufficient to cushion the fallout from "stress events", which are the outlier events that normal distribution models used in finance do not capture.

Elsewhere in this book we have discussed the value of contingent capital instruments that can convert to equity at any time should the issuing bank's capital ratio fall below a pre-specified level. Going forward, this should be the only "sophisticated" financial instrument in the bank's capital structure. It will assist efficient capital management, as well as investor transparency, if a bank's capital is held in the form of simple instruments only, essentially common equity and retained profits (reserves). Of course, long-dated debt instruments can also form part of capital, but again it is more transparent if these are vanilla instruments.

Capital itself on its own is an insufficient protection against firm failure. Bank management must take additional measures, over and above capital buffers, to safeguard the institution in the event of systemic stress or other market crash events, because the capital base on its own will be insufficient to preserve the firm as a going concern. Hence, leverage ratio limits and robust liquidity management is as important as capital buffers. A report from the BoE (2009) suggests that on average a Tier 1 capital ratio of 8.5% would have been needed by banks to avoid falling below the Basel minimum of 4% during the last crisis. This suggests that the current requirement is far too low to act as a genuine risk-based capital reserve. Of course, a financial crisis will affect different banks in different ways; the BoE report goes on to state that even if all the banks in its study sample had indeed possessed a Tier 1 ratio of 8.5%, as much 40% of those banks would still have breached their 4% limit during the crash. For some firms the "in hindsight" sufficient level of capital was as high as 18%.

The implications of the BoE report are clear: minimum capital requirements must be higher, and banks also need to build in an element of flexibility into their capital structure, perhaps by means of contingent capital instruments. Contingent capital is any instrument that would convert into common equity on occurrence of a pre-specified trigger. This is illustrated in Figure 16.4. An issue of bonds by Lloyds Banking Group in 2009, Enhanced

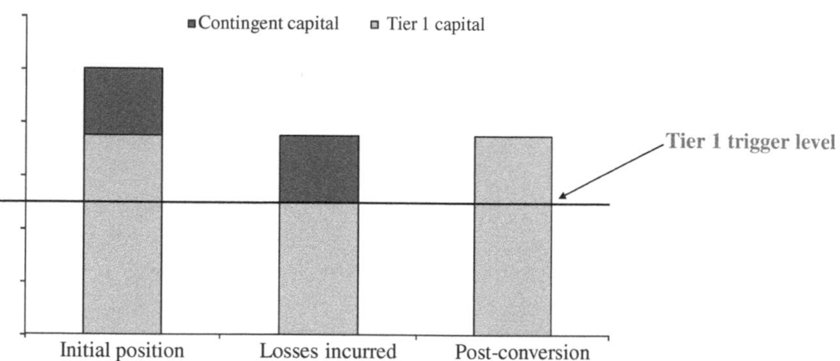

FIGURE 16.4 Illustration of contingent capital note triggering.
Source: Bank of England (2009).

Capital Notes, was of this type. Such instruments enable a bank to purchase catastrophe insurance from the private sector, rather than from the public sector via the lender of last resort. They also allow a bank to hold a Tier 1 equity reserve at a lower cost, in theory at least, than equity itself.

EXAMPLE 16.1 FUTURE BANK CAPITAL STRUCTURE

The financial crash resulted in a major review of the hitherto conventional bank funding model, with results that were exemplified by the UK FSA's consultative papers of 2008 and 2009 on liquidity and the publication of the Basel III guidelines in 2010. Further regulatory reform impacting the liquidity structure of banks is inevitable. An example of this is the FSA's Bail-In regime for UK banks, designed to ensure an orderly wind-down of banks that have become a "gone concern". The impact of such regulatory changes, together with the change in emphasis for bank funding away from short-term wholesale funding to long-term funding and more core customer funding, means that the future bank capital structure will look different in some respects from what it has done recently.

The following factors are influencing change:

- a move away from short-term unsecured wholesale funding: the liquidity crisis of 2008 reinforced the lessons from earlier bank liquidity crises, that an excess reliance on wholesale funding is overly risky;
- a move towards secured funding away from unsecured funding: the experience of 2008–2009 demonstrated that, provided collateral quality was acceptable, repo funding remained available for banks where unsecured funding had frozen. A greater share of the bank funding model will comprise secured funding in the form of repo, TRS, ABS/RMBS and Covered Bonds;
- the FSA Bail-In regime will classify senior unsecured debt as a class of liabilities that absorbs losses following the erosion of Tier 1 equity. While this simply reinforces what was always in legal theory the case (senior debt lies above equity and subordinated debt in the capital structure, so would be expected to absorb losses at some point), the expectation now is that the Central Bank backstop or taxpayer-funded bailout will not be invoked so

(*continued*)

readily, thus the risk premium demanded from investors to hold such liabilities will increase;

- subordinated debt may be difficult for most banks to place with investors, in which case it will be discontinued. Senior unsecured debt would be issued, at a relatively higher yield spread than previously, in the 1- to 10-year tenor; longer dated issuance is more likely to be the preserve of high-rated banks.

For all but the most well-capitalised and/or highest rated banks, we can expect to see a capital structure on the liabilities' side as illustrated in Figure 16.5.

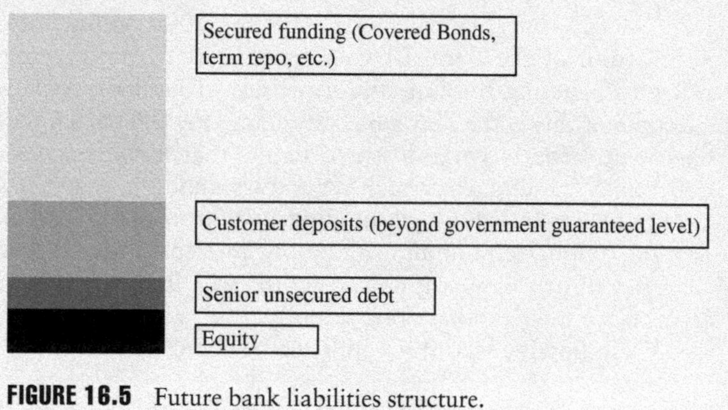

FIGURE 16.5 Future bank liabilities structure.

Core Competence: "Know Your Risk"

Regulatory authorities noticed a considerable decline in cross-border lending flows in the aftermath of the Lehman bankruptcy; for instance, see the BoE's *Financial Stability Report* dated June 2009. This is significant. During the bull market of 2001–2007, international lending volumes had expanded steadily (see Figure 16.6), as banks grew their balance sheets and sought higher yield opportunities overseas.

It is evident that during and after the bank crisis, when inter-bank market liquidity had dried up, banks pulled back from overseas markets, irrespective of whether these were deemed peripheral or not, and concentrated on core markets. This reflects informational advantages in core markets compared to overseas and non-core markets. The UK corporate lending sector makes a case in point: between 2002 and 2009, lending volume from UK banks fell by approximately 16% (the figure between 2006 and 2009 was a decline of 14%). However, the equivalent figures for foreign subsidiaries was a fall of 10.5% and 20%, while for foreign branches the decline was even more

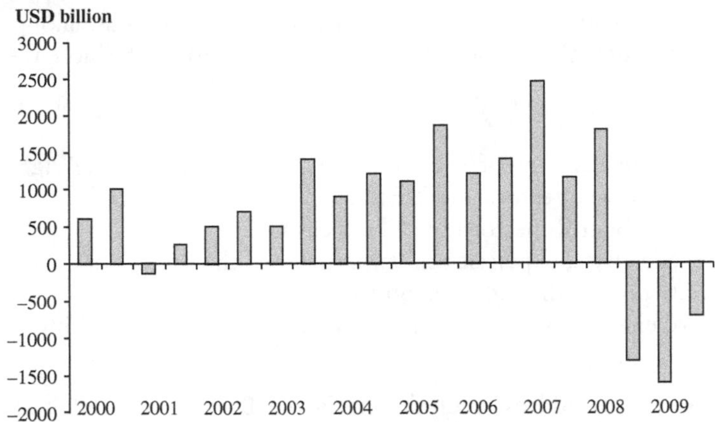

FIGURE 16.6 Cross-border bank lending volumes, 2000–2009.
Source: Bank of England (2009).

dramatic, at 17% and 46%.[2] Foreign banks would, on average, have less depth and breadth of corporate relationships, while branches would be expected to have even less developed relationships in the domestic market.

The lessons for the bank business model are clear: during an expansionary phase, it is important to remain focused on areas of core competence, and sectors in which the bank possesses actual knowledge and strength. Concentrating on areas in which the bank carries competitive advantage makes it less likely that loan origination standards will decline, resulting in lower losses during an economic downturn. There is also a technical reason for ensuring that overseas lending standards are maintained strictly, and limits set carefully, because it is often undertaken in foreign currency. A bank's ability to fund such lending is more dependent on external markets and wholesale counterparties relative to domestic currency lending, thus making the bank more vulnerable to a market downturn. For example, the cross-currency swap market in US dollars came under pressure, resulting in higher swap prices, following the Lehman default, and many banks struggled to obtain dollar funding during this period.

Corporate Governance

We introduce here bank corporate governance in the context of bank strategy; the subject is discussed in greater detail in Chapter 18. The governance structure of a bank is a vital part of ensuring effective overall control and risk

2 Source: Bank of England (2009).

management. An inadequate set-up will result in ineffective decision-making. The crash has highlighted the importance of addressing, in robust fashion, the following:

- What should the makeup of the Board itself be? What is the right number of executive directors and NEDs?
- How should the Board's performance be measured?
- Is the knowledge base, expertise and experience of the Board adequate? Does the CEO possess the right background in banking?[3]
- Are the board executives actually challenged in their decision-making?

Other questions to address include: (i) Is the Board provided with sufficient and adequate management reporting, in accessible fashion, on the bank's performance and risk exposures? (ii) Are there controls built into the firms' cultures such that they are adhered to when the bank's business strategy is in conflict with them?

The role of NEDs came under scrutiny in the wake of the 2008 crash. That some NEDs were not up to the standard required is evident; however, this should not detract from the vital function, in theory at least, that they do undertake. In the first instance, business best-practice dictates that the risk management function should report to a NED on the Board. This clearly implies that the NED in question must be sufficiently experienced and capable. The national regulator should always interview the relevant NED to ensure that this person meets the standards required.

It is rare to observe genuine control at all levels of a bank that also boasts true innovation, creativity and efficiency. It may be, for instance, that some institutions are simply too big to manage effectively, especially when things start to go wrong. However, this does not mean we should not attempt to implement an effective strategy at the top level and still maintain efficiency at the "coal face". The bank crisis demonstrated that in some cases bank boards were not able to maintain effective control of the business as they expanded. Certain desks originated risk that went beyond the stated (or believed) risk-appetite of the parent banks; in other cases, the risk management department was marginalised or ignored, and at board level there was a "rubber stamp" mentality. These instances have significant implications for bank corporate governance.

3 In 2008 the CEOs of two failed British banks, HBOS and Bradford & Bingley plc, had backgrounds in supermarket retail and not banking. They also had management consulting backgrounds.

Countercyclical Funding

One additional lesson learned from the crash is that banks should take advantage of "benign" conditions to improve their funding structures. Figure 16.7 shows the rise and fall in Libor spreads during 2007–2009, giving an idea of the market conditions that may prevail and suggesting when a bank may wish to take on more funding to take advantage of Libor rates.[4] In the first instance this would involve reducing the reliance on short-term funding. The definition of "short-term" is not universal; depending on which person one asks, it may mean up to one week or up to three months. Irrespective of the view that an individual bank takes, and this should reflect the bank's particular business model and current funding gap, best business practice suggests that a time of low funding spreads is the opportune moment to change the liability structure by increasing average maturity tenor. For instance, in the UK, overall banks had reduced their reliance on funding of up to 1-week from 15% of unsecured wholesale funding in December 2008 to 9% by October 2009. The aggregate customer funding gap (the difference between customer loans and customer deposits) was at GBP610 billion by Q2 2009, compared to GBP842 billion at the end

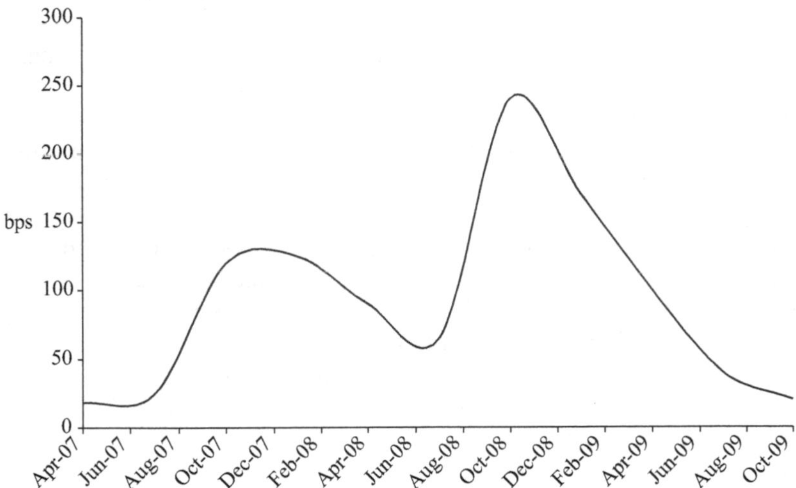

FIGURE 16.7 Sterling Libor–OIS spread, 2007–2009.
Source: Bloomberg L.P.

4 See Chapter 10 in Choudhry (2007a), which discusses the fair value of the Libor term premium.

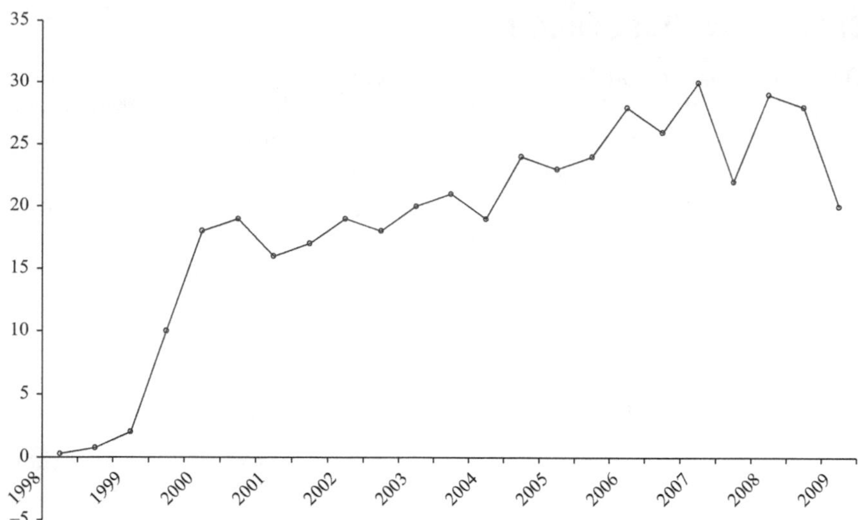

FIGURE 16.8 UK banks customer funding gap 1998–2009, median value.
Source: British Bankers Association.

of Q4 in 2008. This was 18% of all loans, the lowest proportion since 2003.[5] This is shown at Figure 16.8.

This is a critical feature of the new bank business model. The main lesson of the 2007–2009 crisis was the importance of liquidity risk management. To mitigate the impact of the next recession, bank funding structures need to be set up to reduce the reliance on short-term funding and unstable wholesale funding. They also need to extend the maturity of the liability side of the balance sheet. Excluding notable exceptions such as the banks in Australia and Canada, many country banks' customer funding gaps are uncomfortably high (see Figure 16.9). Banks must address two requirements, which are (i) to reduce the reliance on wholesale funding, which is not "sticky" and is less stable than retail customer deposits, and (ii) to increase the average tenor of their liabilities. The UK bank sector, for example, remains vulnerable in this regard: the BoE reported in 2009 that about 50% of UK bank aggregate wholesale funding was lower than six months in maturity.[6]

Bank funding strategy should therefore include targeting increased use of retail funding. Retail deposits are treated by regulators as being more stable, with greater expectation of being rolled over and not withdrawn on

5 Source: Bank of England (2009).
6 Source: Ibid.

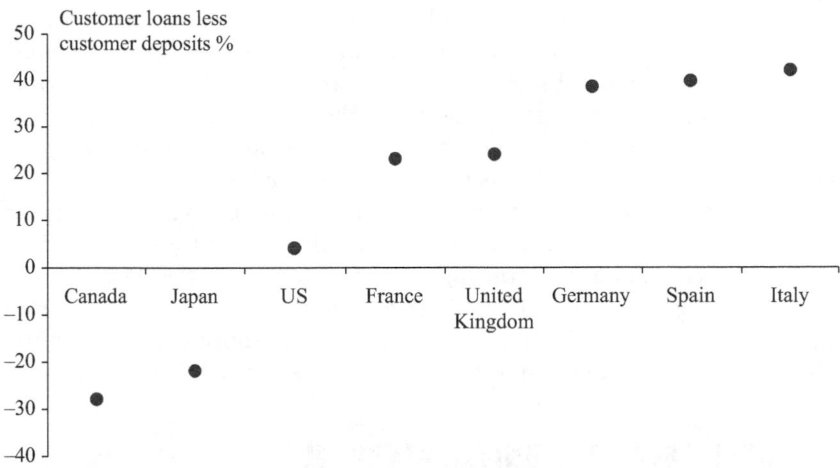

FIGURE 16.9 Selected country bank funding gaps.
Source: Bank of England (2009).

maturity. To reduce its funding gap (whatever it is), a bank would seek to grow its retail deposits.

At a tactical level, this raises the question of what interest rate to pay to attract more such deposits. Figure 16.10 shows the change in average spread on retail savings products offered by UK banks from 2005 to 2009.

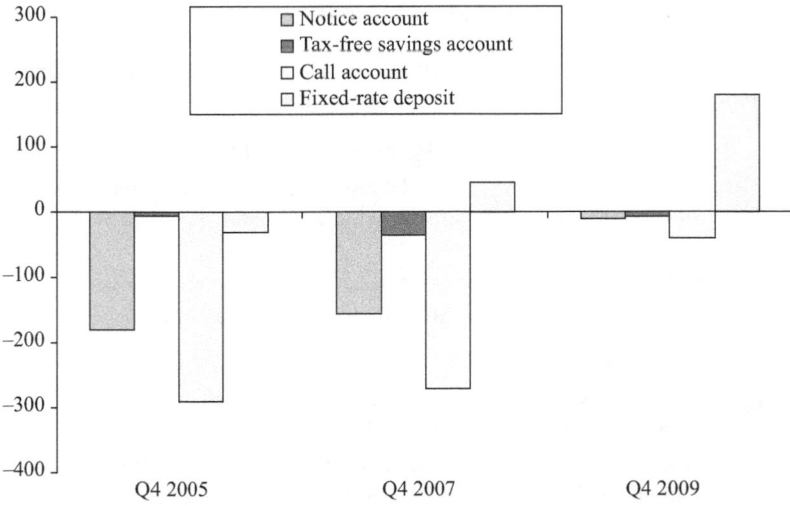

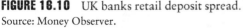

FIGURE 16.10 UK banks retail deposit spread.
Source: Money Observer.

From a spread below Libor, the spread was increased to almost 200 bps over Libor. Partly this reflects the fact that absolute base interest rates had fallen to a very low level, but it also reflects the increased demand for such deposits from banks. It is important not to pay a rate that is excessively above that in the market, partly for reputation reasons, but also so as to not convey the impression that the bank is in difficulty and desperate for funds.

The overall impact of the new modified strategy will be a higher funding cost. In adopting a more robust funding structure, there will be added costs associated with raising longer dated liabilities (assuming a positive-sloping yield curve) and paying more to attract stable retail deposits. However, the object of this strategy is to reduce the vulnerability of the bank should there be another external shock, or systemic instability.

EXAMPLE 16.2 THE UNITED KINGDOM INDEPENDENT COMMISSION ON BANKING (ICB)

The UK ICB was set up by the UK government to provide recommendations on the future of banking, and published its report in September 2011. Its high-level objective was to describe a framework that ensured a more stable banking system in the UK. Its highest impact findings can be summarised as follows:

- establishment of a "ring-fence" separating the retail arm of a bank from an investment banking (IB) arm;
- a higher minimum required loss-absorbing capital base.

For banks that operate in both retail and IB sectors, the ring-fencing must be organised along the following business lines:

- mandatory businesses: individual deposits; SME deposits; overdrafts;
- permitted businesses: corporate banking; private banking; trade finance and project finance; retail assets; European Economic Area (EEA) business;
- prohibited business (and therefore outside ring-fence): trading and wholesale markets; proprietary derivatives trading; non-EEA business.

The organisation must ensure that each part of the bank, inside and outside the ring-fence, is able to meet capital and liquidity requirements on a stand-alone basis. The part inside the ring-fence can deal with the part outside up to a 25% of Tier 1 capital large exposure limit, and otherwise as simply another third-party entity.

Under the ICB regime UK banks will have to set aside a higher core Tier 1 equity level and also a higher total capital base, referred to as the primary loss absorbing capacity (PLAC), which includes other Tier 1 capital and required buffers. This is illustrated in Figure 16.11. The PLAC can include up to 3.5% of "bail-inable" debt; in practice, it is likely to be senior unsecured bonds designated as such, and which would absorb losses after equity has been wiped out (in other words, once the bank is no longer a going concern), and CoCo bonds. If there is no resolution regime in place for the bank, the so-called "Living Will" that describes the mechanism for an orderly wind-down of a bank that is now a gone concern, then a further 3.0% buffer is required.

The date for UK banks to demonstrate implementation of the ICB's requirements will be in 2019. Of course, irrespective of the changes in the UK banking market as a result of the ICB report, the principles of banking described in this book will remain unchanged.

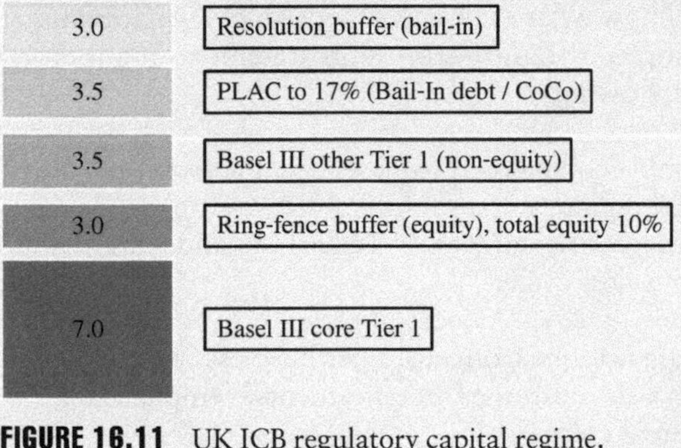

FIGURE 16.11 UK ICB regulatory capital regime.

STRATEGY INPUTS

Notwithstanding that all banks are ultimately similar beasts, the strategy formulated for an individual bank will be unique to it and reflects its particular market, business model, customer base and operating environment. Unlike some of the other subjects dealt with in this book, it would be difficult (and of questionable value) to come up with a "template" strategy document. Instead, in this section we will illustrate business best-practice with a description of the relevant inputs to a coherent strategy. These would then be modified for each specific case.

It is important that a bank articulates its strategic vision, and publicly announces its quantitative and qualitative targets. This may sound obvious, but one would be surprised how many financial institutions do not actually do this beyond bland platitudes, and simply bumble along from one year to the next.

Vision Statement

The concept of a vision statement is beloved of management consultants and therefore care must be taken to avoid writing one that is simply verbiage and platitudes, and thereby a worthless, pointless document. To be of value, it should capture succinctly and accurately what the bank aspires to be. In a top-down strategy origination process, it would drive the quantitative and qualitative elements of the bank strategy; hence, if the statement is well formulated it becomes a worthwhile input to the strategy. It can set the risk-reward culture at the bank. If the bank wishes to deviate from this culture, it would then look to revise the statement (and its strategy). In other words, a vision statement serves as a statement of intent, so that all the bank's stakeholders know what its business model and objectives are.

For example, a framework vision statement might encompass one or more of the following:

- to be a stable commercial bank serving the requirements of customers in the EMEA region;
- to achieve a consistent RoE of 12%–14% and RoA of 4%–5% throughout the business cycle;
- to maintain an AA–/Aa2 credit rating;
- to generate revenue from customer business, within core business lines;
- to focus on customer requirements, emphasising a robust risk management culture;
- to limit cost base, including employee remuneration, to [ ]% of revenue base.

Note how the above almost explicitly restricts proprietary trading business. A bank whose primary focus lay outside some or all of the above would craft a different vision statement. Equally, if the bank that drafted the above statement wished to move into new businesses or products that were not covered by its current vision, it would modify it, thereby giving intent of its new focus.

With the vision set, the bank should drill down from it and articulate its strategic plan. This is still a general statement; it is the next layer down that will describe detailed target metrics. For example, the hypothetical bank that drafted our vision statement above might describe its strategic plan in the following terms:

BANK STRATEGIC PLAN

- Business focus
  - home market, euro-zone and Gulf Co-operation Council (GCC) region;
  - customer base for corporate and institutional banking: corporate and financial institutions;
  - customer base for retail banking: high net worth individuals (HNWIs) in home market and GCC region;
  - limit balance sheet to EUR [ ] billion;
  - limit wholesale funding share to 20%.
- Management focus
  - limit cost base to [ ]% of revenue base;
  - explicit metric for balance sheet usage;
  - return target set at 12%–14% on a sustained basis;
  - robust risk management organisation, policy and reporting line;
  - incentivise long-term customer-focused business.

The above would be built on and developed into greater detail. The next input to the strategy is the next level down, the target metrics.

Strategy Setting: Performance Parameters

The second tier of strategy development is the formulation of a bank-wide business plan and target return metrics. This should set key performance indicators (KPIs) in actual quantitative terms. The base KPIs are:

- capital: return on capital; RAROC; assets-to-capital ratio;
- liquidity: loan-to-deposit ratio; liquidity ratio; wholesale funding ratio;
- cost base: front-office/back-office ratio; cost–income ratio;
- risk appetite: provisions/lending; NPLs/lending; VaR;
- growth: asset growth; liability growth.

We emphasise that the targets are not necessarily minimum levels, and in some cases they can be maximum levels. A sustained performance of 12% RoC over a 10–15-year period is infinitely preferable, from an aggregate market viewpoint (or from society's viewpoint), to several years of 22% RoE followed by losses for a year or two. Equally, a market share target of 10% does not mean that a level of 20% is desirable: an emphasis on market share as a KPI was one of the forces that drove Northern Rock

TABLE 16.1 Bank strategy setting: quantitative targets.

Bank level		
Core Tier 1 capital		
Return on equity		
Return on assets		
Wholesale funding share		
Leverage ratio		
Cost–income ratio		
Treasury	**Corporate banking**	**Retail banking**
Return on capital	Return on capital	Return on capital
Return on equity	Return on equity	Return on equity
Liquidity ratio, 1-week and 1-month	Loan-to-deposit ratio	Weighted average cost of deposits
Front office/Back office cost ratio	Front office/Back office cost ratio	Front office/Back office cost ratio
Cost–income ratio	Cost–income ratio	Cost–income ratio
VaR limit	Provisions/Lending ratio	Loan growth
Securities growth year-on-year (y-o-y)	Loan growth	Deposit growth
Sharpe ratio	Deposit growth	
	Unfunded asset growth	

and Bradford & Bingley to their demise. In any case, market share is not a value-added KPI for banks. It should have no place in bank strategy.

The next level down is quantitative target setting. We imagine a medium-sized commercial bank with three business lines: Treasury, corporate banking and domestic retail banking. Table 16.1 shows the elements of quantitative returns targets that would be set into the strategy, at the bank-wide level and at the individual business unit level. These are not set in stone; they should be set as part of 1-year and 3-year plans, but reviewed on an annual basis. Note how some of them are control targets (such as the Treasury department's liquidity ratio) and cost targets. Not all the elements of the strategy are revenue or returns orientated. The control and cost elements are an important part of the strategy.

The extent of the bank's achievement against the 3-year strategic target should be reported on a regular quarterly basis, as shown at Table 16.2. Given the dynamic situation of the markets and the need to respond to events, there is less worth in setting a longer term (say 5-year) strategic target in anything but the broadest terms; that is, at the level of the vision statement. However, some banks still do this. One would be right to

TABLE 16.2 Performance against strategy: example quarterly report.

	Quarter-end actual	3-year target
Core Tier 1 capital	7%	10%
Return on equity	9.80%	11%
Wholesale funding share	33%	20%
Leverage ratio	23:1	15:1
Cost–income ratio	66%	50%

question the actual practical value of such targets on a day-to-basis, although they do serve a purpose in communicating to stakeholders a coherent view of the Board's strategic vision and direction.

FORMULATING SUSTAINABLE BANKING

The requirements of Basel III standards and those of national regulators will play a major role in bank strategy. The Board should seek to have its own view on sustainable banking nevertheless, and consider the regulatory standards to be a minimum requirement. The specific areas of capital and liquidity, as well as sound asset origination policy, must be set by the Board in line with its own beliefs and understanding. To summarise, the basic strategy is identical for all banks and meets regulatory requirements. At the individual level, strategy should reflect core competence and strengths.

Setting Through-the-cycle Strategy

Inherent to the strategic thinking of the bank is the belief that the strategy should be sustainable. That is, it should focus on preserving returns and capital strength through the business cycle. This belief needs to be a genuine part of the Board's thinking. In other words, the bank needs to stick to its core strengths and ignore KPIs such as balance sheet growth or market share during a bull market phase in the economic cycle. Allied to this is governments' and regulators' conversion to the idea of "macroprudential" strategy; although the practical impact of this sort of thinking is not new, it has just been forgotten in recent years.

Viewed from this perspective, bank strategy falls into two categories:

- Macroprudential: banks should strengthen their balance sheets and liquidity ratios during the expansionary period of the economic cycle, while profits are growing and conditions are benign. This can be done by:

- limiting the asset-side growth of their balance sheet;
- retaining a greater proportion of profits as reserves during the bull market phase;
- setting a leverage ratio limit.

- Microprudential: at all times increasing the level, and quality, of capital and liquid asset buffers; and increasing the average tenor of liabilities.

Both elements of strategy work towards preserving a bank as a going concern irrespective of the state of the economy. Higher capital ratios and absolute levels *per se* should act as a more effective buffer to cushion the impact of an economic downturn, when business volumes decrease and loan losses increase; at the same time, a more conservative liquidity regime, with limits on use of wholesale funding and larger gaps, means that a bank will be less able to grow rapidly during a boom period in the cycle.

The importance of emphasising a macroprudential approach to maintaining the pre-specified strategy reflects the fact that the practice of corporate governance, in all industries, often adopts a "herd mentality". It may be difficult to resist a prevailing trend even if that runs counter to one's better instincts. We illustrate this using Figure 16.12, sourced with data from the European Central Bank. This shows the increase in the funding gap, measured as customer loans less customer deposits, on an aggregate

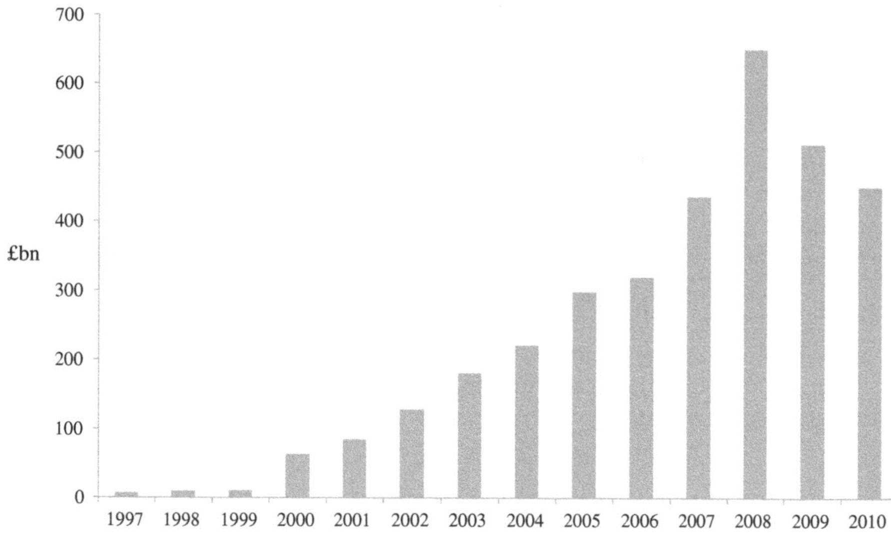

FIGURE 16.12 UK banks customer funding gap, 1997–2009.
Source: European Central Bank.

basis for four large UK banks during the period 1997–2009. The worsening LTD ratio during this time, which was mirrored at the individual bank level, is a perfect example of how banks can end up adopting the same approach when the latest fad becomes viewed as business best-practice. Bank management needs to be mindful of this danger during a bull market.[7]

In assessing what factors should form part of strategy formulation, it is also worth noting those factors that should be expressly left out of the process. The bank crisis of 2007–2008, as well as banking failures throughout history such as the US bank crash of 1980–1982 and the zombie-like experience of Japanese banks in the 1990s, all resulted from banks adopting a management approach that allowed them to become over-extended through:

- ever-greater risk taking and leverage levels;
- over-reliance on wholesale funding;
- increasing exposure to higher risk product classes, such as 100LTV mortgages, adjustable-rate mortgages, buy-to-let mortgages or derivatives trading;
- poor management decisions on acquisitions and new business lines;
- an emphasis on market share and high RoE as KPI targets.

Understanding that these areas should *not* form any element of bank strategy is part of understanding how strategy itself feeds into sustainable banking.

Basel III Impact On Strategy Setting

The Basel III requirements can be viewed as the base element of a bank's strategy. Given that they are minimum requirements, strategy should be set to ensure that they are adhered to at all times. By definition this means preserving the bank as a going concern at all times.

The first element is the capital ratios. We repeat these here for readers' convenience, at Table 16.3.

As well as increasing the level of regulatory capital, implementing Basel III results in a higher quality of capital. There is a stricter definition of "common equity", and a more conservative definition of Tier 1 and Tier 2 capital.

The countercyclical capital buffer is a nod to the post-crash thinking on the need for macroprudential strategy and regulation. It is designed to

7 The four banks whose customer funding gaps are aggregated in this sample are Barclays Bank, HBOS, Lloyds TSB and Royal Bank of Scotland. The figure for 2009 and 2010 includes the combined Lloyds Banking Group entity.

TABLE 16.3 Basel III capital levels, %.

	Common equity	Tier 1	Total capital
Minimum	4.5	6	8
Conservation buffer	2.5		
Minimum + conservation buffer	7	8.5	10.5
Countercyclical buffer range	2.5		

Source: BCBS.

protect the banking sector as a whole during periods of growth, or more realistically excessive growth, which would otherwise result in higher aggregate systemic risk. The exact size of the buffer is set by the national regulator, within the Basel guidelines. It is the responsibility of the regulator to ensure transparent communication and reporting by each bank; however, business best-practice is for a bank to set the procedures required to meet this buffer requirement itself, without waiting for regulatory pressure. Because it is not necessarily apparent when one is approaching, or already in, a period of "excess" economic growth, the bank should place a number of indicators under observation, and monitor these for early warning signs. It can then take appropriate action in a number of areas, including capital buffering, but also loan origination standards (which tend to deteriorate in a bull market and/or period of excess liquidity). These indicators might include the:

- level of private sector credit to GDP ratio;
- credit to GDP gap (that is, the gap between the ratio and its trend).

We discuss the issue of countercyclical capital and "through the cycle" regulation again in the next chapter. From the point of view of individual bank strategy, it is important that a bank monitors macro-level "early warning" indicators on a regular basis, to be aware of the state of the economy and thereby take measures to guard against the impact of overheating. These indicators should form part of the regular MI monitored at the ALCO and other relevant high-level management committees such as the Balance Sheet Management Committee and ExCo.

The choice of which indicators to monitor is open to debate. For example, in a discussion paper the BBA recommended the following:

- the overall level of lending in the economy, both as an absolute level and as a percentage of GDP;

- the rate of increase in retail lending; for example, credit card and residential mortgage approvals, as well as the rate of increase in lower credit-quality lending;
- the rates of return on equity on bank capital, and whether this is running at above long-run averages;
- aggregate economic indicators such as the rate of growth of GDP and asset prices, compared to medium-term average rates.

However, there is an argument that these are as much lagging as leading indicators, and their forecasting ability may be limited. Other possible indicators to monitor for macroprudential reasons include:

- the Baltic Dry Index, which is an index of bulk carrier shipping prices. Again, the forecasting ability of this index may be limited. For example, it reached an all-time high in May 2008, which was right at the start of the UK and (some parts of the) EU recessions. As with the other indicators, it may be viewed more as a hindsight high-water or low-water mark of the business cycle;
- world trade volumes, rate of growth month-on-month: a fall is viewed as a good leading indicator.

Example 16.3 describes the use of the Leading Economic Indicator (LEI) statistic, developed by Stock and Watson (1989). The author recommends using this methodology as the principle forward-looking forecasting metric, and it should be reported monthly in the ALCO and ExCo packs. Where a bank organises a BSMCO as part of its governance structure, the statistic should be reported to it as well. The Example box illustrates the LEI time series for the UK economy, from a calculation spreadsheet developed by the author and Zhuoshi Liu.

EXAMPLE 16.3 EARLY WARNING INDICATOR METRICS

Banks monitor credit card spending and other customer data to provide market intelligence on the state of the economy, as a proxy indicator of distress or recovery.

The main drawback of such observable market factors, however, is that they are generally lagging indicators, and would prove inadequate as forecasting tools; for example, see Figure 16.13 and Figure 16.14 for UK credit card spending data against UK GDP

(*continued*)

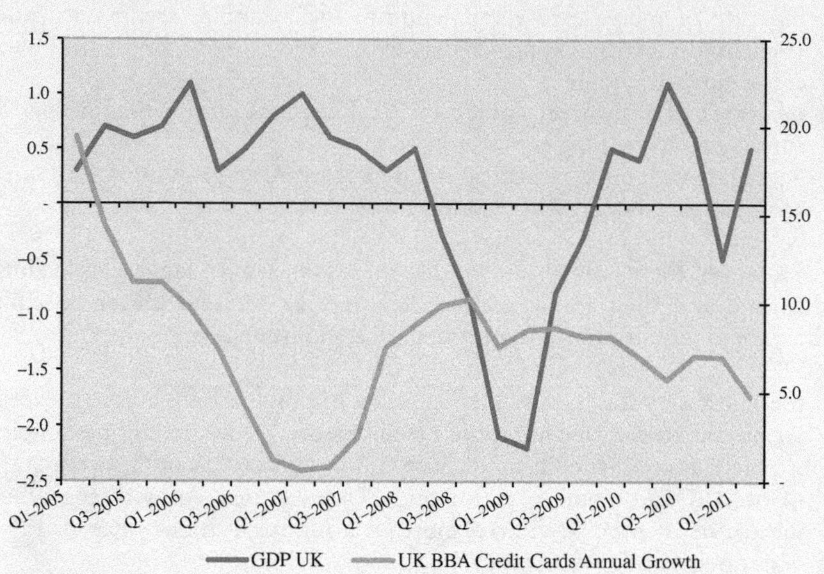

FIGURE 16.13 UK credit card growth and UK GDP 2005–2011.
Source: BBA.

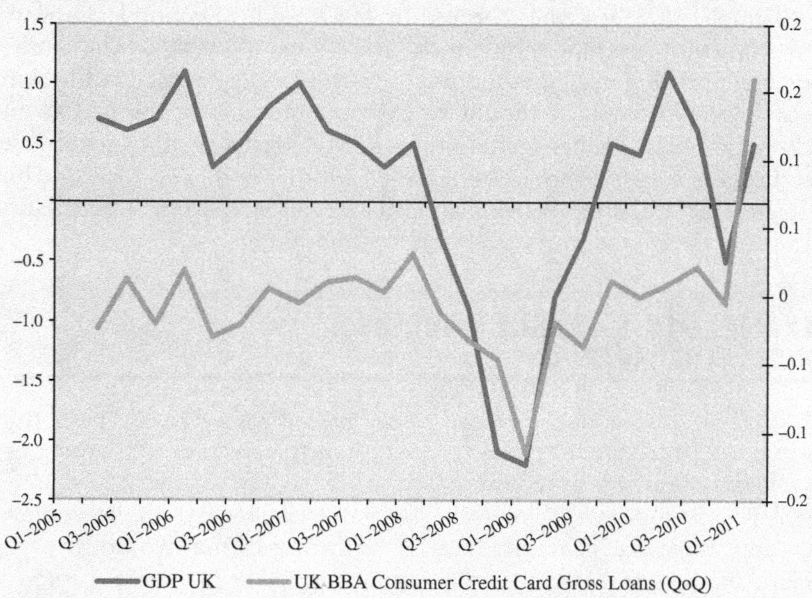

FIGURE 16.14 UK credit card gross loans and UK GDP 2005–2011.
Source: BBA.

output. Not only is consumer spending not sufficiently correlated with the state of the economy, it can also act as a contra-indicator.

A more effective measure for planning purposes is a composite index constructed from a set of transparent underlying macroeconomic variables. The following observations apply to the UK economy only, but the methodology can be extended without loss of effectiveness to any defined economic space for which statistical parameter input data are readily available, such as the eurozone.

Objectives of an Economic Indicator

For use as a strategic decision-making and/or forecasting tool, a statistical metric should be observed to be a leading rather than lagging indicator. In other words, we require it to highlight an impending slowdown in the market before that slowdown occurs "officially"; or at least as the slowdown is taking place. This is not possible with baseline data such as GDP output increase/decrease statistics, which are by definition lagging indicators. Given that the technical definition of a recession is two successive quarters of negative GDP growth, we require a leading indicator to imply a contracting economy before the economy actually starts to contract as defined by this measure. An indicator that tracks the economy is by definition dependant on its statistical inputs, which are snapshots in time and therefore already historic on publication. However, a composite measure has an advantage over one-dimensional indicators in at least attempting to cover a broader swathe of the economy.

Observation and Assessment of Conventional Indicators

In practical terms, for ALCO purposes we assume that any statistic will be monitored on a monthly basis. The most straightforward way to present this is as a graphical time series. Visual inspection of time series charts is a valid form of analysis (see Hatanaka 1996). To be of use as an early-warning indicator, we would require the metric to flag the onset of recession as early as possible.

Recommended Forecasting Indicator

A tractable and simple construction is the coincident and leading economic indices recommended by Stock and Watson (1989). We constructed these indices and observed that it was a leading

(*continued*)

forecasting indicator for the UK economy for both the 1990–91 and 2008–09 recessions. Its construction method and form of output makes it an accessible metric for gauging the future direction of the economy, particularly when the index value moves from positive to negative (or vice-versa). That said, it also reflects the lagged nature of its input parameters and this manifests itself in a delayed reaction when emerging from recession, as observed at a number of points in the time-series illustration.

Nevertheless it is worthwhile to monitor this statistic monthly at ALCO for all the regions in which the bank has business interests, and for which economic statistics are available.

Methodology

A description of the LEI is given in Appendix 16.1. The LEI is designed to provide an advance warning of movements in the business cycle, and not just changes in GDP growth. In truth, it is incorrect to define a recession purely in GDP output terms (see Burns and Mitchell, 1946), although because this view is common we take that as the main yardstick. That said, the LEI input parameters reflect different forms of economic activity.

The inputs to the LEI are user-defined. We specified the model with the following:

1. UK Building Societies – New Commitments (semi-adjusted)
2. UK CBI Monthly Enquiry: Order Book Volume – Balance (non-adjusted)
3. UK CBI Monthly Enquiry: Volume of Expected Output – Balance (non-adjusted)
4. UK FT All Share Index (EP) (non-adjusted)
5. UK Gilt 10 year-3 month yield spread
6. UK Productivity – Whole Economy (semi-adjusted)
7. UK Total Gross Operating Surplus of Corporations (current prices) (semi-adjusted)
8. UK Money Supply – Broad Money (M2) (current prices)
9. UK Coincident Economic Indicator (CEI)

The CEI is constructed from the following inputs:

1. UK Index of Production
2. UK Unemployment Rate (semi-adjusted)
3. UK Household Disposable Income (real terms)
4. UK Retail Sales (including Automotive + Fuel)

Stock and Watson describe two approaches to constructing the index; namely, principal component analysis (PCA) and a factor model. The model is summarised in Appendix 16.1.

LEI1 and LEI2 use PCA analysis, in which the CEI is a principal component of the four macro variables. For LEI1 we use the lagged coincident variable, plus the 8 macro variables; for LEI2 we use only the 8 macro variables, together with the CEI input as independent variable. LEI3 and LEI4 are factor models, given by equations (A16.1.1–A16.1.3) in Appendix 16.1. All four indicators are described by Equation (A16.1.4).[8]

Empirical observations

The LEI for the period July 1983 to April 2011 for the UK economy is shown in Figure 16.15A and Figure 16.15B (illustrated using monthly and quarterly time steps).

The arrows in Figure 16.14A indicate the start of the 1990–1991 and 2008–2009 recessions in the UK. Note that all versions of the LEI are advance indicators of the change in the business cycle, as well as lagging indicators of the recovery (as given by GDP statistics). Be aware that a return to positive GDP growth is not indicative of recovery in all economic sectors, nor of a definitive turnaround in the business cycle.

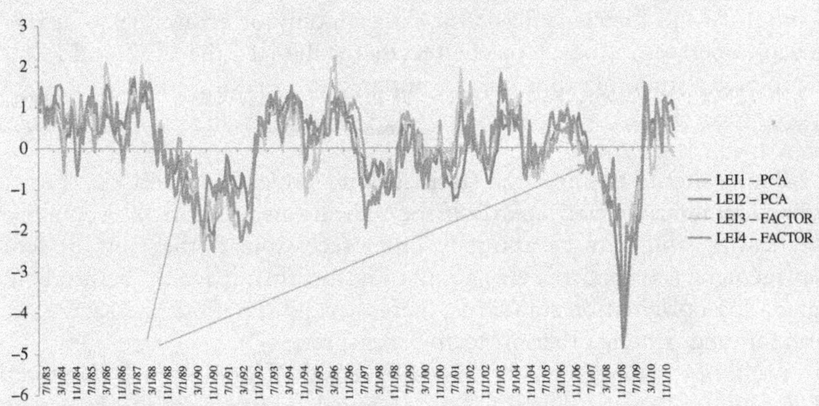

FIGURE 16.15A UK LEI 1983–2011, monthly time steps.

(*continued*)

8 Note that the lambda term in Equation (4) is estimated for LEI1, and is zero for LEI2, LEI3 and LEI4.

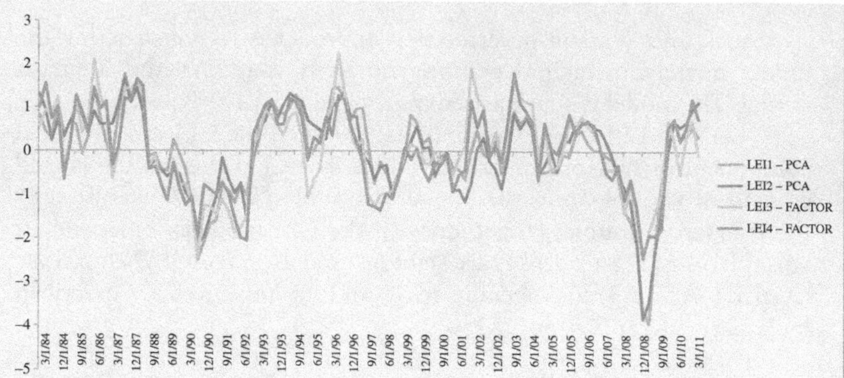

FIGURE 16.15B UK LEI 1983–2011, quarterly time steps.

Therefore the LEI may also be suggesting a slower return to true recovery than what was implied by GDP output data.

Conclusions

On the basis of the empirical evidence, the LEI appear to be effective early warning indicators of the direction of the economy, particularly when the index value moves from positive to negative or vice-versa. The author recommends that a bank ALCO monitors the LEI on both monthly and quarterly basis for the economy or economies that the bank operates in. Based on the results for the UK, the LEI2 and LEI3 produce a smoother time series compared to LEI1 and LEI4.

Banks should monitor the statistics they understand and use them for policy formulation, particularly if the indications are that the economy is overheating and may be about to enter recession. If the view of senior management was that this was going to occur, then it would be prudent to tighten loan origination standards, increase capital buffers and secure more term funding, among other protective measures.

Liquidity management is driven by Basel III minimum levels for the LCR and the NSFR. The LCR is designed to make banks better able to withstand a liquidity shock, by ensuring that they possess sufficient high-quality liquid assets that can offset cash outflows in a stressed environment (the time of this stressed period is viewed as being 30 days. The UK FSA has a metric that extends this period to 90 days). The NSFR promotes funding resilience at a bank over the longer term by ensuring that stable sources of liabilities are in place to support long-dated illiquid assets.

EXAMPLE 16.4 CALCULATION OF COUNTERCYCLICAL CAPITAL BUFFER

The countercyclical capital buffer (CCB) is a function of the credit exposure of a bank in each different national regulatory jurisdiction, weighted by this exposure. It is given by

$$CCB = \sum_{i=1}^{N} W_i \times CCB_i$$

where W is the weighting, or proportion of total capital exposure, and CCB is the countercyclical capital buffer for each jurisdiction i. Assume that a bank has credit exposure in the following markets,

Domestic market	50%
France	20%
US	20%
GCC	10%,

and that the national regulators in these regions set the CCB level as 2%, 2.5%, 1.5% and 2%. The CCB required by the bank would be

$$\begin{aligned} \text{CCB} &= [50\% \times 2\% + 20\% \times 2.5\% + 20\% \times 1.5\% + 10\% \times 2\%] \\ &= 2.000\%. \end{aligned}$$

The LCR and NSFR requirements are minimum standards. Individual bank boards should look to run a more conservative regime than that required under the Basel III rules. For example, the LCR can be applied to a 90-day rather than 30-day stressed cash outflow period, while the NSFR can be set at 110% or 120%, rather than the 100% Basel requirement.

Basel III also sets a leverage ratio limit. This is a straightforward non-risk-based measure, based on the accounting balance sheet. Again, a bank can set its own, more conservative limit.

LIQUIDITY AS ASSET CLASS

As this book states on a number of occasions, an emphasis on capital levels is a necessary but not sufficient condition to maintain sustainable banking. Liquidity levels are as important as capital; hence, liquidity preservation is an essential element of bank strategy. From the vision statement downwards, liquidity should be viewed as the cost of doing business, and therefore never compromised in the desire for higher returns or easier access to new business areas. It can also be viewed as an asset class in its own right. Banks that preserve liquidity are (i) viewed as better quality counterparties, so leading to a reduction in their funding costs (ii) able to generate revenue from this liquidity strength position.

Thus, at the strategy level liquidity must be viewed independently of credit risk and interest rate risk. There is no one precise measure for liquidity, consequently no set measure of its value. Notwithstanding this, it is worthwhile using a number of proxy measures to measure the level of liquidity in the market, and thereby attempting to obtain a measure of its value.[9] For example, in the repo market the lenders of cash will require collateral from the borrower to reduce their counterparty credit exposure. The higher the quality of collateral, typically the lower the margin (haircut) required. The ratio of the repo cost over the asset spread is one proxy measure of the price of liquidity.

To measure this in practical terms, we can value liquidity by calculating the ratio of the repo margin on ABS bonds over the yield spreads on the ABS securities themselves. This is not easily observable in the market, but a bank can use Bloomberg and/or Reuters as well other data sources to check the yield spread on AAA RMBS securities, and also ask its investment bank what repo margin would be to fund such assets. If this ratio is increasing, then the value of liquidity is increasing. As a yardstick, this ratio was approximately 1:5 or 20% during 2005–2007 (a 5% haircut on AAA RMBS, which themselves returned on average 20–25 bps over Libor), but had increased to 1:10 or 10% by Q1 2009.[10]

Another proxy measure of the value of liquidity involves looking at structured finance securities. Collateralised bonds such as mortgage-backed securities or covered bonds are bonds secured against specific pools of assets. For the euro-zone a general measure of their return is given by the iBoxx Euro Collateralised Bonds benchmark yield. Prior to the 2008 crash the spread was stable at around 20 bps during 2003–2007. Subsequently, this spread increased dramatically, hitting over 200 bps in Q1 2009.[11] Of course, this spread measure was simply undervalued before the crash; however, it is worthwhile to keep it under observation, as an indicator of the value of liquidity.

---

9 See Choudhry (2007b) for a discussion of the different proxy measures.

10 Source: Author's notes, from KBC Financial Products and Europe Arab Bank plc.

11 Source: Bloomberg L.P.

The author recommends the CDS and ASW basis as an alternative proxy measure of the cost of liquidity. The academic community is not entirely convinced of this measure, but the case for it is strong. A CDS contract is in theory the price of pure credit risk, with no element of cash funding liquidity. An asset swap is a cash product, requiring the investor to invest actual cash, and thus incorporates a funding element as well as a credit risk exposure element. The difference between these two levels must therefore, by definition, include a factor for the value of cash liquidity. Bank ALM and Treasury managers should always monitor the CDS basis for their most relevant markets, to gauge an idea of the cost of liquidity.[12] An increasing basis indicates (but is not limited to indicating) a higher premium for liquidity.

The importance of liquidity management in the high-level strategy process reflects the view that liquidity is best viewed as an asset class in its own right. We take this further with a look at funding products and at the right policy to apply in derivatives funding.

Funding Tools

The bank Treasury desk can make use of a number of financial instruments to meet liquidity objectives, as opposed to revenue objectives. The use of these instruments should be described in the lower level strategy document, to ensure that management understands the motivation behind their use. That is not to say that such products cannot be used as part of normal customer revenue-generating business; rather, the bank should describe the full range of liquidity instruments that can be used to enhance its liquidity position.

In addition to vanilla funding instruments such as deposits, CDs, MTNs and so on, the following can also be considered:

- tri-party repo;
- TRSs;
- existing assets "collateral upgrade";
- liquidity option transactions.

The option facility is described in Example 16.5.

12 A detailed discussion of the CDS-ASW basis is given in the author's book *The Credit Default Swap Basis* (Bloomberg Press 2006).

EXAMPLE 16.5 LIQUIDITY OPTION FACILITY

The common liquidity-raising transactions, repo and TRS, are described in the existing literature, including the author's book *Bank Asset and Liability Management*. Other means by which banks can generate liquidity for strategic purposes, for example to assist with meeting long-term funding plans or regulatory requirements, are via collateral upgrade and liquidity option trades. These can be medium- or long-dated (say, up to 5-year) facilities.

In a liquidity option facility the bank pays a premium that grants it the option to swap portfolios with a counterparty any time during the term of the facility. This gives access to high-quality collateral.

The transaction is illustrated at Figure 16.16. The counterparty places a portfolio of liquid assets, such as AAA sovereign bonds, into an account managed by a third-party custodian. It continues to retain economic interest in the assets. The bank enters into an option facility for either a fixed period, say three years, or in the form of a rolling "evergreen" facility. This might be in the form of a 366-day facility that continually increases its term by one day every day. Should the bank exercise the option, it pays an upgrade fee and receives the high-quality bonds from the custodian, in return for putting up a portfolio of its assets as collateral.

For liquidity metrics purposes, this facility counts as term funds equal to the term of the upgrade. For example, the trade may specify

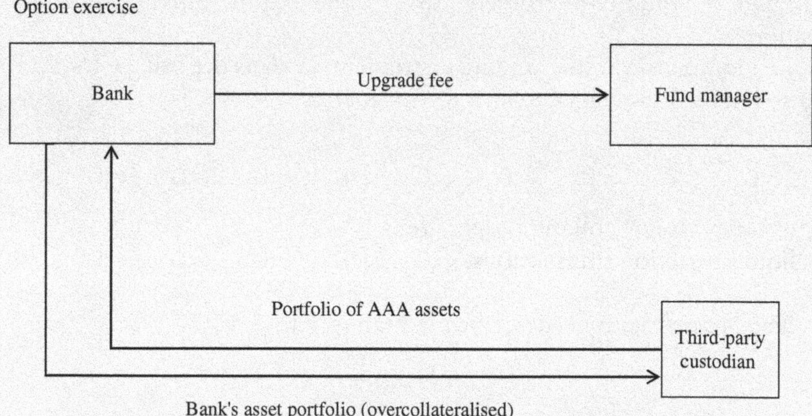

FIGURE 16.16 Liquidity option facility.

that the bank can receive the liquid securities for a period of 95 or 180 days on exercise; this will count as permanent 3-month funding for the bank during the life of the option, thus reducing its LAB requirement by the same amount. For banks that have to fund their LAB with greater than 1-year money, the exercise option will have to specify a 366-day upgrade tenor.

The bank will pay an option premium for the life of the trade, as well as an upgrade fee should it exercise the option. Again, the bank has access to a pool of high-quality securities, while the counterparty enhances the return it receives on its existing holding of sovereign securities.

Funding Policy

The emphasis on liquidity management being as important as capital management in the formulation of strategy means that all aspects of funding policy must be reviewed, and reset to optimum, at the highest level. We discussed liquidity policy in Part III of the book, and there is no need to consider it again here. However, we do note that asset funding requirements have a significant impact on the liquidity position of most banks, and should be considered at the strategy level. Practitioners should be in no doubt as the importance of funding policy in bank strategy, and it is equally important to allow for the impact of securities and derivatives trading, and the collateral requirements thereof, in this funding policy.

CONCLUSION

A neutral observer of the world's economic system would conclude fairly quickly that the financial markets, and banks, are an indispensable part of the economy and societal well-being. It is vital therefore that any regulatory system should incorporate the means of enforcing stability in the banking market. It should also allow for financial market innovation, because it has been largely through innovation that many of the benefits of finance have been made available to the wider population. But the key priority is effective regulation, so that even if individual banks are forced into liquidation, market stability is maintained. In other words, regulation must seek to preserve stability but also recognise that the main business of banks involves taking risk: the act of maturity transformation, the cornerstone of banking, creates risk exposure.

Bank senior management and the Board should accept that the institutions they run are a pivotal part of society, and in the post-crisis era they will be closely regulated. Contributing to the stability of the market is as important an objective for a Board as is achieving shareholder RoE targets. To this end, an understanding and appreciation of market stability is vital. In the first instance, increasing bank capital levels is a necessary but not sufficient means to ensure a stable banking system: liquidity management is as important. In this regard, the UK FSA's requirement that all UK-regulated banks must maintain an LAB is a correct one. Forcing every bank to invest a proportion of their assets in cash, central bank deposits and liquid AAA-rated sovereign securities is the best insurance protection against future liquidity crises.

The exact proportion of the balance sheet that should be placed in the LAB is a function of the liquidity gap that the bank runs, and the diversity and security of its funding arrangements. But a form of LAB is business best-practice and all banks should seek to have one in place. In itself this is not a new suggestion; a truly liquid portfolio was commonplace in banks around the world 15 or 20 years ago. However, banks started to unilaterally relax their own requirements and remove liquidity portfolios, or move them into assets that were not truly liquid (such as bank FRNs), to the point where such portfolios had become rare even in supposedly conservative institutions such as the UK building societies. It is evident that the prevailing orthodoxy has now reverted to its original one.

Bank boards should seek to simplify their capital structures, in the interests of transparency and investor comfort. The simplest structure may well be the most efficient, with a liability base comprised of: pure equity, retained profits, senior unsubordinated bonds and deposits. Deposits are part of the country's deposit guarantee scheme, so such a structure leaves no ambiguity about what stakeholders are at risk should the bank fail.

The nature of bank liquidity management has been transformed, although many of the "new" requirements in regimes such as those implemented by the FSA are more of a return to basics than actual new practices. The bank business model for the next 10 or 20 years will incorporate these practices, with boards recommended to pay close attention to their bank's liability structure. The basic tenets of the new liability model are (i) less reliance on wholesale funding, (ii) less reliance on short-term funding, (iii) a more diversified funding base, and (iv) genuine self-sufficiency in funding. Under this new model, banks will be considerably less likely to suffer failure at the time of the next market crash or systemic stress event.

Sustainable bank strategy should be designed to be just that: pertinent throughout the business cycle. An obsession with maximising return on capital or market share, and their even less logically tenable cousin, the bank's position on the "league table" of transaction volume, cannot be part of such a through-the-cycle strategy.

APPENDIX 16.1: THE LEADING ECONOMIC INDICES

We describe here the factor model proposed by Stock and Watson (1989), referred to as the LEI (the actual model used to calculate results shown in Example 16.1 has been adapted for use with specific parameter inputs by Zhuoshi Liu and Moorad Choudhry).

Coincident and leading economic indicators are designed to track, and in the latter case forewarn, of swings in the broad-based economy given by the business cycle. The CEI changes at approximately the same time as the whole economy, thereby providing information about the current state of the economy. The LEI is a short-term predictor of the future state of the economy.

The basic model states that the business cycle is measured by observing movements across a number of different time series, which are captured by a single variable C_t that describes the state of the economy. This variable is unobserved, and we assume that changes in it drive all movements in the economic input indicators. In other words, the dynamics of each coincident time series is described as being driven partly by changes in this unobserved variable, and partly by a specific "idiosyncratic" factor. The idiosyncratic factor is assumed to be uncorrelated with the other idiosyncratic factors as well as with the common unobserved factor.

The coincident indicator model that we specify is thus a dynamic factor model, which has strong precedent in the academic literature. We specify an $n \times 1$ vector X_t of the logarithms of the macroeconomic variables that (we assume) are driven by the "state of the economy" factor measure. The single index model X_t is comprised of the unobserved common factor C_t and the n-dimensional idiosyncratic factor u_t. Both components are assumed to follow a linear stochastic path. Stock and Watson specify the model in terms of ΔX_t and ΔC_t, as follows:

$$\Delta X_t = \beta + \gamma(L)\Delta C_t + u_t \qquad \text{(A16.1.1)}$$

$$D(L)u_t = \varepsilon_t \qquad \text{(A16.1.2)}$$

$$\phi(L)\Delta C_t = \delta + \eta_t \qquad \text{(A16.1.3)}$$

where L denotes the lag operator, and $\phi(L)$, $\gamma(L)$ and $D(L)$ are scalar, vector and matrix lag polynomials.

The model implies that the unobserved common factor C_t is the sole causal factor driving all the dependent variables X_t. The practical impact of this is minimal if one assumes that the relative movements of the components of ΔX_t to any combination of external factors is identical to ΔC_t.

The LEI model seeks to estimate the dynamics of the unobserved factor over the next six months. This is done using A16.1.1 to A16.1.3 and adjusting by $C_{t+6} - C_t$. We construct the LEI by modelling the variables (Y_t) and the unobserved factor C_t as a vector auto regressive system in the form of the following simultaneous equations:

$$\Delta C_t = \mu_c + \lambda_{CC}(L)\Delta C_{t-1} + \lambda_{CY}(L)Y_{t-1} + \nu_{C_t} \quad \text{(A16.1.4)}$$

$$Y_t = \mu_\gamma + \lambda_{\gamma C}(L)\Delta C_{t-1} + \lambda_{\gamma\gamma}(L)Y_{t-1} + \nu_{Y_t} \quad \text{(A16.1.5)}$$

where v_{ct}, v_{yt} are serially uncorrelated error terms.

To calculate LEI we regress ΔC_{t+6} against the other observed economic indicators as well as the current CEI for each of the macroeconomic indicators X_t. Thus the LEI is given as

$$L_t = K + \beta_i X_{i,t} + \gamma\Delta C_t \quad \text{(A16.1.6)}$$

where K is a constant.

REFERENCES

Bank of England (December 2009), *Financial Stability Report*, Issue No. 26.

Choudhry, M. (2007a), *Bank Asset and Liability Management*, Singapore: John Wiley & Sons (Asia) Pte Ltd.

Choudhry, M. (2007b), *The United Kingdom Government Bond Market: The Impact of the Introduction of Structural Reforms on Market Liquidity*, PhD thesis, Birkbeck, University of London.

Burns, A.F. and Mitchell, W.C. (1946), *Measuring Business Cycles*, New York: NBER.

Engle, R.F. and Watson, M.W. (1981), "A One-Factor Multivariate Time Series Model of Metropolitan Wage Rates", *Journal of the American Statistical Association,* 76: No. 376, 774–81.

Hatanaka, M. (1996), *Time-Series-based Econometrics: Unit Roots and Cointegration*, Oxford: Oxford University Press, p. 9.

Sargent, T. J., and Sims, C.A. (1977), "Business Cycle Modeling without Pretending to Have Too Much A Priori Economic Theory", in C. Sims et al., *New Methods in Business Cycle Research*, Minneapolis: Federal Reserve Bank of Minneapolis.

Stock, J.H. and Watson, M.W. (1988), "Testing of Common Trends," *Journal of the American Statistical Association*, 83, No. 404, 1097–1107.

Stock, J.H. and Watson, M.W. (1989), "New Indexes of Coincident and Leading Economic Indicators", in Blanchard, O.L. and Fischer, S., (editors), *Macroeconomics Annual 1989*, Vol. 4, New York: National Bureau of Economic Research.

CHAPTER 17

Bank Strategy II: Capital and Funding Management

We continue the theme of bank strategy with a look at business best-practice capital and funding management. We first consider the textbook treatment of a bank's capital, which is also business best-practice for how capital should be managed. We then look at:

- capital management policy, and capital strategy;
- systemic risk and macroprudential strategy, and benchmarking against one's peer group;
- funding management policy.

The last part of the chapter includes a review of derivatives collateral funding management. Collateral funding requirements can be a significant part of the overall liquidity exposure of a bank, and so it is important that this area is included within the discipline of the firm's overall approach to liquidity risk management.

TEXTBOOK TREATMENT OF BANK CAPITAL

The core Tier 1 capital base of a bank comprises its initial capital, or start-up capital, and retained earnings that have been placed in the reserves. The accounting and regulatory treatment apart, this capital is in most cases actual cash that needs to be placed somewhere. Generally, the simplest and most transparent model is to consider that the complete capital base is left untouched, and used as part of a leveraged business model in which it represents equity backing for borrowed funds, which are invested in risk-bearing assets. The return on the assets covers for the cost of borrowing, and the surplus over this and all other costs is the shareholder value-added for the equity owner.

The bank's capital itself is not used. It must be placed in an instantly liquid risk-free asset, with zero counterparty risk, so that it is not in danger of erosion and can be retrieved easily if needed, either to cover losses or to fund further expansion and investment. The only assets that fit this category are a deposit at the central bank or an investment in the sovereign bonds of the same currency. All other investments carry an element of counterparty and/or liquidity risk and are not suitable assets in which to park the bank's capital.

The capital base itself is not expected to generate a return. Where it does, for example the coupon return from a holding of government bonds, this income accrues to a central ALCO book, and not to any business line. Neither is it allocated on a pro-rata basis to the business lines, otherwise the calculation of shareholder value-added by the businesses will be skewed. The business lines do not utilise the capital base to fund their operations; hence, there is no explicit cost to allocate. However, the businesses will cover the cost of maintaining the capital through the rate of return. The target return on equity, set by the shareholder, sets the hurdle rate for each of the business lines, which benefit indirectly from the existence of the capital base. This hurdle rate can be a minimum for all the businesses, or it can be modified to suit the differing requirements of each business. We thus show how important it is for the bank's RoE target to be set at board level, reflecting the needs of the shareholder and thereby the "cost" of that equity.

Example 17.1 describes further the treatment of share capital. The treatment and allocation of capital we describe here represents business best-practice and sounds obvious; however, it is not applied universally. In some cases a deviation from the above is justified where a portion of the capital base is allocated for use as "working capital"; for example, in a start-up situation to cover cash requirements such as office rent and salary expenses. In this case the amount to be allocated should be identified in advance, and once the business has declared a profit the same amount should be restored to the capital base, or the bank needs to adjust its reported capital base. No other treatment of the capital base is justified. However, that does not mean that some banks do not still deviate from the above.

CAPITAL MANAGEMENT POLICY

Bank capital management should be articulated formally in a policy standard in the same way that liquidity management is (described in Part III). The objective of the policy is to describe how the bank will:

- meet its regulatory and other legal obligations;
- maintain its capital resources and buffer as required, and in line with the stated risk profile of the business;
- manage its capital planning in an efficient and cost-effective manner.

In the next section we provide a benchmark standard template for a bank's capital management policy.

EXAMPLE 17.1 SHARE CAPITAL[1]

Allocating Share Capital

The share capital of a legal entity represents a source of funding like any other, except it has one main defining characteristic: it bears no real *actual* interest cost. That said, there is a cost that is imputed, this being the shareholder's targeted return on equity. This "cost" must be attributed to the equity base, otherwise there is a risk that it ends up representing "free capital" to the benefit of the business lines. This would result in an incorrect and inaccurate reporting of genuine SVA.

What we describe is business best-practice for the treatment and allocation of equity capital. There are different approaches as to where the share capital is booked and where the benefit of this "free" source of funding is assigned; however, best-practice is for any benefit to be allocated to a central ALCO book. That said, often in reality, because the share capital is a specific type of external funding source, it is often booked in the Treasury book of the entity in which the capital resides, with the cash forming part of the general cash funding pool of the entity that is then managed by Treasury.

The net interest benefit of the utilisation of this "free" cash should then be subject to the same internal funds pricing (Transfer Pricing) rules as any other funding in the bank (see Chapter 15). In any case, the treatment of capital should be consistent with the treatment of retained earnings: since retained earnings and share capital are both similar sources of funding in that neither have a real interest cost, it is

(*continued*)

1 This is based on the section of the same name from Chapter 28 of the author's earlier book, *Bank Asset and Liability Management* (John Wiley & Sons, 2007). It has been updated for this book.

important that the benefit of retained earnings is allocated to a central ALCO book, and not any of the business lines.

Subordinated Debt

Subordinated debt issued by a financial institution forms part of the mechanism of capital structure management. This type of liability has characteristics of both share capital and term funding.

It has characteristics of share capital in that it ranks below senior debt holders in the order of priority of net asset distribution in the event of a wind-up. In order to compensate the subordinated debt holder for this perceived increase in credit risk relative to senior debt holders, the entity must pay an interest premium on the subordinated debt. Additionally, it has characteristics of term funding in that it is generally of a longer maturity term.

Therefore, the rate paid on the subordinated issue will have three elements:

- the base short-term Libor rate for short-term *senior* debt;
- the *term premium*: this will initially be captured within the Treasury P&L, and then reallocated to business lines (see Chapter 15).
- the *subordinated premium*: this will also initially be captured within the Treasury P&L, and should be treated consistently with the return on initial share capital noted above.

What we state here may seem obvious, but it is not universal practice. However, any variation of the treatment of capital described here is not business best-practice.

In a Basel III environment, subordinated debt may be a rarer element of a bank's capital structure.

Capital Management

The starting point for capital management policy is the regulatory capital ratio. The requirements of any overseas regulators, from jurisdictions that the bank also operates in, are also included. This is followed by a description of the monitoring process and escalation process for limit breaches.

A suitable policy template might cover:

Capital Targets

The bank will monitor and report its forecast regulatory capital base and RWAs per business line to Finance and Treasury. The responsibility for regulatory reporting lies typically with the Finance department. The bank may set operational targets such as:

Core Tier 1:	[ ]%
Total Tier 1:	[ ]%
Total capital:	[ ]%

The Finance department will maintain a 3-year rolling forecast and report this to the ALCO. Forecast or actual breaches of the regulatory capital ratios will be reported to the Head of Treasury and to the ALCO and regulatory authority.

The Treasury department will undertake capital stress testing to assess the potential capital impact of changes in firm-specific and market-wide business conditions. Where the test results indicate a potential breach of target rations, this must be reported to ALCO; mitigating action should then be undertaken after approval from ALCO.

Risk-weighted Assets

RWA balances must be reported on a weekly basis to Finance, Treasury and the business lines. RWA forecasts are prepared at month-end; any inconsistency with the Finance general forecast must be reported to the ALCO. The RWA forecast should be in line with the bank's capital allocation process. The impact of any business line transaction, whether asset or liability, that is likely to result in a reduction in capital must be reported immediately to the ALCO.

Capital Approval Process

The allocation of balance sheet capital must be applied for by the business line and approved in advance. Approval is granted by Treasury or the ALCO; this is dependent on the size of the capital impact. The current signing authority limits are:

ALCO	Unlimited
Finance Director	$[ ] million
Head of Treasury	$[ ] million
Business line head	$[ ] million

Business Restructuring

The transfer or disposal of any asset or business line, or any such reorganisation that has an impact on regulatory capital and/or RWAs, must be approved in advance by the ALCO.

Business Line Profit Remuneration

The net profit after direct and indirect costs of each business line must be transferred to the Treasury ALCO book at year-end. This is a direct cash transfer.

Capital Resource Management

A subset of the capital management policy is the capital resource management policy. The object of this document is to articulate formally how each business line will meet its requirements with regard to adherence to the capital management policy standard, and to ensure that use of capital at the business level is at an optimum in terms of allocation, planning and management. The efficient use of capital is also a metric in business performance evaluation; the capital resource management policy is part of the process to ensure that capital is allocated efficiently and as part of the bank's strategy.

Capital Allocation

The Finance department sets targets for RWAs and capital usage as part of the budget forecast and allocation process. Capital is allocated to produce optimum return, in line with the strategy and risk appetite of the bank. The strategy and risk appetite will drill down to each business line. Treasury will present capital usage limits at month-end, for approval by the ALCO, and report current and forecast capital usage to the ALCO on a weekly basis. See Figure 17.1 for an example of a capital usage RWA report.

If a forecast exceeds a limit, the business line will submit a request for mitigating action to be taken or for an increase in limit.

Performance Metrics

The Board, delegated authority to the ExCo, will set performance metrics targets for each business line. This will include RoE and

RISK WEIGHTED ASSET REPORT – SUMMARY	TOTAL RWA 28-Sep-10 $000	TOTAL RWA 27-Oct-10 $000	Basel II Total Combined Final 31-Aug $000
Fixed income	76,163	76,169	80,709
Equities	6,496	6,515	5,911
Corporate sales	66	66	70
Debt capital markets	822	804	919
TOTAL MARKETS	83,547	83,555	87,609
Balance sheet advisory	10	10	10
Corporate loan portfolio	38,062	38,062	38,814
Real estate finance	3,792	3,791	3,820
TOTAL CORPORATE BANKING	41,865	41,863	42,644
Treasury securitisation and term funding	−1254	−1189	−1670
Liquidity buffer	12,654	12,675	12,898
TOTAL TREASURY	11,400	11,486	11,228
Retail lending book	55,689	56,121	56,955
Private banking	10,094	10,124	10,387
TOTAL RETAIL BANKING	65,783	66,245	67,342
TOTAL RWAs	202,595	203,149	208,823

FIGURE 17.1 Example of capital usage RWA report.

capital usage (RWA) metrics, against which the performance of each business is evaluated.

Portfolio Credit Risk Management

The ALCO is responsible for reviewing and approving the asset pool for credit risk management purposes. This is to ensure that provisions are signed off in a consistent manner, that all transactions are in line with the business strategy and risk profile, and that they follow policy on capital usage and regulatory requirements.

CAPITAL MANAGEMENT, SYSTEMIC RISK AND MACROPRUDENTIAL STRATEGY

In this section we examine the nature of regulation and bank systemic risk, which will influence a bank's strategy and capital management policy.

Systemic Risk: Defining Systemic Importance

The economic importance of banks is evident from the reaction of Western governments to the financial crisis following the collapse of US firms AIG and Lehman Brothers. Banks such as Citibank, Lloyds TSB/HBOS, UBS and KBC Bank were partly nationalised and/or received large cash injections from their governments. These were the institutions deemed "too big to fail" (TBTF), and whose bankruptcy, it was viewed, would have been catastrophic for the world economy because of the high systemic risk such bankruptcy represented.

This raises the question as to exactly which banks are systemically risky. The events of 2007–2009 suggest that not only large banks present systemic risk. Prior to September 2008, the experience of Bear Stearns in the US and Northern Rock in the UK had shown that banks not necessarily defined as TBTF could nevertheless create significant market turbulence when they failed. This implies that in a globalised economy with many interconnections, the collapse of almost any bank, and certainly any bank with cross-border interests, can destabilise the economy. Banks therefore must not only manage their own risks adequately, they also have to be aware of the potential risk exposure of their counterparties. Bear Stearns, for example, had large exposure to hedge funds that had invested in low-grade assets. In other words, an understanding of macro-level market risk is vital for a bank that wishes to know its own risk.

The UK FSA has suggested that a firm be defined as systemically important:

> *. . . when its collapse would impair the provision of credit and financial services to the market with significant negative consequences for the real economy.*[2]

Thus the precise definition of systemic importance is no longer purely a reflection of the size of the bank. The FSA view of the factors that make firms systemically important is:

2 FSA, *Policy Statement 09/16*, October 2009.

- systemic by size: the absolute size of the bank is relevant, but so is its size relative to a particular financial market or product;
- systemic by interconnection: the importance of the firm to the interbank market and clearing systems;
- systemic by association: where the market views one company as representative of a group, whereupon failure by one is seen as a potential failure by all (an example would be the UK building society sector).

The above is a logical approach. However, it remains the judgement of financial regulators to determine the extent to which a particular firm falls into one or more of the three categories and can be specified as systemically important. For maximum risk mitigation it is necessary to minimise the amount of judgement required. In this regard, therefore, the author believes that there is a strong case for suggesting that almost all banks fall into at least the last category above, making virtually all banks potential areas of material systemic risk. If we accept this, then there are significant implications for banks and regulatory authorities.

Living With Moral Hazard

One result of the 2007–2009 financial crisis is that governments and central banks are now playing a pivotal role in maintaining moral hazard. A reaffirmation of their position as "lender-of-last resort" creates a dual principle. First of all it gives a strong signal to deposit holders not to withdraw their money from banks, as they should expect that the central bank will place unlimited resources at the disposal of private banks to keep the credit process going. Second, it encourages deposit holders to place their money at the bank with the highest deposit interest rate.

Banks in turn compete against each other to attract deposits. The bank that is able to pay the highest deposit rate will, all else being equal, attract most deposits. This is only sustainable from a bottom-line viewpoint by taking on more risk on the asset side of the balance sheet. This happened with the UK bank Northern Rock plc. In part, due to its more aggressive credit portfolio, the bank was able to pay out a higher rate on its clients' deposit accounts compared to that paid by the big "high street" banks, noted in Cooper (2008).

However, the existence of a LoLR safety net creates an unconscious reflex in bank senior management to take on more risk. Due to competitive pressures in banking a higher risk-reward profile becomes a self-fulfilling prophecy, as banks seek to generate more customer business and attract deposits. Continuing moral hazard is an issue that needs to be resolved if we are to avoid a reoccurrence of the crisis. However, this is not an easy task. The principle of LoLR has merit. The Great Depression in the 1930s could have been more contained if the US central bank had played a more dominant role. In essence, we have a conundrum that is not easily solved.

For the foreseeable future the LoLR concept will not disappear. It is necessary for the safe operation of the financial system. We observed during the Lehman collapse the effects when a government and central bank let market forces act freely: at one stage in October 2008 it appeared as if the entire Western banking system might collapse, with disastrous consequences for the global economy, if governments had not stepped in to guarantee liabilities. It is an economic law that in this case the fall in asset prices relative to current output prices would have been greater but for state intervention. Furthermore, the drop in investments and consumption would be substantial and the decline in income and employment would be larger as well. So it appears apparent that the public sector must step in for the "greater good", in a way that does not apply to other industrial sectors.

Mitigating Moral Hazard Risk at Individual Bank Level

Thus, moral hazard has seemingly become an inescapable fact of life. The ultimate solution to the problem may be no more ambitious than reducing (rather than attempting to eliminate) moral hazard, without curtailing risk taking. This requires that individual banks set their strategies and business models to generate the conditions for sustainable banking. This is the "through-the-cycle" banking strategy, and macroprudential regulation, that Basel III and national regulators are emphasising, and to which bank boards should adhere. To that end, bank strategy needs to incorporate higher level issues of market systemic risk and a sustainable banking business model.

The Interconnection of Financial Markets and Systemic Risk

The reason why a LoLR facility is put in place is to avoid spill-over effects towards other banks and to prevent a bank run. Banking is ultimately a business based on confidence. The instant that customers start withdrawing their deposits on a large scale, a bank is in trouble and will need to be bailed out (either by takeover or merger with another bank or by outright support from the LoLR). The basic bank business model relies on leverage, with only a small fraction of a bank's liabilities held in reserve at the central bank. As bank funding is based on borrowing in the inter-bank market, systemic risk is inherent in the model. Therefore, a bank's strategy and approach to business must, above all, place the highest priority on stakeholders and the wider market maintaining confidence in it as a going concern institution. This overrides all other strategy considerations.

Addressing this risk is a current management issue for banks and regulators. The focus extends to the following:

- setting strict liquidity ratio limits, imposed by the regulator, as well as requirements to diversify funding sources, reduce reliance on single funding sources, and increase the average tenor of liabilities. This is in place under the UK FSA and Basel III liquidity regime for banks;
- the establishment of a global central clearing agency for OTC derivatives – efforts are already underway to set this up for credit derivatives, and such a system would help to reduce bilateral counterparty risk. The Dodd-Frank legislation in the US will result (among other things) in a centralised clearing counterparty for derivatives. An alternative solution would be for regional clearing centres based on currency;
- the establishment of a clearing house for the money markets, a so-called "International Money Exchange" for the inter-bank market that would work similarly to an exchange clearing house. This is noted in Choudhry (2009); such a facility would serve to make the inter-bank market more robust during times of crisis or illiquidity, because it is at these times that banks withdraw credit lines with other banks. A central clearing mechanism that eliminated bilateral counterparty risk would make it less likely that banks would withdraw lines;
- reducing leverage – a leverage limit is in place for Basel III; see BoE (2009a);
- higher capital ratios – this is in place for Basel III;
- developing new capital instruments that absorb losses in distressed situations. Our recommendation is that banks promote a product that has similar features to a classic reverse convertible bond. Banks would issue so-called reverse convertible debentures, which would automatically convert into equity once the minimum capital ratio level of a bank is breached. We discuss this issue elsewhere in this chapter.

The above measures all address moral hazard, and so collectively could be expected to reduce the likelihood that a central bank or government would have to bail out the banks during the next economic downturn. Note, however, that while they are macro-level issues, they are implemented at individual bank level. In other words, it is imperative that they feed into each bank's strategy setting and business model.

Alternative to a Public Sector LoLR

We noted that the LoLR arrangement exists to maintain market stability, but that systemic risk and moral hazard are inherent in this model. The preceding section discussed how banks can set policy at an individual level to decrease the possibility that the LoLR will need to be called upon. In certain circumstances, however, such as a market-wide liquidity crash, certain banks will need to be bailed out by a higher authority. It is possible for the industry itself to set up such a higher authority in the private sector.

An arrangement for a non-taxpayer-funded liquidity support mechanism lies in the origins of central banks themselves (the BoE excepted), which paradoxically were created to maintain bank stability. In 1907 the United States experienced the collapse of a number of banks in the aftermath of a deep recession. Inter-bank liquidity evaporated and there was a bank run. J.P. Morgan and a number of other banks injected their own private money to guarantee market liquidity and avoid any further collapse of the system. To help prevent such market stress in the future, the US Federal Reserve was founded six years later.

The alternative to a public sector LoLR is an industry-funded liquidity mechanism. In this, all banks would contribute to a pool of money that exists as a safety net for the market. There are a number of ways this could be done, but the most workable would be similar to an IMF-style funding arrangement, with the biggest users of the inter-bank market and inter-bank funding contributing the most to the liquidity fund. This fund would act as a liquidity backstop whenever an individual bank member experienced liquidity difficulties. To be an effective means of maintaining confidence, every institution with a banking licence and which operated in the money markets would have to be obliged to be a member of the liquidity fund. A private sector trade association-type body could operate and manage the facility.

In theory, by setting up such a liquidity backstop we withdraw the public sector safety net from the market. As well as removing the taxpayer liability, it also has an added benefit in that banks themselves have an interest in market stability, and so going forward would be expected to be more conservative in their approach to wholesale funding and leverage levels. Although a private sector liquidity fund will not completely eliminate the possibility that the central bank LoLR may be called upon to act – for example, if three or four large banks all experienced difficulties at the same time, the private fund would probably not be large enough – it would certainly reduce it, and it could take the place of the central bank for firm-specific crises and elements of wider crises.

Macroprudential Regulation

The events of 2007–2009 demonstrated clearly how the failure of one bank can have significant implications for other banks as well as the entire market. As a generalisation, banks are identical entities. Large numbers of them operate in the same markets, with the same customers and with each other. It is this interconnection that means that when one bank fails, the entire industry (and by extension the entire economy) is potentially at risk. Hence, it is not sufficient for financial regulators to aim to ensure that each bank is properly managed and has sufficient capital and liquidity arrangements in place. They also have to oversee the soundness of the industry as a whole. Thus "macroprudential" regulation is now the main focus for bank regulators. Bank boards will need to incorporate regulators' thinking into their *modus operandi*, because it has a direct impact on bank capital management.

The framework within which macroprudential regulation would be undertaken remains under discussion; for example, see BoE (2009). It has also been incorporated into the Basel III rules, which specify a "countercyclical buffer" for regulatory capital, although only for the larger banks. The broad objective of such regulation is to ensure the continued safe running of the financial system in the event of individual bank failure. A number of steps can be taken by regulators to assist with this.

There is a sound logic to this approach. When the economy is growing steadily and risk aversion is decreasing, banks fall into a pattern of lowering loan origination standards and easing the supply of credit. A booming economy and tightening credit spreads alter bank risk-taking behaviour. The typical reaction is a lowering of loan origination standards and a change in banks' strategy to the extent that market share and higher RoE targets become emphasised, sometimes to the detriment of liquidity and capital management. This was the error made by UK banks such as Northern Rock, Bradford & Bingley and HBOS.

Because banks operate in the same markets and with each other, this cyclical pattern is exacerbated during any significant market event. The supply of plentiful and cheap credit helps boost the price of assets such as equities and real estate. At the end of the cycle and in a recession, banks then as a group withdraw credit on a large scale, widening the impact of the recession and also causing a fall in asset prices.

The first requirement of macroprudential regulation therefore is for banks to operate in less cyclical a manner. This can be enforced by altering bank capital and liquidity requirements in the course of the business cycle. At any time when the market is viewed as pursuing ever more risky asset generation, and/or credit is seen as too easily available, the regulator can require banks to:

- increase their level of capital, particularly Tier 1 equity capital;
- adjust their liquidity ratio to ensure that there is less reliance on short-term funding and wholesale inter-bank funding.[3]

Both of the above steps would increase the cost of doing business for a bank, and thereby lead to decreased lending levels during a boom period. The broad framework for this approach is now included in Basel III, although its implementation, as well as the level of the countercyclical buffer itself, is left to the individual national regulators.

The difficulty of course is the judgement call of when exactly a bull market is underway, or the precise moment when a market is, to borrow an earlier phrase, irrationally exuberant. While it is easy to see in hindsight at what point a market crash began, it is harder to call such an event beforehand. Measures that regulators may wish to consider include:

- the overall level of lending in the economy, both as an absolute level and as a percentage of GDP;
- the rate of increase in retail lending; for example, credit card and residential mortgage approvals, as well as the rate of increase in lower credit-quality lending;
- the rates of return on equity on bank capital, and whether this is running at above long-run averages.

In practice, the regulator may wish to use a combination of these measures when making this assessment, which will always remain a judgement call. It would also need to monitor aggregate economic indicators such as the rate of growth of GDP and asset prices, compared to medium-term average rates.

The BoE has suggested that particular types of loan activity need to be targeted when capital requirements are raised.[4] Otherwise, there is the risk that banks will merely pull back from lower risk business lines and use the capital saving created to continue business in higher risk activity. This is logical, and we would suggest that it may be addressed by focusing – not at

---

3 The liquidity ratio is essentially the asset–liability "gap". A good idea of this gap can be determined by calculating the ratio of average maturity of assets to average maturity of liabilities. A higher ratio is indicative of a higher gap and higher liquidity or funding rollover risk. See Chapter 12.

4 BoE (2009).

the macroprudential level, but at the direct individual bank level – on RoE targets and leverage levels. If regulators place limits on these two values, and alter them to suit the business cycle, this will also drive more counter-cyclical behaviour. What is apparent is that a reliance on higher capital requirements alone may not be a sufficient safeguard against systemic risk, because it would be difficult to ascertain what level of capital was enough.[5] The liquidity ratio for a bank is a key risk measure and regulators can use it to influence macroprudential behaviour. By setting a more conservative liquidity ratio requirement for banks that run large asset–liability gaps, and therefore greater liquidity risk, the regulator can ensure that asset origination cannot exceed by too much the ability of the bank to fund such assets more robustly.

Notwithstanding the view that essentially all banks pose a systemic risk of a kind, due to their interconnectivity, the risk from larger multinational banks may be mitigated by specific stringent treatment. The UK FSA has required that each legal entity in the large UK banking groups set up a "living will", so that they can be easily and safely unwound without affecting the capital base of the rest of the group. This does not mitigate risk, however, it is merely a means by which the impact of failure can be concentrated into a shorter timescale. To effectively control the risk of TBTF banks, one approach could be to require them to ensure that their overseas operations are separately capitalised and that their liquidity is self-sufficient. This would reduce the risk that an economic crisis in one country was not imported into another via the banking system.

More stringent macroprudential and micro-level regulation would provide for greater financial market stability at the time of the next recession, more so because the nature and size of the next crisis cannot be estimated with any certainty. At the micro level, systemic risk will be mitigated by requiring all banks to adhere to a more stringent capital and liquidity regime, and one that has a counter-cyclical emphasis. Both of these requirements will increase the cost of doing business, and thus reduce lending volumes in the long run, but regulatory authorities and governments will view this as a desirable result because it will reduce the ability for a bank to grow rapidly during a bull market as well as reduce the need for it to cut lending during a recession. As the natural inclination for a private company is to maximise return and minimise operating costs, counter-cyclical behaviour would not occur in a completely free market. To enforce this therefore will require regulatory fiat. However, it is still logical for banks to adopt this approach in their strategy

5 Lehman Brothers was capitalised at 11% Tier 1 at the time of its collapse, a level that was acceptable to regulatory authorities while it was still in operation.

and capital management policy in any case, because this would have a beneficial impact in terms of stakeholder and investor confidence, as well as credit rating reviews.

BENCHMARKING WITH THE MARKET

Regulatory authorities conduct peer group analysis on a regular basis, as part of their review of the state of the financial markets. For related reasons every a bank should, where possible, undertake a review of its peer group. This provides additional indications on what may be business best-practice, as well as a level against which the bank can set benchmarks. As part of its general procedures on liquidity risk management therefore, peer group review should be carried out by the bank's ALCO and BSMCO. If the ALCO is fully occupied with operational matters, we recommend that this process be undertaken by the BSMCO, the remit for which was described in Chapter 10.

Comparison Metrics

Where possible a bank should determine where it sits on a liquidity metrics scorecard. An hypothetical example is given at Figure 17.2, for five peer group banks, one of which is "Our Bank". The choice of which banks one considers to be in one's peer group is dictated by external investor opinion, as well as the views of BSMCO.

From the chart we see that "Our Bank" ranks highly in terms of structural liquidity strength. We can conclude that we are following business best-practice in liquidity risk. Equally, Bank 2 and Bank 4 are not at benchmark levels. This may reflect their business model as much as any underlying management beliefs or practice; nevertheless, the national regulator may wish to monitor these two banks more closely than the market leaders.

Where the data can be obtained, it is worthwhile drilling down into the data revealed in Figure 17.2. For example, the MI pack for BSMCO may include Figure 17.3, which shows the funding mix for customer deposits. If we are familiar with the bank's operating model, we might conclude that the funding mix is consistent with the business models of each bank, with those banks possessing stronger retail franchises having the highest customer funding. We note that Bank 3 has the highest proportion of time deposits, which are the most valuable to a bank for liquidity metrics purposes; this may reflect corporate time deposits raised by its Corporate Banking arm.

Liquidity metrics as at 30 Dec 2010	"Our Bank"	Bank 1	Bank 2	Bank 3	Bank 4
Structural liquidity position					
Customer LTD ratio	81%	78%	114%	125%	135%
Customer funding gap (EUR bln)	150	140	–80	–90	–145
Leverage ratio[1]	15x	10×	22x	19x	20x
Net stable funding ratio	125%	120%	90%	102%	98%
Liquidity buffer ratio	40%	35%	22%	26%	20%
Liquidity reserves					
Liquidity reserves (EUR bln)	190	155	121	185	134
Short-dated wholesale funding (<90 days) EUR bln	130	175	240	195	180
% coverage of <90-day wholesale funding outflow	146%	89%	50%	95%	74%
Short-dated wholesale funding (<1-year) EUR bln	199	210	280	270	150
% coverage of <1-year wholsale funding outflow	95%	74%	43%	69%	89%
Debt securities weighted-average maturity[2]					
WAM of debt securities in issue (years)	10.9	6.8	4.2	4.9	4.1
Total debt securities to total funded assets	19%	15%	14%	16%	17%

[1]Calculated as (Funded assets + Net OBS)/(Owners' equity + Minority interest)
[2]Or WAM

Key
Best ; Worst

FIGURE 17.2 Liquidity metrics scorecard, peer-group comparison.

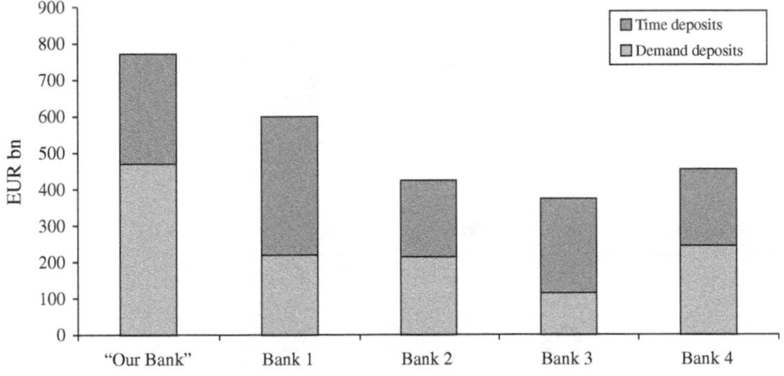

FIGURE 17.3 Customer funding mix, peer-group comparison.

Rating Agency Comparison

Leaving aside the debate on whether the influence of credit rating agencies is desirable or not, it is a fact that the rating agencies are within a bank's stakeholder space. Investors always consider rating agency opinions, so is it important for banks to manage the relationship with the agencies carefully. The agencies' opinion is also a useful, publicly available source of data to use in peer group comparison.

Moody's Criteria

Moody's Bank Financial Strength Ratings (BFSR) are its opinion of a bank's intrinsic financial strength, relative to all other banks rated globally. The BFSR is a measure of the likelihood that a bank will require assistance in order to avoid a default, taking account of the following:

- structure of a bank's assets and liabilities; degree to which a bank's illiquid assets are funded by core liabilities that are stable. The latter comprise customer deposits, long-term debt and equity. This metric is a reflection of the "principles of liquidity" that we described in Chapter 12;
- liquidity risk associated with the extent to which illiquid assets are funded with non-sticky liabilities such as wholesale/inter-bank funds or short-term capital markets funds. These funds are "confidence sensitive", in that they are likely to be withdrawn if investor perception of the bank erodes;
- extent to which a bank can access short-term market funding in the event that its access to markets is disrupted due to a credit or liquidity event;
- effectiveness of a bank's internal liquidity risk management framework. Moody's assigns this a score from A to E, with A being the highest.

Moody's calculates its own liquidity ratio metric, given by:

$$\frac{(\text{Market funds} - \text{Liquid assets})}{\text{Total assets}}$$

where

Market funds: Long- and short-term debt + inter-bank liabilities
Total assets: As at period end.

The liquidity ratio assigns a score of liquidity strength, which is:

Excellent:	<−10%
Very good:	>−10% to 0%
Satisfactory:	0% to 10%
Modest:	> 10% to 20%
Poor:	> 20%.

Liquidity metrics as at 30 Dec 2010	"Our Bank"	Bank 1	Bank 2	Bank 3	Bank 4
Moody's ratio					
Moody's liquidity ratio	−15%	−5%	0%	3%	11%
Moody's liquidity ratio score	Excellent	Very good	Satisfactory	Satisfactory	Modest

FIGURE 17.4 Peer-group scorecard, Moody's liquidity strength.

The BFSR methodology assigns 50% of the final result to qualitative factors, which include the bank's liquidity risk management framework and its relative risk appetite, and 50% to financial factors that include the liquidity ratio and liquidity management. Liquidity itself accounts for 8% of the total 50% assigned to financial factors. Moody's actually places a larger weight on the strength of a bank's liquidity management framework than it does on the liquidity ratio. The former has a risk-weighting of 5.1%, compared to the weighting of 2.8% assigned to the liquidity ratio.

The addition to the peer-group comparison scorecard shown at Figure 17.2 would look like Figure 17.4.

Standard & Poor's Criteria

S&P does not publish a separate liquidity risk assessment methodology for banks such as Moody's BFSR. Instead it describes liquidity strength within the overall rating category that it assigns for the bank. This approach makes use of a liquidity model to measure the survival horizon of a bank during a name-specific liquidity crisis, and benchmarks this against the bank's peers. Thus S&P creates a scenario in which there is a "run" on the bank, under a standard set of assumptions for asset haircuts and liability run-off rates, with the following two levels of analysis:

- Level 1: primary liquidity sources only, including cash, bank deposits, government securities, asset-backed securities and investment-grade corporate bonds;
- Level 2: primary and secondary liquidity sources. Secondary liquidity is the bank's ability to monetise assets through securitisation, syndications, loan sales and other contingent liquidity facilities.

S&P applies a higher run-off rate to less stable funding sources such as wholesale funding and local authority (municipal) deposits.

Fitch Criteria

Fitch also does not publish a separate liquidity risk assessment rating such as Moody's BFSR. However, it does publish the following five metrics as an indication of a bank's structural funding strength:

- Customer loans/Customer deposits;
- Customer loans/Customer deposits and short-term funding;
- Liquid assets/Total assets;
- Liquid assets/Wholesale funding;
- Wholesale funding/Total funding and capital.

As with the Moody's peer-group comparison, both external investors and the banks themselves can see where they stand relative to the market, and can plan appropriate action to address any perceived weakness if deemed necessary.

AN INTEGRATED CAPITAL AND LIQUIDITY MANAGEMENT STRATEGY

In the Basel III environment, banks will wish to ensure that their high level strategy setting integrates both capital management and liquidity management. We describe a template of objectives for banks to consider when formulating strategy.

Capital Management Issues: Strategy Level

As a strategic imperative a bank should review its complete business model and identify which businesses have the most attractive funding and cost base under Basel III, and remain viable, and which do not. The result of this exercise is then an action plan that describes which businesses in the bank's portfolio it should be growing, maintaining, and exiting.

Other considerations include:

- ensure that an appropriate and sustainable incentive scheme is in place to drive correct senior management behaviour and optimise use of capital;
- ensure that specified, consistent, quantified capital objectives are explicitly stated and applied throughout every business line in the bank or group;
- ensure the bank is set up with the infrastructure to enable senior management to measure and report on the capital position and requirements on a sufficiently timely basis;
- review whether existing business models, if they are being retained, should continue in the form they are currently organised or should be

re-modelled on a more efficient basis (for example, branch versus subsidiary) in a way that makes better use of capital;
- prepare to be able to meet more accelerated implementation timescales if required.

The above should not be a worthless management consultant-style strategy document, but rather a working document that sets out exactly how the bank's businesses should be set up in a way that uses capital the most effectively.

Capital Management Issues: Tactical Level

Capital management at the tactical level is first and foremost about ensuring that senior management is intimately familiar with the capital requirements and return on assets of every business line. This requires efficient and timely MI.

The main considerations are:

- ensure that business lines are charged the correct level for the capital costs of their activity;
- ensure that Basel III capital implications are taken into account for new business proposals;
- review all long-dated business on the balance sheet from a capital efficiency and RoA viewpoint, and consider whether this is still SVA business. If not, can it be divested efficiently?
- maintain focus on Basel II as well as Basel III implications of all business lines, because Basel III amplifies any increases in RWAs arising from Basel II;
- review performance of existing regulatory capital calculation methodologies where these are internal models (for example, IRB under Basel II);
- ensure procedures are in place that enable Treasury and the business lines to consider the pricing implications arising from changes in the capital requirements for specified product lines.

The above process is a regular review, and not a one-off exercise.

Liquidity Management Strategy

Liquidity management at the detailed technical level was considered in Part III of this book. For senior management it should be closely integrated into capital management strategy. Liquidity management strategy should be contained in an up-to-date policy document that includes the CFP and liquidity risk tolerances, as well as the strategy and tactical plan for diversifying sources of funds.

The principal considerations for liquidity management strategy are:

- bank senior management must be aware of the current liquidity position at all times, as well as what the forward stress points are. This knowledge must be to sufficient detail;
- the incentive structure for management should ensure optimal use of liquidity. This demands an appropriate and effective internal funds pricing policy (FTP policy);
- ensure that regulatory requirement for liquidity are always taken into consideration when assessing profitability and RoA on existing business and on new business proposals;
- ensure robust and wide-ranging stress testing and scenario planning, and review results regularly. Test results must be acted on through mitigating action and an enhanced CFP;
- review regularly the bank's liquidity strategy and ensure that infrastructure and MI adequately meet all requirements.

The liquidity strategy document should drill down to detailed metric requirements. For example, it could be stated along the following lines:

- the bank will maintain sufficient liquidity buffer to address 115% of 90-day regulatory stressed cash outflows;
- specified liquidity metrics will be:
  - loan-to-deposit ratio of 95%;
  - an LAB size of $10 billion;
  - maximum short-term wholesale funding usage of $1 billion;
- liquidity risk appetite should be made explicit.

Bank senior management should strive to ensure that their liquidity management strategy is always business best-practice. Regular peer-group review and comparison will assist with this. Industry practice should be reported at ExCo and ALCO level.

EXAMPLE 17.2 A CAPITAL ADEQUACY AND LIQUIDITY TRADE-OFF

Figure 17.5 is reproduced with permission from the UK FSA and shows an hypothetical arrangement with two different banks, posing the question "Which is riskier?". The bank on the top is

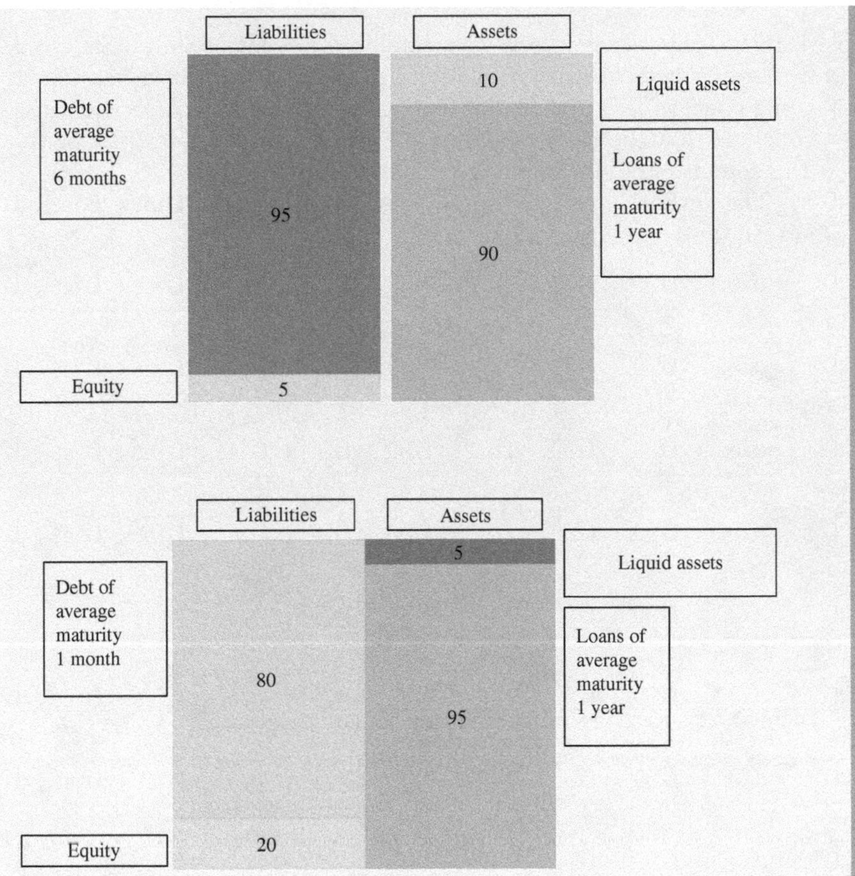

FIGURE 17.5 Capital and liquidity trade-off.
© FSA 2010. Reproduced with permission

running a more conservative liquidity policy, with longer dated liabilities as well as a larger liquidity buffer. The bank on the bottom is running a higher risk liquidity policy, but has a larger capital buffer. Its higher capitalisation would, all else being equal, make it higher rated than the other bank and thereby able to access cheaper funding.

There is not necessarily one right answer to the question. If the first bank has a high risk appetite and has acquired higher risk assets on the balance sheet, then it is in the riskier position because its capital base is low and may be reduced to below regulatory minimum should it start to experience losses. That said, in the event of a liquidity crisis it is in the better position. A liquidity event will finish a bank as a going concern if it cannot roll over liabilities, so ultimately we must conclude that the riskier bank is the second, well-capitalised bank. This sounds paradoxical but we can understand it.

The author's preferred solution is "neither of the above", and is instead shown at Figure 17.6.

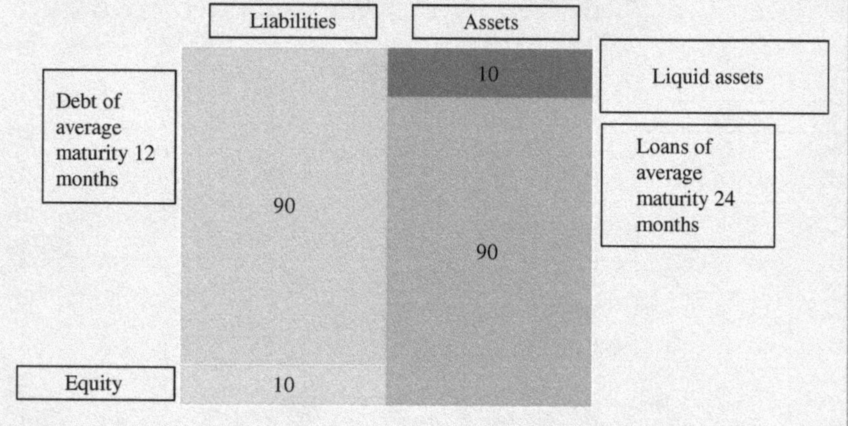

FIGURE 17.6 Recommended capital and liquidity position.

CAPITAL MANAGEMENT: CAPITAL INSTRUMENTS

A key feature of bank capital that appeared to have been forgotten and was re-learned in the aftermath of the 2008 crash was that capital buffers, and hybrid capital instruments that are designed to supplement core Tier 1 capital of equity and retained reserves, need to be loss-absorbing *on a going concern basis*. That is, this element of the capital base needs to be able to absorb losses without this in itself leading to a loss of confidence in the bank. For example, coupons should be able to be cancelled, and the capital on hybrid notes written down, without the act of so doing resulting in the cessation of the bank as a going concern. If this is not possible, then these elements of capital serve no ultimate purpose. As part of their capital management strategy therefore, banks should issue contingent core Tier 1 capital instruments that can be triggered into equity at certain specified points. This triggering action should then result in a restoration of the bank's capital base to its minimum regulatory levels, without also triggering any loss of confidence in the bank itself.

Hybrid capital instruments have, in theory, a role to play in the build-up of the countercyclical capital buffer required under Basel III. The UK FSA limits the share of Tier 1 capital that can be comprised of hybrid capital instruments. They can form up to 15%, 35% or 50% of total Tier 1 capital, depending on their type.[6] Going forward, banks issuing capital-building debt instruments must ensure that they allow principal loss absorbency and coupon cancellation. This ability to cover losses has to be at issuer election; that is, it cannot arise only from being subordinated to other debt. Going concern loss absorbency is a feature of equity capital and retained reserves; hybrid capital instruments need to exhibit this feature, but also they need to be viewed by the market in this way. This is something that is outside the ability of regulators to control. A bank must make clear, in the offering documents describing the hybrid instrument, that this is indeed a feature of the bond. At the point a write-down of a hybrid bond is triggered, the losses should be absorbed on an equivalent basis with core Tier 1 capital. The triggering will have the effect of increasing the reserves by the amount of the conversion. In other words, for practical purposes there is no subordination between the hybrid instrument and common equity. As such, one can expect such hybrid bonds to have to pay a relatively expensive coupon, or investors will believe there is no point holding them and decide that they will either hold equity, or not have any exposure to the bank at all. The one advantage of hybrid capital instruments over equity is that in the future their value can be "written up" back to their original level, from future profits, in a way that equity cannot. The loss is not necessarily permanent.

In 2009 a number of banks issued debt in the form of "contingent capital" liabilities. This is a worthwhile instrument for banks to use as part of their capital management and planning, albeit an expensive one. An example was Lloyds Banking Group's Enhanced Capital Notes (ECN) issued in

6 The 50% bucket is limited to convertible instruments that can convert either at the bank's or regulator's discretion at any time. This can include, but is not limited to, conversion triggered by the issuer breaching a regulatory capital level. It excludes convertibles with a call feature. The 35% bucket is for hybrid instruments that possess going concern loss-absorbency features; for example, write-down or conversion, and do not have any incentive to be redeemed (such as a coupon step-up feature). Hybrids that possess a going concern loss-absorbing capability, but do possess a redemption incentive, such as a step-up coupon if they are not called, can make up to 15% of the total. Hybrids issued by an SPV also fall into this limit bucket.

2009. This was a GBP13.5 billion issue, with a 12% coupon and 10-year maturity.

The key feature of CoCo bonds is that they convert to equity if the issuer's Tier 1 ratio falls to a pre-specified level. The Lloyds' ECN will convert if the Tier 1 ratio falls to 5%, at which point conversion takes place at a pre-specified price (in this case 50% of par issue price). The high coupon reflects the nature of the bond as more equity than debt; in effect, it is a pre-funded rights share issue. If a bank is targeting a Tier 1 level to achieve by a set date, CoCo bonds are an instrument it can consider, provided there is investor appetite for it.

CAPITAL MANAGEMENT STRATEGY

We conclude that bank strategy should focus on serving customers, and driving the business via this customer focus. It should include an RoE/RoC target set in advance, which is aligned to the bank's risk-reward preference. The capital strategy follows on from the overall strategy, and describes how and what capital is allocated to each business line. At that point, the bank sets its core Tier 1 capital target level to achieve. Using CoCo bonds can assist the last stage. The point being made here is that capital strategy is a coherent, articulated and formal plan of action, that builds on a regular review of the business, allocation of capital to those businesses, and desired return on capital. This should all be documented as part of the bank's capital strategy, which feeds into the overall strategy. This may sound obvious, but the layperson would be surprised to see how few banks actually do this.

A bank's management may think that the core Tier 1 ratio to have in place is the starting point of the strategy. In fact, almost the contrary could be true: the desired ratio should be arrived at after consideration of the business lines and the share of capital allocated to each to support the revenue and RoE target that is desired. The bank should compile an annual 3-year and 5-year capital ratio target, aligned to a strategic funding plan, and then target the optimum Tier 1 ratio.

As a key part of strategy, the capital management framework at a bank should address the requirements of all the various stakeholders. It should be communicated in transparent fashion to all internal and external stakeholders, articulating:

- how the risk appetite is aligned to their needs and expectations;
- how and why capital allocation and capital constraints are integrated with funding capabilities and assigned to each business line;
- the extent of tolerance for earnings volatility;

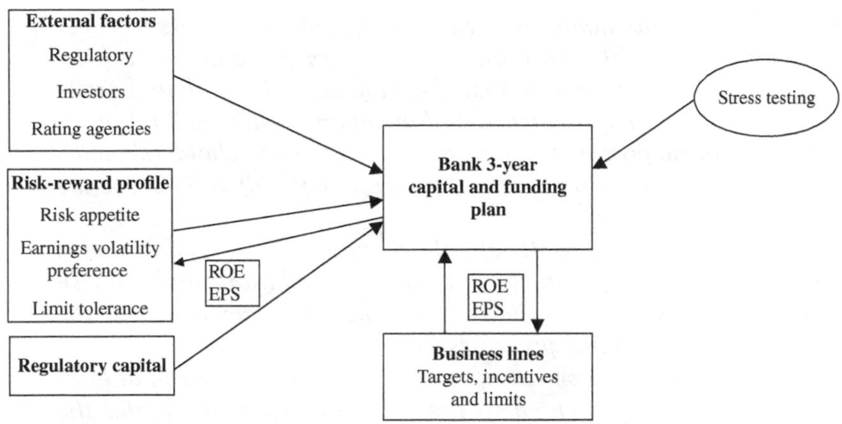

FIGURE 17.7 Formulating capital management strategy.

- the framework in which each of the business lines operate, with respect to risk exposure and the type of business undertaken.

Figure 17.7 is a stylised representation of this strategy formulating process. It reiterates that a bank's capital management process is part of overall strategy and is encompassed in a "capital management framework". This process must be the right way round; in other words, it should reflect the priorities for the bank of maintaining confidence, delivering on its customer-focus strategy, and in optimising risk-adjusted return on capital – and in that order.

THE BASEL PILLAR III DISCLOSURE

In addition to the strategy and capital management setting undertaken by a bank as part of its own governance procedure, a bank will also need to produce capital disclosures for its regulatory authority. We illustrate this with an example of a Pillar III disclosure for a hypothetical medium-sized commercial bank, which is provided with this book. This may be used as a benchmark template for most commercial banks.

An extract from Page 5 of our template is given here:

> *BANK plc has adopted the standardised approach to credit, market and operational risk for calculation of the Basel II Pillar 1 minimum capital requirement.*

> *The bank maintains an actively managed capital base to cover risks inherent in the business. The primary objectives of capital management are to ensure that the bank complies with externally imposed capital requirements, and maintains healthy capital ratios in order to support its business and maximise shareholders' value. In this respect, the Board has set a capital buffer of 10% above the regulatory minimum.*
>
> *BANK plc manages its capital structure and makes adjustments to it in the light of changes in economic conditions and the risk characteristics of its activities. No changes were made in the objectives, policies and processes from the previous year.*
>
> *An internal assessment of capital needs is undertaken at least annually and is presented to the Executive Committee and the Board to review and challenge. This is known as the Internal Capital Adequacy Assessment Process (ICAAP). This is submitted for review to the FSA. The ICAAP describes how risks are assessed, controlled, monitored, mitigated and reported, and helps the management determine what might be required to maintain the Bank's solvency and strategy assuming certain stressed conditions. BANK's assessment during 2010 is that it had more than adequate capital resources to withstand the effects of a severe economic downturn.*
>
> *The minimum amount of capital required is determined in accordance to BIPRU rules, and BANK's opinion is that the Bank complied with the capital requirements set out by the FSA to cover both Pillar 1 and 2 risks.*

The template is provided on the Wiley website (see Chapter 19 for details). For practitioners' information we also include a template, the ICAAP submission, on the website. This form is part of the capital and liquidity adequacy regime in place at the UK FSA. However, as standard good practice it could be applied to most banks, as an example for a starting point of how to formulate one's capital management process.

REFERENCES AND BIBLIOGRAPHY

Bank of England (2009a), *The Role of Macroprudential Policy*, London, November.

Bank of England (2009b), *Financial Stability Report*, London, November.

Bernanke, B. (2007), *Financial Regulation and the Invisible Hand*, remarks at the NY University Law School, April 11.

Choudhry, M. (2009), "A Clearing House for the Money Market?," *Europe Arab Bank Treasury Market Comment*, Vol. 1, No. 9, 6 March.

Cooper, G. (2008), *The Origin of Financial Crises: Central Banks, Credit Bubbles and the Efficient Market Fallacy*, Hampshire: Harriman House Ltd, Petersfield.

United Kingdom Financial Services Authority (2008), *Consultative Paper 08/22*, December.

CHAPTER 18

Principles of Corporate Governance[1]

We conclude this book with a review of the principles of bank corporate governance. As any enlightened study of the economic crash of 2007–2009 would conclude, there were perhaps 10 to 12 significant causal factors, interacting over a number of years, that led to the crisis. However, if one had to identify just one factor specific to the banking industry, it would be that the failures of 2008 were a failure of corporate governance. Poor judgement, allied with not inconsiderable incompetence, led to the financial crash being much worse than it need have been.

In this final chapter we undertake a case study of selected bank failures from the viewpoint of corporate governance, and present recommendations on how best to organise bank governance going forward. These can be taken to be good practice, rather than business best-practice, because they are not universal beliefs and bank managements are free to conduct themselves in a variety of different ways. However, the principles outlined in this chapter have much to commend them and we present them as leading-edge good practice.

In this chapter we review the experience of a sample of failed banks in the period leading up to, and during, the crash. We observe the conduct of boards and senior management, as well as the governance infrastructure in place, to determine lessons for policy going forward. We highlight failures of governance, identify sources of risk as important determinants of a bank's corporate governance structure, and draw conclusions arising from the study to formulate recommendations for policy. We outline a more

1 This chapter was presented by the author at a conference organised by *Corporate Governance: An International Review* at the Wharton School, University of Pennsylvania in September 2010. It was first published in the *Journal of Applied Finance and Banking*, Volume 1, Number 1 (June 2011). It is reproduced here with permission.

effective framework for governance infrastructure, one that is better suited to managing risk under volatile market conditions.

EFFECTIVE BANK CORPORATE GOVERNANCE: CONCLUSIONS FROM THE MARKET CRASH

Banks are the critical infrastructure component in an economy. They provide financing for individuals and corporations, and facilitate the transmission of funds across payment systems. The effective functioning of any economy depends on banks ensuring the supply of credit and liquidity throughout the business cycle and in all market conditions. The importance of banks to human well-being and societal development is recognised by the fact that in virtually every country banking is a regulated industry and protected by taxpayer-funded safety nets. The efficient mobilisation and allocation of funds is dependent on efficient corporate governance at banks. When they are able to undertake this, the cost of capital is lowered for all market participants. This in turn increases capital formation and raises productivity growth. Therefore the management of banks has implications for corporate as well as national prosperity. This in turn highlights the importance, and central function, of bank governance. It is self-evident then, that bank corporate governance must be robust, effective, adaptable to changing circumstances and fit for purpose.

In the banking industry corporate governance refers to the manner in which the business and strategy of the institution are governed by the firm's board and senior management. An accurate and succinct description of it is given in BIS (1999), which describes the mechanics of bank corporate governance as (i) setting the bank's objectives, including target rate of return for shareholders; (ii) setting the control framework that oversees the daily operations of the bank; (iii) protecting customer deposits; (iv) setting strategy that accounts for the interests of all stakeholders, including shareholders, employees, customers and suppliers; and (v) maintaining the bank as a going concern irrespective of economic conditions and throughout the business cycle.

A banking crisis highlights the failure of bank corporate governance with dramatic effect. The financial crash and economic recession of 2007–2009 resulted in the demise of a number of banks, of varying size and systemic importance, in the US and Europe. The evidence from the crash is that corporate governance at many banks failed completely, at least with respect to points (iv) and (v) above, and in many cases with respect to all five governance objectives. This was despite the fact that the banking sector is heavily regulated and subject to internationally agreed rules on capital buffers and accounting transparency.

Related Literature

There is a considerable literature on the subject of bank corporate governance, with the emphasis on the infrastructure of management reporting and board composition. Saunders et al. (1990) conclude that bank ownership and management structure influence risk taking, while Caprio et al. (2009) look at how these factors influence bank valuations. Prowse (1997) and Macey and O'Hara (2003) suggest mechanisms for the governance infrastructure of banks. Barth et al. (2006) consider how regulatory mechanisms influence risk taking.

BIS (1999) is typical of studies from regulatory bodies in proposing a governance outline. It recommends the Board set a strategy and establish accountability of senior management. It points out that governance infrastructure varies by jurisdiction, with some country regimes setting a supervisory role and no executive powers for bank boards; other regimes allow for a broader remit that lays down a general framework for management. In other words, there is no universal set of rules on bank corporate governance. This is still the case.

Levine (2004) notes the importance of strengthening the ability and incentive of private investors to exert governance control over banks, rather than relying excessively on government regulation. Shareholder education is a vital part of this control. The influence of debt holders is post-facto, and dependent on the legal infrastructure and bankruptcy system in place. This is significant, and implies that debt holders do not exert adequate controlling influence on bank strategy and management until the point where the bank ceases to be a going concern. In a bull market environment, managers and shareholders may prefer this, and the finding of Myers (1977) that debt holders are risk averse would support this. However, as a form of macroprudential management and control, the influence of debt holders is vital for effective governance. In a notable pointer for future policy, Levine (2004) finds that state-owned banks are not a solution to the problem of inadequate governance.

Laeven and Levine (2007) is an important contribution to the literature, given the date of publication, which preceded the onset of the crisis. They conclude that bank regulations, including capital requirements and supervisory oversight, do not directly influence risk taking. Their study highlights the need to examine how a bank's ownership and management control structure combines with national regulatory policy to influence bank risk origination. Among their findings the most significant is that traditional regulatory policy does not drive risk aversion; the two key components of Basel II, regulatory capital requirements and supervisory oversight, do not appear to reduce risk taking. They also find that bank shareholders have incentives to increase risk exposure after collecting deposits and debt from investors. This suggests that shareholder presence on the Board is not a risk control device, rather the opposite; and also argues for the presence on the Board of debt holders.

The House of Commons Treasury Committee () makes several observations based on its study of bank governance in the lead-up to the crash. Among its findings is that the system of non-executive director (NED) oversight was flawed, because it had degenerated into a "cosy club", with insufficient time committed to their role by NEDs, who also combined their board responsibilities with full-time employment and directorships at other firms. Critically, NEDs also lacked sufficient relevant expertise. However, the finding that bank boards lacked diversity in their NED complement is difficult to justify, given the wide mix of backgrounds of many board members. If anything, bank boards were over-diversified, at the expense of financial sector expertise and experience. Treasury Committee concludes with recommendations that (i) the talent pool on the Board be enlarged; (ii) NEDs be restricted on the number of directorships they accept; (iii) the Board be supported by a dedicated secretariat; and (iv) all board members, both executive and NEDs, demonstrate sufficient expertise before being appointed.

From the viewpoint of corporate governance, the most significant finding in the Treasury Committee report is that bank shareholders do not subject boards to sufficient scrutiny. In fact, shareholders have an incentive to increase risk exposure, particularly after a period of increasing returns. This was also observed in Laeven and Levine (2007). The experience of KBC Financial Products, discussed later in this chapter, is instructive in this regard.

The Conventional Bank Corporate Governance Framework

We noted in the literature review that there is no universal bank corporate governance model. Differences in organisation and infrastructure differ by regulatory jurisdiction and also within them, depending on the type of institution being considered. The Basel Committee, as noted in BCBS (1998) and BIS (1999), suggest the following, *inter alia*, as elements of strategy and technique that are essential to an effective corporate governance arrangement:

- a coherent and explicit statement of strategy for the business, with stated required return and performance measures;
- clear and transparent outline of responsibilities for the executive management;

- explicit lines of authority and communication, from the Board downwards and from business lines upward;
- strong framework of internal control, and accountability, and review procedures and processes for this control (including internal and external audit arrangements and a Board audit-risk committee);
- an effective risk management framework that also describes the monitoring and reporting of all risk exposures;
- transparent information flows both internally and externally.

These principles would always be required, in any economic environment. In the wake of the crash, it is reasonable to conclude that the above principles were not observed at many banks. However, that does not suggest that these principles need to be changed, but rather observed and enforced more adequately and, in a number of key respects, added to.

Irrespective of the regulatory jurisdiction of a bank, at the top level there are five areas of governance over which strong oversight must be established. These are (i) genuine controlling supervision by the Board of Directors; (ii) supervision by individuals who do not work within the business lines; (iii) direct executive supervision of each business line; (iv) independent audit and risk management sub-boards; and (v) senior personnel who are sufficiently expert in their jobs. In other words, a "rubber stamp" Board is not acceptable.

The Board should establish a coherent, articulated strategy for the bank. This is stated in BIS (1999), but was not always observed. However, strategy objectives must be reviewed on a frequent basis, so that they can be altered as necessary to respond to changes in economic circumstances. Such macroprudential oversight is perhaps the most difficult aspect of a Board's responsibilities. Further, board directors must be qualified to perform their role and must be able to access all necessary information, on a timely basis, to enable them to perform their duties. The events during the crash suggest that this was not always the case.

Board Structure and Role

The most effective composition of a bank board remains an issue for debate. Heidrick and Struggles (2009) define three different forms of board structure that are common in Western Europe and North America, which we summarise at Figure 18.1.

The fully unitary system is common in UK banks, as well as in Spain, while the two-tier format is required by law in Germany, and also observed in Switzerland and Holland. The mixed system is observed in Belgium. All these countries, with the exception of Germany, suffered a banking crisis of

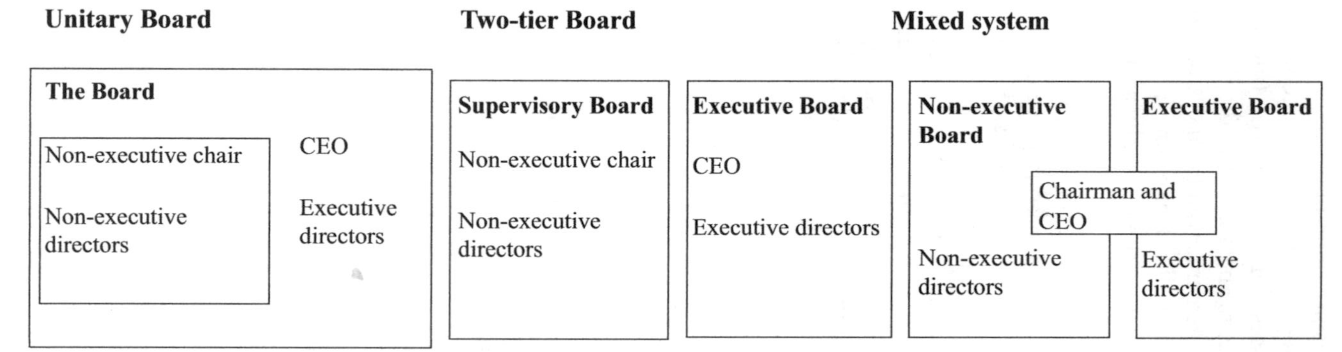

FIGURE 18.1 Examples of board structure.

one type or another in 2008, while a number of German *landesbanks* had to be rescued by the federal government. On anecdotal evidence therefore we conclude that the form of the Board itself does not have a bearing on the ability of a bank to survive a capital or liquidity crisis. A checklist of accepted business best-practice operating mechanisms, as contained in Heidrick and Struggles (2009), confirms further that simple observation of form for board supervision did not prevent banks from failing to meet the challenges of the crisis. For instance, UK banks are reported as exhibiting the highest rating on corporate governance in the study, yet suffered possibly the most serious banking crisis. A country ranked in the study with a low governance rating, such as Denmark, experienced fewer bank liquidity and capital problems in the crash.

Other metrics reported in the study are also uncorrelated with the experience of banks during the crisis; for instance, the average number of board members at European banks is 11.8; however, countries above this figure (Belgium, with 12.7 on average) and below it (the UK, with an average of 8.5) both suffered banking crises. Yet, the issue of the most effective size of a Board remains contentious. Advocates of large boards believe that these allow scope for representation of diverse interests, as well as a wider range of expertise. The experience of banks in the crisis, however, suggests that large boards are unwieldy, as well as unable to react quickly enough to fast-moving events.

Board Objectives and Senior Management

The composition and objectives of the Board should be set to prevent a specific interest group from gaining overall control. Levine (2004) notes that concentrated shareholders can act to exert control over diffuse shareholders and debt holders. Thus board objectives must be set with this in mind. Transparency in operation and reporting is a key requirement.

The performance of senior management is as important to corporate governance as that of the Board. The same principles of independent supervisory oversight, relevant experience and suitable expertise are required of management as they are of the Board. BIS (1999) noted situations to be avoided by senior management, but which were nevertheless evident at certain banks during the crisis, such as (i) senior managers involved insufficiently in business line decision-making; (ii) senior managers lacking sufficient expertise; and (iii) managers unwilling or unable to maintain control over so-called "star" performers.

The BIS report also suggests more frequent board meetings, and meetings of board sub-committees, than is generally the norm. Of the bank failures we observe in this study, we note that no bank conducted board and

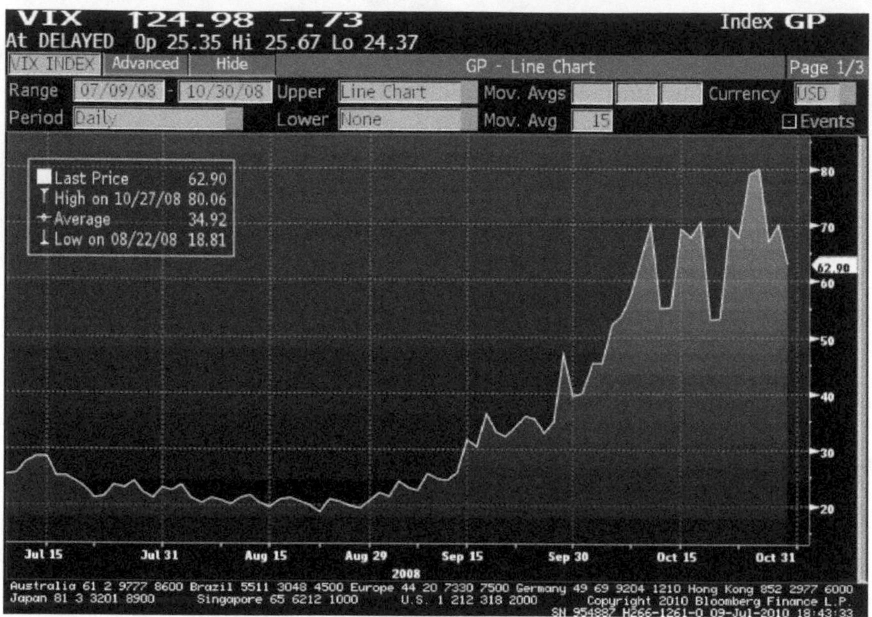

FIGURE 18.2 VIX contract price history, July–October 2008.

sub-committee meetings more than once a month, with an average frequency of one meeting every eight weeks. The pace of events in 2008 suggests that such a frequency is insufficient to meet risk management demands during a stressed period. We illustrate the speed at which events occurred with two charts. Figure 18.2 shows the Chicago Board Options Exchange VIX contract, an indicator of market volatility in the S&P500 equity index, for the period July–October 2008. From a stable level we note the sudden increase in volatility from September, following the collapse of Lehmans, which took markets by surprise (although the funding and capital issues at that firm had already been under scrutiny). Figure 18.3 shows the CDS price for Morgan Stanley during the same period; it also illustrates the same sudden rise in volatility. A meeting of senior management at no more than a monthly basis may not be sufficient. However, the diary complexities and administrative support required for board and senior management meetings may make it problematic to hold them at greater frequency, thus a less unwieldy sub-committee structure is required. This would make senior management better able to respond to changing events.

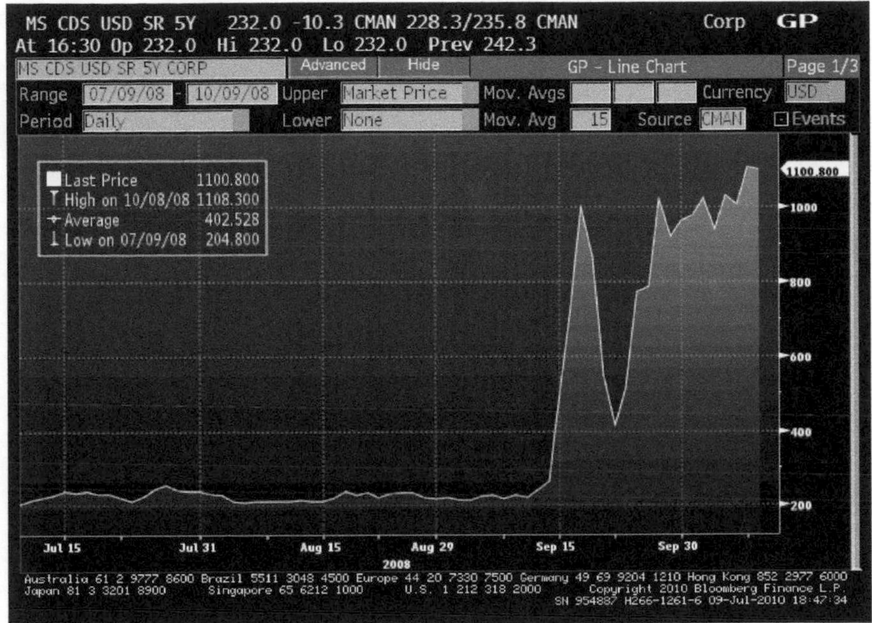

FIGURE 18.3 Morgan Stanley CDS price history, July–October 2008.

MARKET OBSERVATIONS

In a memorandum to its membership inviting the formulation of a response to the Basel Committee for Banking Supervision's latest proposals, the British Bankers' Association notes that "principles are being reviewed in the light of apparent failures in corporate governance that emerged during the credit crisis" (BBA 2010). The events of 2007–2009, when the US and certain European banking sectors were saved from bankruptcy only after the infusion of state aid, imply a failure of corporate governance at individual banks that exacerbated the problems created by a falling market. The diverse nature of the banks that failed or required government bailout, from a Wall Street investment bank to a UK building society, suggests that inadequate and incompetent management was also a factor in the crash. The banks observed in this study reflect failures in:

- the role of the Board, and its approving and overseeing the implementation of the bank's market and risk strategy;
- the Board's qualifications, and having relevant knowledge and experience;

- the existence of an independent risk management function, including a chief risk officer or equivalent with sufficient authority, and the ability to confront senior line management up to CEO level;
- the ability to identify, monitor and manage risks on an ongoing firm-wide and individual entity basis.

The observations in this section provide a selection of failure in corporate governance and control at the banks that failed or required government bailout. We concentrate on those issues of governance that can be addressed directly with practical recommendations for improvement.

United Kingdom Banks

The UK was the first country to experience difficulties in its banking sector, beginning with Northern Rock plc in 2007, which suffered the first bank run in the UK for over 140 years, and culminating with the nationalisation of Royal Bank of Scotland and Lloyds Bank (following its takeover of HBOS), and the government bailout of Bradford & Bingley and Dunfermline Building Society, among others, by the end of 2008. We examine the failures at some of these institutions from the corporate governance perspective.

Northern Rock plc

This bank exhibited a classic failure of best-practice corporate governance in two respects: the inability of the Board to exercise sufficient checks and balances on a senior director; in this case, the CEO, and insufficient banking expertise within the Board itself, principally the Chair.

The UK banking sector was characterised by a high level of competition. Banks competed against each other to attract deposits. All else being equal, the bank that is able to pay the highest deposit rate will attract most deposits. This is only sustainable from a bottom-line viewpoint by taking on more risk on the asset side of the balance sheet. This happened with the UK bank Northern Rock plc, and was stated by the Chairman of Dunfermline Building Society as a factor in its demise. In part due to its more aggressive credit portfolio, Northern Rock was able to pay out a higher rate on its clients' deposit accounts compared to that paid by the big "high street" banks, as noted in Cooper (2008).

The institution began with conservative beginnings, as a building society concentrating solely on regional mortgages and deposits. In 1997 it converted to a bank, and pursued an aggressive policy of growth and geographical expansion. However, the deposit base was not extended significantly beyond its regional roots. CEO Adam Applegarth was the driving force behind the growth strategy.

Muradoglu (2010) notes that in the first half of 2007, Northern Rock originated GBP10.7 billion of mortgages, an increase of 47% from one year previously. This represented 19% of all new mortgages during that period, elevating the firm to market leader. At the time, the bank was ranked the eight largest in the UK, and this share of the mortgage market arose from aggressive marketing and an extension of the risk-reward profile. Northern Rock, for example, was a key supplier of both 100% LTV and 125% LTV loans, the central premise behind which is that house prices will never fall. This was not an assumption restricted to Northern Rock; the credit ratings agencies implicitly assumed continuously rising house prices, on a national scale, in the methodology of their rating models for structured finance securities (noted, for example, in Landuyt (2010)). However, unlike credit rating agencies, banks have direct personal experience of their mortgage markets, including in Northern Rock's case the recession of 1990–1991, during which house prices fell. That the CEO and Board did not consider this risk, and also assumed continuous rising prices, is a failure of board judgement and the bank's governance.

By any standards the bank's growth performance in 2007 was phenomenal, and reflected a key part of Northern Rock strategy: the desire for increased market share. This concentration on market share, at the expense of the funding side of the balance sheet, was the second failure in governance and the one that caused the bank's demise. Northern Rock expanded beyond its deposit base, so the expanded volume of assets was funded in the wholesale markets, including the securitisation market. When rumours of the bank's loan book quality reached the inter-bank market, credit lines were withdrawn in August and September 2007. The shortfall in funding could not be made up without recourse to the central bank, which resulted in the bank being unable to continue business, shortly after which it was nationalised by the UK government.

The overarching component of Northern Rock strategy was a desire for balance sheet growth, and an ever-increasing market share, a strategy put in place shortly after the bank floated on the stock market. This was driven by the CEO, with acquiescence from the Board. The Board failed to notice signs of overheating in the housing market; for instance, the large write-down by a HSBC US subsidiary, together with widening credit spreads in ABS markets, at the start of 2007. Also, Chairman Matt Ridley did not have prior banking experience, with a background as a zoologist and science writer.

HBOS plc

The experience of HBOS plc, a UK bank formed by the merger in 2001 of Halifax plc and Bank of Scotland, illustrates the risks inherent in appointing senior management to banks that do not have backgrounds in banking, and exhibit a lack of experience continuously over the business cycle. The CEO of HBOS plc during the time leading to its takeover by Lloyds TSB (to forestall imminent bankruptcy) was Andy Hornby. He had joined Halifax as chief executive of Halifax Retail in 1999, after periods at a consulting company, Blue Circle (a manufacturing company), Asda (a supermarket) and George (a clothing retailer). He was then chief operating officer of the merged HBOS before being appointed CEO in 2006. During his tenure the firm expanded into corporate lending, and it was the corporate loan book that was revealed to have suffered losses of GBP6.7 billion by the end of 2008, a majority of the total GBP10 billion losses reported by the end of 2008 (quoted in *The Daily Telegraph* on 13 February 2009). The key statistic is the rate of growth in this market, which saw the HBOS balance sheet expand from GBP12 billion of corporate loans in 2005 to over GBP70 billion in such assets by the end of 2008, noted in *Property Week* (2009).

During the entire time that the CEO had been involved in banking (1999–2008), the business environment had been essentially benign; the dot.com crash and events of 9/11 had not impacted seriously bank liquidity levels, and the economy did not suffer recession. In such an environment, an emphasis was placed on market share and balance sheet growth, with a consequent negative impact on loan origination standards. Market share and rate of growth are key elements of strategy in the retail industry, where they are viewed as a benchmark by ratings agencies and shareholders. A successful background in this sector would, one expects, predispose an individual to apply the same principles in the banking industry. However, market share and growth in market share are not natural elements of a banking strategy, which in general incorporates more conservative elements related to loan quality and return on capital. Furthermore, a sustainable strategy would also allow for market slowdown and recessions, knowledge and expertise that a banking professional with experience across the entire business cycle would have been expected to possess.

HBOS was acquired by Lloyds TSB in January 2009. Once the extent of its losses was known, Lloyds TSB was partly nationalised by the UK government.

Dunfermline Building Society

Building societies in the UK are retail savings and loans institutions, and therefore inherently conservative in culture and strategy. Dunfermline

Building Society (DBS) was located entirely in Scotland, with no branches and negligible business interests in England or elsewhere in the UK, and would have been expected to have had mortgage exposure only to this geographical region. That it did not was the result of a change in strategy by the Board from 2004 onwards, and which resulted in the cessation of the firm as a viable independent entity. The failure of DBS at the height of the financial crisis exposed the poor misjudgement, risk management ability and leadership credentials of the Board. The firm was nationalised by the government in 2009, and its deposit business taken over by the Nationwide Building Society the same year.

HM Treasury (2009) reports that Jim Faulds, chairman of DBS until March 2009, stated in testimony to parliament that "the responsibility for the plight that Dunfermline found itself in is solely the responsibility of the Board of the society". He further stated that DBS had "no toxic assets, no sub-prime loans and no USA loans". It is a fact, however, that DBS was holding MBSs during 2007 and 2008, and losses on these assets depleted the capital base of the company to the point where it was no longer solvent.

In 2004 DBS adopted a new strategy that involved diversifying away from the traditional building society business of retail savings and prime loans made against residential property, into the higher risk market of commercial property lending and MBS assets. Testifying to a government committee in 2009 (see HM Treasury 2009), Mr Faulds stated that the Board had felt that DBS had to change its structure, its business and its IT system in order to remain competitive. To quote,

> *Dunfermline's systems and its structure were uncompetitive and out of date. We had right on our doorstep giants of retail financial services who were engaged in a price war, we had to compete with Northern Rock who were making offers which we could not understand how they could make (and history has shown how they did it).*

This comment raises an important governance issue, that of the *raison d'être* of a banking institution. The owners of DBS (the savers and borrowers, as building societies do not have shareholders) may have believed that the firm existed to provide financial services to its regional community, and nothing more. Expansion for its own sake was not on the members' agenda. Faulds' quote also reveals the common mistake of equating absolute size and market presence with genuine shareholder (or membership) added value. The desire to gain market share had been a factor in Northern Rock's failure, and it would appear that this was the case for DBS as well. Furthermore, the comment suggests a short-term strategy of instant growth, in what was seen as a rising market, rather than attempting to follow a coherent policy of long-term value and growth in a sector the firm was expert in.

As part of the new strategy, DBS invested in MBS bonds and lower quality mortgages such as self-certified loans, purchased from two "sub-prime" mortgage providers, GMAC and a subsidiary of Lehman Brothers. These assets suffered write-downs of over 50% of their notional value during 2008. At the same government testimony, when asked whether members were aware of the risks involved in engaging in MBS and commercial lending, Mr Faulds stated, "the members did not know that at the time. We knew that but we believed that we managed those risks reasonably well [sic]." The self-certified loans purchased from GMAC and Lehmans "were performing but not as well as loans we found ourselves". The DBS chairman stated further, "In retrospect I would rather we had not taken on self-certified loans". The spectre of this series of events is that of a Board that was drawn into a sector with which it was unfamiliar and inexpert in, and was outside its core business area.

A further loss, resulting from the failure of an IT project, highlights breakdowns in board transparency and communication. In 2002 DBS set up a subsidiary called Dunfermline Solutions, as part of a strategy to generate fee business from the provision of software solutions and back office services to deposit-takers and mortgage lenders. The firm invested GBP31.4 million in the project, a considerable sum for an institution with a capital base of less than GBP300 million. The system was not implemented, and DBS wrote off GBP9.5 million in respect of the IT development costs; this reduced operating profits in 2007 from GBP11.5 million to GBP2 million. Parliamentary testimony from Chairman Faulds described the project thus:

> *We went for a system that we thought would make us extremely competitive. It was too challenging, it took too long, it took too much money and we made a mistake.*

This in itself is not a failure of corporate governance. What is significant, however, is the manner in which this event was communicated to members, which did not highlight that it was due to management failure; instead, the losses were written off as "excellent progress" in the annual report (*DBS Members Review*, 2008). The Chairman's statement included the following:

> *We made excellent progress last year in many areas of IT by focussing on those areas that deliver the greatest benefits. Over*

> *time the technology market changes and our business priorities and requirements also change, which is why we made the decision to suspend the development and implementation in some areas of our investment, particularly those relating to the origination and administration of retail mortgages and in systems integration. This has resulted in a requirement to make an exceptional provision of £9.5m against those areas where work has been suspended. This re-focussing of technology investment towards Savings and Investments, management information systems and the mortgage intermediary market means the Society is in a better position to deliver in 2008 those areas of our investment that are of greatest benefit to our members.* (p. 4)

The parliamentary commission concluded that the DBS board lost direction, and in allowing the increased costs possibly committed a breach of the duties owed to DBS members. It also described as "disingenuous" the description of the GBP9.5 million loss written off on the IT project in the *Members Review* as "excellent progress", as referred in HM Treasury (2009).

UBS AG

The Swiss bank UBS was the recipient of a USD59 billion government bail-out at the end of 2008, after reporting large losses in its structured credit business (see Bloomberg 2008). This included a USD5.2 billion capital injection. The experience of UBS mirrored that of other banks that were rescued by their governments, in that the failure of specific business lines was exacerbated by failures in governance. In the case of UBS, the senior directors of the bank did not identify a flaw in the internal funding arrangement in place, which allowed the structured credit business to book artificial profits. This demonstrated a lack of expertise by senior management, as well as an inability to involve itself at a sufficient level of detail in what was an important discipline and control mechanism.

As a key driver of the economic decision-making process, the cost at which funds are lent from central Treasury to a bank's business lines needs to be set at a rate that reflects the true liquidity risk position of each business line. If this is unrealistic, there is the risk that transactions are entered into which produce an unrealistic profit. This profit will reflect the artificial funding gain, rather than the true economic value-added of the business. Evidence of the damage that can be caused by artificially low transfer pricing can be found in UBS's own annual shareholder report. As we note in Chapter 15, Blundell-Wignall and Atkinson (2008) discuss the losses at UBS AG in its structured credit business, which originated and invested in CDO products. As Chapter 15 makes clear, the bank operated a flawed internal funding regime. A more realistic funding model was viewed as a "constraint on the growth strategy". We observe again the pursuit of growth and market share for its own sake, rather than genuine shareholder added value.

This lack of funding discipline played an important role in the decision-making process, because it allowed the desk to report inflated profits based on low funding costs. A correct transfer pricing mechanism would have enforced greater discipline on the business lines. That senior management was not aware of this flaw in the internal funding process reflects poorly on its expertise in this area (a fundamental ingredient of banking), and on its knowledge of the bank's core processes.

KBC Bank NV

Excessive losses during 2008, principally in its KBC Financial Products (FP) derivatives trading arm, resulted in KBC Bank NV receiving an injection of EUR2.5 billion in October 2008 from the Belgian government. As it is a high-street retail bank in Belgium, the government had been forced to act to prevent the firm's bankruptcy. A second tranche of EUR2 billion equity cash was paid by the regional Flemish government in January 2009. Taxpayer support was also extended in the form of government guarantees of up to EUR20 billion to cover expected losses in the CDO portfolio. The extent of these losses had not been expected at board level, which had been accustomed to excess profits from the FP subsidiary. These profits, generated during 2002–2007, had helped create a culture of complacency at bank senior management.

For instance, at the outbreak of the US sub-prime crisis in 2007, certain members of the Board were unaware of an SPV called Atomium, which held ABS securities on its balance sheet that included sub-prime mortgage assets. This was a USD5 billion securitisation structure, and its existence was raised by journalists at a press conference in August 2007. The finance director (CFO) was not able to provide details on it. FP's CDO business had grown to over EUR20 billion, but the Board was unaware of this exposure. It was this business that was the cause of FP's losses in 2008.

Insufficient shareholder scrutiny was evident, in part the result of five years of RoE exceeding 22%, up until the crash. The implication is that management oversight was one of complacency, having observed excess profits during the bull market of 2002–2007. At the FP level, trade and business ideas returning less than 20% were rejected, even if they were potentially sound sustainable business ideas, because they did not match the excess returns of the main business lines. The lack of board scrutiny was reported by Donovan (2009), who noted the departure of both the KBC Bank CEO and the board member responsible for overseeing the FP business, shortly after the government bailout.

FP was another institution that had implemented an inadequate internal funds pricing mechanism. The majority of its liquidity came from the parent, a AA-rated bank at the time, which was lent to the subsidiary at a rate of Libor plus a uniform transfer price. This transfer price was 12.5 bps (noted in Choudhry 2009). However, one particular business line at FP, the funds derivative desk, originated assets in partnership with hedge fund of funds. This involved lending to investors in hedge funds via a leveraged structured product. These instruments were illiquid, with maturities of two years or longer. Once dealt, they could not be unwound, thus creating significant liquidity stress for the lender. FP funded these business lines from central Treasury at the standard low transfer price, rolling over the liabilities on a short-term basis. The liquidity problems that resulted became apparent after the fall of Lehmans, when inter-bank liquidity disappeared.

Many banks (including UBS, noted earlier) operated on a similar model, with a fixed internal funding rate of Libor plus a few basis points for all business lines, and for any tenor. But such an approach did not take into account the differing liquidity profiles of the businesses. This resulted in excessive risk taking heavily influenced by an artificial funding gain at the business line level. Senior management was unaware, or unable to understand, the risks inherent in an inadequate transfer price mechanism.

The failure of KBC Bank, which would have moved into administration without state intervention, was a failure of governance. The Board did not possess the expertise and knowledge necessary to effectively supervise its derivatives subsidiary, and was not aware of the extent of its risk exposure. Furthermore, the years prior to the crash, which had seen FP report excess profits, had created a complacent attitude that further eroded adequate board oversight.

Lehman Brothers

The failure of the US investment bank Lehman Brothers is covered abundantly in the existing literature. From the corporate governance viewpoint, what is instructive is the cult of personality of the CEO, Dick Fuld, and the negative impact this had on the firm's management. In this respect, it provides lessons for regulators and policymakers.

The remuneration structure at Lehman's placed significant emphasis on employee share ownership. The annual bonus of all staff was paid partly in the form of stock options, vested over a period of two, three or five years, and not realisable if the individual left the firm's employment. The performance and risk-taking culture of the company suggests that a personal stake in the company at agent level (the senior management), does not reduce the desire to originate risk. In the case of Lehman's therefore, it is difficult to conclude that the compensation and bonus culture was a factor in the firm's demise. It appears instead that the dominance of certain "eccentric personalities" at senior management was the prime factor. This is evident from Sorkin (2009) and McDonald and Robinson (2009). The authors suggest that the CEO and his president, Joe Gregory, did not fully understand the risks involved in the new investment banking environment in place from the 1990s onwards.

In the two references noted above, the words "remote" and "denial" appear frequently when describing the personality of the two Lehman executives. What is implied is that these shortcomings were due to megalomania, ego and envy. An example of this is given in McDonald and Robinson (2009), who describe the way Dick Fuld dealt with the success of the private equity firm Blackstone. This firm was managed by two ex-Lehman managing directors, Peter Peterson and Stephen Schwarz, who it appears were not on speaking terms with the Lehman CEO. Rather than focus on the core business, as advised by the senior investment banking team (Larry McCarthy, Mike Gelband and Alex Kirk), which had warned about the growing risks in private equity and high-risk leveraged finance, the authors suggest that Mr Fuld was driven by frustration and envy to start investing in hedge funds, energy companies, commodities and leveraged mortgages, apparently not only to match the success of Blackstone, but also because of a desire to top the league tables published on Wall Street. This obsession arose to such irrational levels that at certain times when high-risk strategic acquisitions were being discussed at the executive committee, the head of risk management was asked to leave the room. Clearly, if we accept this story as fact, it is not only worrying but also dangerous for any firm.

The example of Lehman is another one of failed corporate governance, and again it results from the drive and excessive influence of one particular individual. Like Northern Rock, it has implications for how bank boards can improve their policies and procedures so that they are not at risk from this type of behaviour in future.

CONCLUSION

The sample of failed firms in this study, all of whom required taxpayer support or in the case of Lehmans was allowed to go bankrupt, is notable for its diversity. The size, culture, market participation and strategy of these banks differed considerably; what the firms appear to have exhibited in common was a failure of corporate governance. The senior management of these firms acted in a way that suggests that their firm's failure would follow inevitably in the event of market correction.

A critical component of effective corporate governance is transparency. The existence of large volumes of off-balance sheet exposures, whether direct or via third-party liquidity backing arrangements, was an issue during 2007–2008. Muradoglu (2010) notes that the opacity of balance sheets to reflect accurately the extent of assets such as securitisations and other complex transactions was a major factor behind the crisis. This is a lesson for bank boards, to be able to understand better the actual risk exposures of the bank, and the reality of the reported management information. An incorrect assessment of risk by senior management is a behavioural issue; we noted the impact of personalities in the observation of Lehman Brothers. Muradoglu states:

> *. . . herding and underestimation of low probability high impact events are all parts of human nature. Human nature will not change. Thus, we need better regulations.* (p.13)

In other words, regulation and governance need to be enforced by fiat to take account of weaknesses caused by human nature. We noted earlier the lack of transparency in the corporate governance of DBS, and the personality cult at Lehman's that made effective board oversight of company direction difficult. De Bondt et al. (2010) suggest that in the pursuit of short-term super profits, current regulations and governance culture were not sufficient to prevent bank management from "bending financial reports in their favour". These examples lead to a conclusion that bank governance needs to be organised formally with stronger, more effective controls and oversight regulation, at the risk of further failure due to behavioural factors at the time of the next crash.

The behavioural issues we have identified in the case studies are a factor because of the nature of financial markets. The paradox of financial assets is that their price behaviour is different to other assets, in that rising prices lead to rising demand. Other assets, goods and services, as well as commodities (but excepting gold), all experience a fall in demand if their prices rise, all else being equal. This leads to short-term behaviour among investors as well as bank management. It is also a principal reason why "market share", while a perfectly acceptable corporate key performance indicator in industries such as clothing, retail and air travel, is an inappropriate measure for banks. Increasing market share is simply a strategy for higher losses at the point when financial markets experience a correction. The influence of management consultants, and their emphasis on market share, is clear here; it is notable that the CEOs of two failed UK banks, HBOS plc, and also Bradford & Bingley plc, both had backgrounds in the consulting industry. The experience of the crash also suggests that it is not best practice to appoint CEOs with a background in retail, where market share is an important KPI.

The financial crash of 2008 exposed the weakness of bank corporate governance. The failure of the banking sector, which required government bailout in the US and Europe, was a failure of governance. Our observations of a sample of failed firms, and the way in which decision-making was taken within them, suggests that the nature and composition of bank boards was not robust enough to provide adequate supervisory oversight of management strategy, or sufficient independent direction. Board members were not geared towards a long-term view of the bank's development, and in some cases lacked sufficient expertise to carry out the function they were entrusted with. An emphasis on peer-level comparisons of market share was allowed to shape strategy, an approach that places low emphasis on shareholder added-value and the firm's core strengths.

POLICY RECOMMENDATIONS

From our observation of a number of failed banks, we conclude that current bank corporate governance culture and legislation is insufficient to deal with the risk of failure when markets crash. We recommend a number of measures designed to strengthen the infrastructure of corporate governance, and to increase the effectiveness of boards when dealing with dynamic and volatile market environments. If necessary, these measures should be imposed by regulatory fiat:

Correct board representation. At none of the failed firms was a representative of the major debt holders placed on the Board. Market observations suggest that risk behaviour is related to the type of representative on the Board, and insofar as they represent any stakeholder, NEDs usually represent the shareholders. Increased scrutiny of company earnings has forced listed companies to report their results on a quarterly basis; the short-term focus on corporate results makes boards focus overmuch on share price and peer comparison. A board membership representing solely the management and shareholders, and concentrating on such performance parameters, will be predisposed to lower risk discipline in a rising market. Furthermore, Levine (2004) suggests that shareholders "have incentives to raise the bank's risk profile. Debt holders, however, do not enjoy any upside potential from risk-taking, but do suffer on the downside if the bank cannot service its debts." Rarely, however, if ever, are bondholders represented on the Board. If they were, the accent on policies and strategies would be more risk averse. Therefore we recommend that bank boards be required to appoint at least one member who is a representative of the major debt holders in the company.

Expert knowledge of board members. In our observation of the events at KBC Bank, we noted that board members were not familiar with securitisation techniques and structured credit products, and with specific structures in use within their own group. For board membership, financial services expertise is a prerequisite. Non-executive directors must have financial services expertise, and executive directors – including CEOs – must have direct relevant experience. We noted that Bradford & Bingley and HBOS, two failed UK banks, appointed CEOs from the retail sector. We recommend therefore that the regulator approve only suitably qualified persons for board membership. The expertise of board members must be reviewed annually by bank regulators.

Management understanding of core strategy. A frequent refrain in risk management principles is to know one's risk. This maxim is also relevant for senior management from a governance point of view. We observed that a Board that has no clear understanding of the bank's direction, beyond a simple one of growth in absolute size and market share, can be easily influenced into higher risk business. This was the case at Northern Rock and DBS. We recommend that boards articulate a clear, coherent definition of strategy and *raison d'être* that explicitly outlines the areas of business competence the bank should engage in.

Board size. We observed that direction and risk management can easily stray into higher risk and inappropriate business sectors without effective checks and balances on management. Bank boards would be more effective with fewer but more committed members. Large-size boards diminish a sense of personal responsibility, with each board member taking refuge in the collective position. This makes it harder to restrain management and the cult of personality. As long as there are sufficient checks and balances to ensure that business lines cannot force their own agenda, we recommend that a Board of 6–10 persons rather than the norm of 12–20 would make for more effective supervision and control.

Frequency of board meetings. The frequency of board meetings was not able to meet the challenge of a dynamic market environment, of the kind observed in 2008. However, it may be administratively difficult for a full board to meet more frequently than once every 4–6 weeks. We recommend that a smaller sub-group of the Board, an "alpha-team" of key executive directors (the CEO, CFO, one business line head, Treasury head and one or two non-executive directors) meet more often – say one or two days every month rather than 6–12 days every year. This would provide more solid direction and awareness of bank business, especially during times of crisis or negative sentiment when markets are fast-moving.

Expertise of board sub-committees. It is common practice for boards to appoint an independent risk committee of non-executive directors; for example, the Board Audit & Risk committee. However, while such committees have an important function, they are ineffective unless the membership is composed of market experts able to understand the nature of the bank's risk exposures. Otherwise, the role is more effectively undertaken by an internal board sub-committee. We recommend therefore that such board sub-committees consist only of those with proven bank experience and expertise gained over the business cycle.

Transparency. We observed that frequently senior management did not issue transparent notices of strategy, intent and risk exposure to shareholders. In the case of DBS, the description of events in the annual report was kept opaque. We recommend that regulators enforce a requirement, reviewed annually, that management communicate to shareholders in a precise and clear fashion the extent of the bank's risk and losses.

At many banks the performance of senior management and boards during the crisis of 2008 was unsatisfactory. It is apparent that current corporate governance infrastructure is not sufficiently robust to handle market corrections. We have outlined a range of recommendations that should, if implemented by banks and enforced by regulators, assist management to better handle events during the next crash.

MANAGEMENT STRUCTURE

There is no one right way for a bank to organise its governance structure; rather, there is an optimum way that best suits the particular bank's business model. The basic structure might follow the principles first outlined by Coase (1937), his treatise that founded the discipline of industrial economics. However, banks often arrive at what they believe to be their optimum governance structure after a period of trial and error and learning from experience. The purpose of this section is to describe what we consider to be business best-practice. It should be viewed as a benchmark template that is suitable for implementation at any medium- or large-size commercial bank, with detail modifications applied relevant to its specific environment.

Figure 18.4 illustrates the typical bank management structure. We add the Board "Alpha Team" as well to it, to manage decision-making during

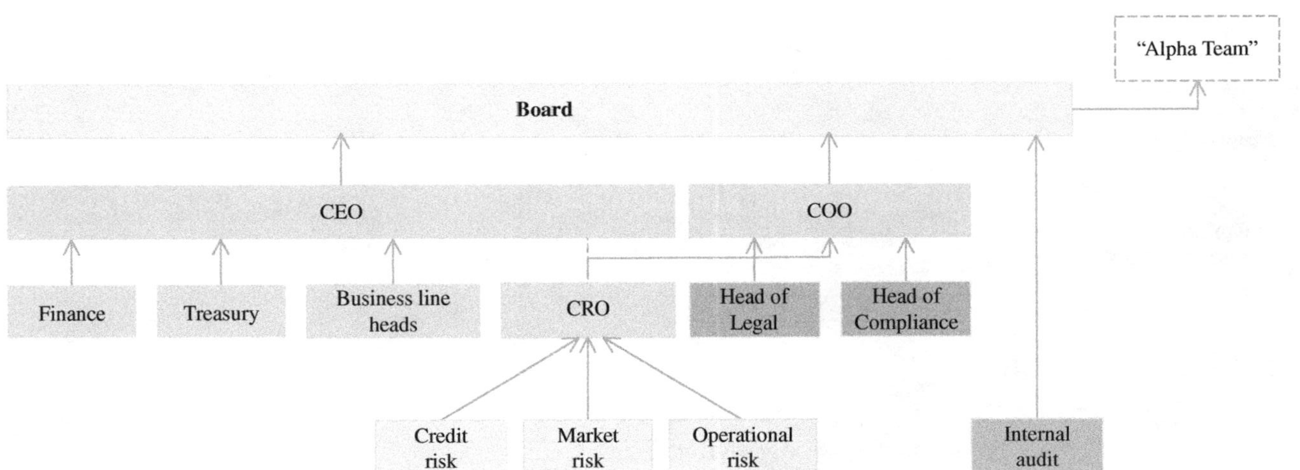

FIGURE 18.4 Standard organisation structure.

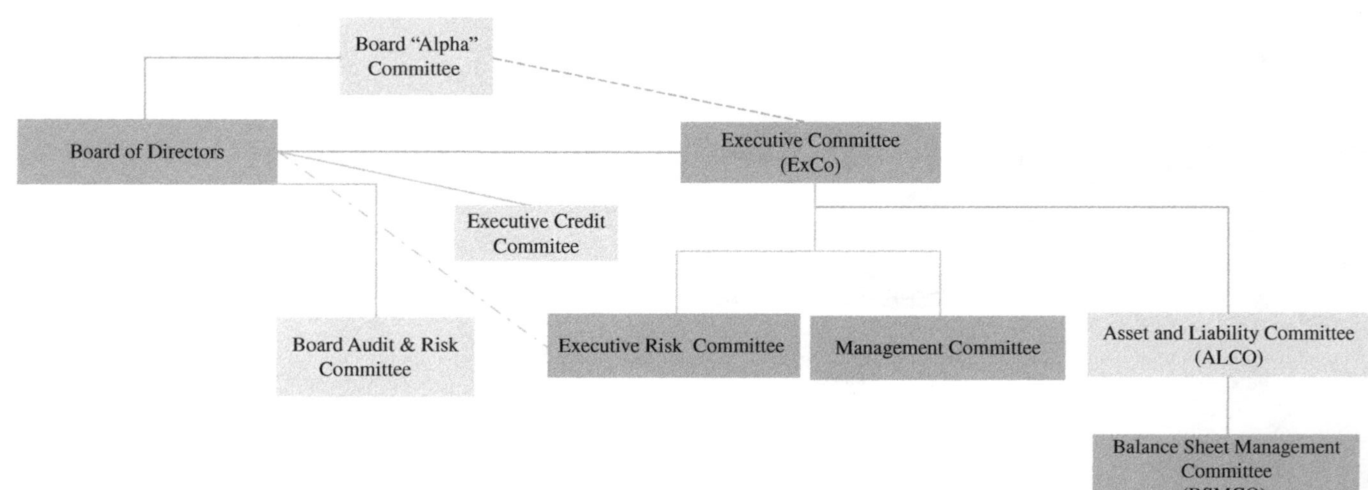

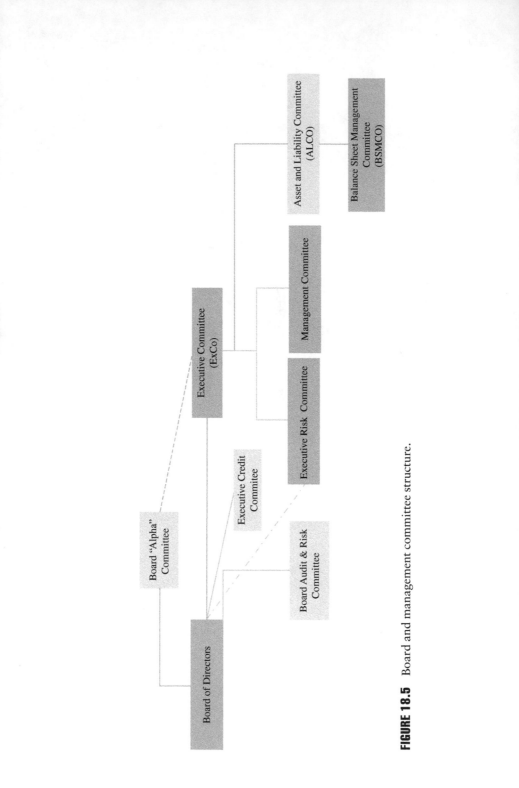

FIGURE 18.5 Board and management committee structure.

TABLE 18.1 Bank governance: committee overview.

Board of Directors	■ Sets the bank's medium- and long-term strategy and objectives, and monitors performance ■ Defines and describes the bank's high-level business model ■ Sets the bank's target ROE/ROC/ROA and approves the desired risk-return profile ■ Monitors the risk exposure and stress scenarios, ensures they are within a specified risk profile ■ Identifies medium- and long-term opportunities and threats to the bank's business operations ■ Assumes overall responsibility for managing liquidity risk for the bank, and specifying liquidity risk tolerance
"Alpha" Committee	■ Smaller committee of principal executives and non-executive directors, meets during crisis or stress periods ■ Executive authority from the Board to manage the bank as and when required ■ Organised to meet on a frequent basis
Executive Committee (ExCo)	■ Implements the Board-approved strategy across the business lines ■ Responsible for management of the balance sheet ■ Manages risk exposure and ensures risk stays within specified tolerance ■ Sets risk limits at business line level ■ Manages the regulatory relationships ■ Manages the liquidity risk position under the delegated authority of the Board ■ Responsible for stewardship of the bank's capital ■ Approves capital allocation to business line transactions
Board Audit & Risk Committee	■ Delegated board authority to oversee and control all aspects of bank finance and accounting policies, internal control and regulatory reporting functions ■ Executive and implementation assistance to the Board on any business matters referred to it by the Board ■ Undertakes the role of audit committee for the bank ■ Oversees every aspect of the bank's business on an investigative basis and reports to the Board with recommendations for improvement ■ Responsible for reporting on all risk and control issues across the bank, at a both strategic and tactical level, including financial, capital, liquidity and operational risk

(*continued*)

TABLE 18.1 *(Continued)*

Executive Credit Committee	▪ Reviews decision-making on all capital allocation issues, as well as the approval of requests for credit limits ▪ Delegated authority from the Board ▪ Delegates authority to the ALCO and relevant Credit Committees as required ▪ Approves credit and loss provisions
Executive Risk Committee	▪ Delegated authority from the Board with responsibility for overseeing risk and control issues at the strategic and tactical level ▪ Review risk tolerances for regulatory, funding and liquidity risk exposures
Management Committee	▪ Delegated authority from ExCo to implement and manage the bank's business lines' strategy ▪ Monitors and reports on capital and revenue targets ▪ Reports on bank's performance against business lines' strategy and budget ▪ Recommends strategy and implementation therefore to ExCo for board approval ▪ Not necessary for smaller banks and/or non-group structures
Asset and Liability Committee (ALCO)	▪ Discussed in Part II of the book ▪ Meets on a more frequent basis than the Board, and on a weekly basis if the Alpha Committee is meeting
Balance Sheet Management Committee	▪ Technical advisory committee that feeds in to ALCO ▪ Reviews all strategic, external market, peer group and regulatory developments of relevance and/or those expected to impact the bank ▪ Reviews the current and forecast state of the bank's balance sheet and the impact of external developments ▪ Monitors trends and forecasts on capital state, capital requirements, customer deposits, customer funding gap, net interest margin and net interest-rate risk ▪ Monitors external macroeconomic indicators and uses this to recommend policy to ALCO and ExCo ▪ Meets on a more frequent basis than the Board and other committees, and on a weekly basis if the Alpha Committee is meeting

stress events. The independence of the chief operating officer (COO), and hence CRO function is paramount here, to ensure the avoidance of the Lehmans-type situation that was recounted in Sorkin (2009). However, in some cases a "dotted line" reporting connection to the CEO, for communications and policy setting, is logical.

This structure drills down to a committee arrangement that is kept as simplified and transparent as possible. It is important to avoid overlap and to minimise drag on decision-making, as experience of the crash demonstrates that these factors prevent effective control during a stress period. We illustrate the recommended committee structure at Figure 18.5.

The matrix diagram at Table 18.1 describes the terms of reference and objectives of each of the committees shown in Figure 18.5.

GOVERNANCE AND SUSTAINABLE BANKING

We conclude this chapter with a request to readers to remember the reasons why banks originated, and why it is important that banks be managed on a footing that is sustainable throughout the business cycle.

The "paradox of aggregation" is a concept in economics that states essentially that what one can do, all cannot do. When there is a market correction, the efficient market hypothesis does not hold and prices all head the same way. It becomes difficult for banks to maintain or raise liquidity, and the prices of their assets fall below previously deemed fair value. At such times therefore it is essential that banks have in place a liquidity management system that enables them to remain liquid. This demands, at a minimum, observation of the liquidity principles described in this book.

Banks are not like other corporate entities. They have an implied social contract with the rest of the economy, which states that in return for a banking licence and the use of lender-of-last-resort facilities and other taxpayer-funded schemes such as deposit insurance, they agree to manage their business in a way that prevents a bank run. A complex set of regulatory rules and requirements is in place to ensure such an occurrence never happens, but in an ideal world they would not be required because the social contract suggests that banks should act prudently anyway. Banks should not need to be required by law to operate in a way that is sensible; rather, they should seek to ensure they do in any case. In other words, it does not matter what the regulator is demanding or whether other banks are following the rules; every bank should wish to do the right thing. And the right thing is not exclusively a profit target.

REFERENCES

Bank for International Settlements (BIS) (1999), "Enhancing Corporate Governance for Banking Organisations," *Working Paper*, September.

Basel Committee for Banking Supervision (BCBS) (1998), "Framework for Internal Control Systems in Banking Organisations", *Consultative Document*, September.

Barth, J.R., Caprio, G. and Levine, R. (2006), *Rethinking Bank Regulation: Till Angels Govern*, New York: Cambridge University Press.

Bloomberg L.P. (2008), "UBS Gets $59.2 Billion Bailout; Credit Suisse Raises Capital". Available at: http://www.bloomberg.com/apps/news?pid=newsarchive&sid=ah0AFa2SEHhw, 16 October.

Blundell-Wignall, A. and Atkinson, P. (2008), "The Sub-Prime Crisis: Causal Distortions and Regulatory Reform", *OECD Working Paper*, July.

Boyd, J.H. and Gertler, M. (1994), "The Role of Large Banks in the Recent U.S. Banking Crisis", *Federal Reserve Bank of Minneapolis Quarterly Review*, Vol. 18, No. 1.

British Bankers' Association (BBA) (2010), "BCBS Issues Principles for Enhancing Corporate Governance", *Memorandum*, 17 March.

Caprio, G., Laeven, L. and Levine, R. (2009), "Ownership and Bank Valuation", *Journal of Financial Intermediation*, 2007, Vol. 16, pp. 584–617, Nov.–Dec.

Choudhry, M. (2009), "Maintenance from Within", *World Finance*, Nov.–Dec. 2009, pp. 64–5.

Cooper, G. (2008), *The Origin of Financial Crises: Central Banks, Credit Bubbles and the Efficient Market Fallacy*, Hampshire: Harriman House Ltd.

Coase, R.H. (1937), "The Nature of the Firm", *Economica*, Vol. 4 No. 16, pp. 386–405.

DeBondt, W., Forbes, W., Hamalainen, P. and Muradoglu, Y.G. (2010), "What Can Behavioural Finance Teach Us about Finance?", *Qualitative Research in Financial Markets*, Vol. 2, No. 1, pp. 29–36.

Donovan, L. (2009), "Troubled Belgian Bank Reshuffles Management", *The New York Times*, July 1.

Dunfermline Building Society, (2008) *Members Review 2008*. Available at: http://www.parliament.the-stationery-office.co.uk/pa/cm200809/cmselect/cmscotaf/548/54805.htm.

Heidrick and Struggles (2009), *Corporate Governance Report 2009*, London.

HM Treasury (2009), "Report Looks at Collapse of Dunfermline Building Society", report on http://www.parliament.uk/business/news/2009/07/report-looks-at-collapse-of-dunfermline-building-society/, 30 July.

House of Commons Treasury Committee (2009), *Banking Crisis: Reforming Corporate Governance and Pay in the City*, Ninth report of session 2008–2009, *Hansard*, London.

Laeven, L. and Levine, R. (2007), Corporate Governance, Regulation, and Bank Risk Taking, IMF Working Paper, Washington, 14 April.

Landuyt, G. (2010), "The 2007–2009 Financial Market Crisis", chapter 24 in Choudhry, M., et al. *Capital Market Instruments: Analysis and Valuation*, 3rd edition, Basingstoke: Palgrave MacMillan.

Levine, R. (2004), "The Corporate Governance of Banks: A Concise Discussion of Concepts and Evidence", *World Bank Policy Research Working Paper 3404*, September.

Macey, J. and O'Hara, M. (2003), "The Corporate Governance of Banks", Federal Reserve Bank of New York *Economic Policy Review*, 9, pp. 91–107.

McDonald, L. and Robinson, P. (2009), *A Colossal Failure of Common Sense: The Inside Story of the Collapse of Lehman Brothers*, New York: Crown Business.

Muradoglu, Y.Z. (2010), "The Banking and Financial Crisis in the UK: What is Real and What is Behavioural?", *Qualitative Research in Financial Markets*, Vol. 2, No. 1, pp. 6–15.

Myers, S. (1977), "Determinants of Corporate Borrowing", *Journal of Financial Economics*, 5, pp. 147–75.

Property Week (2009), "Lloyds Regroups to Tackle £60 Billion Property Loan Book". Available at: http://www.propertyweek.com/lloyds-regroups-to-tackle-%C2%A360bn-property-loan-book/3139625.article

Prowse, S. (1997), "The Corporate Governance System in Banking: What do we know?", *Banca del Lavoro Quarterly Review*, pp. 11–40, March.

Saunders, A., Strock, E. and Travlos, N. (1990), "Ownership Structure, Deregulation and Bank Risk Taking," *Journal of Finance*, 45, pp. 643–54.

Sorkin, A.R. (2009), *Too Big to Fail: The Inside Story of How Wall Street and Washington Fought to Save the Financial System and Themselves*, New York: Viking Penguin.

Rod Eddington spent his first ninety days in charge at British Airways almost exclusively asking questions. "Most bad business decisions stem from a failure to understand the nature of the problem", he says. "Before you can work out where you want to go – let alone get there – you have to know where you are starting from. The bad coach jumps in after watching only a few balls in the nets. The good one first goes to watch from a number of angles." Eddington [has an] understanding that before you can lead people, you have to have formed a connection with them.

— Ed Smith, *What Sport Tells Us About Life*,
Penguin Viking 2008.

PART

V

Applications Software, Policy Templates and Teaching Aids

The last part of the book introduces the supplementary material available on the Wiley website.

To access and download policy templates, lecture materials, PowerPoint files and spreadsheet models that have been referenced in this book, please go to www.wiley.com/go/principlesofbanking. When prompted, please enter:

User name: WileyChoudhry

Password: principlesofbanking

Note that user name and password are case-sensitive.

The content of the website includes templates that can be applied at most commercial banks, and is straightforward to follow. We hope the content is of value to readers.

CHAPTER 19

Applications Software, Policy Templates and Spreadsheet Models

In this chapter we describe the software applications, Excel spreadsheets and PowerPoint presentations that are available on the Wiley website (www.wiley.com/go/principlesofbanking). The methods and techniques associated with these applications are relevant to material that has been covered in various parts of the main text.

The files that are available are grouped into the following categories on the website link:

- Excel spreadsheets;
- lecture material: PowerPoint slides;
- liquidity metrics spreadsheets;
- policy document templates;
- reporting template spreadsheets;
- stress testing report templates;
- a yield curve construction model.

For each application described below we also identify for the reader the relevant part and/or chapter in the book that is related to it, shown in square brackets.

EXCEL SPREADSHEETS

This section holds those general Excel spreadsheets that are not otherwise located in the liquidity metrics or reporting spreadsheets. The Monte Carlo instructional spreadsheet was written by Abukar Ali.

The relative value funding trade repo calculator was written by Didier Joannas. This spreadsheet calculates the net funding gain or loss for a 2-bond relative value position. In effect, it shows the net break-even, in terms of basis points, that the trade must make to be profitable. It is currently set up for US Treasury securities; however, the user may easily adjust the relevant cells to bring the worksheet up to date. The list of non-business days is maintained in the Visual Basic module. The user enters the bond price, coupon and maturity date in columns B, F and G. Long positions are entered separately to short positions. The repo rate applicable to the bond position is entered at column Q. The net funding gain or loss is shown for each bond against all the other bonds in column S. Note that this means a long position against all short positions, and vice-versa.

The Excel spreadsheets are designed to be educational tools and instructional models. They may easily be adapted for users' own particular requirements. To load any application, in Windows Explorer go to the "Excel Spreadsheets" directory and then open the Excel file from there.

[Part I]

LECTURE MATERIAL: POWERPOINT SLIDES

This section holds pdf versions of slides used in lectures by the author. The main section holds the presentations for the:

- ALCO policy summary;
- internal funds pricing policy;
- liquidity risk policy statement.

[Part II, Chapters 5–9; Part III, Chapters 12, 15]

These three presentations are part of a course on bank ALM run by the author. A selection of further presentations from this course is included in the subsection of this section.

LIQUIDITY METRICS SPREADSHEETS

This section holds two spreadsheets, namely:

- Deposit tracker and forecaster: a simple spreadsheet that tracks the balance of customer deposits, and is used to forecast the LTD.

- Liquidity ratio calculation: an instructional spreadsheet that demonstrates how to calculate the bank's ALM gap liquidity ratio. This spreadsheet is also used to report the firm's liquidity ratio against the regulator's limit.

  [Chapter 13]

POLICY DOCUMENT TEMPLATES

This section contains a number of templates that can be used for the various policy documents that describe the foundation of the bank's ALM and liquidity risk policy. This includes policy statements on the:

- ALCO agenda;
- ALCO terms of reference
- banking book policy statement;
- liquidity contingency plan;
- liquidity policy statement;
- trading book policy;
- market risk policy.

These policy templates are applicable for most commercial banking institutions.

[Part II, Chapters 5–10; Part III, Chapter 12]

REPORTING TEMPLATE SPREADSHEETS

We provide here examples of spreadsheets used to report on various liquidity positions. This includes a sample of the ALCO pack, Treasury reporting pack, cash flow survival horizon and liquidity book securities portfolio.

[Chapters 12, 13]

STRESS TESTING REPORT TEMPLATES

This section contains policy templates for stress testing procedures and reporting.

YCF CUBIC B-SPLINE YIELD CURVE APPLICATION

Included on the Wiley website is a yield curve calculation function. Yield curve fitting (YCF) 3.0 is a Cubic-Spline yield curve fitting application for both bond and money market instruments, written by Zhuoshi Liu and Moorad Choudhry. It has a Microsoft Excel front-end for accessibility and user-friendliness. YCF3.0 is a Microsoft Excel VBA program that is easy to learn and use. The application enables users to construct the current spot/forward rate yield curves from government bond prices or money market rates (for example, Libor rates and swap rates). It also calculates the fair prices of bonds and swap contracts, as well as the fair-value swap rates. In addition, users may utilise the application for calculating the fair value of a cross-currency swap or its fair-value rate.

In YCF3.0, the instantaneous forward rate curve is modelled as a natural cubic spline. We choose the forward rate value at each knot point to minimise the difference between market bond/swap data and the model implied values. A smoothing penalty can be added in the objective function to smooth the forward rate curve. Users are given three smoothing options: heavy smooth, light smooth and no smooth. Please note that there is always a trade-off between a smoother forward curve and a better fit of the market data.

YCF3.0 follows a similar methodology to the "VRP" cubic spline methodology used at the Bank of England, for which see Anderson and Sleath (2001). The paper can be accessed here: http://www.bankofengland.co.uk/publications/workingpapers/wpabst01.htm.

The VRP method is itself based on the model used at the US Federal Reserve, described in Waggoner (1997).

The tab "Instruction" in the spreadsheet provides a step-by-step guide on how to use the application, as well as other relevant information. We recommend users to read this before starting.

[Chapter 5]

REFERENCES

Anderson, S. and Sleath, J. (2001), "New Estimates of the UK Real and Nominal Yield Curves", Bank of England, *Working Paper Number 126*.

Waggoner, D. (1997), "Spline Methods for Extracting Interest Rate Curves from Coupon Bond Prices", Federal Reserve Bank of Atlanta, *Working Paper series, 97–10*.

Afterword

The profession of banking is an honourable one. To be given a responsibility at any level of a banking institution is to be entrusted with a valuable part of society's well-being. Bankers should never let this thought stray far from their minds.

Sound judgement requires knowledge and experience, of the right kind, if it is to be exercised during both good and bad economic times. This is not always a core belief of those in senior management. In his book *Bounce: The Myth of Talent and the Power of Practice*, (London: Fourth Estate 2010), Matthew Syed notes that:

> *For years, knowledge was considered relatively unimportant in decision-making . . . This was the presumption of top business schools . . . They believed they could churn out excellent managers who could be parachuted into virtually any organisation and transform it through superior reasoning . . . Experience was irrelevant, it was said, so long as you possessed a brilliant mind and the ability to wield the power of logic to solve problems . . .*
>
> *This is nonsense . . . successful decision-making in any situation characterised by complexity – whether in sport, business or wherever – is propelled not by innate ability but by the kind of knowledge that can only be built up through deep experience.*

An understanding of the core principles of banking, acquired over time, is an essential prerequisite of successful banking.

The risk management principles we have discussed in this book are identical whichever way one looks at them: be it from a shareholder-value perspective, hedging or fair-value perspective, regulatory requirement perspective or societal well-being perspective. It is important for bank management to incorporate them into their strategy, even if they think that other banks are ignoring them.

The underlying message remains: the first principle of good banking is to have principles. Or, as the motto of the London Stock Exchange puts it: *my word is my bond.*

List of Terms and their Abbreviations

asset-backed commercial paper (ABCP)
asset–backed securities (ABS)
asset–liability committee (ALCO)
asset-liability management (ALM)
advanced measurement approach (AMA)
asset-swap spread (ASW)

Balance Sheet Management Committee (BSMCO)
Basel Committee for Banking Supervision (BCBS)
Bank Financial Strength Ratings (BFSR)
Bank for International Settlements (BIS)
Bank of England (BoE)
basic indicator approach (BIA)
basis points (bps)
basis point value (BPV)
British Bankers' Association (BBA)
business as usual (BAU)

capital adequacy directive (CAD)
Capital Requirements Directive (CRD)
certificates of deposit (CDs)
cheapest-to-deliver (CTD)
Chicago Board of Trade (CBOT)
Chicago Board Options Exchange (CBOE)
chief executive officer (CEO)
chief operating officer (COO)
chief risk officer (CRO)
collateralised debt obligations (CDO)
collaterised loan obligations (CLOs)
commercial mortgage-backed securities (CMBS)
commercial paper (CP)
Committee of European Banking Supervisors (CEBS)
consumer price index (CPI)
contingency funding plan (CFP)
contingent convertible (CoCo)

cost of capital (CoC)
cost of funds (COF)
countercyclical capital buffer (CCB)
credit default swap (CDS)
credit-linked note (CLN)
credit rating agencies (CRA)
credit support annexe (CSA)
credit value adjustment (CVA)

debt service coverage ratio (DSCR)
debt value adjustment (DVA)
discount window facility (DWF)
dollar value of a basis point (DVBP)

earnings-at-risk (EAR)
earnings before interest and tax (EBIT)
earnings before interest, taxes, depreciation and amortisation (EBITDA)
earnings per share (EPS)
Economic Cycle Research Institute (ECRI)
Enhanced Capital Notes (ECN)
EuroCommercial Paper (ECP)
European Central Bank (ECB)
European Economic Area (EEA)
Executive Credit Committee (ECC)
Executive Management Committee (ExCo)
expected loss (EL)
expected negative exposure (ENE)
expected positive exposure (EPE)
expected spread (ES)
exposure-at-default (EAD)
external credit assessment institutions (ECAIs)

Financial Services Authority (FSA)
firm liquidity pricing (FLP)
first-to-default (FtD)
floating rate notes (FRNs)
foreign exchange (FX)
forward rate agreements (FRAs)
funds transfer pricing (FTP)

Generally Accepted Accounting Principles (GAAP)
general collateral (GC)
Global Financial Crisis (GFC)
Global Master Repurchase Agreement (GMRA)
Global Master Securities Lending Agreement (GMSLA)
Group Asset–Liability Committee (GALCO)

guaranteed investment contract (GIC)
Gulf Cooperation Council (GCC)

high net worth individuals (HNWIs)
hold-to-maturity (HTM)

independent and identically distributed (iid)
Independent Commission on Banking (ICB)
individual liquidity adequacy assessment (ILAA)
individual liquidity adequacy standards (ILAS)
internal assessment approach (IAA)
internal capital adequacy assessment process (ICAAP)
internal funding rate (IFR)
internal ratings-based (IRB) approach
International Financial Reporting Standards (IFRS)
International Monetary Fund (IMF)
International Accounting Standards (ISA)
International Swap and Derivative Association (ISDA)
interest-rate-risk (IRR)
interest-rate swap (IRS)
intra-group lending (IGL)
integrated group (IG)
investment banking (IB)

key performance indicators (KPIs)

leading economic indices (LEI)
lender-of-last-resort (LoLR)
letter of credit (LoC)
liquid asset buffer (LAB)
liquidity coverage ratio (LCR)
liquidity risk factor (LRF)
liquidity risk profile (LRP)
loan-to-deposit ratio (LTD)
loan-to-value (LTV)
London Clearing House (LCH)
London inter-bank bid rate (Libid)
London inter-bank offered rate (Libor)
London International Financial Futures and Options Exchange (LIFFE)
long term (LT)
Long Term Capital Management (LTCM)
loss-given-default (LGD)
loss volatility (LV)

management information (MI)
medium-term notes (MTMs)

Monetary Policy Committee (MPC)
mortgaged-backed securities (MBS)

net interest income (NII)
net interest margin (NIM)
net present value (NPV)
net stable funding ratio (NSFR)
non-executive directors (NEDs)
non-integrated group (NIG)
non-interest bearing liabilities (NIBLs)
non-performing loans (NPLs)

observed behavioural forecasting (OBF)
ordinary least squares (OLS)
Organisation for Economic Cooperation and Development (OECD)
over-collatereralisation (OC)
over-the-counter (OTC)
overnight index swap (OIS)

payment-to-income ratio (PTI)
present value (PV)
present value of a basis point (PVBP)
primary loss absorbing capacity (PLAC)
principal component analysis (PCA)
probabilities of default (PD)
profit and loss (P&L)

ratings-based approach (RBA)
recovery rate (RR)
research and development (R&D)
residential mortgage-backed securities (RMBS)
return on risk-adjusted capital (RORAC)
return on assets (RoA)
return on capital (RoC)
return on capital employed (ROCE)
return on equity (ROE)
revolving credit facility (RCF)
risk-adjusted return on capital (RAROC)
risk-sensitive assets (RSA)
risk-sensitive liabilities (RSL)
risk-weighted assets (RWA)

sample regression function (SRF)
shareholder value-added (SVA)
short term (ST)
significant risk transfer (SRT)

small and medium-size corporates (SMEs)
special purpose company (SPC)
special purpose entity (SPE)
Standard & Poor's (S&P)
special purpose vehicle (SPV)
standardised approach (SA)
stress testing and scenario analysis (STSA)
stressed VaR (SVaR)
structured investment vehicle (SIV)
supervisory formula (SF)
systemically important financial institutions (SIFIs)

term asset-backed loan facility (TALF)
term liquidity premium (TLP)
terms of reference (ToR)
total return swap (TRS)
too big to fail (TBTF)
Treasury bill (T-bill)

UK Independent Commission on Banking (ICB)
US Commercial Paper (USCP)

value-at-risk (VaR)

weighted-average cost of capital (WAC or WACC)
weighted-average cost of funds (WACF)
weighted-average life (WAL)
weighted-average maturity (WAM)

year-on-year (yoy)
yield curve fitting (YCF)
yield-to-maturity (YTM)

Index

A

B

D

M

Q

R

S

Y

Z